# Modern Banking

**Shelagh Heffernan**

*Professor of Banking and Finance,*
*Cass Business School, City University, London*

John Wiley & Sons, Ltd

**Other Wiley Editorial Offices**

John Wiley & Sons Inc., 111 River Street, Hoboken, NJ 07030, USA

Jossey-Bass, 989 Market Street, San Francisco, CA 94103-1741, USA

Wiley-VCH Verlag GmbH, Boschstr. 12, D-69469 Weinheim, Germany

John Wiley & Sons Australia Ltd, 42 McDougall Street, Milton, Queensland 4064, Australia

John Wiley & Sons (Asia) Pte Ltd, 2 Clementi Loop #02-01, Jin Xing Distripark, Singapore 129809

John Wiley & Sons Canada Ltd, 6045 Freemont Blvd, Mississauga, ONT, L5R 4J3, Canada

Wiley also publishes its books in a variety of electronic formats. Some content that appears
in print may not be available in electronic books.

*British Library Cataloguing in Publication Data*

A catalogue record for this book is available from the British Library

ISBN 13: 978-0-470-09500-3 (PB)

Typeset in 10/12pt Goudy by Laserwords Private Limited, Chennai, India
Printed and bound in Great Britain by Bell & Bain Ltd., Glasgow

This book is dedicated to my parents, GRH and GJH, in their Diamond Anniversary Year

# ABOUT THE AUTHOR

**Professor Shelagh Heffernan** is currently Professor of Banking and Finance at Cass Business School, City University, London and has been a visiting Professor at several universities. *Modern Banking* is her fourth book.

A former Commonwealth Scholar at Oxford University, Professor Heffernan is also a past beneficiary of a Leverhulme Trust Research Award, which funded new research on competition in banking, and recently received a second award from the Leverhulme Trust. She publishes in top academic journals – her paper, 'How do UK Institutions Really Price their Banking Products?' (*Journal of Banking and Finance*) was chosen as one of the top 50 published articles by Emerald Management Review.

Current research includes: SMEs and banking services, the conversion of mutuals to bank stock firms, monetary policy and pass through (funded by an ESRC grant), and M&As in banking. Professor Heffernan is an Associate Member of the Higher Education Academy and has received two Distinguished Teaching and Learning awards.

# CONTENTS

# ACKNOWLEDGEMENTS

Many individuals helped with this book. Anonymous referees made useful suggestions, which were incorporated into the book. Special thanks to Amelia Pais, who read and provided such helpful feedback on several chapters, and in record time! Peter Sinclair was also generous with his time and comments on different parts of the book. I am also grateful to other academics who provided input at various stages (some without knowing it!): Roy Batchelor, Alec Chrystal, Xiaoqing Fu, Ted Gardiner, Charles Goodhart, Alfred Kenyon, David Llewellyn, Shiv Mathur, Phillip Molyneux, Andy Mullineux, Neil Tomkin, Giorgio Questa, Peter Sinclair, Knut Sandal, Giorgio Szego and Geoffrey Wood.

Thanks to participants at seminars and conferences including the LSE Financial Markets Group, European Association of Teachers of Banking and Finance, and SUERF who gave helpful comments on papers, parts of which have found their way into various parts of the book. The stimulating "hands on" debates among (mainly) City practitioners at the seminar sessions organised by the Centre for the Study of Financial Innovation were very helpful over the years. Saadia Mujeeb (a Cass graduate), Mick Green and Tim Thomson of Barclays Bank provided good material for the chapter on risk management. The Leverhulme Trust Foundation has awarded two grants to look at competition in banking – some of the outputs from that research appear in Chapter 9.

Nikki King and James Sullivan did a super job helping out with the references and word-processing corrected chapters. They are part of the team (led by Emma Boylan) who provide the Cass Faculty of Finance with such great support. I am very grateful also to Alec Chrystal, Associate Dean of the Finance Faculty, for his encouragement.

Many students at Cass Business School, City University, assisted with the book in an indirect way by challenging ideas during lectures and case study sessions. However, several stand out for their special contributions such as chasing up data, reading proofs and conducting web searches: Randeep Brar, Olga Bouchina, Katrin Fuchs, Paul Sawh and Olga Vysokova.

Thanks go to the Cass Research Committee, which, through a "Pump Priming" award, funded Katrin Fuchs to help out with data collection for this book. I am grateful to Ingo Walter, Director of the NYU Salomon Center, who gave permission to use case studies from the New York University Salomon Center Case Series in Banking and Finance that appeared in *Modern Banking in Theory and Practice* (Wiley, 1996). The cases in Chapter 10 have been substantially revised and updated since then.

Finally, very special thanks to my dear partner Peter, for his tremendous support while I was writing this book. An intellectual "guru", his capabilities are such that I learn something new from him every day. Such an environment cannot but help but inspire and improve the quality of any book.

All errors and omissions are my responsibility.

Shelagh Heffernan
Cass Business School, City University, London, UK
November, 2004

# PREFACE

This book is a sequel to *Modern Banking in Theory and Practice* published by John Wiley & Sons in 1996. It is a sequel rather than a second edition, because it does substantially more than merely update the 1996 text. In fact, this book has taken much longer to write than the 1996 book! In the eight years since *Modern Banking in Theory and Practice* was published, many aspects of banking have changed considerably, though the key characteristics that distinguish banks from other financial institutions have not. Some might question the need for a book on banking rather than one on financial institutions. While banks remain special and unique to the financial sector, books need to be devoted to them.

*Modern Banking* focuses on the theory and practice of banking, and its prospects in the new millennium. The book is written for courses in banking and finance at Masters, MBA or advanced undergraduate level. Bank practitioners who wish to deepen and broaden their understanding of banking issues may also be attracted to this book. While they often have exceptional detailed knowledge of the areas they have worked in, busy bankers may be all too unaware of the key broader issues and lack perspective. Consider the fundamental question: what is unique about a bank? What differentiates it from other financial institutions? Answering these questions begins to show how banks should evolve and adapt – or fail. If bankers know the underlying reasons for why profitable banks exist, it will help them to devise strategies for sustained growth.

Unlike many other books in this field, the focus of the book is on the microeconomic issues related to banks, covering key areas such as what singles a bank out from other financial institutions, the diversification of banks into non-banking financial activities, different types of banks within a banking structure, bank failures, and so on. There are many excellent books that study the role banks play in the macroeconomy, and/or the contribution of financial institutions/financial sector to an economy. There are also numerous excellent books with detailed descriptions of the financial system in the United States, Britain and other countries, but they cover other types of financial firms and markets, which gives them less space to devote to banking issues. While recognising that banks are an integral part of any financial system, this book is concerned with the key *banking* topics: why they exist, investment, commercial and other types of banks, how they have diversified, risk management, global regulation, banking structures/regulations in key economies, bank failure and crises, banks in emerging markets, and competitive issues. The final chapter provides some case studies – practical applications of many of the ideas and themes covered in the book. Few books provide readers with a systematic treatment of the key micro banking issues, and it is hoped this volume goes some way to rectifying the deficiency.

These are some of the main themes running throughout the text:

- Information costs, and the demand for liquidity, explain why banks find it profitable to intermediate between borrower and lender. Banks undertake two core functions which single them out from other financial institutions: they offer intermediary and liquidity services. Often, a byproduct of these core functions is the provision of a payments service. Given that banks' core activities involve money, it also means banks play a special role in the monetary economy – their actions can even affect the money supply.

- For shareholder owned banks profits are the prime concern. So too are risks. The way banks earn their profits, through the management of financial risks, further differentiates them. The organisation of risk management, and the development techniques and instruments to facilitate risk management, are crucial to the successful operation of all banks.

- The central intermediary role played by a bank is evolving through time, from the traditional intermediation between borrowers and lenders, through to more sophisticated intermediation as risk managers.

- The objective functions of managers and bank regulators are quite different. Banks are singled out for close regulation because bank failures and crises can, and do, have social as well as private costs associated with them. However, as parts of banking become more complex, regulators increasingly rely on the banks' own risk management models to handle the associated risk. Given that bank managers do not allow for the social costs of bank failure, is the increasing use of banks' own internal risk management models by regulators a development to be welcomed? Another issue: are regulators sophisticated enough to monitor the complex models of risk management in place at the top western banks? Finally, regulation contributes to moral hazard problems, so the regulatory environment needs to give the correct incentives to minimise these problems.

- The international regulation of banks is growing in importance but controversial. Its importance stems not only from the globalisation of banking, but also, because many of the "Basel" rules agreed by the Basel Committee are increasingly seen as the benchmark for good banking regulation by all countries and all types of banks, even though the Basel agreements were originally directed at international banks headquartered in the major industrialised nations.

- Identification of the causes of bank failure and financial crises should help to reduce their incidence, thereby saving taxpayers from expensive bailouts.

- Banks in emerging markets are engaged in the core activities of intermediation and the provision of liquidity. But they have a different agenda from those in the developed world because most face a different set of challenges. No single model of banking applies to all "emerging markets", though many share similar problems such as shortages in capital and trained labour. They have their fair share of crises, too. In addition, there are different forms of banking. Islamic banking is one of the most important. Though not limited to emerging markets, Islamic banking has developed most in countries such as Pakistan, Iran and Malaysia.

- The production function for banks is less clear cut than for firms in other sectors. Are deposits and loans inputs, outputs, or both? How can cost X-efficiency, scale and scope economies, technical progress and competition be measured?
- Mergers and acquisitions, and the formation of financial conglomerates, need not necessarily result in scale economies and synergies. Measurement problems abound, and the empirical evidence is mixed. In the 1990s, there was an unprecedented jump in the mergers and acquisitions among banks, though the trend has slowed somewhat. What are the reasons which encourage merger activity and are they set to continue?
- Even though many banks tend to underperform in the stock markets, the outlook for the highly profitable, innovative banks is good, provided they can create, maintain and sustain a competitive advantage in the products and services (old and new) they offer. Like firms in any sector, banks need to plan how, in the future, existing competitive advantage is going to be sustained and extended.

Chapter 1, The Modern Banking Firm, begins with a review of the traditional theory of banking. A bank is a financial firm which offers loan and deposit products on the market, and caters to the changing liquidity needs of its borrowers and depositors. There are many other types of financial institution, and some banks offer other products and services, but it is these two functions which are banks' distinguishing features and explain why banks exist in modern economies. This definition, in turn, raises another question. Why can't borrowers and lenders come to an arrangement between each other, without intermediaries? There are two reasons. First, any lender confronts a variety of information costs – provided a bank can act as intermediary at a lower cost than an individual or a pool of lenders, a demand for banks' intermediary services should emerge. Second, the liquidity preferences of borrowers and lenders differ. If banks can offer a liquidity service at a lower cost than what borrowers and lenders would incur if they attempted to meet their liquidity demands through direct negotiation, there will, again, be an opportunity for banks. The payments services offered by banks are a byproduct of these intermediary and liquidity functions. As the brief review of payment systems suggests, though banks, historically, have been associated with payments, other parties could provide this service.

Another question relates to the organisational structure of a bank. Chapter 1 draws on Coase's (1937) theory to explain why a firm provides an alternative to market transactions. Loans and deposits are internal to a bank, so the intermediary and liquidity roles are conducted more efficiently under a command organisational structure. Unfortunately, the structure itself creates principal–agent problems, between depositor and bank, shareholders and management, the bank and its employees, and the bank and its borrowers. Differences in information between principal and agent give rise to adverse selection and moral hazard. Relationship and transactional banking can, in different ways, help to minimise these problems in a bank–client relationship. Neither arrangement is without its problems, and different countries display varying degrees of these two types of banking. A separate section identifies the key contributors in the development of the theory of banks, dating back to Edgeworth (1888).

The second part of Chapter 1 provides a brief overview of banking structure, using data from the USA and UK to illustrate the variation in banking systems. The chapter also looks at the main organisational forms in banking, such as: universal, commercial, investment, merchant banks, holding companies and financial conglomerates.

The final part of Chapter 1 reviews the relationship between banks and central banks. Central banks are usually responsible for price stability, and depending on the country, have been associated with two other roles, prudential regulation and the placement of government debt on favourable terms. These objectives can be at odds with each other, especially price control and financial stability. By the close of the 20th century, more and more governments assigned responsibility for the regulation of banks to another entity, independent of the central bank. Some countries, such as Germany and Canada, have had separate regulatory bodies for decades, but it is a relatively new phenomenon for others as diverse as the UK, Japan and China. The reason for the change may be related to the increased number of financial conglomerates, where banking is one of several key services – central banks have no expertise when it comes to the regulation of other parts of the conglomerate, such as securities and insurance. The argument for bringing the regulation of all financial firms under a separate roof is a powerful one. Nonetheless, it is worth remembering that should a bank (or any other financial group) encounter difficulties that undermine and threaten market liquidity, the central bank will have a critical role to play.

Though intermediation and liquidity provision are the defining functions of banks, regulations permitting, banks usually offer other non-banking financial products and services, or expand their intermediary and liquidity functions across national frontiers. Chapter 2 reviews the diversification into non-bank financial services, including their role in securitisation. The continued growth of securitisation and derivatives has added new dimensions to banks' management of financial risk. While banks continue to address issues arising from the traditional asset liability management, off-balance sheet risk management has become at least as important for some banks. Yet only the major banks and some specialist financial institutions use these instruments extensively. For the vast majority of banks, intermediation and liquidity provision remain the principal services on offer. Also, poor asset management continues to be a key cause of bank failure, making credit risk management as important as ever, alongside the management of market, operating and other financial risks.

Chapter 2 also considers the banks' growing reliance on non-interest income by banks. But does diversification increase income and profitability? How should banks react to the development of new financial methods, such as securitisation, instruments such as derivatives, or technology such as the internet with e-cash? Next, the chapter looks at international financial markets and the growth of international banking. Attention then turns to the relationship between multinational and wholesale banking and the Japanese and American banks that dominate global markets. What do empirical studies reveal about the factors that explain multinational banking activity? What do financial data for banks' profitability, asset growth, relative operating expenses and relative share price performance actually imply? Lastly, Chapter 2 asks how banks can turn potential threats into opportunities. What is the future for cash? More generally, could IT developments threaten core bank functions or will the 21st century see the end of banks as we know them?

While the first two chapters concentrate on why banks exist and the challenges they face, the next three turn attention to related key managerial issues in banking: financial risk management and the prudential regulation of banks. Though there is risk in any business operation, banks face a number of risks that are atypical of most non-financial firms. These financial risks are the subject of Chapter 3, which defines the various risks faced by banks, including credit, counterparty, liquidity (and funding), settlements (or payments), market (or price), interest rate, foreign exchange (or currency), gearing, sovereign/political and operational risks. The chapter covers asset liability management, duration gap analysis and other standard approaches to managing financial risk, as well as derivatives, including futures, forwards, options and swaps. Do the newer methods and instruments reduce risks in the banking system, or, perversely, raise them?

The management of market and credit risk is singled out for special attention, examining issues such as whether techniques like risk adjusted return on capital (RAROC) and value at risk (VaR) quantify and contain risk. The chapter concludes with a review of how risk management is organised in a major bank and the key tools it employs. Appropriate risk management techniques, both on- and off-balance sheet, are absolutely crucial to banks' profitability, and their long-term survival.

The way a bank manages its risk and how it is regulated are increasingly interdependent. Hence, Chapter 3 is followed by two chapters on regulation. Chapter 4 concentrates on international regulation; Chapter 5 covers the structure and regulation of banks in countries with the key financial centres of the developed world. A section on the European Union is also included because of its increasing influence on its members' structure and regulation.

Chapter 4 provides a comprehensive review of the global regulation of banks, signalling the growing importance of international regulations, such as "Basel 1" and "Basel 2". Why are banks singled out for special regulation? Should they be? It also looks at how the enormous increase in global capital flows and the spread of multinational banking has increased the need for the international coordination of prudential regulation. It reviews the logic and content of Basel 1 in 1988, as well as the likely consequences of the new Basel 2. While the Basel Committee's main concern is with the supervision of international banks, other organisations have focused on international financial stability. The respective roles played by these organisations are reviewed. Chapter 4 concludes with a discussion of the key issues now facing policy makers in the area of financial stability and international bank supervision.

Chapter 5 looks at bank structure and regulation in the UK, USA, Japan and the EU. Regulation can have an important impact on the structure of the banking system in a given country, and vice versa. It begins with the United Kingdom when, in 1997, the newly elected Labour government announced that responsibility for bank supervision was to be transferred from the Bank of England to a single regulator for all financial institutions. To understand the reasons behind this major change, it is necessary to look at the recent history of bank regulation in the UK, which is covered in this section.

The idiosyncrasies of the American banking structure are traced to numerous 20th century banking regulations. Over time American banks have been subject to an extensive range of statutes, which govern everything from bank examination and branch banking, to the functional separation of banks. The USA was the first country to introduce deposit protection legislation in 1933. Many of the laws enacted reflect a commitment to discourage collusive behaviour and regulatory capture. The legacy of these laws is a unique banking structure.

There are over 20 000 deposit-taking firms in the USA, but about half of them are credit unions. Banking systems in most industrialised countries normally have three to five key banks, offering a wide range of wholesale and retail banking services nation-wide. There are some leading global commercial and investment banks located in the USA, they do not dominate the national banking system in the way that leading banks do elsewhere. The US banking structure is fragmented, inward-looking, and showing its age. Take, for example, the payments system. In 1994, this author sent a US dollar cheque (drawn on a US dollar account held in Toronto) to one of the Federal Reserve banks, in payment for an annual conference hosted by them. Payment by credit card was not an option. The cheque was returned several weeks later with an "unable to clear" stamp on it, and an accompanying remark, "*unable to process an international check*"! Reform of the US system has been a long and slow process. It was not until July 1994 that key obstacles to interstate banking were lifted. The old 1933 laws that separated commercial and investment banking were rescinded as recently as 1999. This part of the chapter looks at the likely consequences of these changes.

Until a number of reforms in the 1990s, culminating in Big Bang, 1996, the Japanese banking system was known for its high degree of segmentation along functional lines, and the close supervision of banks by the Ministry of Finance, in conjunction with the Bank of Japan. Many of these regulations helped to shape a Japanese banking structure that has been under serious threat since the 1989 collapse of the stock market. Taxpayer funds and mergers have helped keep the largest Japanese banks afloat. Four mega banking groups now dominate the Japanese banking system. Will these changes be enough to save it?

The European Union's single market programme reached fruition in 1993. However, the 15 – now 25 – member countries' banking systems, especially at the retail level, are not yet integrated. This part of Chapter 5 looks at the reasons for this fragmentation, covering questions such as the role of the EU Commission, its feasibility, and whether the objective is a desirable one. It also reviews the role of the European Central Bank and the issue of whether supervision of the EU should remain the responsibility of member states.

Chapter 6 covers banking in emerging markets. They are the source of many financial crises that reverberate around the world. They are also under growing pressure to adopt western regulatory standards. Some developing economies suffer bouts of financial instability; others do not. Foreign banks play an active role in a few developing countries, but they are banned in others. Why, and with what consequences? Why are informal, unregulated financial markets so common? What are the main problems that these countries face? The first section provides a detailed overview of financial repression and reform, with its main focus on Russia, China and India.

The next part of Chapter 6 reviews the principles and practice of Islamic banking. Iran and Pakistan operate Islamic banking systems and ban conventional western banking. Other predominantly Muslim countries display mixed systems, where both Islamic and conventional banks can be found. The main characteristic is the absence of interest payments on deposits and loans, because the *Holy Quran* forbids it. How does this work in practice? What new products and methods have been devised to ensure the transfer of capital from those in surplus to households and firms in need of it without charging interest? The section concludes with a review of the challenges faced by Islamic banking.

The final topic in Chapter 6 covers sovereign and political risk analysis. This section addresses questions such as why do emerging market economies require external finance? What causes some of them, periodically, to default? What is the nature of sovereign risk and how is it linked to and compounded by political risk?

Having looked at the fundamentals in banking, risk management, regulation, the interaction between regulation and structure, and banking in emerging markets, the book turns to bank failure and financial crises. Chapter 7 considers the causes and consequences of bank failures. It begins with a brief historical review of bank failures, including Overend Gurney (1866), Baring Brothers (1890), and the collapse of more than 3000 US banks during 1930 to 1933. Modern cases of bank failures range from Bankhaus Herstatt (1974) to Barings Bank (1995). Crédit Lyonnais, which resulted in one of the most expensive bank rescues to date, is discussed briefly here, because it forms the basis for a case study in Chapter 10. Looking at individual case details helps to identify common themes and derive lessons from these bank failures. Chapter 7 also reports on quantitative models used to identify the determinants of bank failure. A quantitative approach gives more precise answers to questions such as the link between failure and asset management, inadequate capital, low profitability, general managerial incompetence, fraud and macroeconomic factors.

A sufficient number of bank failures can lead to a banking crisis and, ultimately, if not kept in check, a financial crisis. At the close of the 20th century, a financial crisis in Thailand triggered a set of crises throughout the region. Are crises becoming more frequent, and if so, what policies should be used to contain them? Chapter 8 begins with a review of the debate over what constitutes, characterises and causes a financial crisis. Most of the chapter focuses on modern day crises. There is extensive coverage of the South East Asian and Scandinavian financial crises. The ongoing problems with Japan's banks and financial system are used to illustrate how a financial bubble can expand and burst, this time in the world's second largest economy. The circumstances surrounding the near collapse of the hedge fund, Long Term Capital Management (LTCM) are reviewed to illustrate how problems in a small non-bank can, some think, threaten the world financial order. In view of intervention by central banks, the IMF and other official bodies, the final section of this chapter looks at the arguments for and against a lender of last resort, and in some quarters, proposals for an international lender of last resort.

To survive, a bank must be competitive. Chapter 9 asks what factors govern the competitiveness of banks. The chapter reviews the results of tests on productivity, X-efficiency, economies of scale and scope, and technical progress. The chapter also explores the key competitive issues as they relate to banking markets. Most of the empirical tests focus on the structure–conduct–performance (SCP) hypothesis and relative efficiency models. Other researchers have used empirical models to examine the extent to which banking is a contestable market. Recent work on a generalised pricing model is reviewed. Using this approach, the question is: what variables influence the price setting behaviour of banks with respect to their core products, and is there any evidence of Cournot or other types of behaviour? The final section notes the growing trend in mergers and acquisitions in banking, which was especially pronounced in the 1990s. Some of the extensive empirical literature on bank M&As is reviewed, exploring the causes and consequences of bank mergers.

In Chapter 10, readers can apply the concepts and ideas covered using case studies. The cases cover a range of different themes, which should serve to enhance the reader's understanding of different subjects covered in the text. The *Goldman Sachs* case reviews the lessons learned in the prolonged transition from being a small, private investment bank to a shareholder bank, and the implications it had for governance and performance. It covers a diverse set of topics such as the differences between relationship and transactional banking, how diversification into off-balance sheet banking may still leave a bank exposed to volatile interest rates, and corporate culture. The *Kidder Peabody* case concerns a private American investment bank, but this time, the lessons are quite different. The *Sakura to Sumitomo Mitsuo FG* case gives readers an insight into the workings of a key bank within the tightly regulated Japanese financial structure, and the problems in that sector following the collapse of the stock market. The Sakura case provides a good example of the effects on a bank of a speculative bubble; and some of the practical issues raised when two poorly performing banks merge to form a very large financial group.

The *Bancomer* case pinpoints the potential problems with banking in a developing or emerging economy. It covers issues as diverse as privatisation, political risk, and how too much financial liberalisation can upset a fledging market oriented banking system, creating serious problems for relatively strong banks like Bancomer. Also, the tesobonos swap deals illustrate the need for banks to recognise and remove any deficiencies in risk management, especially after years of operating in a nationalised banking system. Finally, the takeover of most of Mexico's key banks, including Bancomer, by foreign banks raises issues about whether foreign ownership is the best route for emerging market banks in need of capital and skills.

Causes of bank failure and issues relating to bank regulation are demonstrated in the *Continental* and *Crédit Lyonnais* (CL) cases. The CL case also touches on a difficult issue which the European Union will, eventually, have to confront – the extent to which EU states should be allowed to support failing banks. CL also shows how nationalised banks tend to be subject to government interference – for example, CL was used to provide indirect subsidies to other, troubled, state enterprises. Both cases illustrate how management can be a critical factor in the failure of the bank.

The final case is *Bankers Trust: From a Successful(?) Investment Bank to Takeover by Deutsche Bank*. It portrays a bank that underwent a comprehensive change in strategy in a bid to become a global investment bank. The case charts how the bank went about implementing strategic change, and illustrates the problems a bank might encounter if customer focus takes a back seat to product focus. It also reviews how Bankers Trust revised its risk management systems to reflect the growth of off-balance sheet business and derivatives. The case demonstrates why it is vital for a bank to understand how derivatives and other off-balance sheet instruments are used, especially when advising large corporate customers. BT was weakened by its failure to do so, a contributory factor in its takeover by Deutsche Bank. Has Deutsche Bank succeeded where Bankers Trust failed?

# Guidelines on How to Use this Book

The presentation of this book is organised to give the reader/instructor a flexible means of reading and/or teaching. The material is largely non-technical – it is the ideas and concepts that are challenging, not the statistics. It is advisable to cover Chapter 1 and, possibly, Chapter 2 first, but subsequent chapters can be taken in the order chosen by the reader/instructor. If the course is being taught to undergraduates with little or no relevant work experience, then Chapters 1 & 2 and 3 to 8 should be taught first, though the subject order can be varied and used over two single semester courses. Most of the chapters are self-contained, enabling instructors to pick and choose the material they wish to cover. Inevitably, this means there is some overlap, but giving flexibility to lecturers is important.

The case studies may be taught either concurrently, or as a separate set of exercises at the end of subject lectures. Course leaders of Masters/MBA modules may have students with a background in the financial sector who are capable of covering the case studies without doing much background reading. However, for most groups it is advisable to use the relevant chapters to back up the cases, because most classes have some students with good practical banking experience, but little in the way of a formal training in the micro-foundations of banking; others will have completed related courses in economics and finance, but will not have looked at banking issues *per se* and have little or no exposure to banking in the "real world".

It is worth emphasising to the student group that the "real world" nature of case studies means they involve a variety of themes, concepts and issues that affect different parts of bank/financial firms. Cases are likely to cut across subject boundaries. Students may come across a term/topic that the lectures have not yet covered – ideas and themes arising in a particular case do not fall neatly into lecture topics. Students should be encouraged to use new ideas to enhance their learning skills. Overall the learning experience from the case study should include: practical and general applications of topics which reinforce lecture material, learning to think laterally, and learning to work effectively in a group. Students should be encouraged to treat such challenges as part of the learning experience, following up on the new material when necessary.

The questions at the end of each case study are set to test the reader's command of the case, and ability to link these cases to the ideas covered in the text. Students with background courses in introductory economics and quantitative methods will be able to progress more quickly than those without. It is possible to cover the material in the absence of an economics and/or quantitative course, by deviating to teach some basics from time to time. For example, in Chapter 1, if a group has no economics, the instructor may find it useful to explain the basic ideas of supply, demand and the market, before progressing to Figures 1.1 and 1.2. To fully appreciate some parts of Chapters 7, 8 and 9, it may be necessary to give a brief review of basic econometric techniques.

> Important Note: Throughout the book, the $ (dollar) sign refers to nominal US dollars unless otherwise stated. When a local currency is reported in dollars, it is normally converted at that date's exchange rate.

# **WHAT ARE BANKS AND WHAT DO THEY DO?**

1

## 1.1. Introduction[1]

The term "banking" can be applied to a large range of financial institutions, from savings and loans organisations to the large money-centre commercial banks in the USA, or from the smallest mutually owned building society to the "big four" shareholder owned banks in the UK. Many European countries have large regional/cooperative banks in addition to three to five *universal* banks. In Japan, the bank with the largest retail network is Sumitomo Mitsui Banking Corporation,[2] but its main rival for savings deposits is the Post Office.

The objective of this chapter is to provide an overview of banking and the role played by banks in an increasingly complex financial world. It begins with a review of the meaning of banking, identifying the features of banks that distinguish them from other financial institutions. The most common forms of organisational structure for banks in the developed world are reviewed in section 1.3. Section 1.4 considers the relationship between the central banks and commercial banks, including key debates on the functions and independence of a central bank. The chapter ends with a brief summary of the major theoretical contributions to the banking literature, followed by conclusions.

## 1.2. The Meaning of Banking

The provision of deposit and loan products normally distinguishes banks from other types of financial firms. Deposit products pay out money on demand or after some notice. Deposits are *liabilities* for banks, which must be managed if the bank is to maximise profit. Likewise, they manage the *assets* created by lending. Thus, the core activity is to act as *intermediaries* between depositors and borrowers. Other financial institutions, such as stockbrokers, are also intermediaries between buyers and sellers of shares, but it is the taking of deposits and the granting of loans that singles out a bank, though many offer other financial services.

To illustrate the traditional intermediary function of a bank, consider Figure 1.1, a simple model of the deposit and credit markets. On the vertical axis is the rate of interest ($i$);

---

[1] © No part of this chapter is to be copied or quoted without the author's permission.
[2] This banking giant is the result of a merger between Sakura and Sumitomo Mitsui Banks in April 2001.

Figure 1.1   The Banking Firm–Intermediary.

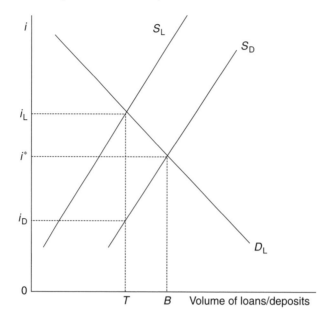

$i_L - i_D$: bank interest differential between the loan rate ($i_L$) and the deposit rate ($i_D$) which covers the cost of the bank's intermediation

$S_D$: supply of deposits curve

$S_L$: supply of loans curve

$D_L$: demand for loans curve

0T: volume of loans supplied by customers

$i^*$: market interest rate in the absence of intermediation costs

the volume of deposits/loans appears on the horizontal axis. Assume the interest rate is exogenously given. In this case, the bank faces an upward-sloping supply of deposits curve ($S_D$). There is also the bank's supply of loans curve ($S_L$), showing that the bank will offer more loans as interest rates rise.

In Figure 1.1, $D_L$ is the demand for loans, which falls as interest rates increase. In Figure 1.1, $i^*$ is the market clearing interest rate, that is, the interest rate that would prevail in a perfectly competitive market with no intermediation costs associated with bringing borrower and lender together. The volume of business is shown as 0B. However, there are intermediation costs, including *search*, *verification*, *monitoring* and *enforcement* costs, incurred by banks looking to establish the creditworthiness of potential borrowers. The lender has to estimate the riskiness of the borrower and charge a premium plus the cost of the risk assessment. Thus, in equilibrium, the bank pays a deposit rate of $i_D$ and charges a loan rate of $i_L$. The volume of deposits is OT and OT loans are supplied. The interest margin is equal to $i_L - i_D$ and covers the institution's intermediation costs, the cost of capital, the risk premium charged on loans, tax payments and the institution's profits. *Market structure* is also important: the greater the competition for loans and deposits, the more narrow the interest margin.

Intermediation costs will also include the cost of administration and other transactions costs related to the savings and loans products offered by the bank. Unlike individual agents, where the cost of finding a potential lender or borrower is very high, a bank may be able to achieve *scale economies* in these transactions costs; that is, given the large number of savings and deposit products offered, the related transactions costs are either constant or falling.

Unlike the individual lender, the bank enjoys *information economies of scope* in lending decisions because of access to privileged information on current and potential borrowers with accounts at the bank. It is normally not possible to bundle up and sell this information, so banks use it internally to increase the size of their loan portfolio. Thus, compared to depositors trying to lend funds directly, banks can pool a portfolio of assets with less risk of default, for a given expected return.

Provided a bank can act as intermediary at the lowest possible cost, there will be a demand for its services. For example, some banks have lost out on lending to highly rated corporations because these firms find they can raise funds more cheaply by issuing bonds. Nonetheless, even the most highly rated corporations use bank loans as part of their external financing, because a loan agreement acts as a *signal* to financial markets and suppliers that the borrower is creditworthy (Stiglitz and Weiss, 1988).

The second core activity of banks is to offer *liquidity* to their customers. Depositors, borrowers and lenders have different liquidity preferences. Customers expect to be able to withdraw deposits from current accounts at any time. Typically, firms in the business sector want to borrow funds and repay them in line with the expected returns of an investment project, which may not be realised for several years after the investment. By lending funds, savers are actually agreeing to forgo present consumption in favour of consumption at some date in the future.

Perhaps more important, the liquidity preferences may <u>change over time</u> because of unexpected events. If customers make term deposits with a fixed term of maturity (e.g., 3 or 6 months), they expect to be able to withdraw them on demand, in exchange for paying an interest penalty. Likewise, borrowers anticipate being allowed to repay a loan early, or subject to a satisfactory credit screen, rolling over a loan. If banks are able to pool a large number of borrowers and savers, the liquidity demands of both parties will be met. *Liquidity* is therefore an important service that a bank offers its customers. Again, it differentiates banks from other financial firms offering near-bank and non-bank financial products, such as unit trusts, insurance and real estate services. It also explains why banks are singled out for prudential regulation; the claims on a bank function as money, hence there is a "public good" element to the services banks offer.

By pooling assets and liabilities, banks are said to be engaging in **asset transformation**, i.e., transforming the value of the assets and liabilities. This activity is not unique to banks. Insurance firms also pool assets. Likewise, mutual funds or unit trusts pool together a large number of assets, allowing investors to benefit from the effects of diversification they could not enjoy if they undertook to invest in the same portfolio of assets. There is, however, one aspect of asset transformation that is unique to banks. They offer savings products with a short maturity (even instant notice), and enter into a loan agreement with borrowers, to be repaid at some future date. Loans are a type of finance not available on organised markets.

Many banking services have non-price features associated with them. A current account may pay some interest on the deposit, and offer the client a direct debit card and cheque book. The bank could charge for each of these services, but many recoup the cost of these "non-price" features by reducing the deposit rate paid.[3] On the other hand, in exchange for a customer taking out a term deposit (leaving the deposit in the bank for an agreed period of time, such as 60 days or one year), the customer is paid a higher deposit rate. If the customer withdraws the money before then, an interest penalty is imposed. Likewise, if customers repay their mortgages early, they may be charged for the early redemption.

Figure 1.1 does not allow for the other activities most modern banks undertake, such as off-balance sheet and fee for service business. However, the same principle applies. Figure 1.2 shows the demand and supply curve for a fee-based product, which can be anything from

**Figure 1.2   The Banking Firm – Fee Based Financial Products.**

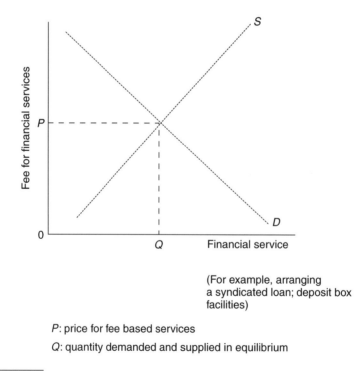

(For example, arranging
a syndicated loan; deposit box
facilities)

*P*: price for fee based services

*Q*: quantity demanded and supplied in equilibrium

---

[3] In some countries, banks charge for each item, such as statements, cheques, etc., or offer customers a package of current account services (monthly statements, a fixed number of "free" cheques per month, etc.) for a monthly fee. In the UK, banks do not normally charge personal customers for writing cheques, statements, etc.

deposit box facilities to arranging a syndicated loan. The demand and supply curves are like any other product, and the market clearing price, $P$, is determined by the intersection of the demand and supply curves. Again, market structure will determine how competitive the price is. Banks will operate in other "non-banking" financial markets provided they can create and sustain a competitive advantage in each of them.

Banks do not necessarily charge a direct price for their services, as suggested by Figure 1.2. Many modern banks offer stockbroking services to their customers, and "make markets" in certain equities. In this case, some or all of the "fee" may be reflected in the difference between the *bid* and *offer* price, that is, the price the bank pays to purchase a given stock and the price the customer pays. The difference between the two is the spread, which is normally positive, since the bid price will always be lower than the offer price, so the bank, acting as a market maker, can recoup related administrative costs and make a profit. Again, the amount of competition and volume of business in the market will determine how big the spread is. When the bank acts as a stockbroker, it will charge commission for the service. Suppose a bank sells unit trusts or mutual funds.[4] Then the price of the fund often consists of an initial charge, an annual fee, and money earned through the difference between the bid and offer price of the unit trust or mutual fund.

This discussion illustrates how complicated the pricing structure of banks' products/services can be. Non-price features can affect the size of the interest margin or the bid–offer differential. Hence, assessing the pricing behaviour of banks is often a more complex task compared to firms in some other sectors of the economy.

## 1.3. Organisational Structures

The intermediary and payments functions explain why banks exist, but another question to be addressed is why a bank exhibits the organisational structure it does. Profit-maximising banks have the same objective as any other firm; so this question is best answered by drawing on traditional models. Coase (1937), in his classic analysis, argued that the firm acted as an alternative to market transactions, as a way of organising economic activity, because some procedures are more efficiently organised by "command" (e.g., assigning tasks to workers and coordinating the work) rather than depending on a market price. In these situations, it is more profitable to use a firm structure than to rely on market forces.

The existence of the "traditional" bank, which intermediates between borrower and lender, and offers a payments service to its customers, fits in well with the Coase theory. The core functions of a bank are more efficiently carried out by a command organisational structure, because loans and deposits are internal to a bank. Such a structure is also efficient if banks are participating in organised markets. These ideas were developed and extended by Alchian and Demsetz (1972), who emphasised the monitoring role of the firm and its creation of incentive structures. Williamson (1981) argued that under conditions of uncertainty, a firm could economise on the costs of outside contracts.

---

[4] Mutual funds (USA) or unit trusts (UK) offer the investor a package of shares, bonds, or a combination of both. The investor purchases units in the fund, as do many other investors. It is managed by the bank or investment firm offering the fund.

## 1.3.1. Banks and the Principal Agent Problem

The nature of banking is such that it suffers from *agency* problems. The *principal agent* theory can be applied to explain the nature of contracts between:

- the shareholders of a bank (principal) and its management (agent);
- the bank (principal) and its officers (agent);
- the bank (principal) and its debtors (agent); and
- the depositors (principal) and the bank (agent).[5]

Incentive problems arise because the principal cannot observe and/or have perfect information about the agent's actions. For example, bank shareholders cannot oversee every management decision; nor can depositors be expected to monitor the activities of the bank. Bank management can plead bad luck when outcomes are poor.

*Asymmetric information,* or differences in information held by principal and agent, is the reason why banks face the problem of *adverse selection* because the bank, the principal, normally has less information about the probability of default on a loan than the firm or individual, the agent. Though not shown in Figure 1.1, adverse selection may mean, for *certain borrowers,* that the bank's supply of loans is discontinuous or backward bending indicating a bank's reluctance to lend as interest rates rise and attract an even greater proportion of risky borrowers. The problem of *adverse incentives* (higher interest rates encouraging existing borrowers to undertake riskier activities) is another reason why banks will reduce the size of a loan or even refuse loans to some individuals or firms.

---

**Box 1.1   Example of Adverse Selection: Robert Maxwell**

In the 1980s, most of the major American and British banks in the City of London had dealings with Robert Maxwell. At the time of his death in 1991, Mr Maxwell owed £2.8 billion to a large group of banks. Little, if any, of it was recovered. The Department of Trade and Industry had censured Robert Maxwell for his business practices in 1954. In 1971, they declared him unfit to run a public company. Despite Maxwell's background, and secrecy about the links of over 400 firms within the publicly owned Maxwell Communication Corporation, banks were attracted to Maxwell because he was prepared to pay high fees and comparatively high rates of interest on his loans, a classic example of *adverse selection. Herd instinct* was also evident. Goldman Sachs, the prestigious investment bank, accepted Mr Maxwell's custom in the late 1980s, originally to buy/sell MCC shares; the loans, options and forex dealings came later. The bank was well known for a high moral tone, which included refusing to take on clients with even a hint of bad reputation, but the New York Committee overruled the misgivings expressed by the London office, possibly because the business was confined to the sale and purchase of MCC shares. For many banks, Goldman Sachs' acceptance of Maxwell as a client was a signal that he was financially sound, and they agreed to lend to him.[6]

---

**Moral hazard** is another problem if the principal, a customer, deposits money in the agent, a bank. Moral hazard arises whenever, as a result of entering into a contract, the

---

[5] For a more theoretical treatment, see Bhattahcharya and Pfleiderer (1985), Diamond (1984) and Rees (1985).
[6] For more detail, see the Goldman Sachs case (Chapter 10).

incentives of the two parties change, such that the riskiness of the contract is altered. Depositors may not monitor bank activities closely enough for several reasons. First, a depositor's cost of monitoring the bank becomes very small, the larger and more diversified is the portfolio of loans. Though there will always be loan losses, the pooling of loans will mean that the variability of losses approaches zero. Second, deposit insurance schemes[7] reduce depositors' incentives to monitor the bank. If a bank can be reasonably certain that a depositor either cannot or chooses not to monitor the bank's activities once the deposit is made, then the nature of the contract is altered and the bank may undertake to invest in more risky assets than it would in the presence of close monitoring.

Shareholders do have an incentive to monitor the bank's behaviour, to ensure an acceptable rate of return on the investment. Depositors may benefit from this monitoring. However, even shareholders face agency problems if managers maximise their own utility functions, causing managerial behaviour to be at odds with shareholder interest. There are many cases of bank managers boosting lending to increase bank size (measured by assets) because of the positive correlation between firm size and executive compensation. These actions are not in the interests of shareholders if growth is at the expense of profitability.

## 1.3.2. Relationship Banking

*Relationship banking* can help to minimise principal agent and adverse selection problems. Lender and borrower are said to have a **relational contract** if there is an understanding between both parties that it is likely to be some time before certain characteristics related to the contract can be observed. Over an extended period of time, the customer relies on the bank to supply financial services. The bank depends on long-standing borrowers to repay their loans and to purchase related financial services. A relational contract improves information flows between the parties and allows lenders to gain specific knowledge about the borrower. It also allows for flexibility of response should there be any unforeseen events. However, there is more scope for borrower opportunism in a relational contract because of the information advantage the borrower normally has.

The Jürgen Schneider/Deutsche Bank case is a good example of how relationship banking can go wrong. Mr Schneider, a property developer, was a long-standing corporate client of Deutsche Bank. Both parties profited from an excellent relationship over a long period of time. However, when the business empire began to get into trouble, Schneider was able to disguise ever-increasing large debts in his corporation because of the good record and long relationship he had with the bank. Schneider forged loan applications and other documents to dupe Deutsche and other banks into agreeing additional loans. In 1995, he fled Germany just as the bank discovered the large-scale fraud to cover up what was

---

[7] Deposit insurance means that in the event of the bank going out of business, the depositor is guaranteed a certain percentage of the deposit back, up to some maximum. Normally banks pay a risk premium to a deposit insurance fund, usually administered by bank supervisors.

essentially a bankrupt corporation. After nearly 3 years in a Florida prison, Mr Schneider gave up the fight against extradition and was returned to Germany to face the biggest corporate fraud trial since the end of the Second World War. In 1998, he was convicted of fraud/forgery and given a prison term of 6 years, 9 months. The judge criticised German banks for reckless lending. Outstanding loans amounted to $137 million. Deutsche Bank apologised for improper credit assessment, especially its failure to follow proper procedures for loan verification.

### 1.3.3. Transactional or Contract Banking

An arms-length *transactional* or *classical contract* is at the other extreme and gives rise to *transactional banking* – where many banks compete for the customer's business and the customer shops around between several banks to find the best deal. Little in the way of a relationship exists between the two parties – both sides stick to the terms of the contract. A transactional contract deters opportunistic behaviour and because each contract is negotiated, both parties can bargain over terms. On the other hand, information flows will be significantly curtailed and the detailed nature of the contract reduces the scope for flexibility.

It is important to treat the definitions given above as two extremes, at either end of a spectrum. In reality, most banks will offer a version of relationship banking to some customers or apply it to some products, while contract-like banking is more appropriate for other clients and/or services. For example, virtually all customers who enter into a loan agreement with a bank will sign a legally binding contract, but if the customer has a good relationship with the manager and a good credit history, the manager is likely to allow a certain degree of flexibility when it comes to enforcing the terms of the contract. For new clients, the manager will be more rigid.

Relationship banking is most evident in countries such as Japan and Germany, where there are cross-shareholdings between banks and non-financial corporations. In other countries, including the USA and the UK, classical contracts are the norm. In Japan and Germany, the close bank–corporate relationships were, in the 1970s and 1980s, praised as one of the key reasons for the success of these economies. However, in the 1990s, relationship banking declined because of global reforms and innovation, which increased the methods for raising corporate finance and the number of players in the market.

Furthermore, the serious problems in the Japanese financial sector that began in 1990 have undermined *keiretsu*, the close relationship enjoyed by groups of firms, including a bank. The bank plays a pivotal role in the group because it provides long-term credit to the main firm and its network of suppliers, as well as being a major shareholder. The bank also gives the keiretsu advice and assistance in overseas ventures. With the steady rise in the number of key banks facing bankruptcy, primarily as a result of problem loan portfolios, and a drastic reduction in the market value of banks' equity portfolios due to the prolonged decline in the stock market, the relationships between banks and corporations have been seriously undermined.[8]

---

[8] See Chapter 8 for more detail.

## 1.3.4. Payment Systems: A By-Product of the Intermediary Process

One theme of this chapter is that banks differ from other financial firms because they act as intermediaries and provide liquidity. Banks require a system for processing the debits and credits arising from these banking transactions. The payment system is a byproduct of intermediation, and facilitates the transfer of ownership claims in the financial sector. Credits and debits are transferred between the relevant parties. In the UK alone, there were over 28 billion cash payments in 2001, but they are expected to decline to 24 billion by 2010. £113 billion was withdrawn from the 34 300 Automatic Teller Machines (ATMs) in 2000.[9] In the same year, there were 3 billion plastic card transactions with UK merchants.

However, there are two key risks associated with any payment. Banks must manage the following.

- *Liquidity risk*: The settlement is not made at the expected time so that assets/liabilities cannot be transferred from one agent to another via the system.
- *Operational risk*: Arising from the threat of operational breakdowns, preventing timely settlement. For example, the hardware or software supporting the system may fail. System breakdowns can create liquidity risk. Given the open-ended nature of the term, it is difficult to provide a precise definition, which makes measurement problematic.

The international payments system is described in the section on international banking in Chapter 2. In the UK, payments are organised through the following.

- **APACS** (Association for Payments Clearing Services): An umbrella organisation formed in late 1984, and made up of BACS, CCCL and CHAPS. It was supposed to allow relatively easy entry of banks into the UK payments system. Membership is offered to all participants with at least 5% of total UK clearing. Financial firms that do not qualify for membership but offer products requiring clearing and payments are made associate members.
- **BACS** Limited: An automated clearing house for non-paper-based bulk clearing, that is, standing orders, direct debits and direct credits. Fourteen direct members sponsor about 60 000 other institutions to use the system. As can be seen from Table 1.1, BACS clearing volumes stood at 3.7 billion in 2002.
- **CCCL** (Cheque and Credit Clearing Company Limited): Responsible for paper-based clearing, i.e., cheques. In 2002, there were 2.4 billion cheque transactions (see Table 1.1), which is forecast to fall to 800 million by 2012.[10]
- **CHAPS**: Provides Real Time Gross Settlement (RTGS) for high value payments, and is the second most active in the world. In 1998, the average value of transactions processed was £2.3 million, compared to £552 for BACS. In 2000, there were some 25 million

---

[9] *Source*: APACS (2003).
[10] *Source*: APACS (2003).

Table 1.1   UK: total transactions by volume (millions)

|  | 1990 | 1995 | 2000 | 2003 |
|---|---|---|---|---|
| Cash payments | 28 023 | 26 270 | 27 910 | 25 859 |
| Cheques | 3 975 | 3 203 | 2 699 | 2 251 |
| ATM withdrawals | 1 045 | 1 471 | 2 027 | 2 373 |
| Number of ATM cards | 47 | 55 | 73 | 88 |
| Plastic cards* | 1 741 | 2 413 | 3 914 | 5 317 |
| BACs clearing | 1 820** | 2 476 | 3 527 | 4 060 |
| CHAPS clearing | 9** | 13 | 25 | 33 |
| Cheque & credit | 2 513** | 2 314 | 1 981 | 1 660 |

* Includes debit, credit, charge and store cards.
** 1992 figures.
*Source*:  APACS (2003), "Payments: Facts and Figures", www.apacs.org.uk

transactions worth £49.1 billion; transactions had risen to 31 million by 2002. CHAPS Euro was formally launched in January 2001, to process euro payments between members, with monthly volumes of 280 000, valued at 3600 million euros.[11] It also provides the UK link to TARGET (see below). The real time nature of the settlement eliminates settlement/liquidity risk, unlike BACS, which settles payments in bulk.

- **CLS**: Created to reduce risks associated with payments involving another currency. It will gradually replace the standard foreign exchange settlement method, where a correspondent bank is used. In 2002, CLS introduced real time payment for foreign exchange transactions.
- **CREST**: Settlement of Securities. Central bank-related transactions moved to real time in 2001, and the idea is to introduce it for all money market instruments – payments are still made at the end of the day on a net settlement basis. The London Clearing House (LCH) acts as a central counterparty for transactions on the financial exchanges, and for some over the counter markets. At the end of 2003, LCH merged with its Paris counterpart Clearnet, creating Europe's largest central counterparty clearing house. It will go some way to creating a pan-European clearing house, reducing the cost of cross-border trading in Europe.

## 1.3.5. Use of Cards and ATMs

In the mid to late 1990s, there was a continued rapid growth in the use of cards instead of cheques. This point is illustrated in Table 1.1. This table also illustrates that cash payments over the decade and into the new century are fairly stable, and ATM withdrawals have more than doubled. Cash payments remain the dominant payment method, making up three-quarters of all payments, and their dominance will continue, though there might be a slight decline once social security benefits are paid directly into accounts. The use of cheques as a form of payment has fallen dramatically, as households and businesses switch

---

[11] The source for all figures cited for CCCL and CHAPS is APACS (2003).

to the use of plastic cards or direct debit/credit. About 3% of card transactions were via the internet in 2002, and by 2012, APACs is forecasting this to grow to 10%.[12] The ATM network in the UK is run by LINK, which is jointly owned by the banks and building societies. Via LINK, customers have access to over 34 000 ATMs. There are two credit card schemes: Mastercard, owned by Europay, and Visa, part of Visa International. There are also two debit card schemes: Switch and VisaDebit.

Cruickshank (2000) reports that the payment schemes (APACS, Visa, etc.) and ATM network are dominated by the "big four" banks[13] because the size of shareholdings is normally determined by the volume of transactions in a given scheme. Cruickshank criticised the consequences of this control, which was to take advantage of their monopoly position. Other users of the network were being charged excessive amounts, which had to be passed on to their customers or absorbed in their costs. For example, internet banks had to pay twice as much for access to the system as the big four, and retail outlets were charged excessive prices to offer a direct debit/credit card service to their customers. Cruickshank reported that the fee charged bore no relation to the cost of the investment undertaken by the big four. The big four banks paid the lowest prices to use the system, and, for a brief period, account holders faced charges if they used a rival's machine, though a vociferous public campaign forced banks to largely abandon this practice.

Cruickshank recommended the establishment of an independent regulator for the payment systems: Paycom. Access would be via a licence, the price of which would reflect the cost of use by a given bank. It could also ensure entrants were financially sound, to minimise settlement and liquidity risk. For example, with the exception of CHAPS, the systems are not based on real time gross settlement,[14] so any bank that failed while it was still using the payments system could strain the liquidity of the system. The British government accepted the need for reform, and referred the matter to the Office of Fair Trading. It has announced the introduction of PaySys, a rule-based system to regulate the payments industry (the Treasury will draft the relevant details), which does not go as far as the "public utility" approach represented by Paycom. An alternative is the "competing network" model,[15] whereby there are several large networks that compete for banks to join them.

The clearing system in the United States is quite different. The Federal Reserve Bank operates a number of cheque clearing centres, which are responsible for about 35% of US cheque clearing, which amounted to $13.4 billion in 1998.[16] Private centre arrangements made between banks account for another 35%, and about 30% is cleared by individual banks. In 1998, $16 billion worth of electronic payments were processed through one of 33

---

[12] The source of these projections is APAC (2003).

[13] At the time, National Westminster Bank, Hong Kong and Shanghai Banking Corporation (HSBC), Barclays and LloydsTSB. NatWest was taken over by the Royal Bank of Scotland in 2000, and Lloyds dropped to fifth position after the merger between Halifax and the Bank of Scotland (to form HBOS) in 2001. It is no surprise that the largest banks control the network. Only very large banks are able to finance the associated costly technology.

[14] It normally takes 3 to 5 working days for a transaction to be completed. For example, if a customer withdraws money from an ATM, it may not be debited from the account for 2 days; in the case of debit cards used at retailers, or a transfer of funds from one account to another, it can take up to 5 working days.

[15] These terms are from Anderson and Rivard (1998).

[16] *Source*: BIS (2000), tables 8 and 9 (pp. 95–96). All 1998 figures for ACHs, CHIPS and Fedwire are from the same tables.

automatic clearing houses (ACHs) run by the Federal Reserve or one of the private ACHs. International interbank transactions are handled by CHIPS, the Clearing House Interbank Payments System. It is run by the privately owned New York Clearing House Association. CHIPS uses *multilateral netting*. Until 2001, all net obligations were cleared at the end of the day, but a new bilateral and multilateral algorithm means most payments will be settled promptly through a given day, thereby reducing settlement risk. In 1998, there were roughly 60 million settlements, with a total value of about $350 trillion.

*Fedwire* is operated by the Federal Reserve and allows banks (that keep deposits or have a clearing facility with the Federal Reserve) to send and receive payments. With more than 11 000 users (1998) there were over 98.1 million transactions worth $328.7 trillion. Fedwire has offered net settlement facilities since 1999, which has reduced members' exposure to settlement risk.

In Europe, TARGET (Trans-European Automated Real Time Gross Settlement Express Transfer System) was set up in response to the European Monetary Union. It means central banks can transfer money within each EU state. It consists of 15 national RTGS systems, the European Central Bank Payment Mechanism (EPM) and SWIFT,[17] which interconnects these systems. Since the settlement is immediate, in real time, it eliminates settlement risk, because the payments are deducted from and credited to the relevant accounts immediately.

TARGET is viewed as a harmonised system, and greater harmonisation is expected in the future. According to BIS (2003f), TARGET processes over 211 000 payments each day, valued at €1.3 trillion. Though TARGET eliminates settlement risk, operational risk is considerable. For example, in 1999, a system error at one of the very large banks meant it was unable to process payment orders for foreign exchange, money market transactions, securities settlement and customer payment. The backup system also broke down because it relied on the same software. Manual systems could not cope, so that many large value payment and securities orders were not settled until the next day – this operational breakdown effectively recreated settlement risk.

Apart from the TARGET arrangement for central banks, the situation in Europe looks bleak. With the introduction of the euro in 2002, there is a need for a payments system that allows for quick settlement within Euroland. Instead, there is a plethora of bilateral agreements between different banks. Eurogiro was set up in 1992 by 14 countries' giro clearing organisations, and a similar system, Eufiserv, operates among the European savings banks. Some moves have been made to link CHAPS with its equivalent in France (SIT), Switzerland (SIS) and Germany (EAF), but no formal agreement has been reached. The large number of independent arrangements (that do not include all banks) will hamper cross-border settlement even if banks are all using one currency, the euro. The cost of cross-state settlement in Europe is estimated to be substantially higher than in the United States.

Increasingly, the responsibility for payments and securities clearing is being unbundled from the traditional bank functions, and given to a third entity, which is not necessarily

---

[17] SWIFT (Society for World-wide Interbank Financial Telecommunications): Established in Belgium in 1973, it is a cooperative company, owned by over 2000 financial firms, including banks, stockbrokers, securities exchanges and clearing organisations. SWIFT is a messaging system, for banking, foreign exchange and securities transactions, payment orders and securities deliveries. The network is available 24 hours a day, every day of the year.

another bank. These firms are providing a service to banks: processing settlements and securities for a large number of banks, reducing banks' back office operations. In other words, back office functions are becoming the sole activity of certain firms, which the banks pay, rather than having their own back office operations. According to BIS (2001, p. 310), in the USA, the top five non-bank service providers make up 20% of the outsourcing market.

## 1.3.6. An International Comparison of Payments Technology

Figures 1.3–1.6 illustrate how the pace and form of payments-related technological innovation has varied widely among the different industrialised countries. Figure 1.3 shows that ATMs are more plentiful in Japan and North America than in Western Europe. In Europe, Denmark has the fewest ATMs relative to population, followed by the UK and the Netherlands. The other European countries are roughly the same. The change in the UK is surprising because, in the 1980s, it was one of the leading ATM countries in Europe. It is consistent with the large number of branch closures in the UK, and ATMs have not spread in sufficient numbers to other sites, such as supermarkets, rail and petrol stations.

Turning to Figure 1.4, Germany stands out as having relatively few Electronic Funds Transfer at Point of Sale (EFTPOS) machines, followed by Italy, the USA and Portugal. However, while the ratio of population to EFTPOS is 466 in Germany, it is half that in the USA. Countries with relatively more machines include Spain, Switzerland, Canada and France.

Switzerland, Japan and the USA have relatively high paperless credit transfers (Figure 1.5), while some of the continental European countries rank at the bottom – France, Portugal, Italy and Belgium. Figure 1.6 shows the USA, Canada and the UK have the highest value of payments by credit and debit cards, with some of the continental countries lagging

**Figure 1.3   Average population per ATM.**

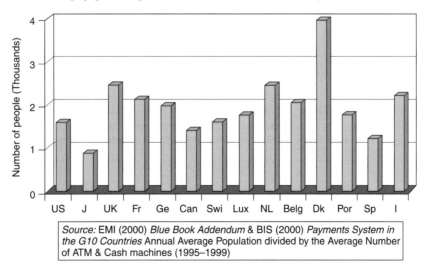

Source: EMI (2000) *Blue Book Addendum* & BIS (2000) *Payments System in the G10 Countries* Annual Average Population divided by the Average Number of ATM & Cash machines (1995–1999)

Figure 1.4   Average population per EFTPOS machine.

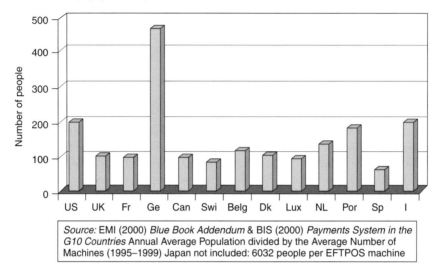

*Source:* EMI (2000) *Blue Book Addendum* & BIS (2000) *Payments System in the G10 Countries* Annual Average Population divided by the Average Number of Machines (1995–1999) Japan not included: 6032 people per EFTPOS machine

Figure 1.5   Ratio of value of paperless credit transfers to nominal GDP.

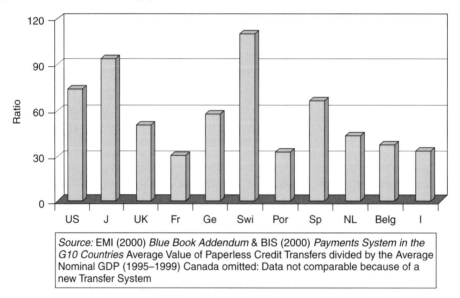

*Source:* EMI (2000) *Blue Book Addendum* & BIS (2000) *Payments System in the G10 Countries* Average Value of Paperless Credit Transfers divided by the Average Nominal GDP (1995–1999) Canada omitted: Data not comparable because of a new Transfer System

behind – especially Germany, Italy and Spain. The use of credit and debit cards in Japan is also low, compared to other countries.

*Correspondent banking* and *custody services* are also part of the payments system. *Correspondent banking* is an arrangement whereby one bank provides payment and other services to another bank. Reciprocal accounts, which normally have a credit line, are used to facilitate

Figure 1.6   Ratio of value of payments by debit and credit cards to nominal GDP.

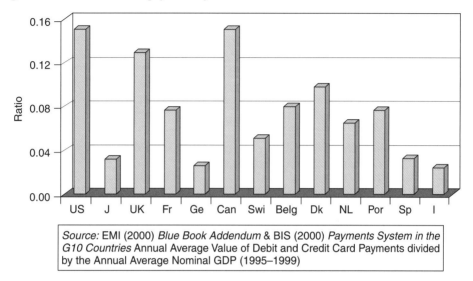

Source: EMI (2000) *Blue Book Addendum* & BIS (2000) *Payments System in the G10 Countries* Annual Average Value of Debit and Credit Card Payments divided by the Annual Average Nominal GDP (1995–1999)

payments through the correspondent bank. *Custody services* involve the safekeeping and administration of securities and other instruments on behalf of other banks or customers. Globally, the number of banks offering these services has declined, as a small number of large banks dominate an increasingly consolidated market. For example, the Bank of New York has opted to be a niche player, offering global custody services to other banks, managing $6.3 trillion worth of custody assets in 2000. Banks specialising in these services normally have sound reputations, offer a fairly large range of products and services that are easily obtainable, participate in key payment and settlement systems, and can raise liquidity.

## 1.4. Banking Structures

### 1.4.1. Some Comparative Figures

The structure of banking varies widely from country to country. Often, a country's banking structure is a consequence of the regulatory regime to which it is subject, a topic that is covered in some detail in Chapter 5. Below, different types of banking structures are defined. These different banking structures do not alter the *core functions* of banks, the provision of intermediation and liquidity, and, indirectly, a payment service, which are the *defining* features of banks.

Table 1.2 shows the top 10 banks by assets and, in recent years, *tier 1 capital*, defined as equity plus disclosed reserves. The USA leads the way in 1996, when seven of its banks were in the top 10. In the 1990s, US banks were hard hit by global, then domestic, bank debts. By 1997, Japanese banks had replaced US ones, with six leading banks,

Table 1.2 The Top 10 banks, 1969–2003

| | 1969 (assets) | 1994 (assets) | 1997 (assets) | 1997 (tier 1 capital) | 2001 (assets) | 2001 (tier 1 capital) | 2002 (tier 1 capital) | 2002 (assets) | 2003 (tier 1 capital) |
|---|---|---|---|---|---|---|---|---|---|
| USA | 7 | 1 | 0 | 3 | 3 | 3 | 3 | 2 | 3 |
| Japan | 0 | 6 | 6 | 3 | 2 | 3 | 3 | 3 | 3 |
| UK | 1 | 1 | 1 | 1 | 1 | 1 | 1 | 1 | 2 |
| France | 1 | 1 | 1 | 1 | 1 | 1 | 1 | 1 | 2 |
| Germany | 0 | 0 | 1 | 1 | 2 | 1 | 1 | 0 | 0 |
| Netherlands | 0 | 0 | 0 | 1 | 0 | 0 | 0 | 2 | 0 |
| Switzerland | 1 | 0 | 0 | 0 | 1 | 0 | 0 | 1 | 0 |
| China | 0 | 1 | 1 | 0 | 0 | 1 | 1 | 0 | 0 |

*Source: The Banker*, various July issues.

measured by assets, though the figures are less dramatic when banks are ranked, for the first time, by tier 1 capital. Note how Japanese banks shrink (by asset size) between 1997 and 2001/2. This partly reflects the serious problems in the Japanese banking sector, a topic to be discussed at greater length in Chapter 8. What is surprising is that Japan's tier 1 capital hardly changes in the period 1997–2000, when the Japanese banks were suffering from serious problems. The reason there is little change in the rankings is because of mergers among the top, but troubled, Japanese banks, especially in 2000/1. Consolidation also took place in the USA during the same period, albeit for different reasons.

Dramatic differences in banking structure can be seen by comparing the UK and USA. Tables 1.3 and 1.4 illustrate this. Table 1.3, which gives figures for the UK, is divided into

Table 1.3 UK Banking Structure, 1997 and 2002
(a) 2002

| Financial institutions | Number | Assets (£bn) |
|---|---|---|
| All banks resident in UK, of which: | 517 | 4 663 |
| Foreign (branches & subsidiaries) | 281 | 2 161 |
| UK incorporated, of which: | 236 | 2 472 |
| (1) Commercial | 35 | 1 455 |
| (2) BS + mortgage banks | 78 | 683 |
| (3) Other UK owned | 53 | 52 |
| (4) Foreign owned | 70 | 281 |
| Insurance companies, of which: | 782 | 1 018 |
| Life | 182 | 942 |
| Non-life | 600 | 76 |

BS: building societies.
*Source:* IMF (2003), which claims sources from the Bank of England, BIS, FSA, and their own estimates.

Table 1.3 (*continued*)
(b) 1997

| Financial institutions | Number | Assets (£bn) |
|---|---|---|
| All banks in the UK | 466 | 2 643 |
| UK owned banks | 112 | 1 254 |
| EU owned banks | 110 | 608 |
| US owned banks | 39 | 207 |
| Japanese owned banks | 19 | 186.3 |
| Building societies | 141 | 167.7 |
| Building Societies | 141 | |

*Sources for assets of banks and building societies*: Bank of England (2000), Statistical Abstract, tables 3.2.1– 3.2.6; 16.2.
*Sources for number of institutions*: Bank of England website, http://www.bankofengland.co.uk/mfsd/abst/ab1ukbks.doc and British Bankers Association (2000), *Abstract of Banking Statistics*.

Table 1.4   US banking structure, 1997 and 2004

| Type of bank | US assets ($bn) | | Number | | % of total assets | |
|---|---|---|---|---|---|---|
| | 1997 | 2000 | 1997 | 2004 | 1997 | 2004 |
| Commercial* | 4 771 | 6 239 | 9 308 | 7 769 | 77.6 | 79 |
| Savings institutions | 1 030 | 1 223 | 1 852 | 1 413 | 16.7 | 15 |
| Credit unions | 349 | na | 11 328 | 9 529 | 5.6 | 6 |
| Total | 6 150 | 7 462 | 22 488 | 18 711 | 100 | 100 |
| Securities firms & investment banks | Capital – 30* | | 7 776* | 5 286 | | |

*Sources*: Table constructed from 1997 figures quoted in Saunders (2000), *Financial Institutions Management*, London: McGraw Hill, chapters 1, 3, which in turn are supplied by the FDIC (second table) and the Federal Reserve Bulletin. 2004 figures obtained from the FDIC website.
*1996 figures.

parts (a) and (b) because the figures are not strictly comparable between 1997 and 2002. Of 420 banks in the UK in 1997, 88 were UK owned,[18] compared to nearly 22 500 US banks. US bank numbers, due to consolidation, are falling – they fell by about a quarter between 1997 and 2000. Even so, compare the 35 commercial banks in the UK in 2002 to over 7700 in the USA.

Table 1.5 shows that in 1996 and 1999, the USA had 10 000 more deposit-taking institutions than the other 10 major western countries combined. At the same time, it does not appear to be over-banked compared to some other countries with much smaller populations. In 1999, the USA had nearly 3500 inhabitants per branch, compared to its

---

[18] Along with 67 building societies, which are mutually owned.

Table 1.5   Number of Depository Institutions and Population per Branch

| | No. of Inhabitants per Branch | | No. of Institutions | |
|---|---|---|---|---|
| | 1996 | 1999 | 1996 | 1999 |
| Belgium | | 1221 | | 121 |
| Canada | 1857 | 2233 | 2497 | 2108 |
| France | | 2350 | | 1672 |
| Germany | 1169 | 1481 | 3509 | 2995 |
| Italy | | 1400 | | 878 |
| Japan | 1634 | 1961 | 4635 | 3169 |
| Netherlands | 2277 | 2523 | 126 | 123 |
| Sweden | 2291 | 2249 | 125 | 123 |
| Switzerland | 946 | 1097 | 372 | 336 |
| UK | 1611 | 1743 | 561 | 506 |
| USA | 2772 | 3469 | 23123 | 21070 |

Source: BIS (1998, 2001), Statistics on Payment Systems in the Group of 10 countries.

neighbour, Canada, with a tenth of the population and 2233 inhabitants per depository institution.

The figures for Canada, France and Germany should be treated with caution. The Canadian banking structure in Canada is similar to that of the UK, with four banks holding a very large percentage of assets and deposits. Caisses populaires in Quebec, along with a large number of credit unions, make the numbers look big. In fact, these organisations have a tiny market share, by any measure. The figures also mask the importance of the cooperative movement in certain countries, especially France and Germany. Furthermore, Germany has a large number of regional banks, which somewhat dilute the dominance of the big universal banks such as Deutsche Bank and Dresdner, but again, their respective market shares are quite high. Together with the large number of "thrifts" (savings and loans), the USA has many more deposit-taking institutions, mainly because of the regulatory structure that discourages interstate and intrastate branching, and the Glass Steagall Act (1933) that required banks to be either investment or commercial, but not both. However, reforms in the 1990s should increase consolidation and could lead to nation-wide banking.[19]

Japan displays a lower population per bank branch than some countries in Western Europe. In Table 1.5, it ranks seventh – Germany, Italy, Belgium and Switzerland all have fewer inhabitants per branch. However, the figure for Japan may be biased downwards because it excludes the 24000 Post Office outlets in that country, where on average about 35% of the country's deposits are held. Western European countries differ widely, with extensive branch networks in Switzerland and Belgium, but relatively few in Denmark, the Netherlands and France. The main organisational banking structures are discussed below.

---

[19] For more detail, see a brief discussion in section 4 and the detailed review of US bank regulation in Chapter 5.

## 1.4.2. Definitions of Types of Banking

### *Universal banking*

Universal banks offer the full range of banking services, together with non-banking financial services, under one legal entity. In addition, the banks have direct links between banking and commerce through cross-shareholdings and shared directorships. Financial activities normally include the following.

- Intermediation and liquidity via deposits and loans; a byproduct is the payments system.
- Trading of financial instruments (e.g., bond, equity, currency) and associated derivatives.
- Proprietary trading, that is, trading on behalf of the bank itself, using its own trading book.
- Stockbroking.
- Corporate advisory services, including mergers and acquisitions.
- Investment management.
- Insurance.

Germany is the home of universal banking (the *German hausbank*), with banks such as Deutsche Bank and Dresdner offering virtually all of the services listed above. Though German banks may own commercial concerns, the sum of a bank's equity investments (in excess of 10% of the commercial firm's capital) plus other fixed investments may not exceed the bank's total capital. In addition to a German bank lending to commercial firms, it will also exert influence through the Supervisory Board.[20] Seats on a supervisory board are for employees and shareholders. Most of the shareholder seats are held by bank executives because the bank normally has a large shareholding. The influence of the bank is increased because smaller shareholders nominate the bank to represent them when they deposit their shares at the bank for safekeeping. Deutsche Bank has major holdings in Daimler-Benz (automobiles), Allianz (the largest insurance company), Metallgesellshaft (oil industry), Philip Holzman (construction) and Munich Re (a large re-insurance firm), to name a few. The bank also purchased a firm of management consultants (Roland Berger) and is represented on more than 400 Supervisory Boards. In 1986, Deutsche Bank undertook an important strategic expansion outside Germany when it purchased Morgan Grenfell in London. Subsequent purchases have included Banca America d'Italia,[21] McLean McCarthy, a Canadian stockbroker, and Bankers Trust. It is a truly universal bank, which, together with its subsidiaries, can offer every type of financial service in Germany and, increasingly, in other major countries.

### *Commercial and Investment banks*

These terms originated in the United States, though they are used widely in other countries. The four Glass Steagall (GS) sections of the Banking Act, 1933, became known as the Glass Steagall Act. Under GS, commercial banks were not allowed to underwrite

---

[20] German companies have two boards. The membership of the Executive Board consists of full-time executives of the company. It is where the main decisions are taken. The Supervisory Board must approve the Executive Board's financial decisions.

[21] A subsidiary of Bank of America in Italy, with 105 branches.

securities with the exception of municipal bonds, US government bonds and private placements. Investment banks were prohibited from offering commercial banking services. The objectives of the Act were twofold, to discourage collusion among firms in the banking sector, and to prevent another financial crisis of the sort witnessed between 1930 and 1933.

The early US investment banks: (a) raised capital for large corporations and government, by acting as underwriters for corporate and government securities and (b) for a fee, arranged mergers and acquisitions (M&As). Modern investment banks engage in an expanded set of activities:

- underwriting
- mergers and acquisitions
- trading – equities, fixed income (bonds), proprietary
- fund management
- consultancy
- global custody

The expansion of activities helps to diversify these firms but has not been problem-free. For example, at Lehman Brothers, Goldman Sachs and others, the growth of the trading side of the bank created tensions between the relatively new traders and the banking (underwriting, M&As) side of the firm. At Lehman's, at one point, 60% of the stock was distributed to the bankers even though banking activities contributed to less than one-third of profits.

Controversy broke out in 2002, beginning with an investigation of Merrill Lynch by the New York Attorney General,[22] Eliot Spitzer, and concluding in April 2003 when 10 of the top US investment banks settled with several regulatory bodies for just over $1.4 billion in penalties and other payments, for alleged conflicts of interest between banks' analysts and their investment bank divisions. The probe began in 2002 when Henry Blodget, considered the top technology analyst at Merrill Lynch, was accused of recommending certain technology companies (thus sending up their share price) who were also clients at Merrill Lynch's investment bank. Mr Spitzer uncovered emails sent by Mr Blodget saying many of the stocks he recommended to investors were "junk" and "crap". Other documentation indicated the practice was widespread. The brokerage head of Citigroup was caught claiming that the research produced by Salomon Smith Barney was "basically worthless". Mr Weill, recent past Chairman of Citigroup, had asked an analyst at Salomon Smith Barney to reconsider the advice given on AT&T.[23] There was a potential conflict of interest because the profits of the investment bank financed banks' research departments. Thus, banks' analysts were under pressure to support a particular company that was also giving underwriting, consulting or other business to the banks' investment banking division.

The $1.4 billion settlement consists of:

- $487.5 million in penalties to be distributed between state regulators, the SEC, the New York Stock Exchange (NYSE) and the National Association of Securities Dealers (NASD);

---

[22] The New York Attorney General is also the state's securities regulator.

[23] Mr Blodget and Mr Grubman (Salomon Smith Barney) were fined $4 and $5 million, respectively and banned for life from working in the securities sector.

- $387.5 million to be returned to investors;
- $432.5 million to set up an independent research body – firms must supply their clients with this independent research for the next five years;
- $92.5 miscellaneous.

Though the banks never admitted to any wrong-doing, they agreed to make the following payments:

- Citigroup–Salomon Smith Barney $400 million;
- Merrill Lynch $200 million (including the $100 million fine it paid in 2002);
- Credit Suisse First Boston $200 million;
- Morgan Stanley $125 million;
- Goldman Sachs $110 million;
- Bear Sterns, JP Morgan, Lehman Brothers, UBS Warburg $80 million each;
- Piper Jaffray $32.5 million.

In addition, the investment banks have agreed to a number of new rules.

1. Their research and banking divisions will be supervised separately and issue separate reports.
2. Investment banking divisions are not allowed to rate research analysts.
3. A firewall[24] was erected – the compensation of analysts cannot be linked to the performance of the investment banking arm of the bank.
4. Research analysts may not participate in the marketing of the bank, e.g., share sales, deals for institutional investors.
5. No unnecessary communication is allowed between analysts and the investment banking group.
6. Banks must make public any companies that are investment bank clients and are analysed by the bank's research department.
7. "Spinning" or giving favoured clients opportunities to purchase shares in top initial public offerings (in exchange, it is hoped, for consulting or other investment banking business) was banned.

Prior to the payout being made public, Merrill Lynch announced it would insert a Chinese wall between its research and corporate finance divisions. Citigroup revealed that its research and retail broking business would be turned into a separate subsidiary. However, other conflicts of interest issues continue to surface. Banks are accused of fraud[25] for inflating prices on stock firms and initial public offerings (IPOs). For example, some banks are cited in a $30 billion damages issue for ignoring problems at Enron, and there are a number of class action lawsuits. At the time of writing, however, early judgements suggest these may not succeed: they are being dismissed for lack of evidence and because of the views of at

---

[24] See p. 28 for a formal definition.

[25] Under the 1934 Securities Act, a bank is liable for fraud if it is negligent and/or ignored problems on a firm's balance sheet that is subsequently promoted.

least one judge (Milton Pollack, who is ruling on 25 class action lawsuits – he has described the plaintiffs as "high risk speculators" and has already dismissed several cases).[26]

Washington politicians have criticised the settlement as being far too low, which banks will treat as the cost of doing business. For example, Mr Richard Shelby[27] noted that Citigroup (parent of Salomon Smith Barney) earned $10.5 billion in investment banking revenues from 1999–2001, so its share of the fine is under 4% of its revenue for the period. Self-regulation has also come under fire because the NYSE and NASD regulate their own members but failed to spot the problem, nor did the SEC, though they are a powerful government regulatory body.

## Merchant banks

Barings, the oldest of the UK merchant banks, was founded in 1762. Originally a general merchant, Francis Baring diversified into financing the import and export of goods produced by small firms. The financing was done through bills of exchange. After confirming firms' credit standings, Barings would charge a fee to guarantee (or "accept") merchants' bills of exchange. The bills traded at a discount on the market. Small traders were given much-needed liquidity. These banks were also known as "accepting houses" – a term employed until the early 1980s. They expanded into arranging loans for sovereigns and governments, underwriting, and advising on mergers and acquisitions.

Financial reforms,[28] including the Financial Services Act (1986), changed merchant banking. The reforms allowed financial firms to trade on the London Stock Exchange, without buying into member firms. Fixed commissions were abolished, and *dual capacity* dealing for all stocks was introduced. This change eliminated the distinction between "brokers" and "jobbers". Most stock exchange members acted as "market makers", making markets in a stock *and* brokers, buying and selling shares from the public.

These changes made it attractive for banks to enter the stockbroking business, and most of the major banks (both clearing and merchant) purchased broking and jobbing firms or opted for organic growth in this area. The majority of the UK merchant banks began to offer the same range of services as US investment banks, namely, underwriting, mergers and acquisitions, trading (equities, fixed income, proprietary), asset or fund management, global custody and consultancy. As merchant banks became more like investment banks, the terms were used interchangeably and, in the new century, "merchant bank" has all but disappeared from the vocabulary.

The UK's financial regulator, the Financial Services Authority (FSA), has been more sanguine on the conflict of interest issue, even though many of the US investment banks that are party to the April 2003 agreement have extensive operations in London. In a July 2002 discussion paper, the FSA acknowledged the presence of US banks operating in London. The study also identifies a number of conflicts of interest, the main one being when the remuneration of research analysts is dependent on the corporate finance or equity brokerage parts of an investment bank, which generate revenues from underwriting and

---

[26] *Source:* "Dismissed", *The Economist*, 5 July 2003, pp. 81–82.

[27] Republican Senator and Chairman of the Senate Banking Committee.

[28] Collectively known, along with other reforms, as Big Bang, 1986.

advisory or brokerage fees. There were no specific accusations of bias, and the FSA noted that institutional investors, who are well informed, are more dominant in the UK markets. However, the paper reports the results of a study by the FSA comparing recommendations on FTSE 100 companies made by firms acting as corporate broker/advisor to the subject company to those made by independent brokers with no such relationship. The main finding was that the firms acting as corporate brokers/advisors to the subject company made nearly twice as many buy recommendations as the independent brokers.

Having identified potential conflicts of interest, the FSA noted that many are currently covered under Conduct of Business rules, Code of Market Conduct and insider trading laws. The paper concluded by suggesting four possible options: (1) the status quo; (2) all research reports from investment banks or related firms to be clearly labelled as advertising; (3) following the US route, though this option would require a far more prescriptive approach, which is at odds with the UK's emphasis on principles; or (4) letting market forces do their job, because investors know who the client firms of investment banks are, and discount any reports coming from their research department. These options were put forward for further discussion, and in 2003 the FSA published a consultative paper (CP171, 2003). It appears the FSA will continue with a principles-based approach, but like the US authorities, recommends analysts should not be involved in any marketing activities undertaken by the investment bank, nor should the investment banking department influence the way analysts are paid. The FSA also suggests that analysts working for a bank underwriting a share issue for a firm should be banned from publishing any research on this firm. There are objections to the last proposal: it is argued that the analyst at the underwriting firm is the best informed about the firm about to go public, so stopping the publication of their reports will mean the market is missing out on a good source of information. Also, what if more than one bank is underwriting a rights issue?

Unlike the USA, the banks will not be required to fund independent research. Nor will analysts be required to certify that any published report reflects their personal opinion. However, the FSA has announced plans to educate the public on the risk associated with stock market investments, which is in line with their statutory duties.

## Is an investment bank a bank?

This chapter has stressed that the features which distinguish banks from other financial firms are the combined function of acting as an intermediary between savers and borrowers (either retail or wholesale) and offering liquidity as a service. Payment facilities are a byproduct of these two services.

Investment banks act as intermediaries when offering services such as underwriting, advice on mergers and acquisitions, trading, asset management and global custody. However, it is a different form of intermediation. Nor do investment banks offer liquidity as a service in the same way as a standard bank. They contribute to increased liquidity in the system by arranging new forms of finance for a corporation, but this is quite different from meeting the liquidity demands of depositors. Indeed, the functions of the investment bank differ so much from the traditional bank that the term "bank" may be a misnomer. The US National Association of Securities Dealers (NASD) does not officially recognise the term "investment bank", and uses "broker dealer" to describe investment banks and securities firms. However, many investment banks, including Goldman Sachs, do offer the core/traditional deposit, chequing, ATM and loan facilities to very high net worth individuals. Merrill Lynch, in 2000, obtained permission from the Federal Reserve Bank to offer FDIC insured deposits. Though these services form a small part of their business, it does mean they are banks, and in most countries they report to both bank and securities regulators.

### 1.4.3. Commercial Banking

Commercial banks offer wholesale and retail banking services. In the USA, commercial banking excludes, by the 1933 Glass Steagall Act, investment banking activities. *Wholesale banking* typically involves offering intermediary, liquidity and payment services to large customers such as big corporations and governments. They offer business current accounts, make commercial loans, participate in syndicated lending[29] and are active in the *interbank* markets to borrow/lend from/to other banks. Global integration, technological advances and financial reforms have made parts of the wholesale market highly competitive. Most US commercial banks also have retail customers.

Retail banking offers the same services to numerous personal banking customers and small businesses. Retail banking is largely intrabank: the bank itself accepts deposits and makes many small loans. It tends to be domestic, though the information technology revolution has the potential to break down national barriers, an issue discussed in the next section.

### 1.4.4. Bank Holding Companies

The term "bank holding company" originated in the United States. The Bank Holding Company Act (1956) defined a BHC as any firm which held at least 25% of the voting stock of a bank subsidiary in *two* or more banks. BHCs are commercial banks, regulated by the Federal Reserve Bank.[30] Having been granted legal status, bank deposits under the control of BHCs grew from 15% in the 1960s to over 90% by the 1990s. Each BHC owns banking (and in some countries, non-banking financial) subsidiaries, which are legally separate and individually capitalised.

In the United States, BHCs were used to circumvent laws which placed restrictions on interstate branching, that is, having branches in more than one state. Through the BHC structure, a bank might own several bank subsidiaries in a number of states.

### 1.4.5. Section 20 Subsidiaries

In 1981, the US Supreme Court ruled that section 20 of the Glass Steagall Act did not extend to subsidiaries of commercial banks. They could offer investment banking activities, provided they were not "engaged principally" in the said activities. Since 1987, BHC

---

[29] Syndicated lending is when a lead bank persuades a number of other banks to contribute to a loan; normally very large loans to finance massive projects such as upgrading a railway network, or sovereign loans to developing/emerging markets.

[30] The definition of BHCs under the 1956 Act led to banks forming *one* bank holding company, with non-banking subsidiaries. A 1970 Amendment stopped BHCs from owning non-bank subsidiaries and gave the Federal Reserve the authority to approve all BHC activities, which had to be closely related to banking. BHCs even had to seek permission from the Fed to expand into credit card operations.

subsidiaries have been authorised by the Federal Reserve Bank to engage in securities activities, and became known as "section 20 subsidiaries". They could underwrite corporate debt and equities provided it was limited to 5% of the bank's total revenue, which was raised to 10% in 1989 and 25% in 1996. With the passage of the Gramm Leach Bliley Act (see below), these subsidiaries are expected to gradually disappear.

## 1.4.6. Financial Holding Companies

The Gramm Leach Bliley Financial Modernisation (GLB) Act was passed in late 1999 and effectively repeals the Glass Steagall Act. The GLB Act allows US bank holding companies to convert into financial holding companies (FHCs), which can own subsidiary commercial banks, investment banks and insurance firms. Likewise, investment banks and insurance firms may form FHCs, subject to the approval of the Federal Reserve.

The GLB Act means, for the first time, that US banks can become *restricted universal banks*. They can engage in commercial and investment banking and insurance businesses but, unlike the German banks, are *restricted* because, as subsidiaries, they must be separately capitalised, which is more costly than if they are part of a single legal entity. Also, the cross-share ownership of non-financial firms is largely prohibited. In the USA, BHCs are allowed to own up to a 5% interest in a commercial concern.

Different versions of restricted universal banks are found around the world. Canada also has legislation to stop banks from owning commercial firms. In the UK, Italy and Switzerland, there is virtually no integration of banking and commerce. It is discouraged by the regulatory authorities in the respective countries, but not prohibited by law. Under the financial reforms of the late 1990s, Japanese banks may also be part of a FHC, though FHCs may not own insurance subsidiaries. However, cross-shareholdings and shared directorships are an integral part of the Japanese financial and commercial structure.[31]

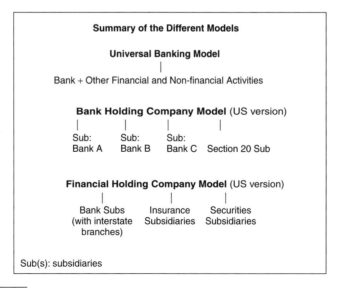

---

[31] See Chapter 5 on bank structure and regulation for more detail.

## 1.5. Financial Conglomerates

Briault (2000) defined a financial conglomerate as a firm that undertakes at least two of five financial activities: intermediary/payments, insurance, securities/corporate finance, fund management and advising on or selling investment products to retail customers. He reports that while in 1978 the vast majority of UK banks engaged in just one of these five activities, by 1998, 8 firms were authorised to offer all five functions, 13 were authorised to offer four, and more than 50 were authorised to offer three.

The Briault figures are for the UK, but rapid growth of financial conglomerates is taking place in the world's key financial sectors. Financial reform (e.g., "big bangs") in many countries eliminating (to some degree, depending on the country) segmented financial sectors has encouraged banks to become part of financial conglomerates. Given the nature of most activities listed above, virtually all conglomerates are global.

Briault identified the advantages and disadvantages of financial conglomerates. First, the efficiency of the financial system is improved if these conglomerates can achieve economies of scale and scope. *Economies of scale* is a long-run concept, where all factors of production (e.g., labour, capital, property) are variable. An equiproportional increase in factor inputs leads to a greater than equiproportional increase in output. Firms operate on the falling part of their average cost curves. For example, suppose there are three factor inputs: deposits, labour, property and one output: loans. Then, in the presence of economies of scale, the doubling of deposits, labour and property would result in loans more than doubling.

*Economies of scope* are said to exist if the joint production of two or more goods or services is cheaper than if they are produced independently, resulting in higher output. Suppose there are two products, $x =$ loans and $y =$ deposits. Then economies of scope exist if $C(x, y) < C(x) + C(y)$, where C is defined as the cost of production. Put another way, average cost falls with an increased number of outputs produced jointly rather than separately.

However, it has proved difficult to produce definitive evidence for the existence of scale and scope economies.[32] Furthermore, any increased efficiency may be offset by the effects of increased monopoly power if the growth of financial conglomerates reduces the number of firms operating in banking and other financial sectors. This will have the effect of raising "prices".[33] The reduced amount of competition in the market could, in turn, increase inefficiency. Hence, it is unclear whether the net effect of financial conglomerates is to raise or lower efficiency.

Second, it is argued that if financial conglomerates locate in countries with emerging financial markets, they can apply their expertise to assist in the development of a country's

---

[32] See Chapter 9 for a more detailed discussion of this issue.

[33] In the case of core banking products, higher prices would be reflected in lower deposit rates; higher loan rates and fees for financial services.

financial markets. Often these economies are short of trained labour in their respective financial sectors. The foreign firm can bring in expertise from other countries, but also train and educate the host country labour force.

A third argument is that financial conglomerates usually diversify their financial functions, with branches/subsidiaries around the world, making them less vulnerable to downturns in one economy or region. Likewise, a decline in securities activity may be accompanied by a rise in banking activity. However, as Staikourous and Wood (2001) have shown, diversification may actually increase the financial institutions' income volatility.

Others have argued that large, diversified financial firms encountering difficulties may "go for broke", adopting high risk/return strategies. If the gamble pays off, the conglomerates survive. If not, their size makes it likely a government might attempt to rescue them should they get into trouble. If, in the absence of a government bailout, they fail, it can trigger the collapse of financial institutions world-wide. Hence, the systemic threat to the global financial system is increased.

Functional supervision normally means independent regulators oversee different functions of the conglomerate – meaning different parts of the conglomerate *may* be answerable to different regulators. The problem with functional supervision is that damage to the reputation of one part of the firm could cause a loss of confidence in other parts of the firm, including its banking arm. The problem is illustrated by the collapse of British Commonwealth Holdings (BCH), a financial services group, in 1990. After news of serious financial problems in the computer leasing subsidiary of BCH (Atlantic Computers) in April 1990, there was a run on the British and Commonwealth Merchant Bank. Two months later, the Securities and Investment Board[34] removed the merchant bank from its approved list, and to prevent a further run, depositors' funds were frozen by the courts and an administrator appointed. The subsequent report by the administrators found the merchant bank to be financially sound.

In 2003, the UK Financial Services Authority created a Major Financial Groups Division (MFGD), which is responsible for approximately 50 complex financial firms operating in London but headquartered in the UK, USA, Japan or Europe. It includes the big four/five UK commercial banks, along with major banks and investment banks from the USA, Europe and Japan. They have been chosen according to size, systemic importance and the complexity of the business within the financial group. The MFGD assigns a "micro-regulator" to each financial conglomerate, responsible for coordinating communication among supervisors from different divisions in the FSA, assessing the group's overall management and monitoring capital adequacy. A lead regulator is assigned to any firm engaged in several activities but not deemed to be a major financial conglomerate.

In June 1989, the Federal Reserve Bank (Fed) introduced a unique system for large complex banking organisations (LCBOs). Teams of 2–12 supervisors will be assigned to America's 50 largest LCBOs, most of which operate in global markets. The emphasis is on

---

[34] The Securities and Investment Board was one of the self-regulatory organisations set up after the Financial Services Act was passed in 1986. See Charts 5.1 and 5.2 for more detail.

daily supervision (replacing periodic examinations) of both the banking *and* trading books. The teams will use an organisation's risk management and information systems, provided the regulator is satisfied with the quality of internal audit, compliance, risk management and top management.

The main concern with the LCBO arrangement is the risk of *regulatory forbearance*, when the supervisor puts the interest of the regulated firm ahead of public/taxpayer interest. To counter this problem, teams will be rotated to new LCBOs every 3 years, and other Fed specialists will double-check particularly vulnerable areas.

Managers of financial conglomerates have expressed concern that compliance costs are too high, because most regulators require them to allocate capital (known as *dedicated capital*) to each of their major operations. For example, if they have businesses in investment banking, stockbroking and intermediary banking, capital must be set aside for each of these divisions. As was noted earlier, in the United States, the FHCs are required to keep insurance, investment and commercial banking activities as separate subsidiaries, which means each subsidiary will have separate capital requirements.

There is also the potential for conflict of interest between the different firms held by the conglomerate. In the UK and elsewhere, the regulatory authorities require firms to erect *Chinese walls* to prevent sensitive information flowing between the departments (or subsidiaries) of firms, which could create problems such as insider trading. For example, if a mergers and acquisitions department knows of an upcoming bid on a target firm and those working in the trading division are informed of the bid before it becomes public information, the traders who act on such information would be accused of insider trading. Investigations by US regulators in 2002 uncovered other serious conflicts of interest among modern investment banks that had expanded into brokerage and sales in addition to their traditional activities of underwriting/mergers and acquisitions. The record $1.4 million payout by New York investment banks was discussed earlier in the chapter, but it is worth recalling the reason for the fines, etc. There was evidence of spinning and of bank analysts "talking up" the share price of companies that were also clients of the investment banking division. Thus, the expansion of modern investment banks into the broad range of activities listed previously may bring diversification benefits, but it has also created serious conflicts of interest. Financial conglomerates are also required to impose *firewalls* to counter the threat of *contagion* between their different operations. Regulators are especially anxious to keep core bank activities separate from those of other subsidiaries. *Firewalls* are legal restrictions placed on information flows and financial transactions between subsidiaries, branches, departments or other firms. For example, the Federal Reserve imposed 28 firewalls on section 20 subsidiaries. The main purpose of the firewall is to protect one unit of a holding company from funding problems associated with another subsidiary within the holding company. However, as will be seen below in the "NatWest" case, there are problems with firewalls that tend to arise if one of the subsidiaries gets into trouble. To quote Walter Wriston (Chairman of Citicorp in the 1980s) testifying before a Senate Committee in 1981, "*It is inconceivable that any major bank would walk away from any subsidiary of its holding company*".

**Box 1.2    County National Westminster Bank**

Even though the incident occurred some time ago, the case continues to illustrate the problems that can arise within a financial conglomerate. County National Westminster Bank (County NatWest or CNW) was a wholly owned subsidiary of National Westminster Bank (NWB) in London. CNW itself had a subsidiary, County National Westminster Securities (CNWS), which acted as market maker for CNW.

CNW was handling a rights issue for Blue Arrow, an employment agency, which was due to expire on 27/9/87. On 28/9, it was found that the shareholders of Blue Arrow had taken up just 49% of the share issue. As the underwriter of the shares, CNW sought out buyers of the additional shares, namely the following.

**CNWS**: According to CNWS, they were asked to purchase 4.6% of the shares in exchange for an indemnity with CNW. The market maker would be reimbursed for any losses on the shares when trading commenced, and CNW would meet all financing costs. If the share proved to be profitable, CNW would take 30% of the profits. County NatWest claims there was no indemnity: the market maker simply agreed to purchase the shares. The shares did not appear on either the trading or bank books of CNWS, and dealers were unaware the shares were being held. There was no public disclosure of the shareholding. Under section 209 of the UK Companies Act, disclosure is not necessary if the shares are held in the normal course of business.

**Phillips and Drew**: a subsidiary of the Union Bank of Switzerland (UBS), P&D were acting stockbrokers for Blue Arrow. Both firms took some of the shares, as did other corporate clients of CNW. A total of 60% of the shares were acquired by CNW-related firms. UBS obtained a written indemnity that CNW would meet any losses arising from the share issue. The Bank of England was informed of the indemnity, though it was kept a secret within CNW.

The October 1987 stock market crash caused the Blue Arrow share price to drop to 60p from 166p. CNW had to unwind its indemnity with UBS, which was done through its parent, National Westminster Bank, at a cost of $30 million. In December, CNW announced it was holding 9.6% of the shares, declaring a provisional loss of £49 million and an overall annual loss of £116 million. It required an injection of £80 million from the parent bank. In February 1988, the two top executives at CNW resigned.

The Bank of England persuaded the Department of Trade and Industry to allow NatWest Bank to conduct an internal investigation, but public pressure eventually resulted in an independent investigation by the DTI. A year later, four CNW individuals were found guilty of conspiracy to defraud; some convictions were overturned on appeal.

There are several issues raised with respect to the County NatWest case.

1. The Chinese walls (erected to prevent sensitive information flowing between the departments or firms) failed because information passed from the corporate finance division of CNW to the market makers at CNWS. Firewalls (legal restrictions placed on information flows and financial transactions between subsidiaries, branches, departments or other firms) also failed under pressure. For example, the secret indemnity with UBS (possibly CNWS), the possible violation of the Companies Act – see below – and the failure of the parent, NatWest, to act when it was aware of financial malpractice by at least one of its subsidiaries. CNW also manipulated the markets by getting other players to purchase shares, to make the share issue appear successful.
2. The UK Companies Act requires public disclosure if one firm owns more than 5% of the shares of another firm. Including shareholdings by CNW's private clients, NatWest's exposure exceeded 5%.
3. The parent, National Westminster Bank, was aware of financial malpractice in CNW, one of its subsidiaries, but failed to take action.
4. The Bank of England failed to query the UBS indemnity, and showed signs of *regulatory capture/forbearance*[35] because it was prepared to allow National Westminster Bank to conduct its own internal enquiry.

National Westminster Bank was purchased by the Royal Bank of Scotland group in March 2000.

# 1.6.  Central Banking

Though most central banks began life as commercial banks with responsibility for special tasks (such as note issue), the modern central bank is a government institution and does not compete with banks operating in the private banking sector. Two key debates dominate

---

[35] In the NatWest incident, the taxpayer did not fund any of the cash injections.

the central banking literature. The first relates to the functions of the central bank, the second to the degree of autonomy enjoyed by it.

Modern central banks are normally responsible for monetary control and, in addition, may be involved in prudential regulation and placing government debt on the most favourable terms possible. These three functions are now considered in more detail.

### 1.6.1. Monetary Control or Price Stability

A country's money supply is defined as currency in circulation outside the banking system plus deposits held at banks.[36] Banks play an important role in creating money, but so does the money supply. Banks create money by lending out deposits, hence their activities can affect the central bank. The *traditional* methods[37] for controlling the money supply include the following.

1. Open market operations: traditionally, this was done by buying and selling gilts (UK government Treasury bills) but since 1996, the Bank of England has also used gilt *repos*, i.e., a gilt sale and repurchase agreement – the Bank of England sells a gilt with an agreement to buy back the gilt at a specified date, at an agreed rate of interest.

2. Buying or selling securities in the financial market: this causes the monetary base (the quantity of notes and coins in circulation plus the quantity held by the banking system) to be affected. For example, if the Bank of England prints new money to purchase government securities (a Treasury bill or more recently a repo), then the monetary base will increase. Most of it will be deposited in the banking system, which the commercial banks, in turn, lend out.[38] Or, if the bank sells government securities, the monetary base is reduced.

3. Reserve ratios: in some countries, banks are required to hold a certain fraction of deposits as cash reserves, and the central bank can influence the money supply. If the reserve ratio is raised, it means banks have to reduce their lending, so the money supply is reduced. This method was standard procedure until the 1980s, and was designed to encourage banks to reduce their amount of credit. In most western countries, the reserve ratio is no longer used as a key monetary tool. For example, in the UK, the reserve ratio in 1971 was 12.5% but in 1981, the government abandoned its use as a means of controlling the growth of credit. It was replaced by a cash ratio, the sole purpose of which is to finance the operations of the Bank of England, and that is currently 0.15%[39] of eligible liabilities for all credit UK institutions.

4. Discount rate: the rate charged to commercial banks when they want to borrow money from the central bank. Again, by raising the discount rate above the general

---

[36] The term "bank" used here refers to any financial institution authorised to hold deposits. In the UK it will include banks, building societies, investment banks, and so on.

[37] These methods were practised in industrialised countries up to the mid-1980s, but have been largely abandoned. In some developing economies, they are still used.

[38] A bank will loan out a large percentage in deposits, holding only a fraction of deposits on reserve. This action, in turn, increases the money supply via the money market multiplier. See any good introductory text or dictionary of economics for a detailed explanation.

[39] This system of raising funds for the Bank of England was formalised in the 1998 Banking Act; eligible liabilities are not defined, except to say they can be in sterling or foreign currencies.

market interest rate, it is more expensive for commercial banks to borrow in the event that withdrawals suddenly rise. The banks hold more cash in reserves to avoid the "penal rate", which again reduces the money supply because it means fewer deposits are loaned out.

Thus, a central bank can stabilise the price level by the exercise of monetary policy, through control of the money supply and/or the use of interest rates. By the late 1970s and early 1980s, many governments singled out price stability as the key objective of the central bank. Some central banks were given a zero inflation target, or more commonly a range of acceptable inflation rates. For example, in the UK, the Bank of England, through its powerful Monetary Policy Committee, is required to exercise monetary control to meet an inflation rate target of 2.5% plus or minus 1%. Some bank governors (e.g., New Zealand) have their salaries and even job renewal dependent upon their success in meeting targets.

A simplified version of the monetarist version of the link between the money supply and inflation is summarised as follows:

$$\hat{P} = \widehat{MS} - \hat{y}$$

where $\hat{P}$ is the rate of inflation, i.e., the rate of change in the price level over a given period of time (month, year), $\widehat{MS}$ is the rate of growth in the money supply, where the money supply can be defined as "narrow" money (e.g., cash + sight deposits at banks) or "broad" money (narrow money + time deposits, CDs, etc.), and $\hat{y}$ is the rate of growth of real output (e.g., real GNP).

According to this simple equation, if the money supply growth rate exceeds the growth rate of national output, then inflation results. The version can be made more complex by, for example, adding the velocity of money (the number of times money turns over in a given year), but the above is a fairly good representation of the basic ideas. In the 1980s, most countries tried to target the money supply growth rate to match the growth rate in output, but when this largely failed to control inflation, policymakers switched their focus to the interest rate.[40] If the central bank believes the economy is beginning to overheat or will do so in the near future, it will raise a base interest rate, or reduce rates if it concludes the opposite. The change in the base rate is expected to be passed on, via the banking system, to consumers and producers, in the form of higher retail and wholesale rates. By raising (lowering) the interest rate, aggregate demand is reduced (raised) which, in turn, reduces/raises the rate of inflation.

It is fairly straightforward to extend this simple model to include exchange rates. Define $\hat{e} > 0$ as the rate of depreciation in a country's exchange rate. Then:

$$\hat{e} = \hat{P} - \widehat{P*}$$

where $\widehat{P*} > 0$ is the rate of inflation for a country's major trading partners. The home country's exchange rate will depreciate if the rate of inflation at home is greater than the

---

[40] Japan and Germany (until it became part of the European Monetary Union) employed both monetary targets and the interest rate.

rate of inflation for the country's major trading partners. Also, if exchange rates are fixed between countries,[41] then $\hat{e} = 0$ and all these countries must follow the same monetary policy, to produce identical inflation rates and ensure a fixed exchange rate. If one country's inflation rate (e.g., Ireland) is higher than those of the other country's, either Ireland will have to do something to remedy its inflation rate, or the other countries will have to raise theirs, since the exchange rate between these countries is fixed. This issue is at the heart of the debate about the UK joining the euro. If it were to do so, responsibility for monetary policy would shift from a directly elected government (delegated to an "independent" Bank of England) and would be set by the European Central Bank (ECB).

It must be stressed that the methods for controlling the money supply described above have been largely abandoned by countries in the developed world. In its place, most central banks have a committee that meets on a regular basis and decides what interest rate should be set to ensure the country's inflation rate meets some government target. Any change in the interest rate should affect aggregate demand, which in turn will keep inflation in check. For example, if a central bank announces a lower rate, it signals that it is trying to raise demand, in order to keep the inflation rate from falling *below* the set target. Targeting the money supply growth rate is no longer fashionable, though in some countries, notably Japan, it continues, but in addition to setting interest rates to control demand.

## 1.6.2. Prudential Control

The central bank (or another government institution – see below) is expected to protect the economy from suffering the effects of a financial crisis. It is widely accepted that the banking system has a unique position in the national economy. A widespread collapse can lead to a decline in the intermediation, money transmission and liquidity services supplied by banks, which will, in turn, contribute to an inefficient allocation of resources in the economy. There are additional macroeconomic ramifications if there is a continuous reduction in the money supply growth rate or rise in interest rates.

A bank run begins when customers withdraw their deposits because they fear the bank will fail. Immediately, the bank finds it is unable to supply one of its key services: liquidity. The banking system is particularly vulnerable to *contagion* effects: a lack of confidence associated with one poorly performing bank spreads to other, healthy, banks because agents know that once a run on deposits begins, liquidated bank assets will decline in value, so everyone will want to withdraw their deposits before the run gains any momentum. In the absence of perfect information about the quality of each bank, the sudden collapse of one bank often prompts runs on other, healthy, banks.

The vulnerability of banks to contagion creates *systemic risk*: the risk that the economic system will break down as a result of problems in the banking sector. To expand on this theme, disturbances in a financial institution or market could spread across the financial system, leading to widespread bank runs by wholesale and retail depositors, and

---

[41] Prior to the introduction of the euro in 2002, participating countries joined the European Monetary System and effectively fixed the exchange rate between countries.

possibly collapse of the banking system. This will severely hamper money transmission which, in the extreme, could cause a breakdown in the economy as it reverts to barter exchange.

The threat of contagion and systemic risk has meant governments are inclined to treat banks as special and to provide, through the central bank, *lender of last resort* or *lifeboat* facilities. By acting as lender of last resort, a central bank can supply liquidity to solvent banks threatened by contagion effects. Increasingly, central banks have pressured healthy banks to assist the bailout of troubled banks – known as a *lifeboat rescue* operation. If the central bank intervenes to assist weak or failing banks, it will be concerned as to how these banks are regulated and supervised because of the moral hazard that inevitably arises when private institutions know they have a chance of being bailed out by government funds if they encounter difficulties. Some central banks operate a "too big to fail" policy, whereby large banks are bailed out but smaller ones are left to collapse.[42] This gives all banks an incentive to expand their assets, even if it means taking very risky lenders onto their books.

## 1.6.3. Government Debt Placement

If a central bank has this responsibility, it is expected to place government debt on the most favourable terms possible. Essentially, a government can instruct the central bank to raise *seigniorage* income[43] through a variety of methods, which include a reserve ratio (requiring banks to set aside a certain percentage of their deposits as non-interest-earning reserves held at the central bank – an implicit tax), interest ceilings, issuing new currency at a rate of exchange that effectively lowers the value of old notes, subsidising loans to state owned enterprises and/or allowing bankrupt state firms that have defaulted (or failed to make interest payments) on their loans to continue operating. Or, the inflationary consequences of an ongoing liberal monetary policy will reduce the *real value* of government debt.

This third objective is important in emerging markets, but by the close of the 20th century had become less critical than the other two functions in the industrialised world, where policies to control government spending reduced the amount of government debt to place. Recently however, surpluses have turned into deficits in key economies: Japan, the USA and the UK. In emerging markets, central banks are usually expected to fulfil all three objectives – ensuring financial and price stability, and assisting the government in the management of a sizeable government debt. While all three are critical for the development of an efficient financial system, the central banks of these countries face an immense task, which they are normally poorly equipped to complete because of inferior technology and chronic shortages of well-trained staff.

The Bank of England had a long tradition of assuming responsibility for all three functions, but in 1997 the Chancellor of the Exchequer announced the imminent separation of the

---

[42] Banks are classified as "too big to fail" if the cost of disruption to or even collapse of the financial system is considered higher than the cost of bailing it out.

[43] Income earned through, for example, printing money.

three functions, leaving the Bank of England with responsibility over monetary policy the FSA[44] regulates financial institutions, including consumer protection and prudential control of the banking sector. The Japanese government created the Financial Supervisory Agency in 1997, to supervise banks and other financial institutions. Part of the Prime Minister's office, this Agency has taken over the job previously undertaken by the Ministry of Finance and Banking of Japan.

The United States assigns responsibility for prudential regulation to several organisations including the Federal Reserve, Comptroller of the Currency and the Federal Deposit Insurance Corporation. The Federal Reserve also sets an independent monetary policy. Until France became part of Euroland, the 20 000 plus employees of the Banque du France played a dual role: implementing monetary policy and regulating/supervising the banking system. In Germany, since the advent of the euro, the Bundesbank has lost its raison d'être, and has lobbyied hard to assume a regulatory role.

There are potential conflicts if one institution is responsible for the three objectives of price stability, prudential regulation and government debt placement. Given the inverse relationship between the price of bonds and interest rates, a central bank with control over government debt policy might be tempted to avoid raising interest rates (to control inflation) because it would reduce the value of the bank's debt portfolio. Or, it might increase liquidity to ease the placement of government debt, which might put it at odds with an inflation policy.

Consider a country experiencing a number of bank failures, which, in turn, threaten the viability of the financial system. If the central bank is responsible for the maintenance of financial stability in the economy, it may decide to inject liquidity to try and stem the tide of bank failures. It does this by increasing the money supply and/or reducing interest rates, so stimulating demand. The policy should reduce the number of bankruptcies (personal and corporate), thereby relieving the pressure on the banking system.

However, if the central bank's efforts to shore up the banking system are prolonged, this may undermine the objective of achieving price stability. Continuous expansionary monetary policy may cause inflation if the rate of growth in the money supply exceeds the rate of growth of national output. The central bank may be faced with a conflict of interest: does it concentrate on the threat to the financial system or is priority given to control of inflation? The dilemma may explain the recent trend to separate them. If the central bank is not responsible for financial stability, it can pursue the objective of price stability unhindered.

Under the Maastricht Treaty (agreed in 1991, signed in 1992), the euro is controlled by the European Central Bank, which has sole responsibility for one goal: price stability.

---

[44] Responsibility for the regulation of banks and other financial institutions was given to the newly formed Financial Services Authority, bound by the Financial Services and Markets Act (2000). The 1998 Bank of England Act makes the Bank responsible for price stability but also has a division focused on the reduction of systemic risk and undertaking official operations to prevent contagion. A Memorandum of Understanding (Appendix 5 of the 1998 Act) makes the Bank of England, the FSA and the Treasury jointly responsible for financial stability. The 1998 Act also transfers responsibility for the management of government debt from the Bank of England to an executive agency of government, the Debt Management Office. Treasury officials set the agenda for the Chief Executive of the DMO in the annual Debt Management Report. See Blair (1998).

However, if a central bank is the ultimate source of liquidity it must, even if only indirectly, play a role in the regulation and supervision of banks. Consider the position of the European Central Bank. Suppose Italian banks came under threat after EU citizens moved their deposits to what they perceived to be safer, more efficient banks offering better rates in other member states. The Italian government will have to approach the ECB for an injection of liquidity, which means the ECB will want to be involved in prudential regulation and supervision, even if these functions have been devolved to the "state" central banks.

Canada and the USA are examples of countries with long histories where responsibility for monetary control lies with the Bank of Canada and the Federal Reserve Board, respectively. As noted above, the supervisory function is shared among several agencies in the USA, including the Federal Reserve. In Canada, the Superintendent of Financial Institutions has responsibility for inspection and regulation. The Bank of Canada is responsible for monetary control. However, in every instance where a bank has been threatened with failure, the Bank of Canada has taken part in the decision about whether it should be supported or allowed to fail. So even in a country where the monetary and supervisory functions are officially separate, the central bank plays a pivotal role in the event of problem banks.

A study by Goodhart and Schoenmaker (1995) looked at the arguments for and against the separation of monetary policy from supervision. They could not find overwhelming support for either approach, consistent with their finding that of the 26 countries examined, about 50% assign the functions to separate bodies. Since the research was published, several countries have changed policy and the computations would show the majority separate the two responsibilities. Nonetheless, given the current trends, it is interesting that neither model was found to be superior.

Another key issue is the extent to which central banking is given independence from government. There is a general view that an independent central bank, unfettered by government directives, can better achieve the goal of price stability. For a government, the control of inflation will be one of several macroeconomic objectives; others are unemployment and balance of trade or exchange rate concerns. If a government decides that the rate of unemployment must be brought down because it is unacceptably high, one option is to stimulate the economy through lower interest rates, which, in turn, has implications for future inflation. It is argued that the goal of price stability requires a long-term, reputable commitment to monetary control, which is at odds with the short-term concerns of politicians. Inflation targets, etc., are seen as more credible if a central bank, independent of government interference, is given sole responsibility for price stability.

In countries where the central bank is independent, the government cannot use it in the manner described above. Under the 1998 Bank of England Act, the Bank acquired some degree of independence from the Treasury over monetary policy. The Act created the Monetary Policy Committee, consisting of the Governor, two deputies and two senior Bank employees. The Bank does not enjoy full autonomy because the Treasury appoints the four outside experts and approves all members of the Monetary Policy Committee. The target inflation rate (currently 2.5%), which the MPC must meet, is also set by the Treasury. The Governor is obliged to write to the Chancellor of the Exchequer if the target is not met, give or take 1%.

The Bank of Japan Act (April 1998) granted the Bank independence to a degree;[45] it has sole responsibility for ensuring price stability. The Governor, Vice-Governor and Policy Board are appointed by Cabinet, but it cannot dismiss them. The final decision on monetary policy is taken by the Policy Board, though in a country of deflation, it has no inflation targets *per se* to meet. The once powerful Ministry of Finance and Economic Planning Agency no longer has members on the Policy Board, but their representatives can express opinions at meetings.

Independence is also an issue if a country is committed to a regime of fixed, managed or targeted exchange rates. It is the central bank that buys or sells foreign currency on behalf of a government committed to, say, a quasi-fixed exchange rate, only allowing fluctuation within a narrow band. In this situation, the central bank (or banks) will be trading against the market – trying to restore the value of a currency threatened with depreciation or appreciation. While the central bank or the coordinated efforts of several central banks might be able to stabilise a currency in the short term, the position cannot be sustained indefinitely. Attempts to shore up a currency may also come into direct conflict with monetary policy, as was illustrated earlier. Under a fixed exchange rate regime, the central bank will find its monetary policy is dependent on the monetary regimes (and inflation rates) of other key economies.

## 1.7. Summary: Why are Banks Special?

A key objective of the preceding sections of this chapter has been to identify the key features of banks, with an emphasis on the reasons why banks differ from other financial institutions. Before moving on to related topics, it is worth summarising the main reasons why banks are special. First and foremost, unlike other financial firms, they act as intermediaries between borrowers and lenders and, in so doing, offer a unique form of asset transformation. Second, liquidity is an important service offered to customers. A byproduct of intermediation is participation in the payments system. Finally, banks play an important role in the macroeconomy, and have a special relationship with the central bank because the process of lending creates money.

Before moving on to Chapter 2, it is important to credit the authors responsible for developing the ideas discussed in earlier sections. Only the key contributors are cited here; readers wanting a more complete list are referred to comprehensive reviews by Baltensperger (1980) and Santomero (1984).

---

[45] By the 1998 legislation, the Bank of Japan's enjoys a qualified independence, because:

- The MoF is responsible for the maintenance of currency stability.
- The Finance Minister has the right to approve the Bank of Japan's budget; and the BJ's semi-annual report is sent to the Diet but via the MoF.
- The Finance Minister can require the BJ to make loans to troubled banks and other financial institutions.

As early as 1888, Edgeworth identified the distinguishing feature of banks: holding less than 100% of deposits as reserves, and making a profit from the positive margin arising from the difference between loan and deposit rates. According to Edgeworth, since the optimal level of reserves grows less than proportionately to deposits, larger banks (measured by deposits) will be more profitable than smaller banks. The outcome is an imperfectly competitive market structure, meaning banks could exert monopoly power. These themes were later formalised by Klein (1971) and Monti (1972). Sealey (1983) showed banks earned monopoly rents because their charters gave them the right to issue sight deposits. The emphasis was on the intermediary function, with little attention paid to price or credit risk. The view was that by borrowing short and lending long, in an environment where interest rates were steady, banks incurred little in the way of credit risk. Tobin (1963) was one of the first to question this view, though his main contribution was describing the role of banks in a macroeconomic setting.

Leland and Pyle (1977), Campbell and Kracaw (1980) and Diamond (1984) formally extended the intermediary function of the bank as information gatherer and monitor. Firms were able to raise finance through loans, and this finance was not, in many cases, available on organised (e.g., bond) markets, because of high verification, monitoring and enforcement costs. Banks were specialists in credit risk analysis, and the internalised information meant they could profit from informational economies of scale (Lewis, 1991). Fama (1985) also identified the unique nature of bank loans, and the bank's need for inside information on a firm to effectively monitor the borrower. As was mentioned earlier, Stiglitz and Weiss (1988) showed that bank loans can convey important signals to the organised markets about the creditworthiness of the firm, which could help the firm raise external finance via bonds or an initial public offering.

The main contribution by Diamond and Dybvig (1983) and Gorton (1988), among others, was to recognise that in the presence of asymmetric information, banks may be inherently unstable. If deposits are paid on demand, any market view that a bank's assets are unsound can precipitate a bank run, which spreads to healthy banks. As was noted earlier in this chapter, if banks are unable to offer a core service, liquidity, they can quickly become insolvent.

Fama (1980, 1985) focused on the assets side of banking and portfolio management: banks that acquire a risky asset portfolio need to generate the expected returns to finance monitoring costs and benefit from a diversified portfolio. More generally, in addition to taking deposits, banks could profit by diversifying risk to earn significant returns through diversified capital investments.

Though Klein (1971), Monti (1972) and others developed monopolistic models of bank behaviour, the approach was criticised for its failure to incorporate the production or supply side of banking. In response, Niehans (1978) used a production function where the volume of loans and deposits depends on factor inputs (capital and labour) together with the interaction between resource costs and factors influencing a bank's portfolio choices. Baltensperger (1980) also explores this idea, building upon earlier contributions by Pesek (1970) and Sealey and Lindley (1977), among others.

The introduction of government-backed deposit insurance to discourage bank runs alters the incentives of banks, to the detriment of the taxpayer. In the presence of less than perfect information about loans and other assets acquired by banks, deposit insurance (and lender of last resort/lifeboat facilities) creates moral hazard problems and encourages banks to assume a riskier portfolio than they otherwise would. Risk is underpriced in a system backed by explicit or implicit guarantees; points argued by, among others, Benston *et al.* (1986) and Kane (1985). Hence the need for regulation, which the banking sector will accept, provided the benefits of mispricing outweigh the cost of compliance – see Buser *et al.* (1981).

In the 19th century, Thornton (1802) distinguished between credit and money, and Keynes (1930) highlighted their importance in a macroeconomy, showing the role of banks in relation to monetary policy. Gurley and Shaw (1956), Pesek and Saving (1969) and Tobin (1963) extended these themes. By the 1950s, the role of banks in the creation of money had become standard fare in introductory economic textbooks.

## 1.8. Conclusion

The main purpose of this chapter has been to review the traditional model of the bank. Banks are distinguished from other financial firms by the intermediary and payments functions they perform. The organisational structure of banks is consistent with Coase's classic analysis of the firm, and extensions of these ideas by authors such as Alchian, Demsetz and Williamson. Information plays an important role in banking; the presence of information costs helps to explain why banks act as intermediaries. Asymmetry of information gives rise to adverse selection and moral hazard, and the classic principal–agent problem between depositors and shareholders and a bank, and the bank and its officers and debtors.

After a review of payments systems and related technology, section 1.3 identified the main organisational structures of banks, including universal and restricted universal banks, holding companies and the difference between commercial (wholesale and retail) and investment banking. The growth of financial conglomerates was also discussed. It was noted that the US banking system has a structure quite unique to the western world, and as will be shown in Chapter 5, is largely the product of the statutes passed by Congress to regulate the banking sector.

Section 1.6 introduced central banking, explaining the link between a country's private banks and the central bank. The various functions of the central bank were reviewed. Concepts such as bank runs and contagion were introduced, in relation to the need for a central bank to provide liquidity when banking systems are threatened. These terms receive more detailed attention in Chapters 4 and 8. Also discussed were the important issues of central bank independence from government, and allocation of responsibility for the prudential regulation of banks to an agency that is separate from the central bank.

In this chapter different types of banking structure, such as universal, commercial and investment banking, were introduced, along with a discussion of the growth of financial conglomerates. These topics prepare the ground for Chapter 2, which looks at the diversification of banking activities. By the end of the 20th century, all but the smaller or specialised banks expanded into other financial activities, while continuing to offer the core banking functions. Chapter 2 also reviews aspects of international financial markets and the growth of international banking. The final section considers the thorny issue of whether the growth of information technology and other developments threaten the very nature of banking.

# DIVERSIFICATION OF BANKING ACTIVITIES

## 2.1. Introduction

In the 21st century, banks remain a central component of well-developed financial markets, though, as was noted in Chapter 1, some banks have expanded their activities beyond the traditional core functions. The banking sector normally consists of specialist banks operating in niche markets, and generalist banks offering a wide range of banking and other financial products, such as deposit accounts, loan products, real estate services, stockbroking and life insurance. For example, "private bankers" accept deposits from high net worth individuals and invest in a broad range of financial assets. Modern investment banks have a relatively small deposit base but deal in the equity, bond and syndicated loan markets. Universal banks, even the restricted form, offer virtually every financial service, from core banking to insurance. This chapter begins with a review of the diversification of banks into non-banking financial activities. There has also been a rapid growth of *global banking* activities, international extensions of the core banking functions discussed in Chapter 1. Section 2.4 reviews trends in the international trade of banking services and multinational banks. Section 2.5 looks at the performance of the banking sector and considers the key issues facing banks in the new century. Section 2.6 concludes.

## 2.2. The Expansion of Banks into Non-banking Financial Services

While Chapter 1 focused on the core banking functions, this section looks at the growing diversification of banks. Of course, many of the savings banks or small British building societies continue to focus mainly on the core banking activities. However, the norm is for the key 5 to 10 banks in any western country[1] to be diversified financial institutions, where traditional wholesale and retail banking are important divisions, but a wide range of financial services are also on offer. For example, universal banks, even if in the restricted form, offer virtually every other financial service, from core banking to insurance.

*Non-bank financial services* include, among others, unit trusts/mutual funds, stockbroking, insurance, pension fund or asset management, and real estate services. Customers demand a bundle of services because it is more convenient to obtain them in this way. For example,

---

[1] The US banking system is different; a point noted in chapter one. However, the top 20 or so US banks (in terms of tier one capital or assets) have also diversified.

buying a basket of financial services from banks helps customers overcome information asymmetries that make it difficult to judge quality. A bank with a good reputation as an intermediary can use it to market other financial services. Thus, some banks may be able to establish a competitive advantage and profit from offering those services.

Most banks are also active in *off-balance sheet* (OBS) business to enhance their profitability. OBS instruments generate fee income and are therefore typical of the financial products illustrated in Figure 1.2, and do not appear as assets or liabilities on the traditional bank balance sheet. Some OBS products have been offered by banks for many years. They include, among others, credit cards, letters of credit,[2] acceptances, the issue of securities (bonds, equity), operation of deposit box facilities, acting as executor of estates, fund management, global custody and sales of foreign exchange. In addition, over the last 20 years, an increasing number of banks have been using or advising on the use of derivatives and securitisation.

## 2.2.1. Derivatives

The rapid growth of OBS activities of major global banks increased from the mid-1980s onward, largely due to the expansion of the derivatives markets and securitisation. Derivatives are briefly described here, but covered in more detail in Chapter 3. The growth of global banking and other financial markets exposed investors and borrowers to greater currency, market and interest rate risks, among others. Derivatives, which are *contingent instruments*, enable the banker/investor/borrower to hedge against some of these financial risks. Their growth has been phenomenal. They increased 13-fold between 1980 and 2000, at an average annual rate of 29.4%, though the growth rate had slowed to about 10% per annum by the new century.

A *derivative* is a contract that gives one party a contingent claim on an underlying asset (e.g., a bond, equity or commodity), or on the cash value of that asset, at some future date. The other party is bound to meet the corresponding liability. The key derivatives are futures, forwards, swaps and options, which are defined in Chapter 3. Table 2.1 shows that in 1988, outstanding traded derivatives stood at $2.6 trillion, rising to $165.6 trillion by 2002. Some of these derivatives are traded on organised exchanges, such as the London International Financial and Futures Exchange (LIFFE), the Chicago Board of Options Exchange, the Chicago Mercantile Exchange, the Philadelphia Board of Trade, the Sydney Futures Exchange or the Singapore Monetary Exchange. All *organised exchanges* have clearing houses, which guarantee the contract between the two parties; traders must be members of the clearing house. In the early years (1988) about half the derivatives were traded on organised exchanges, compared to just over 14% in 2002, testifying to the phenomenal growth in the over the counter market.

*Over the counter* (OTC) instruments are tailor-made for particular clients. In 1988, the size of the exchange traded and OTC markets was about the same. By 2002, OTC instruments accounted for about 86% ($141.7 trillion) of the total derivatives market. Note how interest rate contracts (swaps, options and forward rate agreements) are the predominant OTC contract. In 2001, interest rate options overtook interest rate futures as the leading exchange traded derivative.

---

[2] An undertaking by the bank that it will meet the obligations of the agent carrying the letter of credit should that agent fail to pay for goods or services, etc.

Table 2.1    The Size of the Global Derivatives Market

| | Notional Principal Outstanding (US$bn) | | | | | | | |
|---|---|---|---|---|---|---|---|---|
| | 1988 | 1990 | 1995 | 1998 | 1999 | 2000 | 2001 | 2002 |
| *Exchange-Traded Instruments* | | | | | | | | |
| Interest rate futures | 895 | 1 455 | 5 876 | 8 031 | 7 925 | 7 908 | 9 265 | 9 951 |
| Interest rate options | 279 | 595 | 2 742 | 4 624 | 3 756 | 4 734 | 12 493 | 11 760 |
| Currency futures | 12 | 17 | 34 | 32 | 37 | 74 | 66 | 47 |
| Currency options | 48 | 57 | 120 | 49 | 22 | 21 | 27 | 27 |
| Stock market index futures | 27 | 69 | 172 | 292 | 344 | 377 | 342 | 334 |
| Stock market index options | 43 | 94 | 338 | 908 | 1522 | 1163 | 1605 | 1755 |
| Total | 1 304 | 2 286 | 9 282 | 13 936 | 13 606 | 14 278 | 23 798 | 23 874 |
| *Over-the-Counter Instruments* | | | | | | | | |
| Foreign exchange contracts[a] | 320 | 1 138 | 1 197 | 18 011 | 14 344 | 15 666 | 16 748 | 18 469 |
| Interest rates contracts[b] | 1 010 | 2 312 | 16 516 | 50 015 | 60 091 | 64 668 | 77 568 | 101 699 |
| Equity-linked contracts[c] | – | – | – | 1 488 | 1 809 | 1 891 | 1 881 | 2 309 |
| Commodity contracts[d] | – | – | – | 415 | 548 | 662 | 598 | 923 |
| Other | – | – | – | 10 389 | 11 408 | 12 313 | 14 384 | 18 337 |
| Total | 1 330 | 3 450 | 17 713 | 80 318 | 88 202 | 95 199 | 111 178 | 141 737 |
| Overall total: | 2 634 | 5 736 | 26 995 | 94 254 | 101 808 | 109 477 | 134 976 | 165 611 |

[a] Includes outright forward and forex swaps, currency swaps and currency options.

[b] Includes forward rate agreements, interest rate swaps and interest rate options.

[c] Includes equity-linked forwards, swaps and options.

[d] Includes gold and other commodities forwards, swaps and options.

*Sources*: http://www.bis.org/statistics/derstats.htm (table 23A); BIS (1996) 64th Annual Report p. 112; BIS (1999) 69th Annual Report p. 132; BIS (June 2001) Quarterly Review, p. 89; BIS (June 2003) Quarterly Review, p. 99.

Derivatives can be used to hedge against financial risks and are an important part of banks' risk management techniques, thereby enhancing profitability and shareholder value-added. Derivatives may also assist the bank to meet capital standards and avoid regulatory taxes, which stem from reserve requirements and deposit insurance levies. A bank may also give clients advice on the use of (or arrange) derivatives to hedge risks in their portfolio.

The other side of hedging is speculation on the derivatives market, with features typical of speculation on any market. One concern is the absence of a clearing house in the OTC markets, which could be a source of financial instability. The Group of 30[3] has singled out the risks arising from OTC instruments, and called for self-regulation, with member banks adhering to guidelines on the role of senior management, the way risk is valued and measured, and satisfactory systems for operations, accounting procedures and disclosure. These issues receive a more detailed treatment in Chapter 3.

## 2.2.2. Securitisation

The growth of securitisation has also been very rapid. The term includes the issue of bonds, commercial paper and the sale of asset backed securities. Banks are usually involved in these securities issues, but play an indirect role, unlike the direct intermediation identified as a core banking activity.

### Bonds and commercial paper

A bond is an agreement to pay back a specified sum by a certain date. Short-term bonds have a maturity of up to 5 years, a medium-term bond matures in 5–15 years, while long bonds mature after 15 years or even longer, such as the 30-year US Treasury bonds. Bonds can be placed privately – sold privately to a group of professional investors. It is common for a bonds issue to be handled by a syndicate of banks, with one bank acting as lead manager. For a fee (since they incur the risk that investors don't buy the bond), the banks underwrite the placement of the bond on the market. Government bonds are often sold by auction. For example, the Ministry of Finance auctions 60% of government bond issues in Japan.

Bonds can also be issued by corporations, largely in the USA, where the market is very large. There is a weaker tradition of bond issues in Europe, though the market is growing. If the bond is backed by security, it is known as a *debenture*, and a *convertible bond* is one that can be converted into another instrument (e.g., another type of bond or equity). In Japan, the falling stock market (since 1990) has meant bonds issued in 1990, to be converted 10 years later, face a situation where the conversion price is higher than the current share price. *Foreign bonds* are issued by non-residents. For example, if a US company issues a bond in the Australian market. They differ from *eurobonds*, which are issued by some firms but in a market outside the country where the firm is headquartered. For example, a US firm with headquarters in Miami may issue dollar bonds on the London market. *Junk or high yield bonds* originated in the United States in the 1970s. They consist of bonds with a

---

[3] The Group of 30 is a private organisation of senior members from banks, academia and government, concerned with improving the understanding of global economic issues. See Group of 30 (1993, 1994).

credit rating of less than BBB. They were used to fund some hostile takeovers in the United States, but the market collapsed in 1990, and again after the Asian crises and Russian default (1997, 1998). They continue to be issued from time to time.

**Commercial paper**, as the Goldman Sachs case study shows, dates back to the 1800s. Corporations issue a promissory note, which agrees to repay the bearer at some specified date in the future. The USA has outstanding commercial paper issues of more than $1 trillion, but they have only been issued in European countries since the 1980s, and the size of the market is much smaller, amounting to about $17 billion in the UK.

## Asset Backed Securities

The issue of asset backed securities is the process whereby traditional bank assets (for example, mortgages) are sold by a bank to a trust or corporation, which in turn sells the assets as securities. The bank could issue a bond with the pooled assets acting as collateral, but the credit rating of the bank is assigned to the new security, the proceeds of the bond are subject to reserve requirements, and the assets are included in any computation of the bank's capital ratio.

The bank can avoid these constraints if a separate entity is established (special purpose vehicle, SPV, or trust). The bank sells the asset pool to the SPV, which pays for the assets from the proceeds of the sale of securities. Effectively, while the process commences in an informal market (the bank locates borrowers and makes the loans), asset backed securitisation means a large number of homogeneous loans (in terms of income streams, maturity, credit and interest rate risks) are bundled together and sold as securities on a formal market.

The process involves the following steps.

- **Origination**: Locating the customer, usually via the bank.
- **Credit analysis**: Estimating the likelihood of the potential borrower paying off the loan.
- **Loan servicing**: Ensuring the debt and interest is paid off on time by the agreed schedule, i.e., enforcing the loan contract.
- **Credit support**: In the event of the debtor encountering difficulties, deciding whether the loan should be called or the debtor given a grace period until he/she can pay.
- **Funding**: Loans themselves must be financed, usually through reliance on retail/wholesale deposits, or in the case of finance companies, borrowing from banks.
- **Warehousing**: Ensuring loans with similar characteristics (e.g., risk, income streams) are in the same portfolio.

Many of the above functions continue to be performed by the bank. However, the portfolio of loans is sold to a special purpose vehicle (trust or corporation), which engages an investment banker (for a fee) to sell them as securities. Assets are moved off-balance sheet *provided* a third party assumes the credit risk. Also, manufacturing firms with their own finance companies (e.g., General Electric, General Motors and Ford) offer loans which they securitise. Some banks have dropped out of the auto loan market because they cannot obtain a large enough interest rate spread to stay in business.

Banks undertake asset backed securitisation for a number of reasons. First, they can reduce the number of assets on the balance sheet and so boost their risk assets ratio or

Basel capital ratio,[4] *provided* the credit risk is passed to a third party. If a bank continues to have recourse in the process of securitising assets, then regulators will require them to hold capital against the credit risk exposure of the OBS item. A problem could arise if low-risk assets are securitised, which, in turn, could lower the quality of a bank's balance sheet. However, Obay (2000), based on a 1995 comparison of 95 securitising banks matched with 105 non-securitising banks, could find no evidence to support the idea that banks securitise their best assets, thereby reducing the quality of the loan book. Thus, the riskiness of loan portfolios does not increase among the securitising banks. Obay also found that banks engaging in securitisation have significantly lower risk-based capital ratios, which is consistent with one motive behind securitisation by banks: it helps them comply with the Basel capital ratio standards.

Second, asset backed securitisation raises liquidity because it frees up funding tied to existing loans, thereby allowing new loans to be funded. An extreme case is that of the troubled Bank of New England, which sold its credit card receivables to raise liquidity and prevent closure.[5] Third, assets are made more marketable, because they can be traded on secondary markets, unlike assets on a bank's balance sheet which are not traded.

Finally, securities issues based on an asset pool often have a higher credit rating than the bank holding them as loans. For example, banks often hold US government backed or US government agency backed securities because it lowers their Basel capital requirement.

In the USA (Obay, 2000), securitisation is concentrated among a relatively small number of US banks – the top 200 commercial banks accounted for 85% of securitisation in 1995. Of these, five banks were involved in 60% of the securitised assets.[6] Of securitised assets in the USA, 25% are credit card receivables.

## Mortgage Backed Securities

The Federal National Mortgage Association (Fannie Mae) was set up in 1948 by the government to encourage home ownership in the United States. Fannie Mae supported saving and loans banks (S&Ls)[7] in the USA, by buying mortgages which local (but federally chartered) S&Ls could not fund through deposits. In 1968, the organisation was split into Fannie Mae and Ginnie Mae (the Government National Mortgage Corporation). Ginnie Mae is a wholly owned corporation of US government departments. It claims to have introduced the first mortgage backed security (MBS) in 1970. Though shareholder-owned, Fannie Mae is a US government-related agency, along with Freddie Mac (the Federal Home Loan Mortgage Corporation), also created in 1970. Their respective charters do not say the US government guarantees their debt but as government-sponsored enterprises, they can expect to be bailed out.

[4] The Basel risk assets ratio is defined as (tier 1 + tier 2 capital)/assets weighted for their risks. Tier 1 capital is equity plus disclosed reserves; tier 2 capital is all other capital. International banks are asked to meet a minimum capital ratio of 8%, that is, to back every £100, £8.00 of capital is set aside. The riskier the asset, the higher the weight, and the more capital is needed to back it. For a detailed discussion, see Chapter 4.
[5] The bank failed in 1991. See Chapter 7.
[6] These were MBNA America, Citibank Nevada (a subsidiary of Citigroup), Greenwood Trust, First USA and South Dakota bank.
[7] Created as part of Roosevelt's New Deal.

Fannie Mae and Freddie Mac share the same charters and regulation but claim to compete with each other and to have separate business strategies. These government agencies are subject to a number of restrictions. Mortgages must be for residential property and may not exceed a limit of up to $332 700. Freddie and Fannie are prohibited from originating mortgages – they must buy them from banks and S&Ls.

After the 1970 issue, MBSs grew rapidly. Currently they hold or guarantee nearly half the US outstanding residential mortgages, and have close to $3 trillion in liabilities.[8] Their success encouraged financial institutions to securitise commercial mortgages, mobile home loans, credit card receivables, car loans, computer and truck leases, and trade receivables.

## Collateralised Mortgage Obligations

CMOs originated in the USA in 1983 after they were introduced by First Boston and The Federal Home Mortgage Loan Corporation. They go through the same stages as MBSs (e.g., origination, pooling, placement of the pooled mortgages with a SPV, etc.) until the security reaches the investment bank. Instead of selling the MBS/ABS to investors, the investment bank places the security as collateral in a trust, and, essentially, splits it, offering groups of investors a series of tranches (a portion of the payments) associated with the security – a CMO. Suppose the investment bank creates three tranches or investment classes. Each class has fixed coupon, which may be paid monthly, quarterly or semi-annually. In addition, the investor is holding a bond – they are owed a certain amount. Mortgagees in the pool pay their monthly principal and interest, but there will always be some who unexpectedly prepay (or default on) the full amount of the mortgage. The investment bank issuing the CMO will pay out the interest owed to the first group, plus all the principal paid by the mortgagees, including those who have prepaid. The second class of investors is also paid the fixed interest owed, but does not get any of the principal until the first class has been paid in full and the bond retired. Likewise for the third tranche – no principal is repaid until the second class has been paid off in full, and the associated bond retired. The number of tranches can vary from 3 to 30. There can also be a zero or Z-tranche, where the investor is not paid interest[9] or principal until all the other classes are retired.

The CMO is an example of a **pass through security**: cash flows, interest and principal, from the underlying security (e.g., a mortgage) are passed through to the investor. There are other forms of security apart from mortgages – the generic term is collateralised debt obligation (CDO). A CDO is backed by a pool of debt obligations, such as corporate loans or structured finance obligations. Once pooled, like an MBO, they are split into a number of security tranches, and offered to different groups of investors. The performance of the underlying pool of debt obligations determines the payment of interest and principal, and when the security is actually retired. They are attractive because they offer investors a greater range of risk/return choices than the standard MBS/ABS. For example, with a MBO, the investor can choose to incur a high degree of prepayment risk (by opting for the first

---

[8] *Source*: Wallison (2003).

[9] As with the coupons in other classes, a fixed interest rate is quoted but no interest paid until all the other classes are retired.

tranche) or very little such risk (by investing in the third class). Also, an investor in the first class will find the security is retired relatively quickly, but the debt can be retired 20+ years later for the higher tranches.[10]

Other CDOs include *collateralised bond obligations* (CBOs), consisting of collateralised bonds and collateralised loan obligations (CLOs), which involve collateralised pools of corporate loans or other credit facilities. After being pooled and turned into a security, they are split into different investment classes or security tranches. The bank loans used as collateral for CLOs are typically at investment grade level, whereas the CBOs are usually a mix of investment grade and sub-investment grade, but collateralised by higher yielding securities. CLOs originated in the 1990s and consist of a pool of investment grade revolving/term loans, standby letters of credit and even derivatives. Unlike the original ABS/MBS, the components of the pool can be quite diversified, and the originator remains the owner of the underlying portfolio.

For the bank arranging them, CDOs offer a number of benefits:

- release of core capital and thus increased efficiency of the capital allocation;
- illiquid loans become liquid, tradable securities;
- investors are attracted to the bank because they can have a choice of different tranches to meet their risk/return needs.

The tables below summarise the US data for various types of securitisation.

In 2002, the outstanding volume of US agency mortgage backed securities was $3.2 trillion, compared to $1.5 trillion for US agency backed securities (excluding MBSs). These can be compared to $110.9 billion for MBSs in 1980. In 1995, US ABSs were valued

**US Asset Backed Securities, 2002**

| Type of security | Value (US$bn) | % of total |
|---|---|---|
| Credit card receivables | 397.9 | 25.8 |
| Home equity | 286.5 | 18.6 |
| Auto | 221.7 | 14.4 |
| CMO/CDO | 234.5 | 15.2 |
| Other | 215.4 | 14 |
| Student loan | 74.4 | 4.8 |
| Equipment leases | 68.3 | 4.4 |
| Total (2002) | 1543.2 | |
| Total (1995)* | 316.3 | |

* The percentage breakdown among the different ABS types was largely unchanged between 1995 and 2002.
*Source:* Bond Market Association (2003), *Bond Market Statistics* (www.bondmarkets.com).

---

[10] In the USA, a CMO with three classes: the first class bond retired in an average of 1–3 years, the third class in about 20 years. This type of CMO is typical of the US market, where mortgage interest rates are fixed and mortgagees can prepay the debt at any time, without penalty.

**Agency\* Mortgage Backed Securities ($bn)**

|      | Volume of agency MBS | Issuance of agency MBS |
| ---- | -------------------- | ---------------------- |
| 1980 | 110.9                | 45.6                   |
| 1990 | 1024.4               | 469.8                  |
| 2002 | 3156.6               | 2921.4                 |

\* Agency: Figures for GNMA, FNMA, FHMLC. *Source:* Bond Market Association (2003), *Bond Market Statistics* (www.bondmarkets.com).

**Agency\* Collateralised Mortgage Obligations ($bn)**

|      | Volume of agency CMO | Issuance of agency CMO |
| ---- | -------------------- | ---------------------- |
| 1987 | 0.9                  | 0.9                    |
| 1990 | 187.7                | 101.4                  |
| 1995 | 540.9                | 132.6                  |
| 2002 | 926.0                | 540.9                  |

\*Agency: Figures for GNMA, FNMA, FHMLC.
*Source:* Bond Market Association (2003), *Bond Market Statistics* (www.bondmarkets.com).

at $316.3 billion, rising to $1.5 trillion by 2002. Credit card receivables had 26% of the ABS market in 2002, followed by home equity (19%) and auto ABSs (14%). The market share has remained largely unchanged since 1995. The CMO market grew from $0.9 billion in 1987 to $926 billion by 2002.

Compared to the USA, the market for ABSs in Europe is relatively new and smaller.[11] In 2002, ABS issuance stood at €31.7 billion; MBS issuance was €42.5 billion. Securitised assets in the UK, with by far the largest market, was €34.5 billion, virtually all of which was MBS securities. The market leader in Europe is the *Pfandbrief*, which originated in Germany[12] – the first jumbo Pfandbrief (minimum of €500 million) was issued in 1995. Unlike the standard ABS, the Pfandbrief remains on the balance sheet of the issuing institution, and there is no prepayment risk, so the spread over a sovereign bond will be determined by credit and liquidity issues alone. There are two types, the Hypotheken or mortgage backed bonds and Offentliche or public sector bonds. Most of the jumbo Pfandbriefs are backed by public sector loans. Issues were worth €160 billion in 2002. Compare this to the value of US asset backed securities in 2002 – $1.5 trillion.[13]

---

[11] ABS issues in Australia and Japan amounted to $10 and $20 billion, respectively, in 1999, according to a Merrill Lynch report by de Pauw and Ross (2000). Although a small part of the world market share, Merrill Lynch expects these markets to continue to grow.

[12] Pfandbriefs are issued in most of the key European financial markets, including the UK, but on a much smaller scale compared to Germany.

[13] *Source:* Bondmarkets Online (2002).

One key reason for the difference in size of the American and European markets is the number of subsidies enjoyed by Ginnie Mae, Fannie Mae and Freddie Mac. First, though the government has never provided formal guarantees, the public is under the impression that their loan portfolios and MBSs enjoy implicit government guarantees. These agencies do not pay state or local income taxes, and are exempt from SEC[14] fees and disclosure requirements. Their assets receive a risk-reduced risk weighting under Basel, and these securities qualify as eligible collateral. Freddie and Fannie are regulated by the Office of Federal Housing Enterprise Oversight (OFHEO), avoiding the tough system of multiple regulation faced by banks and other financial institutions in the USA.

Fannie and Freddie argue that their large share of the MBS market has reduced mortgage rates for home owners by one-quarter to three-eighths of 1%. They purchase and hold mortgages originated by mortgage lenders and guarantee the MBSs, which are taken to be a government backed guarantee. It means they are assuming the credit risk associated with loans in the MBS and loans held in their own portfolio.

Some experts advocate the withdrawal of the *implicit* government guarantee because these agencies crowd out the private sector, tax-paying competitors. A study by the Congressional Budget Office in 2002 estimated the cost of implied government backing was about $10.6 billion per year,[15] and about 40% of this goes to the managers and shareholders of the two organisations. There are concerns over their credit and interest rate exposure, because Freddie and Fannie, recognising that the implied guarantee means they can raise finance more cheaply, have, in recent years, opted to profit from holding the high yield mortgages on their own balance sheets rather than turning them into securities and selling them on, as they have done since they were established. As a result, they hold increasing amounts of debt in their portfolio, leaving them highly exposed in the mortgage market. It is estimated that by 2003 they will carry over one-third of the related interest rate risk and three-fifths of the credit risk for the mortgages they are authorised to buy. Though derivatives are used to hedge against interest rate risk, comprehensive risk management systems were not in place until 2002. With the sharp decline in US interest rates (2002/3), the number of prepayments has soared as householders opt for a new mortgage at lower, fixed rates. This has increased the mismatch between revenue from mortgage bonds and their debt obligations.

The combined on balance sheet debt of Freddie and Fannie in 2003 was (roughly) $1.5 trillion, which puts them in the category of "too big to fail" (TBTF). US regulators can deem a bank to be a "systemic risk exception".[16] A bank is placed in this category if it is thought to pose a threat to the US financial system, and will be rescued not by taxpayers but through high risk premia paid by banks. Fannie and Freddie are not banks, so the taxpayer may be left to bail them out. Long Term Capital Management (LTCM) was a hedge fund, not a bank. Though its rescue in 1998 was organised by the Federal Reserve Bank of New York, it was the banks with a vested interest in LTCM that financed it, at

---

[14] Securities and Exchange Commission.

[15] *Source:* "Crony Capitalism", *The Economist*, 23 June 2003.

[16] Part of the Federal Deposit Insurance Corporation Improvement Act (FDICIA), passed in 1991. See Chapter 5 for more detail.

a cost of $3.6 billion. The bill will be considerably greater should Freddie and Fannie fail, and it is unclear whether any body other than the government/taxpayer will pay.

In June 2003, Congress began formal hearings on the way Freddie and Fannie are regulated. In the same month, the OFHEO replaced the entire management team at Freddie Mac after an internal audit revealed questionable practices. Serious problems in Freddie's accounting practices soon came to light. The regulator assured the public that Freddie is not in financial difficulty, but in late 2003 fined it $ 125 million, and recommended numerous changes, especially in the area of corporate governance.

As was explained at length in Chapter 1, a traditional bank acts as intermediary between depositors and lenders. As a consequence, the focus is on their banking book – management of assets and liabilities. The growth of derivatives and securitisation has expanded the intermediary role of some banks to one where they act as *intermediaries in risk management*. In subsequent chapters, it will be observed that as banks continue to find new ways of transferring their credit risk to non-banking financial institutions, the 21st century may witness further changes in the traditional lending function.

## 2.3. The Effect of Non-interest Income on Banks' Total Income

The rapid expansion of new forms of off-balance sheet activity means many banks are diversifying, and as a result, non-interest income is an increasingly important source of revenue. The ratios of net interest income and net non-interest income to gross income, for the period 1990–99, are shown in Figures 2.1 and 2.2. Looking at the averages for the

**Figure 2.1    Ratio of net interest income to gross income.**

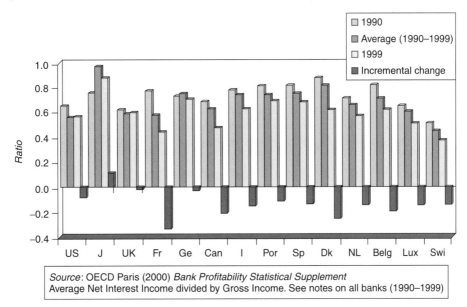

*Source*: OECD Paris (2000) *Bank Profitability Statistical Supplement*
Average Net Interest Income divided by Gross Income. See notes on all banks (1990–1999)

Figure 2.2 Ratio of non-interest income to gross income.

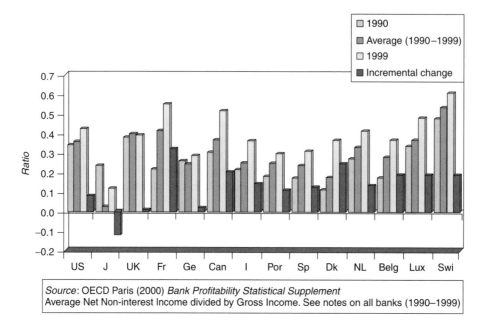

Source: OECD Paris (2000) *Bank Profitability Statistical Supplement*
Average Net Non-interest Income divided by Gross Income. See notes on all banks (1990–1999)

period, for most countries, at least two-thirds of banks' gross income comes from net interest income. Notable exceptions are Japan, where, on average, 97% of income comes from net interest income, and at the other extreme, Switzerland, where net interest income makes up only 45% of gross income. In all countries except Japan, the ratio fell over the decade, as it had in the 1980s.

As Figure 2.2 shows, the opposite is true of non-interest income, except for Japan. Japan's ratio was highly volatile through the period, reflecting the decline in share values for Japanese banks holding substantial amounts of equity. These dramatic changes explain why non-interest income is such a tiny proportion of gross income. In other countries, about one-third of gross income comes from non-interest income. There are exceptions: in Switzerland it is 55%, and about 19% in Denmark. Thus, there is a slow but steady shift towards non-interest sources of income in most countries, reflecting increased diversification as interest margins on traditional banking products narrow, and banks seek new sources of revenue.

Davis and Touri (2000) look at the changing pattern of banks' income for EU countries and the USA.[17] They report a decline in the ratio of net interest income to non-interest income for EU states, from 2.9 in 1984–87 to 2.3 in 1992–95. The respective figures for the USA are from 2.6 to 1.8. Italy is the main exception, where the ratio of net interest to non-interest income rises from 2.9 in 1984–87 to 3.7 in 1992–95. However, the source

---

[17] The study relies on two data sets: OECD data on bank profitability for banks from 28 countries in the period 1979–95 and the Fitch/IBCA Bankscope CD-ROM that provides individual bank data (e.g., balance sheet, financial ratios) for over 10 000 banks from all key industrialised countries for the period 1989–97.

of the non-interest income varies, when it is divided into fees and commissions, profit and loss from financial operations and "other". In the USA and UK, the main source (in 1995) is fees and commission. For France, Italy and Austria, the "other income" source of non-interest income is roughly as important as fees and commissions. Denmark is the only country where profit and loss from financial operations is a key source of non-interest income.[18]

An important question is whether the diversification implied by the growth of non-interest income has made banks' total income more stable, which it should be if the correlation between the two types of income sources is negative. In a recent paper, Wood and Staikouras (2004) consider this issue for EU banks. They reviewed numerous studies based on US data and concluded that they produce mixed findings. For example, Gallo *et al.* (1996) found profitability increased in those banks with a high proportion of mutual fund assets managed relative to total assets. Other studies showed diversification increased profit stability.

Sinkey and Nash (1993) showed that specialising in credit card lending (often generating fee income through securitisation) gave rise to higher but more volatile income compared to banks undertaking more conventional activities. According to Demsetz and Strahan (1995), even though bank holding companies tend to diversify as they get larger, this does not necessarily reduce risk because these firms shift into riskier activities and are more highly leveraged. Lower capital ratios, larger loan portfolios (especially in the corporate sector) and the greater use of derivatives offset the potential gains from diversification. De Young and Roland (1999) reported that as banks shift towards more fee-earning activities, the volatility of revenues, earnings and leverage increases.

Wood and Staikouras (2004) looked at a large "balanced" sample of 2655 EU credit institutions[19] for the period 1994–98. It excludes "births and deaths" and any bank that does not report data for the whole period. A larger unbalanced sample includes these other banks, and runs for the period 1992–99, with gaps in some data. Data are from commercial banks, savings banks, coops and mortgage banks (UK building societies). The authors found the composition of non-interest income to be heterogeneous, consisting of the following.

- Traditional fee income: intermediary service charges (deposit, chequing, loan arrangements), credit card fees and fees associated with electronic funds transfer, trust and fund management, and global custody services.
- Newer sources of fee income: securities brokerage, municipal securities, underwriting, real estate services, insurance activities.
- Fee income from off-balance sheet business such as loan commitments, note issuance facilities, letters of credit and derivatives.
- Management consulting.
- Data processing or more generally, back office work.
- Securitisation.
- Proprietary trading.

---

[18] See table 13 of Davis and Touri (2000).

[19] "Credit institution" is the official European Commission term given to all institutions that take deposits and make loans.

The authors reported non-interest income has increased in relative importance compared to interest income. With few exceptions, throughout the period 1994–98 there is a decrease in the level of interest income as a percentage of total assets, with a corresponding increase in non-interest income. They found the proportionate increase in non-interest income corresponded with a decline in profitability, suggesting the growth in non-interest income sources did not offset the fall in the net interest margin, and/or operating costs for the new activities were higher.

Using measures of standard deviation, Wood and Staikouras (2004) show that through the 1990s the variability of non-interest income increases. In Germany and France, non-interest income was found to be more volatile (measured by standard deviation, SD) than net interest income, but this did not appear to be the case for the other countries: Austria, Belgium, Denmark, Finland, Greece, Ireland, Italy, Luxembourg, the Netherlands, Portugal, Spain, Sweden and the UK. However, using the coefficient of variation,[20] the variability of non-interest income is almost always larger than that for net interest income.

For several countries, a positive correlation between interest and non-interest income was found, suggesting that income diversification may not result from expanding into non-interest income activities. The combined findings of a higher correlation between the two income sources, the rise in the proportion of non-interest income and the greater volatility of non-interest income suggests the diversification may have increased the overall variability of EU banks' income.

Overall, the increased emphasis on non-interest income means the operational and strategic risks of the banks will increase. Their findings support the view that there should be specific capital requirements for several categories of risk, not just credit and market risks.

Using return on equity (ROE) as the measure of profitability, Davis and Tuori (2000) show that for the EU, average bank ROE declined between 1984–87 and 1992–97, from 0.15 to 0.08. The UK bucks the EU trend (rising from 0.18 to 0.21) and ROE rises in the USA, from 0.11 to 0.20. Thus, in a period where the ratio of non-interest income to income rose, profitability has declined – the UK and the USA being notable exceptions. Davis and Touri report a negative correlation between interest and non-interest income for Germany, France, Greece and Luxembourg. For banks in these countries, it appears that diversification into non-interest income sources should help banks in periods when margins are narrow. For example, in a regime of falling interest rates, when margins tend to narrow, banks in these countries could expect to sustain profitability by selling bonds and other assets. French and German banks have substantial shareholdings in non-financial commercial concerns, and falling interest rates (when margins tend to narrow) are often associated with rising equity prices. For the EU as a whole, the correlation is positive (0.08), as it is for the UK (0.45) and USA (0.5). A correlation close to 0.5 is consistent with the Staikouras and Wood finding: diversification may well be associated with an increase in the volatility of banks' income and profits.

Econometric work by Davis and Tuori showed that for the USA, UK, Germany, Spain, Italy and Denmark, and the EU as a whole, the larger the bank, the more dependent it

---

[20] The coefficient of variation is defined as standard deviation of a distribution/mean (M), multiplied by 100, i.e. (SD/M) × (100). It is used as a measure of relative dispersion, when two or more distributions have significantly different means or they are measured in different units.

is on non-interest income. They also find a strong positive relation between non-interest income and the ratio of cost to income. The positive relationship is likely explained by the need for more highly trained, costly staff to generate non-interest income, compared to the traditional core activities.

## 2.4. Global Markets and Centres

International banking is a logical extension of domestic banking, and will include diversification away from the traditional core activities. However, before exploring this topic in detail, it is useful to provide a sketch of the international financial markets.

### 2.4.1. International Financial Markets

In economics, a market is defined as a set of arrangements whereby buyers and sellers come together and enter into contracts to exchange goods or services. An international financial market works on exactly the same principles. Financial instruments and services, which include diverse items such as currencies, private banking services and corporate finance advice, are traded internationally, that is, across national frontiers.

Below, the different types of global financial markets and key international financial centres are identified, followed by a discussion of the different ways of classifying markets, and how imperfections and trade impediments affect market operations.

Financial markets are classified by several different criteria as follows.

1. The markets are global if instruments and services are traded across national frontiers and/or financial firms set up subsidiaries or branches in different national markets. For example, while the trade in *futures* for pork bellies is global, the actual buying and selling of pork bellies themselves is likely to be confined to national or even local markets. Wholesale banking (banking services offered to the business sector) might include international trade of financial instruments on behalf of a client, or the establishment of branches and subsidiaries of the financial firm in other financial centres, to enable it to better assist home clients with global operations, and to attract new clients from the host and other countries.

2. The maturity of the instruments being traded. Maturity refers to the date when a financial transaction is completed. For example, any certificate of deposit that repays its buyer within a year is classified as a *short-term* financial instrument. If a bank agrees to an international loan to be repaid in full at some date that exceeds a year, it is a *long-term* asset for the lender; a liability for the borrower. Sometimes, an instrument is designated *medium-term* if it matures between 1 and 5 years. Short-term claims are normally traded on *money* markets, and long-term claims (bonds, equities, mortgages) are usually traded on *capital* markets.

3. Whether the instruments are primary or secondary. A primary market is a market for new issues by governments or corporations, such as bonds and equities. An example would be **initial public offerings** (IPOs) of shares in firms. Securities that have already been issued are traded on secondary markets. Financial institutions are said to be *market*

*makers* if they buy/sell ("make markets") in existing bonds, equities or other securities; they are acting as intermediaries between buyers and sellers.

4. How the instrument is traded. In the past, almost all instruments were traded in a physical location, a trading floor. However, the advent of fast computer and telephone links means almost all instruments, including derivatives, equities and bonds, are traded electronically, without a physical floor. One notable exception is the New York Stock Exchange where, through "open outcry", equities are traded on the floor of the exchange. It is also common to observe these traditional methods in some of the developing and emerging markets.

## Key international financial markets

In the new millennium, nearly all financial markets in the main industrialised economies are international. The main exceptions are retail banking markets and personal stockbroking, but even here there are some global features. Obtaining foreign exchange for holiday makers is a long-established international transaction, and now debit cards issued by banks may be used world-wide, allowing customers to withdraw cash in a local currency. Some foreign banks, if permitted by the authorities, are expanding into retail markets, though currently these institutions tend to offer a few niche products and/or target high net worth individuals. In Europe, under the Second Banking Directive (1989, effective 1993), approved credit institutions from one EU country can set up banks in any other EU state and undertake a list of approved activities they offer in their home state. In 2000, the Financial Services Action Plan was launched, to bring about the integration of financial markets by 2005. Likewise, personal customers effectively invest in foreign shares by buying or selling unit trusts (mutual funds), which include shares in foreign firms. Some financial firms hoped to use internet technology to enter established financial markets rather than physical locations or branches, but this option is proving more difficult than was first envisaged.[21]

There are several reasons why most financial markets are global. First, investors are able to spread risks by diversification into global markets to increase portfolio returns. A bigger pool of funds should mean borrowers are able to raise capital at lower costs. With an increased number of players, competition is increased. Funds can be transferred from capital-rich to capital-deficient countries. Hence, global markets bring about a more efficient distribution of capital at the lowest possible price.

At the same time, there are impediments to free trade in global financial markets – they are by no means perfect. Market imperfections are caused by the following factors.

1. Differences in tax regimes, financial reporting and accounting standards, national business cycles, and cultural and taste differences.
2. Barriers to free trade including tariffs (e.g., governments imposing higher taxes on domestic residents' income from *foreign* assets), non-tariff barriers (e.g., restricting the activities of foreign financial firms in a given country), and import or export quotas (e.g., nationals are prohibited from taking currency out of the country).

---

[21] For a more detailed discussion of the EU, see Chapter 5 .

3. Barriers to factor mobility, such as capital controls, or restrictions on the employment of foreign nationals.
4. Asymmetric information, when one party to a financial contract has more information relevant to the contract than the other agent. For example, borrowers typically have more information than lenders on their ability to repay, which can cause a bank to make inappropriate lending decisions. The problem is more pronounced in the case of foreign loans if it is more difficult to obtain information on prospective foreign borrowers. Banks try to counter the problem by restricting the size of loans, requiring a potential borrower to obtain a minimum score on a credit risk check list, and so on. More generally, the greater the transparency in a financial market, the more efficient it is. Imperfect information is a central cause of inefficient financial markets.

The main financial markets are listed below.

## Money markets (maturity of less than 1 year)

Money markets consist of the discount, interbank, certificate of deposit and local (municipal) authority and eurocurrency markets. The eurocurrency and interbank markets are wholly international, whereas the other markets listed are largely domestic. In the 1950s, the Soviet Union used the Moscow Narodny bank in London for US dollar deposits. The euromarket grew out of the eurodollar market later in the 1950s, after US regulators imposed interest rate ceilings on deposits and restrictions on US firms using dollars to fund the establishment of overseas subsidiaries. This increased the use of eurodollar deposits and loans in London, with funding from US investors wishing to escape US domestic deposit rate ceilings. Likewise, in other countries with exchange and other capital controls, eurocurrency markets were a way of getting around them. Although many of these regulations have long since been abandoned, the euromarkets continue to thrive. Interbank markets exist because, at the end of a trading day, banks may find themselves long on deposits or short on loans. The interbank market allows surplus banks to make overnight deposits at other deficit banks.

## Currency markets

The foreign exchange markets are, by definition, global, consisting of the exchange of currencies between agents. As demand for the currency rises relative to all other currencies, it is said to be appreciating in value; depreciating if the reverse is true. This topic is mentioned for completeness. It is discussed elsewhere in specialised texts and courses, and for this reason is not analysed here.

## Stock markets

Stock markets are part of the capital markets (maturity in excess of 1 year), as are the bond and mortgage markets. The mortgage market remains largely domestic and is not discussed here. Stocks purchased on these markets help diversify investor portfolios. Portfolio risk is thereby reduced, provided the correlation between stock returns of different economies is lower than that of a single country. Institutional investors and pension fund managers (if permitted), managing large funds, are likewise attracted to foreign shares.

The growth of global unit trusts or mutual funds has also increased the demand for foreign equity. Fund managers select and manage the stocks for the trust/fund, using their (supposedly) superior information sets compared to the majority of individuals. Also, transactions costs are lower than they would be with an independent set of investments.

The euroequities market has grown quite rapidly in recent years, and caters to firms issuing stocks for sale in foreign markets. Investment banks (many headquartered in New York) underwrite the issues, which, in turn, are purchased by institutional investors around the world. Secondary markets for these foreign issues normally emerge.

Firms issue equity on foreign stock markets for several reasons.

- To increase their access to funds without oversupplying the home market, which would depress the share price. Foreign investors, with a different information set to home investors, may also demand the stock more.
- To enhance the global reputation of the firm.
- To take advantage of regulatory differences.
- To widen share ownership and so reduce the possibility of hostile takeovers.
- To ensure that their shares can be traded almost continuously, on a 24-hour basis.
- Funds raised in foreign currencies can be used to fund foreign branches or subsidiaries and dividends will be paid in the currency, thereby reducing the currency exposure of a multinational enterprise.

However, foreign equity issues are not without potentially costly problems. First, foreign equity investments may expose some investors to currency risk, which must be hedged. Second, to list on a foreign exchange, a firm must comply with that country's accounting rules, and there can be large differences in accounting standards. For example, German firms have found it difficult to list and trade shares on the New York Stock Exchange because accounting rules are so different in the two countries. Attempts to agree on common accounting standards made little progress for over 30 years, but the problem may be largely resolved if new IAB standards are adopted by 2005 (see Chapter 5), which will make it much easier for firms to list on foreign exchanges. Third, governments often restrict the foreign equity share of managed funds; these regulations tend to apply, in particular, to pension funds.

With the dawn of the new century, a number of important changes are occurring in stock markets around the globe. A major change in the equity markets is the merger or alliance of stock exchanges in an attempt to offer 24-hour global trading in blue chip firms. In the United States, the trend has gone still further: electronic broker dealers have become exchanges in themselves and have applied to be regulated as such. To quote the Chairman of NASDAQ (taking its name from its parent, the National Association of Securities Dealers and the "alternative" US stock exchange for technology and new high growth firms), "*in a few years, trading securities will be digital, global, and accessible 24 hours a day*".[22] NASDAQ itself merged with the American Stock Exchange in 1998 and is also affiliated with numerous exchanges, for example, in Canada and Japan.

---

[22] *The Economist*, 3/02/01, p.102.

However, European stock exchange mergers are in a state of flux, due partly to the failure to integrate European cross-border payments and settlements systems. The cost of cross-border share trading in Europe is 90% higher than in the USA, and it is estimated that a central counterparty clearing system for equities in Europe (ECCP) would reduce transactions costs by $950 million (€1 billion) per year.[23] The cost savings would come primarily from an integrated or single back office. With a single clearing house, acting as an intermediary between buyers and sellers, netting is possible, meaning banks could net their purchases against sales, reducing the number of transactions to be settled and therefore the amount of capital to be set aside for prudential purposes. The plan is backed by the European Securities Forum, a group of Europe's largest banks.

The existence of EU state exchanges is increasingly an anachronism with the introduction of a single currency. London is in the unusual position of being the main European exchange, even though the UK is outside the eurozone. There are plans to create a pan European trading infrastructure (to include common payment and settlement facilities) for the large, most heavily traded European stocks. It would involve an alliance among the 6 key euro exchanges, together with Zurich and London.

Like the eurocurrency markets, the emergence of the **eurobond** markets was a response to regulatory constraints, especially the imposition of withholding tax on interest payments to non-resident holders of bonds issued in certain countries. For example, until 1984, foreign investors purchasing US bonds had to pay a 30 per cent withholding tax on interest payments. Financing subsidiaries were set up in the Netherlands Antilles, from which eurobonds were issued and interest payments, free of withholding tax, could be made. Investment banks are the major players in the eurobond markets. Many are subsidiaries of US commercial banks which were prohibited, until recently[24] from engaging in these activities in the USA. Normally a syndicate of investment banks underwrites these bond issues.

*Repos or repurchase agreements* have grown in popularity over the last decade. A bond or bonds are sold with an agreement to buy them back at a specified date in the near future at a price higher than the initial price of the security, reflecting the cost of funds being used, and a risk premium, should the seller default. Thus, a repo is equivalent to a collateralised loan with the securities acting as collateral but still owned by the borrower, that is, the seller of the repo.

Another important trend in the bond markets is the reduced issue of debt by key central governments, shifting borrowing activity to the private sector. It means the traditional benchmarks (e.g. government bond yields) are less important, leaving a gap which has not been filled.

## 2.4.2.  Key Financial Centres: London, New York and Tokyo

London, New York and Tokyo are the major international financial centres. Among these, London is pre-eminent, because most of the business conducted in the City of London is global. The London Stock Exchange has, since 1986, allowed investment houses based in

---

[23] *Source: The Economist*, 20/01/01, p. 90.

[24] The creation of section 20 subsidiaries and the Gramm Leach Bliley Act (1999) have partly ended the separation between US investment and commercial banks.

New York and Tokyo to trade in London, meaning one of the three exchanges can be used to trade equity on what is nearly a 24-hour market.

Compared to London, the activities of financial markets in Tokyo and New York are more domestic. Though London's falling share of traditional global intermediation is associated with the general decline in direct bank intermediation, there is a great deal of expansion in markets for instruments such as euroequities, eurocommercial paper and derivatives.

## *Competitiveness: Key Factors*

An important question is: what are the factors that make a centre competitive? A survey of experts undertaken by the CSFI (2003)[25] identified six characteristics considered important to the competitiveness of a financial centre. The score beside each attribute is based on a scale of 1 (unimportant) to 5 (very important).

- Skilled labour: 4.29
- Competent regulator: 4.01
- Favourable tax regime: 3.88
- Responsive government: 3.84
- A "light" regulatory touch: 3.54
- Attractive living/working environment: 3.5

Using the characteristics listed above, respondents were then asked to rank four centres, London, New York, Paris and Tokyo, on a scale of 1 to 5. London or New York placed first or second in all but the environment attribute, where Paris came first. From these figures it was possible to derive an index of competitiveness,[26] where 1 is least competitive and 5 is most competitive. The scores were as follows.

- New York: 3.75
- London: 3.71
- Paris: 2.99
- Frankfurt: 2.81

London comes a very close second to New York, and the slight difference is mainly due to London's third place position in terms of working/living environment. There were concerns about transport, housing and health care.

Looking at figures on market share in a number of key financial markets (Table 2.2), London appears to be a leading centre. Ignoring the "other" category, which is the rest of the world, the UK has the highest market share for most activities listed in the table, the exceptions being fund management, corporate finance and exchange traded derivatives,

---

[25] 727 questionnaires were sent out to banks, insurance firms, fund managers, professional firms and other institutions. There were 274 responses (38%) all with offices in "the City" – 55% were headquartered in other countries. For more detail on the methodology, see Appendix 1 of CSFI (2003).

[26] Once the six key characteristics were identified, respondents were asked to score each city by these features, and the scores were weighted by the importance attached to each attribute.

Table 2.2   Market share–Key Financial Markets (% share)

| % Share | UK | USA | Japan | France | Germany | Other |
|---|---|---|---|---|---|---|
| Cross-border bank lending | 19 | 9 | 9 | 6 | 10 | 47 |
| Foreign equities turnover | 56 | 25 | na | na | 5 | 36 |
| FOREX dealing | | | | | | |
| Derivatives turnover | | | | | | |
|   Exchange traded | 6 | 30 | 3 | 6 | 13 | 42 |
|   OTC | 36 | 18 | 3 | 9 | 13 | 21 |
| International bonds | | | | | | |
|   Primary | 60 | na | na | na | na | na |
|   Secondary | 70 | na | na | na | na | na |
| Insurance net premium income | | | | | | |
|   Marine | 19 | 13 | 14 | 5 | 12 | 37 |
|   Aviation | 39 | 23 | 4 | 13 | 3 | 18 |
| Fund management | 8 | 51 | 10 | 4 | 3 | 24 |
| Corporate finance | 11 | 60 | 2 | 2 | 3 | 15 |

*Source:* CSFI (2003), Appendix 3 and CEBR (table 2-2, 2003) for fund management (stock of managed assets) and corporate finance (proxied by total M&As). All figures are for 2001or 2002; except insurance – 1999. na: not available.

areas where the USA has a leading position. Compared to 1995, London's position remained roughly unchanged in most categories, though it did lose about 6% in some market shares in foreign equity turnover (6%), exchange traded derivatives (6%) and insurance. Its market share for OTC derivatives increased by 9%.

Since monetary union, London's percentage share of cross-border euro-denominated claims has risen by 4% since 1999, bringing it to 25% in 2001. The respective figures for Frankfurt, Paris, Luxembourg and Switzerland are 20%, 12%, 9% and 7%. London's net exports of financial services (1997) stood at $8.1 billion, followed by Frankfurt ($2.7 billion), New York ($2.6 billion), Hong Kong ($1.7 billion) and Tokyo ($1.6 billion).

Tokyo's position as an international financial centre has declined in the 1990s. During the 1980s the trading volumes on the New York and Tokyo stock markets were roughly equal but by 1996, Tokyo's volume was only 20% of New York's, with 70% fewer shares traded. Some of this decline is explained by Japan's recession, but other figures support the idea that the Tokyo stock market is no longer as important as it was. In London, 18% of Japanese shares were traded in 1996, compared to 6% in 1990. Singapore conducts over 30% of Japanese futures trades. In the first half of the 1990s, the number of foreign firms with Tokyo listings fell by 50%.

Table 2.3 shows London as the key international centre if measured by the number of foreign financial firms. Though Frankfurt briefly overtook London in 1995, by 2000, the numbers had declined quite dramatically, as they had in Japan, suffering from a recession which has lasted over a decade, and hit its financial sector particularly hard. After European laws on the transfer of deposits around Europe were eased, London gained from the consolidation of foreign operations, at the expense of Frankfurt.

Table 2.3   Number of Foreign Financial Firms in Key Cities

|         | London | New York | Tokyo | Frankfurt |
|---------|--------|----------|-------|-----------|
| 1970    | 181    | 75       | 64    | na        |
| 1975*   | 335    | 127      | 115   | na        |
| 1985**  | 492    | 326      | 170   | na        |
| 1995    | 450    | 326      | 160   | 560       |
| 2000    | 315    | 250      | 118   | 104       |

* Big Bang, New York.
** Big Bang, London in 1986.
*Sources*: Tschoegal (2000), p. 7 and *The Banker* for the early years. Terry Baker-Self, Research Editor at *The Banker* kindly supplied the 2000 figures.

Frankfurt is hoping to usurp London's leading position. There is a trivial time zone difference of just one hour, and the European Central Bank is located in Frankfurt, making it the heart of Euroland. However, the powerful Federal Reserve Bank is located in Washington, but this did not stop New York from emerging as the key financial centre in the North American time zone. London leads Frankfurt in terms of size of employment in the financial sector, the volume of turnover and the ability of London to innovate to meet the needs of its global clients. As Tables 2.2 and 2.3 show, Frankfurt has some way to go before it knocks London from its financial perch. The major challenge for Frankfurt is to turn itself into a key financial cluster, a phenomenon observed in the other international centres.

## *Clustering*

It is argued that clustering is the main explanation for the competitive success of a financial centre. Porter (1998) defines a *cluster* as geographical concentrations of interconnected-firms, specialist suppliers of goods and services, and firms in related industries. **Clustering** is made possible and sustained by the availability of factor inputs, such as capital, labour and information technology, the demand for the financial instrument/service, firm-specific economies of scale (in some cases) and external economies arising from the operation of related institutions in the same location, which can reduce some costs of information gathering.

Financial firms want to locate with other related financial institutions for a number of reasons. These include the following.

1. **Thick** labour markets may be of particular importance for the financial sector. Marshall (1860/1961) showed the benefits of producers sharing specialised inputs. In the financial sector these include legal, accounting, information technology and executive search skills, among others. Individuals can invest in human capital skills and firms can employ them more quickly. A mix of mathematics and physics PhDs with bankers illustrates the more general point that a diversity of knowledge concentrated in one place will speed up innovation.

2. In a sector where information is an important component of cc
   external economies may be created from the nearby operation (
   which reduces the cost of information gathering. For example, Stı
   firms producing similar but not identical products will reduce seaı
   therefore increase the size of sellers' markets.

3. Defensive strategy: firms may enter the home market of rivals because it is easıc
   to their competitors' actions, which could challenge their profitable operations.

4. Some services require face-to-face contact. Walter and Saunders (1991) reported a
   costly error made by an investment bank when it moved its corporate finance team
   to the suburbs of New York. Prospective clients looking for an investment bank
   confined their search to New York's financial district, unwilling to use time to travel
   to the suburbs. Tschoegal (2000) argues that the type of legal system can influence the
   attractiveness of a centre. Countries such as the USA and UK use common law, which
   facilitates financial innovation more than codified law systems. In common law, it is
   taken that an action is permitted if not explicitly forbidden; but the opposite is true
   in countries (e.g. Japan) with a system of codified law. Tschoegal notes the need for
   financial legal expertise, and cites a study of 47 countries by La Porta et al. (1997), where
   a direct link was found between common law countries and the development of capital
   markets. Rosen and Murray (1997) found a preference for financial transactions based
   on US or UK law.

5. Joint services, including clearing houses, research institutions, specialised degree courses
   and sophisticated telecommunications[27] systems, improve the flow of information, ease
   access to knowledge and make the centre more attractive.

6. Political stability and a reputation for liberal treatment of financial markets with, at the
   same time, sufficient regulation to enhance a centre's reputation for quality.

All of the above points mean every financial firm in the cluster enjoys positive externalities.
Each firm benefits from the proximity of the others. Once established, such positive
externalities reduce the incentive to locate elsewhere, even if operating costs appear to be
lower. Pandit et al. (2001) report that financial service firms have a higher than average
growth rate if they locate in a cluster, and a disproportionately large volume of firms will
locate in a cluster.

Taylor et al. (2003) identified four clusters of London financial firms. The first was a highly
integrated group of banks, insurance, law and recruitment firms located in the "City", with
Canary Wharf viewed as an extension of it, a less cohesive sector in the West End of London,
a law cluster in the "City" and the West End, and a more general cluster immediately north
of the "City", with architecture and business support firms. The authors identified a number
of benefits for financial firms locating in London, which are consistent with the points made
above. These include having a "credible" address, proximity to customers, skilled labour
and professional/regulatory organisations, access to knowledge, and wider attractions such
as a cosmopolitan atmosphere, arts, entertainment and restaurants. The main disadvantages

---

[27] Tan and Vertinsky (1987) report a survey of bankers which showed they thought excellent communication
links with the rest of the world were crucial to the success of an international financial centre.

were property costs, poor transport infrastructure and government-related problems such as increases in taxation, onerous regulation and lack of policy coordination.

### Offshore centres

Offshore financial centres are primarily concerned with global financial transactions for on-residents; nationals are usually prohibited from using these services. Some centres (for example, Switzerland and Hong Kong) are "offshore" because foreign banks locate there to avoid certain national regulations and taxation, thereby reducing the costs of raising finance or investing. Other centres such as the Grand Cayman Islands, Guernsey and Bermuda go further and exempt global activities of registered firms from all taxes and regulations.

Recently there has been pressure for these centres to come into regulatory line by eliminating exemptions. It is argued that they attract very high net worth private clients and the large multinationals. As a result, legitimate centres lose business and tax revenues, which in turn raises the tax burden for smaller firms and average net worth individuals. Some centres offering clients a high degree of secrecy (as opposed to confidentiality, where official regulators are given access to client files) are accused of encouraging the growth of money laundering rather than legitimate business and finance. In the wake of 11 September 2001, a few have come under special scrutiny because they are thought to harbour terrorist funds; all are under pressure to freeze the assets of any account thought to be linked to terrorist organisations.

The Financial Stability Forum (FSF, for the G-8 finance departments) has called for the IMF to offer international financial policing, and for sanctions to be applied to offshore centres with tax regimes that can undermine the fiscal objectives of the major industrialised countries and/or allow money laundering. Switzerland has been one proactive centre, suspending secrecy laws which had protected clients. Other offshore centres are fighting back, arguing that as very small fish in the global economic pond, their views will never be properly represented by organisations such as the IMF, OECD or FSF. Williams (2000) and Francis (2000), governors of the central banks of Barbados and Bahamas, respectively, put forward convincing arguments that they have, through due diligence and careful regulation, granted offshore licences to high quality financial firms which are seeking out tax-efficient regimes for their clients rather than engaging in anything illegal.

## 2.5. International Banking

International banking has been singled out for special attention because although its origins date back to the 13th century, there was a rapid increase in the scale of international banking from about mid-1975 onward. The main banks from key western countries established an extensive network of global operations.

There are varying opinions as to what constitutes an international bank. For example, a bank is said to be international if it has foreign branches or subsidiaries. Another alternative definition is by the currency denomination of the loan or deposit – a sterling deposit or loan by a UK bank would be "domestic", regardless of whether it was made in Tokyo, Toronto or Tashkent. A third definition is by nationality of customer and bank. If they differ, the bank is said to be international. All of the above definitions are problematic. To gain a full understanding of the determinants of international banking, it is important to address two questions.

1. Why do banks engage in the *trade* of international banking services; for example, the sale of foreign currencies? Below, it is argued that the trade in global banking services is consistent with the theory of comparative advantage.
2. What are the economic determinants of the multinational bank, that is, a bank with cross-border branches or subsidiaries? Multinational banking is consistent with the theory of the multinational enterprise.

## 2.5.1. International Trade in Banking Services

**Comparative advantage** is the basic principle behind the international trade of goods and services. If a good/service is produced in one country *relatively* more efficiently than elsewhere in the world, then free trade would imply that, in the absence of trade barriers, the home country exports the good/service and the COUNTRY gains from trade.

Firms engage in international trade because of **competitive advantage**. They exploit arbitrage opportunities. If a firm is the most efficient world producer of a good or service, and there are no barriers to trade, transport costs, etc., this firm will export the good from one country and sell it in another, to profit from arbitrage. The FIRM is said to have a competitive advantage in the production of that good or service.

If certain banks trade in international banking services, it is best explained by appealing to the principle of competitive advantage. Banks are exploiting opportunities for competitive advantage if they offer their customers a global portfolio diversification service and/or global credit risk assessment. The same can be said for the provision of international money transmission facilities, such as global currency/debit/credit facilities. Global systems/markets that facilitate trade in international banking services are discussed below.

### The International Payments System

A payments system is the system of instruments and rules which permits agents to meet payment obligations and to receive payments owed to them. It becomes a global concern if the payments system extends across national boundaries. Earlier, the payments systems (or lack thereof) for the UK, USA and EU were discussed. The payments systems of New York and London take on global importance because they are key international financial centres.

### The Euromarkets

The eurobond and euroequity markets were discussed earlier in this chapter. However, their contribution to the flow of global capital is worth stressing. Prior to their development, foreign direct investment was the predominant source of global capital transfers between countries. The euromarkets enhanced the _direct_ *flow of international funds*.

## The Interbank Market

Used by over 1000 banks in over 50 different countries, the growth of interbank claims has been very rapid. In 1983, total interbank claims stood at $1.5 trillion, rising to $6.5 trillion by 1998 and, early in the new century, $11.1 trillion, with interbank loans making up over half of this total. Among the developed economies, cross-border lending in the first quarter of 2001 reached an all time high of $387.6 billion, a 70% increase over the previous quarter.[28] On the other hand, banks continued to reduce their claims in emerging economies, especially Turkey and Argentina.

Interbank trading in the euromarkets accounts for two-thirds of all the business transacted in these markets. The interbank market performs six basic functions.

1. Liquidity smoothing: banks manage assets and liabilities to meet the daily changes in liquidity needs. Liquidity from institutions with a surplus of funds is channelled to those in need of funds.
2. Global liquidity distribution: excess liquidity regions can pass on liquidity to regions with a liquidity deficit.
3. Global capital distribution: deposits placed at banks are on-lent to other banks.
4. Hedging of risks: banks use the interbank market to hedge exposure in foreign currencies and foreign interest rates. With the emergence of the derivatives markets, the role expanded, giving banks tools to manage market risk.
5. Regulatory avoidance: reduce bank costs by escaping domestic regulation and taxation.
6. Central banks use the interbank markets to impose their interest rate policies.

While the emergence of the euromarkets and interbank markets has been instrumental in changing the way capital flows around the world, there is concern that the interbank market exacerbates the potential instability arising from contagion effects. However, Furfine (1999), using simulations, found the risk to be very small. On the other hand, Bernard and Bisignano (2000) identify a fundamental dilemma with the interbank market. Implicit central bank guarantees are necessary to ensure the liquidity of the interbank market, but one consequence is moral hazard because lending banks have less incentive to scrutinise borrowers.

## 2.5.2. Portfolio Diversification

Another reason why firms engage in international banking is to further diversify their portfolios. Canadian banks are a case in point. The major Canadian banks increased the foreign currency assets from the end of World War II on, so that by the early 1990s, international assets accounted for 32% of Canadian bank assets; 80% of these assets are held by the big five.[29] A bank undertakes international lending for one of two reasons. First, to increase external returns and second, to diversify portfolios and reduce risk. In a study of

---

[28] *Source*: Bank for International Settlements, *Quarterly Review*, various issues.
[29] Royal Bank of Canada, Bank of Nova Scotia, Canadian Imperial Bank of Commerce and Toronto Dominion Bank.

Canadian banks over the period 1978–85, Xu (1996) uses a mean variance framework to test why banks diversify their assets internationally. He finds that Canadian banks diversify to reduce risk (variance), thereby increasing the stability of their asset returns. Making international loans meant the banks could reduce the systematic risk arising from operating in a purely domestic market.

## 2.5.3. The Multinational Bank

A multinational enterprise (MNE) is defined as any firm with plants extending across national boundaries. A multinational bank (MNB) is a bank with cross-border representative offices, cross-border branches (legally dependent) and subsidiaries (legally independent). Multinational banks are not unique to the post-war period. From the 13th to the 16th centuries, the merchant banks of the Medici and Fugger families had branches located throughout Europe, to finance foreign trade. In the 19th century, MNBs were associated with the colonial powers, including Britain and, later on, Belgium, Germany and Japan. The well-known colonial MNBs include the Hong Kong and Shanghai Banking Corporation (HSBC), founded in 1865 by business interests in Hong Kong specialising in the "China trade" of tea, opium and silk. By the 1870s, branches of the bank had been established throughout the Pacific basin. In 1992, the colonial tables were turned when HSBC acquired one of Britain's major clearing banks, the Midland Bank, and HSBC moved its headquarters from Hong Kong to London, in anticipation of Hong Kong's transfer from colonial status, and its return to China in 1997.

The National Bank of India was founded in 1863, to finance India's export and import trade. Branches could be found in a number of countries trading with India. The Standard Bank was established in 1853 specialising in the South African wool trade. Headquartered in London, it soon expanded its activities to new developments in South Africa and Africa in general. Presently it is known as the Standard Chartered Bank, and though it has a London head office, its UK domestic business is relatively small. By 1914, Deutsche Bank had outlets around the world, and German banks had 53 branches in Latin America. The Société Générale de Belgique had branches in the Belgian African colonies, and the Mitsui Bank established branches in Japanese colonies such as Korea. Known as "colonial" commercial banks, their primary function was to finance trade between the colonies and the mother country. Branches were normally subject to tight control by head office. Their establishment is consistent with the economic determinants of the MNE, discussed earlier. Branches meant banks could be better informed about their borrowers engaged in colonial trade. Since most colonies lacked a banking system, the banks' foreign branches met the demand for banking services among their colonial customers.

A number of multinational merchant banks were established in the 19th century, such as Barings (1762) and Rothschilds (1804). They specialised in raising funds for specific project finance. Rather than making loans, project finance was arranged through stock sales to individual investors. The head office or branch in London used the sterling interbank and capital markets to fund projects. Capital importing countries included Turkey, Egypt, Poland, South Africa, Russia and the Latin American countries. Development offices associated with the bank were located in the foreign country. Multinational merchant banks are also consistent with the economic determinants of the MNE. Their expertise lay in the finance of investment projects in capital-poor countries; this expertise was acquired through knowledge of the potential of the capital importing country (hence the location of the development offices) and by being close to the source of supply, the London financial markets.

There was a rapid expansion of American banks overseas after the First World War. In 1916 banks headquartered in the USA had 26 foreign branches and offices, rising to 121 by 1920, 81 of which belonged to five US banking corporations. These banks were established for the same purpose as the 19th century commercial banks, to finance the US international trade and foreign direct investment of US corporations, especially in Latin America. In the 1920s, these banks expanded to Europe, in particular Germany and Austria. By 1931, 40% of all US short-term claims on foreigners were German.

A few American and British banks established branches early in the 20th century, but the rapid growth of MNBs took place from the mid-1960s onwards. As expected, the key OECD countries, including the USA, UK, Japan, France and Germany, have a major presence in international banking. Swiss banks occupy an important position in international banking because the country has three international financial centres (Zurich, Basel and Geneva), the Swiss franc is a leading currency, and they have a significant volume of international trust fund management and placement of bonds. The Canadian economy is relatively insignificant by most measures but some Canadian banks do have extensive branch networks overseas, including foreign retail banking; they are also active participants in the euromarkets.

_Locational_ efficiency conditions[30] in a given country are a _necessary but not sufficient condition_ to explain the existence of MNEs. Locational efficiency is said to exist when a plant is located in a certain place because it is the lowest cost producer (in global terms) of a good or service.

Given locational efficiency is present, there are two important reasons why a MNE rather than a domestic firm produces and exports a good or service.

First, _barriers to free trade_, due to government policy. The most obvious example is when a government imposes a tariff or quota on the imports of a good or service. A form of tax, the tariff/quota raises the relative price of the good, discouraging consumption of the import and acting as a barrier to trade. Firms can often avoid the tariff through foreign direct investment in the country or countries erecting the trade barrier.

Second, _market imperfections_, such as monopoly power in a key global market. If one firm has control over the supply of a commodity (iron-ore, oil) which is a critical factor input in the production process of key goods, it can affect many industries around the world. For example, in the 1970s, OPEC[31] members formed a cartel, controlling much of the world's oil supply. They agreed to restrict production, which raised the price of oil, with serious negative consequences for the production processes of oil-dependent industries.

Market imperfections also arise because the market mechanism fails if the trade of some products, such as knowledge, is attempted. Superior knowledge about a production or swap

---

[30] Locational efficiency refers to a country which has a comparative advantage in the production and export of the good or service; in relative terms, the country is the lowest cost producer.

[31] Organisation of Petroleum Exporting Countries.

technique is not easily traded on an open market. One way of profiting from it is to expand overseas and use the knowledge advantage there. Hirtle (1991) observed that certain US commercial banks, US securities firms and some European universal banks are key players in the global swap markets. Though the consumer base is multinational, the banks and securities firms tend to deal in swaps denominated in their home currency.

The presence of multinational banks may be explained using this paradigm. MNBs establish themselves because of trade barriers and/or market imperfections. In the 1960s, US banks met locational efficiency conditions, but this is not enough to explain their expansion overseas. US regulation at the time strongly discouraged foreigners from issuing bonds in the USA, and American banks were not allowed to lend US dollars to finance foreign direct investment by US multinationals. US banks set up overseas branches to help American companies escape these restrictions. For example, Nigh *et al.* (1986) confirm that US bank branching overseas is correlated with US business presence in a particular country.

Branching restrictions also meant US banks could not easily extend their activities to other states, and in a few states such as Illinois, banks were not allowed to have more than one branch. Thus, domestic regulation was a major contributory factor to the expansion of US multinational banks in the 1960s. For example, Citibank set up operations in London to take advantage of the eurodollar market, lending and borrowing on its own account and to assist US multinational firms to fund their foreign direct investment overseas.

Darby (1986) looked at the factors behind the growth of American MNBs from the 1960s onwards, when the number of foreign branches of US banks rose from 124 in 1960 to 905 in 1984. He argues that the motivation for US foreign bank subsidiaries was domestic banking regulations such as deposit interest ceilings, reserve requirements, various capital controls and restrictions on investment banking.[32]

However, there was a decline in US MNB activity from the late 1980s onwards, which, argued Darby (1986), can be explained by a number of factors. In 1978, US banks were authorised to use international banking facilities (IBFs). An IBF allows a US bank to participate directly in the eurocurrency market. Prior to IBFs, they had to use foreign branches or subsidiaries. The international competitiveness of US banks also declined and interest in foreign expansion waned as earnings from global sources contracted.

Darby also identified several factors explaining foreign bank entry into the American market. First, there was a differential between US and eurodollar interest rates; banks were able to fund their dollar-denominated assets more cheaply in the presence of a large differential. Second, the price–earnings ratios for American banks were relatively low, so purchasing an existing US bank was a cheap way to enter the market.

Generally, MNBs tend to focus on wholesale rather than retail banking. One exception is Citibank, which operates as a wholesale and retail commercial bank in the UK, Spain and Germany. Likewise, it has a significant presence in some Latin American countries. In Mexico, Citibank offers retail and wholesale banking. The two large banks, BBVA Bancomer and Banamex, hold about 30% and 20% of total deposits, respectively, while Citibank holds roughly 6%. However, its attempts to establish a British retail banking

---

[32] US banks had to opt for either commercial or investment banking status under the 1933 Glass Steagall Act. Citibank, Bank of America and other US banks used their London subsidiaries to offer investment banking services.

network in the 1960s and 1970s was unsuccessful. The explanation was the presence of the big four clearing banks, together with a number of smaller banks and building societies. Citibank found it was unable to establish a branch network that could compete with the big four clearing banks, and the building societies were mutually owned. At the end of the 1990s, Citibank did establish a limited presence in UK retail banking, using remote delivery channels (telephone and internet banking, with a shared ATM network) to provide services to a select group of middle and high net worth individuals.

In the 1980s, Japanese banks entered the global banking scene to follow their corporate customers overseas. The growth of Japanese multinational enterprises is, in turn, explained by two factors. The first was to overcome barriers to trade. By locating plants in the UK or other European states, firms (e.g. Japanese car and, later, electronic good manufacturers) could escape onerous tariffs imposed on imports from outside the EU area. The second key reason is unique to Japan. As the size of the Japanese current account surplus and the strength of the yen increased from the mid-1970s onwards, the country came under extreme pressure from the USA and other western governments to do something to reduce the size of the current account, and the strength of the yen. Foreign direct investment and the international use of the yen would help to offset this surplus. From 1983 onwards, the Japanese government introduced measures designed to increase the international use of the yen. For example, restrictions on foreign entry into the country's domestic financial markets were eased, which put pressure on domestic banking markets and encouraged banks to expand internationally.[33] Some Japanese banks used their London and New York offices to gain experience in new markets (e.g. derivatives), to be in a good position to take advantage of any regulatory reform in Japan, which finally came with "Big Bang" in 1996.

Japanese foreign branches engaged in two types of loan business in the global markets. Credit is granted to Japanese firms, including trading houses, auto producers, consumer electronics firms, stockbrokers and the banks' own merchant banking subsidiaries. In addition, loans are made to non-Japanese institutions with a very low default risk. In the UK, these are building societies, governments and utility companies. Both involve large volume simple loan instruments, supplied at low cost. Japanese foreign branches and subsidiaries are not important players in foreign domestic markets. Their foreign presence is greatest in London, but Japanese banks have experienced severe problems since 1990. Their difficulties at home throughout the decade may explain the decline in their share of total UK bank assets, from 7.6% in 1997 to 4.3% in 1999.

Ter Wengel (1995) sets out to identify the factors which explain international banking, including multinational banking. The sample consisted of 141 countries with a MNB presence in the form of representative offices, branches and subsidiaries of the home bank. A number of explanatory factors were found to be highly significant. They include: regulations such as restrictions on capital movements, the size of the exporting country (measured by GNP), the presence of home country MNBs, and countries with designated banking centres.[34]

---

[33] Bank of England (1997).
[34] Bahamas, Bahrain, Windward and Leeward islands (e.g. Anguilla, Nevis, Montserrat, Antigua. St. Kitts, Barbados, Grenada and others), Hong Kong, the Grand Cayman Islands, Channel Islands, Netherlands Antilles, Panama, Singapore and the Pacific Ocean Islands (e.g. Kiribati, Fiji, Solomon Islands, Guam and others).

As was noted earlier, the presence of market imperfections is another reason for the growth of multinational enterprises. In the case of MNBs, the knowledge factor is a critical component for successful banking, but difficult to trade on open markets. For example, the expertise of the top US commercial banks in securitisation can be used by their subsidiaries in Europe as this activity grows. Since it cannot normally be traded,[35] expansion through MNBs allows the banks to profit from the knowledge factor.

A paper by Alford *et al.* (1998) provides an interesting illustration of the importance of knowledge transfers. The authors were looking at the reasons why joint ventures were chosen as a means of building up a merchant banking industry in Singapore. The government had signalled its plan to turn Singapore into a key regional and international financial centre. Merchant banking was viewed as an important component of any key centre, and the first merchant bank was established in 1970. By 1982, 45 merchant banks had been established. The sample consisted of 79 banks, 56 of which were wholly owned; 23 spent at least a year as a joint venture in the period 1974–91. There were 85 partners in the 23 joint ventures – 67 were from outside Singapore. Of the 56 wholly owned merchant banks, 52 were foreign, i.e. headquartered outside Singapore.

The paper compares the performance of the joint venture and wholly owned merchant banks. Alford *et al.* identify the potential benefits of joint ventures, such as knowledge creation and learning, limiting entry into product markets, or bypassing government regulations. There are also costs. There is an incentive for partners to free-ride on each other because each one shares the output of the firm regardless of the resources invested to make the venture a success. Communication problems between partners can be aggravated if they are international.

Alford *et al.* (1998) argue their findings are consistent with two theoretical reasons for joint ventures. First, they are created to transfer knowledge among partner firms. In one case, the commercial banking partner learned about merchant banking from the international partner, and the foreign partner obtained connections with blue chip Singaporean firms. Once these learning/networking advantages were realised, the organisational form of the bank changed and it became wholly owned.

Second, a large number of partners were international. Entering into joint partnerships limited their exposure to economic and political uncertainties. As these uncertainties are alleviated over time, it became optimal to buy out the Singapore partners. The results of this study suggest cautious foreign banks may enter a new country via a joint venture, to reduce exposure to economic and political uncertainties. Over time, some of these concerns are alleviated and knowledge is gained. The response is to buy out the host country partner (e.g. the Singapore firm), leaving an independent MNB. Thus, by 1991, only 6 (out of 23) joint ventures remained – 15 became wholly owned and 2 were dissolved.

Other factors explain the growth of MNBs. First, reputation is important: the US money centre banks can set up subsidiaries in Europe and take advantage of their good reputation – though there are limits to this, as Citibank found to its cost. Also, following corporate activities overseas means banks can monitor the credit risk of their MNE

---

[35] It has been known for an individual or a team of specialists at one firm to be "bought" (by offers of better pay packages, etc.) by a rival bank, an example of a successful trade in knowledge.

borrowers by assessing the performance of overseas operations, in addition to supplying banking services.

Finally, foreign bank entry may stimulate economic development in emerging markets. Some countries limit foreign bank entry, usually to protect the national banking sector, for reasons related to national sovereignty. However, the foreign banks can stimulate competition in this sector, and in emerging markets provide services that would not otherwise be available. He and Gray (2001) use the relaxation of controls on foreign banks in China to demonstrate the point. After China announced it would allow foreign bank entry in December 1990, the number of foreign banks doubled, rising from 12 in 1990 to 24 in 1997 in the Shenzhen Special Economic Zone (SSEZ). Using data on inward foreign direct investment and GDP in the SSEZ, the authors show that the presence of multinational banks improved the financial infrastructure, which in turn encouraged more foreign direct investment, raising SSEZ GDP.

## 2.6. Banking Issues in the 21st Century

A recent, popular opinion is that the contribution of banks to the economy will diminish significantly or that banks will even disappear, as the traditional intermediary and liquidity functions of the bank decline in the face of new financial instruments and technology.

Rybczynski (1997) argued that financial systems evolve through time, passing through three phases. Phase one is *bank oriented*, where most external finance is raised through bank loans, which in turn is funded through savings. Banks are the most important financial intermediaries in the financial system, and interest income is the main source of revenue. Phase two is *market oriented*. Households and institutional investors begin to hold more securities and equity, and non-bank financial institutions may offer near-bank products, such as money market accounts. Banks themselves reduce their dependence on the traditional intermediary function, increasing their off-balance sheet activities, including proprietary trading, underwriting and asset management. The market or securitised phase is established when the financial markets are the source of external finance for both the financial and non-financial sectors. Corporate bank loans are largely replaced by corporate bonds and commercial paper; mortgages and consumer credit originate in banks but are securitised. In this third phase, trading, underwriting, advising and asset management activities become more important for banks than the traditional core banking functions.

Bill Gates, the IT guru, is well known for an alleged remark he made in 1994 that banks were "dinosaurs",[36] which could be bypassed. In 1995, after much consternation among the banking sector about his intentions, Mr Gates subsequently claimed he meant that banking *systems* were dinosaurs. In a 1997 article published in *The New York Times*, he said:

> "These changes [referring to the internet] won't come at the expense of the banking industry... the future is bright... for institutions that evolve. Technology will let banks get

---

[36] Reported in Culture Club, *Newsweek*, 11 July 1994, p. 38.

*closer to customers, deliver a wider range of services at lower costs and streamline internal systems so that all customer data is integrated and can be used to spot trends that can lead to new products. . . The Web will offer banks great opportunities – It will be interesting to see which banks step up to this opportunity. . ."*[37]

The key word is "evolve", to be discussed at the end of the section. Before doing so, the performance of the banking sector is reviewed, together with a discussion of how banks might (and have) turned potential threats into opportunities.

Most studies show that the banking sector underperforms compared to other sectors; and a few argue banks are in an irreversible decline. Some go further, claiming that governments' (or central banks') control over interest rates, and therefore price stability, is under threat.

It is useful to begin by looking at some general figures to establish the position of the banking/financial sector at the beginning of the new century. Begin with the performance of banks measured by bank profitability. Figures 2.3(a) and (b) show, respectively, the ratio of pre-tax and post-tax profits to gross income for all banks over the period 1989–99. In the 1980s, Japanese banks, already very profitable, became even more so. But banks' profits elsewhere were either trendless or slipping. The late 1980s were marked by sharp swings in the profits of Anglo-American banks. After 1990, the situation in Japan changed substantially. There were steady falls in profits from 1990, with a dramatic decline in 1996–98. The recovery to average levels in 1999 was short-lived. These figures are an indication of the serious problems encountered by Japan's banks, discussed in detail in Chapters 5 and 6. Banks in France underwent steady declines in profitability in the early period, but profits have gradually improved since 1996. Like the previous decade, banks in the other major OECD countries show slight rises in the late 1990s, after some declines in the early 1990s.

Turning to the growth of bank assets, in the 1970s, bank assets grew rapidly in nominal terms across the 14 countries, but with wide dispersion, as shown in Table 2.3 and Figure 2.4. Luxembourg exhibited the fastest growth rate, which was more than three times faster than the slowest, the USA. More restrictive monetary policies and lower inflation contributed to the sharply lower growth almost everywhere in the 1980s and 1990s. The lower growth rate of assets also reflected a move away from the strategy of asset expansion to create large banks, or growth for growth's sake, to an emphasis on maximising profits and shareholder value-added. Belgium was the only country where bank assets grew more quickly in the 1990s than the 1980s; and in Portugal, bank asset growth was faster in the 1990s than in the 1970s. Japan's financial difficulties in the 1990s underline the collapse in bank asset growth – Japan saw the largest rise in the 1980s of the 14 countries, dropping to the lowest in the 1990s.

Figure 2.5 refers to banks' foreign assets. Though there were some exceptions, foreign asset growth rates tended to outpace domestic assets in all three decades, as a comparison of Figures 2.4 and 2.5 reveals. In the UK, the foreign asset growth rate more than halved

---

[37] Bill Gates (1997), "No one is really living a Web Lifestyle – Yet", *New York Times*, 29 July 1997; available at www.htimes.com/today/access/columns/0729bill.html.

Figure 2.3 (a) Ratio of pre-tax profit to gross income.

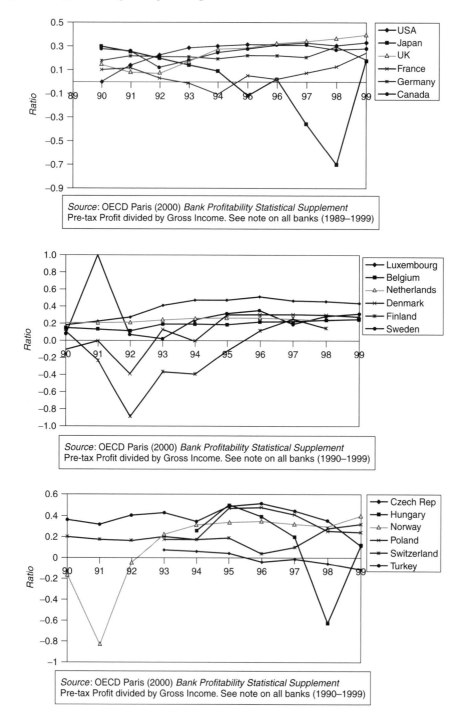

*Source*: OECD Paris (2000) *Bank Profitability Statistical Supplement*
Pre-tax Profit divided by Gross Income. See note on all banks (1989–1999)

*Source*: OECD Paris (2000) *Bank Profitability Statistical Supplement*
Pre-tax Profit divided by Gross Income. See note on all banks (1990–1999)

*Source*: OECD Paris (2000) *Bank Profitability Statistical Supplement*
Pre-tax Profit divided by Gross Income. See note on all banks (1990–1999)

Figure 2.3    (b) Ratio of post-tax profits to gross income.

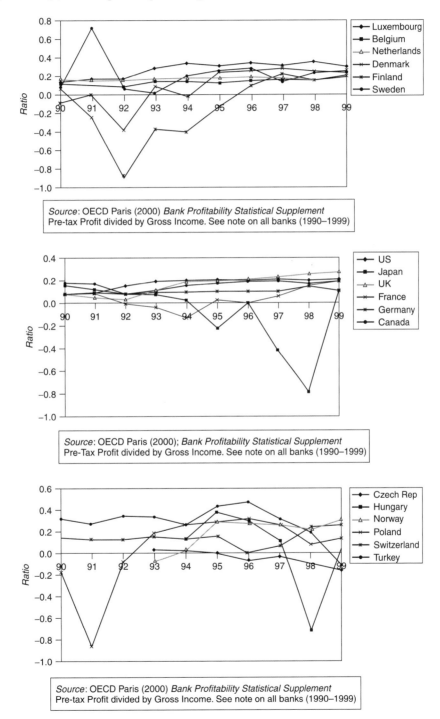

Source: OECD Paris (2000) Bank Profitability Statistical Supplement
Pre-tax Profit divided by Gross Income. See note on all banks (1990–1999)

Source: OECD Paris (2000); Bank Profitability Statistical Supplement
Pre-Tax Profit divided by Gross Income. See note on all banks (1990–1999)

Source: OECD Paris (2000) Bank Profitability Statistical Supplement
Pre-tax Profit divided by Gross Income. See note on all banks (1990–1999)

Figure 2.4   Average annual growth rate of domestic bank assets.

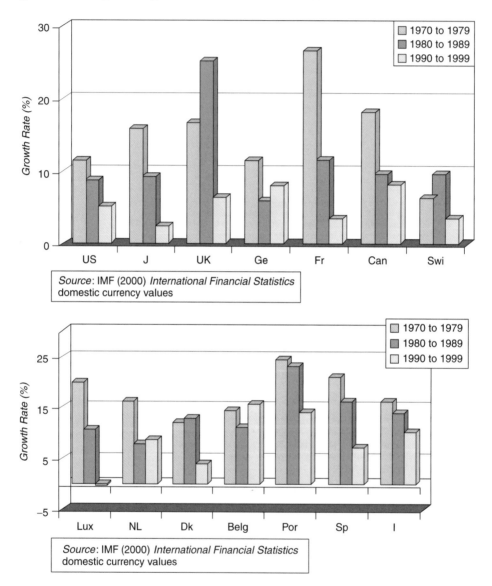

between the 1980s and 1990s but in Switzerland, it doubled. Again, Portugal stands out for high and rising growth rates of foreign assets during the two decades.

The average ratio of total assets to nominal GDP for most industrialised countries since 1970 appears in Figure 2.6. For Switzerland, banking assets have been more than 100% of national income since the 1970s, and very nearly so for Japan and Germany. In other

Figure 2.5  Average annual growth rate of foreign assets.

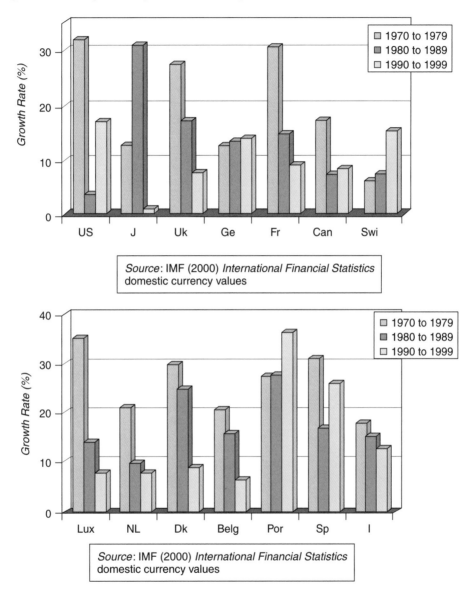

Source: IMF (2000) International Financial Statistics
domestic currency values

Source: IMF (2000) International Financial Statistics
domestic currency values

countries, there has been a steady rise from 40% to 60% of national income in the 1970s, to well over 100% by the 1990s. The notable exception is the United States, where the 1990s figure is barely higher than the 1970s one. Including foreign assets (Figure 2.7) makes the figures more pronounced, but the trends are unchanged. Thus, even though, in absolute terms, asset expansion has slowed since the 1970s, in most countries banks' assets as a

Figure 2.6   Ratio of total domestic bank assets to nominal GDP.

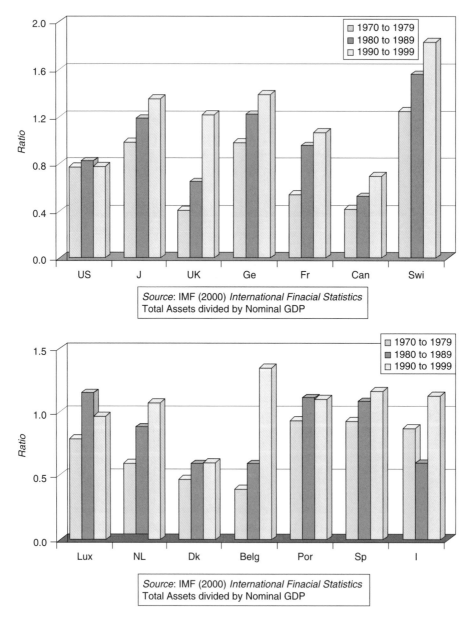

*Source*: IMF (2000) *International Finacial Statistics*
Total Assets divided by Nominal GDP

*Source*: IMF (2000) *International Finacial Statistics*
Total Assets divided by Nominal GDP

percentage of GNP have risen, which contradicts a general view that traditional banking is in decline.

Relative operating expenses in the 1990s are shown in Figures 2.8 through 2.11. Figure 2.8 illustrates that operating expenses as a percentage of total income changed little over the

Figure 2.7 Ratio of total bank assets (including foreign assets) to nominal GDP.

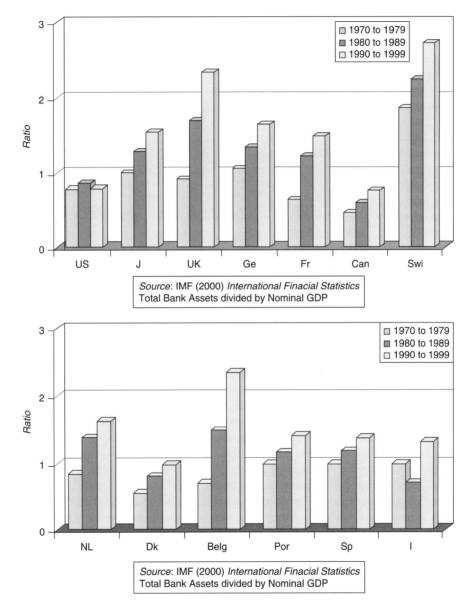

decade; falling slightly by 1999 for 8 of the 14 countries. Beginning from a comparatively low level, the ratio increased in Portugal and Luxembourg. The opposite was the case for Belgium and France. For most of these countries, the ratio remained high through the decade, usually over 65%. Nor has the ratio changed much since the 1980s.

**Figure 2.8  Ratio of operating expenses to gross income.**

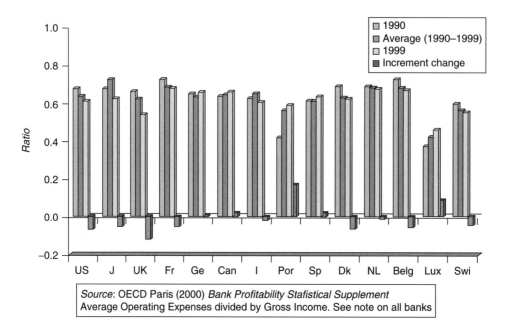

Source: OECD Paris (2000) *Bank Profitability Statistical Supplement*
Average Operating Expenses divided by Gross Income. See note on all banks

A typical ratio of staff costs to income (Figure 2.9) is about 0.35. The exceptions are the USA and Luxembourg, which averaged 0.27 and 0.21, respectively. The figures moved slightly downward over the period, except for Spain and Luxembourg. Figure 2.10 shows that average staff costs per employee rose over the decade in all countries except for Italy, where they fell slightly. The rise is consistent with the idea that more skilled staff are required as banks move into off-balance sheet activities. The differences between countries are notable. They were lowest in Portugal, the UK and the USA (averaging $33 000 to $43 000 but highest in Switzerland (about $89 000), the Netherlands ($83 000) and Japan ($78 000). The average for Germany was just under $50 000.

Figure 2.11 illustrates the average number of employees per branch in the 1990s.[38] Again, there is quite a variation from country to country. Luxembourg has the highest, which corresponds to the relatively high staff costs shown in Figure 2.10. They are relatively high for the UK, largely because Britain has fewer branches in relation to population than elsewhere in Europe. Employee numbers are quite high for Japan and Switzerland, in line with their high staff costs.

Figure 2.12 gives the financial sector share of total employment through the 1990s. The share has been quite steady throughout the decade in most countries – in the UK it has not changed over the period. Switzerland has by far the highest, averaging 3.11% over the period compared to figures between 1.5 and 2% for most other countries. In Japan, the share

---

[38] Figures for the USA are not available.

Figure 2.9   Ratio of staff costs to gross income.

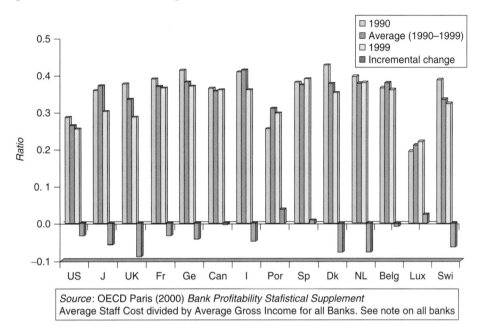

*Source*: OECD Paris (2000) *Bank Profitability Stafistical Supplement*
Average Staff Cost divided by Average Gross Income for all Banks. See note on all banks

Figure 2.10   Average staff costs per employee.

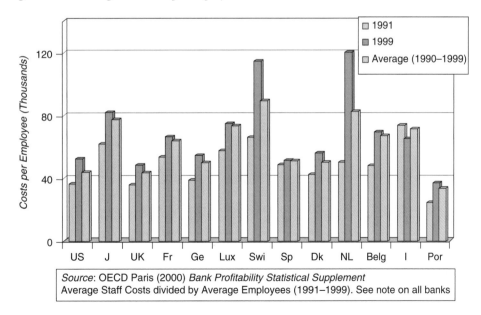

*Source*: OECD Paris (2000) *Bank Profitability Statistical Supplement*
Average Staff Costs divided by Average Employees (1991–1999). See note on all banks

Figure 2.11  Number of employees per branch.

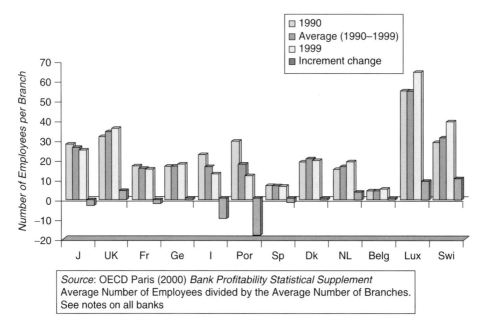

Source: OECD Paris (2000) Bank Profitability Statistical Supplement
Average Number of Employees divided by the Average Number of Branches.
See notes on all banks

Figure 2.12  Financial sector share of total employment.

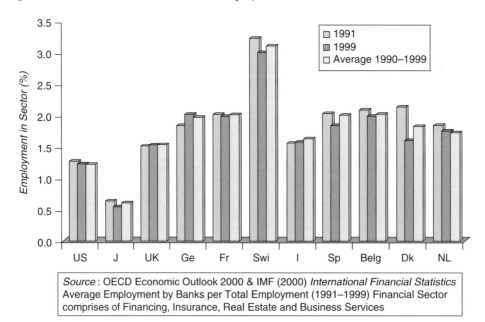

Source: OECD Economic Outlook 2000 & IMF (2000) International Financial Statistics
Average Employment by Banks per Total Employment (1991–1999) Financial Sector
comprises of Financing, Insurance, Real Estate and Business Services

is exceptionally low, averaging just 0.60% for the decade. It should be stressed that these figures relate to the financial sector as a whole, and not just banking.

A final exercise is to review the relative share price performance of banks, which gives an idea of what the markets think about the future prospects of banks compared to other sectors. Figures 2.13 through 2.15 show the performance of a bank share price index against the general market index for the USA, UK and Europe, based on the share price at the beginning of each month. The longest series is for the USA, for 1976–2001. With the exception of the mid-1980s, the US share prices were below the general share price index from the 1970s until about 1992, when they began to track the index in most years, rising above it in 2002. The performance of US investment banks was more volatile, but with the exception of 1999–2000 they outperformed the general price index from 1998 onwards.

UK banks consistently underperformed against the FTSE 100 until January 1994. From the beginning of 1996, banks do better than the blue chip firms, suggesting investors have a more favourable view of the prospects for British banks.

The European bank index is available from 1987 onwards (see Figure 2.15). Bank share prices closely track the index, until January 1994. The bank share price index is below the general index through most of the period 1994–2001, then more or less tracks the index through to 2003.

A special index for Japanese banks (Figure 2.16) begins in 1989; it was in December 1989 that the stock market began a steady decline which lasted over a decade and began to show signs of recovery in 2003, the time this book was written. It is unclear whether or not this is the beginning of a sustained recovery. From the information on the Japanese

**Figure 2.13   US bank indices compared to the S&P500 index.**

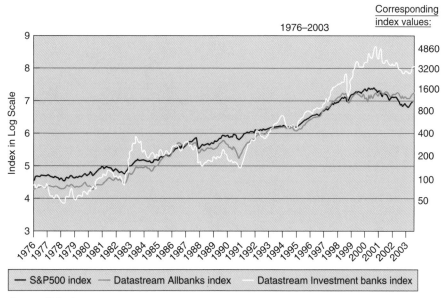

*Source*: Datastream.

Figure 2.14   UK bank index compared to the FTSE100 index.

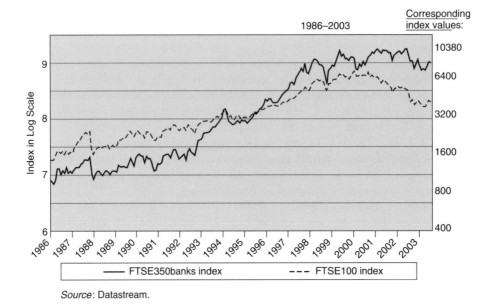

Source: Datastream.

Figure 2.15   European bank index compared to the Eurostoxx index.

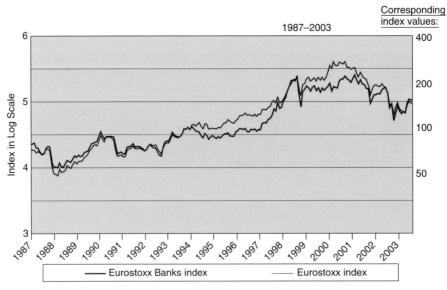

Source: Datastream.

Figure 2.16  Japanese Nikkei 500 banking index compared to the Nikkei 225 index.

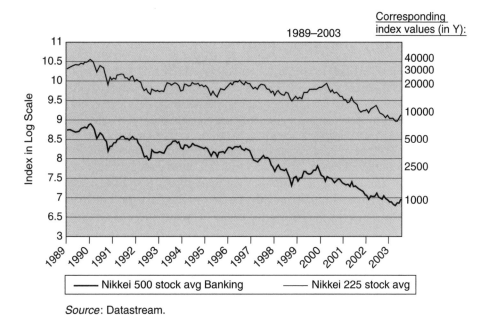

Source: Datastream.

bank index in Figure 2.16, it is clear that investors take a dim view of the prospects for the Japanese banking sector – the index consistently underperforms the Nikkei 225 throughout the period. This result is exactly what would be expected, given the severity of the problems experienced by Japanese banks over the last decade. The Japanese case is analysed in some detail in Chapter 8.

## 2.6.1. Turning Threats into Opportunities

The figures on the performance of banks are mixed. While profitability was fairly static, it appears banks are looking for other sources of income by expanding into non-interest income areas. However, the ratio of cost to income remained largely unchanged, and average costs per employee rose through the 1990s. During the 1970s, 1980s and early 1990s, the share price performance of banks was relatively poor when compared against general price indices in the USA, UK, Japan and Europe. From the mid to late 1990s, British commercial and US investment bank share price performance improved, though the latter was somewhat volatile. By the new century, US, EU and UK banks were either tracking or outperforming the relevant index, suggesting investors have a more positive outlook with respect to banks' future prospects. Japanese banks are the notable exception to this trend. There are several major changes which the existing highly capitalised banks can (and must) turn into opportunities if they are to survive. They are by no means independent, and include electronic and financial innovations including the introduction of "e-cash", the growth of "non-banks" and the trend towards consolidation within national banking sectors.

## New technology and innovation

Begin with the emergence of electronic (e-cash) or digital cash and assume, for the moment, that it has replaced currency in circulation – a cashless society [the *likelihood* of the advent of a cashless society is discussed later in the section]. Based on the development of technology to date, e-cash can consist of stored value cards, network money and e-wallets. Stored value cards store prepaid funds electronically on a chip in the card. Mondex[39] and Visa Cash are good examples. The "smart card" is another example of a stored value card, used widely in some parts of Continental Europe. Customers can download cash from their accounts into the card, so they can be used like cash, but are more secure than cash because personal information is stored in the chip, so only the owner can use the card. The reduced chance of fraud (compared to a debit or credit card) makes them attractive to customers and shop owners alike.

Network money is also prepaid but stored on a computer hard disc and transferred between agents via some network such as the internet. Also, assume agents use the e-cash to purchase goods and services by post, the internet or at physical shops. The e-wallet is an electronic version of a credit or debit card. Money is transferred from an individual's account to the e-wallet, which can be used for internet purchases. All transactions can be traced back to the owner because the e-wallet contains the information.

Some experts have questioned whether the bank intermediary function will be challenged by the growth of e-cash. In this hypothetical world, could the presence of e-cash make banks redundant in the provision of core banking functions? To answer this question, consider each of these functions in turn. First, take payments facilities. To quote King (1999):

> "...there is no conceptual obstacle to the idea that two individuals engaged in a transaction could settle by a transfer of wealth from one electronic account to another in real time... Eligible assets would be any financial assets [with] a market clearing price in real time... the key to such developments is the ability of computers to communicate in real time... enabling private sector real time gross settlement." (p. 48)

King is referring to the settlement of transactions – there is no mention of credit. As Freedman (2000) stresses, the world of settlement envisaged by King would require a population of 6 billion having accounts, with funds transferred between them via the purchase or sale of assets.

---

[39] Mondex is an electronic purse – it uses a smart card to store electronic cash. Smart cards have a microchip rather than a magnetic stripe. The chip can store a large amount of information. It is not easily copied (unlike a strip), reducing the opportunity for fraud. An ATM or adapted telephone transfers cash from a bank account to the card. Retailers use a terminal to download cash from the card. A number of pilots took place in the late 1990s – some successful, some not. NatWest has sold all but 5% of Mondex to other firms. Mastercard International bought a 51% shareholding in 1997. Mondex trials in Swindon (UK), Guelph (Canada) and Hong Kong failed. See Tomkin and Baden-Fuller (2000).

Central banks play an important role in the settlements function. Most of the daily payments made by the household, business and government sectors involve a claim on a bank, and through a given working day, net payments are made to and received from the different banks. Some banks will find their settlement balances at the central bank have increased, others will have declined because they have experienced a net outflow of payments. Banks will use each other or the central bank to ensure their settlement balances at the central bank are kept at some minimum level. The central bank has assumed this role for numerous reasons. It issues the currency, and therefore cannot fail, and it also acts as lender of last resort.[40] However, in the event of real time transfers, payments between banks would no longer be necessary (for the reasons given above) and this settlements function could, in theory, disappear.

Turning to the other core functions of the bank, taking deposits and making loans, the chance of banks being replaced is even more remote. With the most advanced technology the chances are slim, because of the time and cost of collecting the information required to locate the optimal place for a deposit, to pool risks with other depositors or to locate the most suitable borrower(s). Any software programme written to undertake these tasks is only as good as its author, and will quickly become dated. Banks are likely to be able to sustain a competitive advantage in an e-cash world because it would be more costly for individuals to replicate the banks' global risk and information pooling role.

Banks also provide liquidity as a service to their customers. Though technology makes it possible to procure on-line liquidity in the absence of a third party intermediary, *changes* in liquidity preferences are a different matter. Suppose suitable borrowers are found for depositors, and a term of repayment dates, with interest, is agreed. During the term of agreement, the position of one party is altered: he/she wants the cash earlier or later than agreed. Banks, with a large pool of funds, are able, at a relatively low cost, to satisfy any changes in preferences and to profit from it, either by charging a penalty rate of interest on loan extensions or by reducing the interest paid on deposit, but in cyberspace, in the absence of an intermediary, satisfying changes in consumer preferences becomes far more difficult and costly.

However, the dominance of the payments system by major banks is under threat. Traditionally, the payments system has been a by-product of intermediation, which facilitates the transfer of credits and debits between agents. The growth of electronic delivery of core banking services has already given rise to the emergence of a payments system independent of banks. PayPal is a California-based company that offers business and personal customers a secure means of sending and receiving payments via email. Customers use PayPal if they are reluctant to provide credit card details to unknown internet merchants. Also, for tiny internet firms that cannot afford the cost of offering credit or debit card facilities, PayPal credits them for any purchases made via PayPal. PayPal takes the credit card number and pays for any item on behalf of the customer. Its main source of revenue is fees earned from transactions charges. Its early success was largely due to one major customer – PayPal arranges payments on behalf of e-Bay, an electronic auction site with

---

[40] Another reason would be the traditional use of reserve ratio as a monetary policy tool, which has been abandoned in the developed economies.

a large customer base. However, the company is trying to attract a wide customer base. In 2002, just as many banks were prohibiting customers from using their cards for on-line gambling; these casinos have been signing up to accept PayPal. Attempts are being made to pass federal legislation to ban on-line gambling in the USA.

The average fee per transaction is $1.78, and the average PayPal customer has seven to eight transactions per year. By early 2002, PayPal had over 15 million customers, giving it a substantial revenue source which is profitable, given that the cost of processing an email payment is well below $1.[41] The firm successfully went public in early 2002, despite the "tech" stock fallout at the time. In April 2002, it reported a first quarter profit of $1.2 million. It competes against payment providers such as credit card firms which charge higher fees, due to the cost of fraud, among other factors.

It is too early to judge whether PayPal will be a success. Payments are made via a credit card, from a bank account or a PayPal account. A website called PaypalWarning.com has anecdotal reports that PayPal pressures customers for access to their bank accounts. It offers a cash payment if customers transfer funds from their bank accounts to a PayPal account – deposits earn the money market rate. However, any attempt to withdraw the funds is costly and difficult. The FDIC[42] has made it clear PayPal is not a bank, meaning funds held in PayPal accounts are not covered by deposit insurance. However, PayPal transfers its customers' deposits into FDIC insured banks, which, according to PayPal, means the deposits are covered by insurance, even though PayPal makes them on behalf of customers.

On the PaypalWarning website, there are unverified reports of accounts being debited by PayPal in the absence of any purchase. Yet another threat comes from Mastercard. In April 2002, it announced it would not allow credit card payments to go through outlets like PayPal because the credit card firm has far less control over its high risk customers who use PayPal. However, PayPal is confident of gaining an exemption from the exclusion. A number of states are questioning whether PayPal is, *de facto*, a bank, especially as it expands its services, offering credit and debit cards, money market accounts, international payments and on-line bill payments. Louisiana has asked PayPal to cease offering services to its residents until the firm has obtained a state licence to transmit money. Like any website, it attracts viruses and worms. In the first two months of 2003, several email worms have been part of bogus messages on security changes, purporting to be from PayPal.

Some would argue the growth of firms outside the banking system offering payments is a healthy development. Recall the concerns expressed by Cruickshank (2000) over the monopoly power of the "big four" banks in the United Kingdom. Firms such as PayPal will undermine this monopoly and improve prices for consumers, though it is worth remembering that PayPal's services are confined to e-commerce. If payments are offered by non-banks, it does not follow that the core intermediary functions are under threat. Furthermore, if organisations such as PayPal expand to the point that they are effectively banks, the regulators will almost certainly demand they be registered as banks, subject to all bank regulations.

---

[41] Source of figures: Platt (2002).

[42] FDIC: Federal Deposit Insurance Corporation, a government agency which is responsible for deposit insurance in the United States. See Chapter 5 for more detail.

The above discussion indicates that the traditional intermediary and liquidity functions of banks appear reasonably secure. However, some off-balance sheet subsectors are potentially more vulnerable. Large non-banking corporations engaging in the direct trade of financial instruments, such as swaps, just as corporate bonds or commercial paper are used to raise finance instead of loans – both challenge this intermediary role. Likewise, medium sized and large corporates could use the internet to successfully bypass banks when searching for loans and trade finance. However, for banks to lose their competitive advantage, these firms need a more cost-effective way of dealing with credit, settlement, liquidity and other financial risks arising from these transactions: to date, it is the banks which have excelled in financial risk management. Also, established banks are anticipating these new threats and finding new ways to keep this business. For example, Barclays Bank is experimenting with a new service which offers their risk management expertise and, in addition, a business-to-business exchange whereby corporate customers can get information on a large range of products and services, from cheap sources of office equipment to recruitment.

A number of small, specialised on-line investment banks have been established in the USA, though their focus on the technology sector meant they were hit badly by the burst of the technology bubble. On a more positive note, some of the traditional investment banks are taking advantage of the opportunities offered by the internet. An established investment bank has developed a system to put initial public offerings (IPOs) on-line. The prospectus is posted on the internet, and videos replace traditional visits to investors to sell the new issue. Traditionally, an IPO was underwritten by a well-known investment bank. In some cases, a very small percentage of the IPO is released on the market, thus creating excess demand and raising the price. The underwriter (investment bank) profits from the sale of their shares before official trading begins. Most retail investors have to wait until the official markets open. Access to the internet means a much larger pool of investors has access to the IPO information, which could erode the dominance of the institutional investor in this market. For example, one American investment bank reports institutional investors have dropped from holding 80% of the issues to just 27% in one year. The more direct access will benefit the retail or smaller wholesale investors. Thus, the presence of IT will challenge the current favourable position of institutional investors, but banks will continue in their intermediary role. However, there are fewer barriers preventing firms from arranging their share issues independently. Again, the question is whether the bank can remain competitive, arranging the IPO at a lower cost than the issuing firm could. For example, if a firm declines the services of an investment bank, it runs the risk of being unable to place the shares at the expected price; an investment bank would normally underwrite the share issue. Large corporations may have the expertise to arrange an in-house IPO, which is unlikely to be the case for smaller firms.

The rapid growth of the internet is also likely to change the way the bond market functions. In 2000, the World Bank employed two investment banks to issue new bonds direct to investors via the internet – *e-bonds*. Other key borrowers have announced their intention to do the same. An e-bond creates greater transparency in the market because the borrower knows the end investors, and the size of their commitments. Like the internet IPOs, it also opens the market to new investors, so reducing the dominance of institutional investors in these markets. For example, the e-bonds issued by the World Bank attracted investments ranging from $1000 to $250 million worth of bonds.

The influence of institutional investors is also being challenged as the secondary markets go on-line, with well-established investment banks leading the way. Goldman Sachs, together with some other well-known investment banks, set up TradeWeb in 1998, which trades US Treasury bonds. A European equivalent was established in 2000, called Bondclick. There are also on-line services providing information on the prices of bonds issued from all over the world. However, to date, only frequently traded highly liquid bonds have been targeted for electronic issue and trading.

The impact of the above trends should be a reduction in the fees charged for the issue of new shares and bonds, and a narrowing of the bid–offer spread in the secondary markets, which could undermine the profitability of these activities. At the same time, however, related costs should be lower once the IT investment has been made. For example, the use of interactive TV to market new issues could replace expensive sales teams. It is also important to stress that it is the well-known investment banks leading the way with respect to on-line investment banking.

The development of e-cash also has macro/monetary implications. In separate papers, Goodhart (2000) and Freedman (2000) considered the issue of e-cash from the standpoint of the central bank. Both authors argue there is still a role for the central bank in setting monetary policy via short-term interest rates, even if it is accepted that a cashless society will emerge. The central bank only need raise/lower the rate by offering to borrow money at a rate higher/lower than the going market interest rate. These operations (and possible losses arising from its intermediary role) would be backed by government. Alternatively, Goodhart noted, a government could require all taxes be settled in a currency issued by the central bank if it wanted to keep a monopoly over the currency. Freedman makes a similar point: the central bank, especially if it continued to act as banker for the government, could refuse any alternative settlement mechanism and insist on settlements in the currency or a government digital currency. These points demonstrate that sovereign states, should they choose, can undertake very simple measures to have a currency alternative to e-cash and will have sovereignty over monetary policy even in a digital cash world.

Drehmann et al. (2002) ask whether an e-cash society is imminent. They cite qualitative evidence showing a strong demand for currency. In the UK, cash holdings per capita rose from $470 in 1990 to $695 in 1995. In the USA, the respective figures were $998 and $1908; in Japan, $2003 and $4594. Similar trends were found for the major OECD countries. The authors identify several reasons for the sustained demand for cash. Cash is easier for certain small transactions, and is sometimes needed for the occasional one-off large payment. "Hoarders" hold certain foreign currencies (the dollar or Swiss franc) to hedge against inflation in their home countries or political uncertainty. The desire for anonymity, for legitimate reasons or otherwise (black markets, money laundering), also preserves the demand for non-digital cash. Some people, on a point of principle, will not succumb to the lure of e-cash because all transactions are traceable. Even if it became possible to eliminate the trail, there is no guarantee the other party will keep the transaction secret.

The authors also show (where data are available) that the cost of cash as a payment method for retailers is considerably lower. In the Netherlands, the cost per transaction (in euros) of cash is 0.095, compared to 0.22 for on-line debit, 0.25 for an e-purse and 2.5 for a credit card. In the USA (in dollars), the figures are 0.12 for cash, 0.34 for an on-line direct debit, 0.36 for a cheque and 0.72 for a credit card. E-purse costs are not available for the USA.[43]

Drehmann et al. (2002) produce figures showing the demand for products giving electronic access to bank accounts (credit/debit cards) has been much greater than the demand for e-money. The number of debit card transactions per capita in the UK was 0 in 1988, rising to 35 by 1999. Canada's and Denmark's per capita card use rose to 54 and 68, respectively. Credit card transactions underwent similar increases, though their growth rates have been overtaken by debit cards. For the few countries reporting figures, e-cash transactions per capita, at its highest, was 4.45. However, the figures should be treated with caution because e-cash, like the debit card in 1988, is relatively new.

Drehmann et al. claim the threat of counterfeiting is a serious security issue for e-cash issuers. While counterfeit currency is a relatively minor problem,[44] the costs incurred to protect e-cash from counterfeit are considerably greater. Providers must bear the cost of frequent technical updates, limiting the amount stored on cards and the duration of e-money balances. Such costly security precautions will limit demand; for example, hoarders or those seeking anonymity would not want to use e-cash.

Using econometric analysis, Drehmann et al. provide convincing evidence that the replacement of currency by digital cash is some way off. The authors identify two separate markets for currency; the illegal group who demand cash for large value payments, and another group wanting small bills to pay for incidentals such as newspapers, sandwiches or bus tickets. The sample consisted of panel data for 16 OECD countries over the period 1980–98. Two separate equations were tested, one with log(cash[large]/GDP per capita) as the dependent variable and the second using log(cash[small]/GDP per capita). Each equation was regressed against a number of independent variables. The main findings were as follows. First, both the demand for large and small bills was found to be interest sensitive, with a significantly negative coefficient. As interest rates rise, the demand for large/small bills falls. The demand for currency was found to be positively related to increases in real expenditure, though the degree of significance varied from country to country. An increase in taxes (taxes:GDP) increases the demand for large bills in the pooled sample, and in some of the individual country equations. Card payments should be easier with EFTPOS, meaning the demand for currency would fall. The sign is negative but insignificant. The ATM coefficient was positive but not significant for small cash holdings; negative and insignificant for large cash holdings.[45] The authors conclude that EFTPOS reduces the demand for currency, but this has been somewhat offset by ATM usage, which eases

---

[43] See table C1 of the Web Appendix in Drehmann et al. (2002). The figures reported are taken from different studies. They report studies in the Netherlands, Germany, the USA and UK all show cash to be the cheapest means of payment at point of sale.

[44] In the USA, the Federal Reserve reports only 0.0075% of notes in circulation are counterfeit – see Drehmann et al. (2002), table 4.

[45] The effect of ATMs on the demand for cash is ambiguous because while it reduces the cost of transferring funds between accounts (so the demand for money should decline), the ease of access may increase the use of cash for what might have been non-cash payments.

payment by cash. However, the overall impact of card technology is relatively minor. The main factors which discourage the growth of a cashless society, the authors argue, are the need for anonymity, the hoarding of certain foreign currencies, the cost of keeping digital cash secure and inconvenience, for example, the need to remember PIN numbers.

## E-banking and other remote delivery channels

"*According to Good (1998), electricity was invented in 1873 and took 46 years for mass adoption... throughout the world. It took 35 years for telephones, 25 years for radio, and 16 years for PCs. For the World Wide web, it has taken only 6 years.*"[46]

It is important to draw a distinction between the question of whether digital cash will replace banks and the presence of electronic products which change the way intermediary banking services are delivered. They are two quite separate issues. The main attraction of IT-based remote delivery/distribution of banking services is lower costs. There have been a number of estimates.

- A survey undertaken by Booz, Allen and Hamilton[47] (US accounting firm) reported comparative costs per transaction

  – branch banking: $1.07
  – telephone: 54 cents
  – ATM: 27 cents
  – internet: 1.5 cents

- Wood (2002) cites similar figures

  – branch transaction: $1 per transaction
  – on-line transactions: 1 cent per transaction

- Bainbridge *et al.* (2001) report that including the IT systems required, internet transaction costs are 10% of those incurred by a traditional branch.

The Scandinavian countries, especially Finland and Sweden, have been very successful in attracting customers to e-banking. Suominen (2001) reports that 30% of bank customers in these countries either use the internet or engage in PC banking via a modem. In Sweden, tax incentives mean 65% of households are on the internet. The proportion of internet customers is treble that of the European average. Nordea[48] is often cited as the world's leading internet bank because it customers complete 7.2 million on-line transactions per month, twice that of the Bank of America identified (at the time) as the second most internet active bank. The leading Scandinavian banks have also integrated stockbroking

---

[46] Pyun *et al.* (2002), p. 75.
[47] Quoted by Nathan (1999).
[48] Nordea was formed by the mergers of Merita (Finland), Nordbanken (Sweden), Unidanmark (Denmark) and Christiania bank (Norway). In 2001, 25% (2.4 million) of its customers banked on line.

and e-shopping (over 900 shops in one case) with their internet banking. Mobile banking, with the use of a smart card, is also on offer. To date, no serious breaches in security have been experienced. These banks have managed to produce a high quality deposit product and to cross-sell a diverse set of services.

Suominen identifies several reasons for the success of e-banking in Finland and Sweden. First is the use of account transfers through a centralised clearing system in place of a cheque-based or direct debt/credit clearing system, which meant the technology was in place for on-line banking. The account transfer system involves the real time transfer of credit/debits from one account holder to another. The person making the payment provides not only his/her account number, but also the account details of the recipient to the bank, and the transaction is settled.

A second reason for the success of Finnish and Swedish internet banking is due, Suominen argues, to a concentrated banking sector. In 1999, the combined market share of household deposits for the five largest banks was 90% in Finland and 83% in Sweden, compared to an EU average of 58%. The high degree of consolidation and lack of competition meant banks could set fee structures and price deposits/loans to attract customers to on-line banking. Once the technology is in place, the marginal cost of e-banking is nearly zero, making for a profitable operation. Though fees were reduced to attract customers to on-line banking, their more frequent use of the system has boosted operating income. Linked to the rapid increase in e-banking was a fall in the cost-to-income ratios for the banks in both countries. In Finland, the cost-to-income ratio in 1999 was just below 60%, compared with a G-5 average of about 65%. The Swedish banks experienced a temporary increase in the C–I ratio towards the end of the century,[49] but by 2001 it was also below 60%.

Suominen cites additional factors contributing to the success of e-banking. Opting to offer e-banking by the bank rather than a separate subsidiary gives branch managers an incentive to sell this form of banking to their customers. Major security breaches have been avoided, increasing consumer confidence. At Nordea bank, customers use both a permanent password and a list of passwords that are only used once. A new list of passwords is sent to the customer once the list is exhausted.

Suominen acknowledged the use of e-cash is still quite low but expects demand to grow with electronic identification cards (SIM cards), along with m-banking, banking via the mobile phone.[50] However, whether the growth of e-cash will be as successful as the emergence of internet banking is unclear. In both these countries, the per capita value of cash holdings actually rose between 1990 and 1999; from $1224 to $1303 in Sweden and from $472 to $506 in Finland. As in other western countries, per capita debit card and credit card transactions rose during the 1990s – in Finland debit card transactions increased from 11.4 in 1987 to 51 in 1999. By contrast, there were only 0.1 e-money transactions per capita in 1999; the equivalent figure for Sweden was 0.02.[51]

According to Pyun *et al.* (2002), Scandinaviska Enskilda Banken (SEB) of Sweden introduced (European) cross-border internet banking in 1998 – its first targets were Germany

---

[49] The Swedish banks had to invest heavily in technology to offer on-line banking to retail customers because, unlike Finland, it was largely confined to business customers until the mid-1990s.

[50] Deutsche Telekom partly own a mobile payment service, PayBox.

[51] *Source*: Drehmann *et al.* (2002), table 2.

and Denmark. However, penetration of different EU states will remain difficult because of the poor integration of European payment systems mentioned in Chapter 1. Retail interbank cross-border payments are costly and slow, hampered by problems such as the absence of a single standard for processing direct debits, cheques, etc. Until a single interbank payments system is adopted (the EU has agreed to introduce a common international bank account number and international payments instructions but no date has been set for their implementation), the integration of European retail banking will be difficult, be it via the internet or more traditional methods. Diverse computing systems in the EU will also have to be integrated, requiring a substantial outlay. Cultural differences, labour laws and European directives on the use of the internet put more obstacles in their way.

Internet banking has had some success in the United States. Between 1997 and 1999 the number of US banks offering some form of internet banking increased from 100 to 1100. Just under 40% of US banks (regulated by the Office of the Comptroller of the Currency) offered internet banking services in January 2001.[52] Regulators expect about half the US banks will offer this service by 2002. The top 120 banks (with about 75% of the US bank assets) offer some form (e.g. checking balances, paying bills and transferring money between accounts) of interbank access. The number of customers using the service remains small (proportionately, compared to Scandinavia) – about 13 million households banked on-line in 2000. But the figure doubled in one year, and if this growth rate continues, large numbers of Americans will be using it.

Pyun *et al.* (2002) report that both NetBank and E*Trade have been able to attract relatively low cost deposits and profit by transforming them into high yield assets. NetBank, opened in 1996, is the largest of the branchless internet banks, operating in 50 states and 20 other countries. E*Trade began as an on-line discount broker but opened a subsidiary, E*Trade Bank. Both banks offer a full range of internet retail banking, but other innovative services suggest both have found a formula to be profitable internet banks. For example, NetBank customers can use their website to view accounts held at other banks, brokers or credit card firms. E*Trade opened a branch in New York City, benefiting from some forms of P2P (person-to-person) relationship banking. Others have fared less well, and interbank subsidiaries have recently been integrated with the parent bank's internet banking division. These include Wingspan, now a part of its parent, Bank One,[53] and Security First Network Bank, part of the Royal Bank of Canada's on-line (US) bank subsidiary.

Pyun *et al.* (2002) identify two major internet banks in Japan. In 2000, Japan Net Bank (JNB) was established by a consortium of financial institutions, including an insurance firm. JNB offers the standard retail banking services (with access to cash via over 100 000 ATMs), mutual funds and insurance. In 2001, Sony Corporation set up Sony Bank, another bank with no branches, offering all the standard transaction banking services. There are also two relatively minor internet banks, eBank and IY, and a number of on-line brokers offering securities trading. At the time of writing no internet bank was reporting profits.

In the UK, virtually all the (11) major banks offer on-line banking; many of them through subsidiaries. For example, Smile, Egg and Cahoot are subsidiaries of, respectively,

---

[52] *Source:* Hawke (2001), p. 17.

[53] Bank One is the fourth largest (by tier 1 capital) US bank, headquartered in Chicago.

the Cooperative Bank, Prudential (an insurance firm) and Abbey National. In the early years of operation, most UK e-banks reported losses, though in the second quarter of 2002, Egg reported pre-tax profits, a first for a UK internet bank. Security breaches plagued Egg in the first year of its operation. Customers found they could read the details of other customers' accounts; later some hackers were able to access their systems. Barclays Online opened in 2000, but suffered serious operational and security problems. Heavy use slowed transactions and at one point, the system crashed. Following work done on the computer software, customers found large amounts missing from or wrongly deposited in their accounts; others entered their passwords only to obtain another client's account.

Customer concern over the security of the systems may slow the growth in demand for these new forms of delivery. Information technology literate clients are probably the most suspicious of any claim that an internet-based service is secure; and there is also the challenge of convincing new users of PCs and the internet/iTV that a system is secure. Nor is the track record for resolving these problems very good: a common complaint is of "phantom" withdrawals of money from accounts via ATMs. Yet for 20 years, British banks appeared unwilling or unable to deal with the problem and, in the absence of hard evidence, usually blamed the customer for a security lapse. Recently, it became possible to video all transactions, enabling banks to identify the true phantom withdrawals, though the problem itself remains. With the advent of on-line and iTV banking, where a client's information is available at multiple sites, security breaches have the potential of rising at an exponential rate. These security concerns, together with consumer inertia, may explain why banks world-wide (with the exception of the Scandinavian countries and possibly Japan, where electronic innovation is popular) are taking a measured or "click and brick" approach in the transformation of delivery from branch (brick) to IT (click) banking. However, the success of Sweden and Finland suggests security concerns can be overcome.

Consumer groups have expressed concern about the potential for financial information on individuals to be passed between financial firms without the client's knowledge. This is not a new problem – just think of the numerous complaints to banking ombudsmen (or equivalent) that a customer has discovered he/she has been given a poor credit score because of a past misunderstanding with a financial firm that turned out to have nothing to do with the client's creditworthiness. In the absence of adequate data protection laws, the potential for mistakes will rise with the number of electronic transfers of information.

Like internet/on-line banking, digital interactive television banking presents the banking sector with an opportunity for a complete overhaul of the way it delivers or distributes core banking services. The interactive nature of iTV banking makes it attractive; an added bonus is that virtually every household (98% in the UK) owns one, and is television literate. In the UK, there is a government initiative to have all households on digital TV by 2010. The existing banks (with the capital to back the very high start-up costs) have opened up the television banking market. HSBC, the third largest bank in the world (ranked by tier 1 capital – see *The Banker*, July 2003) launched the first interactive banking service in the UK in October 1999. The Woolwich and Abbey National (Cahoot) have since followed. Barclays should gain immediate expertise in this, after purchasing the Woolwich in 2000. One outcome may be that on-line banking remains a limited service offered to a select group, while television banking appeals to the masses. However, it is worth emphasising that on-line and iTV banking have been offered almost exclusively by existing banks or their subsidiaries, not new entrants.

De Young (2001) is one of the first researchers to study the financial performance of groups of banks, what he calls "pure play" internet banks compared to standard branch banks or thrifts. The study uses quarterly US data for the period 1997Q2 to 2000Q2. Only six banks/thrifts met the strict criteria[54] to qualify as pure play, giving an unbalanced sample of 38 observations, against 3225 for the benchmark banks/thrifts. Both groups are *de novo* (newly chartered) banks that commenced operations in the period 1997–99. Using 17 measures of financial performance in a multiple regression model, De Young found that the internet banks were significantly less profitable than the branch banks of similar age, offering similar bank services. Several factors contributed to the lower profitability. The internet group's relatively low physical overheads were more than offset by high non-interest expenses – largely in the form of high staff costs. Hence overall, overhead costs were not lower. Furthermore, there is no evidence that these banks pay higher than average deposit rates. He found non-interest income ratios were significantly lower than for the benchmark banks, suggesting the absence of "P2P" contact makes the cross-selling of other services more difficult, which in turn will lower revenues. Finally, the internet group had higher asset growth rates which outstripped the growth of deposits, forcing them to draw on relatively expensive equity capital to fund the growth.

De Young acknowledged the limitations of his study, such as a very small sample size of pure play banks. Furthermore, critics might argue that these banks (and e-commerce firms in general) simply take longer to become profitable. Finally, it may be that internet banking is more successful if offered with traditional branch banking. Furst *et al.* (2000) employ a large database of US commercial banks, but use a broader definition, i.e. any bank which offers an internet service. They find the typical internet bank is more profitable than non-internet banks, and generates more non-interest revenue.

The amount of capital required to offer PC, internet or iTV banking will require deep pockets for existing banks and new entrants. Innovations such as on-line banking and iTV banking should reduce the need for banks to have a global presence, because they can offer banking services via the internet without setting up costly branches or subsidiaries in other countries. In Europe, cross-border mergers continue apace, though attempts at cross-border internet banking have not proved successful to date. There are problems to overcome, especially with the payments system. Chapter 5 discusses European integration problems in more detail.

To summarise, most of the evidence to date suggests the emergence of a cashless society is unlikely. Cash remains attractive because of the considerable costs associated with making e-cash secure, it is convenient, ensures anonymity and provides residents of unstable countries with an opportunity to hoard safe, foreign currencies. Even if digital cash could overcome these considerable hurdles, governments are unlikely to be willing to lose their sovereignty over currency issue, and will establish measures to safeguard their control over monetary policy.

---

[54] The banks had to be newly chartered, and offer a complete range of banking services. The Federal Deposit Insurance Corporation had to identify them as banks that used the internet for primary contact with customers.

The use of the internet, interactive digital television and other new forms of delivering core banking services should be embraced by the banks because of opportunities related to the substantial change in the way banking services are distributed. The weight of evidence suggests the new delivery methods will substantially reduce the cost of delivering core banking, even after the capital investment required is taken into account. Security issues must be addressed (the Scandinavian experience with internet banking demonstrates they can be) to alleviate consumer concerns. Banks also must be proactive in dealing with consumer inertia, offering the right combination of incentives to persuade consumers to adopt the new technology. Experience in the USA and Scandinavia suggests this can be done without offering high deposit rates that eat into profits. Banks must also be ready to face increased competition in certain off-balance sheet activities, such as their intermediary role in initial public offerings and bond issues. All these remarks point to the need for banks to evolve in the face of new technology, a point which is hardly unique to the banking sector.

## The growth of non-banks

There has been much discussion on the threat posed to traditional banks by the growth of non-banks. *Non-banks*,[55] by definition, are firms which do not offer a complete core banking service but are very similar to banks. For example, personal loan or mortgage corporations specialise in loans or mortgages that are funded through bond issues and/or by turning a bundle of assets into asset backed or mortgage backed securities and selling them to raise liquidity. Though they offer a "banking" product, loans/mortgages, they are not banks because they are not funded by deposits. General Electric Capital (GE Capital) is the financial services subsidiary of General Electric. It issues the largest amount of commercial paper in the USA, supplies credit card facilities to department stores, is the largest insurer of private homes and, for nine years, owned a securities firm, Kidder Peabody. In the UK, Marks & Spencer, well known for its retail clothes, food and home furnishings, began to offer a selection of financial services in the 1980s, starting with an in-house credit card business and expanding into personal loans, unit trusts, personal equity plans and, from 1995, insurance and pensions. Marks & Spencer is able to fund its asset requirements because it is top-rated by key rating agencies. It has since been followed by some well-known shop/brand names such as Virgin, Direct Line Insurance, Tesco and Sainsbury.

However, virtually all of these non-bank firms have chosen to enter niche markets – they do not offer the core activities that define a bank, intermediation and the provision of liquidity. Usually, if one or more of their products includes part of the core functions (e.g. personal loans and/or deposits), these services are supplied to them by existing banks. For example, Tesco, Sainsbury and Virgin have their banking products supplied to them by either the Royal Bank of Scotland or the Halifax Bank of Scotland (HBOS). First Direct, the highly successful telephone bank (now offering on-line services) is a wholly owned

---

[55] In the United States, a loophole in the law made the growth of "non-bank" banks possible: because they accepted deposits requiring notice of withdrawal, as opposed to being payable on demand. See chapter five for more detail.

subsidiary of HSBC. Also, there are notable examples of failed entry into these markets. In 1999, Marks & Spencer allowed the use of rival credit cards in its shops for the first time, part of an overall strategy to revive profits. In 2003, it abandoned its in-house card for a Mastercard issue which rewards loyalty. Sears Roebuck was one of the first large retail firms to offer financial services, but it has recently scaled back its activities. Westinghouse wound up its credit arm after it lost nearly $1 billion in property loans. GE Capital purchased Kidder Peabody for $600 million in 1986 but, in 1994, after losses on the mortgage backed securities portfolio and dubious trading activities in government bonds, sold it to Paine Webber (an investment bank) for $90 million plus a 25% stake in Paine Webber. In the UK, the poor performance, to date, of the telephone/on-line bank Egg illustrates the difficulties of setting up a whole new bank, even if the bank offers customers attractive deposit rates.

### Consolidation

Another important trend is increased consolidation of the national banking sector through mergers and acquisitions. European bank mergers rose from 49 in 1990 to 184 in 1999; for US banks they rose from 113 to 381 in 1995, but had fallen back to 255 by 1999. Mergers of securities firms followed a similar trend.[56] It is unusual for banks to merge because of difficulties related to hidden skeletons in their balance sheets. The rapid pace of mergers, which had begun to tail off by 2001, is discussed in detail in Chapter 9.

## 2.7. Conclusion

This chapter began with a review of the diversification of banks into "non-banking" financial services. New forms of off-balance sheet activity, in particular, derivatives and securitisation, enabled banks to expand their intermediary role in risk management. This theme will be developed further in Chapter 3. The second part of the chapter looked at the effects of this diversification on bank income. Though diversification is thought to be value-enhancing for firms, including banks, there is some evidence that movement into OBS activities has increased the volatility of bank income.

In light of the above finding, a number of bank performance measures were reviewed, to provide an idea of the position of the banking sector in the 21st century. The evidence was mixed: some was indicative of healthy bank performance; other measures indicated the opposite. The relative performance of banks on the stock market was consistent with this mixed evidence; UK bank stocks outperformed the average in most years, European banks tracked the average, falling below it for some years in the 1990s. US banks were relatively poor performers.

The final parts of the chapter considered the issue of whether the rapid advancements in information technology might undermine the ability of banks to offer core functions, or even replace them. To maintain a competitive advantage in the financial market place, banks will have to adapt to the changing nature of intermediation, and compete with

---

[56] *Source*: Group of 10 (2001), and tables A4, A5.

new technology which narrows information asymmetries (thereby reducing the need for an intermediary). At the same time, once the IT investment is made, it should reduce banks' administrative and delivery costs, freeing them from the costly maintenance of extensive branch networks. Furthermore, high IT costs should deter new entrants. Banks will also be challenged by changing consumer preferences, as TV or computer-literate customers demand value for money on intermediation, payments and a wide range of financial services via the internet. Competition may heighten and, in common with other sectors, banking markets will evolve over time. However, banks themselves are here to stay unless they prove unable to maintain a competitive advantage in the core and other products they offer.

The banks most likely to survive are those which embrace the rapid progress of information technology, consolidation of the banking/financial services sector and for European banks, the advent of the euro together with a single European financial market. Treating these changes as a threat, for which defensive action must be taken, will guarantee decline. Thus, one can conclude that Gates' remarks were largely correct, but the emphasis should be on the word evolve. Banking and banks will survive, provided they treat these dramatic changes as opportunities to strengthen their position in the financial sector. In this sense, banks are no different from firms in any other sector. Firms remain in business only if they can evolve over time, spotting the new technology and changes in consumer culture to sustain a competitive advantage over other firms. The surviving banks may not be the household names of today (how many banks can claim to have the same name/functions as they did at the close of the 19th century?), but they are likely to continue to supply the core banking functions.

# MANAGEMENT OF RISKS IN BANKING

*"The fact is that bankers are in the business of managing risk. Pure and simple, that is the business of banking."* (Walter Wriston, former CEO of Citibank; *The Economist*, 10 April 1993)

*"Banks have an ingrained habit of plunging headlong into mistakes together where blame minimising managers appear to feel comfortable making blunders so long as their competitors are making the same ones... VaR is the alibi that bankers will give shareholders (and the bailing out taxpayer) to show documented due diligence."* (Taleb, in Jorion and Taleb, 1997, p. 3)

## 3.1. Introduction

Any profit-maximising business, including banks, must deal with macroeconomic risks, such as the effects of inflation or recession and microeconomic risks like new competitive threats. Breakdowns in technology, commercial failure of a supplier or customer, political interference or a natural disaster are additional potential risks all firms face. However, banks also confront a number of risks atypical of non-financial firms, and it is these risks which are the subject of this chapter.

In Chapter 1, it was argued that banks perform intermediary and payment functions that distinguish them from other businesses. The core product is intermediation between those with surplus liquidity, who make deposits, and those in need of liquidity, who borrow from the bank. The payments system facilitates the intermediary role of banks. For banks where intermediation is the principal function, risk management consists largely of good asset–liability management (ALM) – in the post-war period, right up to the early 1980s, whole books were devoted to ALM techniques.

The role of banks in the financial system changed substantially from the late 1970s onwards. The bank environment was relatively stable and characterised by close regulation; rules which limited the scope of operations and risk; cartel-like behaviour which kept competition to a minimum, and given steady, if not spectacular returns, little incentive to innovate. In most developed countries during the 1980s, regulatory reforms and innovation broke down barriers in financial markets and eliminated the high degree of segmentation, which in turn, increased competition. Japan was the notable exception. The 1990s saw the continued demarcation of financial markets which had begun in the 1980s, and banks faced new risks to manage as a result of continued disintermediation, innovation and greater competition, especially in wholesale markets, where globalisation further eroded barriers.

In Chapter 2 the movement of banks into new areas of off-balance sheet banking, such as the switch from interest income generating sources to non-interest income activities, was discussed.[1] As a consequence, risk management has expanded to include not just ALM, but the management of risks arising from off-balance sheet activity. Furthermore, some new techniques developed to manage market risk are increasingly applied to credit risk management. Risk management involves spotting the key risks, deciding where risk exposure should be increased or reduced, and identifying the methods for monitoring and managing the bank's risk position in real time. Though Walter Wriston's quote is more than a decade old, it summarises the key role of the 21st century bank. At the same time, Nassim Taleb, a PhD with many years of trading experience and author of a book on options, cautions against excessive reliance on value at risk (VaR), one of the new models used to manage not only market risk but, in some banks, credit risk.

Though the risks faced by banks in the 1970s appear straightforward compared to what they are now, there are examples of spectacular collapses in every decade. In the 1970s it was Franklin National Bank and Bankhaus Herstatt, and in the UK, the secondary banking crisis.[2] In the 1980s, over 2000 thrifts and banks in the United States either failed or were merged with a healthy bank. The Spanish and Scandinavian banks also experienced severe problems, which led to a notable amount of bank consolidation. In the 1990s, it was the turn of Bank of Credit and Commerce International, Barings and the Japanese banking system as a whole. For the first time, problems with a non-bank, a hedge fund, to which many key global banks were exposed, threatened global financial stability. In the early 2000s, it may be the turn of the German banking system, where a crisis appears to be looming at the time of writing. Though these failures are the exception rather than the rule in most cases, it demonstrates that no matter what the structure of the banking system, poor risk management can cause insolvency, which may be endemic in a particular country.

Credit risk, the risk that a borrower defaults on a bank loan, is the risk usually associated with banks, because of the lending side of the intermediary function. It continues to be central to good risk management because most bank failures (see Chapter 6) are linked to a high ratio of non-performing loans to total loans. However, as banks become more complex organisations, offering more fee-based financial services and using relatively new financial instruments, other types of financial risk have been unbundled and made more transparent. The purpose of this chapter is to outline the key financial risks modern banks are exposed to, and to consider how these risks should be managed.

---

[1] Though it is unclear whether this has made banks' income more or less volatile.

[2] The secondary banking crisis was caused by financial liberalisation which began with competition and credit control in 1971. The reforms led the banks to lower loan rates quite sharply and bid more aggressively for deposits. A subsequent tightening of monetary policy caused an increase in interest rates, which contributed to a sudden souring of the urban real estate market (which had been booming for 18 months) in late 1972. Many of the loans granted by the smaller banks were for property development and bankruptcies followed, together with liquidity injections by the central bank. See Chapters 7 and 8 for a more detailed discussion of this and the other bank failures/crises mentioned here.

The chapter is organised as follows. Section 3.2 provides brief definitions of the different financial risks banks face, and section 3.3 reviews the traditional asset and liability management approach. The next section looks at derivatives as tools of risk management. The management of market and credit risk is discussed in sections 3.5 and 3.6, including a review of RAROC, VaR and other approaches used in the management of risks. The final section looks at how a major commercial bank organises risk management in the new century. Section 3.8 concludes.

## 3.2. Key Financial Risks in the 21st Century

Risk management involves identification of the key financial risks, deciding where risk exposure should be increased or reduced, and finding methods for monitoring and managing the bank's risk position in real time. Throughout this chapter, readers should bear in mind that for all banks, from the traditional bank where ALM is the key activity to the complex financial conglomerate offering a range of bank and non-bank financial services, the objective is to maximise profits and shareholder value-added, and risk management is central to the achievement of this goal. Shareholder value-added is defined as earnings in excess of an "expected minimum return"[3] on economic capital. The minimum return is the risk-free rate plus the risk premium for the profit-maximising firm, in this case a bank. The risk premium associated with a given bank will vary, depending on the perceived risk of the bank's activities in the market place. The average risk premium ranges from 7% to 10% for banks in most OECD countries. The risk-free rate refers to the rate of return on a safe asset, that is, a rate of return which is guaranteed. The nominal rate of return on government bonds is normally treated as a risk-free rate, provided there is a low probability of the government defaulting on its obligation.[4] Suppose an investor purchases equity in a bank and expects a minimum return of 15%. If, when the shares are sold, the return is 20%, then an extra 5% is added to the value of the investment, and shareholder value-added is positive. If the return is less than 15%, the outcome for the investor is a negative shareholder value-added.

There is a link between shareholder value-added and other performance measures, such as return on assets or return on equity. ROA, ROE and profitability are widely reported for publicly quoted firms, including banks, and are known to influence share prices. Thus, if bank shareholders treat these measures as indicators of performance, and act upon them, they can affect shareholder value. For example, if a firm turns in an unexpectedly poor report for several quarters and shareholders act by dumping the shares, the price of the shares will fall. A prolonged decline will lower shareholder value-added and it could even turn negative.

### 3.2.1. Formal Definitions
### *Risk*

Risk is defined as the volatility or standard deviation (the square root of the variance) of net cash flows of the firm, or, if the company is very large, a unit within it. In a profit-maximising

---

[3] From the standpoint of the company, shareholders' expected minimum return is the firm's cost of capital, which can be computed using the Capital Asset Pricing Model (CAPM).

[4] There is a possibility that a positive inflation rate will reduce the real return, but investors usually have the option of purchasing index-linked bonds, where the return on the bond is linked to the rate of inflation.

bank, a unit could be the whole bank, a branch or a division. The risk may also be measured in terms of different financial products. But the objective of the bank as a whole will be to add value to the bank's equity by maximising the risk-adjusted return to shareholders. In this sense, a bank is like any other business, but for banks, profitability (and shareholder value-added) is going to depend on the management of risks. Large universal banks will focus on the management of risk on the banking book (the traditional asset–liability management), the trading book (where banks are buying and selling bonds, equity, etc.), and in the risk management advice they give to corporate customers. Corporate treasurers of non-financial firms can incur large losses as a result of poor financial risk management. But it rarely leads to insolvency, if the core business operations are sound. By contrast, for banks, risk management is their core business. In the extreme, inadequate risk management may threaten the "solvency" of a bank, where insolvency is defined as a negative net worth, that is, liabilities in excess of assets.

The risks specific to the business of banking are:

- Credit
- Counterparty
- Liquidity or funding risk
- Settlements or payments risk
- Market or price risk, which includes
  - currency risk
  - interest rate risk
- Capital or gearing risk
- Operational risk
- Sovereign and political risk

## *Credit risk and counterparty risk*

If two parties enter into a financial contract, **counterparty risk** is the risk that one of the parties will renege on the terms of a contract. **Credit risk** is the risk that an asset or a loan becomes irrecoverable in the case of outright default, or the risk of an unexpected delay in the servicing of a loan. Since bank and borrower usually sign a loan contract, credit risk can be considered a form of counterparty risk. However, the term counterparty risk is traditionally used in the context of traded financial instruments (for example, the counterparty in a futures agreement or a swap), whereas credit risk refers to the probability of default on a loan agreement.

Banks are in business to take credit risk, it is the traditional way banks made money. To quote a former chairman of the US Federal Reserve System:

*"If you don't have some bad loans you are not in the business."*[5]

If a borrower defaults on a loan or unexpectedly stops repayments, the present value of the asset declines. Losses from loan default should be kept to a minimum, since they are charged against capital. If losses are high, it could increase the bank's cost of raising finance, and in

---

[5] P. Volker, former chairman of the Board of Governors of the Federal Reserve System.

the extreme, lead to bank insolvency. The bank would avoid credit risk by choosing assets with very low default risk but low return, but the bank profits from taking risk. Credit risk rises if a bank has many medium to low quality loans on its books, but the return will be higher. So banks will opt for a portfolio of assets with varying degrees of risk, always taking into account that a higher default risk is accompanied by higher expected return. Since much of the default risk arises from moral hazard and information problems, banks must monitor their borrowers to increase their return from the loan portfolio.

Good credit risk management has always been a key component to the success of the bank, even as banks move into other areas. However, as will become apparent in Chapter 6, the cause of the majority of bank failures can be traced back to weak loan books. For example, Franklin National Bank announced large losses on foreign exchange dealings but it also had many unsound loans. Likewise many of the "thrift" and commercial bank failures in the USA during the 1980s were partly caused by a mismatch in terms between assets and liabilities, and problem loans. In Japan, it was the failure of mortgage banks in 1995 that signalled major problems with the balance sheets of virtually *all* banks.

## *Liquidity or funding risk*

These terms are really synonyms – the risk of insufficient liquidity for normal operating requirements, that is, the ability of the bank to meet its liabilities when they fall due. A shortage of liquid assets is often the source of the problems, because the bank is unable to raise funds in the retail or wholesale markets. Funding risk usually refers to a bank's inability to fund its day-to-day operations.

As was discussed in Chapter 1, liquidity is an important service offered by a bank, and one of the services that distinguishes banks from other financial firms. Customers place their deposits with a bank, confident they can withdraw the deposit when they wish, even if it is a term deposit and they want to withdraw their funds before the term is up. If there are rumours about the bank's ability pay out on demand, and most depositors race to the bank to withdraw deposits, it will soon become illiquid. In the absence of a liquidity injection by the central bank or a lifeboat rescue, it could quickly become insolvent since it can do nothing to reduce overhead costs during such a short period.

The liquidity of an asset is the ease with which it can be converted to cash. A bank can reduce its liquidity risk by keeping its assets liquid (i.e. investing in short-term assets), but if it is excessively liquid, its returns will be lower. All banks make money by having a gap between their maturities, that is, more short-term deposits and more long-term loans: *"funding short and lending long"*. They can do this because of fractional reserve lending – only a fraction of deposits are held in reserve, and the rest are loaned out. Liquidity can be costly in terms of higher interest that might have been earned on funds that have been locked away for a specified time.

Maturity matching (or getting rid of all maturity gaps) will guarantee sufficient liquidity and eliminate liquidity risk because all deposits are invested in assets of identical maturities: then every deposit is repaid from the cash inflow of maturing assets, assuming these assets are also risk-free. But such a policy will never be adopted because the bank, as an intermediary, engages in asset transformation to make profits. In macroeconomic terms, provided there is no change in the liquidity preferences of the economy as a whole, then the withdrawal of a deposit by one customer will eventually end up as a deposit in another account somewhere in the banking system. If banks kept to a strict maturity match, then competition would see to it that the bank which invested in assets rather than keeping idle deposits could offer a higher return (and therefore, greater profitability) compared to banks that simply hold idle deposits.

At the microeconomic level, the maturity profile of a bank's liabilities understates actual liquidity because term deposits tend to be rolled over, and only a small percentage of a bank's deposits will be withdrawn on a given day. This is another argument for incurring some liquidity risk. Given that the objective of a bank is to maximise profit/shareholder value-added, all banks will have some acceptable degree of maturity mismatch.

## Settlement/payments risk

Settlement or payments risk is created if one party to a deal pays money or delivers assets before receiving its own cash or assets, thereby exposing it to potential loss. Settlement risk can include credit risk if one party fails to settle, i.e. reneges on the contract, and liquidity risk – a bank may not be able to settle a transaction if it becomes illiquid.

A more specialised term for settlement risk is **Herstatt risk**, named after the German bank which collapsed in 1974 as a result of large foreign exchange losses. The reason settlement risk is closely linked to foreign exchange markets is because different time zones may create a gap in the timing of payments. Settlement of foreign exchange transactions requires a cash transfer from the account of one bank to that of another through the central banks of the currencies involved. Bankhaus Herstatt bought Deutschemarks from 12 US banks, with settlement due on 26th June. On the 26th, the American banks ordered their corresponding German banks to debit their German accounts and deposit the DMs in the Landesbank (the regional bank was acting as a clearing house). The American banks expected to be repaid in dollars, but Herstatt was declared bankrupt at 4 p.m. German time – after the German market was closed but before the American market had closed, because of the 6-hour[6] time difference. The Landesbank had already paid DMs to Bankhaus Herstatt, but the US banks had not received their dollars. The exposed US banks were faced with a liquidity crisis, which came close to triggering a collapse of the American payments system.

Settlement risk is a problem in other markets, especially the interbank markets because the volume of interbank payments is extremely high. For example, it can take just 10 days to turn over the annual value of the GNP of a major OECD country – in the UK, it is roughly £1–£1.6 trillion. With such large volumes, banks settle amounts far in excess of their capital. Netting is one way of reducing payments risk, by allowing a bank to make a single net payment to a regulated counterparty, instead of a series of gross payments partly offset by payments in the other direction. It results in much lower volumes (because less money flows through the payments and settlement systems), thereby reducing the absolute level of risk in the banking system. Netting is common among domestic payments systems in industrialised countries. At the end of each day, the central bank requires each bank

---

[6] On the east coast of the USA; 9 hours on the west coast.

to settle its net obligations, after cancelling credits and debits due on a given day. If the interbank transaction is intraday, the exposure will not appear on a bank's balance sheet, which is an added risk.

However, settlement risk is still present because the netting is multilateral. The payments are interbank, and banks will not know the aggregate exposure of another bank. Any problem with one bank can have a domino effect. If one bank fails to meet its obligations, other banks along the line are affected, even though they have an indirect connection with the failing bank, the counterparty to the exchange. Given the large volume of transactions in relation to the capital set aside by each bank, the central bank will be concerned about systemic risk – the failure to meet obligations by one bank triggers system-wide failures. Most central banks/regulators deal with this problem through a variety of measures, including a voluntary agreement to conform to bilateral limits on credit exposures, capping multilateral exposures, requiring collateral, passing the necessary legislation to make bilateral and multilateral netting legally enforceable, or imposing penalty rates on banks which approach the central bank late in the day.

Increasingly, there has been a move from netting to real time gross settlement. Real time gross settlement (RTGS), defined in Chapter 1, allows transactions across settlement accounts at the central bank (or a clearing house) to be settled, gross, in real time, rather than at the end of the day. By the late 1990s, most EU countries, Japan, the USA and Switzerland had real time gross settlement systems in place for domestic large value payments. In the EU, the plan is for the domestic payments systems to be harmonised, commencing with RTGS in all countries for large value payments, with cross-border participation in the payments systems. Under a single currency, it is likely there will be an EU-wide RTGS.

Some private netting systems have been established. ECHO is an exchange rate clearing house organisation set up by 14 European banks. Its business has diminished with the advent of the euro, because there is no foreign exchange risk in the eurozone. However, foreign transactions with countries outside Euroland continue. Multinet serves a similar purpose for a group of North American banks. Both commenced operations in 1994 to facilitate multilateral netting of spot and forward foreign exchange contracts. The clearing house is the counterparty to the transactions they handle, centralising and offsetting the payments of all members in a particular currency. Some central bank regulators are concerned the clearing houses lack the capital to cover a member's default on an obligation, in other words, that there is some counterparty risk.

## *Market or price risk*

Market (or price) risk is normally associated with instruments traded on well-defined markets, though increasingly, techniques are used to assess the risk arising from over the counter instruments, and/or traded items where the market is not very liquid. The value of any instrument will be a function of price, coupon, coupon frequency, time, interest rate and other factors. If a bank is holding instruments on account (for example, equities, bonds), then it is exposed to price or market risk, the risk that the price of the instrument will be volatile.

*General* or *systematic market risk* is caused by a movement in the prices of all market instruments because of, for example, a change in economic policy. *Unsystematic* or *specific market risk* arises in situations where the price of one instrument moves out of line with other similar instruments, because of an event (or events) related to the issuer of the instrument. For example, the announcement of an unexpectedly large government fiscal deficit might cause a drop in the share price index (systematic risk), while an environmental law suit against a firm will reduce its share price, but is unlikely to cause a general decline in the index (specific or unsystematic market risk).

A bank can be exposed to market risk (general and specific) in relation to:

- Equity
- Commodities (e.g. cocoa, wheat, oil)
- Currencies (e.g. the price of sterling appreciates against the euro)
- Debt securities (fixed and floating rate debt instruments, such as bonds)
- Debt derivatives (forward rate agreements, futures and options on debt instruments, interest rate and cross-currency swaps, and forward foreign exchange positions)
- Equity derivatives (equity swaps, futures and options on equity indices, options on futures, warrants)

Thus, market risk includes a very large subset of other risks. Two major types of market risks are currency and interest rate risk. If exchange rates are flexible, any net short or long open position in a given currency will expose the bank to *foreign exchange* or *currency risk*, a form of market risk. In this case, it is the market for foreign exchange, and the "price", the relative price of currencies given by the exchange rate. A bank with global operations will have multiple currency exposures. The currency risk arises from adverse exchange rate fluctuations, which affect the bank's foreign exchange positions taken on its own account, or on behalf of its customers. For example, if a bank is long on dollars and the dollar declines in value against other currencies, this bank is going to lose out. Banks engage in spot, forward and swap dealing, with large positions that can undergo big changes within minutes. Mismatch by currency and by maturity is an essential feature of the business – good mismatch judgements can be profitable and signal successful risk management.

If rates between two currencies are fixed, there is no currency risk, provided the arrangement lasts. Fixed exchange rate regimes were the norm from after World War II[7] to the early 1970s. Some countries, such as Hong Kong and Argentina, chose to fix their currencies against the dollar. Unfortunately, Argentina's peg[8] unravelled after it declared it could not repay its international debt in 2001. As part of the transition towards a single currency in Europe, countries entered into a fixed exchange rate regime – the ERM or exchange rate mechanism.

Though there is no currency risk while exchange rates are fixed, investors or banks can be suddenly exposed to very large risks (and losses or gains) if the fixed rate arrangement comes under so much pressure that one of the currencies is devalued or it collapses. An example is when the UK came out of Europe's exchange rate mechanism. In the days leading up to the collapse the UK government vowed sterling would stay in the ERM,[9] and increased interest

---

[7] Part of the Bretton Woods agreement in 1944.

[8] Pegs vary in degree. Both Hong Kong and Argentina (until late 2001) have currency boards, a hard peg.

[9] Under the rules of the exchange rate mechanism, currencies could fluctuate with a band of (+) or (−) 15% since August 1993. Before that, it was as low as (+) or (−) 2.5.%.

rates twice in one day – they peaked at 15%. By late afternoon of the same day (16/9/92), £10 billion had been used to support sterling. The UK left the ERM, quickly followed by Italy. Spain was forced into a parity change. For banks long in any of these currencies, the losses were substantial.

The only way of eliminating currency risk altogether is to adopt a common currency, the most recent example being the introduction of the euro by all but three member states of the European Union. Euro states share the same currency, getting rid of foreign exchange risk, though trade outside Euroland does expose these states to currency risk.

While an important risk consideration for banks, to do justice to the subject would require an extensive diversion. Whole books are devoted to the determinants of exchange rates and the management of currency risk, and it will not be considered in further detail here.

## Interest rate risk

Interest rates are another form of price risk, because the interest rate is the "price" of money, or the opportunity cost of holding money in the narrow form. It arises due to interest rate mismatches. Banks engage in asset transformation, and their assets and liabilities differ in maturity and volume. The traditional focus of an asset–liability management group within a bank is the management of interest rate risk, but this has expanded to include off-balance sheet items, as will be seen below.

## Capital or gearing risk

Banks are more highly geared (leveraged) than other businesses – individuals feel safe placing their deposits at a bank with a reputation for soundness. There are normally no sudden or random changes in the amount people wish to save or borrow, hence the banking system as a whole tends to be stable, unless depositors are given reason to believe the system is becoming unsound.

Thus, for banks, the gearing (or leverage) limit is more critical because their relatively high gearing means the threshold of tolerable risk is lower in relation to the balance sheet. This is where capital comes in: its principal function is to act as a buffer by supporting or absorbing losses. Banks which take on more risk should set aside more capital, and this is the principle behind the Basel risk assets ratio (see Chapter 4). Banks need to increase their gearing to improve their return to shareholders. To see the link, consider the equation below:

$$\text{ROE} = \text{ROA} \times (\text{gearing multiplier})$$

where:
ROE: return on equity or net income/equity
ROA: return on assets or net income/assets
Gearing/leverage multiplier: assets/equity

As will be discussed in detail in Chapter 4, Basel requires a bank's risk assets ratio to be 8% (i.e. [capital/(weighted risk assets)] = 0.08). If a bank satisfies this requirement, it means its equity is about 8%, its debt must be 92%, giving a gearing/leverage ratio of 92/8, or 11.5.

Contrast this with a typical debt to equity ratio for non-financial firms, of, for example, $60/40 = 1.5$.

Since the bank's ROA is typically very small, the ROE can be increased by higher leverage or raising the ratio of assets to equity. But with higher leverage comes greater risk, because there are more assets on the bank's balance sheet. Generally, a bank is said to be *highly geared/leveraged* when a large exposure is associated with a small capital outlay. This can occur in the more traditional activities such as fractional reserve lending (they only keep a small fraction of their deposits as reserves), or because of newer types of business, such as the use of derivatives.

Capital risk is the outcome of other risks incurred by the bank, such as credit, market or liquidity risk. Poor earnings, caused by high loan losses, or inappropriate risk taking in other areas puts the bank's capital at risk. Banks perceived to have an insufficient amount of capital will find it difficult to raise funding. Two ratios will be monitored by agents funding or considering funding the bank:

- The bank's capital ratio or its Basel risk assets ratio – capital/weighted risk assets;
- The bank's leverage ratio – debt/equity.

## Operational risk

The Bank for International Settlements defines *operational risk* as:

> *"The risk of direct or indirect loss resulting from inadequate or failed internal processes, people, and systems, or from external events."* (BIS, 2001, p. 27)

The definition of operational risk varies considerably, and more important, measuring it can be even more difficult. The Basel Committee has conducted surveys of banks on operational risk. Based on Basel (2003), the key types of operational risk are identified as follows.[10]

(1) **Physical Capital:** the subsets of which are: damage to physical assets, business disruption, system failure, problems with execution and delivery, and/or process management. Technological failure dominates this category and here, the principal concern is with a bank's computer systems. A crash in the computing system can destroy a bank. Most banks have a duplicate system which is backed up in real time, in a secret location, should anything go wrong with the main computer system. When banks and other financial institutions had their premises damaged or destroyed as a result of "9/11", they were able to return to business quite quickly (in alternative accommodation), relying on the back-up computer systems. More generally, the loss of physical assets, such as buildings owned, is a form of operational risk. However, banks take out insurance against the risk of fire or other catastrophes, and to this extent, they have already hedged themselves against the risk. To the extent they are fully hedged, there should be no need to set aside capital. Problems with physical capital may interfere with process management and contribute to a break down in execution and/or delivery.

---

[10] This classification of operational risk is based on identifying four general categories, and using the various loss events reported in table 3 (among others) in Basel (2003).

(2) **Human Capital**: this type of risk arises from human error, problems with employment practices or employees' health and safety, and internal fraud. An employee can accidentally enter too many (or too few) zeroes on a sell or buy order. Or a bank might find itself being fined for breach of health and safety rules, or brought before an employment tribunal accused of unfair dismissal. In addition, employees can defraud their bank, but this is discussed in a separate category below.

(3) **Legal**: the main legal risk is that of the bank being sued. It can arise as a result of the treatment of clients, the sale of products, or business practices. There are countless examples of banks being taken to court by disgruntled corporate customers, who claim they were misled by advice given to them or business products sold. Contracts with customers may be disputed. One of the most recent and costly examples of shoddy treatment of clients is the implicit[11] admission, in 2003, by all the major investment banks that they failed to control the conflict of interest between research and investment banking divisions. In addition to fines summing up to hundreds of millions, these banks face civil law suits from angry clients who claim they acted on paid advice from research departments to invest in certain stocks, only to find there was no solid research to back the recommendations, but rather, pressure from corporate finance divisions to bid up the price of one or more shares.

(4) **Fraud**: the fraud may be internal or external to the bank. For example, the looting of his company's pension by Mr Maxwell affected the banks because they were holding some of the assets he had stolen from the funds as collateral. Another illustration of this form of risk is the Hammersmith and Fulham Council case. This London borough had taken out interest rate swaps in the period December 1983 to February 1989. The swaps fell into two categories, one for hedging and one for speculation. With local taxpayers facing a bill of tens of millions of pounds, the House of Lords (in 1991) declared all the contracts null and void, overturning an earlier decision by the appeal court. Barclays, Chemical, the Midland,[12] Mitsubishi Finance International and Security Pacific were the key banks left facing £400 million in losses and £15 million in legal fees. Examples of internal fraud include rogue trading. Nick Leeson brought down Barings with losses of $1.5 billion, and John Rusnak was convicted of fraud at a US subsidiary of Allied Irish Bank, which cost it $750 million.

As can be seen from the classification above, factors contributing to operational risk are not necessarily independent of each other. Internal fraud could be classified as a human capital risk. If an employee sues because of breaches in health and safety, it falls in both the human capital and/or legal risk subclassifications. Certain payment risks may also fall into the operational risk category. For example, in 1985, a major US bank experienced computer problems which prevented it from making outgoing payments. It was forced to borrow $20 billion from the Federal Reserve to meet these payments. Simultaneously, payments to this bank from other banks could not be made, so they flooded the interbank markets, forcing down the federal funds rate by 3%. Thus, an operational failure created settlement and liquidity risks. Or if a borrower is granted a loan based on a fraudulent loan application and subsequently defaults, it will be recorded as a loan loss, and therefore, a credit risk issue, even though the fraud was the original source of the problem.

---

[11] As part of the deal struck with New York's Attorney General's Office, the banks were not obliged to admit any wrongdoing, but paid considerable sums in fines and related costs.

[12] The Midland Bank was subsequently purchased by Hong Kong and Shanghai Bank (HSBC) in 1992.

Classification issues alone make quantification of operational risk difficult, so it should come as no surprise that the "Basel 2" proposals for the treatment of the operational risk proved highly controversial. Operational risk is reviewed at length in Chapter 4.

## Sovereign and political risks[13]

*Sovereign Risk* normally refers to the risk that a government will default on debt owed to a bank or government agency. In this sense, it is a special form of credit risk, but the bank lacks the usual tools for recovering the debt at its disposal. If a private debtor defaults, the bank will normally take possession of assets pledged as collateral. However, if the default is by a sovereign government, the bank is unlikely to be able to recover some of the debt by taking over some of the country's assets. This creates problems with enforcing the loan contract. Sovereign risk can refer to either debt repudiation or debt rescheduling. Since the end of the Second World War, only China, Cuba and North Korea have actually repudiated their debt obligations. Some of the poorest countries had their debt forgiven after a 1996 agreement reached by western countries and their banks, the IMF and the World Bank.

Some countries (e.g. Argentina, Russia) have threatened to repudiate their debt, but in the end, were persuaded by the World Bank and the IMF to reschedule the debt. Other countries announce they cannot meet an agreed payment schedule and renegotiate new terms; usually with the IMF acting as an intermediary. The banks agree to restructure debt repayments and make new loans. Normally the IMF acts as broker or intermediary. The rescheduling agreement is made in exchange for the country agreeing to meet new macroeconomic targets, such as reductions in inflation and subsidies and/or an increase in taxation. The World Bank may also participate in rescheduling negotiations.

*Political Risk* is broadly defined as state interference in the operations of a domestic and/or foreign firm. Banks can be subjected to sudden tax hikes, interest rate or exchange control regulations, or be nationalised. For example, since the Second World War, France has vacillated between nationalisation and privatisation of its banking sector. All businesses are exposed to political risk, but banks are particularly vulnerable because of their critical position in the financial system.

## Interaction among risks

All of the various risks discussed above are interdependent, and as was noted earlier, there are other risks, common to all businesses including banks. These other risks are often more discrete or event-type, affecting a bank's profitability and risk exposure. They include sudden, unexpected changes in taxation, regulatory policy or in financial market conditions due to war, revolution or market collapse, and macroeconomic risks such as increased inflation, inflation volatility and unemployment.

Regulators have identified three key risks related to banks: credit, market (including risks arising from changes in interest rates, exchange rates, equity prices and commodity prices)

---

[13] The term "country risk" appears in some of the literature. It can refer to sovereign risk as defined above, or some form of political interference, or both. To avoid confusion, this book adopts the terms "sovereign" and "political" risk.

and operating risk. The rest of this chapter will focus on the management of interest rate, credit and market risks. Much of the discussion on operating risk is reserved for the next chapter, because it is the regulators who have singled it out for special treatment – most bankers argue they have been taking this risk into account for years. Sovereign and political risk will be reviewed in Chapter 6.

## 3.3. Approaches to the Management of Financial Risks

Though risk management was always central to the profitability of banks, its focus has changed over time. In the 1960s, the emphasis was on the efficient employment of funds for liabilities management. In the 1970s, with the onset of inflation in many western countries and volatile interest rates, the focus shifted to the management of interest rate risk and liquidity risk, with a bank's credit risk usually managed by a separate department or division. Asset–liability management (ALM) is the proactive management of both sides of the balance sheet, with a special emphasis on the management of interest rate and liquidity risks. In the 1980s, risk management expanded to include the bank's off-balance sheet operations, and the risks inherent therein. In the new century, managers are answerable not only to shareholders but to national and international regulators. The emphasis is on the use of models to produce reliable risk measures to direct capital to the activities that offer the best risk/return combination. Scenario and stress tests are employed to complement the models.

In this section, the traditional ALM function is reviewed but it also explores how new instruments have changed the risk management organisational structure within banks, to accommodate all the risks a modern bank incurs. In particular, it should be emphasised that while traditional risk management focused on a bank's banking book (that is, on-balance sheet assets and liabilities), modern risk management has been extended to include the trading book, which consists mainly of off-balance sheet financial instruments. The financial instruments of a bank's trading book are taken on either with a view to profiting from arbitrage, speculation or for the purposes of hedging. Financial instruments may also be used to execute a trade with a customer. The bank and trading books can be affected differently for a given change, say, in interest rates. A rise in interest rates may cause a reduction in the market value of off-balance sheet items, but a gain (in terms of economic value) on the banking book. Also, while the market value gain/loss on the trading book normally has an immediate effect on profits and capital, the effect on the banking book is likely to be realised over time.

### 3.3.1. Interest Rate Risk and Asset–Liability Management

Traditionally, the ALM group within a bank has been concerned with control of interest rate risk on the balance sheet. For some banks it may be equally or even more important to manage interest rate risk arising from off-balance sheet business, but it is instructive to look at the traditional methods and progress to the relatively new procedures. To provide an example of the complexities of interest rate risk management, consider a highly simplified case where a bank, newly licensed by the relevant regulatory authority, commences operations as follows.

1. Liabilities consisting of one deposit product of £1000 and equity equal to £100, which gives the bank total capital of £1100. It plans to lend money to an unsecured borrower. The amount it can lend, given a risk assets ratio of 8%, is £1012.[14]
2. The loan has a maturity of six months, when all interest and principal is payable (a "bullet" loan). It will be priced at the current market rate of interest, 7%, plus a spread of 3%. So the annual loan rate is 10% on 1 January 2000. The loan is assumed to be rolled over every six months at whatever the new market rate is, with an unchanged risk premium of 3%.
3. A customer wishes to purchase the deposit product, a certificate of deposit (CD) on 1 January. The market rate is 7%, and because of highly competitive market conditions it is this rate which is paid on the CD. The bank has to decide what the maturity of the CD is going to be and once the maturity is set, the bank is committed to rolling over the CD at the same maturity.
4. The "yield curve"[15] for the CD is assumed to be flat, that is, the same rate of 7% applies, independent of the maturity. On 1 February 1994 there is an unexpected one-off shift in the yield curve, to a new flat value of 9%, because the market interest rate rises, suddenly, to 9%. There are no further shifts during the year.
5. Ignore all issues related to dividends and operating costs, with the exception of the requirement to conform to a risk assets ratio of 8%.

The ALM group may measure their performance in terms of net interest income (loan income less cost of deposit), the market value of equity (the market price of bank stock) or the economic equity ratio (new equity value/new loan value) for an unexpected change in interest rates. To the extent that changes in net interest income affect bank stock market valuations, the three measures will be very closely linked.

As was noted earlier, there is a 2% increase in market rates on 1 February 1994. To examine what happens to a number of bank performance measures, it is necessary to use a compounding formula to compute the monthly interest rate from the annual rates, because of the potential mismatch in the timing of cash flows for the six-month loan and the CD, the maturity of which is not determined.[16] Thus, for the six-month loan, the monthly interest rate is 0.79741% when the annual rate is 10%, and 0.94888% when the annual rate is 12%. If interest rates rise by 2% on 1 February, the borrower pays monthly interest of £8.07 until 30 June (remember, the loan rate is fixed for six months), and £9.60 from 1 July.

For the deposit product, once the bank decides on the maturity of the deposit, it incurs interest rate risk. In this simple example, the size of the deposit (£1000) and loan (£1012)

---

[14] The risk asset ratio is defined in full in chapter four, but it is the ratio of bank capital to weighted risk assets. Suppose the risk weight for the loan is 100%. Then with total capital of £1100, the bank has to set aside 8% of the capital, or £88. So the maximum it can lend out is £1012.

[15] The yield curve normally refers to the relationship between the rate paid on a bond and time to maturity, and is normally positive, reflecting a higher risk associated with a bond which matures at a later date, and, if unindexed, inflation risk.

[16] To calculate a monthly rate using an annual rate, a compounding formula is used: $[(1 + i)^{x/12} - 1]$, where i = the interest rate and x = the number of months. Using the example in the text, if the annual loan rate is 10%, then the monthly interest rate is $[(1.1)^{(1/12)} - 1] = 0.79741\%$

**Table 3.1  The Effects of an Unexpected Rise in Interest Rates**

*Case A:* an unexpected 2% rise in rates with a three-month deposit product and a six-month loan

|  | Q1 | Q2 | Q3 | Q4 |
|---|---|---|---|---|
| Loan rate (per annum) | 10% | 10% | 12% | 12% |
| Monthly loan income | £8.07 | £8.07 | £9.60 | £9.60 |
| Deposit rate (per annum) | 7% | 9% | 9% | 9% |
| Monthly interest cost of deposit | £5.65 | £7.21 | £7.21 | £7.21 |
| Monthly net interest income | £2.42 | £0.86 | £2.39 | £2.39 |
| Net interest margin per month[a] | 2.42% | 0.86% | 2.39% | 2.39% |

*Case B:* an unexpected 2% rise in rates with a six-month deposit product and a six-month loan

|  | Q1 | Q2 | Q3 | Q4 |
|---|---|---|---|---|
| Loan rate (per annum) | 10% | 10% | 12% | 12% |
| Monthly loan income | £8.07 | £8.07 | £9.60 | £9.60 |
| Deposit rate (per annum) | 7% | 7% | 9% | 9% |
| Monthly interest cost of deposit | £5.65 | £5.65 | £7.21 | £7.21 |
| Monthly net interest income | £2.42 | £2.42 | £2.39 | £2.39 |
| Net interest margin per month[a] | 2.42% | 2.42% | 2.39% | 2.39% |

[a] Net interest margin = (net interest income/equity) × 100%.

are almost equal, so if the bank offers a six-month deposit product, its losses as a result of the interest rate change on 1 February are considered using two maturities for the deposit product. In Case A, the bank opts for a three-month CD. Then the monthly interest rate on the deposit product is 0.56541% when the annual rate is 7%, rising to 0.72073% after the market rate rises to 9%. A three-month maturity on the deposit product will mean the monthly interest paid until the end of March will be £5.65, and, from 1 April, £7.21. These points are summarised in Table 3.1 for Case A. Here, there is a drop in the net interest margin per month (compare the first and second quarters) because of the sudden rise in interest rates. The fall in the net value of equity is calculated using the new market value for assets and liabilities, which is obtained by discounting the value of the asset and liability. The original loan rate of 10% is assumed to be the discount rate for the purposes of equity valuation.

## Loan (assume no change in interest rate)

The value of the loan on 1 July is £1012.00 + 49.39, given the half-yearly interest rate of 4.88088%. Future payments are ignored. So the value of the asset discounted back to 1 February is:

$$[1012 + 49.39/(1.1)^{5/12}] = £1020.07.$$

### Deposit (assume no change in interest rate)

If the deposit is of three-months duration, then an interest income of £16.12 is payable at the end of each quarter (e.g. end March, end June, ignore future payments on 30/09, 31/12). So the value of the liability, discounted back to 1 February, is:

$$[1000 + 16.92 + (16.92)(1.1)^{3/12}]/(1.1)^{5/12} = £994.38.$$

Therefore, the net value of the equity (with no change in interest rates) is: 1020.066 + 88.00 (the reserve asset) $-994.3819 = £113.6841$. If the loan rate rises to 12%, because of an increase in the market rate by 2%, then:

### Loan (after loan rate rises by 2% to 12%)

$$[1012 + 49.39]/(1.12)^{5/12} = £1012.44.$$
$$\text{New Total Assets} = 1012.44 + 88 = £1100.44$$

### Deposit (three-month deposit product)

$$[1000.00 + 21.78 + 16.92(1.12)^{3/12}]/(1.12)^{5/12} = £991.26$$

**New Total Liabilities** = £991.26

**Net Value of Equity:** 1100.44 − 991.26 = £109.18

**Change in Net Value of Equity:** 109.18 − 113.68

$$= -4.5 \text{ or} - 3.96\% \ (4.5/113.68)(100\%).$$

With a six-month deposit product, the bank does not experience the sudden drop in net interest income or net value of equity in the second quarter, as in Case A. The table is reworked assuming a six-month maturity. If the deposit product had the same maturity as the loan (six months), then the six-month deposit liability would be £986.62 after the interest rate jump. Hence the net value of equity would be £1100.44 − £986.62 = £113.82. The change in net value of equity is (113.82 − 113.68) = 13p, or 0.11%.

In Cases A and B, the economic equity ratio, defined as new equity value/new loan value is, for Case A: 109.18/1100.44 = 9.92%. For Case B with a six-month deposit product, it is 113.82/1100.44 = 10.34%.

The above results are obtained because the *volume* of this bank's loans and deposits is roughly equal, which makes the case for matching the maturity of the deposit with that of the loan, if the objective is to minimise interest rate risk. In reality, most banks have a loan portfolio which is a fraction of their deposit base. In this situation, matching maturities will lead to sizeable net effects, depending on the direction of the interest rate change. To see this point, suppose that the deposit product is £1000, equity is £1000 and there are no regulations (for example, no risk assets ratio). The bank decides to lend out all of its capital, i.e. £2000. The six-month loan is now £2000, and the deposit product is £1000. Suppose the maturity on the deposit is three months, and market interest rates rise by 2%. The outcome is summarised in Table 3.2.

As can be seen from Case C, there is a sharp drop in the net interest margin per month, compared with the earlier case where the sizes of the deposit and loan were very

**Table 3.2   An Unexpected Rise in Interest Rates**

*Case* **C:** three-month deposit product, six-month loan of £2000.00

|  | Q1 | Q2 | Q3 | Q4 |
|---|---|---|---|---|
| Loan rate (per annum) | 10% | 10% | 12% | 12% |
| Monthly loan income | £15.95 | £15.95 | £18.98 | £18.98 |
| Deposit rate (per annum) | 7% | 9% | 9% | 9% |
| Monthly interest cost of deposit | £5.65 | £7.21 | £7.21 | £7.21 |
| Monthly net interest income | £10.30 | £8.74 | £11.77 | £11.77 |
| Net interest margin per month | 1.03% | 0.87% | 1.18% | 1.18% |

similar. A three-month deposit will cut the discounted present value of the net assets by 1.15%. A six-month deposit would reduce the discounted present value of net assets by 0.76%, assuming the loan rate rises from 10% to 12% on 1 February. This is an example of a "liability" sensitive strategy, where liabilities reprice faster than assets, so net interest earnings fall with an increase in interest rates. If an asset sensitive strategy had been adopted, interest earnings would rise. It should be stressed that interest rate changes can affect the "economic value" of a bank in a way that is different from the short-term profit and loss accounts. The current earnings perspective will focus on the sensitivity of the profit and loss account in the short term (for example, a year) to a change in interest rates. Over the longer term, the effect on net economic value will be considered, where *net economic value* is defined as the difference between the change in the present value of the bank's assets and the present value of its liabilities, plus the net change in the present value of its off-balance sheet positions, for a given change in market interest rates.[17] The difference between the two will be pronounced if marking to market instruments are not a major part of the bank's portfolio.

The above cases refer to the interest rate risk caused by a shift in the yield curve, that is, *yield curve repricing risk*. There are other types of interest rate risk related to bank products. The interest rate is not necessarily determined by a market yield curve. For example, prime based loans and money market accounts may be linked to central bank or interbank rates, but it may not be a one-for-one relationship. Competition in the market and monetary policy will determine the extent to which this relationship is one-for-one. However, even if it is not one-for-one, provided it is not volatile, there will be little in the way of additional risk. Also, banks will find the balance of their liabilities change in a period of fluctuating interest rates. For example, as interest rates rise, customers will be reluctant to hold cash in non-interest-bearing deposit accounts because of the rising opportunity cost of holding money in these accounts. In a period of falling rates, customers may shift deposits into other assets that yield a higher rate of return.

There can also be one-sided interest rate risk associated with bank products that have options attached to them, which gives rise to different types of customer behaviour

---

[17] This definition of net economic value is from Basel (1993).

depending upon whether interest rates rise or fall. For example, **prepayment risk** arises with fixed rate mortgages. A prepayment[18] option will result in different outcomes; if interest rates rise, mortgage prepayments decline and the expected average life of the portfolio increases. On the other hand, if rates fall, prepayment increases (because the fixed payments are less attractive) and the average life of the portfolio declines. In some countries (e.g. the UK), the borrower is charged a penalty for early repayment of a mortgage. In others, such as the USA, there is no penalty charge on prepayment of mortgages.

## 3.3.2. Gap Analysis

Gap analysis is the most well known ALM technique, normally used to manage interest rate risk, though it can also be used in liquidity risk management. The "gap" is the difference between interest sensitive assets and liabilities for a given time interval, say six months. In gap analysis, each of the bank's asset and liability categories is classified according to the date the asset or liability is repriced, and "time buckets": groupings of assets or liabilities are placed in the buckets, normally overnight–3 months, >3–6 months, >6–12 months, and so on.

Analysts compute incremental and cumulative gap results. An incremental gap is defined as earning assets less funding sources in each time bucket; cumulative gaps are the cumulative subtotals of the incremental gaps. If total earning assets must equal total funding sources, then by definition, the incremental gaps must always total zero and therefore, the last cumulative gap must be zero. Analysts focus on the cumulative gaps for the different time frames. The above points are demonstrated in a simplified interest rate ladder, in Table 3.3.

Table 3.3 separates the assets and liabilities of a bank's balance sheet into groups with cash flows that are either sensitive or insensitive to changes in interest rates. An asset or liability is said to be **interest rate sensitive** if cash flows from the asset or liability change in the same direction as a change in interest rates. The "gap" (see Table 3.3) is the sterling amount by which rate sensitive assets (RSA) > rate sensitive liabilities (RSL). A **negative gap** means RSA < RSL; a *positive gap* means RSA > RSL. The **gap ratio** is defined as RSA/RSL. If the gap ratio is one, then the rate sensitivity of assets and liabilities is matched, and the sterling gap is zero.

Most banks have a positive gap, that is, rate sensitive assets exceed rate sensitive liabilities, because most banks borrow long and lend short, so their assets will mature later than their liabilities. For example, a bank will have rate sensitive deposits, which can be withdrawn any time, but the majority of its rate sensitive loans are not due to be paid back anywhere from a year up to 25 years in the case of a mortgage.

Suppose a bank has a positive gap (RSA > RSL). Then a rise in interest rates will cause a bank to have asset returns rising faster than the cost of liabilities, but if interest rates fall, liability costs will rise faster than asset returns.

---

[18] Prepayment refers to the repayment of the principal and any outstanding interest on a loan before the maturity date. For example, fixed rate mortgages may be repaid early because interest rates decline and the mortgagee wants to get a better rate, or because the circumstances of the borrower change: they move house or need to refinance the loan.

Table 3.3  Gap Analysis for Interest Rate Risk (£m)

| | Overnight–3 months | >3–6 months | >6–12 months | >1–2 years | >2–5 years | 5 years or not stated[a] |
|---|---|---|---|---|---|---|
| **Earning Assets** | | | | | | |
| Notes & coins | £5 | | | | | |
| 3-Month bills | £5 | | | | | |
| Interbank loans | £20 | | | | | |
| 5-Year bonds | | | | | | |
| Overdrafts | | £20 | | | | |
| 5-Year loans | | | | | £20 | |
| Property | | | | | | £30 |
| **Funding Sources** | | | | | | |
| Retail and term deposits | (−£100) | | | (−£50) | (−£45) | |
| 3-Month wholesale deposits | (£5) | | | | | |
| Capital | | | | (−£10) | | |
| Net mismatch gap | £15 | £20 | (−£50) | (−£55) | £20 | £30 |
| Cumulative mismatch gap[b] | 0 | (−£35) | (−£55) | (−£5) | £50 | £30 |

[a] Not stated normally includes a bank's equity because there is no maturity associated with the bank stock.
[b] Cumulative mismatch: cumulated/summed from long to short.

Defining $E$ as the equity value or net worth of the bank, then

$$E = A - L$$
$$\Delta E = \Delta A - \Delta L$$

where:
$\Delta E$: change in the net worth of the bank
$\Delta A$: change in the value of assets
$\Delta L$: change in the value of liabilities

On this banking book, if the maturity of its assets exceeds the maturity of its liabilities, then a parallel rise in all interest rates will reduce the market values of both assets and liabilities of the bank. However, the value of the assets will fall by more because they *mature later* than the bank's liabilities. The term **maturity gap** is used to emphasise the point that it is the difference in maturity that is affecting both sides of a bank's balance sheet.

The assets and liabilities on the banking book, as illustrated in Table 3.3, can also be summarised with a formula for a **maturity gap**:

$$\text{Maturity gap} = W_A \text{RSA} - W_L \text{RSL}$$

where:

$W_A$: weighted average of rate sensitive assets

$W_L$: weighted average of rate sensitive liabilities

The bigger the maturity gap, the more a bank's net worth will be affected by a change in interest rates. Suppose the bank wants to *immunise* itself, i.e. hedge against this type of interest rate risk. If it structures the banking book such that the weighted average of RSA equals the weighted average of RSL, so $M_A - M_L = 0$, then it will substantially reduce, but not eliminate, interest rate risk on the banking book. The bank is not fully hedged against; it ignores the following.

- The extent to which a bank is geared or leveraged, that is, the extent to which loans are funded by deposits (as opposed to equity).
- Duration – to be discussed below.

The maturity gap analysis presented above provides the ALM group with a picture of overall balance sheet mismatches. While this type of analysis still takes place in most banks, it is used in conjunction with other risk management tools, for a number of reasons.

1. Mismatches that fall within each time bucket are ignored. Returning to the case study examples, suppose the deposit product had a term of 3.5 months, so that it was repriced after this time. The loan will not be repriced until after six months, making the >3–6 month time bucket liability sensitive, though in the gap analysis it appears to be asset sensitive, because the loan was £1012, funded by a £1000 deposit and £100 in equity; equity is in the "not stated" time bucket because it has no stated maturity.
2. Interest rates on deposit accounts, some loans and credit card receivables are not solely determined by the market interest rates. Some banks offer "free" bank services with a current account but compensate for it by paying a lower rate.
3. It ignores the bank's exposure to prepayment risk, the risk that long-term fixed rate mortgages and loans will be repaid early if interest rates fall.
4. Some bank products, such as non-maturity accounts, non-market rate accounts and off-balance sheet items, cannot be handled in a gap analysis framework, though part of this problem has been overcome through duration gap analysis (see below).

### 3.3.3. Duration Analysis

Duration analysis expands on the gap analysis presented above by taking duration into account. Again, the objective is to consider the impact on shareholders' equity if a risk-free rate, for all maturities, rises or falls, but takes the procedure one step further. **Duration analysis** allows for the possibility that the average life (duration) of an asset or liability differs from their respective maturities. Suppose the maturity of a loan is six months and the bank opts to match this asset with a six-month CD. If part of the loan is repaid each month, then the duration of the loan will differ from its maturity. For the CD, duration is identical to maturity if depositors are paid a lump sum at the end of the six months. However, if only part of the loan is repaid each month, and depositors are paid a lump sum, a duration gap is created, exposing the bank to interest rate risk.

Duration is the present value weighted average term to repricing, and was originally applied to bonds with coupons, correcting for the impurity of a bond: true duration is less than the bond's term to maturity. The duration of an "impure" bond (that is, one with a coupon) is expressed as follows:

$$\text{Duration} = T\{1 - [\text{coupon size}/(MV \times r)]\} + [(1+r)/r][1 - (DPVR/MV)] \qquad (3.1)$$

where:
 $T$: time to redemption
 $r$: market (nominal) interest rate
 MV: market value
 DPVR: discounted present value of redemption

For example, suppose the problem is to compute the duration of a 10-year £100.00 bond with a fixed £5.00 coupon. The coupon is paid annually, the first one at the end of the first year of the investment, and the last one at the time the bond is redeemed. The current market price for the bond is obtained by computing the present value, using the formula

$$(c/r)[1 - (1+r)^{-T}] + R_T(1+r)^{-T} \qquad (3.2)$$

where:
 $c$: coupon value (£5.00)
 $r$: market interest rate, with a horizontal term structure, assumed to be 10%
 $T$: date of redemption
 $R_T$: amount redeemed (£100.00)

In the example, the current market price of the bond is:

$$£100(1.1)^{-10} + £50[1 - (1.1)^{-10}] = £50[1 + (1.1)^{-10}] = £69.277$$

There is a cash flow associated with the bond, and the idea is to discount each cash flow to the present value. To compute the duration, the formula from equation (3.1) is used:

$$\text{Duration} = 10[1 - (£5/£6.9277)] + (1.1/0.1)\{1 - [£100(1.1)^{-10}/£69.277]\}$$
$$= 7.661 \text{ years}^{19}$$

As can be seen from the example, duration analysis emphasises market value, as opposed to book value in gap analysis. All cash flows are included in the computation, and there is no need to choose a time frame, unlike gap analysis.

---

[19] As opposed to a 10 year maturity.

Duration analysis has been widened to include other assets and liabilities on a bank's balance sheet with flexible interest rates, and paid by borrowers or to depositors at some point in the future. In these cases, the duration of the equity is computed as:

$$D_E = [(MV_A \times D_A) - (MV_L/D_L)] \div (MV_A - MV_L) \qquad (3.3)$$

where:

$D_E$: duration of equity
$D_A$: duration of rate sensitive assets
$D_L$: duration of rate sensitive liabilities
$MV_A$: market value of asset
$MV_L$: market value of liability

The computed duration of equity is used to analyse the effect of a change in interest rates on the value of the bank, because it will approximate a zero coupon bond with the given duration.[20] The greater a bank's duration mismatch, the greater the exposure of the bank to unexpected changes in interest rates.

## 3.3.4. Duration Gap Analysis

Duration gap analysis estimates a bank's overall interest rate exposure on the balance sheet, taking into account that duration gaps are present. The key question is, in the presence of a duration gap, how is the value of shareholders equity affected for a given change in interest rates?

The duration of the assets and liabilities are matched, instead of matching time until repricing, as in standard gap analysis. The on- and off-balance sheet interest sensitive positions of the bank are placed in time bands, based on the maturity of the instrument. The position in each time band is netted, and the net position is weighted by an estimate of its duration, where duration measures the price sensitivity of fixed rate instruments with different maturities to changes in interest rates. If the duration of designated deposits and liabilities are matched, then the *duration gap* on that part of the balance sheet is zero. This part of the balance sheet is said to be immunised against unexpected changes in the interest rate. In this way, immunisation can be used to obtain a fixed yield for a certain period of time because both sides of the balance sheet are protected from interest rate risk. Note, however, that the protection is less than 100%, because market yields can change in the middle of an investment period, and other risks are still present, such as credit risk. Furthermore, the duration measure used assumes a linear relationship between interest rates and asset value. In fact the relationship is normally convex. The greater the convexity of the interest rate−asset value relationship, the less useful is the simple duration measure.

---

[20] Another way of interpreting duration is that it shows how sensitive the value of assets and liabilities are to changes in interest rates, i.e. it measures the interest elasticity of the value of an asset or liability. Saunders derives an algebraic formula showing the link between duration and interest sensitivity of an asset (or liability). See Saunders (2002), ch. 9. His work, in turn, is based on Kaufman (1984).

Hence, the use of duration to measure interest rate sensitivity should be limited to small changes in the interest rate.

Saunders (2002)[21] shows how a duration model can be used to measure the overall gap of the bank's exposure to interest rate risk, i.e. the duration gap. Begin by summing up the bank's duration of, respectively, its assets and liabilities portfolio.

$D_A$: the market value weighted average of the individual durations of each asset in the portfolio
$D_L$: the market value weighted average of the individual durations of each liability

$$\Delta E = \Delta A - \Delta L \qquad (3.4)$$

where:
$\Delta E$: the change in net worth of the bank
$\Delta A$: the change in market value of assets for a given change in interest rates
$\Delta L$: the change in market value of liabilities for a given change in interest rates

Saunders (2002, pp. 208–211) shows the net worth of the bank can be expressed as:

$$\Delta E = -(\text{adjusted duration gap}) \times \text{asset size} \times \text{interest rate shock}$$

where

$$\text{interest rate shock} = \Delta R/(1 + R)$$

where $R$ is the yield to maturity, and will change, for example, as a result of a change in the interest rate set by the central bank:

$$\text{adjusted duration gap} = \text{duration gap } D_A - GD_L$$

where $D_L$ is adjusted for the proportion of assets funded by liabilities (e.g. deposits, or other borrowed funds) rather than equity. That is, $D_L$ is adjusted for gearing or leverage: $G = L/A$, where $A$ is total assets and $L$ is the bank's liabilities, excluding equity.

Thus:

$$\Delta E = -[D_A - GD_L] \times A \times \Delta R/(1 + R) \qquad (3.5)$$

## Example:

Assume $D_A = 4$ years and $D_L = 2$ years.

Assets on the balance sheet are £200 million; liabilities consist of £150 million of borrowed funds and £50 million of equity. So $L/A = 150/200 = 0.75$ and $GD_L = (0.75)(2) = 1.5$.

Suppose the bank expects interest rates to rise by 0.5% from 5% to 5.5%. Then $\Delta R = 0.005$ and $(1 + R) = 1.05$, so $\Delta R/(1 + R) = 0.00476$.

---

[21] Saunder's work, in turn, is based on Kaufman (1984).

So $\Delta E = -(4 - 1.5) \times £200\,000\,000 \times 0.00476 = -£2\,380\,000$ or $-£2.4$ million.

Thus, as a result of an increase in interest rates, the net worth of equity holders will fall by £2.4 million.

The Basel Committee (see Chapter 4) recommends that banks using the standardised approach for market risk also adopt this method for monitoring their interest rate exposure.

### 3.3.5. Liquidity Risk and Asset–Liability Management

The ALM group in a traditional bank is also responsible for the management of liquidity risk. As defined earlier, it is the risk that a bank is unable to meet its liabilities when they fall due. Liquidity risk is normally associated with the liabilities side of the balance sheet when depositors unexpectedly withdraw their financial claims. Assuming the liquidity preferences of a bank's customers are roughly constant, the problem usually arises if there is a run on the bank as depositors try to withdraw their cash. A bank liquidity crisis is normally triggered either by a loss of confidence in the bank or because of poor management practices, or the bank is a victim of a loss of confidence in the financial system, caused, possibly, by the failure of another bank. Contagion and systemic risk are discussed in detail in the next chapter. However, if the bank experiences an unusually high deposit withdrawal rate, and lacks the cash or is unable to borrow the money quickly, it is faced with liquidating its longer-term investments, possibly in a market where other banks and investment houses are also selling, pushing down prices.

A bank can also experience liquidity problems on the asset side of the balance sheet, caused by large numbers of unexpected loan defaults. Banks have also been caught out granting credit lines which they do not expect to be drawn down, but which are subsequently used by the borrowers. If an economy goes into recession relatively quickly, these banks may see firms drawing down their credit lines all at once, which will put pressure on their liquidity. There is also liquidity risk linked to off-balance sheet transactions, and to a slow-down or collapse in the payments system.

If a bank does experience liquidity problems, the central bank is usually willing to lend to them at some penal rate, which is costly for the bank. Also, the central bank will have to be reasonably certain that the problem is one of illiquidity and not insolvency. Banks will borrow funds on the interbank markets or from other sources before they approach the central bank, but again, this is costly for the bank, and undermines its profitability.

The objective of liquidity risk management should be to avoid a situation where the net liquid assets are negative. Gap analysis can be used to manage this type of risk. The gap is defined in terms of net liquid assets: the difference between net liquid assets and volatile liabilities. Liquidity gap analysis is similar to the maturity ladder for interest rate risk, but items from the balance sheet are placed on a ladder according to the expected time the cash flow (which may be an outflow or an inflow) is generated. Net mismatched positions are accumulated through time to produce a cumulative net mismatch position. The bank can monitor the amount of cash which will become available over time, without having to liquidate assets early, at penal rates.

Table 3.4   Liquidity Funding – Maturity Ladder Approach (£000)*

|  | Week 1 | Week 2 | Week 3 | Week 4 |
|---|---|---|---|---|
| *Cash inflows* | 12 000 | 10 000 | 10 000 | 8 500 |
| Assets (week they mature) | 1 500 | 8 000 | 2 000 | 1 000 |
| Sales planned | 10 000 | 1 000 | 3 000 | 2 500 |
| Agreed credit lines | 500 | 1 000 | 5 000 | 6 000 |
| *Cash outflows* | 11 700 | 9 500 | 10 700 | 8 900 |
| Liabilities due | 7 000 | 3 000 | 9 000 | 4 000 |
| Contingent liabilities (e.g. credit lines) | 4 500 | 6 000 | 1 500 | 4 500 |
| Unplanned cash outflows | 200 | 500 | 200 | 400 |
| **Net funding needs** | −300 | −500 | 700 | 400 |
| **Cumulative net funding needs** | −300 | −800 | −100 | 300 |

* It is assumed that each week is 5 working days, and all sums are received on the last working day of each week (Fridays).

The Bank of International Settlements (2000) has outlined a maturity ladder approach, which consists of monitoring all cash inflows and outflows, and computing the net funds required. A simple version of this type of ladder appears in Table 3.4.

The ALM group in a bank is not normally responsible for risk management in other areas, though how risk management is organised does vary from bank to bank. In some banks, the ALM group has been replaced by a division with overall responsibility for risk management, but credit risk continues to be managed separately. Increasingly, 21st century banks have a division with overall responsibility for coordinating risk management.

The management of interest rate risk has moved beyond the traditional gap and duration analysis because banks have increased their off-balance sheet business and the use of derivatives. Derivatives were discussed briefly in Chapter 2, but the next section provides a more detailed coverage of derivatives and their role in risk management.

## 3.4. Financial Derivatives and Risk Management

### 3.4.1. Types of Financial Derivative

Before looking at how banks manage credit and market risk, this section considers the role of financial derivatives in risk management, because they are part of a bank's tool kit for managing risk. Derivatives were touched upon briefly in Chapter 2, which provided some basic definitions and noted the rapid growth in the derivatives market after 1980.

*Financial Derivatives* (or derivatives for short) are instruments that allow financial risks to be traded directly because each derivative is linked to a specific instrument or indicator (e.g. a stock market index) or commodity.[22] The derivative is a contract which gives one party a claim on an underlying asset (e.g. a bond, commodity, currency, equity) or cash value of the asset, at some fixed date in the future. The other party is bound by the contract

---

[22] From Gray and Place (1999), p. 40.

to meet the corresponding liability. A derivative is said to be a contingent instrument because its value will depend on the future performance of the underlying asset. The traded derivatives that are sold in well-established markets give both parties more flexibility than the exchange of the underlying asset or commodity.

Consider the case of the pig farmer who knows that in six months' time s/he will have a quantity of pork bellies to sell. The farmer wishes to hedge against the fluctuation in pork belly prices over this period. He/she can do so by selling (*going short*) a six-month "future" in pork bellies. The future will consist of a standard amount of pork bellies, to be exchanged in six months' time, at an agreed fixed price on the day the future is sold. The agent buying the pork belly future *goes long*, and is contractually bound to purchase the pork bellies in six months' time. The financial risk being traded is the risk that the value of pork bellies will change over six months: the farmer does not want the risk, and pays a counterparty to assume it. The price of the future will reflect the premium charged by the buyer for assuming the risk of fluctuating pork belly prices. The underlying asset (or "underlying") is a commodity, pork bellies, and the futures contract is the **contingent claim**. If the actual pork bellies had been sold, the farmer would face uncertainty about price fluctuations and might also incur some cost from seeking out a buyer for an arm's-length contract. The future increases the flexibility of the market because it is sold on an established market. Similarly, in the currency markets, futures make it unnecessary for the actual currency (the underlying instrument) to be traded.

The key derivatives are futures, forwards, forward rate agreements, options and swaps. Table 3.5 summarises the different types of derivatives, and shows how they are related to each other.

Recall from Table 2.1 that exchange traded instruments grew from $1.31 trillion in 1988 to $14.3 trillion in 2000. The main organised exchanges are the London International Financial and Futures and Options Exchange (LIFFE), the Chicago Board Options Exchange and the Chicago Mercantile Exchange. Smaller exchanges include France's Matif and

**Table 3.5  Summary of Derivatives**

| Transaction | Traded on an Exchange | Over-the-Counter (or non-standardised contracts, not traded via an exchange) |
| --- | --- | --- |
| The purchase or sale of a commodity or asset at a specified price on an agreed future date | Future | Forward |
| Cash flows (linked to currencies, bonds/interest rates, commodities, equities) are exchanged at an agreed price on an agreed date | | Swaps |
| A right but not an obligation to engage in a futures, forward or swap transaction | Option | OTC option Swap option: an agreement to transact a swap |

*Source:* Gray and Place (1999).

Germany's Deutsche Terminbörse. These exchanges also act as clearing houses. If a trader from Barclays Capital sells a future to the Royal Bank of Scotland Group (RBS), LIFFE will buy the future from Barclays and sell a future to RBS. This way, neither bank need be concerned about counterparty risk, that is the failure of one of the two banks to settle on the agreed future date. However, LIFFE does incur counterparty risk, which it minimises by requiring both banks to pay initial and verification margins. An *initial margin* is paid at the time the contract is agreed. However, between the time of the agreement and its expiry date, the price of the future will vary. The future will be marked to market each day, and based on the daily movement in the price, a *variation margin* is paid and settled, i.e. if losses are incurred, the bank has to pay the equivalent amount of the loss to the clearing house, while the other bank has made a profit, which it receives from the clearing house. Some banks will have millions of futures (and options) being traded on a given day, so at the end of the trading day, traders will receive their net profits, or pay their net losses to the clearing house.

Over the counter (OTC) market instruments, tailor-made for individual clients, consist of forwards, interest rate and currency swaps, options, caps, collars and floors, and other swap-related instruments. Table 2.1 shows they grew 50-fold, from $1.3 to $61.4 trillion between 1988 and 2000. Note the share of the OTC market as a percentage of the total market has risen from just over 50% in 1988 to 81% by 2000. OTC derivatives are attractive because they can be tailor-made to suit the requirements of an organisation. They are also the principal source of concern for regulators, because of the added risks inherent in this type of market. For example, in the absence of an exchange, there is no clearing house, so the two parties incur counterparty risk. For this reason, an increasing number of OTC markets do require margins to be paid.

Though Table 2.1 indicates a rapid growth in the derivatives markets, their use by banks is concentrated among a few of the world's largest banks. A 1998 BIS survey reported that 75 market players are responsible for 90% of activity in financial derivatives. This confirms earlier studies (e.g. Bennett, 1993; Sinkey and Carter, 1994). The key US and European banks such as Deutsche, Dresdner, Citigroup, JP Morgan Chase and Nations Bank dominate the derivatives market. Sinkey and Carter found that within the USA, 13 members of the International Swaps and Derivatives Association accounted for 81.7% of derivatives activities. Other banks have access to risk management opportunities offered by derivatives market through correspondence relationships with one of the main players.[23] The survey was reviewing OTC markets, and reports that interest rate instruments (mainly swaps) make up 67% of the market, followed by foreign exchange products (30% – forwards and foreign exchange swaps); equities and commodities make up 2% of the market.

The capital needed to finance the derivative is lower than it would be if the bank were financing the instrument itself. The main difference between the risk associated with derivatives and traditional bank risk management is that prior to these financial

---

[23] Correspondent banking can involve other activities such as loan syndication, or the sale of part of a loan portfolio to a larger bank.

innovations, banks were concerned mainly with the assessment of credit risk, and after the Third World debt crisis (1982), a more specialised form of credit risk, sovereign risk. Banks continue to lend to countries, corporations, small businesses and individuals, but banks can use derivatives to:

- Hedge against risk arising from proprietary trading;
- Speculate on their trading book;
- Generate business related to transferring various risks between different parties;
- Use them on behalf of clients, e.g. putting together a swap arrangement, or advise clients of what instruments they should be using;
- Manage their market (including interest rate and currency risk) and credit risk arising from on- or off-balance sheet activities.

The growth in the use of derivatives by banks has meant management must consider a wider picture, that is, not just on-balance sheet ALM, but the management of risks arising from derivatives. These OBS commitments improve the transparency of risks, so risk management should be a broad-based exercise within any bank.

## Futures

A future is a standardised contract traded on an exchange and is delivered at some future, specified date. The contract can involve commodities or financial instruments, such as currencies. Unlike forwards (see below), the contract for futures is homogeneous, it specifies quantity and quality, time and place of delivery, and method of payment. The credit risk is much lower than that associated with a forward or swap because the contract is marked to market on a daily basis, and both parties must post margins as collateral for settlement of any changes in value. An exchange clearing house is involved. The homogeneous and anonymous nature of futures means relatively small players (for example, retail customers) have access to them in an active and liquid market.

## Forwards

A forward is an agreement to buy (or sell) an asset (for example, currencies, equities, bonds and commodities such as wheat and oil) at a future date for a price determined at the time of the agreement. For example, an agreement may involve one side buying an equity forward, that is, purchasing the equity at a specified date in the future, for a price agreed at the time the forward contract is entered into. Forwards are not standardised, and are traded over the counter. If the forward agreement involves interest rates, the seller has the opportunity to hedge against a future fall in interest rates, whereas the buyer gets protection from a future rise in rates. Currency forwards allow both agents to hedge against the risk of future fluctuations in currencies, depending on whether they are buying or selling.

Forwards are customised to suit the risk management objectives of the counterparties. The values of these contracts are large, and both parties are exposed to credit risk because the value of the contract is not conveyed until maturity. For this reason, forwards are largely confined to creditworthy corporates, financial firms, institutional investors and governments. The only difference between a future and a forward is that the future is a standardised instrument traded on an exchange, but a forward is customised and traded over the counter. To be traded on an exchange, the market has to be liquid, with a large volume. For example, it will be relatively easy to sell or buy dollars, sterling, euros or yen for three or six months on a futures market. However, if an agent wants to purchase dinars forward, then a customised contract may be drawn up between two parties (there is unlikely to be a ready market in dinars), which means the transaction takes place on the forward market. Or, if a dollar sale or purchase is outside one of the standardised periods, it will be necessary to arrange the transaction on the forward market.

Banks can earn income from forwards and futures by taking positions. The only way they can generate fee income is if the bank charges a client for taking a position on behalf of a client.

## *Options*

At the date of maturity, if an agent has purchased yen three months forward (or a future), he/she must buy the yen, unless they have traded the contract or closed the position. With options, the agent pays for more flexibility because s/he is not obliged to exercise it. The price of the option gives the agent this additional flexibility. The first type of option traded on an exchange (in 1973 in Chicago) was a *call option*. The holder of a *European* call option has the right, but not the obligation, to buy an asset at an agreed *(strike) price*, on some specified date in the future. If the option is not exercised, the buyer loses no more than the premium he/she pays plus any brokerage or commission fees. The holder of a call option will exercise the option if the price of the asset rises and exceeds the strike price on the date specified. Suppose an investor buys a call option (e.g. stock in IBM) for $100 two months later. The underlying asset is equity, namely, one share in IBM stock. The agreed price of $100 is the strike price. If IBM stock is more than $100 on the specified day it expires, the agent will exercise the option to buy at $100, making a profit of, for example, $10.00 if the share price is $110. The call option is said to be *in the money* because the strike price is below the stock price. If the strike price exceeds the market price – the call option *is out of the money* because money is lost if the option was exercised. Though there is no point in exercising the option, the holder does not necessarily lose out because the whole point of buying the call option was to gain some flexibility, which in turn could have been used as a hedge during the life of the option.

The underlying asset upon which the option is written can be a currency, commodity, interest rate (bonds) or equity. As Table 2.1 shows, in 2000, they made up about 33% of exchange traded derivatives, though some are traded on the OTC markets. The buyer has the potential to gain from any favourable net movements between the underlying market and the strike price. The seller of the option obtains any fees but is exposed to unlimited loss should the option move so that the strike price is below the current spot price. *American* call options work exactly the same way but give the holder more flexibility because the option can be exercised during a specified period, up to the expiration date. Both types of options are traded in the European, American and other markets.

Exchange traded **put options** first appeared in 1977,[24] and give the holder the right (but not the obligation) to sell an underlying asset at an agreed price at some specified date in the future. This time, if, on the specified date, the price of the asset is less than the strike price, the holder will profit by exercising the option and pocketing the difference between the strike price and the share price (if an equity). Suppose an agent buys a put option for a barrel of wheat, at an agreed price of $50.00 in three months' time. On the specified date three months later, the price of wheat has fallen to $45.00 per barrel. Then the option is exercised: the holder buys wheat in the market at $45.00 and sells it for $50.00.

The subject of options pricing can fill an entire book, and the objective here is to identify the factors influencing the price of options and return to the main theme of this chapter, risk management. One can summarise it reasonably simply. To understand how an option is priced, think what buyers pay for. They are buying flexibility and/or to hedge against risk exposure. This is because stock, commodity and other financial markets can be volatile, and like the farmer selling wheat three months in the future, the agent is hedging against losing money as a result of volatility. So the more volatile the asset, the higher the price of the option.

The time to expiry also affects the price of the option, and the relationship is non-linear. Suppose an option expires in 60 days. Then when the option was agreed only one or two days before, the price is not affected much – there is a small decline in price because the exercise date is still quite far away. As the option ages, the fall in price will be much steeper between two days than it is when the option was only one or two days old. After two days, 2/60ths of the time value has eroded but after 50 days, 5/6ths of the time has eroded, and there is less time for the instrument underlying the option to move in a favourable direction. The loss of time value as the option ages is known as **time decay**, hence the option price tends to decay while $T$ is positive, then vanishes on the expiry date. The final, direct influence of the price of the option is the difference between the strike price ($S_k$) and the spot price, i.e. the current price of the underlying instrument ($S_p$).

To summarise:

$$\text{call option price} = f[\max\{(S_p - S_k, 0); V, T\}]$$

$$\text{put option price} = f[\max\{(S_k - S_p, 0); V, T\}]$$

where:
$S_k$: strike price
$S_p$: spot price
$V$: volatility, always a positive influence on the call or put option price
$T$: time to expiry, the option price tends to decay when positive and vanishes on expiry
The value of an option can never be negative

Options can be bundled together to create option-based contracts such as caps, floors or collars. Suppose a borrower issues a long-term floating rate note, and wants partial

---

[24] The Chicago Board Options Exchange was where call and put options were first traded on an exchange.

protection from a rise in interest rates. For a premium, the borrower could purchase a **Cap**, which limits the interest to be repaid to some pre-specified rate. A **Floor** means the lender can hedge against a fall in the loan rate below some pre-specified rate. **Collars**, where the buyer of a cap simultaneously sells a floor (or vice versa), mean the parties can reduce the premium or initial outlay.

*Currency Options* are like forward contracts except that as options, they can be used to hedge against currency fluctuations during the bidding stage of a contract. Purchasers of options see them as insurance against adverse interest or exchange rate movements, especially if they are bidding for a foreign contract or a contract during a period of volatile interest rates.

Call options for assets have, in theory, unlimited scope for profit because there is no ceiling to the price of the underlying instrument, such as a stock or commodity. For example, unexpected news of a widespread failure of the cocoa crop can cause the price to soar, or there can be bubble-like behaviour in certain shares, such as the technology stocks in the 1990s. Provided the option is exercised before the bubble bursts, option holders can make a great deal of profit. At the same time, their losses are limited to the premium they pay on the option.

For put options, the price of the underlying instrument can never fall below zero, so there is a ceiling on profits for puts. To see the contrast, return to the cocoa example. Suppose an agent buys a call option with a strike price of $60, that is, a right to buy a unit of cocoa for $60. In the event of widespread crop failure, the price soars to $100 per unit, giving the holder of the call option a profit of $40. The agent's profit is unlimited because the price, in theory, can keep on rising. But for a put option, where the holder has a right to sell a unit of cocoa, the profit is limited. If the strike price for the put option is $50, in the event of a cocoa glut, profits are limited to $50 because the cocoa price cannot fall below zero.

Consider the example below, taken from *The Financial Times*. Table 3.6 is part of the figures reproduced from *The Financial Times*. The table states that the index is "£10 per full index point". It is possible to buy a call or put option for the FTSE 100 index at different levels. All profit and loss figures are multiplied by 10 to give the appropriate sterling sum. C reports the call units and P the put units, for a given FTSE index level, for July to December – each is priced at £10 per unit. On 24 June, the volume of puts (29 273) far exceeded that of calls (12 965), possibly because it had risen strongly in the spring of 2003, and many more agents are looking for the right to sell rather than buy options on the FTSE index, anticipating a greater downside than upside risk in the coming months.

Suppose the agent decides to purchase a call option on the FTSE 100 at 3725, to expire in July. On 24 June, the agent buys 351 units at £10 per unit for the right to buy at 3725 in July. The right is exercised if the index exceeds 3725 in July, but not otherwise. At 3726, the agent recoups £10 from the £3510 paid, so exercises the call, even though s/he makes an overall loss. The break-even point is 4076: $(3725 + 351) = 4076$. Suppose the index is 4276 in July. The agent can sell at 3725, and makes $(4276 - 3725 - 351)(£10) = £2000$.

All these computations exclude any interest foregone, between the time an agent buys/pays for the call and exercises it. The call price rises with time because the greater the time between when the call was purchased and its expiry, the greater the chance the index will move in the agent's favour.

Table 3.6 FTSE 100 Index Option (£10 per full index point)

| | 3725 | | 3825 | | 3925 | | 4125 | |
|---|---|---|---|---|---|---|---|---|
| | C | P | C | P | C | P | C | P |
| Jul | 351 | 10 | 259.5 | 34 | 175.5 | 104 | 48.5 | 106.5 |
| Aug | 362 | 29 | 277.5 | 67.5 | 200.5 | 134.5 | 80.5 | 147.5 |
| Sept | 382 | 55 | 301.5 | 101 | 230 | 166 | 113.5 | 182.5 |
| Oct | 404.5 | 71.5 | 331.5 | 125 | 259 | 190 | 135 | 201 |
| Dec | 446.5 | 112 | 373 | 168 | 306 | 245 | 188.5 | 207 |

C: call units
P: put units
Source: *The Financial Times*, 24 June 2003, p. 38.

Consider the put prices, given by the P column. Again, they rise over time, i.e. from July to December, for the same reason as the call prices. Here, the agent chooses to buy a put (the right to sell the option), to be exercised in July. S/he pays (10)(£10) = £100 for the right to sell the index at 3725. The break-even is (3725 − 10) = 3715. If, in July, the index is >3725, the option is not exercised. For example, if the FTSE is at 3730, the agent will lose money: (3725 − 3730 − 10)(£10) = £150, the option would NEVER be exercised – the agent loses the initial £100 plus the £50 implicit in the FTSE indices!

If the index is <3715, the agent will not just exercise the right to sell, but will earn an overall profit. Suppose the index has declined to 3615 in July. Then, for an initial stake of £100, the agent makes (3725 − 3615 − 10)(£10) = £1000.

In December, the price of the put is 112, and the agent will pay £1120 for the right to sell at 3725. The option will be exercised at any price below 3725. The break-even is 3725 − 112 = 3613. If the index falls to 3724, the agent will exercise because even though a loss is made, it is a loss of £1110 rather than £1120. If the index is at 3613, then exercise, but no profit is made; if the index is below 3613, then the profit is positive. For example, at 3600, the profit is:

$$(3613 − 3600)(£10) = £130$$

The risk is borne by the **writers** of options, the other party, who agrees to deliver/buy the underlying asset, and receives the premium for entering into the agreement. For a call option, the larger the difference between the strike and spot prices of the underlying asset, the bigger the losses, because the writer is committed to deliver the asset at the strike price. If the spot rises by a large amount, the writer, in theory, has to buy the asset at this high spot price, then deliver it to the agent who has exercised the option to purchase at the lower strike price. For a put option, the risk of loss is limited, since the price cannot fall below zero.

Just as in theory, profits for some options are unlimited for the holder, the downside is the losses incurred by the writer of the option, usually a bank or other type of financial institution. In the cocoa case, the writer has to buy the cocoa unit for $100 but sell it to the holder for $60. So the writer's losses are $40 less the premium. On the other hand, for a put option and a glut in the cocoa market, losses are limited to $50, less the cost of the premium. If there is a crop failure, then the put option won't be exercised and the writer makes a profit equal to the premium.

While option writing can be highly profitable, the potential for losses on options written for equities and commodities is unlimited – option writers will need to have a large amount of capital available to cover the institution. Given that the downside of writing a call option is potentially large, clearing houses (exchanges for traded options) that register and settle options will require a writer to make a deposit to cover an initial margin when the option contract is initiated. In addition, the exchange will specify an amount that must be deposited as a maintenance margin, and writers must ensure the deposit never falls below this level. In the case of rising cocoa prices, this margin would fall as the spot price increased, so the writer would have to top up the margin to keep it at maintenance level.

As can be seen from Table 2.1, some options are traded on exchanges, while others are OTC. There is no clearing house for OTC options but increasingly, parties are imposing margin-type requirements.

## Swaps

*Swaps* are contracts to exchange a cash flow related to the debt obligation of two counterparties. The main instruments are interest rate, currency, commodity and equity swaps. Like forwards, swaps are bilateral agreements, designed to achieve specified risk management objectives. Negotiated privately between two parties, they are invariably OTC and expose both parties to credit risk. The swap market has grown rapidly since the late 1980s, for a number of reasons. Major financial reforms in the developed countries (see the next two chapters), together with financial innovation, has increased the demand for swaps by borrowers, investors and traders. This in turn has increased liquidity in these markets, which attracts more users. It is also a means of freeing up capital because it is moved off-balance sheet, though as will be seen in the next chapter, banks also have to set aside capital for off-balance sheet activity.

Table 2.1 also shows that interest rate swaps and foreign exchange swaps are the most common type, and the value of interest swaps increased nearly 50-fold between 1988 and 2000. The basis for an interest rate swap is an underlying principal of a loan and deposit between two counterparties, whereby one party agrees to pay the other agreed sums – "interest payments". These sums are computed as though they were interest on the principal amount of the loan or deposit in a specified currency during the life of a contract.

The most common type of interest rate swap is also known as the **vanilla interest rate swap**, where the two parties swap a stream of future fixed rate payments for floating rate payments. Suppose Jack owns SINCY plc and has a fixed rate liability. Gill owns HEFF plc and has a floating rate liability. If they agree to swap future interest payments, then Jack will commence making a net floating rate payment; Gill a net fixed rate payment. The principal on the two respective loans is not exchanged, and both are still liable to make interest payments to their respective creditors. Why enter into a swap agreement? Often it is because there is an opportunity for arbitrage, if each party borrows in markets where they have a comparative advantage. Suppose HEFF plc has a better credit rating than SINCY plc. They can use the difference in credit rating to save on interest payments. Both Jack and Gill want to borrow for 5 years by issuing 5-year bonds. Jack has a better credit rating, and can get the 5-year loan at either 10% fixed rate or a floating rate equal to Libor + 0.5%. Gill can borrow the same amount but, respectively, for 12.5% or Libor + 1%. If they take full advantage of the arbitrage opportunity before them, Jack borrows at the fixed rate of 10%; Gill borrows at the floating rate of Libor + 1%. Jack borrows at a fixed rate, even though he wants floating rate. Gill does the reverse. Together, these two save 2% (the difference between the fixed and floating rate differentials), and they agree to split the saving. If Jack gets 0.75% and Gill gets 2.5%, Jack's loan is 0.75% cheaper than if he had borrowed on the flexible rate market, and Gill saves 1.25% because she has borrowed on the fixed rate market.

To summarise:

|  | Credit Rating | 5-year Fixed Debt | 5-year Floating Debt |
|---|---|---|---|
| HEFF plc | AA | 10% | Libor + 0.5% |
| SINCY plc | AB | 12.5% | Libor + 1% |
| Difference (credit) |  | 2.5% | 0.5% |
| Arbitrage saving: 2% |  |  |  |

Note that both these firms must be large enough to be able to issue bonds and to be rated by agencies. HEFF may have a better credit rating because it is an older firm, and has never defaulted, and therefore there is more information than for SINCY plc. But Jack has to be reasonably certain that Gill won't renege on the contract (counterparty risk), and may agree to the swap because they have had dealings before and Jack knows Gill is good for the payments. Put another way, Jack has more information about the creditworthiness of Gill than the market does. Also, they will only undertake the swap if transactions costs do not reduce the arbitrage to zero. Note that they are exposed to market risk in the form of interest rate changes, and the bondholders continue to be exposed to credit risk and interest rate risk if they invested in the floating rate notes.

Many banks are attracted to interest rate swaps because they tend to borrow short and lend long. Many deposits are paid a variable rate of interest; many loans are at fixed interest. This exposes banks to the risk of loss if there is a rise in short-term interest rates. A bank can hedge against this risk with an interest rate swap. The bank agrees a contract with a counterparty, to pass fixed interest payments over a certain period in return for a stream of variable interest receipts.

A **basis rate swap** involves the floating part of the swap being defined in terms of two different interest rates. For example, it could be the Bank of England base rate and Libor. A bank seeking this type of swap may have to pay depositors the base rate less some percentage, but loans are linked to Libor. It exposes the firm to basis risk: the risk that the relationship between the two interest rates will change over time. More generally, **basis or correlation risk** is the risk of a change in a typical gap between the movement in futures prices and the price of the underlying asset, or, more generally, the price(s) of the instrument(s) to be hedged is less than perfectly correlated with the price(s) of the instrument(s) used for hedging. For example, the yield curve for a bond is normally positive, and a future will be priced according to the relationship between interest rates and the maturity of the bond.

Basis risk is the risk that the yield curve turns negative, thereby affecting the relationship between the future price and the bond, which in turn will affect the value of the portfolio.

In the foreign exchange markets, there are two main types of swaps. An **FX swap** involves the exchange of principal on a debt obligation (in different currencies) at the beginning and end of the transaction. The equivalent would be for the two parties to enter into a spot currency exchange, and a foreign exchange rate forward: they agree to swap back the currencies at a fixed price and on a specific date.

A **currency swap** is a contract between two parties to exchange both the principal amounts and interest rate payments on their respective debt obligations in different currencies. There is an initial exchange of principal of the two different currencies, interest payments are exchanged over the life of the contract, and the principal amounts are repaid either at maturity or according to a predetermined amortisation schedule.

The need for currency swaps arises because one party may need to have its debt in a certain currency but it is costly to issue that debt in the currency. For example, a US firm setting up a subsidiary in Germany can issue US bonds but not eurobonds because it is not well known outside the United States. A German company may want to issue dollar debt, but cannot do so for similar reasons. Each firm issues bonds in the home currency, then swaps the currency and the payments. Unlike an interest rate swap, the principal is exchanged, which creates additional risks. These are credit risk (risk of default on the debt) and settlement or Herstatt risk if there is a difference in time zones.

The market for **credit swaps** began to grow quickly in the early 1990s. There are two main types: a credit default swap and a total return swap, discussed below. Both are examples of credit derivatives. **Credit derivatives** are OTC contracts, the value of which is derived from the "price" of some credit instrument, for example, the loan rate on a loan. Credit derivatives allow the bank or investor to unbundle or separate an instrument's credit risk from its market risk. This is in contrast to the more traditional credit risk management techniques (discussed below), which manage credit risk through the use of security, diversification, setting the appropriate risk premium, marking to market, netting, and so on. By separating the credit risk from the market risk, it is possible to sell the credit risk on, or redistribute it among a broad class of institutions. Credit derivatives are used to protect against **credit events**, which can include:

- A borrower going bankrupt;
- A default on the payments associated with a particular asset.

The credit derivatives market grew very rapidly in the later half of the 1990s. It has risen from 0 in 1996 to $800 billion in 2000 to $2 trillion in 2002, measured by the amount of net sold[25] protection. At the time of writing, it is expected to double again to $4 trillion by 2004. The main players are the top seven US banks, which have a market share of 96%.[26] Based on a survey by Fitch ratings undertaken in 2003:

- Banks and brokers are net buyers of protection – $190 billion, a tiny percentage of total loans.

---

[25] Net sold position = sold positions minus bought positions
[26] By value of outstanding contracts. These figures are from Carver (2003) and BIS (2003e).

- Insurance firms are net sellers of protection – $300 billion.
- European regional banks are net sellers of protection – $76 billion.

These figures leave a gap of about $186 billion, which may be explained by the refusal of hedge funds to participate in the Fitch (2003) survey. The smaller regional banks that are net sellers of insurance include Germany's Landesbank. This has raised concerns among regulators, especially for the lack of transparency in the treatment of credit derivatives on the accounts of banks and insurance firms. In their defence, the positions are quite small, and they are getting a higher yield for relatively little risk. They are also a way for these banks to diversify into US firms.

The key issues arising from the growth of this market include:

- Improvements in disclosure of credit risk details.
- Information on positions taken by hedge funds.
- Is the market dispersing credit risk or concentrating it? The findings reported by Fitch (2003) tend to support the idea that the market is spreading credit risk across a greater number of players.

There are two main types of credit derivatives/swaps.

A *Credit Default Swap* (CDS): all bonds and loans carry a risk premium. Here one party A (e.g. a bank) pays the risk premium on a loan to party B, an insurance against the risk of default. If the borrower defaults on the bond or loan, then party A gets a cash payment from B to cover the losses. If there is no default, counterparty B keeps the risk premium. For example, a bank might make an annual payment to another agent, who pays the bank for the default should there be a default on a loan (or loans), equal to the par value of the defaulted loan, less its value on the secondary market.

The Fitch survey found single name CDSs made up 55% of the market, rising to 80% if insurance firms are included. Portfolio products (synthetic collateralised debt obligations, basket trades) made up most of the rest of the market. The respective market shares are 63% for the North American market; 37% for Europe/Asia.

An issue that could undermine the growth of this market is the debate over what constitutes a credit event, that is, default. The main problem is with restructuring, and when it constitutes default. For example, with a syndicated loan, participants could enter into a restructuring with a plan to trigger a default and collect payments from the buyer of the CDS. In Europe, buyers of credit protection favour a broad definition of restructuring because when a borrower encounters payment difficulties, the problem is usually resolved through informal negotiation between the two parties. In the USA, a more narrow definition is acceptable to those buying credit risk because firms that file for Chapter 11 protection from bankruptcy have a chance to restructure before being declared insolvent.

Fitch (2003) reported 42 credit events, few of which were controversial. However, Railtrack (in the UK – nationalised by the British government in 2002) and Xerox in the USA have been challenged. The Xerox case prompted some sellers (e.g. insurance firms) to refuse to agree on a CDS if restructuring was included as a credit event. They were of the view that Xerox's loan financing was not due to problems with its financial position, yet swaps were triggered. Other credit events included Enron and Argentina, and no financial institution found its solvency threatened as a result of exposure, which indicates this market is fulfilling its role of spreading credit risk. However, some experts take a less sanguine view. Credit risk is being transferred away from banks, which have the most sophisticated models for analysing it, to other financial institutions, such as insurance firms (or pension funds), with little or no expertise in the area. This issue is discussed in more detail in Chapter 4.

A *total return swap* involves two parties swapping the total returns (interest plus capital gains or minus capital losses) related to two assets. Consider a simple example. Asset A is on bank A's balance sheet, and the bank receives a fixed interest rate from that asset. Asset B is held by a counterparty, call it Bank B. This asset is linked to a floating rate, that is, Bank B receives a stream of income at some variable market rate (e.g. Libor or some other benchmark rate). In a total return swap, Bank A makes periodic payments[27] to Bank B, which are linked to the total return of the underlying asset A, in exchange for, from Bank B, periodic floating payments which are tied to a benchmark such as Libor (e.g. semi-annual cash flows linked to a six-month Libor), that is, the total return on asset B. Usually the swap agreement is for three to five years, but the maturity of the underlying asset may be much longer. A total return swap may involve a bond or portfolio of bonds, a loan or loan portfolio, or any other type of security. The receiving party need not be a bank. It could be an institutional investor, insurance firm, or some type of fund specialising in these type of swaps.

Suppose Bank A lends money to a borrower at a fixed rate, and some time during the period of that loan, the borrower begins to encounter difficulties repaying the loan, increasing the credit risk associated with it, resulting in a lower credit rating on the loan. This is an adverse credit event for Bank A because the value of its asset, the loan, falls. The bank has agreed a total return swap with Bank B, to hedge against the possibility of this adverse credit event. Bank A pays the counterparty the initial interest rate charged on the loan plus any change in the value of the loan, if the credit event occurs. This is a cash outflow for Bank A, and represents income for the counterparty, Bank B, the fee paid to B because it is taking on the credit risk associated with Bank A's loan. If the adverse credit event occurs, then Bank A pays less: the fixed interest rate minus the reduction in the loan value. Thus, Bank B receives a reduced cash inflow. Its cash outflow to Bank A is based on an asset paying a flexible rate (e.g. interest rate plus Libor). In the absence of an adverse credit event, the swap becomes a standard (pay fixed/receive floating) interest rate swap.

If Libor is correlated with the adverse credit event, and rises, then the payment made by Bank B to A will rise if the adverse event occurs, which further compensates for the reduced value of A's loan. However, Libor could fall, depending on the nature of the credit event (see below). Furthermore, unlike the pure credit swap, there is some basis risk because if Libor changes, the net cash flows of the total return swap change, even in the absence of a credit event.

Bank A may opt for this type of swap if the bank has had a long relationship with the borrower, but is concerned that the borrower could default on the loan (e.g. because of

---

[27] For example, if asset A is a bond, the payments will consist of the coupon payments plus any change in the value of the bond itself.

political upheaval in the borrower's country, adverse currency movements, or because there is an unexpected decline in demand for that firm's product). In these situations, the bank may want to preserve the relationship, perhaps because the firm is a customer for other types of bank business. Since the loan never leaves Bank A's loan book, the borrower need never know of the bank's concern, yet Bank A has hedged against any possible adverse outcomes. Bank B is attracted to the swap because it gets an unchanged cash inflow if there is no adverse credit event, and because the fixed interest rate may prove higher than the average variable rate it pays to Bank A.

An *equity swap* is an agreement to exchange two payments. Party A agrees to swap a specified interest rate (fixed or floating) for another payment, which depends on the performance (total return, including capital gains and the dividend) of an equity index. An *equity basis swap* is an agreement to exchange payments based on the returns of two different indices.

A *cross-currency interest rate swap* is a swap of fixed rate cash flows in one currency to floating rate cash flows in another currency. The contract is written as an exchange of net cash flows which exclude principal payments. A *basis interest rate swap* is a swap between two floating rate indices, in the same currency. Coupon swaps entail a swap of fixed to floating rate in a given currency.

Like forwards and options, hedging is one reason why a bank's customers use swaps. In a currency, interest rate or credit swap market, a customer can restructure and therefore hedge existing exposures generated from normal business. In some cases, a swap is attractive because it does not affect the customer's credit line in the same way as a bank loan. Currency swaps are often motivated by the objective to obtain low cost financing. In general, swaps can be a way of reducing borrowing costs for governments and firms with good credit ratings.

## Hybrid derivatives

These are hybrids of the financial instruments discussed above. Variable coupon facilities, including floating rate notes, note issuance facilities and swaptions, fall into this category. A *swaption* is an option on a swap: the holder has the right, but not the obligation, to enter into a swap contract at some specified future date. Variable coupon securities are bonds where the coupon is revalued on specified dates. At each of these dates, the coupon rate is adjusted to reflect the current market rates. As long as the repricing reflects the current interest rate level, this type of security will be less volatile than one with a fixed rate coupon. The *floating rate notes (FRNs)* have an intermediate term, whereas other instruments[28] in this category will have different maturities. All the periodic payments are linked to an interest rate index, such as Libor. A FRN will have the coupon (therefore the interest rate payments) adjusted regularly, with the rates set using Libor as a benchmark. **Note issuance facilities** are a type of financial guarantee made by the bank on behalf of the client, and have features similar to other financial guarantees such as letters of credit, credit lines and revolving loan commitments.

---

[28] Other variable coupon securities include variable coupon bonds (a longer maturity than FRNs) and perpetual floaters, which never mature.

### 3.4.2. Why Banks Use Derivatives

It is important to be clear on the different uses of these instruments by the banking sector. Banks can advise their clients as to the most suitable instrument for hedging against a particular type of risk, and buy or sell the instrument on their clients' behalf. This may help the bank to build on relationships and open up cross-selling opportunities. Additionally, banks employ these instruments to hedge out their own positions, with a view to improving the quality of their risk management.

Banks also use derivatives for speculative purposes and/or proprietary trading, when trading on the banks' own account, with the objective of improving profitability. It is the speculative use of derivatives by banks which regulators have expressed concern about, because of the potential threat posed to the financial system. Chapters 4 and 6 will return to this issue. They may also use them for purposes of hedging, which can increase the value of a bank by reducing the costs of financial distress or even compliance costs when meeting regulatory standards.

Non-financial corporations are attracted to derivatives because they improve the management of their financial risks. For example, a corporation can use derivatives to hedge against interest rate or currency risks. The cost of corporate borrowing can often be reduced by using interest rate swaps (swapping floating rate obligations for fixed rate). Banks are paid large sums by these firms to, for example, advise on and arrange a swap. However, some corporations, whether they know it or not, end up using derivatives to engage in speculative activity in the financial markets. There have been many instances where corporate clients have used these derivative products for what turned out to be speculative purposes.

One customer of Bankers Trust, Gibson Greetings, sustained losses of $3 million from interest rate swaps that more than offset business profits in 1993. The case was settled out of court in January 1995, after a tape revealed a managing director at Bankers had misled the company about the size of its financial losses. In December 1994, Bankers Trust agreed to pay a $10 million fine to US authorities, and was forced to sign an "agreement" with the Federal Reserve Bank of New York, which means the leveraged derivatives business at Bankers Trust is subject to very close scrutiny by the regulator. Bankers Trust was also bound by the terms of the agreement to be certain that clients using these complex derivatives understand the associated risks.

In 1994, the chairman of Procter and Gamble (P&G) announced large losses on two interest rate swaps. The corporate treasurer at Procter and Gamble had, in 1993, purchased the swaps from Bankers Trust. The swaps would have yielded a substantial capital gain for Procter and Gamble had German and US interest rates converged more slowly than the market thought they would. In fact, the reverse happened which, together with another interest rate swap cost the firm close to $200 million. The question is why these instruments were being used for speculative purposes by a consumer goods conglomerate, and whether the firm was correctly advised by Bankers Trust. Procter and Gamble refused to pay Bankers Trust the $195 million lost on the two leveraged swap contracts. P&G claimed it should never have been sold these swaps, because the bank did not fully explain the potential risks, nor did the bank disclose pricing methods that would have allowed Procter and Gamble to price the product themselves.

The publication of internal tapes which revealed a cynical attitude to the treatment of customers was unhelpful for the bank. In one video instruction tape shown to new employees at the bank, a BT salesman mentions how a swap works: BT can "get in the middle and rip them (the customers) off", though the instructor does apologise after seeing the camera; another said how he would "lure people into that total calm, and then totally f- - - them".[29] An out of court settlement was reached in May 1996 but only after an opinion given by the judge, who considered both parties to be at fault. P&G's argument that swaps came under federal jurisdiction was rejected, as was their claim that BT has a fiduciary duty to P&G. The court also opined that Bankers Trust had a duty of good faith under New York State commercial law. Such a duty arises if one party has superior information and this information is not available to the other party.[30] Bankers Trust was acquired by Deutsche Bank in 1998. (See case study in Chapter 10 for more detail.)

Other well-known US banks, namely Merrill Lynch, Credit Suisse First Boston (CSFB) and some smaller banks, were sued by a local government in Orange County, California, after it was forced into bankruptcy in late 1994. The county borrowed money from Merrill to purchase securities for its investment fund. Merrill also underwrote and distributed the securities. CSFB underwrote an Orange County bond issue. The fund made a $700 million profit, but losses quickly mounted after an unexpected rise in interest rates. Orange County's borrowing costs soared and the value of the securities in the investment fund collapsed. Merrill, CSFB and other banks found themselves being accused by Orange County, and in a separate case filed by 14 other governments that were part of the investment pool (the so-called "Killer Bs"), of encouraging the Treasurer, Robert Citron, to invest in speculative securities, and making false statements about the health of the county's investments. Some litigants even claimed the banks had a duty to inform them that the Treasurer's actions were inappropriate. The county also sued KPMG, its auditor, Standard and Poor's (for giving its bonds too high a rating), and 17 other banks.

The case never had its day in court because all the parties settled out of court. Merrill Lynch paid Orange County $420 million, and two years later (in 2000), settled with the "Killer Bs" for $32.4 million. Substantial settlements were also reached with KPMG, CSFB and the other banks. In total, the settlement reached roughly $800 million. Given the $700 million in profit the fund made before the interest rate collapsed, the county was almost fully compensated for the $1.8 million loss. The banks were probably concerned they might be convicted by a jury, though they claimed they settled to avoid mounting legal costs.

The question is whether the banks were guilty, given the interest rate products were not particularly complex, and the Treasurer's conviction for securities fraud – he seemed to be knowledgeable about the investments. Also, local governments collect taxpayers' money to fund expenditure. The norm is for the money to be invested in relatively safe assets, such as Treasury bills and certificates of deposit, not to run an investment fund in the hope of making capital gains in the financial markets.

In Japan, the currency dealers of an oil-refining company, Kashima Oil, entered into binding forward currency contracts, buying dollars forward in the 1980s (in anticipation of

---

[29] *Source: The Economist*, "Bankers Trust Shamed Again", 7 October 1995.

[30] A third criterion for duty of good faith was noted by the court: the informed party knows the other party is acting on the basis of misinformation, though the duty would arise even if this one did not apply.

future purchases of oil), which led to losses of $1.5 billion. Metallgesellschaft, a German commodities conglomerate, lost $1.4 billion in oil derivatives because they sold long-dated futures, hedging the exposure with short-dated futures. It left the firm exposed to yield curve repricing risk, a type of basis risk – the price of the long-dated futures increased but the short-dated prices declined.

Other examples of non-financial firms reporting significant losses because of trading on the financial markets include: Volkswagen, which lost $259 million from trades in the currency markets in the early 1980s; Nippon Steel Chemical, which lost $128 million in 1993 because of unauthorised trading in foreign exchange contracts; and Showa Shell Seikiyu, which lost $1.05 billion on forward exchange contracts. Allied-Lyons plc lost $273 million by taking options positions, and Lufthansa lost $150 million through a forward contract on the DM/US$ exchange rate. Barings plc, the oldest merchant bank in the UK, collapsed after losing over £800 million after a trader's dealings in relatively simple futures contracts went wrong (see Chapter 7).

The above cases illustrate the need for managers to ask why an instrument is being used – that is, is it for hedging or speculative purposes? Additionally, as illustrated by the Metallgesellschaft case, all parties to a hedging arrangement must ask whether an instrument used to hedge out one position has exposed a party to new risks.

Any bank dealing in derivatives is exposed to market risk, whether they are traded on established exchanges, or, for OTC instruments, there is an adverse movement in the price of the underlying asset. For options, a bank has to manage a theoretically unlimited market risk, which arises from changing prices of the underlying item. Banks will usually try to match out option market risks, by keeping options "delta neutral", where the delta of an option indicates the absolute amount by which the option will increase or decrease in price if the underlying instrument moves by one point. The delta is used as a guide to hedging. In swap contracts, market risk arises because the interest rates or exchange rates can change from the date on which the swap is arranged.

Derivatives expose banks to liquidity risk. For example, with currency options, a bank will focus on the relative liquidity of all the individual currency markets when writing them, especially if they have a maturity of less than one month. Swap transactions in multiple currency markets also expose banks to liquidity risk. Additional risks associated with derivatives include operational risk – e.g. system failure, fraud or legal problems, where a court or recognised financial authority rules a financial contract invalid.

To summarise, once banks begin to deal in derivatives, they confront a range of risks, in addition to credit risk. Most of these risks have always been present, especially for banks operating in global markets, where there was a risk of volatile interest or exchange rates. What these instruments have done is unbundle the risks and make each of them more transparent. Prior to their emergence these risks were captured in the "price" of a loan. Now there is individual pricing for each unbundled risk. In the marketing of these new instruments, banks stress the risk management aspect of them for their customers. Essentially, the bank is assuming the risk related to a given transaction, for a price, and the bank, in turn, may use instruments to hedge against these risks. The pricing of each option, swap or forward is based on the individual characteristics of each transaction and each customer relationship. Some banks use business profit models to ensure that the cost of capital required for these transactions is adequately covered. In a highly competitive environment, a profitable outcome may be difficult to achieve, in which case the customer relationship becomes even more important.

## 3.5. Management of Market Risk

### 3.5.1. Background

Recall that, from the mid-1980s, as major investment and commercial banks rapidly expanded into trading assets, new management techniques for market risk were needed, and as a result a great deal of academic and practitioner attention has been devoted to improving the management of market risk. An offshoot of this research has been the development of new methods to manage credit risk, especially at the aggregate or portfolio level. For example, JP Morgan's Riskmetrics™ was published in 1994, and outlined the bank's approach to the management of market risk. Similar principles were developed for the management of aggregate credit risk, and the outcome was Creditmetrics™, produced in 1997. For this reason, this section begins with a review of the relatively new approaches for managing market risk, followed by a discussion of credit risk management techniques. Once readers acquire a general knowledge of key terms in the context of market risk, it is reasonably straightforward to apply the same ideas to credit risk, though credit risk, as will be seen, presents its own unique set of problems.

The central components of a market risk management system are RAROC (risk adjusted return on capital) and value at risk (VaR). RAROC is used to manage risk related to different business units within a bank, but is also employed to evaluate performance. VaR focuses solely on giving banks a number, which, in principle, they use to ensure they have sufficient capital to cover their market risk exposure. In practice, the limitations of VaR make it necessary to apply other techniques, such as scenario analysis and stress tests.

### 3.5.2. Risk Adjusted Return on Capital

Bankers Trust introduced RAROC in the late 1970s, to assess the amount of credit risk embedded in all areas of the bank. By measuring the risk of the credit portfolio, the bank could decide on how much capital should be set aside to ensure that the exposure of its depositors was limited, for a given probability of loss. It was subsequently expanded to include all the business units at Bankers Trust, and other major banks adopted either RAROC or some variant of it. The difference between RAROC and the more traditional measures such as return on assets (ROA) or return on equity (ROE) is that the latter two measures do not adjust for the differences in degree of risk for related activities within the bank.

RAROC on the *risk adjusted return on capital* is defined as:

$$\text{Position's Return Adjusted for Risk} \div \text{Total Capital}$$

Position's Return: usually measured as (revenue – cost – expected losses), adjusted for risk (volatility)
Capital: the total capital (equity plus other sources of external finance)

Other, related measures of RAROC are used, though it is increasingly the sector standard.[31]

A bank wants to know the return on a position (e.g. a foreign exchange position, or a portfolio of loans or equity). RAROC measures the risk inherent in each activity, product or portfolio. The risk factor is assigned by looking at the volatility of the assets' price – usually based on historical data. After each asset is assigned a risk factor, capital is allocated to it. For example, a trader is assigned a risk adjusted amount of capital, based on the risk factor for the type of assets being traded.

Using RAROC, capital is assigned to a trader, division or centre, on a risk adjusted basis. The profitability of the product/centre is measured by returns against capital employed. If a unit is assigned X amount of capital and returns are unexpectedly low, then the capital allocation is inefficient and therefore, costly for the firm. An attraction of RAROC is that it can be employed for any type of risk, from credit risk to market risk.

A bank's overall capital will depend on some measure of volatility, and if looking at the bank as a whole, then the volatility of the bank's stock market value is used. Capital allocations to the individual business units will depend on the extent to which that unit contributes to the bank's overall risk. If it is not possible to price the asset or marking to market is irregular, then the volatility of earnings is one alternative that can be used. It will also depend on how closely correlated the unit's earnings are with the bank as a whole. Some units will have a volatility of market value that moves inversely with the rest of the firm, and this will lower the total amount of equity capital to be set aside. For example, suppose the bank is universal, and owns a liquidation subsidiary which deals with insolvent banks. Its market value is likely to be negatively correlated with the rest of the bank.

Once computed, RAROC is compared against a benchmark or *hurdle rate*. The hurdle rate can be measured in different ways. If it is defined as the cost of equity (the shareholder's minimum required rate of return), then provided a business unit's RAROC is greater than the cost of equity, shareholders are getting value for their investment, but if less than the cost of capital, it is reducing shareholder value. For example, if the return is 15% before tax, then if RAROC > 15%, it is adding value. The hurdle rate may also be more broadly defined as a bank's weighted average cost of funds, including equity.

To compute RAROC, it is essential to have measures of the following.

(1) *Risk*. There are two dimensions to risk: expected loss and unexpected loss. *Expected loss* is the mean or average loss expected from a given portfolio. Suppose a bank makes "home" loans to finance house repairs. Then, based on past defaults on these types of loans, the bank can compute an expected loss based on an average percentage of defaults over a long time period. The risk premium charged on the loan plus fees should be enough to cover for expected losses. These losses are reported on a bank's balance sheet, and their operating earnings should be enough to cover the losses. A bank will set aside reserves to cover expected losses. A bank also sets aside capital as a buffer because of *unexpected losses*, which, for home improvement (or any other type of loan) is measured by the volatility (or standard deviation) of credit losses. For a trading portfolio, it will be the volatility of returns, i.e. the standard deviation of returns. Figure 3.1 illustrates the difference between expected and unexpected loss and the relationship between variance and unexpected loss.

---

[31] An example of a related measure is RORAC (return on risk adjusted capital), where the adjustment for risk takes place in the denominator, i.e. (position's return)/(risk **adjusted** capital).

**Figure 3.1**  **Expected Loss and Unexpected Loss (Variance).**

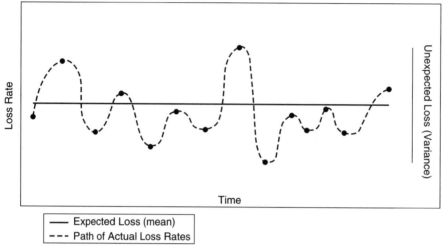

Source: Zaik *et al.* (1996).

(2) *Confidence intervals*. Capital is set aside as a buffer for unexpected losses, but there is the question of how much capital should be set aside. Usually, a bank estimates the amount of capital needed to ensure its solvency based on a 95% or 99% confidence interval. Suppose the 99% level of confidence is chosen. Then each business unit is assigned enough capital, on a risk adjusted basis, to cover losses for 10 out of 100 outcomes. Investment banks may opt to use a less restrictive confidence interval of 95% (covers losses for 5 out of 100 outcomes) if most of their business involves assets which are marked to market on a daily basis, so they can quickly react to any sudden falls in portfolio values.

(3) *Time Horizon for Measuring Risk Exposure*. Ideally, the risk measured would be based on a 5 or 10-year time horizon, but there are problems obtaining the necessary data. Usually there is an inverse relationship between the choice of confidence interval and the time horizon. An investment bank may have a higher confidence interval but a short holding period (days), because it can unwind its positions fairly quickly. A traditional bank engaged primarily in lending will normally set a time horizon of a year for both expected and unexpected losses, recognising that loans cannot be unwound quickly. Since it cannot react quickly, it sets a lower confidence interval of 99%.[32] Note that if RAROC is being used to compare different units in the banks, the same time horizon will have to be used.

(4) *Probability Distribution of Potential Outcomes*. It is also necessary to know the probability distribution of potential outcomes, such as the probability of default, or the probability of loss on a portfolio. The prices of traded assets are usually assumed to follow a normal distribution (a bell-shaped curve), though many experts question the validity of this assumption, to be discussed later in the chapter. Furthermore, loan losses are highly skewed, with a long downside tail, as can be observed for the distribution of credit

---

[32] Some major US commercial banks use a confidence interval of 99.97%. In this case, enough capital is assigned, on a risk adjusted basis to each business unit, to cover losses in all but 3 out of 10 000 outcomes.

**Figure 3.2  Comparison of Distribution of Market Returns and Credit Returns.**

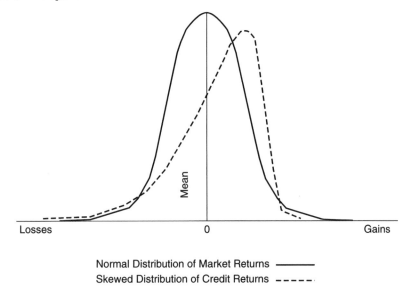

Normal Distribution of Market Returns  ———
Skewed Distribution of Credit Returns  – – – –

*Source*: JP Morgan (1997), *CreditMetrics – Technical Document*, New York, JP Morgan, p. 7.

returns shown in Figure 3.2. The skew on the loss side is due to defaults, indicating that there is a large likelihood of earning quite small returns, together with a really small chance of very large losses. If a bank has a large portfolio of loans, these two possibilities explain why the distribution is skewed. Figure 3.2 shows the contrast between normally distributed market returns and the skewed distribution of credit returns. However, if different distributions are allowed for, then it is not possible to compare one business unit against another.

RAROC has its limitations. First, the risk factor for each category is assigned according to the **historic** volatility of its market price, using something between the past two to three months and a year. There is no guarantee that the past is a good predictor of the present/future. Second, it is less accurate when applied to untraded assets such as loans, some of which are difficult to price. The choice of the hurdle rate or benchmark is another issue. If a single hurdle rate is used, then it is at odds with the standard capital asset pricing model (CAPM), where the cost of each activity reflects its systematic risk, or the covariance of the operation with the value of the market portfolio – the $\beta$s in standard CAPM. Furthermore, if RAROC is used as an internal measure, there are no data to compute the covariances. This means the returns on the activity being screened are considered independently of the structure of returns for the bank. Any correlation between activities, whether positive or negative, is ignored.

To summarise, a RAROC measure can assess what areas a bank should be allocating more resources to, and where they should be divesting from. RAROC is also used to measure performance across a diverse set of business units within a bank and different parts of the business can be compared. However, the problems mentioned above mean RAROC is a somewhat arbitrary rule of thumb, not ideally suited to complex financial institutions. On the other hand, making some adjustment for risk is better than ignoring it.

### 3.5.3. Market Risk and Value at Risk

The VaR model is used to measure a bank's market risk, and it therefore serves a different purpose from RAROC. It has since been adapted to measure credit risk, which is briefly reviewed in the next section.

Though VaR was originally used as an internal measure by banks, it assumed even greater importance after the 1996 market risk amendment to the 1988 Basel agreement – regulators encouraged banks to use VaR. The Basel agreement was mentioned briefly in Chapter 2. Where appropriate, some references to the Basel requirements are made in this chapter, but Basel is discussed at length in Chapter 4.

The distinguishing feature of VaR is the emphasis on losses arising as a result of the volatility of assets, as opposed to the volatility of earnings. The first comprehensive model developed was JP Morgan's Riskmetrics™, and the discussion throughout this chapter is based on their model.

The basic formula is:

$$VaR_x = V_x \times dV/dP \times \Delta P_t \qquad (3.6)$$

where:

$V_x$: the market value of portfolio $x$
$dV/dP$: the sensitivity to price movement per dollar market value
$\Delta P_t$: the adverse price movement
(in interest rates, exchange rates, equity prices or commodity prices) over time $t$

Time $t$ may be a day (daily earnings at risk or DEAR), a month, etc. Under the Basel market risk agreement, the time interval is 10 days.

Value at risk estimates the likely or expected maximum amount that could be lost on a bank's portfolio as a result of changes in risk factors, i.e. the prices of underlying assets over a specific time horizon, within a statistical confidence interval. VaR models of market risk focus on four underlying instruments, and their corresponding prices: bonds (interest rates at different maturities), currencies (exchange rates), equity (stock market prices) and commodities (prices of commodities such as oil, wheat or pork bellies). The principal concern is with unexpected changes in prices or price volatility, which affects the value of the portfolio(s).

VaR answers the question: how much can a portfolio lose with $x$% probability over a stated time horizon? If a daily VaR is $46 million, and the confidence interval is 95%, the value of the portfolio could fall by at least $46 million in an average of 5 out of every 100 trading days (a 95% probability), or daily losses would not be less than $46 million, on average, on 5 out of every 100 trading days. The **exact amount** of the average daily trading losses on each of these 5 days is unknown – only that it will be in excess of $46 million. Or, more conservatively, if the daily VaR measure for a portfolio is €25 million, at a 99%

confidence level, there is a 99% probability that the daily losses will, on average, be €25 million or more on 1 out of every 100 trading days. If a 10-day VaR measure is €200 million at the 99% confidence level, then on average, in 1 out of every 100 10-day trading periods, the losses over a 10-day trading period will be not less than €200 million.[33]

Any VaR computation involves several critical assumptions.

1. How often it is computed, that is, daily, monthly, quarterly, etc.
2. Identification of the position or portfolio affected by market risk.
3. The risk factors affecting the market positions. The four risk factors singled out[34] are: interest rates (for different term structures/maturities), exchange rates, equity prices and commodity prices.
4. The confidence interval. The confidence interval chosen is usually 99% (as required by Basel) and one-tailed, since VaR is only concerned with possible losses and not gains. If the loss level is at 99%, the loss should occur 1 in 100 days or 2 to 3 days a year. The choice of 99% is a more risk averse or conservative approach. However, there is a trade-off: a choice of 99% as opposed to 95% means not as much historical data (if it is a historical database being used – see below) is available to determine the cut-off point.
5. The holding period. The choice of holding period [$t$ in equation (3.6)] will depend on the objective of the exercise. Banks with liquid trading books will be concerned with daily returns, and hence the daily VaR or daily earnings at risk, DEAR. Pension and investment funds may want to use a month. The Basel Committee specifies 10 working days, reasoning that a financial institution may take more than 10 days to liquidate its holdings.
6. Choice of the frequency distribution. Recall this issue was raised when RAROC was discussed. The options for VaR include the following.

**(a) Non-Parametric Method**. This method uses historical simulations of past risk factor returns, but makes no assumption on how they are distributed. It is known as a _full valuation model_ because it includes every type of dependency, linear and non-linear, between the portfolio value and the risk factors. Basel requires that the historical data used date back at least one year.

In the non-parametric approach, the researcher must specify the period to be covered, and the frequency, e.g. daily, monthly or annually. It is assumed that the contents of the portfolio is unchanged over the period, and the daily return (loss or gain) is determined. These are ranked from worst loss to best gain. Based on a chosen tolerance level, the loss is determined. If the frequency chosen is 2 years or 730 days, and the tolerance threshold is 10%, then the threshold bites at the 73rd worst daily loss, and VaR is the amount of this loss. A low tolerance threshold is more conservative and implies a larger loss and bigger VaR.

**(b) Parametric Method**. Use of a variance–covariance or _delta normal_ approach, which was the method selected by Riskmetrics™. Risk factor returns are assumed to follow a certain

---

[33] Under the 1996 Basel market risk amendment, the required VaR measure is for every 10 days, and the banks must use a confidence level of 99%. See Chapter 4.

[34] As readers will see in Chapter 4, Basel requires banks to include these four risk factors, one reason why they are normally modelled.

parametric distribution, usually a multivariate normal distribution. It is a *partial valuation* model because it can only account for linear dependencies (deltas) and ignores non-linear factors, for example, bond convexities or option gammas. This is why it is sometimes called the correlation or "delta-var" variation.

If this frequency distribution is chosen, then VaR is estimated using an equation which specifies portfolio risk as a linear combination of parameters, such as volatility or correlation. It provides an accurate VaR measure if the underlying portfolio is largely linear (e.g. traditional assets and linear derivatives), but is less accurate if non-linear derivatives are present.

Banks that use variance–covariance analysis normally make *some allowances* for non-linearities. The Basel Amendment requires that non-linearities arising from option positions be taken into account.

In approaches (a) and (b), a *data window* must be specified, that is, how far back the historical distribution will go. The Basel Committee requires at least a year's worth of data. Generally, the longer the data run, the better, but often data do not exist except for a few countries, and it is more likely the distribution will change over the sample period. In approach (b), there is the question of which variances–covariances of the risk factor returns are computed.

**(c) Monte Carlo[35] approach**. Another full valuation approach, involving multiple simulations using random numbers to generate a distribution of returns. Distributional assumptions on the risk factors (e.g. commodity prices, interest rates, equity prices or currency rates) are imposed – these can be normal or other distributions. If a parametric approach is taken, the parameters of the distributions are estimated, then thousands of simulations are run, which produce different outcomes depending on the distributions used. The non-parametric approach uses *bootstrapping*, where the random realisations of the risk factor returns are obtained through iterations of the historical returns. In either approach, pricing methodology is used to calculate the value of a portfolio.

Unlike (a) and (b), the number of portfolio return realisations is much greater in number, from which the VaR estimates are derived. Even though large numbers of computations are involved, falling costs means Monte Carlo techniques are commonly used by banks and/or trading houses.

## 3.5.4. VaR, Portfolios and Market Risk

It is possible to show simple applications of VaR for individual trading positions involving two currencies or equities. However, banks compute VaR for large portfolios of equities, bonds, currencies and commodities. Management will want an aggregate number showing the potential value at risk for the bank's entire trading position. This aggregate VaR is not just a simple sum of the individual positions because they can be positively or negatively correlated with each other, which will raise or reduce the overall VaR. The components of

---

[35] Generally, a Monte Carlo approach models different cash flows of a particular deal, and subjects them to thousands of simulations involving different scenarios to generate the risk parameters. For example, if a bank agrees a loan for a particular venture, detailed cash flow models are subjected to thousands of simulations to assess how changes in the economy will affect the probability of default, exposure at default and loss given default.

any portfolio are sensitive to certain fundamental risks, the so-called "Greeks". These are as follows.

**Delta or Absolute Price Risk:** the risk that the price of the underlying asset will change (e.g. the stock or commodity price, exchange rate or interest rate). The delta risk is the effect of a change in the value of an underlying instrument on the value of the portfolio.

**Gamma or Convexity Risk:** the rate of change in the delta itself, or the change in the delta for a one point move in the underlying price. It allows for situations where there is a non-linear relationship between the price of the underlying instrument and the value of the portfolio.

**Vega or Volatility Risk:**[36] this risk applies when an option is involved, or a product has characteristics similar to an option. It is the sensitivity of the option price for a given change in the value of volatility. An increase in volatility of the underlying asset makes the option more valuable. Therefore, if the market's view of the volatility of the underlying instrument changes, so too will the value of the option.

**Rho or Discount Risk:** this risk applies primarily to derivatives, or any product which is valued using a discount rate, i.e. the value is determined by discounting expected future cash flows at a risk-free rate. If the risk-free rate changes, so too does the value of the derivative.

**Theta or Time Decay Risk:** the time value of the option. A change in the value of a portfolio because of the passage of time. For example, in an option theta rises with the length of time to the strike price.

To arrive at a VaR, the components of the portfolio are disaggregated according to the above risk factors (if they apply), netted out, then aggregated together.

Suppose a bank computes daily earnings at risk for its foreign exchange, bond and equity positions. Then it will end up with an interest DEAR, a foreign exchange DEAR and an equity DEAR. These will be summarised on a spread sheet, and if the bank operates in more than one country, their respective DEARs are reported too. Assume the bank is headquartered in Canada but also operates in the USA and the UK. Then a simplified version of the spread sheet will look like in Table 3.7. The interest rate column is highly simplified, for ease of exposition. Normally the interest rate risk would appear for a number of time buckets, with a column for each bucket. "Portfolio effects" is another name for benefits arising from diversification, which will depend on the degree to which various markets and assets are correlated with each other. There are two to account for. The first is the diversification effect arising from having a portfolio of currency, bonds and equity in one country. The other allows for the effects of holding bonds, foreign exchange and equity in more than one country. The portfolio/diversification effects will be calculated in a separate matrix and depend on numerous intercorrelations. In the table, it has been assumed that the diversification effects allow a total of $30 million to be reduced from the summed DEAR, giving a total DEAR of $45 million.

To show how VaR is reported by banks, the figures from Merrill Lynch's *Annual Report* are provided. Merrill's differentiates between trading and non-trading VaR, as can be seen from

---

[36] As was noted in Heffernan (1996), vega is NOT a Greek letter, and a plea was made for a replacement. Unfortunately, as was feared, vega is now accepted as a Greek letter! Even prestigious researchers of the Bank of England have to include vega in "the Greeks", from which this excellent description of "the Greeks" is drawn. See Gray and Place (1999).

Table 3.7   A Hypothetical Daily Earnings at Risk for a Canadian bank (CDN$m)

| Country | Interest rate Risk DEAR* | Forex Risk DEAR | Equity Risk DEAR | Total |
|---|---|---|---|---|
| Canada | 20 | | 10 | 30 |
| USA | 5 | 10 | 10 | 25 |
| UK | 5 | 5 | 10 | 20 |
| Total | 20 | 5 | 30 | 75 |
| **Gross Portfolio Effect** | | | | −30 |
| Total DEAR | | | | 45 |

*DEAR: Daily Earnings at Risk

Table 3.8   Merrill Lynch: value at risk ($m)

| | 2001 | 2000 | Daily/quarterly Average 2001** |
|---|---|---|---|
| *Trading VaR of which:* | 256 | 215 | 194 |
| Interest rate & credit spread | 113 | 81 | 64 |
| Equity | 94 | 77 | 61 |
| Commodity | 2 | 9 | 3 |
| Currency | 3 | 14 | 11 |
| Volatility | 44 | 34 | 35 |
| Diversification benefit | (144) | (116) | (92) |
| *Firm-Wide Trading VAR* | 112 | 90 | 102 |
| *Non-Trading VaR\*of which:* | 165 | 140 | 155 |
| Interest rate & credit spread | 77 | 67 | 76 |
| Currency | 20 | 23 | 19 |
| Equity | 57 | 47 | 51 |
| Volatility | 11 | 3 | 9 |
| Diversification benefit\*\*\* | (59) | (44) | (45) |
| *Firm-Wide Non-Trading VaR* | 106 | 96 | 110 |

Overall VaR is based on a 99% confidence interval and 2-week holding period.
* VaR for non-trading instruments excludes US banks.
** Daily average figures for traded VaR; quarterly average figures for non-traded VaR.
*** Diversification benefit: the difference between aggregate (firm-wide) VaR and the VaR summed from the four risk categories. The difference arises because the four market risk categories are not perfectly correlated. For example, the simulations of losses at a 99% confidence interval show the losses from each category will occur on different days. There are similar benefits within each category.
( ): negative.
*Source:* Merrill Lynch (2002), *Annual Report*, pp. 34–35.

Table 3.8. The daily trading VaR for 2001 is $256 million, which says, with an assumed volatility of $44 million, that average trading losses could exceed $256 million in 1 out of every 100 trading days. Had the confidence interval been 95%, average trading losses could exceed $256 million in 5 out of every 100 trading days. Again, the actual size of the losses on these 5 days is unknown, and could be much higher than $256 million. Table 3.8

shows that both trading and non-trading VaR at Merrill Lynch rose between 2000 and 2001 because (according to the *Annual Report*, 2002, p. 35) of increases in interest, equity and credit spread risk VaR. The figure would have been higher but for a partial offset due to the diversification effect. Commodity trading VaR also increased more than fourfold between the two years.

### 3.5.5. Problems with the VaR Approach

Danielsonn (2000, 2002) has been one of the most vociferous critics of value at risk, to be discussed below. Other authors[37] have voiced similar concerns.

The first problem with VaR is that it does not give the precise amount that will be lost. For example, if a bank reports VaR $\geq$ \$1 million at the 99th percentile, it means that losses in excess of VaR would be expected to occur 1% of the time. However, it gives no indication as to how much VaR will be exceeded – it could be \$2.5 million, \$450 million or \$1 billion – there is no upper bound on what can be lost. Statistically, rather than giving the entire tail, it is giving an arbitrary point in the tail.

Second, the simpler VaR models depend on the assumption that financial returns are normally distributed and uncorrelated. Empirical studies have shown that these assumptions may not hold, contributing to an inaccurate VaR measure of market risk.

Anecdotal evidence and remarks from traders suggest it is also possible to manipulate VaR by up to a factor of five. A trader might be told to lower VaR because it is too high. By lowering VaR the bank can increase the amount of risk, and expected profit.

VaR does not give a probability of bank failure, only losses that arise from a bank's exposure to market risk. On the other hand, it was never meant to. It is only a measure of the bank's exposure, reflecting the increased trading activities of many banks.

If all traders are employing roughly the same model, then the measure designed to contain market risk creates liquidity risk. This point was illustrated by Dunbar (2000), commenting on the 1998 Russian crisis. Market risk had been modelled using VaR, based on a period of relatively stable data, because for the previous five years (with the exception of the Asian crisis, which was largely confined to the Far East) volatility on the relevant markets had been low. Financial institutions, conforming to regulations, employed roughly the same market risk models. The default by Russia on its external loans caused the prices of some assets to become quite volatile, which breached the risk limits set by VaR-type models. There was a flight from volatile to stable assets, which exaggerated the downward price spiral, resulting in reduced liquidity. Hence if all banks employ a similar VaR, it can actually escalate the crisis.

The above example also illustrates that statistical relationships applied to VaR which hold during a period of relative stability often break down and cannot be used during a crisis. While there may be little in the way of correlation between asset prices in periods of stability, in a crisis, all asset values tend to move together. This means any portfolio/diversification effects will disappear.

---

[37] See Taleb (1996, 1997), an experienced trader with an MBA and a PhD, is also highly critical of the use of VaR. For an alternative view, see Jorion (1997).

Variations in the model assumptions with respect to the holding period, confidence interval and data window will cause different risk estimates (Beder, 1995). Likewise, Danielsonn (2000) demonstrates the VaR models lack robustness, that is, the VaR forecasts across different assets are unreliable. To illustrate, Danielsonn employs a violation ratio. **Violation** is defined as the case where the realised loss is greater than the VaR forecast. The **violation ratio** is the ratio of realised number of VaR violations to the expected number of violations. If the V-ratio >1, the model is under-forecasting the risk; if V-ratio <1, it is over-forecasting. Put another way, over-forecasting means the model is thick tailed relative to the data; under-forecasting means the model is relatively thin tailed. Danielsonn reports disappointing results using this test. Different estimation methods produce different violation ratios, but all vary between, for example, 0.38 and 2.18 (using variations of Riskmetrics™).

For the above reasons, it is necessary to test the actual outcomes with the VaR predictions of losses. However, such tests also have a problem (Kupiec, 1995) because if the period over which the performance of the VaR model is relatively short,[38] the tests lack statistical power. It is difficult to evaluate the accuracy of the model on the basis of a year of data. The choice of a 99% confidence interval allows for a loss to occur very 2.5 days in a year. Danielsonn (2000) argues such an allowance is irrelevant in a period of systemic crises, or even for the probability of a bank going bankrupt. If VaR violations occur more than 2.5 times per year under a 99% confidence interval, it does not usually indicate the bank is in any difficulty, and in light of this point, when are VaR breaches relevant? In defence of VaR, it was never meant to indicate that a bank was in difficulty. It is a benchmark number for banks to use to track their market risk exposure.

Both the parametric and non-parametric frequency distributions produce measures which rely on historical data, an implicit assumption is that they are a good predictor of future returns. But historical simulation is sensitive to the sampling period (Danielsonn and de Vries, 1997). For example, in an equity portfolio, the VaR outcomes will be quite different if the October 1987 crash is included than if it is excluded. Or, looking at US share price data from mid-1983 to mid-2000 would suggest sizeable index price falls were the exception, and if they happened, quickly reversed themselves. Agents armed with this information would think the future was like the past (a popular assumption in many models of VaR) and would have found the subsequent share price declines completely mystifying, and outside anything remotely predictable.

However, the non-parametric or historical simulation approaches are superior to the variance–covariance approach (advocated by Riskmetrics™) for two reasons. First, financial market returns do not always follow a normal distribution – large movements in the market (fat tails) occur more often than indicated by the normal distribution. Second, historical simulation allows for non-linearities between the position and risk factor returns, which are important when the VaR being computed includes derivatives, especially options.

There are other criticisms of the use of VaR which relate to the actual 1996 Basel Amendment and "Basel 2" agreement, but these will be discussed in Chapter 4. However,

---

[38] For example, the 250 days specified by the Basel Amendment – see Chapter 4.

to conclude this section, some quotes from Jorion (defending VaR) and Taleb (rejecting its use) are helpful.

First, comments in favour of VaR by Philippe Jorion:[39]

*"First, the purpose of VaR is not to describe the worst possible outcomes. It is simply to provide an estimate of the range of possible gains and losses. Many derivatives disasters have occurred because senior management did not inquire about the first-order magnitude of the bets being taken. Take the case of Orange County, for instance. There was no regulation that required the portfolio manager, Bob Citron, to report the risk of the $7.5 billion investment pool. As a result, Citron was able to make a big bet on interest rates that came to a head in December 1994, when the county declared bankruptcy and the portfolio was liquidated at a loss of $1.64 billion. Had a VaR requirement been imposed on Citron, he would have been forced to tell investors in the pool: Listen, I am implementing a triple-legged repo strategy that has brought you great returns so far. However, I have to tell you that the risk of the portfolio is such that, over the coming year, we could lose at least $1.1 billion in one case out of 20."* (Jorion, 1997, p. 1)

*"VaR has other benefits as well. By now, all U.S. commercial banks monitor the VaR of their trading portfolios on a daily basis. Suppose a portfolio VaR suddenly increases by 50 percent. This could happen for a variety of reasons – market volatility could have increased overnight, a trader could be taking inordinate risks, or a number of desks could be positioned on the same side of a looming news announcement. More prosaically, a position could have been entered erroneously. Any of these factors should be cause for further investigation, which can be performed by reverse-engineering the final VAR number. Without it, there is no way an institution can get an estimate of its overall risk profile."* (Jorion, 1997, p. 1)

*"Still, VaR must be complemented by stress-testing. This involves looking at the effect of extreme scenarios on the portfolio. This is particularly useful in situations of 'dormant' risks, such as fixed exchange rates, which are subject to devaluations. Stress-testing is much more subjective than VAR because it poorly accounts for correlations and depends heavily on the choice of scenarios. Nevertheless, I would advocate the use of both methods."* (Jorion, 1997, p. 2)

*"A second misconception raised in the discussion is that VaR involves a covariance matrix only and does not work with asymmetric payoffs. This is not necessarily the case. A symmetric, normal approximation may be appropriate for large portfolios, in which independent sources of risk, by the law of large numbers, tend to create normal distributions. But the delta-normal implementation is clearly not appropriate for portfolios with heavy option components, or exposed to few sources of risk, such as traders' desks. Other implementations of VaR do allow asymmetric payoffs. VAR is an essential component of sound risk management systems. VaR gives an estimate of potential losses given market risks. In the end, the greatest benefit of VAR lies in the imposition of a structured methodology for critically thinking about risk. Institutions that go through the process of computing their VAR are forced to confront their*

---

[39] Comments from Jorion and Taleb (1997).

*exposure to financial risks and to set up a proper risk management function. Thus the process of getting to VAR may be as important as the number itself. These desirable features explain the widespread view that the 'quest for a benchmark may be over'."* (Jorion, 1997, p. 2)

Nassim Taleb opposes the use of VaR:[40]

*"... the professional risk managers I heard recommend a 'guarded' use of VaR on the grounds that it generally works or 'it works on average' do not share my definition of risk management. The risk management objective function is survival not profits and losses. One trader, according to Chicago legend, made \$8 million in eight years and lost \$80 million in eight minutes. According to the same standards, he would be 'in general' and 'on average' a good trader."* (Taleb, 1997, p. 3)

*"VaR has made us replace about 2500 years of market experience with a co-variance matrix that is still in its infancy."* (Taleb, 1997, p. 1)

*"[VaR can measure] the risks of common events, perhaps. Those that do not matter, but not the risks of rare events."* (Taleb, 1997, p. 2)

*"VaR players are all dynamic hedgers and need to revise their portfolios at different levels. As such they can make very uncorrelated markets become correlated. In 1993 hedge funds were long in seemingly independent markets. The first margin call in the bonds led them to liquidate their positions in the Italian, French, and German bond markets. Markets therefore became correlated."* (Taleb, 1997, pp. 2–3)

### 3.5.6. Stress Testing and Scenario Analysis to Complement VaR

Given the limitations of VaR, most banks apply scenario analysis and stress testing to complement estimates of market risk produced by VaR. Banks begin by identifying plausible unfavourable scenarios which cause extreme changes to the value of one or more of the four risk factors, i.e. interest, equity, currency or commodity prices. These might include an event which causes most financial agents to act in a similar manner, prompting severe illiquidity, as illustrated by the LTCM case, discussed earlier. Or the unexpected collapse of Enron and WorldCom (two American financial conglomerates in 2002), creating widespread fears about the quality and accuracy of company financial statements which, in turn, contributed to unexpected, dramatic declines in a key or several stock market prices. Other scenarios might be ill-founded rumours which prompt unexpected cash margin calls or changes in collateral obligations.

The **stress test**, based on a scenario, computes how much a bank's portfolio could lose. Note the difference from VaR, which estimates the maximum amount that a portfolio, security or business unit (of the bank) could lose over a *specified time period*. In VaR, the third and fourth moments are assumed to be zero. Some forms of stress testing go beyond the

---

[40] Comments from Taleb (1997) and Taleb and Jorion (1997).

second moment of the distribution (volatility) and consider the third (skewness) and fourth moment (kurtosis) of the distribution. Skewness will include the worst case outcomes. Kurtosis describes the relative thinness or fatness of the tails of a distribution compared to a normal distribution. For example, in a credit portfolio, if the loss distribution is leptokurtic (i.e. has fat tails), meaning extreme events are more likely than in a normal distribution (e.g. one large credit default results in massive losses). Thin (platykurtosis) tails suggests the opposite.

The size of the change in key risk factors will have to be computed. One group[41] recommended changes in volatility such as currency changes of plus or minus 6%, or a 10% change in an equity index. The bank must also choose the frequency with which the stress tests should be conducted.

As a practical example, suppose there are two scenarios: (1) a 40% decline in UK and world equity prices or (2) a 15% decline in residential and commercial property prices. If these are the scenarios, the next step is to decide what stress tests should be conducted. Banks could be asked to identify the potential impact of (1) and (2) on market risk, credit risk and interest rate risk. In addition (or alternatively), building societies could be asked to compute the impact of (1) and (2) on the retail deposit rate, the mortgage rate and the income of building societies. The complexity of the stress tests that must be performed is immediately apparent. Complicated models are required if the banks or building societies are going to produce realistic answers to the questions.

A final task is to decide how to use the results. This presents a very difficult problem for the bank because, by definition, a bank cannot forecast "surprises" or unexpected events. Nor can it judge how frequently they will occur, and therefore, whether or not a special reserve should be created. Furthermore, if such a reserve is kept, how much should the bank be setting aside?

## 3.6. Management of Credit Risk

### 3.6.1. Background

Market risk has received an inordinate amount of attention in recent years but managing credit risk is the "bread and butter" of most commercial banks. Every commercial bank, by definition, has a loan portfolio. Increases in credit risk will raise the marginal cost of debt and equity, which in turn increases the cost of funds for the bank. Techniques for credit risk management are well known because the banking sector has had a long history of experience in this area. Nonetheless, loan quality problems are an important cause of bank failure, as will be seen in Chapter 6. For this reason, all bankers, not just those in a credit risk department, should be aware of the key factors affecting the quality of a loan portfolio, and the methods for managing it.

### 3.6.2. Credit Risk Decisions: Retail versus Corporate

If a bank is looking to minimise its aggregate credit risk, then good risk management of retail and corporate lending is essential. The approaches taken for retail and corporate loans

---

[41] Derivative Policy Group (1995).

differ considerably, mainly because a corporation is able to produce a variety of financial ratios, which are not available when the suitability of an individual or a small firm for a loan is being assessed. Most bankers concede that lack of information makes retail lending more difficult than corporate lending. On the other hand, loans to corporates which turn out to be bad can be very serious for the bank because of the large sums involved. Countless cases abound: Maxwell and a number of London-based banks; Schroder and Deutsche Bank; and the collapse of Enron and WorldCom. The number of incidents where retail loan defaults have had serious consequences for a bank is very much lower, and usually occurs if a bank is over-exposed in one area such as mortgages, and property prices collapse at the same time as interest rates rise.

The principles used to model credit risk, and the methods used to minimise credit risk for the retail and corporate sectors, are discussed below.

### 3.6.3. Minimising Credit Risk

There are five key ways a bank can minimise credit risk: through accurate loan pricing, credit rationing, use of collateral, loan diversification and more recently through asset securitisation and/or the use of credit derivatives. The weights applied to each of the methods will vary, depending on whether the loan is commercial or retail.

(1) **Pricing the loan**: any bank will wish to ensure the "price" of a loan (loan rate) exceeds a risk adjusted rate, and includes any loan administration costs, that is:

$$R_L = i + ip + \text{fees} \tag{3.7}$$

where:

$R_L$: interest rate charged on the loan

$i$: market interest rate, such as LIBOR or an equivalent term[42]

$ip$: risk premium, negatively related to the probability of the loan being repaid ($ip = 0$ if repayment is certain)

In the above equation, $ip$ and $i$ are positively related, for one of two reasons. In the case of a variable rate loan, if the market rate rises, so will the interest rate charged on the loan, and the borrower will find it more difficult to repay the loan, so the probability of default increases. Or, at very high market rates, the loan rate will rise, attracting riskier borrowers (due to adverse selection), so the chances of the loan being repaid fall.

Other factors also influence the loan rate. If there is any collateral or security backing the loan, the rate charged should be lower than in the absence of security. In addition, there are non-price features: the bank may charge a high fee for arranging the loan but the interest rate will be lower. Or, some central banks impose reserve ratios, which means a percentage of a bank's deposits is held at the central bank, often earning no interest. This is effectively a tax on deposits, which banks will try to make up by imposing higher loan rates.

---

[42] The loan rate set will also depend on the term of the loan. Normally (but not always) the longer the term the higher the loan rate. This will be in the risk premium and will depend on the term structure of interest rates, which is often but not necessarily upward sloping.

Thus, the loan rate should include a "market" rate, risk premium and administration costs. The riskier the borrower, the higher the premium. Should the risk profile of the loan be altered, the rate should change accordingly, though if increased, it should be borne in mind that the potential for adverse selection or adverse incentives is greater. The guidelines may also be difficult to implement in highly competitive markets.

(2) *Credit Limits*: another method for controlling credit risk. Given the potential for adverse selection, most banks do not rely solely on loan rates when taking a lending decision. Instead, the availability of a certain type of loan may be restricted to a selected class of borrowers, especially in retail markets. Branch managers are given well-defined credit constraints (and checklists – see below), and borrowers usually discover they may not borrow above some ceiling. In retail markets, banks normally quote one loan rate (or a very narrow range of rates) and then restrict the amount individuals or small firms can borrow according to criteria such as wealth or collateral. However, in the United States, legislation prevents banks from discriminating against certain retail customers. The Community Re-investment Act (1977) requires banks to provide evidence to the regulator that loan decisions do not discriminate against the local community. Under the Home Mortgage Disclosure Act (1975) regulators must be satisfied mortgage decisions by banks do not discriminate on the grounds of race, income, age or income status.

By contrast, in the wholesale markets, credit limits are of secondary importance; loan rates (and the risk premium) normally vary from business to business because banks have more information on the value of a firm, such as independent auditor reports on a company's financial performance.

(3) *Collateral or Security*: Banks also use collateral to reduce credit risk exposure. However, if the price of the collateral (for example, houses, stock market prices) becomes more volatile, then for an unchanged loan rate, banks have to demand more collateral to offset the increased probability of loss on the credit. Another problem that can arise is if the price of collateral is negatively correlated with the ability of the borrower to repay, that is, as the probability of default among a borrower class increases, the price of the collateral declines. For example, in the 1980s, Texan banks made a large number of loans to firms in the booming oil industry, and the collateral was often the oil well(s) or Texan real estate. When oil prices collapsed, the value of the collateral also collapsed. In the late 1980s, over a quarter of US banks that failed were located in Texas.

In Britain, building societies and banks tend to enter into flexible rate mortgage agreements with homeowners, using the property as collateral. In the early 1990s, interest rates began to rise to counter inflation. The housing boom came to an abrupt end, and house prices fell rapidly. Householders who had borrowed up to 100% mortgages found themselves holding *negative equity*: the value of the house was less than the cost of the total outstanding mortgage. Many households were unable to make the mortgage repayments as recession set in and the unemployment rate rose. The banks/building societies realised they would end up having to dispose of real estate at very low prices. So many accommodated distressed borrowers, by allowing interest repayment holidays and other measures which meant increased arrears. Though costly, losses would have been far higher if houses were repossessed and sold. These examples illustrate an important point. Collateral tends to be a more effective means of managing risk for short-term (e.g. overnight loans) because the risk of its value changing is quite low. In this context, for big corporates and other banks, a bank will often use *haircuts*: an extra amount of collateral (in the form of a margin) applied to a loan, i.e. collateral plus a margin. Even with an overnight loan, there is a chance the value of the collateral will decline. A haircut is the amount by which the collateral exceeds the principal of a loan. For example, for an overnight loan the banks may ask for collateral, the value of which is 5% greater than the amount loaned.

(4) **Diversification**: Additional volatility created from an increase in the number of risky loans can be offset either by new injections of capital into the bank or by diversification. New loan markets should allow the bank to diversify and so reduce the overall riskiness of the loan portfolio, provided it seeks out assets which yield returns that are negatively correlated. In this way, banks are able to diversify away all non-systematic risk. Banks should use correlation analysis to decide how a portfolio should be diversified. An example of a lack of lending diversification was the US savings and loans sector, or "thrifts" in the 1980s. Regulations required a high percentage of their assets to be invested in home mortgage loans and mortgage-related securities. The thrifts tried to diversify by moving into commercial real estate financing, and later got involved with new financial innovations about which they knew little, resulting in a costly debacle – over 1000 failed. (see Chapter 6). Banks can help to ensure they are properly diversified by setting **concentration limits**: the bank sets a limit on the amount of exposure in relation to a certain individual or sector.

(5) **Credit Derivatives and Asset Securitisation**: recall from Chapter 2 that asset securitisation is a method of reducing credit risk exposure, provided a third party assumes responsibility for the credit risk of the securitised assets. As discussed earlier in the chapter credit risk derivatives can be used to insure against a loan default.

## 3.6.4. Assessing the Default Risk of Individual Loans

Most banks have a separate credit risk analysis department – their aim is to maximise shareholder value-added through credit risk management. Managerial judgement always plays a critical role, but a good credit risk team will use qualitative and quantitative methods to assess credit risk. The use of different methods will be determined by the information the bank can gather on the individual.

If a bank is unable to obtain information on a potential borrower (using, for example, annual reports), it is likely to adopt a **qualitative approach** to evaluating credit risk, which involves using a checklist to take into account factors specific to each borrower:

- Past credit history (usually kept by credit rating agencies).
- The borrower's gearing (or leverage) ratio – how much the loan applicant has already borrowed relative to his/her assets.
- The wealth of the borrower.
- Whether borrower earnings are volatile.
- Employment history.
- Length of time as a customer at a bank.
- Length of time at a certain address.
- Whether or not collateral or security is part of the loan agreement.
- Whether a future macroeconomic climate will affect the applicant's ability to repay.

For example, a highly geared flexible rate borrower will be hit hard by rising interest rates. Thus, the credit risk group will have to consider forecasts of macroeconomic indicators such as the interest rate, inflation rate and future economic growth rates.

Along a similar vein, Sinkey (2002) singled out what he calls the "fives Cs" to be used in a qualitative assessment of credit risk.

- Character: Is the borrower willing to repay the loan?
- Cash flow: Is the borrower reasonably liquid?
- Capital: What assets or capital does the borrower have?
- Collateral or security: Can the borrower put up security (e.g. deeds to a house, share certificates which will be owned by the bank in the event of default)?
- Conditions: What is the state of the economy? How robust will the borrower be in the event of a downturn?

## Quantitative models

A quantitative approach to credit risk analysis requires the use of financial data to measure and predict the probability of default by the borrower. Different models include the following.

*Credit scoring.* Here, the data from observed borrower behaviour are used to estimate the probability of default, and to sort borrowers into different risk classes. The type of information gathered is listed above but here, a weight is applied to each answer, and a score obtained. The weights are obtained from econometric techniques such as discriminant or logit analysis. Here a large amount of historical data from two populations are obtained, from the population that defaults and a group which does not default.

Discriminant analysis assumes that a borrower will come from one of two populations: those that default are in one population (P1) and population 2 (P2) consists of firms that do not default. Data from past economic performance are used to derive a function that will discriminate between types of firms by placing them in one of two populations. Thus, if Z is a linear discriminant function of a number of independent explanatory variables, then

$$Z = \sum a_i X_i, \quad i = 1, 2, \ldots, n \tag{3.8}$$

where $X_i$ are the independent explanatory variables, such as credit history, wealth, etc. Sample data are used to test whether the discriminant function places the borrower in one of the two populations, with an acceptable error rate.

Logit analysis differs from discriminant analysis in that it does not force borrowers into separate populations but instead assumes that the combined effect of certain economic variables will serve to push a borrower over a given threshold. In this case, it would be from the non-arrears group into the arrears group. Note that in logit analysis, the dependent variable is a binary event, and the objective is to identify explanatory variables which influence the event. The logit model may be written as follows:

$$P\{(y_{it} + 1) = 1 | x_{it}\} = [e^{b+c'xu}]/[1 + e^{b+c'xu}] \tag{3.9}$$

where:

$x_{it}$: value of the explanatory variable $i$ at time $t$

$P(y_{it} + 1)$: probability of a firm being in arrears at time $t + 1$; $y = 0$ implies the firm is not in arrears

See Chapter 7 for a further discussion and diagram (figure 7.1)

In either the discriminant or logit models, the estimates obtained are used together with out of sample data, to forecast which borrowers will or will not default on their loans. The number of forecasting errors is determined. A type-I error occurs when the borrower is not forecast to go into arrears but does and a type-II error when a borrower is forecast to go into arrears but does not. The average costs of the two types of errors will differ. A type-I error means the value of the lender's assets will fall, whereas with a type-II error a profitable lending opportunity has been missed – the bank loses in terms of opportunity cost. For this reason, it is normally assumed that a type-I error has a higher average cost for creditors than a type-II error. However, it is necessary to decide where the cut-off is going to be; the optimal cut-off will depend on the value of the cost ratio, defined as:

$$C = \text{average cost of type-I error} \div \text{average cost of type-II error}$$

For example, if a bank is very risk averse and puts a high weight on type-I errors, then C will be high (e.g. 2.5) and the bank will require very high scores if an individual or firm is to be approved a loan.

Individuals or corporations can be credit scored, though the variables used to determine the score will differ. For example, an individual will be scored based on age, income, employment and past repayment records, etc. Not all personal loans or firms are subject to credit scoring – it can only be done if there are enough data, which requires a sufficiently high volume of standardised loans that have been granted for some time.

Different financial ratios (such as debt to equity) are used to score corporations, as well as any external ratings of the firm, if is creditworthy enough to be issuing its own securities.[43] The **Altman (1968)** *Z-score* model is derived from discriminant analysis and is used for larger corporations. Based on financial/accounting ratios,[44] each firm is assigned a Z score and, depending on that score, either the loan is granted or it is refused. The higher the Z score, the lower the probability of default; If Z is lower than 1.81,[45] the default risk is considered too high and no loan is made.

For example, suppose SINCY corporation is applying for a loan. Its credit rating by the Good Rating Company is AB. The bank also requests that it provide extensive financial information: a business plan on what the loan is for, return on assets and equities, the ratio of debt to equity, and so on. This information is fed into a program, where every financial

---

[43] Critical to any bond issue is a good credit history, so most firms will seek out some loans, which acts as a signal to the market place that they are creditworthy.

[44] The accounting ratios used in Altman (1985) are the working capital, retained earnings, current earnings (before taxes and interest) and sales–each expressed as a percentage of total assets and the market to book value of equity. The original paper upon which future models are based is Altman (1968).

[45] In the Altman model, the $Z = 1.81$ is the average of Z scores of the defaulting and non-defaulting firms.

variable is weighted, then summed into a Z score. If it is very high, the loan is granted. If the score is borderline (for example, 2) then the relationship the firm has with the bank may be quite important, as well as Z scores on any previous loans which had been repaid.

Relationship banking also plays its part, especially in countries such as Germany and Japan. If a corporation has done business with a bank for a long period of time, then an application for a new loan will involve a combination of banker judgement and credit scoring. This may also apply to personal customers with a long-standing credit history at a bank.

Small businesses are more difficult. They vary considerably in their activities, and failure rates among small and medium-sized enterprises can be as high as 95%. This makes it difficult to apply credit scoring models to this group.

## Problems with Credit Scoring Models

These models are not fail safe. They are only as good as the original specification, and one limitation is that the data are historical. Though the original discriminant analysis may have produced a Z score which was fairly accurate, unless it is frequently updated either the variables or the weights (assumed to be constant over time) make it less accurate. For example, the relevant financial ratios are likely to change, and may even differ depending on the industry being evaluated. The same remarks apply to the weights. This problem can be minimised if the bank keeps records of their type-I and type-II errors, and acts to implement a new model to address any necessary changes. An extensive list of variables must be subject to regular testing in the discriminant model, and any insignificant variables discarded. However, even a comprehensive list cannot take into account variables not easily quantified, such as the length and nature of the relationship between borrower and bank.

A more difficult problem is that the model used imposes a binary outcome: either the borrower defaults or does not default. In fact, there is a range of possible outcomes, from a delay in interest payments to non-payment of interest, to outright default on principal and interest. Often the borrower announces a problem with payments, and the loan terms can be renegotiated. These different outcomes can be included, but only two at a time. For example, the discriminant function can contain the default and no-default outcomes or the no-default and rescheduling outcomes, but not both.

## 3.6.5. Aggregate Credit Risk Exposure and Management

Up to this point, the discussion has focused on loans to individuals or firms. All banks will want to manage their aggregate credit exposure. A heavy concentration of loans in one sector has the potential of threatening the survival of the bank. There are many examples of banks getting into problems precisely because of over-exposure in one sector. The case of the Texan banks has already been mentioned. Not only did the value of their collateral (oil wells and real estate) fall when the oil industry began to encounter difficulties, but these banks were over-exposed in the oil sector as a whole. In the UK, excessive lending in the commercial property markets resulted in the illiquidity (and later, insolvency, in some cases) of secondary banks.[46] In late 1972 secondary banking problems prompted a Bank of

---

[46] The secondary banks were established in the 1960s. They borrowed on the wholesale markets to fund long-term loans to property developers and construction firms. Problems began after the government tried to stem inflation by raising interest rates and reducing government expenditure.

England-led lifeboat rescue to prevent a general crisis of confidence. In Japan, the *jusen* or mortgage corporations collapsed in 1995 after over-exposure in the property markets, five years after they had been instructed by the regulators to curtail their lending to this sector – a directive they ignored at their peril, prompting a public outcry (public taxes were used to fund a government rescue).

When assessing aggregate credit exposure, four factors should be taken into account in any model of credit risk. They are:[47]

1. Compute the expected loss levels over a given time horizon, for each loan and for the portfolio as a whole.
2. Compute the **unexpected** loss for each loan, i.e. the volatility of loss.
3. Determine the volatility of expected loss for the portfolio as a whole.
4. Calculate the probability distribution of credit loss for the portfolio, and assess the capital required, for a given confidence level and time horizon, to absorb any unexpected losses.

In the United States, where many corporations are rated by agencies such as Standard and Poor's or Moody's, it is possible to apply standard modern portfolio theory (PT) to get a measure of aggregate exposure. Assume the banks hold traded loans and bonds. The basic principle is diversification: provided returns on loans are not highly correlated, the bank can raise its expected return on a portfolio of assets by diversifying across asset classes. Put another way, suppose a bank has a portfolio consisting of two loans. The bank can achieve the same expected return on its portfolio of assets and reduce its overall risk exposure, provided the returns on two loans are negatively correlated.

Outside the United States, there are not many corporations which are externally rated. Even within the USA, the majority of banks' main portfolios consist of non-traded loans. New methods are being developed to deal with this problem. Below, two approaches – the KMV model and Credit Riskmetrics™ – are discussed.

### 3.6.6. Default Mode Approach

The default model approach draws on modern portfolio theory to measure a bank's aggregate credit exposure for non-traded assets, such as loans on the banking book. In PT, to obtain a measure of the risk–return trade-off between a portfolio of assets, there must be data on the expected return on the assets, the risk of the asset (measured by the standard deviation), and the correlation between the risks of the assets. If these assets are loans, then this translates into the expected return on each loan, $E(R_i)$, where $i$ goes from 1 to $n$ loans, the risk of each loan $\sigma$ and the degree to which the risk of each loan is correlated ($\rho_{ij}$ if there are two loans, $i$ and $j$).

The emphasis is on loan loss rates. CreditRisk Plus™ (developed by Credit Suisse Financial Products) uses a default mode model. The "KM" model, developed by the KM Corporation, also takes this approach.[48] The advantages over credit VaR (discussed below) are that less data are required, and there is no assumption of a normal distribution, which, as was noted earlier, is unrealistic for a portfolio of non-traded loans.

---

[47] This discussion is partly from a summary by Matten (2002).
[48] The firm was acquired by Moody's in 2002. See its website: www.moodyskmv.com

Some important assumptions are necessary.

1. Either there is a default on the loan, or there is no default. Thus any **migration**, which measures the probability of a loan being downgraded, upgraded or defaulted on over a specified period of time, is assumed to be zero.[49]
2. When considering a portfolio of loans (e.g. auto, home, personal), the DM approach assumes the probability of one loan default is independent of the probability of default on all other loans.
3. The risk being measured. Here the focus is on credit risk – the risk of the debt not being repaid as agreed at the time agreed, where all loans are held to maturity. Recall from the discussion on RAROC that the unexpected loss on a loan is how the risk of the loan is measured, and differs from expected loss which is covered in the risk premia charged. Banks can compute the expected loss on a given loan category based on historical data. It will be known from past experience the proportion of borrowers who will default on home loans, car loans, etc. It will also be possible to calculate loss given default, based on past experience. If a borrower either repays the loan, or does not, then the standard deviation or **risk** of the $i$th borrower is the square root of the (probability of default)(1 − probability of default). This will be incorporated into equation (3.11), below.
4. The holding period. In common with what most banks do, the holding period is defined as one year. While a loan agreement may be for many years, specifying a holding period of a year means the bank can take stock of the status of the loan portfolio on an annual basis, because firms report their annual (sometimes quarterly) performance figures, and the bank can take action should the loan appear to be in trouble.
5. **Loss Given Default (LGD):** The amount the bank loses if the borrower defaults. If there is no security on the loan, and the loan is completely written off, this loss will be in excess of the amount loaned if the book value of the loan is less than the current value of the loan, due to compounding. If the bank is able to cash in on collateral, the LGD can be quite low. Some defaults may involve relatively small sums, others involve substantial losses. For example, losses on a personal loan may amount to £5000, but losses when a business goes bankrupt can be in the hundreds of millions, which was the case with the collapse of Maxwell Communications Corporation, LTCM and Enron.
6. **Potential Credit Exposure (PCE):** Refers to the amount of credit outstanding at the time of default. If all of the loan is taken at the time it is granted, then the repayment schedule makes it relatively straightforward to compute what the PCE is. It is assumed that 100% of any credit line (or agreed overdraft) has been used at the time of default. Hence, the PCE is assumed to be fixed over time.[50]

To compute a loan loss value, it is necessary to compute expected loss (EL) and unexpected loss. Recall from the earlier discussion on RAROC that the risk premium of a loan covers

---

[49] It is also assumed that the probability of default is independent of the economic cycle. It is well known that the mean default rate rises when there is a macroeconomic downturn, and falls as the economy recovers and goes into a boom. This additional uncertainty is allowed for in the more sophisticated DM models.

[50] However, it can vary – for example, borrowers may exceed the agreed overdraft or credit line, or if it is related to an exposure arising from a derivative.

the expected loss, and capital is set aside as a buffer for the unexpected loss:

$$EL = AVG(EDF) + AVG(LGD) + AVG(PCE) \qquad (3.10)$$

where:
AVG: average of ( )
EDF: expected default
LGD: loan loss given default
PCE: potential credit exposure

EL, or expected loss, is the average expected loss on a loan or set of loans over a specified length of time. Since EL is an average, averages (AVG) are used for each of the three terms on the right-hand side of the equation.

For the portfolio of loans as a whole:

$$EL(portfolio) = \sum_{i=1}^{n} EL_i \qquad (3.11)$$

where $EL_i$ is the expected loss on the $i$th loan, $i = 1, \ldots, n$.

Recall that unexpected loss will be determined by the volatility (standard deviation) of the expected loss. If PCE and LGD are assumed constant, then the volatility will only depend on the expected default rates, and since there is either default or no default, the unexpected loss is:

$$UL_i = \sqrt{EL_i\,(LGD - EL_i)} \qquad (3.12)$$

7. Correlation between default risks. Suppose a bank has a portfolio made up of car loans and mortgages, or the loans are to firms in different sectors. Then the likelihood of a default occurring at the same time is quite low, unless there is severe depression or recession which affects the majority of firms and individuals.

To obtain the unexpected loss for an entire portfolio, assume the unexpected default on loans will be correlated. Thus, for the portfolio as a whole:

$$UL(portfolio) = \sum UL_i \rho_i \qquad (3.13)$$

where:
$\rho_i$: correlation between the loss on the $i$th loan and the loss on the portfolio as a whole
UL(portfolio): standard deviation of the losses on the $i$th facility
$UL_i$: standard deviation of the loss on the $i$th loan

Historical data are one way of computing the average correlation of each part of the loan book. For example, a 10-year series on loan losses for each of autos, personal loans, house loans, different categories of commercial loans can be used to estimate the standard deviation of the portfolio's losses. With knowledge of the standard deviations, and the unexpected losses for each segment, then the average correlation can be obtained, i.e.

$$UL(portfolio) = \sqrt{\rho_s} \left( \sum UL_i \right) \qquad (3.14)$$

where:

$\rho_s$: average correlation of one loan segment (e.g. personal loans) to the whole loan portfolio

This simpler approach assumes that the average correlation remains unchanged over time, and therefore, that the mix of different loan types is unchanged. Nor does it allow for the effects of concentrated risks. If a bank concentrates 90% of its loans in one industry, then its unexpected losses will be far greater than that indicated by the equation above.[51]

The KMV Corporation report that default correlations vary from 0.002 to 0.15. Such low correlation figures mean a bank can reduce their aggregate credit risk by spreading the loans across many firms and individuals.

Example:

Assume:

- Super-Specialised Bank grants 100 unsecured bullet loans (principal and interest paid in full when the loan matures) of £2 million each, giving a total loan portfolio of £200 million.
- The probability of default on each loan is 1%.
- LGD is the value of the loan if a borrower defaults. So LGD will be £20 000 for a given default, rising to £2 million for the whole portfolio if every borrower defaults.
- Based on KMV estimates, the correlation between each loan default and the portfolio as a whole is 0.02.

Then:

$$EL_i = £20\,000 \text{ on each loan, i.e. 1\% of £2 million}$$
$$LGD = £2 \text{ million for the portfolio (1\% of £200 million)}$$
$$UL_i = \sqrt{EL_i\,(LGD - EL_i)} = \sqrt{(20\,000)(2 \text{ million} - 20\,000)}$$
$$= £198\,997.4874 \text{ or about £200\,000}$$

The computations show the unexpected loss for the loan portfolio as a whole is roughly £200 000. The correlation between each of the 100 loans and the whole portfolio is 0.02. Then the risk contribution of one loan to the unexpected loss of the portfolio is £3979.95 or approximately £4000[52] per loan. For the entire portfolio, the loan loss is £397 995, or approximately £400 000.

The objective is for the bank to hold enough capital to absorb unexpected losses from the loan portfolio. To determine the appropriate confidence interval, the bank's own rating is normally used. Suppose the bank has an AA rating, and the bank is conservative, with a confidence interval of 99.99%, meaning the bank is focusing on all but the worst outcome

---

[51] KMV Portfolio Manager uses stock price correlation to deduce $\rho i$. KMV was taken over by Moody's in 2002. See www.KMV.com
[52] (0.02) X (£198, 997.48) = £3979.95, or approximately £4000.

in 10 000. So enough capital needs to be set aside to be 99.99% certain that losses arising from loan defaults will not cause the bank to fail. If the credit losses are normally distributed, then 3.89 standard deviations from the mean are needed for a 99.99% confidence interval. Then the capital to be set aside for the whole portfolio is:

$$(£397\,995)(3.89) = £1\,548\,200.55, \text{ or about £1.6 million}$$

Remember, however, that for loan portfolios in particular, the assumption of a normal distribution does not hold – see Figure 3.2. With this type of distribution, the 99.99% confidence interval lies between 6 and 10 standard deviations from the mean. The higher the proportion of commercial loans in a bank's portfolio, the less likely the returns will approach a normal distribution, because there tend to be very large losses associated with one default, and the probability of default is more closely correlated with the economic cycle, compared with personal loans.

Suppose this portfolio is not too heavily skewed because there are proportionately more personal loans in the portfolio, and the 99.99% confidence interval lies 8 standard deviations from the mean, or 8 standard deviations are needed for the 99.99% confidence level. Then the capital to be set aside is:

$$\text{Risk contribution} \times 8 = £397\,995 \times 8 = £3\,183\,960, \text{ or approximately £3 million}$$

Note the amount of capital to be set aside has risen because the bank, by assuming a skewed distribution, has adopted a more conservative, or it could be argued, a more realistic, attitude.

### 3.6.7. Credit Value at Risk

Unlike the KMV and DM approaches, a credit VaR, e.g. Creditmetrics™, is a marked to market approach, focusing on a loan loss value and/or a risk–return trade-off for a portfolio of debt. In the VaR approach there is more than one single credit migration. Instead of an asset either being a good asset or in default, in credit VaR, there is the possibility of multiple migration, that is, a range of upgrades or downgrades. Figure 3.3 illustrates the difference between credit migration in the two approaches. With multiple credit migration, any upgrade or downgrade will affect the spread changes, which in turn changes the discount rate.

VaR for market risk was covered in some detail, and space constraints preclude an in-depth treatment of credit VaR. Suffice to say that to obtain a credit value at risk for a given portfolio, it will be necessary to address the same list of issues raised in the section on market VaR. The overall approach which must be taken to obtain a credit VaR is summarised in Chart 3.1.

Credit VaR is also the target of criticisms raised with respect to market VaR. Indeed, some of the underlying assumptions, such as a normal distribution, become even more problematic. For detailed accounts of VaR, readers are referred to the Creditmetrics™ *Technical Document*, originally published in 1997 but updated on their website: http://www.riskmetrics.com/. In addition, Saunders (2003) explains a range of credit portfolio models, including Creditmetrics™ and CreditRisk Plus™. Many banks use a version of the default mode model, which is most useful when applied to portfolios of untraded personal or commercial

**Figure 3.3   Comparison of Credit VaR and Default Mode.**

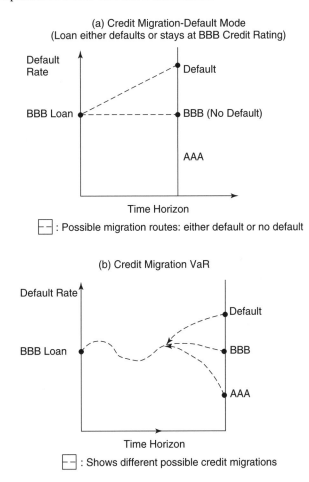

**(a) Credit Migration-Default Mode**
**(Loan either defaults or stays at BBB Credit Rating)**

Default Rate

Default

BBB Loan — — — — — — — — BBB (No Default)

AAA

Time Horizon

☐—☐ : Possible migration routes: either default or no default

**(b) Credit Migration VaR**

Default Rate

Default

BBB Loan                    BBB

AAA

Time Horizon

☐—☐ : Shows different possible credit migrations

loans. The credit VaR models are more appropriate for bond portfolios, which are traded on the market, receive a debt rating and are reasonably liquid.

One final point. All models are just that: models. To work out a problem, simplifying assumptions must be made. When applying these models in the real world, any such assumptions must be borne in mind. In May 2003, JP Morgan Chase admitted to serious credit problems in the investment banking arm. Yet JP Morgan's research department, which produced Riskmetrics™ (1994), is the home of Creditmetrics™ (1997). However, these procedures did not prevent it from becoming "excessively" over-exposed in some industries, especially telecommunications. Credit losses in investment banking more than doubled from $1.2 billion to $2.4 billion between 2001 and 2002, and lending in the telecommunications and cable sectors accounted for more than half of those losses ($1.5 billion); 10 corporate deals were blamed for most of the losses. To prevent the problem

**Chart 3.1   Credit Value at Risk.**

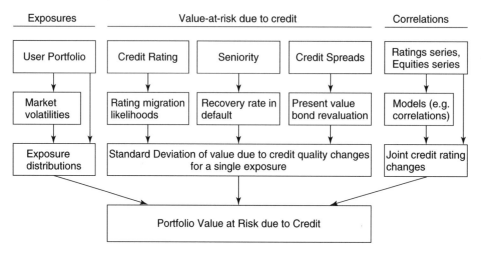

*Source*: JP Morgan (1997), *CreditMetrics – Technical Document*, New York: JP Morgan, p. 41.

from arising again, a more centralised structure has been put in place to oversee all credit decisions and assess risk across all asset classes. Based on their models, it might be expected that the bank would already be doing the latter. One interesting observation is that the bank announced it will use equity prices to assess credit risk, which is an approach developed by KMV Moody's.[53]

## 3.6.8. Financial Innovation and Risk Management

The financial products discussed above are examples of recent financial innovations. Like the manufacturing sector, financial innovation can take the form of process innovation, whereby an existing product or service can be offered more cheaply because of a technological innovation. Product innovation involves the introduction of a new good or service. The new financial instruments discussed above are examples of where technological changes resulted in product innovations.

Silber (1975, 1983) argued that product innovation arises because of constraints placed on a bank – namely, regulation, competition and risk. Kane (1984) thought it important to observe the regulatory and technological factors behind any financial innovation. However, it is more useful to think of financial innovation, regulation and risk management as being interdependent. For example, regulations (such as exchange controls) can be a catalyst for financial innovation which allows bankers to bypass the rules. The eurocurrency markets developed in just this way – US interest rate restrictions and limits placed on foreign direct investment by US multinationals, together with UK exchange controls, created a demand for and supply of an offshore dollar market, the eurodollar market. As technology advanced,

---

[53] Source of this information: Silverman (2003), *The Financial Times*.

this became the eurocurrency market, allowing bankers to trade in all the key currencies outside any domestic regulations. Even though most of the offending regulations have since been relaxed, the market continues to thrive.

Risk management and financial innovation are also interdependent. Financial innovation has made it possible to unbundle the different types of risks which, in turn, has led to measurement of different types of risks. At the same time, financial innovation has forced banks to re-examine their risk management systems, because banks are increasingly exposed to new forms of risk, which are quite different in nature from the traditional credit risk. For example, Bankhaus Herstatt collapsed in 1974 because of inexperience in dealing with foreign exchange risk. However, to date, very few bank collapses can be said to have been caused by a failure to understand risk exposure associated with a new instrument.

## 3.7. Risk Management by Major Global Bank

Barclays Bank plc very kindly agreed to provide information on how a major global bank actually manages its risk.[54] Barclays is a long-established British bank, headquartered in London but with major global operations. By tier 1 capital, it is the fourth largest UK bank, and ranks 14th in the world, according to the July 2003 edition of *The Banker*. Chart 3.2 shows the way Barclays organises its risk management. Essentially, risk is managed along two lines, by type of risk and by different business units. Four directors, each in charge of a certain type of risk (e.g. credit risk, market risk) report to a group risk director, as do three directors in charge of functional support, such as regulatory compliance. Seven "business risk" directors also report to the group risk director. One business unit is their investment banking arm, Barclays Capital, others include Barclaycard, Business Banking and Barclays Private Clients.

Barclays classifies risk into four categories: credit, market, non-financial and other risk.

**Credit Risk** is defined as the risk that customers will not repay their obligations, and is divided into _retail_ and _wholesale risk_.

**Market Risk** is the risk of loss due to changes in the level or volatility of market rates or prices such as interest rates, foreign exchange rates, equity prices and commodity prices. It is incurred as a result of both trading and non-trading activities.

**Non-financial Risk** consists of *operational risk*, using the Basel definition (see p.110, Chapter 4) and *business risk*, defined as the potential to incur a loss because of an unexpected decline in revenue, which cannot be offset by a corresponding decrease in costs.

**Other risk** includes risks arising from all other sources, such as property, equipment, associates (e.g. risk linked to joint ventures), and so on. Given the diversity of risks in this category, there is no further discussion of it in this section.

Barclays divides market risk into *trading risk* and *retail market risk*. Trading risk is primarily incurred by Barclays Capital and Treasury operations – used to support customer services, such as the sale or purchase of foreign currencies. DVaR, or daily value at risk of the exposure, is the central measure used in Treasury operations and at Barclays Capital. Trading market risk is evaluated through a multiple of the DVaR (e.g. DVaR times some multiple). The same method is employed for Treasury operations but with a higher multiple.

---

[54] The author would like to thank Mick Green, Tim Thompson, and Saadia Mujeeb, of Barclays Bank plc for their assistance in supplying this information.

**Chart 3.2    Barclays Bank plc: How Risk Management is Organised.**

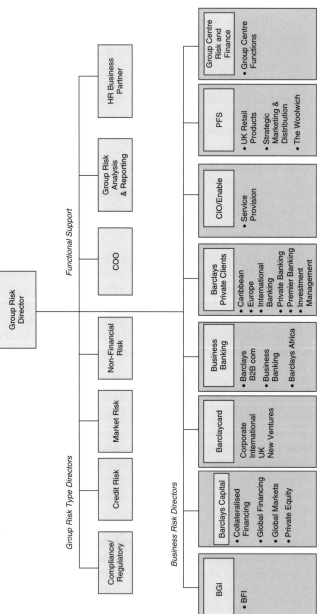

COO – chief Operating Officer; BGI – Barclays Global Investors, Enable – Enable provides the commonly used IT and operations services
everyone in Barclays needs to do their job, PFS – Personal Financial Services (retail banking)
© 2003, Barclays Bank plc

Retail market risk arises from imperfect hedges against customer products, either due to the unexpected customer behaviour or losses arising from residual unhedged positions. It applies to all fixed rate, capped rate or index-linked products, across all business units, except for Barclays Capital. There are three categories. Prepayment risk – the risk that customer repayments or withdrawals are unexpected. Recruitment risk – the risk that the bank fails to sell the expected amount of a fixed rate product (e.g. bond), usually due to an adverse movement in market rates. In this event, the bank has to adjust the hedge, by buying/selling interest rate swaps. It can affect the expected cost of funds. Finally, residual unhedged risk – occurs if the actual hedge positions differ from the hedge positions determined by the hedge models that are used. Again, the risk is estimated based on a multiple of the DVaR of the exposure.

*Wholesale Credit Risk* is the risk of losses arising from default by a wholesale counterparty. Though Barclays uses both Creditmetrics™ and KMV Portfolio Manager. The KMV model, now based on five years of experience, is used to assess wholesale credit risk. The KMV model has been discussed at length. At Barclays, KMV Portfolio Manager is used to compute the capital which should be set aside for each individual exposure, then aggregated over the business unit to provide the overall capital allocation for that unit.

*Retail Credit Risk* employs two methodologies. For the "base level" methodology, it is assumed that the factors affecting the probability of borrower default are factors specific to a borrower (e.g. age, occupation) and the influence of the state of the macroeconomy on the retail sector. The correlation between the systematic and factor-specific variables is also taken into account. This framework was chosen because it is consistent with the KMV model (used to assess wholesale credit risk) and with the approaches recommended by Basel 2. It is also relatively easy to use because it is based on straightforward formulae.

The second methodology for retail credit risk is known as the advanced approach, and is applied to Barclaycard. Here, Monte Carlo techniques are used to estimate a loss distribution.

To reduce concentrations of retail credit risk, Barclays uses securitisation (transferring assets off-balance sheet), credit derivatives and insurance.

Barclays manages *operational risk* beginning with the assumption that OR consists of two independent stochastic components, frequency of loss and severity of loss. Four variables are used to model operational risk: (1) the expected number of loss events over a one-year time horizon, assuming risk controls are in place; (2) the expected size of the loss once it occurs, assuming risk controls are in place; (3) loss mitigation or the use of effective controls to mitigate a percentage of the loss; (4) the degree to which the controls in (3) are effective. Using (1) through (4), Barclays employs a Monte Carlo model to simulate the frequency and severity of the loss events. It also monitors the effectiveness of risk controls over time, using the available data. Once the capital to be set aside is calculated, it can be reduced through a scorecard, which assesses how well the operating risks are being managed/controlled in a given unit.

## 3.8. Conclusion

This chapter reviewed the various aspects of bank risk management. It began by noting that banks differ from other firms in the range of financial risks they assume. The management of these risks will be a crucial determinant of their profitability and shareholder value-added.

The traditional function of an asset–liability management group in banks which involves the management of credit, interest rate and liquidity risks was reviewed, together with the use of gap analysis, duration and duration gap analysis for on-balance sheet items. Increasingly, however, banks act as intermediaries in risk management; a central objective of the modern bank is the management of a whole range of unbundled risks: credit/counterparty, market (including interest rate and currency risks), sovereign and operating risks. The latter two are discussed in Chapters 4 and 6, respectively. As credit insurance grows, some of the key global banks are acting as conduits of risk, shifting credit risk to non-bank financial institutions, an issue to be discussed in the next chapter.

Section 3.5 on market risk introduced many of the new techniques developed to manage market risk. Risk adjusted return on capital (RAROC) can be used both for risk management and to compare relative performance, using a hurdle rate. Value at Risk was originally developed to manage market risk, though it has been modified to measure credit risk exposures. Though VaR offers a new quantitative approach to measuring market risk, a critique of its use followed, illustrated by the quotes from Jorion and Taleb (see p. 153–4). Given the problems with VaR, stress tests under different scenarios are essential, though they have their limitations too. Techniques for managing retail, corporate and aggregate credit risk were also discussed.

Derivatives, introduced briefly in Chapter 2, were reviewed in more detail, together with a discussion of the ways banks use them as tools for risk management. The growth of exchange traded and customised OTC derivatives has meant banks can broaden the type of intermediation they undertake. Banks can use derivatives for proprietary trading and speculation, to hedge, or as part of fee-based risk management services offered to customers. It was argued that banks and customers alike must understand the purpose for which a given instrument is being used. There have been many cases where large corporations have lost enormous sums and have claimed, in some cases correctly, that they were ill-advised by their banks.

Section 3.7 looked at how a major commercial bank organises its risk management function. If the objective is to maximise profits and shareholder value-added, then the way risk management is organised in a bank is as important as the development of risk management tools and techniques. This point assumes even greater importance now that the Basel Committee is proposing to allow banks, subject to the approval of national supervisors, to determine their capital requirements for market and other risks, using their own internal models.

In this chapter, it has been stressed that bank risk management has undergone a profound change since the 1980s, and will continue to evolve in the 21st century. In the next two chapters, the focus shifts to the role of the regulatory bodies, which are trying to introduce systems to encourage the operation of an efficient but stable domestic and global financial system. These chapters should help managers understand how and why governments tend to single out banks for special attention, how the regulations impact on bank structure, and identify the major regulatory challenges of the 21st century.

# GLOBAL REGULATION OF BANKS

*"No bank ever went bust for want of capital says one senior banker. They go bust because of bad management."* (Anonymous, quoted in *The Economist*, 16/8/03, p. 63)

## 4.1. Introduction

The principle objective of this chapter is to review attempts to regulate internationally active banks through global agreements. The chapter begins with a review of the reasons why governments regulate markets in general, and financial markets in particular. It continues with a discussion of why banks, which are part of the financial system, are singled out for additional regulation. Sections 4.3, 4.4 and 4.5 consider different aspects of the international regulation of banks, with a special emphasis on the activities of the Basel Committee. Section 4.6 looks at other international organisations involved in global financial regulation and reform. Many of the rules agreed upon by global organisations have become the drivers for domestic regulation, the subject of Chapter 5. For example, the 1988 Basel agreement ("Basel 1") was for international banks operating in OECD countries but authorities in both the industrialised world and some emerging markets have required their domestic banks to adhere to Basel 1 standards. Likewise, "Basel 2" is expected to become a new benchmark for bank supervision. Having completed a comprehensive study of global regulation, Chapter 5 focuses on bank structure and regulation in, respectively, the United Kingdom, United States, European Union and Japan.

## 4.2. Why Regulate?

### 4.2.1. Rationale for Regulating Financial/Banking Markets

Most markets are subject to some degree of regulation for a variety of reasons.

1. There is a need to protect the consumer: *"caveat emptor"* ("let the buyer beware") is considered insufficient – putting too much responsibility on the consumer for many goods and services that lack transparency.
2. To check the abuse of oligopolistic and monopoly power: there are many markets in which just one or a few firms operate. The degree of monopoly power held by these firms will affect the pricing of their products. For example, in a pure monopoly, the

amount of output produced by the monopolist is lower and the price charged is higher compared to firms operating in a perfectly competitive market. Governments react either by introducing measures to encourage greater competition and/or monitoring the price set by these firms, and if necessary, intervening to force the firms to reduce prices.

3. To protect the public from criminal activity.

4. To deal with the effects of externalities: the effects of the actions of one agent in the economy on others, which is not reflected through the price mechanism. There are positive and negative externalities. If a neighbour's property is kept in good order, other neighbours benefit not just from enhanced property values but because it is pleasant to look at neighbourhood houses and gardens. A classic example of a negative externality is pollution. Industrial output in the USA can pollute the rivers, lakes and air in Canada. Governments intervene to minimise the effects of negative externalities. For example, the Canadian government might try to reach an agreement with the USA to reduce emissions.

In **financial markets**, these principles apply to the following.

1. Protecting the investor: the quality of many financial products is not easily observed, which makes it important for the investor to be kept fully informed about the risks he or she incurs when purchasing a financial product. Investors are expected to assume some of this responsibility, but often, government directives are needed to ensure financial firms provide adequate information.

2. The concentration of financial firms in the market place: the financial sector is made up of many different markets, from retail banking markets to global bond markets. The competitive structure of each of these markets varies considerably. Global markets tend to be more competitive if firms from all over the world are active in them. Some domestic markets have only a few firms offering banking services. Recall from Chapter 1 the concern expressed by Cruickshank over the apparent lack of competition in the UK payments system because it was controlled by only a few firms. In 2001, the UK's Competition Commission ruled against the proposed merger of Lloyds TSB and Abbey National on the grounds that it would leave the retail banking market too concentrated. In 1998, the federal government of Canada refused the proposed mergers of the Toronto Dominion Bank with the Canadian Imperial Bank of Commerce and the Royal Bank of Canada with the Bank of Montreal on the grounds that the Canadian system would be too concentrated.[1]

3. Illegal activities: agents who engage in financial fraud, money laundering and tax evasion.

4. Externalities: the problem is actions by agents which undermine the stability of the financial system. In the financial markets, contagion often results in negative externalities. For example, in 1998, when it became apparent that a hedge fund, Long Term Capital Markets (LTCM), was about to collapse, concern that its failure might threaten

---

[1] Concern was also expressed that if one of the newly merged banks got into difficulty and was closed, it would increase monopoly power, and/or the risk of systemic crises should another failure occur. The possible takeover of a major bank (should it get into financial difficulty) by a foreign concern is also considered undesirable, unlike other countries, such as Mexico and New Zealand.

the stability of global financial markets was so great that New York's Federal Reserve Bank intervened and arranged for its rescue by a consortium of international banks, at a total cost of $3.625 billion. The main contributors were the counterparties with very large exposures, and included Goldman Sachs, Salomon Smith Barney, Bankers Trust, Deutsche Bank, JP Morgan, Merrill Lynch, Morgan Stanley, Credit Suisse, UBS, Chase Manhattan, Barclays Capital ($300 million each); Société Générale, Lehman Brothers, Paribas ($100 million each).[2] Though public (taxpayers') money was not used in the LTCM bailout, it was the Federal Reserve Bank of New York which pressured the banks to bail out LTCM because of potential global knock-on effects.

There are many cases where central banks or other financial regulators have intervened to rescue a bank or banks to protect the rest of the banking system. **Contagion**, or the spread of bank problems from one bank to the banking system, arises for a number of reasons. To the extent that banks offer fairly homogeneous products to customers, they are collectively exposed to the same risk. At the micro level, a marginal borrower will seek out all the banks until one makes the loan. At the macro level, all banks are affected by events such as changes in monetary policy.

The reputation of banks is extremely important because of the lack of transparency on bank balance sheets, their intermediary function and the cost of acquiring information. Any market rumour can undermine depositor confidence. The banking system is particularly vulnerable to contagion effects, when lack of confidence associated with one poorly performing bank spreads to other, healthy banks. It arises because customers know that once a run on a bank begins, liquidated bank assets will decline in value very quickly, so they will want to withdraw their deposits before a run. Thus, even healthy banks may be subject to a bank run.[3] If most banks are affected, the financial system may well collapse.

The vulnerability of banking to contagion creates *systemic risk*; the risk that disturbances in a financial institution or market will spread across the financial system, leading to widespread bank runs by wholesale and retail depositors, and possibly, collapse of the banking system. An extensive collapse will result in the loss of intermediation, money transmission and liquidity services offered by banks which, in turn, will cause an inefficient allocation of resources in the economy. In the extreme, the economy could revert to barter exchange.

Systemic banking risks are aggravated by the interbank and euromarkets, which, as was noted in Chapter 2, play a crucial role in the global banking scene. The interbank market acts as a risk absorber and risk spreader but at the same time makes the global banking system vulnerable to certain exogenous shocks.

Additional problems arise because of the macroeconomic role played by banks; they help to implement government monetary policy. For example, the government may use the banks (changing a reserve ratio or setting a base rate) to achieve certain inflation and/or monetary growth targets. If the banking system collapses, there may be a dramatic reduction in the money supply, with the usual macroeconomic implications.

---

[2] *Source*: Dunbar (2000), *Inventing Money*, pp. 221–223.
[3] Diamond and Dybvig (1983) provide a rigorous treatment of bank runs.

Thus, bank failures can create substantial negative externalities or **social** costs,[4] in addition to the obvious private costs of failure. So in most countries, to minimise the chance of governments having to rescue a bank or banks, the national banking systems are singled out for special regulation, known as **prudential regulation**, which is typically more comprehensive than regulation of other sectors of the economy, even other parts of the financial sector. The prudential regulation of banks is concerned with minimising the social costs of bank failure (which lead to the collapse of the financial system) but at the same time, ensuring that banks do not take advantage of the fact they are singled out for special regulation, and possibly protection. For example, many countries offer some form of deposit protection to bolster confidence and counter bank runs. Experience has shown that to be fully effective, 100% deposit insurance is often required. These schemes escalate moral hazard problems, and part of the regulatory role will be to ensure such problems are minimised.

As this chapter proceeds, it will become apparent that prudential regulation focuses on bank regulation at the micro level, i.e. ensuring each bank behaves in a prudent manner, to prevent systemic failure arising from contagion if one bank fails. Boreo (2003), among others, has called for more attention to be paid to "macroprudential regulation" – preventing the banking system as whole from getting into trouble because they are exposed to the same collective risks – so an entire banking system can encounter problems simultaneously. For this reason, Boreo argues, equal attention should be paid to the aggregate exposures of banks. The macro component is considered in Chapter 8, which includes a review of financial crises, where banks' exposure to collective risks is often found to be a key contributor to the crisis itself.

To summarise:

- _Financial fragility_ can provoke a loss of confidence in a bank/banks and provoke a bank run, preventing the bank/banks from offering an important product/service: _liquidity_.
- The banking system is vulnerable to _contagion_: contagion occurs when a lack of confidence associated with one bank (e.g. a bank that has just failed) causes a run on other banks as depositors, fearing the worst, withdraw their cash. The problem here is one of incomplete information – depositors do not have the information to distinguish between healthy and failing banks.
- The presence of contagion contributes to _systemic risk_: the risk that problems in one bank will spread throughout the entire sector, via contagion. Once the entire financial system collapses, there is no mechanism for money transmission and in the extreme, the absence of a payments system, the country reverts to a barter economy.
- Bank failures have obvious private costs, but there are _social_ costs too.
- The issue of microprudential regulation shifts to macroprudential regulation if banks in one or more countries are collectively exposed to the same risks, a point which is taken up in Chapter 6.

---

[4] _Social cost_ refers to the total cost of an activity, including private costs borne by the main party and all "external" costs borne by others. The private costs from collapse of a financial firm are incurred by investors, depositors, employees and, in some cases, customers of the bank. Social costs are incurred if the financial sector collapses because the economy loses its system of financial intermediation and money transmission.

Unfortunately, the special treatment of banks has a downside. Not only does it divert government resources away from other activities, it can create **moral hazard** problems. The concept of moral hazard was introduced in Chapter 1. In the regulation of the banking system, the traditional line is that moral hazard can arise for one of two reasons. First, if deposit insurance is offered to discourage runs on banks and second, if a bank is considered so important to the economy that they are deemed by regulators to be "too big to fail". The existence of one or both these conditions can alter the incentives of depositors and bank management. Most governments offer some degree of insurance. Customers with deposit insurance know their capital is safe, giving them little incentive to monitor the activities of their bank. It is even possible that bank managers' behaviour will be affected – some may be inclined to undertake riskier activities, especially if the bank is encountering difficulties. Here, the manager may go for broke, hoping the gamble pays off and the bank survives. If not, at least depositors are protected. The same points apply if depositors or bank management know (or think it likely) their bank is considered too big to fail, making it probable the bank will be rescued by the state.

Or so the standard argument goes. However, the logic is somewhat flawed. Managers will worry about loss of jobs and status if a bank fails, but why should they have any special concern for depositors once the bank collapses? Any bank manager trying to undertake riskier activities because of deposit insurance and/or the attraction of "too big to fail" status will encounter objections from well-informed shareholders who stand to lose their capital. Even some depositors have an incentive to monitor managerial behaviour because insurance is normally capped at some deposit level, their type of deposit does not qualify for insurance,[5] there is *co-insurance*, or all three.

A more likely scenario is the **looting hypothesis**, first described by Akerlof and Romer (1993). Consider the situation where a bank has, for whatever reason, got itself into serious problems, and senior management has enough inside information to know there is a good chance the bank could fail within a few years, at which time they will lose their jobs. They could respond by undertaking riskier activities[6] to boost short-term profits, which enhance their status and salary, and boosts the bank's share price, which they can take advantage of by cashing in stock options. Well-informed shareholders may also sell their shares when prices are high, turning a blind eye to the reasons for the sudden increase in short-term profits. There is a small chance the risky undertakings might restore the bank to economic health, in which case, all parties are better off. However, if the strategy is unsuccessful and the bank fails, then senior managers (and possibly, major shareholders) have used the breathing space to feather their nests. To make matters worse, managers have every reason to undertake sizeable gambles because the downside is truncated. It is someone else's problem whether the bank collapses with losses of £1 or a million pounds.

---

[5] For example, most regulators exclude deposits held in foreign currencies. In Japan, the 100% deposit insurance introduced in 1998 is gradually being withdrawn, and now only applies to "liquid" deposits.

[6] E.G. Managers could raise short-term rates to attract more deposits, thereby expanding the balance sheet and making more loans. Or they can invest in junk bonds, where immediate interest payments are high even if the issuers defaults in the longer term. In both cases, short-term profits rise, along with salaries and stock option values.

## 4.2.2. Free Banking

An alternative school of thought advocates free banking. In the 19th century, free banking was unregulated by government authorities, they did not need a charter or licence to operate, and issued their own bank notes. There were periods of free banking in Scotland (1716–1844), Sweden (1831–1903), Switzerland (1826–1907) and Canada (1867–1914). Cameron (1972) argued that Scottish free banking fostered economic growth because of the intense competition between the banks, which forced them to innovate. He credits the banks as being the first to introduce branch banking, interest paid on deposits, and overdraft facilities. Dowd (1993) argued the free banking episodes in Scotland, Sweden and Canada were highly successful.

Modern-day usage of the term "free banking" refers to a highly competitive system operating without a central bank or regulations. Proponents of free banking claim central banks have the potential to encourage collusive behaviour among banks, thereby increasing their monopoly power. In the absence of government regulation, private banks have a collective interest in devising a framework to prevent runs. It could take the form of private deposit insurance and/or a private clearing house, which acts as lender of last resort. See, among others, Dowd (1993), Friedman and Schwartz (1986), White (1986). However, a private clearing house could also encourage collusion among banks. In Chapter 1, recall Cruickshank (2000) claimed that the private settlements system in the UK has resulted in the big banks exercising monopoly power, resulting in higher settlement charges for banks and customers. Furthermore, private deposit insurance and/or lender of last resort institutions merely replicate what a central bank does, so the same monitoring problems exist, creating incentives to free-ride.

Free banking also raises macroeconomic issues, because banks issue their own notes. No bank should have an incentive to issue too many notes because they will be exchanged for specie at that bank, thus running down its reserves. However, Nelder (2003) argues the above is only true if holders of the notes have to return to the bank where they are issued. However, if the notes issued by the different banks are perfect substitutes (or perceived to be by the public), then smaller banks have an incentive to issue an excessive supply of notes because there is a greater chance they will be redeemed at the larger banks. He argues that in the Swiss case, this resulted in an over-issue of notes, causing the depreciation of the Swiss franc. As a result, the banks agreed to give up their right of issue, and approved the establishment of a central bank, controlled by the federal government. Nelder argues Sweden and Scotland also experienced periods of excess issue, but Canada escaped it because there was little in the way of effective price competition between the banks.

Though the free banking idea is interesting in theory, it is very unlikely that the regulatory systems of western countries will be dismantled to allow an experiment.[7] For this reason,

---

[7] New Zealand introduced a form of free banking in the 1990s, removing all deposit insurance and requiring banks to publish detailed information on their financial status so that all agents are kept fully informed. However, given that all but one savings bank is foreign owned, it could be argued that the New Zealand government saves money by importing prudential regulation from abroad, since the foreign banks are regulated by the governments of the countries in which they are headquartered. In 2003, the Reserve Bank of New Zealand (RBNZ) Amendment

the issue is not explored any further. The rest of this chapter is devoted to issues related to the global regulation of banks.

## 4.3. International Regulation

The international coordination of prudential regulation at global level is increasingly important. As was discussed in Chapter 2, there has been a rapid growth of international banking, and financial conglomerates. A number of arguments favour global coordination of prudential regulations.

First, policy makers, bank management and regulators recognise that problems with the global institutions and markets could undermine the stability of the international financial system, and therefore the environment in which all banks operate.

Second, if a branch or subsidiary of a bank is located in another country, there is the question of which supervisory authority should have jurisdiction over the branch. Home country regulators will want to ensure a bank's overseas operations meet their supervisory standards because foreign operations will be difficult to monitor but affect the performance of the parent. Host country authorities are concerned with the effect the failure of a foreign bank could have on the confidence in its banking system. They will want to see the foreign branch to be adequately supervised, but will lack information about the parent operations. For these reasons, effective international coordination will only be achieved if there is good communication between the supervisory authorities.

Third, if all multinational banks are required to meet the same global regulations, compliance costs will be similar. Hence a global approach to regulation can help to level the competitive playing field for banks with international operations.

It is worth noting that decisions taken by international regulators are increasingly being used as benchmarks for other banks. For example, the Basel Committee's (see below) 1988 agreement on capital standards was adopted by not only the member countries, but also by governments that were not signatories to the agreement. Also, many regulators impose the Basel agreements on domestic banks.

On the other hand, it could be argued that international banking is largely wholesale, making prudential regulation less important from the standpoint of consumer protection, depending as it does on interbank and corporate business. However, the performance of a global bank will affect the confidence of depositors and investors located in the home country. Unprotected wholesale depositors are capable of starting bank runs, and the enormous size of the interbank market creates the potential for a rapid domino effect. Often, the first indication of a problem bank is when it has trouble raising interbank loans – wholesale depositors will be the first to withdraw their money.

An excellent example of this phenomenon is Continental Illinois Bank, rescued by a "lifeboat" in 1984. The bank was highly dependent on the interbank markets for funding,

---

Act introduced some additional controls, which include a requirement that the Reserve Bank consider whether managers are "fit and proper" when registering a bank, any buyer of more than 10% of a bank must seek approval, and more information must be included in the disclosures. See Bollard (2003).

which was quickly cut off once rumours about its health began to circulate. The rapid loss in liquidity merely exacerbated the problems, prompting a rescue organised by the Federal Reserve. Furthermore, if a global bank acquires a bad reputation as a result of some international transaction, and has a retail presence in its home country, it may find itself the target of a run. Finally, global financial conglomerates, if they get into difficulties, can cause problems in more than one country.

## 4.3.1. The Basel[8] Committee

Two major international bank failures in 1974 (Bankhaus Herstatt and Franklin National Bank[9]) resulted in the formation of a standing committee of bank supervisory authorities, from the G-10 countries (Belgium, Canada, France, Germany, Italy, Japan, Netherlands, Sweden, the UK and USA) plus Luxembourg and Switzerland. It has a permanent secretariat (of 15) based at the Bank for International Settlements in Basel, and meets there about once every three months.

The **Bank for International Settlements** is owned by the central banks – it does not participate in Basel's policy-making, provides a venue for the Committee's secretariat and for membership meetings. Traditionally, members came from western central banks but since 1994, there are 13 member central banks from emerging markets.

The main purpose of the Basel Committee is to consider regulatory issues related to activities of international banks in member countries. Their objective is to use concordats and agreements to prevent any international banking operation from escaping effective supervision.

The **1975 Basel Concordat** was the first agreement. The home and host countries were given supervisory responsibilities as follows:

|  | Country supervisor |
|---|---|
| Liquidity – foreign bank subsidiary | Host |
| Solvency – foreign bank subsidiary | Host |
| Liquidity – foreign branch | Home |

The Concordat stressed that consolidated data should be used to supervise the activities of a global bank, and provide an accurate picture of performance. Offshore banking centres (see Chapter 2) are not party to this agreement – the Committee did not consider them to pose a major threat to international financial stability because their operations are relatively minor.

In 1983 the Committee approved a **Revised Basel Concordat**, when gaps in the supervision of foreign branches and subsidiaries came to light after the Banco Ambrosiano affair. Banco Ambrosiano Bank failed in 1982, after its Chairman, Roberto Calvo, was found hanging from Blackfriars Bridge in London. Depositors panicked upon hearing the news; a lifeboat rescue was launched by the Bank of Italy ($325 million), but the bank was declared

---

[8] Readers will note the change in spelling compared with Heffernan (1996). In 1998, the city of Basel voted to adopt this German spelling, rather than the English (Basle), French (Bâle) or Italian (Basilea) versions.

[9] See Chapter 7 for more detail on these failures.

bankrupt in late August 1982. The bank's Italian operations were taken over by a new bank, Nouvo Banco Ambrosiano.

The Luxembourg <u>subsidiary</u> (BA in Milan owned 69% of Banco Ambrosiano Holdings) also suffered a run on deposits, but the Italian central bank refused to inject any cash. Nor would the Luxembourg Banking Commission. It, too, failed. As a result of this case, the Concordat was revised so that home and host supervisors now have *joint* responsibility for solvency problems of subsidiaries and liquidity problems from either a subsidiary or branch. Solvency problems associated with any foreign branch are dealt with by the parent country's central bank.

A number of issues were not addressed by either Concordat. First, no reference was made to lender of last resort (LLR) responsibilities. Recall a lender of last resort normally aids a bank in the event of a liquidity crisis. Lifeboat operations serve a similar purpose, where the central bank persuades other healthy, private banks that it is in their interest to inject liquidity into the ailing bank.

However, the Basel Committee did not feel able to offer guidelines because the LLR function is normally assumed by central banks, and the Basel Committee members do not necessarily come from the central bank.[10] However, LLR intervention or lifeboat rescues have been quite frequent in most westernised countries in the post-war period. There will be problems with achieving satisfactory international coordination if a run on foreign branches or subsidiaries occurs because the parent has run into difficulties. Guttentag and Herring (1983) identified three types of banks that are vulnerable under the current arrangements: banks headquartered in countries with no LLR facilities (such as Luxembourg); banks headquartered in countries with non-convertible currencies or a shortage of foreign exchange reserves; and subsidiary banks with ambiguous access to the parent bank facilities.

The Basel Committee also side-stepped another issue related to financial stability – the extension of deposit insurance to all deposit liabilities. Normally deposit insurance excludes wholesale and interbank deposits, on the grounds that these depositors are better informed about the financial health of a bank and therefore do not need it. Foreign currency deposits tend to be excluded because of the concern that deposits might be shifted between the foreign bank and its parent, to the detriment of the former. However, if deposit insurance was expanded, its effects on moral hazard would have to be considered.

## 4.3.2. The 1988 Basel Accord (Basel 1)

The 1988 Basel Accord was a watershed because it established Basel's main *raison d'être*: to focus on the effective supervision of international banking operations through greater coordination among international bank supervisors and regulators. Improved international financial stability would be a key consequence of the Committee's actions.

---

[10] Some countries, such as the UK, have representatives from both the Financial Services Authority and the Bank of England.

The 1988 Basel Accord established a single set of capital adequacy standards for international banks of participating countries from January 1993.[11] With the arrival of a new revised accord (see below), the 1988 Accord will be known as Basel 1 henceforth. **Basel 1** requires all international banks[12] to set aside capital based on the (Basel) risk assets ratio:

$$\text{Basel risk assets ratio} = \text{capital/weighted risk assets}$$

Specifically:

$$\frac{\text{Capital (tier 1 \& 2)}}{\text{Assets (weighted by credit type)} + \text{credit risk equivalents (weighted by counterparty type)}}$$

where capital is defined as follows.

- Tier 1 or core capital: common equity shares, disclosed reserves, non-cumulative preferred stock, other hybrid equity instruments, retained earnings, minority interests in consolidated subsidiaries, less goodwill and other deductions.
- Tier 2 or supplementary capital: consisting of all other capital but divided into (1) *upper tier 2* – capital such as cumulative perpetual preferred stock, loan loss allowances, undisclosed reserves, revaluation reserves (discounted by 55%) such as equity or property where the value changes, general loan loss reserves, hybrid debt instruments (e.g. convertible bonds, cumulative preference shares) and (2) *lower tier 2* – subordinated debt (e.g. convertible bonds, cumulative preference shares).

Risk weights are assigned to assets by credit type. The more creditworthy the loan, the lower the risk weight.

- 0%: cash, gold, bonds issued by OECD governments.
- 20%: bonds issued by agencies of OECD governments (e.g. the UK's Export and Credit Guarantee Agency), local (municipal) governments and insured mortgages.
- 50%: uninsured mortgages.
- 100%: all corporate loans and claims by non-OECD banks or government debt, equity and property.

Off-balance sheet instruments (e.g. letters of credit, futures, swaps, forex agreements) were converted into "credit risk equivalents",[13] and weighted by the type of counterparty to a given claim. Again, OECD government counterparties receive a 0% weight; 20% for OECD banks and public sector agencies.

---

[11] Basel 1 originated from the risk assets ratio, originally known as the Cooke Ratio, adopted by the UK and US regulatory authorities in 1980. See for example, the Bank of England (1980) "Measurement of Capital".

[12] Many countries adopted the standard for all banks, both domestic and international. For example, in the EU, the ratio applies to all credit institutions.

[13] Since credit risk equivalents were abandoned with the introduction of market risk measures in 1996, the method of conversion is not discussed.

<u>Example</u>: <u>Simple Bank</u>

Simple Bank plc has the following balance sheet (£ billions):

| Liabilities | Assets |
| --- | --- |
| Equity: £15 | Cash: £2 |
| Disclosed reserves: £2 | OECD government bonds: £30 |
| Subordinated debt: £5 | Interbank loans*: £20 |
| Customer funding (e.g. deposits): £180 | Mortgages (uninsured): £50 |
| Loan loss reserves: £3 | Company loans: £103 |
| **TOTAL**: £205 | TOTAL: £205 |

* All interbank loans are to banks located in OECD countries.

From the information given in the balance, tier 1 and tier 2 capital are:

$$\text{Tier } 1 = £15 + £2 = £17 \text{ billion}$$

$$\text{Tier } 2 = £5 + £3 = £8 \text{ billion}$$

Assuming capital is defined as tier 1 + tier 2, total capital = £25 billion.
A simple capital assets ratio, with assets unweighted, would be capital (tier 1&2)/assets = $25/205 = 12.195\%$.
Assuming the Basel 1 agreement applies, the use of weightings would change the denominator of the risk assets ratio for Simple Bank:

$$2(0) + 30(0) + 20(0.2) + 50(0.5) + 103(1) = 4 + 25 + 103 = £132 \text{ bn}$$

The Basel 1 risk assets ratio is $25/132 = 18.9\%$.

This ratio is higher than the simple capital assets ratio because assets are now weighted, hence some assets (cash and OECD government bonds) go to 0 or are lower than if unweighted.

So far, off-balance sheet items have been ignored. Suppose the off-balance sheet items of Simple Bank have been computed and equal £13 billion. Then the denominator of the risk assets ratio becomes $132 + 13 = 145$, and the risk assets ratio is $25/145 = 17.24\%$.

The Basel Accord requires banks to set aside a <u>minimum</u> of 8% capital; 4% for core capital. At least half the capital must be tier 1, and is set aside as a safeguard against bad credit or counterparty risk. As any July edition of *The Banker* shows, the average risk assets ratio for the top UK, US and other OECD banks is in fact much higher. *The Banker* ranks the top 1000 banks by tier 1 capital and reports other performance data, including the Basel risk assets ratio. Of the bottom 25 banks measured by the Basel ratio, it ranges from just over 8% to slightly below 4%. The vast majority of the top 50 banks (ranked by the Basel ratio) are reporting double digit risk assets ratios, some even exceed 100%.[14] Many OECD

---

[14] *Source*: see the July edition of *The Banker* in recent years.

regulators ask for higher ratios. For example, in the USA, to be labelled "well capitalised" banks must have a Basel ratio $\geq 10\%$ – see Chapter 5.

Before the agreement was even implemented, Basel 1 was being criticised for a number of reasons. Some argued using equity as a measure of capital fails to recognise that different countries allow their banks varying degrees of access to the stock market. For example, French nationalised banks in the 1980–90s had no access and relied on government injections of capital. Though privatisation has largely resolved this issue, it does demonstrate the potential problem with using equity. On the other hand, ignoring equity would be unthinkable because it is a key source of capital for shareholder owned banks. A more serious debate is whether the book or market values should be used in the computation of tier 1 and 2 capital.

The difference between market and book values of equity is more pronounced in periods of interest rate and stock market volatility, and, indirectly, if changes in credit ratings raise or lower asset values. Regulators opted to use the book rather than the market value to compute the capital assets ratio largely because of the potential for volatility. Using market values can be the source of wild fluctuations in tier 1 capital from year to year. In the Japanese case, tier 1 would have soared in the 1980s, only to fall dramatically from late 1989 onwards, thereby adding to the pressure to find new capital (and/or reduce assets) to meet the 8% minimum.

Ambiguity about the constituents of tier 1 and 2 capital has encouraged agents to innovate to get round the regulations. Also, different standards apply in each country. Take tier 2 capital as an example. In the 1990s, Japanese banks could not issue subordinated debt but US banks did. Also, Japanese regulators allowed their banks to treat 45% of unrealised capital gains on cross-shareholdings as reserves for tier 1 capital, though regulations have since been tightened.[15] Nonetheless, these points illustrate that it is difficult to obtain comparable measures of tier 1 and 2 capital. Scott and Iwahara (1994) argued differences in tax and accounting rules cause the measurement of capital to vary widely among countries, rendering different countries' risk assets ratios incomparable.

Second, the Accord alone could never achieve the objective of a level playing field among international banks, because the degree of competition in a system is determined by other factors, such as the structure of the banking system and the degree to which a government is prepared to support its banks. Until recently, Japan's well-known "safety net" meant Japanese banks could borrow capital more cheaply from wholesale markets than banks from countries where failures have been allowed. Also, they received substantial capital injections throughout the 1990s and into the early 2000s (see Chapter 8).

The use of credit risk equivalents for off-balance sheet instruments was considered far too simplistic. Effectively all on- and off-balance sheet items were treated the same, and the market or price risk associated with the growing off-balance sheet activities of many banks were largely ignored. The credit risk equivalence measure took account of the possibility of default on corporate bonds but no capital had to be set aside to allow for the possibility that

---

[15] Since September 2001, Japanese regulators have required banks to subtract any equity losses from their capital base, which will adversely affect their Basel ratios. Until 2002, unrealised profits on equity holdings were reported on a mark to market basis, but historical costs were used for unrealised losses. Since 2002, equity holdings have had to be marked to market even if they are showing a loss.

the price of bonds might fall with a rise in market interest rates. Or, an OECD government bond maturing in 30 years time carries a higher interest rate risk than one maturing in a year. In Basel 1, both receive a 0% weighting in the computations, which is acceptable from the standpoint of credit risk, but the different interest rate risks (arising from differences in maturity) are ignored. Nor are liquidity, currency and operating risks accounted for. For this reason, the 1996 Market Risk Agreement replaced the use of credit risk equivalents – it applies a capital charge for the market risk associated with all traded instruments, whether on- or off-balance sheet.

It should be remembered that national bank supervisors are monitoring banks' exposure to these risks. For example, most regulators use a liquidity ladder to estimate liquidity exposure, and monitor short and medium-term foreign exchange exposure of the banks they regulate. Also, the Basel 2 proposals (see below) deal with some of the risks largely ignored by Basel 1.

The weightings used in Basel 1 are simplistic. Commercial bank loans have a 100% weighting while OECD government debt is given a 0% weight, and OECD bank claims have a 20% weight even though some corporations have a higher external credit rating than the banks they do business with. For example, a loan to Marks & Spencer or General Electric, with AAA rating, receives a 100% weight, while loans to Italian or Japanese banks are weighted at 20%, even though the long-term debt rating for the top 5 Italian banks ranges from A+ to AA−; likewise for Japanese banks – long-term debt ratings for the top 5 vary from A to A−. [16] All corporations get the same weight, independent of whether their rating is AAA or BBB.

The weight for corporations and other counterparties is 50% for off-balance sheet items converted into credit risk equivalents, just half the risk weight assigned to corporate loans. Basel reasoned that only the most sophisticated banks were involved in off-balance sheet activity, hence the weight could be lower.

Such anomalies can and do tempt banks to engage in *regulatory capital arbitrage* – using a financial instrument or transaction to reduce capital requirements without a corresponding reduction in the risk incurred. For example, a bank may agree to a 364-day credit facility on a rollover basis because no capital need be set aside for credit arrangements between banks and a customer that are rolled over within a year. If the maturity of the agreement is a year or more, it is subject to the same capital regulations as a loan that matures in 30 years. More generally, banks are tempted to keep their capital charges to a minimum by exploiting loopholes even though the overall risk profile of the bank is higher.

Basel 1 does not reward banks which reduce their systematic risk – that is, no recognition is given for risk diversification of a bank's loan portfolio. While the Accord limits the concentration of risk among individual customers, over-exposure in a particular sector is ignored. A bank which lends €500 million to two sectors will set aside the same amount of capital as a bank lending €1 million to 500 different firms. In general, banks with a highly diversified portfolio set aside the same amount of capital as a bank with the same total value of commercial loans concentrated in just one industry. Nor is there any reward for geographical diversification.

Basel 1 is accused of being a "one size fits all approach" – there is little recognition that banks undertake different financial activities. A US/UK investment bank in the USA has

---

[16] *Source: Bankscope*, annual reports of top 5 banks (by assets), 2002.

quite different risk profiles from universal banks engaged in wholesale and retail banking activities. The balance sheets of a UK building society or German savings bank will be quite unlike the large universal (e.g. Deutsche Bank) or "restricted universal" banks (e.g. Barclays Bank plc). Yet all these banks are expected to conform to the same risk assets ratio requirements.

The regulations act as a benchmark, which could give some banks a false sense of security, causing them to make sub-optimal decisions. For example, since loan concentration in a specific industry is ignored by the ratio, banks may become complacent about the lack of portfolio diversification across sectors. They may also allocate too many resources to satisfy the Basel requirements (or find ways of getting round them), at the expense of other types of risk management.

In defence of Basel 1, it is worth emphasising that the Accord called for a *minimum* amount of capital to be set aside. As was noted earlier, many of *The Banker*'s top 1000 banks by tier 1 capital have ratios far in excess of 8%. Furthermore, banks are subject to additional supervision in their own countries. For example, as will be shown in the next chapter, the UK's Financial Services Authority applies a "risk to objectives" approach to all financial institutions, including banks. It also requires banks to satisfy other criteria. American banks are subject to scrutiny by multiple regulators, and pay different deposit insurance premia depending on the size of three different ratios. Finally, managers of publicly owned banks must answer to their shareholders. If a stock bank were to engage in excessive amounts of regulatory arbitrage which substantially increases its risk profile, it would not be long before concerns were voiced by shareholders and national regulators.

### 4.3.3. Basel Amendment (1996)[17] – Market Risk

The Basel Committee began to address the treatment of market risks in a 1993 consultative document, and the outcome was the 1996 Amendment of Basel 1[18] to be implemented by international banks by 1998. It introduced a more direct treatment of off-balance sheet items rather than converting them into credit risk equivalents, as was done in the original Basel 1.

As defined in Chapter 3, market risk is the risk that changes in market prices will cause losses in positions both on- and off-balance sheet. The "market price" refers to the price of any instrument traded on an exchange. The different forms of market risk recognised in the amendment include: equity price risk (market and specific), interest rate risk associated with fixed income instruments,[19] currency risk and commodities price risk. Debt securities (fixed and floating rate instruments, such as bonds, or debt derivatives), forward rate agreements,

---

[17] The details of the agreement can be found in Basel Committee (1996).

[18] In total, there were five amendments to the 1988 Accord – in 1991, 1994, 1995 (allowed for more netting, two counterparties could offset their claims against each other; these changes were prompted by the 1990 BIS Committee/Lamfalussy Report on Interbank Netting Schemes), 1996 and 1998 – some securities firms which fulfilled certain criteria were recognised as OECD banks, and thus their risk weighting was reduced to 20%. The amendments in 1991, 1994 dealt with, respectively, loan loss provisions and any OECD country which rescheduled its external sovereign debt in the past 5 years.

[19] A change in interest rates will affect the value of a fixed income security, such as a bond.

futures and options, swaps (interest rate, currency or commodity) and equity derivatives will expose a bank to market risk. Market and credit risk can be closely linked. For example, if the rating of corporate or sovereign debt is upgraded/downgraded by a respected credit rating agency, then the corporate or sovereign bonds will rise/fall in value.

In the numerator of the Basel ratio, a third type of capital, **tier 3** capital, can be used by banks but only when computing the capital charge related to market risk, and subject to the approval of the national regulator. Tier 3 capital is defined as short-term subordinated debt (with a maturity of less than 2 years), which meets a number of conditions stipulated in the agreement, including a requirement that neither the interest nor principal can be repaid if it results in the bank falling below its minimum capital requirement.

Whether the Amendment raises or lowers the capital charge of a bank depends on the profile of its trading book. However, as will be shown below, banks using the "standardised" approach are likely to incur higher capital charges, unless positions are well hedged or debt securities are of a high investment grade.[20] Under the Amendment, one of two approaches to market risk can be adopted, internal models or standardised.

## Market risk – the internal model approach

Banks, subject to the approval of the national regulator, are allowed to use their own internal models to compute the amount of capital to be set aside for market risk, subject to a number of conditions. The market leader is JP Morgan's Riskmetrics™. Value at risk was discussed at length in Chapter 3. This subsection shows what Basel requires of banks if they use a VaR model. Throughout, it will be assumed they are using the Riskmetrics™ model, so the key equation is:

$$\text{VaR}_x = V_x(dV/dP)\Delta P_t \tag{4.1}$$

where

$V_x$: the market value of portfolio $x$
$dV/dP$: the sensitivity to price movement per dollar market value
$\Delta P_t$: the adverse price movement (in interest rates, exchange rates, equity prices or commodity prices) over time $t$

There are several critical assumptions underlying any VaR computation, which were outlined in Chapter 3. Basel has certain specific requirements to be satisfied.

1. Bank models must compute VaR on a daily basis.
2. The four risk factors to be monitored are interest rates (for different term structures/maturities), exchange rates, equity prices and commodity prices.
3. Basel specifies a one-tailed 99% confidence interval, i.e. the loss level is at 99%; the loss should occur 1 in 100 days or 2 to 3 days a year. Recall the choice of 99% is a more risk averse/conservative approach. However, there is a trade-off: a choice of 99% as opposed

---

[20] This treatment of market risk was also adopted by an EU second capital adequacy directive, CAD-II (1997).

to 95% means not as much historical data (if it is a historical database being used – see below) are available to determine the cut-off point.

4. The choice of holding period ($t$ in the equation above) will depend on the objective of the exercise. Banks with liquid trading books will be concerned with daily returns and compute DEAR, daily earnings at risk. Pension and investment funds may want to use a month. The Basel Committee specifies 10 working days, reasoning that a financial institution may need up to 10 days to liquidate its holdings.

5. Basel does not recommend which frequency distribution should be used. Recall that Riskmetrics™ employs a variance–covariance approach. Banks that use variance–covariance analysis normally make *some allowances* for non-linearities, and the Basel Amendment requires that non-linearities arising from option positions be taken into account. For either approach, Basel 2 requires the specification of a *data window*, that is, how far back the historical distribution will go, and there must be at least a year's worth of data. Generally, the longer the data run the better, but often the data do not exist except for a few countries, and it is more likely that the distribution will change over the sample period.

## Computation of the capital charge using the internal model

If the bank is employing its internal model once VaR is computed, the capital charge is set as follows:[21]

$$[\text{MRM}(10\text{-day market risk VaR}) + \text{SRM}(10\text{-day specific risk VaR})][\text{trigger}/8] \qquad (4.2)$$

where

MRM: a market risk multiplier, which is 3 or 4 depending on the regulator – the lower the multiplier, the greater the reward for the quality of the model in its treatment of systematic risk

SRM: a specific risk multiplier, which can be 4 or 5 – a lower multiplier indicates a greater reward for the way a given bank's model deals with specific risk

trigger: the number assigned is based on the assessment of the quality of a bank's control processes, it can vary between 8 (assigned to US and Canadian international banks) and 25 – the higher the trigger number the higher the overall capital charge

If an internal market model is used, it is estimated that a bank could reduce its capital charge by between 20% and 50%, depending on the size of the trading operations and the type of instruments traded, because the bank's model will allow for diversification (or model for correlation between positions) whereas the standardised model does not.

The 1996 Market Risk Amendment also introduced restrictions on the total concentration of risk. If the risk being taken is greater than 10% of the bank's total capital, the

---

[21] This equation is taken from Crouhy *et al.* (2000), p. 65.

regulator must be informed, and advance permission must be obtained for any risk that exceeds 25% of the bank's capital.

Unlike the standard approach, banks using an approved internal model can allow for the correlation between four market risk categories: interest rates (at different maturities), exchange rates, equity prices and commodity prices. Thus, banks are rewarded for portfolio diversification that reduces market risk, and so reduces the capital they must set aside.

In a theme that continues in the Basel 2 proposals (see below), the Committee is encouraging banks to have a risk management system that not only satisfies regulatory requirements, but ensures the bank has a framework to manage all the risk exposures generated by its business activities. To be approved by the regulators, in addition to a VaR model (which meets the criteria discussed above), the risk management system should:

- Allocate the capital to various business units.
- Use RAROC to track the performance of each business unit and the bank as a whole.
- Record all positions in a centralised system.
- Conduct regular stress testing and scenario analysis (see Chapter 3) to ensure their risk management systems can cope with extreme market conditions, such as a sudden loss in liquidity or exchange rate crises.
- All models should be subject to a system of continuous evaluation, and tests of the risk management system should be done independently of traders and the front office.

## 4.3.4. Basel and Related Problems with the VaR Approach

The numerous problems arising from the use of VaR, many of which derive from the assumptions underlying the model, were discussed in Chapter 3. One, perhaps unjust, criticism is that VaR does not give a probability of bank failure. However, it was never meant to because it is designed to establish a capital requirement for *market* risk, one of many types of risk the bank faces. Due to the amount of attention it has received, there is a tendency to forget that it deals with just one aspect of a bank's risk. Nonetheless, there are other problems related to the use of the Basel VaR.

Under the current Basel rules, the more sophisticated banks may employ their own advanced risk models if the country regulator approves. However, all banks will have to meet the minimum VaR standards. In a crisis, all will react the same way.

Just as Goodhart (1974) demonstrated that statistical relationships break down once employed for policy purposes, Danielsson (2000, p. 5) argues that a model breaks down once regulators use a model like VaR to contain risk.

As shown in equation (4.2), Basel requires VaR to be multiplied by 3 (sometimes 4 if there are large differences between the actual and predicted outcomes) to determine the minimum capital requirement. The larger banks have objected because the incentive to use sophisticated models is reduced. Basel justifies the requirement because of the problems with the VaR approach. In the absence of strong evidence, Shin *et al.* (2001) recommend a reduction in the multiplication factor, to be increased if it is found that losses are under-predicted.

Basel requires capital to be set aside for market risk based on a 10-day time horizon, Danielsson (2002) demonstrates that the production of 10 (working) day VaR forecasts is technically difficult, if not impossible. For example, suppose 1 year (250 days) is used to produce the daily VaR. To compute a 10-day VaR, 10 years' data would be needed. To get round this problem, Basel recommends taking the daily VaR and multiplying it by the square root of 10. However, Danielsson shows the underlying assumptions with respect to distribution are violated if the square root method is used.

Most banks employ very similar VaR models, or use the standard approach. However, banks differ widely in their objectives and exposure to market risk. A small savings bank or building society in the EU is unlikely to be exposed to much market risk but must adopt the standard approach nonetheless, which is costly. Other banks may be exposed to types of market risk not well captured by VaR methods.

### Market risk – the standardised approach

Banks without an approved internal model for estimating market risk exposure are required to use Basel's standardised approach. Recall the objective: to replace the credit risk equivalents used in Basel 1 with a more sophisticated treatment of off-balance sheet items. No VaR computation is used. Instead, the amount of capital to be set aside is determined by an additive or building bloc approach based on the four market risks, that is, changes in interest rates (at different maturities), exchange rates, equity prices and commodity prices. In every risk category, all derivatives (e.g. options,[22] swaps, forward, futures) are converted into spot equivalents. Once the capital charge related to each of these risks is determined, it is summed up to produce an overall capital charge. The computation does not allow for any correlation between the four market risk categories. Put another way, portfolio diversification is not accepted as a reason for reducing the capital to be set aside for market risk.

### Equity risk

Determining the market risk arising from equities is a two-stage process, based on a charge for specific risk (X) and one for market risk (Y). To obtain the specific risk the net (an offset of the long and short of the spot and forward position) for each stock is computed. The net exposure of each share position is multiplied by a risk sensitivity factor, which is 8% for specific and market risk, but if the national regulator judges the portfolio to be liquid and well diversified, the systematic risk factor is reduced to 4%. In the example below, it is assumed to be 4%.

_____

[22] Option positions are converted at their delta equivalents. Recall from Chapter 3 that delta measures the sensitivity of the option price to a change in the underlying asset. If a bank has 500 call options on an equity, each with a delta of 0.5, then the equivalent is 250 shares. A further allowance is made for gamma risk, i.e. the sensitivity to a change in delta.

### Example:  Computing the Capital Requirement for Equity Risk

Assume the bank holds three equities in its portfolio, and the regulator has judged it to be well diversified. Then:

| Equity | Long positions ($m) | Σ Short positions ($m) | $X$ factor specific risk (net* × 8%) | $Y$ factor market risk (gross** × 4%) | Capital required $X + Y$ ($m) |
|---|---|---|---|---|---|
| 1 | 100 | 25 | 75* × 0.08 = 6 | 125 × 0.04 = 5 | 11 |
| 2 | 75 | 25 | 50 × 0.08 = 4 | 100 × 0.04 = 4 | 8 |
| 3 | 25 | 50 | 25 × 0.08 = 2 | 75 × 0.04 = 3 | 5 |

*Net: column 1 − column 2.
**Gross: columns 1 + 2.

Though there is some allowance for diversification (depending on the regulator), the method assumes the $\beta$s (i.e. systematic/market risk) is the same for all equities.

## Foreign exchange and gold risk

Recall that all derivatives have been converted into the equivalent spot positions. A bank's net open position in each *individual* currency is obtained – all assets less liabilities, including accrued interest. The net positions are converted into US$ at the spot exchange rate. The capital charge of 8% applies to the larger of the sum (in absolute value terms) of the long or short position, plus the net gold position.

Alternatively, subject to approval by national regulators, banks can employ a simulation method. The exchange rate movements over a past period are used to revalue the bank's present foreign exchange positions. The revaluations are, in turn, used to calculate simulated profits/losses if the positions had been fixed for a given period, and based on this, a capital charge imposed.

## Interest rate risk

The capital charge applies to all debt securities, interest rate derivatives (e.g. futures, forwards, forward rate agreements, swaps) and hybrid instruments. The *maturity approach* involves three steps.

1. Obtain a net overall weighted position for each of 16 time bands. Before they are summed, the net position in each time band is multiplied by a risk factor, which varies from 0 at the short end to 12.5 at the long end.
2. 10% of each net position in each time band is disallowed to take account of the imperfect duration mismatches *within* each time band – known as *vertical disallowance*.

3. There is another problem: the interest rates in the different time buckets may move together, which is resolved through several *horizontal disallowances*, which vary from between 30% and 100% (i.e. no disallowance) in recognition that the degrees of correlation will vary. The matched long and short positions between the time buckets can be offset, but:
   - a 40% disallowance applies in the first set (0–1 year);
   - a 30% disallowance applies to the other two sets of time bands, i.e. 1–4 years and over 4 years;
   - there is a 40% disallowance for adjacent time buckets, and a 100% disallowance between zones 1 and 3.

Duration, explained in Chapter 3, is an *alternative* approach banks can employ to determine the capital to be set aside for interest rate risk. In each time band, the sensitivity of each position is computed by employing the duration for each instrument. The horizontal disallowance is 10% but the charge related to vertical disallowance is lower because duration allows sensitivity to be measured more accurately.[23]

### Commodities risk

This risk is associated with movements in prices of key commodities such as oil, natural gas, agricultural products (e.g. wheat, soya) and metals (e.g. silver, copper, bronze) and related risks such as basis risk, or changes in interest rates which affect the financing of a commodity. The capital charges are obtained with a methodology similar to that used for the other three categories, but it will not be discussed here.

This outline[24] of the standardised approach has been kept brief for several reasons. First, depending on their activities, banks using this approach are more likely to incur substantially higher capital charges than if they opt for the internal model approach, because offsetting correlations between the four risk categories are ignored. Banks with a large trading book would be the hardest hit. Second, a bank will incur substantial costs because it still has to change its systems to comply with the standardised model. Taken together, these points provide a strong incentive for most banks to invest in a risk management system which ensures their internal model is approved.

## 4.4. Basel 2 – The Three Pillar Approach

*"New Capital Regulation Rules, known as Basel 2, will more closely align regulatory requirements with economic risk, and will have a profound effect on banking industry structures and practices."* (Citigroup/Smith Barney, *Basel II Strategic Implications*, October 2003, p. 3)

---

[23] Recall from Chapter 3 that unlike the maturity approach, duration distinguishes between the average life of an asset or liability and their respective maturity.

[24] Readers interested in a more detailed description of the standardised approach, with worked examples, are referred to Crouhy *et al.* (2000), pp. 137–150 and Basel (1996). Some of the material used above is based on their book.

In response to criticism of the 1988 Accord, a number of changes were made, culminating in the 2001 proposal.[25] The original plan was for the proposal to be discussed among bankers and members of the Basel Committee, agreed on by January 2002, and adopted by 2004. However, over 250 (largely negative) comments from banks, together with the Committee's three impact studies, prompted it to make substantial changes to the original document. A final consultative document was published in April 2003, with comments invited until the end of July 2003. The new agreement was reached in May 2004, and is published in full (251 pages!) by the BIS on behalf of the Basel Committee on Banking Supervision (2004). The standardised approach will apply to the G-10 countries by the end of 2006 and the "advanced" approaches will take effect from the end of 2007. During the first year of implementation, banks and national regulators are expected to run parallel computations, calculating capital charges based on Basel 1 and 2.

However, US regulators have thrown a spanner in the works. In February 2003 it was announced that just 10 of the most active global US banks would adopt the advanced IRB approach (see below); another 10 or so are expected to abide by the Accord. In addition, it will apply to the largest broker dealers in the USA, according to new rules recently proposed by the Securities and Exchange Commission. The rest of the American banks will continue to use Basel 1. The matter is discussed later in the chapter, but the decision does undermine the potential impact Basel 2 will have.

It is also worth emphasising that though the Basel agreements apply to the international banks in member countries, many countries require all their banks to adhere to the Basel rules. For example, part of the European Union's Capital Adequacy Directive II (CAD-II) requires all EU credit institutions to adopt the Basel 1 standards. Basel 2 will be part of the new Capital Requirements Directive, which must be passed by the EU Parliament. Elections were held in June 2004, and included the 10 new countries for the first time. The first opportunity for the Directive to be put to the EU Parliament is in late 2004/5. Once passed by the EU, each of the 25 member states incorporate the Directive into their respective laws. For example, it becomes part of UK law once it is ratified by parliament.

Finally, since the membership of the Bank for International Settlements (and the Basel Core Principles Liaison Committee) has expanded to include key developing countries, and regulators from these countries often require their banks to adopt Basel 1/2, many countries with no direct representation on the Basel Committee aspire to treat the Basel rules as a benchmark for their banks.

The new Accord seeks to achieve the following objectives.

1. It moves away from the "one size fits all" approach characteristic of Basel 1. The emphasis is on "mix and match". That is, each bank can choose from a number of options to determine its capital charge for market, credit and operational risk. Table 4.1 illustrates the choices open to banks.
2. Recognition that in terms of credit risk, lending to banks or corporates can be more *or less* risky than to OECD sovereigns. As a result, risk weightings have been changed

---

[25] The market risk amendment of Basel 1 and the contents of the first consultative document on Basel 2 was heavily influenced by the Group of Thirty (G-30) (1993) report on derivatives. The G-30 is an influential group of senior representatives from academia, the private and public sectors.

Table 4.1    Basel 2's Risk Pillar 1: Summary of Approaches

| Credit risk | Operational risk | Market risk (unchanged from 1996 amendment) |
|---|---|---|
| (1) Standardised approach<br>(2) Foundation IRB approach<br>(3) Advanced IRB approach | (1) Basic indicator approach<br>(2) Standardised approach<br>(3) Advanced measurement<br>    approaches | (1) Standardised approach<br>(2) Internal model |

*Source:*  Part of the table comes from BIS (2003a), p. 3.

to such an extent that a bank or corporation can receive a lower risk weight than the country where it is headquartered.

3. Explicit recognition of operational risk, with capital to be set aside, though overall the amount of capital set aside should remain at 8% of total risk assets.

4. Subject to the approval of national regulators, banks will be allowed to use their own internal rating models for the measurement of credit, market and operational risk. Otherwise, banks will have to adopt a standardised approach drawn up by the Basel Committee.

5. In addition to the new "risk pillar", new "supervisory" and "market discipline" pillars have been introduced.

Thus, the proposal consists of three *interactive*, "mutually reinforcing" pillars:

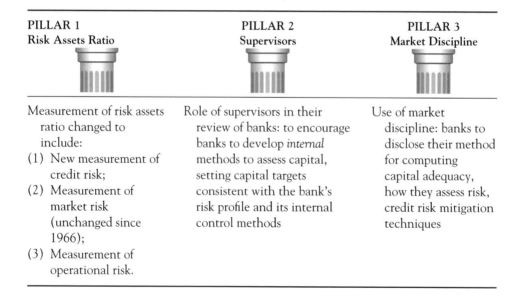

| PILLAR 1<br>**Risk Assets Ratio** | PILLAR 2<br>**Supervisors** | PILLAR 3<br>**Market Discipline** |
|---|---|---|
| Measurement of risk assets ratio changed to include:<br>(1) New measurement of credit risk;<br>(2) Measurement of market risk (unchanged since 1966);<br>(3) Measurement of operational risk. | Role of supervisors in their review of banks: to encourage banks to develop *internal* methods to assess capital, setting capital targets consistent with the bank's risk profile and its internal control methods | Use of market discipline: banks to disclose their method for computing capital adequacy, how they assess risk, credit risk mitigation techniques |

## Pillar1 – Minimum Capital Requirements

| Basel 1(with 1996 Amendment) | Basel 2(2006/7) |
|---|---|
| Capital (tier 1 & 2) | Capital (tier 1 & 2) |
| Credit risk + market risk | Amended credit risk + market risk +operational risk |

The definition of tier 1 and 2 capital used in Basel 1 is retained. However, over the longer term the Basel Committee plans to review what constitutes eligible tier 1 capital. The minimum requirements to set aside, 4% of capital (for tier 1) or 8% (for tier 2), remains unchanged.

The market risk measure introduced in the 1996 amendment is part of the new risk assets ratio, and was discussed at length earlier in the chapter. The only change proposed is to have one system for determining the trigger charge [see equation (4.2)]. There are important changes in the measurement of credit risk and, for the first time, an attempt to measure and impose a capital requirement for operational risk.

### 4.4.1. Pillar 1 – Credit Risk Measures

Measures of credit risk have been changed to deal with some of the criticisms of Basel 1. Banks must adopt one of three measurements: Standardised (modification of existing approach); "Foundation Internal Ratings Based Approach" and "Advanced Internal Ratings Based Approach".

### *The standardised approach to credit risk*

Banks lacking sophisticated models for assessing risk will be required to adopt the standardised approach under Basel 2. Even with the standardised approach, the Basel Committee has recognised the need for more flexible treatment with respect to credit risk. The major modification involves the use of a wider band of risk weightings, from 0% for very low risk to 150% for high risk loans. The credit risk weights for loans to countries, banks, corporates and securitised assets are summarised in Table 4.2. There is no longer a distinction between OECD and other sovereigns – a sovereign risk weighting will be determined by external rating agencies or a qualified export credit agency (see notes below Table 4.2).

Weightings for other assets are as follows.

(a) Residential mortgages: 35%
(b) Commercial mortgages: 100%
(c) Personal loans: 100%
(d) Venture capital: the decision of the national regulator
(e) All other assets: 100%[26]

The above changes mean, for example, that if a corporation is rated BB–by a rating agency, the bank may be asked to assign a risk weight of 150% to that asset, so it will have to

---

[26] This list is not exhaustive. The Committee also specifies weights for past dues loans, higher risk categories, commitments and some other categories. See paragraphs 41–56 of Basel (2004) for more detail.

Table 4.2   Credit Risk Weights Under the Standardised Approach

| Credit Rating | AAA to AA− | A+ to A− | BBB+ to BBB− | BB+ to B− | Below B− | Unrated |
|---|---|---|---|---|---|---|
| Sovereigns & central banks* | 0% | 20% | 50% | 100% | 150% | 100% |
| Banks[1] | 20% | 50% | 100% | 100% | 150% | 100% |
| Banks[2] | 20% | 50% | 50% | 100% | 150% | 50% |

| Credit Rating | AAA to AA− | A+ to A− | BBB+ to BB− | Below B− | Unrated |
|---|---|---|---|---|---|
| Corporate | 20% | 50% | 100% | 150% | 100% |

| Credit Rating | AAA to AA− | A+ to A− | BBB+ to BBB− | BB+ to BB− | Below BB− | Unrated |
|---|---|---|---|---|---|---|
| Securitised assets** | 20% | 50% | 100% | 150% | Deducted from capital | Deducted from capital |

* For sovereigns, supervisors may opt for the credit scores produced by qualified Export Credit Agencies, in which case the risk weight (in brackets) for ECA risk scores is as follows: risk score = 1 (0%), 2 (20%), 3 (50%), 4–6 (100%), 7 (150%).

** For more detail on how Basel 2 proposes to treat securitised assets, see section IV of Basel (2003a).

[1,2] Supervisors can use one of two options for all banks in their respective countries. Option 1: banks are assigned a risk weight one category less favourable than the weight given to the country, except for countries where the sovereign rates B+ to B−, in which case the score is capped at 100%. Option 2: banks are assigned a risk weight based on the external credit ranking of the bank itself. Securities firms are ranked as banks provided they are subject to comparable supervision and regulation. If not, they are treated as corporates.

set aside 12% of the value of the loan as capital. On the other hand, firms with treble A ratings carry a risk weight of 20%, meaning the bank need set aside only 1.6% of the value of the loan. The changes give banks an incentive to loan to more highly rated corporations, whereas under Basel 1, the amount of capital to be set aside was always the same, independent of corporations' risk profiles. Small and medium-sized enterprises are generally not rated at all. The German government, among others, expressed concern at higher capital charges imposed on the *mittelstand*. However, in the final version, the approach taken has satisfied the critics, and the consensus is that Basel 2 is unlikely to result in a reduction in the availability of finance for small and medium-sized enterprises (SMEs) (see below).

Some on-balance sheet netting is to be allowed on the banking book provided it meets specified standards. However, there is no provision that would encourage banks to spread their risks across a group of loans.

## Credit risk: foundation and advanced internal ratings based approach

Subject to the approval of the national supervisor, these banks may use their own internal ratings and credit information to determine how much capital is to be set aside for credit

Table 4.3   Foundation vs Advanced IRB

| Data Input | Foundation IRB | Advanced IRB |
|---|---|---|
| Probability of default (PD) | Supplied by bank-based on own estimates | Supplied by bank-based on own estimates |
| Loss given default (LGD) | Supervisory values set by Basel | Supplied by bank-based on own estimates |
| Exposure at default (EAD)* | Supervisory values set by Basel | Supplied by bank-based on own estimates |
| Maturity (M)** | Supervisory values set by Basel or at the discretion of national supervisors, supplied by bank-based on own estimates, with an allowance to exclude some exposures (e.g. make them fixed maturity) | Supplied by bank-based on own estimates, with an allowance to exclude some exposures (e.g. make them fixed maturity) |

\* EAD: refers to loan commitments – the amount of a loan or credit line that is likely to be drawn at the time of default, and equivalent to potential credit exposure (PCE) discussed in Chapter 3.
\*\* In IRB, the average maturity is assumed to be 3 years, though under special cases, adjustments will be possible: a minimum of 1 year and a maximum of 7.
*Source:* BIS (2003a), p. 5.

risk. Basel has introduced these options to reward banks with sophisticated risk weighting systems, which should lower the capital to be set aside to cover credit risk. It also increases the likelihood that ratings will be based on *economic capital*, the capital set aside to cover unexpected losses. This is considered an improvement over *regulatory capital*, which is set aside based on regulatory dictates such as the Basel 1 or 2 risk weightings. The difference between the foundation and advanced IRB relates to the data supplied by a bank, and the data provided by the supervisor. Table 4.3 summarises the differences.

A bank must satisfy some minimum requirements to be approved for use of the internal ratings approach (IRB). The conditions include:

- Differentiation of credit risk.
- Clear criteria for the internal ratings system and a complete ratings assignment.
- The probability of default (PD) is estimated for each group of borrowers assigned to internal grades.
- PD data: banks must have at least 2 years of data from the time Basel 2 takes effect, rising to 5 within 3 years.
- LGD: advanced IRB banks are to supply 7 years of data for loss given default (LGD), though they are encouraged to develop a database covering a complete economic cycle. Banks can use data from other sources, such as rating agencies or other banks.
- Internal validation.

- Risk components: the bank uses its own. Supervisors are to approve the method by which the risk components are converted into risk weights for the computation of risk weighted assets.
- A bank's internal ratings and VaR must be part of an integrated risk management system. For example, while VaR is used to assess market risk and the regulatory capital to be set aside, the risk management system must determine the economic capital (used to set limits), look at performance via a risk adjusted return on capital (RAROC), etc.
- Satisfy the disclosure standards specified under pillar 3.

## Risk weights under foundation IRB

Table 4.3 applies for all corporate, sovereign and interbank exposures. Once the supervisory authorities approve a bank's use of the foundation IRB approach, there is the question of how the risk weights will be applied. Basel assigns two risk weights. The first risk weight is a function of PD, which is supplied by the bank; the second a function of LGD.[27] The values for LGD, along with EAD, are supplied by Basel, and will depend on the nature of the exposure.

Basel had intended to include expected losses in the risk weightings but the final agreement (June 2004) replaced this with a requirement that if a bank finds the actual provisions it set aside is less than expected losses, it must be deducted from tier 1 and tier 2 capital, subject to a maximum cap.

For _retail_ exposures, _no_ distinction is drawn between IRB and advanced IRB. All IRB (foundation and advanced) banks are expected to supply internal estimates of PD, LGD and EAD based on pools of exposures.[28] Retail loans are divided into three categories: (1) residential mortgages; (2) revolving retail loans – mainly unsecured revolving credits, such as that incurred by agents who roll over most of their credit card payments; and (3) other retail – non-mortgage consumer lending including loans to SMEs with annual sales of less than €5 million. Basel provides the risk weight formula to obtain risk weighted assets in each of the three categories. The risk weight is obtained using a Basel specified risk correlation, and formulae using PD, LGD and EAD.[29]

The loan loss rates on different types of loans are used to obtain estimates of the loss given default, LGD. Once LGD is known, together with PD, a risk weight is derived. The risk weight for retail exposures is assumed to be about 50% of corporate exposures, based on the reasoning that personal loan portfolios are more highly diversified.

In the original proposals, loans to small and medium-sized enterprises (SMEs – defined as firms with annual sales of <€50 million) were to be treated like retail loans, but in the final document,[30] the IRB risk weight formula for corporates is to be used, adjusted for firm

---

[27] While PD and LGD will be used to determine the risk weights, Basel also intends to impose an additional multiplier of 1.5 to allow for further cover in case of model errors. At the time of writing, there is strong opposition to it, and it may not appear in the final document.

[28] Unlike corporate exposures, where the values are estimated for individual exposure.

[29] For the detailed formulae, readers are referred to Basel (2003a, paragraphs 298–301).

[30] See Basel (2004).

size. The corporate risk weight is adjusted using the formula: $0.04 \times 1[(S - 5)/45]$, where $S$ is the annual sales in € millions. If €50 $\geq S \geq$ €5 million, then the formula is used. €5 million is a floor: anything less is treated as €5 million, or the firm can opt to have the loan treated as a retail loan. SMEs are treated as retail loans if their total exposure to the banking group is less than €1 million–the bank in question treats these loans the same way as other retail exposures.

## Securitisation

For IRB banks *originating* securitisations, a bank must calculate $K_{IRB}$, which is the amount of capital that would have been set aside if the underlying pool of assets had not been securitised. If the bank is in a first loss position (i.e. in the event of a default on the securitised assets it has to absorb the losses that are a fraction of (or equal to) $K_{IRB}$), then the position must be deducted from capital. In other words, banks that do not pass on the full credit risk to a third party will have to set aside capital. The amount set aside is determined by a ratings based approach if the security is externally rated. If IRB banks *invest* in securitisations, a formula is used to estimate how much capital is to be deducted based on the external rating given, or, if they are unrated, other factors. However, in the June 2004 agreement, it was acknowledged that some aspects of the treatment of securitisation was under review.

## *Credit risk mitigation: collateral, guarantees and credit derivatives*

Basel recognises collateral, guarantees and credit derivatives as "credit risk mitigants", because the presence of any three may mean that in the event of default, some assets are recovered, which reduces the size of a loss for the bank. However, certain restrictions apply, depending on the risk management approach adopted by a bank.

## Collateral

Collateral backs a loan, and in the event of default, is used to recover some assets, Thus, collateral affects LGD – the higher the quality and amount of collateral, the smaller the LGD. Under Basel 2, what is accepted as recognised collateral depends on the approach adopted by the bank.

- *Standardised approach*: The main components of recognised financial collateral include cash (held on deposit at the bank granting the loan[31]), gold, government securities rated BB− and above or at least BBB (when issued by non-government entities, including banks and securities firms); unrated securities if they are issued by a bank, are traded on a main exchange and qualify as senior debt, equities (or mutuals/UCITS[32]) that are part of a main index (e.g. the FTSE 100).

---

[31] This type of cash collateral is an example of *netting* – it effectively means banks are offsetting assets and liabilities of a given counterparty, provided the bank has recourse to the deposits in the event of default.

[32] UCITS: undertakings for collective investments in transferable securities (e.g. unit trusts).

- *IRB*: the main components are all collateral under the standard approach, equities (or mutuals/UCITS) traded on a main index, receivables, and some types of commercial/residential and property.
- *Advanced IRB*: all forms of physical collateral are accepted, in addition to the collateral listed under IRB.

## Guarantees

A guarantee is provided through a backer. For example, another bank can guarantee a loan. The key risk is the quality of the guarantor. Thus, a guarantee, depending on its quality, will affect the probability of loan default (PD). Ischenko and Samuels (2001) show that for a given expected loss, the risk weight on LGD will be lower than that on PD. It means banks are likely to opt for lending with collateral rather than guarantees, because the risk weight will be lower.

## Credit derivatives

Though excluded as a possible credit risk mitigant in the earlier consultative documents, in the third paper (BIS, 2003c), Basel accepted that credit derivatives, in the form of credit default swaps (CDSs), can give a form of insurance against loss. The main issue surrounds what constitutes a credit event, i.e. what constitutes default, and in particular, what types of restructuring constitute default. Basel's current position is that banks can use them to lower capital requirements provided the credit default swap includes restructuring as a form of default event if it results in credit losses, unless the bank has control over the decision to restructure.

### *Advanced internal ratings based approach and credit risk*

As Table 4.4 shows, if a bank's credit risk management system is approved for the advanced internal ratings based approach (AIRB), the bank supplies its own estimates for PD, LGD, EAD and maturity. There are no rules on what factors should be used for the purposes of risk mitigation. Furthermore, all physical collateral is recognised, unlike the limited recognition of property and equity under IRB. Basel 2 proposals reward more sophisticated risk management systems by reducing the amount of capital to be set aside. The reasoning is that their models account for economic capital sufficiently well to satisfy regulatory capital requirements. Ischenko and Samuels (2001) estimated that for some banks, adopting an AIRB will reduce capital requirements by 10–20% compared to IRB.

A more recent publication by Citigroup Smith Barney (2003) concluded there was little difference by way of capital relief if the AIRB was used in place of IRB, but AIRB is significantly more costly to introduce.

### 4.4.2. Pillar 1 – Operational Risk

Operational risk (OR) is a new controversial addition to the denominator of the risk assets ratio. Recall Basel's definition of operational risk from Chapter 3, which in more recent documents has changed very slightly:

*"... Operational Risk is defined as the risk of losses resulting from inadequate or failed internal processes, people and systems, or external events."* (BIS, 2003a, p. 8)

Based on the most recent Basel publications at the time of writing, a bank may adopt one of three approaches (or a variant of the basic standardised approach) in the measurement of operational risk.

- *Basic indicator*: A capital charge based on a single indicator for overall risk exposure, the average (positive) annual gross income over the previous 3 years. Then the capital set aside is 15% (the *alpha* factor) of this, i.e.
  capital charge $= (0.15) \times$ (average annual gross income).
- *Standardised*:[33] To qualify for the use of this approach, banks must have in place an operational risk system, which complies with minimum criteria outlined by Basel. This approach requires banks to identify income from eight business lines. The capital charge for each business line is gross income multiplied by a fixed percentage (*beta* factor), which varies between 12% and 18%. The total capital to be set aside is the sum of these capital charges. The business lines and accompanying beta factors are summarised in Table 4.4. The total capital to be set aside is a three-year average of the regulatory charges calculated for each year. Negative capital charges (arising from negative income) for a given business line can be used to offset positive capital charges from other business lines in that year. However, if the aggregate capital charge for a given year turns out to be negative, it is entered as a 0 in the numerator of equation (4.2). The total capital charge[34] is then:

$$K_{TSA} = \left\{ \sum_{1-3} \max \left[ \sum (GI_{1-8} \times \beta_{1-8}), 0 \right] \right\} / 3 \qquad (4.3)$$

where

$K_{TSA}$: capital charge using the standardised approach
$\sum_{1-3}$: sum over 1 to 3 years
$GI_{1-8}$: annual gross income in a given year for each business line
$\beta_{1-8}$: fixed percentage of the level of gross income for each business line,
    given in Table 4.5.

- *Advanced measurement approaches (AMAs)*: AMAs are for banks meeting more advanced supervisory standards. Banks use their own methods to assess their exposure to operational risk, and from this, determine the amount of capital to be set aside. Banks are allowed to purchase insurance against operational risk, and use it to reduce the OR capital charge by up to 20%. However, to use insurance, banks must meet certain conditions. The most important is that the insurer is A-rated (by external agencies) in terms of its ability to

---

[33] An alternative standardised approach may also be used, subject to the approval of the national supervisor. It is similar to the standardised approach but for retail and commercial banks, loans and advances, multiplied by a fixed factor (0.035) is used instead of gross income. The other business lines remain unchanged. See Basel Committee on Banking Supervision (2004), p. 139.

[34] Source of equation (4.3) and Table 4.4: Basel Committee on Banking Supervision (2004), p. 140.

Table 4.4  Operational Risk – Standardised Approach

| Business lines | Beta factors (%) |
| --- | --- |
| Corporate finance, $\beta_1$ | 18 |
| Trading & sales, $\beta_2$ | 18 |
| Retail banking, $\beta_3$ | 12 |
| Commercial banking, $\beta_4$ | 15 |
| Payment & settlement, $\beta_5$ | 18 |
| Agency services, $\beta_6$ | 15 |
| Asset management, $\beta_7$ | 12 |
| Retail brokerage, $\beta_8$ | 12 |

meet claims. In addition, the insurance coverage must last at least a year, be explicit in terms of the OR it is covering, and may not have any exclusions or limitations arising from regulatory action.

For banks with global operations and numerous subsidiaries, the final agreement notes that a "hybrid approach" to operational risk may be used. Subject to the approval of a national supervisor, a parent bank with international operations, when employing AMAs for calculating capital to be set aside, can allow for diversification gains *within* its own operation but is not allowed to include group-wide benefits. Significant subsidiaries can use the head office model, parameters, etc. to compute their operational risk but the amount of capital set aside must be based on the same criteria as those used by the parent bank. Subsidiaries deemed of minor significance to the group's operations can (subject to agreement by the supervisor) be allocated a charge for OR from the group-wide calculation, or use the parent's methodology to compute the charge.

## 4.4.3. Pillar 2 – Responsibilities of National Supervisors

This pillar identifies the role of the national supervisors under Basel 2. Basel has identified four principles of supervisory review:

1. Supervisors are expected to ensure banks use appropriate methodology to determine Basel 2 ratios, and have a strategy to maintain capital requirements.
2. Supervisors should review banks' internal assessment procedures and strategies, taking appropriate action if these fall below standard.
3. Banks should be encouraged by supervisors to hold capital above the minimum requirement.
4. Supervisors are expected to intervene as early as possible to ask a bank to restore its capital levels if they fall below the minimum.

To fulfil these objectives, an ongoing dialogue between supervisors and banks is necessary. Also, supervisors are likely to focus on banks with a history of taking higher than average risks.

Pillar 2 does not give explicit detail on how supervisors should behave, and is likely to be used to back up pillar 1, and possibly, deal with some of the more controversial aspects of pillar 1. For example, the Committee has recently emphasised the importance of conservative stress testing for banks adopting the IRB approach. Supervisors should require these banks to devise a conservative stress test in order to test how their capital requirements might increase given a particular scenario. Based on the test results, banks should ensure they have a sufficiently robust capital buffer. If capital falls below the necessary amount, supervisors would intervene and require the bank to reduce its credit and/or market risk exposures until it can cover the capital requirements implied by the relevant stress test.

### 4.4.4. Pillar 3 – Market Discipline

The main purpose of pillar 3 is to reinforce pillars 1 and 2. Providing timely and transparent information, or even knowing they have to provide it, gives the market a role in disciplining banks. Participating banks are expected to disclose:

- Risk exposure.
- Capital adequacy.
- Methods for computing capital requirements.
- All material information, that is, information which, if omitted or mis-stated, could affect the decision-making of the agent using the information.
- Disclosure should take place on a semi-annual basis; quarterly in the case of risk exposure, especially if the bank engages in global activities.

The Committee plans to issue templates banks can use to ensure the disclosure principles are adhered to. It considers pillar 3 an important component of Basel 2, especially for banks using the IRB approaches in credit risk, AMA for operational risk and their own internal models for market risk. These banks have far greater discretion in terms of computation of capital charges they incur, and it will be difficult for supervisors to master every detail of the approach they take. Market discipline should discourage attempts by banks to cut corners in their risk assessment.

### 4.4.5. A Critique of Basel 2

There were numerous criticisms of Basel 2, but some were addressed during the consultative process (e.g. SMEs). The problems with the use of VaR were discussed earlier. Here, the more general problems related to the Basel 2 framework are reviewed. Perhaps the most serious is that it moves with the economic cycle, i.e. it is pro-cyclical. To the extent that the creditworthiness of financial and non-financial firms moves with the cycle, the method for calculating the amount of capital to be set aside in a given year means less will be needed during an economic boom; more during a downturn. The nature of recession (falling stock markets, downgrading of firms experiencing falling profits by independent rating agencies, and higher loan losses as a result of increased default rates) will reduce banks' risk assets ratios. Since raising capital, even if possible, will be more costly, banks are likely to cut back on their activities (e.g. reduced lending, less trading), which in turn will aggravate the downturn.

Hawke (2001) gives an interesting example of the effect of pro-cyclicality. When Basel 1 was being implemented in the late 1980s/early 1990s,[35] the US banking system was in the throes of a crisis. Banks were facing mounting losses – even the Deposit Insurance Corporation was threatened with insolvency. Many US bank supervisors thought Basel 1 aggravated the crisis as banks struggled to get their Basel risk assets ratios up to 8%, either by reducing lending and/or trying to raise new capital in a depressed market.

The Basel Committee addressed this criticism in several ways. Compared to earlier proposals, the *risk curve*, or the relationship between capital charges and the probability of default, has been flattened for corporate and retail loans. Also, banks have been asked to take a long run view (rather than just one year) when they determine the internal ratings of borrowers. This means the ratings should reflect conditions over a number of years, taking the whole business cycle into account. If banks are estimating their probability of default (which in turn feeds into the capital to be deducted), they are advised to use the full economic cycle. When making loan decisions, banks should note the stage of the economic cycle and employ stress tests to identify economic changes that will affect their portfolio. The information can be fed into the determination of their capital requirements. However, it is often difficult to assess how long a stage of the cycle will last. There is also a more general challenge: to collect sufficient data, especially in the early years.

A recent study suggests that the external ratings of the creditworthiness of firms could also fuel the problem of pro-cyclicality. Amato and Furfine (2003) reported that it is rare for the rating of a large corporation or bank to change. This finding is consistent with the general claim that credit ratings are not related to the cycle because they are relative measures. A bond rated AAA signals that it is less risky than a bond rated BB. Nonetheless, it has been shown that ratings move with the business cycle,[36] though this alone does not necessarily mean the ratings themselves are influenced by the cycle. This is the question Amato and Furfine set out to address, using data on the economic cycle, financial ratios and the ratings themselves. The ratings data include both investment and speculative grade; from Standard and Poor's monthly ratings of all firms – January 1981 to December 2001. Amata and Furfine report that for small changes in business risk, ratings remain unchanged. However, they find evidence of "overshooting" when a rating is changed. Upgradings were found to be excessive; downgradings too severe. Furthermore, the excessive optimism/pessimism is directly correlated with the state of the macroeconomy, meaning the upgrade/downgrade will aggravate a boom/recession.

Perversely, Basel 2 could raise the amount of systemic risk for banks using the standardised approach. They have little incentive to diversify because they are not rewarded for it, though this was also true in the case of Basel 1.

Recall the original purpose of the Basel 1 accord was to establish a level playing field for international banks in terms of regulatory capital to be set aside. Banks can pick and choose from different parts of Basel 2, which means all banks have an equal opportunity to

---

[35] Recall the Basel 1 accord was reached in 1988 but international banks had until 1993 to implement it.
[36] See Graph 1 of Amato and Furfine (2003) and Nickell *et al.* (2000).

determine the amount of regulatory capital to be set aside. However, the complex details and/or proportionately higher compliance costs for some banks means the playing field is no longer level.

As was noted earlier, Basel 2 will be used by 10 to 20 of the most internationally active US banks, but the rest of the American banks will use Basel 1. This has important competitive implications. The US banks which do adopt Basel 2 are the ones with sophisticated in-house models, so they will employ advanced approaches to the treatment of credit, market and operational risks, i.e. internal ratings for market risk, advanced IRB for credit risk and AMA for operational risk. Therefore it is likely their overall capital requirements will fall. Furthermore, there are no onerous new compliance costs for the thousands of US banks which continue to employ Basel 1, which may give them a cost advantage if the capital charge based on Basel 1 is lower. This gives US banks a competitive edge over their European or Japanese counterparts. On the other hand, banks adhering to Basel 1 will not experience a reduction in the capital they must set aside, while banks in other countries may. Also, the US sets quite rigorous regulatory standards (see Chapter 5), which may offset any cost advantage they achieve because they do not adopt Basel 2.

The big European banks which see the major US banks as their main competitors in wholesale markets will have their competitive position further undermined, for two reasons. First, it was noted earlier that Basel 2 is to be part of the Capital Adequacy Directive III before it is implemented in Europe. According to Milne (2003), contrary to expectations, the fast track Lamfalussy option[37] will not be used for the CAD III, which means that most of Basel 2's technical details will have to be passed by the European parliament, a process that will take, at the minimum, three to four years. US banks which adopt Basel 2 will do so immediately after their regulators approve its use. Their capital requirements are likely to be lower, while the European competitors will have to set aside larger amounts of capital under the old Basel 1 accord. This competitive edge for the top US banks will continue until the Capital Adequacy Directive III is passed. Second, once Basel 2 is part of a European directive, any component of it that dates or is affected by financial innovation will be extremely difficult to update/amend because it is part of a European law.

The problems outlined above will hit London's financial district particularly hard, and could undermine its leading international position in financial markets. The UK's Financial Services Authority may be forced to take unilateral action, and require banks in London to implement Basel 2 ahead of the EU's CAD III.

Some commentators have suggested that there is a danger of banks that are part of financial conglomerates moving their credit risk to another non-bank financial subsidiary to reduce the amount of capital they have to set aside. For example, credit derivatives might transfer the credit risk related to a loan to an insurance company. Or assets could be securitised and sold to third party insurers. However, the final version of Basel 2 (BIS, 2003c; Basel Committee, 2004) has tightened up many loopholes and should prevent some aspects

---

[37] After the development and qualified acceptance of the Lamfalussy fast track procedure for securities law, the expectation was that it be used for Basel 2. However, only the Annexes of Basel 2 are deemed "level 2", that is, they can be amended by a special committee. The main document of Basel 1 is classified as "level 1", and therefore will be part of a directive – any amendment will require approval by the European parliament, and then adopted by the national legislatures.

of regulatory arbitrage that occurred under Basel 1. Also, such behaviour is unlikely to be ignored by national regulators: this is an example where pillar 2 could re-enforce pillar 1.

A related concern is that the Basel requirements are encouraging banks to transfer credit risk off their balance sheets. As was documented in Chapter 3, the credit derivatives market grew from virtually nothing in the early 1990s to $2 trillion by 2002. These are forms of **credit risk transfer**: banks originate the loan (agree to lend money to firms and individuals) but transfer the risk from the bank to purchasers of loans or securities. The trend to move loans off-balance sheet began with the issue of mortgage backed securities in the 1970s, followed by, in the 1980s, the sale of sovereign debt, syndicated loans and corporate debt. However, now it is credit risk which is being transferred. Most of the institutional investors assuming this credit risk (as a consequence of securitisation or the use of credit derivatives) do not have in-house credit risk departments and rely on credit rating agencies. The agencies have expertise in assessing personal, firm or country risks, but do not look at the aggregate picture (the techniques for portfolio credit risk analysis were discussed in Chapter 3), even though institutional investors typically purchase, or insurance is written for, bundles of loans or bonds. Banks no longer hold risk but are conduits of risks.[38]

On the other hand, only a few of the top global banks are active in this market. Recall BIS (2003e) reported that 17 (19) US banks sold (bought) credit protection and only 391 out of 2220 banks supervised by the Office of the Comptroller of Currency held any form of credit derivatives. *Risk Magazine* reported 13 firms were behind 80% of transactions in credit derivatives.[39] Finally, *The Economist* claimed roughly 8% of US commercial and industrial loans were insured ($60 billion).[40] All of these figures indicate responsibility for the majority of the credit risk associated with lending remains in the banking sector.

The emphasis on the use of external ratings raises other issues. To reduce capital requirements, banks using the standardised approach will want to lend to rated firms. Most rated corporations are headquartered in the USA, and to the extent that corporations do business with their own national banks, it gives US banks an additional competitive advantage, at least in the short run. Another problem is the absence of a strong ratings culture in Europe and Japan. For example, Moody's rates 554 corporates in Europe; 221 of these are in the UK, another 121 in the Netherlands. In France and Germany, the numbers are as low as 43 and 45; respectively. That leaves just 127 other firms spread throughout Europe. In Japan, just 191 corporates are rated.[41] However, given the importance Basel will place on rating agencies, it is likely their business will spread rapidly in Japan and Europe. Regulators will have to identify the most accurate, requiring them to meet a set of criteria to be accepted as a recognised agency.

Small and medium-sized enterprises, and firms located in emerging markets, may find it more difficult to raise external finance because they are not rated. To address this issue, the

---

[38] The term "conduits of risk" first appeared in *The Economist* (2003b), p. 62.

[39] These figures were reported by *Risk Magazine* and the OCC to BIS researchers. See BIS (2003d).

[40] *The Economist*, 5 July 2003, p. 81.

[41] *Source*: Ischenko and Samuels (2001), table 12, which took the figures from Moody's. Note the figures are for Moody's only – other rating agencies offer their services, so the totals will be higher. However, if the proportions are the same, it means that only $\frac{1}{3}$ of European firms are rated, and about 10% of Japanese firms, compared to the USA.

final document (2004) confirmed the use of an adjusted formula based on the IRB corporate risk weight for SMEs with sales revenues ranging from €5 to €50 million. Otherwise, if SMEs are classified as retail, they could benefit from the flatter risk curve noted earlier.[42] However, there is no allowance for portfolio diversification through SME exposure.

In the USA, only four agencies (Standard and Poor's, Moody's, Fitch IBCA and Dominion Bond Ratings) are officially recognised by the Securities and Exchange Commission (SEC), giving them effective control over the US market. This raises the issue of monopoly power in the ratings sector. A US congressional subcommittee has asked the SEC about its relationship with these agencies. The subcommittee has expressed concern that the arrangement could limit the operation of a free market and prevent consumer interests from being served. Just three of these rating agencies are global players, meaning they are exposed to even less competition outside the USA.

There is also a potential for conflict of interest because increasingly, ratings firms advise banks on their risk management systems. The ratings agency may be tempted to give higher ratings to banks acting on their advice, though this is unlikely provided there are effective firewalls between the ratings agency and its offshoot offering the advice. However, it could increase the number of banks using similar risk management techniques. The degree to which they are correlated will mean banks react in similar ways to changes in the financial markets/macroeconomy, thereby aggravating any boom or recession.

Excessive prescription is another problem. The final agreement (2004) is 251 pages, with detailed instructions given for the implementation of Basel 2, especially the new risk assets ratio. To quote Hawke, who was referring to the (2003c) document:

> "When I complained to the Basel Committee about the complexity of the paper, I am roundly admonished... 'We live in a complex world. Don't quibble if we try to fashion capital rules that reflect that complexity'. But... the complexity we have generated goes far beyond what is reasonably needed to deal with sensible capital regulation. It reflects, rather, a desire to close every loophole, to dictate every detail, and to exclude to the maximum extent possible any opportunity for the exercise of judgement or discretion by those applying and overseeing the application of the new rules... Any effort to simplify runs the danger {of upsetting} compromises that have been hammered out." (Hawke, 2001, pp. 48–49)

The detailed computations needed if banks adopt either of the IRB approaches could discourage financial innovation and expansion into new markets because of the paucity of historical data necessary to compute PD and LGD. Also there are many recent examples where national regulators have encouraged healthy banks to merge with problem banks to avert a failure. Under Basel 2, any bank with IRB status will be reluctant to agree to such a merger if it means their IRB status is removed for several years because it will take that long to improve the risk management system of the weak acquisition. Thus, regulators could lose a useful tool in the resolution of banking problems, which could increase systemic risk.

Milne (2003) identifies another problem arising from too many rules. He argues that regulators may find it difficult to oversee the actions of banks that opt for the advanced

---

[42] German banks are developing their own internal ratings of SMEs, using both financial ratios and measures such as quality of management. The ratings will influence a SME's loan rate but will be internal to the bank.

approaches and compute their capital obligations in Basel 2. For example, if using the IRB approach they will compute PD and LGD using sophisticated models and a considerable amount of judgement. Independent analysts or supervisors may find it difficult to assess the quality of the risk management input at this level of sophistication, and it will pose a considerable challenge to their resources. There are ways of dealing with this problem, such as requiring external auditors to verify the quality of the capital adequacy requirements as assessed by the banks, or to have supervisors monitor the work of other national supervisors. However, these are costly options. Another possibility is to tighten up disclosure requirements so that banks (after some lapse in time to preserve confidentiality) had to disclose the detailed computations of PD and LGD. But by this time, it might be too late.

The treatment of operational risk (e.g. capital to be set aside based on gross income) is considered unworkable, and OR itself is difficult to quantify. These views are shared by academics and practitioners alike. The Americans rejected Basel 2 for most of its banks because, they argue, it is too costly for them to switch. Also, their regulators believe it is impossible to quantify operational risk,[43] making the resulting capital charge inherently subjective. They argue operational risk should be part of pillar 2 – monitored by regulators, with no explicit charge. European officials want all banks to be able to use insurance on operational risk to reduce the OR portion of the capital charge, independent of the approach they adopt.

Ischenko and Samuels (2001) claim the Basel Committee's remarks indicate they are focusing on two risks. *Rogue trader risk*: such as Barings (1995) and Allied Irish Bank (2002). If banks were required to set aside explicit capital for this type of risk, it would give them a greater incentive to monitor their positions. *IT risk*: relates to the concern on the reliance of computer systems to complete large numbers of banking transactions. However, there have been no real disasters arising from computer failure, though liquidity has been strained in certain cases; "9/11" is a good example. Back-up systems meant, relative to the scale of the disaster, there was no serious disruption and minimal loss of data.

Ischenko and Samuels (2001) estimated that for some banks, adopting the Advanced IRB will reduce capital requirements by 10–20% compared to IRB. Citigroup Smith Barney (2003) concluded there was little difference by way of capital relief if the AIRB was used in place of IRB, but AIRB is significantly more costly to introduce. More generally, Ischenko and Samuels (2001) argue the banks primarily engaged in investment banking, asset management, proprietary trading, custody and clearing will be the most adversely affected by capital charges for operational risk (OR), because of the emphasis placed on setting aside capital for rogue trading or the collapse of a bank's IT system. For the more traditional bank with proportionately large amounts of credit related business, the OR charge will be small and the capital savings made from the new proposals for credit risk (especially if the bank adopts an advanced internal ratings approach) could be substantial.

Three quantitative impact studies were conducted by the Basel team. The results of the first two indicated higher capital charges (compared to Basel 1) in the majority of cases, and in response to these findings, the proposals were revised. The final quantitative study was

---

[43] Even though the Basel third quantitative impact study (Basel, 2003b) indicates quantification is feasible.

Table 4.5   Percentage Change* in Capital Requirements

| | Standardised (%) | | | IRB Foundation (%) | | | IRB Advanced (%) | | |
|---|---|---|---|---|---|---|---|---|---|
| | Mean | Max | Min | Mean | Max | Min | Mean | Max | Min |
| G-10 group 1 | 11 | 84 | −15 | 3 | 55 | −32 | −2 | 46 | −36 |
| G-10 group 2 | 3 | 81 | −23 | −19 | 41 | −58 | | | |
| EU group 1 | 6 | 31 | −7 | −4 | 55 | −32 | −6 | 26 | −31 |
| EU group 2 | 1 | 81 | −67 | −20 | 41 | −58 | | | |
| Other groups 1&2 | 12 | 103 | −17 | 4 | 75 | −33 | | | |

* The percentage change in minimum capital requirements, compared to the current Basel 1 Accord.
*Source:* BIS (2003b), table 1.

initiated in October 2002, and the results (BIS, 2003b) published in May 2003. 188 banks from 13 G-10 countries, and 177 banks from 30 other countries took part in the third study. Banks were divided into group 1 (globally active, diversified, large banks, with tier 1 capital in excess of €3 billion) and group 2 (smaller, more specialised). Table 4.5 summarises the key findings. After the revisions implemented from the consultation documents, the findings were much more positive, especially if banks adopt one of the two advanced procedures which rely on their own internal ratings system. Table 4.5 shows that the average capital reduction is between 2% and 6% for globally active banks.

Compared to the previous two quantitative impact studies, the findings were much more positive, especially if banks adopt one of the two advanced procedures which rely on their own internal ratings system. As can be seen from the Min and Max columns, the variation is considerable. Recall the objective of Basel 2: to bring in more sophisticated systems of risk measures so that banks could set aside capital for market, credit and operational risk, but with no change to overall capital burden (compared to Basel 1) or even a reduction in it. For banks using the standardised approach, column one shows the capital charge is higher, especially for the G-10 group 1 and the "other" category – countries including Australia, Hong Kong, Norway, Singapore and a large number of emerging market countries such as China, Russia, Hungary, the Czech Republic, India, Malaysia, Thailand and Turkey. While most G-10 group 1 banks are likely to have systems in place to qualify for the IRB foundation or advanced approaches,[44] this is not the case for many of the banks headquartered in countries from the "other" category.

If the IRB foundation approach is used, the capital charge will fall for most banks, but again, it increases for the G-10 group 1 banks and the "other" category. The report notes that G-10 group 1 banks have, on average, less retail activity than group 2 banks – banks with large retail exposures tended to do better because the new risk weightings are lower compared to Basel 1, with the exception of past due assets. Furthermore, the standardised approach was used by most of the banks to compute operational risk figures; a few used the basic indicator approach; only one used the advanced approach.

[44] In addition, the report notes that G-10 group 1 banks have far less retail activity than group 2 banks – banks with large retail exposures tended to do better because of the new risk weightings.

Table 4.5 shows that for banks adopting the IRB advanced approach, average capital charges will fall. Note, however, that very few banks in the "other" category will have the systems in place to qualify for this approach. Indeed, there were so few banks from the IRB category that they could not be reported because of fears they could be identified.

Basel 2 could prove most onerous for the "other" group, many of which come from emerging markets, not necessarily because they are inherently riskier but because they do not have sophisticated risk management systems in place.

The Min and Max columns show the wide variation of impact the Basel 2 framework will have. No matter what approach is used, some banks stand to gain a great deal, while others will suffer a large increase in the capital charge.

For the more sophisticated banks that experience a reduction in their capital requirements, more capital will be released. If, overall, more capital is released than set aside, "surplus" capital will emerge. Too much capital will increase competition, encourage consolidation (capital surplus banks will be looking for capital weak banks), and possibly greater risk taking. The latter outcome would be a bit of an irony: regulators, by creating a situation of surplus capital, end up encouraging the banks to engage in riskier activities.

It appears that banks in most of the G-10 countries are quite advanced in their preparations to adopt pillar 1 of Basel 2. In a recent survey,[45] over 75% of large (assets in excess of $100 billion) and medium-sized (assets ranging from $25 to $99 billion) banks in North America, Europe and Australia are planning to be using IRB by 2007 and to have IRB Advanced by 2010. Over 60% of European banks report being at the "implementation" stage, compared to 12% in the USA and 27% in Asia and the emerging markets. Progress on meeting Basel 2 operational risk requirements has been slower, with less than half the North American, European and Australian banks expecting to be using the Advanced Measurement Approach (AMA) by 2007, rising to 70% by 2010. About 62% consider their preparations for pillars 2 and 3 to be "poor" or "average". For the larger banks the cost of complying with Basel 2 ranges from between €50 million (60%) and €100 million (33%). The majority of medium-sized banks (more specialised) are expecting the cost to be less than €50 million.

# 4.5. Alternative or Complementary Approaches to Basel

The Basel Committee claims that Basel 2 has been designed to encourage banks to use their own internal models to compute a capital charge. Critics argue the incentives are not there, the approaches discussed in this section are examples of *incentive compatible regulation*: the objective is to improve the incentive of individual banks to have accurate risk management systems, either through use of the market or regulators, or both.

## 4.5.1. The Pre-commitment Approach

This proposal would deal with private banks' criticism of Basel, that if a bank is allowed to use its own internal model, the minimum capital requirement is too high because it is

---

[45] All the figures in this paragraph come from *The Banker* (2004), pp. 154–165. The article is based on a survey of 200 global leading banks undertaken by FT Research for Accenture, Mercer Oliver Wyman and SAP.

based on VaR multiplied by 3 or even 4. The larger banks claim this requirement creates a disincentive to use more sophisticated models of risk management.

The Fed's *pre-commitment* proposal (1995): The Federal Reserve suggested that banks and trading houses "pre-commit" a level of capital they believe to be necessary to cover losses arising from market/trading risks. The amount pre-committed would be based on the bank's own VaR model.

At the end of a specified period, the regulator would be able to impose penalties (e.g. a fine or a non-monetary fine, such as not being able to incur certain types of market risk over a period of time) on a bank which failed to set aside enough capital. If the bank over-commits, it penalises itself by setting aside too much capital.

Such a system would remove the responsibility of the regulator to endorse a particular model, which is necessary in Basel 2's internal model approach. It gives each firm an incentive to find the best model and to add the appropriate multiplication factor to the estimate of possible losses to ensure against incurring a penalty.

The problem with pre-commitment is that banks are penalised at a time when they are under-capitalised – similar to the pro-cyclical problem discussed in Basel. Also, if all banks failed to meet their target because of an unexpected event, it could create systemic problems itself.

## 4.5.2. Subordinated Debt

Another example of an incentive based approach is that all banks be required to have a certain percentage of their capital in *subordinated debt*: uninsured, unsecured loans which are junior to all other types of lender, that is, the lenders would be the last to be paid off in the event of bankruptcy. However, a number of issues need to be dealt with if it is to be successful. A clear signal that these creditors will not be bailed out is necessary. Thus, only well-informed buyers, such as institutional investors, should have access to it, which could be done if the debt is issued in very high denominations. The choice of correct maturity is also important. If too short, there is a reduced incentive to monitor. If too long, banks would issue the debt at infrequent intervals, and the market would be unable to give an indication of its view on that debt, which would undermine market discipline. Most proposals suggest a maturity of at least 1 year. The amount suggested is between 2% and 5% of total assets, with a reduction in capital contributions to ensure a fair capital burden. Some propose quarterly debt issues so the market can adequately signal the banks' debt value. However, there is a question of whether even the largest banks could issue this debt so frequently. Subordinated debt is most likely to work with the largest banks, i.e. with assets of at least $10 million. For smaller banks, the transactions costs would be high and it is unlikely there would be enough liquidity for small bank issues, meaning the spreads would convey very little information. To be effective, regulators must take punitive action if the yield on the debt falls below a certain level, e.g. the equivalent of BBB corporate debt or junk bond yields on the secondary market. The regulators would then intervene and declare the bank insolvent.

There are a number of advantages arising from the use of subordinated debt. The holders of the subordinated debt, sophisticated creditors, have a strong incentive to monitor the actions of the bank because they lose all their investment in the event of failure. If traded, the debt would be a means of providing a transparent, market price of the risk a given bank is taking. Finally, regulators in some countries (e.g. the USA) are required to take prompt, corrective action or a least a cost approach when dealing with a problem bank. Regulators would be concerned about runs on debt if there were any rumours about the condition of the bank, which would reinforce this requirement.

There are also disadvantages. First, the same rules would apply to all banks above a certain size, independent of the type of bank, its management and the riskiness level. The use of such debt also implies that bank regulators have access to less information than the market place, since the idea is to use sophisticated investors to provide early warning of problems via the sale of the debt. In some developed economies, such as the USA, the opposite is true. Ely (2000) states that a US bank with assets of $100 billion pays bank regulators over $4 million in fees, which should be enough for all the bank's financial information to be carefully examined. By contrast, the market relies on the publication of quarterly indicators, and does not have access to detailed information that regulators have. Second, if each bank subsidiary in a financial holding company structure was required to issue subordinated debt, there would be two-tier disclosure with the regulator: at the FHC consolidated level and at subsidiary level. This would be costly for the banks. Next, in the case of a financial conglomerate the issue arises as to which parts of the conglomerate would have to comply with the requirement to issue such debt. Also, problem banks would be tempted to avoid full disclosure or massage the figures at the time the debt was issued. However, with the Sarabane Oxley rules, the bank executives run a high risk of jail or heavy fines. As was noted above, if the debt was issued quarterly, it would be costly for the bank and could mean the market was flooded with bank debt, thereby forcing up yields, which merely indicated excess supply rather than anything inherently wrong with the bank. Yields would also be forced up in times of systematic problems, for example, in 1998 with the LTCM and Russian government debt default.

Finally, requiring banks to issue subordinated debt might cause market manipulation. For example, an institutional investor could buy up a large portion of a bank's subordinated debt and short sell its common stock at the same time. The speculators would then dump the debt in an illiquid market, forcing up the yields, which could trigger intervention. This would be likely to cause the stock price of the bank to fall, at which time the investor closes out the short position: the gain would exceed the loss on the sale of the SD. Bank management could do nothing about it – a bank can buy back its own common stock but its management would not be allowed to buy subordinated debt.

## 4.5.3. Cross-Guarantee Contracts

Ely (2000) argues this is another market oriented method to encourage banks to be safe and sound. A cross-guarantee contract is a form of private insurance against insolvency. The guarantors provide unconditional guarantees of the financial firms' (including banks) liabilities. It would be negotiated on a firm by firm basis, and to operate in the financial sector, a firm would be required to find a guarantor. The guarantor would be paid a premium that would reflect how risky each bank's activities were. In a simplistic example, a retail bank offering a diversified range of intermediary services would be far less risky than a firm specialising in proprietary trading.

The guarantor and guaranteed firm would jointly agree on a supervisor to monitor compliance with the cross-guarantee contract; hence supervisory arrangements would apply to a particular bank according to the risk profile of that particular bank's assets. It would get rid of the "one size fits all" approach, though so do the Basel 2 proposals. Also the large universal banks would need a group of guarantors, and close monitoring of the guarantors would be necessary to ensure they have the funds to cover an insolvency.

## 4.6. International Financial Architecture

### 4.6.1. The Meaning of International Financial Architecture

Though the term "international financial architecture" is relatively new, institutions such as the Basel Committee have been working towards a common system of regulating global banks for over two decades. National bodies concerned with containing national crises, such as Sweden's central bank and the Bank of England, have been around for centuries.

However, the agenda for *international financial architecture* is much broader, bringing together the various organisations dealing with international finance in an attempt to regulate banks, other global financial institutions and the financial system as a whole. The objectives are to design a global financial structure, and a means of regulating and coordinating institutions within that structure, to minimise the probability of a major financial crisis occurring. Also, to have in place methods for dealing with a crisis, should it occur.

Table 4.6 shows the key global institutions concerned with preserving the stability of the international financial system. These organisations focus on the international coordination of regulations in a particular area, including banking, securities, insurance and accounting. The exception is the Financial Stability Forum, which is trying to ensure the *effective implementation* of all these rules. For example, at its September 2003 meeting, the FSF identified a number of areas which, in their view, required close monitoring and/or action. The issue of credit risk transfer (CRT) from the banking sector to non-banking financial areas, notably the insurance sector, which is arising from the use of credit derivatives (see Chapter 3). It reported that a work plan had been set up to investigate the issue and address concerns about financial stability posed by CRT. The need for greater transparency in the reinsurance industry was also discussed, as was the role of offshore financial centres in an increasingly integrated global financial market. It looked forward to stronger arrangements by these centres in the areas of supervision, information exchange and regulation. Other areas considered were corporate governance and auditing standards.[46]

There are other organisations which also focus on the broader picture, including the IMF and the World Bank. The *International Monetary Fund* (IMF) was created by the 1944 Bretton Woods Agreement. With a membership of 182 countries, its primary concern is with the balance of payments, exchange rate and macro stability, with a responsibility for economic surveillance around the world. Member countries are encouraged to meet

---

[46] BIS (2003), "The Financial Stability Forum Holds its 10th Meeting", *Bank for International Settlements Press Release*, 11 September 2004. Available at www.bis.org

Table 4.6   International Organisations Concerned with Financial Stability

| Name | Date Established | Objective | Who Meets | Membership |
|---|---|---|---|---|
| Basel Committee on Banking Supervision | 1975 | Supervision of international banks but many countries (e.g. EU states) apply standards to all banks | Supervisors + central bankers from G-10 | 12 countries + observer status: E Commission, ECB, BIS Financial Stability Group |
| International Organisation of Securities Commission (IOSCO) | 1990 | Pre-dates 1990 but membership increased after that date. Supervisors of securities firms | Supervisors of securities firms (e.g. SEC, FSA) | 91 countries |
| International Association of Insurance Supervisors (IAIS) | 1994 | Supervisors of insurance firms | Supervisors of insurance firms | 80 countries |
| International Accounting Standards Committee (IASC) | 1973 | To harmonise accounting rules world-wide. Set up the IASB to implement agreed global accounting standards. | 3 or 4 day meetings per annum | 16 delegations – each with 3 members plus observers |
| International Accounting Standards Board (IASB) | 2001 | To implement a set of global accounting standards. Advised by a 49 member Standards Advisory Council | Monthly meetings | 14 members from 9 countries |
| Financial Stability Forum (FSF)* | 1999 | To advocate stronger development & implementation* of international standards; to access, identify and take joint action on vulnerable points that could undermine the stability of the international financial system; to improve information flows, coordination and cooperation among the various members. No executive role but rather, to encourage the other groups to take action | Supervisors + international supervision bodies, central banks (+ECB), finance ministries, IMF, World Bank, OECD, BIS | G-7 + Australia, Hong Kong, Netherlands, Singapore (42) |

* FSF: emphasis on EFFECTIVE implementation of standards, rather than devising them.
G-7: Canada, France, Germany, Japan, Italy, UK, US.
G-8: as above + Russia.
OECD: G-10: G-7 plus Netherlands, Belgium and Sweden + Switzerland – joined in 1984.
G-30: The Group of 30: a private group of very senior representatives from the private and public sectors and academia.
Objective: to improve understanding of international economic issues.

macroeconomic targets. Also, since the 1980s, the IMF has been involved in rescheduling loans/facilitating new ones in the event of major problems (e.g. default or requests by sovereign countries to reschedule debt repayments). If a country is having problems repaying its external debt (private, public, or both), it puts pressure on lenders to extend financing in exchange for the Fund increasing its lending; and on problem debtor countries to implement macroeconomic adjustment programmes including meeting inflation targets and reducing the size of government debt relative to GDP.

The *World Bank* was also created by the 1944 Bretton Woods Articles of Agreement. The Bank is a development agency, arranging external finance for developing and emerging markets with little or no access to private lending. The external finance consists of project finance or loans, granted on condition that certain structural adjustments, etc. be made. It also encourages private foreign direct investment.

Both institutions have expanded their financial policy departments and are concerned with financial stability, but mainly at the macro level. The *Financial Sector Assessment Programme* (FSAP) is a joint programme run by the IMF and the World Bank. Introduced in 1999, it signalled that these institutions were intending to play a greater role monitoring and trying to preserve global financial stability. By April 2003, approximately 95 countries (both developed and emerging market) have either been, or are about to be, assessed. The assessments cover the macroeconomy, identification of points of vulnerability in the financial systems, arrangements for managing financial crises, regulation, supervision and soundness of the financial structure. There is a direct link with the Basel Committee and the WB/IMF through the *Core Principles Liaison Group*: its remit is to draw up methods for assessing different aspects of the financial sector and for setting up new capital standards. In its most recent public statement (IMF, 2003), concern was expressed that the programme is turning out to be costly, stretching IMF/World Bank resources. Though these reports are thorough, there is a question about their necessity, especially among the G-10 countries, which are reported on by the organisations such as the OECD and produce their own extensive statistics and analyses.

## 4.6.2. Ongoing Issues Related to International Bank Supervision

International coordination of banking regulation and supervision has come a very long way since the formation of the Basel Committee in 1975. However, there continue to be a number of outstanding issues to be addressed.

### *Harmonisation of national supervisory arrangements*

Increasingly, bilateral meetings are being used to improve harmonisation between supervisors of different countries. They are used to exchange information and draw up memoranda of understanding (MOU). The MOU broadly defines the areas in which the information exchange takes place, dealing with ongoing financial issues and firms. For example, Evans (2000) reports the UK's FSA has over 100 MOUs with other supervisors. Keeping the lines of communication open in the event of serious cross-border problems is very important, and requires contact and communication at both the formal and informal level.

### Improved compliance

Improved compliance with agreed standards set by bodies such as the Basel Committee. The traditional approach has been the assumption that once a standard (e.g. the Basel risk assets ratio) has been agreed upon, the members of the group would implement the new standard. However, there are problems with this method:

- Failure to apply the rules.
- Different interpretation of the rules (e.g. tier 2 capital – Basel 1).
- In the case of Basel, a membership limited to developed countries, though this is changing.
- For organisations such as IOSCO and IAIS, the membership is so large and the secretariat so small (6 and 5, respectively with 91 and 80, respectively country members) that the rules are impossible to enforce, even if these organisations saw enforcement as part of their remit, which they do not.
- Basel and IOSCO have attempted peer review but abandoned it for lack of resources, issues related to confidentiality (e.g. how much information does a member pass to the peer member conducting the review?) and a reluctance on the part of one member to pass judgement on another because it could upset bilateral relationships. The IMF and World Bank may be able to monitor compliance to standards laid down by the international supervisors because they have the expertise and resources, and already have detailed knowledge of most countries' financial sectors. The FSAP is a good example, though these bodies are already concerned that the assessments are stretching their resources. There is a more fundamental issue about whether the IMF/World Bank can be policy advisors/assessors and also act as neutral intermediaries, should a sovereign nation encounter problems repaying their external debt.
- Incentives could be put in place to encourage countries to cooperate with a compliance assessment and make the results public. Incentives could include using the assessments to reinforce attempts at financial reform by a government, getting better ratings from external agencies and the markets, obtaining lower risk weights for government and bank borrowing in a given country, and being given better access to IMF and World Bank loans. Finally, the market would form a poor opinion of countries that did not publish their reports.

### Improved disclosure

Improved disclosure by financial firms is an important component of effective international supervision because it can improve market discipline. The disclosure can be direct, provided by the firms themselves (e.g. pillar 3 of Basel 2) or indirect, where the ratings published by independent rating agencies are used. A more radical suggestion is to use spreads on subordinated debt as an indicator of the health of a financial firm. The Federal Reserve Bank of Chicago has provided some evidence that these spreads are a significant indicator of the creditworthiness of banks but to date, there is no serious move to use them for supervisory purposes.

The Financial Stability Forum (2001) reported the results of a working group looking at disclosure by banks, hedge funds, insurance firms and securities firms. The purpose of the exercise was to issue recommendations on an improved regime of disclosure and the incentives needed to ensure firms participate. The main recommendations called for timely disclosure (at least semi-annual and preferably quarterly) of financial data drawn from a firm's risk management practices. In addition to data on market risk, credit risk, liquidity risk, etc. qualitative information should be provided. The report also called for more information on intra-period disclosures or issues such as the methodology behind the production of statistics.

However, it is important to bear in mind the costs and benefits of disclosure. For example, supervisors rarely disclose the overall assessment of the riskiness of a particular bank because of the effect it might have on the markets if a bank is pronounced "high" risk. This in turn would adversely affect the incentives of the bank to fully disclose its position to the supervisors, and/or to go for broke in the hope of getting the bank out of a problem before the supervisor finds out.

## Participation and cooperation by developing countries/emerging markets

All of the key international bodies concerned with prudential supervision have their memberships dominated by the industrialised countries, while the developing nations are normally the recipients of aid and loan packages by the IMF, World Bank, etc. However, greater participation of the emerging market countries is vital if international financial stability is to be achieved, and this is beginning to happen. For example, 13 emerging market central banks are members of the Bank for International Settlements, in contrast to its predominantly western focus at the time of its establishment. The Basel Core Principles Liaison Committee has members drawn from developing nations.

## Harmonisation of accounting standards

There are significant differences in the application of accounting standards, even among industrialised countries. In the United States, pre-Enron, the standards were used to ensure that those looking at a firm's accounts would get a "true and fair view" of the firm. The result was a proliferation of accounting rules which, in Europe, are regarded as too onerous. Also, many non-Anglo Saxon countries view firms' accounts as serving a different purpose, such as providing information to creditors and employees. For example, in Germany, methods (e.g. for depreciation) using published accounts must be approved by the tax authorities because tax is determined from the published profits. By contrast, tax authorities in Anglo Saxon countries do not use these accounts to assess tax. In the USA, the Sarbanes–Oxley Act (2002) introduced new, stricter rules designed to prevent a repeat of the poor accounting practices discovered after the spectacular problems uncovered at the bankrupt Enron and WorldCom. External auditors for a firm may no longer offer consulting services, and there are strict new corporate governance rules which apply to all employees and directors of a company. CEOs and CFOs must certify the health of all reports filed with the Securities and Exchange Commission, and face stiff fines/prison sentences if they certify false accounts. A new independent board is to oversee the accounting profession. While the US experience prompted authorities in other countries to re-examine their laws, no country has introduced new laws similar to Sarbanes–Oxley.

There has been significant progress in the resolution of differences, and a convergence of global standards in accounting. In May 2000, IOSCO agreed to allow the International Accounting Standards Committee (IASC) to produce a set of 30 core accounting standards, that would apply globally. After some debate over structure, the International Accounting Standards Board (IASB) was formed in 2001, with 14 members, from 9 countries: 5 from the USA, 2 from the UK, and 1 member each from, respectively, Australia, Canada, France, Germany, Japan, South Africa and Switzerland.[47] A Standards Advisory Council (SAC) was established to advise the IASB. The IASB has produced one set of international accounting standards (IAS) so that a transaction in any country is accounted for in the same way. A firm meeting these standards could list themselves on any stock exchange, including, it is hoped, the New York Stock Exchange.

In June 2002, the European Commission (EC) agreed that all EU firms listed on a regulated exchange would prepare consolidated accounts in accordance with the IAS from 2005 onwards. In October 2002, it was announced that the IASB and the US Financial Accounting Standards Board (FASB) were committed to achieving convergence between their respective standards by 2005. Should convergence be achieved, the Securities and Exchange Commission (SEC) could accept financial statements from non-US firms which use IAS – they would not have to comply with the US GAAP (Generally Accepted Accounting Principles). However, the issue of whether foreign firms operating in the USA will have to conform to Sarbanes–Oxley remains unresolved – many countries are seeking to have their companies exempted. A separate dispute has arisen over one standard, IAS 39. Banks' financial assets and liabilities are currently reported on the accounts at book value. In earlier periods when few bank assets and liabilities (e.g. loans, deposits) were traded, holding them at book value was not controversial. IAS 39 would make accounting statements more transparent with respect to derivatives – many of the markets for futures, options, etc. are large and liquid due to the growth of derivatives and securitisation. The IASB proposes to replace book value with "fair value" – the market price of the financial instrument. European banks, especially the French, objected on two grounds. Not all financial instruments are traded in liquid markets, so obtaining a market value is difficult. For options, futures, etc. that are traded frequently, the concern is that fair value would lead to more volatile accounts. In late 2004, the European Commission and its Parliament agreed to adopt IAS 39 but removed two of its provisions to assuage the banks' concerns. However, in the USA, the Securities and Exchange Commission (SEC) will not allow European firms to use international rules unless there is greater transparency. The FSAB has threatened to halt its efforts to converge GAAP and international standards. As this book goes to press, the issue has not been resolved, though HSBC has announced it will adopt the new rules independent of what the EC does. It joins UBS, Dresdner, and other key banks which already use them.

---

[47] See Table 4.6. The IASB is an independent foundation with a board and group of trustees. The trustees include, among others, Paul Volcker (former Fed Chairman) and a former chairman of the US SEC. Board members are chosen according to technical expertise.

## 4.7. Conclusion

This chapter began with a review of the reasons for regulating financial markets, and explained why banks tend to be singled out for special regulation. The reader was introduced to key terms such as financial fragility, contagion and systemic risk. The bulk of the chapter focused on the Basel Committee, and its efforts to establish common global regulatory standards for international banks. Rapid financial innovation, together with obvious gaps and inconsistencies in Basel 1, resulted in a major amendment on the treatment of market risk. Proposals for a new "Basel 2" were put forward in 2000, with a recommendation to change the treatment of credit risk, and introduce a new capital charge for operational risk. Pillars 2 and 3, dealing, respectively, with supervisory practices and market disclosure, were added to create a comprehensive system of global bank regulation. It would allow banks to "mix and match" the way capital charges are assessed for credit, market and operational risk. Basel 2 gives banks incentives to employ their own internal models, to achieve convergence in the amount of regulatory and economic capital set aside by banks. The original proposals were attacked by practitioners and academics alike, and Basel's own quantitative impact studies indicate many banks will experience a net increase in the amount of capital they are required to set aside. Additional consultative documents made substantial concessions in response to critics, and Basel 2 was adopted by the Basel Committee in June 2004.

The United States has already declared its hand. An announcement by its regulators means only 10 to 20 US banks will use the most advanced methods to compute their capital charges; the other 8000 or so will continue to use Basel 1, and the 1996 market risk amendment. Failure to bring the USA on board could undermine the authority of the Basel Committee. Whatever its fate, the protracted debate over the content of Basel 2 illustrates the complexities of trying to regulate 21st century banks.

The final sections of the chapter showed that while the objectives of the Basel Committee are important, other organisations are involved in global regulation and there are other key issues, such as the need for a global set of accounting standards.

Chapter 5 looks at the regulation of banks in countries with key international financial centres. The EU is also included, to round out the coverage of banking regulation in the developed world. All of these countries (except the US) plan to integrate the Basel 2 into their domestic regulations, which is why the global regulations were examined first. However, national prudential regulations are also important, and either influence or are influenced by the structure of their respective banking systems. Furthermore, a study of the different systems raises a number of diverse issues, ranging from the optimal number of regulators to problems achieving a single banking market within the EU.

# BANK STRUCTURE AND REGULATION: UK, USA, JAPAN, EU

## 5.1. Introduction

Having reviewed international regulation in Chapter 4, this chapter looks at bank structure and regulation in the United Kingdom, the United States, the European Union and Japan. The UK is singled out for special scrutiny (section 5.2) for a number of reasons. London is a leading international financial centre. It has also undergone major financial reforms twice in just over a decade. Big Bang, 1986, ushered in a period of functional but self-regulation, though the Bank of England was responsible for the prudential regulation of banks. However, by 1997 it was "all change" again: supervision was divorced from the central bank, and a monolithic single regulator created. Scrutiny of the British experience provides a unique insight into many of the debates on different types of financial regulation.

Section 5.3 reviews the structure and regulation of the American banking system. New York is a key international financial centre, but the approach to regulation (and the resulting structure) provides a stark contrast with the United Kingdom and many other countries. The Japanese system is discussed in section 5.4. The world's second largest economy underwent major financial reforms in the late 1990s, largely in response to a severe financial crisis.

The situation in the European Union introduces a whole new set of issues. What is the optimal form of regulation in an economic union which, in 2004, will begin the process of admitting ten new diverse countries? As Europe struggles to integrate its banking and financial markets, American reforms make the emergence of nation-wide banking more likely. Why is it proving so difficult to achieve a single financial market, especially at the retail level, with a free flow of financial services across frontiers? There is also the question of the European Central Bank's role in the event of financial crisis in one or several EU states, when prudential regulation is the responsibility of individual member states.

This chapter also looks at how bank and other financial regulations have influenced bank structure, and vice versa. New trends appear to be emerging; such as the separation of responsibilities for monetary control and regulation, though the USA is an important notable exception. It is evident that no country has yet struck an optimal balance between the application of free market principles in the financial sector and protection of the public interest.

## 5.2. Bank Structure and Regulation in the UK

### 5.2.1. Background

The structure of the UK banking system was covered briefly in Chapter 1. The UK's banking system falls into the "restricted universal" category, because banks are discouraged from owning commercial concerns. It is made up of: *commercial banks* consisting of the "big four" UK banks, HSBC (Hong Kong & Shanghai Banking Corporation), the Royal Bank of Scotland group, HBOS (Halifax-Bank of Scotland) and Barclays,[1] with tier 1 capital in 2002 ranging from $35 billion (HSBC) to $18 billion (Barclays),[2] and the Group, together with about a dozen or so other major banks including Lloyds-TSB ($13.3 billion), Abbey National, Standard Chartered and Alliance and Leicester ($2.5 billion). The big four, and some of the other banks, engage in retail, wholesale and investment banking, and some have insurance subsidiaries. By the turn of the century, many of the traditional English *merchant banks* had been bought by foreign concerns, beginning with Deutsche's purchase of Morgan Grenfell bank in 1988. Kleinwort-Benson was bought by Dresdner, and Warburgs by the Union Bank of Switzerland. Barings, having collapsed in 1995, was bought by ING, but later closed.

Some building societies converted to banks following the **Building Societies Act, 1986**. Effective January 1987, the Act allowed building societies to convert to bank plc status,[3] to be supervised by the Bank of England, and protected from hostile takeover for five years. Most of the top ten (by asset size) building societies in 1986 had, by the new century, given up their mutual status. The early conversions were Abbey National (1989), Bristol and West, Cheltenham and Gloucester (1992; a subsidiary of Lloyds-TSB). Building societies that converted between 1995–7 were the Halifax (after a merger with Leeds BS), Alliance & Leicester, Northern Rock and the Woolwich (taken over by Barclays in 2000). Birmingham Midshires was purchased by the Halifax in 1999; Bradford & Bingley converted in 2000.

*Building societies* have a long history in British retail finance. Members of a society paid subscriptions, and once there was enough funding, a selection procedure determined the member who would receive funds for house purchase or building. The early societies were attached to licensed premises (e.g. the Golden Cross Inn in Birmingham, 1775) and were wound up after all members had paid for their houses. The first legislation on them was passed in 1836.[4] In 1845, permanent societies began to form, such as the Chesham Building Society. Members kept a share (deposit) account at a society and could, after a period of time, expect to be granted a mortgage. Over time, depositors and mortgagees were not necessarily from the same group.[5]

As mutual organisations, every customer (depositor or borrower) has a share in the society, with the right to vote on key managerial changes. Each vote carries the same weight, independent of the size of the deposit mortgage or loan.

---

[1] With the merger of the Halifax and the Bank of Scotland, Lloyds TSB dropped to fifth place in 2002.

[2] *Source: The Banker*, "Top 1000 by Country", July 2002.

[3] Two-thirds of a building society's "shareholders" (each with one vote) had to approve the conversion.

[4] The Benefit Building Societies Act in 1836, followed by the Building Societies Acts in 1874 and 1894.

[5] See Boddy (1980) and Boleat (1982) for more detail on the background to building societies.

In 1984, an informal but effective cartel linking the building societies dissolved after Abbey National broke ranks. By this time, many of the larger societies viewed the "big four"[6] and other banks as their main competitors. The Building Societies Act (1986) took effect in January 1987, and allowed building societies to offer a full range of retail banking services typical of a bank. The Act specified the financial activities a building society could undertake, namely:

1. Offering a money transmission service through cheque books and credit cards.
2. Personal loans, unsecured.
3. Foreign currency exchange.
4. Investment management and advice.
5. Stockbroking.
6. Provision and underwriting of insurance.
7. Expansion into other EU states.
8. Real estate services.

However, there were important restrictions: 90% of a building society's assets had to be residential mortgages, and wholesale money plus deposits could not exceed 20% of liabilities, subsequently raised to 40%, then 50%.

The 1986 Act also gave these organisations the option of converting to bank status, and as a result, the number of building societies fell dramatically as Table 5.1 shows. The conversions between 1995 and 1997 resulted in two-thirds of the assets being transferred out of the sector.

**Table 5.1  Number of UK Building Societies, 1900–2002**

|      | Societies | Branches |
|------|-----------|----------|
| 1900 | 2286      | na       |
| 1960 | 726       | 985      |
| 1980 | 273       | 5684     |
| 1984 | 190       | 6816     |
| 1988 | 131       | 6912     |
| 1992 | 105       | 5765     |
| 1996 | 88        | 4613     |
| 1999 | 67        | 2502     |
| 2001 | 65        | 2101     |
| 2002 | 65        | 2101     |
| 2003 | 63        | 2100     |

*Sources*: BuckleThompson (1998). Figures for 1999–2002 from Building Societies Association (2003), *Building Societies Yearbook*, London: Building Societies Association.

---

[6] In 1984, the "big four" consisted of Barclays, the Midland, National Westminster and Lloyds.

Table 5.2   A Selection of UK Building Societies, 2003–2004

| Rank (by Asset Size) | Society | Assets* (£bn/mn) |
|---|---|---|
| 1 | Nationwide | 85.41 bn |
| 4 | Portman | 14.09 bn |
| 18 | Scarborough | 1.29 bn |
| 52 | Buckinghamshire | 116 mn |
| 63 | Century | 18 mn |

*Source:* The Building Societies Association, www.bsa.org.uk/Information – "Assets of Authorised UK Building Societies". *Some firms reported in 2003, others during 2004.

A *revised Building Societies Act* was passed in 1997 to make mutual status a more attractive option. It relaxes the prescriptive 1986 Act by allowing mutuals to undertake all forms of banking unless explicitly prohibited. In addition, any converted building society which attempts a hostile takeover of another building society loses its own five-year protection from takeover. Nonetheless, important restrictions continued to be placed on their assets and liabilities. At least 75% of their assets must be secured by residential property, and 50% of funding has to come from shareholder deposits.

There is considerable variation in the size of the remaining building societies, as Table 5.2 shows. In 2003, the building society sector had 18% of the outstanding household mortgage market and 18% of personal deposits.

Building societies had been regulated by an independent Building Societies Commission (BSC). Under the *Financial Services and Markets Act* (2000), the BSC was subsumed by the Financial Services Authority (FSA – see below), and large parts of the previous legislation relating to building societies became redundant, though similar rules have been imposed by the FSA.

An increasing number of *non-bank firms* offer some retail banking services. Good examples are the supermarkets, Sainsbury, Tesco and Safeway. They offer basic deposit and loan facilities. Virgin plc is one of several firms that offers a product whereby savings and mortgages (a condition of holding the account) are operated as one account. All these firms either operate as a separate subsidiary, subject to regulation by the FSA, or use an established bank to offer these services (e.g. as a joint venture), such as the Royal Bank of Scotland, HBOS and Abbey National. For this reason, it is debatable whether these firms are genuine non-banks. Insurance firms such as the Prudential and Scottish Widows offer a retail banking service without branches, relying on postal, telephone and internet accounts to deliver their services.

*Finance Houses* or non-bank credit institutions account for a tiny proportion of UK funding. They borrow from banks, etc., provide instalment credit to the personal and commercial sectors, and are involved in leasing and factoring (purchase all or some of the debts owed to a company – the price is below the book value of the debt (assets)).

### Box 5.1   Mutual Status versus Shareholder Ownership

As the number of building societies fall, the question arises as to whether a mutual organisation in financial services is superior to a firm with plc (public limited company) status, that is, one owned by shareholders. The answer is equivocal. Mutual status means that each "member" of the building society (and in the UK, insurance firms) has a single vote on matters involving major changes in strategy. By contrast, plc or stock bank status means bank customers can "purchase" financial products from the firm without necessarily holding equity shares in the bank, making the ownership of the bank independent of the customers using it. Furthermore, the greater the number of shares held, the greater the voting power of that shareholder. This means mutual banks are less dependent on external finance than stock banks, which can be advantageous to management for a number of reasons.

(1) Management has the choice between keeping interest margins high, thereby increasing the revenue for the firm, allowing it to increase reserves OR increasing market share with very narrow interest margins (subject to costs being covered).

(2) Depositors and borrowers can be shielded from fluctuating interest rates, in the short to medium term, because managers can respond more slowly to changes in market rates of interest. For example, if interest rates are thought to be temporarily rising, homeowners can be protected by not raising mortgage rates in line with the rising market rate. Likewise, depositors can be protected in periods of falling rates. Even if the

### Box 5.1   (Continued)

rate changes are thought to be long-term, borrowers or depositors can be cushioned from the changes for a period of time. Since the customers are also the owners of the society, they are likely to support this type of action, though any shielding of depositors will be at the expense of mortgagees, and vice versa. It is less easy to justify such action if it is at the expense of profits and shareholders are not necessarily the customer.

More generally, the presence of mutual financial institutions increases the diversity of the retail financial sector, creating more competition and giving consumers greater choice. On the other hand:

(3) Agency problems are present, independent of ownership structure. It means the interests of the customer–shareholder (building societies) or shareholder (banks) may be undermined by the manager trying to maximise his or her utility. In both cases, the source of the problem is asymmetric information (managers know more about the state of the firm) and incomplete contracts (owners can never draw up a contract with managers which specifies every action to be taken given that future events are unpredictable). Nonetheless, it is likely that the managers will be more accountable in a stock company, given that they are bound by some minimum profit constraint because of the threat of takeover. The constraint on the building society manager is less pronounced because depositors/mortgagees, with less information and higher switching costs,[7] are less likely to move their accounts elsewhere. Also, management of the mutual is less concerned about the possibility of takeover, which again reduces the accountability of decisions and action compared those of the plc bank.

(4) In the UK, the option to convert under the 1986 Building Societies Act left building societies vulnerable to "carpet baggers". These agents would open an account with a small deposit, then, as a "shareholder", demand that the society allow their members to vote on conversion to plc status. If the resolution is put forward by the required number of members, only a 50% majority of those voting is required. If put forward by the directors, then the resolution to convert is passed only if 50% of investing members vote, and 75% of those vote in favour. If there is a vote to convert, reserves of the society are divided up and distributed equally among members, meaning the new account holders could earn between £300 and £500, sometimes more. Most remaining building societies have tried to stop the practice by imposing restrictions on new members. For example, Nationwide, should it go plc, explicitly states that new shareholders (opening accounts or taking out mortgages, etc. after a certain date) would have their part of the windfall go to charity. Other societies restrict conversion windfalls to those who have been members for at least 2 years. Over 20 building societies agreed in 1999 general meetings that any resolution to convert would require a 75% majority to pass.

(5) "Mutual" shares are not tradable on a secondary market, unlike shares held in the plc bank, making them far less liquid.

*Friendly Societies* were first defined in law in 1793. As mutual organisations, members make contributions to a fund which in turn can provide relief for a member in times of hardship – e.g. sickness, old age, unemployment. Some provide a form of insurance,

---

[7] Shares can be sold with relative ease; switching accounts is more difficult, especially for customers with mortgages.

and often provide disproportionate amounts (in terms of the amounts paid in) to those who encounter hardship. Since the 2000 Financial Services and Markets Act, they have been regulated by the FSA, though many of the rules have been carried over from the 1992 Friendly Societies Act. In 2001, 104 societies were authorised to engage in new business, and another 247 not authorised because of declining membership or their very small size.

There are also *investment institutions* such as pension funds, insurance firms, unit trusts, investment trusts, and so on. These are not banks in any sense of the term, but investment tools, often managed or offered by banks.

Table 5.3 provides a snapshot of the UK financial structure in 2002. Table 5.4 reports the key ratios for the top 5 banks in the UK.

Table 5.3   UK Banking Structure 2002

| Financial institutions | Number | Assets ($bn) |
| --- | --- | --- |
| All banks resident in UK | 517 | 4663 |
| *Foreign* (branches & subsidiaries) | 281 | 2161 |
| *UK incorporated* | 236 | 2472 |
| (1) Commercial | 35 | 1455 |
| (2) BS + mortgage banks | 78 | 683 |
| (3) Other UK owned | 53 | 52 |
| (4) Foreign owned | 70 | 281 |
| Insurance companies | 782 | 1018 |
| Life | 182 | 942 |
| Non-life | 600 | 76 |

*Source:* IMF (2003), which claim sources from the Bank of England, BIS, FSA, and their own estimates.

Table 5.4   Top UK Banks (by tier 1 capital) in 2003

| Bank | Tier 1 capital ($m) | Assets ($m) | Cost:income (%) | ROA (%) | Basel risk assets ratio (%) |
| --- | --- | --- | --- | --- | --- |
| HSBC Holdings | 38 949 | 759 246 | 59.44 | 1.27 | 13.30 |
| Royal Bank of Scotland | 27 652 | 649 402 | 55.65 | 1.18 | 11.70 |
| HBOS | 23 836 | 512 168 | 50.70 | 0.92 | 10.43 |
| Barclays Bank | 22 895 | 637 946 | 58.48 | 0.81 | 12.85 |
| Lloyds TSB Group | 15 297 | 334 329 | 55.40 | 1.26 | 9.60 |

*Source: The Banker,* July 2003.

## 5.2.2. UK Financial Reforms in the late 20th Century

In 1986, the "City"[8] of London underwent "Big Bang", or a series of financial reforms to change the structure of the financial sector and encourage greater competition. The reforms gave UK banks and other financial firms opportunities to expand into new areas. At the same time, London wanted to maintain its reputation for quality, and new financial regulations were introduced, designed to ensure continued financial stability within a more competitive environment. Just over a decade later, banks and other financial sectors were subject to major changes in regulation again. One objective of this section is to explore how and why regulation changed in such a dramatic fashion.

The Financial Services Act (1986) was the culmination of a number of radical reforms of the UK financial system, known as "Big Bang". The government put pressure on the London Stock Exchange to get rid of cartel-like rules. The first reform was in 1982 when ownership of stock exchange firms by non-members was raised from 10% to 29.9%. By 1986, new firms could trade on the stock exchange without buying into member firms. *Dual capacity* dealing was introduced, eliminating the distinction between "brokers" and "jobbers". Stock exchange members became "market makers", that is, making markets in a stock *and* acting as brokers: buying and selling shares from the public. Minimum commissions were also abolished.

These reforms made it attractive for banks to enter the stockbroking business, and most of the major banks (both commercial and merchant) purchased broking and jobbing firms or opted for organic growth in this area. Around the same time, the traditional merchant banks became, effectively, investment banks by expanding into other areas, such as trading: equities, fixed income [bonds] and later, proprietary trading, asset management, global custody and consultancy.

Some commercial banks purchased investment banks (e.g. the Trustee Savings Bank bought Hill Samuel) while others, having purchased firms to offer stockbroking services, used them as a base to expand into other areas of investment banking. The only exception was Lloyds Bank, which opted to focus largely on retail banking, with some commercial banking.

There were other important reforms of the UK financial system that affected banking and the financial structure.

- Competition and Credit Control (1972): terminated the banking cartel, among other changes. The cartel was an agreement among banks that the deposit rate would be 2% below base rate; personal loan rates would be 1–3% above base, and no interest was paid on current accounts.
- The Special Supplementary Deposit Scheme:[9] if interest earning deposits grew beyond a certain limit, banks were subject to an increasing reserve ratio (a tax on banks). The objective was to reduce deposit rates on accounts, which in turn would help to keep down building society mortgage rates and government debt servicing charges.

---

[8] London's financial district is known as "The City" or "Square Mile". For many years, financial firms were concentrated in the square mile of the City of London, but over the past 20 years, have spread to Canary Wharf, east of the City. However, the term, "the City" continues to apply to all firms in the financial services sector.

[9] Also known as the "corset", it was used on and off from December 1973–74, December 1976–77 and 1978–80.

- End of exchange controls on sterling (1979).
- The collapse of an informal but effective building society interest rate cartel (1984).
- The Building Societies Act (1979; amended 1987).
- The Banking Act (1979; amended 1987).
- Financial Services Act (1986).
- The 1998 Banking Act.
- The Financial Services and Markets Act (2000).

The legislation on Building Societies has already been discussed, and the last four acts listed are discussed below, to illustrate how the regulation of UK financial institutions evolved over a relatively short period of time.

### 5.2.3. The Financial Services Act, 1986

The main objective of this Act was the protection of investors in the "Big Bang" era. *Self-regulation* was introduced for all financial firms. A two-tier system, the lower tier consisted of SROs or self-regulatory organisations, which would regulate different functions. Originally, there were six SROs, each responsible for the regulation of futures dealers, securities dealers, investment managers, personal investment, life insurance and unit trusts. The number was later reduced to three: the Securities and Futures Association (SFA), IMRO (the Investment Managers Regulatory Organisation) and PIA (the Personal Investment Authority). These SROs reported to the Securities and Investment Board (SIB), the upper tier, which was an umbrella organisation with statutory powers. Chart 5.1 shows the organisational structure under this regulatory regime. Together, they were responsible for ensuring the proper conduct of business by the investment community.

The Act required all firms belonging to a SRO to adhere to a number of rules. Managers had to meet "fit and proper" standards. Depending on the nature of the business, adequate capital was to be set aside. General conduct of business rules set by the relevant SRO had to be met. All members contributed to a compensation scheme for investors should a member go bankrupt and/or default on their obligations. Claims up to £30 000 were met in full, and for sums between £30 000 and £50 000, 90% of losses were reimbursed, for a maximum payout of £48 000.

In addition to the SROs, there were three prudential regulators, the Bank of England for banks, the Building Societies Commission for building societies, and the Department of Trade and Industry for insurance regulation. The self-regulating bodies were thought to be the best judges of the standards and rules of conduct for their members because they have more information and knowledge about the operations of the financial business in question (e.g. insurance companies, stockbroking, etc.). State regulators will always be less well informed. It was also argued that public regulators can develop a close relationship with the firms they regulate, causing laxity in their enforcement of regulations, and in some instances, a vested interest in trying to protect insolvent firms from closure, known as *regulatory forbearance* (or *regulatory capture*). The SRO system would prevent this problem from arising. However, though there is substantial evidence of this problem occurring among

Chart 5.1   UK Self-Regulatory, Functional regulation (based on the Financial Services Act, 1986).

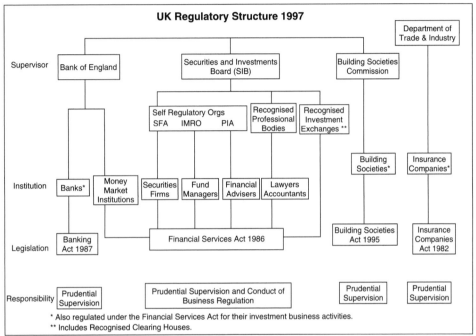

*Source*: Jackson, P. (2000), Unified Supervision the UK Experience, *Financial Regulator*, **5**(3), 50–59.

SFA: Securities and Futures Association
IMRO: Investment Managers Regulatory Association
PIA: Personal Investment Authority
DTI: Department of Trade and Industry

state regulators (for example, US regulators in the 1980s), there is no reason why it may not occur under self-regulation. Cynics often argue that SROs and the firms they regulate are more like a club.

There are also arguments which favour regulation by government bodies. Though a SRO may have better information with which to draw up an impressive set of regulations, their enforcement powers are minimal, though the British system granted statutory powers to the SIB. Public regulators can resolve the information problem by hiring individuals with extensive experience in the relevant financial business, though normally salaries in the public sector are lower, making it difficult to attract the best expertise. Another potential problem is that self-regulation might encourage collusive behaviour among firms because of the close connections between the practitioners who regulate, and the regulated. The increase in the number of financial conglomerates is also cited as a factor which favours state regulation. Under self-regulation conglomerates face costly compliance – having to satisfy the requirements of multiple regulators rather than just one single body. But this point is more an argument in favour of a single, but not necessarily state, regulator.

## 5.2.4. The 1979 UK Banking Act (Amended, 1987)

Prior to this Act there was no specific banking law in the UK. Prompted by the secondary banking crisis in 1972, the Bank of England, for the first time in its history, was assigned *formal* responsibility for the prudential regulation of UK banks. The Bank of England was nationalised in 1946, and had been responsible for price and general financial stability, answering to Her Majesty's (HM) Treasury. The 1979 Act covered clearing[10] and merchant banks, finance and discount houses, and foreign banks. The Bank of England decided on whether a firm was given bank status.[11] To qualify for bank status, the firm had to offer facilities for current and deposit accounts, overdraft and loan facilities to corporate/retail customers, and at least one of: foreign exchange facilities, foreign trade documentation and finance (through the issue of bills of exchange and promissory notes), investment management services, or a specialised banking product. Also, the Bank of England had to be satisfied that the "bank" had an excellent reputation in the financial community, the affairs of the bank were conducted with integrity and prudence, the bank could manage its financial affairs, and "fit and proper" criteria were applied to all directors/controllers/managers. These conditions ensured an ongoing supervisory function for the Bank, because it could revoke bank status at any time.

A *Depositors Protection Fund* was established under the 1979 Banking Act – all recognised banks contribute to the fund. In line with EU policy the current protection is: compensation for up to 90% of any one deposit, for deposits up to a maximum of £35 000 or the equivalent in euros. The 10% *co-insurance* means no individual depositor is ever repaid the full amount of the deposit held in a bank that fails – the maximum payout is £31 500. The reason for co-insurance is to give each depositor an incentive for monitoring the health of his/her bank.

The key *1987 amendments* to the Banking Act included the following.

1. A clause "encouraging" auditors to warn supervisors of bank fraud, with auditors being given greater access to official information.
2. Exposure rules were changed – the Bank was to be informed if the exposure of any single borrower exceeded 10% of the bank's capital, and was to be consulted if a loan to a single borrower exceeded 25% of its capital.
3. Any investors with more than 5% of a bank's shares must declare themselves.
4. The purchase of more than 15% of a UK bank by a foreign bank may be blocked by the authorities.

---

[10] This book does not use the term "clearing bank". It was originally used for the "high street" banks which were members of the London Clearing House, that is the "big four" banks at the time, the Midland, National Westminster, Barclays and Lloyds. There were also a few smaller banks. The term is largely redundant now, because some of these banks fit the definition of commercial banks and some are financial conglomerates, offering commercial and investment banking services to varying degrees, along with insurance, real estate, stockbroking and other services.

[11] The 1979 Act recognised two classes of financial institution – banks and licensed deposit institutions – but the 1987 amendment eliminated any distinction between the two.

5. A Board of Bank Supervision was established, the result of a recommendation of a committee set up after the rescue of the failing Johnson Matthey Bankers[12] by a Bank of England led lifeboat. The new Board assists the Bank of England in its bank supervisory role. It is chaired by the Bank's Governor but includes a number of independent members with a background in commercial banking.

There was no single disaster or scandal which prompted demands for a reform of the system, though the closure of BCCI (1991) and the collapse of Barings (1995) raised questions about the supervisory abilities of the Bank of England. Nor was there evidence of collusion between the Bank of England and regulated banks. However, practitioners and regulators alike recognised that the system was increasingly cumbersome, and ill-fitted to financial firms which had to answer to more than one of the SROs. After 1986, banks expanded into securities, stockbroking, insurance and a host of other financial activities. A major bank could find itself having to report to the Bank of England, comply with the rules set by different SROs, and answer to other prudential regulators. Lead regulators were designated for certain large banks. For example, the Bank of England had sole responsibility for the supervision of Barings Bank because Barings had *solo consolidation* status. The parent bank and its subsidiary, Barings Securities, produced one set of capital and exposure figures. With greater expertise in the securities area, the SFA might have demanded explicit changes in the Singapore operations had they been regulating Barings Securities.[13]

Thus, it seems a number of factors were responsible for another major shake-up of the British financial sector. In just over a decade, the UK financial sector was the target of more regulatory change than it had experienced over the entire century. In May 1997 the Chancellor of the Exchequer announced that the Bank of England was to be "independent" of the Treasury. A Monetary Policy Committee, chaired by the Governor of the Bank, would meet monthly and announce what the central bank interest rate is to be, with a view to meeting inflation targets set by the government. Less than a fortnight later an end to self-regulation by function was announced. Responsibility for all aspects of financial regulation (e.g. prudential regulation and conduct of business) was given to a single state regulator, the Financial Services Authority or FSA. The role of the FSA is discussed below.

The *1998 Bank of England Act* transferred the Bank of England's supervisory and related powers to the newly created Financial Services Authority. Though the Bank of England's <u>formal</u> role as prudential regulator was short-lived, it continues to share responsibility for financial stability, with the FSA and HM Treasury under a Memorandum of Understanding (see below). As a consequence of the Act, the FSA took over responsibility for the authorisation, and, where applicable, the prudential regulation of all financial institutions, and the supervision of clearing and settlements and financial markets.[14]

The 1998 Act also transfers responsibility for the Deposit Protection Board, which administers the Deposit Protection Fund, to the FSA. The Deputy Governor of the Bank of

---

[12] See Chapter 6 for more detail.

[13] See Chapter 7 for more detail.

[14] The 1998 Act also transferred responsibility for the management of government debt from the Bank of England to an executive agency of government, the Debt Management Office. Treasury officials set the agenda for the Chief Executive of the DMO in the annual Debt Management Report. See Blair (1998).

England responsible for financial stability is a member of the board but the FSA Chairman chairs it.

The membership of the Board of Banking Supervision was changed by the 1998 Banking Act. It now consists of six independent members (with no executive responsibility in the FSA) and two *ex officio* members from the FSA. The independent members[15] decide who among them will act as Chair.

The **Financial Services and Markets Act** (FSM Act) was passed on 12 June 2000, after a record 2000 amendments, and established the Financial Services Authority as the sole regulator of all UK financial institutions. The FSA assumed its full powers by November 2001. It is bound, by statute, to:

- Maintain confidence in the UK financial system.
- Educate the public – with special reference to the risks associated with different forms of investing.
- Protect consumers but encourage them to take responsibility for their own financial decisions.
- Reduce financial crime.

The FSA is also obliged to be cost effective. It is required to use cost benefit analysis to demonstrate that the introduction of a regulation will yield benefits that outweigh any costs (e.g. compliance costs for banks).

The government has instructed the FSA to adopt some recommendations made by the Cruickshank (2000) bank review team. They include the introduction of CAT (charges, easy access, reasonable terms) standards for credit cards. The FSA is also reviewing the Banking Code, which sets the standards of service for personal banking. The banks' adherence to the code is thought to be weak. It is likely to be extended to include small business.

Cruickshank recommended the FSA be given an additional statutory objective of minimising any anti-competitive effects in markets arising from FSA regulations. Instead of imposing a fifth statutory obligation, the Financial Services and Markets Act emphasised the need to minimise any such effects, which will be monitored by the Office of Fair Trading, the Competition Commission and the Treasury. The need for the FSA to encourage competition among the firms it regulates was also noted in the Act, and it was given responsibility for developing a set of disclosure of information rules for mortgage lenders.

In May 2001, the FSA employed just over 2000, with regulatory responsibility for about 660 banks, 7500 investment firms, insurance firms with annual premiums of £48 billion, and over 40 000 investment advisors. The business generated by the firms regulated by the FSA accounts for just under 6% of UK GDP. The FSA is a private company, funded by levies paid by the financial firms it supervises.

The regulators merged to make up the FSA (see Chart 5.2) included the following.

- The Self-Regulatory Organisations: Securities and Investment Board, Securities and Futures Association, Personal Investment Authority and Investment Management Regulatory Organisation.

---

[15] Chosen by the Chancellor and the Chair of the FSA.

**Chart 5.2   A Single Financial Regulator in the UK (based on the Financial Services and Market Act, 2000).**

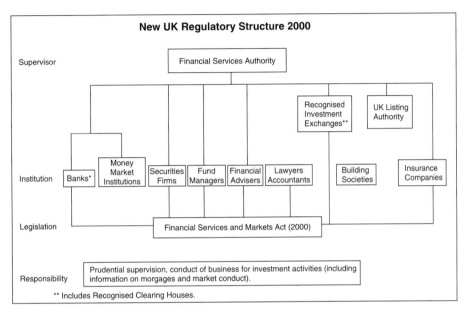

**New UK Regulatory Structure 2000**

*Source* : Jackson, P. (2000), Unified Supervision the UK Experience, *Financial Regulator*, **5**(3), 50–59.

- The banking supervision division of the Bank of England.
- The Register of Friendly Societies, Friendly Societies Commission.

In addition, in 2000, the FSA was given responsibility for:

- The Building Societies Commission.
- The Insurance Directorate at the Department of Trade and Industry.
- The UK Listing Authority, which regulates solicitors, accountants and actuaries, if their businesses offer financial services to a substantial degree.
- Credit unions.

The FSA reduced the 14 rule books associated with the different regulators to one FSA *Handbook*. The *Handbook* is more than several feet thick, and therefore, difficult to grasp! However, it is smaller than the sum of the 14 books it replaced. There are four prudential regulation regimes: banks, building societies, friendly societies and insurance.

To date, FSA rules focus on three areas: to ensure firms have the right systems and controls, to require management, especially senior management, to be responsible for complying with FSA rules, and to make staff aware of the FSA's view of what constitutes desirable behaviour. Tables 1 through 3 of the FSA Discussion Paper (2002) illustrate what the financial firms (e.g. banks, building societies, insurance) report in relation to financial information, systems and controls, and conduct of business. The large differences and discrepancies identified by the FSA is one of the reasons why it favours adopting a risk based approach to regulation (see below).

An inevitable consequence of a rule based regulatory system is the use of lawyers hired by firms not only to ensure compliance but also to look for any loopholes that might benefit the firm, which will lead to more rules. Their presence at meetings will discourage the free flow of information. Firms are reluctant to reveal information about their activities (especially those which are problematic) for fear of having new rules imposed on them. This problem is potentially very serious for contagion inclined sectors, such as commercial and retail banking.

The success of the "City" (London's financial district) has been partly due to getting regulation correctly balanced, that is, being adequately regulated but at the same time, allowing various firms to innovate, to maintain a competitive edge over other financial centres. However, a rule based system discourages innovation. When new ideas have been put to the FSA for approval, firms have to answer extensive lists of questions, and, it is reported, some are confronting long delays before a decision is taken.

Finally, though the FSA is considered a "one stop" integrated regulator of financial firms, there are other regulators. For example, there are numerous ombudsmen, the Office of Fair Trading, consumers groups and, in the case of non-investment markets such as foreign exchange dealing, firms still have to comply with codes laid down by the Bank of England.

## 5.2.5. Prudential Regulation by the FSA

The FSA's *Handbook of Rules and Guidance* consists of very long volumes, which cannot be covered in any detail here. For example, in the *Handbook*, the section on standards consists of a 686 page document, "The Interim Prudential Sourcebook for Banks", together with sourcebooks for building societies (503 pages), friendly societies, insurers and investment businesses.

Even though the FSA deals with the prudential concerns of all financial firms, the emphasis here is on how it regulates banks. The interim sourcebook for banks and building societies includes many of the regulations derived from the Banking Act, and its amendments. However, readers are reminded that regulation of banks (and other financial firms) is increasingly being driven by the European Union's directives and the Basel agreements and accords. Thus, rules governing capital and liquidity adequacy are largely determined by the EU and Basel agreements. Also, as a member of the European Union, the UK is committed to adopting the IASB accounting standards by 2005 for listed companies in the first instance (see Chapter 4 for more detail). However, there is nothing to stop the FSA from imposing additional rules and regulations. One of the most important is the risk based approach to regulation.

### The FSA's Risk Based Approach to Regulation: RTO

As supervisor for all financial institutions, the FSA is trying to move away from specific rules for each of the different types of financial institution. Of course, it is not possible to introduce a single system of supervision, because the prudential concerns vary depending on the institution. For banks, the issue is contagion caused by a problematic bank or banks which causes liquidity to dry up, leading, in time, to insolvency. For insurance firms, customers worried about the value of their policies will try to cash them in early. Keeping the financial markets liquid is critical to the success of the securities sector. So while some aspects of the regulation are unique (hence the different sourcebooks), the FSA is keen to introduce rules which apply across all financial institutions. They have done this by introducing a *risk based*, as opposed to *competition based*, approach to regulation.

The competition based approach has been adopted by the telecommunications and utilities sectors in the UK. After these industries were privatised, the decision was taken to place competition and good value for customers ahead of security of service supply (electricity, gas, water, etc.). This was achieved by creating several suppliers (e.g. gas, electricity, telephones) and encouraging competition. Firms are allowed to increase prices by the rate of inflation less some predetermined percentage, announced by the regulator.[16] The idea was to have the real price of these services fall over time.

The FSA opted for the risk based route, also known as **RTO** *(risk to our objectives)*, indicating that they consider the financial sector to be of such importance to the economy that risk management must take priority. According to the FSA, such an approach is necessary because of its statutory responsibility for maintaining the financial sector,[17] including minimising any adverse effects of competition between FSA regulated firms.

The RTO approach involves computing a score for each firm supervised by the FSA. The score will show the probability of the firm having an impact on the ability of the FSA to meet its four statutory objectives outlined earlier. The score is obtained from a simple equation:

**IMPACT SCORE = [Impact of the problem] × [Probability of the problem arising]**

A firm's score will determine how closely the FSA monitors it. If the impact score is low, then the firm is likely to be monitored through the completion of various checklist forms, while a high impact firm will require continuous meetings and regular visits made by the FSA.

Each firm is scored varying from A (very high risk) to D (low risk). The risk is not confined to the risk of financial instability, but any risks that might prevent the FSA from meeting its statutory obligations. So for example, firms might be designated high risk because:

- As deposit takers, the firm could be the target of panics about the quality of the bank.
- The firm conducts a business that could prevent the FSA from protecting consumer interests. For example, for the average consumer, valuation is difficult for products such as unit trusts, insurance and endowment mortgages.

---

[16] The formula used is the well-known "RPI – X", where RPI is the retail price index and X is determined by the regulator.
[17] However, as Farrant (2000) and others argue, the collapse of the electricity grid would pose as serious a problem to the infrastructure of an economy as would the collapse of the financial system. So why treat the financial sector (in particular, banks) as special?

- The activities of a firm might encourage a financial crime, such as money laundering and/or insider trading. After "9/11", banks, bureau de change outlets, and other financial firms have been asked to tighten procedures to guard against money laundering. In 2003, Northern Rock was fined £1.25 million by the Financial Services Authority for failing to comply with the rules on money laundering set out in the FSA's *Sourcebook*.

Note the emphasis on high impact financial firms in terms of how their actions affect the FSA's ability to fulfil its statutory obligations; NOT, say, systemic risk. However, any threats to systemic risk are dealt with through the special rules applied to different types of firms such as banks, building societies, insurance firms, and so on. For example, in Chapter 2, the special approach adopted for the supervision of financial conglomerates was discussed. In addition, the FSA has a memorandum of understanding with the Bank of England and HM Treasury – see below.

The FSA anticipates that 85% of the firms supervised by it will be given the lowest risk rating, D. High impact groups will include: major banks, the large insurance firms, the big broker-dealers, stock exchanges and big networks of independent financial advisors.

When the Bank of England was responsible for the supervision of banks, it was well known for employing a **consensus** approach to bank supervision. There was no formal examination of a bank's books by the supervisor, and ratios (with the exception of the Basel minimum and European directives) were negotiated rather than imposed. The BE relied on guidelines rather than strict rules. This approach had been eroding over time with the large increase in the number of banks.

In addition to computing an impact score, the FSA makes a number of specific demands on banks.

- The FSA sets the criteria for licensing banks and can reject an application or withdraw an existing licence.
- "Fit and proper" criteria are applied to key positions. The FSA must be notified if any person plans to take (or increase) control of a bank, and can refuse to sanction the change.
- In addition to the Basel risk assets ratios and requirements, the FSA sets an individual capital ratio for each bank, based on its risk profile. Capital requirements must be satisfied on a consolidated and solo basis. The risks of each bank are assessed by a firm-specific model.
- The FSA is in the process of developing a new approach to monitor banks' liquidity which is closely aligned to the systems used by the banks themselves.
- As part of the EU, UK banks must comply with the EU's large exposures directive (see section 5.5).
- There are no explicit rules on credit/investment policies, which is considered the domain for each bank's management group. However, the FSA must be satisfied with banks' procedures for taking, monitoring and controlling risk.
- Banks can be asked to supply regular information on asset quality if there is a reason to be concerned about them, but there is no established system for supplying data on classified or non-performing loans.
- Each bank must be externally audited, and have a system for independent internal audits. The FSA or external auditors can examine the internal audits, and external auditors must

inform the FSA of any concerns they might have. The FSA has the power to dismiss external auditors.

- On-site examinations are reserved for high impact firms. FSA supervisor staff may be supported by its risk management specialists and/or it may call in "skilled persons" (normally from an independent accounting firm) to help with any inspection. As has been noted, high impact banks may expect regular visits and frequent contact with senior management and directors. By contrast, low impact banks will be supervised off-site through monitoring of key ratios unless some event or revelation of excessive risk taking prompts site visits/contact with bank management. The FSA defends this approach on the grounds that this group of banks account for only 0.02% of deposit liabilities.
- Banks will face restrictions on overseas activities if the FSA is not satisfied with a bank's risk management system in one of its foreign business units.
- Banks are required to appoint a money laundering reporting officer who is approved by the FSA.

## 5.2.6. The Bank of England and Financial Stability

A central bank will always be involved in the preservation of financial stability because it will act as the lender of last resort, and/or play a key role in any lifeboat rescue, injecting any liquidity needed to stabilise markets. Financial stability is also a statutory obligation of the FSA, hence a **Memorandum of Understanding** was deemed essential. The MOU (Appendix 5 of the 1998 Bank of England Act) is between the Treasury, the FSA and the Bank of England. These organisations are jointly responsible for financial stability, including the reduction of systemic risk and undertaking official operations to prevent contagion. A tripartite standing committee was established, consisting of the respective heads of the three organisations, and chaired by the Chancellor. Though their deputies meet on a monthly basis, additional meetings take place in the event of any problem (e.g. a threatened bank failure) which could exacerbate systemic risk.

Under the MOU, an information sharing system has been put in place to ensure the FSA fulfils its obligation to supply the Bank with all the information needed to allow the Bank to meet is responsibilities in this area. In a recent IMF report (2003), the MOU is praised for its information sharing and clear line of responsibilities for each player. However, the report recommended that the FSA require banks to submit data (regularly) on classified/non-performing loans, pay greater attention to the supervision of market risk, improve the supervision of low impact firms, and address the issue of the potential for conflict of interest because it has to meet four statutory objectives.

## 5.2.7. A Single National Regulator?

There is a wide variety of regulatory systems around the world. In addition to the UK, Sweden, Denmark, Norway, Germany, Greece and Austria have single regulators for all financial firms. Canada has combined the supervision of financial and insurance firms (Office of the Superintendent of Financial Institutions) but securities firms are regulated by the provinces. Australia employs a "twin peaks" model, where the Australian Prudential Regulation Authority is separate from the central bank but conduct of business is the responsibility of the Australian Securities and Investment Commission. In Italy, the Banca d'Italia is responsible for prudential regulation and financial stability for banks and securities houses, while another body (CONSOB) deals with conduct of business issues. The Netherlands adopted a similar approach in 2002, but cross-sector activities are jointly regulated by the central bank and the insurance supervisor. In Japan, after recent reforms, the central bank shares bank supervision with the new regulator (since 2001), the Financial Services Authority; the system is reviewed in section 5.5.

In the United States, numerous bodies, both state and national, but including the central bank (the "Fed"), are responsible for prudential regulation with separate agencies regulating securities and insurance firms. Multiple regulation is regarded as an important means of guarding against collusion within the financial sector. However, some aspects of "self regulation" have come under fire. Recall from Chapter 1 the discussion of the settlement between the authorities and investment banks, following findings of a serious conflict of interest between banks' research departments and their investment banking divisions. The banks are members of the NYSE and NASD – both groups have been criticised for failing to spot the problem. The US system is discussed at length in the next section.

The UK introduced a single regulator relatively recently, as have other countries, though the UK has gone further in terms of the different types of financial firms the FSA supervises, and the wide range of objectives it must fulfil. This prompts the question of which regulatory model, if any, is superior. There are two issues. The first is the extent to which the central bank should be involved in the regulation of banks. The debate on the role of a central bank was aired in Chapter 1. The second issue to be discussed here is whether a single body should be given responsibility for regulation of the financial sector. First, as was noted earlier, the growth of financial conglomerates favours a single regulator, because functional regulation is not only costly for conglomerates but may leave gaps. Functional supervision is also less effective as product boundaries become less well defined: securitisation and the growth of derivatives means risks can be unbundled and traded, weakening the distinction between equity, debt and loans, and the firms which supply them. Subjecting firms to a system of functional regulation could create difficulties. In the UK prior to the creation of the FSA, a lead regulator was often assigned to the financial firms engaging in multiple financial activities, but this arrangement did not prevent regulatory failures such as the mis-selling of pensions, the Maxwell theft of pension funds, and a spectacular case of fraud at Barings. A single authority may be better at spotting potential difficulties at an earlier stage, and the adoption of a risk based scoring system should contribute towards integrated supervision. However, there is a danger that supervision will continue along functional lines when there is a single regulator employing about 2000.

The main case for a single regulator is that greater efficiency is achieved because of economies of scale and scope. These include:

- A single system of reporting for all firms. On the other hand, the data reported vary according to activities a given firm engages in. For example, the statistics for a bank are quite different from those of a stockbroking firm.

- Financial firms only need answer to a single regulator, which allows for a more effective system of communication, cooperation and coordination. This should mean the regulator can promote a public understanding of the financial services sector. In the UK, it is one of the FSA's statutory obligations.
- A single point of contact for regulated firms and consumers.
- A common approach can be adopted for issues which affect all firms; an example is the FSA's risk based approach.
- More efficient resource allocation is also achieved if the single regulator can pool resources for the regulation of firms and activities. The risk points system developed by the FSA is one example but there are also many instances where separate rules must be developed for specific sectors. In the case of the FSA, this point is illustrated by the numerous, lengthy sourcebooks that have been produced for each major financial sector.
- The FSA has developed a single framework for authorisation, supervision and investigation/discipline, training and competence, consumer relations and central services. However, it is too early to judge whether the obvious advantages from such a framework will be realised.
- A single regulator is more likely to be able to recruit from the pool of experts, who, for example, are able to assess market risk models and other bank systems.

Bannock (2002) argues three types of costs must be included to obtain an accurate measure of the cost of regulation. These are:

- Direct administration costs incurred by the FSA;
- Compliance costs borne by different parts of the financial sector; and
- Deadweight losses arising from market distortions created by regulation.

For example, the higher cost of regulatory compliance by independent advisors increases the cost of advice, which makes it uneconomic for them to assist the lower income groups, which may have the most to gain from such advice. There is also the potential for welfare gains (not mentioned by Bannock) if more financial firms are attracted to the UK because of the perception that the regulatory regime improves market quality and reputation. It is very difficult to measure deadweight losses (or gains). Excluding deadweight gains/losses, Bannock estimates the cost of UK regulation is £200 million (the FSA budget, 2001–2) plus £800 million in compliance costs, or in excess of £1 billion. These figures are at odds with those cited below, and disputed by Sykes (2002).

However, costs will be incurred by any type of regulation, and the challenge of the FSA/single regulator is to minimise the costs. The FSA must eliminate areas of overlap which existed under functional regulation with its multiple regulators. One of the FSA's statutory obligations is to be cost effective. The FSA's budget for 1999/2000 was lower in real terms than the sum of all the regulatory bodies that existed in the previous two years.[18] Its actual budget for 1999/2000 was £154.5 million, which rose to £164 million in 2001/2, an annual increase which is well below the rate of inflation. The budget is lower

---

[18] *Source:* Sykes (2002).

than Canada's Office of the Superintendent of Financial Institutions,[19] and less than 10% of US regulatory costs. Certainly, in these early years, it appears to be cost effective. Costs are met by fees charged to the supervised firms: determined by the size of the business and the number of financial activities in which it is engaged – the more diversified the firm, the higher the fees.[20]

Under multiple regulation, inconsistencies are more likely to arise, and a single regulator can ensure any differences reflect the unique features of a given financial sector. For example, retail banks or credit institutions face different types of liquidity risk, and the single regulator needs to ensure that more liquidity resources are allocated to the retail bank rather than being spread through the entire organisation.

There are a number of arguments against a single regulator. First, as a government agency, it lacks the expertise found in a system of self-regulation, where practitioners run the regulatory body. Government salaries tend to be low, making it difficult to attract experts from financial firms. One way to counter this problem is to establish a body similar to the Board of Banking Supervision, which has a large number of independent practitioners. The FSA could set up the equivalent in other areas such as securities and insurance.

Anticipating concern about accountability, the Financial Services and Markets Act has built in certain procedures to deal with this issue. The FSA Chairman and board members appointments are controlled by the Treasury, and the majority of its board members are non-executive. It is required to submit an annual report to Parliament on the extent to which it has met its objectives, and public meetings must be held to discuss the report. Consumer and practitioner bodies can examine the FSA's performance, and any firm affected by FSA decisions (e.g. sanctions, excessively onerous regulations) can appeal to an independent tribunal.

Multi-function firms have expressed concern at the cost of building up new systems to meet new rules of compliance under the FSA. In the short run, these costs offset the gains from having a single regulator, but only in the short run, as firms adjust to the new regulatory regime. Smaller firms may have a more legitimate concern because for the first time, they are having to employ compliance officers full-time, which was not necessary in the past.

Another issue the FSA has to confront is the danger of imposing too many rules to ensure equitable treatment of different firms it supervises. As a counter to this problem, the FSA must employ cost benefit analysis to evaluate whether the benefits of introducing a new regulation will outweigh the costs.

A single regulator can be so large that the accompanying bureaucracy makes it unwieldy and inefficient. It also has a great deal of power over financial institutions which can prove dangerous if not checked. Furthermore, any benefits from competition between regulators are lost.

There is also the potential for regulatory forbearance, especially with the FSA's determination to focus most of its resources on high impact firms. Regulators adopt policies which favour the regulated firms at the expense of the consumer and/or taxpayer, because the regulator, over time, begins to have a vested interest in the survival of the firms it regulates.

---

[19] Canada's population is just over half that of the UK.
[20] Source of these figures: Lascelles (2001).

Various US authorities have been accused of regulatory forbearance (e.g. the US thrift crisis of the 1980s) and there is no reason why a single regulator might escape the problem.

The size of the FSA has caused it to be organised along the lines of functional supervision (see Chart 5.2), i.e. divisions are allocated responsibility in terms of insurance, banking, securities and futures, etc. While this type of organisational form may improve information flows, it increases the danger of regulatory forbearance or collusion between the two parties, if the same regulator(s) are assigned to firms. However, investor protection is a statutory objective, which should counter any tendency for FSA officials to try and protect or collude with badly run financial firms. But the FSA has more contact with the firms it regulates than the public, which could tip the balance away from protection of the consumer.

The statutory objective of investor protection has raised concerns that the FSA may attempt to apply new rules in the wholesale markets, which would undermine London's international position. To date, the view has been that wholesale customers are financially sophisticated, and therefore, the principle of *caveat emptor* (let the buyer beware) applies. If considerably less monitoring and regulation is needed for the wholesale markets, compliance costs will be minimised. However, there are many cases where sophisticated investors have found themselves in trouble. For example, corporate finance/treasurers of non-financial firms, on the advice of investment banks, have entered into complex swaps which have subsequently resulted in significant losses. Also, as has been pointed out before, if deposit insurance is limited to retail customers, wholesale depositors will withdraw their money at the first hint of financial trouble.

The FSA is required to meet four quite diverse statutory objectives, and has added duties imposed more recently. Given its limited (especially human) resources, the potential for conflict of interest is high because the FSA may have to sacrifice one of its objectives for another. For example, scarce management resources could result in consumer protection and financial crime being given priority over maintaining stability in financial markets. As a result, firms are less closely monitored than they should be, which could cause more firms getting into difficulty, thereby undermining confidence in the financial sector.

The potential for moral hazard among consumers and financial firms may arise because they believe the FSA is ensuring that risks posed to a sector and the system as a whole is minimised. The incentive to monitor these firms by customers is reduced. Financial firms may think they are fully protected if they implement the regulator's rules because of a false sense of security. Though moral hazard will be a problem under any type of regulatory regime, it is more likely to arise in a rule based system.

Finally, the MOU between the Bank of England, HM Treasury and the FSA has yet to be tested. Even though the Bank of England is no longer directly involved in regulation, since it is the Bank which will be supplying liquidity in the event of systemic problems, it is critical that the memorandum ensures the requisite information flows between the FSA and the Bank if the Bank is to head off any potential crisis.

Some experts advocate the introduction of a *systemic regulator*. Banks and other financial institutions would be singled out for special regulation if their failure is likely to pose a systemic risk to the financial infrastructure of the economy. If adopted (at national, European or international level), and the firms falling into this category were made public, then everyone would know which firm was going to be bailed out. Again, moral hazard could be a serious problem if the "systemic risk" firms engaged in led to greater risks and depositors or shareholders were less vigilant in their monitoring.

Is there an optimal way of supervising banks and other financial institutions? The answer is no – most countries mentioned in the opening paragraphs of this chapter have experienced varying degrees of bank crises and/or other problems at some point over the last two decades – these problems are discussed in greater detail in Chapter 8. Japan's reforms (see below) are largely a reaction to the financial collapse in that country which began in late 1989. Until "Big Bang", Japan had, effectively, a single regulator. The United States, home of the multiple regulators, experienced serious problems with its thrifts and some banks in the 1980s. Most banks in the Nordic countries came close to being insolvent in the 1980s. The UK and Canada, to date, are part of a small group of countries with no recent history of serious banking problems, though the UK has witnessed some spectacular collapses, notably BCCI (1991) and Barings (1995). These collapses partly contributed to the decision to overhaul the system. It is too early to judge the success or otherwise of the relatively new FSA. The UK's system of a separate monolithic regulator, which is required to meet four potentially conflicting statutory objectives, has yet to be tested.

## 5.3. Bank Structure and Regulation in the USA

### 5.3.1. Background

The central bank and bank supervisory functions in the USA have evolved to create a US banking and financial structure which, by the late 20th century, was notably different from those in other western countries. Several factors explain its unique structure. First, US regulators have been far more inclined to seek statutory remedies in the event of a new problem, resulting in a plethora of legislation. Second, the protection of small depositors has been considered an important objective since the 1930s. Third, concern about potential collusion among banks and between banks and regulators has received as much weight in the USA as measures were put in place to preserve the stability of the banking system. However, two important financial reforms could result in gradual but major changes in the structure of US banking over the first decade of the new century.

As Table 5.5 shows, the most striking feature of the US banking system is the large number of banks, despite recent consolidation. In 2000, there were about 7770 commercial banks, down from approximately 14 500 in 1984. Until the Gramm Leach Bliley Financial Modernisation Act of 1999 (GLB), these banks were severely constrained in the amount of securities related business they could undertake. Unlike most other western economies, the banking system is not highly concentrated. Commercial banks hold over 80% of total US banking assets, 50% of the commercial banking assets are held by 107 banks, and just under 80% of commercial bank assets are controlled by 373 commercial banks. By contrast, in the United Kingdom, the five largest banks[21] control up to 80% of the country's assets.

Table 5.6 shows the "big 6" American banks by tier 1 capital. Citicorp has assets in excess of $1 trillion and tier 1 capital of just over $39 billion. By contrast, Wachovia, the

---

[21] HSBC, Royal Bank of Scotland Group, HBOS, Barclays and Lloyds TSB.

Table 5.5   US Banking Structure, 1997 and 2004.

| Type of Bank | US Assets ($bn) | | Number | | % of Total Assets | |
|---|---|---|---|---|---|---|
| | 1997 | 2004 | 1997 | 2004 | 1997 | 2004 |
| Commercial | 4 771 | 7 603 | 9 308 | 7 769 | 77.6 | 79 |
| Savings institutions* | 1 030 | 1 474 | 1 852 | 1 413 | 16.7 | 15 |
| Credit unions | 349 | 599 | 11 328 | 9 529 | 5.6 | 6 |
| Total | 6 150 | 9 676 | 22 488 | 18 711 | 100 | 100 |
| Securities firms | | | 7 776 (1996) | 5 286 | | |

* Savings and loan or thrift associations and savings banks.
*Sources*: Table constructed from 1997 figures quoted in Saunders and Cornett (2003), chapters 1, 3, which in turn are supplied by the FDIC (www.fdic.gov – FDIC Quarterly Banking Profile) and the Federal Reserve Bulletin. 2000 figures obtained from websites for the FDIC.gov and the National Association of Securities Dealers Regulation (NASDR.com) and National Credit Union (www.ncua.com). In the USA, the official term for securities firms, including investment banks, is "broker dealer", and virtually every firm operating in the USA is registered with NASD and NASDR.

Table 5.6   Top US Banks (by tier 1 capital) in 2003

| Bank | Tier 1 Capital ($m) | Assets ($m) | Cost:Income (%) | ROA (%) | Basel Risk Assets Ratio (%) |
|---|---|---|---|---|---|
| Citigroup | 59 012 | 1 097 190 | 54.99 | 2.08 | 11.25 |
| Bank of America Corp. | 43 012 | 660 458 | 53.45 | 1.97 | 12.43 |
| JP Morgan Chase & Co. | 37 570 | 758 800 | 76.87 | 0.33 | 11.95 |
| Bank One Corp. | 23 918 | 277 383 | 57.30 | 1.72 | 13.71 |
| Wells Fargo & Co. | 21 512 | 349 259 | 56.78 | 2.55 | 11.31 |
| Wachovia Corp. | 21 411 | 340 788 | 65.53 | 1.37 | 12.01 |

*Source*: *The Banker*, July 2003.

sixth largest, is about a third of Citicorp's size, measured by assets. Commercial banks with assets of less than $1 billion are known as **community banks** – controlling just over 20% of commercial bank assets. Commercial banks with assets in excess of $1b are known as **regional** or **super-regional banks**. There is virtually no nation-wide banking, i.e. banks with branches throughout the US, but this may change due to recent reforms (see below).

In common with other industrialised nations, the USA has savings banks and "thrifts" – savings and loans associations. Some are mutually owned, others are stock banks. Their original function was to make long-term residential mortgages funded by short-term savings deposits. Changes in regulations in the early 1980s allowed them to offer money market accounts, current or notice of withdrawal (NOW) accounts, flexible rate mortgages (in addition to the traditional fixed rate) and some commercial and personal loans. Mortgages make up just under 80% of their assets.

Serious problems with savings and loans/thrift associations (see Chapter 7) throughout the 1980s led to a sharp reduction in their number, from 2600 in 1987 to 1481 in 1989 and

1230 in 2000. Over 700 were closed by the Resolution Trust Corporation, which operated from 1989 to 1995. Deposits are insured by the FDIC controlled Savings Association Insurance Fund.

In the 1980s and 1990s, most of the mutual savings banks converted to stock banks under state charters, and a few under federal charter. Nearly three-quarters of their assets are in the form of mortgages, though they have been allowed to offer corporate bonds and stocks. In 2004, there were 1413 savings institutions;[22] their deposits are insured by the FDIC.

There were just under 10 000 **credit unions** in 2004, which are owned by members (e.g. employees, police and fire associations, teachers). A member's salary is paid into the credit union, which provide customers with basic deposit and loan facilities. In common with British building societies, deposits are known as shares. As non-profit maximising firms, net income is tax exempt, allowing them to offer more attractive deposit and loan rates than commercial or savings banks.

Regulatory reforms in the 1980s resulted in just over 4000 new **investment banks and securities firms**. They numbered about 9500 in October 1987, but the stock market crash (October 1987), together with higher capital requirements, gave rise to mergers so that by 1996 their number had dropped to under 8000. Further consolidation reduced their numbers to 5286 by 2004. There was a correspondingly large increase in concentration. For example, the largest investment bank in 1987 (Salomon's) had capital of $3.21 billion, but a decade later, the largest is Merrill Lynch with $33 billion of capital.

It is increasingly difficult to distinguish between these firms. As was noted in Chapter 1, US investment banks tend to specialise in underwriting and new issues of bonds and equity (IPOs), though they have expanded into trading, research and consultancy, among other activities. Though Morgan Stanley is often thought of as a typical investment bank, it also offers stockbroking services. Securities firms such as Merrill Lynch have a large number of retail outlets, as well as offering investment banking services to corporate clients.

Other financial firms in the USA include insurance firms and finance companies. Over the last two decades, the finance company sector has grown rapidly. As in the UK, they are not banks, because they rely on loans from banks to fund short and long-term lending. In 1997, total assets stood at about $900 billion (larger than the thrifts), with the top 20 firms controlling more than 80% of these assets. They consist of sales finance firms which lend to a particular retail or wholesale group (e.g. Sears Roebuck Acceptance Corporation and Ford Motor Credit), personal credit firms such as Household Finance Corporation, which make loans to consumers and business credit firms that specialise in finance to corporations in the form of equipment leasing or factoring. General Motors Acceptance Corporation is involved in several activities. For example, they purchase debt from firms at a discount, then collect the debt. Another one of its subsidiaries is the largest commercial mortgage lender in the USA.

## 5.3.2. Bank Regulation in the USA

The USA has been inclined to seek statutory remedies whenever a serious problem in the banking/financial sector arises, which is one reason for its somewhat unique financial

---

[22] Savings Institutions: Savings and Loan (or Thrift) Associations and Savings banks.

structure. Given the extensive amount of legislation passed since the 1930s, and related litigation, US regulation is best understood if reviewed under a number of subject headings.

## Creation of a central bank and bank supervision

The National Bank Act was passed in 1863 and amended in 1864. It outlined the power, duties and regulations covering national banks, which are federally chartered by the Comptroller of the Currency (and the US Treasury Department). The Federal Reserve Act, 1913, created a central bank for the US banking system, following panics over a number of banks and trust companies, which originated in New York, in October 1907. Concerns about other banks spread to different parts of the USA, causing banks to restrict payments in New York and in other states. The 1913 Act allowed the Federal Reserve Bank to provide an "elastic" currency, that is, to supply liquidity in the event of crises. In 1934, the Federal Reserve Bank (or Fed) was granted the authority to adjust its reserve requirements, independent of the legislators.[23]

In contrast to most other countries, there has always been a great deal of concern that a central bank with lender of last resort/lifeboat functions could add to and/or encourage oligopolistic banking behaviour, going against the American philosophy of free competition in all sectors. As a result, the Federal Reserve System (FRS) had a number of checks and balances built into it to discourage the development of cartel-like tendencies. The emphasis was placed on decentralisation – the FRS consists of 12 regional Federal Reserve Banks and a Board of Governors. The primary function of the Federal Reserve Bank was to pool the reserves of each of these banks.

The Federal Reserve System is one of several regulators of US banks. To operate as a bank, a firm must obtain a national or state charter (hence the term **dual banking system**), granted by either the Comptroller of the Currency or by a state official, usually called the Superintendent of Banks. The origin of the charter determines the banks' main regulator. In a national charter, the bank must be regulated by the FRS, which is optional for state chartered banks. Regulations applied to state chartered banks are historically less stringent than for national banks. In 2004, about 2000 banks held national charters, and just under 6000 (75%) were state chartered. The top 10, with national charters controlled 55% of assets; the top 5 controlled 66% of assets.[24]

There are costs and benefits arising from membership of the FRS. The costs are bank examination, conducted by officers from the Comptroller of the Currency at least three times every two years. Bank examiners use composite scores from the CAMEL scores system to evaluate banks. Banks are scored on a scale of 1 (the best) to 5 (the worst), using five criteria.

- **C**: capital adequacy
- **A**: asset quality

---

[23] This authority was part of the Glass Steagall Banking Act, 1934, discussed below. Friedman and Schwartz (1963) dispute that there was any inelasticity of the currency (pp. 168–173) during the panic.
[24] *Source*: FDIC: www.fclic.gov.

- **M**: management quality
- **E**: earnings performance
- **L**: liquidity

A composite score is produced and banks with scores of 1 or 2 are considered satisfactory. Additional supervision is indicated if the score falls between 3 and 5. Banks scoring 4 or 5 are closely monitored, and a 5 signals that examiners think the bank is likely to fail. The examinations are meant to prevent fraud and to ensure a bank is complying with the various rules and regulations related to its balance sheet and off-balance sheet holdings. For example, banks can be ordered to sell securities if they are considered too risky, or to write off dud loans. Bank examiners may declare a "problem bank" if it is deemed to have insufficient capital, has too many weak loans, an inefficient management or is dishonest. Since the 1991 Federal Deposit Insurance Corporation Act (see p. 44), regulators are obliged to undertake a well-defined set of actions if banks are deemed to be under/significantly/critically under-capitalised.

Three organisations have the authority to examine banks, and the Federal Deposit Insurance Corporation has the right to examine insured banks. To avoid duplication, the Fed, Comptroller of Currency and FDIC normally examine, respectively, state member banks, national member banks and the non-member (of the FRS) insured banks.

Banks which are members of the Federal Reserve System must meet a tier 1 capital assets or leverage ratio of at least 5%. An unweighted version of the 1988 Basel ratio, it is defined for a given bank as:

$$\frac{\text{Tier 1 capital (i.e. equity capital + long-term funds)}}{\text{Total assets}}$$

The higher the ratio of capital to assets, the more secure the bank. If a bank's capital ratio is 5% of its assets, then the bank can afford to lose 5% of these assets (for example, unsound loans) without undermining its ability to repay depositors. Only shareholders will lose. This ratio is one of several banks report; others are used to assess the premium a bank pays for deposit insurance, and are reviewed below.

Federal Reserve membership for larger banks means they can attract deposits from smaller banks, in a correspondent relationship. FRS membership confers an image of quality and reputation, because of the requirements to which all members must conform.

Over the years, the piecemeal legislation has resulted in complex bank supervision in the USA, with a great deal of overlap between supervisory authorities. Table 5.7 summarises the key national supervisors and their responsibilities. However, there are also state supervisors, too numerous to list here. They include, for example, the State of New York Banking Department, the different regional reserve banks (e.g. Federal Reserve Bank of Boston, the Federal Reserve Bank of St. Louis, The Federal Reserve Bank of Cleveland), each with some supervisory responsibilities in their respective regions.

## *Separation of commercial and investment banking*

The Glass Steagall sections (20, 32) of the Banking Act (1933), which became known as the Glass Steagall Act, separated commercial and investment banking from 1933

Table 5.7  Key Regulators of Financial Firms

| Regulators | Financial Firms |
| --- | --- |
| OCC (1863) | National commercial banks – includes foreign branches, branches of foreign banks, Edge Act* corporations |
| FED (1913) | FHCs/BHCs, national commercial banks (includes foreign branches), foreign banks, state banks which are members of the Fed |
| FDIC (1933) | Any bank (national/state) covered by FDIC insurance – may/may not be members of the Fed |
| OTS (1989) | Savings & loans (national or state) |
| NCUA (1970) | National Credit Union Administration: for national or state credit unions |
| State regulators | State chartered banks licensed by the state |
| FTC | Uninsured state banks or savings & loans, credit unions, US banks' foreign branches, branches of foreign banks |
| SEC (1934) | Securities firms/investment banks, investment advisors, brokers |
| NAIC, DTI | Insurance firms |

Abbreviations: ( ) : year established; OCC: Office of Comptroller of the Currency, part of the Treasury; FED: Federal Reserve System/Federal Reserve banks; FDIC: Federal Deposit Insurance Corporation; OTS: Office of Thrift Supervision; NAIC: National Association of Insurance Commissioners – NAIC insurance firms are state chartered but the NAIC coordinates supervision and regulation; NCUA: National Credit Union Administration – state regulators, for banks licensed/chartered by a state rather than the FED; FTC: Federal Trade Commission; SEC: Securities and Exchange Commission; DTI: Department of Trade and Industry.
* Edge Act Corporations: banks allowed to set up out of state subsidiaries which can take deposits and make loans provided they were related to international trade and finance. Took effect after the 1919 **Edge Act**, and extended to foreign banks after 1978.

until it was repealed in 1999. It was largely responsible for the somewhat unique structure of banking that prevailed in the United States for the rest of the 20th century. Under the Act, the securities functions of commercial banks were severely curtailed: they were limited to underwriting and dealing in municipal government debt. Investment banks can engage in securities and underwriting, but are prohibited from taking deposits.

The Glass Steagall Act was passed during the Great Depression, after a special Commission persuaded Congress that separation of commercial and investment banking would prevent another financial crisis arising from the large number of bank failures (over 10 000) between 1929 and 1933.[25] The Act also reflects the American obsession with the potential for collusion and anti-competitive practices. In this instance, the Act prevented the possibility of collusion between bank and customer which could arise if a bank both held a firm's equity and underwrote its securities.

---

[25] The case for separating the two types of banking is not supported by empirical evidence. White (1986) showed that, before the Act was passed, banks offering both commercial and investment banking services were less likely to fail.

## Bank holding companies

Until the 1960s, bank holding companies (BHCs) were a minor part of the US banking scene, controlling about 15% of total bank deposits. By the 1990s, 92% of banks were owned by BHCs. They became popular in the 1950s when banks found they could establish a bank holding company to circumvent the regulations: only wholly owned banking subsidiaries were required to conform to banking regulations.

The Bank Holding Company Act, 1956, defined a BHC as any firm holding at least 25% of the voting stock of a bank subsidiary. It required BHCs to be registered with the Federal Reserve. The purpose of the Act was to restrict BHC activity but by granting them legal status, it actually encouraged their growth. BHCs could circumvent the interstate branching laws, via "multi-bank" holding companies. The BHC organisational framework also meant banks could diversify into non-bank financial activities such as credit card operations, mortgage lending, data processing, investment management advice and discount brokerage. They were also attractive for tax reasons. However, they could not engage in certain financial businesses (for example, securities) excluded by Glass Steagall, or in businesses not closely related to banking, as specified in the regulations.

The Amendment (1970) to the 1956 Act increased control by the Federal Reserve over BHCs, which in turn tried to limit BHCs to offering banking products, and engaging in non-banking financial activities. However, the bank holding company structure continued to expand, with BHCs acquiring domestic and overseas banks.

In 1987, the Supreme Court ruled that section 20 of the Glass Steagall Act did not extend to subsidiaries of commercial banks. It meant they could offer investment banking services, provided they were not "engaged principally" in the said activities. In 1987, the Federal Reserve allowed BHCs (see below) to create *section 20 subsidiaries* which could undertake securities activities if the revenues generated did not exceed 5% (later raised to 10%, then 25% in 1996) of total BHC revenue. These subsidiaries captured substantial market share in some areas. For example, in 1997, JP Morgan and Chase were in the top 10 underwriters of domestic equity and debt.

Pressure to repeal the Glass Steagall Banking Act increased, especially in the 1990s. In June 1991 a key House of Representatives Committee, considering a Banking Reform Bill, voted in favour of breaking down barriers between banking and commerce. But most aspects of this legislation collapsed in November 1991. In October 1993, Lloyd Bentsen, the Treasury Secretary, set out an agenda for banking reform. Unlike the failed attempt at reform in 1991, the Bentsen agenda did not call for a repeal of Glass Steagall, but did support reforms for interstate banking (see below). The Chairman of the House banking committee (Mr Leach) claimed his top priority was to repeal Glass Steagall. Finally, in November 1999, the **Gramm Leach Bliley Financial Modernisation Act (GLB)** was signed into law by President Clinton.

The GLB Act was passed at a time when technology and other factors were eroding the boundary between commercial and investment banking. Investment banks had been able to enter retail banking through money market funds, cash management accounts and non-bank banks – though legislation put an end to the latter (see below). Merrill Lynch, an investment bank, owns two thrifts, and together with other subsidiaries engages in a limited amount of deposit taking and lending. From 1987, commercial banks began to offer some investment banking services through section 20 subsidiaries. According to Sweeney (2000), 43% of banks offered insurance products in 1998, a year before the new legislation (see below) was passed. Perhaps the greatest pressure was competitive: it was increasingly difficult for US banks to compete in global markets with the European universal banks.

## Financial holding companies

Under the GLB Act, US bank holding companies can convert into financial holding companies (FHCs) which, in turn, can own commercial banking, investment banking and insurance subsidiaries, but are prohibited from cross-share ownership or directorships of non-financial firms.

Supervision of the FHCs is *functional*, i.e. insurance firms continue to be supervised by the Department of Trade and Industry, investment banks (securities activities) by the Securities and Exchange Commission, and the banking subsidiaries by the Federal Reserve Bank (Fed). However, the Fed acts as an "umbrella" regulator because it has the power to approve the conversion of the bank holding company into a financial holding company. Nonetheless, for the insurance and securities activities, the Fed is expected to defer to the supervisory authority of the other regulators.

US banks may convert from BHC to FHC status provided the Fed has deemed them to be "well capitalised" and "well managed" – see below. In addition, they must be rated "satisfactory" under the 1977 Community Reinvestment Act.[26] FHCs can engage in a broad range of financial activities listed in the GLB Act; they must seek the permission of the Federal Reserve and Treasury should they wish to offer services not explicitly listed. However, unlike the German universal banks, FHCs fall into the *restricted universal* category, for a number of reasons. As subsidiaries, they must be separately capitalised, which is more costly than if they are part of a single legal entity. In addition, the cross-share ownership of non-financial firms is largely prohibited. In the USA, BHC/FHCs may not own more than 5% of a commercial concern. Furthermore, a firewall has been imposed between the commercial and securities subsidiaries – they are prohibited from cross marketing with each other, and a bank can sell but may not underwrite insurance.

As of July 2003, 636 (up by 76 since 2001) BHCs converted to FHCs, leaving just over 2000 bank holding companies at the end of 2003, nearly four years after the legislation was passed.[27] Of the 636 FHCs, 39 are foreign banks – they include the six big Canadian banks, four from the UK,[28] Deutsche Bank, Dresdner Bank, ABN Amro, Credit Suisse Group and Union Bank of Switzerland.

The large American BHCs (e.g. Citigroup, JP Morgan Chase, Bank of America) have converted. Citibank, an insurance firm, Travelers and Salomon Smith Barney, a securities

---

[26] The 1977 Community Reinvestment Act requires all commercial and saving banks to demonstrate (through records) that loans granted in the local community are not discriminatory. The 1975 Home Mortgage Disclosure Act was passed to stop discrimination in mortgage lending; since 1990 banks are required to supply reasons for all mortgage decisions to their main regulator.

[27] *Source*: Federal Reserve Board, Financial Holding Companies as of 11.07.03 website www.federalreserve.gov/ General.

[28] Abbey National, Barclays, HBOS plc, HSBC Holdings.

house, began merger talks in 1998 and subsequently merged to form Citigroup.[29] Some insurance firms, such as the State Farm Insurance Company, have set up a bank subsidiary, State Farm Savings Bank, to offer some banking products through their insurance offices, located across the USA.

Merrill Lynch has not converted to a FHC, but was one of the first investment banks to offer a cash management account, that is, a money market account with a cheque book and loan options. Nor has ING (a universal Dutch bank) sought FHC status even though it launched ING Direct in 2000, a savings bank which offers FDIC insured deposit accounts, mortgages and personal loans. Many on-line brokerage houses also offer banking services, and banks offer brokerage services and mutual funds.

Not many insurance firms or securities houses have sought FHC status, for a number of reasons. Unlike the FHC banks, the Fed becomes their umbrella supervisor for the first time, which is a considerable change in the way they are regulated, and compliance costs increase. If they fail to meet the "well capitalised" and other criteria, they are likely to be required to divest of any banks, loan companies and other depository institutions. Also, there are cases where securities or insurance firms engage in banking activities without becoming a FHC, as Merrill Lynch and ING illustrate. There are notable exceptions. The insurance giant MetLife used its new FHC status to purchase a small bank and Charles Schwab (a discount broker) became a FHC after purchasing a firm offering private banking.

The GLB Act has a potential drawback for banks engaged in securities or investment advisory. Before the Act, they were not required to register with the Securities and Exchange Commission as broker dealers or investment advisors. The Act emphasises functional regulation which means any banks which underwrite or broker corporate securities must, or so the SEC claimed, set up separate broker/dealer subsidiaries, subject to SEC regulation, and become members of the National Association of Securities Dealers (NASD).[30] This will raise their compliance costs because they are subject to SEC regulations, and their employees face examinations to acquire the appropriate licences. After complaints from bankers and regulators, the SEC extended the deadline for compliance to May 2002.

To understand the potential complexity of functional regulation, consider Citigroup.[31] It is keeping its banking operations, which means it continues to have a BHC. The BHC is regulated by the Fed, but the various banking subsidiaries, etc. are regulated by state and federal bank authorities including the FDIC and relevant state regulators (for state chartered bank subsidiaries and thrifts), the Office of the Comptroller of the Currency (for nationally chartered bank subsidiaries), and the Office of Thrift Supervision (for federal savings subsidiaries). In the USA, insurance is regulated at state level, which means Citigroup's insurance subsidiaries must comply with all the state insurance regulators. The broker-dealer subsidiary, Smith Barney, is regulated by the SEC, the exchanges where they trade (e.g. the New York and London stock exchanges), and the National Association of

---

[29] The creation of Citigroup put pressure on Congress to pass the GLB Act, since it involved the merger with an insurance firm.

[30] If a firm's activities are limited to government or municipal securities, trust, safekeeping or custody, then they continue to be exempt from registering with the SEC.

[31] Part of the Citigroup discussion is from Soifer (2001), p. 78.

Securities Dealers (NASD). In addition, Citigroup is subject to the regulations of other countries where it has subsidiaries.

## Branch banking regulations

To discourage concentration in the banking sector, the United States has a long history of limiting the extent to which banks could set up branches, unlike most of the other banking systems in the industrialised world. Heffernan (1996) reviews the relevant legislation, which discouraged interstate branching, that is the branching across states, and in some states, intrastate branching or branching within the state.

Since 1933, legislation meant the regulation of branching was largely a matter for individual states, and as a result, each state had different degrees of restrictions. Most states prohibited out of state banks from collecting retail deposits, which effectively excluded them from setting up branches. Bank holding companies might establish bank subsidiaries in each state, but each was an individual legal entity, which had to be separately capitalised. In most western countries, such as the UK, Australia, Canada, France and Germany, customers with an account at one branch of a bank can do business in other branches throughout the country. For example, a customer with an account at a London branch of HSBC could also bank at a branch in Manchester or Leeds. Or a customer with an account at the Bank of Montreal in Quebec City could attend one of the branches in Vancouver.[32] However, in the United States, a customer with an account at the subsidiary of a bank holding company in one state cannot bank at another subsidiary of the same bank holding company. There are exceptions. For example, California has a history of liberal intrastate branching laws, and with few branching restrictions. At the other extreme there are states such as Illinois, where no branching was allowed until very recently.

The failure of thousands of banks and thrifts during the 1980s put pressure on individual states to revise their legislation to allow out of state bank entry through the merger of healthy bank holding companies with unsound local banks and thrifts. Also some neighbouring states entered into regional reciprocal agreements to allow branching across state lines.

The passage of the *Riegle Neal Interstate Banking and Branching Efficiency Act* in 1994 (henceforth, the RN Branching Act or Riegle Neal) largely eliminated these restrictions. The Act allowed all US banks to acquire banks in other states from September 1995, and from June 1997 BHCs could convert subsidiaries into branches. Any out of state bank taken over by another bank can be converted into a branch. State laws requiring out of state BHCs to enter by acquisition only continue to apply, though the BHC may opt to take over an existing branch or branches rather than an entire bank. States have the option of passing legislation to stop *de novo* branching (setting up a new branch) by out of state banks, but the FDIC can override these restrictions if a bank has failed or is failing. The Federal Reserve has a final say over interstate bank acquisitions. To prevent excessive concentration, a BHC/FHC may not hold more than 30% of total deposits in any given

---

[32] Customers might be subject to an additional charge if they bank at a branch other than where their account is based. With the advent of debit cards and ATMs, customers with suitable identification could conduct business at any branch, free of charge.

state,[33] and 10% nationally. The changes make nation-wide banking possible in the USA for the first time in its history.[34] Nationwide bank, after its merger with Bank of America in 1998, claimed to be America's first national bank, with branches in 22 states and a share of insured deposits of just over 8%.

The general view of several studies is that the Act conveys benefits such as increased efficiency and lower costs as subsidiaries become branches. Using a sample of bank holding companies, Carrow and Heron (1998) report that the Act had a positive welfare effect. Jayaratne and Strahan (1997) show that the reciprocal/regional agreements (1978–1992) which deregulated branching laws resulted in substantial permanent increases in economic growth in these states. However, Freeman (2002) cautions that the Jayaratne and Strahan findings are over-estimated because, in the sample they used, real incomes in the states that deregulated were on average 4% below trend, and recovered slowly. The states deregulated branching laws to encourage new bank entry because their own state banks were severely troubled or failing as a result of poor economic conditions. The authors conclude Riegle Neal did not have a powerful impact on growth rates. Nippani and Green (2002) looked at the performance of banks (in six different asset categories) pre- and post-Riegle Neal, using measures such as return on equity, return on assets, net interest margins and the ratio of non-performing loans to total loans. Their findings confirm a significant increase in the degree of consolidation in the US banking sector following the RN Act. However, the improvement in most performance measures was largely due to a stronger macroeconomy, as shown by the significance of real gross domestic product and the bank prime rate in their regression analyses. The finding that the new Act had little impact on the economy or bank performance may be due to a simultaneous increase in consolidation. The reduced competition that accompanies increased consolidation can offset any efficiency gains.

However, the two reforms together, Riegle Neale and GLB, make it highly likely the new century will see a major change in the structure of the American banking system. Universal banking, albeit restricted, together with nation-wide branching, creates new opportunities for financial institutions. But caution should be used when predicting the impact on performance of banks or economic growth rates. Branching across states comes just when banks in other countries are cutting back on bank branches, because new technology makes the remote delivery of most banking services possible. With GLB, financial institutions opting for FHC status face substantial compliance costs, a consequence of functional regulation. Other countries with universal banking tend to have a more concentrated banking system, with all the potential drawbacks arising from reduced competition. However, the reforms make an important contribution: they increase banks' choice of financial structures within the USA, with greater opportunities for a mixed banking system, ranging from highly specialised banks to mammoth financial supermarkets.

---

[33] States can opt to waive the 30% limit.

[34] The Act allowed individual states to opt out of the second part of legislation on interstate branching, i.e. the 1997 provisions, and to date, Texas and Montana have, though both states added provisions in their statutes which would allow them to opt in quickly. For more details of this Act, see Carrow and Heron (1998).

## Deposit insurance

Deposit insurance has been an important part of the US system since the Federal Deposit Insurance Corporation (FDIC) was set up after the 1933 US Banking Act. The FDIC was created to protect small depositors from ever experiencing the losses which were a consequence of massive bank failures that occurred between 1929–33. All member banks of the Federal Reserve System are required to join the FDIC; non-members may join if they meet the FDIC admission criteria. Membership is important for any bank if it is to attract depositors, effectively giving the FDIC veto power over the formation of almost any new bank. 97% of US banks, representing 99.8% of deposits, are insured by the FDIC.

The FDIC member banks pay an insurance premium to the FDIC, which is used to purchase securities to provide the insurance fund with a stream of revenue. With these funds, the FDIC insures deposits of up to \$100 000.[35] Initially, the FDIC was allowed to borrow up to \$3 billion from the Treasury, but in the 1980s FDIC resources were seriously threatened because of the increase in bank failures, and for this reason the limit was raised by Congress (see below).

From 1933 until the savings and loans/banking problems in the 1980s (see Chapter 7), there was little in the way of debate about the need for deposit insurance in the USA. The scheme was devised with a view to protecting small depositors to prevent them from initiating runs on banks thought to be in trouble. It is argued that small personal and business depositors are most inclined to initiate runs, because of the absence of detailed information about the quality of the bank, which is too costly for small depositors to obtain, even if the information were available. Unlike the UK, small depositors do not bear some of the cost of failure through co-insurance. Large depositors are expected to have the information necessary to make an informed judgement and to impose market discipline on the banks. However, runs are still possible. For example, when Continental Illinois got into trouble in the 1980s, it was the very large depositors who withdrew their money first, because their deposits would not be protected by insurance if the bank failed. Two years earlier, wholesale depositors had lost deposits held at Penn Square bank when the authorities made no attempt to rescue it.[36]

Looking at US commercial bank failures as a percentage of healthy banks in the period 1934–91, the annual average was 0.38% from 1934–39 and did not rise above 0.08% between 1940 and 1981. In 1981 it jumped to 0.29%, rising steadily to peak at 1.68% in 1988. The FDIC tried to reduce demands on its insurance funds by merging problem banks with healthy banks.

The Federal Savings and Loan Insurance Corporation (FSLIC), the insurance fund for the thrift industry, was declared insolvent in early 1987, because of the large number of thrift failures during the 1980s. The FDIC was also on the brink of insolvency. Under the 1989 *Financial Institutions Reform, Recovery, and Enforcement Act* (FIRREA), the FSLIC was dissolved, as was its regulator, the Federal Home Loan Bank Board. Two new deposit

---

[35] In 1933, the amount insured was \$2500. Over the years, this was gradually increased, to the current amount of \$100 000.

[36] See Chapter 7 and the Continental Illinois case study.

funds were created, the Bank Insurance Fund and the Savings Association Insurance Fund (SAIF) – both administered by the FDIC, even though it, too, was bordering on insolvency. The law also imposed higher deposit premiums for commercial banks and thrifts, to raise the reserves for the respective insurance funds. Under the Act, the regulation of thrifts was tightened by creating the Office of Thrift Supervision, modelled after the Comptroller of the Currency. The Act also authorised $50 billion of government-backed bonds, to help pay off depositors at insolvent thrifts.

A system of 100% deposit insurance is the only way to stop banks being threatened from runs by depositors, but it can create serious moral hazard problems, a point discussed in Chapter 4. Protected depositors have no incentive to monitor a bank's activities, and a bank with difficulties is likely to undertake riskier activities. In fact, the looting hypothesis (see Chapter 4) was developed to explain the behaviour of managers during the US thrift crisis in the 1980s. The experience of costly rescues of banks and thrifts (the rescue of the savings and loans sector alone cost the taxpayer $160–$180 billion in the 1980s[37]) increased the pressure for reform of deposit insurance schemes.

In 1991, the *Federal Deposit Insurance Corporation Improvement Act* (FDICIA) was passed by Congress to reform the role of the FDIC. The Act requires the FDIC to take *prompt corrective action* should a bank fail to meet the criteria for being well capitalised (see below). A "least cost" approach (from the standpoint of the taxpayer) must be adopted to resolve bank failures. The FDIC must use a present value approach to evaluate the costs of alternative ways (e.g. closure, merger with a healthy bank, etc.) of dealing with the problem bank. The new changes were introduced to reduce regulatory forbearance and give the FDIC clear rules for dealing with troubled banks. Collusion between banks/thrifts and their regulators and the absence of clear guidelines were thought to be contributory factors in the 1980s bank and thrift crises (see Chapter 7 for more detail).

However, if an insured bank's failure poses a threat to the US financial system (because, for example, it initiates runs on other banks, etc.) then it is exempt from the least cost criteria. Known as the *systemic risk* exemption, it is really "too big to fail" by the back door. With the rapid rate of consolidation in US banking and reforms allowing restricted universal banks with nation-wide branches, the number of banks qualifying for the exemption is likely to rise. To limit its use, the exemption can only be applied if the boards of the FDIC and the Fed agree by a two-thirds majority, with subsequent approval by the US Treasury Secretary and the US President. The cost of any rescue is funded by higher premia on other FDIC member banks.[38]

Under the FDICIA, the FDIC had to establish a system of risk based deposit insurance premia, based on the risk category of the bank, and the size of the FDIC fund.

Three ratios are used to categorise banks:

- **Tier 1 Capital Assets or Leverage Ratio:** tier 1 capital/assets
- **Tier 1 Risk Assets Ratio:** tier 1 capital/weighted risk assets
- **Total Risk Assets Ratio:** tier 1 & 2 capital/weighted risk assets

---

[37] See Chapter 7 for more detail.
[38] The bigger the bank (measured by size of deposits and borrowed funds), the greater the premium.

The different categories include:

### Well capitalised banks
Total risk assets ratio $\geq$ 10%
AND tier 1 risk assets ratio $\geq$ 6%
AND tier 1 leverage $\geq$ 5%

### Adequately capitalised banks
Total risk assets ratio $\geq$ 9%
AND tier 1 risk assets ratio $\geq$ 4%
AND tier 1 leverage $\geq$ 4%

### Under-capitalised banks
Total risk assets ratio < 6%
OR tier 1 risk assets ratio < 4%
OR tier 1 leverage < 4%

### Significantly under-capitalised banks
Total risk assets ratio < 6%
OR tier 1 risk assets ratio < 3%
OR tier 1 leverage < 3%

*Critically under-capitalised banks*
Equity: assets < 2%

Under the Act, a receiver must be brought in if the tier 1 leverage ratio is $\leq$2%. There is also a list of mandatory and discretionary actions to be taken if any bank falls into a group below well capitalised. For example, brokered deposits[39] may only be accepted by well-capitalised banks and, subject to FDIC approval, by adequately capitalised banks.

The prompt corrective action clause also requires supervisors to ensure action is taken if capital ratios fall, even if this means re-capitalisation. Capital trigger points were set, but Hawke (2003) identifies a flaw that could give rise to forbearance. The supervisor determines what constitutes capital, which makes it relatively easy to move the goal posts.

In addition to the risk category dimension, banks are also ranked by regulators, based on the supervisor's view of a bank's financial health, determined by the quality of assets and other risk indicators. For example, suppose two banks fall into the category "well capitalised". If one is designated a regulatory concern, it will pay a higher premium than the other bank.

Basis points are assigned to determine the premium rates; in January 1996, the premia ranged from 0 to 0.27% of deposits.[40] Risk classifications are kept confidential and based

---

[39] Brokered deposits are deposits which are spread among banks by deposit brokers, to take advantage of the deposit insurance scheme, which operates per bank. In the 1980s, weak banks used higher deposit rates as a means of raising funds and staying liquid because they were unable to attract funds from the wholesale markets.

[40] Initially (January 1993), the premia ranged from 23 to 31 cents per $100 of deposits. The premia were reduced because the FDIC's funds improved. The same rates were introduced in 1997 for thrifts insured under the Savings Association Insurance fund.

on supervisory evaluations, rather than credit ratings from private agencies. It is notable that banks wishing to be in one of the first two categories will have to conform to more stringent requirements than the 8% risk assets ratio laid down in the Basel 1 accord. This may explain why US banks have declared that only ten US mega banks will be required to comply with Basel 2, and the rest with Basel 1. Regulators are confident of their own systems, and do not consider it worth subjecting the majority of banks to the high costs of switching to a new system of risk management.

By the late 1990s, about 92% of insured banks paid no premium to the FDIC – the premia were lowered in 1996 because under FDICIA (1991), the FDIC cannot charge premia to highly rated banks provided their fund reserve exceeds 1.25% of insured deposits. Effectively, although the USA has a risk based system, the vast majority of banks are exempt from it because the fund reserve is large enough under FIDCIA rules. It means the Act has an element of procyclicality built into it; the fund reserve is likely to fall during a downturn in the economy,[41] and will have to resume its contributions during a period of recession, when credit losses are higher and profits are being squeezed. The FDIC, anxious to have a bigger reserve, has proposed that some premium be paid based on additional measures of banks' risk levels, such as CAMEL and other financial ratios.

The purpose of these reforms was to reduce moral hazard problems by computing deposit insurance premia on a risk-related basis, thereby effectively curbing bank risk-taking. It is hoped that the "least cost" requirement will expose depositors to greater risks than was true in the past, which in turn should increase their incentive to monitor bank activities. However, explicit co-insurance continues to be absent.

Another proposal to combat the problems created by deposit insurance is to limit coverage to *narrow banking* activities. Insurance, with no upper limit, would be available for transactions-related purposes or a minimum level of non-transactions deposits (e.g. $250 000). Banks would be required to invest these liabilities in safe government bills and top-rated commercial paper. Any other activities undertaken by banks would not be covered by deposit insurance. Effectively, this would mean banks could become financial conglomerates, but without the special protection of insurance, except for their transactions-related deposit business. To date, this proposal has not been implemented.

## Regulation of foreign banks

The International Banking Act (1978) eliminated some of the differences in the way domestic and foreign banks were regulated in the US market. For the first time, foreign banks were bound by the McFadden,[42] Bank Holding Company and Glass Steagall Acts. Foreign bank branches and agencies were to be regulated by the Fed. Foreign subsidiaries could apply for a federal charter, which would give them access to federal services such as the discount window, cheque collection and clearing.

---

[41] Marginal borrowers will default on their loans and the weakest banks/savings and loans could be declared insolvent, leading to closure or a drawing down of the fund as insured deposits are paid off.

[42] The McFadden Act (1927) allowed national banks to have branches but required them to obey state branching regulations. Hence the proliferation of different rules on interstate and intrastate branching, until the Riegle Neal Interstate Banking and Branching Efficiency Act (1994).

Reserve requirements were imposed on all federal and state licensed foreign bank branches and agencies which had a parent with more than $1 billion in international assets, thereby covering virtually all foreign banks based in the USA at the time. FDIC insurance was made mandatory for all foreign banks that accepted deposits. Finally, the Act introduced a reciprocity principle for foreign bank entry; foreign banks were only permitted to enter US banking markets to the degree that US banks could enter into the foreign market.

The Foreign Bank Enforcement Supervision Act (1991) was passed to establish uniform federal standards for entry and expansion of foreign banks in the USA. The Act extended the supervisory powers of the Federal Reserve over foreign banks, in response to their rapid growth – their numbers had more than doubled in the 1980s. The Act also ensures that foreign bank operations are regulated, supervised and examined in the same way as US banks. For example, foreign banks wanting to set up state licensed branches/agencies or purchase an existing bank must obtain approval from the Federal Reserve Board, and are subject to examination and supervision by the Board.[43] The principle of reciprocity was replaced by *equal treatment*: foreign and domestic banks receive identical regulation and supervision, provided US banks are treated the same way (i.e. subject to the same regulations as domestic banks) if they have subsidiaries in the foreign bank's country of origin.

The 1991 Act gave the Fed the right to close any foreign bank which violates US laws or if the bank's home country regulation is deemed inadequate. In 1996, the Fed used the Act to stop Daiwa Bank from operating in the USA[44] after one of its bond dealers lost over $1 billion in bond sales. The trader had concealed the losses from Daiwa for a considerable period of time, but what angered the US authorities was Daiwa's failure to report the matter until six weeks after the trader owned up. In addition, the bank was fined $340 million. In 2001, the State Bank of India was fined for what the Fed considered unsound practices in some of its branches.

US banking activities overseas are regulated by the Federal Reserve. US banks are required to seek permission to open foreign branches, and may only invest in foreign banks through bank holding companies. Edge Act corporations can invest in financial activities such as leasing, trust businesses, insurance, data processing, securities and dealing in money market funds.

### 5.3.3. A US National Banking Structure?

US regulatory authorities have largely abandoned trying to regulate bank interest rates or bank products,[45] accepting that it is not possible to do so in an environment of rapidly changing technology and financial innovation. Foreign banks can expect to be

---

[43] For more detail, see the *Federal Reserve Bulletin* (1993).

[44] Sumitomo bank purchased Daiwa's US operations in January 1996. At the time it was ranked the 14th largest Japanese bank by tier 1 capital; Sumitomo was the 2nd largest. (*Source: The Banker*, July 1998.)

[45] There are numerous examples of US legislation which illustrate attempts to control interest rates and new products. Under regulation Q, the Federal Reserve Bank could set ceilings on interest rates offered on savings and time deposits, and the 1933 Banking Act prohibited banks from paying interest on demand deposits. The Fed allowed thrifts to pay $\frac{1}{4}$% more interest than commercial banks, which gave them a competitive advantage. Banks reacted by introducing new products which were not classified as savings or time deposits; such as Notice of Withdrawal (NOW) accounts, money market mutual funds and sweep accounts. In 1980, under the Depository

subject to the same regulations as US domestic banks provided the foreign country applies the principle of equal treatment. More important, the RN Branching (1994) and GLB Financial Modernisation (1999) Acts, taken together, mean that the US banking and financial structure could change beyond all recognition in the 21st century.

For the first time, there are few barriers to prevent the development of a nation-wide banking system (e.g. the ceiling on state (30%) and nation-wide (10%) deposits one bank can hold), which has eluded the USA to date, but is taken for granted in most other countries. Now that BHCs (and the banking subsidiaries of FHCs) can have a national branch structure and FHCs can cross-sell some financial services through those branches, there is an increased likelihood that a national banking system could emerge. The large number of mergers and acquisitions among BHCs, commercial banks, investment houses and insurance firms over the last 15 years should bring about a more consolidated national banking system. New technology will mean the scale of national branching is smaller but at the same time, US banks do not have to face the unpopular branch closure programmes witnessed in many countries such as Canada, the UK, France and Germany.

## 5.4. Bank Structure and Regulation in Japan

### 5.4.1. Background

In the post-war period, Japan faced a severe shortage of capital and weak financial infrastructure. World War II virtually wiped out the household sector's financial assets. The priority of the US occupying force and the new Japanese government was to increase assets, which in turn could finance recovery of the real economy. The outcome was a highly segmented financial system, with strong regulatory control exerted by the **Ministry of Finance (MoF)**, backed by the Bank of Japan. Domestic and foreign and short and long-term financial transactions were kept separate, interest rates regulated, and financial firms organised along functional lines. Table 5.8 illustrates this high degree of functional segmentation. This arrangement fitted in with the *keiretsu* system. A keiretsu is a group of companies with cross-shareholdings and shared directorships which will normally include a bank, trust company, insurance firm and a major industrial concern such as steel, cars, property and construction. The bank supplies services to the other keiretsu members, including loans.

The MoF was the key regulator, through three MoF bureaux: Banking, Securities and International Finance.[46] Responsibilities included all aspects of financial institution supervision: examination of financial firms, control of interest rates and products offered by firms, supervision of the deposit protection scheme, and setting the rules on activities to be undertaken by financial firms.

The MoF used *regulatory guidance* (combining the statutes with its own interpretation of the laws) to operate the financial system. Banks, in exchange for providing low interest

---

Institutions Deregulation and Monetary Control Acts (DIDMCA), regulation Q was to be phased out by 1986 (it had been largely ineffective since 1980), NOW accounts were allowed and restrictions on the use of remote terminals lifted.

[46] The MoF also had tax and budget bureaux.

**Table 5.8  The Functional Segmentation of the Japanese Banking Sector, pre-Big Bang**

| Financial Institutions | Numbers (1997) | Geographical Area | Funding | Loans to/Key Customers | Other Links/Comment |
|---|---|---|---|---|---|
| **Ordinary or Commercial Banks\*** | | | | | |
| (1) City | 10 | HQ in Tokyo/Osaka – national branch networks | Deposits with maturity<3 yrs; may not raise capital using long-term debt | Large corporates, especially keiretsu affiliates | Securities; cross-shareholding via keiretsu |
| (2) **Regional + former sogos** | 139 | In one or neighbouring regions (prefectures) | As above but confined to a certain region | Regional clients and public utilities | |
| (3) Foreign banks | 94 | Tokyo | As with city | As with city | Securities & trust business through partly owned affiliates |
| Long-term credit | 3\*\* | Tokyo | Deposits from client fund and government bodies; issue long-term debentures with maturity up to 5 yrs | Long-term loans to industry | |
| Trusts | >30 | Various | Long-term deposits | Long-term loans & money trusts; trust-related business | |
| Japanese Post Office | 24 000 branches | Cross-country | A cheap source of funds for MoF; savings attracted by regulated deposit rates and products until 1994/5; continue to offer attractive rates, etc. | | Subsidised by government therefore not constrained to maximise profits\*\*\* |
| Public Financial Institutions | Six key Japanese development banks, export–import banks, small business corporations, agriculture, forestry & fisheries, housing loans | Various | MoF fiscal and loan programme; may not accept deposits | To supplement private sector loans to industry | Have outgrown their purpose |
| Savings & Loans | 395 Shinkin credit associations | Various | Short-term deposits from small business & individuals | Loans to small business and individuals | Mutual organisations |
| Cooperative Banks | >3000 agriculture & fisheries coops, credit unions, rokin banks | Various | Mutual organisations, so finance cannot be raised via shareholders | | Largely exempt from regulation |

\*Article 65 of the 1948 Securities and Exchange Law restricted banks from engaging in the securities business and vice versa.

\*\*1949 Foreign Exchange Law: separated domestic and international banking and finance.  The Bank of Tokyo was the designated foreign exchange bank.

\*\*\*One estimate of the state subsidy to the postal system is ¥730 billion per year, equivalent to 0.36% on postal savings deposits.

*Source:*  Ministry of International Trade and Industry, as quoted in Ito *et al.* (1998), p. 73.

loans to large industrial firms, were protected from foreign competition, and the highly segmented markets (see Table 5.8) limited domestic competition. In return, until 1995, there was an implicit guarantee that virtually any financial firm getting into trouble would be protected – a 100% safety net. MoF officials were often given jobs by banks when they retired – evidence of the cosy relationship between the MoF and regulated bankers.

The **Bank of Japan** (BJ) was responsible for the implementation of monetary policy, but was not independent. MoF officials exercised strong influence through its membership on the Bank's policy board. The Bank and MoF conducted on-site inspections of banks in alternate years. The Bank of Japan also acted as banker for commercial banks and government, regulated the interbank market and was consulted about regulatory issues, though the MoF took all final decisions.

Functional segmentation and restrictions on international capital flows resulted in an excessive dependence on the banking sector compared to other major industrialised countries. In 1998, 60% of domestic corporate finance in Japan consisted of loans, compared to just over 10% in the USA. Capital markets were underdeveloped. Participation by foreign financial firms in the Japanese markets was also low compared to other financial centres, mainly because the Japanese believed their interests were best served if foreign firms were kept out. Token gestures were made, to avoid criticism from the world community. In 1997, there were 94 foreign financial firms, compared to 290 in New York, 533 in London and 560 in Frankfurt.

## 5.4.2. Japan's Big Bang, 1996[47]

Following the crash of Japan's stock market in late 1989, Japan's financial sector went into severe decline, so that by the beginning of the 21st century most Japanese banks were insolvent. In an attempt to revive the financial sector, "Big Bang" was announced in 1996. The programme of reforms was designed to fulfil two objectives. First, the financial sector was to be restructured, putting an end to functional segmentation. Second, to restore financial stability, the Financial Supervisory Agency and Financial Reconstruction Commission were established. The Bank of Japan was granted independence.

Big Bang was announced in November 1996 by Prime Minister Hashimito. The somewhat optimistic objective was to place Tokyo on a level playing field with New York and London by 2001.[48] The package of reforms is based on three principles: FREE, FAIR and GLOBAL.

**FREE**: Free market principles were to apply to the financial sector. Integration of the banking, securities and insurance markets was encouraged. Financial products and prices were to be liberalised. Rules which prohibited banks from jointly engaging in short and long-term operations were to be abolished. Fees and commissions, especially on the stock market, would be liberalised.

**FAIR**: A transparent, fair financial market was to be created through the complete disclosure of information at all levels, including government, with clear rules on market operations. Investors were to be encouraged to take responsibility for their actions, but at the same time, new laws of investor (especially retail) protection were to be introduced.

---

[47] Some financial reforms were introduced earlier, such as the deregulation of deposit rates in 1994.

[48] Financial deregulation was part of a larger package of reforms in telecommunications, property and labour markets, and an overhaul of the medical and welfare systems.

**GLOBAL**: Tokyo was to become an international financial centre, raising Japan's international profile. Accounting, legal, supervisory and tax procedures would be changed to meet global standards set by international organisations such as the Basel Committee and the International Organisation of Securities Commissions.

Space constraints prevent a detailed outline of the reforms; for more detail, see Heffernan (2001) or Appendix 8.1 in Chapter 8. The thrust of the reforms was to largely eliminate the segmented markets characteristic of the Japanese financial sector since the end of World War II. In its place is a form of "restricted"[49] universal banking. Using the financial holding company structure introduced in the United States, banks are able to own separately capitalised securities firms and vice versa. Global expansion is largely unrestricted and foreign firms are given improved access to Japan's financial markets. In addition, Japan is party to the key international agreements, such as Basel 1 and Basel 2. However, as was noted in Chapter 4, Japan's interpretation of tier 1 and tier 2 capital means the ratios are not strictly comparable with those produced by other countries.

The combination of reform and financial difficulties caused a large number of mergers, even among the top banks. Table 5.9 reports the top 5 Japanese banks (by tier 1 capital), together with a few key ratios. The banks listed did not exist a few years ago, and testify to the large amount of merger activity. These mergers will affect the keiretsu system – some of the banks which have merged belonged to different keiretsu (e.g. Sumitomo and Mitsui). Note the negative ROAs, and the high cost:income ratios, compared to other major countries.

The regulatory system was also reformed. The MoF (given a new name, "Zaimisho"), blamed for much of Japan's financial malaise, had its responsibilities sharply curtailed. The opaque system of regulatory guidance was replaced with transparent rules. The **Bank of Japan Act, 1998** gave the Bank a large degree of autonomy, with a remit to focus on price stability. The Cabinet appoints the Governor, Vice-Governor and Policy Board, but it cannot dismiss them. The MoF is no longer a member of the Policy Board, though

Table 5.9  Top Japanese Banks (by Tier 1 Capital) in 2003

| Bank | Tier 1 Capital ($m) | Assets ($m) | Cost:Income (%) | ROA (%) | Basel Risk Assets Ratio (%) |
|---|---|---|---|---|---|
| Mizuho Financial Group | 29 092 | 1 080 764 | 55.40 | −1.74 | 9.53 |
| Sumitomo Mitsui Financial Group | 27 099 | 844 764 | 94.54 | −0.58 | 10.10 |
| Mitsubishi Tokyo Financial Group | 26 039 | 781 060 | 110.37 | −0.36 | 10.84 |
| UFJ Holding | 21 310 | 641 523 | 129.69 | −0.80 | 9.96 |
| Norinchukin Bank | 12 695 | 411 726 | 76.99 | 0.17 | 10.02 |

*Source: The Banker, July 2003.*

[49] It is restricted because unlike the German model, insurance firms cannot be subsidiaries of financial holding companies, and there is an upper limit on the percentage of commercial (i.e. non-financial) companies that a FHC can own. Insurance firms can offer banking and other financial products, and banks are allowed to sell their own insurance.

representatives can express their opinions at meetings. In addition to maintaining price stability, the Bank of Japan, together with the Financial Services Authority, conducts bank examinations. The power of the Finance Minister to issue directives to the Bank of Japan has been revoked. However, the MoF has been left with responsibility for the yen's stability. The Finance Minister also has the right to approve the Bank's budget, and can require the Bank to make loans to troubled financial institutions.

After an interim arrangement, the Financial Services Agency (JFSA) was formed in 2001, through a merger of the Financial Reconstruction Commission and the Financial Supervisory Agency. It reports to the Prime Minister's Office (_not_ the MoF). The FSA both formulates policy and regulates the financial sector. As new institutions, establishing creditability is a major challenge for both the Bank of Japan and the Financial Services Agency.

### 5.4.3. Deposit Insurance

Temporary changes in the deposit insurance scheme were also designed to restore financial stability. Established in 1971, the Deposit Insurance Commission (DIC) currently reports to the Financial Services Agency. The Deposit Insurance Act was amended in response to the large number of bank failures in 1998. Levies on banks' deposits fund the DIC,[50] but ¥17 trillion was injected into the fund to assist banks and allow for 100% deposit insurance coverage. A temporary measure, it expired in March 2002,[51] and reverted to the original scheme, that is, each depositor of a failed bank is paid a maximum of ¥10 million (plus interest). The only exception was liquid or settlement (used for direct debits, etc.) deposits, which earn no interest, where the 100% deposit insurance would not expire until March 2003. However, in the period leading up to March 2002, there was a notable transfer of funds to protected deposits and gold. In September 2002, fearing new bank runs, Japan's FSA announced the 100% guarantee would continue to apply to all liquid deposits until April 2005.

The DIC can draw on a special fund for banks if failure is deemed to threaten overall financial/economic stability at a local or national level. A Conference for Financial Crises (chaired by the Prime Minister) will decide which banks pose a systemic risk. However, it is often very difficult to distinguish between illiquid and insolvent banks, and a weak economy will make the job tougher.

# 5.5. Bank Structure and Regulation in the EU

## 5.5.1. Background

In common with the United Kingdom and Japan, the European Union has adopted the key global recommendations and agreements reached by various international committees. For example, it is expected that Basel 2 will be integrated with the EU's new Capital Adequacy Directive III. This section begins with a brief review of the banking systems in Germany,

---

[50] Since 1996, the premium has been 0.048% (raised from 0.012%) of insured deposits, with an extra premium of 0.036% to apply until March 2001. By contrast, in the USA, the premium paid is based on risk-related points scored by each bank; premia range from 0 to 0.27%.

[51] Originally, this temporary measure was due to expire in April 2001.

France, Italy and Scandinavia, before turning to three issues central to the European Union: the achievement of a single market, the European Central Bank, and the extent to which regulation should be integrated at European level.

## 5.5.2. Bank Structure – Germany

As was noted in Chapter 1, Germany is the home of the universal bank, and the *hausbank* system. Not only do they engage in retail and wholesale commercial and investment banking but, as in Japan, they will hold equity in commercial entities, to whom they also grant loans. Like the keiretsu in Japan, Germany's *hausbank* system involves close relationships between these commercial concerns and their banks, with cross-shareholdings and shared directorships. Normally senior bank executives sit on the supervisory boards of these companies. The big three to five national banks or *Grosßanken* (e.g. Deutsche Bank, Dresdner) date back to the 19th century and offer a full range of banking services, as do 200 regional banks, which have their headquarters and branches concentrated in a particular region.[52] The 13 *Landesbanken* began as regional girobanks in the 1900s – clearing was their primary function, though by the 21st century they too offer a full range of banking services, making them effectively universal banks. There are just under 600 saving banks (*Sparkassen*), with links to local or regional governments. The post office, *Deutsche Postbank*, also accepts savings from individuals and small firms, which are used to fund finance for the local/regional infrastructure, as well as lending to clients who might be turned away by other banks – hence the guarantee extended to them. There are just under 1800 mutual credit cooperatives. As in Canada and the USA, they are linked to particular professions and trades, and provide basic banking services – accepting deposits and making loans. There are also privately owned mortgage banks (*hypothekenbanken*) and mutual building and loan associations (*Bausparkassen* – some are state owned). Both focus largely on arranging mortgages for home ownership.

Just as the UK has recently undergone major reforms, Germany is considering what to do with its Bundesbank, which up to 2000 set monetary policy to achieve price stability. However, with Germany part of the eurozone, this role is somewhat diminished, though the Bundesbank Governor is part of the ECB interest rate setting committee.

The central banking system in Germany consists of the Bundesbank and nine regional Landeszentralbanken. Until the introduction of the euro, its remit was to maintain price stability. There is a proposal (by the Pohl Commission) to reduce the number of Landeszentralbanken to five. The Bundesbank proposed that **BAKred** (Bundesaufsichtsamt fur das Kreditwesen), the independent bank supervisor, be subsumed under the reorganised Bundesbank. However, in March 2001, the finance minister called for the creation of a new agency, with responsibility for the supervision of the entire financial sector, including banks.

The Bundesanstalt für Finanzdienstleistungsaufsich (**BaFin** – see www.bafin.de) began operations in May 2002. A legal entity within the Ministry of Finance, BaFin merges the functions of the former offices for banking supervision (BAKred) with the equivalent organisations in insurance and securities, creating a single body with responsibility for supervising all firms in the financial sector, including issues as diverse as solvency and

---

[52] Regional banks will also have branches in all the major German cities.

Table 5.10  Top German Banks (by Tier 1 Capital) in 2003

| Bank | Tier 1 Capital ($m) | Assets ($m) | Cost:Income (%) | ROA (%) | Basel Risk Assets Ratio (%) |
|---|---|---|---|---|---|
| Deutsche Bank | 23 849 | 795 255 | 78.75 | 0.47 | 12.60 |
| HypoVereinsbank | 20 057 | 724 787 | 69.10 | −0.12 | 9.20 |
| Commerzbank | 12 260 | 442 674 | 77.30 | −0.09 | 12.30 |
| Bayerische Landesbank | 9 951 | 357 904 | 48.40 | 0.06 | 10.30 |
| Dresdner Bank | 8 989 | 433 562 | 87.58 | −0.28 | 10.60 |

*Source: The Banker*, July 2003.

consumer protection. BaFin supervises 2700 banks, 700 insurance companies and 800 other firms offering financial services. At the time of writing, it employed about 1000 people, with offices in Bonn and Frankfurt/Main. The Bundesbank continues to represent German interests at the European Central Bank.

There is some uncertainty regarding the future structure and soundness of the German banking system. In 1999 the private banks complained to the European Commission that the public bank sector (Landesbanken, Sparkassen, Deutsche Postbank) had an unfair competitive advantage because they are backed by public guarantees. The complaint was upheld by the EC's Competition Commission. In 2001, the Commission and German government agreed that by July 2005, the loan guarantees for the Landesbanken would be phased out,[53] along with reform of some general guarantees. There is increasing concern about the health of German banks because prolonged recession has forced them to increase their loan loss reserves. Table 5.10 summarises the key ratios for the top 5 German banks. Three of the five are reporting a negative ROA in 2003 and some banks' cost to income ratios are high by European standards.

## 5.5.3. Bank structure – France

The French financial system, including its banks, has developed at a relatively slow pace, due partly to the relatively high degree of state interference in this sector. France is characterised by numerous regulations, even though it has recently shed some of its more onerous rules. For example, before 1985, France had no money market to speak of, apart from an interbank market.

The key banks in France are the 400 members of the AFB or Association Française des Banques. The system was highly segmented until the 1984 Banking Act. After 1984, AFB member banks became universal banks, offering retail, wholesale and investment banking, together with an intermediary service and investment banking.

The French banking system experienced episodes of bank nationalisation during the last half of the 20th century. The Socialist governments which nationalised banks thought it

---

[53] For existing assets, loan guarantees will apply for up to 10 years.

the only way to offer "fair" banking services to small and medium-sized industries. The more cynical saw it as a means by which the government could control the banking system to meet the industrial goals set by the socialists. The privatisation of banks began after the Gaullists took control of the National Assembly in 1986, but was suspended in 1988. They resumed again in the 1990s, so that by the new century, all the major banks were in the private sector.

There is also a strong mutual and cooperative movement. Typically, they are owned by the depositors, each with a single vote, independent of the size of the deposit. Membership is usually drawn from a particular industry – they can make deposits and apply for loans. The local offices are members of regional offices, which offer clearing and intermediary facilities. The two national organisations are the Caisse Central de Crédit Mutuel, which offers banking services to the regional groups, and the Confédération Nationale de Crédit Mutuel, which acts as a political lobby for this group. Unlike the UK, these groups are very large, as Table 5.11 illustrates. In 2002, Crédit Agricole, a mutual organisation, was the largest bank by tier 1 capital; Crédit Mutuel was the fourth largest.

There is a substantial savings bank movement, the Caisses d'Epargne, which, as a group, represents the fifth largest banking organisation by tier 1 capital. Interest on deposits is tax free, up to a limit. As cooperatives, they offer a full range of banking services to the retail sector. They are not allowed to make loans to commercial or trade concerns. Again, the local banks use regional centres for clearing purposes and two national bodies, one which manages funds collected by the local saving banks and the other which both regulates and represents the savings banks.

The other banks which appear in Table 5.11 are effectively universal banks.

The French banking system has also been subjected to more extensive regulation when compared to other EU states. Though the Banque de France gave up control over lending rates in 1967, restrictions on deposit rate setting, fees and commissions were not lifted until 1996. Even now no interest is paid on current accounts, in exchange, it is claimed, for free bank services. However, as pressure of the single market, particularly in Euroland, increases, it is unlikely that any control over rates will last. For example, in 2000, the Dutch financial group, ING, began to offer interest paying deposit rates on all accounts in credit via the internet. With the implementation of financial reforms, a great deal of consolidation has

Table 5.11   Top French Banks (by Tier 1 Capital) in 2003

| Bank | Tier 1 Capital ($m) | Assets ($m) | Cost:Income (%) | ROA (%) | Basel Risk Assets Ratio (%) |
|---|---|---|---|---|---|
| Crédit Agricole Groupe | 35 661 | 609 055 | 62.21 | 0.62 | 11.70 |
| BNP Paribas | 24 119 | 744 882 | 65.20 | 0.75 | 10.90 |
| Société Générale | 16 001 | 525 655 | 72.00 | 0.50 | 11.13 |
| Crédit Mutuel | 13 156 | 364 389 | 69.00 | 0.56 | 10.10 |
| Groupe Caisse d'Epargne | 13 084 | 374 510 | 72.52 | 0.46 | 143.00 |

Source: *The Banker*, July 2003.

taken place, causing the number of French financial institutions to fall from 2000 in 1990 to just over 1000 at the end of the decade.

## 5.5.4. Bank structure – Spain[54]

Spanish depository institutions include banks, mutual savings banks and credit cooperatives. All of them operate under a similar regulatory regime. There are also "Specialised Credit Institutions" (SCIs), which are confined to granting credit to specific sectors of the economy and may not be funded through deposit taking.

The Spanish banking system was gradually liberalised during the second half of the 1980s. Prior to liberalisation, the financial market was geographically segmented and there was little competition. In 1987, controls on interest rates were relaxed. In 1991–2, credit restrictions and investment targets were eliminated.

These reforms created a very competitive environment; commercial banks and mutual savings banks fought to attract deposits and borrowers by offering very cheap products (e.g. "la supercuenta" and "la superhipoteca"[55]). The reforms generated two types of institutions: those focused on growth, and banks which gave priority to increased returns rather than size. There was a wave of mergers and acquisitions among both commercial and mutual savings banks. State owned banks were also affected. Until 1990, state credit institutions depended on the government's Official Credit Institute. In 1991 the Banking Corporation of Spain, Argentaria, was created by merging the Official Credit Entities: the Banco Exterior de España and the Postal Savings Bank (Caja Postal de Ahorros). Argentaria was gradually privatised between 1993 and 1998, then merged with Banco Bilbao Vizcaya[56] in 1999. The two largest Spanish institutions (see Table 5.12), Banco Santander Central Hispano and Bilbao Vizcaya Argentaria, are the result of mergers between Spain's bigger banks.[57]

These mergers have increased the degree of concentration in the market. The private commercial banks and the mutual savings banks are the key players in the Spanish banking system. Commercial and mutual savings banks have, respectively, about 49% and 46% of total deposits; credit cooperatives have 5%. In recent years mutual savings banks have progressively increased their share of the deposit market, at the expense of the commercial banks. The change could be due to the restructuring of the commercial banks over the past 10 years, which resulted in the closure of numerous branches (e.g. nearly 600 closed in 2002). At the same time, mutual savings banks have expanded their branch networks.

The major Spanish banks moved into Spanish South America (Hispano-América). There are cultural and political links between the two regions[58] (common history, language and very similar legal systems), reducing some of the risks normally related to multinational

---

[54] Thanks go to Amelia Pais for contributing the material for the section on Spain.

[55] The super current account and the super mortgage.

[56] Banco de Bilbao had merged with Banco Vizcaya in 1988.

[57] In 1991 Banco Central merged with Banco Hispano, then Central Hispano merged with Santander in 1999 (which acquired, by state auction Banco Español de Crédito in 1994 – this bank was in trouble due to fraud, and some of its directors were imprisoned). Santander Central Hispano also owns Banco Español de Crédito.

[58] Spain, after the USA, is the second investor in South American countries. In 1999, 63% of the total Spanish foreign investment was in South America.

Table 5.12  Top Spanish Banks (by Tier 1 Capital) in 2003

| Bank | Tier 1 Capital ($m) | Assets ($m) | Cost:income (%) | ROA (%) | Basel Risk Assets Ratio (%) |
|------|------|------|------|------|------|
| Santander Central Hispano | 15 556 | 339 983 | 61.75 | 1.08 | 12.64 |
| Banco Bilbao Vizcaya Argentaria | 14 346 | 293 144 | 54.44 | 1.12 | 12.50 |
| Caja de Ahorros y Pen. de Barcelona - la Caixa | 7 212 | 108 033 | 71.23 | 0.01 | na |
| Caja de Ahorros y Monte de Piedad de Madrid | 4 240 | 74 072 | 57.46 | 1.00 | 12.87 |
| Banco Popular Espanol | 3 402 | 44 049 | 35.54 | 2.51 | 11.00 |

*Source: The Banker*, July 2003.

banking. Hispano-América is also a big market (more than 500 million inhabitants), with good growth. Spain plays a leadership role in Hispano-América – many see Spain as the "Mother country". As a result, the Argentinean financial crisis affected the big Spanish banks with significant exposure in Hispano-América.[59]

In November 2002, a financial law was passed to modernise the Spanish financial system. The main objectives are to increase the efficiency and competitiveness of the financial system, and to encourage the use of new channels of distribution and technologies in banking, by authorising the creation of e-cash institutions which will issue e-cash, to be used as a means of payment.[60] The law also calls for greater protection of the consumers using financial services. The central bank is responsible for bank supervision; and the new law gave its risk agency expanded powers to centralise and supervise financial risks incurred by all financial institutions.

## 5.5.5. Bank Structure – Scandinavia

Though four independent countries, Norway (not a member of the EU), Denmark, Sweden and Finland make up the region of Scandinavia,[61] recent mergers of banks across the region have increased the degree of financial integration between the countries. In fact, it could be argued that this region is closer to achieving a single financial market than the EU as a whole.

---

[59] In 2002 Santander Central Hispano, Banco Bilbao Vizcaya Argentaria and La Caixa suffered, respectively, a 9.62%, 27.3% and 29.1% drop in profits due to their exposure to Hispano-América (*Source*: LaBolsa.com 31st January 2003).

[60] To date, the use of new technologies and online banking is relatively low compared to other countries. Only 17% of Spanish have internet at home compared to an European average of 40% (Anuario de Economía y Finanzas 2003 – Ediciones El País)

[61] Iceland is often considered part of this region, but there are few banking ties, and it will be excluded from the discussion.

The area experienced quite a severe banking crisis in the early 1990s, which led to a large number of mergers, giving this region the most concentrated banking system in Europe. Universal banking is the norm; there are savings and "union" banks, but on a much smaller scale (compared to Germany or France), and no regional banks.

The degree of concentration is quite striking. The five largest banks in each country accounted for, respectively, as a percentage of the banking sector's aggregate balance sheet, 96% in Finland, 94% in Sweden, 84% in Denmark and 71% in Norway.[62] One example of the increased concentration which crosses national boundaries is Nordea – the name should be familiar to readers from the discussion on e-banking in Chapter 2. Nordea is a large universal bank, headquartered in Sweden, which, following a number of acquisitions, became a Scandinavian financial group. In 1993, Nordbanken took over the sickly Gota bank, and shortly after merged with Merita Bank of Finland, to form Merita Nordbanken. Other acquisitions included two Danish banks, Tryg-Baltica and Unibank. It purchased Christianiana Bank og Kreditkasse (K-bank) and Den Norske Bank in Norway, both of which had to be rescued by the government in the early 1990s. Insurance firms were also purchased, reflecting the trend to "all finance" or *bankassurance* – whereby one bank offers every financial service, from insurance to e-banking.

Scandinavia has some of the oldest central banks in the world, some even preceding the growth of commercial banks, in contrast to the trends in the UK, USA and many European countries, where the central bank was set up after the emergence of a private/public commercial banking sector. The Bank of Sweden or Sveriges Riksbank was created in 1668, replacing the Stockholm Banco, which had been formed to issue bank notes. The Financial Supervisory Authority is responsible for individual bank soundness; the Riksbank controls the payment system and ensures financial stability prevails. The Dansmarks Nationalbank originated as a private bank in 1736, but insolvency led to its nationalisation 37 years later. Though Dansmarks Nationalbank has been independent of government since 1936, its monetary policy is driven by the fixed exchange rate regime it has with the euro, because it is part of the Exchange Rate Mechanism. There is a separate supervisory authority, though both institutions have joint responsibility for financial stability. Soumen Pankki (the Bank of Finland) was formed in 1811, followed by the Norges Bank (Bank of Norway) in 1816. Norges Bank implements monetary policy set by the government. It also controls the investments of the Government Petroleum Fund, which receives the profits from the oil and gas sector. Norway's banks are supervised by a separate institution, the Kredittilsynett.

In Finland, banks are supervised by a Financial Supervision Group, which is located at the Bank of Finland, but independent of it. Finland has adopted the euro, so its monetary policy is largely determined by the European Central Bank. Finland has 343 banks (1999 figures), which is high compared to other countries in this region. There are just eight commercial banks, and a group of 246 union banks making up Okobank, Merita, a commercial bank, and Leonia, a state owned bank (the product of a 1998 merger between the Postal Bank and the Export Bank). These three banks have 90% of bank assets; 85% of bank liabilities.

There is a fairly strong movement of savings and union banks in Finland – about 130 (out of 152 banks in total) in 2000. In the other countries, these sectors have largely integrated

---

[62] *Source*: Dansmarks Nationalbank (2000), *Monetary Review*, **2**, p. 69.

with the commercial banks. There are also some non-bank financial firms in the region, including specialised mortgage banks, state lending firms, investment companies, mutual funds, insurance and pension funds, but most are either subsidiaries or linked to domestic banks, in keeping with the bancassurance approach.

## 5.5.6. Bank Structure – Italy

The banking structure in Italy underwent major changes in the 1990s, the result of financial reform in preparation for operating in a single market. By 2000, the number of banks in Italy had more than halved due to the 561 mergers and takeovers during the 1990s. The proliferation of large numbers of small, local branchless uncompetitive banks was the outcome of the 1936 Banking Act, which allowed commercial banks to take short-term (18-month) deposits and loans, while investment banks were restricted to long-term finance. No bank could own a commercial concern. The central bank, the Banca d'Italia, had a great deal of power in terms of approving products offered by banks; it also discouraged branch banking. In addition, because of frequent bank failures and crises before and during the 1930s, large numbers of banks were either state owned or run by non-profit organisations, all closely supervised by government.

Given that the Italian industry consists largely of family or state owned firms, there was little demand for finance via an equity market or a more sophisticated banking system. There was pressure for reform in the 1980s, coming from the banking association itself and groups representing firms and employees. The Banca d'Italia responded by relaxing what restrictions it could, and in 1990 began to encourage mergers and branch networks. The Banking Act of 1993 effectively allowed the formation of bank holding companies, and got rid of the distinction between short and medium-term deposits and loans. Banks were allowed to hold up to 15% of a commercial concern. The outcome was subsidiaries of the BHCs which offered a full range of financial services, including insurance.

From 1993 onward, there was a steady stream of privatisations, beginning with the sale of 64% of the ordinary shares of Credito Italiano followed by Banca Commerciale Italiana, Mediobanca, and in the late 1990s, Banca Nationale del Lavoro, Banco di Napoli and Banca di Roma, among others. By 1999, the share of the banking sector held by the state or organisations supervised by the state had fallen to 12%, from 70% in 1993. The trend has been to form banking groups; in 2000 there were 79 such groups with 267 bank subsidiaries, controlling just under 90% of the country's assets. There are 8 *maggiori* or very large banks, and 16 *grandi* (large) banks. In 2000 there were 284 limited banks with over 20 000 branches, 44 cooperative banks with nearly 5000 branches, and 499 mutuals with just under 3000 branches. Unlike other western countries (with the exception of the USA), the number of bank branches expanded through the 1990s, following the relaxation of the laws by the central bank.

Table 5.13 shows the top 5 Italian banks, with some key ratios. As can be seen from the table, despite considerable consolidation, the top Italian banks are much smaller than their British, German or French counterparts in terms of tier 1 capital and assets.

Like the Bank of England, the Banca d'Italia was founded as a private bank in 1893 and given responsibility for maintaining price stability in 1947. It is also the key bank regulator.

Table 5.13   Top Italian Banks (by Tier 1 Capital) in 2003

| Bank | Tier 1 Capital ($m) | Assets ($m) | Cost:Income (%) | ROA (%) | Basel Risk Assets Ratio (%) |
|---|---|---|---|---|---|
| Banca Intesa | 14 151 | 294 393 | 69.31 | 0.08 | 11.12 |
| UniCredito Italiano | 11 300 | 223 730 | 54.29 | 1.54 | 11.64 |
| SanPaolo IMI | 10 240 | 213 688 | 65.10 | 0.50 | 10.70 |
| Capitalia Gruppo Bancario | 6 380 | 147 800 | 71.76 | 0.05 | 9.77 |
| Banca Monte dei Paschi di Siena | 5 411 | 135 154 | 72.83 | 0.69 | 8.79 |

*Source: The Banker*, July 2003.

Since the introduction of a single currency in 1999, it participates in running European monetary policy via the European Central Bank.

## 5.5.7. Directives for a Single EU Financial Services Market

The review of individual bank structure and regulation for a selection of continental European states and the UK illustrates considerable differences in the respective banking systems. In France and Spain, the savings banks are major players; France also has an extensive cooperative movement. Germany is the home of some very large universal banks, but also has some important regional and savings banks. A traditionally fragmented system in Italy is gradually disappearing but has some way to go to match the high degree of consolidation in Scandinavia. The UK and Germany have recently introduced monolithic financial regulators but in Italy, France and Spain, banks continue to be supervised by the central bank. Within this somewhat diverse framework, the EU is seeking to integrate EU financial markets, creating a single market in banking and other financial services.

The objective of this section is to address the issue of achieving a single banking market in the European Union. The Single European Act (1986) was considered essential if EU markets, including the banking and financial markets, were to become sufficiently well integrated to be called "single" markets. It was hoped the Act would speed up the integration of European markets through the introduction of qualified majority voting and the replacement of harmonisation with mutual recognition. The 1st of January 1993 was designated "single market day", i.e. the day the single internal market was to be completed, in all sectors, including banking. Yet, as this text goes to press, more than a decade later, achieving an integrated banking and/or financial market continues to be an elusive goal. The Financial Sector Action Plan has set 2005 as the date to achieve a single financial market in Europe. What happened? After reviewing the background to the current state of affairs, the problem of existing barriers to the completion of a single market is discussed.

### *The internal market: background*

The **Treaty of Rome** *(1957)* was a critical piece of legislation because one of its key objectives was to bring about the free trade of goods and services throughout EU member states.[63] This was to be achieved through the harmonisation of rules and regulations across all states. However, by the 1980s, it was acknowledged that progress towards free trade had been dismally slow. The **Single European Act** *(1986)* was another milestone in European law. To speed up the integration of markets, qualified majority voting was introduced and the principle of mutual recognition replaced the goal of harmonisation. The Act itself was an admission that it would be impossible to achieve **harmonisation**, that is, to get states to agree on a single set of rules for every market. Instead, by applying the principle of **mutual recognition**, member states would only have to agree to adopt a minimum set of standards/rules for each market. Qualified majority voting, where no member has a right of veto,[64] would make it easier to pass directives based on mutual recognition.

These acts applied to all markets, from coal to computers. In this subsection, the European directives or laws which were passed to bring about integrated banking/financial markets are reviewed. The **First Banking Directive** *(1977)* defined a credit institution as any firm making loans and accepting deposits. A Bank Advisory Committee was established which, in line with the Treaty of Rome, called for harmonisation of banking in Europe, without clarifying how this goal was to be achieved. The **Second Banking Directive** *(1989)* was passed in response to the 1986 Single European Act. It remains the key EU banking law and sets out to achieve a single banking market through application of the principle of mutual recognition. Credit institutions[65] are granted a **passport** to offer financial services anywhere in the EU, provided member states have banking laws which meet certain minimum standards. The passport means that if a bank is licensed to conduct activities in its home country, it can offer any of these services in the EU state, without having to seek additional authorisation from the host state. The financial services covered by the directive include the following.

- Deposit taking and other forms of funding.
- Lending, including retail and commercial, mortgages, forfaiting and factoring.
- Money transmission services, including the issue of items which facilitate money transmission, from cheques, credit/debit cards to automatic teller machines.
- Financial leasing.
- Proprietary trading and trading on behalf of clients, e.g. stockbroking.
- Securities, derivatives, foreign exchange trading and money broking.
- Portfolio management and advice, including all activities related to corporate and personal finance.
- Safekeeping and administration of securities.
- Credit reference services.
- Custody services.

This long list of financial activities in which EU credit institutions can engage illustrates Brussel's strong endorsement of a universal banking framework.

---

[63] The EU has 15 member countries. Free trade extends to members of the European Economic Area (EEA): Iceland, Liechtenstein and Norway. Switzerland is a member of the European Free Trade Association but not the EEA. In 2005, 10 new members will join.

[64] With the exception of directives on fiscal matters, which could be vetoed by any member state.

[65] In the EU, a credit institution is any firm which is licensed to take deposits and/or make loans.

Prior to the Second Directive, the entry of banks into other member states was hampered because the bank supervisors in the host country had to approve the operation, and it was subject to host country supervision and laws. For example, some countries required foreign branches to provide extra capital as a condition of entry. The Second Directive removes these constraints and specifies that the home country (where a bank is headquartered) is responsible for the bank's solvency and any of its branches in other EU states. The home country supervisor decides whether a bank should be liquidated, but there is some provision for the host country to intervene. Branches are not required to publish separate accounts, in line with the emphasis on consolidated supervision. Host country regulations apply to risk management and implementation of monetary policy. Thus, a Danish subsidiary located in one of the eurozone states is subject to the ECB's monetary policy, even though Denmark keeps its own currency.

The Second Directive imposes a minimum capital (equity) requirement of 5 million euros on all credit institutions. Supervisory authorities must be notified of any major shareholders with equity in excess of 10% of a bank's equity. If a bank has equity holdings in a non-financial firm exceeding 10% of the firm's value and 60% of the bank's capital, it is required to deduct the holding from the bank's capital.

The Second Directive has articles covering third country banks, that is, banks headquartered in a country outside the EU. The principle of *equal treatment* applies: the EU has the right to either suspend new banking licences or negotiate with the third country if EU financial firms find themselves at a competitive disadvantage because foreign and domestic banks are treated differently (e.g. two sets of banking regulations apply) by the host country government. In 1992, a European Commission report acknowledged the inferior treatment of EU banks in some countries, but appears to favour using the World Trade Organisation to sort out disputes, rather than exercising the powers of suspension.

Other European directives relevant to the banking/financial markets include the following.

- **Own Funds and Solvency Ratio Directives (1989):** The former defines what is to count as capital for all EU credit institutions; the latter sets the Basel risk assets ratio of 8%, which is consistent with the 1988 Basel accord and the 1996 agreement on the treatment of market risk. The EU is expected to adopt the Basel 2 risk assets ratio (see Chapter 4).
- **Money Laundering Directive (1991):** Effective from 1993, money laundering is defined to include either handling or aiding the handling of assets, knowing they are the result of a serious crime, such as terrorism or illegal drug activities. It applies to credit and financial institutions in the EU. They are obliged to disclose suspicions of such activities, and to introduce the relevant internal controls and staff training to detect money laundering.
- **Consolidated Supervision Directives:** Passed in 1983 and 1993. The 1993 directive requires accounting reports to be reported on a consolidated basis. The threshold for consolidation is 20%.
- **Deposit Guarantee Directive (1994):** To protect small depositors and discourage bank runs all EU states are required to establish a *minimum* deposit insurance fund, to be financed by banks. Individual EU states will determine how the scheme is to be run, and can allow alternative schemes (e.g. for savings banks) if they provide equivalent coverage.

The minimum is 20 000 euros,[66] with an optional 10% co-insurance. Foreign exchange deposits are included. The UK is one of several states to impose the co-insurance, the objective of which is to give customers some incentive to monitor their bank's activities. For example, the maximum payout on a deposit of £20 000 is £18 000; £4500 for a £5000 deposit. Branches located outside the home state may join the host country scheme; otherwise they are covered by the home country. However, if the deposit insurance of the home country is more generous, then the out of state branch is required to join the host country's scheme. The host country decides if branches from non-EU states can join.

- **Credit Institution Winding Up Directive:** Home country supervisors have the authority to close an institution; the host country is bound by the decision.

- **Large Exposures Directive (1992):** Applies on a consolidated basis to credit institutions in the EU from January 1994. Each firm is required to report (annually) any exposures to an individual borrower which exceeds 15% of their equity capital. Exposure to one borrower/group of borrowers is limited to 40% of bank's funds, and no bank is permitted an exposure to one borrower or related group of more than 25%. A bank's total exposure cannot exceed eight times its own funds.

- **The Consolidated Supervision Directives:** There have been two directives. The original was passed in 1983 but replaced by a new directive in 1992, which took effect in January 1993. It applies to the EU parents of a financial institution and the financial subsidiaries of parents where the group undertakes what are largely financial activities. The threshold for consolidation is 20% of capital, that is, the EU parent or credit institution owns 20% or more of the capital of the subsidiaries.

- **Capital Adequacy Directives (1993, 1997, 2006(?)):** The capital adequacy directives came to be known as CAD-I (1993), CAD-II (1997) and CAD-III (2006?). CAD-I took effect from January 1996 but CAD-II replaced it, adopting the revised Basel (1996) treatment of market risk. It means trading exposures (for example, market risk) arising from investment business are subject to separate minimum capital requirements. As in CAD-I, to ensure a level playing field, banks *and* securities firms conform to the same capital requirements. Banks with securities arms classify their assets as belonging to either a trading book or a banking book. Firms are required to set aside 2% of the gross value of a portfolio, plus 8% of the net value. However, banks have to satisfy the risk assets ratio as well, which means more capital will have to be held against bank loans than securities with equivalent risk. For example, mortgage backed securities have a lower capital requirement than mortgages appearing on a bank's balance sheet. This gives banks an incentive to increase their securities operations at the expense of traditional lending, which could cause distortions. The European Commission published a working document on CAD-III in November 2002. Consultation and comments on the document were completed in 2003. The plan is to publish a draft CAD-III in 2004, and by the end of 2006 it should have been ratified by European Parliament and the EU state legislatures. It will coincide with the adoption of Basel 2 by the banks. As was pointed out in Chapter 4, the Commission has made it clear that the main text of Basel 2 will form part of the CAD-III directive. In other words, the Basel guidelines will become statutory for all EU

---

[66] In the UK, banks can opt to insure for £35 000 or the euro equivalent.

states. This means it will be very difficult to adjust bank regulation to accommodate new financial innovations and other changes in the way banks operate. EU banks will have a competitive disadvantage compared to other countries (notably the USA), where supervisors require banks to adopt Basel 2 but do not put it on their statute books.

- **The Investment Services Directive:** Passed in 1993, and implemented by the end of 1995. It mirrors the second banking directive but applies to investment firms. Based on the principle of mutual recognition, if an investment services firm is approved by one home EU state, it may offer the same set of services in all other EU states, provided the regulations in the home state meet the minimum requirements for an investment firm set out in the directive. The firm must also comply with CAD-II/III. The objective of the ISD was to prevent regulatory differences giving a competitive edge to banks or securities firms. It applies to all firms providing professional investment services. The core investment products covered include transferable securities, unit trusts, money market instruments, financial futures contracts, forwards, swaps and options. The directive also ensures cross-border access to trading systems. A number of clauses do not apply if a firm holds a banking passport but also meets the definition of an investment firm.

Three other directives are relevant to the operations of some EU banks. The UCITS (Undertakings for the Collective Investment of Transferable Securities) Directive (1985) took effect in most states in 1989, other states adopted it later. Unit trust schemes authorised in one member state may be marketed in other member states. Under UCITS, 90% of a fund must be invested in publicly traded firms and the fund cannot own more than 5% of the outstanding shares of a company.

- **Insurance Directives for Life and Non-Life Insurance:** Passed since 1973. The Third Life Directive and Third Non-Life Directives were passed in 1992, and took effect in July 1994. These directives create an EU passport for insurance firms, by July 1994. Provided a firm receives permission from the regulator of the home country, it can set up a branch anywhere in the EU, and consumers can purchase insurance anywhere in the EU. The latest Pension Funds Directive was approved by Parliament in late 2003. It outlines the common rules for investment by pension funds, and their regulation. Though silent on harmonisation of taxes, a recent ruling by the European Court of Justice states that the tax breaks for pension schemes should apply across EU borders. States have two years to adopt the new directive, and it is hoped that during this time, they will remove the tax obstacles which have, to date, prevented a pan-European pension fund scheme, and transferability of pensions across EU states. It is also expected that restrictions on the choice of an investment manager from any EU state will be lifted and it will be possible to invest funds anywhere in the Union.
- **Financial Conglomerate Directive (2002):** This directive harmonises the way financial conglomerates are supervised across the EU. A financial conglomerate is defined as any group with "significant" involvement in two sectors: banking, investment and insurance. More specifically, in terms of its balance sheet, at least 40% of the group's activities are financial; *and* the smaller of the two sectors contributes 10% or more to the group's balance sheet and the group's capital requirements. By this definition, there are 38

financial conglomerates in the EU (2002 figures), and most of them have banking as their main line of business. These financial conglomerates are important players, especially in banking, where they have 27% of the EU deposit market; their market share in the insurance market is 20%, in terms of premium income. Market share (in terms of deposits or premium income) varies widely among EU states.[67] The directive bans the use of the same capital twice in different parts of the group. All EU states must ensure the entire conglomerate is supervised by a single authority. The risk exposure of a financial conglomerate is singled out for special attention – risk may not be concentrated in a single part of the group, and there must be a common method for measuring and managing risk, and the overall solvency of the group is to be computed. American financial conglomerates are supervised by numerous authorities, even though the Federal Reserve Bank is the lead supervisor. The US authorities have expressed concern at the plan for an EU coordinator, who will decide whether the US system of regulation is "equivalent"; if not, then the compliance costs for US financial conglomerates operating in the EU will increase, leaving them at a competitive disadvantage. A compromise is being sought. Analysts have speculated that the trade-off may be achieved by a relaxation of the Sarbanes–Oxley[68] rules for EU firms operating in the United States. Europe, like Japan, Mexico and Canada, is seeking exemption from parts of the Act.

- **Market Abuse Directive (2002):** This directive is part of the Lamfalussy reform of the EU securities markets (see below), and introduces a single set of rules on market manipulation and insider dealing, which together, make up market abuse. The directive emphasises investor protection with all market participants being treated equally, greater transparency, improved information flows, and closer coordination between national authorities. Each state assigns a single regulatory body which must adhere to a minimum set of common rules on insider trading and market manipulation.

## 5.5.8. Achieving a Single Market in Financial Services

A single financial market has been considered an important EU objective from the outset. A study on the effects on prices in the event of a single European financial market was undertaken by Paolo Cecchini (1988), on behalf of Price Waterhouse (1988). The study looked at prices before and after the achievement of a single market for a selection of products offered by banks, insurance firms and brokers.[69] The banking products studied

---

[67] Source of data: EU-Mixed Technical Group (2002), p. 2.

[68] The Sarbanes–Oxley Act was passed by Congress in July 2002, in the wake of the Enron and Worldcom financial disasters. External auditors are no longer allowed to offer consulting services (e.g. investment advice, broker dealing, information systems, etc.) to their clients. Internal auditing committees are responsible for hiring external auditors and ensuring the integrity of both internal and external audits. There are strict new corporate governance rules which apply to all employees and directors. CEOs and CFOs are required to certify the health of all quarterly and annual reports filed with the Securities and Exchange Commission. Fines and prison sentences are used to enforce the Act. For example, a CEO convicted of certifying false financial reports faces fines in the range of $1 million to $5 million and/or prison terms of 10–20 years. The accounting profession is to be overseen by an independent board.

[69] The Cecchini/Price Waterhouse study covered key sectors of the EU economy, but the discussion here is confined to findings on the financial markets.

included the 1985 prices (on a given day) for consumer loans, credit cards, mortgages, letters of credit, travellers cheques/foreign exchange drafts, and consumer loans. Post-1992, it was assumed that the prices which would prevail would be an average of the four lowest prices from the eight countries included in the study. Based on these somewhat simplistic assumptions and calculations, the report concluded that there would be substantial welfare gains from the completion of a single financial market, in the order of about 1.5% of EU GDP. Germany and the UK would experience the largest gains, a somewhat puzzling finding given that the UK, and to a lesser extent Germany, had some of the most liberal financial markets at the time.

Heinemann and Jopp (2002) also identified the gains from a single financial market. They argue that the greater integration of retail financial markets will encourage financial development, which stimulates growth in the EU and will help the euro gain status as a global currency. Using results from another study[70] on the effect of financial integration on growth, Heinemann and Jopp (2002) argue growth in the EU could be increase by 0.5% per annum, or an annual growth of €43 billion based on EU GDP figures for the year 2000.

As was noted earlier, the original objective was to achieve a single market by the beginning of 1993. The grim reality is that integration of EU financial markets, especially in the retail banking/finance sector, is a long way from completion, and any welfare gains are yet to be realised. The **Financial Services Action Plan** (2000) is an admission of this failure, and sets 2005 as the new date for integration of EU financial markets.

## Barriers in EU retail financial markets

Heinemann and Jopp (2002) examined the retail financial markets and identified a number of what they term "natural" and "policy induced"[71] obstacles to free trade. Eppendorfer *et al.* (2002) use similar terms; "natural" barriers refer to those arising as a result of different cultures or consumer preferences, while different state tax policies or regulations are classified as "policy induced" barriers.

Before proceeding with a review of the major barriers, it is worth identifying an ongoing problem which hinders the integration of EU markets. EU states have a poor record of **implementation** of EC directives. There are two problems – passing the relevant legislation AND enforcing new laws. The problem is long standing. Butt-Philips (1988) documented the dismal performance of EU states in the period 1982–86, especially for directives relating to competition policy or trade liberalisation. *The Economist* (1994) also reported a poor implementation rate, though the adoption of directives had improved. For example, in 1996 one country was taken to the European Courts before it would agree to pass a national law to implement the Investment Services Directive. It has also been difficult to get some countries to adopt the 1993 CAD-II Directive. The European Commission website has

---

[70] De Gregorio (1999), who found a positive impact on growth as a result of greater financial market integration, using a sample of industrial and developing countries.

[71] One policy induced barrier, they claimed, was the failure of Denmark, Sweden and the UK to agree to adopt the euro in place of their national currencies. However, there are many examples of free trade agreements among countries with different currencies, such as the North American Free Trade Agreement (NAFTA), and the Mercosur (Brazil, Argentina and other countries).

a long list of actions being taken because some EU states have failed to adopt and/or implement a variety of directives.

Heinemann and Jopp identify *policy induced barriers*, which, they argue, could be corrected by government changes in policies. They include the following.

- Discriminatory tax treatment or subsidies which favour the domestic supplier. For example, tax relief on the capital repayment of mortgages was restricted to Belgian lenders, which gave them a clear cost advantage. This barrier has since been removed but the European Commission had cases against Greece, Italy and Portugal because of similar tax obstacles. In Germany, pension funds are eligible for subsidy but only if a long list of highly specific requirements are met, which means that any pan-European supplier of pension products faces an additional barrier in Germany. Either the firm will not qualify for the subsidy or compliance costs will be higher than their German competitors, unless the rules imposed by the home state are very similar. If every state has different requirements, compliance costs soar, discouraging the integration of an EU pensions market.

- Eppendorfer *et al.* (2002) provide an example of where the principle of mutual recognition creates problems. Banco Santander Central Hispano, Nordea, HSBC and BNP Paribas all reported problems when they tried to extend their respective branch network across state frontiers because of the split in supervision: the home country is responsible for branches but the host deals with solvency issues.

- Lack of information for customers on how to obtain redress in the event of a legal dispute or problem with a product supplied by an out of state firm.

- Additional costs arising from national differences in supervision, consumer protection and accounting standards. For example, the e-commerce laws[72] in the EU mean all firms are subject to country of origin rules: if an internet broker is planning to offer services in other EU states, then the broker must follow the internet laws of each state. It is illegal to use a website set up in France for French customers in Germany – a new website has to be created for German customers. Likewise, the EU directive on distance marketing of financial services allows each member state to impose separate national rules on how financial services can be marketed, advertised and distributed. The myriad of different rules makes it almost impossible to develop pan-EU products which can be sold in all states. Nonetheless, Nordea (see Chapter 2) used the internet to successfully capture market share in several Scandinavian countries, which shows the internet can bypass some entry barriers.

- Conduct of business rules can be used as a way of preventing other EU firms from setting up business in a given EU state. For example, there may be a rule which does not make a contract legally binding unless written in the said state's language(s). Though there is increasing convergence on the professional markets, this is not the case for retail markets.

- The "general good" principle is used by EU states to protect consumers, and cultural differences influence consumer protection policy. However, these rules can deter competition from other EU states: the principle is interpreted in different ways across the

---

[72] The E-Commerce Directive was passed in June 2000, to be implemented by member states by June 2002.

EU states. The outcome is 15 to 25[73] different sets of rules on, for example, the supply of mortgage products, which raises costs for any firm attempting to establish a pan-EU presence. There is a fine line between the use of the general good clause to protect consumers, as opposed to domestic suppliers.

- There are 15 to 25 different legal systems, each with different contract and insolvency laws, and so on. For example, trying to sell loans across EU frontiers is extremely difficult because of different definitions of collateral across the member states.[74]

- It is acknowledged that it is much harder to raise venture capital in the EU than in the USA. The **Risk Capital Action Plan** was endorsed by the European Council in June 1998, to be implemented by 2003. The point of the plan is to eliminate the barriers which inhibit the supply of and demand for risk capital. It will focus on resolving cultural differences (e.g. lack of an entrepreneurial culture), removing market barriers, and differences in tax treatment. However, the plan is ambitious and may prove too difficult to implement.

- Reduced cross-border information flows can also create barriers. New entrants to state credit markets face a more serious problem with adverse selection than home suppliers because they have less information. In many EU states central banks keep public credit registers, but access to them is restricted to home financial institutions that report domestic information to the central bank. The same is true for some private credit rating agencies. It creates barriers for out of state lenders and even if they do manage to enter the market, it increases the risk of them being caught out with dud loans.

- Domestic suppliers, especially state owned, often have special privileges. Or, the costs of cross-border operations, such as money transfers, may involve costly identification/verification requirements. For example, on-line brokers (or any financial service) have to verify the identity of the client they are dealing with. This is done through local post offices, the relevant embassy, or a notary. Such cumbersome procedures discourage the use of foreign on-line broking/financial firms.

- The existence of national payments systems for clearing euro payments is cumbersome and costly. In July 2003, a new EU regulation requires that the charges for processing cross-border euro payments be the same as for domestic payments up to €12 500, rising to €50 000 by 2005. The goal is to create a single European payments area. Banks have done well from extra charges for cross-border payments, and one estimate is that this regulation will cause lost revenues of around €1.2 billion.

- Though the integration of EU stock exchanges continues apace through mergers and alliances, clearing and settlement procedures remain largely national. This means, for example, that on-line brokers must charge additional fees for purchasing or selling stocks listed on other EU exchanges (even if there is an alliance), or they do not offer the service. The demand side is also affected: customers are deterred from choosing a supplier in another EU state. The cost of cross-border share trading in Europe is 90% higher than in the USA, and it is estimated that a central counterparty clearing system for equities in

---

[73] The EU is set to expand to include up to 10 additional states from 2004.
[74] *Source*: Eppendorfer *et al.* (2002), p. 16.

Europe (ECCP) would reduce transactions costs by $950 million (€1 billion) per year.[75] The cost savings would come primarily from an integrated or single back office. A central clearing house for European equities acts as an intermediary between buyers and sellers. Netting would also be possible, meaning banks could net their purchases against sales, reducing the number of transactions needing to be settled, and therefore the capital needed to be set aside for prudential purposes. Real time gross settlement would help to eliminate settlements risk. The plan is being backed by the European Securities Forum, a group of Europe's largest banks.

- There are more than 50 related regulatory bodies with responsibility for regulation of financial firms in the EU, and the number will continue to rise as new member states join. This makes it difficult for them to cooperate. This issue will remain while individual states have the right to decide how to regulate home state financial firms. Different reporting rules for companies and different rules on mergers and acquisitions are just two examples of how regulations can create additional barriers to integration. A new directive on takeovers (the 13th Company Law Directive) was supposed to be ratified by the EU Parliament in July 2001. The directive would have brought in standard EU-wide rules on how a firm can defend itself in the event of a hostile takeover bid. Hostile bids would have been easier to launch because it would require management wishing to contest a bid to obtain the support of their shareholders. German firms believed the directive did not give enough protection,[76] and lobbied German MEPs to vote against it. The result was an even number of votes for and against with 22 abstentions, so it was not passed.[77] Though unprecedented, it meant 12 years of work on a directive had been wasted. The failure to ratify this directive has encouraged banks to enter into strategic alliances or joint ventures rather than opting for a full merger. Recent examples include Banco Santander Central Hispano (BSCH) with Société Générale, Commerzbank, the Royal Bank of Scotland Group and San Paolo-IMI, and Dresdner Bank with BNP Paribas.[78]

**Natural barriers** identified by Heinemann and Joppe include the following.

- Additional costs due to differences in language and culture. For example, the barriers to trade caused by the e-commerce directive were noted earlier. But there are natural barriers arising from the use of the internet as a delivery channel across European frontiers. Fixed costs are created by the need for a specific marketing strategy in each EU state because of differences in national preferences, languages and culture, together with the need to launch an advertising campaign to establish a brand name. IT systems must be adapted for local technical differences and sunk costs can discourage entry. Consumer access to some products may also be limited if certain EU states are ignored because their market is deemed to be too small.

---

[75] *The Economist*, 20/01/01, p. 90.

[76] Certain firms in Germany (e.g. Volkswagen) are protected in German law against a hostile takeover. With the directive defeated, the German government announced it would bring in new legislation on takeovers.

[77] For a directive to be passed into law, there must be a majority over those against plus any abstentions.

[78] *Source*: Eppendorfer *et al.* (2002), p. 16.

- Consumer confidence in national suppliers. For example, a real estate firm may refer clients to the local bank for mortgages.
- The need to have a relationship between firm and customer, which makes location important. This point is especially applicable for many banking products. Relationship banking may be used to maximise information flows, which can in turn, for example, improve the quality of loan decisions.

Heinemann and Jopp (2002) surveyed seven European banks and insurance firms to ascertain how important they considered these obstacles to be, using a scale from 1 (not relevant) to 10 (highly relevant). In retail banking,[79] the most important barriers were differences in tax regimes (6.8/10) and regulation (supervision, takeover laws, etc.) 5.8/10. Consumer loyalty and language barriers came next (5.2/10 and 5.1/10), followed by unattractive markets (4.8/10) and poor market infrastructure (3.2/10).

An earlier survey by the Bank of England (1994) reached similar conclusions. About 25 firms, mainly banks and building societies, were surveyed. Cultural and structural barriers were found to be the most difficult to overcome, including cross-shareholdings between banks and domestic firms, consumer preferences for domestic firms and products, governments choosing home country suppliers, and a poor understanding of mutual organisations, which made it difficult for British building societies to penetrate other EU markets. Others included fiscal barriers due to different tax systems, regulatory barriers due to different regulations (e.g. the pension or mortgage examples identified by Heinemann and Jopp), and legal and technical barriers. Note the perception that notable barriers exist has not changed, even though the two surveys (albeit small) were done nearly 10 years apart.

## The Lamfalussy report: February 2001

Though this report dealt with EU securities markets, the ratification of its key recommendations by the EU Parliament in February 2002 may have important implications for the future integration of banking and other financial markets.

The report made a number of recommendations, most of which were eventually endorsed by Parliament. The key proposal was that rules for EU securities markets would be formulated by expert committees. They consist of a Committee of European Securities Regulators (ESRC), to be made up of national financial regulators. Based on advice from the ESRC, a European Securities Committee (ESC) made up of senior national officials (chaired by the European Commission) will employ quasi-legislative powers to change rules and regulations related to the securities industry. Though these arrangements represent a radical change in the EU legislative process, they are considered essential for Europe to keep up with the rapid pace of change in the financial markets. It normally takes at least three years (an average of five) to have rule changes ratified by the EU Parliament, which undermines Europe's competitive position in global securities markets.[80]

---

[79] The retail banking results appear in table 9 of a background paper by Eppendorfer *et al.* (2002).

[80] The legislative system works in this way: the European Commission will propose a change. The European Council can approve it by a majority of 71%. Then Parliament must either accept, make amendments, or reject.

The Lamfalussy report recommended that the home country principle (of mutual recognition) apply to securities markets, with a single passport for recognised stock markets. International accounting standards should be adopted, with an EU-wide prospectus for Initial Public Offerings.

Lamfalussy also called for the European Commission to act on the failure of certain states to either implement and/or enforce new EU directives. The Committee noted that the failure to integrate the retail financial services sector is preventing the development of a pan-EU retail investor base, which in turn undermines the development of a single securities market.

In February 2002, the European Parliament voted to accept the Lamfalussy report, to ensure a fast track for securities market legislation, even though it undermined their power somewhat. The European Securities Committee can implement legally binding rules, subject to a "Sunset" clause. Each new regulation imposed by the ESC expires within four years unless approved by Parliament. Both Parliament and the Council of Ministers have the right to review any regulation they are dissatisfied with.

Hertig and Lee (2003) are pessimistic about whether the success of the Lamfalussy reforms will work. State members of the ESC will attempt to act in the interests of their home state, and the Council of Ministers or Parliament can always intervene with regulatory decisions. Thus, they predict the ESC will be less powerful than its US equivalent, the Securities and Exchange Commission. For this reason, when the Lamfalussy model comes up for review in 2004, it could be ruled unworkable and ineffective.

These arrangements for the securities markets are important for banking because a similar model could be used to get new rules passed through quickly, to deal with many of the long-standing problems which have inhibited the emergence of a single financial market. However, as was noted earlier, the Commission's plan to put the main text of Basel 2 (part of CAD-III) through the standard ratification process is a source of concern. Only the Basel 2 annexes will be put on the fast track. Not only will this delay its adoption, it means excessively prescriptive components of Basel 2 will become part of EU law, and therefore, very difficult to change.

## *Will a Single Market Ever be Achieved?*

As was noted earlier, the objective of the Financial Services Action Plan is to achieve a single financial market in Europe by 2005. However, it is open to question whether the plan will succeed. As has been documented, major barriers continue to exist. The question is the extent to which a single market can be achieved in view of the cultural, language and legal differences within the EU, especially now it has expanded to include up to 10 new countries. Application of the Lamfalussy approach to retail financial markets is considered one solution to achieving a more integrated retail financial market, but if Hertig and Lee are correct, it will not succeed.

Instead, perhaps policy makers should concentrate on removing blatant policy induced entry barriers and accept that some markets will never be fully integrated, particularly in the retail banking and some other financial markets. The wholesale financial markets are already global in nature, and a key objective of the European regulators should be to ensure that no legislation is passed which hinders the competitive advantage of Europe's financial firms operating in wholesale markets. The earlier section on the USA showed that, like in Europe, the wholesale markets are highly integrated, but the retail markets are not. The US insurance sector is regulated by individual states, so insurers face similar problems – there are 51 different sets of rules. It is only very recently that nation-wide branch banking became a possibility. Thus, even though it is one country, parts of retail banking and finance are still highly fragmented. The EU is a collection of 25 independent nations. From 2004, it is 76% bigger than the USA in terms of population, and has a somewhat higher GDP. If a country with just one official language has not achieved a single market in certain sectors, how can the EU, with its many different languages, cultures and legal systems be expected to succeed?

Evans (2000) is one of several experts calling for an increase in the harmonisation of rules across Europe in the banking, capital and securities markets. However, the whole point of the 1986 Single European Act was to introduce mutual recognition because the goal of harmonisation was inhibiting the achievement of internal markets. As the early history of the EU demonstrates, attempts at achieving harmonisation will be even less successful than efforts to bring about a single market through mutual recognition. However, the time has come to recognise that like any country, some markets will be easier to integrate than others.

## 5.5.9. The European Central Bank

The European Central Bank was formed as part of the move to a single currency within the European Union. The objective of the **Maastricht Treaty (1991)** was to achieve European Monetary Union (EMU), with a single European central bank and currency, the "euro". The UK and Denmark were allowed to ratify the Treaty but reserve their decision on monetary union. Denmark ratified the Treaty after a second referendum in 1992 and is part of the Exchange Rate Mechanism (ERM). The British Parliament approved Maastricht, but after 22 months in the ERM, left in September 1992. The UK has yet to join the euro; Denmark voted against it by referendum in 2000. Sweden joined the Union in 1995 but has neither entered the ERM, nor adopted the euro,[81] though it is technically required to do so, as will the ten new countries who commence the process of joining the EU in 2004, once they have met the economic criteria. These are a budget deficit/GDP ratio of 3%, a debt/GDP ratio of 60%, inflation and interest rates which have converged to the EU average, and two years of participation in the ERM, with no parity changes.

In January 1999, having satisfied these economic criteria,[82] 11 countries entered into monetary union. They were: the Bene-Lux countries (Belgium, Luxembourg, the Netherlands), Germany, France, Italy, Spain, Portugal, Finland, Austria and Ireland. Greece joined later in 2000. The European Central Bank (its precursor was the European Monetary Institute until 1999) became the central bank for all union members. In January 2001, dual pricing was adopted for all EMU currencies: all prices were to be quoted in

---

[81] Finland and Austria joined the EU at the same time, and have adopted the euro.

[82] Many commentators at the time argued there was some "fudging" of figures/interpretation of objectives to ensure the 11 states could join, and also when Greece was allowed to adopt the euro in 2000.

euros and the state currency. The euro was launched in January 2002, to operate alongside state currencies (e.g. the Deutsche mark, the French franc). A few months later, the state currencies were gradually withdrawn from circulation.[83]

The Maastricht Treaty included the statutes for the European Central Bank, the primary one being that the inflation rate within the monetary union was limited to a maximum of 2%. The inflation target is met through interest rates, which are set by a committee consisting of 18 members, 12 Governors from each EMU state central bank, the Governor of the ECB, and 5 ECB officials. The Committee decides on the euro interest rate about every six months, but no minutes are taken nor are votes publicised. This lack of transparency is in contrast to the Bank of England's Monetary Policy Committee, where votes and the minutes of meetings are made public. The Bank of England is of the view that transparency improves the information analysts have when trying to predict what the Bank will do. Thus any subsequent decisions by the Bank are already discounted in asset prices by the time they are announced. It means the markets help the Bank achieve its monetary objectives, and it also reduces volatility in the financial markets.

While the principal function of the ECB is to achieve price stability, articles in the Maastricht Treaty refer to the possibility of the ECB undertaking more formal tasks related to the prudential supervision of financial institutions (excluding insurance). However, the treaty requires these tasks to be specific, and there is <u>no</u> provision for *federal* supervision of the sort observed in the USA, with the SEC and Federal Reserve Bank.

Nonetheless, these articles[84] are sufficiently ambiguous to allow for the possibility that the ECB may one day undertake the joint functions of ensuring price *and* financial stability through some form of prudential regulation. There is an ongoing debate about whether the EMU should have a single regulator and if so, whether it would be part of or independent of the central bank. The pros and cons of a multi-function central bank were reviewed in Chapter 1 and will not be repeated here.

Likewise, many of the arguments for and against a single European financial regulator, independent of central banks, are similar to those raised when the issue of a UK single regulator was discussed. However, there are additional points to be aired in the case of a proposed pan-European regulator. One important consideration is that two member states, the UK and Denmark, can opt out of joining Euroland, and Sweden, to date, has kept her own currency. The ten new prospective members are obliged to join the monetary union, but only after the conditions (outlined on p. 284) are met. There would need to be close coordination between the euro regulator and those outside Euroland. Also, a single regulator is at odds with the principle of mutual recognition, whereby passports are granted (subject to each state enforcing minimum standards) and a single market is eventually achieved through a competitive process. A pan-EU regulator (Euro-supervisor) would also require greater harmonisation of the EU states' legal/judicial systems, if the body is going to be able to enforce any rules.

---

[83] At the launch of the euro in 2002, the $/euro exchange rate was €1 =$1.20, but over the year it fell by 30% to €1 = 88 cents; for the UK, it was €1 = 72p but fell to €1 = 58p in 2000. Since December 2000, it has recovered somewhat, and reached a record high in the winter of 2003.

[84] Articles 105(5), 105(6).

Any pan-European regulator would also have to confront the significant cultural and language differences among the states it supervised. Successfully dealing with these would probably mean any regulator would have to have offices in all the states; otherwise, it would be distant from the firms and activities it regulates. An alternative is to use existing regulators, but employ procedures for sharing information, and agree on how to organise financial institutions operating in multiple states. For example, it might be necessary to appoint lead regulators, responsible for collecting the consolidated accounts, etc.

Davis (1999) and others have identified several existing bodies which could be used to facilitate coordination and cooperation among EU supervisors, with the objective of ensuring financial stability throughout the Union. These groups are organised by function. Three organisations deal with issues related to bank regulation:

- **The Groupe de Contact**, established in 1972 by bank supervisors from the European Economic Area to exchange information and focus on micro-prudential issues, such as problem banks.
- **The Banking Advisory Committee** (1977), consisting of EU banking supervisors and finance ministers. The committee discusses EU directives, regulation and policy affecting EU banks.
- **The Banking Supervision Committee** (ECB, 1998), consists of EU central bank governors and national banking supervisors. It is concerned with matters which affect financial stability across the EU.

In the securities markets the Committee of European Securities Regulators (ESRC) and the European Securities Committee (ESB) were both established as recommended by the Lamfalussy report, and discussed earlier. For the insurance sector, there is an EU Insurance Committee which considers insurance regulation, and an EU Conference of Insurance Supervisory Authorities, set up to exchange information among supervisors.

Should there be any systematic challenge to the EU's banking financial infrastructure, there would need to be a good, timely flow of information between these bodies, the state supervisors and the ECB. Memoranda of understanding (similar to those developed in the UK between the FSA, the Bank of England and the Treasury) may also be important. However, in Euroland equivalent memoranda would be less likely to succeed (it has yet to be tested in the UK), because the two or three different institutions involved would be multiplied by up to 25 states in the EU – the makings of a logistical nightmare. With such an enormous bureaucracy, it is doubtful whether the relevant information could be passed on fast enough for the ECB to act appropriately, given the circumstances. Any uncertainty of this sort would exacerbate the growing financial instability, because the ECB would play a critical role – it is the only institution in Euroland which can inject liquidity into the system, and would be central to any LLR or lifeboat rescue in Europe.

There is the added problem of undue pressure put on the ECB by one of the member states if any of its key banks was facing illiquidity/insolvency. The threatened failure of a few banks headquartered in the EU, such as HSBC or Deutsche Bank, would have global implications. However, the majority of banks will be of key importance to the home state (and its taxpayers), but relatively minor for the EU as a whole. These issues are complex and have yet to be addressed by the EU authorities, apart from the proliferation of memoranda of understanding.

Similar debates have arisen at the global level – calls for an international lender of last resort go in and out of fashion. However, it is widely accepted there needs to be international *cooperation* AND *coordination* of supervisors across countries and markets of the different financial services and institutions. For example, in April 1999 the G7 Financial Stability Forum was formed, and brings together supervisors of banking markets (Basel Committee of Banking Supervision), capital markets (International Organisation of Securities Commission) and insurance markets (International Association of Insurance Supervisors).

To conclude, the issue of an integrated approach to supervision and rescue of financial institutions in EU states is a long way off. Both the EU (and global) agencies must resolve the problem of national legal frameworks which still apply in a supposedly integrated European financial system. Also, there is the issue of whether a single EU regulator should be created, and if not, how to overcome information sharing problems among numerous bodies. The possibility of a pan-European systemic risk regulator has been raised as an alternative, but faces the same problems identified earlier when the issue of a British systemic risk regulator was discussed. Whatever the framework adopted, a good working relationship with the ECB is essential because only the ECB can supply liquidity in the event of a crisis in the eurozone.

## 5.6. Conclusions: Structure and Regulation of Banks

The last two chapters have reviewed regulation at the global level, in the European Union and in the three countries with key international financial centres, the UK, Japan and the United States. All three underwent substantial financial reform in the 1990s. These changes will affect the banking structure and financial systems in the respective countries.

Until 1996, Japan had, *de facto*, a single regulator (the Ministry of Finance), overseeing a highly segmented and protected financial sector. A stock market collapse followed by serious problems with banks and other financial firms prompted major regulatory reforms, which have structural implications. "Big Bang" (1996) marked the beginning of the end for segmented markets. At the same time, a new rule driven single financial regulator was created, with an independent Bank of Japan assuming responsibility for monetary policy.

In the UK, self-regulation by function was replaced with a single financial supervisor. While the Bank of England gained its independence over the conduct of monetary policy, it lost its established role as prudential regulator of UK banks. Unlike Japan, no single event prompted these quite radical changes, just a view that self-regulation was not working as well as it might, and a recognition that the changing nature of financial institutions required a new approach. It is too early to judge whether these changes will improve the regulatory regime. For example, the Memorandum of Understanding between the Bank of England, the Financial Services Authority and the Treasury in the event of a financial crisis has yet to be tested. The FSA must prove that the enormous power it wields is justified and show that it can control its costs while meeting four demanding statutory objectives.

By contrast, the United States continues with a system of multiple regulation, but recent reform has created the opportunity for the development of a nation-wide universal (albeit restricted) banking system. Though the legislation means the US banking market can never be as concentrated compared with some other nations, its unique structure, which has evolved over time, is likely to change and become more like that of other countries.

The European Union faces multiple challenges in the new century. It has been aiming to achieve the free trade of goods and services since the Treaty of Rome in 1957. However, its record of progress towards this goal in financial services, especially the retail sector, is dismal. Given the continued obstacles, perhaps the real challenge is to accept that *if* preserving languages and cultural diversity is high on the agenda; not only will progress towards achieving a single market be slow, but the objectives themselves may have to be less ambitious. On the other hand, multilingual Scandinavia has achieved a high degree of integration, even in the absence of a single currency.

Monetary union is now a reality in most of the EU, but as the American case illustrates, it is neither necessary nor sufficient for a high degree of integration, or a nation-wide system of banks. The maintenance of price stability will remain the central focus of the European Central Bank, but the Maastricht Treaty leaves room for it to play a limited role in regulation. There is increasing support for a single regulator (though it is unlikely to be the ECB given current trends), even though it could be at odds with the principle of mutual recognition, a central component of the 1986 Single European Act.

However, as this book goes to press, the status quo is to depend on coordination among multiple regulators within the EU. This is an enormous challenge, especially as the union expands. It is doubtful whether good, timely information flows could continue with so many organisations involved, and thus, whether a financial crisis in the EU could be prevented or contained.

# BANKING IN EMERGING ECONOMIES

## 6.1. Introduction

The objective of this chapter is to review some of the key issues related to banking in developing or emerging market economies. The first thing to be clarified is nomenclature. In the 1980s, economists divided the world into developed/industrialised or less developed countries (LDCs). However, it grew increasingly difficult to classify some of the Asian countries (e.g. South Korea) as LDCs, and the term "newly industrialised countries" (NICs) was adopted. With the break up of the Soviet Union, labels such as transitional and emerging market economies were used to describe the financial systems of former communist countries which were trying to transform their highly centralised directed economies to ones that operated on market principles. In this chapter, the terms developing countries/economies, emerging economies, emerging market countries (EMCs) and emerging market economies (EMEs) are used interchangeably, and include all countries that are not part of the developed world.

It would be impossible to do justice in one chapter to a subject that has enough of its own material to fill a book itself.[1] The objective is to supply the reader with the basic tools to understand the key debates in this area of banking. Section 6.2 sets the stage by reviewing the key features of financial repression, something that all these countries suffer from to some degree, though most are aiming to liberalise their financial markets, including banks. Section 6.3 reviews reform programmes in China, Russia and India and the extent to which they have reduced financial repression. Other countries are mentioned where relevant.

Section 6.4 provides an overview of Islamic banking, which has been included in this chapter for two reasons. First, in a few emerging market countries, Islamic banking is the only form of banking allowed, while in others, it runs in tandem with conventional banking systems of the sort discussed in this book. Second, banks in the west are using the experience gained from these countries to develop and offer Islamic financial services to their Muslim customers. It is an interesting example of where some emerging market countries are passing on their expertise to western banks.

Section 6.5 considers the key issues related to sovereign risk. Though risk management was the subject of Chapter 3, it was noted then that its quite unique features make it more appropriate to discuss it here. The underdeveloped nature of the financial systems of

---

[1] See, among others, books by Beim and Calomiris (2001), Fry (1995). Gros and Steinherr (2004) examine the development of transition economies in Eastern Europe.

most emerging market countries makes them reliant, to some degree, on external finance. Many incur external debt in the form of loans or bonds. The lending banks are often exposed to sovereign risk and there are special problems for a country with external loans. Section 6.6 concludes the chapter.

## 6.2. Financial Repression and Evolving Financial Systems

### 6.2.1. Introduction

Banks in developing countries/emerging markets reflect diverse political and economic histories, but all share two characteristics. The first is that banks are the key (and in some cases only) part of the financial system by which funds are channelled from saver to investor. As noted in Chapter 1, banks in the industrialised world have evolved over the last two decades in the face of disintermediation. As a financial system matures, agents find there are alternative ways of raising finance, through bond issues and the stock market. Banks find they are competing with other financial houses for wholesale customers by offering alternative means of raising finance through bond issues and/or going public – selling stocks in the firm to the public. One consequence of disintermediation is that while all banks continue to profit from offering retail and wholesale customers the core intermediary and liquidity services, universal banks have expanded into off-balance sheet activities, investment banking and non-banking financial services such as insurance.

In emerging market economies the fledgling bond and stock markets are very small, if there at all. Commercial banks are normally the first financial institutions to emerge in the process of economic development, providing the basic intermediary and payment functions. They are the main channel of finance. For example, in several socialist economies, the central bank also acted as the sole commercial bank. With the break up of the Soviet bloc and the introduction of market reforms in Russia and China (see below), the commercial and central bank functions were separated. Stock and bond markets have begun to emerge to varying degrees, but they remain small. This means traditional banking continues to dominate the financial systems of emerging market economies.

Developed economies constitute quite a homogeneous group. Emerging countries do not. For example, national income per head, at current exchange rates, is up to 100 times higher in the richest emerging countries than the poorest. In the most prosperous emerging economies, banking is extensive and sophisticated, sharing much in common with North American or Western European banking systems. In the world's poorest societies, most people live on the land and have little use of money, let alone banks. Banking there is urban and very limited. These countries are at different stages of financial evolution. They also vary widely in their degree of financial stability. Some, such as Malaysia and Thailand, have experienced relatively short-lived periods of financial instability while others in Latin America (Mexico, Argentina, Brazil) and some former Soviet states suffer from chronic bouts of crises. Many of the transition countries (e.g. Kazakhstan, Estonia, Latvia and Lithuania) emerged from the post-Soviet era and quickly transformed their financial systems – with relatively stable banking sectors and reasonably liquid, transparent stock and bond markets. In China, financial reforms have encouraged the development of small stock and bond markets. Under the World Trade Organisation (WTO) agreement reached in 2001, all trade barriers, including those in the banking sector, are to be lifted by 2006/2007. Yet China's banking system is probably the only one in the world that is both insolvent and highly liquid, one of several issues to be examined in more detail later in this chapter. After reviewing the characteristics of financial repression, the banking systems of three key developing economies are assessed in terms of how far they have come by way of reforms aimed at eliminating features of financial repression, and many of the problems that accompany it.

## 6.2.2. Financial Repression

The term *financial repression* refers to attempts by governments to control financial markets. There are varying degrees of it, from complete repression at the height of the Soviet era, to much milder regimes. Nor is financial repression exclusive to EMEs, as will be observed below.

Beim and Calomiris (2001) provide an excellent summary of the characteristics of financial repression. These include:

1. Government control over interest rates, which usually take the form of limits imposed on deposit rates. This in turn affects the amount banks can lend. If the deposit rate ceilings reduce deposits, banks curtail their loans.
2. The imposition of high reserve requirements. If the reserve ratio (see Chapter 1) is set at, for example, 20%, banks must place 20% of their deposits at the central bank. Normally no interest is paid. Effectively it is a tax on bank activities, which gives the government a reserve of funds.
3. Direction of bank credit to certain (often state owned) sectors: the Soviet Union, China and India have all promoted these policies to some degree.
4. Interfering with the day to day management of bank activities, or even nationalising them.
5. Restricting the entry of new banks, especially foreign banks, into the sector.
6. Imposing controls on borrowing and lending abroad.

In addition banks in EMEs have a number of problems, most of them the consequence of financial repression. In some emerging markets, the growth of an unregulated **curb market** becomes an important source of funds for both households and business. It becomes active under conditions of a heavily regulated market with interest rates that are held below market levels. In South Korea, it was estimated that in 1964, obligations in the curb market made up about 70% of the volume of total loans outstanding. By 1972, this ratio had fallen to about 30%, largely due to interest rate reforms. However, intervention by the monetary authorities in the late 1970s caused another rapid expansion. Since then, the curb market has all but disappeared, not only because of deregulated interest rates but also because business shifted to the rapidly growing non-bank financial institutions which offered substantially higher returns. In pre-revolutionary Iran there were money lenders in the bazaar who set loan rates between 30% and 50%. In Argentina, the curb market grew after interest rate controls were reimposed. Most of the credit was extended to small and medium-sized firms by the curb market and did not require collateral, probably because most lenders are reputed to have used a sophisticated credit rating system. As a conservative estimate, the average annual curb loan rate can be two to three times higher than the official rate.

Pay is lower in EMCs than in developed economies, and dramatically lower in some of the poorest. So bank operating costs should be correspondingly lower, too. But a number of factors mitigate this. In poorer countries, bank staff tend to earn incomes far above the local average. Banking is more labour intensive and much less computerised; and banks and branches are small, so economies of scale are not reaped as they might be elsewhere. Furthermore, government restrictions and regulations (e.g. interest rate ceilings, high reserve requirements) tend to raise bank operating costs.

Inflation rates vary widely among emerging market economies. In a few, it is both high and variable. To the extent that higher inflation encourages people to switch out of cash into bank deposits (where at least some interest is earned), it can strengthen bank finances, especially if reasonable interest is paid on reserves held at the central bank. However, variable inflation exposes banks to serious risks and rapid inflation is costly for them in other ways, not least because of the government controls that so often accompany it.

Another problem for many emerging markets is the percentage of arrears and delinquent loans, often because of state imposed selective credit policies, and/or named as opposed to analytical lending.

The financial sectors of developing economies and their rates of financial innovation are inhibited by poor incentives, political interference in management decisions and regulatory systems which confine banks to prescribed activities.[2] In the absence of explicit documented lending policies, it is more difficult to manage risk and senior managers are less able to exercise close control over lending by junior managers. This can lead to an excessive concentration of risk, poor selection of borrowers, and speculative lending. Improper lending practices usually reflect a more general problem with management skills, which are more pronounced in banking systems of developing countries. Lack of accountability is also a problem because of overly complicated organisational structures and poorly defined responsibilities. Staff tend to be poorly trained and motivated. Ambiguities in property and creditor rights, and the lack of bankruptcy arrangements, create further difficulties.

Staikouras (forthcoming) looks at annual data on 20 emerging market economies between 1990 and 2000. He examines a number of questions, including testing for factors that affect a country's probability of default and whether economic "jitters" can be shown to be a function of economic signals. One of his key conclusions is that emerging markets need to develop stable market oriented financial systems to minimise the number of credit crashes, raise their credit ratings and avoid excessive borrowing costs.

---

[2] Though regulations can sometime encourage financial innovation, especially if bank personnel are well educated and experienced. For example, deposit rate controls in the USA led to the development of money market sweep accounts. Other restrictions encouraged the growth of the eurocurrency markets – see Chapters 1 and 2.

## 6.2.3. Foreign Bank Entry: Does it Help or Hinder Emerging Financial Markets?

The role foreign banks are allowed to play is an important differentiating characteristic of banking systems in emerging market economies. Branches and/or subsidiaries of foreign commercial banks dominate the banking systems in a variety of countries, such as the Bahamas, Barbados, Fiji, the Maldives, New Zealand, St Lucia, Seychelles, the Solomon Islands and, in recent years, Hungary, Mexico and Kazakhstan. The new banking systems in some of the former Soviet bloc economies have strongly encouraged the entry of foreign banks. In others, such as China (pre-2007) and pre-crisis (1997) Thailand, foreign banks have been prohibited from offering certain banking services (e.g. retail) and/or their activities are confined to certain parts of the country.

Terrell (1986), in a study of OECD countries, found that banks in countries which exclude foreign banks earned higher gross margins and had higher pre-tax profits as a percentage of total assets, but exhibited higher operating costs compared to countries where foreign banks are permitted to operate. He showed that excluding foreign bank participation reduces competition and makes domestic banks more profitable but less efficient. The entry of foreign banks is seen as a rapid way of improving management expertise and introducing the latest technology, through their presence. However, the presence of foreign banks can be an emotive political issue.

Clarke *et al.* (2001) conduct an extensive review of the literature on this issue, and summarise a number of findings based on these studies. First, foreign banks that set up in developed economies are found to be less efficient than domestic banks. The opposite finding applies to developing countries: foreign banks are found to outperform their domestic counterparts, suggesting that cross-border mergers will improve the overall efficiency of a banking system in emerging markets. There is also evidence indicating that in addition to following clients abroad, foreign banks seek out local business, especially lending opportunities.

Though foreign banks tend to be selective in the sectors they enter, empirical evidence from a number of studies finds their entry makes the market more competitive, reducing prices (e.g. raising deposit rates and lowering loan rates). However, the increased competition may give weaker home banks an incentive to take greater risks – a contributory factor to failure. Other inefficient domestic banks could lose business and fail. Both outcomes would be destabilising for the banking sector as a whole. The crisis could be aggravated if foreign banks react by reducing their exposure, and/or depositors switch to foreign banks perceived as safer. However, Clarke *et al.* report that tests using Latin American data show foreign banks are more likely than domestic banks to extend credit during a crisis. Another concern about foreign bank entry is that their presence will make small and medium-sized enterprises worse off because borrowing opportunities will be reduced. While it is true that larger banks have a smaller share of their loan portfolios in SMEs and foreign banks tend to be large, more recent studies suggest that technical changes (e.g. the development of risk scoring models for SMEs) will increase lending to this group. These authors call for more research in this area. Finally, tests on the organisational form of banks indicate that subsidiaries are likely to have the best impact in a developing country because they can offer a wider range of services, and enhance stability. Again, more research is needed.

Even developed countries have had features of financial repression until recently, especially interest rate and credit controls. Until 1971 UK banks operated a cartel which agreed limits on deposit and loan rates. The UK government used the "corset" in the 1980s to limit the availability of credit. In the USA, regulation Q allowed the Federal Reserve Bank to impose ceilings on deposit rates paid to savers with accounts at thrifts and banks until as late as 1986. Canada differentiates between domestic and foreign banks, and subjects the two groups to different regulations. Britain did not eliminate capital controls until 1979. France has a long history of nationalising banks, and during the Mitterand years (1980s) all the major French banks were nationalised. Crédit Lyonnais was not fully privatised until 2001 and only after the European Commission threatened fines if the French government did not sell off its shares. As the case study (see Chapter 10) shows, Crédit Lyonnais was used by the state to fulfil a variety of objectives, including propping up state owned firms, such as the steel company. However, these economies normally have one or two features of financial repression and most have been phased out. By contrast many emerging market countries exhibit all six types of financial repression in varying degrees.

Beim and Calomiris (2001) produce an index of financial repression and compare it to real growth rates for the periods 1970–80 and 1990–97. Part of their work is reproduced in Table 6.1. The higher the financial repression index, the more liberalised the country is. Beim and Calomiris define a severely repressed economy as one with an index of <45; a highly liberalised one has an index >70. None of these economies are classified as severely

Table 6.1  Financial Repression and Growth, 1990–97

|  | FR index[1] | Growth[2] | Income[3] (US$) |
|---|---|---|---|
| Industrial countries | 67.8 | 1.5 | 18 518 |
| East Asia | 58.7 | 4.7 | 4 779 |
| N-Africa & M-East | 52 | 2.1 | 5 736 |
| Latin America | 51.3 | 1 | 755 |
| Transition countries | 47.2 | −3 | 543 |
| Africa (Sub-Saharan) | 46.2 | −0.9 | 775 |
| South Asia | 45.7 | 2.1 | 238 |
| UK | 77.2 | 1.2 | 16 827 |
| USA | 70.7 | 0.8 | 21 989 |
| Hungary | 66.7 | −2.6 | 2 191 |
| India | 54 | 4.4 | 216 |
| Indonesia | 52.6 | 6.4 | 503 |
| China | 49.3 | 9.2 | na |
| Russia | 48.4 | −7.3 | na |

*Note*: 1. The financial repression (FR) index is constructed by Beim and Calomiris (2001, p. 78), averaging the indices of six measures of financial repression such as real rates of interest, liquidity, bank lending, etc. 2. Growth: the mean annual growth rate in real GDP, 1990–97. 3. Income: GDP per capita in 1997, in dollars, converted by the year-end exchange rate.
*Source*: Beim and Calomiris (2001), table 2.A2.

repressed, though South Asia and Latin America were in 1990. A better positive correlation is found between the wealth measure and the index: In a formal regression, the wealth coefficient is found to be highly significant. The $R^2$ is low, which is not surprising, since there are other factors contributing to a country's GDP per capita. However, the test does show more repressed economies have much lower levels of income. The causation could run from income to financial liberalisation,[3] but Beim and Calomiris reject this argument because of the lack of correlation between GDP growth (which would create income) and financial repression. Countries such as China illustrate the point: it is the most repressed but has one of the highest growth rates. This is partly explained by the fact that China's financial and other sectors were repressed but at the same time, sheltered from competition by the authorities.

Beim and Calomiris acknowledge the limitations of their work, and cite more sophisticated econometric research that makes a similar point. The classic works by McKinnon (1973) and Shaw (1973) are cited to back up the case that financial liberalisation promotes growth. The main argument is that by depositing money in a banking system (rather than hoarding it under a mattress or keeping it in gold), wealth is generated because all but a fraction of deposits are loaned out, as explained in Chapter 1. Financial institutions try to overcome information asymmetries and other market imperfections, which should contribute to higher growth. Most of the evidence shows that financial liberalisation promotes economic development.[4] This is not to say it is all plain sailing. If the legal system and human resources are deficient, financial reform can cause serious problems, as a review of the country cases will demonstrate.

Below, the attempts to liberalise the financial sectors in Russia, China and India are reviewed. The theme throughout is the extent to which these countries have liberalised their financial systems, the positive and negative aspects of the changes, and the policy lessons to be learned.

## 6.3. Banking Reforms in Russia, China and India

### 6.3.1. Russia[5]

Most readers are familiar with the collapse of communism throughout Eastern Europe in the late 1980s and early 1990s. The USSR[6] (with 15 republics) was dissolved and Russia became an independent state in 1991. After the creation of the Commonwealth of Independent States (CIS) in the early 1990s, separate banking systems emerged in each of the new countries. All the former Soviet bloc countries had used a socialist banking model. In the Soviet Union, the USSR State Bank had been a monopoly which undertook

---

[3] Greater income implies higher tax receipts and less pressure on government to contain their debt charges through financial repression; it might also imply a better educated electorate, more aware of costs of distortionary financial policies, and more suspicious of politicians' competence and motives.

[4] For more detail on the evidence, see Beim and Calomiris (2001), pp. 69–73 and Fry (1995).

[5] I should like to thank Olga Vysokova for her helpful input in parts of this section.

[6] USSR: Union of Soviet Socialist Republics, also known as the Soviet Union.

all central and commercial banking operations. The central government channelled all available funds into the central bank. The USSR State Bank was responsible for allocating these funds in a planned economy consisting of 5-year economic plans announced by the government. In 1987, five state controlled banks were created from the existing system, and linked to specific sectors. The new banks were USSR Promstroybank (industry), USSR Agroprombank (agriculture/industrial), USSR Zhilsotzbank (housing and social security), USSR Vnesheconombank (foreign trade) and the savings bank, USSR Sberbank.[7] Existing loans from the portfolio of the central bank were transferred to these commercial banks, hence, they commenced operations with an overhang of doubtful assets, highly concentrated by enterprise and industry. Banks were confined to doing business with enterprises assigned to them, stifling competition.

In 1990, a new law "On Banks and Banking Operations" created a *two-tier* banking system. The Central Bank of Russia (CBR) was established with the sole right to issue currency, and a statutory obligation to support the rouble. In the early 1990s, Agroprombank, Promstroybank, Sberbank, Vnesheconombank and Zhilsotzbank became universal joint stock commercial banks, which were supposed to diversify across all sectors of the economy but most remain concentrated in their specialist areas.

In July 1996, the number of Russian commercial banks peaked at 2583. Most were created after 1990. One reason for the rapid proliferation was the near absence of a regulatory framework until 1995, and a desire to dismantle all parts of the old communist economic system as quickly as possible, to reduce the chance of it being resurrected. The amount of capital required for a banking licence was several hundreds of thousands of dollars[8] – compare this to the UK minimum of at least £5 million.

By 1998, the number of banks had dropped to 1476 and, as a result of numerous reforms, the system consisted of the following.

- *State owned/controlled banks*: Sberbank, Vnesheconombank, Vneshtorgbank, Rosex-imbank, Eurofinance and Mosnarbank. Some have other shareholders, but are state controlled. For example, in 2003, 61% of Sberbank was owned by the CBR, 22% by corporates, 5% by retail, and the rest by smaller groups.[9] There is a potential serious conflict of interest because the CBR is both a major shareholder and acts as supervisor/regulator. Though the state, via the CBR, is the majority shareholder, Sberbank, with assets of $34.2 billion, is the only joint stock state bank with shares traded on the stock market. The next two largest banks, by asset size, are Vneshtorgbank ($7.3bn) and Gazprombank ($4.9bn). Overall, the state (including the central bank) has a majority holding in 23 banks.

In 2002, Sberbank had 1162 branches (18 980 "sub-branches"), compared to a total of 2164 branches for the rest of the commercial bank sector. Sberbank's share of household deposits has varied considerably, from a low of 40% in 1994 (newly licensed private banks offered more attractive rates) to a high of 85% in 1999 (after a large number of bank failures/closures). Since then, deposits have levelled off somewhat, but by any measure are still extremely high. In 2002 Sberbank had 75% of household deposits, and 25%

---

[7] *Source*: World Savings Bank Institute and European Savings Banks Group (2003).
[8] Gros and Steinherr (2004).
[9] *Source*: World Savings Bank Institute and European Savings Banks Group (2003).

($34.2 billion) of Russia's banking assets. With its unique combination of an extensive branch network, a state deposit guarantee and a near monopoly on pension payments,[10] Sberbank has major advantages over other banks. For example, in 2004 it paid a deposit rate of 7%[11] for 12-month term deposits, when other banks are paying 12–14%. Its large pool of funds means it can make long-term loans more easily than other banks. In 2003, 50% of Sberbank's loans exceeded a year, and another 48% of loans were granted for a period of 3 to 12 months. The other top 20 banks have a portfolio consisting of loans with a maturity of more than one year (35.5%), short-term loans (i.e. one month to a year) (50%), "call loans" (13%)[12] which Sberbank does not offer, and 1.1% in overdraft credit.[13] Most of these banks are carrying the bad debt of the old state owned enterprises, and for this reason are proving difficult to sell, to either domestic or foreign investors. In 2002 the government assumed ownership of Vnesheconombank (VEB) and Vneshtorgbank (VTB). VEB's banking activities were transferred to VTB, leaving VEB as the government debt agency.[14] In 2004, VEB assumed responsibility for managing the entire state pension fund.

- *Former state specialised banks*: The privatisation scheme (see below) included a number of banks. Agroprombank (which was bought by the SBS Argo group – now called SBS Argo Bank), Promstroybank, Moscow Industrial Bank, Mosbusinessbank and Unicombank. They were specialised banks serving the loss making agricultural and industrial sectors (e.g. machinery, steel) of the economy. The consequent debt overhang has made it difficult to diversify because their customers are the previously heavily indebted state owned enterprises (SOEs).

- *Bank oligarchies or bank industrial groups*: Some of the banks (e.g. Alfa-Bank) hold controlling shares in industrial groups. Their main function is to provide services to the firms under their control. Other banks were founded and owned by large industrial groups such as Gazprom bank, Guta Bank, NRB and Nikoil (recently merged with UralSibBank). MDM Bank provides a good example of the way these banks are structured. It is part of the MDM Group holding which is involved in energy and coal mining and metallurgy. The connection with industrial/commercial sectors is similar to German and Japanese bank practice. The banks manage the cash flows of their shareholders, which include the large commodity exporters in Russia. None of them offer intermediary services to the public, apart from the banking services for employees of the firms. Many of the original banks including Oneximbank, Rossijskij Credit, Incombank Menatep, Mapo bank lost their licences due to insolvency.

- *Municipal banks*: These banks are owned and controlled by municipal governments, and include the Bank of Moscow and the Industrial Construction Bank in St. Petersburg.

---

[10] Sberbank is involved with the non-state pension fund (established in 1995). It receives pension payments, invests them and distributes payments to the pensioners.

[11] Effectively, a negative real rate, with an annual inflation rate of 11% in 2004.

[12] In April 2004, the CBR declared that call loans would not be treated as assets, making them unprofitable for banks, so they are likely to disappear. Call loans were short-term loans (e.g. 7 days) which were continually rolled over, thereby disguising what were effectively long-term loans.

[13] *Source*: World Savings Banks Institute and European Savings Banks Group (2003), p. 17.

[14] *Source*: Barnard and Thomsen (2002).

Their sole function is to provide banking services to their respective local government owners, managing their budgets and revenues.

- **Small unit banks**: Owned and controlled by a few individuals, they offer services to small private firms.

- **Banks with a high proportion of foreign shareholders**: These include Autobank, Tokobank, International Moscow Bank and Dialog Bank. They offer personal and corporate banking services.

- **Subsidiaries of foreign banks**: Since 1995, foreign banks have been allowed to operate in Russia after a delegation from the European Union persuaded the former President Yeltsin to lift the decree restricting their operations. By 1998, there were 29 foreign banks. In 2001, their overall market share stood at 10%, though their operations tend to be confined to the major cities. They include Credit Suisse First Boston, Deutsche Bank, ABN Amro, Raiffeisen Bank and Citibank. Their main function is to supply banking services to foreign corporations operating in Russia. They are also active in trading Russian government securities and foreign exchange.

Between 1996 and 1998, the concentration of the top 50 banks increased from 63% to 74%. Since then, it has remained largely unchanged, as can be seen from Table 6.2. Note the tiny share of the market held by the 1000 or so banks which, in 2003, account for about 76% of the total number of banks.

Effectively, the centralised communist system was abandoned overnight before anything replaced it. It proved a disaster. The macroeconomy collapsed. GDP fell steadily between 1991 and 1994 (an annual average of 14.5% per year); the annual inflation was 2510% in 1992. This rapid economic collapse prompted further government action. A massive privatisation scheme was launched, even though, at the time, there was no clear concept of property rights in Russian law. In June 1992, the government announced a voucher scheme, to sell off state enterprises – with the exception of oil and some other natural resource based industries. Every adult was given a free voucher worth 10 000 roubles (then $14) to bid for shares in state enterprises. Obliged to change their corporate structure, most of these

Table 6.2  Russian Banks' Share of Assets in the Banking System

| Banks | 1996 | 1998 | 2003 |
|---|---|---|---|
| Top 20 | 51.3 | 60.2 | 62.6 |
| 21–50 | 11.6 | 13.8 | 10.9 |
| 51–200 | 18 | 14.5 | 15 |
| 201–1000 | 16.4 | 10.6 | 11.2 |
| From 1000* | 2.6 | 0.9 | 0.3 |

* The number of banks stood at 2029, 1097 and 1319 in 1996, 1998 and 2002, respectively. *Source*: World Savings Bank Institute and European Savings Banks Group (2003), p. 19.

state-owned firms opted for a scheme whereby employees would own 51% of the firm, and another 29% could be purchased by vouchers. In a country where most citizens had no knowledge of how firms operated in a capitalist system, the majority failed to appreciate how the vouchers were to be used. Most were sold at deep discounts to managers of the state firms, who used them to buy up more of their enterprises. Roughly 16 500 SOEs were sold off between 1992 and 1995, but insiders obtained between 55% and 65% of the shares.

A second phase of privatisation took place after 1994, which, in the opinion of most experts, was more distortionary than the first stage. It involved a loan for shares scheme (**collateral auctions**) and resulted in fraud on a large scale. In the face of a growing budget deficit, the government took out loans worth about $1 billion. The collateral was state shares held in the 12 profitable firms operating in the energy and other natural resource sectors. The banks, in the event of non-repayment, could sell the shares and keep 30% of the capital gains. The value of the shares far exceeded that of the loan, and there was virtually no chance of the loan being repaid in the stipulated nine months. The banks making the loans were close to the government and ended up with the shares – which they were obliged to sell. To maintain control of them, the shares, held in trust, were bought by either the trust holders or some front company – all were linked to the banks. Other outsider bidders found themselves disqualified for technical reasons. The result was a number of large conglomerates, each with an oligarch and linked to certain banks. In return this group supported the re-election of Mr Yeltsin in 1996.[15]

For some Russians the privatisation scheme had benefits: private property is recognised and tradable, whereas before the state owned everything. However, the privatisation programme failed to achieve broader objectives. Most state enterprises were sold too cheaply to the "oligarchs". Managers used their political influence to avoid taxes and other obligations, and therefore lacked the usual incentives to maximise and distribute profits. The concentration of economic power in a few conglomerates exacerbated the problem.[16]

In 1995, though inflation was still high (120%), it was falling, the rouble had stabilised, and the CBR implemented closer supervision of the banking sector. However, the economy, with the exception of a few export led industries (e.g. oil), had ground to a halt. The government found its debts rising, and needed to borrow. Bonds were issued to the banks via the Finance Ministry and CBR. Banks bought these bonds, safe in the knowledge that it was government debt. State securities investments rose by 171% between 1996 and 1998, compared to a 33% increase in loans. Commercial banks were also active in foreign exchange operations. The problems began in late 1998. Throughout 1997, prices in world commodity markets had been falling. Oil prices declined from $25 per barrel in January 1997 to less than $12 by August 1998. The worsening outlook for the Russian economy together with the Asian financial crisis (see Chapter 8) caused the rouble and short-term government bonds (GKOs) to come under intense speculation – the catalyst for a severe crisis in Russia. The return on GKOs reached 120%. The government could not protect

---

[15] This account is from Gros and Steinherr (2004), p. 239.

[16] Beim and Calomiris (2001) are of the view that the presence of Russia's nuclear arsenal prevents the IMF (which by 1999 had loaned Russia $18 billion) from exercising its normal tough line on countries that fail to adhere to its loan conditions (see Chapter 8). This judgement may be too harsh: the IMF did impose tough monetary targets which, for example, led to salaries not being paid and rising social problems.

the rouble, which was devalued four times. Unable to service its debts, Russia defaulted on its _domestic_ debt and declared a moratorium on the repayment of _foreign_ debt.

The short-term government bonds had been a major share of banks' assets up to August 1998, and the default announcement created severe liquidity problems among banks, which in turn prompted a series of defaults. Customers panicked and withdrew their deposits: in the month of August, rouble deposits declined by 20% and foreign currency deposits by 24%. Since the end of the Soviet era, Russians had favoured holding foreign (mainly US dollar) cash or deposits,[17] but withdrew any dollar deposits because of a concern they would be frozen.

In response to the crisis, the central bank sought to restore liquidity by buying the debt in exchange for loans to banks. Sberbank, trusted by most Russian depositors, was able to honour the demands of its domestic and foreign customers and, for this reason, the assets of weak commercial banks were transferred to it. In late 1998, the Agency for the Restructuring of Credit Organisations (ARCO) was established and staffed by the government and CBR. Its remit was to manage all problem banks, and by 2000 the banking crisis had been largely resolved.

With a devalued rouble, the Russian economy began to recover in 1999, and subsequently experienced five years of sustained growth, for the following reasons:

- A devalued rouble made exports more competitive, and import substitution stimulated demand for Russian goods at home. With a sharp appreciation of the rouble in 1999, import volumes began to rise, and doubled by 2003.
- The rising price of oil, and growth in export revenues. The dependence on oil and other commodities has been a major factor in Russia's economic recovery but at the same time, is a cause for concern. In 2002, 85% of private sales of the top 64 Russian companies were by enterprises belonging to eight conglomerates, all of them based in commodities – mainly oil and metals. State owned firms (Gazprom and RAO UES) accounted for 43% of total sales. Russia's economic recovery is therefore largely due to a few commodity based conglomerates.[18]

The situation in the banking sector improved in the post-crisis period. Between 1999 and 2003, bank assets, bank credit to the economy and household deposits more than doubled; and there was a fourfold increase in capital. Post-crisis, the central bank was criticised for its ad hoc approach to problem banks and its dealings with some of their managers – allowing them to continue even if the bank was failing. In 2001 the government and central bank announced a reform plan for the banking sector, including improved supervision by the central bank, the application of more sophisticated risk management techniques, greater corporate governance/transparency, setting up credit bureaux so all banks have access to credit histories, and a deposit insurance scheme for private banks. The main changes to date include the following.

---

[17] According to Barnard and Thomsen (2002), about half of household savings are held in US$ cash.

[18] _Source_: Barnard and Thomsen (2002), p. 4. They also note that the share of SMEs in GDP is about 10–15%, compared to 50% in other transition economies.

- The legal framework has been improved, with new laws on bank insolvency and restructuring. In the event of insolvency of a bank with retail deposits, ARCO (the restructuring agency) will act as liquidator. Amendments to the banking laws have been introduced to ensure secured creditors receive priority if a bank is declared bankrupt. Once in place, they should encourage more lending with collateral, which will help to raise the level of bank intermediation. The development of the legal system has some way to go.
- In 2001, new amendments introduced more stringent "fit and proper" criteria for bank owners and management.
- A new anti-money laundering law was passed in 2001 and as a result, Russia was removed from the list of countries failing to undertake sufficient measures to stop international money laundering. Banks can refuse or close accounts if money laundering is suspected.
- The banking sector was to adopt international accounting standards (IAS) by 2004, ahead of the 2005 date set for EU banks. Sberbank claims to have met these standards since 1996, publishing two sets of accounts – one according to Russian procedures and the other using IAS rules. The CBR asked all banks to publish two sets of accounts in 2005, and by 2006 it is hoped they can use the IAS accounts to show compliance with the Basel rules. It is reported that by the end of 2003, 120 banks (controlling 70% of the assets and capital of the sector) were preparing accounts according to IAS standards, and many are using foreign auditors to sign them off.[19] However, there are a number of problems with its implementation. Russian civil law recognises Russian standards, and will have to be changed to accommodate IAS accounts and statements. A draft law is being prepared, but could take some time because of notable differences between Russian and IAS accounting rules. International audit standards are to be adopted. However, there are very few Russian accountants or auditors trained to prepare and inspect accounts using the IAS procedures. On the other hand, the greater transparency of Russian accounts will result in more reliable information on the banks' financial positions, which is important for potential depositors, investors and supervisors. It is also likely to help encourage the acquisition of very small banks by domestic or foreign banks.
- In 2002, corporate tax was lowered to 24%, for banks and all other firms. Prior to this, banks had paid a higher rate of tax. However, it is claimed that the elimination of tax relief on interest expenditure by corporations is causing them to use internal funds to finance expenditure, reducing the demand for corporate loans.
- A law "On Deposit Insurance" was passed in 2003. At the moment, only Sberbank's retail deposits, and those of other state banks, are protected – the state guarantees the deposits of all banks where it has at least 50% of the voting shares. As this book goes to press, the Russian Duma is considering a change in deposit insurance. All banks would be required to pay a quarterly premium of 0.15% of eligible deposits to a fund. In the event of bank failure, retail deposits of Rub 20 000[20] would be 100% insured, with 75% coverage for deposits in excess of Rub 20 001 up to Rub 120 000. Thus the maximum amount any depositor could get back would be Rub 95 000 (or $3000). Banks will not be allowed to hold retail deposits unless they participate in the scheme. The

---

[19] World Savings Banks Institute and European Savings Banks Group (2003).
[20] About $700 given the exchange rate in late 2003.

"safer" banks are objecting to subsidising depositors at weak banks who will receive insurance if they collapse. This criticism is often made by the large dominant banks in countries (e.g. the UK) where all banks pay the same premium. The USA is notable in setting premia according to the risk rating of the bank (see Chapter 5). Concern about moral hazard problems has also been expressed, though a more serious problem could be the limited nature of coverage. In the event of another crisis, wholesale depositors and those holding more than $700 in their accounts will be the first to "run". However, 100% coverage could cause serious moral hazard problems unless there is much closer supervision of banks. The proposed changes would help to create a level playing field for private banks, which have had to pay a risk premia to attract deposits away from the state banks, especially Sberbank. It comes as no surprise that Sberbank and other state banks are objecting to the scheme because their depositors will be worse off.

## Issues and problems in the Russian banking sector

The Russian banking system remains underdeveloped, even when measured against other emerging markets. Keeping in mind Russia's fledgling bond and stock markets, the banking sector is central to financial intermediation. Table 6.3 shows monetisation and bank lending as a percentage of GDP is much lower than other transition economies. The bond market

Table 6.3 Banking and Financial Market Indicators (expressed as a percentage of annual GDP).

| | M2 (%) | Bonds (%) | Equity market capitalisation (%) | Aggregate assets (%) | Loans to private sector (%) |
|---|---|---|---|---|---|
| Russia | 24 | 3 | 27 | 35 | 17 |
| China* | 165 | 26 | 45 | 173 | 125 |
| India** | 63 | 36 | 43 | 50 | 29 |
| Czech Republic | 71 | 15 | 16 | 94 | 36 |
| Slovak Republic | 66 | 13 | 3 | na | na |
| Hungary | 43 | 26 | 20 | na | na |
| Poland | 43 | 20 | 15 | 51 | 21 |
| Brazil | 29 | na | na | 67 | 35 |
| Mexico | 45 | na | na | 37 | 13 |
| S. Korea | 84 | na | na | 134 | 114 |
| Turkey | 51 | na | na | 19 | 21 |
| USA | 64 | 115 | 137 | 91 | 78 |
| UK | 113 | 43 | 153 | 145 | 143 |
| Japan | 123 | 107 | 92 | 153 | 102 |
| Germany | 71 | 56 | 57 | 168 | 119 |

*Sources:* Barnard and Thomsen (2002) for columns (1) to (3) – 2001 figures. World Savings Banks Institute and European Savings Banks Group (2003) for columns (4) and (5) – 2003 figures.
\* Columns (1), (2) and (3) for China come from *Almanac of China's Finance and Banking* (2002).
\*\* Columns (1), (2) and (3) for India come from Bhattacharya and Patel (2004).

is even smaller, and though the stock market looks relatively more important, the figure is due to privatisation in the 1990s, which created a few large concentrated firms. The banking sector is even less developed than the figures suggest because some banks are linked to a particular industry, so that much of the lending is **connected**, that is, within the group.

Just under 65% of corporate loans made by the large banks have a maturity of less than a year. The short-term nature of the lending is partly due to a civil code which requires all retail deposits to be available on demand,[21] even though about 14% of deposits at large banks are for more than one year, and 57% are on deposit for six months or more. This rule leaves the banks highly liquid, as does a liquidity ratio of 7–10% of liabilities which banks are obliged to place with the CBR. There are calls to reduce this ratio or to exempt liabilities of a longer maturity. The limitations on long-term sources of finance are a problem – foreign banks, or very large corporate bond issues, are the only options for long-term finance.

The performance of Russian banks appears to be highly variable. Take Sberbank: its cost to income ratio (C:I) was in excess of 90% between 1999 and 2002, and in 2003 it dropped to 83%, with a ROA of 3.3%. These figures vary considerably from bank to bank. Vneshtorgbank reported one of the lowest cost to income ratios (39%) in 2003, with a ROA of 5.37%. Compare that to Citibank (Russia): its C:I ratio is 58% with a ROA of 4.6%. The spreads between loan and deposits rates are high. These variations are probably due to the different market niches of these banks. However, it is notable that Sberbank, which operates under such favourable conditions, has such high cost to income ratios, suggesting that protectionism breeds inefficiency.

The low level of market capitalisation of most banks is a cause for concern. According to Goryunov (2001), roughly 80% of the banks operating in Russia have (questionable) capital of less than $5 million, and about half of these have less than $1 million. Based on scale economy estimates (see Chapter 9), the figures suggest most of these banks are unable to benefit from scale economies because of their current size. Many question whether banks have as much capital as they claim. For example, banks can borrow from another bank and treat the loan as a capital injection. The CBR has recently imposed rules to stop this activity, but there is a general feeling that capital is over-reported by most Russian banks.

It was noted earlier that Russia lacks IAS trained auditors and accountants, which highlights a more general problem. Russia continues to be deficient in trained and experienced banking staff, both in the private and state (central bank) sectors. Few staff have experience in credit or other forms of risk analysis because so little of it was practised in the 1990s, where connected or named lending was the norm, up to and during the crisis. The absence of restrictions on the operation of foreign banks should help to alleviate the problem more quickly.

A major obstacle to the further growth of Russian banking has been the failure of the banks to instil confidence among potential and existing customers. This lack of trust is not surprising, given the events of the early 1990s and during the 1998 crisis. Recall the reluctance of the central bank to close some insolvent banks. In the early

---

[21] According to this civil code, depositors withdrawing the deposit before the term is up are entitled to the interest paid on a call deposit.

1990s, investment funds were introduced, but these became vehicles for criminals to steal assets. Pyramid funds advertising extremely high rates of return attracted unsophisticated investors, and proved extremely popular, even after they began to collapse when some clients attempted to cash in on their investment. They continue to exist in a variety of forms, even though many originators of funds launched in 1995 have been tried for fraud and other crimes.

In the summer of 2004, the central bank revoked the licence of Sodbiznesbank following an investigation into money laundering. Less than a month later a run on another Moscow bank, Credittrust, forced it to suspend business and negotiate with the CBR how to meet its debt obligations. One analyst claims that only 30 of 1200 banks in Russia are financially viable, and if the crackdown on money laundering persists, there will be more bank runs.[22] Once the banking system rids itself of the problem banks, greater stability should improve confidence in the system, though it could take many years. If and when the banks do overcome this lack of trust, the growth potential for household deposits at banks is considerable. Russian retail bank savings as a percentage of GDP is just under 11%, compared with 30% in Poland and 43% in the Czech Republic. It exceeds 50% in Western Europe and 40% in the USA.

There is also a lack of trust between Russian banks (which may explain the tiny interbank market) and foreign banks do not have much confidence in Russian borrowers; foreign banks make up about 12% of US dollar loans to Russian corporates, while their share of the rouble market is just 1.3%. However, many of the financially viable Russian corporates borrow from the head offices of foreign banks, which is classified as cross-border lending. In 2002 it accounted for about 30% of total corporate lending in Russia. This substantial (dollar) loan market is largely due to cash flows arising from imports and exports. Loans to individual customers are a very small part of the market, with under 3% of total bank assets in 2003.[23]

The CBR is criticised by banks and observers for focusing on adherence to form rather than substance in their supervision of banks. The number and length of forms banks are required to complete for the CBR and other federal agencies is estimated to take up 10–15% of bank time. All would benefit from a reduction in the duplication of forms and the number of agencies banks must report to. If the CBR were in sole charge of bank supervision and adopted the practices of western regulators, supervision would improve, which in turn should help build trust.

There is also concern about whether the authorities will be able to implement many of the planned reforms effectively. The major banks are part of powerful industrial groups. Their close connection with big conglomerates and/or business people with political clout could lead to pressure on the CBR to, for example, keeping failing banks open. Since the crisis, there has been no major test of the new system and reforms. The CBR answers to the Duma (parliament), depending on it for adequate supervisory powers. Yet when the Duma was considering amendments to CBR law in 2003, it actually reduced the number

---

[22] Nick Holdsworth, "Russian Bank Falls Victim to Crime Fears", *The Daily Telegraph*, 5.6.04, p. 34.
[23] The figures cited in this paragraph are from the World Savings Banks Institute and European Savings Banks Group (2003).

of inspections the central bank is allowed. Also, having recently introduced restrictions on single large credit exposures, the CBR, under political pressure, exempted both Sberbank and VTB.[24] Another vulnerable point is deposit insurance. If and when the new system is introduced, the CBR must be given the power to refuse entry by weak banks into the scheme, and there must be strict, transparent criteria for admission to the scheme itself. The amendments also include changes in the way the National Banking Council (which oversees the CBR) members are appointed – half will be appointed by the Duma or the Kremlin, which again makes the CBR vulnerable to political interference. Nor do members of the Duma have time to manage the fine details of the CBR's supervisory functions, which makes them highly susceptible to the influence (and money) of the powerful banks. Likewise, the low-paid staff of the CBR may easily be persuaded by the same banks to engage in regulatory forbearance should a bank or banks get into trouble.

The state still owns a considerable number of banks, including Sberbank. Sberbank's special privileges give it unfair advantages, which should be phased out. It appears that some of them (e.g. guarantees of retail deposits) will be in the near future. The position of Sberbank must be dealt with very carefully because it is the one bank that depositors do trust, and it would be unwise to create panic among householders. The CBR has decided Sberbank's status should be left unchanged until other banks erode its dominant position. This should be possible if the new deposit scheme is introduced, and its other privileges are gradually removed. The other state banks are more of a problem. The proposed reforms say nothing about privatising them but there is little interest in taking them over because they are saddled with the bad debt of former state owned enterprises. This problem must be resolved by the state, but it requires dealing with politically sensitive, but unprofitable, sectors.

To conclude this section, how has Russia fared in terms of reducing financial repression? After nearly 70 years of a communist regime, where a central bank reallocated funds between sectors according to a centralised economic plan, Russia has come a long way in a short period. There are now virtually no controls on interest rates or capital. Russia has sensibly allowed foreign banks to enter the market with few restrictions. Banks have a free hand over the direction of credit, though this is stifled by the expectation that banks be able to repay all retail deposits on demand, regardless of their maturity. In the absence of such a requirement, reserve ratios of 7–10% would not be unreasonable, but with it they are on the high side.

Despite the 2002–3 financial sector reforms, a number of problems remain.

- Political interference in the banking sector – for example, the central bank's supervisory authority can be undermined by members on the National Banking Council.
- The oligopolistic power of the bank/financial conglomerates, and their close political connections.
- State ownership of a considerable share of the banking sector.
- The potential for a large number of bank failures, if analysts' assessments about the viability of most of the banks prove correct.

---

[24] It has since instructed them to reduce their exposures to the permitted limits.

- **Named**, as opposed to analytical, lending, which has grown because of close connections between individual banks and financial conglomerates. It reduces the available capital for small innovative firms.
- Human resource problems – the need to train staff in risk management techniques, IAS accounting and auditing. The expertise brought by the foreign banks should help, as will the good educational system.

Amendments to the Russian Civil Code are slowly changing the banking landscape, enabling the CBR to more effectively supervise banks, subject to the constraints noted above. However, Russia has some way to go before its financial system can support a forward-looking, growing economy. As this book goes to press, the CBR and government are expected to announce a new strategy for the banking sector.

## Performance of the transition economies

How does banking in the other ex-communist countries compare? Space constraints prevent a detailed review, but a few points are worth making. The figures in Table 6.3 indicate some are doing considerably better than Russia, especially in terms of monetisation, aggregate assets and private lending. Countries such as the Czech Republic, Hungary and Poland, which joined the European Union in 2004, have made great progress very quickly. An investigation by the World Bank (2002) considers the effect of liberalisation on economic growth between 1990 and 1999 in the Eastern European states and Russia. This study assessed the extent to which the initial conditions or changes in economic policy affected annual rates of growth. The authors used the World Bank's liberalisation index, which quantifies progress from a transition to market economy. They found that initial economic conditions were the most important factor explaining the decline in output in the period 1990–94, though the liberalisation index was also significant in this early period. Also, certain distortions (such as the absence of pre-transition reforms, high repressed inflation and high black market exchange rates) were found to be more significant than other indicators in explaining most of the early decline in output. As transition progresses, policies begin to take over as the principal explanation for the growth in output. The overall conclusion is that market reform helps to cushion the effects of transition on the fall in output in the early period, and over the medium term (1995–99) contributed to a faster rate of recovery and promoted growth.

Grigorian and Manole (2002) used data envelope analysis (DEA) to estimate an efficiency frontier, and to identify how close banks are to that frontier. This is not the appropriate place to explain DEA in detail,[25] but it involves using linear programming techniques to identify efficient production units, and constructing a piecewise linear efficiency frontier. The most efficient bank is on the frontier and less efficient ones will be inside it. Using data from *BankScope*, these authors look at the period 1995–98 for 15 Central and East European countries, including Russia, the Czech Republic, Slovakia, Hungary, Poland and the Ukraine. Looking at the results by region, the Central European countries were, on

---

[25] See Chapter 9 for a more detailed explanation of DEA.

average, closest to the efficiency frontier. Banks in the Czech Republic came closest to the efficiency frontier – 79% efficient, followed closely by Slovenia (77%). Banks in Hungary (68%) and Poland (69%) were roughly 10% less efficient. Slovakia (61%) was found the least efficient, i.e. Slovakian banks would have to improve their efficiency by 39% to reach the frontier. Among the Commonwealth Independent States, Kazakhstan (59%) and Belarus (52%) do best. Russian banks were found to be 49% efficient. Then there is a large gap with Armenia (34%), the Ukraine (29%) and Moldova (27%) coming at the bottom. Moldova's banks would have to become 73% more efficient to reach the frontier. Banks in the Baltic region and South Eastern European countries ranged between 51% (Romania) and 71% (Bulgaria), with an average score of 59%.

Grigorian and Manole (2002) used these measures of output efficiency as the dependent variable to test a number of explanatory variables. Since the dependent variable varies between 0 and 1, they used a Tobit[26] model rather than ordinary least squares. They find well capitalised banks are relatively more efficient, as are banks with a larger share of the market. The authors suggest that the latter finding indicates a high concentration may lead to greater efficiency in transition economies. Once the economy is stronger, greater competition among banks might be encouraged, without an efficiency loss. Foreign controlled banks were found to be more efficient than domestically owned banks (private or state), which is consistent with the argument that these banks bring with them superior technology, risk management, management and operational techniques. Also, because of the perception that they are likely to be backed by their parent, they can pay a lower deposit rate than domestic banks, making their funding cheaper.

Certain prudential regulations (e.g. capital adequacy rules) were found to affect efficiency, but not others. Also banks in countries with less stringent foreign exchange exposure rules were more efficient, possibly because in transition economies, foreign exchange business and earnings are a big component of banks' non-interest income. GDP per capita was the only macroeconomic variable found to influence bank efficiency, probably because the high income countries attract more deposits, contributing to a higher level of intermediation.

## 6.3.2. China[27]

As a communist country, China operated an economic and financial system similar to the USSR. The People's Bank of China (PBC) not only issued currency, but was the financial hub of each State Economic Plan. All funds were channelled to the PBC, which, taking its cue from the state, allocated the funds in accordance with each plan. The PBC controlled currency in circulation, managed foreign exchange reserves, set interest rates, collected all deposits (via 15 000 branches and sub-branches) and made loans, almost exclusively to state owned enterprises. In addition, there were three specialised banks. The Bank of China[28] became a subsidiary of the PBC, responsible for all foreign exchange and international

---

[26] Tobit is similar to the logit model, but rather than the outcome being binary (0 or 1), it is specified to be any number between 0 and 1. See section 6.5 and Chapter 7 for more detail on the logit model.
[27] Special thanks to Xiaoqing Fu for her assistance with this section.
[28] Originally established as a private bank in 1912.

transactions. The Agricultural Bank of China (ABC), set up in 1951, operated under the PBC, dealing with the agricultural side of the economy. Rural credit cooperatives, which pre-dated the PBC, provided basic banking services for their members – mainly peasant farmers. These coops became units of the ABC after it was formed, collecting deposits in rural areas and confining lending to farmers. In 1954, the China Construction Bank (CCB) was established as a fiscal agent for the Ministry of Finance, with control over the administration of funds for major construction projects, in line with the relevant economic plan.

## Chinese bank reforms: 1979–92

In 1978, China opted for major economic reforms with the objective of increasing economic efficiency and improving resource allocation. Emphasis was placed on decentralisation and the gradual introduction of a market based economy to replace the old system. Unlike the USSR there has been no political disintegration, and the plan is to create a market-like economy operating within a communist political system.

The banking system was to be reformed, with banks acting as intermediaries between savers and borrowers, together with the provision of a payments system to ensure the transfer of funds between economic units. To date, two stages of reform have been undertaken, from 1979 to 1992 and 1993 to present. Stage one began with the creation of a "two-tier" banking system. Between 1979 and 1984 the specialised banks were separated from the direct control of the PBC/Ministry of Finance and became state owned, national commercial banks, each operating in a certain sector of the economy, which effectively ruled out any competition between them. For example, the CCB was now independent of the Finance Ministry, and acted as banker to state construction firms, as well as managing the fixed assets of all state enterprises.[29] In 1984, the Industrial and Commercial Bank of China (ICBC) was established, to assume the PBC's deposit taking function as well as granting loans to state owned industrial and commercial enterprises in urban areas.

Gradually the lines of demarcation that separated these banks were removed, reducing the amount of functional segmentation. In 1985, in addition to the ICBC, the ABC, BOC and CCB were allowed to accept deposits and make loans to households and corporates (mainly SOEs), via nation-wide branches.[30] As universal banks, by 1986, most had expanded to include trust, securities and insurance affiliates.

In 1984, the People's Bank of China officially became the central bank. It was assigned the tasks of formulating monetary policy and supervising all financial institutions. Though responsible for monetary policy and supervision, it differed from its western counterparts because of its continued role in economic development. Under a credit quota system, the PBC imposed credit ceilings on the state and so-called independent commercial banks, though they could exceed their limits by borrowing from the PBC. The length of the

---

[29] The Ministry of Finance had allocated funds for physical plant and equipment to state owned enterprises so when the banks were separated the CCB assumed this role for all fixed assets.

[30] At the end of 1992, each bank had an average of about 30 000 branches and sub-branches, though there were large variations. The ABC had over 56 000 and at the other extreme the Bank of China had 1352. The ICBC had just under 32 000.

loans could be for days, months, or up to 1–2 years. Wu (1998) argues that the PBC's role in economic development took precedence over monetary policy until 1995. For example, in 1992 it loaned 678 billion renminbi to other banks, making up 26% of the total bank lending.

Between 1985 and 1992, to promote more competition, the Chinese government permitted the establishment of new "small and medium-sized" commercial banks, which initially offered universal banking services to households and firms, mainly in the regions and cities.[31] Total loans cannot exceed total deposits, and they are allowed to borrow short-term funds from the PBC. This group included the Shenzhen and Guangdong Development Banks, the CITIC Industrial Bank, Bank of Communications, China Merchants Bank, China Everbright Bank and Hua Xia Bank. Many are joint stock, i.e. shareholder owned – but the state is a key player in their operations, because either central or local governments and/or state owned enterprises are major shareholders. For example, the respective provincial governments own shares in Shenzhen and Guangdong Development Banks and China Everbright Group Limited, a SOE, owned China Everbright Bank. Between 60% and 70% of these banks' shares are either owned directly by the state (or indirectly via SOEs) and cannot be publicly traded. Thus, when the Shenzhen Development Bank became the first bank to list its shares on the Shenzhen Stock Exchange in 1991, only a minority were listed. Likewise for the three other banks that listed their shares in 1999.

Rural credit cooperatives have a long history of offering basic banking services in their respective agricultural communities. Since 1979 they had been required to place a certain percentage of their deposits with the Agricultural Bank of China, which provided clearing services to them. The ABC also acted as supervisor until 1996, when this responsibility was transferred to the PBC. City based urban credit cooperatives were introduced in 1979, but most were established after 1987. The idea is to offer banking services to households, urban collectives and small firms. Though these cooperatives raise some equity capital, local government owns most of the shares. Unlike the west, where members of coops or mutual organisations each have one vote independent of the size of their deposits and loans, in China the state, as majority shareholder, has much more power and influence over the way the cooperatives are run than individual customers.

The attitude towards foreign bank operations remained quite restrictive in this period. In 1979, the authorities allowed Japan's Export and Import Bank to establish a representative office in Beijing, and in 1982, a Hong Kong bank was allowed a subsidiary, but was restricted to offering foreign exchange services to firms and individuals in Shenzhen, one of the special economic zones China had established.

This first stage of banking reform led to a rapid growth in the banking sector's assets and liabilities. Deposits increased by 25 times; there was a 15-fold increase in loans. However by 1992 the market share of the state owned banks was still very high: 84% of loans and 78% of deposits. The rural credit cooperatives had higher deposit (13%) and loan (9%) shares than the small/medium-sized commercial banks, with, respectively, 6% and 4% of the deposit and loan markets. Foreign banks had no deposits, and just 1% of the loan market.

---

[31] Later, two of these banks expanded beyond their regions, with nation-wide branches.

## *Chinese bank reforms, 1993–present*

In 1993 the State Council[32] announced a second stage of banking reforms which had three objectives:[33]

- To further refine the central bank functions of the PBC.
- To create a competitive commercial banking sector where state banks coexisted with other forms of banking institutions.
- To ensure a sound financial market.

In 1995, the People's Bank of China was reformed by the Central Bank Law. The PBC was to control the money supply, formulate and implement monetary policy, act as the government's fiscal agent and supervise the financial system. From 1992, its role as financial supervisor was gradually reduced,[34] culminating in 2004 when bank supervision was transferred to a new body, the China Banking Regulatory Commission.

There have also been major reforms to address the problem of the increasing amount of bad debt held by the "big four" state banks. These banks are, by any measure, effectively insolvent, but they continue to function because of the ongoing injection of funds by central government. Their bad debt problem is largely due to the loss-making state owned firms they lend to, and the banking system is used to support them. According to official estimates, non-performing loans as a percentage of total loans is about 25%, but Whalley (2003) puts unofficial estimates as high as 50–60%. China is in the unique position of having a largely insolvent banking sector which is highly liquid, with liquidity ratios averaging about 57% for the big four, about 1% higher than the big four UK banks.[35] Not only is the savings rate high (30% of GDP), but customers are content to keep their deposits at these banks because they are confident the state will always support the banks. Likewise, even though required to lend to loss-making SOEs, the state banks are not too concerned about it because the loans are considered "safe" – the state will bail them out. This situation has created serious moral hazard problems – bankers have virtually no incentive to practice good risk management techniques. Depositors think it is the job of the state to protect their deposits. Borrowers, in turn, have little motivation to make their firms profitable and repay the loans. The World Bank (2002) estimates that to restore the banking system to financial health, the stock of government debt will have to increase from 20% to 75% of GDP, and its servicing is likely to be a serious burden for the government.[36]

Part of the second stage of reform attempts to address the issue of the critical condition of these state owned banks. Since 1993, a number of reforms have been put in place:

---

[32] "The Decision on Financial System Reform".

[33] Wu (1998).

[34] Supervision of insurance and securities firms was gradually transferred to, respectively, the China Insurance Regulatory Commission (established in 1998) and the China Securities Regulatory Commission (set up in 1992).

[35] *Source: BankScope.* The liquidity ratio is defined as net loans to total assets, and has been averaged over 2000 to 2002.

[36] *Source:* World Bank (2002), p. 36.

- Creation of new policy banks (1994): to encourage the state banks to act like commercial banks, the government created three new state owned policy banks to assume the development goals of the state banks, freeing them to meet commercial banking objectives. The new policy banks are the Export–Import Bank of China, the Agricultural Development Bank of China and the China Development Bank. All three provide financial support for key projects designated by government to be of central importance to the nation. The first two banks grant policy loans to the agricultural and trade sectors, respectively, and the China Development Bank covers industries not included by the other two.

- The Commercial Bank Law (1995): this law formalised the prohibition of universal banking, a rule the PBC had imposed since 1993. Financial firms can only operate as banks or securities firms or insurance companies. Banks had to terminate all insurance and securities operations. The reasons given were that in an emerging market where bank finance accounts for 85% of finance, the system is not mature enough to cope with universal banking. It is blamed for many of the problems banks have, especially a real estate "bubble" created when some banks used their investment and trust affiliates to invest in property. When the bubble burst, they incurred a substantial amount of debt. However, the main source of the bad debt is from loans to state owned enterprises. The authorities are also worried about contagion effects, but in a country full of insolvent banks where there have been no bank runs,[37] this concern seems unwarranted unless the authorities are planning to let one of the major state banks fail without compensation.

- The 1995 Commercial Banking Law also made banks responsible for profits and losses, and set explicit prudential ratios, but at the same time required state banks to make loans according to the needs of the national economy and social development as outlined in the state's industrial policy. The law sends out conflicting signals: be profitable, but at the same time, make what are effectively policy loans when called upon to do so, even though the three development banks were established for this purpose.

- At the end of 1997, the credit quota system was terminated. Under this system, the central bank had set a limit on the amount of new loans, and specified how the loans were to be allocated among the different sectors of the economy. In 1998, a new system was introduced by the PBC, which requires banks to satisfy various constraints on their balance sheet ratios. In China these are collectively referred to as **asset liability ratios**, consisting of a number of ratios including a liquidity ratio of at least 25%;[38] the Basel 1 capital adequacy ratios ($\geq 4\%$, $\geq 8\%$ – see Chapter 4); and a reserve ratio of at least 5% for local and foreign currency deposits. There are also limits on loan exposure to an individual ($\leq 4\%$) and a bank's top ten clients ($\leq 8\%$) which commercial banks are

[37] The Hainan Development Bank is the only bank that has been closed since 1949. Created as a joint stock bank in 1995, it had been profitable until the Hainan provincial government, which held 30% of its shares, asked it to take over 28 credit unions – about two-thirds of their debt was non-performing. This proved a disaster for the bank, and it was closed by the central bank in 1998. It was never declared bankrupt: all the creditors were paid off, and the government repaid depositors. This type of record explains why Chinese depositors have so much confidence that they will be protected by the state.

[38] The liquidity ratio is defined as liquid assets/liquid liabilities. Liquid assets must account for at least a quarter (25%) of liquid liabilities (e.g. demand deposits). The foreign currency liquidity ratio must be at least 60%.

supposed to use.[39] In addition banks are given a non-binding annual loan target to provide guidance on the total volume of loans they can make.

- Widening the ownership of the joint stock banks (1993–96): during the first stage of reform, the joint stock banks were largely regional, with a small number of owners. For example, the China Merchants Group Company Limited, a SOE, owned the China Merchants Bank. Between 1993 and 1996, these banks were allowed to operate nation-wide and their ownership was widened, which increased their capital base. For example, a company with the same name had wholly owned China Everbright Bank, but by 1996, the China Everbright Group Limited had reduced its shareholding to 51%. Institutions such as the Asian Development Bank and other domestic firms (130) hold the other 49%, which more than doubled its capital base. Two new joint stock banks were created during this period. By the end of 2002, some shares of four joint stock banks were being traded on the stock exchange. However, these banks are still controlled by the state, despite the joint stock label, because for all but one of them,[40] the government remains a majority shareholder, usually via the shares held by state owned enterprises. According to Sun *et al.* (2002), the arrangement preserves the communist principle of public ownership. The Communist Party officially recognised private ownership in 2004,[41] though within the banking sector the state will continue as a major player.

- Recapitalisation of state owned commercial banks (1998): a new Treasury bond was issued. The reserve ratio was permanently reduced from 13% to 8% (for all banks), freeing up funds to enable the state banks to purchase the bond. The yield from the bond would raise these banks' income streams. The aim was to recapitalise them so their capital asset ratios would rise to the Basel requirement of 8%, though in 2002, only one of these banks, the Bank of China, met this target, with a Basel ratio of 8.15%.[42] In 2003 another government injection worth $45 billion raised the capital adequacy ratios of the Bank of China and the China Construction Bank to 16.4% and 14.4%, respectively. In early 2004 the China Regulatory Commission stated that all commercial banks must meet a minimum capital ratio of 8% by 2007. There are reasons for being pessimistic about these plans. There have been no changes to curtail directed lending, and these banks are used to government rescues – since 1998, they have received about $200 billion to boost their capital. Further-more, the injection of $45 billion is quite low when bad debt of the big four is estimated to be just under $300 billion and analysts think it could be as high as $420 billion.[43]

- Asset management corporations (AMCs)[44] (1999): even by official estimates, the per-centage of non-performing loans is high. The government created four asset management corporations, each affiliated with one of the four state owned banks. Bonin and Huang (2001) argue that having one AMC for each bank could create the expectation that the

---

[39] Other ratios place limits on international borrowing, the percentage of medium and long-term loans in the portfolio and limits on interbank borrowing.

[40] The China Mingsheng Banking Corporation created in 1996.

[41] In 2004, at a session of the Communist Party of China, the constitutional ban on the ownership of private property was removed.

[42] *Source: The Banker*, July 2003.

[43] The capitalist injection figures are from 'Botox Shot', *The Economist*, 10/01/04, p. 65.

[44] For more on AMCs, including their pros and cons, see Box 8.1 in Chapter 8.

bank can dump bad loans with its AMC. However, the AMCs are supposed to close within 10 years. Also, they may only deal with debt incurred before 1996. This cut-off was chosen because under the Commercial Bank Law, these banks were supposed to be responsible for loans made from 1996 onwards. However, as was noted above, the Law has not freed the state banks from involvement in policy type loans. Another problem is that by 2001, the AMCs had reduced the state banks' NPLs by 10%, quite a low percentage by the standards of other countries that have created AMCs (see Chapter 8). These AMCs have used a variety of means to manage/offload this debt, including restructuring, sales/auctions and collecting the principal and interest. By 2002, an average of 36% of the NPLs had been recovered. The AMCs also entered into debt equity swap agreements with just over 1100 state owned enterprises, to help alleviate the debt burden of the state banks. The central bank loaned the AMCs funds to purchase enterprise debt from the state bank, then swapped them for equity in the enterprises. The plan is for the equity to be sold by the AMC, and the funds used to repay the PRC loan. In 2004, Shi Jiliang, Vice Chairman of the China Banking Regulatory Commission, admitted bad loans for the four major state commercial banks averaged about 20%.[45]

- Organisational changes (1998–2002): by merging or closing branches, these banks refocused their operations on city based construction and medium to large-sized firms. During the period the number of branches was reduced by 36%, from 154 051 to 55 324. Staff cuts were less successful – just 362 900 employees (18%) were reduced from a total of 2 001 300 workers in 1998.

- Shareholder restructuring (2002): a three-stage plan to transform the state owned banks into first, joint stock banks and eventually for them to seek a public listing. The $45 billion capital injection for the Bank of China and the China Construction Banks is a pilot scheme to convert them into joint stock banks by 2005 and encourage a more competitive environment. They have been told to implement an efficiency drive to ensure a return to profitability within three years. It is unclear what the sanction is if these banks fail to meet the target. In the past, managers have been let go only if they fail to be profitable over a number of years.

Many credit cooperatives, like their banking counterparts, found themselves burdened with a large amount of debt. The credit coops were never bound by the PBC's credit quota system. Though the coops were supervised by the PBC, the power of local governments (majority shareholders in the coops) was such that the central bank cannot control their lending decisions. No attempt was made to apply the basic principles of asset liability management, and many of them are effectively insolvent. For example, 49% of the rural credit coops had liabilities exceeding assets by 1996. At the end of 2003, the official estimate of the ratio of non-performing loans to total loans was 12.9% for urban credit coops and 29.7% for their rural equivalents.[46] It is unclear whether the new regulation will be able to make a difference. In 1992, there were more than 4000 urban credit coops. After 1995, 2000 were converted into 111 city commercial banks with local shareholders (e.g. urban firms, residents and local

---

[45] *Source*: channelnewsasia.com, 27 May 2004. He was referring to the Bank of China, the China Construction Bank, the Industrial and Commercial Bank of China and the Agricultural Bank of China.
[46] *Source*: cbrc.gov.cn/chinese/module/viewinfo.jsp?

government), serving small and medium enterprises in the cities where they operate. The remaining 2000 were reduced to just 758 by 2002 through mergers and some closures.

In 2001, China became a member of the World Trade Organisation. China is committed to allowing foreign banks completely open access to Chinese markets by the end of 2006. The government has a long way to go, though there has been some progress. By 2000, foreign financial institutions had 233 representative offices and 191 subsidiaries in 23 cities, with assets worth $34 billion.[47] Foreign banks have been allowed to offer foreign exchange services to residents and non-residents since 2001. In Pudong and Shenzen, they have been allowed to convert offices into branches and engage in renminbi businesses. Some have also been allowed to acquire small shareholdings in the joint stock banks. Newbridge Financial now owns 15% of Shenzen Development Bank, and Citicorp has a 5% share in Pudong Development Bank. Geographical restrictions are due to be lifted in 20 cities/provinces by 2005.

Loan classification has also been reformed. Until 1995, the PBC placed a ceiling on the percentage of loans that could be classified as bad debt, independent of a bank's asset quality. From 1995, the system was changed: loans were to be classified as past due, doubtful or bad debt, though banks could still classify a loan as past due even if the firm had closed down! To bring China up to international standards, it was announced (in 1998) that by 2002, banks had to place loans in one of five categories: normal/pass (the borrower is repaying on schedule), special mention (the loan is being repaid but there may be factors which interrupt the loan repayment), substandard (the income from the firm's business is insufficient to service the loan), doubtful (debtor unable to repay the loan; even with the guarantees, the bank will incur losses) and lost (either the principal and interest cannot be recovered or, with legal action, a very small amount may be recovered).

External examination of the banks has been improved. Since 2000, state supervisory boards have been supervising state owned banks. External auditing has been introduced, and external agencies have the duty to sign off bank statements as reflecting true and fair value.

Until very recently, the government, through the PBC, maintained a tight control over interest rates: they were seen as a key instrument of political control. However, in 2002 two State Council announcements began a protracted, gradual process of interest rate reform, with liberalisation of:

- Long-term funds followed by short-term funds;
- Foreign rates to precede domestic rates; and
- Domestic loan rates before domestic deposit rates.

Small interbank money markets have operated in different provinces since the 1980s. In 1996 the money market was centralised, with rates to be determined by market supply and demand. Since then, it has become quite active – a major source of liquidity for banks, depositing and lending funds at a CHIBOR rate. The inter-rate bond market was also opened in 1996. Bond and long-term deposit rates were liberalised between 1998 and 1999.

Deposit rates are fixed by the PBC and remain so, though longer term deposits are paid a slightly higher rate than short-term deposits. Banks have always had some discretion in

---

[47] *Source: Almanac of Chinese Finance and Banking* (2002).

setting rates for loans to small and medium sized enterprises (SMEs). Until 1998 it was the central bank rate plus a rate added by the bank, up to a limit of 10%, with the exception of rural credit cooperatives, where it was 40%. The banks' ceiling was raised in 1998 and again in 1999, to 20%, then to 30%. For the rural credit cooperatives, it was increased to 50%. Rates on foreign deposits have also been liberalised. Since 2000, the bank and customer have been able to negotiate the rate paid on foreign exchange deposits in excess of $3 million; the same privileges were extended to small foreign exchange deposits in 2003.

The decade between 1992 and 2002 saw many changes in China's banking sector, leaving a system consisting of the following components.

- The central bank, PBC: responsible for implementation of monetary policy, though the State Council sets interest rates (China's equivalent of a cabinet). The Governor of the PBC is on the committee that advises the State Council. When its supervisory functions were reassigned to separate authority, a financial stability bureau was established at the PBC to take decisions about liquidity support in the event of bank runs.
- The China Banking Regulatory Commission: established in 2003, it is the bank supervisory authority.
- Three policy banks were established and are funded through issues of state bonds and loans from the PBC.
- Four state owned commercial banks offer nation-wide wholesale (to large and medium-sized enterprises) and retail banking services. Overseas branches have been established to serve Chinese customers abroad.
- Eleven[48] joint stock banks, with shares owned by the state, private sector and some foreign concerns. A portion of shares of four of these banks is traded on the stock market. Retail and wholesale banking services are offered to firms and residents in large and medium-sized cities.
- City commercial banks (111) owned by local government, local enterprises and households. Commercial banking services (intermediary, settlements, money transfers, etc.) are offered to city based small and medium-sized enterprises and residents, though they are also trying to attract larger firms headquartered in their city, which would normally do business with a state bank. There is some customer overlap with the Commercial Credit Cooperatives (758), though the coops offer basic banking services (taking deposits, making small loans) to residents and small local firms in urban areas.
- Rural commercial banks (3): like their urban counterparts but offering commercial bank services in rural areas.
- Rural credit cooperatives (35 544 in 2002): each coop offers basic banking services to residents and local enterprises based in a particular rural area.
- In 2004, there were 204 foreign bank subsidiaries, which offer nation-wide foreign exchange services to foreigners and Chinese citizens, and renminbi bank services to all customers (Chinese nationals and others) in Pudong and Shenzen. By 2006/7, restrictions on offering renminbi services will be lifted.

Despite all these changes, two indicators suggest that their impact, to date, has been nominal. First, the banking system remains highly segmented, as indicated by the above

---

[48] In 2003, the Yantai House Savings Bank became a new joint stock bank, the China Evergrowing Bank.

Table 6.4  Market Shares of Chinese Banks: 1992 and 2002

| Banks | Deposits 1992 | Deposits 2002 | Loans 1992 | Loans 2002 |
|---|---|---|---|---|
| Policy banks | na | 0 | na | 13% |
| State owned commercial | 78% | 66% | 84% | 59% |
| Joint stock commercial | 6% | 13% | 4% | 11% |
| City commercial | na | 7% | na | 6% |
| Urban credit coops | 3% | 1% | 2% | 0.005% |
| Rural credit coops | 13% | 12% | 9% | 10% |
| Foreign banks | 0.004% | 1% | 1% | 1% |
| Total | RMB2742 bn | RMB16 861 bn | RMB2759 bn | RMB13 528 bn |

Source: Fu (2004) and Almanac of China's Finance and Banking.

list. Second, the distribution of shares of total loans and deposits has changed, but not significantly so. Table 6.4 illustrates how, since 1992, the market shares of the state owned banks and rural credit cooperatives have declined, partly due to a redistribution of loans to the policy banks, but also because of the growth of the joint stock banks. However, the market share of the big four state banks continues to be very high. The shares of the foreign banks remain low, though these figures were compiled just as some of the restrictions on foreign banks began to be lifted.

## China and financial repression

In 1979, China's banking system was financially repressed by any measure used. The banking system is undergoing reform as part of a bigger plan to move to a market based economy, while conforming to the political ideals of communism. To what degree have these reforms removed the characteristics of financial repression from the Chinese banking system?

One interesting figure is China's ratio of M2 to annual GDP, reported in Table 6.3. In 2002, it stood at 165%, higher than any country listed, including the UK and USA, and it has exceeded 100% for a number of years. Part of the explanation relates to financial repression. Residents of China have a dearth of alternative assets to hold. The stock market is underdeveloped and thin, and access to real assets (e.g. property) has been very limited, though private ownership of assets should begin to rise, now that it is officially recognised in the Constitution. In this environment, the large savings (prompted by China's very rapid rate of growth) will accumulate substantially in (interest bearing) financial assets, included in M2. The confidence in Chinese banks reassures savers that they are a safe place for their deposits. Other factors have contributed to this unusually high figure. Inflation (and nominal interest rates) are very low, and expected to remain so, which builds real M2. By contrast, other countries on the list have much slower growth, a worse inflation record and prospects and (in many cases) more access to alternative assets in which savings can be held.

The state used the central bank to administer the credit quota system, which involved control over all deposit and loan rates, domestic and foreign. This meant credit was directed where the state wanted it to go – the third feature of financial repression. Plans to ease control began with the interbank market in 1996, and since then controls have been relaxed (though not removed) on a variety of loan rates. Renminbi deposit rates remain fixed and determined by the PBC.

The degree of financial repression was reduced after China's reserve ratio was lowered from 13% to 8%, as part of a programme to recapitalise the debt ridden state owned banks. Unlike other emerging economies, it had never been used as a major policy tool, and though it is on the high side by western standards, the PBC pays banks a small amount of interest on the reserves.[49] Chinese banks are subject to a large number of "asset liability" ratios, but most of these are used by supervisors in the developed world, and the ratio requirements are not particularly restrictive.

The reorganisation of the banking system after 1992, with its emphasis on corporate governance and profitability, is indicative of a move away from government interference with the day to day management of bank activities. However, as can be seen from Table 6.4, the nationalised banks continue to control a large portion of deposits and loans, giving the state an option to interfere with how they are run. Also, the central, provincial and local governments hold sizeable stakes in the joint stock and city commercial banks. Traded shares make up just a small proportion of total shares, and until this arrangement is changed, the potential for state interference in running the majority of Chinese banks is high. The influence of powerful local governments on the lending policies of credit coops is unhealthy. Nor does there appear to be any mechanism that allows new private banks to enter the system.[50]

Finally, as the discussion and Table 6.4 shows, foreign banks have been largely barred from operating in Chinese banking markets. In anticipation of its obligation to the World Trade Organisation to allow full foreign bank participation by 2006/7, controls on foreign bank participation are gradually being lifted. However, given the state of the Chinese banks, as shown by their high rates of non-performing loans and other indicators, if foreign banks are accorded the equal treatment expected by the WTO, they could emerge as a dominant force in Chinese banking. Whalley (2003) notes that such a prospect will give China the incentive to keep the renminbi inconvertible,[51] to deny access of foreign banks to renminbi deposits, which in turn will limit their participation in local currency lending. However, foreign banks could bypass this type of restriction (assuming the WTO conditions are satisfied) by accepting domestic currency deposits. The more efficient foreign banks, unencumbered by the debts of state owned firms, could offer higher deposit rates to attract Chinese depositors and fund renminbi loans from these deposits.[52] This would aggravate the problems of most Chinese banks and the government – a major stakeholder in these

---

[49] The banks are paid 1.89% on their reserves (2002 figures).

[50] There is a plan to allow new private banks, but to date the government has shelved all new applications.

[51] The renminbi is currently fixed against the US dollar with convertibility restrictions. For over a decade, the rate has been $1 = 8.3 RMB.

[52] Under the principle of "equal treatment" (see Chapter 5), provided foreign and domestic banks are subject to the same regulations, the Chinese government is not violating WTO conditions. This means it could require foreign banks to adhere to the same deposit and loan rate controls as the local banks, which would considerably reduce the foreign banks' competitive advantage.

banks. They could either restrict foreign bank business (reneging on their WTO agreement) and/or reorganise the entire banking sector, a costly exercise, as was noted earlier. However, given the ongoing economic boom, tax revenues should rise which will help to finance the restoration of the banking sector. Also, the presence of foreign banks means they can pass on their expertise in risk management and other areas, a crucial consideration if the Chinese banks are to operate efficiently in a market based economy. Nonetheless, it appears the Chinese government must act to resolve a major policy dilemma: it either protects its bankrupt state banking sector, which currently dominates the entire banking system, or it adheres to the conditions of the WTO agreement.

Other features of financial repression remain. Although inflation (a key problem in many financially repressed regimes) is low, some restrictions on capital inflows and outflows remain. Limitations have been placed on inward FDI – all foreign investors must have a local partner. Also, Chinese nationals have limited access to foreign equity markets and foreign currency.

To summarise, the approaches taken to banking reform in Russia and China could not have been more different. China has adopted a very gradual approach while many of the changes in Russia can be described as haphazard and ad hoc. The reforms of the Russian banking system mean it is largely free of financial repression whereas in China, the opposite is true. Yet both countries have ended up with concentrated, inefficient banking sectors, a high percentage of non-performing loans, poor risk management systems and incentive/moral hazard problems among depositors, borrowers, and the banks themselves.

### 6.3.3. India

Since India's independence in 1947 (it became a republic in 1950), this democratic nation has never operated a centralised economic system to the degree witnessed in the USSR and China (until 1979). Its private sector is well established in some areas of the economy and the financial system was quite unrestricted at the time of independence. However, by the 1960s, the economy was characterised by rigid state controls designed to meet the objectives of national 5-year economic plans. The state effectively assumed control of the financial sector to raise saving and investment rates and channel funds to priority sectors, agriculture and heavy industry. In 1969 the 14 largest commercial banks were nationalised to ensure that funds were allocated in line with the economic plan, and to create branches in rural and semi-urban areas which, at the time, had no direct access to bank services. To increase the amount of agricultural credit, the regional rural banks were established in 1975. In 1980, another six commercial banks were nationalised. Specialised development financial institutions (DFIs) were created in the 1980s, such as the National Bank for Agricultural and Rural Development, established in 1982 to coordinate and supervise the rural credit cooperatives. Other DFIs included the Export Import Bank of India and the National Housing Bank.

India, like China, did not experience any serious upheaval but in 1991 severe balance of payments problems emerged because of the effects of the first Gulf War in 1990–91[53]

---

[53] Oil prices soared which was a serious problem for oil importing countries like India.

and a large, rapidly growing fiscal deficit. The government responded with a systematic programme of economic reform. The objectives were to increase the role of the private sector in a more open economy (including easing controls on foreign direct investment), allow market forces (rather than the state) to play a greater role in resource allocation, and redefine the role of the government in economic development. Reforms included new measures to improve fiscal discipline and sweeping changes in industrial, trade, foreign direct investment and agricultural policies, together with a plan to overhaul the infrastructure. Not all the changes were implemented but the plan was most successful in the removal of controls in the industrial sector, abolishing import licensing, allowing foreign ownership (either 100% or majority) in most sectors, and dismantling the tariff structure. The reforms appeared to pay dividends. India became one of the fastest growing emerging markets in the 1990s, averaging about 6.7% per annum between 1992 and 1997. Gordon and Gupta (2003) produce econometric evidence (using data from the 1980s and 1990s) showing that in the 1990s, the growth of India's service sector was due to rapid growth in communications, IT, financial services and community services (education and health). Though a high income elasticity of demand and the growth of service exports partly explains this growth, economic reforms were also found to be statistically significant. Nonetheless, between 1997 and 2002, the growth rate slowed to an average of 5.4%, which increased pressure for more reform.

This section concentrates on reforms to the financial sector,[54] and in particular banking, the dominant form of financial intermediation. As Table 6.3 shows, India, like China (but unlike Russia) has functioning bond and equity markets. However, the bond market is largely made up of government bonds – corporate issues make up about 9% of the total market.

Reforms in the financial sector were based on "*pancha sutra*" or five principles:

- A gradual process of sequential changes;
- Measures to reinforce each other;
- Changes in the banking sector to complement macroeconomic policy;
- Financial markets to operate on market principles; and
- Development of the financial infrastructure.[55]

Key reforms included the establishment of the National Stock Exchange (1992) – India's first screen based exchange[56] – the introduction of an auction system for government securities (1992), and improved regulatory powers for the Securities and Exchange Board of India. In banking, the objectives were to keep banks financially sound while encouraging more competition, and reducing government ownership of state banks.

- A commitment to adopt the Basel 1 supervisory standards (see Chapter 4).
- Increased supervision of banks. In 1994, the Board for Financial Supervision was established, and though part of the Reserve Bank of India (RBI), is supposed to be autonomous.

---

[54] For a general discussion of the economic reforms, see Ahluwalia (2002), Acharya (2002) and Dreze and Sen (1995). For a discussion of the Indian financial system pre- and post-reform, see Mohan (2004).

[55] Mohan (2004), p. 122.

[56] Stock exchanges in Mumbai, Calcutta, Dehli, Bangalore and others throughout the country were well established.

- Freeing up (complex) controls on interest rates: for example, rates on loans over Rs 200 000 were deregulated, as were deposit rates on term deposits if maturity exceeded two years. Deposit rates were further deregulated over time.
- A reduction in the cash reserve ratio and statutory liquidity ratios.
- A plan to reduce government ownership of banks.
- Removal of the requirement that large loans had to be approved by the Reserve Bank of India.
- Granting new bank licenses, and easing restrictions on the operations of foreign banks. Foreign banks could accept deposits and make loans subject to the same regulations as domestic banks. A committee made up of members from several government departments approves all applications for entry. Roughly 25 foreign banks have been licensed to operate, with about 150 branches. In 2004, the limit on foreign direct investment in the banking sector was raised from 49% in 2002 to 74%. According to Mohan (2004), by 2003 the new private sector banks accounted for 11% of the assets and 10% of net profits of commercial banks;[57] the figures for foreign banks were, respectively, 7% and 11%.
- Free entry of private firms into the mutual fund business.
- A commitment to reduce government shareholdings of the state owned banks from a minimum of 51% to one of 33%.

However, there has been general dissatisfaction with the slow pace of these reforms – most experts think changes in the banking sector have been insignificant. The current structure of the Indian banking system is as follows:

- Scheduled commercial banks: 92.
- Regional rural commercial banks: 200 – operating in rural areas not covered by the commercial banks.
- Development financial institutions (DFIs): includes *development* institutions such as the Industrial Development Bank of India, *specialised* institutions such as the Export Import Bank, *investment* institutions such as the Unit Trust of India (UTI), the Life Insurance Corporation of India (LIC), and *refinance* firms such as the National Housing Bank. The government owns 100% of UTI and LIC and has shares in three others. As part of the reform programme, DFIs no longer have access to low cost funds and must compete with banks for long-term lending. The DFIs responded to the increased competitive pressure by diversifying into merchant banking and investment advisory services.
- Rural banks and credit cooperatives: these banks are nationalised and focus on rural related activities such as development and agriculture. They do not base loans on the prime lending rate, and tax concessions help to keep costs down which means they can offer slightly higher deposit rates.
- Cooperative banks: there were 1951 urban credit coops in 2002, which differ from their 29 rural counterparts. Most are urban or regional based – some cater to high net worth clients, others specialise in areas such as auto finance and home finance. There are also

---

[57] Excluding the regional rural banks.

group focused coops, such as the Air Corporation Employees Coop Bank, the Zoroastrian Cooperative Bank and the Bassein Catholic Coop Bank.
- Non-bank financial institutions (NBFIs).

Banks were nationalised in 1969 and 1980 to enable the government to channel funds into certain priority sectors and minimise the cost of state borrowing. About 85% of commercial banks are state owned, but 27 dominate the banking sector. In the 1990s, concern about these banks' lack of profitability, their high percentage of non-performing loans and lack of capital prompted some of the reforms listed above. They have been successful in some respects. For example, by 2001, all but two of the state banks met the minimum capital ratio of 9%, set by the RBI.

Since 1996, 13 state banks have been partially privatised but the government owns between 60% and 80% of them. Fourteen remain wholly owned by the state. Two new acts were submitted to Parliament in 2000, which, once they become law, will reduce the state's minimum shareholding in state banks to 33%. To date, these new laws have not been passed, and the newly elected Prime Minister Manmohan Singh has said strategically important enterprises, including banks and oil companies, would remain state owned.[58] Even if the laws are introduced, it has been made clear that the state will maintain management control by ensuring widespread ownership of newly issued shares, and/or through state owned enterprises that own shares. Evidence of this commitment was illustrated when the government intervened to save a troubled financial institution even though it owns just 44% of this bank. Furthermore, Bhattacharya and Patel (2002) infer that the partial privatisation allowed to date has little to do with a genuine commitment to privatise the banking system. Faced with the need for more capital to raise capital ratios to international standards, the state opted for partial privatisation to avoid having to use government funds for costly capital injections.

As part of their liberalisation policy, the government allowed the entry of nine new private banks, in addition to the 25 that existed before. The Reserve Bank has permitted the new entrants to concentrate up to 70% of their business in the more profitable urban areas. Superior technology and greater productivity have, apparently, allowed them to capture a 4% share of the deposit market.

There are concerns about the performance of Indian banks and financial institutions, and state ownership. The major problems with the Indian banking sector include the following.

- **_Poor Asset Quality_**: There are a number of related problems that have contributed to relatively high non-performing loans. Like Russia and China, much of the bad debt can be traced back to traditional heavy industries: agriculture, cars and steel. In 2001, as a percentage of total loans, NPLs are estimated to range between 14% (based on reports from the RBI) and 17% – estimates from independent agencies. Though the NPL percentages are low compared to China and Russia, they are high by international standards – in a healthy bank they would be between 1% and 3%. There are a number of reasons for thinking they are even higher. Under pressure to meet capital adequacy standards, banks have rolled over the interest due (and principal) on doubtful loans,

---

[58] P. Watson, "Reforms with a Human Face for India", _Los Angeles Times_, 21 May 2004.

so they need not be classified as bad debt – known as **evergreening**.[59] Also, the loan classification system used is below international standards.

Despite introducing risk management systems and committees in some banks, many have been unwilling to force corporate borrowers to repay their loans. This is because of an ineffective legal system with opaque bankruptcy laws, especially in the area of foreclosure. However, a securitisation bill[60] was passed in 2002 and allows secured creditors to recover the security more easily without judicial interference, making it easier for financial institutions to act on overdue loans. A set of clear guidelines on recovery of assets has been issued, resulting in several banks establishing asset reconstruction companies and debt recovery tribunals.

- **Priority Sector Lending**: For years, the government has identified certain sectors that must receive 40% of total loans made by commercial banks. The state banks actually exceed the requirement and allocate more than 40% of their loans to these groups. They include agriculture, textiles, steel, SMEs, transport operators, export firms and, more recently, parts of the information technology sector. It has reduced incentives for due diligence and monitoring, thereby increasing the likelihood that these loans will, in time, become problem assets. The figures bear this out. The percentage of NPLs among the priority sector loans is about 23%. Private and foreign banks have tried to avoid them, for example, by opting to invest in government bonds. A knock-on effect is the crowding out of loans to creditworthy firms in other sectors.

- **Weak Financial Institutions and "Destructive Unambiguity"**: Not only is the percentage of non-performing loans high, but, according to Mohan (2004), productivity is lower and operating costs high (due to high wage costs) compared to other developing countries. A working party looked into the financial health of the state banks, reviewing indicators in three areas: performance (e.g. efficiency, as measured by the ratio of cost to income, operating profit as a percentage of working capital), earning capacity (e.g. return on assets, net interest income) and solvency (capital adequacy and other ratios). Of the 27 major state banks, three failed to meet any of the criteria, two met all the criteria and the rest met some criteria, an indication of weaknesses among state owned banks.[61] The authorities have an ostrich-like attitude to the problem, hoping it will go away or at least be contained through capital injections. However, banks will have to change their modus operandi by cutting costs and increasing earnings. State banks will be unable to attract new equity capital if they remain weak, and even if they could raise private capital, they will always be constrained by the law requiring that the state own (at the moment) at least 51% of the concern. Bhattacharya and Patel (2002, 2003) describe the government attitude as one of "_destructive unambiguity_"; while they continue to be major shareholders, the public impression (as in China) will be that these banks will never be allowed to fail. Bhattacharya and Patel (2002) document cases of government bailouts (by the Reserve Bank of India

---

[59] Bhattacharya and Patel (2002), p. 19.

[60] The Securitisation and Reconstruction of Financial Assets and Enforcement of Security Interest Act (SAR-FAESI), April 2002.

[61] Bhattacharya and Patel (2002), p. 24.

or the Ministry of Finance), ranging from large banks to small cooperatives. With such a wide safety net, there is little incentive for depositors to monitor or pressure the banks by voting with their feet. These attitudes encourage borrowers to use these loans for their more risky projects, knowing a reprieve is likely if they prove unable to service the debt. Likewise, managers have no reason to work to improve bank performance.

There is a system of deposit insurance, run by the Deposit Insurance and Credit Guarantee Corporation.[62] As its name suggests, it offers credit guarantees on loans to the priority sectors and to small enterprises. Just under 75% of commercial bank deposits are insured. All banks pay the same annual premium of 0.5% of total deposits. Depositors are paid a maximum of Rs 100 000 (about $2000[63]). Though a working party recommended (1999) the use of risk based premia (as in the USA), no action has been taken. However, given the high percentage of state ownership with what appears to be an implicit guarantee, it is unclear why an insurance scheme is necessary.

- *Reserve Requirements and Lending Restrictions*: Though controls on interest rates have been liberalised, the government has a high statutory liquidity ratio (SLR, 25%) and cash reserve ratio (4.5%[64]), though they have been reduced from the 1991 pre-reform requirements which, combined, were 63.5%.[65] The average SLR for banks was 45% in late 2003, because they are choosing to use the high level of savings (deposits) to purchase government securities. This means the traditional intermediary function of banks, making loans, has been largely curtailed. There are number of reasons for this:
- Interest rates have declined. At the same time, a floor on deposit rates may have discouraged lending.
- Increased prudential standards have made government securities attractive because they carry a lower risk weight than most loans. A related distortion is the tendency for state owned banks and financial institutions to buy each other's paper, in an attempt to raise tier 2 capital to required levels.
- Employees of state banks are considered to be civil servants, which means they can be prosecuted under the anti-corruption law. There is a tendency by institutions such as the Central Vigilance Commissioner to prosecute managers responsible for loans that are not repaid instead of looking at the question of whether the loan was a good calculated risk and/or for evidence of corruption. This discourages them from taking reasonable risks – fewer loans reduce the risk of being prosecuted. It also encourages managers to lend to government institutions or those backed by government because this group of firms is likely to be protected by the state.
- *Bank Supervision*: Just as too many cooks spoil the broth, "too many supervisors make for regulatory sloth!". India suffers from excessive numbers of supervisors. Bhattacharya and Patel (2003) note that the problems of multiple regulators and jurisdiction overlap. Following fraud on the stock market, a recent official report criticised the Reserve Bank of India for ineffective bank supervision and noted that the RBI and the supervisors of

---

[62] Created in 1978 by the merger of the Deposit Insurance and Credit Guarantee Corporations.
[63] Calculation based on the exchange rate in 2004.
[64] As of 2004 – applies to scheduled commercial banks except rural banks.
[65] *Source*: Mohan (2004), p. 122.

cooperative societies often issued counter directives. This raises another problem with the central bank – the large number of hats it wears. It is responsible for:

- Supervision of banks.
- Monetary policy and price stability, the issue of notes and coins and the supervision of the financial system (not just banks).
- The implementation of the 1999 Foreign Exchange Management Act that means it must monitor the balance of payments and undertake any measures to keep the currency stable.
- "Banker" to the state and federal government, including the placement of government debt on the most favourable terms possible.
- Assisting with the promotion of national objectives.

Chapter 1 discussed the potential for conflict of interest if a central bank assumed three of these functions; adding two more merely aggravates the problem.

The equity markets have grown rapidly in the 1990s, with 23 stock exchanges and 9413 listed companies in 2003, up from 6229 in 1991. Market capitalisation as a percentage of GDP rose from 12.2% in 1991 to 43% in 2001. Compared to the banking sector, some attempt is being made to instil a greater sense of responsibility among investors in equity markets. The state owned Unit Trust of India is the largest mutual fund, with 54% share of the total assets invested in mutual funds, down from 80% in the mid-1990s. Since private mutual funds have been allowed, UTI has twice been bailed out by the state, in 1998 and 2001. The fund has never been given an official government guarantee and it has been made clear that it will not be bailed out again. Investors are expected to bear the full risk of their investment. However, it is doubtful whether any government would allow its own mutual fund to fail, resulting in losses for so many small investors.

To conclude, India's economic "miracle", with its impressive growth rates, was largely the result of reforms which made key sectors of the economy more market based. Currency convertibility and capital controls were reformed at the early stages, and have been in the process of relaxation over a long period of time. External finance in the form of foreign direct and/or portfolio investment is being encouraged. The currency has moved gradually over the years from a sterling peg, through a basket peg, to its current regime of a managed float, which is consistent with moves away from financial repression. However, the banking reforms, while notable in some respects (e.g. liberalising many rate controls and allowing foreign bank entry), have some way to go. There are several ongoing features of financial repression, the most serious being the continuation of state ownership and control in the banking sector and other parts of the economy, too many rules on lending, and the absence of laws in bankruptcy. Given these restrictions, it is surprising that the percentage of non-performing loans is not higher, though this probably reflects a more serious problem: not enough loans are being made in an economy still largely dependent on its banking sector for finance.

# 6.4. Islamic Banking

## 6.4.1. The Basic Principles and Key Products

The countries where Islamic banking plays a central role are classified as emerging economies, though they vary considerably in terms of living standards, income and level of development. It is estimated that there are roughly 250 Islamic financial institutions (IFIs) operating in more than 48 countries, with combined assets of somewhere between $200 and $250 billion, though some estimates are as high as $400 billion.[66] To put this in perspective, the top 10 banks (measured by tier 1 capital) in 2003 had assets ranging from just over $1 trillion for Citibank to about $745 billion for BNP Paribas.[67] Clearly Islamic banking is a fringe activity in global terms. However, it has been growing at a rate of 10% per annum and is thought to have a market potential of close to 10% of annual global GDP.[68]

Islamic banking provides some interesting contrasts to the standard modern bank which is the subject of most of this book, and raises fundamental questions about the role of interest and how a bank functions if the payment or receipt of interest is banned. If, as predicted, it attracts 40–50% of Muslim savings in the coming years, it could be an important source of profit for the established banks, provided they create divisions able to cater to Muslim needs. Furthermore, having devoted a good deal of space to the role of the state controlling interest rates, a cornerstone of financial repression, this section looks at several nations which have, for religious reasons, banned banks from paying or charging interest on their deposits and loans. How banks operate if they cannot use the interest rate to intermediate between borrowers and lenders is a question this section attempts to answer. Do these countries, which have developed Islamic products and systems, have something to teach the west? Some of the major western banks, including Citibank, HSBC, Goldman Sachs and UBS, certainly think so. All have opened Islamic banking divisions relatively recently.

Iran, Pakistan and the Sudan run banking systems solely based on Islamic principles, and interest based banking is prohibited by law. Others, including Turkey, Saudi Arabia, Indonesia, the UAE, Yemen and Malaysia, operate mixed systems. Malaysia is particularly proud of its dual system.

The *Holy Quran* forbids the charging of riba, defined as any interest:

> "*Allah has permitted trade and forbidden interest*" (Qu'ran, 2:275)

The above quote shows that for Muslims, earning a return for bearing risk is acceptable (to promote trade) but charging interest is not.

The roots of recent Islamic banking are usually traced back to the Mitghmar Egypt Savings Association, established in 1963. A village bank, it attracted rural people, most of whom did not use financial institutions, due to lack of trust and the absence of facilities in their community. The Association offered savings and investment accounts in keeping with Islamic principles. Deposits were on-lent on a profit/loss basis (see below), thereby mobilising what had been "mattress" savings to finance small businesses and trade. It was later nationalised and merged with the Nasser Savings Bank.

The Mitghmar Savings Association illustrates the point that Islam accepts the need for financial intermediation, but rejects the idea that interest is the core means by which it

---

[66] The estimate of $200–$250 billion is from Institute of Islamic Banking and Insurance, www.islamic.banking.com. However, Karim (2004) suggests it could be as high as $400 billion because the assets of the Islamic banking divisions of conventional banks such as HSBC or BNP Paribas are usually excluded from the calculations. To quote Karim (2004, p. 48): "These are all guesses".

[67] *Source: The Banker*, July 2003, p. 187.

[68] *Source:* El-Hawary *et al.* (2004), p. 39.

should be facilitated. Money is not a commodity, and must be used for productive pursuits: the risk of any investment should be *shared* not *traded*. The main distinguishing characteristic of Islamic banking is the absence of fixed interest rates on deposits and loans. Returns from lending are usually earned through mark-up pricing or profit/loss sharing. Islamic financial principles extend beyond banking applications to broader areas of finance. For example, Islamic equity funds are offered which exclude investment in companies producing alcohol, tobacco and other goods or services prohibited by the *Holy Qu'ran*, but this section focuses on banking.

Organisationally, the President Director of an Islamic bank is responsible to a Board of Commissioners, which has responsibilities and duties similar to that of a Board of Directors. In addition there is a Board of Auditors, which is responsible for the financial monitoring of the bank, and reports to the Commissioners. However, the key difference from a conventional bank is that the Shariah Supervisory Board, which is governed by Islamic law, must approve decisions made by these boards. The Board of Commissioners appoints religious scholars to the Shariah Board. Once they become board members these scholars have complete autonomy and can reject anything deemed to be contrary to Islamic law.

In theory the Islamic financial system is based on contracts, of which there are two types, intermediation and transactional.

## Intermediation contracts

The main intermediation contracts are as follows.[69]

- **Mudaraba** or a trustee finance contract. This is an example of the well-known profit and loss approach which, in theory, is at the heart of Islamic banking. The profits and losses (PLS) are shared among all the concerned parties. The bank or owner of the capital provides all the capital to finance a project; and in return a prearranged percentage of the profits are returned to it. However, the bank incurs all the risk of financial loss. The liability of the firm is the time, labour and expertise put into the project. If it makes losses, the firm has lost these valuable inputs and for this reason does not have to meet any of the financial losses. The drawbacks are problems with monitoring and control, especially when the lending is to small businesses. Double bookkeeping for tax evasion can occur, making it difficult for the bank to discover the actual profit made.
- **Kifala**: when the debtor assumes full liability for the debt, pledging to repay it to the creditor without interest. A third party acts as guarantor and repays the debt should the debtor, for whatever reason, be unable to pay.
- **Amana**: these are demand deposits, held at the bank for security. The bank guarantees the repayment of capital on demand but pays no interest. The Amana account is to facilitate transactions. Though depositors share no profit, the bank can invest the funds. Often,

---

[69] Excluded from the list are *Ju'ala*, a service charge paid by one party for specific services, such as fund management or acting as a trustee and *Wikala*, which is an agency contract – this is covered in the discussion of the Iranian system, see p. 58.

prizes are offered to attract custom. Depositors may approach the bank for short-term interest-free loans. The bank can levy a charge to cover administration costs.

- **Takaful**: mutual insurance, based on collective protection. Members paying into the scheme are its owners, and benefit from the fund should the event they have insured against occur.

## Transactions contracts

El-Hawary *et al.* (2004) identify three categories of transactions based contract.

### (a) Equity Participation

**Musharaka**: this is an equity agreement between the bank and one or more partners to share the risks of an investment project. The returns/losses are determined by the percentage contribution each party makes. For example, if a bank puts up 60% of the capital and two investors provide 20% each, the bank will get 60% of the profits or bear 60% of the losses, and each of the other two parties will gain/lose 20% of the profits/losses.

### (b) Asset Backed Transactions

- Securities for Trade Finance: the most common one is **Murabaha**, a form of mark-up financing. The bank purchases the good/service and sells it to the client at cost, plus an agreed mark-up charge. The mark-up covers the risk the bank incurs between buying the good and selling it to the firm. Other factors affecting the mark-up are the size of the transaction, the reputation of the buyer, and the type of good or service. Normally the repayments are made in instalments, or payment is deferred (**Bay mu'ajal**[70]), and there is no charge for the deferment. The price is agreed upon at the time the product is sold.
- Collateralised Securities: of which the main product is **Ijara**, a lease or lease/hire purchase – the bank (or another party) leases out the good or service and demands a user fee, which is a fixed regular charge over a period of time. Ownership (title of the goods) passes to the lessee once the final payment is made. This category also includes **Istisna**, where delivery and payment are deferred. One party agrees to deliver the good (e.g. a house) at a future date for a price agreed now. Payment may be made at the time of delivery of the final product or in instalments, depending on the nature of the contract.
- One form of loan permitted is the **Qard Hassana**, whereby a lender provides a loan to a needy borrower at no charge, repayable when the borrower is able. The lender can impose a service charge to cover the cost of administering the loan, but it cannot be linked to the size or length of the loan. The loan is repaid when the borrower is able to do so. Personal, health and education loans fall into this category.

---

[70] Or payment is made at the time of the sale, but delivery takes place at a later date, known as **Bay Salam**.

Many of these products resemble asset backed securities in the sense they are all claims on an asset. The difference between the "western" ABS and the Islamic one is that in the west, the claim is against a pool of assets; for the Islamic product described above, it is against an individual.[71] Note that the bank can bring two parties together, or the bank is the investing party. In this sense, it acts as both an investment bank and a commercial bank, but unlike a conventional universal bank, there are no firewalls between the two groups of activity.

As an example, consider Islamic bank products offered in the UK. In 1997, the Allied United Bank of Kuwait brought in the Manzil Murabaha Plan, an Islamic mortgage. The buyer finds a house and agrees the price with the seller, the bank purchases the house, then resells it at a mark-up. The householder repays the bank in equal monthly instalments, for up to 15 years. During this time, the property is registered in the consumer's name but the bank holds the legal title, which is passed to the client once the price is paid. This plan was phased out for all but a few clients because of property price risk incurred by the bank. It was replaced with an Ijara[72] plan: once the householder has found the house, the bank purchases the property and agrees to resell[73] it to the customer after 25 years. The customer makes a monthly payment to the bank, but the rent is reassessed once a year and changed to reflect any changes in the value of the property. Customers can purchase the property at any time.

There is also a conversion plan to allow clients with a conventional mortgage to switch to an Islamic one. The bank makes its profit from the rent, which changes to reflect the state of the property market and risk. However, it is more costly for several reasons. First, there is the large deposit the householder must make, between a fifth and a quarter of the purchase price, compared to 5% or even nothing in a conventional mortgage. Also, two sets of legal contracts must be drawn up. In the UK, stamp duty is payable each time a property changes ownership. For this type of mortgage, it was paid twice (when the bank purchased the property and after the owner paid the bank in full) until 2003, when the Chancellor of the Exchequer agreed to stop imposing this double stamp duty. Finally, the relatively small number (compared to conventional mortgages) means proportionately higher administrative costs for the bank. The only attraction compared to a conventional mortgage is the absence of a charge for repaying early.

The HSBC Islamic subsidiary, HSBC Amanah Finance, based in Dubai, operates in several countries, including the UK. In 2003, it announced the availability of Shariah compliant[74] consumer finance products, available in 25 HSBC branches where the Muslim population is high. It offers an Ijara mortgage, similar in features to the one described above, where the rent is reviewed bi-annually and a 10% downpayment is required. The rent is determined using LIBOR as a benchmark plus a profit margin. HSBC argue the rent is not a substitute for interest payments but rather, a charge for use of the property. The Amanah bank account is a basic deposit account with no overdraft, credit/debit interest. The customer is issued with a cheque book and debit card. The deposits are not used for

---

[71] El-Hawary *et al.* (2004), p. 8.

[72] Most banks have shifted from Murabaha to Ijara, not only for mortgages but for other forms of lending too.

[73] Or payment is made at the time of the sale, but delivery takes place at a later date, known as **Bay Salam**.

[74] HSBC has a Shariah Supervisory Board, which approves and monitors all its Islamic banking and finance products.

HSBC interest based activities such as lending. One drawback is that the minimum credit balance is £1000 – a conventional basic account usually does not require more than £1 in deposits. Also, it is unclear what bank charges, if any, the client will incur.

Given the range of products, a hypothetical balance sheet is shown in Table 6.5. Note the differences compared to a standard bank balance sheet. Though the investment accounts are listed as liabilities, they involve using deposits to finance some form of equity investment, either in the bank itself or some other project. Deposits in a conventional bank finance loans. On the asset side, there are no loans, apart from Qard Hassana, and these do not involve any interest payments. Fee based activities would be off-balance sheet in the western system.

In terms of risk, Islamic banks should face a reduced chance of getting into problems, because the risk is, in principle, shared among more agents. Banks bear the risk of project investment, and holders of investment accounts can lose out. In practice, however,

**Table 6.5    Balance Sheet of an Islamic Bank**

| Assets | Liabilities |
|---|---|
| Asset Backed Transactions/Trade Finance:<br>　Murabaha<br>　Bay mua'jal<br>　Bay salam | Demand/Transactions/Current Account:<br>　Amana |
| Collateral-Based Products:<br>　Ijara<br>　Istisna | |
| Syndication:<br>　Mudaraba (special purpose)<br>　Musharaka (venture capital/private<br>　equity) | General Investment Accounts :[1]<br>　Mudaraba<br><br>Specialized Investment Accounts:<br>　Mudaraba<br>　Musharaka |
| Fee-Based Services (e.g. letters of credit,<br>　safety deposit boxes, etc.):<br>　Ju'ala<br>　Qard Hassana | Equity |

[1]A general investment account would be like an investment or term deposit, whereby customers share in the profits (or losses) of the bank but do not have any management control. The formula for profit-sharing is usually regulated by the central bank and agreed by both parties at the time of the agreement: typically the investor gets 80%; the bank 20%.
*Source*: Grais and Iqbal (2003).
Specialised investment accounts involve a specific investment opportunity the bank offers clients – e.g. private equity, join ventures or a fund.
*Source*: El-Hawary *et al.* (2004).

Islamic bank managers often opt for the relatively risk-free products such as ijara (leasing) and murabaha, rather than the riskier PLS finance such as mudaraba and musharaka. In a mixed system, the capital on investment accounts may be effectively protected from downside risk. This creates another risk, fiduciary risk: banks face legal action if found in breach of their fiduciary responsibility towards depositors (with investment accounts) or for failing to comply with Shariah law. They also face institutional risk, arising from a divergence between product definition and practices (El-Hawary *et al.*, 2004, p. 48).

Iqbal and Mirakhor (2002) estimated that these products make up 80% or more of the assets side of most Islamic banks. The other 20% involve profit sharing (musharaka) projects. It is a conservative approach because some form of collateral implicitly backs most of the banks' assets. However, these banks lose out on the benefits of diversification. Furthermore, the mark-up often involves a formula based on the return a project would get if market interest rates applied.[75] Dar and Presley (2003) report exceptions to the dominance of murabaha and Ijara. In Iran and Switzerland, Islamic banks and financial institutions use PLS when arranging Islamic finance, and use very little in the way of mark-up type products. In Iran the **wikala** contract is used instead of the mudaraba contract – the agent receives a fixed fee rather than a share of the profits.

High reserve ratios, in the order of 30–40%, are maintained because of the short-term nature of the banks' liabilities. The risky nature of the ventures causes banks to confine their loans to well-established, valued clients. Also, a bank will monitor closely the employment of capital it has financed.

Another issue relates to investment accounts. The idea is that both the bank and depositors share in the profits and *losses* of the investment. El-Hawary *et al.* (2004) argue that in practice, in mixed systems where Islamic and conventional banks are competing for the same customers, if asset values fall, the value of the deposit may not be written down, leaving other parties to subsidise this group of investors. El-Hawary *et al.* (2004) cite the example of Egypt's International Islamic Bank for Investment and Development. The bank, during hard times, paid no dividends to its shareholders in the late 1980s, allocating them to investment account holders. In 1988, this amount exceeded profits – the difference was reported as a loss carried forward. Also, individuals tend to hold these accounts, even the high value ones, with little control over what is done with their funds, adding to potential moral hazard problems. The onus is on regulators and the Shariah Boards to ensure that their rights are protected.

An additional problem for these banks is the lack of standard contracts for Islamic bank services, together with an ineffective legal system to enforce contracts. Usually procedures for resolving disputes are inadequate. This has led to impromptu solutions to problems. For example, Shariah law forbids penalties being imposed if there is late or non-payment by the party concerned. The banks have responded by imposing penalties, but giving them away to charitable causes.

---

[75] Dar and Presley (2003) identify other approaches to mark-up, including an arrangement for profit/loss sharing, a fixed rate determined and agreed upon by parties to the transactions, or a mark-up based on the average profit from a similar investment in a certain industry.

Islamic banks face many of the risks of conventional banks, including the following.

- Counterparty risk: reneging on a contract.
- Market risk in relation to murabaha contracts: when there is a change in the benchmark mark-up upon which the contract was based. To price their financing facilities, the banks often use an underlying market interest rate such as LIBOR. A change in LIBOR is the source of the market risk.
- Currency risk: assets or liabilities are denominated in foreign currencies.
- Operational risks: a breakdown in internal systems, fraud, IT problems, etc.
- Business commercial risk: there is a chance the investment will not perform according to expectations. This risk can be very serious in the face of mudaraba arrangements.
- Withdrawal risk: if depositors are concerned about the quality of a bank (e.g. in relation to investments), or in mixed systems, conventional banks pay a better rate.
- Risk of a mismatch in assets and liabilities.
- Liquidity risk: banks are unable to meet their payments as they fall due.

However, Islamic banks are distinctly safer than their western counterparts in some respects. First, since depositors receive no (nominal) interest they can represent a large source of revenue to the bank itself in at least a modestly inflationary environment under conditions where a western bank might have to offer them a return. Second, investment account depositors are, effectively, "quasi" shareholders in a unit trust. They cannot "run" if the bank is in trouble because "selling" just reduces the value of their holdings. Third, in a conventional bank, a great pyramid is constructed around a small equity base. An Islamic bank's equity base, and its buffer against shocks, is far larger.

Third, the western bank's main asset, loans, suffer from the problem that the borrower bears all the upside risk on the project while the bank has all the downside risk. This gives the borrower (if he/she can get away with it because monitoring is deficient) a big incentive to take on more risk. By contrast, an Islamic bank that participates in an equity sharing contract assumes some of the upside risk, somewhat dulling the incentive for the firm to take more risk.

## 6.4.2. Regulation of Islamic Banks

Recall from Chapter 4 that experts differ in their opinion as to how closely the banking sector should be regulated. A few argue in favour of "free banking" but the majority accept the need for some regulation and the debate centres around what the extent of regulatory intervention should be. The same is true in Islamic banking. Some Shariah Boards are of the view that their presence is sufficient – a form of self-regulation. Most parties favour some external regulation. However, applying the regulatory regime imposed on conventional banks is not straightforward. For example, in a system where investment depositors face downside risk, a system of deposit insurance would be inappropriate. A survey of Islamic banks by Moody's (2001) suggests the majority do not see their deposits as being PLS.

Likewise, the 1993 Malaysia Islamic Banking Act treats investment accounts as liabilities. Clearly this is an issue requiring further clarification.[76]

El-Hawary *et al.* (2004) argue in favour of a segmented approach to Islamic regulation that centres on the degree of risk aversion. Segment A would be for highly risk averse depositors using the bank for transaction purposes and/or to ensure their capital is protected. This group's funds would be invested in Shariah compliant low risk securities. The arrangement is similar to the "narrow bank" idea explained in Chapter 4. The second segment would be for less risk averse investors who are prepared to risk some capital in exchange for some expected return. The bank would use the funds for medium to long-term instruments, such as ijara or istina. Or a mudaraba fund could be set up with the investors holding shares. They would operate like mutual funds and could be traded if the market was sufficiently liquid and deep. This segment would be for investors prepared to take a significant degree of risk – their deposits would be used to fund musharaka or mudaraba, which are backing riskier projects, akin to private equity or venture capital. For musharaka funded projects, the bank itself has the right to participate directly in the way the venture is run, and would be expected to develop a long-term relationship with the musharaka enterprises, with a seat on a firm's board – not unlike the German and Japanese approaches. For all three segments, the regulator would ensure the depositors' and investors' funds were being directed to the appropriate instruments. Regulators would also monitor a bank's overall exposure to make certain it is well diversified.

There are other regulatory issues in the area of transparency and market discipline. The difference in standards across states with Islamic banking is widely acknowledged. The Accounting and Audit Organisation for Islamic Financial Institutions (AAOIFI) was established in 1991 and has 105 members in 24 countries.[77] A self-regulatory organisation, to date it has issued 50 standards on accounting, auditing, governance, ethical and Shariah law related issues. It has also encouraged harmonising accounting and auditing standards. In 2002, an Islamic Financial Services Board was set up by the central banks of Islamic countries. Its objective is to agree on a set of international standards in corporate governance, transparency and disclosure for the Islamic financial services sector, covering banking, insurance and securities.[78]

The International Islamic Rating Agency (IIRA) was established in 2002. The Bahrain agency rates Shariah compatible banks and mutual funds. Assuming the IIRA is able to establish a credible reputation, it will help to persuade investors of the attractions of Islamic banks and funds.

## 6.4.3. Islamic Banking in Malaysia, Iran and Pakistan

*Malaysia* operates both a conventional and an Islamic banking system. The first Islamic bank was established in 1983, and dual banking, where a bank can offer both conventional and Islamic banking services, was introduced in 1993. Banks offering both types must have

---

[76] Archer and Ahmed (2003) identify the areas of Islamic banking which require explicit attention with regard to prudential regulation, accounting and corporate governance.

[77] Accounting and Audit Organisation for Islamic Financial Institutions (AAOIFI), www.aaofi.com, 2004.

[78] See Karim (2004) for more detail on the activities of the IFSB.

a firewall between their Shariah compliant Islamic bank and their conventional bank. Also, a standard system is required for computing the rate of return to determine the distribution of profit on the relevant products and ensure a satisfactory capital adequacy framework for the Islamic bank portfolio. The latter point is part of the drive by the Bank Negara Malaysia (the central bank) initiated to ensure that all Malaysian banks, including Islamic ones, comply with international prudential and supervisory standards. Transparency in accounts is considered to be even more important because investment accounts carry a downside risk, unlike conventional deposits. By the end of 2002, Islamic banking assets reached 9% of total assets, deposits stood at 10% of total deposits and the market share for Islamic financing was 8%. Based on these figures the system is on course to meet the market share targets of 20% in assets, deposits and financing by 2010.[79]

By contrast, **Iran** nationalised its banks after the 1979 revolution. In 1983, the Usury-Free Banking Act limited the activities domestic banks could undertake. Savings and current accounts must be interest-free, though prizes and bonuses are allowed. There are short and long-term investment accounts, operated on a PLS basis, unlike most other systems, such as Pakistan, which rely heavily on mark-up. Banks charge fees for loans. Iran's overseas banking operations are exempt from the Act. Iran's Supreme Council of Banks determines rates of return and loan fees. Until 1990, the Supreme Council insisted all banks have the same rate of return on investments, but has since relaxed this rule to promote competition.

**Pakistan** introduced Islamic banking in 1984. Over the period, the banks introduced new products to conform to Shariah law. Until the Shariah court intervened, the interest-free banking system that evolved in Pakistan was fairly typical of systems found in other countries operating an Islamic system. It included loans where no interest is charged (Quard-e-Hasan), trade related modes of financing such as Isira or a buy back agreement, and investment type financing such as musharaka – profit and loss sharing. However, the Federal Shariat Court judged a number of key products offered by Islamic banks to be inconsistent with Islam, i.e. riba was, indirectly, being paid. There were 55 appeals against the judgement but in 1999 the Supreme Court dismissed them. The government decided not to appeal against this dismissal and began a wholesale transformation of the economy which would be necessary if the Supreme Court's vision of true Islamic banking was to be implemented. One of the affected banks did appeal the judgement, which the government eventually supported because it was proving very difficult to implement the large-scale changes that were necessary. In June 2002, the Supreme Court quashed the 1999 "riba" judgement. It meant Pakistan would revert to its original system of interest-free banking until the courts had sorted out the question of what constitutes riba.

## 6.4.4. Expansion into Global Markets

Some Islamic banks have attempted to expand into the global markets since the early 1980s, to capture a Muslim market overseas and diversify their portfolio, but have faced a number of challenges. There are difficulties with being recognised as banks, because they

---

[79] *Source*: "Malaysia IBS deposits Hit 10% Market Share", *Islamic Banker*, 90, July 2003, pp. 8–11.

cannot hold interest-earning government securities, such as bonds.[80] The profit/loss-sharing nature of their deposit and lending business is at odds with a western system, which protects depositors and emphasises the importance of a transparent portfolio, where all assets can be valued. Furthermore, in cases where a bank lends money and shares in the profits, the borrower repays the bank out of profits after tax. Those banks that do establish themselves in the west usually have to adapt their deposit-taking and lending rules to gain recognition. A few western institutions have also entered the Islamic banking market, including HSBC and Citicorp – both have Shariah advisors. To date a large proportion of the resulting assets are short-term, and the banks are focusing on the development of long-term instruments that are compatible with Islamic banking.

## 6.5. Sovereign and Political Risk Analysis

### 6.5.1. A Review of Terminology

The final section of this chapter undertakes a brief review of sovereign and country risk. Again, whole books have been written on the subject. The purpose here is to explore the key ideas and findings in this area. The section provides the definitions of standard terms, reviews why emerging market economies tend to be net importers of external finance, and investigates models designed to identify the factors which increase the risk of sovereign defaults, The impact of political risk is also reviewed.

It is helpful to begin by reviewing the terminology used.

*Sovereign Risk*: definitions vary but generally it is the risk that the government of a country will default on its external debt, which may be in the form of loans or bonds. It is known as sovereign debt because it is either owed or guaranteed by a sovereign government. For example, in 1998 the Russian government declared a moratorium on the repayment of their foreign debt and defaulted on its domestic debt. Sovereign risk is a special type of credit risk, but unlike a conventional loan, lenders cannot seize a country's assets if they default on external debt.

*Country Risk*: this term is more general, and usually means sovereign risk plus the *political risk* foreign investors are exposed to. To understand the term country risk, it is important to recognise the three types of foreign investment.

(1) **Foreign Loans**: these include loans to businesses headquartered in another country, which may or may not be guaranteed by the state. They also include loans to any foreign government, at any level, e.g. national or local.

(2) **Foreign Direct Investment**: when a foreign national sets up business operations in another country. These firms will face all the normal business risks plus the *political risk* that arises because the operation is based in another country. In stable countries that do not discriminate against foreign operations, the risk is trivial. In other countries,

---

[80] Nor can Islamic governments issue bonds. Public funds are raised through profit sharing loans made by banks to state owned enterprises. Tax exempt loan certificates are used to meet any government requirements for short-term funds.

it may be very high, for a variety of reasons. The government may be unstable, the country may have a reputation for nationalising foreign firms, or there may be the threat of a government coup d'etat, high crime rates, red tape, and so on.

(3) **Foreign Equity or Portfolio Investment**: when an investor buys shares in foreign firms. Again, there are the standard risks associated with any equity investment but with foreign shares, the degree of political risk may vary from nil to quite substantial. If the portfolio includes shares in countries such as Canada or Australia, there is virtually no political risk. On the other hand, foreign shareholders with a stake in a large profitable mine in Siberia face more substantial risk, as a group recently discovered. They tried to attend a shareholders meeting but were unable to after being confronted by armed bouncers at the door. This group soon found the other shareholders had agreed to an increase in capital, which diluted the value of the foreign shareholding, leaving the foreigners with a minority stake.[81]

Thus, *country risk* is a measure of the perceived probability that a country will be unable or unwilling to meet its obligations, with respect to foreign debt, equity or foreign direct investment. The responsibility to meet these obligations does not always rest with the state but with private borrowers, firms and even employees engaged to work there. The political situation may enhance or detract from a country meeting its obligations, and therefore its country risk profile. Sovereign risk, as defined above, is a type of country risk. Political risk can raise a country's risk profile. Given the focus of this book, the rest of this section is concerned with sovereign risk, including the effect of politics on sovereign risk.

## 6.5.2. Why do Developing Nations Demand External Finance?

Capital-importing developing nations demand capital in excess of their own domestic capital base. The demand for external finance is explained by the "development cycle" hypothesis. Countries demand capital based on expectations of higher future income streams. By borrowing capital, the country can finance a more rapid rate of economic growth and smooth consumption paths over time. Provided the country's domestic capital base is insufficient to meet its growth rate targets and the expected marginal productivity of the domestic endowment of capital exceeds the rate of interest charged for the borrowed capital, it will borrow capital from the international capital markets, that is, it will import capital. Financial repression is likely to increase the need for foreign finance because the absence of a well-developed money capital market will exacerbate the shortage of domestic finance, on the part of both government and domestic firms. Financial repression can involve restrictions on private international capital flows, and usually means that governments have to try to borrow more from abroad.

External finance comes in a number of different forms: short and long-term private and official loans made by foreign banks/governments, foreign direct investment and portfolio investments, consisting of debt securities (private or state backed bonds and other securities issued by the LDC) and equity, acquired when non-residents purchase shares on the LDC's

---

[81] *Source*: Gros and Steinherr (2004), pp. 239–240.

stock markets and/or private shares. Emerging market countries also receive official finance from other governments, the IMF and the World Bank, which may be concessionary or non-concessionary. As net importers of finance, these countries are leveraged (or geared), just like firms. A country's *foreign leverage (or gearing) ratio* is defined as the ratio of foreign debt or equity of the capital-importing nation. Foreign debt consists of loans made plus bonds purchased by non-residents, and foreign equity includes direct and portfolio investment by non-residents.

In the 1960s, foreign direct investment as a percentage of external finance was, on average, 39%. Official finance and commercial loans each contributed about 30% to external finance in developing countries. From the late 1960s onwards, the growth rate in the real value of foreign direct investment was very slow. Commercial medium and long-term lending increased at an annual average real rate of just under 10% per annum, most of it in the form of sovereign loans. By the late 1970s, foreign direct investment had fallen to less than 15% of the total external finance component; sovereign loans peaked at 75%, falling after 1982, the year Mexico announced it could no longer service its external debt. This triggered defaults by a large number of developing countries. The phenomenon tends to come in waves: the early 1980s, the early 1990s (e.g. Mexico, 1994), with new problems in Russia in 1998 and Argentina in 1995, and again in 2001. External finance from official sources also fell steadily until 1982, and then from 1982–88 it increased to over 50% of the total. Issues of foreign bonds and foreign equity were negligible until the late 1980s.

On the supply side, the increased sovereign lending accompanied a rise in *syndicated lending* (where a lead bank arranges the loan, but involves a syndicate of other banks). The syndicated loan market peaked in 1982, with the majority of the loans arranged for sovereign borrowers. After a decline of several years, 1987 saw a rapid increase in the volume of syndicated loans arranged, but these were largely confined to the private sector. Normally, the loans are in US dollars and subject to a variable rate of interest.

Thus, throughout the 1970s, there was a dramatic rise in developing country foreign gearing/leverage ratios (FGRs/FLRs). At the same time sovereign debt became the predominant form of lending. Three parameters play a crucial part in the determination of a country's optimal foreign gearing (leverage) ratio. These are risk attitudes, moral hazard and interference costs.[82]

### Risk Attitudes

Suppose borrower and lender are risk neutral, that is, the agents are indifferent to a fair bet with even odds. In this case, foreign debt and equity are perfect substitutes, and neither party has preference for one instrument over another. If one of the parties is risk averse, the agent will refuse a fair bet with even odds. To isolate the importance of risk attitudes in international debt, assume there are no costs associated with moral hazard or interference, borrower and lender treat foreign equity as a risky asset (the returns on foreign equity are proportional to domestic output) and foreign debt is considered a safe asset (the returns to debt are guaranteed, payable at a fixed rate and independent of what happens to domestic

---

[82] For a more technical treatment of these ideas, see Heffernan (1986).

output). Under these assumptions, the composition of external finance will be 100% equity if the borrower is risk averse and the lender risk neutral, 100% debt if the lender is risk averse and the borrower is risk neutral, and a combination of debt and equity if both parties are risk averse.

Risk attitudes provide a partial explanation for the rise in developing country external debt through the 1970s. Lenders treated sovereign loans as safe assets, because banks, drawing from their experience of credit analysis for individual and corporate borrowers, focused the probability of a debtor remaining solvent. Bankers correctly assumed the probability of default on a sovereign loan was very low because a country could not go bankrupt. However, the subsequent debt crisis taught them that when it comes to sovereign loans, the solvency issue is not enough. If a nation encounters a long period of illiquidity (that is, it has a positive net worth but lacks the means to meet its maturing liabilities as they fall due), the true book value of the lender's assets will be lower. Banks made the mistake of assuming sovereign loans had zero or little risk, but the risk of illiquidity turned out to be as serious as the risk of default.

### Interaction between Moral Hazard and Interference Costs

Recall from Chapter 1 that moral hazard arises whenever an agreement between two parties alters the incentive structure for either party. In the case of the loan, the borrower may choose a more risky production technique unless the bank closely monitors the use of funds. The problem is aggravated if the borrower thinks the loan agreement may be altered when the country encounters debt servicing problems. The lender usually reacts to borrower moral hazard by demanding a higher risk premium on a loan and/or a higher yield in the equity. A bank moral hazard problem can arise if there is a "too big to fail" policy or a lender of last resort. For the moment, ignore this aspect of moral hazard and assume only the borrower exhibits it.

Asymmetry of information explains why moral hazard may affect the foreign gearing ratio. The lender should know how borrower incentives have been affected by looking at choice of production technique or for signs of reduced effort. But often, these cannot be observed, and the bank is unable to penalise the behaviour. One remedy is for the bank to choose a premium to cover the estimated cost of borrower moral hazard. Alternatively, the investor may use *sighted investment* to minimise asymmetry in information. Here, managers are sent to the country to discourage underperformance of local staff. Project finance is a type of sighted investment, as is monitoring the developing country more closely, in the event of repayment problems.

However, "sighted" investment by a lender may be considered an interference cost by the capital-importing country – the government may be concerned about the degree to which the sighted investment impinges upon the microeconomic sovereignty of the country. Interference costs are difficult to measure because of the value judgements associated with them. However, during the 1970s, many Latin American countries placed a heavy weight on what they perceived as a loss of "microeconomic" sovereignty if they allowed foreign direct investment; most countries in the Far East were less concerned. External loans did not seem to involve any loss of sovereignty, because virtually no conditions were attached to the loans, and bankers did not monitor their use very closely. However, developing nations failed to impute the hidden costs arising from IMF macroeconomic stabilisation conditions imposed when debt was rescheduled (see below).

The attraction of sovereign lending over other forms of investment is exacerbated if there is a bank-related moral hazard problem. The argument here is that banks will engage in riskier investments if they think they are going to be bailed out by a lender of last resort, or assisted by the state. However, in the 1970s banks were attracted to sovereign loans because they genuinely thought they were low-risk assets. How, after all, could a government default on its debt? Subsequent intervention by the IMF did not give bankers an easy time of it. Hence, the moral hazard problems generated after the 1982 sovereign debt crisis were probably kept to a minimum.

To summarise, the three factors discussed above help to explain why developing countries allowed themselves to become highly geared by sovereign borrowing in the 1970s and early 1980s. First, western banks were willing to make sovereign loans because they thought they were low-risk; risk premia and monitoring were kept to a minimum. Developing countries were willing to borrow from private banks to finance development and because interference costs were thought to be comparatively small. Both parties ignored the impact of random economic shocks on their borrowing and lending decisions. For example, many countries borrowed on the strength of wildly optimistic forecasts about future commodity prices. In the cases where commodity prices did rise as forecast (e.g. oil), they were far more volatile than had been anticipated. Subsequent oil price declines prompted serious debt servicing problems for some countries. By definition, it is not possible to forecast random shocks, but in this situation scenario analysis might have helped the banks better assess the impact of possible changes in the global macroeconomic situation.

After Mexico defaulted on its debt in 1982, Brazil and other countries soon followed. Between 1980 and 1993, 64 developing nations experienced problems repaying their sovereign external debt and negotiated multilateral debt relief agreements totalling $6.2 billion. In the late 1980s and early 1990s, global banks began to increase their exposure in emerging markets, though sovereign loans were largely replaced by the use of debt securities and equities. Thus, the early 1990s (as in many previous years) saw a net financial transfer towards emerging market economies, peaking at $66 billion in 1993. However, in December 1994, Mexico was forced to devalue its currency because of rising trade deficits and falling reserves. Fears of another default escalated, with drastic effects for emerging capital markets around the world. Investors began dumping emerging market debt and equity. The Clinton government and IMF calmed the markets by intervening to sort out the Mexican problems. Mexican debt was restructured with the help of $20 billion in loan guarantees by the US government, IMF loans totalling just under $18 billion and BIS loans of $10 billion. Mexico worked with the IMF and international bankers to restructure the country's debt. Rising oil revenues meant that by 1997, Mexico was able to repay the US government loans in full.

Though the intervention calmed the markets, the provision of external finance to the developing world began to fall off. After 1996 these economies made, in aggregate, a net financial transfer *to* the "Rest of the World", so financial flows out of developing countries

Table 6.6   Net Financial Flows to Developing Economies (US$bn)

| | 1991–1996 (annual average) | 1997–2001 (annual average) |
|---|---|---|
| Net financial flows to emerging market countries | 169 | 74.7 |
| (1) Net official | 22.7 | 25.7 |
| (2) Net foreign direct investment | 62.8 | 136.9 |
| (3) Net portfolio investment[1] | 58.9 | 4.2 |
| (4) Other net investment[2] | 24.6 | −92.1 |

[1] Includes portfolio debt and equity.
[2] Short and long-term lending.
Source:  United Nations (2002), *Trends and Policies in the World Economy*, New York: United Nations, table II.3.

exceeded those coming in. This dramatic change reflected a reduced willingness to lend to emerging markets, which worsened after the Asian (1997) and Russian crises (1998).[83]

Table 6.6 documents these changes. In the period 1997–2001, net financial flows to developing countries were positive, much lower than in 1991–96. Note the large rise in net FDI: it accounted for just over one-third in the early 1990s, but over 180% in the second period. Cross-border lending collapsed between the two periods. In 1990–96 it accounted for nearly 50% of total net financial flows, but in the second period its contribution was negative: (−) 118%! Official financing flows rose from 13% to nearly 80%, reflecting the IMF and other agreements put in place to deal with the Asian and Russian meltdowns – see Chapter 8 for more detail.

## 6.5.3. Sovereign Risk Analysis

Quite a substantial academic literature on sovereign risk analysis has built up, though it tends to be cyclical. Hoti and McAleer (2003) reviewed 50 published papers on the subject and found three types of explanatory variables are tested: economic, financial and political. The number of economic and financial variables used ranged from 2 to 32 (mean: 11.5). Debt rescheduling as a proxy for default (since outright default rarely occurs) was used in 36 studies, followed by country risk ratings[84] (18) and debt arrears (4). The use of other variables tailed off to between 1 and 3. Some of the more recent studies used the secondary market price of foreign debt, stock returns and relative bond spread. In 30 of the 50 studies, no political variables were used, but when they were, the number ranged from 1 to 13 with an average of 1.86.

This subsection centres on recent empirical work in the area, to illustrate what the key issues are, and for bankers, the critical question of how to decide on whether a loan is worth making. Manasse *et al.* (2003) derive a model of how best to predict a debt crisis, using information from 47 countries for the period 1970–2001. Out of these 47, 16 did not

---

[83] See Chapter 8 for more detail.
[84] These are ratings produced by *Institutional Investor, Euromoney, Standard & Poor's, Moody's,* the *Economist Intelligence Unit.*

default. Here "default" is defined as any country that has received a large, non-concessional IMF loan in excess of its 100% quota,[85] or if Standard and Poor's classifies the country as being in default, which occurs if a country's government fails to pay interest or principal on an external obligation when it is due.

Table 6.7 is a partial reproduction of table 1 from Manasse *et al.* (2003)–22 countries (including China and India) which did not default were dropped from the original table. It is notable that Russia is the only former Soviet bloc country that has defaulted. Some appear

Table 6.7   Country Debt Problems, 1970–2002

| | Number of Crises | Average Length | Years in Crisis | Crisis Episodes (entry–exit) |
|---|---|---|---|---|
| Algeria | 1 | 6 | 6 | 1991–97 |
| Argentina | 3 | 5 | 15 | 1982–94, 1995–96, 2001– |
| Bolivia | 2 | 6.5 | 13 | 1980–85, 1986–94 |
| Brazil | 3 | 5.3 | 16 | 1983–95, 1998–2000, 2001– |
| Chile | 1 | 8 | 8 | 1983–91 |
| Costa Rica | 1 | 10 | 10 | 1981–91 |
| Dominican Republic | 1 | 22 | 22 | 1981– |
| Ecuador | 2 | 8 | 16 | 1982–96, 1999–2001 |
| Egypt | 1 | 1 | 1 | 1984–85 |
| Guatemala | 1 | 1 | 1 | 1986–87 |
| Indonesia | 2 | 2.5 | 5 | 1997–2001, 2002– |
| Jamaica | 3 | 4.7 | 14 | 1978–80, 1981–86, 1987–94 |
| Jordan | 1 | 5 | 5 | 1989–94 |
| Mexico | 2 | 5 | 10 | 1982–91, 1995–96 |
| Morocco | 2 | 3 | 6 | 1983–84, 1986–91 |
| Pakistan | 1 | 2 | 2 | 1998–2000 |
| Panama | 1 | 14 | 14 | 1983–97 |
| Paraguay | 1 | 7 | 7 | 1986–93 |
| Peru | 3 | 6.3 | 19 | 1976–77, 1978–81, 1983–98 |
| Philippines | 1 | 10 | 10 | 1983–93 |
| Russia* | 1 | 3 | 3 | 1998–2001 |
| South Africa | 4 | 1.8 | 7 | 1976–78, 1985–88, 1989–90, 1993–94 |
| Thailand | 2 | 1 | 2 | 1981–82, 1997–98 |
| Trinidad and Tobago | 1 | 2 | 2 | 1988–90 |
| Tunisia | 1 | 1 | 1 | 1991–92 |
| Turkey | 2 | 3.5 | 7 | 1978–83, 2000–02 |
| Ukraine* | 1 | 3 | 3 | 1998–2001 |
| Uruguay | 3 | 2 | 6 | 1983–86, 1987–88, 1990–92 |
| Venezuela | 3 | 3.3 | 10 | 1983–89, 1990–91, 1995–98 |

* Data from 1993.

*Source*: Manasse *et al.* (2003), table 1. Note the table is not exhaustive – it does NOT include every country that defaulted during this period, only those the authors included in their study.

[85] More explicitly, if a large non-concessional loan is approved and some of the loan is disbursed over the first year.

to be chronic defaulters – South Africa was in default four times (though not since 1994) Argentina, Brazil, Jamaica, Peru, Uruguay and Venezuela have each had three episodes of default. Ecuador, Mexico and Turkey have defaulted twice and the majority have defaulted just once. The average length of time to resolve the problem is 5.5 years, though the Dominican Republic (22 years), Panama (14 years) and Costa Rica (10 years) took longer. Egypt, Guatemala, Thailand and Tunisia managed to settle the problem within a year, and only encountered difficulties of this magnitude just once.

Manasse *et al.* used a multinomial logit model to identify the variables significant in explaining why a country defaults, and once identified, to set up an early warning system (EWS). The use of logit is the most common econometric method used to assess sovereign risk.[86] The logit approach is explained in detail in Chapter 7, but essentially it is an econometric procedure that deals with binary outcomes, that is, in situations where the event, default, happens or does not happen. In logit analysis, the dependent variable is the binary outcome and the objective is to identify the explanatory variables that influence the event. The right-hand side of the regression contains the explanatory variables.

In common with most of the work in this area, Manasse *et al.* test for the significance of a large list of possible explanatory variables, some of which are listed in Table 6.8. Column (3) gives the expected sign. If positive, it means a rise in the variable will raise the probability of rescheduling/default; if negative, an increase should reduce the probability of default. Manasse *et al.* also use two political indicators, a dummy for years with an election (in the country) and an index of freedom.

The list in Table 6.8 is not exhaustive, Manasse *et al.* test a total of 47 variables providing indicators of liquidity, solvency, external and public debt, and general macroeconomic indicators. Many of these are not independent of each other, and are tested in separate regressions – the researcher decides on the optimal set of variables based on the model's diagnostics and the degree of significance of the variables tested.

The logit early warning system (or logit EWS) is estimated for 37 countries over the period 1976–2001, using a total of 594 observations. Acting on evidence suggesting that the defaults after 1990 differ in character to those in the 1970s and 1980s, the authors test the model in the two different periods. The variables found to be significant are reported in Table 6.9.

When it comes to prediction, the focus of attention is on the number of type I and type II errors. A type I error occurs when a country is not predicted to default but does; a type II error arises when a country is predicted to default and does not. Too many type I errors, and the value of the lender's assets will fall. Too many type IIs, and profitable lending opportunities are missed. Normally, the average cost of a type I error is assumed higher than type II because losses will affect the bank's balance sheet. The Manasse *et al.* logit EWS model correctly predicted 74% of the defaults for the whole sample, but post-1990 this drops to 69% with, respectively, 6% and 5% type II errors. However, for roughly half the error cases, default did occur two years later – the model is set up to predict a problem one year ahead.

---

[86] In the review by Hoti and McAleer (2003), logit (or some variant of it) was used in 43 of the 50 studies they report on.

Table 6.8    Economic Variables Commonly Tested for Significance in Models used to Predict the
Probability of Rescheduling (a proxy for default on external debt)

| Explanatory variable | Definition | Effect on probability of default or rescheduling |
|---|---|---|
| DSR (the debt service ratio) | The ratio of scheduled external debt service payments to exports | (+): As DSR rises, so does the probability of default |
| External debt: GNP | The ratio of external indebtedness to GNP | (+): The higher the ratio the greater the probability of default |
| External debt: exports | | (+) |
| Growth rate of exports | | (−) |
| Reserves: imports (the coverage ratio) | Normally this is expressed in terms of months – the number of months the reserves are available given the value of the import bill. A rule of thumb is that the availability of reserves of less than three months is a sign of short-term illiquidity | (−): The higher the ratio, the lower the probability of default or rescheduling |
| Foreign direct investment: GDP | | (−) The more FDI, the lower the probability of default |
| Growth of Foreign Direct Investment | | (−) |
| Current Account Balance: GDP | The ratio of net trade in goods and services to GDP | If in surplus (−) If in deficit (+) |
| Public External Debt: GDP | The higher this ratio, the more debt the government has to finance, and the more likely it is to require external loans | (+) |
| Public External Debt: Revenue | | (+) |
| Inflation Rate | A high inflation rate is a sign of economic mismanagement, which would raise the probability of default | (+) |
| Real GDP Growth Rate | | (−) |
| Unemployment Rate | Again, a sign of economic problems | (+) |
| LIBOR | London Interbank Offer Rate: studies have found that as LIBOR or the US treasury bill rate rises in the years preceding a default of rescheduling, so does the probability of default by an emerging market economy | (+) Tighter credit conditions in the developed world reduce capital flows to the emerging market economies, which, combined with other factors, can give rise to debt servicing problems |

Table 6.9   Significant Explanatory Variables in the Logit EWS

| Variable | Pre-1990 | Post-1990 | Remarks |
| --- | --- | --- | --- |
| External Debt/GDP | Yes (+) | Yes, even more so | |
| Short-term Debt/Reserves | Yes (+) | Yes (+) | |
| Interest Payments/GDP | No (+) | Yes (+) | |
| External Debt Service Ratio | Yes (+) | Yes (+) | |
| Current Account Balance (CAB) | Yes (−) | Yes (−) | The higher the CAB, the lower the probability of default |
| Economy Open | No | Yes (−) | |
| Treasury Bill Rate | Yes (−) | Yes (−) | Very pronounced significance in the early 1980s |
| Real GDP Growth Rate | Yes (+) | Yes (+) | |
| Inflation Volatility | Yes (+) | Yes (+) | |
| Inflation Rate | Yes (+) | Yes (+) | |
| Election Year | Yes (+) | Yes (+) | The probability of default rises with an election year |
| Political Freedom Index | Yes (+) | Yes (−) | Pre-1990, the higher the index, the greater the probability of default. Post-1990, the reverse is true |

*Source:* (Manasse *et al.*, 2003).

Post-1990, there were some important type I errors: Argentina (1995), Brazil (2001), Tunisia (1991) and Venezuela (1995). There are various reasons why these were not picked up, but Argentina is perhaps the most interesting case. The Mexican problems in 1994/95 gave rise to what has become known as the "*tequila*" effect: essentially, Mexico's difficulties prompted concerns among investors/creditors that other countries with a similar economic profile would also get into trouble, and they reacted by withdrawing or cutting back on their investments. For example, Argentina found it was refused lines of credit it had been expecting to receive. This in turn aggravated economic problems in that country, and provoked a debt crisis. The Manasse *et al.* model did not include contagion as an explanatory variable due to the problems of getting an objective measure of contagion, which explains why the model failed to predict Argentina's default. Readers will find a more comprehensive discussion of the contagion effect in Chapter 8.

## 6.5.4. The Political Aspects of Risk Analysis

Manasse *et al.* (2003) included two political explanatory variables in a model of sovereign default. In the 50 papers reviewed by Hoti and McAleer (2003), 30 included at least one political variable. In contrast to the number of economic variables tested in these models, political influences get far less attention, possibly because it is difficult to obtain objective measures. Yet the political risk aspect of banking in a foreign country (or even the home country) is a major concern to bankers. If the banks (or their clients) are exposed in lending to a foreign country, they will want to assess the effects of the political situation on the ability and/or willingness of the country to repay its debt. This section reviews the quantitative models that have been developed to test the influence of politics on the probability of a debtor country going into arrears or rescheduling.[87]

Brewer and Rivoli (1990) tested for the effects of political instability on banker perceptions of the creditworthiness of the country in question. They expected to find negative relationships between political stability and a country's capacity to service its debt or perceived creditworthiness. They also wanted to identify the types of political stability which affect creditworthiness perceptions.

The authors considered three types of political instability, including government regime change (the frequency of regime change, assumed to be inversely related to political stability), political legitimacy (as measured by the degree to which a country's political system is democratic as opposed to authoritarian, arguing that while authoritarian regimes may be stable in the short run, they are unstable in the long run) and internal (civil wars) or external armed conflict. Several measures of political instability were used because, the authors argued, political risk is not a single phenomenon that can be measured by a single variable.

A least squares regression technique was used to test for the effects of proximate instability and chronic instability on perceived creditworthiness. The study employed 1986 data for the 30 most heavily indebted countries. The dependent variable, perceived creditworthiness of a country, was taken from the 1987 *Institutional Investor* (II) and *Euromoney* (EM). The II scores come from a survey of bankers who are asked to grade a country (0 to 100) according to the probability of it going into arrears.[88] The EM ranking is based on the weighted average spread borrowers are able to obtain from the euromarket.[89] Thus, the II scores represent banker assessments of the countries' creditworthiness and the EM scores reflect the actual market conditions. The scores of II and EM were interpreted as probabilities, which allows logistic transformation of the credit rating.

The independent variables tested were as follows.

- *PHI, CHI:* The number of changes in the head of government between 1982–86 (proximate head instability) or, for CHI, 1967–86 (chronic head instability).

---

[87] Much has been written on the methods for assessing the risk of expropriation of foreign firms with branches or subsidiaries located in foreign countries. However, a detailed discussion of the literature on expropriation and political interference lies outside the scope of this chapter. It has a limited impact on banks, via their loan exposure in foreign branches or subsidiaries of a multinational firm. For more discussion of these aspects of country/political risk, readers are referred to Calverley (1990) and Shapiro (1988), Moran (2003) and Bouchet and Clark (2004).

[88] Their responses are weighted according to the bank's exposure in a country and the level of sophistication in risk assessment.

[89] The weighted average spread for country $i = \sum(\text{volume} \times \text{spread} \times \text{maturity}) / \sum(\text{volume} \times \text{maturity})$, where volume is the volume of loans signed by country $i$ during a given year, spread is the margin over LIBOR and maturity is the length of the loan to repayment.

- *PGI, CGI:* The number of changes in the governing group between 1982–86 (proximate group instability) or, for CGI, 1967–86 (chronic group instability).
- *PPL, CPL:* Political rights scores for 1986 (for proximate instability) and 1975–86 (chronic instability). These variables are the proxy for political legitimacy and are taken from the annual reports on human rights.
- *PAC, CAC:* Armed conflict scores indicating proximate armed conflict at the end of 1986 (0, 1) and chronic armed conflict – the number of years the country had been involved in armed conflict.
- *CAB:* The 1986 current account balance (CAB) expressed as a percentage of GNP.
- *TED:* Total external debt as a percentage of GNP in 1986.

Brewer and Rivoli found perceptions of creditworthiness had a greater sensitivity to proximate head instability as measured by regime change, suggesting lenders focus on short-term recent changes rather than considering a country's experience from a longer term perspective. Regime change was a better measure of political instability than either armed conflict or political legitimacy. The findings should be treated with caution, for two reasons. Compared to related published studies, the economic variables were not given much attention. Furthermore, perceptions of political risk may already be included in the II and EM scores.

In a second study, Rivoli and Brewer (1997) address these concerns. They employ a logit model to test political and economic variables. The dependent variable is whether a country reschedules its debt in a given year. The political variables tested were changed to allow for short and long-term instability as follows:

- *SCH, LCH:* The number of times the head of government changes in 5 years (S) and 20 years (L).
- *SPOLEG, LPOLEG:* A political rights score for year $t$ (S) and a score for the preceding 12 years (L).
- *SCG, LCG:* The number of times the governing group (e.g. political party or military) changes over the past 5 years (S) and past 20 years (L).
- *SCONFL, LCONFL:* A dummy variable indicating the presence or absence of armed conflict in year $t$ (S) and the number of years the conflict had been taking place by the end of year $t$ (L).

They also test a number of economic variables, drawn from variables found to be significant in other studies, plus a lagged value for the rescheduling variable.

Rivoli and Brewer (1997) also looked at the question of whether the model is as effective in predicting rescheduling in the late 1980s and early 1990s as it was in the early 1980s. They estimate the model over the period 1985–89 to predict reschedulings between 1986 and 1990. These results are compared with estimates of the model for the period 1980–85. For this part of the investigation, only the economic variables are included. The economic variables found to be significant at the 1% level with the correct sign were the debt service ratio, the ratio of reserves to imports, and the ratio of external debt to GNP. The ratio of scheduled debt service to external debt is correctly signed and significant at the 10%

level.[90] A rescheduling variable (RESC), the dependent variable lagged by one year, was also included as an explanatory variable, and found to be significant at 1%, indicating the presence of positive serial correlation, Thus, if a country rescheduled one year, it is likelier to do so the next.

When the model is estimated for the later period, Rivoli and Brewer find its overall explanatory power falls. The parameter estimates are smaller, so their usefulness as explanatory variables is reduced, and the ratio of reserves to imports is no longer significant. The correct overall prediction rate was found to be 20% higher in the earlier period.

The next step of the investigation involved introducing the political variables. When added to the earlier model (1980–85), they are found to have little impact on overall performance. The only political variables found to be significant are the presence and length of armed conflict. According to the authors, armed conflict will place heavy demands on government budgets and often require large-sum hard currency expenditures, hence it could raise the probability of rescheduling. Adding the short and long-term political variables improved the prediction rate for rescheduling by 18% and 35%, respectively.

Overall, the explanatory power of the economic and political variables was greater for the early period, 1980–85, compared to the later period. However, by adding the political variables (a political economic model), the correct rescheduling prediction rate improved by 9% (short-term measures of political instability) and 12% (long-term measures) in the early period. For the later period (1986–90) the correct prediction rate rose by 18% (short-term measures) and 35% (long-term measures).

Recall that armed conflict was found to be the significant variable in the current study, which differs from the authors' 1990 results, when government instability was found to affect bankers' perceptions of a country's creditworthiness and armed conflict did not. Part of the findings may be explained by the differences in dates of estimation: the early and late 1980s. Also, the dependent variable was different. More research is needed on how political factors affect a country's probability of default.

Balkan (1992) used a probit[91] model of rescheduling to examine the role of political (in addition to economic) factors in explaining a developing country's probability of rescheduling. Two political variables were included in the model. A "political instability" variable is an index which measures the amount of social unrest that occurred in a given year. The "democracy" variable, reflecting the level of democracy, is measured by an index which, in turn, is captured by two components of the political system: participation (the extent to which the executive and legislative branches of government reflect popular will) and competitiveness (the degree of exclusion of political parties from the system and the ability of the largest party to dominate national elections). Balkan also included some standard economic variables in his model, such as the ratios of debt service to exports, interest payments to exports, and so on. In common with most studies all the explanatory variables were lagged by one year to minimise simultaneity problems. The sample period ran from 1970 to 1984 and used annual data from 33 developing nations. Balkan found

---

[90] The lower the ratio, the smaller the amount of external debt being repaid, which means interest accruals will be building up.
[91] Probit differs from logit in that it assumes the error terms follow a normal distribution, whereas in logit the cumulative distribution of the error term is logistic.

the democracy variable was significantly negative: the probability of rescheduling fell as democracy levels rose. The probability of rescheduling rose with the level of political instability. The number of type I and type II errors fell when the political variables were included in the model.

## 6.5.5. Rescheduling and Debt Conversion Schemes

Once a country has defaulted on sovereign debt, banks can hardly foreclose on the loans, put the country into receivership or insist on collateral – some of the nation's assets. Though "gunboat diplomacy" was not unheard of as a means of putting pressure on a sovereign state in earlier centuries, it has not been considered an acceptable way of resolving such matters for many years. Since the Mexican announcement in August 1982, many indebted countries have entered into or completed renegotiations for the repayment of their loans. The International Monetary Fund (and, to a lesser extent, the World Bank) plays a critical intermediary role. Rescheduling agreements share a number of features in common:

- The agreement is reached between the debtor, the borrowing bank and the IMF. It typically involves rescheduling the total value of the outstanding external debt, with the debt repayment postponed.
- Bridging loans often feature, as does an IMF guarantee of interbank and trade facilities, sometimes suspended when a country announced that it was unable to service its external debt.
- The private banks normally agree to provide "new money" to allow the debtor country to keep up interest payments, raising the total amount of the outstanding debt. The IMF usually insists on increased exposure by the banks in exchange for IMF loans.
- The debtor country is required to implement an IMF macroeconomic adjustment programme, which will vary according to the economic problems the country faces. Governments are required to remove subsidies that distort domestic markets, meet strict inflation and budget deficit targets, and reduce trade barriers. Note the country loses some "macroeconomic sovereignty" because its government is now limited in its choice of economic policy. Thus, *ex post*, it can be argued that sovereign borrowing exposed these countries to high interference costs.

*Debt–equity swaps* are another means of dealing with a sovereign debt problem, usually as part of or to complement an IMF rescheduling package. A debt–equity swap involves the sale of the debt by a bank to a corporation at the debt's secondary market price. The corporation exchanges the debt for domestic currency through the central bank of the emerging market, usually at a preferential exchange rate. It is used to purchase equity in a domestic firm. It has proved unpopular with some countries because it can be inflationary, and the country loses some microeconomic sovereignty. Similar debt conversion schemes in the private sector have allowed firms to reduce their external debt obligations.

Other types of swaps include *debt–currency swaps*, where foreign currency denominated debt is exchanged for the local currency debt of the debtor government, thereby increasing the domestic currency debt. A *debt–debt swap* consists of the exchange of LDC debt by one bank for the debt of another LDC by another bank. **Debt–trade swaps** grew between emerging markets as a means of settling debt obligations between them. They are a form of counter-trade because the borrower gives the lending country (or firm) home-produced commodities. Alternatively, a country agrees to buy imports in exchange for the seller agreeing to buy some of the country's external debt on the secondary markets.

**Debt–bond swaps** or "**exit**" **bonds** allow lenders to swap the original loan for long-term fixed rate bonds, reducing the debtor's exposure to interest rate risk. In a period of sustained rising interest rates, the fixed rate bonds will lower debt servicing costs for the borrowing country. The Mexican restructuring agreement of March 1990 was an early example of the new options offered to lenders. In addition to the option of injecting new money, banks could participate in two debt reduction schemes; either an exchange of discount bonds against outstanding debt or a par bond, that is, an exchange of bonds against outstanding debt without any discount, but with a fixed rate of interest (6.25%). The bonds are to be repaid in full in 2019 and the principal is secured by US Treasury zero-coupon bonds. Participating banks can also take part in a debt–equity swap programme linked to the privatisation of state firms – 13% opted for the new money, 40% the discount bond (at 65% of par) and 47% the par bond.

**Exit bonds** are now known as **Brady bonds**, because they were an integral part of the Brady Plan introduced in 1989. This plan superseded the earlier Baker Plan (1985), which had identified the "Baker 15", the most heavily indebted LDCs, as the key focus of action.[92] The Baker Plan also called for improved collaboration between the IMF and the World Bank, stressed the importance of IMF stabilisation policies to promote growth, and encouraged private commercial lenders to increase their exposure. The Brady Plan reiterated the Baker Plan but explicitly acknowledged the need for banks to reduce their sovereign debt exposure. The IMF and World Bank were asked to encourage debt reduction schemes, either by guaranteeing interest payments on exit bonds or by providing new loans. The plan called for a change in regulations (e.g. tax rules) to increase the incentive of the private banks to write off the debt.

Brady bonds are now a common part of loan rescheduling, and very simply, are a means by which banks can exchange dollar loans for dollar bonds. These bonds have a longer maturity (10 to 30 years) and lower interest (coupon) payment than the loan they replace – the interest rate can be fixed, floating or step. They can include warrants for raw materials of the country of issue and other options. The borrowing country normally backs the principal with US Treasury bonds, which the bond holders get if the country defaults. However, as the Mexican case in 1995–96 illustrates all too well, outright defaults are rare. As of 2001, about $300 billion worth of debt had been converted into Brady bonds.

In 1996, the first **sovereign bonds** were issued by governments of emerging market countries after their economic conditions improved. Essentially this involves buying back Brady bonds: they are either repurchased or swapped for sovereign bonds. A secondary market for trading emerging market debt including Brady and sovereign bonds emerged in the mid-1980s. Most of it is traded between the well-known commercial and investment

---

[92] Both Richard Baker and Tom Brady were Treasury Secretaries in the 1980s. They played no formal role in resolving emerging market debt problems but their ideas were influential.

banks based in London and New York, as well as hedge funds and other institutional investors. The market allows banks to move the assets off their balance sheets, and for those with continuing exposure, it is possible to price these assets.

## 6.6. Conclusion

This chapter focused on several areas of banking in emerging market countries. The objective was to provide the reader with an insight into several key issues: attempts to resolve problems arising from financial repression through reform of banking systems, sovereign and political risk analysis, and a review of Islamic banking.

Until the last decade of the 20th century, almost half of the world's population lived under communism. Communist regimes had extinguished the conventional, private sector, independent commercial bank. In country after country, throughout the former Soviet Union and its Warsaw Pact allies in Central and Eastern Europe, the 1990s were to see private banks return. China, still led by the Communist Party, also underwent profound financial changes as part of a broader economic reform, starting as early as 1979 and gathering pace in the new millennium. In India, the world's largest democracy where banking has been subject to a high degree of state control, regulation and ownership, some cautious steps have been taken in the same direction as Russia and China.

If the demise (or reinterpretation) of communism and socialism has been a great victory for the concept of the conventional western bank, the later 20th century saw two other developments that posed it challenges. One of these is the growing perception in many Muslim countries – and beyond – that the whole basis of the conventional western bank's operations, lending at interest, is inconsistent with religious principles. The other was the periodic but serious issue of how western banks should respond to many emerging market governments that could not or would not service or repay the debt owed to them: the problem of non-performing sovereign loans.

This chapter has chronicled these massive emerging market changes and their effects on the global financial landscape, especially banking. It began by analysing the phenomenon of financial repression, and exploring the question, a pressing policy issue for many countries, of whether foreign banks should be allowed to operate within their borders.

Next came a survey of financial systems of Russia, China and India. Each are classic, but different, examples of financial repression in the late 1990s. The key question was whether the reforms they introduced were enough to alleviate some of the more serious problems arising from financial repression. All three countries have enjoyed some degree of success. Though Russia experienced the economic equivalent of a roller coaster ride, it has gone the furthest in terms of financial liberalisation, followed by China, provided it lives up to its promises to allow foreign bank entry by 2007 and liberalises interest rates. India is the laggard here, with no clean plans to reduce state control of the banking sector, though other parts of its financial sector have been liberalised.

However, these countries are also experiencing a common problem: the difficulty each government faces in reducing or eliminating state ownership and control of banks. There is nothing wrong with state ownership *per se*, provided banks are free from government interference, have no special privileges which give them an unfair advantage, and have to compete with private banks. Though India has allowed some private banks to open, it has signalled its intention to maintain a strong state presence in banking with very few policies aimed at encouraging the development of a vibrant competitive private sector able to take on the state banks.

Russia has made the most advances – the banking sector was part of its privatisation programme. Unfortunately, the outcome is unappealing: bank oligarchies which confine their banking activities to the industrial group they serve/own, and state owned banks that will be difficult to privatise until something is done about the high percentage of non-performing loans. The state owned Sberbank has special privileges, which give it advantages over any potential rivals, especially in retail banking. If it is true that about 30 of the thousand plus banks are financially viable, Russia faces a future of unstable banking periods, which will do nothing to build up trust in the system, a key ingredient for a successful banking sector. One ray of light is the absence of restrictions on foreign bank entry, though efficient foreign entrants could imperil short-term financial stability if they are a contributing factor to the speedy collapse of costly, inefficient local banks.

In China, scratch the surface of a joint stock bank and state control of the bank is quickly revealed. Most of China's banks have a high percentage of non-performing loans, and the overt political interference by local governments in the credit coops is a symptom of a more serious dilemma. How can the central bank and regulatory body teach Chinese banks the rudiments of risk management when policy objectives (be they local, provincial or national) interfere with lending decisions? If unfettered foreign bank entry is allowed from 2007, their presence will contribute to the development of a more efficient banking system, but the price could be high in the short run as domestic banks are forced out of business. It is likely a one-party Communist State will intervene if Chinese banks face closure, which could threaten some of the market oriented policies it has introduced.

Developing economies and emerging markets in Eastern Europe share similar structural problems, including inadequate monitoring by supervisory authorities and poorly trained staff, which have compounded general problems with credit analysis, questionable accounting procedures and relatively high operating costs. Many developing countries exhibit signs of financial distress; the problem for banks in the emerging East European markets is debt overhang from the former state owned enterprises. A stable financial structure is some way off for Russia, but many of the transition economies that adopted a gradualist approach to financial reform have created workable and stable structures. These banks were found to be much closer to an efficiency frontier compared to Russian banks.

Most Islamic banking is located in emerging markets, and this is the reason it has been discussed in this chapter. Its growth is important because it relies on a financial system where the payment of interest is largely absent. The development of financial products that conform to Shariah law has been impressive, and in this respect, Islamic banking has something to teach the conventional banking system. Nonetheless, there are several problems that need to be addressed, such as the tendency to concentrate on one or two products, which discourages diversification. Also, although moderated in some ways, the potential for moral hazard remains. Finally, the regulatory authorities and banks need to work together to come up with an acceptable framework to deal with the unique aspects of regulation associated with Islamic banking.

The underdeveloped financial systems of emerging market economies make them dependent on external finance. Bankers face unique problems when it comes to the management of sovereign risk. The key lesson is that bank managers must assess properly the risks associated with any given set of assets. The sovereign lending boom of the 1970s demonstrated how bankers failed to acknowledge that illiquidity can be as serious as insolvency if there is no collateral attached to the loan, and this in turn led to poor assessment of sovereign risk. Since then practitioners and academics have worked to improve sovereign risk assessment by identifying the significant variables contributing to the probability of default and developing early warning systems. The protracted process of IMF led rescheduling agreements rather than a swift bailout of the indebted countries (and associated private banks) serves as a lesson to bankers and developing countries that even though a sovereign default may undermine the stability of the world financial system, official assistance comes at a steep price. The more recent episodes of sovereign debt repayment problems underline these lessons, though political factors appear to have become more important.

Suspension of interest flows on sovereign loans all too often reflects an economic/financial crisis in the country that does it. It also triggers difficulties for the creditor banks overseas. Financial crises were, however, omitted from this chapter. They can affect any country, developed or emerging, and are the subject of Chapter 8, while Chapter 7 explores the causes of individual bank failure.

# BANK FAILURES

## 7.1. Introduction

Bank managers, investors, policy makers and regulators share a keen interest in knowing what causes banks to fail and in being able to predict which banks will get into difficulty. Managers often lose their jobs if their bank fails. The issue is also important for policy because failing banks may prove costly for the taxpayer; depositors and investors want to be able to identify potentially weak banks. In this chapter, the reasons why banks fail are explored, using both a qualitative approach and quantitative analysis. Since bank failures often lead to financial crises, the chapter also looks at their causes, undertaking a detailed examination of the South East Asian and Japanese financial crises.

After defining bank failure, section 7.3 discusses a range of key bank failures, from the collapse of Overend Gurney in 1866 to the well-publicised failures such as the Bank of Credit and Commerce International and Barings bank over a century later. Based on these case studies, some qualitative lessons on the causes of bank failure are drawn in section 7.4. A review of econometric studies on bank failure is found in section 7.5, most of which use a logit model to identify the significant variables that increase or reduce the probability of a bank failing. The quantitative results are compared to the qualitative contributors. Section 7.6 concludes.

## 7.2. Bank Failure – Definitions

Normally, the failure of a profit-maximising firm is defined as the point of insolvency, where the company's liabilities exceed its assets, and its net worth turns negative. Unlike certain countries that default of their debt, some banks do fail and are liquidated. Recall from the discussion in Chapter 5 that the USA, with its prompt corrective action and least-cost approach, has a well-prescribed procedure in law for closing and liquidating failed banks. In other countries, notably Japan (though it is attempting to move towards a US-type approach) and some European states, relatively few insolvent banks have been closed in the post-war period, because of real or imagined concerns about the systemic aspects of bank failure. Thus, for reasons which will become apparent, most practitioners and policy makers adopt a broader definition of **bank failure**: a bank is deemed to have "failed" if it is liquidated, merged with a healthy bank (or purchased and acquired[1]) under central government supervision/pressure, or rescued with state financial support.

There is a wide range of opinions about this definition. Some think a failing bank should be treated the same way as a failing firm in any other industry. Others claim that failure justifies government protection of the banking system, perhaps in the form of a 100% safety net, because of its potential for devastating systemic effects on an economy. In between is support for varying degrees of intervention, including deposit insurance, a policy of ambiguity as to which bank should be rescued, merging failing and healthy banks, and so on.

The debate among academics is reflected in the different government policies around the world. The authorities in Japan (until very recently) and some European states subscribe to the view that virtually every problem bank should be bailed out, or merged with a healthy bank. In Britain, the tradition has been a policy of ambiguity but most observers agree the top four or five commercial banks[2] and all but the smallest banks would be bailed out. The United States has, in the past, tended to confine rescues to the largest commercial banks. However, since 1991, legislation[3] has required the authorities to adopt a "least cost" approach (from the standpoint of the taxpayer) to resolve bank failures, which should mean most troubled banks will be closed, unless a healthy bank is willing to engage in a takeover, including taking on the bad loan portfolio or any other problem that got the bank into trouble in the first place.

There are three ways regulators can deal with the problem of failing banks.

1. Put the bank in receivership and liquidate it. Insured depositors are paid off, and assets sold. This approach is most frequent in the USA, but even there, as will be observed, some banks have been bailed out.
2. Merge a failing bank with a healthy bank. The healthy bank is often given incentives, the most common being allowing it to purchase the bank without the bad assets. Often this involves the creation of an agency which acquires the bad assets, then attempts to sell them off. See the "good bank/bad bank" discussion in Box 8.1 of Chapter 8. A similar type of takeover has emerged in recent years, known as purchase and acquisition (P&A). Under P&A, assets are purchased and liabilities are assumed by the acquirer. Often a state or state-run resolution pays the difference between assets or liabilities. If the P&A is partial, uninsured creditors will lose out.
3. Government intervention, ranging from emergence of lending assistance, guarantees for claims on bad assets or even nationalisation of the bank.

These different forms of intervention are discussed in more detail below.

The question of what causes failure will always be of interest to investors, unprotected depositors and the bank employees who lose their jobs. However, if the state intervention school of thought prevails, then identifying the determinants of bank failure is of added

---

[1] See Table 7.1.

[2] The big four: HSBC, Barclays, Royal Bank of Scotland and HBOS. Lloyds-TSB has been in fifth place (measured by asset size and tier 1 capital) since the merger of the Halifax and Bank of Scotland – HBOS.

[3] This rule is part of the Federal Deposit Insurance Corporation Improvement Act, 1991 – see Chapter 4 for more detail.

importance because public funds are being used to single out banks for special regulation, bail out/merge banks and protect depositors. For example, the rescue of failing American thrifts in the 1980s is estimated to have cost the US taxpayer between $250 and $300 billion. In Japan, one reason the authorities shied away from early intervention was a hostile taxpaying public. However, the use of public funds to inject capital into weak banks and nationalise others, together with the need to extend "temporary" 100% deposit insurance well past its "end by" date, had raised the cost of the bailout to an estimated 70 trillion yen ($560 billion).[4] Posen (2002) estimates the direct cost of the Japanese bailout to the year 2001 to be 15% of a year's GDP, compared to just 3% for the US saving and loan debacle.

## 7.2.1. How to Deal with Failed Banks: The Controversies

Most academics, politicians (representing the taxpayer), depositors, and investors accept the idea that the banking sector is different. Banks play such a critical role in the economy that they need to be singled out for more intense regulation than other sectors. The presence of asymmetric information is at the heart of the problem. A bank's managers, owners, customers, regulators and investors have different sets of information about its financial health. Small depositors are the least likely to have information and for this reason, they are usually covered by a deposit insurance scheme, creating a moral hazard problem (see pp. 6–7 for more detail). Regulators have another information set, based on their examinations, and investors will scrutinise external audits.

Managers of a bank have more information about its financial health than depositors, regulators, shareholders or auditors. The well-known *principal agent* problem arises because of the information wedge between managers and shareholders. Once shareholders delegate the running of a firm to managers, they have some discretion to act in their own interest rather than the owners'. Bank profits depend partly on what managers do, but also on other factors unseen by the owners. Under these conditions, the best managerial contracts owners can devise will lead to various types of inefficiency, and could even tempt managers into taking on too much risky business, either on- or off-balance sheet.

However, these types of agency problems can arise in any industry. The difference in the banking sector, it is argued, is that asymmetric information, agency problems and moral hazard, taken together, can be responsible for the collapse of the financial system, a massive *negative externality*. Though covered in depth in Chapter 4, it is worth summarising how a bank run might commence – recall a core banking function, intermediation. Put simply, banks pay interest on deposits and lend the funds to borrowers, charging a higher rate of interest to include administration costs, a risk premium and a profit margin for the bank. All banks maintain a liquidity ratio, the ratio of liquid assets to total assets, meaning only a fraction of deposits is available to be paid out to customers at any point in time. However, there is a gap between socially optimal liquidity from a safety standpoint, and the ratio a profit-maximising bank will choose.[5]

---

[4] *Sources*: "Notes", *The Financial Regulator*, 4, 2000, p. 8 and *The Banker*, January 1999, p. 10.

[5] For example, in the UK, mutually owned building societies maintain quite high liquidity ratios, in the order of about 15–20%, compared to around 10% for profit oriented banks.

Given that banks, even healthy ones, only have a fraction of their deposits available at any one time, an unexpected sudden surge in the withdrawal of deposits will mean they soon run out of money in the branches. Asymmetric information means rumours (ill-founded or not) of financial difficulties at a bank will result in uninsured depositors withdrawing their deposits, and investors selling their stock. *Contagion* arises when healthy banks become the target of runs, because depositors and investors, in the absence of information to distinguish between healthy and weak banks, rush to liquidity.

Governments may also impose a reserve ratio, requiring banks to place a fraction of non-interest earning deposits at the central bank. This is, effectively, a tax on banking activity. The amount paid is the interest foregone multiplied by the volume of funds held as reserves. Since the nominal rate of interest incorporates inflation expectations, the reserve ratio is often loosely thought of as a source of inflation tax revenue. In recent decades many western governments have reduced or eliminated this reserve ratio. For example, in the UK, the reserve ratio has been reduced from a cash ratio of 8% before 1971 to one of just 0.4% today. In developing and emerging markets, the reserve ratio imposed on banks can be as high as 20%, as an inexpensive source of government revenue.

Asking all banks to set aside capital as a percentage of their assets (capital assets ratio) or risk weighted assets (the ratio of capital to weighted risk assets) is now the preferred method for ensuring banks have a cushion against shocks to credit, market and operational risks which could threaten the viability of the bank. The Basel 1 and 2 agreements are examples of an application of this approach. They were discussed at length in Chapter 4 and are noted here to illustrate the role they play in averting bank failures and crises.

In the absence of intervention by the central bank to provide the liquidity necessary to meet the depositors' demands, the bank's liquidity problem (unable to meet its liabilities as they fall due) can turn into one of insolvency, or negative net worth. Normally, if the central bank and/or other regulators believe that but for the liquidity problem, the bank is sound, it will intervene, providing the necessary liquidity (at a penalty rate) to keep the bank afloat. Once depositors are satisfied they can get their money, the panic subsides and the bank run is stopped. However, if the regulators decide the bank is insolvent and should not be rescued, the run on deposits continues, and it is forced to close its doors.

If the authorities do intervene, but fail to convince depositors the problem is confined to the one bank, contagion results in systemic problems affecting other banks, and perhaps all banks, putting the sector in danger of collapsing. In the extreme, the corresponding loss of intermediation and the payments system could reduce the country to a barter economy. A "bank holiday" may be declared in an effort to stop the run on banks, using the time to meet with the stricken banks and decide how to curb the withdrawals, usually by an agreement to supply unlimited liquidity to solvent banks when their doors open after the holiday.

If the bank holiday agreement fails to reassure depositors, or no agreement is reached, the outcome is a classic negative externality because what began as a run on one bank (or a few small banks) can lead to the collapse of the country's financial system. The economic well-being of all the agents in an economy has been adversely affected by the actions of less than perfectly informed depositors and investors, who, with or without good reason, decided their bank was in trouble and sought to get their funds. The negative externality is a type of market failure, as is the presence of asymmetric information. Market failure is a classic argument for a sector to be singled out for government intervention and regulation.

The evidence on whether bank contagion is a serious matter is mixed and controversial. In a comprehensive paper, Kaufman (1994) reviews a number of contagion theories, and related evidence. His main findings are as follows.

- Bank contagion spreads faster in the banking sector compared to other sectors. Based on US studies, compared to non-banks, there is evidence that contagion appears faster and spreads to a larger proportion of the sector.
- Bank contagion is both industry and/or firm-specific because compared to other industries, depositors tend to be less well informed about the performance of their bank or the banking sector. Kaufman's survey of the evidence suggests that bank contagion and bank runs are largely firm-specific and rational, that is, depositors and investors can differentiate between healthy and unhealthy banks.
- Bank contagion results in a larger number of failures: compared to other sectors, contagion does cause a larger percentage of failures.
- Contagion results in larger losses for depositors, but the evidence suggests the losses are smaller than losses to creditors in other sectors. For example, during the 1980s when there were a large number of thrift and bank failures in the USA, the solution of the problem was more efficient when compared to the closure of insolvent non-bank firms through bankruptcy procedures.
- Kaufman's review finds little evidence to support the view that runs on banks cause insolvency among solvent banks; nor does it spread to other parts of the financial sector or the rest of the macroeconomy.

These findings might lead the reader to conclude that an inordinate amount of resources may be directed to the protection of a sector that does not need it. However, it is worth stressing that most of Kaufman's evidence comes from the United States, which has one of the most generous deposit insurance schemes in the world,[6] about which customers are well informed. But even with deposit insurance, some failing US banks are rescued, and "too big to fail" policies often apply. Such an environment naturally instils confidence among depositors and creditors, which reduces the likelihood of contagion and makes it difficult to quantify its effects.

Close supervision by regulators, and perhaps intervention too, contributes to managerial incentives to gamble. Senior management is normally the first to recognise their bank is, or will be, in serious trouble. They have the option of taking no action, letting it fail, and losing their jobs. However, if they are the only ones with information on the true state of the bank, downside risk is truncated. If a gamble fails, the bank fails with a larger net loss, but bad as this event is for managers, its marginal effect on them is zero. If a gamble succeeds, the bank, and their jobs, are saved. Returns are convexified, encouraging gambling to increase their survival probability and resurrect the bank. Thus, they will undertake highly risky investments, even with negative expected returns. Likewise, "looting" (defined

---

[6] The USA was the first country to introduce deposit insurance, in 1933.

in Chapter 4) may be seen as a way of saving the bank, and if not, providing a comfortable payoff for the unemployed managers. Given the presence of contagion in the sector, such behaviour should be guarded against through effective monitoring.

Lack of competition will arise in a highly concentrated banking sector and can also be a source of market failure. Depositors are paid less interest and borrowers are charged more than marginal operating costs could justify. However, anti-competitive behaviour occurs in other sectors, and is usually monitored by official bodies with the power to act, should the behaviour of a firm (or firms) be deemed insufficiently competitive. Chapter 9 explores competitive issues in banking.

To summarise, the banking system needs to be more closely regulated than other markets in the economy because of market failure, which can be caused by asymmetric information and negative externalities. The special regulation can take a number of forms, including deposit insurance (funded by bank premiums being set aside in an insurance fund), capital requirements (e.g. Basel 1 and Basel 2), the licensing and regular examination of banks, intervention by the authorities at an early stage of a problem bank, and lifeboat rescues.

In fact, the transition from the failure of an individual bank to the complete collapse of a country's banking/financial system is rare. The US (1930–33) and British (1866) cases have already been discussed in some detail. Proponents of special regulation of banks, and timely intervention if a bank or banks encounter difficulties, would argue that the presence of strict regulation of the banking sector has prevented any serious threats to financial systems of the developed economies (with the arguable exception of Scandinavia and Japan – see Chapter 8). However, there have been frequent systemic crises in developing and emerging market economies. As will be seen in Chapter 8, contagion was responsible for the spread of the threat of financial crises from Thailand to Korea, Indonesia, Malaysia, the Philippines and beyond, to Russia and Brazil.

Unfortunately, there is a downside to the regulation of banks. The key problem is one of moral hazard, defined and discussed in Chapters 1 and 4. In banking, moral hazard arises in the presence of deposit insurance and/or if a central bank provides liquidity to a bank in difficulties. If a deposit is backed by insurance, then the depositor is unlikely to withdraw the deposit if there is some question raised about the health of the bank. Hence, bank runs are less likely, effectively putting an end to the possibility of systemic failure of the banking system. Blanket (100%) coverage of depositors (in some cases, creditors too) is often deemed necessary to stop bank runs. However, deposit insurance is costly, and normally governments limit its coverage to the retail depositor, on the grounds that this group lack the resources to be fully informed about the health of a bank.

Restricted forms of deposit insurance do not eliminate the possibility of bank runs because wholesale depositors and others (e.g. non-residents, or those holding funds in foreign currencies) are usually excluded. For example, in 1998 the Japanese authorities had to extend the insurance to 100% coverage of most deposits because of its persistent banking problems, which reduced depositor confidence and caused runs (see Chapter 8 for more detail). The next section gives the background to the rescue of Continental Illinois Bank in 1984. This bank was heavily dependent on the interbank markets, and suffered from a withdrawal of funding by uninsured wholesale depositors.

On the other hand, the more extensive the deposit insurance coverage and/or central bank intervention, the more pronounced the moral hazard problem because if agents know a bank will be supported in the event of problems, they have little incentive to monitor the banks, making it easier for senior management to undertake risks greater than they might have in the absence of closer scrutiny by their customers. The looting hypothesis, discussed in Chapter 4, is more likely to be a problem, especially if bank managers who know their bank is in trouble undertake highly risky investments in an attempt to rescue themselves from the problem.

Counter-arguments made by proponents of deposit insurance are that even in its presence, the incentives of senior management are not altered to such a degree that they undertake riskier investments. Management is still answerable to shareholders, who do have an incentive to monitor their investments, which are unprotected in the event of failure. Also, if the bank does fail, it is the managers and employees who lose their livelihoods.

A final argument relates to the fund itself. Normally it is the banks which pay the insurance premia to fund the deposit insurance. In most countries, all banks pay the same premium but in the United States, regulators rank banks according to their risk profile, which is kept confidential. The riskier the bank, the higher the premium paid (see Chapter 5 for more detail). Being answerable to shareholders, linking the deposit insurance premium to banks' risk profiles and loss of employment will help to reduce the problem of moral hazard on the part of bank management.

Another way of dealing with bank runs is for the central bank to supply liquidity to illiquid banks caught up in bank runs, provided most of the deposits are denominated in the home currency. This is discussed in more detail in the section on lender of last resort in Chapter 8. It is raised here for completeness, and because some interesting work has been done on the fiscal costs of resolving bank crises. Hoggarth *et al.* (2003) look at the impact of liquidity support and government guarantees on output losses, controlling for the degree of bank intermediation in a given country. They find open-ended liquidity support has a significantly negative effect on output, that is, during a banking crisis, the greater the liquidity support, the bigger the fall in output. By contrast, the deposit guarantees appear to have no effect on output. This result is similar to the findings reported by Bordo *et al.* (2001), who looked at crises in 29 countries from 1973 to 1997. They suggest open-ended liquidity support could mean more insolvent banks survive, increasing moral hazard, encouraging banks to increase risk-taking activities in the hope the gamble is successful, and allow loss-making agents to continue to borrow.

This section reviewed the controversies related to the methods used to rescue banks in the event of a banking crisis. Proponents of government intervention are by far the majority, though some researchers argue that intervention is only justified if the benefits should exceed any costs. The work by Hoggarth *et al.* (2003) and Bordo *et al.* (2001) suggests the type of intervention is important. Their results indicate deposit guarantees have no impact on output, whereas liquidity support reduces output. These findings indicate the type of bank rescue needs to be carefully considered, keeping in mind that while intervention may have fiscal costs, the absence of any support also has consequences – conceivably, systemic meltdown.

Table 7.1  Failed Bank Resolution Strategies and Who Loses

| Resolution options | Shareholders – Lose Money | Creditors – Lose Money[5] | Taxpayers – Government Injection | Managers – Lose Jobs | Employees – Lose Jobs |
|---|---|---|---|---|---|
| Capital injection by shareholders | Yes – in the short term, but could be made up if the bank recovers | No | No | Yes – likely | Possibly if shareholders demand cost cuts |
| Government injection[1] | Likely | Likely | Yes | Likely | Likely |
| M&A – state funded[2] | Partly | Possibly | Yes | Yes | Likely |
| M&A – private | Likely | Likely | No | Yes | Yes |
| P&A[3] | Yes | Yes – if uninsured | Possibly | Yes | Yes |
| Bridge bank/nationalisation[4] | Yes | Possibly | Yes | Yes | Possibly |
| Liquidation | Yes | Yes – if uninsured | No | Yes | Yes |

*Notes:*

[1] Government injection usually comes with conditions for bank restructuring which are likely to cause managers and some employees to lose their jobs. Some creditors could lose out in any financial restructuring.

[2] Some merger or acquisitions involve the state agreeing to take on the dud assets and/or inject funds.

[3] P&A: purchase and acquisition. Assets are purchased and liabilities are assumed by the acquirer. Often the state/state run resolution pays the difference between assets or liabilities. If the P&A is partial, uninsured creditors will lose out.

[4] The state will take over the bank temporarily (the bridge bank) until a strategy for resolving the bank's problems is agreed. The bank is later sold, though it may be several years later. Uninsured creditors may lose out, depending on the option, unless a government issues a blanket guarantee for depositors and creditors.

*Source:* Hoggarth *et al.* (2003), table 1.

Hoggarth *et al.* (2003) provide a useful table summarising the different options available for troubled banks, and the trade-offs involved. The table is reproduced here (Table 7.1), with some adaptations.

At the other extreme are the free bankers, discussed in Chapter 4. Those who support special regulation of the banking sector expect governments/regulators to use the determinants of bank failure to achieve an optimum where the marginal benefit of regulation/rescue is equal to its marginal cost. Even free bankers have an interest in what causes a bank to fail, if only because investors and depositors lose out when a bank goes under. Either way, it is an important question, and the next few sections attempt to answer it.

## 7.3. Case Studies on Bank Failure

Bank failures, broadly defined, have occurred in virtually every country throughout history. In the 14th century the Bardi family of Florentine bankers was ruined by the failure of

Edward III to meet outstanding loan obligations – the only time in history, to date, that an English government failed to honour its debts. Some failures seriously undermine the stability of the financial system (as happened, for example, in the UK in 1866 and the USA in 1933). Others do not. In some cases, state support of problem banks proves costly. For example, the taxpayers' bill for the US thrift bailout is put at around $250–$300 billion, while recent problems with the Japanese banking system has cost the taxpayer about $560 billion to date. In this section, bank failures are examined on a case by case basis, the objective being to identify the qualitative causes of bank failure. After a brief historical review, the main focus is on modern bank failures, commencing with the failure of Bankhaus Herstatt in 1974.

## 7.3.1. Historical Overview

This subsection is a selective, brief review of well-known bank failures in Victorian England and between 1930 and 1933 in the USA. In England, there were two major bank failures in the 19th century: Overend Gurney and Company Ltd[7] in 1866, and Baring Brothers in 1890. Overend Gurney originated as a discount house but by the 1850s was a prosperous financial firm, involved in banking and bill broking. After changes in management in 1856 and 1857 it began to take on bills of dubious quality, and lending with poor collateral to back the loans. By 1865 the firm was reporting losses of £3–£4 million. In 1866, a number of speculative firms and associated contracting firms, linked to Overend Gurney through finance bills, failed. London-based depositors began to suspect Overend was bankrupt; the consequence was a drawing down of deposits and a fall in the firm's stock market price. On 10 May 1866 the firm sought assistance from the Bank of England, which was refused. The bank was declared insolvent the same afternoon.

Overend Gurney was a large bank: by balance sheet it was about ten times the size of the next largest bank in the country – the Midland.[8] Its failure precipitated the collapse of a number of country banks and firms associated with it. Contagion spread: country banks withdrew deposits from other London banks and finance houses, which in turn caused a run on the Bank of England. Several banks and finance houses, both unsound and healthy, failed. The 1844 Bank Charter Act was suspended to enable the Bank of England to augment a note supply, which was enough to allow the panic to subside. Overend Gurney was liquidated, and though the Bank Act was not amended, the episode made it clear that henceforth the Bank of England was to intervene as lender of last resort in situations of severe panic.

Baring Brothers was a large international merchant bank which failed in 1890. Barings had been founded in 1762, largely to finance the textile trade in Europe. After the Napoleonic wars, Barings began to finance for public projects in foreign countries; initially the long-term lending to foreign governments was concentrated in Europe and North America, but in 1821–22 the loan portfolio was expanded to include Mexico and Latin America, notably Chile, Colombia and Brazil. Even though these loans were non-performing, Barings granted

---

[7] Legislation passed in 1858 allowed limited liability and Overend Gurney became a limited liability company in 1862.
[8] Wood (2003), p. 69.

additional, large loans to the governments of Argentina and Uruguay between 1888 and 1890. By the end of 1890, these loans made up three-quarters of Barings' total loan portfolio. Problems with key banks in Argentina and Uruguay led to suspended payments and bank runs. Barings' Argentine securities dropped in value by one-third; the firm also faced a drop in income from loan repayments and liabilities arising from a failed utility. Barings borrowed heavily from London banks in an effort to contain the problem, but in November 1890 was forced to report the crisis to the Bank of England. The Governor of the Bank of England organised subscriptions to a fund – London's key merchant banks contributed, and the fund guaranteed Barings' liabilities for three years. Eight days after Barings reported its problems to the Bank, its illiquidity had become public knowledge. But there was no run of any significance, and no other banks failed. Though put into liquidation, Barings was refloated as a limited liability company, with capital from the Baring family and friends.

Both banks underwent notable changes in bank management in the years leading up to the failures. The collapse of the banks was due largely to mismanagement of assets, leading to a weak loan portfolio in the case of Barings, and for Gurneys, the issue of poor quality finance bills. Batchelor (1986, pp. 68–69) argued that, unlike Barings, the Gurney failure caused a serious bank run because the public lacked crucial information about the state of the bank's financial affairs. The Latin American exposure of Barings was well known, but there was no run because of its historical reputation for financial health in the banking world.

One of the most important series of bank failures occurred in the USA between 1930 and 1933.[9] The stock market crash of October 1929 precipitated a serious depression and created a general climate of uncertainty. The first US banking crisis began in November 1930, when 256 banks failed; contagion spread throughout the USA, with 352 more bank failures in December. The Bank of the USA was the most notable bank failure. It was the largest commercial bank, measured by deposits. It was a member of the Federal Reserve System, but an attempt by the Federal Reserve Bank of New York to organise a "lifeboat" rescue with the support of clearing house banks failed. It was followed by a second round of failures in March 1931.

Other countries also suffered bank failures, largely because the depression in the USA had wide-reaching global effects. The largest private bank in Austria, Kreditanstalt, failed in May 1931, and in other European states, particularly Germany, banks were closed. Meanwhile, in the USA, another relapse followed a temporary recovery, and in the last quarter of 1932 there were widespread bank failures in the Midwest and Far West of the USA. By January 1933 bank failures had spread to other areas; by 3 March, half the states were required to declare bank holidays to halt the withdrawals of deposits. On 6 March 1933, President Roosevelt declared a nation-wide bank holiday, which closed all banks until some time between the 13th and 15th of March, depending on location. There were 17 800 commercial banks prior to the bank holiday period, but fewer than 12 000 were allowed to open, under new federal/state authority licensing requirements. About 3000 of the unlicensed banks were eventually allowed to remain open, but another 2000 were either

---

[9] The details of US bank failures in the early 1930s are taken from Friedman and Schwartz (1963), pp. 332–349, 351–353.

liquidated or merged with other banks. The suspended operations and failures caused losses of $2.5 billion for stockholders, depositors and other creditors. Friedman and Schwartz (1963) argued a poor quality loan book and other bad investments was the principal cause of some bank failures in 1930,[10] but later on, the failures were due largely to bank runs, which forced banks to divest their assets at a large discount. Many failures were caused by the FRS refusing to inject liquidity into the system aggravating the depression.

## 7.3.2. Bankhaus Herstatt

This West German bank collapsed in June 1974 because of losses from foreign exchange trading, which were originally estimated at £83 million but rose to £200 million. At the time it was unclear how the bank had managed to run up such losses. The bank's failure is famous because it exposed a weakness in the system related to liquidity risk. Bankhaus Herstatt was due to settle the purchase of Deutsche marks (DMs, in exchange for dollars) on 26 June. On that day, the German correspondent banks, on instruction from the American banks, debited their German accounts and deposited the DMs in the Landes Central bank (which was acting as a clearing house). The American banks expected to be repaid in dollars, but Bankhaus Herstatt was closed at 4 p.m., German time. It was only 10 a.m. on the US east coast, causing these banks to lose out because they were caught in the middle of a transaction. The US payments system was put under severe strain. The risk associated with the failure to meet interbank payment obligations has since become known as Herstatt risk. In February 1984, the chairman of the bank was convicted of fraudulently concealing foreign exchange losses of DM 100 million in the bank's 1973 accounts.

## 7.3.3. Franklin National Bank

In May 1974 Franklin National Bank (FNB), the 20th largest bank in the USA (deposits close to $3 billion), faced a crisis. The authorities had been aware of the problem since the beginning of May, when the Federal Reserve refused FNB's request to take over another financial institution and instructed the bank to retrench its operations because it had expanded too quickly. A few days later, FNB announced it had suffered very large foreign exchange losses and could not pay its quarterly dividend. It transpired that in addition to these losses, the bank had made a large volume of unsound loans, as part of a rapid growth strategy.

These revelations caused large depositors to withdraw their deposits and other banks refused to lend to the bank. FNB offset the deposit outflows by borrowing $1.75 billion from the Federal Reserve. Small depositors, protected by the FDIC, did not withdraw their deposits, otherwise the run would have been more serious. In October 1974, its remains were taken over by a consortium of seven European banks, European American.

---

[10] Friedman and Schwartz (1963), pp. 354–355 distinguish between the *ex ante* and *ex post* quality of bank assets. *Ex ante*, banks' loan and other investment decisions were similar in the early 1920s and the late 1920s. The key difference was that the loans/investments of the late 1920s had to be repaid/matured in the Great Depression. Thus, they argue, with the exception of foreign lending, the number of bank failures caused by poor investment decisions is debatable.

FNB had been used by its biggest shareholder, Michele Sindona, to channel funds illegally around the world. In March 1985 he died from poisoning, a few days after being sentenced to life imprisonment in Italy for arranging the murder of an investigator of his banking empire.

### 7.3.4. Banco Ambrosiano

Banco Ambrosiano (BA) was a commercial bank based in Milan and quoted on the Milan Stock Exchange. It had a number of foreign subsidiaries and companies located overseas, in Luxembourg, Nassau, Nicaragua and Peru. The Luxembourg subsidiary was called Banco Ambrosiano Holdings (BAH). The parent, Banco Ambrosiano, owned 69% of BAH. BAH was active on the interbank market, taking eurocurrency deposits from international banks which were on-lent to other non-Italian companies in the BA group.

The parent bank, BA, collapsed in June 1982, following a crisis of confidence among depositors after its Chairman, Roberto Calvi, was found hanging from Blackfriars Bridge in London, 10 days after he had disappeared from Milan. Losses amounted to £800 million, some of them linked to offshore investments involving the Vatican's bank, the Institute for the Works of Religion. The Bank of Italy launched a lifeboat rescue operation; seven Italian banks provided around $325 million in funds to fill the gap left by the flight of deposits, and BA was declared bankrupt by a Milan court in late August 1982. A new bank, Nuovo Banco Ambrosiano (NBA), was created to take over the bank's Italian operations. The Luxembourg subsidiary, BAH, also suffered from a loss of deposits, but the Bank of Italy refused to launch a similar lifeboat rescue operation, causing BAH to default on its loans and deposits.

The main cause of the insolvency appears to have been fraud on a massive scale, though there were other factors whose contribution is unclear. The BA affair revealed a number of gaps in the supervision of international banks. The Bank of Italy authorities lacked the statutory power to supervise Italian banks. Nor was there a close relationship between senior management and the central bank, as in the UK at the time. It appears that Sig. Calvi's abrupt departure may have been precipitated by a letter sent to him by the surveillance department of the Bank of Italy seeking explanations for the extensive overseas exposure, asking for it to be reduced and requesting that the contents of the letter be shown to other directors of the bank. This activity suggests the regulatory authorities were aware of the problem. The Bank of Italy refused to protect depositors of the subsidiary in Luxembourg because BA was not held responsible for BAH debts; it owned 69% of the subsidiary. The Bank of Italy also pointed out that neither it nor the Luxembourg authorities could be responsible for loans made from one offshore centre (Luxembourg) to another (Panama) via a third, again in Latin America.

In 1981, the Luxembourg Banking Commission revised some of its rules to relax bank secrecy and allow the items on the asset side of a bank's balance sheet to be freely passed through the parent bank to the parent authority, though bank secrecy is still upheld for non-bank customers holding deposits at Luxembourg banks. The authorities in Luxembourg also obtained guarantees from the six Italian banks with branches in Luxembourg that they would be responsible for the debts of their branches. The 1975 Basel Concordat was revised in 1983 (see Chapter 5) to cover gaps in the supervision of foreign branches and subsidiaries. In July 1994 the former Prime Minister of Italy, Bettino Craxi, was convicted of fraud in relation to the collapse of Banco Ambrosiano.

Over 20 years later, questions relating to the death of Roberto Calvi continue. The first Coroner's Inquest judged the death to be suicide, but the family has always protested this verdict, pointing to evidence such as bricks stuffed in the pockets of the deceased. A second inquest recorded an open verdict. The City of London police decided to investigate and in 2003, one woman was arrested on suspicion of perjury and conspiring to pervert the course of justice.

In March 2004,[11] four people went on trial in Rome for the murder of Roberto Calvi. One of them, a former Mafia boss, is already in prison. A member of the Mafia turned informer named the four accused. The prosecution claims the Mafia ordered his murder because Mr Calvi bungled attempts to launder bonds stolen by the Mafia and was blackmailing associates with links to Vatican and Italian society. A masonic lodge (P2) where Mr Calvi was a member also appears to be involved.

## 7.3.5. Penn Square and Continental Illinois

As will become apparent, the collapse of these two banks was connected. Penn Square Bank, located in Oklahoma City, had opened in 1960, as a one-office retail bank.[12] On 5 July 1982, the bank collapsed, with $470.4 million in deposits and $526.8 million in assets. It embarked on an aggressive lending policy to the oil and gas sector – its assets grew more than eightfold between 1977 and 1982. It sold the majority interest in these loans to other banks, but remained responsible for their servicing. From the outset, loan documentation was poor and loan decisions were based solely on the value of the collateral (oil and gas) rather than assessing the borrower's ability to repay. From May 1977 onward, the Office of the Comptroller of Currency (OCC), the main regulatory authority, expressed concern about a host of problems: poorly trained staff, low capital, lack of liquidity, weak loans and increasing problems with the loan portfolio. The external auditors signed qualified opinion in 1977 and 1981.

The way Penn Square's failure was dealt with marked an apparent change in FDIC policy. Of the 38 banks that failed since 1980, only eight were actually closed with insured depositors paid off. The other 30 had been the subject of purchase and assumption transactions, whereby the deposits, insured and uninsured, were passed to the acquiring institution. Of the $470.4 million in deposits at Penn Square, only 44% were insured. The uninsured deposits were mainly funds from other banks. The FDIC paid off the insured depositors, and in August 1983 the Charter National Bank purchased the remaining deposits.

At the time of its collapse, Continental Illinois National Bank (CI) was the seventh largest US bank and the largest correspondent bank, involving about 2300 banks.[13] Though its problems were well known by regulators, they were caught out by the speed of the bank's collapse. In the summer of 1984, a number of CI customers were having trouble repaying

---

[11] "Four go on Trial for the Murder of God's Banker", *The Guardian*, 17 March 2004.

[12] At the time, branching was prohibited in the State of Oklahoma. The details on Penn Square come from FDIC (2001). Penn Square was one of the early failures – one of many between 1980 and 1994. See below.

[13] Kaufman (1994, 2002).

their loans because of the drop in oil prices. The decline in oil prices also undermined the value of the collateral securing these loans, much of it in real estate in centres of oil production.

Penn Square had a close connection to Continental Illinois. The bank was one of five large banks around the country that purchased participations in oil and gas loans. Shortly after the collapse of Penn Square, CI announced a second-quarter loss of $63.1 million and revealed its non-performing loans had more than doubled to $1.3 billion. In subsequent quarters, the bank was slow to recover and its non-performing loans held steady at approximately $2 billion, even though the non-performing loans related to the Penn Square connection had declined.

The first-quarter results of 1984 (17th April) revealed the bank's non-performing loans had risen to $2.3 billion, representing 7.7% of its loans. Increasingly, CI had been relying on the overseas markets to fund its domestic loan portfolio. On the eve of the crisis, 60% of its funds were being raised in the form of short-term deposits from overseas. This reliance on uninsured short-term deposits, along with its financial troubles, made it especially vulnerable to a run.

Rumours about the solvency of the bank were rife in the early days of May 1984, thereby undermining the ability of the bank to fund itself. On 10 May the rumours were so serious that the US OCC took the unusual step of rebutting the rumours, though the normal procedure was a terse "no comment". The statement merely served to fuel more anxiety and the next day, CI was forced to approach the Chicago Reserve Bank for emergency support, borrowing approximately $44.5 billion. Over the weekend, the Chairman of Morgan Guaranty organised US bank support for CI: by Monday 14 May, 16 banks made $4.5 billion available under which CI could purchase federal funds on an overnight basis. However, the private lifeboat facility was not enough. The run on the bank continued and the bank saw $6 billion disappear, equivalent to 75% of its overnight funding needs.

On 17 May the Comptroller, the Federal Deposit Insurance Corporation (FDIC) and the Federal Reserve Bank announced a financial assistance programme. The package had four features. First, there was a $2 billion injection of capital by the FDIC and seven US banks, with $1.5 billion of this coming from the FDIC. The capital injection took the form of a subordinated demand loan and was made available to CI for the period necessary to enhance the bank's permanent capital, by merger or otherwise. The rate of interest was 100 basis points above the one-year Treasury bill rate. Second, 28 US banks provided a $5.5 billion federal funds back-up line to meet CI's immediate liquidity requirements, to be in place until a permanent solution was found. It had a spread of 0.25% above the Federal funds rate. Third, the Federal Reserve gave an assurance that it was prepared to meet any extraordinary liquidity requirements of CI. Finally, the FDIC guaranteed *all* depositors and other general creditors of the bank full protection, with no interruption in the service to the bank's customers.

In return for the package, all directors of CI were asked to resign and the FDIC took direct management control of the bank. The FDIC bought, at book value, $3.5 billion of CI's debt. The Federal Reserve injected about $1 billion in new capital. The bank's holding company, CI Corporation, issued 32 million preference shares to the FDIC, that on sale converted into 160 million common shares in CI and $320 million in interest-bearing preferred stock. It also had an option on another 40.3 million shares in 1989, if losses on doubtful loans exceeded $800 million. It was estimated they exceeded $1 billion. Effectively, the bank was nationalised, at a cost of $1.1 billion. A new team of senior managers was appointed by the FDIC, which also, from time to time, sold some shares to the public. By 1991 it was back in private hands, and in 1994 it was taken over by Bank America Corp. (Kaufman, 2002, p. 425).

Continental Illinois got into problems for a number of reasons. First, it lacked a rigorous procedure for vetting new loans, resulting in poor-quality loans to the US corporate sector, the energy sector and the real estate sector. This included participation in low-quality loans to the energy sector, bought from Penn Square. Second, CI failed to classify bad loans as non-performing quickly, and the delay made depositors suspicious of what the bank was hiding. Third, the restricted deposit base of a single branch system forced the bank to rely on wholesale funds as it fought to expand. Fourth, supervisors should have been paying closer attention to liability management, in addition to internal credit control procedures.

Regulators were concerned about CI's dependence on global funding. This made it imperative for the FED and FDIC to act as lender of last resort, to head off any risk of a run by foreign depositors on other US banks. Continental Illinois was also the first American example of regulators using a "too big to fail" policy. The three key US regulatory bodies were all of the view that allowing CI to go under would risk a national or even global financial crisis, because CI's correspondent bank relationships left it (and the correspondent banks) highly exposed on the interbank and Federal funds markets. The regulators claimed the exposure of 65 banks was equivalent to 100% of their capital; another 101 had between 50% and 100% of their capital exposed. However, Kaufman (1985, 1994) reports on a Congressional investigation of the collapse, which showed that only 1% of Continental's correspondent banks would have become legally insolvent if losses at CI had been 60 cents per dollar. In fact, actual losses turned out to be less than 5 cents on the dollar, and no bank suffered losses high enough to threaten its solvency. *The Economist* (1995) argues that regulators got their sums wrong, and reports that some privately believed the bank did not need to be rescued. However, it is worth noting that the correspondent banks were not privy to this information at the time of the crisis, and would have been concerned about any losses they incurred, even if their solvency was not under threat. Given the rumours, it was quite rational for them to withdraw all uninsured deposits, thereby worsening the position of CI.

Furthermore, the episode did initiate a too big to fail policy, which was used sporadically throughout the 1980s. Some applications were highly questionable. For example, in 1990 the FDIC protected both national and off-shore (Bahamas) depositors at the National Bank of Washington, D.C., ranked 250th in terms of asset size. The policy came to an end with the 1991 FDIC Improvement Act (FDICIA), which required all regulators to use prompt corrective action and the least cost approach when dealing with problem banks. However, the "systemic risk" exception in FDICIA has given the FDIC a loophole to apply too big to fail.[14]

---

[14] See Chapter 5 for more detail on FDICIA.

## 7.3.6. Johnson Matthey Bankers

Johnson Matthey Bankers (JMB) is the banking arm of Johnson Matthey, dealers in gold bullion and precious metals. JMB was rescued in October 1984, following an approach to the Bank of England by the directors of JM, who believed the problems with JMB might threaten the whole group. During the original lifeboat rescue, the Bank of England wrote off a large proportion of JMB's assets after it purchased the bank and its subsidiaries for the nominal sum of £1.00. The bullion dealer, Johnson Matthey, was required to put up £50 million to allow JMB to continue trading. Charter Consolidated, a substantial investor in JM, contributed £25 million. Other contributors were the clearing banks (£35 million), the other four members of the gold ring (£30 million), the accepting houses which were not members of the gold ring (£10 million) and the Bank of England (£75 million).

On 7 November 1984 an agreed package of indemnities was announced to cover the possibility that JMB's loan losses might eventually exceed its capital base of £170 million. In May 1985 the Bank of England declared that provisions of £245 million were necessary to cover the loan losses. With this increase in loan provisions, all lifeboat contributions were raised to make up the shortfall; the Bank of England and other members of the lifeboat contributing half the amount of the shortfall each. On 22 November 1984, the Bank of England made a deposit of £100 million to provide additional working funds.

JMB got into trouble because it managed to acquire loan losses of £245 million on a loan portfolio of only £450 million, so it had to write off over half of its original loan portfolio. Compare this to the case of Continental Illinois, where non-performing loans were only 7.4% of its total loans. Press reports noted that most of these bad loans were made to traders involved with Third World countries, especially Nigeria, suggesting a high concentration of risks. The Bank of England's guideline on loan concentration (banks should limit loans to a single borrower or connected group of borrowers to 10% of the capital base) appears to have been ignored. The Bank of England was aware of some problems in 1983 but did not act until the full extent of the problems emerged after a special audit in 1984.

The auditors also appeared to be at fault. Under the UK Companies Act, their ultimate responsibility lies with the shareholders and they are required to report whether the accounts prepared by the bank's directors represent a "true and fair view". In assessing the bank, the auditor reviews the internal audit and inspections systems, and on a random basis examines the record of transactions to verify that they are authentic, and discusses with the directors decisions made in highly sensitive areas such as provisions against bad and doubtful debts. Auditors are not permitted to discuss the audit with bank supervisors, without the permission of the clients. The auditors can either agree with the directors that the accounts represent a true and fair view, or they can disagree with the directors, in which case they must either resign or qualify the accounts. The auditors at JMB signed unqualified reports, implying all was well. On the other hand, if the auditors had signalled problems by signing a qualified report or resigning, it might have precipitated a bank run, and the authorities may not have had enough time to put together a lifeboat operation.

As was noted in Chapter 5, the Bank of England's system of supervision was flexible. However, the JMB affair revealed two gaps in the reporting system. First, auditors had no formal contact with the Bank of England and were unable to register their concerns, unless they either resigned or qualified their reports. Second, the statistical returns prepared for the Bank of England, based on management interviews, were not subject to an independent audit. The 1987 amendment to the Banking Act addressed these problems partially; auditors were encouraged to warn supervisors of suspected fraud, and were given greater access to Bank of England information.

The JMB affair prompted the establishment of a committee involving the Treasury, Bank of England officials and an external expert, to review the bank supervisory procedures, especially the relationship between the auditor and supervisor. The result of the review of the affair was an amendment of the Banking Act (1987). However, the effectiveness of private auditing was again questioned after the BCCI closure (see below).

The JMB case illustrated the use of a lifeboat rescue by the Bank of England, and is a rare example of where the too big to fail doctrine was extended to protect non-banking arms of a financial firm. The main point of a rescue is to prevent the spread of the contagion effect arising from a collapsed bank. Johnson Matthey was one of the five London gold price fixers. Obviously, the Bank of England was concerned that the failure of the banking arm would spread to JM, thereby damaging London's reputation as a major international gold bullion dealer. The episode suggests the Bank is prepared to engage in a lifeboat rescue effort to protect an entire conglomerate, provided it is an important enough operator on global financial markets.

## 7.3.7. The US Bank and Thrift Crises, 1980–94

Between 1980 and 1994 there were 1295 thrift failures in the USA, with $621 billion in assets. Over the same period, 1617 banks, with $302.6 billion in assets, "failed" in the sense that they were either closed, or received FDIC assistance. These institutions accounted for a fifth of the assets in the banking system. The failures peaked between 1988 and 1992, when a bank or thrift was, on average, failing once a day.[15] This section will begin with a review of the thrift failures, followed by the commercial bank failures.[16]

### *Failing thrifts*

Thrifts are savings and loan (S&L) banks, either mutuals or shareholder owned, though by the end of the crisis, the majority were stock owned. Until 1989, they were backed by deposit insurance provided by the Federal Savings and Loan Insurance Corporation (FSLIC). The FSLIC was in turn regulated by the Federal Home Loan Bank Board. Both institutions were dissolved by statute in 1989.

In 1932, Congress passed the Federal Home Loan Bank Act. The Act created 12 Federal Home Loan Banks, with the Federal Home Loan Bank Board (FHLBB) as their supervisory agent. The aim was to provide thrifts with an alternative source of funding for home mortgage lending. In 1933, the government became involved in the chartered savings

---

[15] These figures are from FDIC (2001). "Failure" includes thrifts that were either closed by the Federal Savings Loan Insurance Corporation (FSLIC) or the Resolution Trust Corporation (RTC), or received financial assistance from the FSLIC. For a detailed account of the crisis, see White (1991).

[16] The author's account used two excellent publications by the Federal Deposit Insurance Corporation, FDIC (1997) and FDIC (1998).

and loans firms. The Home Owner's Loan Act was passed, authorising the Federal Home Loan Bank Board (FHLBB) to charter and regulate the savings and loan associations. The National Housing Act, 1934, created a deposit insurance fund for savings and loan associations, the Federal Savings and Loan Insurance Corporation (FSLIC). Unlike the FDIC, which was established as a separate organisation from the Federal Reserve System, the FSLIC was placed under the auspices of the FHLBB. S&L depositors are insured for up to $100 000.

The first signs of trouble came in the mid-1960s, when inflation and high interest rates created funding problems. Regulations prohibited the federally insured savings and loans from diversifying their portfolios, which were concentrated in long-term fixed rate mortgages. Deposit rates began to rise above the rates of return on their home loans. In 1966, Congress tried to address the problem by imposing a maximum ceiling on deposit rates, and thrifts were authorised to pay 0.25% more on deposits than commercial banks (regulation Q), thereby giving them a distorted comparative advantage. Unfortunately, the difference was not enough because market interest rates rose well above the deposit rate ceilings. The system of interest rate controls became unworkable and aggravated the thrifts' maturity mismatch problems.

The 1980 Depository Institutions Deregulation and Monetary Control Act (DIDMCA) took the first significant step towards reforming this sector. The DIDMCA allowed interest rate regulations to be phased out, and permitted thrifts to diversify their asset portfolios to include consumer loans other than mortgage loans, loans for commercial real estate, commercial paper and corporate debt securities. But lack of experience meant diversification contributed to a widespread loan quality crisis by the end of the 1980s.

DIDMCA came too late for thrifts facing the steep rise in interest rates that began in 1981 and continued in 1982. Federally chartered S&Ls had not been given the legal authority to make variable rate mortgage loans until 1979, and then only under severe restrictions. Variable rate mortgages could not be freely negotiated with borrowers until 1981. By that time, deposit rates had risen well above the rates most thrifts were earning on their outstanding fixed rate mortgage loans. Accounting practices disguised the problem because thrifts could report their net worth based on historic asset value, rather than the true market value of their assets.

Policies of regulatory forbearance aggravated the difficulties. Kane and Yu (1994) defined forbearance as:

> *"a policy of leniency or indulgence in enforcing a collectable claim against another party"*
> (p. 241)

To repeat the definition used in other chapters, regulatory forbearance occurs when the supervisory/regulatory authorities put the interests of the firms they regulate ahead of the taxpayer. In the case of the thrifts, supervisory authorities adopted lenient policies in the enforcement of claims against thrifts, because they had a vested interest in prolonging the S&Ls' survival: fewer thrift failures reduced the demands on the FSLIC's fund. In 1981 and 1982, the FHLBB authorised adjustments in the Regulatory Accounting Principles, thereby allowing thrift net worth to be reported more leniently than would have been the case had Generally Accepted Accounting Principles (GAAP) been applied. In 1980 and 1982, the

FHLBB lowered minimum net worth requirements. These changes reduced the solvency threshold and meant thrifts could record inflated net worth values.

The FSLIC also introduced an income capital certificates programme, to counter any crisis of confidence. Thrifts could obtain income certificates to supplement their net worth – they were reported as a part of equity. Since the FSLIC did not have the funds to cover the certificates, it usually exchanged its own promissory notes for them. S&Ls included these notes as assets on their balance sheets. Effectively, the FSLIC was using its own credit to purchase equity in an insolvent thrift. The certificates reduced the number of thrift failures, but heightened the FSLIC's financial interest in preventing troubled thrifts from failing.

The Garn-St Germain Depository Institution Act of 1982 created a net worth certificate programme, a derivative of the income capital certificates. The net worth certificates differed from the income capital certificates in that they did not constitute a permanent equity investment but were issued only for a set time period, authorised by the legislation. These certificates could not be used to reorganise insolvent thrifts or to arrange mergers, because they were not transferable. The Act also allowed troubled savings and loans with negative net earnings to obtain interest-free loans from the FSLIC.

The Garn-St Germain Act also liberalised the investment powers of federally chartered thrifts – they were allowed to offer money market accounts at an interest rate competitive with money market funds. Additionally, some states (for example, California) took the initiative to deregulate savings and loans even further. Though many of these changes disappeared with two new acts, FIRREA (1989) and FDICIA (1991). With the benefit of hindsight, it is now acknowledged that granting new powers to the FSLIC allowed thrifts to expand into areas where they had little expertise worsened the crisis.

From late 1982, interest rates were lower and less volatile, but this failed to reduce the difficulties because of increasingly poor credit quality. For example, by 1984 asset quality problems explained 80% of the troubled thrifts. In 1985, the FHLBB introduced a "Management Consignment Program", designed to stem the growing losses of insolvent thrifts. Usually, it resulted in a thrift's management being replaced by a conservator selected by the Bank Board. It was to be a temporary measure, until the FSLIC could sell or liquidate the thrifts. However, it became increasingly apparent to financial market participants that the FSLIC lacked the resources to deal with the heavy losses accumulating in the troubled savings and loan industry. They became reluctant to accept the promissory notes which backed the income capital certificates. By 1985, the deteriorating condition of the insolvent thrifts strained the resources of the FSLIC to the point that it needed outside funding. Despite efforts to recapitalise it, the FSLIC's deficit was estimated to exceed $3 billion at the end of 1986. The 1987 Competitive Equality Banking Act (CEBA) authorised the issue of $10.8 billion in bonds to recapitalise the FSLIC, but in 1988 its deficit stood at $75 billion. The possibility of a taxpayer-funded bailout of the FSLIC appeared in the financial press. All of these events heightened concern about the creditworthiness of the FSLIC's promissory notes.

In 1988, the General Accounting Office (GAO) estimated that the cost of dealing with more than 300 insolvent thrifts (that the FSLIC had yet to place in receivership) was $19 billion. By the end of 1988, the estimate was raised to over $100 billion, as the GAO recognised the problem was far more extensive than had first been thought. The final bill was approximately $150 billion. Unlike the commercial bank failures (see below), the thrift failures were more evenly spread throughout the country. Texas (18%), California (9.8%), Louisiana (7%), Florida and Illinois (6.5%) each, New Jersey (4.55) and Kansas (3%) accounted for 55% of the failures from 1989 to 1995. The rest were spread throughout the states and just six (including DC) had no failures.[17]

To deal with the crisis, the Bush Plan was unveiled on 6 February 1989, and became the model for the Financial Institutions Reform, Recovery and Enforcement Act (FIRREA), 1989, which was discussed in Chapter 5. The parts of the Act relevant to the thrift crisis include:

- New restrictions on the investment powers of S&Ls, requiring them to specialise more in mortgage lending, thereby reversing the earlier policy. Under the qualified thrift lender (QTL) test, at least 65% of their assets must be mortgage related.
- An attempt to stop the regulatory forbearance witnessed in the 1980s by abolishing the institutions which promoted it. The Act dissolved the FSLIC and established the Savings Association Insurance Fund (SAIF) under the auspices of the FDIC. The Federal Home Loan Bank Board was closed and replaced with the Office of Thrift Supervision (OTS), under the direction of the Secretary of the Treasury.
- Thrifts are required to meet capital requirements at least as stringent as those imposed on commercial banks, and the Act set out new rules on higher minimum net worth.
- The Resolution Trust Corporation (RTC) was established to take over the case-load of insolvent thrifts. The RTC was allocated funds to pay off the obligations incurred by the FSLIC, and subsequently received $50 billion in additional funding, to be used by the Corporation to take over 350 insolvent thrifts, and either liquidate or merge them.
- Commercial banks were allowed to acquire healthy thrifts – prior to this Act, they could only take over failing savings and loans.

FIRREA left a number of problems unresolved. Requiring savings and loans to specialise more in mortgage lending limited opportunities for diversification. Though capital requirements became more stringent, risks have been concentrated in home loans. However, as the experience in the 1980s showed, greater diversification could only be profitable if staff had the experience and training to manage a more diversified portfolio. No measures were introduced to prevent the massive fraud that occurred throughout the industry from recurring.

The Federal Deposit Insurance Corporation Improvement Act (FDICIA), 1991, addressed the issues of closing insolvent institutions more promptly and of funding the FDIC. The Act requires the FDIC to undertake prompt corrective action and a least cost approach to problem and/or failing thrifts. The Act was quite specific in what action the FDIC must undertake. A risk based deposit insurance premium was also introduced, to ensure adequate funding of the FDIC and to give banks and S&Ls an incentive to manage their risks better. See Chapter 5 for more detail.

---

[17] *Source*: FDIC (1998), table 1.3-11, p. 108.

Perhaps the most notable contribution of FIRREA was the creation of the Resolution Trust Corporation because it introduced the concept of a *good bank/bad bank*.[18] The RTC was the first to apply this idea, which involves a separate corporation dealing with the bad assets of a problem bank. Usually the problem loans of the troubled bank are sold, at a discount to the corporation (**the "bad" bank** or asset management company), which has the responsibility of disposing of the assets for the best possible price. This cleans up the balance sheet of the troubled bank (it becomes **the good bank**), which might then recover or be sold to a healthy bank. Though its initial remit was to deal with 350 insolvent thrifts, the RTC, by the end of 1990, had become conservator of 531 thrifts, with $278.3 billion in assets. The statutory duties of the RTC included:[19]

1. Dealing with all the insolvent thrifts which had been insured by the FSLIC, for which a conservator or receiver was appointed between January 1989 and August 1992, later extended to June 1995.
2. To ensure they got maximum value when the failed thrifts and their assets were disposed of. FIRREA required the RTC to sell property for at least 95% of its market value. The Act had to be amended to reduce this to 70% because of low sales and the rising costs of maintenance for property on the RTC's books. However, some of the commercial real estate loans proved very difficult to sell – they were valueless.
3. To ensure 2 had a minimal effect on the local property market and financial markets.
4. To use some of the houses acquired by the RTC to provide low income housing units.

These obligations conflicted with each other, posing a real challenge for the RTC. When other countries adopted this approach, the role of the asset management company (as they came to be known) focused on the second objective – obtaining the maximum net present value of the disposed assets.

The RTC used private asset management and disposal firms to help with disposal of the assets. National sales centres were established to sell certain assets and it securitised assets, which at the time were considered unconventional, such as commercial loans. It also would sell packages of good and bad loans to deal with the problem that some assets, especially in commercial real estate, were valueless. All of these techniques helped the RTC to dispose of a very large volume of assets at reasonable prices. By the time the RTC was wound down (31 December 1995) it had dealt with 750 insolvent thrifts, disposed of more than $400 billion in assets (just $8 billion in assets were transferred to the FDIC) and sold over 100 000 of units of low cost housing. The RTC received a total of $90.1 billion in funding, though Ely and Varaiya (1996) argue the cost could be as high as $146 billion once the opportunity cost of using taxpayers' funds is taken into account. However, the RTC's (and the FDIC's) management and disposal of assets appears to have been good value for money, because they reduced the cost of resolving the crisis. Initial estimates ranged from $350 to $500 billion, but in the end, though still staggering, it was resolved at a cost of $150 billion.

However, the cost of the crisis is likely to rise still further following Supreme Court judgement that the reversal of accounting rules in 1989 effectively moved the goal posts

---

[18] See Box 8.1 for a discussion of the pros and cons of this approach.
[19] This account is taken from FDIC (1998), chapters 1, 4.

for investors who were persuaded to inject new capital or merge a healthy thrift with a new one. As a result of the ruling more than 120 thrifts or failed thrifts are suing the US government for compensation.

To summarise, the thrift industry suffered as a result of concentration of credit risk in the real estate market and exposure to interest rate risk through long-term fixed interest loans and mortgage backed securities, valued on their books at the original purchase price. Rising interest rates reduced the value of these securities and forced the thrifts to bear the burden of fixed interest loans. The problem was compounded by policies of regulatory forbearance because the FSLIC and the Bank Board had a vested interest in keeping the thrifts afloat. Though the cost of resolving the crisis was considerable, the success of the RTC and FDIC in the management and disposal of the assets was instrumental in significantly reducing these costs. Some of the duties of the Resolution Trust Corporation have become a model for the "good bank/bad bank", and one of the standard tools for resolving bank crises. In the USA, the RTC was a public corporation (though private firms assisted), but other countries have opted for a private firm or a mix of public and private. The good bank/bad bank approach is critically assessed in the section on financial crises (see Box 8.1 in Chapter 8).

### *Failing US commercial banks*

During 1980–94, more banks (over 1600) than thrifts failed, but less than half the assets (by value) were involved. The key point is that the bank failures were concentrated in regions of the USA at different points in time, as Chart 7.1 illustrates. The crisis can be divided into three phases.

Chart 7.1   US Bank Failures in the Northeast and Southwest, 1986–1995. copyright FDIC.

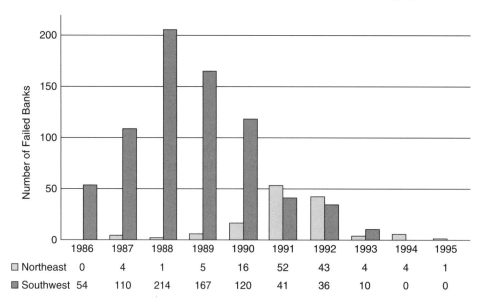

| | 1986 | 1987 | 1988 | 1989 | 1990 | 1991 | 1992 | 1993 | 1994 | 1995 |
|---|---|---|---|---|---|---|---|---|---|---|
| ☐ Northeast | 0 | 4 | 1 | 5 | 16 | 52 | 43 | 4 | 4 | 1 |
| ■ Southwest | 54 | 110 | 214 | 167 | 120 | 41 | 36 | 10 | 0 | 0 |

*Phase 1*: The early 1980s. Between 1980 and 1984, there were 192 bank failures, about 12% of the total between 1980 and 1994. The main problem arose because of interest rates. Many of the failing or problem banks had high quality loan portfolios, but were hit by adverse economic conditions. Since they were few in number, regulatory forbearance was used to see them through the crisis period.

*Phase 2*: 1984–91. In 1984, there was a shift in bank failures to some southern states, Arkansas, Louisiana, New Mexico, Oklahoma and Texas, officially defined as the south-west by the FDIC (1997, 1998). 1985 marked the beginning of the shift, but the problem was most acute between 1986 and 1990. In 1986, 37% of bank failures in the USA took place in the south-west, rising every year to a peak of 81% in 1989, falling to 71% in 1990. By 1991, it was down to 32%. Within this region, by far the greatest number took place in Texas (522),[20] followed by Oklahoma (122) and Louisiana (70).[21] During this phase, the number of bank failures was so high that forbearance was no longer an option. The FDIC, used to dealing with a few bank failures each year, suddenly found itself dealing with well over a 100 per year, peaking at 279 in 1988.

There were several contributory factors. First, volatile oil prices. They rose very rapidly between 1973 and 1981, fell between 1981 and 1985, with a steep decline of 45% in 1986. During the boom years of the 1970s and early 1980s, banks were keen to lend to firms in the energy related sectors, backed by what was thought to be safe collateral – real estate.

Once oil prices began to fall in the 1980s, the banks also increased direct lending to the commercial real estate sector, apparently oblivious to the idea that if the oil economy was in trouble, property prices there would soon be affected. The property boom prompted building and more buying – pushing up property prices and encouraging more lending, especially between 1981 and 1988. What the (Texan) banks saw as a "win win" situation quickly became "lose lose", i.e. loan quality deteriorated and so did the value of collateral when the property market, following the energy sector, slumped. Between 1986 and 1989, there was a 25% office vacancy rate in Texan cities.

The problems were aggravated by bank regulations. Problem banks were not spotted early enough because bank examinations were infrequent.[22] Laws placed severe limits on branching by Texan banks and prohibited out of state banks from purchasing Texan banks. The former limited expansion into the retail sector (and hence narrowed the funding base for banks); the latter discouraged mergers in the early days of the problem loans. As soon as there was a hint of problems, uninsured wholesale depositors switched to safer banks, further restricting growth.

Another problem was increased competition from deregulated S&Ls,[23] and an increase in the number of new banks. Bank charters in the "SW" rose from 62 in 1980 to 168 by 1984, and the vast majority of these were in Texas. A third of these banks were to fail between 1980 and 1994, compared to 21% of the established banks. But among the long-standing banks, the largest in the state failed. The percentage of non-performing loans to total loans

---

[20] For a discussion of the Texan banking crisis, see O'Keefe (1990).

[21] These last three figures are for the period 1980–94.

[22] FDIC (1998), p. 85.

[23] The 1982 Garn-St Germain Depository Institutions Act allowed the S&Ls to expand into new areas.

Table 7.2   Large Bank Failures in the South-West, 1980–90

| Bank | Failure Date | State | Assets ($m) | Resolution Cost As a % of Assets |
|------|------|------|------|------|
| Penn Square | 5.7.82 | OK | 436 | 14.9 |
| Abilene National | 6.8.82 | TX | 437 | 0 (open bank assistance given) |
| First National Bank of Midland | 14.10.83 | TX | 1 410 | 37.3 |
| First Oklahoma | 11.7.86 | OK | 1 754 | 9.6 |
| BancOklahoma | 24.11.86 | OK | 468 | 16.9 |
| BancTexas | 17.7.87 | TX | 1 181 | 12.7 |
| First City Bancorp | 20.4.88 | TX | 12 374 | 8.9 |
| First Republic | 29.7.88 | TX | 21 277 | 12 |
| Mcorp | 29.3.89 | TX | 15 641 | 18.2 |
| Texas American | 20.7.89 | TX | 4 665 | 21.1 |
| National Bancshares | 1.6.90 | TX | 1 594 | 13.4 |

TX: Texas; OK: Oklahoma.
*Source:* FDIC (1997), table 9.2. The FDIC defines a bank as large if its assets exceed $400 million.

grew steadily, peaking at over 10% in 1987. Likewise, the percentage of banks reporting negative net income rose from 8% in 1982 to 39% in 1987.[24] Table 7.2 reports the largest bank failures in the south-west between 1980 and 1990 – seven banks were from Texas; the other three from Oklahoma.

Note the failure of the bigger Texan banks took place relatively late. First Republic Bank was the biggest bank in Texas, and called in the FDIC for restructuring talks in March 1988. Other Texas state banks also required large amounts of federal support, namely First City (1988) and MCorp (1989).

*Phase 3*: 1991–94. In this phase, the concentration of troubled banks shifted from the south-west to the north-east (see Chart 7.1), i.e. New England,[25] New Jersey and New York State. In 1989, there were just five failed banks in the north-east, compared to 167 in the south-west. Though proportionately much smaller in the NE, by 1991, with 52 bank failures, it overtook the SW (41), and also remained higher in 1992. In 1994, there were four failures in the NE, none in the SW. It appears that these banks did not take the opportunity to learn the lessons of the SW.

Rapid economic growth in the northeast region until the late 1980s resulted in booming retail and commercial property markets, though the subsequent problems with loan quality was largely due to difficulties in the commercial market. The banks were only too happy to participate in the bonanza. The median ratio of real estate loans to total loans rose from 25% in 1983 to 51% in 1989.[26]

---

[24] Source of these figures: FDIC (1997), p. 329.
[25] The FDIC report defined "New England" to include the states of Connecticut, Maine, Massachusetts, New Hampshire, Rhode Island and New York.
[26] *Source*: FDIC (1997), p. 338.

One reason some of the banks could expand their asset base relatively quickly was because of the change in the status of mutual banks in this region. Between 1985 and 1990, 40% of mutual savings banks converted to joint stock ownership. Conversion increased their capital, and loan growth was an obvious way to maintain returns on equity. As mutuals, the banks had concentrated on retail property loans and mortgages but post-conversion, seeking new opportunities for asset growth, they moved into commercial real estate, an area where their managers had little experience. This strategy was a contributing factor to the problem of excessive exposure in the commercial property markets.

In 1986 a major tax reform removed tax concessions on property. However, even the property markets remained healthy through 1987. By 1988, the region was in a slump, reflected by increasingly high vacancy rates and falling property prices. The recession of 1990–91 halted construction altogether. Heavily exposed in real estate, banks in the NE experienced a sharp decline in the quality of their loan portfolios and collateral. Between 1990 and 1992, the percentage of non-performing loans peaked at just over 8%, well above the average (3–4%) for other US banks. This was reflected in the percentage of banks with negative net income, peaking at 40.2% in 1990, up from 9.2% in 1988. In 1989, only five NE banks failed, representing 2.4% of the total. In 1990, this figure rose to 9.5%, then jumped to 50% in 1991 and 35% in 1992.

In 1991, 52 NE banks failed, making up 78% of failing assets and responsible for 91% of FDIC resolution costs. Between 1990 and the end of 1992, 111 FDIC insured banks in the NE failed. Though they made up 27% of total bank failures, these banks represented 67% of the total assets of failing banks and 76% of the FDIC resolution costs. By this time, the toll on FDIC finances was increasingly evident. For the first time in its history, the fund had a deficit of $7 billion in 1991.[27]

## The Bank of New England

Several large savings banks failed in the New York area, but it was the Bank of New England group that was the most spectacular. At one point, the Bank of New England was the 15th largest in the USA, but it failed in 1991 due to a large number of non-performing loans. The Bank of New England Corporation (BNEC) was formed in 1985 through a merger of the Bank of New England (BNE) with Connecticut Bank and Trust. With $14 billion in assets, analysts were optimistic about the merger because it combined the Bank of New England's expertise in property lending with retail banking, the Connecticut bank's speciality. A remarkable growth spurt meant that by 1989, BNEC had $32 billion in assets, and eight subsidiary banks. However, the decline in the real estate markets hit the BNEC subsidiary banks hard. At the Bank of New England, one of the subsidiaries, non-performing loans climbed to 20% by the end of 1990. There was a run on the BNE on 4 January 1991 – depositors withdrew $1 billion. Two days later the OCC declared BNE and

---

[27] The FDIC had set aside $13.3 billion for future bank failures. *Source*: FDIC (1998).

two other subsidiaries bankrupt.[28] BNEC's failure was the third largest, after First Republic Bank and Continental Illinois.[29]

On 6 January, the OCC appointed the FDIC as receiver. The FDIC announced that three new "bridge banks" had been chartered to assume the assets and liabilities of the three insolvent banks, and they would run a normal banking business on Monday 7th January. *All* depositors of the three BNEC banks (independent of deposit size) were protected, but shareholders and bondholders suffered heavy losses. The House of Representatives Banking Committee expressed concern that this decision was disadvantageous for savers at small banks, and undermined incentives for depositors to monitor their banks' activities.[30] When the FDIC Improvement Act was passed in 1991 this "too big to fail" episode was one of the incidents which influenced legislators to impose tighter restrictions to limit the protection of uninsured depositors.

The Senate Banking Committee asked the General Accounting Office to investigate the causes of BNEC's failure. The GAO identified the extremely rapid growth in assets, liberal lending policies, and a concentration of commercial property loans as the main factors behind its demise. Though the OCC was continually monitoring BNE from September 1989, the GAO concluded losses would have been lower had the OCC conducted more intensive examinations of the bank's assets when it was growing so rapidly.[31]

In April 1991, the FDIC announced that the bridge banks would be purchased by Fleet/Norstar Financial group, and by investment managers KKR (Kohlberg, Kravis, Roberts & Co.). This was another "first": a non-bank financial institution providing capital to purchase a failed commercial bank.

## Freedom National Bank

A small community bank based in Harlem, founded to give American blacks their own bank, Freedom National Bank was one of the largest minority owned banks in the country. On 9 November 1990, it was closed by the OCC, with $78 million in deposits and $102 million in assets. The FDIC liquidated the bank; account holders with deposits in excess of $100 000 only got 50% of their deposits back, prompting accusations of racism, because in the Bank of New England failure, all depositors were paid in full.

## 7.3.8. Bank of Credit and Commerce International

On Friday, 5 July 1991, the Bank of England (which had responsibility for bank regulation and supervision at the time), together with the Luxembourg and Cayman Islands authorities,

---

[28] The BNE's failure triggered the collapse of Connecticut Bank and Trust (CBT) and the Maine National Bank of Portland (MNB). The CBT had loaned $1.5 million in federal funds to the BNE, which it could not recover, and the FDIC charged the loss against CBT's capital accounts, resulting in negative equity of $49 million. MNB was unable to make a payment to the FDIC equal to the amount the FDIC was expected to lose as the BNE's receiver. This was an application of cross guarantee provision of the 1991 Financial Institutions Reform, Recovery and Enforcement Act, which makes a bank liable for losses incurred by the FDIC if another bank fails and they are part of a commonly controlled set of insured banks (FDIC, 1997, pp. 375–376).

[29] *Source*: FDIC (1997), p. 377.

[30] As reported by the FDIC (1997), p. 376.

[31] FDIC (1997), p. 377.

closed all branches of the Bank of Credit and Commerce International (BCCI) and froze all deposits. Though BCCI was not incorporated in the UK, once the winding-up order was made, sterling deposits in branches of the UK were eligible for compensation from the Deposit Protection Fund, which then covered 75% of a deposit, up to a maximum of £15 000. The first reaction of many of the Asian community with deposits and loans was that the Bank of England was being unduly harsh, and its closure prompted accusations of racism because it was the first developing country bank to become a global concern. It was also widely claimed that the regulatory authorities had failed to act early enough.

In 1972 BCCI was founded by the Pakistani financier Agha Hasan Abedi and incorporated in Luxembourg, with a small amount of capital, $2.5 million (below the Bank of England's £5 million requirement). The Bank of America took a 25% stake. By the time it was wound up, its debts amounted to £7 billion. BCCI, which has come to be known as the "Bank of Cocaine and Criminals International", had a long history of fraud and illegal dealings. In 1975 the US authorities blocked BCCI's attempt to take over two New York banks, criticising Abedi for failing to disclose details about the company. In 1977, Abedi and BCCI joined forces with a Saudi billionaire, Ghaith Pharon. BCCI launched a hostile takeover bid for Washington's largest bank, Financial General Bankshares. The bid was blocked by the US Securities and Exchange Commission. In 1981, Bankshares was taken over by Middle East investors closely associated with BCCI, though the authorities were assured there was no connection between the banks.

In 1983, BCCI bought a Colombian bank, with branches in Medellin and Cali, centres for the cocaine trade and money laundering. Manuel Noriega, the Panamanian dictator, was a prominent customer of the bank from 1985 to 1987. It later transpired that the bank had laundered $32 million of drug money. BCCI was indicted in Florida for laundering drug money in 1988. In London, one of the branches was raided by British customs, who seized evidence of Noriega's deposits, and by 1989 BCCI was announcing losses from bad loans amounting to nearly $500 million. In 1988, senior BCCI executives in Florida were charged with money laundering and in 1990 five of them were imprisoned after they pleaded guilty. The bank was fined $15 million and taken over by Sheikh Zayed Bib Sultan al-Nahyan, ruler of Abu Dhabi. An audit showed large financial irregularities. Bankshares reported a loss of $182 million – it had come to light that BCCI was the secret owner of Bankshares in 1989. In January 1991, John Bartlett of the Bank of England was sent a copy of the "Project Q" interim report. The report identified a core group of 11 customers and 42 accounts linked to the international terrorist, Abu Nidal. No immediate action was taken, but in March the Bank ordered a section 41 investigation by the auditors.

A number of regulatory gaps and problems came to light as a result of the BCCI scandal. In 1979, the Bank of England granted BCCI licensed deposit taking (LDT) status, preventing it from having a branch network in England. When the Banking Act was amended in 1987, the distinction between banks and LDTs was eliminated – BCCI now had full banking status. The change gave BCCI the opportunity to extend the branch network, giving the bank access to less sophisticated personal and small business customers, who used the bank to make deposits and obtain loans. A countless number of innocent, but ill-informed small firms such as newsagents banked at BCCI and lost access to their deposits when it failed. Some local authorities had also placed the proceeds of the council tax on deposit at BCCI because it was offering higher interest rates. Western Isles Council lost up to £24 million when the bank was closed, which it had to borrow from the Scottish Office (to be repaid over 30 years) to finance the provision of local council services. In different parts of the world (BCCI had offices in 73 countries), such as Pakistan and Hong Kong, where the bank was not closed immediately, there were runs on BCCI branches. Many depositors lost all their savings.

During the Florida criminal case, it was revealed that top BCCI managers knew about and approved of the money laundering. Therefore, BCCI management failed the "fit and proper" test. The Bank of England did not suspend management, even though it had the discretionary power so to do. The Florida drug case prompted the establishment of a College of Regulators because of concern about BCCI. The original group consisted of regulators from the UK, Switzerland, Spain and Luxembourg. Hong Kong, the Cayman Islands, France and the United Arab Emirates joined later. However, it was largely ineffective. In July 1989 Manhattan District Attorney staff attended an international conference on money laundering, held in Cambridge, UK. They discovered BCCI had an international reputation for capital flight, tax fraud and money laundering. Assuming the Bank of England also knew about it, there is the question of why BCCI was not closed earlier. Furthermore, it is alleged the Bank of England and Price Waterhouse failed to cooperate with the US authorities. For example, investigators from the New York District Attorney's office claim they were refused access to BCCI London documents in July 1989. Also, the Manhattan District Attorney and the Federal Reserve were unsuccessful when they tried to get a copy of the Price Waterhouse special audit report. In the autumn of 1990, the Federal Reserve demanded a copy of the audit.

Price Waterhouse (PW) had been BCCI's sole auditor since 1988, and submitted 10 reports to the Bank of England. Two Price Waterhouse reports were published in April and October 1990, indicating large-scale fraud. The Price Waterhouse evidence to the British House of Commons (February 1992) confirmed that as early as April 1990, they had been informed by the Bank of England at BCCI, "certain transactions have either been false or deceitful". In October 1990, PW reported fictitious loans and deposits to the Bank of England. By December, the auditors told the Bank the main shareholders in Abu Dhabi were aware of the fraud. The Bank of England admits that it received its first indication of fraud in January 1991, but it did not activate section 41 of the Banking Act until March. The section 41 investigation carried out by Price Waterhouse confirmed large-scale fraud, but it was a further four months before BCCI was closed.

Two people appeared in a UK court, charged with conspiring to mislead BCCI's auditors. Mohammed Abdul Baqi, a former managing director of a London based trading group, was convicted in April 1994 and given a custodial sentence. In 1997, Abbas Gokal was found guilty on two counts of conspiracy – one to defraud, the other to account falsely, which involved the secret removal of £750 million from the bank. He was fined £2.9 million and sentenced to 14 years in prison. In the USA, two Washington "super lawyers", Clark Clifford and Robert Altman, were accused of concealing BCCI's ownership of Bankshares, fraud, conspiracy and accepting $40 million in bribes, but the charges were dropped against Clifford in early 1993, and Altman was acquitted in 1994. In Abu Dhabi, 14 ex-BCCI managers were convicted in 1994 and one was extradited to the USA in 1994 to face further charges.

The Bingham Report (October 1992) criticised the Bank of England for failing to act after receiving a series of warnings, over many years, of fraud and other illegal activities at BCCI. Price Waterhouse was accused of not fully briefing the Bank of England about the extent of the fraud it had found in early 1991. A US Senate report (from a Senate foreign operations subcommittee, October 1992) claimed the Bank of England's supervision of BCCI was wholly inadequate, and singled out Price Waterhouse for its lack of cooperation with the US authorities. Two accounting firms acting on behalf of BCCI, Price Waterhouse and Ernst and Whinney, were sued for negligence by Deloitte and Touche (the BCCI administrators). The matter was settled out of court in 1998 when the two firms agreed to pay £106 million ($195 million) in damages.

The UK government imposed new measures following the Bingham Report. The Bank of England set up a special investigations unit to look into suspected cases of fraud or financial malpractice. A legal unit was established to advise the Bank on its legal obligations under the Banking Act. The Banking Act was amended to give the Bank of England the right to close down the UK operations of an international bank if it feels the overseas operations of the bank are not being conducted properly. All of these responsibilities have since been passed to the Financial Services Authority, which in 1998 became the supervisory body for all financial institutions operating in the UK (see Chapter 5).

As a result of the Bingham recommendations, auditors have a legal duty to pass on information related to suspected fraud to the Bank of England (now FSA).[32] Auditing firms in the UK objected to the change, claiming it would no longer be profitable for them to conduct bank audits, though no accounting firm has, to date, withdrawn from this market.

With respect to international supervision, the Bingham enquiry recommended a method for international monitoring of supervisory standards and an international database of individuals who have failed to pass a "fit and proper" criterion. If a financial centre permits a high degree of bank secrecy, regulators in other countries should be able to close down foreign branches or subsidiaries. There has been notable progress on this front, but largely because of the post "9/11" measures to halt the use of banks by terrorist organisations for money laundering and other illicit financial activities.

In January 2004, the case against the Bank of England finally reached the courts; Western Isles Council is one of many creditors hoping to gain from the law suit. The liquidators, Deloitte and Touche, claim the Bank of England failed to protect depositors for two reasons. First, it granted BCCI a licence to operate in London when the bank was registered and headquartered in Luxembourg, and therefore subject to Luxembourg regulations. BCCI was originally a licensed deposit taker (which prevented it from having branches in the UK) but under the 1987 Amendment to the 1979 Bank of England Act, the distinction was withdrawn, enabling BCCI to set up branches across the UK. Second, the Bank stands accused of failing to revoke the licence once it was clear BCCI was engaging in fraudulent activity. The Bank of England cannot be sued for negligence, and the onus of proof is on Deloitte to prove misfeasance, that is, to show that the Bank of England acted in bad

---

[32] Building society and insurance companies are subject to similar requirements.

faith – "knowingly and recklessly" failing to supervise the bank properly, thereby subjecting customers to unreasonable amounts of risk. Failure to forecast an imminent collapse is not enough. The case is expected to last for up to two years.

## 7.3.9. UK Small Bank Failures and Liquidity Problems, 1991–93[33]

This episode is reported here because it began before the failure of BCCI but appears to have been exacerbated by it. It shows how regulators can contain the problem if it is largely one of liquidity. The Bank of England opted to keep the liquidity difficulties of up to 40 small[34] banks a secret until after the crisis had passed. The banks faced problems on both sides of the balance sheet. The British economy enjoyed a boom until 1988, then recession: commercial property prices fell 27% between 1989 and 1993; residential by 14%. Many of these small banks specialised in property lending. Recession reduced the quality of their assets and the value of collateral, which was largely in property. These banks also depended on wholesale funding. At the end of 1990, US, Japanese and other foreign banks began to reduce their sterling deposits because of increased concerns about the UK's unexpectedly prolonged recession. By the end of 1992, they had fallen over sevenfold. The Bank of England closely monitored 40 small banks from mid-1991. Many were told either to reduce their assets and/or increase their liquidity. There were virtually no systemic effects after three small banks failed in early 1991.

The collapse of BCCI and the losses incurred by the Western Isles Council exacerbated the problem, as local authorities shifted their funds into the bigger banks, which they considered to be too big to be allowed to fail. In 1991, the Bank of England supplied liquidity in the form of loans to a few small banks, and had to provision for it – provisions peaked at £115 million in 1993. The Bank decided to take action because it believed contagion was the main culprit, which could spread to larger banks if not kept in check. Not all banks survived. Auditors of the National Mortgage Bank could not sign it off as healthy because of concerns about its illiquidity. The Bank of England purchased it for £1 in 1994, and it was sold in 2000. In total, 25 small banks failed in the first half of the 1990s, but there was no contagion or systemic crisis, no doubt due to the willingness of the Bank to support the small banks that were illiquid but solvent.

## 7.3.10. The Secondary Banking Crisis, 1973

The events of the early 1990s share some features with the UK's secondary banking crisis. In the early 1970s, several small banks were rescued by the Bank of England. A number of so-called "secondary" banks were established in the UK in the 1960s. Unlike the mainstream banks, which relied on relatively cheap, stable retail deposits, most of the funding for the new banks came from the growing wholesale money markets, which they

---

[33] This account is from Hoggarth and Soussa (2001) and Logan (2000).
[34] According to Logan (2000), there were 116 authorised small banks and 92 of them had a full data set. Their average size, by assets, was £166.4 million, compared to a mean of £11.8 billion for the UK's major banking group. Within the small bank group, the smallest had assets of £1 million; the largest stood at £3.2 billion.

used to fund long-term loans, mainly to property and construction companies. A tightening of monetary and fiscal policy in 1973, together with the first OPEC oil price hike, caused interest rates to increase and declines in property prices and the stock market. The balance sheets of the secondary banks suddenly began to look quite weak, especially because much of the collateral backing their loans was stocks or equity. Some suffered from a withdrawal of deposits. The Bank of England organised a lifeboat rescue: 26 secondary banks were given £1.3 billion in loans, 90% of which came from the major UK commercial banks. The Bank of England was able to persuade shareholders and creditors not to take action that would cause a failure. Some of the insolvent banks were either taken over by other banks or the Bank of England itself. At the time there was no deposit insurance, but depositors (not shareholders) were protected. The lessons from the crisis were reflected in the UK's first major piece of banking legislation, passed in 1979 (see Chapter 5), which included a deposit insurance scheme and tighter restrictions on bank licensing.[35]

## 7.3.11. Barings

*"The recovery in profitability has been amazing following the reorganization, leaving Barings to conclude that it was not actually terribly difficult to make money in the securities markets."*
(A 1993 remark attributed to the Chairman of Barings plc, speaking to Mr Brian Quinn, Director of the Bank of England at the time)

*"People at the London end of Barings were all so know-all that nobody dared ask a stupid question in case they looked silly in front of everyone else."* (Nick Leeson, *Rogue Trader*, 1996)

On Sunday, 26 February 1995, the oldest merchant bank in the UK, Barings (founded in 1762) ceased trading and was put into administration.[36] It owed over £800 million on financial derivatives contracts, but had a capital base of just £540 million. On Friday, 24 February, Barings' senior management became aware of large losses in its Singapore office and requested support from the Bank of England. Auditors' reports came in suggesting Barings was highly likely to be insolvent, raising the question of whether contagion effects arising from the bank's failure were serious enough to warrant the central bank's intervention. It was decided the risk of contagion was small because Barings was a small merchant bank; the exposures were largely bilateral (see below), and it was due to fraud.

The next question to be addressed was whether other banks, concerned about the reputation of other merchant banks or the City of London as a financial centre, might be willing to purchase Barings. The decision whether to provide support had to be taken by Sunday evening London time before the Japanese markets opened because insolvent firms are not allowed to trade. So the Bank of England spent the last weekend of February 1995

---

[35] This account is taken largely from Davis (1992), but see also the Bank of England (1978) and Reid (1982).

[36] Under the 1986 Insolvency Act, a firm can be put into administration, and an administrator appointed to try and prevent a failing business from being liquidated, and to keep it operating as a going concern. Administration automatically freezes the enforcement of creditors' rights. By contrast, the receiver's duty is to protect the interests of the creditors.

trying to put together a lifeboat rescue package involving other banks, but it conceded defeat late on Sunday night. The Bank could not persuade a bank or banks (both domestic and foreign) to close futures contracts entered by a trader, Mr Nick Leeson, in Barings' Singapore offices. A syndicate of commercial and investment banks was ready to recapitalise Barings (at an estimated cost of £700 million), but none would accept a fixed fee in exchange for closing these trading positions. The Bank of England announced it was ready to provide liquidity to the markets if necessary, but refused to use public funds to bail out Barings. As it turned out, global market disruptions were minimal, demonstrating the point that the insolvency of a small merchant bank, however famous, was unlikely to provoke systemic collapse.

The Chancellor of the Exchequer, Mr Kenneth Clarke, announced that the Barings collapse would be investigated by the Bank of England's Board of Banking Supervision, but ruled out a public or independent inquiry. This Board was chaired by the Governor of the Bank of England and consisted of six outside members, in addition to Bank of England representatives. In March 1995 the Bank's governor, Mr (later Sir Edward) George revealed that six external members had been asked to make an independent assessment of the Bank of England's supervision of Barings. The Board of Banking Supervision's Report ("The Report") was made public on 18 July 1995.

Before its collapse, Barings was well known in the City of London for mergers and acquisitions and its strength in emerging markets. Roughly half of the bank's employees were based outside the UK – a third in Asia. The broking and market making arm of the bank, Barings Securities, was a leading equity broker in Asia and Latin America. The fund management operation had a reputation for its expertise in Eastern Europe. Just as exposure in Latin America had led to near ruin in 1890, so exposure in the Far East was the cause of Barings' downfall in 1995.

On 6 March 1995, Internationale Nederlanden Group (ING Bank), a Dutch bancas-surance concern, purchased Barings' banking, securities and asset management businesses for one pound sterling. *Bancassurance* is the combination of banking and insurance in one group. ING had been formed as a result of the merger, in 1991, of Nationale Nederlanden (the largest Dutch insurer) with the Netherlands' third largest Dutch bank, NMB Post-bank, known for its lending to small and medium-sized Dutch companies. Bank branches sell insurance and the group was able to offer new financing schemes to corporations by pooling the short and long-term funds from, respectively, the banking and insurance arms of the company. ING took responsibility for Barings' existing liabilities (estimated at £860 million), but any future liabilities will be borne by Barings plc, the holding company, which ING did not buy.

ING was inexperienced in third party fund management, corporate finance and brokerage, and there were high expectations that Barings' expertise in this area would prove beneficial.[37] Just under 5 years later (November 2000), ING announced that its US operation (2000 employees) of ING Barings was to be sold or wound down, while the London office would be integrated into the wholesale operations of ING. At the time of the announcement Barings'

---

[37] To encourage staff to stay on in the aftermath of Leeson, the chairman of ING announced that all senior executives of Barings would be kept on until the publication of the Bank of England report. Staff bonuses of close to £100 million were paid, though senior employees directly involved in the losses were excluded and executive directors of Barings waived them.

return on capital was well below its target and far below that of ING Asset Management. In 2004, just a skeleton remains, Barings Asset Management and Barings Trust, both owned by ING.

Though the downfall of Barings was due to uncovered positions (options – see below) in the derivatives market, there was nothing very complicated about the derivatives that got the bank into trouble. Mr Leeson was an arbitrageur, whose job was to spot differences in the prices of futures contracts and profit from buying futures contracts on one market and simultaneously selling them on another. The margins are small, and the volumes traded large. The procedure does not entail much risk, because a long position is established in one market (speculating on a rise) and a short position in another (betting on a fall), making a profit from the price differences.

Mr Leeson was supposed to have been trying to profit by spotting differences in the prices of the Nikkei 225 futures contracts listed on the Osaka Securities Exchange (OSE) and the Singapore Monetary Exchange (SIMEX). SIMEX attracts Japanese stock market futures because the Osaka exchange is subject to more regulation and hence is more costly.[38] The Report claimed that rather than hedging his positions, Leeson seems to have decided to bet on the future direction of the Nikkei index. By 23 February, when his actions came to light, Leeson had purchased $7 billion in stock index futures and sold $20 billion worth of bond and interest rate futures contracts. Most of the losses came from the stock index futures. Meanwhile, senior management at Barings were under the impression that the extraordinary profits Leeson was claiming came from the relatively risk-free arbitrage, and remained unconcerned. The Report criticised the former chairman and deputy chairman of Barings, respectively Mr Peter Baring and Mr Tuckey, for failing to ensure they were properly informed of Mr Leeson's activities, and the source of his apparent (extraordinary) profits. Mr Peter Norris, chief executive of Barings, was blamed for inaccurate reports being submitted to the Bank of England, the Securities and Futures Authority, and Coopers and Lybrand, the external auditors. Mr Ron Baker, the former head of the financial products group, was criticised for not knowing what Mr Leeson was really doing, and for his general lack of understanding of Singapore's operations.

Though early reports suggested Mr Leeson had acted on his own, it has since become apparent that "rogue trading" does not explain all the events leading up to the collapse. The *Financial Times* reported that an internal audit at Barings Futures in Singapore had been initiated by Barings' management because of the subsidiary's exceptional profitability. The purpose of the audit was to investigate whether rules were being broken and/or exceptional risks taken. The audit report was submitted in August 1994 and concluded the profits had been made by legitimate means – it appeared to accept that the Singapore office had found a method to make exceptional profits through derivatives arbitrage, without assuming much risk.

However, the audit noted Mr Leeson held the position of General Manager, head of both trading (front office) and settlements (back office), thereby making it possible for him to circumvent the controls in place, because he could initiate transactions in the front office and use the back office to ensure they were recorded and settled as per his

---

[38] At the time, investors taking a position on the OSE market must deposit 30% of the initial value of the contract with the exchange. In Singapore, the cost was a fraction of this.

instructions. The report accepted that Barings Futures was a relatively small operation (25 employees) which, in the absence of more experienced staff, would mean Leeson continued to play an active role in both offices. Instead of appointing a full-time risk manager, it was agreed the risk manager in Hong Kong would conduct quarterly reviews of the Singapore operations. The internal auditors suggested Mr Leeson should no longer supervise the back office team, cheque-signing, signing off on the reconciliations of activities at SIMEX, and signing off bank reconciliations. However, it is unclear whether Mr Leeson relinquished any of these duties.

The *Financial Times*[39] was the first to report that Mr Leeson used a secret error account 88888 to hide trading losses. From the Board of Banking Supervision's report,[40] it appears Mr Leeson opened the secret account 88888 ("5-eights") early on, in July 1992, a few months after he arrived in Singapore. Initially the account was included in reports to Barings, London, but at some point Leeson persuaded a computer expert to confine information about this account to just one report. While secretly accumulating losses in the "5-eights" account, Leeson used cross trades to record profits in three public arbitrage trading accounts, numbers 92000, 98007 and 98008. During 1994, Leeson made £28.5 million in false profits and large bonuses for himself and other Barings employees. Meanwhile, losses in the "5-eights" account grew: by year-end 1992, the account had a cumulative loss of £2 million, and it remained at about this level through to October 1993. By the end of 1993, losses had risen to £23 million, and by 1994, to £208 million.

The problems began in January 1994, when Leeson sold put options (conferring a right to buy) and simultaneously sold call options (conferring a right to sell) on the Nikkei 225 index. Up to 40 000 contracts were sold. The deals would have been profitable had the Japanese market proved less volatile than that predicted by the option prices. But Kobe was hit by a devastating earthquake on 17 January, and the Nikkei fell slightly. Mr Leeson needed the Nikkei to stay in the range of 18 500 to 19 500 to stay in profit. In an attempt to bolster the Nikkei, Leeson bought Nikkei futures on an enormous scale, but on 23 January the index lost 1000 points, falling to under 17 800. He continued to buy futures, hoping to influence the market, keeping in mind that bonuses were due to be fixed on 24 February. His attempts failed, leaving Barings with £827 million in losses.

Throughout this time, Barings London was deceived into thinking Mr Leeson had made profits from arbitrage. But losses were accumulating in the 88888 account. For example, Leeson earned a £130 000 bonus in 1993, and in 1994 it was reported he generated £28.5 million in revenues, more than three-quarters of the profits of the Barings Group. It transpires that the London head office had transferred large amounts of funds to Singapore, under the impression it was being used for clients' business, when in fact it was being used for margins, to cover Leeson's options positions.

This account was used again when Mr Leeson went long on the Nikkei 225 index. In a memorandum written by Mr Tony Hawes, Barings Group Treasurer on 24 February 1995, the account had over 61 000 long positions on SIMEX, in the form of futures contracts. It also had 26 079 short positions in Japanese government bonds, and 6485 positions

---

[39] *Financial Times*, 3 March 1995, p. 2.
[40] See Bank of England (1995).

in Euroyen. The total loss on the account came to £84 million. But the writer of the memorandum did not appear to know about further losses on options contracts. Auditors failed to notice its significance, because, it was claimed, it had been disguised as a receivable.

Since the collapse, it has been widely acknowledged that internal controls at Barings were lacking, especially in the area of risk management. On paper, the controls appeared satisfactory. At the end of 1994 a new unit in Barings called Group Treasury and Risk was formed to oversee risks. It reported to an Asset Liability Committee, which was supposed to meet daily to oversee risk, trading limits and capital funding. This new unit was created as part of the effort to integrate the merchant bank, Barings Brothers, with Barings Securities, the broking arm, into a single investment bank. But Barings, it was rumoured, faced the usual problems of trying to merge traditional merchant banking with trading cultures. Barings may have expanded into derivatives trading too quickly, before internal checks were in place. For example, Barings appears to have had no gross position limits on proprietary trading operations in Singapore. The deals undertaken by Mr Leeson aroused little suspicion until it was too late, even though traders at rival firms and regulators at the Bank for International Settlements (BIS) were amazed at the growth of Barings' positions.

Regulatory authorities are also open to criticism. The SIMEX and Osaka exchanges failed to act, despite the rapid growth of contracts at Barings. Mr John Sander, Chairman of the Chicago Mercantile Exchange, noted that such a build-up of contracts would not happen on the CME. A CME trader buying or selling more contracts than allowed by the regulations would be immediately expelled from the exchange. Participants on this exchange are required to have a surveillance team to conduct regular and independent monitoring.[41] SIMEX blamed Barings' management in London, claiming the group had continuously assured SIMEX it could meet any obligations, throughout January and February.

According to the report by the Bank of England's Board of Banking Supervision, the Bank of England was deficient in its supervision of Barings, in several areas. Barings had been granted *solo consolidation* status: the parent bank and its subsidiary, Barings Securities, were required to meet a single set of capital and exposure standards. This meant the Bank of England had sole responsibility for the supervision of all of Barings, even though the Securities and Futures Association (SFA) is much more experienced in the supervision of securities activities. Solo consolidation also meant Barings depositors were exposed to trading losses. The alternative, more common method of supervision is known as *solo plus*, whereby the bank and the securities subsidiary are separated for the purposes of regulation, meaning different capital standards may be applied. Effectively, a firewall is erected between the two parts of the business, so the bank does not have to fund trading losses from the parent bank. These points raise broader questions about the best way to supervise financial conglomerates, an issue that was discussed in Chapters 2 and 5.

The Bank of England will also have to address the question of why a breach of European Union rules by Barings was not detected. Under EU regulations, banks are not allowed to put more than 25% of their equity capital into a single investment without Bank of England approval. The capital for Barings' investment banking operations was £440 million,

---

[41] *Financial Times*, 3 March 1995.

limiting it to a single exposure of no more than £100 million. Yet in the first two months of 1995, Barings transferred a total of £569 million to Barings Futures, Singapore. The losses accumulated in Mr Leeson's account amounted to £384 million. Barings did not report the exposure to the Bank of England. However, the Bank of England should have been able to detect the substantial increase in credit exposure through the monthly liquidity report, supplied by a bank's treasury to supervisors. Though some other banks, including the BIS, noted Barings' increased borrowings on the money market by the end of January 1995, the Bank of England apparently did not. Mr Chris Thomson, the supervisor for merchant banks, resigned from the Bank of England in the week before the Report was published. He had agreed to allow Barings to exceed exposure limits on the Osaka Securities Exchange. This informal concession was granted without any consultation with more senior Bank of England officials. Once discovered, the Bank of England took over a year before it rescinded this concession, in January 1995.

One gets a sense of *déjà vu* when reading the Report's criticism of Barings' external auditors, Coopers and Lybrand. Coopers and Lybrand London was criticised for failing to conduct sufficiently comprehensive tests that would have detected the large funding requests from Singapore, which were inconsistent with the claim that Leeson's profits were coming from arbitrage. Coopers and Lybrand Singapore had audited Barings Futures Singapore in 1994, and had been satisfied that proper internal controls were in place. Coopers London responded that it did find and report a £50 million discrepancy – the documentation for a £50 million receivable was insufficient. The firm also argued it cannot be criticised, because Barings collapsed before it had conducted its 1994 audit. But the Board of Banking Supervision has called for improved communication between internal and external auditors, and regulators – recall that similar conclusions were reached after the JMB and BCCI investigations. As was discussed in Chapter 5, the duties of auditors have been considerably enhanced under the FSA.

Mr Leeson fled to Germany (en route to London) after the losses came to light. He was arrested by the German authorities after Singapore filed an extradition request. In late November 1995, Mr Leeson gave up his fight against extradition, was later convicted of fraud, and sentenced to 6.5 years in a Singapore prison before being released in July 1999.

BCCI's administrators (KPMG) sued Coopers and Lybrand – both the London and Singapore offices were named in the law suit. They settled out of court soon after the trial began in 2001, for a sum of £65 million. In addition, an accounting watchdog (the Joint Disciplinary Scheme) fined Coopers and Lybrand for its role in the downfall of Barings. In April 2002, C&L appealed to a tribunal and lost, though the size of the fine imposed was reduced to £250 000. Of the complaints against two audit partners, one was dismissed but the other was upheld, though the size of the fine was reduced to £25 000 from £65 000. In June 2003, a High Court judge ruled that Deloitte and Touche (Singapore) was not liable for the £850 million in trading losses but was negligent in its audit work at Barings Future Singapore in 1992 and 1993. The fine of £1.5 million was well below the £130 million demanded by KPMG.

The next three cases provide additional examples of rogue trading, although these banks did not actually fail.

## 7.3.12. Daiwa Bank

In September 1995, a senior bond trader, Mr Toshihide Iguchi, lost just over $1.1 billion, over a 10-year period, while working for the New York branch of Daiwa Bank. He covered up the trading losses through the sale of securities stolen from customer accounts, which were replaced by forged securities. The losses remained undetected until Mr Iguchi confessed to Daiwa in July. Japan's Ministry of Finance had given the New York branch a clean bill of health in 1994. The branch had also been subject to joint regulatory scrutiny by the Federal Reserve Bank of New York and state banking authorities since 1991. The auditors in Japan (part of Ernst and Young International) did not conduct a separate audit of the New York branch, so failed to spot any problems. While the parent bank had sufficient capital to absorb the loss, American regulators were furious with Daiwa for a number of reasons.

- Iguchi had worked in the back office for many years before becoming a trader in 1983. However, he did not give up his back office duties. Regulators criticised Daiwa in 1993, and Daiwa had agreed to reorganise the bank to ensure separation of back and front offices. Traders would no longer report to Iguchi, as Head of Securities Custody. However, the bank failed to act on its promise, and Iguchi remained in this post from 1977 to 1995. Iguchi was effectively auditing his own accounts, giving him the opportunity to hide the losses.
- Daiwa used its hidden reserves to purchase and replace the securities that Iguchi had sold off.
- Daiwa management failed to report the losses for two months even though an official at Japan's Ministry of Finance had been informed of the problem in early August.

The bank faced several criminal charges but in a plea bargain, was fined $344 million. More serious, in November of 1995, Daiwa was ordered to cease US operations within 90 days. Sumitomo Bank purchased most of its US assets (worth $3.3 billion), and Daiwa sold its 15 US offices. In December 1996, Iguchi was given a four-year prison sentence and fined $2.6 million. In September 2000, eleven current and former Daiwa board members were ordered (by a Tokyo judge) to pay Daiwa $775 million in damages. The judgement was subsequently appealed.

## 7.3.13. Sumitomo Corporation

In June 1996, the UK Securities and Investment Board revealed that for over a decade, one of Sumitomo's copper traders, Yasuo Hamanaka, hid losses of $1.8 billion, which eventually rose to $2.6 billion. Problems began in 1985 when Saburo Shimizu, Hamanaka's boss, began forward trading on the London Metal Exchange forward market for copper. The trades were an unauthorised attempt to recover earlier losses on physical trades of copper. But the losses mounted to $60 million, at which point Mr Shimizu resigned. Hamanaka continued the trades, in an effort to recoup the losses. It is estimated he conducted up to $20 billion in unauthorised trades. Tried in Tokyo in 1997, Hamanaka pleaded guilty to charges of fraud and forgery.

## 7.3.14. Allied Irish Bank/Allfirst Bank

On 6 February 2002, Allied Irish Bank (AIB) announced it was to take a one-off charge of $520 million to cover losses from a suspected fraud of $750 million involving currency trades at the Baltimore headquarters of its subsidiary, Allfirst Bank. The total losses amounted to $691 million (£483 million) and were due to the illegal actions of John Rusnak, who joined the bank in 1993, and was later promoted to managing director in charge of foreign exchange trading.[42]

AIB gave a former Comptroller of the Currency, Eugene Ludwig, the job of investigating the events leading up to the losses, to report within 30 days. At the beginning of the report Ludwig comments that he considers this amount of time inadequate. Rusnak did not participate in the enquiry. According to the report, the fraud began in 1997 when Rusnak lost money on proprietary trading – using currency forwards to try and make profits from currency trades in yen, dollars and the euro. Ludwig describes these as one-way bets on which way a currency was supposed to move, when he was supposed to be spotting arbitrage opportunities between foreign exchange options and the spot and forward forex markets. To hide his losses, Rusnak:

- Used fictitious options.
- Took advantage of gaps in the bank's monitoring and control systems. For example:
- Rusnak used two bogus options, one involving the receipt of a large premium, the other paying out an identical amount, so there was no net cost to the bank. The first option expired on the day it was written, and Allfirst did not prepare reports on options that expired on the same date.
- Rusnak persuaded the back office that confirmation orders were not needed since they offset each other.
- The value at risk model used information from Rusnak's PC to compute its VaR. This meant Rusnak could manipulate the figures, making it look like the bogus options hedged the real options, thus lowering his VaR.

The true position became apparent when a supervisor in the back office noticed deals were not being confirmed. The back office staff spent the weekend trying to confirm trades in Asia but were unable to do so. Rusnak did not come to work on Monday 4 February.

The Ludwig report criticised senior bankers at AIB and Allfirst for failing to pay close attention to its proprietary trading operations at Allfirst, even after the OCC raised concerns about risk management procedures. The robustness of the controls for Allfirst's trading activities were not reviewed by the group risk management teams, and more generally there was a lack of effective controls in the proprietary trading area. Ludwig also noted the inferiority of the IT systems at Allfirst compared to AIB, but apparently this was part of a deliberate strategy to give Allfirst some independence, to avoid conveying the impression that head office was interfering unduly – thought to be the cause of the poor performance of European owned subsidiaries.

---

[42] Rusnak was hired from Chemical Bank by First Maryland Bancorp. In 1999, Allfirst was formed from the merger of First Maryland and Dauphin Deposit Corporation, which AIB owned.

Allfirst responded by sacking six Allfirst employees. Allfirst's President resigned a few months later, but offers of resignation by the CEO and Chairman were rejected by the Board of Directors. A number of changes were announced, including:

- Cessation of proprietary dealing in subsidiaries, to be centralised in Dublin.
- A new post was created to ensure risk was effectively managed across the AIB group.
- Treasury management to be centralised in Dublin.

In a plea bargain deal, Mr Rusnak pleaded guilty to one charge of bank fraud in October 2002, and was jailed for 7.5 years. There is no evidence he gained financially from these frauds (apart from bonus payments that were bigger than they would otherwise have been) – he was using them to cover up ever-increasing losses.

Though AIB's solvency was never in question, the losses represented 17.5% of their tier 1 capital, and reduced earnings by 60%. In September 2002, Allfirst was sold to M&T Banking Corporation for $886 million and a 22.5% stake in M&T. To appease shareholders angered by the fraud, half the cash from the sale was to be used to buy back AIB shares.

Barings, Daiwa, Sumitomo and AIB/Allfirst all suffered from rogue traders, which resulted in the UK's oldest merchant bank failing, eventually being reduced to a tiny part of the operations of a multinational bank, and another respected Japanese bank being barred from operating in the USA. Management was criticised for dereliction of duty of one sort or another. Perhaps the most lasting effect of these failures is the consternation rogue trading caused among members of the Basel Committee, and their subsequent attempt to include an explicit measure for operational risk in the Basel 2 risk assets ratio (see Chapter 4).

## 7.3.15. Canadian Bank Failures

During the autumn of 1985, five out of 14 Canadian domestic banks found themselves in difficulty. Two banks (Canadian Commercial and Northland) had to close. The problems of Canadian Commercial Bank (CCB), based in Edmonton, originated with its loan portfolio, which was concentrated in the real estate and energy sectors. A formal inspection in early 1982 revealed two-thirds of uncollected interest was on property loans and another 16% on energy related loans. In the summer of 1985 (after CCB had approached the authorities), government investigations revealed that 40% of the loan portfolio was marginal or unsatisfactory. To attract deposits, CCB had to pay above-average rates, as did other regional banks.

In March 1985, CCB informed the authorities it was in danger of collapse. Despite indications of trouble, the inspection system failed to identify the serious problems. A rescue package (CDN $225 million) was put together, the six largest banks contributing $60 million. This action failed to restore the confidence of depositors and contagion spread to other smaller regional banks in Canada; depositors (for example, municipal treasurers) who had been attracted by their higher interest rates began to withdraw their deposits on a large scale, as did the big banks that had participated in the rescue package. The Bank of Canada responded by granting short-term loans to cover these deposit withdrawals but soon had to extend this facility to the Calgary based Northland Bank, because of contagion induced runs on this bank. The Northland Bank had been receiving liquidity support from the major private banks since 1983, but the agreement ran out and the bank turned to the Bank of Canada for support at the same time as the CCB. The two banks were forced to close in September 1985, after the Bank of Canada withdrew its support because of a supervisory report (by the Inspector General of Banks), which indicated insolvency at both banks because of weak loan portfolios.

Two other banks, Mercantile and Morguard, were merged with larger institutions. Mercantile Bank was a Montreal based bank, in which Citicorp had a 24% interest. This bank was involved in wholesale bank business. The bank began to experience trouble attracting deposits. The Bank of Canada did not intervene but persuaded the six large banks to provide short-term loans to Mercantile. A few weeks later, it was purchased by the Montreal based National Bank. In November 1985, Morguard Bank was taken over by California's Security Pacific Bank.

A fifth Canadian bank, Continental, experienced a serious run on deposits. Although this bank had a healthy loan portfolio, it had suffered from low rates of profitability: the return on assets was 0.29% in the 12 months to 31 October 1985. The Bank of Canada and the six largest banks granted Continental CDN $2.9 billion in standby credit lines when it experienced a run, which proved to be short-lived. Some depositors returned after the bank launched a campaign to restore confidence, which included an examination of its loan portfolio by 25 officials from the big six banks.

## 7.4. The Determinants of Bank Failure: A Qualitative Review

The previous section reviewed the details of a large number of bank failures from around the world. These cases make it possible to make a qualitative assessment of the causes of bank failure. The list of causes as they appear below is for ease of exposition – it is rare to find a single cause for bank failure; rather, there are a number of contributing factors. For example, poor management can be the source of a weak loan portfolio or sloppy supervision, and regulatory forbearance can make conditions ripe for rogue traders and fraud.

### 7.4.1. Poor Management of Assets

Weak asset management, consisting of a weak loan book, usually because of excessive exposure in one or more sectors, even though regulators set exposure limits. When these are breached, the regulators may not know it or may fail to react. Examples of excessive loan exposures that regulators failed to control effectively are numerous. Perhaps the most glaring example is the failure of US commercial banks in the south-west, with a similar episode a few years later in the north-east which regulators (and managers) failed to spot, despite a similar build-up of bad loan portfolios in the south-west a few years earlier.

It is possible to look at almost any western country and find examples of excessive exposure by banks in one particular market, which eventually led to failure. In other cases, such as the collapse of Barings (February 1995), the failure was not caused by the excessive loan exposure, but by uncovered exposure in the derivatives market. Usually, the regulatory authorities knew guidelines (or rules) on exposure were being exceeded but took no action. Internal and external auditors also failed to detect any problem. All of these countries tightly regulate their banking sectors, yet no system has managed to resolve this problem. In the USA, the case of the thrifts illustrates how far regulators are prepared to go to protect a sector, even though such action prolongs the pain and raises resolution costs. Japan (discussed in Chapter 8) provides another example where, in the early stages of the crisis, the regulator actually made things worse. In other countries, such as Canada, the authorities seemed to be successful in containing the problem, so it was limited to just a few banks.

Weak asset management often extends to the collateral or security backing the loan, because the value of the collateral is highly correlated with the performance of the borrowing sector. In the case of the Continental Illinois Bank, new loans had been secured by leases on underdeveloped properties, where oil and gas reserves had not been proven. Texan state banks are another example. Key Texan banks – namely First Republic Bank (1988), First City (1988) and MCorp (1989) – required large amounts of federal support; some were merged with healthy banks. Though there were other contributory factors to their problems, a key one was banks lending to the Texan oil and gas industry and accepting Texan real estate as collateral, and, to add insult to injury, increasing lending to the property sector when energy prices began to decline. Banks (and regulators) seemed oblivious of the fact that if the energy sector collapsed, plummeting real estate prices would soon follow. The lessons of the south-west appeared to have been ignored by banks in the north-east, resulting in some notable bank failures in that region.

## 7.4.2. Managerial Problems

Deficiencies in the management of failing banks is a contributing factor in virtually all cases. The Crédit Lyonnais case is a classic example of how poor management can get a bank into serious trouble. It was not discussed in the previous section because it is the subject of a case study in Chapter 10, but a brief review is provided here. Jean Yves Harberer was a typical French meritocrat. He earned an excellent reputation at the Treasury, heading it in his forties. In 1982, after the newly elected socialists had nationalised key banks, President Mitterand asked Harberer to take charge of Paribas, where he was responsible for one of the worst fiascos in Paribas' history. Removed from office when Paribas was re-privatised in 1986, Harberer was appointed chief executive of Crédit Lyonnais (CL), a bank which had been state owned since the end of the Second World War. Harberer's principal goal was growth at any cost, to transform the bank into a universal, pan-European bank. This rapid growth caused CL to accumulate a large portfolio of weak loans, which could not survive the combination of high interest rates and a marked decline in the French property market. By 1993, Harberer had been dismissed and made the head of Crédit National, but the post was terminated after the CL 1993 results were published later that year.

Though weak management was the key problem, it is difficult to disentangle it from government interference in the operations of the bank. The government, through its direct and indirect equity holdings, had a tradition of intervention by bureaucrats in the operational affairs of state owned firms, commonly known as *dirigisme*. It is consistent with French industrial policy where a proactive government role in the economy is thought to be better than leaving it to the mercy of free market forces. Crédit Lyonnais did not escape; the most well-known example was when Prime Minister Cresson asked CL to invest FF 2.5 billion in Usinor-Sacilor, in exchange for a 10% stake in the ailing state owned steel company. By late 1992, 28% of CL's capital base was made up of shares in state owned firms, many of them in financial difficulty.[43] The problem escalated over time because the bank's fate was linked to the deteriorating performance of these firms.

By March 1994, the first of four rescue plans was announced, and the government is committed to privatising Crédit Lyonnais by 2000.[44] It is difficult to calculate the total cost of the bailout because of other aspects of the rescue plans, including creating a "bad bank", which took on CL's bad loans, thereby removing them from the bank's balance sheet. However, estimates of the total cost of resolving CL's problems range between $20 and $30 billion (see case study in Chapter 10).

Although state interference in CL partly explains why the bank got into such difficulties, it is one of the best examples where poor management, based on a strategy of growth at any expense, is the main reason for the bank ending up effectively insolvent.

Continental Illinois, a US bank, would have collapsed in 1984 had it not been for a government rescue. Its problems, too, can be traced back to managerial deficiencies. Managers were unaware one of the senior officers at Continental had a personal interest in Penn Square – he had arranged a personal loan of half a million dollars. There was no change in the internal credit review process, even though there had been repeated criticisms by the Comptroller of the Currency, one of several bank regulators in the United States. Furthermore, Continental's internal audit reports on Penn Square never reached senior management. Finally, management's strategy was growth by assets despite very narrow margins. Continental also relied on the wholesale (interbank) markets for most of its funding, partly explained by an Illinois rule which restricted a bank's branches to one.

Barings was brought down by a "rogue trader", but the underlying problem was bad senior management. For example, head office allowed a trader in Singapore to run the front and back offices simultaneously even though a 1994 internal audit report had recommended Mr Leeson stop managing the back office. His simultaneous control of the two offices allowed him to hide losses in the "5-eights" account. Similar circumstances prevailed at Daiwa's New York office. Managers at Barings failed to question how huge weekly profits could be made on arbitrage, which is a high volume, low margin business. Finally, senior management sanctioned a huge outflow of capital from Barings, London. For example, the bank transferred £569 million (its total capital was £540 million) to Barings Singapore in the first two months of 1995.

Senior management were also criticised in the Daiwa and AIB rogue trader cases. In 1993, two years before Iguchi's confession, management assured US regulators that the back and front office activities at the New York office would be separated but failed to do so, leaving Iguchi as a trader with back office responsibilities. The Ludwig Report (commissioned by

---

[43] By forcing state owned banks to invest in these industries, the state continued to play an indirect role in the management of these firms, even if they were privatised.

[44] The rescue plans led to a formal complaint of unfair competition by other French and European banks. In response, the European Commission agreed to the rescue, conditional upon Crédit Lyonnais being privatised by 2000.

Allied Irish Bank) criticised senior managers at AIB and Allfirst for failing to improve the proprietary trading operations after the Comptroller of the Currency raised concerns about the risk management systems at Allfirst. Thus, in these three major cases, senior management was responsible for sanctioning operations that allowed rogue traders to thrive. Yet the Basel Committee is of the view that rogue trading is one of the reasons for the explicit treatment of operational risk in the Basel 2 risk assets ratio (see Chapter 4).

Mr Leeson subsequently claimed his actions were driven by the imminent decision on bonuses. Had he been able to keep up the charade for only a few more days, he would earn a large bonus, along with his office colleagues. The size of the bonus was a function of net earnings, so Mr Leeson had every incentive to hide losses until they were paid. There have been other instances where bonus driven behaviour was at the expense of the bank in question. For example, there is a tendency to promote individuals associated with innovation or rapid growth in assets. Though this problem also exists in non-financial sectors, it has more serious consequences in the financial sector because of the maturity structure of the assets, both on- and off-balance sheet – what looks profitable today may not be so in the future. It suggests management should seek out more incentive compatible bonus schemes. For example, group responsibility would be encouraged by group bonus schemes. Salomons introduced bonuses determined by a specified post-tax return on profits. A percentage is withheld should the firm do badly in subsequent years. The result was the loss of some of their top performing traders to other firms which continued with schemes to reward the individual. Even ING, the Dutch concern that bought Barings after its collapse, had to pay out bonuses totalling $100 million to prevent Barings staff from going to rival firms.

Senior bank management are also prone to mimicry, copying untested financial innovations by other banks in an effort to boost profits. Again, the source of the problem is asymmetric information in this sector. One consequence is that whereas in other sectors, managers strive to differentiate their product, bankers seem to rush to copy the actions of other banks, the success of which is attributed to financial innovations.

### 7.4.3. Fraud

Benston (1973) noted that 66% of US bank failures from 1959 to 1961 were due to fraud and irregularities, a percentage backed (and indeed higher, at 88%) by Hill (1975) for the period 1960–74. According to Benston and Kaufman (1986), the Comptroller of the Currency cited fraud or law-breaking as the most frequent cause of bank failures in the USA between 1865 and 1931, and the FDIC reported that about a quarter of bank failures in the period 1931–58 were due to financial irregularities by bank officers.

Barker and Holdsworth (1994) cited a study published by a US government house committee,[45] which found about 50% of bank failures and 25% of thrift failures between 1980 and mid-1983 were principally due to fraud. The authors also report the findings of a US interagency working group: fraud was present in a substantial percentage of failures between 1984 and the first half of 1986.

Hard evidence of fraud is apparent in the failures of Allfirst, the Bank of Credit and Commerce International, Bankhaus Herstatt, Banco Ambrosiano Barings, Daiwa and Penn

---

[45] The House Committee on Government Operations.

Square. There were suggestions of fraud in relation to the collapse of Johnson Matthey Bankers, but no one was ever prosecuted. However, it is rare to be able to identify fraud as the principal cause of bank failure – even BCCI had a low quality loan book. In the case of Barings, the Leeson fraud was only possible because of problems with senior management. In Japan (see Chapter 8), there were Mafia links to property firms which borrowed from banks and coops. Illegal activities have been proved in only a handful of cases, though they are thought to be widespread. In Heffernan (2003 – see Table 7.3), using an international database of bank failures, there is only one incident of fraud.

Securing a conviction can be problematic because of the fine line between fraud and bad management. The "looting" hypothesis (Akerlof and Romer, 1993 – see Chapter 1) illustrates this very point. According to Akerlof and Romer, many thrift managers bought risky debt (junk bonds) to profit from short-term high interest payments, when they knew default was likely in the longer term. The authorities had relaxed accounting rules in the early 1980s to encourage wider diversification, which meant managers could move into little known product areas. Finally, thrift managers took advantage of the system. In the USA, deposits of up to $100 000 (per bank) are insured – the thrifts knew they could attract customers by offering high deposit rates, thereby contributing to short-term profitability.

## 7.4.4. The Role of Regulators

Bank examiners, auditors and other regulators missed important signals and/or were guilty of "regulatory forbearance", that is, putting the interests of the regulated bank ahead of the taxpayer. In many cases of failure, subsequent investigation shows stated exposure limits were exceeded, with the knowledge of the regulator. Examples include Johnson Matthey Bankers, Banco Ambrosiano, most of the US thrifts and Barings.

Like all firms, banks pay for external private auditing of their accounts. In every western country banks are also subject to audits by regulators. For example, in the United States and Japan, banks are regularly examined by more than one independent regulator. In the UK, formal examination was introduced relatively recently;[46] before then, the role of the private auditor assumes greater importance. However, Johnson Matthey Bankers, BCCI and Barings had been examined by private external auditors. Some firms are being sued by these banks' liquidators for signing off a bank in good health when, in fact, it wasn't. The official report[47] into the collapse of Barings criticised Coopers and Lybrand, London for failing to detect the discrepancy between the large outflow of funds to Singapore and the claim that the Singapore office was responsible for three-quarters of the bank's profits. Coopers London deny responsibility because the bank collapsed before they could conduct their 1994 audit, and it had questioned the documentation for a £50 million receivable. However, Leeson had been running fictitious accounts for two years. Furthermore, Coopers Singapore had audited the subsidiary in 1994 but did not raise any concerns.

---

[46] In the UK, formal examinations by the regulator are undertaken by the Financial Services Authority, created in 1998. The Bank of England did not carry out formal examinations but did monitor banks very closely. See Chapter 5 for more detail.

[47] The Board of Banking Supervision Report (Bank of England), July 1995.

These failures suggest the presence of communication difficulties between the auditor and the Bank of England. Despite official reports calling for a resolution of the problem (after Johnson Matthey, BCCI and Barings), little action was taken. Since the creation of the Financial Services Authority, the role of the auditor has been clarified and strengthened (see Chapter 5). However, countries with multiple regulators conducting regular examinations seem to systematically either ignore or miss important signals of trouble. The behaviour of US regulators during the thrift/commercial bank failures is a case in point. Largely in response to that period, Congress passed the Financial Institutions Reform, Recovery and Enforcement (1989) and the FDIC Improvement Acts (1991), which have gone some way to tighten the loopholes and provide regulators with a clear set of rules they must follow from the time a bank shows any sign of difficulty.

The US thrifts provide one of the best examples of regulatory forbearance. In 1981–82, the Federal Home Loan Bank Board (since abolished) tried to ease the problems of the thrifts by allowing these firms to report their results using the Regulatory Accounting Rules, which were more lenient than the Generally Accepted Accounting Rules. They also lowered net worth requirements for thrifts in 1980 and again in 1982. The Federal Savings and Loans Insurance Corporation (FSLIC – also since abolished) issued income capital certificates which were treated as equity, so the thrifts could use them to supplement their net worth. Effectively, the FSLIC was using its own credit to purchase equity in insolvent thrifts. Thus, both institutions had a vested interest in keeping thrifts going long after they were insolvent. It was this sort of activity which prompted US legislators to impose a legal requirement on all regulators to adopt a "least cost approach" (see page 254 for more detail).

There is also evidence of regulatory forbearance in the 1984 Continental Illinois case. The Comptroller of the Currency failed to follow up its own criticism of Continental's internal review process and concentration in wholesale funding. The regulator also denied newspaper reports in May 1984 that Continental faced collapse, even though it was true. However, had it admitted the bank was in trouble, it may not have given the authorities time to put together a rescue package.

A final problem relates to confusion over which regulator is in charge. For example, BCCI was a Luxembourg Holding Company. UK operations went through BCCI SA, a Luxembourg bank subsidiary of the holding company. The Bank of England argued it was not the lead regulator because BCCI was headquartered in Luxembourg. Under the Basel Concordat (1975, revised 1983), the principal regulator was the Luxembourg Monetary Institute, even though 98% of its activities took place outside its jurisdiction. In 1987, in an attempt to resolve the problem, the Luxembourg Monetary Institute, together with regulators from Britain, Switzerland and Spain, formed an unofficial College of Regulators for BCCI. However, hindsight showed that the College proved unequal to its task, largely because of the massive web of subterfuges and intersubsidiary transactions, involving many jurisdictions, that concealed the systematic looting of depositors' funds.

## 7.4.5. Too Big to Fail

The policy of "too big to fail" applies in all countries, to some degree. In France and Japan, the safety net was close to 100%, (e.g. allowing only small banks to fail; nationalising large insolvent banks), though recently, the authorities have adopted a tougher line. In the three Nordic countries that encountered severe problems (see Chapter 8), banks were nationalised and later, largely privatised. In Britain and most other countries, the regulators operate a policy of deliberate ambiguity with respect to bank rescues. Lifeboat rescues, where regulators pressure healthy banks for capital injections before agreeing to organise and contribute to the bailout, became the norm. Lifeboats have largely replaced the traditional lender of last resort,[48] which involved the central bank (as regulator or via the regulator) providing a very large proportion (up to 100%) of the capital required to shore up a bank. Even though the central banks try to operate a policy of ambiguity, it is normally clear to analysts which banks will be bailed out. For example, Fitch,[49] a private rating agency, provides its clients with a "legal rating" for each bank, indicating the likelihood, on a scale of A to E, of a bank being rescued by the authorities. In the UK, the Bank of England tried to put together lifeboats even when it was unlikely the failure would have systemic effects. Examples include Johnson Matthey Bankers and Barings. In the case of Barings, however, the Bank failed to assemble a lifeboat. This outcome may indicate an increasing reluctance on the part of healthy banks to accede to requests by the central bank, unless they think their own banks might be threatened by the failure.

Before the introduction of the "least cost approach" for dealing with bank failures, US regulators successfully launched a lifeboat rescue of Continental Illinois in 1984, and several large (e.g. Texan) banks. The argument in favour of bailing out key banks is to prevent runs and systemic failure of the banking system, but it creates moral hazard problems: managers have an incentive to make the bank big by expanding the balance sheet, it aggravates looting tendencies, and can contribute to regulatory forbearance, points discussed at length elsewhere. It effectively gives the large banks a competitive advantage over the smaller ones. It also means supervisors may concentrate on the health of these banks, at the expense of smaller banks, though the Bank of England's liquidity support during the small banks' crisis is evidence to the contrary.

## 7.4.6. Clustering

Looking at failures across a number of cases and countries, there appears to be a clustering effect, that is, bank failures in a country tend to be clustered around a few years, rather than being spread evenly through time. Looking at US commercial bank failures as a percentage of healthy banks in the period 1934–91, the annual average was 0.38% from 1934 to 1939 but did not rise above 0.08% between 1940 and 1981. In 1981, it jumped to 0.29%, rising steadily to peak at 1.68% in 1988.[50] Other nations have experienced these clusters,

---

[48] A lender of last resort is still used to inject liquidity into fragile economies, when systemic collapse threatens. For example, on Black Monday (October 1987), when stock markets around the world appeared to be going into freefall, the central banks of most western countries injected liquidity to prevent the world economy from slipping into depression. Likewise, when the UK withdrew from the Exchange Rate Mechanism (September 1992) and Barings failed (February 1995), the Bank of England stood ready to inject liquidity should there be a run on shares. See Chapter 8 for an extensive discussion of the role of the LLR.

[49] Formerly Fitch IBCA and before that, IBCA.

[50] *Source*: White (1991), table 1.

though comparable figures are not available. In Spain, the period 1978–83 saw a total of 48 out of 109 banks "fail"; the central bank rescued three, 10 banks were taken over, and 35 entered the Deposit Guarantee Fund. In Norway (see Chapter 7), 22 banks were the subject of state intervention between 1988 and 1991, after a post-war period free of bank failures. State support of problem banks also occurred in Canada (1985) and in Japan. Japan's banking problems coincided with the worst, prolonged recession/depression in the post-war era. Britain is well known for highly publicised failures: Johnson Matthey Bankers (1984), BCCI (1991) and Barings (1995), which appear to be isolated incidents over time. However, the secondary banking crisis (1973–74) and the small banks crisis from 1991 to 1994 are consistent with the clustering.

The presence of a herd instinct among depositors and investors (or a contagion effect) helps to explain a run on several banks over a relatively short period, and more recently, this has been coupled with a flight to quality or to banks thought to be too big to fail. However, it does not explain why banking problems can last for up to a decade, suggesting macroeconomic factors are at work.

A related reason for clustering may be the failure of timely intervention by the government/regulatory authorities.[51] The initial reaction of regulators to the problems with US thrifts is an example. Here, a combination of new reforms which allowed these firms to diversify into areas where they had little expertise and relaxation of accounting and other rules certainly prolonged the length of the thrifts crisis. Also recall that in the early 1990s, the Bank of England was quick to intervene to (successfully) stop the spread of contagion from small banks to the wider banking sector. Liquidity was given to some banks, but 25 others failed.

Japan provides another example of a potentially complex link between the absence of timely intervention and macroeconomic factors. Though the stock market collapsed in 1989, there were no immediate injections of liquidity into the economy, and government regulators discouraged banks from provisioning for or writing off bad debt in the early years. This and other factors contributed to a decade long recession, including the collapse (and nationalisation) of some key banks, threatening the soundness of the financial system. The government succumbed to pressure for an overhaul of the financial system by the second half of the 1990s. The result was the announcement of "Big Bang" in 1996, with the reforms to be in place by 2001. The authorities also agreed to blanket deposit insurance of depositors, though it is due to be phased out. Despite these changes, the problems persisted, creating a serious financial crisis, which is discussed at length in Chapter 8.

## 7.4.7. Miscellaneous Factors

The case reviews have revealed a number of factors which do not easily slot into any of the section headings. Gowland (1994) raised the possibility that ownership structure affects the probability of bank failure. He suggested that the decline in mutual ownership of thrifts is a partial explanation for the thrift industry crisis. In a mutual organisation, profits are not paid out to shareholders but are accumulated as reserves. When a mutual firm is sold to

---

[51] I am grateful to an anonymous referee for this point.

shareholders, the reserves become the property of the new shareholders. Since the reserves form part of the funds used to finance risky ventures, investment in relatively risky loans appeared to offer an attractive risk reward combination. Mutuals are more likely to play safe, and know more about their borrowers. Gowland observed that over 60% of the soon to fail thrifts were shareholder owned, compared to just 25% of mutuals.

Second, banking structure can be a contributory factor in the presence of other conditions. In the southwestern USA in the 1980s, the changes in regulations that allowed S&Ls to compete with the banks for retail business put the banks under greater pressure to find new business, which may be one explanation for their eagerness to lend in the property market, especially the commercial area – to keep market share.

In the USA, an unbalanced deposit base was a contributory factor because regulations have limited access to funding. For example, the savings and loans industry, even after the reforms, had restrictions on accessing the wholesale markets; Continental Illinois had to rely on relatively high cost short-term wholesale funding because of branch banking restrictions in Illinois. First Republic Bank in Texas suffered the same problem but to a lesser degree, because 20% of its deposits came from the wholesale markets and 40% from regional companies. Other US banks faced similar branching restrictions, but did not use the CI route to overcome the problem, relying instead on more innovative methods of funding through bank holding companies, Edge Act banks and non-bank banks.

Deposit protection schemes normally cover the small depositor with a view to preventing bank runs. Several of the cases demonstrate the necessity of 100% deposit insurance, if the objective is to eliminate bank runs. However, such a scheme creates moral hazard problems because banks have an incentive to assume greater risks than they would in the absence of deposit insurance, and depositors have less reason to monitor banks. Eliminating or "privatising" deposit insurance would force a bank with a portfolio of assets showing a comparatively high variance in rate of return to pay higher interest on deposits, or to pay higher deposit insurance premia than banks with less risky portfolios. The recent introduction of risk based deposit insurance premia by the FDIC in the USA is an attempt to reduce the moral hazard problems created by deposit insurance. Co-insurance (an option in the EU scheme but not the US one) encourages depositors to scrutinise bank activities more closely.

Finally, lack of experience with relatively new financial products, especially if they have a global dimension, can be a contributory factor. Bankhaus Herstatt and Franklin National Bank collapsed[52] in 1974 after huge losses arising from trading in the (relatively new) foreign exchange markets. The US thrifts had little experience with junk bonds or mortgage backed securities but used them to boost short-term profits. Barings management did not seem to understand that arbitrage would yield modest profits and not normally involve the lodging of funds on an immense scale. It appears that Mssrs Iguchi, Hamanaka and Rusnak did not make personal gains from their rogue trading activities (apart from bonuses), indicating they made mistakes because they did not really understand the markets, then covered up their losses to avoid loss of face and dismissal.

---

[52] What was left of Franklin National Bank was taken over by a consortium of European banks. Bankhaus Herstatt was closed.

To conclude this section, numerous contributory factors to bank failure have been identified in this review. The advantage of a case study approach is the detailed background provided, which is helpful for the practitioner. However, the discussion itself illustrates that most failures are explained by an interaction of the various causes listed above. More precise answers, such as the relative importance of these factors, can be supplied by the quantitative analysis. The drawback is that it is not possible to test all the causes identified in this section. However, having used econometric analysis to identify significant variables, the two approaches can be brought together to form some tentative conclusions as to the causes of bank failures.

## 7.5. Bank Failure: Quantitative Models

Qualitative reviews of bank failure provide some insight into what causes a bank to fail, but these ideas need to be subjected to more rigorous testing. Any econometric model of bank failure must incorporate the basic point that insolvency is a discrete outcome at a certain point in time. The outcome is binary: either the bank fails or it does not. The discussion in the previous section shows that banks (or, in Japan, almost the entire banking sector) are often bailed out by the state before they are allowed to fail. For this reason, the standard definition of failure, insolvency (negative net worth), is still extended to include all unhealthy banks which are bailed out as a result of state intervention, using any of the methods outlined in earlier sections, such as the creation of a "bad bank" which assumes all the troubled bank's unhealthy assets and becomes the responsibility of the state, and a merger of the remaining parts with a healthy bank.

Much of the methodology employed here is borrowed from the literature on corporate bankruptcy, where a firm is either solvent (with a positive net worth) or not. In situations where the outcome is binary, two econometric methods commonly used are discriminant or logit/probit analysis. Multiple discriminant analysis is based on the assumption that all quantifiable, pertinent data may be placed in two or more statistical populations. Discriminant analysis estimates a function (the "rule") which can assign an observation to the correct population. Applied to bank failure, a bank is assigned to either an insolvent population (as defined above) or a healthy one. Historical economic data are used to derive the *discriminant function* that will discriminate against banks by placing them in one of two populations. Early work on corporate bankruptcy made use of this method. However, since Martin (1977) demonstrated that discriminant analysis is just a special case of logit analysis, most of the studies reported in Table 7.1 use the multinomial logit model.

The logit model has a binary outcome. Either the bank fails, $p = 1$, or it does not, $p = 0$. The right-hand side of the regression contains the explanatory variables, giving the standard equation:

$$z = \beta_0 + \boldsymbol{\beta}'\mathbf{x} + \varepsilon \tag{7.1}$$

where

$p = 1$ if $z > 0$
$p = 0$ if $z \leq 0$

$z = \log[p/(1-p)]$

$\beta_0$ : a constant term

$\beta'$ : the vector of coefficients on the explanatory variables

$\mathbf{x}$ : the vector of explanatory variables

$\varepsilon$ : the error term

It is assumed $\text{var}(\varepsilon) = 1$, and the cumulative distribution of the error term is logistic; were it to follow a normal distribution, the model is known as probit.

Readers who are unfamiliar with logit analysis will find it explained in any good textbook on introductory econometrics. However, an intuitive idea can be obtained by referring to Figure 7.1. In a simple application of equation (7.1), if $\mathbf{x}$ consists of just *one* explanatory variable (e.g. capital adequacy), the logit model becomes a two-dimensional sigmoid shaped curve, as shown. The probability of failure is on the vertical axis and the explanatory variable, in this case capital adequacy, is on the horizontal axis. Recall, in the logit model, that a bank either fails ($p = 1$) or it does not ($p = 0$). As the bank's capital adequacy (which could be measured in a number of ways) falls (approaching 0 in Figure 7.1), the probability of bank failure rises. Note the difference between the logistic curve and the straight line of a standard least squares regression.

A potential problem arises from the use of the multinomial logit function in estimating bank failure. These studies rely on a cross-section of failed banks either in a given year, or over a number of years. They are using panel data and, for this reason, an alternative model could be a panel data logit specification first described by Chamberlain (1980). The "conditional" logit model for panel data is:

$$z = \alpha_i + \beta'\mathbf{x} + \varepsilon \qquad (7.2)$$

**Figure 7.1  The logit model.**

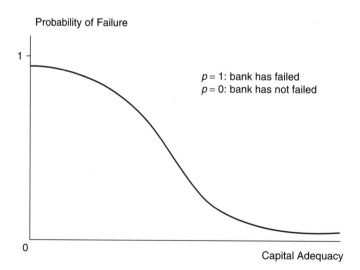

Probability of Failure

1

$p = 1$: bank has failed
$p = 0$: bank has not failed

0

Capital Adequacy

where

$\alpha_i$ : captures individual group effects, and is separate for each group; i = failed or non-failed

$\boldsymbol{\beta'x}$ : as in equation (7.1)

Chamberlain shows that if a multinomial logit regression is used on panel data, and the number of observations per group is small (except in the USA, where the number of failed banks was very high in the early 1930s and throughout the 1980s), the result is inconsistent estimates, arising from omitted variable bias. Furthermore, the $\alpha_i$ allow a test for group effects, addressing the question of whether there is something unique to the group of bank failures. In equation (7.2), the $\alpha_i$ are not considered independent of $\mathbf{x}$. Heffernan (2003), using a Hausman test,[53] shows that the multinomial logit model employed by most studies is superior to a conditional logit model where the $\alpha_i$ are different for the failed and healthy groups.

Table 7.3 summarises the results of a selection of econometric studies testing for the determinants of bank failure, most of which use a logit model, though some use discriminant analysis.[54] The paper by Cebula (1999) employs linear regression analysis, where the dependent variable is the percentage of banks that failed in a given year. Most of the studies are based on US data, mainly because the sample of bank failures is large enough to allow quantitative tests to be conducted. This means caution should be used when drawing inferences from the results from other countries, because, as was noted in Chapter 5, the structure of the American banking system differs from most other countries. An added problem is the difficulty in testing for the effects of macroeconomic variables when only one country is studied. Two of the studies, Heffernan (2003) and Logan (2000), draw on, respectively, international and British data.

These studies test a large number of variables, creating the potential for multicollinearity problems, arising from lack of independence among the variables, making a stepwise (forward and backward) procedure appropriate. A series of regressions is run, and variables are dropped from or added to the model one at a time based on their individual significance (*t*-ratios) and their contribution to the overall fit of the model, as measured by pseudo or McFadden $R^2$ (M$R^2$).[55]

As can be seen from column (5) of Table 7.3, numerous measures of profitability, liquidity, capital adequacy (total loans/total equity capital) and loan quality (reserve for possible loan losses/total loans) were found to be significant with the expected sign in several of the studies reported. In 9 of the 11 studies, the coefficient on a profitability measure (e.g. net income/total assets) is significant and negative: as net income rises, the probability of bank failure declines.

---

[53] The Hausman test (see Hausman, 1978 and Madalla, 1988) was developed to test for specification error, and is used to compare a given model with a hypothesised alternative. If there is no misspecification, there exists a consistent and asymptotically efficient estimator, but that estimator is biased and inconsistent if the model is misspecified.

[54] Martin (1977) showed the linear discriminant function to be a special form of the more general logistic function. See Chapter 6 for a discussion of discriminant analysis.

[55] The McFadden $R^2$ is a pseudo $R^2$ and is defined as {1 − (log-likelihood)/(restricted (slopes = 0) log-likelihood)}. See McFadden (1974).

**Table 7.3   Summary of Results from Econometric Studies of Bank Failure**

| Author | Country, Years of Studies | Sample Size | Method | Variables found to be Statistically Significant with Expected sign* | Remarks |
|---|---|---|---|---|---|
| Altman (1977) | US thrift failures, 1966–73 | 65 S&Ls with serious problems, 65 with temporary problems, 65 healthy | Discriminant analysis | Net op income/gross income (−), net worth/TA (−), property owned/TA (−), earned surplus/TA (−), TL/TS (+), borrowed money/total savings (+), FHLB advances/net worth (+) | |
| Sinkey (1975) | 110 US bank failures, 1972, 1973 | Each failed bank matched with a healthy bank; financial ratios 1969–72 | Discriminant analysis | K-adequacy: loans/(K + reserves for bad debt) (−) Loan volume: loans/TA (+) Efficiency: op expenses/op income (+) | |
| Martin (1977) | US banks, 1970–76 | 58 failed banks out of 5700 Fed member banks | Logit | Net income/TA (−), commercial loans/TL, gross charge-offs/net operating income (+), capital/risky assets (−) | |
| Avery and Hanweck (1984) | US, 1979–83 | 100 failed commercial banks, 1190 healthy banks | Logit | After tax earnings on assets (−), K/A (−), L/A (+), % of commercial and industrial loans (+) | |
| Pantalone and Platt (1987) | US banks, 1983–84 | 113 failed banks, 226 healthy banks | Logit | NI/TA (−), equity K/TA (−), TL/TA (+), % change in residential construction (+) | Authors looked at these ratios 12, 18 and 24 months prior to bank failure and found them to be significant, though the % change in residential construction was only significant 18 months prior to failure |
| Espahbodi (1991) | US banks, 1983 | 48 failed banks, 48 healthy banks | Logit | Loan revenue/total income, interest income/total op income, interest paid on deposits/total op. Income(total time + savings deposits)/total demand deposits: all (−) | Various measures of liquidity, capital adequacy, efficiency, loan quality, loan volume were not found to be significant |

| Study | Sample | Sample details | Method | Variables | Comments |
|---|---|---|---|---|---|
| Barker and Holdsworth (1994) | US banks, 1986–91 | 859 failed and 12 364 non-failed banks | Logit | Concentration of real estate loans (+) ("risk taking"), systemic factors (−) (e.g. condition of local real estate market) | Try to test for fraud – loans to insiders was + and significant |
| Cebula (1999) | US banks, 1963–91 | % of failed banks each year – dependent variable | OLS | Increases with competition in the early 1980s, real cost of deposits, increased deposit insurance; falls with: K/A, real interest rate, real GDP growth rate | One of several studies which find that the bank failure rate increased when the FDIC raised DI from $40 000 to $100 000 in 1980 |
| Hwang et al. (1997) | US, 1985–88 | 131 to 819 failed banks, depending on year, about 500 failed banks each year | Logit by year | Equity K (−), profitability (−), liquidity (−), past-due loans increase (+) | Tested 48 financial variables in all. Found that the significant variables varied with each year, suggesting instability in the contributing factors |
| Logan (2000) | UK banks: 25 small banks failed between 1991 and 1994, matched with surviving banks | | Logit | Loan growth in the year to 1991 (credit risk −), net interest income (+), liquidity risk (short-term assets less short-term liabilities, −), profits (−), leverage (−) | The more leverage a bank has, the lower the probability of failure. These banks rely on wholesale deposits, therefore an indication of market discipline – if thought to be weak, they can't get the capital that would allow them to increase their leverage |
| Heffernan (2003) | International – Aus, Fin, Fra, Ita, Nor, Sp, Sw, UK, 1988–92 | 36 healthy banks, 19 failed banks (choice restricted to banks on FitchIBCA database) | Logit | Net income/TA (−), internal K generation (−) liquidity (−), loan losses (−), bank size (−), growth rate of assets (−), inflation (+), real exchange rate (−), real interest rate (−), IBCA rating (−) | K/A significant (−) in equations where NI/TA was not used, variables reported in previous column estimated in different equations, see text for more comment. Only one case of fraud in the sample: Barings |

*For those papers using discriminant analysis, the variables are chosen when fewer variables reduce accuracy but adding other variables does not improve accuracy (see Chapter 6). K: capital, TA: total assets, TL: total loans, TS: total savings, DI: deposit insurance, FHLB: Federal Home Loan Bank Board.

Measures of capital adequacy feature in 8 of the 11 studies. Martin's early study (1977) is one of the few that used a measure of capital to risky assets. The Basel 1 ratio requirement did not take effect until 1993, making it too early for it to be tested in these studies. But even the ratio of capital to assets, unweighted for risk, appears significant: as capital adequacy rises, the probability of failure declines.

Loan growth rates or loan losses also feature (though studies use different measures), suggesting that too rapid a growth rate in loans will raise the probability of failure. Concentration of loans in real estate, or loans to insiders (which one study treats as a proxy for fraud) was also significantly positive. However, Logan found lower loan growth rates made banks more likely to fail. He argues this is consistent with both demand and supply side factors. On the demand side, borrowers from banks that eventually failed may have suffered more under recession than firms at healthy banks, suggesting poorer screening by the failed banks. On the supply side, weaker banks may be writing off past loans, concentrating staff resources on firms in trouble rather than actively seeking loans, or problems with funding. Logan notes that the deposits of the failed group increased by 1.1% compared to 10% for the survivor group over the same period. The median risk assets ratio was about the minimum required – so capital constraints do not appear to be a factor. In Heffernan (2003), the coefficient on loan losses was negative and nearly significant at the 95% confidence level in the first seven equations. At first this result may appear counterintuitive, but it may be that banks which set aside reserves are explicitly acknowledging loan loss problems and take appropriate action, thereby avoiding failure.

In a minority of studies, other variables are found to be significant with the expected sign. In three of them, increased liquidity reduces the probability of bank failure, and a coefficient on bank size is found to be significantly negative, that is, the larger the bank, the lower the likelihood of failure. Hwang et al. (1997) report that 48 variables were tested year on year from 1985 to 1988, but the significant variables changed every year, which raises some question about being able to use precise measures. For example, profitability appears to be important, but which measure should be monitored? This problem may be less serious than it first appears, because regulators/supervisors are tracking such a large number of measures each year.

As has been noted, it is difficult to test for the influence of macroeconomic variables, if just one country is included in the test. Cebula (1999) overcomes this problem by using the percentage of bank failures over several years as the dependent variable. This approach makes it possible to test for the effects of macroeconomic variables over time. Cebula's least squares regression results find negative coefficients on the real GDP growth rate and real interest rate are negatively signed: as either increases, the percentage of bank failure falls. Heffernan (2003) was able to test several macroeconomic variables in a logit model because the data set was international, with bank failures from eight countries.[56] The inflation and real exchange rate coefficients were, in their respective equations, highly

---

[56] A cross-country data set is beneficial because it permits a broader study of bank failure than that which is possible if one focuses on just one country. However, country accounting differences narrow the range of financial ratios that can be tested. There is a need for consistent international measures of the on- and off-balance sheet activities of banks, and it is hoped the agreement to recognise international accounting standards by 2005 (see Chapter 4) will go some way to rectify this problem.

significant (99% level of confidence) and positive, suggesting that as the rate of inflation increases or the real external value of the home currency rises, the probability of bank failure rose too. The positive sign on the inflation rate (or real appreciation) is consistent with the idea that higher inflation rates prompt fears of future recession (or official policy responses that could provoke it), and hence a rise in problematic banks. The nominal interest and exchange rate coefficients were insignificant, so too was the country's annual growth rate.

Consistent with Cebula (1999), Heffernan reports a significantly negative real interest coefficient, suggesting bank failures rise as the real interest rate falls. A possible explanation for the negative sign on real interest rates could be as follows. The central bank is the first to know when some banks are beginning to experience difficulties. They may be prepared to allow a brief period of lower interest rates, and hence lower real rates, to allow the banking sector to regain control over problem loans. Sometimes the troubled banks recover. In other cases, they do not, with the failure occurring more often than not during the period of lower real interest rates. More generally, banks' loan difficulties may begin in a period of high rates, and build up slowly before generating failure at a point in the cycle when the real interest rate has started to fall. Alternatively, in a recession, nominal (and therefore real) rates decline, hence the link to the increased likelihood of bank failure.

The Fitch[57] ratings variable was also tested in a separate regression. The IBCA individual rating for each bank ranges from A (excellent) to E (the bank has a serious problem and is likely to require external support).[58] The firm rates a bank based on financial ratios, size, macroeconomic variables (to a lesser extent) and on the knowledge of their field experts. To avoid problems of multicollinearity, it was tested in a separate regression, had the expected negative sign, and was highly significant ($t$-ratio of $-5.56$). With a MR$^2$ of 0.723, it did better than any of the models above, even though the number of observations fell to 270 because not all the banks in the sample had been assigned ratings in all years. The findings suggest users of this service are getting value for money when it comes to identifying troublesome banks which could fail. Under Basel 2, corporate ratings from reputable agencies are used to weight loans in the standardised approach to credit risk (see Chapter 5), but bank ratings are not employed.

## 7.6. Conclusion

Bank failures have a long history. This chapter has conducted both qualitative and quantitative analyses of troubled banks, with a view to identifying the chief determinants of bank failure, defined as liquidation, merger with a healthy bank (or purchase and acquisition) under government supervision, or rescue with state financial support. The case studies reveal one of the principal causes of failure to be substandard asset management, usually reflected in a poor quality loan portfolio. Managerial deficiencies were also important, highlighted by the herd instinct, and it is often difficult to distinguish between incompetence and fraud. The clustering phenomenon is suggestive of contributory macroeconomic factors,

---

[57] At the time the data were collected, the firm was known as IBCA, which later merged with another ratings agency, Fitch. The new firm was known as Fitch IBCA for a time, and is now known as Fitch.

[58] For the econometric work, A was converted to 5, down to E, which was set at 1.

though over a short period it could be due to contagion effects. The cases also showed that problems could be aggravated by regulatory forbearance, the absence of blanket deposit insurance, and the apparent inability of supervisors and auditors to pick up important signals of problem banks.

Section 7.4 reported a number of studies which used a logit model to identify variables that are significant in explaining the probability of bank failure. The econometric results are broadly consistent with the findings from the case studies, and provide the reader with greater precision with respect to which variables contribute to failure, namely:

- Falling profitability, most commonly measured by the ratio of net income to total assets. The case studies indicate that falling profitability resulting in bank failure is most likely caused by the deterioration in the quality of a bank's loan portfolio, and different measures of loan losses were found to be significant in some of the econometric work.
- Falling capital adequacy (various measures).
- Rising loan losses.
- Greater illiquidity, though the support for measures of illiquidity in the econometric studies is weaker.
- Macroeconomic indicators, according to the findings in Cebula (1999) and Heffernan (2003), are important explanatory variables which should be tested in any model of bank failure, in addition to financial ratios. The likelihood of bank failure rises with inflation and falls as the real exchange rate, real interest rate or real GDP growth rate rises.
- Heffernan (2003) found the Fitch bank rating variable to be significant, suggesting there is a role for these agencies in the assessment of bank quality.
- The econometric studies found that the larger the bank (in terms of assets) the less likely it is to fail. The finding is consistent with the "too big to fail" hypothesis, which often results in these banks being singled out for close scrutiny by regulators. Or it could also indicate that large banks engage in greater diversification, making them less likely to fail.
- Fraud – one econometric model tested for fraud (indirectly) and found its coefficient to be significant and correctly signed. However, a number of US studies report a high incidence of fraud when bank failures are reviewed over time.
- Moral hazard – several US studies find the bank failure rate increased when US deposit insurance was raised from $40 000 to $100 000, which is suggestive of moral hazard.
- Regulatory forbearance and looting are variables that are difficult to quantify, but the case study review suggests they were contributory factors.

This chapter has taken a detailed look at bank failures, and attempted to assess what caused them using qualitative and quantitative analysis. Chapter 8 turns to the subject of financial crises, which are very frequently associated with too many bank failures. Some may ask why the thousands of bank failures in the USA appeared in this chapter rather than the next. The reason is that though the bank failures were numerous, at no time was the US system under systemic threat, the way it was following the bank failures in 1930–33. The next chapter deals with bank failures (and other events) which lead to financial crises, and in some instances, to systemic collapse.

# FINANCIAL CRISES

## 8.1. Introduction

The previous chapter looked at the causes of bank failures; here, the emphasis shifts to financial crises, often caused by the collapse of a bank or banks. The objective is to explore the definitions, causes and consequences of financial systems in crisis. Section 8.2 looks at the controversies surrounding the different definitions of financial crises, and the costs of resolving more recent crises. Section 8.3 conducts extensive reviews of the crises in three South East Asian economies; those of Japan and Scandinavia are explored in sections 8.4 and 8.5. While there are some similarities in the factors leading up to these crises, the approaches taken to resolve them have been quite different. The choice of countries is deliberate. It covers a continuum, from relatively underdeveloped, such as Indonesia, to newly industrialised (Korea), to small open advanced economies, to the second largest economy in the world. It shows that no country is exempt from crises and their resolution can be complex and costly. The case of Long-Term Capital Management is discussed in section 8.6, to provide another contrast – a non-bank financial institution, the sudden collapse of which, some argue, threatened the world financial order, prompting a lifeboat rescue organised by the US central banking authorities. Given the need for intervention by central banks, other government agencies, the IMF (in the cases of the less wealthy economies) and the private banks to resolve financial crises, section 8.7 discusses the evolution and role of the lender of last resort, together with proposals to establish an international lender of last resort. The chapter concludes with a summary of the key points and findings from the various sections.

## 8.2. Definitions and Controversies

The title of Kindleberger's (1978) first chapter is: "*Financial Crisis: A Hardy Perennial*", an apt description of the problem of crises in the financial sector. This section begins with the question of what constitutes a financial crisis. There is little agreement about this. Economists of a monetarist persuasion employ a narrow definition: they argue that a financial crisis is normally associated with a banking crisis and when the stability of the banking system is threatened, the financial infrastructure could collapse in the absence of central bank intervention. The collapse of a key financial firm normally prompts runs on the banks: customers panic and, unable to distinguish between healthy and problem banks, withdraw their deposits. Fractional reserve lending results in the multiple contraction of deposits once the run begins. In the absence of central bank intervention, providing liquidity to solvent but illiquid banks, healthy banks are also threatened because of the declines in their asset values in the rush to become more liquid.

Schwartz (1986) argued there had been just two genuine or "real" financial crises in Britain and the USA. The first was caused by the failure of Overend Gurney Ltd in 1866, the other was the US crisis which occurred in the USA between 1930 and 1933. The episodes were described in detail in Chapter 7. It was the failure by the respective central banks to supply liquidity in 1866 and 1930–33 which turned failures into crises. According to Schwartz (1986), the solution to a crisis is to ensure a financial safety net is in place, that is, the central bank provides liquidity to solvent but illiquid banks. Schwartz labels all other so-called crises as "pseudo crises", because timely central bank intervention will head off and prevent any threat to the financial system.

One issue with the Schwartz criteria is that it is difficult to distinguish between insolvent and illiquid banks, especially during times of financial upheaval. Kindleberger dismisses the distinction between a real crisis, which involves changes in the money base or high powered money at some stage in the crisis, and all others, which are pseudo because they do not. He argues it is akin to "a cardiologist finding a cancer patient only pseudo sick" (1978, p. 3).

Kindleberger (1978) employs the Minsky (1977, 1982, 1986) model as his framework for explaining financial crisis. Kindleberger's interpretation of Minsky is as follows. Any financial crisis is an endogenous part of the business cycle. There is an exogenous shock to the financial system, which is significant enough to improve profit opportunities in a new or existing sector of the economy, and worsen them in others. The original "shock" initiating the new profit opportunities includes events as diverse as: the beginning or end of war, a new technology which becomes very popular, a surprise financial event (e.g. financial deregulation), or an unexpected shift in monetary policy.

Agents with savings or credit shift their finance to the new profit areas, and provided the profitable sectors (which can be assets, goods or services) dominate the losers, there is an upswing in the economy. An increase in credit finances a boom, and expands the money supply. Investor "euphoria" sets in. The financial system becomes increasing "fragile" (Minsky, 1977), exhibiting a number of features:

- Banks make insufficient provision for risk, possibly because they take an optimistic view of the collateral's value, which allows investors to engage in even more speculative activity.
- In time, demand outstrips supply in the new profitable sectors. Prices increase, creating new opportunities for profit and more investment, which raises incomes, prompting further investment.
- Herd behaviour together with increasingly speculative activity is observed, involving inexperienced agents who do not normally undertake investment.

The object of the speculative behaviour varies, and is often unique to a particular crisis: stock, bonds, currencies, commodities (e.g. oil, silver, sugar, coffee, cotton) or property. *Mania*, or irrational behaviour, sets in – this activity creates the *bubble*, defined by Kindleberger as price increases over an extended range. More precisely, it is caused by prices (e.g. asset, property) rising above those dictated by economic fundamentals.

Minsky (1977, 1982, 1986) wrote about a unit's financing shifting from *hedge* finance (cash flows are sufficient to meet the commitments on outstanding liabilities) to *speculative* finance (receipts are less than payments, making it necessary to roll over the debt) to *ponzi*[1] finance (an unsustainable sequence of ever-increasing borrowing – interest on debt repayments exceeds net income, and agents have to increase the debt to keep up their debt servicing), which heightens financial fragility: the probability of firms and households defaulting on their loans.

The speculative boom continues until it snaps. Some event or signal (e.g. the failure of a key firm in one of the boom areas, a bank collapse or an unexpected shift in government policy) which damages the sector(s) at the centre of speculative activity or the economy as a whole. "Distress selling" (Fisher, 1932) begins when firms or households, unable to repay their debt, are forced to liquidate their assets. More and more people see that at some point, sellers may outnumber buyers, causing prices to fall. Those who borrowed to finance their speculation will find it increasingly difficult to service/repay their debt. The longer the financial distress continues, the greater the realisation that markets are likely to collapse. This new, negative view of the markets might form gradually or very quickly but either way, at some point, there is a rush to liquidate. The bubble implodes, *panic* erupts, and prices collapse: Kindleberger defines a *crash* as an extended negative bubble (1978, p. 16). The above account provides the three words in Kindleberger's (1978[2]) title: *Manias, Panics, and Crashes*.

The panic continues until:

- Agents realise asset prices are so low they are undervalued; OR
- Trading is halted (e.g. closure of a stock exchange, declaration of bank "holidays"); OR
- A lender of last resort restores confidence to the market by making it clear that sufficient liquidity will be supplied to meet demand. Though Kindleberger recognised the need for a lender of last resort, he acknowledged the negative effects of moral hazard arising from rescues – other banks could expect an equivalent response in future crises. Kindleberger emphasised that the authorities must create ambiguity as to when and if they would intervene – easier said than done.
- Kindleberger reports 37[3] (international) financial crises between 1618 (set off by the debasement of coins in several European states) and the East Asian, Russian and Brazilian crises of 1997–98, caused by volatile international capital flows, deregulation and borrowing from overseas lenders. Caprio and Klingebiel (2003) report 116 systemic bank crises[4] since the 1970s. Beim and Calomiras (1999) identify 126 banking crises in developing/emerging market countries during the 1980s and 1990s.

---

[1] The term is named after Charles Ponzi, a Boston swindler who ran a pyramid scheme in 1920. Investors were promised 50% profit 45 days after they purchased his notes. The early buyers were paid off by later investors, but as they began to realise the scheme was unsustainable, it collapsed.

[2] Four editions were published. Here, reference is to the 4th edition (2000).

[3] See Appendix B of Kindleberger, 4th edition (2000).

[4] Caprio and Klingebiel (2003) define a systemic banking crisis as one where most, if not all, of the capital in the banking system is exhausted.

Other definitions and/or explanations of financial crises have appeared in the literature. For example, the banking sector is often identified as the source of the problem. Banks take on increasing amounts of risk by lending to firms and households, which use the loans to finance purchases in assets such as property, equities, etc. Increasingly the purchases are made for speculative purposes. As the proportion of short-term debt finance rises, the risk increases. An event triggers a fall in the value of these assets and increasingly, borrowers find they are unable to repay the banks. Banks have typically accepted the assets as collateral, so they, too, encounter problems, as their ratios of non-performing loans to total loans begin to rise. With lower profit prospects, share prices fall, depleting bank capital. Depositors become concerned and, in the absence of adequate deposit insurance, move their funds to safety. If this transfer is sufficiently widespread, banks could collapse.

Others point to the danger of a pegged exchange rate. A peg means the currency is fixed against some other currency, usually the dollar. There are fixed but adjustable peg regimes, which have a band width, such as Europe's exchange rate mechanism which preceded the adoption of the euro. For example, when the UK was part of the ERM, its band width was $(+)$ or $(-)$ 2.25%, a parity condition of £1 = 2.95 Deutsche marks.[5] A currency board is the most rigid form of fixed exchange rate. Hong Kong has a currency board, as did Argentina until the end of 2001. A crawling peg means the par rate is subject to revisions, usually pre-announced, of, for example, 1% per month. The adjustment is normally downward if the inflation rate in the home country is higher than that of the country it is pegged against. Less developed countries (LDCs) often opt for some type of peg, hoping to stabilise their currencies. Rising inflation rates (well in excess of US inflation) put pressure on the peg, because the LDC currency should be falling against the dollar. This scenario heightens expectations that the currency will be devalued, causing it to be offloaded. World-wide, currency traders, out to make a profit, will go short on the currency, undermining its value still further. At some point the pressure is too great, the peg breaks and the currency plummets. Whether or not the currency crisis leads to a banking/financial crisis depends on the state of the economy.

Lamfalussy (2000), referring to developing economies or emerging markets, defined a crisis as the situation where a nation's central bank has (or is about to) run out of

---

[5] The European case illustrates that currency crises are not confined to developing nations. Britain joined the EU's exchange rate mechanism in 1990, and experienced a currency crisis in September 1992. For two years, the UK had languished in steep recession. By 1991, the inflation rate had been sharply reduced, and the priority for monetary policy was to reduce interest rates. The ERM required member countries to impose German rates (with a small differential) to maintain parity conditions (£1 = 2.95 DM, + or −2.25%). Germany, having just reunified, was facing a construction boom and rising inflation rate. The Bundesbank's priority was to keep interest rates high to maintain monetary stability. The UK authorities pleaded for an interest rate cut. The Bundesbank reacted with understandable irritation, emphasising it did not take instructions from the German government, let alone foreign ones – e.g. Britain, Spain and Italy. These events convinced the Bundesbank that the sterling parity would have to change, and it was unwise for the Bundesbank to intervene on the foreign exchange markets to defend it. The Governor of the Bundesbank went further – he revealed his thinking to a financial news journalist and when asked to retract his words, refused to do so. This provoked gigantic capital outflows from the UK on one day, the 16th September, despite two large interest rate hikes (peaking at 15%). When the interest rate increases failed to stop the fall in sterling, the British government suspended ERM membership the same evening. The cost of defending sterling was £14 billion. The Italian and Spanish parities broke on the same day.

reserves, or cannot service foreign debt obligations, denominated in another currency. Once this unexpected news is made public, there is a rapid outflow of foreign capital,[6] a collapse of domestic equity bond markets, and a sharp decline in the value of the home currency.

Haldane *et al.* (2004) claim a third generation of models of financial crises has emerged, which identify the capital account as the source of the problem.[7] In developing countries or emerging markets, high net inflows of foreign capital can trigger a crisis, which is even more severe if the foreign capital is largely in the form of short-term debt denominated in dollars. Foreign lenders become excessively optimistic, the capital market overshoots, but some event causes concern among lenders, who start cutting back on loans to the country that triggers the crisis. Mexico, South East Asia, Russia, Brazil and Argentina have all recently experienced a financial crisis, where the capital account was a major factor. In the review of crises in the next section, short-term net capital inflows are a major contributory factor to the South East Asian crises, though this is not true for Japan. Nonetheless, if the capital account has become so important, then it has policy implications for resolving the crises. The issue of the capital account is revisited in section 8.7.

All of the above scenarios, including the third generation models, are variations of the Kindleberger theme. The key to his argument is that agents may start by being excessively optimistic about the future price of certain assets, but at some point grow excessively pessimistic. In both cases, the price(s) of the asset(s) (e.g. stocks, property or currencies) will overshoot their equilibrium price. However, the Kindleberger approach suggests agents are irrational, an inconsistency with the efficient markets hypothesis.[8] The EMH states that, in the absence of full information, speculators can make mistakes, but not systematically so, if expectations are rational. Still others, such as Flood and Garber (1994), argue that the efficient markets model is misspecified, and call for further research to identify the variables at work not accounted for in the theory.

In some multiple equilibrium models, expectations are treated as exogenous to the model, so a collapse or overshoot in prices can be consistent with rational behaviour. See, for example, Obstfeld (1986, 1996), Chang and Velasco (1998a,b), among others. Other authors use the presence of incomplete markets to explain bubbles. For example, Schleifer and Vishny (1997) argue that the more prices rise above their true value, the greater the cost of going short (selling borrowed securities), making it difficult to arbitrage away excessively high prices. This would explain why rational informed investors did not, for example, arbitrage away the excessively high dot com prices during the dot com bubble, which finally burst in mid-2000. Ofek and Richardson (2003) argue that the IT firms limited the issue of dot com shares, so there were no new shares to short sell. As a result, as the price of these share rose, the dot com bubble burst.

---

[6] Lamfalussy (2000) acknowledges that domestic residents can initiate capital outflows well before there is news of problems in the central bank. Such behaviour can speed the development of a crisis.

[7] See, for example, Chang and Velasco (1998a,b), IMF (2002) and Krugman (1999). The first generation models argue fundamentals cause crises; while fragility expectations are central to the second generation models.

[8] The seminal papers on the efficient markets hypothesis include Fama (1970, 1991).

Alternatively, the relatively new school of "behavioural finance"[9] acknowledges the possibility of irrational behaviour and uses bubbles to demonstrate the point. For example, Daniel *et al.* (1998) link overshooting in the stock markets to a trader's over-confidence and/or "biased self-attribution", when a trader accepts information and news consistent with his/her beliefs, but screens out information which is inconsistent. The various articles cited above demonstrate that a Kindleberger framework can be made consistent with either the efficient market hypothesis or behavioural finance.

Most experts broaden the definition of financial crisis to include features of financial fragility, bank panics and contagion. For example, Bordo *et al.* (2001) define a crisis as an episode when financial markets experience volatility, and financial firms suffer from illiquidity and insolvency. The authorities normally intervene to contain it. Earlier crises were largely confined to the banking sector, more recent ones can involve currency, banking and other financial markets. Their rate of occurrence appears to have increased. Bordo *et al.*, in a 56 country sample (1973–97), report a crisis frequency rate of 12.2% per annum which, the authors show, is high by historical standards. However, the features vary considerably. The run on the Argentinean peso in early 2002 triggered a financial crisis in that country. In Japan, the crisis has been largely confined to the banking sector.

Financial crises often require costly rescues if stability is to be preserved. Table 8.1 reports the estimated cost of crises for a wide range of countries.

All of the above crises required injections of public funds, together with, in some cases, private funds from banks and international funds. These estimates are *direct* costs, and do not take into account costs arising from subsequent future bad loans which will have to be covered, government guarantees, central bank tactics such as widening the interest rate spread to protect the banks, higher unemployment, and reduced national output and real income. Attempts have been made to measure these indirect costs. Hoggarth *et al.* (2003, table 2) report output losses as a percentage of real GDP, where output losses are defined as the cumulative deviation in the level of output from its pre-crisis 10-year trend. For 33 countries over the period 1979–22, the median output loss was 23.1% of GDP. The costs rise to 32% when both banking and currency crises occur. Honohan and Klingebiel (2003) find that lender of last resort facilities (liquidity support) and deposit guarantees extended to all deposits increase the fiscal costs of resolving the crisis.

The figures on the cost of the crises need to be treated with some caution. Sandal (2004), in a study of the Nordic banking crises, discusses how the fiscal cost (ignoring wider social costs) of a crisis should be measured in some detail. Issues include:

- What is included in the fiscal costs? Sandal's estimate includes direct payments and interest subsidies but excludes guarantees. In Sweden and Finland, the blanket creditor guarantees meant some banks did not need state support, recovered without being nationalised, and their share values increased. An almost impossible question to answer is: how much of the increase in share value was due to the guarantee?
- Whether one is looking at gross fiscal costs, i.e. total government expenditure, versus net costs.

---

[9] See, among others, Sheffrin (2000), Schleifer (2000) and Taffler (2002a,b).

Table 8.1   The Cost of Financial Crises

| Country | Year | Cost (as % of GDP) |
| --- | --- | --- |
| Argentina | 1980–82 | 55 |
| Argentina+ | 1995 | 2 |
| Mexico+ | 1995–97 | 14 |
| Brazil+ | 1995– | 5–10 |
| Chile | 1981–83 | 41 |
| Cote d'Ivoire | 1988–91 | 25 |
| China** | 1990s | 47 (1999) |
| Indonesia** | 1997–99 | 50–60 |
| Korea | 1997–99 | 15 |
| Thailand+ | 1997–99 | 24 |
| Malaysia+ | 1997–99 | 10 |
| Philippines** | 1998–2000 | 7 |
| Russia** | 1998 | 5–7 |
| Spain** | 1977–85 | 17 |
| Finland+ | 1991–93 | 8–10 |
| Norway+ | 1988–92 | 4 |
| Sweden+ | 1991–93 | 4–5 |
| US (thrifts bailout)+ | 1984–91 | 5–7 |
| Japan | 1990–2002 | 17, 20* |
| Israel | 1977–83 | 30 |

*Sources:* Evans (2000); Japan's estimate – Heffernan (2002).
* BIS (2004) estimates the total cost of dealing with Japan's non-performing loans between April 1992 and September 2001 was 20% of GDP or ¥102 trillion.
** Beim and Calomiris (2001).
+ BIS (2001).

- Estimates are not normally done on a present value basis, but if they are computed in this way, what discount factor is used?
- Which measure of GDP is used in the denominator, and from what date are the costs calculated?
- Posing and answering the counterfactual: how differently would GDP have evolved had the crisis been prevented?

The estimates of the costs for Sweden and Finland in Table 8.1 are very close to Sandal's estimate using gross costs, without using present value. Based on net costs, the figures fall to just over 5% for Finland, and 1.9% for Sweden. He does supply a "simple" estimate for Norway. His present value estimates range between 2.6% and 3.4% using gross costs, and 0.4 to 0.9% using net costs. Not surprisingly, the estimates fall once net costs are used.

Below, some actual crises are explored in more detail, to enhance readers' understanding of how they arise, and what might be done to minimise their potentially considerable costs in terms of a country's GDP. The Overend Gurney and US banking crises have already been discussed. Below, the South Sea bubble provides another historical example, followed by analyses of more recent financial crises.

## 8.2.1. South Sea Company[10]

The South Sea bubble is considered by many to be the first major international financial crisis,[11] because it involved investors in England, France, the Netherlands and other parts of Europe. In 1711, the Sword Blade Company (later a bank) assumed some of the government debt issued in the War of the Spanish Succession. In exchange the group, led by Robert Harley,[12] was given a monopoly in South (Atlantic) trade and formed the South Sea Company. Holders of the government debt were to exchange it for South Sea stock, though they would be paid interest by the Treasury. South Sea also sold shares to raise capital to finance what was expected to be lucrative trade with the South American Spanish colonies, after the cessation of hostilities in 1713. In fact there were a few unprofitable slave trades, before the British and Spanish went to war again in 1718. Despite this poor record, investors in South Sea looked to the future and seemingly attractive trade prospects that would be realised once the war was over.

South Sea wanted to emulate the success of the Paris based Mississippi Compagnie des Indes, which had been granted the monopoly of French trade with North America. Mississippi was owned by a Scot, John Law, who used his bank to issue stock and raise capital. By May 1719, the firm was overwhelmed by subscribers: in addition to the French, foreign subscribers, including some from Britain, were trying to buy stock. Investors from all the major Continental cities (e.g. Paris, Amsterdam, Geneva) now clamoured to buy shares in South Sea. The share price rose from £175 in February 1720, and peaked at over £1000 by the end of June.[13] On the Continent, speculation in a number of stocks also took place.

However, there was some unease at the sheer scale of speculation, and a few investors, including some of the South Sea directors, sold their stock. There was no sudden burst in the bubble – but a slow, steady fall in price through the summer months. It finally collapsed at the end of September 1720, when the price dropped to £135. Fortunes had been lost, Parliament was recalled, and a Committee formed to investigate. Many of the key players escaped to other countries with the books, making it difficult to prosecute, though some

---

[10] For a more detailed account see Balen (2002).

[11] Kindleberger, in his 4th edition (2000), discusses an earlier crisis, known as the "Kipper-und Wipperzit". It began with debasement of coinage around 1600, which involved putting baser in low value gold or silver coins used in daily transactions. It grew very quickly after 1618 (to finance the Thirty Years' War, which began in 1618) with a speculative peak and crash in February 1622. It began with the debasement of a nation's own coinage, but spread to other countries after nobles came up with an even better system: taking the bad coins across the border, bringing back good ones, and debasing them. It came to an end when all the coins of low value were treated as virtually worthless.

[12] Harley's group, by assuming some national debt, also hoped to challenge the Bank of England (created in 1694) which was beginning to emerge as the state's banker.

[13] The sale of South Sea shares would also help to stop the drain of capital from London to Paris.

properties were seized. The Bank of England rescued South Sea but refused to assist Sword Blade, which failed, thus ensuring the dominance of the Bank of England.[14]

The next two sections look at financial crises in developed and emerging market economies, the Asian crisis in the late 1990s and the prolonged crisis in Japan, largely confined to its banking sector. The reviews illustrate how economies that appear to be reasonably stable can suddenly shift into crisis mode and, depending on conditions, the frightening speed with which contagion can spread a crisis from one country to another. While they share a few common features, there are many differences, especially the policy responses where, ironically, Japan could have learned a great deal from the Korean experience.

## 8.3. The South East Asian Financial Crisis, 1997–99

### 8.3.1. An Overview of General Contributing Factors

What became known as the Asian financial crisis originated in Thailand, then spread quickly to South Korea, Indonesia, Malaysia, Thailand, other Asian economies and beyond.[15] The onset, speed and seriousness of the crises took experts by surprise – there were no official forecasts of a sudden downturn, let alone crisis. Spreads on Asian bonds had substantially narrowed during 1996 and for most of 1997; likewise, credit ratings remained largely unchanged. Until the onset of problems, fiscal and monetary indicators were relatively stable. While it was acknowledged in some quarters that the growth of the "tiger" economies could not be sustained,[16] there was little reason to think a slowdown would turn into a meltdown.

The first sign of trouble was when prices on the Thai stock market began to fall in February 1997, and by year-end had declined by more than 30%. Pressure on the Thai baht quickly turned into a currency crisis, which spread to the financial sector. Thailand had experienced a massive net capital inflow during the previous three years, especially 1995–96, amounting to 13% of Thai GDP compared to 0.6% for the G-7 economies. The year 1997 saw this inflow at first stop, and by the second and third quarters, sharply reverse. Exports had grown by 25% in 1995, but fell (−1.3%) in 1996. The growth of imports also slowed but not by enough, resulting in a large current account deficit (8% of GDP by 1996). An unexpected fall in exports in early 1997 heightened concerns about the sustainability of the baht.

The Thai baht was pegged to the US dollar. It depreciated through 1996 and 1997, but within the intervention band.[17] From early 1997, despite rising interest rates, the Thai

---

[14] When its charter was renewed in 1792, the Bank of England (known as the Bank of London until the early 1800s) was given a near monopoly over note issue in England – private banks (partnerships of up to six people) could still issue notes.

[15] Taiwan, the Philippines and Hong Kong were also affected, but the discussion here will focus on Thailand, Indonesia and Korea, with some references to Malaysia and the Philippines. It aggravated problems in Russia, which had its own crisis in 1998. By September 1998, Mexico, Brazil, Chile, Colombia and other countries were fighting hard to defend their currency pegs – some were forced to abandon them.

[16] See Krugman (1994), Young (1995) and McKinnon and Pill (1996), among others.

[17] From late 1996 until the onset of the currency crisis in 1997, the baht fluctuated (+) or (−) 3% around a mean of 24.5 baht = $1

Table 8.2   Income and Inflation Indicators

|  | Indonesia | Philippines | Malaysia | Thailand | Korea |
|---|---|---|---|---|---|
| Real GDP growth 1985–97 | 6.6% | 7.6% | 3.8% | 8.5% | 7.6% |
| GDP per head, 1986 | $480 | $530 | $1700 | $820 | $200 (1962) |
| GDP per head, 1996 | $1100 | $1200 | $4600 | $3100 | $9900 |
| Inflation, 1996 | 6.5% | 8.4% | 3.5% | 5.8% | 4.5% |

*Source*: Goldstein (1998); Beim and Calomiris (2001).

central bank intervened heavily, buying baht to maintain the peg. Though the bank fended off two major attacks, the pressure was unrelenting and the Thai government responded by imposing capital controls in May. The overnight interest rate soared, peaking at 20% on 9 May. By July, the government had little option but to allow the baht to float. Meanwhile, pressure was building on other pegged currencies, especially Malaysia, Korea, the Philippines and Indonesia.

In Chapter 6, it was noted that the terms "less developed countries" (LDC) and "emerging market economies" encompass a wide variety of countries at varying stages of development, just as the labels *developed* or *industrialised* do. Here, an interesting aspect of the crisis is the differences in income per head among the crisis countries in South East Asia. Table 8.2 shows a rapid rise in per capita incomes for all of them between 1986 and 1996. However, there is a wide variation in income per head. Korea is highly industrialised and joined the OECD in 1997, though at this time its financial system was less well developed than most OECD members. Compared to Korea, the other four countries in the table have lower per capita GDPs, but there is wide variation among them. By the 1990s, Thailand and Malaysia are classified as "newly industrialising" – note their higher incomes per head compared to the Philippines and Indonesia. Even further down the income ladder (not shown) is China ($750) and India ($380).

Nonetheless, many of the contributing factors were common to all the countries involved, though the emphasis and structural arrangements varied. Below, these institutional features are summarised under two headings, industrial, trade and exchange rate policy, and the role of the financial sector. Where appropriate, examples are drawn from one or more of the countries to illustrate a point. The interaction between these factors combined to produce a crisis which rapidly spread across Asia and beyond. Kiyotaki and Moore (1997), in a powerful analytical model, show how a crisis can arise from the interaction of excess credit granted by banks, land prices and macroeconomic swings. The Asian crisis is a good application of these ideas.

## *Industrial, trade and exchange rate policy*

- All of these economies had experienced rapid, although declining, growth rates. Table 8.2 shows the real GDP growth rate in the decade leading up to the crisis was well in excess of most OECD countries (a weighted average of 3% per annum). With the exception of Indonesia, none of these countries had experienced recent, previous crises.

- In this region, exports (increasingly manufactured goods) trebled between 1986 and 1996 and, on average, made up about 40% of each country's GDP by 1996. These countries, competing with each other in global markets, faced growing pressure from Chinese products and, frequently (except in Korea), the firms were foreign owned.
- Restrictions on capital movements had been liberalised, and by 1996 were completely free. These economies experienced a huge inflow of foreign credit but (see below) inward foreign direct investment had started to decline. Increasingly, foreign firms were looking to China as the Asian base for their manufacturing plants. For the five Asian countries,[18] $75 billion of net international credit was granted in 1995–96, consisting of bank loans (20%), net bond finance (22%) and net interbank (58%), compared to just $17 billion (or 18% of total net capital inflows) for net equity and portfolio investment. In 1997 it fell to $2 billion (just under 4% of net capital inflows), compared to $54 billion in foreign credit.[19]
- Large, indebted corporations exerted strong political influence. Nowhere was this more evident than in Korea. In the 1960s, the Korean government adopted an industrial policy that was to transform it from a largely agricultural economy to one based on manufacturing, which, by 1996, absorbed 90% of capital and accounted for 61% of GDP. The "economic miracle" was achieved through complex, interactive relationships between the government which directed state investment in around 30 *chaebol*: family owned industrial groups, each associated with a financial institution responsible for meeting the chaebol's funding needs. Long-standing relationship banking consolidated the link between chaebol and bank.[20]

Using funds generated from household savings, the government also supported about 30 state owned firms which were largely monopolies. The government promoted key sectors such as steel, vehicles, chemicals, consumer electronic goods and semiconductors. Provided an industry met the goals set by the state, it could expect protection from imports and foreign investors, preferential rates from state controlled interest rates, and cheap financing from the banks. There was significant competition among the four car manufacturers, the five chemical firms and four semiconductor companies. However, the emphasis was on revenue growth and capturing market share, rather than adding value. In the 1990s, return on capital was less than the cost of the debt.

At the onset of the crisis in 1997, most of the chaebol had debt to equity ratios in excess of 500%. Any equity was held by the family, which meant there was little in the way of corporate accountability. In July 1997, the eighth largest conglomerate, the Kia group, collapsed, defaulting on loans of just under $7 billion. Two more chaebol had failed by December, which, together with other factors, undermined foreign and domestic confidence in the economy and contributed to the onset of crisis.

---

[18] Korea, Indonesia, Malaysia, Philippines, Thailand.

[19] *Source*: BIS (1998, table VII.2).

[20] Bae *et al.* (2002) show that relationship banking can be costly to the firm in periods of bank distress. Looking at the bank crisis period, they show that firms which are highly levered experience a larger drop in the value of their equity. By contrast, the drop in share value is less pronounced for firms that rely on several means of external financing, and with more liquid assets.

However, Korea had the legal framework to deal with the chaebol problems. Creditors have been able to use the courts to put the chaebol into receivership. Though the Daewoo crisis did not come to the fore until mid-1999, its creditors negotiated rate reductions, grace periods and debt–equity conversions to stabilise its debt of $80 billion, then proceed with the break-up and sale of its assets. Other chaebol have been stabilised, after debt restructuring agreements with bankers. The state also intervened, requiring gearing ratios to be reduced to at least 200%, and prohibiting cross-guarantees of chaebol members' debt.[21]

The situation is quite different in Indonesia and Thailand, where corporate restructuring has been hampered by the absence of clear legal guidelines on issues such as foreclosure, the definition of insolvency and the legal rights of creditors.

- Exchange rate regimes: these countries had all adopted some type of US dollar peg.[22] In the absence of any serious inflation, real effective exchange rates were stable, with only a slight rise in 1995–96. Trade weighted exchange rates were also stable. Once the Thai baht came under pressure, and floated in July 1997, it depreciated rapidly. The other countries responded by widening their fluctuation bands (depending on the system of pegging), but the runs continued, forcing them, with the exception of Malaysia,[23] to float their respective currencies. The Indonesia rupiah was floated in August; the Korean won in December. All of these governments had used their central banks to defend the currency, exhausting much of their foreign exchange reserves[24] and pushing up domestic interest rates.

## *The financial sector*

- All of the Asian economies were bank dominated, with underdeveloped money markets. Between 1990 and 1997, bank credit grew by 18% per annum for Thailand and Indonesia, 12% for Korea. By way of contrast, credit growth averaged 4% per annum for the G-10, and was just 0.5% for the USA. By 1997, bank credit as a percentage of GDP for Thailand, Korea and Indonesia was, respectively, 105%, 64% and 57% – amounts that were close to, or in the case of Thailand above, those for developed countries. The rapid increase in the supply of credit, in the absence of the growth of profitable investment opportunities, caused interest margins to narrow (to the point that they were roughly equal to operating costs), even though riskier business loans were being made, largely in construction and property. Property was also used as collateral – soaring property prices fooled the banks into thinking the risk they faced from property-backed loans was minimal.

---

[21] This account comes from Scott (2002), pp. 61, 63.

[22] Hong Kong was the only economy in the region with a currency board. Ferri *et al.* (2001), using data on SME borrowers (1997–98), show that during a systemic banking crisis, relationship banking with the banks that survive has a positive value because it reduced liquidity problems for SMEs, and therefore made bankruptcy less likely.

[23] Prime Minister Mahathir of Malaysia blamed speculators for the run on the ringgit and refused to float the currency, though the band was widened.

[24] For example, foreign exchange reserves in Thailand amounted to about $25 billion pre-crisis, but by the time the baht was floated, the central bank had issued about $23 billion worth of forward foreign exchange contracts.

Table 8.3   Bank Performance Indicators

|  |  | Thailand | Indonesia | Korea | Malaysia |
|---|---|---|---|---|---|
| **Weighted Capital Assets Ratio** | 1997 | 9.3 | 4.6 | 9.1 | 10.3 |
|  | 1999 | 12.4 | −18.2 | 9.8 | 12.5 |
| ROA | 1997 | −0.1 | −0.1 | 9.1 | 10.3 |
|  | 1999 | −2.5 | −17.4 | 9.8 | 12.5 |
| Spread* | 1997 | 3.8 | 1.5 | 3.6 | 2.3 |
|  | 1999 | 4.8 | 7.7 | 2.2 | 4.5 |

* Spread: short-term lending rate – short-term deposit rate.
*Source:* BIS (2001), table III.5.

- The build-up of bad credit would not have been possible had foreign lenders been unwilling to lend to these countries. In a First World awash with liquidity,[25] there were a number of reasons why Japanese and western banks found these markets attractive. Until the onset of the currency crises, the economic performance of these tiger economies had been impressive. Through the 1990s, real economic growth rates were high, inflation appeared to be under control, they had high savings and investment rates, and good fiscal discipline: government budgets were balanced. As Table 8.3 shows, the weighted capital assets ratios were, with the exception of Indonesia, respectable. Borrowers (usually local banks) were prepared to agree a loan denominated in a foreign currency (dollars, yen), thus freeing up the lender from the need to hedge against currency risk. Short-term lending was particularly attractive, allowing western banks to avoid the standard mismatch arising from borrowing short (deposits) and lending long to firms. Finally, many foreign lenders were under the impression these banks would be supported by the government/central bank in the unlikely event of any problems (see below).
- Increasing reliance on short-term borrowing as a form of external finance: international bank and bond finance for the five Asian countries between 1990–94 was $14 billion, rising to $75 billion between 1995 and the third quarter of 1996. By 1995, the main source of the loans was European banks, and nearly 60% of it was interbank. By the beginning of 1997, foreign credit made up 40% of total loans in Asia.[26] Of these loans, 60% were denominated in dollars, the rest in yen. Two-thirds of the debt had a maturity of less than a year.[27]
- The almost unlimited availability of bank credit led to over-investment in industry and excess capacity. There was a close link between local bank lending and the construction and real estate sectors, especially property development. In Thailand, by the end of 1996, 30–40% of the capital inflow consisted of bank loans to the property sector, mainly

---

[25] In the west, there was an easing of monetary policy from 1993. However, after the relatively harsh recession between 1990 and 1991, companies were reluctant to borrow or invest until 1997, when the economic boom increased borrowing once again. Japanese banks were keen to gain market share overseas.

[26] Foreign investors were also attracted to the Asian stock markets – about 33% of domestic equities were held by foreigners at the end of 1996.

[27] Source of these figures: Bank for International Settlements (1998, table VII.2).

developers. The figure for Indonesia was 25–30%. The problem was compounded by the use of collateral, mainly property. The loan to collateral ratios stood between 80 and 100%, creating a collateral value effect, that would further destabilise banking sectors once property (and equity) prices began to decline. The role of collateral and collateral values in models of shocks and money transmission has been emphasised by Bernanke and Gertler in various papers.[28]

- Some government policies could inadvertently contribute to the problem. For example, the Thai government introduced the Bangkok International Banking Facility (BIBF) in 1993, to promote Bangkok as a regional banking sector and encourage the entry of international banks. The BIBF was also used by domestic banks to diversify into international banking intermediation by obtaining offshore funds for domestic or international lending. Unfortunately, they gave Thai banks[29] a new way of borrowing from abroad, using BIBF proceeds to invest heavily in property and related sectors.

- Asian banks borrowed in yen and dollars from Japan and the west, and on-lent to local firms in the domestic currency. There was little use of forward cover against the currency risk arising from these liabilities because of the relative success of the peg, up to 1997. For example, the Thai baht had not been devalued since 1984, with only slight fluctuations around the exchange rate (BT25.5:$1). Rising interest rates and a collapsing currency proved lethal. Firms could not repay their debt, and banks found it increasingly difficult to repay the principal and interest on the dollar debt. Non-performing loans as a percentage of total loans soared, especially in Thailand and Indonesia. As Table 8.7 shows, by 1998, the percentage of non-performing loans was just under 40%.

- A tradition of forbearance towards troubled banks, and the widespread impression that governments would support the banking sector – through either implicit or explicit guarantees. For example, in Indonesia, the costly and protracted closing of Bank Summa in 1992 resulted in a policy of no bank closures in the years prior to the crisis.[30] Similar attitudes prevailed in all these countries. An added problem was that even if the authorities had wanted to close insolvent banks, an inadequate legal framework in most of these countries made it very difficult to force firms into insolvency.

- Regulation of the financial sector was nominal, for several reasons. First, **named** as opposed to **analytical** lending, i.e. it was the individual's connections with the bank that mattered. There was little in the way of assessment of the feasibility of proposed projects, nor was the risk profile of the borrower evaluated. Together with a lack of staff training and expertise, it meant no modern methods of risk assessment were used by the banks. In Korea political interference meant some financial institutions were subject to unfair audits and penalties.[31]

- In Thailand, the same group of top officials moved back and forth between business, the banking sector and government. Offices were run to enhance an official's future standing,

---

[28] See for example, Bernanke and Gertler (1995).
[29] In December 1996, 45 financial firms were licensed to handle BIBFs, or, effectively, engage in offshore activities. 15 were Thai banks and 30 were foreign banks or bank branches. The Thai banks used their BIBFs to borrow from abroad and lend locally.
[30] Batunaggar (2002), p. 5.
[31] Casserley and Gibb (1999), p. 325.

and for regulators, this meant avoiding any controversial action which would upset senior bankers and/or politicians. Many of the banks had family connections: a family would succeed in a certain area of business and then expand into banking by buying up its shares. For example, in the early 1900s, the Tejapaibul family began a liquor and pawnshop business in Thailand, and by the 1950s the business was so large that ownership of a bank would ensure a ready source of capital. They established the Bangkok Metropolitan Bank in 1950, and bought controlling stakes in other banks in the 1970s and 1980s. After problems in the 1990s, the central bank appointed the managing director and other staff, while a family member remained as President. In 1996, US regulators ordered it to cease its US operations. In early 1998, with 40% of total loans designated non-performing, the family was forced to accept recapitalisation by the state and loss of management control, with the family losing close to $100 million.[32] It is currently owned by the Financial Institutions Development Fund. Part of the Bank of Thailand, the FIDF was set up in the 1980s as a legal entity to provide financial support to both illiquid and insolvent banks. It normally takes over a bank by buying all its shares at a huge discount.

- The ratio of non-performing loans to total loans illustrates the growing problem of bad debt. Table 8.4 reports the BIS estimates. Even in 1996, they were on the high side if the benchmark for healthy banks is assumed to vary between 1% and 4%. In 1997, Thailand's NPL/TL rose to 22.5%. In 1998, Korea's and Malaysia's percentage of NPLs are high by international standards, but dwarfed by the estimates for Thailand and Indonesia. These ratios are understatements because of lax provisioning practices. In most industrialised economies a loan is declared non-performing after 3 months. In these Asian economies, it is between 6 and 12 months. Bankers also practised *evergreening*:[33] a new loan is granted to ensure payments can be made or the old loan can be serviced.

- Weak financial institutions/sectors, supported by the state. By the time of the onset of the crisis (and in Indonesia's case, long before), it was apparent that these countries' financial sectors were part of the problem. In Thailand there was tight control over the issue of bank licences, but finance companies were allowed to expand unchecked. By 1997, the country had 15 domestic banks and 91 finance companies – their market share in lending grew from just over 10% in 1986 to a quarter of the market by 1997. In response to pressure from the World Trade Organisation, Thailand allowed limited foreign bank

Table 8.4  BIS Estimates of Non-performing Loans as a Percentage of Total Loans

|      | Thailand | Indonesia | Korea | Malaysia | Philippines |
|------|----------|-----------|-------|----------|-------------|
| 1996 | 7.7      | 8.8       | 4.1   | 3.9      | na          |
| 1997 | 22.5     | 7.1       | na    | 3.2      | na          |
| 1999 | 38.6     | 37.0      | 6.2   | 9        | na          |

*Source*: Goldstein (1998); BIS (2001).

---

[32] *Source*: Casserley and Gibb (1999).
[33] See Chapter 6 and Goldstein (1998), p. 12.

entry, with 21 foreign banks in 1997. However, their activities were severely constrained because each one was only allowed a few branches.

- In the Korean financial sector, activities were strictly segmented by function. Specialised banks provided credit to certain sectors, for example, the Housing and Commercial Bank, development banks (e.g. the Korea Long Term Credit Bank and the Export Import Bank), and nation-wide/regional banks. By 1997, there were eight national banks, serving the chaebol and the retail sector. Ten regional and local banks offered services to regional (or local) business and retail clients. Government influence was all pervasive. Not only did they own shares in some banks, but all executive appointments were political. There was directed lending – the government would pressure a bank to grant specific amounts of credit to firms. Political connections, not creditworthiness, was the determining factor in many bank loan decisions.

- There were also investment institutions, which held about 20% of total assets in 1997. They were made up of merchant banks, securities firms and trusts. Merchant banks had no access to retail markets, raising their funding costs. Using funds raised by commercial paper issues, overnight deposits and US dollar loans, they invested in relatively risky assets, including risky domestic loans and Indonesian and Thai corporate bonds. Once these economies collapsed, these banks faced mounting losses. Depositors panicked, especially those who held US dollar accounts. Loan rollovers were also terminated, which forced these banks to buy US dollars.

The central bank tried to defend the won but by late 1997, had used up all of their foreign exchange reserves. An application for IMF standby credit was agreed by early December. It amounted to $21 billion over 3 years, with just under $6 billion for immediate disbursement. A few days later, the won was floated – in 6 weeks it lost 50% of its value against the US dollar.

Indonesia's banking sector aggravated the crisis in that country. It was unique among the countries in allowing foreign bank participation. Foreign banks could own up to 85% of joint ventures. Major banking reforms came into effect in 1988, and between 1988 and 1996, the number of licensed banks grew from 20 to 240. Branch networks grew and new services were offered by banks. This stretched the supervisory services, and banks began to engage in questionable practices. There was intense competition among banks. This contributed to the rapid expansion of credit, much of it named or "connected", 25–30% of it going to the property sector, especially developers.

In 1991, prudential regulation was tightened by Bank Indonesia. Banks had to meet capital ratios, and were rated. Mergers were encouraged, but did not take place, and banks used their political connections to escape the tough new measures. From 1990, Indonesia's private corporate (non-bank) sector borrowed heavily from overseas, with most of the debt denominated in dollars.[34] By 1997, it had grown to $78 billion, exceeding the amount of sovereign external debt by close to $20 billion. Lack of confidence in the banking and corporate sectors caused the currency crisis to deepen, even after the rupiah was floated.

---

[34] The government had stopped banks from taking on much external debt.

## 8.3.2. The Contagion Effect

The Asian crisis provides a classic example of contagion. The previous section illustrates how each country had unique problems which made them prime contagion targets following the rapid decline of the currency and financial markets in Thailand. There were two dimensions: positive feedback mechanisms within each country and rapid geographical spread across national boundaries. Initially, the currency markets bore the brunt of the contagion: the currency crisis spread from Thailand to Indonesia, Malaysia, the Philippines and Korea because investors tended to group these countries together. Table 8.5 shows a degree of correlation between Thai equity prices and those in other Asian markets. The exception is Korea, where, pre-crisis, the correlation was slightly negative. Post-crisis, the correlation strengthens, especially in Korea, where it jumps to just under 60%.

Table 8.5 suggests that overseas investors will have believed that asset returns in these economies would remain positively correlated to a high degree. The currency crisis spread rapidly because of the high substitutability of many of each other's exports, the absence of capital controls, and the perceived similarity of financial conditions. Since these countries competed with each other in world export markets to a high degree, a fall in the value of the Thai baht would mean the other currencies would have to decline to remain competitive. Traders reacted accordingly, selling these currencies in anticipation of their inevitable depreciation. The surprise depreciation wrecked the balance sheets of banks and companies with unhedged foreign exchange liabilities. High interest rates and a deteriorating economic outlook caused a steep decline in the property and equity markets. The hitherto sound loans suddenly looked problematic, causing concern about the viability of the banks with high percentages of non-performing loans, backed by collateral, the value of which was collapsing.

For these reasons, the contagion spread from the foreign exchange markets to the bank sectors very quickly. Indonesia had a history of bank problems, as was illustrated in Chapter 6.

In the absence of bank guarantees, runs on banks quickly follow and include:

- Withdrawals by depositors.
- A run on off-balance sheet products, for example, closing trust accounts, mutual funds.
- Cuts in domestic and international interbank funding.
- Borrowers run down credit lines, in anticipation of not being able to do so in the future.
- Financial assets such as equity, bonds and mutual funds are sold and any proceeds withdrawn from domestic banks.

Table 8.5  The Correlation Coefficients: Thai and Other Asian Equity Markets (weekly equity price movements)

| Equity markets | Philippines | Singapore | Indonesia | Malaysia | Hong Kong | Korea |
|---|---|---|---|---|---|---|
| **Pre-crisis** (1/97–6/97) | 0.66 | 0.38 | 0.35 | 0.34 | 0.26 | −0.06 |
| **Post-crisis** (7/97–2/98) | 0.66 | 0.53 | 0.64 | 0.61 | 0.42 | 0.57 |

*Source:* BIS (1997), table VII.7.

Though domestic and foreign owned banks benefit from early runs, failure to restore confidence in the system means they too can be targeted, as agents take more drastic measures to shift their funds out of the country.

The rapid onset of the severe, systemic Asian crisis was such that to counter the problem with bank runs the authorities had to "temporarily" close/suspend some banks, provide liquidity to solvent financial institutions and guarantee depositors' (and creditors') funds. Korea and Thailand issued guarantees as soon as domestic banks began to experience funding problems. Indonesia's authorities were slower to react and the action taken was incomplete. These points become more apparent by reviewing some of the detailed restructuring which took place in Indonesia, Thailand and Korea.

## 8.3.3. Policy Responses and Subsequent Developments

Thailand, Indonesia and Korea requested credit assistance from the IMF and other agencies.[35] The size of the packages grew with each settlement, as Table 8.6 shows, but only Korea's exceeded the size of the earlier settlement with Mexico in 1995–96 ($51.6 billion). Note the bilateral commitments exceeded the IMF's standby credit. One objective of such large amounts is to restore investor faith in the future of these economies.

Any IMF package comes with a substantial number of conditions, tailored to accommodate the circumstances of the individual country. For the crises in Korea, Thailand and Indonesia,[36] they included:

- Closure of insolvent banks/financial institutions.
- Liquidity support to other banks, subject to conditions.
- Requirements to deal with weak banks, which can include placing them under the supervision of the regulatory authority, mergers or temporary nationalisation.

Table 8.6   Official Financing Commitments (US$bn)

| | IMF | World Bank (IBRD) | Asian Development Bank | Bilateral commitments* | Total |
|---|---|---|---|---|---|
| Thailand | 3.9 | 1.9 | 2.2 | 12.1 | 20.1 |
| Indonesia | 10.1 | 4.5 | 3.5 | 22 | 40 |
| Korea | 21 | 10 | 4 | 22 | 57 |
| Total | 35 | 16.4 | 9.7 | 56.1 | 117.1 |

* Bilateral commitments: agreements between national authorities of different countries (e.g. central banks in the west agree to support and contribute to the refinancing package).
IBRD: International Bank for Reconstruction and Development.
*Source*: BIS (1997).

---

[35] Dr Mahathir, Prime Minister of Malaysia, did not approach the IMF to negotiate a restructuring agreement. Instead, tight capital controls were imposed from September 1998.
[36] For the specific conditions imposed on these countries, see Goldstein (1998) or Lindgren et al. (1999).

- Purchase and disposal of non-performing loans, normally by an asset management company.
- Loan classification and provisioning rules were raised to meet international standards; similar guidelines were applied for rules on disclosure, auditing and accounting practices.
- Bank licensing rules were tightened, with improved criteria for the assessment of owners, board managers and financial institutions.
- Review of bank supervision laws.
- Bankruptcy and foreclosure laws to be amended/strengthened.
- Restructuring/privatisation plans for the banks or other firms that had been nationalised because of the crisis.
- New, tighter prudential regulations.
- Introduction of a deposit insurance scheme if one did not exist.

## *Korea*

From Korea's macroeconomic indicators, pre-crisis, there was little to suggest a crisis was imminent. Real GDP growth rates averaged 8% from 1994–97, inflation was stable at 5% and unemployment was low. Private capital inflows financed a current account deficit of about 5% of GDP in 1996. However, total external debt as a percentage of GDP had risen, from 20 to 30% between 1993 and 1996, and two-thirds of it was short-term debt. After Thailand was forced to float the baht in August 1997, the Philippine, Malaysian, Indonesian and Taiwanese currencies all came under extreme pressure. The stock exchanges in Hong Kong, Russia and Latin America declined sharply. From late October, the Korean won faced grave strains. Despite the widening of the fluctuation band from (+) or (−) 2.25% to 10% on 20 November, and IMF standby credit worth $21 billion agreed on 4 December, the won was floated on 16 December. The crisis quickly spread to the banking sector.

The government moved quickly to deal with the problems in the merchant banking sector. In December 1997, in the same month when the won was floated and an IMF agreement reached, 14 merchant banks were suspended, and 10 of these were closed in January; more closures followed through 1998. The rest were given deadlines for submitting recapitalisation and rehabilitation plans. Since most of these banks were small and many owned by chaebol, the government avoided making capital injections. The surviving 11 banks (see Table 8.7) received capital from their respective owners.

The situation with the commercial banks was a different matter because of the systemic risk widespread closure posed. These banks were either nationalised or merged with other banks. Korea First Bank and Seoul Bank were nationalised in 1998. They had been left highly exposed to chaebol that went bankrupt in 1997, and were targets for deposit runs. Attempts to privatise Seoul Bank failed, and a major foreign bank was contracted to run it. 51% of Korea First was sold; the new investors assumed responsibility for management.

In 1998, five healthy banks each took over an insolvent bank, by government decree. Through "assisted acquisitions" (i.e. with state financial support), 11 banks merged to create five banks in 1999 and 2000. New banks were given put options on the non-performing loans of the banks they were taking over and capital was injected to maintain their capital ratios at pre-acquisition levels. Performance contracts were imposed on top management

Table 8.7    The Korean Banking Sector: pre/post-crisis

| | Pre-crisis (12/96) | | Post-crisis (7/99) | |
|---|---|---|---|---|
| | No. of banks | Market share* | No. of banks | Market share* |
| Commercial banks | 26 | 40% | 12 | 19% |
| Commercial banks – state owned** | 0 | 0 | 5 | 18% |
| Merchant banks | 30 | 6% | 12 | 4% |
| Specialised/development banks | 3 | 20% | 3 | 20% |
| Investment trust companies | 8 | 10% | 4 | 20% |
| Credit unions | 1600+ | 5% | 1600+ | 5% |
| Mutual savings | 230 | 10% | 210 | 7% |
| Life insurance | 33 | 9% | 29 | 7% |

*Source*: Lindgren (1999), p. 76.

* Market share: % share of assets.

** Banks with majority government ownership; the state had a minority interest in six other banks.

to encourage restructuring, which was successful. Staff costs were reduced by 35%, and the number of branches by 20%.

Foreign banks were permitted 100% ownership and in December 1999, Korea First Bank was sold to a US financial holding company, Newbridge Capital. Deutsche Bank was hired to prepare Seoul Bank for privatisation and sale to foreign investors in June 2001. However, despite a respectable bid from an American group, 70% of it was sold to Hana Bank in late 2002.

Non-performing loans were disposed of more successfully than in other countries. The Korean Asset Management Company (KAMCO) had been established in 1962. For a fee, it collected non-performing loans from banks. In 1997, a special fund was set up within KAMCO to purchase all impaired loans from firms covered by the Korean Deposit Insurance Corporation. It was funded by the Korean Development Bank, the Korean Deposit Insurance Corporation, special government guaranteed bonds and the commercial banks. This special fund is, effectively, a "bad bank", discussed earlier in the chapter. It purchased the NPLs at 45%, 3% for unsecured loans, and disposed of collateral. KAMCO sold some of the NPLs to international investors and others at public auction, foreclosed and sold the underlying collateral, and collected on loans. As of June 1999, 7 trillion won was collected from loans with a face value of 17 trillion, or 41% of the face value.[37] By global standards, this is a reasonably successful recovery rate.

As shown in Table 8.7, restructuring cut the number of merchant banks by 60% and the number of private merchant banks by half. The five commercial banks that were state owned in mid-1999 were to be re-privatised by 2002, in accordance with the terms of Korea's agreement with the IMF. At the time of writing, some progress had been made. Of the five state owned commercial banks in Table 8.7, as of 2003:

[37] *Source*: Lindgren (1991), p. 72.

- Cho Hung Bank – *Bankscope*[38] has no information.
- Seoul Bank – absorbed by Hana Bank in December 2002; 30% state owned.[39]
- Hanvit Bank – renamed Woori Financial Holdings; 88% state owned.
- Korea First – 49% state owned.
- Korea Exchange Bank – 65% of the shares were purchased by foreign firms;[40] 20% state owned.

To phase out the pre-crisis segmentation of the Korean financial market, the Financial Holding Company Act was passed in 2000. It allows commercial and merchant banks, securities firms and insurance companies to operate under one holding company. A large number of strategic alliances have since taken place between banks, non-banking financial firms (e.g. securities, insurance), which should help to phase out the segmentation.

## Thailand

Like Korea, Thailand managed to arrest bank runs at an early stage in the crisis, and a key reason for their comparative success in containing the bank crisis was early intervention by the authorities. Intervention was swift. At the height of the currency crisis, from March to June 1997, the Bank of Thailand was secretly supplying liquidity to 66 finance companies,[41] up to four times in excess of their capital, at below market rates. By August, 58[42] out of a total of 91 finance companies were suspended and instructed to draw up a rehabilitation plan.

As part of the IMF restructuring agreement, the Financial Restructuring Agency (FRA) was established in the autumn of 1997 to take (temporary) responsibility for financial restructuring on behalf of the Bank of Thailand and Ministry of Finance. In December, the FRA announced the closure of 56 finance companies – two were reprieved provided new capital was forthcoming. A state asset management company (AMC)[43] was set up to dispose of their assets, and by 2000, most of them had been disposed of, at 25% of their face value.

By mid-1997, problems were such that 7 of the 15 commercial banks required daily liquidity support as depositors shifted funds to the seven state banks, perceived to be safer. The Bank of Thailand had been slow to take action because it was afraid any intervention would be interpreted as confirmation that the banks were in trouble and prompt a run on the whole banking system. In August 1997, the government guaranteed the depositors and creditors at banks and finance companies. Bank runs continued because of uncertainty about the legal status of the guarantee, but once it became law a few months later, a degree of confidence was restored.

Initially, private sector banks were left to fend for themselves. Several formed their own AMCs as wholly owned subsidiaries, but tended to delay the sale of NPLs, hoping the

---

[38] *Bankscope* is an electronic database owned by Fitch Ratings. Information on these banks was obtained from *Bankscope* in February 2004.

[39] Shares are held by one or more of the Korean Deposit Insurance Corporation, the state development banks and the Ministry of Finance. Korea Exchange was owned by the central bank, Bank of Korea.

[40] 51% by Lone Star (USA) and 14.75% by Commerzbank.

[41] These firms dealt with securities.

[42] The operations of 16 were suspended in June, followed by another 42 in August.

[43] An AMC is, effectively, a "bad bank"; see Box 8.1 for more discussion.

economy would recover and/or they could restructure the loans. Also, because an AMC was managed by its bank (rather than independent third party specialists) auditors would not recognise them as true sales. When the slow rate of disposal became apparent, the state took over the funding and management of these private AMCs. However, by late 1999, only about 25% of NPLs had been restructured.

In June 1997, an analysis of data revealed that none of the commercial banks had enough capital to satisfy the 8% minimum. Attempts were made to tighten prudential regulation in 1997 and again in 1998, including strict loan classification, loss provisioning and other rules. As agreed with the IMF, all insolvent financial firms were to be closed or merged, and state banks would, eventually, be privatised. Public funds were set aside to recapitalise viable banks and finance companies, provided they complied with new prudential rules on items such as loan classification, provisioning for losses, and methods for the valuation of collateral. Fearing state interference, most banks did not take up the offer.

Thailand's experience provides a good illustration of how an inferior legal framework can exacerbate the problems. It was not until October 1997 that the Bank of Thailand had legal authority to intervene in troubled commercial banks by changing management, writing down capital,[44] and so on. In western developed nations, bank supervisory authorities take such powers for granted.[45] It was not until January 1998 that the Bank began to intervene, starting with the Bangkok Metropolitan Bank. By May, six banks and nine finance companies had been nationalised, accounting for 33% of total deposits. Bank runs finally subsided – recall a blanket guarantee had been in place since August 1997.

Table 8.8 shows the change in structure of the financial sector pre- and post-crisis. Note the large drop in finance companies, the rise in state owned commercial banks, and the

**Table 8.8  Thailand's Financial Sector, Pre- and Post-Crisis**

|  | December 1996 | | July 1999 | |
| --- | --- | --- | --- | --- |
|  | No. of banks | Market share* | No. of banks | Market share* |
| Finance companies | 90 | 20% | 22 | 5% |
| State finance company | 1 | 0 | 1 | 1% |
| Commercial banks | 14 | 59% | 7 | 39%** |
| State owned banks, specialised | 7 | 7% | 7 | 15% |
| Commercial state owned banks | 1 | 8% | 6 | 6% |
| Foreign banks (branches) | 14 | 6% | 14 | 12% |

*Source:* Lindgren *et al.* (1999), p. 101.

* Market share: % of total assets.

** Two of the private commercial banks have received substantial foreign capital injections – more than 50% of them are foreign owned.

---

[44] In Thailand, the Bank of Thailand would give a bank a short period of time to raise new capital. If it failed to do so, the Bank would order it write down the value of its existing capital and then have it recapitalised by the Financial Institutions Development Fund.

[45] The relevant authorities in Korea and Indonesia did not have the legal power to liquidate banks and repay affected depositors; nor could they transfer deposits from a weak to the healthy bank in a state assisted merger.

corresponding change in their share of total assets. The number of private commercial banks has been reduced by half. The increase in state owned banks is largely due to the merger of many of the banks and finance companies considered non-viable, of which the Bank of Thailand had assumed control in August 1998.

In March 2000, Thailand's largest corporate debtor was declared insolvent, a milestone in what had been relatively slow progress in the restructuring of the corporate sector. A new bankruptcy law, and a procedure for out of court restructuring, were established.

## Indonesia

Indonesia had shown strong growth in 1996, and in 1997 its inflation rate stood at 5%, with a current account deficit at 3% of GDP. The currency crisis led to floating of the rupiah in August 1997. By November 1997, the IMF had approved a programme of reforms, together with standby credit of $10.1 billion, of which $3 billion was available for immediate use. So what went wrong, and how did the country end up with a systemic banking crisis? Even before the currency crisis, there was concern about the highly geared corporate sector, poor supervision of the financial sector, high external debt and the political situation.

Furthermore, unlike Korea and Thailand, the Indonesian authorities were slow to deal with problems in the banking sector. This resulted in a sustained systemic banking crisis. The rupiah was floated in August 1997, but state intervention in the banking sector did not commence until October, and even then, as the account of the events will show, it was controversial, further undermining confidence and initiating a vicious circle of bank runs, attempts at reform, political interference, renewed loss of confidence, runs, and more reform until late 1999.

In the mid-1980s, Indonesia had suffered from balance of payments problems arising from a collapse in the oil market and the depreciation of the US dollar. Its external debt was denominated in non-dollar currencies such as the Japanese yen, but the country relied on dollar based oil revenues. The Suharto government moved away from a nationalistic economic policy to a "technocratic model" with an emphasis on growth led by a broad manufacturing export base and a liberal financial sector.[46] Extensive banking reforms were introduced in 1988 under the "Pakto" package. Restrictions on private banks were lifted, as were limits on domestic bank branching. Foreign banks could form joint ventures with local partners. For the first time, state owned firms could place up to 50% of their deposits outside the state banks. The reserve ratio was lowered to 2% (from 15%). At the same time Bank Indonesia (BI) imposed some new prudential rules designed to limit banks' exposure to single clients and firms. The banking sector changed overnight, with a rapid extension in the number of banks, and credit expansion to match. But much of it was *named* rather than *analytical*. By 1990, the total number of banks had increased from 108 to 147, with 1400 new branches. There were 73 new commercial banks.

The situation deteriorated over the years, so that by November 1997, the government and IMF agreed a plan of action for the banking sector. The package involved 50 banks – 16 small private banks, with a combined market share of 2.5%, were closed. The other 34

---

[46] For more detail on the earlier background, see Anderson (1994), Heffernan (1996) and Schwartz (1991).

were subject to a range of orders, including more intensive supervision for the six largest private banks, rehabilitation plans for ten insolvent banks, recapitalisation, and at least one merger. Deposit insurance was introduced for the first time, to apply to small depositors at the closed banks, covering 90% of these deposits, that is, Rp 20 million ($2000) per depositor per bank. Bank Indonesia made it clear that the remaining banks would be given liquidity support in the event of bank runs.

There was a rapid decline in public confidence, for several reasons. Concern heightened because the 34 banks were not identified. The partial, limited nature of the deposit insurance was considered inadequate. One of the closed banks was effectively re-opened under a new name, suggesting that political connections,[47] not a bank's balance sheet, were influencing decisions as to which banks would be closed. High interest rates and depreciation of the rupiah contributed to an economic slow down, aggravating the positions of the bank balance sheets. Finally there was political uncertainty because of rumours about the health of President Suharto. The high state of anxiety provoked widespread runs on two-thirds of the private banks, which made up half the banking sector. The Bank of Indonesia supplied liquidity but this failed to stop the runs, and exacerbated the flight of capital out of the country, because the liquidity was supplied in rupiah and used by banks for dollar deposits.[48]

A letter of intent signed with the IMF did little to reassure the country because of the failure of the Indonesian authorities to abide by previous agreements. This lack of credibility aggravated the runs on banks and liquidity support from BI reached all time highs. In January 1998, the rupiah was now rapidly depreciating against the dollar[49] – prompting runs not only on banks but on supermarkets as well.

At the end of January 1998, the government announced a new series of reforms to head off complete collapse of the financial system. A blanket guarantee was issued, which was to cover all depositors and creditors, and a corporate restructuring programme announced. The Indonesian Bank Restructuring Authority (part of the Ministry of Finance) was given a broad remit to deal with the problems in the financial and non-financial sectors. This included dealing with problem banks (e.g. closure, nationalisation, etc.) and acting as an AMC, i.e. the management and sale of dud assets. The assets were acquired at book value in exchange for government bonds so they could recapitalise.

These plans calmed the markets, and for the next two months the IBRA undertook a variety of actions in an attempt to stabilise the banking markets. However, under orders of the President, these operations were not publicised, and in late February, the respected head of the IBRA was removed by the President. Any confidence restored by the recent reforms began to wane, leading to renewed runs on banks. So began a cycle of IBRA attempts to restore a credible banking system, political interference, new runs on banks requiring yet more liquidity injections by BI, and riots. These cycles continued through 1998. By August 1998 reviews of 16 non-IBRA banks revealed that most (private and state) were insolvent.

---

[47] The President's son was connected to the closed bank, and was allowed to take over another bank.

[48] Unlike Korea and Thailand, Indonesia was unsuccessful in its attempts to sterilise the huge liquidity injections: BI had no way of recycling the huge deposit withdrawals/capital outflows caused by months of uncertainty, creating fears of hyperinflation, an added problem for the authorities.

[49] In December 1997, the rupiah was trading at 4600 to the dollar. By late January, it had declined to 15 000 rupiah:$1.

Table 8.9  Indonesia's Banking Sector, Pre- and Post-Crisis

| | Pre-crisis, July 1997 | | Post-crisis, August 1999 | |
|---|---|---|---|---|
| | No. of banks | Market share* | No. of banks | Market share* |
| Private domestic banks | 160 | 50% | 82 | 17% |
| State domestic banks | 34 | 42% | 43 | 73% |
| Joint ventures/foreign banks | 44 | 8% | 40 | 10% |

*Source*: Lindgren *et al.* (1999), p. 64.
* Market share: % of assets.

The IBRA and BI persisted with restructuring, in the face of constant political interference. President Suharto resigned from office in May 1998, after 6 months of trying to prop up the business interests of family and friends.

Table 8.9 summarises the dramatic changes in Indonesia's banking sector over the two-year period, from pre-crisis to post-crisis. The number of private commercial banks nearly halved, through closure and nationalisation. The state's share of total bank liabilities swelled to nearly three-quarters. The cost of government intervention to deal with the two crises is estimated at 50–60% of GDP.[50]

The relative success of Korea and Thailand in stopping runs suggests that quick action is advisable, to restore confidence that the system is liquid, especially when compared to the panic and bank runs experienced by Indonesia. The problem with such action (and the reason the Indonesian government was reluctant to intervene) is the effect on future incentives. However, in view of the very real systemic threat, these governments had no other option.

## 8.3.4. Assessment of Policy Responses in Korea, Thailand and Indonesia

This review of the policy responses to crisis and contagion in the three countries illustrates that Korea was the most effective in managing its crisis, followed by Thailand and Indonesia. One way of illustrating this point is to look at peaks in the demand for liquidity from the central bank and the timing of key announcements. Peaks in liquidity demand can be used as a measure of confidence in the banking sector. Banks will have to approach the central bank for liquidity if they are subject to bank runs.

Korea announced a blanket guarantee for bank depositors and creditors in December 1997, the same month the won was floated and the IMF plan agreed. Even so, the demand for liquidity peaked a month later, but fell rapidly once foreign debt was rescheduled. In Thailand, banks' demand for liquidity from the Thai central bank peaked when the suspension of the 16 finance companies was announced, and again when 42 more were suspended. When 100% deposit insurance coverage became law, the demand for liquidity

---

[50] The estimate for Indonesia and the other Asian countries varies depending on the date of computation and what is included. Lindgren (1999) reports the cost of financial sector restructuring was $85 billion or 51% of GDP as of June 1999.

tailed off. Concern about the state of several small and medium-sized banks prompted runs (despite deposit insurance) and caused a third peak in early 1998. It quickly tailed off after the authorities intervened in the banks.

By contrast, Indonesia experienced three peaks in liquidity demand in late 1997, early 1998 and mid-1998. The need for three substantial liquidity injections was likely due to the relatively late intervention in the banking sector by the authorities, a failure to implement agreed IMF reforms in a timely manner, and a sustained general view that unhealthy banks were being allowed to stay open because of political corruption, favouritism and interference. Radelet and Woo (2000) also criticise the IMF for some of the early restructuring. For example, the IMF insisted on the abrupt closure of the 16 banks in November 1997. Done in volatile capital markets, with no plans for dealing with these banks' assets, and no strategy for addressing the problems in Indonesia's banking system, this action was bound to provoke the widespread run observed.

In light of the above, it comes as no surprise that as a percentage of GDP, the cost of dealing with the currency and banking crises was highest for Indonesia (estimated at 50–60% of GDP), followed by Thailand (40%), Korea (15%) and Malaysia (12%). Despite Thailand's prompt intervention, the cost of resolving the crisis is considerably higher than Korea because of the closure of more than 50% of the finance companies, nationalisation of a third of the banking sector, and the considerable delay in dealing with private banks' non-performing loans because they were left to form their own AMCs – in the end, the state had to intervene.[51]

The use of the "good bank/bad bank" approach first appeared when the USA created the Resolution Trust Corporation (RTC) to deal with the mounting bad assets of the increasing number of insolvent thrifts. It was considered highly successful in fulfilling its objectives. Since that time, it has become common for countries experiencing a banking crisis to create an institution with similar objectives. For example, Sweden created Securum, Japan (see below) began with a private initiative, which was later taken over by the state, and in this section, all three countries set up some form of institution to handle bad assets. A critique of the approach is found in Box 8.1.

Indonesia took the decision to inject capital into all state owned banks, no matter what the cost. The plan for the private banks was to preserve an elite of a small group of the best banks. The recapitalisation programme asked private owners to contribute at least 20% of private capital, with the state injecting the rest, to bring tier 1 regulatory capital up to 4% of risk adjusted assets. Private owners would be given first refusal on the sale of government shares after 3 years. However, they had to meet stringent performance targets. In the end, the plan came to nothing. Nine banks appeared eligible, but one of the banks (Bank Niaga) could not raise the capital and was nationalised. Revised audits in March 1999 showed the recapitalisation requirements were much higher than what had been assumed in the initial proposal. The eight banks could not come up with the updated capital outlay in time,

---

[51] Scott (2002) argues that disposal of assets at the best possible price was a secondary consideration for KAMCO and IBRA, the Korean and Indonesian government agencies charged with dealing with the banking sector's dud loans. IBRA was plagued by political interference and an ineffective legal framework. In Korea, the first priority was to strengthen the banks' balance sheets – the debts were purchased in exchange for government bonds.

## Box 8.1 AMCs or Good Bank/Bad Bank

Korea, Thailand and Indonesia all employed a "good bank/bad bank" approach to deal with "dud" assets. A special corporation (e.g. asset management company or AMC) is established which purchases, at a discount, banks' bad assets (usually non-performing loans), thereby cleaning up the balance sheets and allowing "good" banks to start afresh. The corporation tries to sell the assets. The USA established the Resolution Trust Corporation during the US thrift crisis in the 1980s, and was one of the first countries to adopt this method, though it was confined to thrifts that were already insolvent, whereas most other countries have used these corporations to help banks recover.

The main advantages:

- Bank capital needs are reduced for a bank already struggling.
- Bank management has a chance to focus on healthy assets, and attract new, healthy business.
- By selling the assets, the AMC "prices" the loans, making the size of the losses more transparent.
- Provided the organisation buying the assets has the expertise to restructure or dispose of the assets, it can maximise the value of these assets.

The main disadvantages:

- The effect on incentives. The borrowers whose assets are transferred no longer have an opportunity to try and restructure the debt, and any relationship the bank had built up with the borrower is lost, though this can be a positive point if banks made loans on a named rather than analytical basis.
- If key management remains in place, banks might be led to think that any future build-up of bad assets will be passed to a third party to deal with, which is likely to increase moral hazard and risk taking.
- Many asset management companies have found it very difficult to sell bad loans, and end up doing so at a much higher discount than they expected.
- If the percentage of non-performing loans is very high (e.g. Thailand and Indonesia) their sale results in immediate, serious losses, which can reduce the share value of financial institutions still further, and make it essential for them to raise new capital. When this was not forthcoming, the state had to intervene, leading to closure, nationalisation and mergers.
- In developing countries, they are unlikely to have enough skilled individuals who could ensure proper asset management and/or disposal. A weak legal and judicial system aggravates the problems. Debtors soon realised there was little reason to service the debt once the debt had been transferred. All of these weaknesses, which all three countries suffered to a varying degree, prevent the AMCs from maximising the value of bank assets at disposal, and the value of any nationalised banks when they were privatised.
- There is also the question of whether the AMCs should be state owned, as they were in the USA and Korea, or whether banks should be left to organise their own AMCs, as they were in Thailand and in the early years of Japan's crisis.

Advantages of state ownership:

- Additional conditions to the sale of NPLs can be imposed on the state. For example, in the USA, the RTC was obliged to use some of the real estate assets to create low cost housing.
- The agency has control over all the assets and collateral, making for more effective management and disposal of the assets. If allocated to the private sector, the assets and collateral are likely to be divided among several firms.
- The government can insist on a programme of bank restructuring, as a condition for disposal of assets and collateral.
- The state can more easily impose special legal powers to ensure efficient asset disposal.

Advantages of private ownership:

- The private sector has more expertise in asset management, though there is no reason why a state organisation cannot work with private specialists, as the RTC did in the USA. This may be a moot point for emerging markets, where there may not be the expertise.
- AMCs are less likely to be subject to political pressure, since they are independent of government.
- It is less likely that a profit-maximising firm will keep assets and collateral for an extended period of time. It prevents any build-up of loans and collateral over time. A government owned institution will be under less pressure and assets may remain with it over a long period of time.
- In a private firm the assets are actively managed, but this may not happen for a state AMC, again because profits are unlikely to be at stake. This could send the wrong signals to financial firms, increasing credit problems in the financial system as investors take on more risk.
- If the AMC is efficient and used to a competitive environment, their costs of dealing with the dud assets could be lower than in the state sector.

and the government's only option was to nationalise them. All nine banks were nationalised.

Thailand, Korea and Indonesia proved unable to attract enough private investor interest to recapitalise the insolvent banks. It was to be expected in Korea where there were many small shareholders, but in the other two states it proved impossible to entice more capital from existing shareholders or new investors (either domestic or foreign). There was too much downside risk, and the governments provided no explicit protection of the shareholders should the banks fail. The shareholders had already seen creditors compensated when banks were nationalised, but investors got nothing.

# 8.4. The Japanese Banking Crisis

Since 1990, Japan's economy has gone from bad to worse, with the first signs of recovery appearing as this book goes to press. Following the collapse of the stock market in 1989, the early tendency to protect failing firms, both banks and non-financial, aggravated the situation. The subsequent prolonged weakness of the financial sector is largely responsible for the world's second largest economy being in the macro doldrums. This section discusses the background to the current situation and how Japan passed through various stages of a "bubble" economy. The knock-on macroeconomic effects have been very serious. Backed into a corner, Japan should, most observers agree, stimulate the economy through ongoing financial reform and monetary expansion.

## 8.4.1. The Japanese Financial System, 1945–Mid-1990s

To understand how Japan ended up with a chronic, but serious, banking crisis, it is helpful to briefly review the growth of Japan's financial structure from the ruins of World War II. Japan faced a severe shortage of capital and weak financial infrastructure. The financial assets of the household sector were virtually wiped out. The priority of the US occupying force and the new Japanese government was to increase assets, which in turn could finance recovery of the real economy. The outcome was a highly segmented financial system, with strong regulatory control exerted by the Ministry of Finance (MoF), backed by the Bank of Japan. Domestic and foreign and short and long-term financial transactions were kept separate, interest rates regulated, and financial firms organised along functional lines. Table 8.10 illustrates the degree of functional segmentation.

The MoF remained the key regulator until the late 1990s, with three MoF bureaux: Banking, Securities and International Finance.[52] Responsibilities included all aspects of financial institution supervision: examination of financial firms, control of interest rates and products offered by firms, supervision of the deposit protection scheme, and setting the rules on activities to be undertaken by financial firms.

The MoF used "**regulatory guidance**" (combining the statutes with its own interpretation of the laws) to operate the financial system. In the post-war era, banks, in exchange for

---

[52] The MoF also had tax and budget bureaux.

Table 8.10  The Functional Segmentation of the Japanese Banking Sector, Pre-Big Bang

| Financial Institutions | Numbers (1997) | Geographical Area | Funding | Loans to/Key Customers | Other Links/Comment |
|---|---|---|---|---|---|
| **Ordinary or commercial banks\*** | | | | | |
| City | 10 | HQ in Tokyo/Osaka – national branch networks | Deposits with maturity <3 yrs; may not raise long-term debt | Large corporates, especially keiretsu affiliates | Securities; cross-shareholding via keiretsu |
| Regional + former sogos (Regional II) banks | 139 | In one or neighbouring regions (prefectures) | As above | Regional clients and public utilities | |
| Foreign banks | 94 | Tokyo | As with city banks | As with city banks | Securities & trust business through partly owned affiliates |
| Long-term credit | 3\*\* | Tokyo | Deposits from client fund and government bodies; issue long-term debentures with maturity up to 5 yrs | Long-term loans to industry | |
| Trusts | >30 | Various | Long-term deposits | Long-term loans & money trusts; trust-related business | |
| Japanese Post Office | 24 000 branches | Cross-country | A cheap source of funds for MoF; savings attracted by regulated deposit rates and products until 1994/5; continue to offer attractive rates, etc. | | Subsidised by government therefore not constrained to maximise profits\*\*\* |
| Government financial institutions | 10, all state owned except for the Shoko Chukin Bank; 9 are specialised lending institutions | Various | MoF fiscal and loan programme; may not accept deposits | To supplement private sector loans to industry | Have outgrown their purpose |
| Savings & loans | 395 Shinkin credit associations | Various | Short-term deposits from small business & individuals | Loans to small business and individuals | Mutual organisations |
| Cooperative banks | >3000 Agriculture and fisheries coops, credit unions, rokin banks | Local | Mutual organisations, so finance cannot be raised via shareholders | | Mutual organisations |
| Securities firms | 190 (1990) | National | Standard securities activities | | Largely exempt from regulation |

\*Article 65 of the 1948 Securities and Exchange Law restricted banks from engaging in the securities business and vice versa.

\*\*1949 Foreign Exchange Law: separated domestic and international banking and finance. The Bank of Tokyo was the designated foreign exchange bank.

\*\*\*One estimate of the state subsidy to the postal system is ¥730 billion per year, equivalent to 0.36% on postal savings deposits.

*Source:* Ministry of International Trade and Industry, as quoted in Ito *et al.* (1998), p. 73.

providing low interest loans to large industrial firms, were protected from foreign competition, and the highly segmented markets (see Table 8.10) limited domestic competition. In return, until 1995, there was an implicit guarantee that virtually any financial firm getting into trouble would be protected – a 100% safety net. MoF officials were often given jobs by banks when they retired – evidence of the cosy relationship between the MoF and regulated bankers.

The **Bank of Japan** (BJ) was responsible for the implementation of monetary policy, but was not independent. MoF officials exercised strong influence through their membership of the Bank's policy board. The Bank of Japan also acted as banker for commercial banks and government, regulated the interbank market and was consulted on regulatory decisions taken by the MoF. The Bank and MoF conducted on-site inspections of banks in alternate years.

Japan is the world's second largest economy. But functional/geographical/segmentation and restrictions on international capital flows resulted in an excessive dependence on the banking sector unlike other major industrialised countries. In 1998, 60% of domestic corporate finance in Japan consisted of loans, compared to just over 10% in the USA. According to the IMF (2003), the major banks and trust banks hold about 25% of the financial system's assets.

Capital markets remain underdeveloped. In the 1980s, the trading volumes on the New York and Tokyo stock markets were roughly equal but by 1996, Tokyo's volume was about 20% of New York's, with 70% fewer shares traded. Though some of this decline is explained by Japan's recession, other figures underline the structural problems with this sector. For example, market share has declined. In London, about 18% of total shares in Japanese equity were traded in 1996, compared to 6% in 1990. Singapore commands just over 30% of Japanese futures trades.

Participation by foreign financial firms in the Japanese markets was also low compared to other financial centres, mainly because the Japanese believed their interests were best served if foreign firms were kept out. Token gestures were made, to avoid criticism from the world community. The number of foreign firms with a listing on the Tokyo exchange fell by 50% during the first half of the 1990s.[53] In 2000, there were 118 foreign financial firms, compared to 250 in New York, 315 in London and 104 in Frankfurt.

## 8.4.2. Late 1980–1989: A Financial Bubble Grows and Bursts

Financial bubbles and manias were briefly discussed in Chapter 7. A *financial bubble* normally refers to a bubble in asset prices. The events in the Japanese financial sector provide a good description of the three phases of a financial bubble described by Allen and Gale (2000).[54]

*Phase 1*: Financial reforms and/or a policy decision by a central bank/government eases lending. The increased availability of credit increases the property and stock market prices. The phase of rising asset prices can take place for a prolonged length of time as the bubble gets bigger.

---

[53] *Source*: Craig (1999).

[54] Allen and Gale (2000) provide a rigorous theoretical framework to explain these phases. For other theoretical contributions see Allen and Gorton (1993), Camerer (1989), Santos and Woodford (1997) and Tirole (1985).

By the early to mid-1980s, the Japanese government had accepted it would have to deregulate its financial markets, including allowing foreign firms equal access. There were two major reasons for the change in attitude. The United States and other countries were putting pressure on Japan to reduce its trade surplus, which was undermining the value of the dollar. The Ministry of Finance and Bank of Japan loosened monetary policy to reduce the value of the yen against the US dollar. Second, the USA and the European Commission had passed laws on the treatment of foreign firms in their respective financial markets. The principle adopted was one of equal treatment: foreign financial firms would be given free access to the US/European financial markets provided financial regulations in the foreign country did not discriminate against US/EU financial firms (see Chapter 5 for more detail). Japan's regulatory regime did discriminate, which threatened foreign operations of Japanese financial firms. Financial agents in Japan anticipated a future of deregulated markets, together with an increase in the availability of credit as monetary controls were relaxed.

The outcome was the emergence of a bubble economy, as evidenced by a sixfold increase in stock market prices from 1979 to 1989. In 1985, the Nikkei index was approximately 10 000, rising to a peak of 38 916 in September 1989. See Chart 8.1. Property prices followed a similar upward spiral. *Zaitech* behaviour was also evident: non-financial firms were purchasing financial assets using either borrowed funds or issuing securities, often on the eurobond market. In short, companies increased their debt to invest in financial assets, ignoring or underestimating the risk of price declines.

Zaitech's beginnings were innocent enough. Many large Japanese corporations realised they had credit ratings as good as or better than the banks from which they borrowed. It was cheaper to raise finance by issuing their own bonds, instead of borrowing from banks. These firms issued bonds with a low cash payout. At the same time, the return on financial assets was much higher than the returns on reinvesting money in manufacturing firms. Firms unable to issue their own bonds borrowed to finance the purchase of assets, usually

**Chart 8.1   Nikkei index: highs and lows, 1988–2003.**

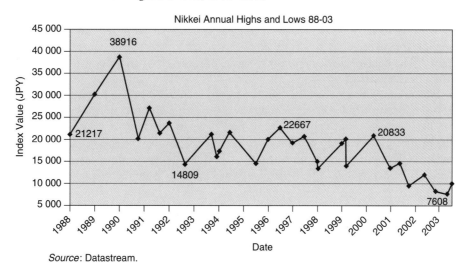

*Source*: Datastream.

pledging real estate as collateral. As the asset and property prices continued on their upward spiral, there was increased *speculative activity*. By the mid-1980s, the money raised was used to speculate in risky stocks, options, warrants, and the booming real estate sector.

In the period 1984–89, Japan issued a total of $720 billion in securities. The new equity financing was twice that of the USA, an economy twice its size which was experiencing a boom over the same period. Just under half were sold on the domestic market, mainly in the form of *convertible debentures* (and new share issues); the rest were sold in the euromarkets as low coupon bonds with *stock purchase warrants*[55].

Banks and securities firms were enthusiastic supporters of zaitech behaviour. Some corporate loan business was being lost to the bond markets, but banks benefited from disintermediation through fee based "commissioned" underwriting. The rise in the stock market increased the value of their cross-shareholdings in keiretsu member firms. Lending patterns also changed. Hoshi and Kashyap (1999) report a dramatic increase in loans to small business and the real estate sector through the 1980s. The proportion of bank loans to property firms doubled between the early 1980s and early 1990s.

The regional and smaller banks were especially keen to lend to firms unable to raise finance through the bond market but in need of cash to finance their own share purchases. These marginal borrowers were charged higher loan rates and supplied "safe" collateral: real estate and/or equities held by the firm.

In the late 1970s and early 1980s, Japanese banks entered the global loan markets, competing with international banks to lend to developing countries. The objective was to increase market share, by lending to these countries at below market rates. Most foreign lending is denominated in US dollars. The resulting currency risk, if uncovered, is costly when the yen depreciates against the dollar. The 1982 Mexican crises hit the Japanese banks hard, but along with other global banks, they were persuaded by the IMF to reschedule the debt. The MoF also discouraged the banks from writing off these loans. It is worth noting not all the lending went to developing countries. Peek and Rosengreen (2003) report an eightfold increase in Japanese loans to the US commercial property markets between 1987 and 1992.

Bubbles add to uncertainty because it is unclear when they will burst. Asset management is made more difficult because of increased marginal borrowers on domestic and international markets.

*Phase 2*: The bubble bursts and prices collapse, a process that can occur within a few days, months or even years.

In 1989, a new Governor at the Bank of Japan, influenced by the Ministry of Finance, expressed concern that Japan's economy was overheating and threatened by inflation. In Japan, like Germany, past episodes of inflation[56] means any hint of inflationary pressure results in strong measures to combat it. In early 1990 the bubble was pricked by tighter monetary policy and a jump in interest rates. Chart 8.1 illustrates the sharp decline in the Nikkei 225. By September 1992, it was less than 15 000, 62% off its 1989 peak.

---

[55] Convertible debentures involve a bond issue where the investor has the option of converting the bond into a fixed number of common shares. Stock purchase warrants are like convertible debentures but the conversion part of the bond, the warrant, can be detached and sold separately.

[56] At the end of World War II and immediately thereafter, Japan experienced a burst of substantial inflation (a 20-fold increase in prices) relative to what they were used to.

Property prices followed the Nikkei in a dramatic spiral downwards – by 1995, property prices were 80% lower than in 1989. According to the IMF (2003, p. 72), in 2002, property prices declined for their 12th consecutive year, by an annual average of 6.4%. Any hope of recovery in 2003 was dampened by the increasing supply of redeveloped office space coming onto the Tokyo market.

Zaitech holdings declined in value, with no change in firms' loan obligations. Firms sold shares to cover loan repayments, prompting further falls in the stock market. Shares fell even faster for companies known to have extensive zaitech holdings. Many share prices fell below the exercise prices of the convertible debentures and warrants, meaning these bonds would not be converted into shareholdings, leaving firms to pay off bondholders once they matured.

*Phase 3*: When the firms that borrowed from banks to purchase the high yielding assets default on their loans, the outcome is a "crisis" in the banking sector, and possibly the financial system as a whole. Volatile foreign exchange rates may prompt a run on the currency. All contribute to recession or depression in the real sector of the economy. To date, there has been no currency crisis in Japan. A serious banking crisis which was left unresolved for several years has contributed to what the IMF (2003, p. 14) calls a "fragile" banking sector, with both *stock* and *flow* problems.

Box 8.2 illustrates the problems Japan has faced and summarises the key banking events and reforms. The box also shows Japan, albeit late in the day, took action characteristic of most countries experiencing a banking/financial crisis. These include:

- The creation of a "bad bank" to improve the balance sheets of solvent banks by buying their poorly performing loans.
- Closure or nationalisation of banks – though few in number and relatively late in the crises.
- New laws and procedures such as prompt corrective action to close banks, though a policy of too big to fail has also been adopted.
- Introduction of blanket insurance coverage to stop runs on banks.
- Recapitalisation and new procedures designed to improve loan restructuring, provisioning and better corporate governance.
- Bank mergers, again relatively late. By 2002, Japan had four mega bank groups: Mizuho Financial Group (Fuji, Dai-ichi Kango and Industrial Bank of Japan), Sumitomo Mitsui Banking Corporation (Sakura and Sumitomo Banks), Mitsubishi Tokyo FG (Bank of Tokyo and Mitsubishi Bank) and UFJ Holding (Sanwa and Tokai Banks). Since virtually all these banks were unhealthy at the time of merger, it was not possible to marry weak banks with solvent ones, unlike other countries. The first three mega banks rank in the top 10 world banks in terms of tier 1 capital, but all four reported negative ROAs and real profits growth in 2003.

Unfortunately, these actions have proved insufficient for dealing with the bank/financial crisis. A recent IMF (2003) report, 13 years after the onset of problems, refers to the "fragility" of the banking system. Why do these problems persist when, in most countries, similar policies have resolved the crises? The IMF report refers to the "stock and flow" problems of the banking sector and it is in this context that the discussion below explores the reasons for the prolonged crisis.

## Box 8.2 Japan: Symptoms of and Solutions to its Problems

- 1991: Toyo Sogo Bank and Toyo Shinkin (part of the Sanwa Bank group) run into problems. Toyo Sogo's were due to excessive exposure to a local shipbuilder and other bad loans, and it was taken over by another bank. Toyo Shinkin Bank ran into problems because of forged certificates of deposit (CDs) issued in its name, and bad debts. The Industrial Bank of Japan (IBJ) was required to forgive 70% of its loans to Toyo Shinkin, because it had allowed Ms Nui Onoue (a restaurant entrepreneur) to take back some collateral (its own debentures), which she used to borrow somewhere else. Fuji Bank had to write off a similar amount, and so did two non-banks. The Deposit Insurance Corporation assisted by loaning the bank money at favourable rates.
- 1991: Financial scandals – the most notable being bad loans to Nui Onoue. She borrowed about ¥14 billion from 12 of Japan's largest banks, including the IBJ. In October 1992 the senior officials of IBJ, including the chairman, resigned.
- Establishment of the Cooperative Credit Purchasing Corporation (CPCC) in the early 1990s, a body similar to the Resolution Trust Corporation in the USA, which helps to bail out troubled banks. Unlike the RTC, the CPCC was privately (bank) owned and bought distressed loans from banks, provided a bank sells a loan to the CPCC at a discount to face value.
- In December 1995, the government announced that seven *jusen* (mortgage lending firms) were insolvent and would be closed. Despite a public outcry, approximately 2000 of the agricultural coops with outstanding loans to the jusen received $6.5 billion in public funds and were bailed out by the banks. The Ministry of Finance subsequently revealed that most of the jusen lending was to property companies controlled by Japanese Mafia, the Yakuza. As early as 1990, the MoF had told banks and coops to stop lending to the jusen. The banks obeyed but the coops ignored the order. The MoF instructed the banks (but not the coops) to write-off all loans made to the jusen. The coops got off lightly because of strong links to the Liberal Democratic Party, which relies on them for support in local campaigns. A new body (the Housing Loan Association) was created to buy the bad assets from the jusen, to be funded by new loans from the banks and coops. Virtually none of these assets has been sold off. The jusen affair was a watershed: it was announced that a committee would be established to look at reform of the supervisors. Soon after, with the creation of the FSA (see below), the MoF had lost all its regulatory power.
- 1996: "Big Bang". See Chapters 5, 8 and Appendix 8.1 for more detail but the key change was the removal of barriers separating the ownership of banks, trusts, securities firms, and insurance companies. Financial Holding Companies allowed. Plan to establish the Financial Supervisory Agency and Financial Reconstruction Commission make the Bank of Japan independent – see below.
- June 1997: The Financial Supervisory Agency was created in June 1997 with responsibility for bank supervision. In January 2001, the functions of the Financial Reconstruction Commission and the Financial Supervisory Agency were merged to create the Financial Services Agency (FSA). It has both a supervisory and policy making role.
- 1998 Banking Law Reform: the Housing Loan Association and the Resolution and Collection Bank (created from the Tokyo Kyodo ["saviour"] Bank) were merged into the Resolution and Collection Corporation (RCC). Modelled after the US Resolution Trust Corporation; its remit is to maximise the recovery on non-performing loans. Distressed loans are purchased by the CPCC or the Resolution and Collection Organisation. CPCC sales of collateral has earned, on average, less than 1% of what it paid for the collateral. This is because much of the collateral was property, and property prices have fallen by approximately 84% in real terms since the 1989 peak.
- 1998 Banking Law Reform: FSA to be allowed to take "prompt corrective action" for problem banks.
- 1998: Bank of Japan Act: created an independent central bank, with a primary duty to ensure price stability. The Cabinet appoints but cannot dismiss the Governor, vice-Governor and Policy Board. The MoF continues to have responsibility for currency stability and fiscal matters.
- 1992–99: over 60 banks (half of them in 1999!), consisting largely of credit cooperatives but also, city, regional, and local credit associations, were given assistance by the Deposit Insurance Corporation of Japan, mainly through subsidised mergers. These figures exclude the large number of securities houses and insurance firms which have also been rescued.
- Between 1997 and 1999, three major banks either failed (Hokkaido Takushoko – the 10th largest commercial bank), or were nationalised (Long Term Credit Bank of Japan in 1998 – later purchased by a US financial consortium, Ripplewood Holdings, and Nippon Credit in 1999 – bought by an internet firm, Softbank). Four regionals were allowed to fail – one, Kofuku, was bought by the Asia Recovery Fund.
- 1998: The Deposit Insurance Act was amended in response to the large number of bank failures, and bank runs. Established in 1971, the Deposit Insurance Commission currently reports to the Financial Services Agency. The DIC is funded by premia on banks' deposits to insure deposits of up to ¥10 million. The 1998 reform introduced 100% coverage. After a delay, all time deposits reverted to the 1971 coverage in March 2002. 100% coverage for ordinary deposits was due to expire in March 2003 but this has been postponed,

---

**Box 8.2  (Continued)**

---

again, to April 2005. ¥17 trillion was injected into the fund to assist banks and to allow for 100% deposit insurance coverage.

- May 2000: Deposit Insurance Law amended to allow for "systemic risk" exceptions. If the failure of a FI is deemed a threat to the stability of the financial system, the Prime Minister can call a meeting of the Financial Crisis Council, chaired by the PM. The DIC is then allowed to inject more capital, provide additional assistance or acquire the bank's share capital. In May 2003, the PM used the law for the first time and ordered the DIC to recapitalise the Resona Group (the 10th largest Japanese Bank by tier 1 capital according to *The Banker*, 2003) to bring its capital adequacy ratio above 10%. The recapitalisation included a revitalisation plan submitted by the bank which meant 70 senior managers would go, and salaries would be cut. This has been interpreted to mean that the largest banking groups are "too big to fail". For all other failing banks, the FSA can appoint a financial administrator to deal with the bank, including the disposal of assets and liabilities.
- The FSA is actively encouraging mergers. By 2002, Japan had four mega bank groups: Mizuho Financial Group (Fuji, Dai-ichi Kango and Industrial Bank of Japan), Sumitomo Mitsui Banking Corporation (Sakura and Sumitomo Banks), Mitsubishi Tokyo FG (Bank of Tokyo and Mitsubishi Bank), UFJ Holding (Sanwa and Tokai Banks). It is hoped the mergers will encourage the cross selling of financial products such as mutual funds and insurance, achieve cost savings (through staff cuts, especially when there are overlapping branches, and by spreading IT costs) and improve corporate governance by getting rid of managers of unhealthy banks.
- 2002: The Government and Bank of Japan set up schemes to purchase bank equity.
- 2003: Industrial Revitalisation Corporation of Japan, established to encourage effective corporate restructuring. Japan Post was created with plans to reform or even privatise it.

## 8.4.3. Japanese Banks: The Stock and Flow Problem

The *Banks' stock problem* is caused by a high percentage of non-performing loans, weak capital, and exposure to the equity and property markets, either directly through cross-shareholdings, or through low value collateral, all of which lower the value of their assets. The contributory factors to the stock problem include the following.

- The value of the equities held on the banks' own books fell dramatically, there were large numbers of zaitech firms unable to repay their debt, and the value of collateral (equity and property) collapsed.
- Early MoF policies discouraged banks from writing off bad loans, a critical mistake. For example, in 1991, non-performing loans were rising (evident from the large number of company failures) but banks *reduced* new reserves set against bad debts! According to Hoshi and Kashyap (1999, p. 27), provisioning began to increase but even in 1995, loan loss reserves covered just 52% of the bad debt of the major banks.
- The FSA's estimates of non-performing loans appear in Table 8.11.

If it is assumed the NPLs of healthy banks lie between 1% and 3%, Table 8.11 shows that banks in every sector are in trouble. The long term credit banks (LTCB) are at or close to 10% and the trust banks are not far behind. The rise of NPLs at city and regional banks in 2002–3 reflect the attitude on the part of the new FSA which, unlike the MoF in the early years, has pressured banks to provision for NPLs. However, there are several reasons for thinking these figures substantially underestimate the percentage of bad loans on the banks' books. First, with such low interest rates, it is relatively easy for firms that are effectively insolvent to find the cash to service their debt. Second, the definition of NPLs omits

Table 8.11   Non-Performing Loans as a Percentage of Total Loans, 1998–2003

|                   | 1998 | 1999 | 2000 | 2001 | 2002 | 2003 |
|-------------------|------|------|------|------|------|------|
| City banks        | 4.8  | 5.2  | 6.1  | 6.6  | 8.9  | 7.8  |
| Regional banks I  | 3.7  | 4.9  | 5.6  | 7    | 7.7  | 7.7  |
| Regional banks II | 5.3  | 5.5  | 6.7  | 8.2  | 9    | 8.9  |
| Trust banks       | 8.4  | 11   | 8.7  | 7.5  | 9.5  | 7.5  |
| LTCB              | 10   | 9.1  | 9    | 10   | 9.6  | 6.2  |
| Average           | 5.4  | 5.8  | 6.1  | 6.6  | 8.9  | 7.8  |

NPL: risk management loans: loans to borrowers who are legally bankrupt, restructured loans, past due loans of $\geq 3$ months.
*Source*: IMF, in turn, FSA and Japanese Bankers Association.

categories of debt that would normally be classified as non-performing.[57] Private analysts claim the debt problem is seriously understated – their estimates of the true percentage of NPLs vary from 16.5% to 25%.

Japanese banks aggravated the problems by remaining loyal to their *keiretsu*. A keiretsu is a group of companies with cross-shareholdings and shared directorships, normally including a bank, trust company, insurance firm and a major industrial concern such as steel, chemicals, cars, property and construction, or electronics. Keiretsus grew up in the post-war period after the US occupation forces had abolished the *zaibatsu* – major holding companies which owned firms in all sectors of the economy. The Americans viewed the zaibatsu as cartels, engaging in anti-competitive behaviour. To discourage ownership of commercial concerns, banks were prohibited from owning more than 5% of any industrial firm, later raised to 10%. To circumvent these rules, one company would buy 5% of other firms in the former zaibatsu; the result was the emergence of the keiretsu. For example, before the major problems of the 1990s, the Mitsubishi keiretsu consisted of 160 firms, which included Mitsubishi Bank, Meiji Mutual Life Insurance and Tokyo Marine and Fire Insurance, Mitsubishi Motors and the Kirin brewery. The ownership structure inevitably led to shared directorships.

Within the keiretsu, relationship banking is the norm and analytical lending of secondary importance. Companies of notable financial strength could borrow at a very thin spread, resulting in low revenues for the bank. Weak keiretsu members can negotiate loan rates that do not reflect their riskiness. Middle sized or small, innovative firms outside the keiretsu circle experience difficulty obtaining loans because banks' capital is tied up in loans to keiretsu members.

The financial arrangements between keiretsu members are rarely revealed. The parent firm files a report, but not the explicit activities of subsidiaries. Often the same collateral is pledged for different loans, with no legal recourse for the lending firms in the event of default. Lax accounting procedures and lack of transparency mean there is little credible

---

[57] For example, there are classified assets based on the financial reconstruction law, which, if included in the NPL definition, would double the percentage. Hoshi and Kashyap (1999) note that in the 1990s, the official definition of bad loans was changed (expanded) three times.

information on pension liabilities, audited cash-flow statements, and the debt loans of subsidiaries.

Peek and Rosengreen (2003) provide evidence for much of the bank behaviour noted above. They employ a panel data set from 1993 to 1999, including firm level data which link each Japanese firm to their individual lenders. Together with other data, their econometric tests confirm three hypotheses. First, banks engaged in a policy of **evergreening**, that is, they extended new credit to problem firms to enable them to make interest payments, and thereby avoid or delay bankruptcy. This policy serves the interest of the bank because they can avoid provisioning for bad loans which would put additional strain on their capital requirements. Second, the incentive to evergreen increased if a bank's capital adequacy ratio was approaching the minimum required ratio. Finally, corporate affiliations (e.g. keiretsu) increase the probability that the loan will be made and, the weaker the affiliated firm, the greater the likelihood of a loan being granted. The authors also confirm the presence of regulatory forbearance: the government, in the face of rising deficits and a public hostile to the bailout of banks, put pressure on the banks to behave in this way.

Japan's Financial Supervisory Agency (see Box 8.2) recently began to encourage banks to evaluate loans based on the cash flows the borrowing firm is expected to generate. Banks agree a new repayment scheme and provision according to the net present value of the loan. Provided the estimated cash flows are accurate, this will improve the quality of a bank's balance sheet and encourage more loan restructuring.

Another problem banks face relates to their substantial holdings of equity, arising from cross-shareholdings. The high value of the equities had provided a capital cushion because market value exceeded book value. The situation was reversed after 1989, when the dramatic decline in the stock market began. It is estimated that Japan's hidden reserves fall to 0 if the Nikkei is below 13 000, which it has been for most of the new century so far. In 2001, banks were estimated to hold shares which exceeded their capital by 1.5 times. To deal with the problem, banks have had to adhere to new regulations:

- From September 2001, they must subtract any equity losses from their capital base, which will adversely affect their Basel ratios.
- Since 2002, banks have had to mark to market their equity holdings, even if these are showing a loss.[58]
- Effective September 2004, equity holdings cannot exceed their tier 1 capital.[59]
- Other accounting changes require bad corporate debts hidden in the books of subsidiaries to be added to bad debt provisions.[60]

Manipulation of bank capital has inflated the size of tier 1 and 2 capital. One example is Deferred Tax Assets, or credits against taxes in future income (IMF, 2003, p. 18). Most DTAs are due to losses carried forward: banks are borrowing from expected future profits

---

[58] To date, unrealised profits on equity holdings were reported on a mark to market basis but historical costs are used for unrealised losses.

[59] The Bank of Japan has a scheme to purchase up to 3 trillion yen of these holdings at market prices but will keep them off the market.

[60] Also, companies have to reveal unfunded pensions, which will reduce their creditworthiness.

but only part of their losses are subtracted from capital. According to the IMF, DTAs make up about half the tier 1 capital, but cannot be used to meet losses should a bank fail. Also, low profitability has meant very little capital has been raised via new share issues. Instead, interest earning securities (e.g. preferred securities) have been issued and usually sold to other financial institutions. They are treated as tier 1 capital. Until banks are more profitable, it is unlikely banks will be able raise capital through equity issues. Finally, tier 2 capital is inflated by treating provisions for category II loans[61] as part of tier 2 capital.

## Banks' flow problem

The banks' flow problem arises because of poor profitability which prevents banks from writing off bad assets and raising new capital. The performance of Japan's banks during the period 1998–2003 was quite poor. Over these 6 years, their ROA and ROE were, on average, negative for all but two years, unlike the other G-7 countries. In terms of financial strength, Moody's rates Japanese banks between D− and E+, compared to AAA to C+ for the other G-7 countries (Canada, France, Germany, Italy, UK, USA).[62] Furthermore, as was observed in Chapter 5 (see Figure 5.9), Japanese banks' cost to income ratios are much higher than is true for leading banks in other countries. This poor performance is likely to continue while the corporate sector remains weak, net interest margins are very low, and banks are crowded out from certain core businesses because of the subsidised post office and government financial institutions (see below). Consolidation (see below) should help to reduce competition and cut costs. However, while the banks' performance remains poor, it will be difficult to raise capital through equity issues.

## Other issues

The shinkin credit associations, credit unions and cooperative movements are very small, and most are exempt from regulation. There are about 1700 all together (see Table 8.12) with total assets in the region of ¥124 trillion ($1.1 trillion). As mutual firms, they cannot raise finance through share issues. Local coops make loans to farms and fishing concerns. Farmers are net savers, and about two-thirds of their deposits are passed to the 47 shinren (prefectural lenders) or the national lender, the Norinchukin Bank. Though Norinchukin appears sound, local shinren approved loans to property developers, non-bank affiliates of big banks and speculators in the stock markets during the 1980s. The number of shinren reporting losses is unknown, but it is thought to be very high. Likewise, agricultural coops are in serious trouble.

Life insurance firms are also in trouble. Nissan Mutual and Toho Mutual, two big life insurance firms, failed in 1998/99. The public reaction was to cancel policies. Four more went bankrupt in 2000. Under Japanese law, once bankrupt, firms can reduce annual payouts and the amount paid out on maturity. Mergers and demutualisation are other possible options.

---

[61] Category II loans are loans which need special attention.
[62] *Source*: IMF (2003), p. 14 and table 4 in Appendix II.

Table 8.12   Japan's Financial Structure 2003

| Financial Institutions | Number of FIs | Branches | Employees per Branch | Deposits as % of Total | Loans as % of Total | Assets as % of Total |
|---|---|---|---|---|---|---|
| City | 7 | 2655 | 40 | 22.7 | 28 | 21.6 |
| Regional | 64 | 7600 | 16.4 | 16.6 | 17.1 | 10.8 |
| Regional II | 53 | 3790 | 14 | 5 | 5.4 | 3.2 |
| Foreign banks | 73 | 111 | 42.3 | 0.9 | 1.3 | 2.3 |
| Long-term credit | 2 | 46 | 66.7 | 0.4 | 0.9 | 0.7 |
| Trusts | 27 | 325 | 65.6 | 3.1 | 3.9 | 3.2 |
| Savings & loans | 325 Shinkin credit associations | 8015 | 15.74 | 11 | 9 | 7.4 |
| Others | 5-1 bridge bank, 4 internet banks | 22 | | 0 | 0 | 0 |
| Credit coops | 192 | 1996 | 12.4 | 1.6 | 1.1 | 3.8 |
| Labour credit coops | 22 | 689 | 16.3 | 1.5 | 1.1 | 1 |
| Agricultural coops | 1085 | | | 11.4 | 3.3 | 6.9 |
| Fishery coops | 510 | | | 0.3 | 0.1 | 0.2 |
| Japan Post | 1 | 24773 | 2.5 | 21.9 | 0.7 | 12.8 |
| Government financial institutions* | | 581 | 19.4 | | 20 | 8.8 |
| Securities firms | 276 | 20697 | 42 | 1.6 | 0.5 | 1.6 |
| Money market dealers | 3 | 7 | 62 | na | na | Na |
| Life insurance | 59 | 15807 | 24 | na | 5.9 | 9.5 |
| Non-life insurance | 276 | 4869 | 18 | na | 0.5 | 1.6 |

* The government financial institutions include the Development Bank of Japan (25 branches, 55.6 employees per branch), Japan Bank for International Co-operation (29 branches, 30 employees per branch), Finance Corporations (257 branches, 35 employees per branch).
*Source*: IMF (2003b), table 1, adapted by author.

Tax rules required firms to offer pensions which guarantee a minimum return, typically 2.75% over 8 years.[63] The "5-3-3-2" rule[64] (lifted in 1997) forced funds to invest in government bonds, property and the stock market. Bond yields have declined with the fall in interest rates, and are now below 2%. Thus, pensions are underfunded with very low rates of return. By one estimate, these firms have made losses since 1992.[65]

Non-life insurance firms do not face difficulties because most of their liabilities are short term, so they were limited to investing in cash instruments. In 2001, insurance markets will no longer be segmented. The problems of the life insurance sector may be alleviated

---

[63] The norm in western countries is a contributory plan: inputs are defined and the final pension payout will depend on portfolio returns.
[64] 50% of funds to be invested in safe assets, less than 30% in shares, less than 30% in foreign currency denominated shares, and less than 20% in real estate.
[65] *The Economist*, 2/9/00, p. 98.

if healthy non-life insurance firms take them over and the fixed returns requirement is terminated, a proposal made in December 2000.

Very few securities firms have been profitable in the 1990s. Yamaichi Securities, the oldest and fourth largest of the securities firms, collapsed in November 1997, with $23.8 billion in liabilities. Total losses were close to $53 billion, because Yamaichi bailed out many of the 40 investment management, property and finance keiretsu affiliates. Sanyo Securities failed in the same month. Since 1990, 112 securities firms have closed or been merged, and 114 new firms created. Thus the overall number of securities firms has remained unchanged at about 190.

The Japanese Post Office (JPO) became a state owned corporation in 2003 and was renamed Japan Post. According to the IMF, it is the world's largest deposit taker (IMF, 2003, p. 69). The JPO is the traditional means by which the government raises cheap funds to finance public institutions. Deposit rates were regulated and higher than the rates banks could offer. In 1994, they were deregulated, and in 1995, the MoF lifted restrictions on the types of savings deposits private banks could offer. However, since the Post Office is not constrained to maximise profits, it has continued to attract deposits by offering higher rates than banks. For example, its main product is the *teigaku-chokin*, a fixed amount savings deposit. Once the designated amount has been on deposit for 6 months, it may be withdrawn without notice. However, it can be held on deposit for up to 10 years, at the interest rate paid on the original deposit, compounded semi-annually.[66] Thus, for example, if a deposit is made during a period of high interest rates, that rate can apply for up to 10 years. In 1996, five of the major banks offered a similar type of savings deposit. However, these banks had to respond to changes in market interest rates, and could never guarantee a fixed rate over 10 years. Also, the JPO enjoys a number of implicit subsidies.

- Unlike banks, the JPO does not have to obtain MoF approval to open new branches. With 24 000 outlets, letter couriers are used to facilitate cash deposits and withdrawals in one day, through the two deliveries. By contrast, Table 8.1 shows there are only 2655 branches for the city banks taken together. Sumitomo Mitsui, one of the more retail oriented mega banking groups, had 462 branches in 2003.
- The JPO is exempt from a number of taxes, including corporate income tax and stamp duty.
- It does not have to pay a deposit insurance premium, nor is it subject to reserve requirements.
- JPO deposit rates are set by the Ministry of Posts and Telecommunications, rather than the BJ/MoF/FSA.

One estimate put the state subsidy to the postal system at ¥730 billion per year, equivalent to 0.36% on postal savings deposits.[67] The result is a disproportionately high percentage (about 25%) of total deposits held at the Post Office, and its market share for life insurance is about 15%. It also offers payments facilities. Another consequence is that the subsidy squeezes the interest spreads and profits of the banks that compete with it.

---

[66] See Ito *et al.* (1998), p. 73.
[67] *Source*: Ministry of International Trade and Industry, as quoted in Ito *et al.* (1998), p. 73.

The Japanese are very big savers compared to the rest of the world. Total deposits as a percentage of GDP rose from 1.58 to 2.06 between 1983 and 1996. By contrast, in the USA, they were 0.57, falling to 0.42 in 1996. The US figures are replicated by other OECD countries, though they tend to be a bit higher, in the region of 0.52 and 0.67 (1997 figures).[68] However, there is a need to channel some of these savings away from Japan Post to banks, and into the new investment trusts (similar to mutual funds), which the banks and insurance firms have been allowed to sell directly to the public since 1998. Hoshi and Kashyap (1999) report on forecasts made by the Japan Economic Research Centre. 59% of household assets were in cash and deposits, and the JERC expects them to fall to 45% by 2010 and 35% by 2020. However, the effects of reduced deposits will be partly offset by an increase in banks' revenues from the sale and management of the equivalent of mutual funds.

Ten Government Financial Institutions, nine of which specialise in some form of lending, crowd out private sector loans. For example, the Government Housing Lending Corporation has 30–40% of the mortgage market in Japan. Small and medium-sized enterprises can borrow from any one of three GFIs created to supply them with loans. The Japan Small and Medium Enterprise Corporation insures guarantees of loans to SMEs made by the private sector. It is estimated that four of these GFIs have 20% of the market share in loans to SMEs. Large corporations can borrow from two of these GFIs, which have a market share of about 19%. The GFIs, other public corporations and local governments are funded by transfers from postal savings and life insurance.[69] There are plans to reform Japan Post and the GFIs, but progress is painfully slow.

Japan's Prime Minister announced a series of financial reforms in "Big Bang", 1996 – see Box 8.2 and the appendices at the end of this chapter.[70] Despite all of these reforms there has been little in the way of obvious changes in the financial structure. Compare Table 8.12 with the pre-Big Bang Table 5.8. There has been no significant reduction in the number of city, foreign, savings and loans (shinkin banks), and regional banks. The difference is that these firms may now be part of financial holding companies, and therefore can expand into new areas of business. However, a major drawback is the existence of Japan Post (compare its branch outlets with those of the city and regional banks) and the government financial institutions in their current form, which are subsidised and have a notable market share of deposits, mortgages and loans to SMEs and corporations, making it difficult for banks to penetrate these potentially lucrative markets. Unlike banks in other industrialised countries, Japan's private banks have little opportunity to profit from many aspects of retail and wholesale banking.

## Japan's macroeconomic situation

The slow pace of reform together with the failure of policy makers to close insolvent corporations and banks contributed to a serious downturn in Japan's macroeconomy. The

---

[68] *Source:* Hoshi and Kashyap (1999), table 10.

[69] Via the Fiscal and Investment Loan Programme.

[70] The Big Bangs in New York (1970s) and London (1980s) took place in comparatively robust economies with healthy financial firms. Neither of these conditions applied to Japan when its version of Big Bang was announced in 1996.

cancer in so many of Japan's financial institutions both reflected and aggravated the country's macroeconomic weakness from the early 1990s on. By 2001, the government had spent about $500 billion in direct support[71] of the banks, or about 17% of Japan's annual GDP, with another $200 billion in credit guarantees. Since then, it is difficult to assess the size of the fiscal injection. The expenditure has been financed by government bond issues: any tax increases would depress the economy still further (and there have been some tax cuts). This has resulted in rising government debt and fiscal deficit. In 1999 government debt as a percentage of annual GDP was 100%, climbing to 113% in 2002, nearly double the average in other G-7 economies. These figures exclude large debts recently incurred by institutions linked to Japan's lower tiers of government.

Unemployment peaked at 5.6% in 2001, double its post-war average. For seven years from 1995, consumer expenditure fell in real terms almost uninterruptedly. It was depressed in a climate of job losses and deflation and possibly, by the prospect of higher future taxes to service the burgeoning debt of the public authorities. Official interest rates have remained very close to zero. The consumer price index fell by an average of nearly 1% a year between 1999 and 2003. Expectations of falling prices are a powerful inducement to postpone spending of all kinds.

The government macro policy options are very limited. Fiscal stimulus has not worked, though about half the increase in government expenditure has gone to the financial sector, shoring up banks and other financial firms that should have been allowed to fail. Since 2002, attempts to lower the external value of the yen, designed to strengthen the trade balance contribution to aggregate demand, have only led to some ¥7 trillion paper losses from the MoF's reserves. Monetary stimulus (expected or unexpected) has been hampered by the zero lower bound to nominal interest rates. Generally, with an increase in the money supply, short-run interest rates will fall but in the current climate, this is not possible. One issue is whether the demand for money has a horizontal intercept or not. If it does, money is held to satiation when the nominal interest rate is zero, and there is no apparent way of inducing people to hold more.[72] This was the view held by the previous Governor of the Bank of Japan, Mr Hayami. However, the new Governor, Mr Fukui, clearly thinks the Bank of Japan has a role to play. He has sent out a strong message that monetary policy will be continuously eased (i.e. printing money) until annual inflation has been positive for a reasonable period of time. This message should create inflation expectations.[73] Government bond yields have risen in 2003–4, suggesting a declining proportion of households expect consumer prices to fall.

As this book goes to press, there are a number of encouraging signs pointing to economic recovery:

- In January 2004, narrow money growth rates increased to 4.1%, up from 1.5% a year ago.
- Real GDP increased by 2.3% in 2003, and is forecast to rise by the same amount in 2004.

---

[71] For example, capital injections, purchase of bad assets, support for the Deposit Insurance Corporation.

[72] In the old Keynesian view, this is because of a liquidity trap: horizontal demand curves for bonds (bondholders expect long-run interest rates to rise). If the government tries to buy them back to increase the money supply, the price of bonds will not change, therefore interest rates cannot fall, so there is no way of stimulating investment.

[73] Even though the price of money is close to zero, increasing notes and coins in circulation will raise liquidity.

- Profits earned by non-financial firms have improved, largely due to rapidly increasing import demand from China, rising domestic demand and cost cutting.
- Higher profits have helped to increase share prices by just over 30% between April 2003 and March 2004, encouraging firms to sell off some of their cross equity shareholdings, and pay off some of their debt.

These recent indicators point to a modest recovery, for the first time in over a decade. The irony is that it will be the non-financial sector, together with inflation, which helps banks recover, as more firms are able to repay their debt, the real value of which will decline if there is some inflation in the economy. Japan must continue to stimulate the economy through ongoing financial reform and monetary expansion.

When Japan's Asian neighbours experienced their crises, they were forced to call in the IMF, because currency crises drained them of foreign exchange reserves, and the weak banking sectors quickly collapsed. With its vast foreign exchange reserves (over $350 billion) and healthy trade surplus, Japan has not suffered from a run on its currency. It was wealthy enough to sustain over a decade of recession following on from what was largely a banking crisis. The IMF made mistakes (especially in Indonesia) but few would dispute the necessity of its involvement in resolving the Asian crises. One can only ponder whether the discipline of IMF intervention in Japan would have hastened the pace of financial reform, led to the closure of many more insolvent banks, and prevented a depression.

Has Japan learned its lesson? It is too early to say. The reforms look impressive, but there is nothing to prevent the re-emergence of strong keiretsu, with banks at their centre, engaging in named, rather than analytical, lending. The close bank–corporate relationships in Japan (and Germany) were once praised as models of good governance which contributed to rapid economic growth. However, the serious problems in the financial sector have illustrated problems arising from keiretsu, which discourage healthy competition. Reducing keiretsu ties could improve corporate governance and boost shareholder returns. Though there is talk of reform, Japan Post and the government financial institutions continue to crowd out the private banks from profitable areas of banking and other financial services.

## 8.5. Scandinavian Banking Crises

Finland, Norway and Sweden each experienced systemic banking crises in the late 1980s and early 1990s. They are included here rather than Chapter 7 because the bank failures were systemic: the largest banks in each country required capital injections – five in Finland, four in Norway and three in Sweden (though two large banks came through the crisis without the need for government support), and countless other smaller banks were affected. Denmark experienced a few problems, but they did not turn into a systemic crisis. They are reported here as a contrast on how crises can be resolved, especially in comparison to Japan, and for this reason a less comprehensive account is provided – readers can find numerous studies on the crisis.[74]

---

[74] The account here is based on Sandal (2004). Readers are also referred to Andersson and Viotti (1999), Englund (1999), Koskenkylä (1994, 2000) and Pesola (2001).

The background to the problems in these three countries shares some features with Japan and South East Asia. Prior to the onset of the crises, real GDP growth rates were steady and averaged between 4% and 6% for each country. The growth of credit had been regulated by the governments, but these were removed in the early to mid-1980s. Many interest expenses were tax deductible, and the real interest rate was low and in some years, negative. Once the quantitative restrictions were lifted, there was a boom in lending, which led to a rapid rise in property and stock market prices.[75] Property was the main collateral, and as property price indices soared, there was more borrowing, which in turn raised property prices. The banks were willing lenders, probably due to a combination of factors: they had just been freed from a significant number of restrictions on their activities, including rationing and controls on risk-taking. It is revealing that staff were promoted for increased loan sales rather than risk adjusted return. Other factors include the illusion that collateral substantially reduces risk, and the 'herd' instinct among banks. Thus, the non-financial firms were highly geared, and when the downturn came, bankruptcies soared. Pesola (2001) notes that in Norway and Sweden, 75% of the banks' loan losses were due to bankruptcies in the corporate sector.

Despite the obvious credit boom, fiscal policy was loose, and monetary policy focused on using the interest rates to keep exchange rates steady – particularly in the case of the Swedish crown, against the German mark. As in Asia, the long period of relatively steady exchange rates meant currency risk was largely ignored. Attracted by lower interest rates, banks and the non-financial sector borrowed in foreign currencies. Sweden was the most exposed: about half of total bank lending was in foreign currencies. Unlike Asia, net capital inflows were not a significant contributor.

The bubbles in all three countries burst as a result of economic shocks. Norway was first in line following a sharp drop in world oil prices in 1985–86. The sudden implosion of the Soviet Union in 1990 caused a crash in exports by Finland and (to a lesser extent) Sweden. This led to more severe recessions in these two countries, which is evident in their GDP growth rates, which were negative between 1991 and 1993. Finland's worst year was in 1991, when real GDP fell by 6.3%. In Sweden, the figures are less dramatic: its GDP fell by 1.1% in 1991 and 2.4% in 1993. Both countries recovered quickly: GDP growth rates were 4% in 1994. Norway's growth rate fell much earlier, but the decline was notably smaller – 0.1% over their crisis period of 1988–92 (see Table 8.13).[76] All three countries were raising their interest rates to protect their currencies after German interest rate increases, which increased the cost of borrowing. In the autumn of 1992, Sweden and Finland experienced serious runs on their currencies. This coincided with the onset of the systemic banking crisis in Sweden, though Finland had already entered its systemic phase.

Table 8.13 summarises the main features of the crisis in the three countries. There are several interesting features to point out. In **Finland**, Skopbank was the first to run into difficulties. A commercial bank, it was important to the banking sector because it acted as central bank to the savings banks. In October 1990 a group of savings banks provided

---

[75] Sandal (2004) points out that personal sector investment in the stock market is of much less importance than the property sector.

[76] Sources for GDP figures: Koskenkylä (2000) and Sandal (2004).

Table 8.13   Features of the Scandinavian Crisis and Resolution*

| | Norway | Finland | Sweden |
|---|---|---|---|
| Crisis period | 1988–92 | 1991–93 | 1991–93 |
| Onset of problem bank | Autumn 1988 | Skopbank, 10/90 | Autumn 1991, Första Sparbanken |
| Onset of systemic crisis | Autumn 1991 | 06/92 | Summer 1992 |
| Currency crisis? | No | Yes | Yes |
| % fall in real GDP over the crisis period | −0.1 | −10.4 | −5.3 |
| NPLs as % of total loans | 9 | 9 | 11 |
| Years from peak of crisis to the restoration of bank profitability | 2 | 4 | 2 |
| % of total assets controlled by failed banks | 61% | 96–97% | >90% |
| Introduction of blanket guarantee | Yes but not in law | Yes | Yes |
| Private insurance scheme | Yes, early stages | Yes | No |
| LLR assistance | Yes | No | No |
| Creation of bank restructuring Agency | Yes | Yes | Yes |
| AMCs | No | Yes | Yes |
| Merger or P&A | Yes | Yes | Yes |
| Nationalisation | Den norske Christina Fokus | Skopbank, Savings Bank of Finland** | Nordbanken*** Gota |
| Liquidation (% of banking assets) | Yes (1%) | No | No |
| Creditor losses | No | No | No |
| Shareholder eliminated or diluted | Yes | Yes, mixed | Yes, mixed |
| Managers/board sacked | Yes | Yes | Yes |
| Targets for cost cuts, improved risk management | Yes | Yes | Yes |
| Changes in prudential regulation and supervision | Yes | Yes | Yes |

* This table was constructed from tables 1 and 2 of Sandal (2004), except the % of assets controlled by troubled banks. The figures were supplied by the Bank of Finland (Sampo Alhonsuo), Bank of Norway (Knut Sandal) and Koskenkylä (2000) for respectively, Finland, Norway and Sweden.
** SBF was established from the mergers of several problem savings banks.
** Nordbanken was majority owned by the state before the crisis.

Skopbank with a capital injection but by September 1991, it faced acute liquidity problems. The Bank of Finland took it over (through a substantial equity capital injection) to maintain confidence in the banking system. Two new asset management companies were created, owned and operated by the central bank. In March 1992 the government offered capital to all banks to ensure there was no sudden cut back in lending. Virtually every bank took up the offer, costing the state FIM 8 billion. A month later, the Government Guarantee Fund was created, financed by the state. The GGF could provide guarantees, capital injections and, in June, the central bank sold its shares in Skopbank to the GGF.

June 1992 marked the beginning of the systemic crisis, when it became evident that 41 savings banks were in trouble. They were merged into the Savings Bank of Finland owned by the GGF. Again, bad assets were transferred to a state owned AMC. As Table 8.13 shows, at the height of the crisis, the troubled banks controlled 97% of Finland's bank assets.[77] In August, the government announced protection of all creditors, and this blanket guarantee soon became law. The GGF also had to intervene in a smaller commercial bank, and provide guarantees for two large commercial banks (Union Bank of Finland and KOP) and the cooperative banks, though these guarantees were never used.

**Norway's** problems began in the autumn of 1988, when middle-sized commercial banks' loan losses resulted in 25% of their equity capital being wiped out, and two regional savings banks lost all their equity. Norway had no government run deposit insurance scheme. Instead, there were two private commercial and savings banks funds, called, respectively, the Commercial Banks' Guarantee Fund and the Savings Bank Guarantee Fund. These two private funds intervened with capital support, followed by mergers. During 1989–90, the savings bank fund provided support to 11 banks, which were merged with healthy banks. As the number of problem banks grew, it was clear the private funds could not provide the necessary support. In January 1991, the Government Bank Insurance Fund (GBIF) was formed. Initially it supplied loans to the two private funds but as these funds began to acquire large debt burdens, the GBIF began to provide direct support.

The crises turned systemic in the autumn of 1991 when Den norske Bank, Christiania Bank and Fokus Bank, the three largest commercial banks, reported large loan losses. The latter two banks lost all their capital; Den norske a substantial proportion. Christiania and Fokus were nationalised – their shareholders received nothing. By late 1992, Den norske suffered the same fate. In October 1991, the government announced that all depositors and creditors would be protected. These banks were gradually returned to the private sector: Christiania bank is now part of the Nordea group (since 2000). In 1995 Fokus shares were privatised and eventually bought by Den danske Bank (Denmark). The state owned just under 50% of Den norske in 2002 and the policy is to own at least a third of it, primarily to keep its head office in Norway. The government maintains an arms-length relationship and is not involved in its daily operations.

In the autumn of 1991, **Sweden's** largest savings bank, Första Sparbanken, announced heavy loan losses and the need for capital injections, followed by Nordbanken, the third largest commercial bank, which was state owned (the state had 71% of its equity). The government introduced guarantees, which later turned into loans. Gota Bank (the fourth

---

[77] Thanks to Sampo Alhonsuo, of the Bank of Finland, for supplying this figure.

largest commercial bank) reported problems in April 1992 – it was given an injection of capital and put up for sale. With no buyers, Nordbanken took it over in 1993. Two state asset management companies (Securum and Retriva) took on the bad assets of, respectively, Nordbanken and Gota Bank.

By the autumn of 1992, the currency crisis, the severity of the recession and a collapse in property prices coincided with the onset of a systemic crisis, as foreign creditors cut off their foreign currency funding. The seven largest banks (which together controlled 90% of the assets) were in trouble because of loan losses. Government intervention was swift, with a 100% creditor guarantee, and a commitment to unlimited liquidity support by the central bank, Riksbanken. In May 1993, Bankstödsnämnden (BSN) was created – nearly 100% of the support, in the form of equity capital, loans and guarantees, went to Gota and Nordbanken – these banks were now effectively nationalised and owned by BSN. Nordbanken eventually became part of the Nordea group, but the Swedish state, as the largest shareholder, owned just under 19% of Nordea. Other large banks, S-E Banken and Sparbanken Sverige, were able to raise capital privately, as were many smaller banks, thanks in part to the strong signal sent out by the Swedish government that the banking system would be supported.

Pesola (2001) used panel data from Norway, Sweden and Finland, and also Denmark (where no crisis occurred), in an econometric study of the causes of the banking crises in the Nordic countries. He used 63 observations for the period 1983–98. Two dependent variables were used: firm bankruptcies per capita and loan losses as a percentage of total lending. The key independent variables tested were as follows.

- Banks' domestic credit/nominal GDP: a proxy for financial fragility.
- Income surprise variable: the difference between the % change in actual GDP volume and its forecast value published in June of the preceding year.
- Interest rate surprise variable: the change in the nominal lending rate.
- Nominal trade weighted effective exchange rate in country.
- Terms of trade: a country's export price index/import price index.
- Regulation dummy coefficient.

Pesola found that the high levels of indebtedness, together with the negative income and interest rate surprise proxies, were all statistically significant with the expected signs. So was the economic regulation proxy, suggesting that financial liberalisation contributed to the crisis: deregulation increased the amount of loan losses by about 1%. However, he is rightly cautious about the regulation variable, because it influences the other independent variables – Pesola surmises that there may be some sort of feedback mechanism operating. Neither the exchange rate nor the terms of trade were found to be significant.

Between 1984 and 1993 seven Danish banks encountered problems, but they avoided a systemic crisis. Pesola argues there were several reasons why Denmark avoided a banking crisis. The financial reforms were introduced earlier and changed to deal with new circumstances. For example, Danish banks had to allow for probable credit losses, and mark to market off-balance sheet items when reporting their profit figures. Hence the debt burden of firms was far lower, and unlike the other three countries, credit losses were spread over a 9-year period. Macroeconomic shocks were also smaller.

There are several interesting observations to make concerning the Nordic crises and the Asian and Japanese crises. Compared to Japan, the crises were rapidly resolved. This appears to be largely due to concerted government intervention as soon as a bank got into trouble, which became all embracing once the crises turned systemic. This, in turn, reduced the cost of resolving the crises in the Nordic countries compared to the Asian economies and Japan.

In the Scandinavian crisis, there were virtually no runs on domestic bank deposits, though interbank lending dried up for all three countries. It is notable that, unlike Asia, blanket creditor guarantees apparently prevented any classic bank runs, even in Norway, where it was not backed by law. This attests to the importance of government credibility. In Japan, a 100% guarantee to depositors was introduced to stop retail runs on banking, which began quite a few years after the crisis began.[78] When it was partially lifted, depositors were quick to move their deposits into gold or accounts that were still guaranteed. This forced the government to twice postpone its return to partial deposit insurance.

The currency crises in Sweden and Finland occurred some time after problems in the banking sectors had begun. So, unlike Asia, there is no clear line of causation from the foreign exchange markets to problems in the banking sector, though there is no doubt that currency problems aggravated growing difficulties in the Swedish and Finnish banking sectors. Finland and Sweden switched exchange rate regimes, from fixed to flexible (though Finland has since adopted the euro), while Norway opted for a pegged regime.

It is notable there was a macro downturn in two of the Nordic countries (see Table 8.13), despite the rapid intervention and resolution of the problem in all three. One of the reasons for the prolonged depression in Japan appears to be the assumption by the authorities and the banks that problems such as the rising proportion of non-performing loans would resolve themselves. These country differences in the role played by the macro/currency sector in the crises raise the issue of the direction of causation: did the banking crises aggravate macro problems or did the state of the macroeconomy worsen the crisis? More research on these causality issues is needed.

## 8.6. Long Term Capital Management (LTCM)

Though not a bank, LTCM is included here because of the implications of the failure of a non-bank financial firm in the banking sector, and also, it demonstrates the increasing importance of having good risk management procedures if a financial firm wants to survive. It shows the deficiencies of excessive reliance on value at risk, which, as seen in Chapters 3 and 4, has become a central component of banks' risk management techniques and regulators' tools for monitoring banks.

Dunbar (2000) wrote an excellent book on LTCM's rise to fame and subsequent demise, and it is not the intention to try and replicate his work here. Rather, the focus is on the key lessons for banks and regulators. LTCM was founded in 1993 by highly regarded practitioners and academics. Five years later, it collapsed.

---

[78] This may have been due to the absence of information that the banking system was in trouble, which in turn was caused by the Ministry of Finance discouraging banks from provisioning for, and writing off, bad debt.

LTCM was a hedge fund, a term with US origins after an investment company was set up to buy stocks and to sell them short, hence the term "hedge". Provided the company was for wealthy investors, it was exempt from the strict regulations imposed by the Securities and Exchange Commission.[79] Until LTCM, the Soros fund was the most famous. It sold sterling short during the ERM crisis of 1992, when the UK authorities spent £14 billion trying, but failing, to keep sterling within the ERM band. John Meriwether was a highly respected trader even though he had left Salomon Brothers under a cloud in 1991. He formed LTCM in January 1993. It consisted of two partnerships. Long Term Capital Portfolio, the actual fund, was registered in the Cayman Islands to minimise taxation and avoid regulation, and Long Term Capital Management (LTCM) was a limited partnership registered in Delaware with offices in Greenwich, CT.

The hedge fund made money from arbitrage opportunities: buying low and selling high. However, the margins are low, so these funds need high volumes and require huge capital backing. The exceptionally good reputations of the founders, Merton Miller and Myron Scholes (who in 1997 jointly shared the Nobel Prize in Economics for their work on option pricing), John Meriwether and others, meant the firm was able to attract capital of over $1 billion, including personal capital committed by the partners.[80]

One source of profit was the "money machines" which had been developed while Meriwether and many LTCM employees who had worked with him were at *Salomon Brothers*. When securities with the same or near identical payoffs have different returns, the arbitrageurs use them to create a *money machine* to provide a risk-free return. One example: at Salomons, Meriwether found that newly issued 30-year US Treasury bills sold at a premium compared to those issued say 1 year earlier, with a term of 29 years. By selling 30-year bonds short and buying the older bonds, a profit could be made when the new bond (sold short) was a year old.

Another money machine was issuing a capital bond which guaranteed investors their capital at the end of say 5 years, plus, for example, the equivalent of their capital plus 110% of the rise in the FTSE 100. The financial institution issuing this instrument could hedge against any rise by buying a zero-coupon bond plus a long-term option which would pay out the equivalent amount if the FTSE does rise. LTCM arranged the option for the financial institution.

Initial profits on trades such as these increased capital to $4.87 billion by 1998. The partners were so confident that they returned $2.7 billion to investors shortly before they began to get into difficulties. In theory, the risks incurred by LTCM should not have been that high. Just before their collapse, liabilities amounted to $124.5 billion, and assets $129 billion. However, LTCM was highly leveraged with off-balance sheet items worth $1.25 trillion (Miller, 2001, p. 323). Investors were unaware of the size of the leverage and were not concerned because the firm was supposed to be profiting from arbitrage opportunities.

---

[79] The Investment Company Act (1940) was another one of the post-depression laws aimed at protecting small investors from mutual funds, which would be strictly regulated by the Securities and Exchange Commission. The company described above was exempt from the rules. Investors typically pay 1–2% annual fee plus 20% of whatever the fund earns.

[80] Investors had to commit at least $10 million for a minimum period of 3 years, pay fees of 2% per annum, earning 25% of the profits.

The arbitrage positions necessitated short sales. The firm making the loan usually gets collateral (securities) plus a "haircut" (see Chapter 5), an additional sum amounting to about 2% of the security's value, so if the borrower defaults, the lender gets something back. Or if the value of the collateral declines, the haircut is there to cover the lender until an additional margin is paid. However, the size and reputation of LTCM meant it did not normally pay haircuts.

A number of factors contributed to the "failure" of LTCM.

- The use of a value at risk model: known as the Risk Aggregator Model (at LTCM), the problems with VaR models were outlined in Chapter 3. However, most other financial institutions using VaR are subject to additional regulations and scrutiny by regulators which complement the VaR contribution. However, LTCM had been set up to minimise regulatory constraints – it was not a bank, and it was registered in the Cayman Islands. So there was no independent body scrutinising their risk control measures. When LTCM lost money early in the summer of 1998, and breached its VaR measures, the firm claimed it was a one-off loss, caused by *Salomon* unwinding all positions related to the bond arbitrage operation, which it decided to close down. Nonetheless, the breach in VaR limits is an indicator, telling a firm to either sell assets or increase capital. Ironically, LTCM had just returned capital to investors. Raising capital would be difficult with increasingly volatile financial markets – this was the time when many of the "tiger" economies of South East Asia experienced currency and banking crises that were affecting markets around the world (see Chapter 5). LTCM took the only course open to it: it reduced its assets. Rather than cut a range of positions, a decision was taken to reduce the most liquid (and least profitable) positions.
- In already volatile markets, under government orders, Russia devalued the rouble and, not for the first time in its history, declared it was suspending its debt repayments. Some banks heavily exposed in Russia experienced large losses, and many financial firms, having breached their VaR limits, were forced to reduce their exposures. They rushed to sell their more liquid swap and bond positions, which caused prices to fall – VaR limits were *exceeded* again, leading to more sell-offs. This episode provides an example of one of the problems with VaR: if most FIs are selling at the same time, there are no buyers, causing a further drop in prices. The only prices that were rising were those of safe, relatively liquid securities. Many LTCM positions involved going short on less liquid securities and purchasing the less liquid securities with about the same risk (e.g. the Treasury bill money machine explained above). The events in Asia and Russia reduced the creditworthiness of developing country/emerging market bonds, and widened the spreads between the prices of these bonds and those issued by creditworthy western governments. LTCM had bet on a narrowing of these spreads. Losses mounted and by the end of August 1998, LTCM's capital shrunk to $2.3 billion. As its asset base declined, its leverage soared to 45.
- The LTCM partners had always assumed their positions were, to a large extent, offsetting, but in a market where most prices are falling, this no longer holds true. Furthermore, LTCM was short on the only securities that were rising in price. LTCM was searching for more capital by August but with a flight to security, hedge funds were the last place investors were willing to place their capital. With losses of $1.85 billion in August,

LTCM's situation worried the banks which had exempted them from haircuts. The counterparties to long-term options can change the mark to market requirements, and raised them in an effort to secure more collateral. For LTCM it meant more capital had to be set aside, making it unavailable for other activities.

It was clear LTCM was effectively bankrupt and little could be done to stop it, short of finding the necessary capital. The LTCM portfolio was in the Cayman Islands, and the country's bankruptcy laws, unlike the USA, did not force the immediate liquidation of all positions. This meant the key investment banks faced big losses if LTCM was declared insolvent because their capital would be tied up for years. Losses also came from the individual banks' own exposures: many had tried to copy what LTCM was doing. For example, the arbitrage activities at Goldman Sachs gave rise to trading losses of $1 billion in the period July to September – most of it lost in August and September. The potential losses faced by the investment banks if LTCM failed prompted fears of major repercussions on world financial markets, which were already being felt. For example, the mortgage and company bond markets had more or less ceased to function because there were no investors willing to buy the high yield (but also more risky) bonds. The President of the Federal Reserve Bank of New York, Mr William McDonough, decided action was needed.

Meriwether had already been to see Jon Corzine, Co-chairman of Goldman Sachs. Corzine was anxious to absorb LTCM and agreed to try and raise the $2 billion in capital Meriwether needed, in exchange for control over LTCM's risk management and 50% ownership of LTCM.[81] On 18 September, McDonough's phone calls to the leading investment banks confirmed his worst fears, but Corzine was able to tell him there could be a way out. Client confidentiality meant Corzine had to get Meriwether's permission before providing details of their agreement. Meriwether refused, and asked to speak with the regulators directly, perhaps sensing that a less painful solution might come via the FRBNY. At his meeting with the FRBNY, Meriwether outlined the scenario if LTCM went under: the main point being that the counterparties to the trades (most of them investment banks) would each lose between $3 billion and $5 billion.[82] Furthermore, these banks would lose even more money when the size of these losses became known, creating turmoil on global financial markets. By Tuesday, 22 September, the FBRNY had a consortium of 13 investment banks reach an agreement. They would inject $3.625 billion, the principals would be allowed to keep their stake, and would be retained at LTCM on a salary of $250 000 per annum.

Meanwhile, Corzine of Goldman Sachs had persuaded Warren Buffet to inject $3 billion into the fund, and another $1 billion came from another investor and Goldman Sachs. The deal was worth $4 billion but Buffet insisted that all the principals at LTCM had to go, along with their stake in the firm, which would be bought for $250 million.

On Wednesday, 23 September, the main investment banks and the FRBNY officials were meeting to finalise their agreement, but Corzine informed McDonough of the Buffet deal. Meriwether was faxed details of Buffet's offer and asked to accept it. According to Dunbar (2000), Meriwether had worked out that if he refused the deal, it was highly likely the

---

[81] Plus other concessions.
[82] According to Dunbar (2000), p. 219, Mr McDonough later reported these figures to Congress.

FRBNY's consortium arrangements would have to be adopted because no one could afford to let LTCM fail. Meriwether had 50 minutes to agree to the Buffet offer, but claimed he had no legal authority to accept it – all the partners would have to agree and it was impossible to do that in the 50 minute time frame, so the deal would, and did, lapse. Losses at LTCM had increased during the week, depleting its capital still further to $400 million. Earlier in the week, Bear Sterns had declared it would not clear LTCM's trades if its capital was less than $500 million. McDonough was not prepared to challenge Meriwether's decision. By evening, the major investment banks[83] agreed to inject $3.625 billion, the principals would stay on at LTCM (supervised by traders appointed by the consortium), and they could keep the $400 million, though it now amounted to just 10% of the fund.[84]

Dowd (1999) and others argue that had LTCM been allowed to fail, the threat to the financial markets would have been minimal. He argues that the losses would have been in the billions, when there are trillions of dollars of capital in the global markets. However, the problems would have been concentrated in the investment banks, which would have seen their capital severely depleted. For example, Goldman Sachs' IPO, which finally took place in May 1999, raised $3.6 billion. It was rumoured that Lehman Brothers was close to bankruptcy. The failure of respected investment banks would have added to the market turmoil. On the other hand, the rescue of LTCM did not quiet the markets, and those banks which were part of the bailout and quoted on the stock market suffered badly in the immediate aftermath. Merrill Lynch lost 75% of their market value between January and October 1998. The markets did not begin to recover until October 1998, when the Fed twice dropped interest rates by 25 basis points, in October and November 1998, and market calm was restored. Even then, the summer of 1999 saw another round of volatility. Countless numbers of hedge funds were forced to close.

By October 1999, LTCM had repaid $2.6 billion of capital to the consortium, after the consortium had sold off the big money machines, and its assets were reduced by 90%.[85] Having repaid its loans, LTCM was liquidated in 2000.

Miller (2001) provides a good summary of the lessons learned from LTCM, and some of his points appear in the discussion here. First, arbitrage may not always be achieved, so trades that depend on price discrepancies between markets narrowing over time may find there are occasions when the differences actually widen, and if a fund is highly leveraged, it may not have the capital to fund the positions. At this point the old question of how efficient the market is arises, a debate that was briefly covered early in the chapter. Also, portfolios which appear to be diversified in normal markets may turn out to be highly correlated if traders want to liquidate their positions at the same time. Linked to this point is the role played by VaR models: if all banks are using similar risk management techniques linked to regulations they must abide by, it will encourage investors to sell at the same time. However, the phenomenon of an event (or events) causing all agents to sell simultaneously has been observed for centuries, so it is difficult to apportion much of the blame to VaR

---

[83] Goldman Sachs, JP Morgan, Merrill Lynch, Morgan Stanley, Credit Suisse, UBS, Salomon Smith Barney, Bankers Trust, Deutsche Bank, Chase Manhattan and Barclays Capital each contributed $300 million; Société Generale, Lehman Brothers and Paribas each contributed $100 million.

[84] The principals had held about 40% of LTCM's equity.

[85] Dunbar (2001), p. 230.

models alone. The issue to tackle is to identify the events which will trigger VaR breaches, and the subsequent downward spiral.

Miller makes a point about the method of financing hedge funds and its effects on the traders. If managers are paid a base sum – e.g. 2% of the assets and a share (25%) of the profits – then they have an incentive to take excessive risks because in good years, they do very well, but it is the investors who cover the losses if the fund fails. The only counter-argument to this point is that the managers (and traders) have often invested most of their own capital in the fund – LTCM is a case in point. Dunbar (2000), p. 223 talks about one of the LTCM traders breaking down because all of his savings had been invested in the firm.

A final point relates to the role of the regulators. It was Mr Buffet's offer that should have been accepted. Meriwether appeared to know he could hold the regulators to ransom because of the financial carnage envisaged if the fund had failed. Surely if McDonough had insisted the Buffet deal be accepted, Meriwether and partners would have been forced to comply. Such remarks are easily made with the benefit of hindsight, and the bailout did not involve any public funds. However, Meriwether (and other partners) ended up as salaried employees (albeit low ones by their standards) rather than certified bankrupt, at the expense of investors of the consortium banks, a difficult pill to swallow. There are no constraints on their actions, and Meriwether is reported to be running another fund.

The actions of the FRBNY (supported by Alan Greenspan at the Federal Reserve) sends out somewhat worrying signals. It suggests that it is prepared to intervene in problem hedge funds (if it is thought they pose a threat to world markets) even though it does not regulate them, which is likely to aggravate the already inherent risk-taking activities of these funds, especially if they get into trouble.

## 8.7. Lender of Last Resort

### 8.7.1. The LLR Debates

The review of the Asian and Japanese crises has shown the domestic lender of last resort in action, i.e. the central bank intervening to supply liquidity to banks being crippled by runs. IMF intervention was needed to help resolve most of the crises in South East Asia, though Japan avoided it due to its wealth and the absence of a run on the yen. This section takes a more formal look at the issues surrounding the lender of last resort (LLR), and the calls for an international LLR (ILLR).

The passage of the Bank of England Act (1844) was a victory for the *Currency School*,[86] which called for the central bank to stabilise the price level through control of the money supply. There was to be adherence to the strict quantity theory of money, reflecting an earlier acceptance of the Palmer Rule (1832), i.e. note issue was strictly limited to the amount of gold held by the Bank. It was thought the 1844 Act would put a stop to manias because agents knew the Bank of England could not intervene should there be a speculative

---

[86] The *Banking School* argued the money supply should grow with output and trade. They opposed any law which restricted the quantity of note issue, no matter what the circumstances. See Andreades (1966) for further discussion.

event. They were soon proved wrong, with a crisis in 1847 and two more in 1857 and 1866. The Act had to be suspended to allow the Bank of England to break the rule, and the panics were brought under control. Despite two investigations by the House of Commons following the first two crises, changing the 1844 Act was not thought necessary. It was not until the 1914 Bank of England Act that the Bank was given a dual role: supplying liquidity in the event of bank crises and using discretionary monetary policy to maintain price stability.

Henry Thornton (1802) had discussed the relative merits of a lender of last resort, but most attention is paid to the writings of Walter Bagehot, editor of *The Economist* and author of *Lombard Street* (1873). Bagehot advocated the Bank of England act as lender of last resort, calling on it to supply cash during banking crises:

> *"Theory suggests, and experience proves that in a panic the holders of the ultimate Bank reserve (whether one bank or many) should lend to all that bring good securities quickly, freely and readily. By that policy they allay a panic; by every other policy, they intensify it."* (1873/1962, p. 85)

> *"The Bank of England. . . in a time of panic it must advance freely and vigorously to the public out of the reserve. . . And for this purpose, there should be two rules:—First. That these loans should only be made at a very high rate of interest. . . This will prevent the greatest number of applications by persons who do not require it. The rate should be raised early in the panic. . . so that the Banking reserve may be protected as far as possible.*

> *Secondly. That at this rate these advances should be made on all good banking securities. . . The object is to stay alarm. . . . But the way to cause alarm is to refuse some one who has good security to offer – if securities, really good and usually convertible, are refused by the Bank, the alarm will not abate, the other loans made will fail. . . and the panic will become worse and worse. . ."* (1873/1962, p. 97)

The classic features of a LLR have hardly deviated from Bagehot's recommendations. From the 1914 Act until 1997/98, the Bank of England assumed responsibility for dealing with runs, panics and financial crises. Though its role as lender of last resort was never formalised, it has, *de facto*, acted in this capacity. Its more recent interventions include:

- The UK's secondary banking crisis (1973).
- The nationalisation of Johnson Matthey Bankers (1984).
- Closing the Bank of Credit and Commerce International (1993) and dealing with the subsequent fallout from its closure, requiring the Bank to supply liquidity to a number of smaller banks.
- Its attempt to launch a lifeboat rescue for Barings Bank in 1995, and when that failed, the Governor's announcement that the Bank stood ready to supply liquidity to the financial markets should they be unsettled by the Barings failure. In the event, it proved unnecessary.

Following the 1998 Bank Act (see Chapter 4), responsibility for financial stability is now shared between the Financial Services Authority, HM Treasury and the Bank of England by a formal Memorandum of Understanding. This arrangement is yet to be tested.

Compared to the UK, the US Federal Reserve System was given more formal responsibility for ensuring the stability of the banking system. A series of panics and runs on banks and trust companies had originated in New York in 1907, and spread to other states. The Federal Reserve Act (1913) created a central bank, and allowed it to provide an "elastic" currency (liquidity) in the event of a crisis. After the Banking (or Glass Steagall) Act was passed in 1934, the Federal Reserve was given the power to change the reserve ratio – up to this time, it could only be changed by Congress. The Act also sanctioned the introduction of bank deposit insurance.

Wood (2000) argues central banks should be confined to supporting troubled but solvent banks during a banking crisis. However, actions by central banks suggest that they have widened their remit to assist in a wide range of financial crises, not just banking crises. Examples include the Bank of England's declared support of the financial markets post-Barings, the Fed-led injection of liquidity by key central banks in the aftermath of Black Monday in October 1987, the package to rescue a *hedge* fund, Long Term Capital Management, organised by the Federal Reserve Bank of New York because of fears that its failure would threaten the solvency of some of LTCM's bank creditors and, more generally, disrupt financial markets, and the numerous interventions in currency markets to support a particular currency.

Thus, the function of the domestic lender of last resort has evolved over time. Central banks (and or another authority, though it is the central bank which supplies the liquidity) may be involved in the rescue of a single bank or substantial parts of the whole domestic banking system. The authorities in most countries supply liquidity during bank runs or financial crises. Apart from restoring financial stability, Kindleberger has identified two other potential advantages of a LLR. First, a LLR appears to have reduced the length of the economic slowdown that follows a crisis. Kindleberger (ch. 12) notes the crises of 1873 (Vienna, Berlin, New York) and 1929 turned into great depressions of the 1870s and 1930s; in both cases there was no LLR. Likewise, the slowdown was prolonged in 1720 (England and France), 1882 (France), 1890 (England) and 1921 (Britain, USA). By contrast, all the other crises from 1763 to 1914 had an LLR (or equivalent), which helped minimise disruption to the real economy.

Second, Kindleberger[87] claims that the number of crises was less frequent in Britain after 1866 and in the USA after 1929, suggesting a LLR reduces the number of crises. But as was noted earlier in this chapter, a substantial increase in systemic crises has been observed, many of them international. These crises have been large, varying and, in some cases, very costly, as Table 8.1 illustrates.

LLR intervention also has a downside: problems related to moral hazard. Agents may be induced to change their subsequent behaviour.

- It signals that future misfortunes for private banks (or countries – see below) may well be followed by future bailouts. The likely consequences are that banks exercise less care in assessing loans, and appraising risks, as do creditors who lend to banks.

---

[87] Kindleberger (1978/2000, p. 211). Also, Kindleberger cites these advantages when he is writing about an international lender of last resort, but they could equally apply to a LLR.

- The wrong (i.e. insolvent) banks are bailed out, either because there is not enough information to distinguish between illiquidity and insolvency, or for other reasons such as political interference. Whatever the cause, it undermines future incentives and weakens market discipline.
- The LLR could be influenced by political considerations (e.g. powerful lobbies persuade government to forbear and bend criteria) that override or distort financing or accounting judgements.

To counter moral hazard problems, most LLR operate under strict conditions, which date back to Bagehot. For illiquid banks, the LLR should accept commercial paper at a discounted rate[88] and/or grant loans at a penal rate of interest, with the borrowing banks required to supply collateral. Insolvent banks should be closed and losses borne by shareholders, holders of subordinated debt, uninsured depositors and the deposit insurance corporations. While few dispute the necessity of these requirements accompanying a LLR facility, they are by no means straightforward.

Begin with the need to distinguish insolvent from illiquid banks. In practice, the boundary between the two can be fickle and unclear. The increased complexity of bank balance sheets can make it difficult to distinguish between the two. Many troubled banks, on the brink of failure, will have assets with a total "real" value (as quantified post-crisis) exceeding liabilities, even though this may well not be the case at the height of the panic. Furthermore, studies such as James (1991) have shown that liquidating insolvent banks is more costly than restructuring them, through, for example, a bailout or merger with a healthy bank, or nationalisation. This may explain why Goodhart and Schoenmaker (1995) found that out of 104 failing banks (in 24 countries), 73 were rescued and the other 31 liquidated. Santomero and Hoffman (1998) report that even though banks had poor CAMEL ratings, they were given access to the Fed's discount window between 1985 and 1991.[89]

Charging a penal rate to illiquid banks can also be problematic, causing runs because of the signal it sends to the market, which will worsen a bank's problems. Managers faced with a penal rate may "go for broke", adopting high risk strategies in the hope that the bank's position will improve. A possible alternative would be to attach conditions to a loan, such as closer monitoring, restrictions on banks' activities, and even changes in top management.

The demand for adequate collateral dates back to Bagehot, and he acknowledged the need to lower standards under certain conditions. The Asian and Japanese crises illustrate how collateral can be a healthy security one day and of no value the next. How can any bank be sure collateral is absolutely safe unless it is reduced to a narrow range of securities such as US Treasury bills or UK gilts? Even with these assets, problems could arise. Japanese government bond issues were once considered on a par with their US equivalent, but have been steadily downgraded in recent years.

---

[88] The central bank could accept banks' commercial paper for delivery at some specified date in the future: If a central bank accepts a $100 bill for $90.91, to be repaid in 1 year, the implicit rate of interest is 10%.

[89] This is unlikely to be repeated. Since the Federal Deposit Insurance Corporation Improvement Act was passed in 1991 (see Chapter 5), the FDIC is required to use the "least cost" approach to resolve bank insolvency. Also, see Chapter 4 for an explanation of CAMEL.

There may be an argument for using a case approach. If the LLR judges that a panic or bank run rather than a bank's balance sheet is the source of the problem, it could lower the standards for collateral required, and/or lower the penal rate of interest. In some ways the case for the LLR is rather like that for a nuclear deterrent: a device aimed to prevent the panics that would occasion its use. Nonetheless, the recurrence of crises in countries where the authorities have granted emergency liquidity assistance, and failed to find other solutions for insolvent banks, does testify to the fact that it may have been misused.

These remarks are not intended to challenge the principle of having a lender of last resort. However, they do suggest that the function brings with it considerable complexities, and certain longer term risks if insolvent banks are assisted. Added to this is the expense of bank rescues and/or the whole system. The subsequent additions to public sector debt could lead to higher distortionary taxes to finance the bailouts, or threaten inflation targets or lower growth rates.

## 8.7.2. International Lender of Last Resort

With the advent of international crises has come the call for an international LLR. Goodhart and Huang (2000) use a theoretical model to show that the central bank, unable to meet the demand for foreign currency, can cause a currency crisis, which triggers a banking crisis. Though an international interbank market can help economies with the necessary liquidity, it also raises the size of the international financial contagion risk. An ILLR could, it is claimed, help to provide the liquidity and reduce this contagion.

The IMF has come closest to playing that role: it intermediates between private banks and countries in crises. Calomiris (1998) and Calomiris and Meltzer (1999) assign the role of an ILLR to the IMF, arguing it should adhere to the strict "Bagehot rules". Fischer also advocates the IMF as ILLR for countries with an external financing crisis, when the central bank lacks the reserves to meet the demand for foreign exchange.

However, the IMF is unlikely to assume the role of ILLR in the traditional sense of the term, because of its budgetary constraints, the absence of arrangements for member country central banks to supply it with liquidity,[90] and its inability to print money.

The IMF is funded through contributions by member countries. Each member is assigned a quota, based on its relative size in the world economy. Quota contributions were last reviewed in January 2003, but kept at their 1998 levels, which means their total quota is just under $300 billion. However, the *one year forward commitment capacity* gives a rough indicator of the amount available for new[91] lending, and as of September 2003, it was $88 billion. In view of the size of recent restructuring packages, the IMF could never be the sole source of finance. It has to rely on funds from development agencies (e.g. the World Bank), and government or private loans from other countries.

Consider the case of Mexico. In August 1982, the government suspended the principal of foreign debt after it became impossible to meet its debt service commitments. Its story is all too familiar. Oil rich, it had borrowed from foreign banks on the strength of the price

---

[90] It is worth stressing that a central bank is likely to supply liquidity in the event of a run or runs on a bank. However, the longer-term restructuring will require government and agency funds.

[91] Non-concessional.

of oil, which rose sharply at the end of 1973 and again in 1978. There were large current account deficits in 1980–81, but the current account surplus almost doubled over the same period, keeping the value of the peso high against the dollar. The growing current capital surplus was largely due to high growth rates in dollar denominated sovereign external debt and commercial loans. Mexico was exposed to two shocks: a drop in the oil price and a rise in real interest rates, and soon found itself unable to service its dollar denominated debt. A moratorium was announced in August 1982. By 1983, the rescheduling agreement was in place. The IMF played a crucial role but it would not have been possible but for the $1 billion loan from the Fed, and the US government purchase of oil, worth $1 billion.

In 1994, a peasant revolt, the assassination of a presidential candidate, an earthquake and high inflation rates prompted a massive capital flight and depreciation of the peso: In April, the USA and Canada rescued Mexico, in view of its special status as a member of the North American Free Trade Agreement (November 1993). Canada contributed $700 million, and the USA $6 billion, to provide Mexico with a line of credit. The calm this restored to the currency markets was short-lived. In December 1994, there was another run on the peso as both domestic and American investors withdrew their capital. The USA led a rescue package totalling $50 billion (short-term loans at a penal rate): $20 billion from the US exchange stabilisation fund, $2 billion from Canada, $10 billion from a group of European banks, and $17.8 billion from the IMF. The size of this package immediately stopped the run on the currency – in the end, only $12.5 billion was drawn down, and repayments of that loan commenced in January 1995. The collateral was oil revenue.

The 1994/95 Mexican package nearly consumed all of the IMF funding available to it. The size of the Mexican rescue, and the Asian packages that followed, illustrate that when it comes to supplying the needed liquidity the IMF faces far more serious constraints (in terms of financial resources) than a domestic central bank.[92]

Nonetheless, the detailed review of the Asian problems shows the IMF can and does play a central role in dealing with global crises. Their activities tend to focus on the developing and emerging markets because these countries are in need of external finance and many tend to borrow. Foreign direct investment makes up a very small proportion of the Asian countries' external finance, and these figures are typical of most developing or emerging market economies. However, when these countries get into trouble, the domestic authorities can supply liquidity to curb runs on local currency deposits, but they can do little about foreign currency deposits and debt or defend the external value of the currency in the face of a large, speculative attack.

Table 8.14 shows the relative speed with which the IMF became involved. Also, note the amounts involved – nearly $77 billion for the three Asian countries, another $64 billion for Russia and Brazil which were to suffer soon afterwards. However, the "support" package typically involves the IMF (including an IMF restructuring programme), together with banks and governments from several countries agreeing to provide credit.

Some of the restructuring programmes themselves are not without controversy. It has been argued that the IMF's insistence that 16 Indonesian banks be closed in November 1997 only aggravated and lengthened the crisis. One bank closed was owned by the President's

---

[92] A domestic bank can always print more money, provided the debt is denominated in the home currency.

Table 8.14   **IMF Rescues**

| | Date of Onset of Currency Crisis | Date of IMF Agreement |
|---|---|---|
| **Thailand** | Jan–May 1997 | 20/8/97: $3.9 bn standby credit<br>20/8/97: $20.1 bn support package |
| **Korea** | Oct 1997 | 4/12/97: $21 bn of standby credit; $5.6 bn disbursed immediately |
| **Indonesia** | 7/97 | 5/11/97: $10.1 bn standby credit & $40 bn support package |
| **Malaysia** | 7/97 | Na |
| **Russia** | 11/97–1/98 | 7/98: support package $22.6 bn |
| **Brazil** | 10/97&9/98, 02 | 12/98: support package $41.5 bn<br>02: $30 billion |

son, leading depositors to think the crisis must be very serious. Soon after, the same son was allowed to open up a bank under a new name, taking much of the business from the closed bank with him, which heightened concern about political interference and cronyism. The partial deposit insurance only applied to the closed banks – no announcement was made for banks that were kept open, nor were the 36 banks under surveillance identified. Not only were funds shifted from private to state banks, but about $2 billion left the banking system. It is reported that an IMF internal document on Indonesia reached similar conclusions.[93] More generally, there is a great deal of resentment of IMF "interference" with the running of a sovereign economy. Many developing/emerging market countries are wary of approaching the IMF, which, in some cases, can delay the intervention needed to resolve the crisis.

A more general problem is increasing evidence that the *catalytic effect* is not working. The IMF packages (see above) are of high value, but conditional on the country adhering to IMF restructuring programmes. The objective is to signal such a show of confidence that these actions act as a *catalyst* for stimulating increased private capital flows, thereby reversing the capital flight that is often a principal cause of the crisis.

Ghosh *et al.* (2002) considered eight countries[94] experiencing capital account crises. They report that capital outflows were larger than the IMF projected, i.e. the catalytic effect failed to restore the private capital inflows. Hovaguimian (2003) extends the study to include the more recent crises in Argentina, Brazil (2001–2), Turkey (2002) and Uruguay (2003), and reports similar findings, though the capital outflow projection error had risen. His own result, together with a survey of other studies which looked at the impact of the catalytic effect, leads Hovaguimian (2003) to conclude that this approach has been largely unsuccessful. In the absence of a catalytic effect, more IMF intervention will be required. As can be seen from Table 8.14, the initial IMF programmes had to be extended.

---

[93] "IMF Now Admits Tactics in Indonesia Deepened the Crisis", *New York Times*, 14/1/98. See also Radelet and Sachs (1998b) and Radelet and Woo (2000).

[94] The countries were Turkey (1994), Mexico (1995), Argentina (1995), Thailand (1997), Indonesia (1997), Korea (1997), Philippines (1997), Brazil (1999).

An additional issue to consider is the effect of these settlements on incentives. Mexico is one of many countries enjoying multiple rescues. Have the IMF rescues contributed to complacency and expectations of future support in Mexico and other countries? Furthermore, IMF-led intervention appears to have done little to minimise contagion effects.

Haldane *et al.* (2004), in an elegant theoretical model, consider the effectiveness, from the standpoint of efficiency, of various types of resolutions to crises. Their model shows that delaying debt repayments and provision of lender of last resort facilities are equally efficient means of dealing with a liquidity crisis. Given the limited resources of the IMF, the former may be preferable to the latter. Both approaches lower borrowing costs for countries compared to a case of no intervention. Surprisingly, their model shows there are no moral hazard implications. By contrast, if dealing with a solvency crisis, then from an efficiency standpoint, rescheduling debt repayments is preferable to bailouts, which are more likely to induce firms and banks to take on riskier projects. In light of this finding, the authors support new approaches to rescheduling such as collective action clauses (CAC: a debt write down agreed at firm level) or a sovereign debt rescheduling mechanism (SDRM), involving an international bankruptcy court. For more on CAC and SDRM, see Taylor (2002), and Krueger (2002), respectively. Though CACs are beginning to appear in some international sovereign bond contracts, little progress has been made on the SDRM proposal. The applied cases of Indonesia and Mexico suggest many issues need to be resolved in terms of the current approaches taken by the IMF. Taken together with the Haldane *et al.* paper (2004), it is clear that the question of the role of an ILLR will continue to be open to both theoretical and empirical debate, and is likely to be for some years to come.

# 8.8. Conclusions

This chapter began with a discussion of the debates over what constitutes a financial crisis and ended with a review of the possible functions of a lender of last resort. Three major crises were deliberately chosen, to illustrate the vast array of circumstances which can provoke these problems, and also the different approaches taken to resolve a crisis. In South East Asia, the crisis originated in Thailand and spread rapidly to neighbouring countries. In Scandinavia, three countries experienced crises but Denmark escaped the problems. Japan provides a good working example of a financial bubble, but banks and authorities alike adopted ostrich-like behaviour for close to a decade. LTCM illustrated how a single firm, left to its own devices, can end up on the brink of insolvency, provoking intervention by the authorities to allay fears that left to fail, it would, at the very least, have provoked costly financial volatility on world markets. What are the main messages coming from this review?

First, financial crises are very costly events in terms of GDP lost. They may be triggered by a sudden drop in export receipts (Finland, Norway), local equity and land prices (Japan), a sharp, adverse change in investor sentiment (Thailand), or contagion between economies with perceived similarities (other South East Asian countries). While the crisis and the accompanying GDP downturn are jointly precipitated by such developments, financial crises leave an aftermath of GDP weakness and depressed lending. A crisis in the banking system often coincides with grave problems in the currency markets, but need not – witness Japan. A grave threat to banks can be posed by a risk miscalculation in a large non-bank financial institution (LTCM), or in banks themselves – Japan, Sweden, Thailand.

Second, though financial crises are costly, they are, fortunately, infrequent. However, they have been much more common since the 1970s than in previous post-war decades. They can also become chronic (Japan) if decisive action is not taken, and unpleasant medicine swallowed. Prolonged crises may be exacerbated by excessively restrictive monetary policy (USA, 1930–33), by tardiness in restructuring or closing illiquid banks (Japan), or by official refusal, or inability, to adopt official changes in fiscal or exchange rate policy – as illustrated by Asian and Latin American examples.

Finally, official guarantees to depositors and/or creditors and emergency lending to banks may prevent a bank run, but can leave an unfortunate legacy of altered incentives for bankers and their customers that increase the likelihood of future crises. Bad decisions can also result when troubled banks exercise undue political influence (Indonesia and Japan). Moreover, despite the global nature of many recent crises, an international lender of last resort could quickly become part of the problem, rather than a solution. Policy makers cannot realistically prevent all financial crises, but prompt action to ensure that banks' owners and managers bear the brunt of any losses whenever possible should help to minimise them and the costs to taxpayers.

## Appendix 8.1. Japanese Financial Reforms (Big Bang, 1996)

Prime Minister Hashimito announced Japan's Big Bang in November 1996.[95] The market reforms are based on "FREE" (emphasising free market entry, free price movements and the removal of restrictions on financial products), "FAIR" (introduction of transparent markets and rules, with an investor protection scheme) and "GLOBAL" (all financial markets to be opened up to global players, with adherence to international legal, accounting and supervisory standards). The key reforms are listed below, in chronological order.

### 1997

- The ban on securities derivatives was lifted. New legislation was passed to allow the trading of options on specified stocks and over the counter derivatives by securities and banking firms.
- Pensions fund management was to be deregulated.
- Investment trust firms were allowed to sell their products at banks.
- Banks were permitted to offer asset management accounts, and could sell investment trust securities without going through subsidiaries.
- The accounting books of financial firms had to separate the assets of their clients from their own.

---

[95] For a discussion of earlier reforms, see Hoshi and Kashyap (1999).

- Legislation was passed to authorise the use of special service vehicles (SPVs) for asset backed securitisation.

## 1998

A new foreign exchange law, passed in 1997, took effect.

- Financial institutions could engage directly in foreign exchange transactions, rather than having to use authorised foreign exchange banks.
- It was no longer necessary to seek permission and/or prior notification for foreign settlements and capital transactions.
- To reduce settlement risk, netting was allowed; with real time gross settlement to be introduced by the turn of the century.

These changes will reduce the cost of foreign exchange related transactions for all firms, financial and non-financial. Cross-border capital transactions were also liberalised, widening the choice of investment and borrowing for households and firms alike.

- Tighter regulations on money laundering were introduced to bring Japan up to international standards. Under the new foreign exchange law, banks and other financial institutions are required to provide the identities of foreign remittances, and custom authorities must be informed if exports or imports are paid for by cash.
- Stockbroking commissions were relaxed. Fixed commissions no longer applied to transaction values above 50 million yen (about $400 000). All fixed commissions were to be abolished by the end of 1999.
- Restrictions on non-life insurance premium rates were removed.
- Financial holding companies were introduced, with bank, securities and trust company subsidiaries, though insurance firms were excluded. It meant FHCs could offer a broad range of financial services to customers. At the same time, new laws were to be passed to protect depositors, investors and policy holders.
- "Prompt corrective" guidelines were to be applied to troubled banks. For banks engaged in domestic and international operations, the Basel risk weighted capital adequacy ratio[96] was to be used as an objective, early warning indicator. External auditors and the Financial Services Agency are required to monitor the banks' computation of their ratio. If a bank is rated as poor, it will be required to improve its management as quickly as possible. Specifically, a capital restoration plan must be submitted if the ratio is between 4% and 8%.[97] Further action must be taken if the ratio falls between 0 and 4%, such as reducing or stopping the payment of dividends and bonuses to directors, closing branches or subsidiaries, and reducing assets and/or higher rate paying special deposits. Banks will be ordered to cease operations partially or completely if liabilities exceed risk weighted assets, i.e. the risk assets ratio is <0.

---

[96] A Japanese capital adequacy ratio is applied to banks if their activities are confined to the domestic markets. No "PCA" is required until the ratio falls below 4%, compared to 8% for banks required to meet Basel standards.

[97] For <u>domestic</u> banks operating in Japan, the respective ratios are 2–4%, 0–2% and <0.

- Similar PCA rules will be applied to securities houses and insurance firms. The Financial Services Agency can order a securities firm to cease operations if its capital adequacy ratio (measured by improved risk weights) falls below 100%, or in some cases 120%. Solvency margin requirements were introduced under the revised Insurance Business Law (1996). From 1998, the MoF can order insurance firms to improve their performance and/or close if solvency margins are breached.

Investor protection laws were tightened. In December 1998, the Securities Compensation Fund (established in 1968) was expanded. Securities firms must keep clients' deposits (margins for margin accounts, and shares) separate from their own. Until March 2001, all funds and shares deposited with a stockbroker are to be protected. The payment scheme was extended, to a maximum payment of 10 million yen for each client.[98]

Likewise, to restore investor confidence in insurance policies, insurance companies are required to join an Insurance Payment Guarantee Scheme. If an insurance company fails and is taken over by another firm, financial aid is extended to it from the protection scheme. If the losses of the failed firm exceed the amount available in the fund,[99] the fund can obtain government guaranteed loans from the Bank of Japan and other financial institutions.

Tougher penalties for financial crimes were introduced, including larger fines and longer periods of imprisonment. For example, for insider trading, a convicted person could go to prison for up to 3 years (compared to 6 months before), and the maximum fine was raised by 2 billion yen to 5 billion yen.

A series of tax reforms was announced:

- The securities transactions tax and bourse tax on futures and options were halved, to be abolished completely in 2000.
- Capital gains on stock options is not payable until they are realised.
- The taxation of stocks involved in the merger of financial institutions would be relaxed to encourage the formation of financial holding companies.
- Private investment trusts, when introduced, will be taxed.

## 1999

- A securities business must be registered, but will not require a government licence to operate.
- Explicit permission for specific activities (such as OTC operations and underwriting) will be granted to banks and securities firms with acceptable systems of risk management.
- Securities firms will no longer be obliged to specialise in certain aspects of the business.
- Off-exchange trading of listed securities to be permitted.
- Securities firms are allowed to sell insurance via a subsidiary.
- Banks to be allowed to sell their own investment trusts/mutual funds.

---

[98] Compared to Yen 2 million for all a firm's clients.
[99] In 1997, Nissan Mutual Life failed with losses of Yen 300 billion, which exceeded the total amount in the protection fund by Yen 100 million.

- Types of investment trusts can be expanded to include corporate and private placement investment trusts.
- Ordinary banks can issue their own bonds.
- Non-bank financial firms to be allowed to issue bonds and take out other commercial loans to fund lending activities.
- Pension fund rules were relaxed:
  (a) Companies may use investment advisors to manage their pension funds, in addition to life insurance and trust companies.
  (b) In April 1999, the "5-3-3-2" rule was abolished. It specified that 50% of funds had to be invested in "safe" assets, less than 30% in stocks, less than 30% in foreign currency denominated assets, and less than 20% in real estate.
  (c) Regulations on the management of public pension funds have been eased.
- Accounting procedures will be tightened:
  (a) Financial firms to be required to report accounts on a consolidated basis.
  (b) Marking to market for securities, derivatives and other financial instruments to be introduced.
  (c) Auditing will comply with international standards. For example, accounts will have to be signed off by an independent auditing firm.

## 2000

- Banks' securities subsidiaries allowed to engage in bond issues, initial public offerings and secondary trading.
- All stockbroking fixed commissions abolished.
- Banks, trusts and securities firms can create area specific securities to enter each other's markets.

## 2001

- Insurance firms are allowed to enter the banking sector and vice versa.
- Life insurance firms may sell other types of insurance such as medical insurance; non-life insurance firms can offer life insurance.
- Banks to be permitted to sell life insurance and insurance taken out with housing loans (e.g. fire and default insurance) through their branches.

# Appendix 8.2.  Reform of the Regulators

In June 1997, new legislation created the Financial Supervisory Agency. It assumed responsibility for bank supervision, which, up to this time, had been shared between the MoF banking bureau[100] and the Bank of Japan (BJ). The Financial Supervisory Agency was empowered to:

---

[100] As a result of the reduced role of the Ministry of Finance, the Banking and Securities Bureaux were merged to form the Financial Planning Bureau, with a consequent reduction in staff. The MoF's Banking Inspection Department and Exchange Surveillance Commission were abolished.

- License, inspect and supervise banks. All banks' loan portfolios are subject to an internal grading, to be certified by a public auditor.
- Close insolvent lenders, issue and revoke financial licences, and arrange mergers.
- Support the Deposit Insurance Commission (DIC). The Agency will examine cases for merging sick with healthy banks, with support from the DIC.
- Supervising the financial sector, i.e. banks, securities firms, insurance companies and some non-bank lenders.

The Financial Supervisory Agency reported to the Financial Reconstruction Commission (FRC), created to manage the financial crisis and institution failures, as well as supervise and examine financial institutions. As non-ministerial agencies, both institutions report directly to the Prime Minister's Office, not the MoF.

The functions of the Financial Reconstruction Commission and the Financial Supervisory Agency were merged on 6 January 2001, to create the Financial Services Agency. The merger was supposed to signal that the problems which have plagued the Japanese financial sector were largely resolved. Independent of the Ministry of Finance,[101] it reports to the Prime Minister's Office. The FSA will carry out all the functions of the former Supervisory Agency *and* assumes an important policy-making role with respect to financial regulation.

The autonomy of the Bank of Japan was increased by the April 1998 Bank of Japan Act. The BJ's Policy Board takes the final decision on monetary policy. The Finance Minister is no longer allowed to issue directives to the BJ or conduct an on-site inspection of the Bank. The Governor, Vice-Governor and Policy Board are appointed by Cabinet,[102] but it cannot dismiss them. The MoF and Economic Planning Agency have been removed from the membership of the BJ's Policy Board, though their representatives can express opinions at meetings.

To encourage greater transparency, the new Act makes it mandatory for the BJ to publish minutes of its meetings and a summary of the proceedings.

These changes fall short of granting complete independence to the Bank of Japan. The MoF continues to have control over the maintenance of currency stability. The Finance Minister has the right to approve the BJ's budget, and the BJ's semi-annual report is sent to the Japanese Diet, but via the MoF. The Finance Minister can also require the BJ to make loans to troubled banks and other financial institutions.

---

[101] Though the FSA has statutory independence from the MoF, many of its workers have been transferred by the Ministry, leading some to question how really independent the Agency is.
[102] Subject to the Diet's approval.

# COMPETITIVE ISSUES IN BANKING

## 9.1. Introduction

This chapter is concerned with a number of related competitive issues in banking, including productivity, efficiency, economies of scale and scope, tests of competition in banking markets, and mergers and acquisitions. These topics are less straightforward in the financial sector than in other industries, because of the intangible nature of banking/financial products, ranging from non-price features associated with virtually all bank services, to the maturity structure of bank assets and liabilities.

The chapter first looks at the definition and measurement of bank output and then reviews key productivity measures used in banking. A selective review of the empirical evidence on X-efficiency, bank scale and scope economies, and technical progress appears in section 9.3. Section 9.4 considers the empirical approaches used to test for competitiveness in banking markets including the structure–conduct–performance and relative efficiency models, contestability in banking, and estimating a generalised linear pricing model. There is also a brief discussion on computing interest equivalences for non-price features of bank products. Section 9.5 looks at consolidation activity in the banking sector, and reviews the reasons why banks get involved in merger and acquisitions, together with their *ex ante* and *ex post* performance. Section 9.6 concludes.

## 9.2. Measuring Bank Output

The definition of output and productivity is not straightforward for a bank. For example, should demand deposits be treated as an input or an output? Are bank services best measured by the number of accounts and transactions, or values of accounts? If it is shown that one bank is more productive than another, as measured by assets per employee, employees per branch, or assets per branch, is it also possible to conclude that the bank is more efficient?

The measurement of "output" of services produced by financial institutions has special problems because they are not physical quantities. Additionally, it is difficult to account for the quality of banking services. For example, customers opting to use cash dispensing machines/ATMs and electronic delivery of standard banking services instead of a bank cashier at a branch usually view these changes as improvements in the quality of banks services, because of greater convenience such as better access and the increased speed of transactions. ATM technology is also known to reduce bank operating costs, but if customers access the machine more frequently than they would visit the branch, the cost savings may be lower than expected. Also, to the extent that visits to a branch help foster a relationship, banks may find that electronic delivery methods reduce their ability to cross-sell other financial products.

As was discussed in Chapter 1, banks provide customers with many services, including intermediation (deposits, loans), liquidity and payment services, and non-banking financial services ranging from management of investment portfolios to protection of valuables. In some bank systems, direct payment for these services is the exception rather than the rule. For example, demand deposits may be paid interest, in exchange for "free" services. Or "free retail banking" may be offered to all customers in credit, but those with an overdraft are charged very high fees and interest, meaning these customers are effectively subsidising those in credit. Corporate clients normally receive a package of banking services to accompany a loan or overdraft facility, but depending on the size of their custom, are often charged for every transaction (direct debits/credits, fund transfers, etc.) they use.

In aggregate, bank output, for the purposes of a country's national accounts, should be based on value-added, that is, adjusted operating profits less the cost of shareholder equity. When looking at the financial sector as a share of GDP, net interest receipts are normally included in value-added; in the USA these are attributed to depositors, while in the UK they include depositors and borrowers. However, empirical studies on banking do not normally use the national accounts definition of bank output. Instead, a "production" or "intermediation" interpretation of bank output is employed.

### 9.2.1. The Production Approach

The production approach measures bank output by treating banks as firms which use capital and labour to produce different categories of deposit and loan accounts. Outputs are measured by the number of these accounts or the number of transactions per account. Total costs are all operating costs used to produce these outputs. Output is treated as a *flow*, that is, the amount of "output" produced per unit of time, and inflation bias is absent. An example of the use of this type of measurement may be found in Benston (1965). There are several problems with this approach. First, there is the question of how to weight each bank service in the computation of output. Second, the method ignores interest costs, which will be important if, for example, deposit rates fall as the number of branches increase. Furthermore, data from banks in countries using different accounting systems may not be comparable, making accurate measures of relative efficiency difficult to obtain. It is hoped the move towards International Accounting Standards (IAS) will address this problem.

The total factor productivity (TFP) approach employs a single productivity ratio, using multiple inputs and outputs. Humphrey (1992) measured productivity and scale economies using flow and stock measures of banking output in identical models. He employed both a non-parametric growth accounting procedure and the econometric estimation of a cost function. A structural model of bank production was used, which incorporated both the production of intermediate deposit outputs as well as "final" loan outputs. Thus, both the input and output characteristics of deposits were simultaneously represented.

With data on 202 US banks from the Federal Reserve's 1989 Functional Cost Analysis survey, Humphrey employed a general production function:

$$Q = Af(K, L, D, S, F) \qquad (9.1)$$

where

$Q$ : bank output
$A$ : efficiency
$K, L$ : capital and labour, respectively
$D$ : demand deposits
$S$ : small time and savings deposits
$F$ : purchased funds

Humphrey used three different measures of bank output

QT: a transactions flow measure – the number of deposits and loan transactions processed
QD: a stock measure – the real $ value of deposit and loan balances
QA: a stock measure of output – the number of deposit and loan accounts serviced

The growth of production efficiency is the residual, obtained after subtracting the growth in inputs from the growth in outputs. The residual from the dual cost function also shows productivity growth: the shifts in the average cost curve after controlling for changes in input prices. Expenditure share weights were estimated rather than being computed directly. A translog cost function[1] was used for the econometric estimation. TFP was derived from these equations, decomposed into cost reductions arising from either technical change over time or scale economies. Humphrey specified scale economies of 0.9 (slight scale economies), 1.00 (constant costs) and 1.1 (slight diseconomies). Humphrey reported on the equation that assumed constant costs because the total factor productivity results did not appear to be sensitive to the scale economies imposed.

Humphrey's key findings are as follows.

- Using the QT definition (number of deposits and loans processed), banking productivity was found to have been flat over 20 years, with an annual average rate of growth of only 0.4%.
- If output is defined as QD (dollar value of loans and deposits), TFP actually fell between 1968 and 1980 but rose thereafter. The overall average rate of TFP growth was 1.8% per annum.
- The real value of total assets (QTA): the average TFP rate fell by about 1.4% per year.

Humphrey finds the TFP result using the parametric/econometric approach is virtually the same as when a growth accounting approach (non-parametric) is used. Nor was there much

---

[1] This is a fairly common specification of a cost function, and the equations for it will not be derived here. Readers are referred to equations (2) and (3) in Humphrey (1992), or see any good introductory textbook on econometrics.

difference in the predictive accuracy of the stock and flow measures of bank output. By the flow measure, productivity growth was slightly positive; it was slightly negative when the stock measure was used. During the 1980s, both measures generated a small positive productivity growth. Two reasons are offered for the relatively low US bank productivity growth. First, banks lost low-cost deposit accounts as corporate and retail customers shifted to corporate cash management accounts and interest-earning cheque accounts. Second, the study largely ignored quality differences in bank output. For example, the quality of bank services may have improved because banks started to pay interest on most accounts but did not raise charges for bank services such as transfer of funds, cheque clearing and monthly statements.

## 9.2.2. The Intermediation Approach

This approach recognises intermediation as the core activity – banks are not producers of loan and deposit services. Instead, output is measured by the value of loans and investments. Bank output is treated as a *stock*, showing the given amount of output at one point in time. Total cost is measured by operating costs (the cost of factor inputs such as labour and capital) plus interest costs. Sealey and Lindley (1977) argued that earning assets (loans, securities, etc.) make up bank outputs, so deposits, capital and labour should be treated as inputs. Others favour deposits being treated as outputs. However, if banks offer an extended range of services, such as trust operations or securities, the intermediation approach will make their unit costs appear higher than for banks that engage in traditional intermediation. The relative importance of different bank products may also be ignored in the computation, unless weighted indices are used. Greenbaum (1967) suggested one method for obtaining weights: he used linear regressions to obtain average interest rate charges on various types of bank assets.

Most bank productivity studies use the intermediation approach because there are fewer data problems than with the production approach. They tend to follow Sealey and Lindley (1977), where earning assets are produced from several factor inputs. In the more recent literature, in an attempt to recognise the multiproduct nature of the firm, outputs typically include loans, other earning assets (e.g. securities, interbank assets), deposits and non-interest income, which acts as a proxy for off-balance sheet "output". Inputs include the price of labour, the cost of physical capital (proxied by non-interest expenses/fixed assets) and the price of financial capital (proxy: interest paid/purchased funds).

The empirical work suffers from a number of difficulties. First, the way output is measured varies considerably. Some studies use the number of deposit accounts because customers are getting services (e.g. intermediation, liquidity) from the account. Though banks incur costs from offering these services, all but a fraction of deposits earn revenue when they are loaned out. Studies that rely on the underlying production and cost functions for banks encounter these problems. The literature on X-efficiency, scale and scope economies and structure–conduct–performance often employ different definitions of output. Furthermore, deposits may be treated either as inputs, outputs or, in some studies, both.

The intermediation and production approaches fail to address a number of issues. No account is taken of the different risks attached to each loan, or, for example, the reputation of the bank in terms of the perceived probability of failure. The maturity structure of loans and deposits, critical in banking, is generally ignored. Finally, any change in the structure of the banking market could distort output measures. For example, increased competition may narrow interest margins, which in turn will reduce output as reported in the national income accounts. In the production approach, the output measure is affected if the change in margins affects the volume of loans – a fall in margins could increase the volume of loans and deposits. If the number of loan accounts increases, the intermediation approach will record a rise in output; but using the flow measure, a decline in margins, all else equal, would trigger a fall in output.

## 9.3. X-efficiency, Scale Economies and Scope Economies

### 9.3.1. Cost X-efficiency

X-efficiency[2] can be measured in terms of cost or profit but the emphasis of much of the banking literature is on cost X-efficiency. Since managers have the ability to control costs (cost X-efficiency) or revenues (profit X-efficiency), greater X-efficiencies can be achieved by superior management. The cost efficiency frontier is shown in Figure 9.1.

**Figure 9.1   Cost and Profit X-efficiency.**

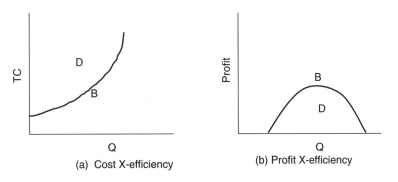

(a) Cost X-efficiency

(b) Profit X-efficiency

Cost efficiency frontier: objective of firms: to be on the frontier, not above it;  not possible to be on points below  the curve

• Profit efficiency frontier: objective of firms: to move to the maximum profit point on the profit frontier curve-point B

Q = output (e.g.bank services)
TC = total cost

---

[2] Farrell (1957) was the first to provide an empirical measure of X-efficiency.

Profit-maximising firms will want to be on the efficiency frontier, but can go no further unless there is technological change which actually moves it downwards. In a perfectly competitive market, any firm that fails to reach the efficiency frontier will be forced out of the market. However, in markets where firms have some degree of monopoly power (due, for example, to entry barriers, scale economies or regulation), some firms are likely located somewhere inside the X-efficiency frontier. X-inefficiencies may be due to expense preference behaviour or when the managers are able to maximise their own utilities,[3] if these diverge from shareholders'. Inefficiency may be registered by higher than minimum total costs [e.g. point D in Figure 9.1(a)]. It will imply a sacrifice of profits – the gap between B and D in Figure 9.1(b). Profits could be even lower if a different output level had been chosen.

Cost X-efficiency gets far more attention than profit X-efficiency. Consider them in relation to scale and scope economies, which were mentioned briefly in Chapter 2 and are discussed in more detail below. Scale or scope economies provide measures of the extent (if any) to which unit costs could be lowered by offering the total volume of production, or range of products, respectively. Allocative inefficiencies are caused by the sub-optimal use of the _input_ mix, and X-inefficiencies are attributed to failures to minimise the cost of producing the given scale and range of outputs, which can be due to administrative costs or deliberate choices by management or staff. Reaping scale economies involves getting bigger, while scope economies are exploited by diversifying outputs. Lowering X-inefficiencies means reducing costs (through, for example, improved management, greater employee productivity), which moves the firm closer to the most efficient way of harnessing a given set of resources. Berger _et al._'s (1993) review of the (mainly US) literature showed that in banking, X-inefficiencies explain about 20% of the costs, and less than 5% of the costs are due to inefficiencies arising from the failure to exploit scale and scope economies to the full. Allen and Rai (1996), looking at banks in 15 countries over the period 1988–92, report that countries which prohibit banks from combining commercial and investment banking have the largest bank X-inefficiency, amounting to 27.5% of total costs. In other countries where integrated banking is allowed, banks are more cost X-efficient: X-inefficiency was about 15% of total costs. Berger and Humphrey (1997) review 122 studies of bank cost efficiency, and report a mean level of 15% for 60 studies using a _parametric_ approach; 28% for the 62 studies which adopted _non-parametric_ techniques – the distinction between these two techniques is discussed immediately below.

### Data envelope analysis

Data envelopment analysis (DEA) is one way of testing for X-efficiencies, and was briefly discussed in Chapter 6. DEA is a "non-parametric" approach because it is not based on any explicit model of the frontier. The methodology was originally developed for non-profit-making organisations, because accounting profit measures are difficult to compute. DEA compares the observed outputs ($Y_{jp}$) and inputs ($X_{ip}$) of several organisations. If

---

[3] For example, spending more on managerial comforts, or awarding themselves higher salaries.

measuring cost X-efficiency, the relatively more efficient firms can be compared against the relatively less efficient by identifying a "best practice" firm or firms. To do this, maximise the following:[4]

$$E_p = \sum u_j Y_{jp} / \sum v_i X_{ip} \qquad (9.2)$$

subject to $E_p \leq 1$ for all $p$; where $p$ represents several organisations and weights $v_i, u_j > 0$. A linear programming model is run repetitively with each firm appearing in the objective function once to derive individual efficiency ratings. Each firm will have a derived rating of $E$, a measure of _relative_ efficiency. The closer $E$ is to 1, the higher the relative efficiency. $E = 1$ is for the "best practice" unit, and will be lower for all other firms in the study. Thus, $E < 1$, which implies _relative_ inefficiency.

Numerous studies have used DEA to measure the cost X-efficiency of banks. Here, only a selection are reported. Rangan _et al._ (1988, 1990) tried to break down the efficiency of 215 US banks into that originating from technical inefficiency (arising from wasted resources) and scale inefficiency (operating at non-constant returns to scale). Bank output was measured using the intermediation approach. In the first study (1988) the results showed the average value of efficiency for the sample was 0.7, implying that, on average, the banks in the sample could have produced the same output using 70% of the inputs. Thus, there was, apparently, much waste, almost all of it due to technical inefficiencies.

In Rangan _et al._ (1990), the study was extended to include a sample of banks from unit banking as well as branch banking states. The pooled sample was split into two subsamples, and separate production frontiers calculated. No sizeable differences in efficiency as between the two types of banking were found. Field (1990) applied the DEA method to a cross-section of 71 UK building societies in 1981–81% were found to be inefficient, due to scale inefficiencies. Unlike Rangan _et al._, Field found technical efficiency to be positively correlated with firm size. Drake and Weyman-Jones (1992) applied DEA to building societies in 1988 after deregulation in 1987–37% were found to exhibit overall efficiency, an increase compared to the Field study.

Berger (1993), Berger and Humphrey (1997) and Bauer _et al._ (1998) identify the advantages of using data envelope analysis and other non-parametric techniques.[5] DEA is advantageous because it can vary over time and all outputs and inputs are handled simultaneously. It produces a true frontier from which relative efficiencies can be derived and no functional form is imposed on the data. However, no allowance is made for a random error arising from measurement problems, such as inaccurate accounting data, random effects which have a temporary effect on outputs or inputs, or specification error (e.g. due to excluded outputs and inputs). Also, the DEA frontier is defined on the outliers rather than on the whole sample and, therefore, is susceptible to extreme observations and measurement error. Data problems also arise because it is necessary to obtain the same output and input measures for all the firms in the sample. Nor is it possible to draw statistical inferences from this approach, and the efficiency scores are not independent of market structure.

---

[4] This equation and some of the discussion is taken from Colwell and Davis (1992). Their working paper provides a more complete review of earlier empirical studies.

[5] Another non-parametric technique is free disposal hull analysis, but DEA is by far the most common approach used.

### *Stochastic frontier analysis and other parametric techniques*

Over the last two decades, the use of parametric techniques to estimate bank efficiency has increased. The most common includes a stochastic frontier approach, which uses a translog cost function. Parametric approaches allow a more explicit breakdown of the constituents of X-efficiency, namely technical inefficiency, which arises from factor inputs being over-used (e.g. expansion of staff) and allocative inefficiency – resources are not allocated efficiently, due to lax management or expense preference behaviour.[6]

The most common parametric method, the stochastic frontier approach, involves estimating a cost (or profit) function for a sector. A bank is inefficient if its costs exceed those of the most efficient bank using the same input–output combination. Or it is profit inefficient if its profits are inside a profit frontier, that is, its profits are lower than the best practice bank. To test for cost inefficiency the stochastic cost model is given as:[7]

$$TC = TC(q, p, y, z, \mu_c, \varepsilon) \tag{9.3}$$

where

TC : variable total costs
$q$ : a vector of quantities of variable outputs
$p$ : a vector of prices of variable factor inputs
$y$ : other variables (environmental or market) which might affect output
$z$ : quantities of fixed inputs or outputs which could affect variable costs
$\mu_c$ : an error term – $\mu_c$ picks up allocative inefficiencies, which can arise because the bank fails to react optimally to the vector of input prices ($w$) plus inefficiencies from employing too many of the inputs to produce $q$
$\varepsilon$ : a random error term

Using natural logs (ln) on both sides of the equation[8] gives:

$$\ln TC = f(q, p, y, z) + \ln \mu_c + \ln \varepsilon_c \tag{9.4}$$

Profit efficiency measures show how close a bank is to producing the maximum profit possible given input prices, output prices and other variables. The standard profit function is:

$$\ln(\pi + \theta) = F(q, x, y, z) + \ln \mu_\pi + \ln \varepsilon_\pi \tag{9.5}$$

where

$\pi$ : variable profits
$\theta$ : constant to ensure the natural log is of a positive number
$x$ : vector of prices of the variable outputs
$\mu_\pi$ : inefficiency that reduces profits

---

[6] This interpretation is taken from Berger and Hannan (1998).
[7] Following Aigner *et al.* (1977).
[8] The inefficiency and random terms are assumed to be multiplicatively separable from the rest of the cost function.

Berger and Humphrey (1997), in a comprehensive survey of 122 cost X-efficiency studies, report that most studies of cost X-efficiency among banks range from 0.7 to 0.9, that is, banks' efficiency ranges between 70% and 90%. Better management would improve efficiency by between 10% and 30%. The X-efficiency scores from other studies include the following.

- Berger and Mester (1997): 0.868, based on 5949 US commercial banks over 1990–95. Thus, US banks could improve their cost X-efficiency by 13.2%.
- Altunbas *et al.* (2001a): for Japanese commercial banks, 0.94 and 0.96 over the period 1993–96, with between 136 and 139 observations per year.
- Hao *et al.* (2001): 0.889 for private banks in South Korea, 1985–95; 19 banks per year, 17 in 1986.
- Isik and Hassan (2002): 0.895 for Turkish banks, 1988 (36 obs), 1992 (50 obs.), 1996 (53 obs.).
- Mertens and Urga (2001): 0.672 for banks in the Ukraine, 79 banks in 1998.
- Hardy and Patti (2001): 0.272 for Pakistan banks, 33 banks in 1981–97; X-efficiency could improve by as much as 73%.
- Fu (2004): 0.35 to 0.44 for 14 major state owned and joint stock banks in China, 1985–2002; within this range joint stock banks were found to be more efficient than state owned; X-efficiency fell in the second stage of banking reform.

The number of banks included in these studies varies considerably, from just under 6000 observations in Berger and Mester (1997), to 14 in the China study, with 187 observations. Note also the higher X-efficiency in Berger and Mester, where 1990s data are used, compared to earlier US studies which relied on 1980s data.

In a 1980s study of 5000 US commercial banks, Berger and Hannan (1998) estimate a translog cost equation for each individual bank to get a measure of efficiency (based on an average of the residuals), then use these efficiency estimates to test the relationship between concentration and efficiency. They were testing the standard "structure–conduct–performance" hypothesis (see p. 13 for details), and find strong evidence that banks in more concentrated markets exhibit lower cost efficiency. The social costs from these extra operating costs were found to be between 3 and 20 times greater (depending on how efficiency is measured) than the welfare losses arising from non-competitive pricing.

Williams and Gardener (2000) review the efficiency studies for Europe, and complete a comprehensive study of cost and profit X-efficiency among regional banks in six European countries, for the period 1990–98. The sample size includes 990 savings banks and 6300 observations. Using the Fourier flexible form[9] and the stochastic frontier approach, they are able to distinguish between cost X-efficiencies arising from operating costs and variable costs. They report a mean operating cost inefficiency of 15.1%, and a variable cost X-inefficiency

---

[9] According to Altunbas *et al.* (2001) the Fourier flexible functional form is a semi-non-parametric approach used when the true functional form of the relationships is unknown (2001, p. 1936). It is used to estimate scale and scope economies, but not X-inefficiency. See Carbo *et al.* (2000) for more detail.

of 8.3%. They argue operating cost inefficiencies are higher because they include the cost of monitoring loans and dealing with bad debt. Profit X-efficiency is estimated at just under 80%, meaning these European savings banks are losing 20% of their profits (relative to what the best bank can earn) because of inefficiency.

Altunbas *et al.* (2001b) use income and balance sheet data from the *Bankscope* database for banks from 15 EU countries between 1989 and 1997, to estimate X-inefficiency using a stochastic frontier approach.[10] The traditional intermediation approach is adopted where labour, physical capital and deposits are used to produce outputs, which includes loans, securities and total off-balance sheet items. They find, on average, X-inefficiency levels ranging between 20% and 25% depending on asset sizes, suggesting that more output could be produced if the banks reduced their inefficiencies by this amount. Table 9.1 summarises the Altunbas *et al.* (2001b) results for 1989 and 1997, the first and last years for which X-inefficiencies are computed. Using their data, the means for the two years were computed – they show X-inefficiencies have declined very slightly between 1989 and 1997. When placed in rank order, UK banks are close to the bottom in terms of X-inefficiency. Though not shown, X-inefficiency peaked in the UK in 1992, at 0.333. Put another way, in 1992, the same output could have been produced with about 67% of current inputs had British banks been able to reduce their managerial and technical inefficiencies. Note Ireland goes from being the most efficient in 1989 to one of the least by 1997.

**Table 9.1  X-inefficiencies for European Countries**

| | 1989 | | 1997 | | 1989 | | 1997 |
|---|---|---|---|---|---|---|---|
| Austria | 0.209 | Austria | 0.181 | Ireland | 0.166 | Italy | 0.126 |
| Belgium | 0.369 | Belgium | 0.322 | Finland | 0.193 | Germany | 0.135 |
| Denmark | 0.222 | Denmark | 0.191 | Sweden | 0.194 | Sweden | 0.165 |
| Finland | 0.193 | Finland | 0.296 | Austria | 0.209 | ALL | 0.179 |
| France | 0.288 | France | 0.244 | Netherlands | 0.213 | Austria | 0.181 |
| Germany | 0.218 | Germany | 0.135 | Italy | 0.217 | Denmark | 0.191 |
| Greece | 0.28 | Greece | 0.238 | Germany | 0.218 | Spain | 0.237 |
| Ireland | 0.166 | Ireland | 0.323 | Denmark | 0.222 | Greece | 0.238 |
| Italy | 0.217 | Italy | 0.126 | Luxembourg | 0.234 | Netherlands | 0.238 |
| Luxembourg | 0.234 | Luxembourg | 0.33 | Spain | 0.234 | MEAN | 0.241 |
| Netherlands | 0.213 | Netherlands | 0.238 | MEAN | 0.245 | France | 0.244 |
| Portugal | 0.335 | Portugal | 0.289 | ALL | 0.245 | Portugal | 0.289 |
| Spain | 0.234 | Spain | 0.237 | Greece | 0.28 | Finland | 0.296 |
| Sweden | 0.194 | Sweden | 0.165 | France | 0.288 | UK | 0.297 |
| UK | 0.298 | UK | 0.297 | UK | 0.298 | Belgium | 0.322 |
| ALL | 0.245 | | | Portugal | 0.335 | Ireland | 0.323 |
| MEAN | 0.245 | | 0.179 | Belgium | 0.369 | Luxembourg | 0.33 |
| | | | 0.241 | | | | |

---

[10] The authors also use a flexible Fourier functional form.

## 9.3.2. Scale and Scope Economies

There is an extensive literature and debate on the degree to which scale economies are present in banking. The term "economies of scale", or "scale economies", is a long-run concept, applicable when all the factor inputs that contribute to a firm's production process can be varied. Thus, if a firm is burdened with any fixed capital, property or labour then, strictly speaking, it is not possible to test for economies of scale. Assuming all factor inputs are variable, a firm is said to exhibit:

*Increasing Returns to Scale or Scale Economies*: if equiproportionate increases in factor inputs yield a greater than equiproportionate increase in output. Firms are operating on the falling part of their average cost curves – the curve shows the average cost per unit of output, and firms with economies of scale can reduce average costs by increasing output. However, at some point scale diseconomies may set in, that is, if a firm/bank increases its output, average costs will rise.

*Decreasing Returns to Scale or Scale Diseconomies*: if equiproportionate increases in factor inputs yield less than equiproportionate increases in output.

*Constant Returns to Scale*: if equiproportionate increases in factor inputs yield an equiproportionate increase in output.

*Product Specific Economies of Scale*: this term applies if the firm produces more than one product (e.g. a bank can produce loans, deposits and securities), and is asking whether there is economies of scale with respect to a particular product. It is determined by looking at average incremental cost (AIC) – the effect on total cost if a product is produced at a specific level rather than not at all. Thus:

$$PSES_i = AIC_i/(\partial TC/\partial Q_i) \tag{9.6}$$

where

$TC$ : total cost

$Q_i$ : output vector for product $i$

$PSES_i > 1$ implies product specific economies of scale; diseconomies of scale if $PSES_i < 1$.

Consider the case of a simple bank, which has three factor inputs: capital from deposits, labour – the bank's employees – and property, in the form of a branch network. The bank produces one output, loans. Then economies of scale are said to exist if, as a result of doubling each of the three factor inputs, the bank is able to more than double its loan portfolio. Even in this simple example, the concept is fraught with difficulties when applied to a financial institution. First, unless a new bank is setting itself up from nothing, not all of its inputs will be completely variable. It is difficult to imagine a bank being able to double the number of deposits at short notice. Second, even if they could there is a potential problem with risk. If a bank more than doubles its loan portfolio the risk profile is bound to change, a critically important consideration for any bank wanting to maximise shareholder value-added. Third, there is a problem of indivisibilities. A bank branch could not add one-third of a bank cashier (teller) or half an ATM. Additionally, in banking, as has been noted, there is the question of what constitutes output. Some authors, including this one, have argued that deposits, in addition to loans, must be treated as bank products, because deposits provide customers with intermediary services. Furthermore, most banks produce multiple outputs, namely, a fairly broad range of financial services. These observations make it difficult to apply the term "economies of scale" in the financial sector, which may partly explain the widely varying empirical evidence on the degree to which economies of scale exist. Yet they are normally cited as one of the key reasons why a merger between financial institutions will be a profitable one for shareholders.

The concept of economies of scope is another one that, employed loosely, can lead to unrealistic expectations of the benefits of a merger or acquisition. **Economies of Scope** exist if the joint production cost of producing two or more outputs is lower than if the products are produced separately. For example, suppose a bank offers three services to its customers: deposit, loans and a payments service. If a bank can supply these services more cheaply through a joint production process it is said to enjoy economies of scope. The core banking business, where the bank intermediates between borrowers and lenders by lending out a percentage of its deposits, is one example of economies of scope. Though the payments service offered by banks is a byproduct of intermediation, it is not obvious that lower costs result from the joint production of this service with intermediation. This may explain why some countries, such as the UK, have a highly integrated payments system while in others (e.g. the USA) it is more fragmented (see Chapter 1).

The business policy term for economies of scope is **Synergy**, though synergy may embrace broader ideas such as the newly formed, larger firm reducing input prices by exploiting its more powerful influence on suppliers, thereby enhancing profitability. Again, among financial firms, where skills and innovation may be the difference between success and failure, synergy may be costly to achieve if it requires a merger of different cultures, or stifles the entrepreneurial spirit typical of small, successful financial firms.

From the strategic standpoint of managers, the question of whether or not economies of scale and scope or synergy are present in the banking is important. Evidence of economies of scale will mean large banks have a cost advantage over small ones. If cost complementarities are present, multiproduct banks will be more efficient than the financial boutique. Though obtaining these measures is fraught with difficulty, it has not stopped a large number of investigators from testing for it. Not surprisingly, empirical studies of economies of scale and scope in financial institutions throw up mixed results for every country which has been tested, though most of the empirical work emanates from the United States. Here, the results of some of the key studies are reported.[11]

Recall Humphrey (1992) looked at productivity growth in US banking using different measures of output. He used the same data to obtain estimates of scale economies. Based on $R^2$ and the predictive accuracy of the different output measures, he concluded that the stock measure QD (the real dollar value of deposit and loan balances) was more accurate than the flow measure of output, QT (the number of deposits and loan transactions processed) in tests for scale economies. Humphrey found slight economies of scale for small US banks (assets of \$10–\$25 million), but slight diseconomies for larger US banks (\$2–\$5 billion).

---

[11] For a comprehensive review of published studies in this area up to the mid-1990s, see Molyneux *et al.* (1996).

Allen and Rai (1996) use their data to test for scale and scope economies. No scope economies are found; scale economies are significant for the smallest banking groups,[12] in the order of 2%. There are significant diseconomies of scale (about 5%) for banks which are prohibited from offering commercial and investment banking. This finding by Humphrey (1992) and these authors are fairly typical for studies of US banks using 1980s data.

One exception is Shaffer and David (1991), who questioned US empirical work that reported diseconomies of scale for very large US multinational banks. These results are inconsistent with the observation that very large banks are financially viable over long periods of time. Shaffer and David used data from the 100 largest commercial banks in the USA in 1984, with assets ranging from $2.5 billion to $120.6 billion. They relied on the Federal Reserve's Call Report data.[13] However, the aggregated nature of these data may obscure some of the factors which differentiate banks, such as output mix, input mix, strategy, regulatory environment, and so on. All of these factors will influence the bank's level of costs. To correct for this problem a hedonic cost function[14] was used. The scale variable in the cost equation is augmented with a vector of variables chosen to reflect qualitative differences (therefore, "hedonic" terms).

Shaffer and David estimated a translog cost function (In TC) (TC: total operating expenses) with the following independent variables.

$y$ : assets
$w_1$ : price of labour
$w_2$ : price of physical capital
$q_j$ : the vector of hedonic terms – funding strategy, off-balance sheet activities, asset quality, the regulatory environment (unit versus branch banking) and target clientele

The translog cost function was estimated, with and without the hedonic terms. In the absence of hedonic terms, they found evidence of economies of scale which were exhausted in the region of $21 billion–$25 billion of assets. $F$-statistics rejected the hypothesis of constant returns to scale at the 1% level. With the hedonic terms included, scale economies were found at slightly lower sizes, between $18.9 and $23.6 billion.[15]

Hardwick (1990) tested for scale and scope economies using UK building society[16] data. The author employed multiproduct statistical cost analysis. Building societies were assumed to supply one type of financial service to borrowers (mortgages) and another type to lenders

---

[12] Small is defined as any bank that falls below the median assets size for banks in that country.
[13] US studies of scale and scope economies normally use data from one of two sources. There is the Federal Reserve's Functional Cost Analysis (FCA) data – supplied (on a voluntary basis) to the Federal Reserve System by commercial and savings banks from across the USA. Or there is data from the banks' call and income reports. The FCA data exclude large banks with deposits in excess of $1 billion. This is why Shaffer and David opted to use call report data. See Molyneux et al. (1996, pp. 158–159) for a critique of the two sources of data.
[14] The hedonic cost function was developed by Spady and Friedlaender (1978).
[15] Shaffer and David (1991) estimated cost functions with each hedonic variable at a time, and a full model that included every hedonic variable.
[16] UK building societies are mutually owned and some engage in functions that are similar to US savings and loans – see Chapter 5 for more detail.

(personal sector savers). Hardwick argued that for a firm producing $m$ outputs, the cost function may be written as:

$$TC = TC(y, p) \qquad (9.7)$$

where

TC : total cost
  $y$ : vector of $m$ outputs
  $p$ : vector of $n$ input prices

Hardwick's definition of overall economies of scale (OES) was $\sum(\partial \ln TC / \partial \ln y_i)$. OES were measured by the elasticity of total cost with respect to a given composite input. If OES $<1$ ($>1$), there are overall economies (diseconomies) of scale. To identify the main sources of economies or diseconomies of scale, it was necessary to estimate the cost saving attributable to the $j$th input as the firm expands. Hardwick employed the following equation:

$$\ln C_j = \ln S_j + \ln TC \qquad (9.8)$$

where

$S_j$ : $j$th input's cost share

The $OES_j$ (input specific overall economies of scale) is given by:

$$OES_j = \sum(\partial \ln S_j / \partial \ln y_i) \qquad (9.9)$$

Hardwick also tested for product specific economies of scale. These measure the effect on the $i$th product's incremental cost of a change in the quantity of product $i$, with the quantities of the other products unchanged. It is captured by the elasticity of the $i$th product's incremental cost with respect to the output of the $i$th product. He used a marginal cost approach; a negative gradient of the marginal cost ($\partial^2 TC / \partial y_i^2$) confirms product specific economies while a positive gradient is indicative of diseconomies.

Economies of scope are said to exist if the total cost of the joint production function is less than the sum of the costs of separate production. If a firm is producing two goods, then the appropriate test is ($\partial^2 TC / \partial y_i \partial y_j$) to be significantly negative. If less than zero, the marginal cost of producing one good decreases with increases in the output of another good, implying cost complementarities and economies of scope.

Hardwick's data come from the 1985 annual returns of a sample of 97 building societies. The variables included in the model were as follows.

TC: total operating cost – the dependent variable, measured by the sum of management expenses and depreciation, where management expenses include all staff expenses, auditors' remuneration, office expenses, advertising and various commission and agency fees
  $y_1$: the average number of outstanding mortgage accounts
  $y_2$: the number of outstanding share and deposit accounts
  $p_1$: the effective wage rate

$p_2$: the effective price of capital – the rental rate on capital, measured as [(annual expenditure on office accommodation and equipment + depreciation)/mean assets] × 100

B: number of branch offices

M: average size of all outstanding mortgages and deposit accounts ($D$), to control for the heterogeneity of accounts

$S_1$: labour's cost share – the dependent variable in the derived share equations

$S_2$: capital's cost share – the dependent variable in the derived share equations

Hardwick used a maximum likelihood procedure to estimate the full cost equation jointly with one of the share equations. Behind these equations lies the assumption that the technology of the building society industry can be represented by a translog multiproduct cost function, where the natural log of total cost is approximated by a quadratic in the natural logs of the two outputs, the two input prices and the other explanatory variables.

To test for overall economies of scale, the 97 building societies were put into one of eight groups, by value of mean assets.

A1: > £5.5 billion
A2: £1.5 billion to < £5.5 billion
B1: £450 million to < £1.5 billion
B2: £280 million to < £450 million
C1: £140 million to < £280 million
C2: £60 million to < £140 million
D1: £15 million to < £60 million
D2: < £15 million

Input specific overall economies of scale were found to be present and significant for all eight size groups except A1. Hence, economies of scale are present for all but the very largest building societies, where economies of scale could not be established (OES > 1 but was not statistically significant from unity), due to the presence of significant diseconomies in the employment of capital. For the other groups, the cost savings attributable to the employment of labour were found to be greater than those from the employment of capital.[17]

Hardwick tested for product economies of scale by looking at the gradient of each product's marginal cost. For output supplied to mortgage borrowers, the marginal cost gradients were negative for all size groups, indicating the presence of product specific economies of scale, though the findings were not significant for groups A1 and A2. For the output supplied to depositors and shareholders ($y_2$), none of the marginal cost gradients were significantly different from zero, so it was not possible to conclude whether there were economies or diseconomies of scale.

[17] In an earlier study where the same methodology and data were employed, Hardwick (1989) reported a finding of significant diseconomies of scale for societies with assets in excess of £1.5 billion if an augmented economies of scale measure was used. The formula was augmented to account for the direct effect on TC of a change in output, and an indirect effect, arising from the induced change in the number of branches.

Looking at the derivative of each product's marginal cost with respect to changes in output of the other product, Hardwick did not find evidence either for or against economies of scope for A1 and A2 firms. For building societies with assets of up to £1.5 billion, Hardwick found significant diseconomies of scope, suggesting diversification could actually raise the average operating costs of the society. Thus, there appeared to be virtually no case for diversification of building societies into the broader banking market.

Drake (1992), using a multiproduct translog cost function, found evidence for economies of scale in the asset value range of £120–£500 million. He could find no evidence to support the earlier Hardwick (1989) finding of diseconomies of scale for building societies with assets in excess of £1.5 billion. Nor did Drake find economies or diseconomies of scope for the building society industry or subcategories of building societies, except for the second largest group (assets in the range of £500 million–£5 billion), which demonstrated significant diseconomies of scope. Drake was also able to test for product economies of scope. Mortgage lending showed significant diseconomies of scope, but scope economies were found for unsecured consumer lending and secured commercial lending.

Numerous US studies have tested for _Economies of Scope_ in banking, with mixed results. Gilligan and Smirlock (1984) used balance sheet data from 2700 unit state banks in the period 1973–78. Two definitions of output were used, the dollar amount of demand and time deposits, and the dollar amount of securities and loans outstanding. Their test results supported the hypothesis of economies of scope, because they found the structure of bank costs to be characterised by jointness, that is, the cost of production of one output depended on the level of other outputs. Lawrence (1989) used a generalised functional form to test for economies of scope in a multiproduct production function. He employed the Federal Reserve's functional cost data for the period 1979–82. The deposit size for banks in the sample ranged between $6 million and $2.6 billion – excluding the largest US banks. Lawrence used three output measures: deposits, investments and loans; and three factor inputs: interest costs, wages and computer rental costs. He found cost complementarities to be present in the joint production of the three outputs.

Hunter _et al._ (1990) used a sample of 311 out of 400 of the largest US banks at the end of 1986. Bank production was analysed using an intermediation approach and multicost production function. Deposits were treated as an output and as an input. The authors found no evidence to support the presence of subadditive cost functions, meaning cost complementarities (and scope economies) were not present. Mester's (1987) review of eight US multiproduct studies published between 1983 and 1986 led him to conclude there was no strong evidence either to support or refute the presence of economies of scope.

Altunbas _et al._ (1996)[18] used the intermediation approach. A translog cost function was estimated to examine the 1988 cost structure in four European countries – France, Germany, Italy and Spain. They use income and balance sheet data from the IBCA database, which includes 201 French, 196 German and 244 Italian banks. The data for 209 Spanish banks came from a Spanish source. The outputs and inputs were defined as:

---

[18] Some of these results (on economies of scale) were reported in Altunbas and Molyneux (1996).

### Outputs

$Q_1$: total loans
$Q_2$: securities

### Inputs

$P_1$: average annual wage per employee (Italy, Spain); average annual wage per branch (France, Germany)
$P_2$: average interest cost per dollar of interest bearing total deposits
$P_3$: average price of capital (capital expenses/total fixed assets)

Economies of scale and scope are tested for banks in different assets categories: $0–$100 million, $100–$300 million, $300–$600 million, $600 million–$1 billion, $1–$3 billion, $3–$5 billion and greater than $5 billion.

The key findings for Molyneux *et al.* (1996) are reported in Table 9.2. The findings on scale economies suggest that for at least some size ranges, French, German and Italian banks

**Table 9.2   Summary of Findings from Molyneux *et al.* (1996)**

| | France | Germany | Italy | Spain |
|---|---|---|---|---|
| Scale Economies | – | – | – | Yes, all asset sizes |
| Constant Returns to Scale | Yes, all asset sizes | – | Yes, all asset sizes | – |
| Scale Diseconomies | – | Yes, all asset sizes | – | – |
| Product-specific Scale Economies in Loans and Securities | Yes | Yes | No | Yes |
| Scale Economies at Branch Level | Yes, except banks with asset size >$5 billion | Yes, for asset sizes of $100–$300 million or >$5 billion | Yes, for asset size >$1 billion | Yes, for assets size <$1 billion |
| Economies of Scope | Yes | Yes, if assets size exceeded $3 billion | No | Yes, for assets size up to $600 million |
| Diseconomies of Scope | No | Yes, for small and medium-sized banks | No | Yes, if assets size >$600 million |
| Branch Economies of Scope | Yes, if asset size >$300 million | Yes | Yes | Yes, for banks with asset size <$300 million |
| Branch Diseconomies of Scope | No, if asset size <$300 million | No | No | Yes, except for banks with asset size <$300 million |

could reduce their costs by expanding the size of their existing branches. The exception is Spain, where costs would fall by increasing the number of branches.

Based on the results for economies of scope, all banks in France, smaller banks in Spain and larger banks in Germany could reduce costs by increasing their output mix. Branches in Italy and Germany, together with those of large banks in France, should do the same. Branches of smaller French and Spanish banks should do the opposite, i.e. specialise more.

Altunbas *et al.* (2001b) estimate scale economies using the same data set (income and balance sheet data from the *Bankscope* database for banks from 15 EU countries between 1989 and 1997) as was used for their X-inefficiency scores. They find average scale economies range from between 5% and 7%, suggesting that if outputs were increased by 100%, total costs would rise by 93% to 95%, on average.[19] If the banks are broken down by asset size, it reveals that the significant economies of scale are being enjoyed by the smallest banks in all countries, with assets ranging between 1 and 99 million ECUs.[20] German and Greek banks also enjoyed economies of scale for most asset size categories. Banks in Germany, the UK, Denmark and the Netherlands with assets in excess of 5 billion ECUs (the largest asset category) have significant economies of scale of just under 5%, but the largest banks in Austria, Belgium, Finland, Greece, Ireland and Luxembourg all had diseconomies of scale: so doubling output would lower average cost for the first group by about one-twentieth, but raise it for the second group. However, when equity capital is removed as a factor input,[21] scale economies are found for the largest banks. Thus, the results here are mixed, but it is notable that the scale economies are found for the UK, Germany and the Netherlands – countries with large banks active in global markets. If it is accepted that equity capital is a weak measure of risk taking, the findings for scale economies are strengthened. These findings are more consistent with US studies using post-1990s data.

Berger and Mester (1997) review the possible reasons for differences in efficiency estimates. They also used their data to examine scale economies. Recall the database: nearly 6000 US commercial banks over the period 1990–95. They use the Fourier flexible cost model to estimate *Scale Efficiency*, defined as the ratio of the predicted minimum average costs to average costs, both adjusted to be on the X-efficiency frontier. They find evidence of scale efficiency at every asset size classification, ranging from 0.851 for banks with assets of up to $50 million to 0.782 for banks with assets in excess of $10 billion. From this, scale economies are computed as the bank's ratio of cost efficient size to its actual size. In column (2) of Table 9.3, the ratio is >1, implying scale economies for all asset sizes. For a given bank's product mix and input prices, the typical bank needs to be over two times larger to maximise cost scale efficiency. Another way of looking at it is based on column (4), the reciprocal of (3), i.e. the ratio of actual to cost efficient size. Given an average of about 0.4, it indicates that the US system would, on average, reach maximum efficiency by reducing the number of its banks by 60%, with each surviving bank producing, on average, 170% more.

---

[19] Except for Finland and France, when scale economies were not found to be significant in most years.

[20] ECU: European currency unit. The term used before the euro was introduced.

[21] By including equity capital as a factor input, the authors argue they are controlling for risk in the cost estimation.

Table 9.3   Key Results from Berger and Humphrey (1997)

| Bank Size (assets) (M/B US$) | No. of Banks | Cost-Efficient Size/ Actual Size | Actual Size/ Cost-Efficient Size |
|---|---|---|---|
| 0–$50M | 2218 | 2.2 | 0.455 |
| $50–$100M | 1794 | 2.363 | 0.423 |
| $100–$300M | 1344 | 2.523 | 0.396 |
| $300M–$1B | 392 | 2.815 | 0.355 |
| $1B–$10B | 171 | 2.986 | 0.335 |
| >$10B | 30 | 2.673 | 0.374 |
| Average | – | 2.723 | 0.389 |

*Source:* Berger and Mester (1997).

In the smallest asset category the number of banks should be reduced by 54% and banks in the second largest category, which would benefit by reducing their numbers by 67%.

These findings differ from most of the US studies that used 1980s data, where scale economies tended to be found for small banks; larger banks exhibited diseconomies or constant returns to scale. Berger and Mester identify a number of factors which could help to explain the difference:

- The Fourier flexible function was used rather than a translog cost function, but they re-estimated using the translog and found the scale economies to be even larger for the bigger banks.
- Open market interest rates were low in this period, about half what they were in the 1980s. The lower rates would reduce interest rate expenses which are normally proportionately higher for large banks because a greater proportion of their liabilities tend to be market sensitive. For example, they use wholesale funds.
- Regulatory changes tending to favour large banks. In the 1980s, with unit banking, or inter/intrastate branching restrictions, and restrictions on activities, it was costly to become large. For example, branching restrictions meant fewer branches for collecting deposits, contributing to scale diseconomies for large banks.
- New technology has altered the way basic services are delivered, making it possible for banks to expand faster rather than having expensive branch outlets.

Drake and Sniper (2002) revisited UK building societies in light of more recent US studies (such as Berger and Mester, 1997) and found more evidence of scale economies. They use a translog cost function but extend it to allow for entry/exit[22] and to estimate two types of technical change. They apply their estimating equation to a sample of UK building societies over the period 1992 to 1997. In their preferred model, the economies of scale estimate is highly significant and indicates that economies of scale exist for all different asset classes. Potential scale economies decline with size. Technical progress is shown to

---

[22] The authors have an unbalanced panel set because the building societies exist through the period. Rather than discarding them, they extend the Dionne *et al.* specification based on the translog cost function.

reduce the costs of larger societies relative to smaller ones, suggesting one strategy: mergers to reduce costs. Smaller societies are particularly vulnerable because they have the largest unexploited scale economies.

Cavallo and Rossi (2001) uses a translog cost function to estimate X-inefficiencies, scale and scope economies for several European countries (France, Germany, Italy, Netherlands, Spain and the UK) between 1992 and 1997. They have an unbalanced panel set of 442 banks and 2516 observations. The banks include commercial, saving and loans, cooperatives, investment, mortgage, non-banks, some government credit institutions. X-inefficiency is present in all the banking systems, with a mean cost X-inefficiency of 15.64%. The small financial institutions are significantly more efficient, especially those involved in traditional activities, and the coop banks do best among those involved in core banking services. They find evidence of economies of scale of similar magnitude, across the banking systems. They also report evidence for economies of scope, though it is not always significant. The best evidence is for large banks, while medium and small banks did not have significant coefficients. While these results are at odds with most other studies, they are similar to the findings of Berger and Mester (1997), which used 1990s data.

All the studies reviewed looked at the question of whether joint production reduces costs because of complementarities in production. Berger *et al.* (1996) used data from US banks over the period 1978 to 1990, looking for evidence of revenue economies of scope, that is, if complementarities in consumption raise revenues. Based on samples of small banks, large banks, specialists and banks offering a wide variety of products, they find no evidence to support this idea. The authors conclude that banks do not gain (in terms of higher revenues) by offering, for example, deposits *and* loans.

### 9.3.3. Technological Change

Altunbas *et al.* (1999) argue a time trend can act as a proxy for technical change.[23] It was found to be significant, and reduced the real annual cost of production by 3%. Also, the bigger the bank, the greater the reduction in costs. In a recent paper, Molyneux (2003) summarises the econometric approach to measuring technical change, which involves using the cost or profit functions summarised in equations (9.3) to (9.5). Using the cost function, estimated with a time trend, technical change is measured by taking the partial derivative of the estimated cost function with respect to a time trend. Following Molyneux (2003, p. 13):

$$\partial \ln TC / \partial T = t_1 + t_2 T + \sum \psi_i \ln P_i + \sum \phi_i \ln Q_i \qquad (9.10)$$

where

$\ln TC$ : natural log of total costs
$\ln Q_i$ : natural log of bank outputs
$\ln P_i$ : natural log of ith input prices (wages, interest rate, price of capital)
$T$ : time trend

---

[23] Though they note it must be treated with caution because of problems identified in the literature when using a time trend for this purpose. Also, technical progress rates are not constant.

Equation (9.10) can be broken down into three types of technical progress.

1. Pure technical progress, $t_1 + t_2 T$: reduces total costs (or raises profits).
2. $\sum \psi_i \ln P_i$: non-neutral technical change, reflects changes in the sensitivity of total cost (or profits) to changes in input prices. If $\psi_i$ is negative then the share of cost of input 1 towards total cost (profits) is decreasing over time.
3. $\sum \phi_i \ln Q_i$: scale augmenting technical progress, reflects changes in the sensitivity of total cost (profits) to variations in the quantities of output produced. If $\phi_i$ is negative, then the scale of production which minimises average cost (or maximises profit) for a given output is rising over time.

Molyneux uses balance sheet income data for 4000 European banks for the period 1992–2000, giving a panel of 20 333 observations. His main findings are:

- There was a reduction in costs of 5.62% arising from pure technical change (1.7%), and non-neutral technical change (3.92%). This was offset by a 1.8% increase in annual costs due to augmenting technical change. Overall annual costs fell by 3.8%.
- Classified by asset size, the small banks (with assets ranging from €1 million to €499.99 million) gained the most from cost reductions due to technical changes. The cooperative and savings banks benefited more than commercial banks, probably because these banks are normally smaller.
- Technical change reduced annual average costs by 2–4% in most EU states. Austria, Denmark, France, Germany, Italy and Spain experienced the largest reduction in costs. The decline in costs was highest in Denmark (6.6%), followed by Germany (4.4%). In the UK, they fell by 2.2%.

The effect of technical progress on the profits/profit frontier is estimated in the same way as equation (9.10), but this time the dependent variable is profits – see also equations (9.3) to (9.5). Based on the estimated profit function, it appears that reduced costs due to technical change have not fed into higher profits.

- The average annual reduction in profits as a result of technical change was 0.45% over the period, brought about by a fall in profits of 3.42% from pure technical change (1.9%) and from non-neutral technical change (1.52%), and an increase in profits (2.966) due to scale augmenting technical progress. In the early period, 1992–95, technical change improved profits but since then, it has reduced them by increasing amounts. Molyneux suggests this is due to "early mover" (p. 14) advantage: banks adopting the early technology earned enough revenue to offset the costs of adopting it but by the late 1990s, profits began to decline because all banks were adopting similar technologies, thereby incurring costs but not improving revenues.
- It appears that the banks that benefited most in terms of cost reduction suffered from reduced profits and vice versa. Commercial banks and banks from the top three asset categories experienced an increase in profits, while technical change reduced profitability of the smaller banks including the savings and cooperative banks. Molyneux suggests there

is a trade-off: banks using technology for large cost cuts (e.g. increasing ATMs and closing branches) ended up with poorer service quality, lower revenues and reduced profits. The commercial banks experience a smaller cost reduction because they use the technology to improve revenues through better services and risk management, etc. – reflected in higher profits.

- Countries that led the way in terms of annual cost reductions as a result of technical progress experienced the biggest declines in profits. For Danish banks, annual profits fell by 2.7% over the period; they also fell for the four other big cost cutters. Austria, Germany, Italy and Spain experienced annual declines in profits, though all except Austria were less than 1%. The other 10 countries experienced a rise in profits as a result of technical change. It is notable that in the UK, which (along with New York) led the way in generating new forms of commercial and investment banking business,[24] technical change led to an annual increase in profits of 0.781, with a small annual cut in costs. Sweden did the best overall, where annual costs fell by 1.8% and profits increased by 1.7%. Luxembourg's profit increase was about the same as Sweden's, though costs fell by just 0.41%.

Berger (2003) and Berger and Mester (2003) use similar cost and profit equations but look at changes in cost productivity (caused by movements in the best practice frontier and changes in inefficiency) and profit productivity. Berger and Mester looked at US banks from 1991 to 1997 and found annual increases in profit productivity of 13.7% to 16.5%, but cost productivity declined by 12.5%. They argue that these findings are consistent with US banks adopting new technologies that improved a range of services (e.g. mutual funds, derivatives, securitisation) such that the rise in revenues exceeded the increase in costs, hence the rise in profit productivity. Their US results are consistent with Molyneux's findings for commercial banks and for some European states.

## 9.4. Empirical Models of Competition in Banking

This section reviews different approaches that have been used to assess how competitive the banking sector is and to identify factors influencing competitive structure. The hypotheses most frequently tested are based on the structure–conduct–performance and relative efficiency models. Attempts to measure contestability in banking markets were briefly popular in the late 1980s/early 1990s, and are still mentioned in many papers. Finally, some studies have been trying to obtain more direct measures of competition by looking at bank pricing behaviour.

### 9.4.1. The Structure–Conduct–Performance Model

Since the Second World War, a popular model in industrial economics has been the structure–conduct–performance (SCP) paradigm, which is largely empirical, that is, it

---

[24] It is unclear whether investment banks were included in the sample, but the large European commercial banks also offer investment banking services. Off-balance sheet business is not included in Molyneux's model, though it would contribute to the profit figures.

relies on empirical data but for the most part, lacks a theoretical base. Applied to the banking sector, SCP says a change in the market structure or concentration of banking firms affects the way banks behave and perform. The more concentrated the market, the more market power banks have, which means they can be inefficient (i.e. avoid minimising costs) without being forced out of the market. This approach assumes a well-defined link between structure, conduct and performance:

Structure of the market: determined by the interaction of cost (supply) and demand in a particular industry

Conduct: a function of the numbers of sellers and buyers, barriers to entry and the cost structure – a firm's conduct is reflected chiefly in its pricing decisions

Performance: the bank's conduct (e.g. its pricing behaviour) will affect performance, often measured by profitability

How the links between the three might work in practice is:

$$\text{Structure} \rightarrow \text{Conduct (higher prices)} \rightarrow \text{Performance (higher profits)}$$

In the actual tests (see below), some authors treat profits as the dependent variable. Others look at the first link and try to explain prices by structure; the argument is that a concentrated market allows firms to set prices (e.g. relatively low deposit rates, high loan rates) which boost profitability.

Several theoretical models predict that fewer firms imply higher prices. Cournot oligopoly and Dixit–Stiglitz monopolistic competition models are examples. However, market structure is normally thought of as being endogenous, not exogenous, as assumed in the SCP model. So the SCP framework depends on the assumption that entry is effectively barred. In banking, the SCP model has been used extensively to analyse the state of the banking market in a given country or countries. Given there is no single generally accepted model of the banking firm, and since entry barriers are often high, emphasis on the SCP paradigm[25] is understandable.

## 9.4.2. The Relative Efficiency Hypothesis[26]

This model challenges the SCP approach. Relative efficiency (RE) posits that some firms earn supernormal profits because they are more efficient than others. This firm specific efficiency is exogenous. Greater efficiency may well be reflected in greater output. When the number of firms is small, bigger efficiency differences between them would imply greater concentration. Though RE predicts a similar (positive) profits concentration relationship to the SCP model, its key claim is that firms' profits should be correlated with this efficiency. Prices and concentration are inversely related, the opposite of SCP. Under the

---

[25] Hannan (1991) developed a theoretical model, from which the SCP relationship is derived.

[26] This model is sometimes known as the efficient markets model, but to avoid confusion with the well-known "efficient markets" hypothesis used in finance, this book uses the term "relative efficiency".

relative efficiency hypothesis, causation runs from greater efficiency, lower prices and higher concentration/market share:

Efficiency → Conduct (Higher Output and/or Lower Prices) → Market Share → Performance (Higher Profits)

The relative efficiency hypothesis can be linked to the X-efficiency hypothesis: some firms have superior management or production technology, which makes them relatively more cost X-efficient with lower costs. They are able to offer lower prices (if products are differentiated), gain market share (which increases concentration) and earn more profit. Likewise the presence of scale economies would mean these firms produce at low unit cost, lower prices and higher profits per unit of output.

The evidence for or against these hypotheses is important because the policy implications are so different. Confirmation of SCP is a case for intervention to reduce monopoly power and concentration. Curbing the exercise of monopoly power may be done by policies to encourage more firms to enter the sector or through a regulator who monitors the prices set by existing firms and/or imposes rules on pricing; e.g. deposit rates may not be more than $x\%$ below the central bank official rate. Strong evidence for the relative efficiency hypothesis suggests policy makers should not interfere with deposit and loan rate setting in the banking markets. Mergers should be encouraged if they improve relative efficiency, but discouraged if all they do is increase concentration and market power (SCP).

## 9.4.3. Empirical Tests: Structure–Conduct–Performance and Relative Efficiency

There are a multitude of studies testing the SCP and/or relative efficiency models in banking, especially for the USA. It would be impossible to do justice to them all. This section does not attempt a comprehensive survey of the published work.[27] Instead, it provides a summary of the findings reported in some recent key papers, which will be discussed below. For the SCP model, the general form is:

$$P = f(CONC, MS, D, C, X) \tag{9.11}$$

where

$P$ : measure of performance (profits or price)

CONC : market structure, with the degree of concentration in the market a proxy for the variable

MS : market share, more efficient firms should have a greater market share

$D$ : market demand

$C$ : variables used to reflect differences in cost

$X$ : various control variables

---

[27] For surveys of SCP and relative efficiency, see Gilbert (1984), Molyneux et al. (1996). Brozen (1982), Smirlock (1985), Evanoff and Fortier (1988), Molyneux et al. (1996) provide studies which have tested SCP. Berger (1995) and Goldberg and Rai (1996) review and extend the debate.

The dependent variable, performance, is proxied by either the price of the good or service, or profitability. In the list of performance measures below, the first number in the brackets gives the number of times these measures have been used in 73 SCP studies between 1964 and 1991 using US data, as reported by Molyneux *et al.* (1996, table 4.1). The second number shows the number of times the performance measure was found to be significantly related to market structure.

Measures for price include:

- Loan rates, such as interest rates and fees on personal loans, business loans or residential mortgages (30;14).
- Deposit rates, for example the interest rate paid on a term or savings deposits, money market accounts (25;10).
- Bank service charges, such as a monthly service charge levied on a current account, or service charges on a standard account (22;6).

Profitability measures include:

- Return on assets: net income/total assets (24;12).
- Return on capital: net income/capital (14;8).
- Return on equity: used in more recent studies, net income/stockholder's equity (NA).

There is an ongoing debate as to which performance variable should be employed. Profitability, it is argued, addresses the issue of banks supplying multiple products/services. However, it combines a flow variable (profit) with stock variables (assets, capital). The use of interest rates (prices, e.g. deposit or loan rate) has been criticised for the same reason (e.g. loan rates over one year and loans outstanding at the end of the year). Using service charges can be fraught with problems; the way they are computed can vary from bank to bank, and account charges will vary depending on the number of times a service is used, and some customers may be exempt provided they maintain a minimum balance.

Some studies employ a price measure as the dependent variable and others used a profit variable. For example, Berger and Hannan (1989) conducted direct tests of the SCP and relative efficiency models using the estimating equation:

$$r_{ijt} = \alpha_{ij} + \beta_j \text{CONC}_{jt} + \sum \delta_{ij} x_{jit} + \varepsilon_{ijt} \qquad (9.12)$$

$r_{ijt}$ : the interest paid at time $t$ on one category of retail deposits by bank $i$
      located in the local banking market $j$
$\text{CONC}_{jt}$ : a measure of concentration in local market $j$ at time $t$
    $x_{jit}$ : vector of control variables that may differ across banks, markets or time periods
    $\varepsilon_{ijt}$ : error term

By the SCP hypothesis, $\beta$ should be less than 0; that is, there is a negative relationship between concentration and deposit rates, the "price" of the banking service.[28] If the relative

---

[28] If loan rates are used as the dependent variable, then $\beta$ should be positive for SCP, and non-positive under RE.

efficiency model holds, $\beta \geq 0$. Berger and Hannan (1989) collected quarterly data from 470 banks in 195 local banking markets over a 2.5-year period, from 1983 to 1985, with 3500–4000 observations in six deposit categories. The dependent variables were retail deposit rates paid by commercial banks, as reported in the Federal Reserve's monthly survey of selected deposits and other accounts.[29] Banks in the sample were assigned to local markets, which were defined as metropolitan statistical areas (MSAs) or non-MSA counties. Banks with less than 75% of their deposits in one local market were deleted from the sample.

Berger and Hannan used two concentration ratios to measure the degree of firm concentration in the banking market. The "three firm" concentration ratio, $CR_3$ is defined as the proportion of output attributed to the top three firms in the industry. More generally, this ratio is written as $CR_n$, where $n$ is the output share produced by the top $n$ firms in the industry. The Herfindahl index[30] was also used, defined as $H = s_i^2$, where $s_i$ is the market share of the $i$th firm. These measures were constructed both with and without the inclusion of saving and loans firms.

The vector $x$ included a number of additional explanatory variables:

- The growth rate of deposits in the bank's market, which may reflect local supply and demand conditions, and could have either sign.
- The number of bank branches divided by total bank branches plus savings and loan branches in the local market – it should have a negative coefficient if costs rise with the number of branches. Local per capita income was included to control for factors affecting the supply of funds to banks – in a non-competitive market, it may reflect a greater or lesser elasticity of deposit supply. The local bank wage, reflecting a cost factor, was another explanatory variable. Its sign is not predicted, because bank wages could also reflect local income differences.
- Whether a state in which a given bank operates prohibits (UNIT) or limits (LIM) branch banking. To the extent that such regulations limit entry, and therefore raise costs, one would expect to observe a negative coefficient.

The different concentration measures yielded similar results, so only the results using $CR_3$ were reported. The $\beta$ coefficient on the concentration variable was found to be negative and significant at the 1% level – that is, the more concentrated the market, the lower the deposit rate, a finding which is consistent with the SCP hypothesis but not the relative efficiency model. For example, *ceteris paribus*, banks in the most concentrated markets were found to pay money market deposit rates which were 25–100 basis points less than what was paid on the less concentrated markets. Similar findings were obtained for all but some certificate of deposit (CD) rates. For the regressions using the short-term CD rates, there were some large and significantly negative rates; a few of the coefficients were insignificant. But for

---

[29] The six rates were: MMDA – money market deposit account, 10 quarters, September 1983–December 1985; SNOW, super now* account, 10 quarters, September 1983–December 1985; CD rates – certificate of deposit rates for 3, 6, 12 and 30 months, nine quarters from January 1983–December 1985 (CD rates had not been deregulated in September 1983).

[30] A more general measure of concentration which does not rely on a single arbitrary cut-off point.

the longer term CD rates (12, 30 months), the $CR_3$ coefficient was mostly negative but insignificant. This finding is not surprising because the longer the CD's maturity, the more substitutes will exist and the greater will be the competition from other financial markets.

The authors argued that the results were robust with respect to the use of separate OLS cross-section estimates in place of pooled time-series cross-section data, the choice of concentration measure and the inclusion of firm-specific variables such as market share, bank branches or bank size. The treatment of concentration under different state branching laws, modelling the deposit rate as a premium (the difference between the deposit rate and the money market mutual fund rate), and the inclusion of savings and loans in the measures of concentration did not affect the results.

Jackson (1992) challenged Berger and Hannan (1989). Jackson reported that a regression conducted for the entire sample period yielded similar results. However, if the sample was divided according to relative degrees of concentration, the findings differed.

- A low concentration group, relatively low market concentration: here the $\beta$ coefficient was negative, large and significant at the 1% level, which is consistent with the SCP finding.
- A middle concentration group: $\beta$ was negative but insignificant.
- A high concentration group: $\beta$ was positive and significant.

These results suggest price is non-linear over the relevant range and appears to follow a U-shaped relationship. This finding supports the relative efficiency type model, where high levels of market concentration signal the gaining of market share by the most efficient firms, but low levels of concentration signal entry of efficient new firms. In their reply, Berger and Hannan (1992) questioned some of Jackson's results,[31] but repeated their earlier work, allowing for the three levels of concentration. They found:

- $\beta < 0$ and significant for the low concentration group;
- $\beta > 0$ but insignificant for the middle concentration group;
- $\beta = 0$ but insignificant for the high concentration group's summary equation (though it was significant for seven out of ten individual periods; changing the control variables in the high concentration group reversed the sign, raising the question of how robust the model actually is)

Berger and Hannan (1992) concluded that the price–concentration relationship is negative for some ranges of concentration (supporting the SCP model), though it does vary across time periods. It is unclear, they claim, whether, at high concentration levels, it turns positive.

More recent studies have used some measure of profitability as the performance variable. Molyneux and Forbes (1996) is typical of the approach taken. They regressed banks' profits in different markets against a concentration ratio for that market (CR), the bank's market

---

[31] Jackson (1992) used monthly rather than quarterly observations, but did not correct the standard errors for serial correlation.

share of the market, its total asset size, and variables capturing market risk and state ownership of banks (if any) in the local market. Schematically:

$$\Pi_{ij} = \alpha_0 + \alpha_1 C_j + \alpha_2 MS + \text{other terms} \qquad (9.13)$$

where

$\Pi_i$ : bank $i$'s profit, measured by return on assets

Note the dependent variable is now a measure of profit rather than price. Molyneux and Forbes pool data from a number of European countries[32] for 1986 (756 banks), 1987 (1217 banks), 1988 (1538 banks) and 1989 (1265 banks). Each European country is treated as a separate local market.

The SCP hypothesis would predict $\alpha_1 > 0 = \alpha_2$. The relative efficiency hypothesis implies $\alpha_1 = 0 < \alpha_2$. When the data were pooled and the measure of market share is given in either deposits or assets, the SCP hypothesis is supported. In the regressions using yearly data, the coefficient on $\alpha_2$ is negative and insignificant, a rejection of the relative efficiency hypothesis. The government dummy coefficient is positive and significant – state owned banks are more profitable. The coefficient on asset (size) is negative and insignificant, suggesting that size does not influence profitability. The significant, positive coefficient on (K/A) indicates that the higher the capital adequacy, the more profitable the bank.

Altunbas and Molyneux (1994) used a three-stage least squares estimator to estimate the structural equations as well as the reduced form equations [like (9.12) and (9.13) above] to test the profits–concentration relationship. The results of OLS regressions favour SCP, as in Molyneux and Forbes. However, the three-stage least squares test results lend some support to both the SCP and the relative efficiency paradigms, and cast doubt on the validity of the OLS reduced form equations. These ambiguous results indicated the need for more sophisticated models and econometric techniques, and the inclusion of direct measures of efficiency in the model. A key issue is simultaneity: there may be more than one link between the coefficients, implying that the regression coefficients are biased.

Berger (1995) introduces two efficiency measures, and tested four hypotheses:

- Hypothesis 1: the traditional SCP model.
- Hypothesis 2: the Relative Market Power Hypothesis. Firms with a higher market share can exert more market power and earn higher profits, independent of how concentrated the market is.

The relative efficiency model is divided into two, to allow for either X-efficiency and/or scale economies.

---

[32] Accounting data from IBCA is used for 18 European countries. The countries were Austria, Belgium, Denmark, Finland, France, Germany, Greece, Ireland, Italy, Luxembourg, the Netherlands, Norway, Portugal, Spain, Sweden. Switzerland, Turkey and the UK.

- Hypothesis 3: Relative X-Efficiency Hypothesis. Firms that are more X-efficient (better management or better technology) have lower costs, higher profits and gain bigger market shares, which may result in greater concentration.
- Hypothesis 4: Relative Scale Efficiency Hypothesis. Firms have similar management skills/production technology but different scale economies.

Berger refers to Hypotheses 1 and 2 as the market power (MP) hypotheses; 3 and 4 are the efficient structure (ES) hypotheses. Berger then derives the structural forms for the ES and MP models, which are used to derive a single reduced form equation that nests all four hypotheses:

$$P_i = f(\text{X-EFF}_i, \text{S-EFF}_i, \text{CONC}_m, \text{MS}_i, Z_i) + \varepsilon_i \qquad (9.14)$$

where

$P_i$ : a measure of performance. ROE, ROA or the net interest margin for bank $i$[33]
$\text{X-EFF}_i$ : X-efficiency measure
$\text{S-EFF}_i$ : measure of economies of scale
$\text{CONC}_m$ : measure of concentration in market $m$
$\text{MS}_i$, market share of bank $i$ in market $m$
$Z_i$ : control variables for each bank $i$
$\varepsilon_i$ : error term for each bank $i$

For the ES hypotheses to hold, both profits [as in (9.14) above] and market structure variables must be positively related to efficiency, so two more reduced form equations are necessary:

$$\text{CONC}_m = f(\text{X-EFF}_i, \text{S-EFF}_i, Z_i) + \varepsilon_i \qquad (9.15)$$

$$\text{MS}_i = f(\text{X-EFF}_i, \text{S-EFF}_i, Z_i) + \varepsilon_i \qquad (9.16)$$

The tests are applied to 30 data sets, each of which has between 1300 and 2000 observations, with a total sample of 4800 US commercial banks. The decade of the 1980s is used to enable Berger to study three types of market structure: unit banking (one branch per state), limited branching, and states that do not impose any restrictions on banking. A number of different measures of concentration were estimated, but the results were similar, so Berger's paper reports the results using the Herfindahl index. Estimates of X-efficiency and scale efficiency were derived in separate tests. The average X-efficiency measure was 0.575, meaning that banks, on average, are about 42% X-inefficient. In terms of scale economies, 90% of banks were found to be operating at below efficient scale – this may be due to the exclusion of interest costs in the computation. The control variables chosen for the three different markets include whether a bank is in a metropolitan area, the real growth of the weighted average market, and dummies for the bank's state.

Berger's (1995) key results are as follows.

- When equation (9.16) is estimated, the results strongly reject the SCP hypothesis: 41 of 60 concentration coefficients are negative, and 16 of these are significant, suggesting a

---

[33] Berger (1995) also uses price measures.

*negative* relationship between profits and concentration. Just one CONC coefficient was found to be positive and significant. He claims that evidence supporting SCP (higher concentration yields higher profit) in earlier papers is likely due to correlations between other variables, such as concentration and market share.

- There is some evidence for the relative market power hypothesis. In estimations of equation (9.16), 45 out of 60 MS coefficients are positive, 22 of these are significant. Only four are significantly negative. Since the efficiency measures are included, it suggests that larger firms have gained market power through advertising, networks, and so on.
- The relative efficiency school argues that it is the efficiency of banks that allows them to capture a higher market share, and therefore perform better. There is some support for the X-efficiency version of this hypothesis – X-efficiency has a significant and positive influence on profits. However, there is little evidence of a significantly positive coefficient for X-efficiency in the market share or concentration equations, which is needed to explain the higher profitability, i.e. greater efficiency (through better management of resources) should increase market share or concentration, which in turn increases profits. While there is evidence of a link between X-efficiency and profits, there is none to support the idea that X-efficiency raises market share or concentration. So while one necessary condition is satisfied, the other is not.
- Berger finds no evidence to support the scale efficiency version of the relative efficiency hypothesis.
- Perhaps the most important conclusion is how small changes in these variables affect a bank's profitability. Based on the size of the coefficients, Berger reports that ROA would rise by 0.142% and ROE by 1.9% if a bank increased its market share, X-efficiency and scale efficiency by 10%, respectively. It is unlikely a bank could achieve these very large increases simultaneously, unless, Berger argues, it is done through a merger. Since most of the rise in profitability comes from an increase in X-efficiency, the acquiring firm should be looking for an inefficient target, which is likely to be able to be made as efficient as the acquiring firm.
- Berger also notes that the $R^2$ on most of the $\Pi$ regressions are low, under 10%. Including the market and efficiency variables raises them to about 13%. With such a low explanatory power, it suggests profitability sources come from elsewhere, such as portfolio choices or other factors not considered here.

Goldberg and Rai (1996) conduct a Berger type exercise for 11 European countries[34] between 1988 and 1991. They use the large banks from each of these countries, most of which have extensive branch networks, where, unlike the USA, deposit and loan rate decisions are taken by head office and are quoted by all the national branches. There are 79 banks, ranging from 1 in Belgium to 15 in Italy. Following Jackson (1992), the authors divide the sample into high and low concentration countries, depending on their Herfindahl index and the three bank concentration ratio scores. The UK, Belgium, Finland, Sweden and Denmark were classified as high concentration countries. Data were pooled over the four years, and dummy variables used for the first three years.

---

[34] Austria, Belgium, Denmark, Finland, France, Germany, Italy, Spain, Sweden, Switzerland, United Kingdom.

The variables tested are similar to Berger (1993), except for the performance measures. In addition to ROA and ROE, they use net interest margin/total assets as a proxy for pricing by banks. They also try NIR: non-interest returns. The control variables include per capita income [(wages + salaries)/number of employees], size (log of total assets) and a measure for risk: total liabilities/total assets. Another difference from the Berger study is the use of stochastic frontier analysis to obtain the efficiency measures.[35] The estimating equations are similar to the three shown above for the Berger study. The main findings from the Goldberg and Rai (1996) study are:

- The results are highly sensitive to the performance measure used.
- There is only evidence to support the scale efficiencies version of the relative efficiency hypothesis in low concentration countries.
- There is no support for the relative market power hypothesis.
- The two concentration measures do very little to explain bank performance.
- The results are at odds with those of Molyneux and Forbes (1996), which support SCP, and Altunbas and Molyneux (1994), though the latter paper finds some evidence to support SCP and relative efficiency. The authors note that based on their findings, there is no reason for regulators to restrict bank mergers or cross-border acquisitions in Europe.

Also similar to Berger (1995), Goddard, Molyneux and Wilson (2001) investigate the SCP hypothesis for 15 European countries from 1980 to 1996. Though the explanatory power is very low, they report evidence to support the SCP hypothesis. Mendes and Rebelo (2003) use Portuguese banking data from 1990 to 1999. For the first half of the 1990s there is evidence of SCP, but in the later half, following regulatory reforms, their results support the relative market power hypothesis, that is, firms with a greater market share can earn higher profits, independent of concentration.

Corvoisier and Gropp (2002) employ a Cournot model of loan pricing, where banks are price makers in the loan market but face a given deposit rate, and show that differences in the deposit rate and loan rate will occur in markets with a low number of banks, $n$. As the number of banks rises to $\infty$, the deposit rate will approach the loan rate, making the loan market perfectly competitive. In the theoretical model, they also show the loan rate depends on aggregate loan demand, the elasticity of aggregate loan demand, the probability of default by borrowers and the ban's operating costs.

They go on to test an empirical version of the model, where:

$$\text{MARGIN}_{ic} = \beta_0 + \beta_{1i}\text{CONC}_{ic} + \beta_{2i}\text{RISK}_c + \beta_3\text{NRISK}_c + \beta_{4i}(C/I)_c + \beta_{5i}\text{DL}_c$$

$$+ \beta_{6i}\text{SM}_c + \beta_6 I + \mu + \nu \qquad\qquad (9.17)$$

---

[35] Berger (1993) uses deviations from an average residual over a time horizon to obtain efficiency measures. Goldberg and Rai (1996) estimate the deviations from the stochastic cost frontier, then use the error terms to obtain measures of X-efficiency for each bank. Scale efficiency measures are also obtained using the SCF model.

where

MARGIN$_{ic}$ : the difference between a bank retail interest rate and a money market rate for product $i$ and country $c$

CONC$_{ic}$ : the Herfindahl index for product $i$ in country $c$ – it declines as $n$, the number of banks, and also as their shares become more similar

RISK$_c$ : a proxy for the probability of default by borrowers, which is the share of problem loans in country $c$. If that is not available, NRISK$_c$, a dummy – valued at 1 if there is no measure for problem loans, 0 otherwise

$C/I$ : the average cost to income ratio in country $c$, a proxy for operating costs

DL : the consumer and producer confidence indices for each country, which act as a proxy for the aggregate demand for loans

SM$_c$ : the extent of stock market capitalisation in a country $c$ – proxies for the elasticity of aggregate loan demand; also uses the ratio to total assets in a country's banking system to GDP

$I$ : indicator dummy – 1 if the Herfindahl index describes concentration in the product market I, 0 otherwise

They test equation (9.17) for a number of loan and deposit categories:

1. Overall, short-term and long-term loans;
2. Mortgage loans;
3. Demand, fixed term and savings deposits.

Corvoisier and Gropp make interesting use of the Herfindahl index. They compute Herfindahl indices (recalibrated) for several bank products in each country: customer loans, short-term loans, long-term loans, mortgages and demand, savings and time deposits. For example, using consumer loans of bank $k$ and the total number of banks in the country, the Herfindahl index is defined as:

$$H = \sum_{k=1}^{K} [L_k / \sum L_k]^2 \tag{9.18}$$

where

$L_k$ : consumer loans of bank $k$
$K$ : total number of banks in the country

They also use the more conventional Herfindahl computation based on total assets. By this measure they find that concentration increases in the period 1995–99, but at a slower rate than in earlier years. On average, it grew by about 10%. The largest countries (e.g. Germany) show the least concentration, while Finland and the Netherlands show the greatest concentration. The product specific indices tend to follow the same pattern. However, the differences between products is notable. In Italy, the Herfindahl indices vary from 25 to 160 for deposits and loans. In Germany, they vary from 5 to 30; in Finland, from 350 to 500. Concentration in deposit markets tends to be higher than in loan markets.

The main objective of the study was to look at the relationship between concentration and margins. The authors estimate equation (9.17) using three models, each of which eases the restrictions on slopes across different products and markets. The results show:

- Concentration has different effects depending on the type of product under consideration.
- The more concentrated the market for loans and demand deposits, the higher the margins, which supports the structure–conduct–performance hypothesis, and supports the presence of collusion.
- For savings and time deposits, the more concentrated the market, the lower the margins, which does not support the SCP model. The authors try to explain the result by arguing that proximity to the bank is important for demand deposits, but not for savings and time deposits. They suggest this difference could make the market more contestable.[36] However, if contestability was determining interest margins, then there should be no relationship between changes in concentration and price, since the number of firms does not matter in a contestable market. Furthermore, during the period studied, the development of technology was such that bank location grew increasingly less important for all products, except for customers who insist on using a branch. A more likely explanation is that current accounts (demand deposits) lack close substitutes, whereas for savings and time deposits, there are alternatives (e.g. sweep accounts, low risk mutual funds, government bonds). This could make the demand for savings and time deposits more price elastic, especially if the amount saved is quite high, say, in excess of $1500, and customers are prepared to lock away their money for a period of time. The presence of close non-bank financial substitutes makes the market less concentrated than it appears.

A related problem may be the use of the interest rate in the computation of margins. Corvoisier and Gropp are somewhat vague on the rates used in the study: the data are reported to come from national central banks of reporting countries. However, it is well known these data tend to be highly aggregated, for example, an average interest rate for the big four or five banks in a country. A more precise measure would be constructed from each bank's deposit or loan rate corresponding to each product, for varying amounts, at different maturities.

Angelini and Cetorelli (2003) look at competition in the Italian banking market from 1984 to 1997. They find evidence of an increase in competition post-1992, the year the European Union's second Banking Directive (see Chapter 5) came into effect, which introduced a single passport for European banks, so banks could branch more easily across Europe. Using firm based balance sheet data on approximately 900 Italian banks over the 14-year period, they compute Lerner indices. A Lerner index is defined as:

$$L^c = v/(\varepsilon n) \tag{9.19}$$

---

[36] See the next subsection for more detail on the meaning of contestable banking markets.

where

$n$ : number of firms
$\varepsilon$ : the elasticity of demand for the industry product, defined as a positive number
$\nu$ : the conjectural variation for output, that is, the representative firm's belief about
   how industry output responds to its own output

Thus, the Lerner index measures the relative mark-up of price over marginal cost. The higher the index, the less competitive the market is. Looking at the results for commercial banks, they find Lerner indices remain largely unchanged in the first part of the period 1984–92, but drop after 1993, suggesting competitive conditions increased post-1992. The authors also compared a group of banks that were involved in a merger/acquisition and those that were not. However, they can find no discernible differences in the two grouped Lerner indices, suggesting consolidation had little effect on market power.

With the Lerner index as the dependent variable, regression analysis is used to test a number of explanatory variables which could have affected mark-ups. Different measures of market structure included the number of banks and the Herfindahl index. As expected, the coefficient on number of firms is positive, that is, as the number of firms increases, the Lerner index falls. A negative relationship is found between the level of concentration and the relative price mark-up, that is, as concentration rises, the mark-up falls – contrary to the prediction of the SCP hypothesis. The finding is, the authors claim, likely due to the fact that the increased consolidation was a strategic reaction by banks anticipating increased contestability. Consolidation and restructuring increased efficiency, which was passed on to consumers, hence the fall in the index.

There are two problems with these arguments. First, if, as the authors claim, contestability was a driving force, then the number of firms in the market should have *no* effect on pricing. Second, using Herfindahl or the number of firms as explanatory variables creates a potential simultaneity problem, because the Lerner index is derived from the number of firms [see equation (9.19)]. Thus, these results must be treated with extreme caution. Overall, their results show increased consolidation in the Italian banking sector coincided with a fall in the Lerner index, suggesting bank mergers have increased bank efficiency, which in part has been passed on to consumers. This could be part of a defensive strategy – becoming more competitive in the face of anticipated entry by banks headquartered in other states.

## 9.4.4. The Panzer–Rosse Statistic and Contestable Banking Markets

Some empirical studies consider the question of whether banking markets are contestable. A contestable market is one in which incumbent firms are vulnerable to "hit and run" entry and exit, and given this threat, behave as though they are price takers, pricing products at average cost (equal to marginal cost with a horizontal cost curve), thereby maximising consumer surplus. This type of entry is possible if the market is one where customers can switch suppliers faster than the suppliers can reprice, if incumbents and newcomers have access to similar technology and factor prices and there are no *sunk* or irrecoverable costs.

Sunk costs are fixed costs which cannot be recovered when a firm leaves the market/industry. Not all fixed costs are sunk costs. For example, if used machinery has a secondary market value, it can be sold, making the costs fixed but not sunk. In the banking industry, some experts argue that most of the costs are fixed but not sunk, making it contestable. New firms enter if incumbent firms are acting as "price-makers", that is, deposit or loan rates are lower (higher) than perfectly competitive rates, "hit" the market and capture market share with lower prices. They remain in the market until profit margins begin to fall when existing firms react by lowering their prices. Having made a quick profit, these firms, with virtually no sunk costs, "run" or exit the market when increased competition narrows profit margins.

Under these assumptions, new entrants capture market share by offering lower "prices". This type of market is known as *contestable*; the mere threat of entry keeps existing banks pricing their products at marginal cost. There are important policy implications if a market is found to be contestable. It will not matter if there are only a few firms in the industry, for example, a banking oligopoly. The mere threat of entry will mean incumbent banks price their products at marginal cost, and consumer surplus is maximised. Hence, there is no need for governments to implement policies to encourage greater entry into the market.

Shaffer (1982) and Nathan and Neave (1989) argue the Panzer–Rosse (1987)[37] statistic (PR) can be used to test for contestability and other forms of competition in, respectively, the US and Canadian banking markets. The technique involves measuring market power by looking at how changes in factor prices affect firms' revenues, quantifying the firms' total revenue reaction to a change in factor input prices. For example, for a given change in factor prices, revenues rise less than proportionately; in the case of monopoly, there should be no response, while in perfect competition, there will be an equiproportionate increase in gross revenues.

In Shaffer (1982) and Nathan and Neave (1989), input prices consisted of the unit price of labour, the unit price of premises, and the ratio of interest expenses to total deposits for banks. PR, the Panzer–Rosse statistic, is defined as the numerical value of the elasticity of total revenue with respect to a chosen vector of input prices.

Shaffer (1982) used data for unit banks in New York, and estimated the PR statistic to be 0.318. He concluded that banks in the sample behave neither as monopolists (their conduct was inconsistent with joint monopoly) nor as perfect competitors in the long run. In Nathan and Neave (1989) a similar methodology was applied, using cross-section data (1982–84) from the Canadian banking system, PR values for 1983 and 1984 were found to be positive but significantly different from both zero and unity. These PR values, they argued, confirmed the absence of monopoly power among Canadian banks and trust companies. Nathan and Neave concluded their results were consistent with a banking structure exhibiting features of monopolistic, contestable competition.

Molyneux, Lloyd-Williams and Thornton (1994) tested for contestability in German, British, French, Italian and Spanish markets, using a sample of banks from these countries, for the period 1985–89. The authors found the PR for Germany (except 1987), the UK,

---

[37] Originally known as the Rosse–Panzer statistic after Rosse and Panzer (1977) used it to test for competition in the newspaper industry. Following Panzer and Rosse (1987), it has come to be known as the Panzer–Rosse statistic.

France and Spain to be positive and significantly different from both zero and unity. They concluded that in these markets, commercial banks operated in a monopolistically competitive market. However, the authors cautioned that the result is different from the type of contestable market implied by the theory because incumbent banks were not undertaking perfectly competitive pricing. For Italy, the authors could not reject a hypothesis of monopoly or a conjectural variation short-run oligopoly for the years 1987 and 1989 because the PRs were found to be negative, and both were significantly different from zero and unity.

Bikker and Haaf (2002) look at competition in the European banking sector using the PR statistic, and compare their European findings with the USA and other countries.

Perrakis (1991) criticised Nathan and Neave and argued the PR may be inadequate as a test for contestability.[38] However, there are more fundamental problems with the use of PR to infer contestability than those raised by Perrakis. There is a potential problem with the timing of the firms' entry and exit decisions. The computations in the studies cited above implicitly assume there were no lags in interest rate adjustments, so interest rates were contemporary with the change in total revenue, and entry and exit by other firms was very rapid and in the same period.

Additional problems arise from the claim that PR is sufficient or necessary for contestability. If firms have flat-bottomed average costs in a perfectly contestable market, the elasticity of total revenue to the input price vector is $(1 - e)$, where $e$ is the price elasticity of demand if no firm actually enters or quits the market. $e$ could be greater or less than unity, and therefore, PR could be negative, even under conditions of perfect contestability. Furthermore, consider a classic, incontestable Cournot oligopoly. In the Cournot model, as the number of firms increases, the price of the good or service will fall. In a contestable market, there should be no sensitivity to firm entry. Assume Cournot applies, with linear demand and horizontal marginal cost. Then PR will be positive if the given number of firms is large and marginal cost is low. If the statistic can be positive under Cournot, then one cannot claim a positive value of PR as evidence of confirmation of contestability.

Furthermore, given the banks' ever-increasing dependence on information technology, which dates within a year if not months, it is hard to argue the case for a contestable banking market on practical grounds alone. For example, secondary markets exist for used furniture but in banking it might be difficult, if not impossible, to sell computer hardware and systems, because of dating or compatibility problems. Indeed the lack of compatibility of IT systems is often cited as a problem for newly merged firms because it prevents them from getting costs down quickly.

## 9.4.5. Testing for Competition Using a Generalised Linear Pricing Model

It was noted that testing for competition using the SCP or relative efficiency hypothesis has numerous difficulties, giving rise to a remark by Berger (1995):

---

[38] Nathan and Neave (1991) reply to this criticism.

*"Despite... it does not appear that any of the efficient structure or market power hypotheses are of great importance in explaining bank profits."* (Berger, 1995, p. 429)

Some studies using more recent data and Berger's techniques have found some evidence to support the relative efficiency hypothesis in some markets, but the results, at best, are patchy. Yet the SCP and relative efficiency hypotheses dominated the literature on microstructure bank behaviour over two decades. The dependent variable was either profitability or "price", for example, a loan or deposit rate. The use of the Panzer–Rosse statistic also has its limitations. As the most recent literature appears to have quietly conceded, it cannot be used to test for contestability, and there are doubts about any result which shows a country's banking system to be perfectly competitive. An alternative approach suggested by Heffernan,[39] yet to be used by other researchers for other countries, possibly because of difficulty obtaining the necessary micro-data.

To look at the competitive behaviour of banks, Heffernan asks: what are the factors influencing the decision to set deposit and loan rates, and from bank price setting behaviour, what if anything can be said about the model that best describes their behaviour? In common with the efficiency, scale/scope economies, SCP and relative efficiency model, the focus is on the retail banking market. It would be possible to conduct a similar exercise for the wholesale markets, data permitting. However, it is generally accepted that the wholesale markets are highly competitive because the customers are well informed, and in some cases, are not dependent on banks for external finance, and there are a large number of players offering a wide range of products. On the other hand, customers in the retail markets tend to be ill-informed and consumers show signs of serious inertia. The presence of scale and scope economies[40] is indicative of imperfect competition. Even the Panzer–Rosse statistic may suggest the presence of imperfect competition in the banking sector.

The work by Heffernan attempts to go a step further by looking at pricing behaviour. It begins with a generalised pricing equation, which can be applied to the key retail banking products: deposits, loans, mortgages and credit cards.

$$Rd_{it} = \alpha_0 + \sum_j \beta_j \text{Libor}_{t-j} + \gamma_t + \delta_i D_i + \varsigma n_t + \varepsilon_{it} \qquad (9.20)$$

where

$$Rd_{it} : \text{gross deposit rate paid by firm } i \text{ at time } t$$
$$\text{Libor}_{t-j}, j = 0, 1, 2, 3 : \text{monthly lags used on Libor, the London interbank offer rate}$$
$$n : \text{number of FIRMS offering the product}$$
$$t : \text{time trend}$$
$$D_i : \text{DUMMY variable for each financial firm } i; \text{ unity for firm } i, 0 \text{ otherwise}$$

For mortgages and loan products, the equation is:

$$Rl_{it} = \alpha_0 + \sum_j \beta_j \text{Libor}_{t-j} + \gamma_t + \delta_i D_i + \varsigma n_t + \varepsilon_{it} \qquad (9.21)$$

---

[39] See, for example, Heffernan (2002).
[40] The evidence is mixed, but more recent studies have suggested their presence.

where

$Rl_{it}$ : loan or mortgage annual percentage rate charged by firm $i$ at time $t$

and for credit cards:

$$Rl_{it} = \alpha_0 + \sum_j \beta_j \text{Libor}_{t-j} + \gamma_t + \delta_i D_i + \varsigma n_t + \eta_t f_{it} + \varepsilon_{it} \qquad (9.22)$$

where

$f_{it}$ : FEE for credit cards charged by firm $i$ at time $t$.

Equations (9.20) through (9.22) were estimated by ordinary least squares,[41] using monthly rates for savings, chequing, mortgage, loan and credit card rates, for the period 1993–99. The rates for the savings and chequing accounts are obtained by using the rate quoted by each bank or building society at representative "high" and "low" amounts.[42] This yields four products: high and low savings and high and low chequing. The savings account includes all firms quoting a rate for a 90-day deposit. An interest penalty is incurred if the deposit is withdrawn within three months. The chequing product is a current account which pays interest on accounts in credit, and offers a range of free services, such as chequing and direct debit/credit facilities, ATM access and monthly statements, among others.

To test for the degree of competition in the banking market, a benchmark for a perfectly competitive rate is required, against which deposit and loan rates can be compared. Libor, the London Interbank Offered Rate, is the rate banks quote each other for overnight deposits and loans. Libor represents the opportunity cost of all of a bank's assets; for a bank that aims to maximise expected profit, it is the basis for determining the marginal revenue for all assets, and the marginal cost of all liabilities. It is an international rate, to which all banks have access, and therefore, is representative of a perfectly competitive rate. For these reasons, Libor is treated as a proxy for the perfectly competitive deposit/loan/mortgage/credit card rates. This study employed a monthly average of the daily 3-month Libor rate available from *Datastream* and other sources. Since retail rates are unlikely to respond to changes in current Libor immediately, the rate was lagged by one, two and three months.[43]

---

[41] OLS is adequate if estimating a pooled data set of firms across a number of years. However, in later studies where more data meant it was possible to run regressions for each bank and pooled regressions, there were unacceptable levels of serial correlation when the OLS procedure was used in the individual firm estimations. The use of an autoregressive error regression model that computes maximum likelihood estimators (i.e. AR(1) or AR(2)) resolved the problem. The time series regressions yield an adjusted $R^2$ of $>0.95$ for most of the FIs, and the Durbin Watson (DW) results show the null hypothesis of no serial correlation can be accepted. The pooled results display predictably lower adjusted $R^2$s.

[42] These representative high and low deposit levels were calculated using data from the British Bankers Association. See Heffernan (2002) for a complete explanation. This gave a high and low amount for each of the years, 1993–99. The average amount for savings was £23 811 (high) and £2107 (low); for chequing it was £2107 (high) and £310 (low).

[43] In Heffernan (1997), an error correction model was used to capture the dynamics of retail deposit and loan rates to changes in a base rate. The results (see, in particular, table 6, p. 223) provide econometric justification for choosing current Libor and Libor lagged by one, two and three months, respectively.

The variable $n$ allows a test for Cournot behaviour, which is present if the coefficient on FIRMS is significantly positive (negative) in the deposit (loan) equations. An indirect test of perfect contestability is also possible. In this study, if the coefficient on FIRMS in equations (9.20) to (9.22) is significant, then contestability is rejected because the number of incumbent firms should not influence deposit or loan rate setting.

The DUMMY variable for each firm permits a direct test of the theoretical model of monopolistic competition with bargains and rip-offs developed by Salop and Stiglitz (1977). Normally, a rise in market demand, or a fall in fixed costs, will attract more firms and, one would expect, generate greater competition. However, despite the large number of players in the market firms in this model are able to offer relatively good or bad buys to the consumer. In the Salop–Stiglitz model, consumers face unseen information costs. Some know the distribution of prices and others don't. The former only buy bargains; the latter buy randomly. A firm can survive either by charging a low price (bargain) or a high one (rip-off). Rip-off firms stay in business as long as there are enough purchases by the ill-informed (or inert) consumers. Firms offering bargain products profit from a higher volume of sales, because well-informed customers buy their relatively cheaper product. Thus, the relative bargains and bad buys co-exist, and there is a twin-peak price distribution.

Some consumers of retail bank products are well informed; others are not, enabling the Salop–Stiglitz theory to be put to the test. The dummy variable captures the competitive behaviour of each individual firm, relative to a default bank. The Royal Bank of Scotland was chosen as the default, thereby acting as a benchmark against which the behaviour of all the other institutions can be studied. The bank was selected because it satisfied a number of criteria: it was important to include the "big four" (Barclays, Lloyds, Midland and National Westminster[44]) and new players in the rankings, and the default firm had to have a complete set of data for all the products over the period of testing, 1993–99. In fact, the choice of default bank (with whose interest rates other banks' rates are compared) has NO significance for the ranking of financial institutions, nor (apart from a common constant) fo the interest rate deviations. Had another comparator bank been chosen, all the deviations from it change by the value of the coefficient on the default bank. However, the *range* of deviations does not change, nor do the ***relative rankings***.

A negative coefficient on a bank offering one of the deposit products means this bank is offering a bad bargain or rip-off relative to the default bank; a positive coefficient indicates a relative bargain. For loan products, the opposite is true; a negative (positive) coefficient confirms the presence of a relative bargain or good buy (rip-off or bad buy).

In the Salop–Stiglitz model, the coefficient on the number of firms offering the product may also be negative for deposit products and positive for loans, the opposite sign expected for the Cournot model. For example, a fall in fixed costs could be one of several reasons why new firms enter the market. Hence, firm entry could rise, and with it, the number of relative rip-offs. On the other hand, a Salop–Stiglitz framework is compatible with the Cournot prediction that as firm entry increases, deposit rates will rise and loan rates will

---

[44] During the period of study (1993–99), Lloyds Bank took over the Trustees Savings Bank in December 1995 and began calling itself Lloyds TSB in 1999. The Hong Kong and Shanghai Bank Corporation took over the Midland Bank in 1992; in late 1999 the Midland branch network was renamed HSBC.

fall. The sign of the coefficient will be determined by the relative influence of the rip-off and bargain firms.

## Analysis of the econometric tests

Space constraints prevent a complete set of regression results for the five products, estimated using equations (9.20)–(9.22), and readers are recommended to read Heffernan (2002). The adjusted $R^2$s range from 0.41 to 0.83, which, given the data are cross-section time series, indicate the overall model is a good fit.

Working through the results gives a picture of the state of UK competition in the retail sector in the 1990s. Sometimes it is possible to compare them with an earlier study which conducted a similar exercise using data for 1985–89. By the mid-1980s, most of the banking reforms, designed to make the market more competitive, were complete. Hence, by the 1990s, there should be evidence of greater competition. Begin with the coefficient on Libor, which would be unity in a perfectly competitive market. The summary in Table 9.4 shows the deposit rates on savings accounts range from 63% to 70% of a perfectly competitive rate, but are much lower for the chequing account: 18–38%. Compared to the earlier study [see Heffernan (1993)], only savings at the high amount have become more competitive, the rates for the chequing account are far less competitive, and low savings has hardly changed. These results illustrate how banks' pricing decisions are very much product based, and depend on how many substitute products there are. High savings, averaging just under £24 000, had many substitutes such as national savings products, tax efficient savings schemes and mutual funds. Savings at the lower amount had far fewer substitutes, reducing the competitive pressure on banks. An interest paying chequing account was offered for the first time in the latter half of the 1980s, but again, had few substitutes. The results suggest that for products with few substitutes, banks introduce new products that offer highly competitive rates to "capture" the consumer and then reduce the rates over time.

Table 9.4 shows the Libor coefficients on mortgages are slightly below unity, suggesting quite competitive rates, especially when compared to deposit products. However, the presence of the large constant terms (not shown) is indicative of smoothing, slowing the rise to the competitive rate which takes place in discrete jumps. Also, the constant term for existing borrowers is twice that of new borrowers – evidence of discrimination against

Table 9.4   Sum of Significant Coefficients for Libor

| Account | Significant Libors | Sum of Significant Coefficients |
|---|---|---|
| Low Saving | Lagged by 1, 2 months | 0.626 |
| High Saving | Current, lagged by 1 month | 0.702 |
| Low Chequing | Lagged by 3 months | 0.184 |
| High Chequing | Lagged by 3 months | 0.381 |
| Mortgages (existing) | Current, lagged by 2 months | 0.848 |
| Mortgages (new) | Lagged by 1, 2 months | 0.714 |

existing borrowers, who are locked in and face high switching costs. Compared with the 1985–89 study, there appears to be little change in this market.

The very high significant constant terms found for personal loans and credit cards are indicative of large margins for the banks. For all products, the prominence of the lagged Libors shows banks respond to a change in Libor over several months. The coefficient on FEE was strongly significant and positive in the credit card regression.[45] As the annual fee rises, so does the credit card rate charged. Financial firms charging annual fees are unquestionably engaging in price discrimination because other credit cards are available with similar non-price features and no annual fee. Either fees and/or the rate charged can be the source of a rip-off.

Current Libor is significant in only one case, existing borrowers using the top financial institutions, indicating there is a partial, immediate rate response to changes in the interbank rate. All the regressions have at least one lagged Libor which is significant.

Table 9.5 shows the results of the bargain rip-off test (column 2) and the sign of the coefficient on n, the number of firms (column 3) offering the product. Taken together, this

Table 9.5  Models of Imperfect Competition by Product (1993–99)

| Product | Size of margin (%) | Sign on no. of firms coefficient | Applicable Model |
|---|---|---|---|
| Mortgages – existing Borrowers | 0.37 (−0.32 to −0.06) | (+) insignificant | Competitive but with some price discrimination |
| Mortgages – new Borrowers | 0.45 (−0.04 to 0.05) | (+) significant | Competitive but not contestable |
| Low Chequing | 0.92 (−0.36 to 0.56) | (−) insignificant | Unclear |
| High Savings | 2.14 (−0.67 to 1.47) | (−) significant | SS Monopolistic competition – bargain/rip-off |
| Low Savings | 2.8 (−2.1 to 2.7) | (−) significant | SS Monopolistic competition – bargain/rip-off |
| High Chequing | 5.08 (−2.7 to 2.38) | (+) insignificant | SS Monopolistic competition – bargain/rip-off |
| Personal loans (unsecured) | 8.17 (−3.8 to 4.9) | (+) insignificant | SS Monopolistic competition – bargain/rip-off |
| Credit Cards | 16.5 (−7.4 to 9.1) | (−) significant | SS Monopolistic competition – bargain/rip-off |

SS: Salop Sitglitz.

---

[45] The coefficient on FEE was 0.166 with a t-ratio of 10.1.

information makes it possible to classify a product according to the model of competition which best describes it.

Begin with column 2. These margins come from the coefficients on the dummy variables which are used to capture the extent of the rate setting differences across banks for a given product. Consider personal loans. The margin of 8.17% indicates there is a difference of 8.17% between the best bargain bank (margin of $-3.8\%$) and the worst rip-off, where the bank earns a margin of 4.9%. The coefficient on firm variable is insignificant. With such a large margin and no evidence of Cournot-like behaviour, this suggests the Salop–Stiglitz model of monopolistic competition, where banks offer relative bargains and rip-offs both survive in the marketplace. The price setting behaviour by banks for all but three of the products is best described by a bargain/rip-off model of monopolistic competition. Mortgage products are the key exception. Recall the earlier evidence suggesting that existing borrowers suffered from price discrimination because they were locked into a mortgage. The lack of support for the Cournot model, and the small margin between the best bargain and worst rip-off, tends to confirm this. For new mortgagees, the margin is also small, but the coefficient on number of firms is significant but the opposite of what would be expected by Cournot – rates rise with more firms. Based on this evidence, it appears the market is competitive but not contestable, because the firm entry coefficient is significant, and in a contestable market, it should not be.

A similar approach[46] was used to examine whether UK building societies, which are mutuals, changed their pricing behaviour once they converted to shareholder owned status. After the 1986 Building Societies Act (see Chapter 5), eight opted to convert between 1995 and 2000.[47] The period covered was 1995 to 2001 for a sample of converted societies and mutuals. The presence of imperfect competition in UK retail banking has already been confirmed, which gave the financial institutions market power. Under these conditions:

- The new stock banks became more price sensitive post-conversion – they were far more likely to respond rapidly to a change in Libor than building societies.
- After they converted to bank status, deposit rates were found to be permanently lower, and mortgage rates permanently higher.
- Using the Salop–Stiglitz test, the new converts were found to offer predominantly rip-off products.

## 9.4.6. Competition in the Canadian Personal Finance Sector

With 3% of the world's bank deposits, Canada provides an example of a nationally integrated banking system with relatively high concentration, much higher than the USA. Historically, the Canadian financial sector consisted of five financial groups. Federally chartered banks focused on commercial lending, and since the late 1950s, personal lending and mortgages. Trust and mortgage loan companies originally offered trust and estate administration services and later, mortgages and long-term deposits. In the 1980s, trust companies expanded into the personal financial sector by offering demand deposit, short-term deposit and personal lending products. Trust companies are normally in possession

---

[46] Heffernan (2005).
[47] Abbey National had converted in 1989.

of a federal charter, though some are chartered by provincial governments and operate in local markets. There is also a cooperative credit movement, consisting of credit unions and caisses populaires. Provincial governments grant charters to the credit unions which service provincial markets, but they do not have national branch networks. Life insurance firms, subject to federal and provincial regulations, have expanded from offering traditional life insurance products into the administration of pension funds and some savings instruments. The securities industry offers the usual products related to underwriting, brokerage, market making and securities investment advice.

From the 1960s through to the 1980s, a number of federal and provincial legislative revisions[48] set the stage for greater competition in the Canadian financial system. Much has been written about the dissolution of the traditional "four pillars" financial system, i.e. the chartered banks, trust and mortgage loan companies, life insurance dealers, and securities firms.

Three empirical studies, Nathan and Neave (1989), Shaffer (1990) and Nathan (1991), conclude that Canadian banking is, at least approximately, contestable. This section briefly reports on the results of a study of competition in Canadian banking which challenges these results. Heffernan (1994) used the generalised pricing methodology similar to that described above.[49] The study looked at pricing behaviour for four products: mortgages, term deposits, fixed rate registered retirement savings plans (RSPs) and registered retirement income funds (RIFs). These products (with the exception of RIFs) are offered by more than one type of financial institution, making it possible to use the data in a test of competitive behaviour among different financial groups in the personal finance sector. There were five financial groups in the database: domestic banks, trust companies, foreign banks, savings and loan firms, and life insurance companies. The data were pooled, cross-section, time-series, for the period 1987–90.

The equations estimated were similar to equation (9.20). The main findings may be summarised as follows.

- When the sample was split between "major" and "minor" firms,[50] the diagnostics indicated the presence of systematic pricing differences between them. Thus, though the "four pillars" may well have been eroded *de jure* in the sense that there is no regulation preventing different types of financial firms from entering a given market, the regression results for mortgages, term deposits and RSPs suggest that *de facto*, a fifth column consisting of 12 major banks and trust companies had emerged, at least in the personal finance sector. Life insurance firms continue to be the major players in the RIF market – only one trust company offered RIFs.
- The finding of a significant, right-signed coefficient number of firms variable in most of the estimations supported the presence of a Cournot-type behaviour, that is, the greater the number of sellers in a market, the lower the "price".

---

[48] The first change in the regulations appeared in the 1967 Bank Act, the 1980 Bank Act, the 1982 revised Quebec Securities Act, "Big Bang" in Ontario in 1987, and legislation in 1990. See Heffernan (1994) for a more detailed discussion.

[49] See Heffernan (1994).

[50] The major firm sample consisted of the 12 major banks and trust companies; minor firms operated in local markets.

- In comparison to the studies of Canadian banking by Nathan and Neave (1989), Nathan (1991) and Shaffer (1990), which cover similar years, this investigation finds no evidence to support a contestable markets model for the Canadian banking market, or one which exhibits features of traditional monopolistic competition. Rather, the findings here are consistent with Cournot-type behaviour of financial firms, where the gap between price and marginal cost is negatively related to the number of firms in the market. In a contestable market, firm entry would not affect prices. Significant coefficients found on the financial group dummy variables mean different financial groups exhibit price-making behaviour for some personal finance products, offering relative bargains for some products, relative rip-offs for others. The presence of systematic pricing differences between the "fifth column" and minor firms operating in local markets is also inconsistent with the predictions from models of contestability and monopolistic competition.

- There were notable, significant differences in the relative pricing behaviour of the different groups. Trust companies were price-makers, setting above-average interest rates on mortgages. The chartered banks were shown to exert a strongly negative influence on term deposit rates in 1987 and 1988, but trust companies had a significantly positive influence on deposit rates in all four years. Domestic banks also exert a negative influence on RSP rates. Foreign banks offered relative rip-off RSPs and mortgages but, in most cases, bargain term deposits.

- The dummy variable coefficients permitted a ranking of the different financial groups according to the degree of bargain/rip-off product on offer. In the case of mortgages, no one group offered a particularly good or bad rate. For term deposits, trust companies offered a relatively good deal, followed by savings and loans, foreign banks and domestic banks. For RSPs, trusts and foreign banks offered the best deal, followed by life insurance firms and banks. Life insurance firms offered a relatively bad deal on RIFs in 1987 and 1990, but a better rate in 1989.

There are some qualifications to the procedures used in the generalised pricing model. First, it is often argued that financial institutions produce financial products jointly, and hence looking at the rates associated with a single deposit or loan product may be misleading. While it is correct to recognise the joint production of deposit and loans, one would have to have detailed data on the relevant cost functions to model it empirically, and they are not available. Furthermore, there is nothing to stop a customer from using a different financial firm for each of the deposit and loan products. The presence of transactions or switching costs may mean customers maximise their utilities by purchasing personal finance products at one firm but if true, such behaviour creates the opportunity for the financial firm to discriminate in prices. Furthermore, practitioners in the field report that when deciding upon, say, a deposit rate for a particular retail product, their principle concerns, among others, are the number of close substitutes, the ease with which consumers can switch, the actual switching rates, range of prices of similar products on the market, and in the case of loans, the credit risk profile. While in aggregate the number of loans are linked to deposits/funding, these other factors determine how loans and deposits are actually priced.

A second caveat concerns risk characteristics. If one bank is considered by depositors to have a higher probability of failure than other financial firms, then the funding costs for the bank will be relatively high. It will have to pay higher rates to attract deposits. Obviously, a difference in bank riskiness would affect the deposit pricing structure. In the case of assets, banks may charge different rates to reflect differences in risk among a class of borrowers. But there is no evidence to suggest banks/trusts in the sample would attract more risky mortgagees than any other firm.

## 9.5. Consolidation in the Banking Sector

In most western economies, the trend is towards increased consolidation of banks and other financial firms. Consolidation is normally defined to include *mergers*: the assets of two or more independent firms are combined to establish a new legal entity and *acquisitions*: where one bank buys a controlling interest in at least one firm but their assets are not integrated, nor do they form a single unit. Firms may also enter into *strategic alliances* which are looser relationships but, as one study has shown (see below), can influence rival banks' competitive behaviour. Most of the literature focuses on mergers and acquisitions – M&As. In this area of banking, the consultant/academic literature is divided, with the consultants/practitioners tending to be strongly supportive of the process. After a merger or acquisition is announced, bankers emphasise the achievement of economies of scale and scope or synergy, and the improved shareholder returns that should follow, but rarely back it up with hard evidence. Academics are more cautious because most of their studies using shareholder returns, performance and other measures give a less favourable verdict on the effects of M&As. Rhoades (1994) provides an example of how both groups can claim to be right. Bankers tend to focus on the dollar volume and/or the percentage of costs that are cut. A banker can claim they have achieved their post-merger goals if costs fall. But economists will argue there has been no change in efficiency if assets or revenues fall more or less proportionately. Depending on the audience one is addressing, both are right.

Additionally, there are also welfare considerations, such as the effects of increased concentration on competition, which is not the concern of a profit-maximising manager, but will be an issue for policy holders. After looking at trends in consolidation, a selection of key academic studies is reviewed, followed by a brief discussion of a case study approach undertaken by Davis (2000).

### 9.5.1. The Trends

Consolidation tends to be periodic. Evenett (2003) documents general trends in mergers and acquisitions in the recent past. He identifies two waves of consolidation, in 1987–90 and 1997–2000. In the first wave, 1987–90, 63% of M&As were in the manufacturing sector, 32% in the tertiary or services sector, and 5% in the primary sector. In the second wave, 1997–2000, 64% of M&As were in services and 35% in manufacturing. In both periods, within the service industry, a good proportion of the M&As were among financial institutions, especially between banks. Rhoades (1994), referring to the USA, noted a marked increase in bank merger activity in the early 1970s, then again in the late 1980s. From the late 1980s to the new century, M&As in the banking sector enjoyed a prolonged boom in both the USA and Europe. To date, there have been few bank mergers in developing/emerging markets, except under duress.

Table 9.6 Number of Mergers and Acquisitions by Country

| | 1990 | 1995 | 1999 |
|---|---|---|---|
| *Banking – Europe*[1] | | | |
| National – intra | 22 | 66 | 113 |
| National – cross | 8 | 33 | 23 |
| Global – intra | 15 | 29 | 36 |
| Global – cross | 4 | 16 | 12 |
| Total | 49 | 144 | 184 |
| Value ($m) | 4 946 | 27 631 | 124 873 |
| *Securities – Europe*[2] | | | |
| National – intra | 18 | 46 | 49 |
| National – cross | 7 | 26 | 28 |
| Global – intra | 5 | 17 | 25 |
| Global – cross | 6 | 8 | 18 |
| Total | 36 | 97 | 120 |
| Value ($m) | 3 036.8 | 4 975 | 16 162 |
| *Banking – USA* | | | |
| National – intra | 107 | 356 | 208 |
| National – cross | 4 | 14 | 34 |
| Global – intra | 2 | 11 | 10 |
| Global – cross | 0 | 0 | 3 |
| Total | 113 | 381 | 255 |
| Value ($m) | 3 986 | 71 417 | 68 399 |
| *Securities – USA* | 22 | | |
| National – intra | 22 | 42 | 45 |
| National – cross | 15 | 30 | 38 |
| Global – intra | 2 | 8 | 10 |
| Global – cross | 3 | 4 | 12 |
| Total | 42 | 84 | 105 |
| Value ($m) | 482.4 | 7 225.2 | 14 237 |

[1] Europe includes: Belgium, France, Germany, Italy, Netherlands, Spain, Sweden, Switzerland, UK.
[2] Securities includes investment banks.
*Source:* OECD (2001), *Report on Consolidation in the Financial Sector, Annex 1.*

According to an OECD (2001) report (covering 13 key industrialised countries[51]), during the 1990s, there were over 7600 deals involving the acquisition of one financial firm by another, with a total value of $1.6 trillion.[52] Between 1990 and 1999, there was a threefold increase in the number of deals, and the total value of M&As increased more than tenfold. More detailed figures for Europe and the USA appear in Table 9.6.[53] This table shows that

[51] Australia, Belgium, Canada, France, Germany, Italy, Japan, the Netherlands, Spain, Sweden, Switzerland, UK and the USA.
[52] *Source:* BIS (2000), p. 33, which obtained the data from the Securities Data Corporation.
[53] The insurance sector is not shown, but the numbers were comparatively small.

while the total number of bank mergers in Europe (1267) was under half that of the USA (2871), by 1999, the value of European mergers was much higher: $124.9 billion compared to $68.4 billion in the USA.

The rise in the number of financial sector M&As with values in excess of $1 billion reflects the general trends:

|  | 1990 | 1995 | 1998 | 1999 |
|---|---|---|---|---|
| **Number** | 8 | 23 | 58 | 46 |
| **Value ($bn)** | 26.5 | 113 | 431 | 291 |

*Source*: OECD (2001), table 1.1.

Of these financial sector M&As, 60% were banks, 25% were securities firms (including investment banks) and about 15% involved acquisitions of insurance firms. In 1998 there were a number of "super mega mergers", i.e. mergers between banks with assets in excess of $100 billion each. They included:

- Citicorp Travelers
- Bank America and Nationsbank
- Bank One and First Chicago
- Norwest and Wells Fargo
- UBS-Swiss Bank Corporation

By 2000, the M&A boom was over – M&As in most countries peaked in 1999 or 2000. In 2001 the total number of US M&A deals (across all sectors) had dropped to 8545, and fell again in 2002 by 13.6% to 7387. In Europe the rate of decline was about the same – 13.2% between 2001 and 2002. Since most of the activity had been in the financial sector, the decline in bank mergers was dramatic. Nonetheless, it is worth investigating the causes and consequences of mergers and acquisitions in banking, since future changes in technology, regulation and other factors are bound to prompt a new round.

## 9.5.2. Reasons for Consolidation in the Financial Sector

The reasons for mergers and acquisitions fall into three broad categories. The first is shareholder wealth maximisation goals. If mergers lead to greater scale/scope economies and improved cost/profit X-efficiencies, the sector as a whole should become more efficient and create value, all of which benefits shareholders. However, consolidation invariably raises the degree of concentration, which could increase market power, leading to higher prices. While shareholders will still gain, consumers could be worse off. The second category is managerial self-interest: managers might see mergers as a way of enhancing or defending their personal power and status.

In the third category are a number of miscellaneous factors that create an environment favourable to M&As. They include changes in the structure of the banking sector, such as increased competition from non-bank competitors – as indicated by the decline in the banks' share of non-financial short-term corporate debt, from about 58% in 1985 to around 48% a decade later (Bliss and Rosen, 2001). However, as was noted in Chapter 1, banks have expanded into new areas (e.g. bancassurance) and increased off-balance sheet activities. Changes in regulation may also be a factor. In the USA, changes to the Bank Holding Company Act in 1970, together with liberalisation of state laws on the treatment of BHCs, increased merger activity. More recently, allowing commercial banks to have section 20 subsidiaries, relaxing the laws on interstate branching, and the repeal of Glass Steagall, so that financial holding companies can have banking, securities and insurance subsidiaries, encouraged greater consolidation and nation-wide banking. In Europe, the Banking and Investment Services Directives, the introduction of the euro, and the Lamfalussy report should have encouraged greater integration of EU markets.[54] Another factor is technological change, which (as was seen in an earlier section) has affected cost and profit X-efficiency, both by encouraging more revenue earning financial innovations (e.g. the derivatives markets) and cutting costs, such as the delivery of retail banking services. It is estimated that IT accounts for 15–20% of total bank costs, and is growing. Mergers can help control these costs and improve IT systems.

## 9.5.3. Empirical Studies on Mergers and Acquisitions in the Banking Sector

The literature on bank mergers and acquisitions is vast, much of it based on US data. Researchers have asked different sets of questions. These include the following.

- **Announcement Effects**: Using event study methodology, researchers have asked: how does the announcement of M&As affect the share price performance of the bidding and target firms, that is, do bank shareholders gain or lose?
- **Performance**: What are the performance characteristics of the banks before and/or after the merger? The most common performance measures include cost ratios, cost-X-efficiency, scale/scope economies and profits.
- **Managerial Motives**: Do bank M&As maximise wealth by creating value and benefiting shareholders or are they undertaken by managers to maximise their own utility? The most common reason given for why managers might pursue managerial utility is because compensation has been shown to rise with the size of a firm.
- **Market Power/Competition**: How will M&As affect competition in the financial sector? Greater consolidation can increase market power of the remaining banks, causing them to raise prices and/or reduce services.
- **Systemic Risk**: Will M&As encourage more diversified, and therefore bigger, less risky banks or could bank managers assume more risks because a merger has made them "too big to fail"?

Some studies test for the effects of M&As indirectly. They examine whether economies of scale or scope are achieved (and if so, at what asset level), or how concentration affects

---

[54] See Chapter 5 for more detail on the changes in US and EU regulation.

prices and profitability, and from these results draw inferences on the effects of M&As. Since these topics were covered in earlier sections, they are not revisited here. The focus is on dynamic studies which consider the behaviour of financial institutions before and/or after the merger or acquisition. Space constraints prevent a comprehensive survey. In what follows, a selection of studies that address the above questions have been chosen, with some attempt to balance the US literature with studies based on European data.[55]

## 9.5.4. Announcements and Event Study Analysis

This group of studies looks at the change in the stock market value for the acquiring and target firms before and after the merger announcement. Event study analysis is used to test whether the merger announcement gives rise to significant cumulative abnormal returns (CAR) over some time interval. The typical estimating equation is:

$$R_{it} = \alpha_j + \beta_j R_{BIt} + \varepsilon_{jt} \tag{9.23}$$

where

$R_{it}$ : return on share $i$ at time $t$

$R_{BIt}$ : the return on a country's stock market bank index $I$ at time $t$

Estimates of $\alpha$ and $\beta$ are obtained using daily returns over a period of time before (usually a year) the event. Then, the expected returns are computed from:

$$E(R_{it}) = \alpha'_j + \beta'_j R_{BIt} \tag{9.24}$$

where

$\alpha'_j, \beta'_j$ : **estimated** coefficients obtained from a regression of equation (9.23)

$E(R_{it})$ : expected returns

Abnormal returns are defined as:

$$AR_{jt} = R_{jt} - (E)R_{jt} \tag{9.25}$$

where

$AR_{jt}$ : abnormal stock returns calculated for one or more event windows. For example, event window $T = [-1, +1]$ is for 3 days: 1 day before the event[56] (in this case the announcement of the merger or acquisition), the event day itself (0), and 1 day after the announcement. $T = [-20, +20]$ is 41 days: 20 days before the event, the event day itself, and 20 days after the event. Studies vary in the number of event windows they use.

---

[55] Readers are referred to a paper by Berger *et al.* (1999), who provide an excellent survey of key studies on consolidation. It appears in a special issue of the *Journal of Banking and Finance* (see references), which is devoted to mergers and acquisitions.

[56] It has been observed that the share prices of the two firms often start to react to rumours of a merger several days before the formal announcement and for this reason, more recent studies compute the cumulative abnormal returns for the seller and the buyer from several days (e.g. 10) before the public announcement is made.

Cumulative abnormal returns (CAR) for the interval $[-t_1, t_2]$ is the sum of the mean of the abnormal returns, and defined as:

$$CAR[t_1, t_2] = \sum_{[t_1, t_2]} (1/n) \times \sum_{j=1}^{n} AR_{jt} \qquad (9.26)$$

where

$n$ : number of shares included in the analysis

The dependent variable, abnormal returns, is usually weighted either by total assets of each firm or by stock market value prior to the announcement. Separate estimates are obtained for the acquirer and acquired firms.

The vast majority of work in this area is based on US data. Rhoades (1994) conducted a survey of 21 US studies that used event study methodology and published results for the period 1980–93. Seven found the merger announcement had a significantly negative influence on the shareholder returns for the bidding firm, another seven found no effect, three report a positive finding, and four find mixed effects. By contrast, eight of the nine studies that look at targets report positive shareholder returns, and one finds no abnormal returns. Four papers measure the net wealth effects: one finds a positive effect, another finds a negative, and two studies reported net gains for some merger announcements. Recently, some studies have used European data. Below, the key findings from relatively recent work using US and European data are reported.[57]

Cybo-Ottone and Murgia (2000; cited as COM below) was one of the first major European studies. Over the period 1988 to 1997, COM include European M&As from 14 countries,[58] involving 54 buyers and 72 target financial firms. The sample includes banks, securities and insurance firms, but at least one party to the merger must be a bank. For the acquiring banks, when a general market index is used as the benchmark, they find significant and positive abnormal returns in the shorter event periods (e.g. 1 or 2 days on either side of the announcement) of 0.99% and 1.4%. Finding a significantly positive return for the bidding bank contrasts with virtually all US studies, which find a significantly negative effect. Table 9.7 summarises the sample details of the studies cited here. Cornett and Tehranian (1992), Houston and Ryngaert (1994), Zhang (1995), Pilloff, (1996), Siems (1996) and Bliss and Rosen (2001) all report an immediate drop in the share price of the acquiring firm in the region of 1.96% to 3.8%. As Table 9.7 shows, the average size of US banks (measured by total assets) is smaller. Of the US studies, Siems (1996), looking at 19 mega bank mergers, had the highest mean size of $61 billion for the bidder, compared to $136.3 billion in COM. Bliss and Rosen (2001) also looked at mega mergers, and found the net percentage share price change in a 3-day window was, on average, −2.4%.[59]

---

[57] Studies based on M&As in other regions are virtually non-existent, though this will change because in Japan and some Asian countries, M&As have increased in recent years.

[58] Austria, Belgium, Denmark, Finland, France, Germany, Italy, the Netherlands, Norway, Portugal, Spain, Sweden, Switzerland and the UK.

[59] A mega merger is defined as one where the target bank is at least 10% the size of the bidder. Bliss and Rosen's sample consisted of the largest US banks by asset size: a bank was in the sample if it was in the top 30 in any of the

Table 9.7  Information on Samples from Different Event Studies

| | Countries | Years | Total Bank Mergers | Bidder Size in Assets* | Target Size in Assets* |
|---|---|---|---|---|---|
| Cornett and Tehranian (1992) | USA | 1982–87 | 30 | $17.7B $17 698M | $6.4B $6399M |
| Houston and Ryngaert (1994) | USA | 1985–91 | 153 | $100M (minimum) | $100M (minimum) |
| Zhang (1995) | USA | 1980–90 | 107 | $13.9B | $2.4B |
| Pilloff (1996) | USA | 1982–91 | 48 | $13B | $3.7B |
| Siems (1996) | USA | 1995 | 19 "mega" mergers | $60.6B | $18.7B |
| Bliss and Rosen (2001) | USA | 1986–95 | 32 | $11.9B** | |
| Cybo-Ottone and Murgia (2000) | 13 EU states plus Switzerland | 1988–97 | 126 | $105.6B | $23.67B |
| DeLong (2003) | US and non-US | 1988–99 | 397 US, 18 non-US | na*** | na*** |
| Beitel et al. (2003) | EU states plus Switzerland, Norway | 1985–2000 | 98 | $181.8B | $37B |

* Average size over the period, in $M (millions) or $B (billions).
** Average assets of sample, in billions (B) – no distinction between bidder and target.
*** DeLong's data are available on request. He notes the non-US acquirers are twice the size of their US counterparts; non-US targets 2.5 times larger.

For the target banks, the results were consistent with findings in most US studies. A positive, significant abnormal return was found for all the event windows (e.g. ranging from 1 or 2 to 20 days on either side of the announcement). The COM return over 5 days is 13%, which is similar to that of Houston and Ryngaert (1994). Likewise, Siems (1996) reported a 13% return in a window of plus or minus a day, which is similar to that of COM at 12.03%. However, other US studies report lower returns. For example, Cornett and Tehranian (1992) report an average CAR for the target of about 8%.

Along with more in-depth analysis of the CAR results, the authors also test for the influence of other factors on M&As using standard regression, with CAR (over 11 days) as the dependent variable. The explanatory variables included size, and dummies for different types of deals, countries and time. The main findings from their investigations may be summarised as follows:

---

years included in the study, from 1986 to 1995. They only report a net percentage change in share prices, not the individual changes for bidding and target banks.

- Dummies for time and country suggest they do not play any role.
- There is evidence of significant excess returns in domestic mergers but not for cross-border deals. Based on this result, COM suggest deals with a large geographical overlap are more likely to improve productive efficiency. The results for cross-border mergers are consistent with Berger and Humphrey (1992) and Rhoades (1993). Mergers with foreign banks do less well.
- They find the combined value increased for M&As among insurance firms and banks. COM suggest this finding is due to scope economies or revenue efficiencies from cross selling – though there is no explicit test of this explanation.
- There is no evidence to support gains from M&As between commercial banks and securities firms. This could be due to a clash of cultures between commercial and investment banks.

DeLong (2003) compared 41 non-US mergers and 397 US mergers between 1988 and 1999. Some findings are similar to Cybo-Ottone and Murgia. Non-US bidders gain, but their US counterparts lose, on average, 2.1% – the difference is significant at the 99% level of confidence. Targets in both groups earn significant, positive abnormal returns but the non-US group earn about 8.6%, less than the US bank group, where the CAR is 15.39%, a difference of 6.8%. DeLong introduces control variables to try and explain these differences. Also, non-US mergers are subdivided into two groups: 18 mergers from "market based" economies, and 23 that are "bank based".[60] This split produces returns that are roughly the same for both the US and non-US banks in market based economies, for bidders and targets. However, if the CAR of the US bank group is compared with the non-US group, the differences remain. DeLong (2003) cautions against concluding that the effects of M&As on shareholders are the same for all banks in market based economies. Some of his control variables suggest differences in structure influence the shareholder wealth effects of a merger. For example, strict anti-trust laws in the USA limit the size of the targets, but in other countries the limits are more relaxed. This could mean the overall gain for shareholders outside the USA is greater. In bank based economies shareholders of bidding and target banks were found to gain more.

Beitel, Schiereck, and Wahrenburg's (2003) sample consists of 98 M&As between large financial institutions[61] in the EU states plus Switzerland and Norway. They find the CAR of both bidders and targets in general rise. The CAR [−20, −2] for targets was 3.68% and 0.36% for bidders. For the event window [−1, +1] it was 12.4% and 0.01% for targets and bidders, respectively. The combined CAR of target and bidder is significantly positive for the majority of the 98 transactions. The net welfare gain of the 98 transactions is estimated to be $6.5 billion on the announcement day. These results are similar to those of Cybo-Ottone and Murgia and DeLong. Using each financial institution's CAR as the dependent variable,

---

[60] DeLong (2003) used the definitions of market and bank based economies developed by Demirguc-Kunt and Levine (1999). The USA and UK are in the market based category because they have well-developed stock markets and securities markets, which means firms can raise finance from several sources, not just banks. Countries such as Germany and Switzerland are more bank based, with large universal banks that can offer customers both on- and off-balance sheet banking services.

[61] Their study included all large financial service providers, for example, insurance and securities firms, and banks.

Beitel *et al.* employ regression analysis to identify which variables explain the success of the bidders, but none is found to be significant. However, significant variables are found by using the targets' CAR of successful and unsuccessful bidders. The results show that successful bidders choose targets which are smaller in size, have relatively high growth rates, and relatively low cost to income (or cost to asset) ratios.

To summarise, most studies employing US data find the net effect of a M&A announcement to be negative for the share price of the bidder, but positive for the shareholders at the target bank.[62] In many cases, there is a wealth transfer from the acquiring bank to the acquired because the stock price of the bidding firm falls and that of the target firm rises. Cyber-Ottone and Murgia (2000), using data from 14 European states, find both groups of shareholders gain, as do Beitel *et al.* (2003). However, the positive CAR is substantially higher for the target than for the bidder – shareholders of the target bank do best. DeLong (2003) found that most differences in CAR disappear once a sample is divided into banks that operate in a market based economy and those from bank based economies. A word of caution is needed on the tendency of many of these studies to draw inferences on the reason for a positive or negative CAR. The abnormal returns reflect market reaction to the announcement of a merger. The reasons for the investor reaction are unknown, unless explicit tests are done. For example, in the absence of econometric evidence, it is incorrect to assert that the presence of positive abnormal returns for domestic bank mergers and their absence among cross-border mergers suggests the former are more likely to improve productive efficiency. In the absence of efficiency tests, little more can be said other than the CAR are found to be positive or negative. There are plausible reasons (all of which require explicit testing) why the prey's shares should outperform the predator at the time of the merger around the event: the possibility of a higher second bid for the target and the fear of "winners' curse" for the bidder. The shares of European predators could outperform US bidders because regulatory changes are causing greater integration in US retail banking and subjecting it to more competitive pressures, leaving the US banks with less scope for widening spreads than in many European countries.

## 9.5.5. Efficiency

Mergers and acquisitions may increase efficiency by:

- Improving economies of scale and scope, which in turn adds to shareholder valued-added.
- X-efficiency may be increased through improvements in organisation and management if an efficient bank merges with and improves an inefficient bank.
- If the merger creates a more diversified bank, then there is an opportunity to raise expected returns for the same amount of risk.

### Effects of M&As on cost X-efficiency

Numerous studies of US M&As which took place in the 1980s find little evidence of change in terms of bank cost X-efficiency, or economies of scale/scope. For example, Berger

---

[62] This is a common finding when tests of the effect of a merger announcement on CAR are done for other sectors of the economy, not just banking.

and Humphrey (1992), in a study of 60 large US commercial bank "mega" mergers in the 1980s, found no evidence of an increase in cost efficiency. Even though there might have been gains from combining back operations, sharing technology, etc., these were offset by problems such as "culture" differences or the inability of management to run larger banks. Likewise, Berger *et al.* (1999) surveyed a large number of studies and report little evidence in the way of scale, scope or cost X-efficiencies.

Wheelock and Wilson (2000) include all US commercial banks with assets of at least $50 million,[63] using quarterly data from 1984(3) to 1993(4). They look at both bank failures and mergers. The part of the paper relevant to this section is the variables which influence the probability of acquisition. A stochastic frontier model was used to test for cost inefficiency. Input and output technical efficiency were measured using DEA. They find that the likelihood of a bank being acquired declines with cost inefficiency, i.e. the more cost inefficient a bank, the less likely it will be acquired, which is consistent with other studies that have found little in the way of gains in cost efficiency as a result of bank acquisitions. Wheelock and Wilson also found the probability of acquisition declines the higher the return on assets, and the higher a bank's capitalisation (measured by equity to assets).[64]

Resti (1998) uses data envelope analysis (therefore non-parametric) to study the impact of 67 Italian mergers (1986–95) on cost efficiency. She measures the efficiency of the bidder and target banks in each of the three years before and after the deal. Banks taking part in a merger had their cost X-efficiency measured against a benchmark. Resti found:

- Bidders were significantly less cost X-efficient than their targets, which suggests achieving greater market discipline does not appear to be a motive.
- On average, merged banks increased their cost X-efficiency in the post-merger years, though efficiency scores tended to decline in the third year after the merger.
- Mergers of large banks did not increase efficiency. Resti suggests this may be due to Italy's strict labour laws on dismissing employees, making it difficult to achieve cost savings.
- There was a marked increase in cost X-efficiency for mergers between geographically adjacent banks.
- No significant change in efficiency was observed if the banks were separated. So there is no support for the idea that the well-known inefficiencies of banks in the south could be improved by mergers with more efficient banks located elsewhere.

Haynes and Thompson (1997) examine mergers between UK building societies in the period 1981–93, when the number of mutuals fell from 200 to 80. All but one was due to intra-sector mergers. Data constraints left a final sample of 95 societies, of which there were 79 mergers.[65] Using an augmented production function, they report significant productivity gains from the mergers, rising from 3% a year after a merger to 5.5% five years later. They argue their findings are consistent with acquirers being more efficient than targets, so the

---

[63] This gives them a bank sample of roughly 4000 banks, depending on the year.

[64] Wheelock and Wilson also found acquisition is more likely in states where branching is permitted.

[65] Of the 79 mergers, 47 took place prior to major reforms that took effect in January 1987 (see Chapter 5) and 31 in the post-reform period.

mergers result in increased efficiency for the merged building societies. However, no explicit econometric test is conducted to verify this claim.

A few studies look at the effects of M&As on profit X-efficiency, i.e. whether the M&A moves the firm closer or further from the optimal profit point. Akhavein *et al.* (1997) and Berger (1998), using data on US M&As from the 1980s and 1990s, found that M&As improved profit efficiency, mainly because of the effects of diversification: these firms could increase their assets (loans) because of diversification.

Calomiris (1998) suggests mergers may be due to inefficiency or may stimulate inefficient banks to become more efficient so they are not taken over. This might reconcile the somewhat negative findings by the authors (above) and the relatively high levels of bank profitability in the 1990s.

## 9.5.6. Performance

Rhoades (1994) surveyed 19 US based studies on operating performance that were published between 1980 and 1993. They used accounting data to look at changes in costs, profits or both, before and after the merger. All but two use a control group of banks not involved in mergers and compare them against the banks involved in mergers. Some employed univariate *t*-tests to compare the performance of ratios before and after, while others used multiple regression analysis. The majority used expense ratios[66] to measure performance, but three estimate translog production functions to test for X-efficiency, scale efficiency and the position of the bank in relation to an efficiency frontier. Virtually all of the studies show no gain in efficiency or profitability. Of the few that do, the results are mixed. For example, one study by Cornett and Tehranian (1992) found higher ROE post-merger but no change in ROA or cost efficiency. Another finds higher ROA but no change in the cost ratios or efficiency. Seven studies also looked at horizontal (or in the market) mergers where the two banks have overlapping branches. Again, there is no change in efficiency as a result of the merger, even though one would expect greater efficiency from closing branches and integrating back office operations and IT. On average, merging banks have not achieved considerable improvements in performance.

Outside the USA, Vander Vennet (1996) examined domestic and cross-border M&As of credit institutions[67] in Europe over the period 1987–93. The sample consists of 422 domestic and 70 cross-border M&As. He conducts a univariate comparison of performance pre- (3 years before) and post-merger (3 years after). The variables included performance (measured by pre- and post-tax ROE and ROA), the ratio of labour costs to total costs, an operating expense ratio and cost efficiency. A translog total cost function is used to estimate cost efficiency. The findings for the four subsamples he looks at are described briefly below.

- *Domestic majority acquisitions*: Pre-merger, the acquirers are profitable, efficient, large banks. The performance of the acquired banks is declining, with falling operational efficiency. Post-merger, the performance of the target banks worsens still further in terms

---

[66] The most common ratios were total expenses/assets, non-interest expenses/assets, revenues/employees and total expenses/total revenues.
[67] Credit institutions is the term used by the EU for deposit-taking firms.

of ROE, ROA. The efficiency frontier slightly worsens, and the cost ratios are rising. Three years post merger, the difference in the performance of the two sets of banks widens. Vander Vennet attributes these results to the fact that the two institutions never become fully integrated.

- *Domestic full acquisitions*: These involve large banks taking over smaller ones. Both are profitable pre-merger, and there is a small improvement in ROE post-merger but it is not significant. Nor is there any significant change in the cost ratios or cost efficiency post-merger.
- *Domestic mergers of equal partners*: Pre-merger, ROE and ROA fall from positive to negative, the cost ratios are worsening, and they move further away from frontier cost efficiency frontier. Post-merger there is a significant improvement in profitability, the cost ratios fall below sector averages. Operational efficiency moves from 67% (pre-merger) to 83%.
- *Cross-border acquisitions*: Pre-acquisition, the acquiring banks have above average profitability but on the cost side, there are no significant differences from the sector's peers. The acquired banks have below average ROE and significantly high cost ratios. The acquirers, on average, operate at 80% in terms of the cost efficiency frontier, compared to 63% for the acquired. In the three-year period after acquisition, the cost ratios and cost X-efficiency for the acquired firms improve to sector averages.

To conclude, Vander Vennet finds there is virtually no improvement in efficiency for domestic acquisitions, whether partial or complete. The post-merger performance of domestic banks is notably better in terms of both profits and operational efficiency. Cross-border, the smaller acquired bank became more efficient, but profitability did not improve, at least in the short run.

Focarelli *et al.* (2002) include all the M&As among Italian banks between 1985 and 1996, but split the sample to analyse mergers (full integration of bidder and target banks) and acquisitions (one bank buys a controlling stake in another but the assets of the two banks are not integrated to form one new entity). There were 135 mergers and 66 acquisitions, reducing the number of Italian commercial banks from 359 in 1984 to 253 in 1996.[68] They consolidate the balance sheet data of all banks involved in a merger or acquisition.[69]

*Ex ante* analysis of the data shows the acquired banks have statistically significantly more lending of lower quality. The authors infer that the primary reason for acquiring a bank is to improve its credit management. The statistical tests on merger group suggest the principal reason for a merger is to expand the customer base. By merging with another bank(s), the bidder will be able to sell its products through the target's outlets.

In an *ex post* analysis, a number of financial ratios are employed as the dependent variables in separate regressions to assess what happens to them in the year during the merger and three years later. For the *merger group*, using measures for size, profitability, productivity, revenues and diversification, the results of regressions show that *ex post* revenues are significantly higher, as a result of an increase in fee income during the year of the merger

---

[68] These figures include new entries and failures, which they adjust for.

[69] The authors argue that event study analysis is not possible because very few Italian banks are listed in this period.

and in the longer run. However, labour and operating costs rise in the first year and remain permanently higher because Italian labour laws make it very difficult to dismiss employees,[70] and salaries at the target firm, which tend to be lower, are raised at the time of the merger. The authors conclude that mergers are unlikely to be motivated by the prospect of cutting costs. Instead, they take place to broaden the consumer base of the bidding bank, which in turn raises revenues. Profitability measured by ROA before taxes falls in the year of the merger and over the next four years. In the longer run, ROA does not change: the higher costs are just offset by the higher revenues from selling more services. There is no change in ROE during the first four years, but it rises in the long run because non-interest income growth more than offsets the growth in operating costs.

For the *acquisition group*, Focarelli *et al.* find no permanent change in the cost structure of the acquired banks – the above average cost of labour before the acquisition does not fall. Nor does its size change. There is a significant decrease in small business loans in the long run. In the acquisition years the bad loan ratio rises considerably but in the long run (three years later) there is a permanent increase in the quality of the loan portfolio, due to the imposition of the acquiring bank's improved credit risk management system. The initial rise in bad loans suggests the acquiring bank is imposing stricter standards on loan classification. There is an increase in both profitability (ROA) and ROE in the long run. ROA drops in the year of the transaction, probably because of higher loan losses. Thus, acquisitions appear to be motivated by an opportunity to improve profitability by improving the quality of the acquired bank's loan portfolio.

Overall, this study of Italian M&As among commercial banks suggests it is important to distinguish between mergers and acquisitions because the motivation and outcome were quite different. Though the data come from Italian banks, the authors suggest that in any European country with inflexible labour markets, merger and acquisition strategies based on cutting costs or achieving scale economies will not succeed.

### 9.5.7. Market Power/Competition

Kahn *et al.* (2000) investigate the market power hypothesis by examining the effect of bank mergers on two types of consumer lending, personal loans and car loans. The US data are weekly personal loan rates and loan rates for new cars, from 1987 to 1997, quoted by the large commercial banks in 10 major cities. They found that mergers led to higher personal loan rates, suggesting an increase in market power in this market. However, in the car loans market, rates fell. The authors suggest the differences in results are due to the existence of economies of scale in the origination of car loans (mainly because most of the loans are securitised) – the merging banks that achieved economies of scale passed them on to borrowers in the form of lower loan rates.

Prager and Hannan (1998) looked at M&As which exceed US Department of Justice guidelines on market concentration, and found that increases in market concentration reduced the deposit rates paid by the banks involved in the M&A. Simons and Stavins (1998) used a larger sample, some of which did not violate Justice guidelines and found that some M&As lowered deposits rates while others raised them.

---

[70] Recall Resti (1998) makes a similar point about rigidities in the labour market.

Based on Italian data, Sapienza (1998) found loan rates declined when there was a substantial degree of market overlap and the market share of the acquired bank was small. However, if market share was large, loan rates increased.

Evenett (2003) takes a different approach. Using the database from the OECD (2001) study of consolidation of the financial sector in 13 industrialised countries, he tests for the effect of different types of M&As/strategic alliances on interest rate spreads. The spread is defined as the difference between the loan rate to prime rate customers less the deposit rate paid by commercial banks on demand, time or savings deposits.[71] The OECD study distinguishes between domestic cross-border strategic alliances and M&As. In the estimating equation, the interest rate spread for each country is the dependent variable. Independent variables include the different types of strategic alliances and M&As, a five-firm concentration ratio adjusted for the number of M&As in each country, the number of banks in the country, and control variables for regulatory changes and macroeconomic effects.[72]

Evenett finds a positive and significant coefficient on the concentration ratio: as concentration rises, so does the interest rate spread, which would suggest that any effects on efficiency brought about by the increase in consolidation have been more than offset by the effects of greater market power. The number of firms has a negative sign (consistent with the Cournot model), but is insignificant. Evenett also finds that domestic M&As raise spreads (coefficient significant and positive) but cross-border M&As do not (coefficient negative but insignificant). The coefficient on domestic alliances is also positive and significant, but for cross-border alliances, it is negatively signed and insignificant. Thus, increases in domestic consolidation and alliances raise spreads but their cross-border counterparts do not.

When the sample is split up and estimated by countries, the only notable change in results comes when Evenett divides the sample into the eight EU countries and the five-nation non-EU group. For the non-EU group, the coefficient on cross-border alliances is the only one that is significant – they reduce the interest rate spread. Cross-border M&As also have a negative coefficient, but it is insignificant. National alliances and M&As are positively signed but insignificant. By contrast, the EU group regression shows cross-border alliances raise spreads but cross-border M&As reduce them – the signs on the coefficients are respectively, positive and negative, and both are significant. Also, the EU regression has a significantly positive five-firm concentration ratio, and significantly negative coefficient on the number of banks.

Evenett's results are interesting but should be treated with caution. Not only is the spread variable likely to be too aggregated and suffer from other problems (see footnote 71), but the controls for regulatory changes are somewhat arbitrary. The control variables do not include the ERM in the lead up to the adoption of the euro by most EU countries. Evenett's results suggest that while efficiency gains appear to have outweighed market power

---

[71] Evenett (2003, p. 16) obtains these rates from the World Bank's *World Development Indicators*. The definition alone is problematic. The "official" deposit and loan rates tend to be highly aggregated, e.g. an average across the main commercial banks. Furthermore, just one rate is provided for demand/time/savings deposits. Finally, the way rates are collected, "averaged", and reported varies among the national authorities.

[72] The macro control variables were real GDP and stock market capitalisation as a percentage of GDP in each country. Regulatory control variables were country-specific – see Appendix table 2 of Evenett (2003).

effects in non-EU countries, cross-border alliances may have been used to frustrate any efficiency gains among the EU states. Moreover, his findings indicate that some takeovers are motivated by the potential for increased efficiency. For example, there is a gain in cost X-efficiency if an efficient bank merges with an inefficient bank.

Akhavein *et al.* (1997) looked at the joint issue of market power and efficiency gains. Based on US data, their study found M&As resulted in very small price changes and very large gains in efficiency, which is consistent with Evenett.

## 9.5.8. Managerial Motivation

Principal agent issues mean managerial behaviour can affect and be affected by the probability of takeover as predator or prey. Managers may want to acquire another bank because compensation is linked to firm size. Or concerned about their future, managers may attempt to diversify risk through a merger to reduce insolvency risk below what is optimal for shareholders. Alternatively, they could engage in takeovers to expand their bank and diminish the chance of receiving a takeover bid.

Milbourn *et al.* (1999) develop a theoretical model in which agency conflicts between managers and shareholders give rise to consolidation. It is cited here to provide the reader with an insight into the complexities of managerial behaviour. Managers want to maximise their own compensation rather than shareholders' wealth. It is assumed that banks' corporate control is weak so managers can pursue consolidation activities exclusively for their own benefit. Another assumption is that more size and diversified activities result in better compensation for the bank's CEO. However, these banks are more difficult to manage. Thus, overconfident managers will want to expand size and/or scope to enhance their compensation, even if the probability of success is lower. Herd instinct amongst bank managers can cause a rush in merger activity.

Bliss and Rosen (2001) conducted one of the most comprehensive econometric studies of the relationship between compensation for the CEO and bank mergers. They use US data for the period 1986–95, with data on bank size, mergers, managerial compensation and stock market performance. The sample consists of 32 banks and 298 bank years. Like many studies they find negative abnormal returns on shares caused by the decline in the stock price on the day of the announcement, but this is more than offset by subsequent increases in salary, so the net effect on compensation is positive.

Compensation is found to rise with size,[73] and mergers may be seen as a quick way of increasing bank size. The authors also find a negative relationship between share ownership and the number of banks acquired: CEOs engaging in numerous mergers have a smaller percentage of their compensation based on shares than CEOs at other banks. CEOs owning a small percentage of shares will be less concerned about the merger's negative effect on the stock price of the acquiring bank. Also, CEOs of banks that merge more frequently are rewarded less per dollar of acquired assets. The authors conclude by stressing that the way CEO compensation is structured is but one contributing factor, and other variables also explain the relatively high number of mergers and acquisitions in the period.

---

[73] Bank size is measured by assets.

Ely and Song (2000) look at 60 US depository institutions with at least $5 billion in assets, operating from 1989 to 1995. These firms completed 449 acquisitions between 1990 and 1995. They test two hypotheses. According to the wealth maximisation hypothesis, in a period of regulatory reform, the most efficient banks will acquire the least efficient, which will create value and benefit the shareholders. By the incentive conflict hypothesis, managers acquire large numbers of banks to pursue their own interests.

A linear equation is estimated, where the dependent variable is the number of acquisitions (or the total assets gained through acquisitions) between 1990 and 1995. The independent variables are size (log of total assets), OWN (the percentage of shares held by insiders at year-end 1989) and the market to book value of equity (M/B), year-end 1989. If takeovers are shareholder wealth-maximising, the coefficient on M/B should be positive, if managers are pursuing their own interest, (M/B) will be negatively signed.

When the equation was estimated with acquired assets as the dependent variable, the wealth maximisation hypothesis is supported for the group of firms with or without an outside blockholder:[74] acquisition activity is found to be positively (and significantly) related to the ratio of market to book value and to insider ownership. The positive coefficient on the insider ownership variable means the most active bidders are those which have minimised costs arising from agency conflicts. The group accounts for 67% of the acquired assets in the sample. However, if the other dependent variable (number of acquisitions) is used, the results are inconsistent with the wealth maximisation hypothesis and weakly support the incentive conflict hypothesis.[75] Overall, shareholder value is more likely to be maximised if a few large acquisitions are made rather than a large number of small acquisitions. These findings are consistent with Bliss and Rosen (2001).

Hadlock et al. (1999) conduct an empirical test of the relationship between management incentives, performance and corporate governance in the target bank, and the likelihood of being acquired, using a sample of 84 acquired US commercial banks between 1982 and 1992, and another 84 that were not involved in a merger. They test a number of competing hypotheses.

- The "irrelevance hypothesis": consolidation activities are not affected by management variables.
- The "financial incentive hypothesis": managers with significant ownership of the bank make financial gains when their bank is acquired and therefore are more likely to be targets.
- The "entrenchment hypothesis": managers who own a significant amount of the bank do not like to lose control and will reject attempts to be taken over, making continued independence likelier.
- The "discipline hypothesis": poorly managed banks are more likely to be acquired. Better managed banks are those where managers have a significant ownership stake or there are

---

[74] A firm is deemed to have an outside blockholder if at least one outside investor owns at least 5% of the total shares.

[75] When the authors changed the dependent variables to year-end 1994, and the number of acquisitions is used as the dependent variable, the wealth maximisation hypothesis is supported, and accounts for about 70% of the 1995 acquisitions. No significant relationships are found if the dependent variable is acquired assets.

a large number of outsiders on the board. Managers' incentives are more in line with the shareholders' incentives and/or the presence of outsiders in the board should ensure that actions are taken in the interest of shareholders. For these reasons, such banks are less likely to be targets.

Hadlock *et al.* find that banks with high levels of management ownership are less likely to be acquired. Furthermore, poor performance does not increase the likelihood of being acquired. They conclude the results are consistent with the "entrenchment hypothesis".

## 9.5.9. Consolidation and Systemic Risk

The subject of systemic risk was covered in Chapters 4 and 5. Mergers and acquisitions can affect systemic risk in a variety of ways. First, mergers and acquisitions generally result in a more diversified firm, which should reduce the risk. However, there is some research showing that the gains from diversification are offset by banks taking more risks, in search of greater expected returns. M&As also increase the size of banks and if these larger firms fail, the systemic consequences are normally greater. Regulators could find themselves with larger banks that come under the financial safety net of the central bank. If managers know a merged bank will be large enough to qualify for "too big to fail" status, they are more likely to take on greater risks, especially if the bank's performance worsens – the "go for broke" syndrome. Thus, welfare costs could rise. The OECD (2001) report on consolidation among the G-10 nations found that the effects of M&As on banks' risk are mixed, and that post-consolidation, banks may be inclined to take on more risks because they choose to or because monitoring of their risk exposure is less effective. The econometric research in this area has produced mixed results.

Berger *et al.* (1999), based on US evidence, found that BHCs move eligible activities from non-bank subsidiaries into bank subsidiaries. Kwast and Passmore (1998) provide the motivation for such action: BHCs are maximising shareholder value by ensuring that every activity they engage in can benefit from the implied subsidy of a financial safety net.

Benston *et al.* (1995) use US data to examine two competing hypotheses. The first is that banks merge to become "too big to fail". This behaviour would be in the interest of shareholders because it ensures all deposits are effectively protected by the financial safety net. Thus, they would expect the data to show that banks are willing to pay more for banks that will increase the post-merger bank risk.[76] The second hypothesis posits that regulatory constraints mean increasing risk is not in the interest of shareholders. Instead, banks merge to diversify earnings and increase cash flow without increasing risk, so they are willing to pay higher prices for banks that will increase cash flow. The hypotheses are tested by looking at the relationship between the premium[77] paid for the target bank and proxies for target's and acquirer's risk, risk diversification opportunities, the value of a deposit insurance put option, and the cash flow of the merged entity. Their findings are consistent with the second hypothesis, which also suggests that managers act in the interests of their shareholders.

---

[76] The preferred targets would be riskier banks whose returns are highly correlated with the acquirer bank.

[77] Measured as the price minus the preconsolidation market value of the target bank.

In a paper based on Italian bank mergers between 1997 and 2001, Chionsini *et al.* (2003) look at the effect of diversification on credit risk among merging banks. Instead of using the standard risk, return approach, these authors use data on the probabilities of default and loss given default for 180 000 non-financial Italian firms to assess the change in the *credit* risk profile of these banks before and after the mergers took place. They find that mergers significantly reduced credit risk because of the diversification of unsystematic risk. This result is likely due to the higher proportion of small and medium-sized enterprises (SMEs) in Italy. In their sample of 180 000 commercial and industrial firms, 80% were SMEs (sales of less than €5 million), accounting for 26% of loans.[78] They argue SMEs are less likely to be affected by the economic cycle, and most of the default risk is firm or industry specific. The authors also studied the change in composition of the loan portfolios two years post-merger. They find no significant change in the banks' portfolio risk, and loans to more creditworthy borrowers had increased. However, two years after the merger the findings indicated a larger diversification of systematic risk.

A paper by Acharya *et al.* (2002) also employed Italian data from 105 commercial banks in the period 1993–99. Though they do not look at the effects of M&As on diversification of risk, their findings are worth citing in light of the Chionsini *et al.* study. Using returns as the dependent variable, they test the effects of loan diversification on banks' risk. For industrial and asset diversification,[79] they find diversification simultaneously increases loan risk and reduces returns, implying an overall decline in bank performance. The opposite is the case if the diversification is geographic. Based on these results, Acharya *et al.* conclude that diversification can reduce returns in some cases, either because of poor monitoring and/or because of problems of adverse selection when banks attempt to move into new areas of activity.

## 9.5.10. Mergers and Acquisitions: A Case Study Approach

Davis (2000) takes a case by case approach on bank mergers and acquisitions, studying 33 mergers around the world that took place in the late 1990s. The discussion that follows embraces Davis' key ideas but updates the information in the banks and provides some further analysis. The conclusions by Davis can be divided into several categories.

### *Strategic and financial targets*

In this group of 33 banks, all had strategic targets, but just two-thirds of the sample gave explicit financial targets for the post-merger period. Many of these targets, such as reduced cost/income or increased ROE, may be the result of factors other than the merger itself, which is one of the problems with a case approach. Nonetheless, it is interesting to review Davis' findings. Davis identified 15 that had been merged for long enough to comment on whether these targets have been met. Of the 15, six have achieved their financial targets.

---

[78] Firms with sales in excess of €50 million had 38% of total loans.

[79] Industrial diversification: expansion across different industrial sectors; asset diversification: expansion of loans across different asset classes.

**Banco Commercial Português (BCP)** – Portugal: merged with Banco Português do Atlântico (BPA) in 1996.

**Chase Manhattan:** in 1991, Chemical merged with Manufacturers Hanover; in 1996, Chase merged with Chemical bank. Since then, Chase merged with JP Morgan, to form JP Morgan Chase in September 2000.

**Den Danske Bank (DDB)** – Denmark: formed in 1990, a three-way merger of Den Danske Bank, Copenhagen Handelsbank and Provinsbanken. It also became a regional Scandinavian Bank in the late 1990s, taking over Ostgoda Enskilda Bank (Sweden), Fokus Bank (Norway) and stockbrokers in Norway, Finland and Sweden.

**Unibank** – Denmark: after DDB, Denmark's second largest bank. Again, it was the product of a three-way merger in 1990. In 1999, it acquired Tryg Baltica, the largest general insurance firm in Denmark.

**Lloyds TSB:** Now the fifth largest UK bank in terms of assets. Lloyds acquired the TSB group in December 1995, though full integration, to comply with the wishes of the regulatory authorities, did not take place until 1999. It also acquired Cheltenham and Gloucester (C&G), a former building society, but it has been kept as a separate subsidiary.

**Svenska Handelsbanken:** based in Sweden, this bank has retail operations in the other Nordic countries: Denmark, Finland and Norway. It took over a state owned mortgage bank, Stadshypotek, in February 1997.

For the other nine banks that failed to meet their financial targets, the reasons are explored in more detail:

**Bank Austria:** took over Creditanstalt in 1997 by purchasing the government's controlling share. Bank Austria had to agree not to change the structure of Creditanstalt for 5 years. As a result, there were two separate retail banking markets. The main reason for the agreement to keep Creditanstalt's structure intact was concern that branches would be closed, causing reduced employment. This is reminiscent of the points made by Resti (1998) and Focarelli *et al.* (2000) – that inflexibility in some labour markets in European states can hinder gains from a merger. A single corporate structure BAC, it operates in global and investment banking. In 2004, it is still known as "BA-CA"; its strategic goal is to become the leading bank in Central and Eastern Europe. Since 2000 it has been part of the German bank group HypoVereinsbank, which holds 22.5% of BA-CA's shares.

**HBV:** Hypovereinsbank, Germany's third largest bank, formed by the merger of two regional banks based in Munich: Bayerische Vereinsbank and Bayerische Hypotheken Bank, which was completed in October 1998. Dominant in mortgage markets in Europe and Germany, HBV was unable to meet its earnings targets because of the need to set aside DM 3.5 billion in provisions to cover losses from Hypo's real estate lending in what was East Germany. As a result, all of the former Hypo executives resigned in October 1999. Hypovereinsbank is now the second largest private bank in Germany, with extensive operations in Austria (see above), Central Europe (with BA-CA) and Greece.

**BBV:** Banco Bilbao Vizcaya, Spain's largest bank, formed in 1988 through the merger of two banks, roughly the same size. After the 1988 merger it invested in a new IT system which raised the cost to income ratio to between 60% and 70%, above the pre-merger level. It has since fallen to 56%. In 1999, it merged with the third largest bank, Argentaria, to become Banco Bilbao Vizcaya Argentaria (BBVA).

**Crédit Agricole Indosuez:** Crédit Agricole is the largest French bank, and until 2001 a mutually owned cooperative, operating through caisses regionales. It is the dominant retail bank. In July 1996 it took over Banque Indosuez, a wholesale and global bank, with special corporate banking strengths in the Middle East and Asia. Due to credit and market losses in Asia (1997) and Russia (1998) arising from Crédit Indosuez, the new group has been unable to achieve its one financial goal of 12% ROE.

In 2001 Crédit Agricole floated on the stock market, ending its tradition of mutual ownership. In 2003 it successfully bid to take over Crédit Lyonnais, and is now known as the Crédit Agricole group. A universal bank, it is a major force in French retail banking through roughly 8000 branches of the caisses regionales, and the former branches of Crédit Lyonnais. In April 2004 the shareholders of Crédit Lyonnais and Crédit Agricole approved the partial transfer of the investment banking arm of the former bank, Crédit Lyonnais Banque de Financement et d'Investissement (BFI) to Crédit Agricole Indosuez. The tender offer was made by Crédit Agricole S.A. for Crédit Lyonnais. It is also consistent with the policy of creating a subsidiary for the Credit Agricole Group's corporate banking activities. The new entity created by the partial merger trades under the brand name "Calyon" (also its legal name) – it is a corporate and investment banking subsidiary of Crédit Agricole. The transaction is part of Crédit Agricole's bid for Crédit Lyonnais.

**UBS AG:** in June 1998, two of the largest banks in Switzerland merged, Swiss Banking Corporation and Union Bank of Switzerland. UBS is Switzerland's largest bank, the largest fund manager in the world, and a key global investment bank. Due to the problems in global investment banking in 1998, the former UBS was left badly exposed due to poor risk management, as was a subsidiary, the Warburg Dillon Read investment bank. The former CEO of UBS, who had become the group's chairman, resigned in 1999 as a result of the losses incurred. Initially known as UBS Warburg, it is now UBS Investment Bank – this subsidiary is headquartered in London.

**First Union:** at year-end 1998, it was the sixth largest US bank in terms of assets. First Union has acquired over 70 banks in the Eastern USA, making it the largest retail bank in the region. The problem acquisition was Core States in April 1998 – it paid five times book value for the firm. It then embarked on a big cost cutting programme which undermined the client focused nature of Core States and resulted in a loss of its key staff and a significant (well above the average for a merger) departure of customers. This is an example of where gains from an efficiency drive can be offset by lost revenues. Another acquisition, The Money Store, produced several earnings warnings in 1999, and its share price was cut by two-thirds from its historical high. In 2001, First Union successfully bid for another US super-regional bank, Wachovia, and trades under the Wachovia name; it remains the sixth largest US bank, by assets.

**Bank One:** in 10/98, Bank One merged with a bank of similar size, First Chicago NDB, to form the fourth largest US bank – a "super-regional". The firm encountered problems with a core credit card business, which resulted in an earnings warning in 1999.

**ABN Amro:** two banks, ABN and Amro, of roughly the same size merged in 1991. It is a leading retail and investment bank in the Netherlands, but has operations in over 70 countries. It lost market share because it took four years to develop a new retail banking system, and the cost income ratio target reduction has not been met because of an unexpected drop in revenues.

## Falling stock prices

Most bank mergers have experienced a post-merger decline in the stock price, by more than 33% in some cases. Wells Fargo, First Union, Bank One, UBS and Swedbank have shown the most dramatic declines, for the reasons noted above. A weak share price can make a bank a target, as Wells Fargo found when it was taken over by Nor West. This is consistent with the findings of many academic studies, especially for US banks, that the stock price of the bidding bank falls. For bank mergers in other countries, see more recent data (e.g. Cybo-Ottone and Murgia, 2000; Beital et al., 2003; DeLong, 2003).

## Unforeseen events

A common post-merger problem, unforeseen events suggest the need for careful due diligence before a takeover, to avoid finding post-merger skeletons in the cupboard. The problems encountered by those banks which failed to meet their financial targets provides a good example.

## Politics

Politics can hamper mergers. For example, in 1998, the Canadian government refused to allow two mergers (Royal Bank/Bank of Montreal and TD Bank/Canadian Imperial Bank of Commerce) citing concern over excessive concentration. In Europe, unions, labour laws and general inflexibility can hamper the achievement of goals, especially when it comes to the closure of branches and staff reductions. In an econometric model using time series data from 1976 to 1996, McIntosh (2002) shows the big five Canadian banks, with multiple branches, have technology characterised by increasing returns to scale, though the source of the scale efficiency is not determined. McIntosh (2002) speculates that it could arise because the cost of acquiring new technology is spread over a multibranch network. In simulations of what would have happened had the banks been allowed to merge, McIntosh shows that post-merger, "prices"[80] fall. He concludes that even though the mergers would have increased concentration, the scale efficiency offsets the effects of any reduced competition, and the post-merger price of banking services falls, and total banking services rise. McIntosh's simulations show a social welfare gain, and the Canadian government should have allowed the mergers to take place. However, Baltazar and Santos (2003) use event study analysis, where the events are the announcement dates of the mergers and the date the government ruled the mergers would not be allowed. They *infer*[81] that market power, rather than efficiencies from scale/scope economies, X-efficiencies or

---

[80] McIntosh uses a price index of banking services, but it is unclear where it comes from.
[81] Like many of these studies, there is no explicit test to confirm that investors reacted the way they did in anticipation of greater market power (and higher profits through higher prices).

a net subsidy from a government safety net, was the principal benefit of the mergers, suggesting the regulators were correct to disallow the mergers.

The longer term (i.e. over 10 years) effects of mergers are more difficult to pinpoint but may be more favourable. Davis (2000) notes that the European banks that merged in 1990 suffered a loss of market share, took longer than expected to get the cost/income ratio down (BBV took seven years before the cost to income ratio returned to pre-merger level), and it can take many years to resolve culture clashes. So shareholder value may suffer for several years, but the key question is: what would happen in the absence of the merger? One can never answer this critical counterfactual question definitively. However, it seems likely that many banks that did merge might well have fallen victim to hostile takeovers otherwise, and some, left on their own, could have drifted into insolvency.

## 9.6. Conclusion

This chapter has explored key competitive issues as they relate to banking markets. Differences in banks prompt a number of questions, the answers to which are important to managers (especially those working in the area of bank strategy) and policy makers. The key questions are:

- How much, if anything, do financial firms stand to gain by expanding their output and/or product range?
- How widely do banks vary in the efficiency with which they use resources?
- How do banks' average costs vary with their size?
- Should banks specialise or produce multiple outputs?
- Is the banking sector dominated by a few large banks that charge higher/lower prices, and if either, why?
- Are bank mergers and acquisitions (M&As) beneficial for shareholders?
- Are bank M&As good or bad for customers?
- To what extent does the possibility of entry keep the banks from overcharging?

The empirical evidence on these issues is complex and rarely clear cut. Some questions are hotly disputed. Others elicit answers that vary according to the country or period studied, or the methodology employed. However, it is possible to summarise a number of points from the material reported in this chapter.

First, there is wide diversity in the degree of "X-efficiency" of banks, both within countries and between them. The Berger and Humphrey (1997) survey found that management could improve X-efficiency anywhere between 10% and 30%. It is worth stressing a major drawback with these measures: they are relative, so an entire banking system could be inefficient even though the cost X-efficiency estimates suggest otherwise.

The presence or otherwise of economies of scale is an important issue for bank managers for several reasons. If they are only present for small banks, as much of the literature using data from the 1980s seemed to suggest, then mergers and/or organic growth could make things worse. Data from the 1990s and more sophisticated econometric techniques have produced evidence of scale economies at much larger asset sizes, for both US and European banks. In other words, increasing their scale of operations will reduce average costs. If economies of scale are present, they can be used by incumbent firms as an entry barrier, which could encourage anti-competitive behaviour, possibly prompting intervention by the authorities.

Evidence of economies of scope is important because they indicate that it would be profitable, all else equal, to jointly produce different bank products and/or diversify into non-bank financial activities, depending on the nature of the scope economies found. US studies using 1980s data found little evidence of them, but as Table 9.2 illustrates, the results for France, Italy, Germany and Spain vary considerably. Research based on 1990s data finds more evidence of scope economies.

Pricing practices were found to deviate from textbook competition in varying respects. Early studies tended to find support for the structure–conduct–performance hypothesis, but Berger (1997) casts doubt on the results of these studies because of problems with the techniques used. The results from Berger's study, and others, suggest the relative efficiency hypothesis may have some merit. Such a mixed bag of evidence is not much help for policy makers because the regulatory implications are so different. Until the issue of correlation between market share and concentration is properly addressed, the results of these empirical studies should be treated with caution.

Though the issue of perfectly contestable markets received some empirical attention in the 1980s, recent work suggests researchers are backing away from testing for it, perhaps because of the flaw in using the Panzer–Rosse statistic for this purpose. Intuition suggests the banking market is unlikely to be perfectly contestable, and studies finding evidence of Cournot-type behaviour (i.e. the number of firms affect pricing) must reject it. Tests using data from the UK and Canada in a generalised pricing model found considerable deviation in retail deposit and loan rates from the competitive rate, and bargains and rip-offs co-exist in retail banking markets. Policies directed at reducing consumer inertia would encourage greater competition among banks.

Studies of mergers and acquisitions address a myriad different questions such as the effects on share prices, managerial compensation, efficiency, competition and systemic risks. Takeovers do not appear to serve the interests of the bidder's shareholders. Banks' customers do not appear to fare particularly well either, but they may be undertaken if managers stand to gain from them. Though there are reasons for arguing that M&As could increase systemic risk, the empirical evidence is mixed. The case study approach taken by Davis (2000) tends to confirm the econometric findings, though over the longer term, i.e. 10 years, the overall effect may be positive. Even though studies of bank mergers and acquisitions may raise more questions than they answer, two important points stand out. One is the fact that merger proposals have often been disallowed when the authorities saw a serious threat to the banks' customer interests. The other is that the fear of takeover will have constrained management and helped to deliver a higher stream of earnings than would have been expected had takeovers been prohibited. Takeovers that *did not* occur may have had more influence than those that did!

# CASE STUDIES

# 10

## 10.1. Introduction

This chapter consists of a collection of eight case studies that are designed to provide readers with working cases of many of the concepts and ideas presented in the book. Unlike a book, case studies do not compartmentalise themselves neatly into an organised set of terms, definitions and analysis. Each case brings out a number of themes and ideas which are drawn from different parts of the text, providing the reader with an integrated approach to key management issues in modern banking. For example, the case study "From Sakura to Sumitomo Mitsui Financial Group" covers areas as diverse as the universal banking (Chapter 1), Japanese bank structure and regulation (Chapter 5), banking crises (Chapter 8) and mergers and acquisitions (Chapter 9).

At the beginning of each case, the reader is directed to chapters which are the most relevant to the case. However, the nature of case work is that the reader is confronted with a wide range of ideas, problems and potential solutions. One of the purposes of the cases is to provide an alternative method of learning which complements the material in the book, and challenges the reader to apply and integrate a cross-section of ideas and concepts. Answering the questions at the end of each case will help readers to apply what they have learned to a series of modern banking issues, in the context of a particular case.[1] As was noted in the Acknowledgements, each case originated from New York University Salomon Center (at the Stern School of Business) Case Series in Finance and Economics. However, the cases have been edited, revised and updated by Shelagh Heffernan; several bear little resemblance to what appeared in the original cases. All the questions have been set by Shelagh Heffernan.

---

[1] It may be helpful to refer to the index and/or a banking/finance/economics dictionary when asked to explain various concepts.

## 10.2. Goldman Sachs

*Relevant Chapters: 1, 2, 3, 9*

### 10.2.1. Introduction – Getting Started

Goldman Sachs was established as a simple commercial paper house in 1869 under the name of Marcus Goldman and Company. Mr Marcus Goldman loaned money to diamond and leather merchants in New York in exchange for a promissory note – the borrower agreed to pay on a fixed date, a sum determined by the amount of the loan plus the going rate of interest and a commission fee. In 1882, Sam Sachs, Mr Goldman's son-in-law and bookkeeper since the age of 15, was made a partner. In 1894, the firm became Goldman Sachs & Company (GS). For the first 50 years, all its partners were drawn from one of the two families – either sons or sons-in-law of the two families. In 1894, the firm's capital was close to $600 000 and by 1906, stood at $4.5 million.

From the outset, the firm had ambitions which spread beyond the New York markets. Goldman Sachs engaged in correspondence banking from as early as 1897 through Kleinwort and Sons, a London merchant bank. The firm saw the advantage of advising some clients to borrow in sterling (despite the currency risk, deemed to be small) from London because UK interest rates were lower during this period.

As more firms sought listings on the New York stock exchange to raise capital from the late 1890s, Henry Goldman, a son of Marcus Goldman,[2] and his good friend, Mr Philip Lehman, from another family based financial firm in New York, agreed a joint expansion into underwriting. After being snubbed by established banks when they tried to enter the business of underwriting railroad firms, Goldman focused on the retail sector. In 1906 GS underwrote a share issue by United Cigar Manufacturers, and later in the year Henry Goldman advised the growing mail order firm Sears Roebuck to raise capital through a stock exchange listing.

Unlike railroads, mining or steel firms, most of the "value" of retail firms was in goodwill rather than physical assets. Goldman argued that for retail firms, earnings and the price earnings ratio were good proxies for value. The terms were new to the investors' vocabulary, and it could take months to place the shares. Over 30 years, GS and Lehmans co-managed the share issues of 56 retail firms, amounting to 114 offerings. The relationship was dissolved in 1936, after deteriorating over a number of years. They became rival "investment banks". At this stage, investment banking consisted largely of issuing commercial paper and underwriting stock market share issues.[3]

Though GS was one of the original US "investment" banks, the connection with Kleinworts meant they were also familiar with merchant banking. From this time up to the 1980s, the two types of banking differed. Merchant banks originated in London in the 18th century. A general merchant, Francis Baring, began financing the imports and exports of small firms based in London. Barings Bank was the first merchant bank, established in 1762. After establishing the creditworthiness of firms, Barings would, for a fee, guarantee

---

[2] Marcus Goldman retired, and died a few years later, in 1904.

[3] The Glass Steagall Act, or more appropriately, sections 16, 20, 21 and 22 of the 1933 US Banking Act, prohibited firms from engaging in investment and commercial banking activities.

or "accept" merchants' bills of exchange, which would be traded in the market. Merchant banks were a also called "accepting houses"; this term was still being used to describe this type of UK bank until the early 1980s.

Though most observers have the impression of GS as being a successful firm with a reputation for steady profits, this is by no means the case. Individuals were responsible for Goldman Sachs' history being somewhat like a rollercoaster ride – some famous names helped the firm soar to unbelievable heights but others were responsible for rapid descents in the bank's fortunes. Though the firm established a first rate reputation in its early years, it was plagued by a series of fiascos, some of which threatened the financial viability of the firm. However, GS always managed to restore its reputation and fortunes, thanks to some key individual. This case will review the early fiascos and the individuals who rescued the firm, before turning to the mid-1980s, and the long road to becoming a listed company.

## 10.2.2. The Peaks and Troughs

Throughout the 20th century, Goldman Sachs suffered a number of difficult episodes, costing its profits, capital and reputation. There were numerous major incidents, followed by internal rescues.

At the outbreak of World War I, Henry Goldman supported the German cause. His father, Marcus, had emigrated from Germany in 1848. He continued to have dealings with German banks, even after the United States had entered the war. His brother-in-law, Sam Sachs, supported the English side. Nonetheless, GS lost all of its London business until after the war because Kleinworts was forbidden by the UK government to have any dealings with Goldmans.

In 1917, Henry Goldman resigned, the last of the Goldman family to serve at the bank. Though he was deemed a liability, his departure deprived the firm of a significant amount of capital and investment banking skills.[4]

A new partner, Waddill Catchings, joined GS in 1918, with a remit to revive the underwriting business. He helped restore the firm's fortunes by the 1920s. However, his real interest was in trading – a number of trading accounts were opened, and GS profited from trading in foreign exchange, though they were still minor players compared to the giants such as JP Morgan.

In 1928, Catchings persuaded the other partners to enter fund management. The firm formed an investment trust, known as the GS Trading Corporation, part of a boom in investment trusts at the time. These speculative times meant the shares in the trust were soon priced at twice the value of the underlying assets.[5] A second trust was created. Trusts could produce revenue from three sources: fees from underwriting and broking, the rising value of shares GS had on its own books, and new investment banking business from some of the firms with shares in the trust. Shares in GSTC were priced at $100 at issue, and peaked at $326.

---

[4] Henry Goldman retired a wealthy man, and continued to support the German cause, planning to make it his permanent home in the early 1930s. However, the rise of the Nazis forced his return to the USA. He died in 1936.
[5] Investment trusts are closed end mutual funds, structured as limited public companies but with fixed shares of capital. Ironically, one of the modern day issues is an apparent anomaly: the shares trade at a discount to the underlying asset value.

In the aftermath of the October 1929 stock market crash, the GSTC share price plummeted to $1.75. GS had leveraged itself to buy shares in these trusts, and was now facing debts of $20 million and another $10 million in obligations. Though the investment trust and GS were separate entities, in the eyes of the public, they were one and the same. Investors in the trading corporations who incurred large losses tried to sue Goldmans. Trading losses and legal costs amounted to $13 million, and the firm's capital dropped to $5 million, only slightly more than it had been in 1906.

Catchings was persuaded to resign in May 1930, and Walter Sachs became President. In June, Sidney Weinberg,[6] with a grade 8 education, became Chairman of Goldman Sachs, a position he held until his death in 1969. Their first task was to unwind the Goldman Sachs Trading Corporation. It was sold for $8.00 per share, a fraction of the share's value when first issued.

From 1930 to 1945, GS suffered not only from loss of reputation, but also from lack of business due to the depression. Weinberg restored Goldman's reputation, and transformed it into one of the leading investment houses of the 20th century. Mr Sachs, as managing partner, focused on the firm's daily operations. Despite the absence of profits, Weinberg had the foresight to buy out other key firms dealing commercial paper, thus emerging as the market leader.

More important, Mr Weinberg also positioned the firm for the post-war boom by building client/personal relationships with top US corporations. At one point, Weinberg was a director on the boards of more than 30 corporations (Endlich, 1999, p. 55). His most famous contribution was the close relationship he developed with Henry Ford II. Weinberg, with another partner, Mr Whitehead, restructured the family firm, taking it public in 1956 with an IPO worth $650 million. Virtually all the major investment banks helped to underwrite the issue. With the Ford Motor Company a key client, Goldman's reputation was fully restored. Weinberg also oversaw a large range of other private and public placements. The emphasis on client service revived the investment banking side of the business, though Weinberg refused to support any move into fund management after the costly, near fatal experience with investment trusts.

In 1961, in a move to reduce the dependency of GS on Weinberg, Whitehead won the partners' approval to organise departments around a particular specialisation. He created an Investment Banking Services department, made up of sales people who were assigned to cultivate relationships with companies throughout the USA. Their job was to persuade them to raise some finance through a commercial paper issue instead of relying solely on loans. Specialist departments were soon the norm in GS, and the firm also became active in underwriting municipal bond issues and acting as a retail broker for very high net worth clients.

## 10.2.3. Entry into Trading

Mr Gus Levy developed the trading side of Goldman Sachs. Hired by Goldmans in 1933, he left for war service, then rejoined the firm, becoming a partner in 1946. Levy re-established the trading floor by creating an arbitrage department, specialising in the trade of railroad and utility bonds. He invented *block trading*, which, to date, is still the main method by which

---

[6] Sidney Weinberg had been a partner since 1927.

very large blocks of shares are traded on the stock exchange. Companies had started to set up pension funds after World War II, and the institutional investor was born. The lessons of the 1929 stock market crash meant these funds restricted their investments to bonds. However, the interest in investing in shares grew as the benefits of diversification became apparent.

The New York Stock Exchange was organised to serve the small investor – there was no mechanism for the huge trades institutional investors would need. Stockbrokers lacked the capital to fund larger trades. Levy agreed to buy large blocks of stock (e.g. 250 000 shares) assuming the market/price risk but confident, given Goldman's position in the market, that it could find buyers for these shares. GS would profit from the difference between the bid–offer price and from the commissions charged for block trading.

In the late 1980s, Goldman Sachs would export its knowledge of block trading to Europe, via its London office. Up to that time, any firm wanting to sell a large block of shares had to do so through its bank, which normally agreed to act on the firm's behalf by purchasing the block of shares at a discount of 10%, even though buyers had already been found. GS used their experience and capital to offer customers a better deal and quickly captured a large share of this market.

Levy the trader succeeded Weinberg the investment banker as senior partner in 1969. However, Levy had to report to a management committee, comprised of more senior partners, created to monitor the trader's activities. This move illustrated the well-known animosity between traders (whose notion of the long run was a full rather than a half day) and investment bankers, who cultivated long-term customer relationships. To quote Sydney Weinberg: "I never traded. I am an investment banker. I don't shoot craps. If I had been a speculator and taken advantage of what I knew I could have 5 times as much [money] as I have today." (Endlich, 1999, p. 64)

The establishment of a management committee was not enough to stop GS from becoming involved in another major crisis when Penn Central Railroad went bankrupt in the 1970s. Penn Central's earnings had been very poor, yet Goldman Sachs, which arranged the issue of the firm's commercial paper, continued to sell the paper and even assured a rating agency that the company was sound. GS was confident the Federal Reserve Bank would provide the liquidity to the railroad company, and had calculated that the firm's assets exceeded its debts. At the same time, GS was reducing its own exposure in this paper. Even though Levy claimed GS had always been confident of Penn Central's securities, it was censured by the Securities and Exchange Commission for its activities and required to provide investors with more information in future issues. Again, GS faced a mountain of law suits, which threatened to wipe out the partners' combined capital. Most were settled out of court but one went to a jury and GS was found guilty of defrauding its customers by selling commercial paper in Penn Central in 1969 and 1970 when the railway was nearly insolvent. The firm was forced to buy back all of the plaintiffs' commercial paper at its initial value plus interest. However, GS also bought back paper from other clients at huge discounts. The losses were far less than expected once the value of the paper began to rise, which helped to cushion the overall losses.

Levy, with the other existing partners, agreed to inject some of their own capital to protect the junior partners from suffering capital deficits. This inspired a great deal of loyalty among members, especially as the firm grew into a much larger partnership.

The 1970s was a period of doldrums for the firm, largely because of the steady decline in the stock markets, which did not recover until 1980. In 1976 Levy died suddenly after a stroke. He was succeeded by two co-leaders, Mr John Whitehead and Mr John Weinberg, the son of Sidney, a partner since 1956.

Levy's development of the trading floor left the firm well positioned to take advantage of the growth in the stock market from 1980. By 1984 there were 75 partners, each earning $5 million per year. The firm appeared to have learned from experience over time, and by this time had a well ingrained corporate culture, with the two co-heads, an eight-partner management committee and the partners. There was a clear hierarchy: senior partners, partners, vice-presidents and associates, who put in long hours in the hope of being made partner. Though there was increasing pressure for the partnership to agree to a public listing, three more scandals would delay the change until the late 1990s.

## 10.2.4. From Partnership to Public Listing?

In 1986, Mr John Weinberg, as senior partner, was responsible for informing those who were to be promoted from being vice-presidents to partners. The firm had grown so large that for the first time, partners did not know every candidate up for partnership. Also, many of the new partners came from trading, illustrating its importance in this traditional investment bank. These were signals that Goldmans had grown so large, it was time to look at alternative methods of corporate governance, to replace the partnership arrangement, which had served the firm since its inception. Before considering the initial attempts to get the partners to agree to a public listing, it is worth reviewing where the bank was in 1986, the year when, for the first time, serious consideration was given to the bank going public.

In 1986, the firm had four divisions:

1. Traditional investment banking: underwriting and M&As.
2. Fixed income (bond trading).
3. Equities: share trading.
4. Currency and commodities trading.[7] Proprietary trading was not yet in a separate division but became one in the early 1990s.

These functions are explained in detail in the Appendix.

Until the mid-1980s, Goldmans had a well-defined, strong corporate culture. Its main features were as follows:

- A traditional recruitment procedure, with in-house training. From the early years, Goldman Sachs tended to hire from a large pool of MBAs. 1500 would apply for 30 places. The chosen few would be intelligent, mature, confident and value teamwork. The motivation of the associates and vice-presidents, in the scramble to become partner, was summarised by a senior partner, Steve Friedman, "No one ever washes a rental car".[8] Most graduates who were hired would expect to spend their whole career with a department, so

[7] GS purchased a commodities partnership, J. Aron, in 1981.
[8] Endlich (1999), p. 19.

every department had a wealth of expertise. Employees were expected to give a lifetime of service. In 1984, almost all of the 75 partners had been with the firm for 10–20 years.
- The firm was insular. It was rare to bring in "outsiders" at senior levels.
- Top priority was given to the customer, and GS was selective in the customers it chose. GS prided itself on moral standards. For example, it would not underwrite shares involving non-voting stock because all shareholders should have voting rights. Nor would they participate in hostile takeovers. As a result, any firm threatened by a possible or actual takeover sought the advice of GS. Giving priority to clients was not just to please clients. A close relationship yielded information, which in turn helped in the development of new products and services, which could be sold at a premium.
- The management committee was the main source of decision making, though departments were encouraged to be innovative.

However, during the 1980s, there was a radical change in the investment banking business, due mainly to the growing importance of the trading side of the business, both proprietary and for clients. As a consequence, the traditional culture at GS was challenged by:

- An increasing tendency to recruit staff at senior levels. Prominent employees from other firms had to be hired if Goldmans was to keep pace with the new parts of investment banking such as the derivative markets. By the end of the 1980s, nearly half of the GS employees had been there less than three years. The newcomers who joined as partners had little time to acquire the firm's "lifetime" values. Employees of long-term standing resented the new entry.
- "Black Monday" (17 October 1987) forced the firm to take the unprecedented step of making a large number of redundancies. Lifetime employment was no longer guaranteed, and the loyalty inspired by it was undermined. The combination of senior level hiring and redundancies led to staff defections and early retirements. The comparatively low compensation levels also encouraged the best staff to leave for firms where compensation was linked to individual performance and short-term profitability.
- The team approach was being undermined by all of the changes noted above. It was no longer possible to place an employee in a department for life.
- Ignoring the competition was no longer an option. For example, in 1989, Weinberg agreed to allow GS to represent a hostile bidder in a takeover attempt. Also, the firm had hoped that by taking on Maxwell as a client, it could position itself in the London markets.

Goldmans tried to address these issues by hiring consultants for advice on management techniques. Management and leadership programmes were introduced for the higher level entrants to encourage them to adopt GS's core values of specialisation and teamwork. Though recruitment at senior level caused resentment, it also meant the firm could quickly move into new areas of the rapidly growing investment banking business.

Overall, however, there were severe pressures on the partnership system of ownership. The unlimited personal liability of partners frightened them, as the number of law suits against Goldmans and other investment banks grew. A better method of compensation was needed if Goldmans was to attract and keep the best. It could no longer rely on individuals working for years as associates and vice-presidents, especially when it began to recruit at senior level.

The first serious attempt to organise an initial public offering (IPO) was in late 1986. Earlier in the year, the management committee had unanimously recommended that the partnership should vote on the question of whether GS should opt for a public listing. There were several reasons for this:

- Other partnerships had opted for mergers or public ownership. The list was growing, and involved nearly all of Goldman's key rivals: Dean Witter was bought by Sears and Salomon Brothers was bought by Philip Brothers in 1981. Lehman Brothers was sold to Shearson American Express (1984) and General Electric bought Kidder Peabody (1986). Bear Stern went public in 1985, followed by Morgan Stanley in 1986. The partners of these firms became immensely wealthy, and much needed capital was raised, allowing them to expand existing activities, and enter new areas. The establishment of a global presence was thought necessary for effective competition. Globalisation would increase diversification.
- More capital was needed to fund expansion into trading and investment in other operating companies.
- As a partnership, each partner faced unlimited personal liability. Earnings were more volatile as the firm invested and traded more. Also, Goldman Sachs had long been a target for law suits, launched by dissatisfied clients and the public (e.g. the Maxwell pension fund trustees). Employment law made it easier for employees to sue the firm for sexual harassment, job discrimination, and so on.
- The firm's capital could not be relied upon as a stable source of finance. If a year of poor results coincided with the retirement of a significant number of partners, with a consequent loss of capital, the financial implications for GS could be very serious.

There were also a number of arguments against going public:

- An IPO, to the extent that it undermines relationship banking (shareholders take precedence over the client), would reduce important information sources.
- In 1986, 37 new partners had been created. They had spent many years working as associates in the hope they would be offered a partnership some day. The financial windfall would be small ($3–$3.5 million) compared to what the senior partners would get.
- There was a division between partners in the traditional investment banking areas and those in trading. Investment banker partners opposed the change because they did not need more capital to run their divisions.
- Shareholders would expect dividends each year. As a public company, the firm would have to adhere to a number of regulations, such as quarterly reporting requirements. It was argued that as soon as a firm went public it, by necessity, would have to focus on strategies that boosted short-term profitability. By contrast, a private firm had no such pressures, and could focus on long-term returns.
- If GS went public, the firm could not protect their privacy from the press.
- There were human resource implications for existing employees. Some partners argued the emphasis on teamwork would suffer as would dedication to serve the client, because the short-term interest of the shareholder would become paramount. Also, new employees could no longer expect a partnership, so the value placed on team effort would disappear.

The firm's unwritten motto, "never say I; say we", and the likelihood of opportunistic behaviour would increase, as would principal agent problems between employees and management. On the other hand, many public firms create the right incentives to encourage teamwork, and minimise agency problems by linking bonuses to long-term profitability – withholding a fraction of the bonus in the event of a subsequent downturn.

- Goldmans might find they could no longer recruit the best graduates, because the attraction of making partner would disappear. On the other hand, the days of the lifetime employee ended when GS was forced to hire senior people from outside the firm to remain competitive, especially in new areas such as proprietary trading, derivatives and, more generally, risk management. The bank could use schemes such as stock options and golden handcuffs to keep the best employees. Also, Goldman's traditional methods of compensation meant they were losing some of the best employees to rival firms.
- It was possible to raise capital in other ways. In 1986, in a secret deal, Sumitomo Bank injected $500 million for a non-voting minority shareholder state, in exchange for 12.5% of annual profits. At the time, Sumitomo was the most profitable Japanese bank, and their long-term goal was to enter the US market in some way. Also, it would give Sumitomo a unique insight into how a deregulated, competitive market works, so that if and when Japan was deregulated, they would have some experience. Originally, Sumitomo had hoped its employees could shadow GS workers, but the Federal Reserve imposed explicit firewalls before it would approve the investment. Sumitomo could not have any directors on the boards of Goldman Sachs; nor could it participate in the selection of partners or policy making. It was not allowed to hold voting shares in Goldmans. Neither firm could solicit business for the other, and explicit contracts were to be used for any business transactions.
- "Weinberg was Goldman Sachs" (Endlich, 1999, p. 7). John Weinberg faced a moral dilemma: why should the money raised by the IPO (estimated at $2–$3 billion) go to the existing partners, when generations of partners had contributed to the growth in the economic value of the firm over 127 years? He reasoned that since partnership injections were based on book value, this should determine what they are paid in the event of an IPO. However, payments based on book value would create a new problem: large surpluses.

Weinberg also believed capital constraints could be useful if they forced the partners to choose the best markets to enter rather than just following the competition. For example, the firm would have to decide whether a big expansion into capital intensive trading was appropriate given the traditional strengths of the firm in areas such as underwriting and mergers and acquisitions. This attitude would mean Goldmans concentrating on niche markets, traditional investment banking. However, the firm always moved with the times, profiting from new areas. The decision to be a niche player would be at odds with its long history of expansion. Perhaps more important, going public does not suddenly convey an endless supply of capital to any firm. For capital to be forthcoming, it has to satisfy its shareholders and lenders that more injections will be profitable.

Five days after the new partners joined the firm, the December meeting was held to decide on the future of Goldman Sachs. Steve Friedman and Robert Rubin (co-vice-chairmen since 1987), who oversaw the daily operations of the firm, expressed support for going public. In the end, no vote was taken. With such strong opposition, especially by John Weinberg and his elder son (Jimmy),[9] there was no chance of a majority vote in favour of an IPO.

In February 1987, Robert Freeman was arrested for insider trading. By November 1991, the Maxwell affair was public knowledge. During these years, the question of seeking a public listing was very much on the back burner.

Goldman's was the leading investment bank for mergers and acquisitions, but in the heady days of the 1980s, until the October 1987 crash, risk arbitrage was the second most profitable division. It specialised in spotting opportunities for making profits from arbitrage among securities: buying/selling equity or bonds because they were considered under/overpriced, For example, a firm that became a target for a leveraged buyout often saw its share price rise dramatically after the announcement. Profits could be made if investment banks spotted potential LBO targets and bought shares before the LBO became public information.

However, in this risky business, there was a fine line between public information and insider information, confidential information held by, say, the M&A department about an upcoming merger, that would yield high profits to the risk arbitrage department. Insider trading is a criminal offence. To ensure compliance, Chinese walls were erected which restricted the flow of information between departments in a bank or securities firm.

In 1986, Mr Robert Rubin (a partner at GS since 1966) was head of the arbitrage department, originally founded by Gus Levy. Robert Freedman, his assistant and a partner since 1978, was chief of arbitrage and head of international equities. In 1987, Dennis Levine of Drexel, Burnham Lambert[10] was arrested for insider trading. Plea bargains led to Levine naming Ivan Boesky, who then identified Martin Siegal, a recent recruit to Drexel from Kidder Peabody. Siegal, in turn, named Robert Freedman, and some former employees from Kidder Peabody.

Robert Freedman was arrested in February 1987. An internal investigation by GS after Boesky's arrest had revealed no evidence of insider trading at Goldmans, so the firm was confident there was no case to answer and stood by their man. To have a relatively senior partner convicted of this crime would seriously damage the reputation of any bank, especially one as august as Goldman Sachs. On 13 May the US government, seemingly unable to prove its case, moved for dismissal, claiming it was preparing a bigger indictment. In 1989, after over two years of legal wrangling, Freedman pleaded guilty to one charge of insider dealing, based on what some would interpret as an innocent remark made to Siegal. During the internal investigation, no one at GS thought the remark constituted insider trading. But in 1989, when reminded of what he had said, Freedman acknowledged that after Siegal had confirmed some information in relation to a leveraged buyout (LBO), he should not have continued to trade in the shares of the target firm, Beatrice Company.

Freedman was ready to plead guilty on this one count, perhaps because he was worn down by the affair and like Goldmans, recognised that the chances of a fair trial were slim. Polls of potential jurors had revealed an innate hostility to investment banks, which were perceived by the average public to be greedy and lacking in morals. Freedman was fined,

---

[9] Weinberg's other son, John, on the management committee, did not voice an opinion.
[10] Drexel, Burnham, Lambert specialised in leveraged buyouts, raising large amounts of finance based on borrowed money (e.g. junk bonds) on behalf of a bidding firm, so it could buy out a target.

spent just over 3.5 months in jail, and resigned his partnership. The whole episode cost GS $25 million (they paid Freedman's legal bills) and a lost reputation.

Goldmans had been slow to make its mark in London, possibly because of its long running relationship with Kleinworts. Though they opened a London office in the 1970s, it was a small, largely unprofitable operation. The firm was anxious to establish itself. Enter Mr Robert Maxwell, a Czech who emigrated to the UK after World War II.

Robert Maxwell had already been censured twice, once in 1954 and again in 1971, when the Department of Trade and Industry declared he was unfit to run a public company. Despite warnings from the London office, the management committee in New York agreed to do business with Maxwell. However, in view of Maxwell's chequered history, the London office was instructed to proceed with caution. All the transactions were to be relatively low risk, such as buying and selling MCC (Maxwell Communication Corporation) shares over the period 1989–91.

Maxwell's champion was Mr Eric Sheinberg, a partner in GS for 20 years and based in the London office. Sheinberg had known Maxwell since the mid-1980s and bid on a block of shares being offered by Maxwell. This was followed by a series of block share (5–20 million shares per purchase) dealings, the most serious of which involved Goldmans unwittingly repurchasing shares Maxwell stole from his company's pension funds. The proceeds, £54.9 million, from the share purchase went to BIT, a private firm in the Maxwell group. BIT used the money to finance the purchase of the shares by two Liechtenstein trusts, indirectly controlled by Maxwell. Using these trusts, Maxwell gained control of the stolen pension fund shares, which could now be used as additional collateral.

During this period, Sheinberg arranged numerous foreign exchange transactions and two call options on Maxwell's behalf, pricing them himself rather than using the experienced option price team. Sheinberg also arranged two loans of £25 and £35 million in, respectively, March and August of 1991. However, the management committee was increasingly concerned about the Maxwell connection, and Sheinberg's role. At an August 1991 meeting, it was decided that two partners, Mr Ken Brody and Mr Robert Katz (a lawyer) should handle the Maxwell affair; Sheinberg was gradually eased out. GS was holding £106 million worth of shares in Maxwell's companies. If they called the loans and tried to offload the shares on the market, they would get very little back. The plan was to get Maxwell to agree to reschedule debts. Maxwell had the firm exactly where he wanted them, because Goldmans would be too embarrassed to call a loan or sell their collateral.

It was not just Goldmans that fell into the trap. Most of the major American and British banks in the City of London had dealings with Maxwell. At the time of his death, he owed £2.8 billion to a large group of banks. Despite Maxwell's bad reputation, withholding crucial financial information and secrecy about the links of over 400 firms within the publicly owned MCC, banks were attracted to Maxwell because he was prepared to pay high fees and comparatively high rates of interest on his loans, a classic example of adverse selection. It also demonstrates the dangers of a herd mentality. A reputable bank such as Goldman Sachs doing business with Mr Maxwell acted as a signal to other banks that perhaps Maxwell was creditworthy.

The GS loans had not been repaid by early October 1991. Deadlines were set, then extended, when no payment was made. GS had had enough but after Maxwell barged into the New York offices, he was given another week to repay the $35 million loan. By 30 October, no payment had been made. Maxwell was informed that GS would begin liquidating collateral. Maxwell left for his yacht, making no attempt to extend the deadline. GS was able to sell 2.2 million shares, leaving them with 24.2 million. They tried to stall further sales, telling Kevin Maxwell they would halt the sales if the loan was repaid. By 5 November, the markets knew that GS was liquidating Maxwell's shares. Two hours later trading was suspended because Maxwell had disappeared from his yacht.

For Goldman Sachs, it was the beginning of three years of law suits and trying to salvage its damaged reputation. The US Securities and Exchange Commission investigated GS but did not charge the firm or Sheinberg with any wrong doing. The pension funds were a different matter. The public perception of the affair was that Goldmans and other reputable banks were guilty of supporting Maxwell and indirectly, of depriving 17 000 British pensioners of £400 million worth of retirement income. Lawyers for the funds' trustees launched a US law suit, presenting GS and Sheinberg with a long list of charges including, among others, fraud, breach of contract and conspiracy. Not willing to risk a hostile jury and public trial, GS settled out of court for $253 million. Not only had the firm's reputation suffered, but many of the partners, especially limited partners[11] who knew nothing of the affair, were angry at having to pay out such a large sum.

In addition, GS faced losses totalling $91 million from defaults on loan and unsecured foreign exchange transactions the firm had conducted on Maxwell's behalf. The Securities and Futures Association (SFA) fined Goldmans for breaching its capital requirements in its commitments to Maxwell. The cost in reputation became clear when the British government excluded GS from underwriting the third flotation of British Telecom shares in 1993.

Profits at Goldmans in 1994 were the lowest in a decade. The fixed income and foreign exchange departments in the London office had lost over $350 million between the beginning of the fiscal year (December) and April 1994. Profits were also undermined by a 40% increase in operating costs between 1992–94, due mainly to overseas expansion.

## 10.2.5. Volatility and Losses from a "Cocktail"

In 1994, GS considered itself to be highly diversified, engaging in commodity trades, underwriting stocks and bonds, mergers and acquisitions, and proprietary trading. Unfortunately, in February 1994, the Federal Reserve Bank raised interest rates by 0.5% – the first of six increases over 6 months. As a consequence, losses in proprietary trading nearly exceeded the gains made in other areas of investment banking.

At this point in time, GS had no risk management system *per se* – the view of Mr Michael O'Brien (head of proprietary foreign exchange trading) was to hire the best in the business and let them get on with the job, with minimal interference, provided he was kept informed. Traders could take very large positions – it was up to them to decide when to close them down. Trading managers were responsible for their own desk; senior management relied on informal channels of communication. Friedman, the co-chairman,[12] was hoping for the

---

[11] Partners who retired but left half their capital with the firm, earning interest on the capital invested.

[12] Stephen Friedman and Robert Rubin were appointed co-vice-chairmen in 1987. They were named senior partners and co-chairmen in 1990, succeeding Mr John Weinberg.

success of one big trade. A trader, Houghton-Berry, had a short sterling position, the result of a "cocktail" (Endlich, 1999, p. 203) of 50 000 options and futures, designed to profit from the timing and size of the Bank of England (BE) future rate changes. HB and the GS economist Davies expected UK rates to rise, but not by as much as the market was anticipating. The HB position would profit provided any rise in UK rates was *less* than the market anticipated. By December 1994, they were to be proved correct, but short-term events resulted in a fiasco.

The position showed marginal profits by September 1994, despite volatility in the markets since July. On 7 September, the Chancellor of the Exchequer would announce any change in official interest rate. There was no announcement, and activity in the markets suggested a rate rise was unlikely. By Monday, 12 September, the position had recouped losses from the previous week[13] and was in profit of $10 million. On the same day, the portfolio lost millions in minutes, because the Chancellor announced a 0.5% increase in UK rates to 5.75%, resulting in *changed* market *expectations* that UK rates could be as high as 8% by Christmas.

Houghton-Berry was instructed to unwind some of the position. GS lost $50 million because the market was illiquid, and the action of unwinding the position depressed the markets even more. Had the position been carried until year-end, these futures and options would have made about $20 million – the rise in interest rates (to 6.25%) was much lower than had been expected after the September announcement. Davies and Houghton-Berry were proved correct, but it was too late.

## 10.2.6. Risk Management: A Formal System

Goldman Sachs responded to these losses by introducing an interdisciplinary, firm-wide risk management committee in 1995. It meets weekly and can "push a button" to see GS's market and credit risk exposure in aggregate. Traders had to defend their positions weekly. Each trader is assigned a "risk limit", an amount which GS will accept as losses before the trader shuts down. Unlike other banks (e.g. Bankers Trust), the limit is not based on a predetermined size for a given position. It is possible that had formal risk management procedures been set up at the time, HB and Davies might have successfully defended holding the position. It would be highly unusual for the Chancellor to raise rates by 2.25% in 3 months – it had taken the Fed 6 months to raise rates by 3%.

This risk management committee has evolved through time in response to the introduction of new risk management techniques and the requirement to meet new demands set by regulators. By 2003, the single committee had expanded into nine risk committees.

1. Firm-wide: Approves new businesses/products, divisional market risk limits, sovereign credit risk limits, credit risk limits, limits based on abnormal/catastrophic events, inventory position limits for some country exposures. Reviews activities of existing businesses, business unit market risk limits, scenario analyses. Also, together with the Controllers Department, regularly reviews internal valuation models and the pricing positions set up by the individual limits.

---

[13] More than $50 million was lost the week before the BE had been unsuccessful in a sale of short-term bills, causing rates to rise by 1% – quickly reversed because there had been no *official* change of interest rate policy.

2. FICC and equities risk committees: Set market risk limits for their respective product lines based on a number of measures including VaR, scenario analyses and inventory levels.

3. Asset management control oversight and asset management risk committees: Oversee issues related to operation, credit, pricing and business practice.

4. Global compliance and control: Develops policies and training programmes to mitigate compliance, operational and reputation risks; assists management in the identification/review of these risks.

5. Capital: Reviews/approves all transactions involving commitment of GS capital, e.g. extensions of credit risks, bond underwritings and any unusual transactions or financing arrangements which involve significant capital exposure; also, maintenance of capital standards on a global basis.

6. Commitments: Reviews and approves underwriting and distribution activities; sets policies to ensure standards (e.g. legal, reputation, regulatory, business) in relation to these activities are maintained.

7. Credit policy: Establishes/reviews broad credit policies.

8. Operational risk: Development/implementation of policies on operational risk; monitors their effectiveness.

9. Finance: Oversees GS's capital, liquidity and funding needs; sets inventory position limits.

All the risk committees report to the powerful management committee, which takes ultimate responsibility for risk management and control.

GS also has departments ("non-revenue" producing) that perform risk management functions: firm-wide, controllers, treasury, global operations, internal audit and legal.

Goldman Sachs' integrated approach to managing risk involves:

• Manage the exposures through diversification of exposures, controlling the size of trading positions, and using securities and derivatives to hedge positions.

• Use quantitative tools which includes:

– Use of VaR to set risk limits. Use of scenario analyses to set risk limits: scenario analysis involves looking at how certain market events affect GS's net trading positions. The market events include: an unexpected, large widening of credit spreads, substantial decline in equity markets, and significant changes in emerging markets.

– Setting limits on inventory positions for certain country exposures and business units.

– Value at risk, scenario analysis and stress tests are explained in some detail in Chapter 3.

GS has started to review its approach to VaR, and some related VaR numbers in its *Annual Report*. Recall from Chapter 3 that a number of assumptions are needed to compute value at risk. In the *Annual Report*, the VaR numbers reported are based on a 95% confidence interval and a 1-day time horizon. So there is a 1 in 20 chance that daily net trading revenues will fall below expected net trading revenues by an amount that is at least as large as the reported VaR. Or, on average, about once a month, shortfalls from the expected

Table 10.1   Goldman Sachs: Average Daily VaR ($m)

| Risk categories | 2002 | 2001 | 2000 |
|---|---|---|---|
| Interest rates | 34 | 20 | 13 |
| Equity prices | 22 | 20 | 21 |
| Currency rates | 16 | 15 | 6 |
| Commodity prices | 12 | 9 | 8 |
| Diversification benefit* | (38) | (25) | (20) |
| Firm-wide | 46 | 39 | 28 |

* Diversification effect: the difference between the firm-wide or aggregate VaR and the VaRs for the four risk categories. Arises because the four market risk categories are not perfectly correlated. For example, the losses from each category will occur on different days.
*Source: Goldman Sachs 2002 Annual Report*, p. 49.

daily trading net revenues can be expected to be greater than the daily VaR.[14] GS reports that it uses weighted historical data to compute VaR, with more recent observations given a higher weight. The VaR number includes the product positions taken plus any related hedges which require positions taken in other product areas. The VaR numbers are reported for the four major risk categories: interest rate, equity, currency and commodity. Table 10.1 reproduced from the 2002 *Annual Report*.

The table shows that in aggregate, Goldmans' average daily VaR has increased since 2000, and most of the increase can be traced back to higher interest rate risk. According to the *Annual Report* (2003), greater interest rate volatility and increased exposure contributed to the increase between 2000 and 2001, but between 2001 and 2002, it is caused by increased "market opportunities" and more customer activity which raised interest rate risk. Goldman Sachs reports that one day in 2002, trading losses exceeded its 95% daily VaR.

The paragraphs above are a brief description of how risk is managed at GS, with a special emphasis on market risk. As the outline of the committee system showed, the company also has systems in place to manage non-trading risk, credit risk, and operational risk.

## 10.2.7. Go for an IPO?

On 6 September 1994, Mr Friedman informed the management committee that he wanted to resign and become a limited partner. The public announcement came on 12 September, hours after the Chancellor unexpectedly announced the rise in interest rates and GS lost $50 million as a result of the Houghton-Berry/Davies "cocktail". Though a coincidence, the markets perceived that Friedman was being asked to resign because of the losses in proprietary trading, which suggested there were management problems at the top. Morale appeared to be low. In 1994, 35 partners opted for a limited partnership.

When Mr Friedman resigned in November 1994, Mr Corzine was made senior partner and chairman, and Mr Paulson sub-chairman. After the firm was restructured, they became co-chairmen. By 1996, Goldman Sachs had fully recovered, with profits restored to their

---

[14] Goldman Sachs, *Annual Report 2002*, p. 48.

1993 levels, and in 1997 profits increased again. Several factors contributed to the improvement. Corzine and Paulson recognised the need for increased diversification. They increased overseas operations and revived the fund management business. Goldman Sachs had withdrawn from fund management in 1976 but in the 1980s, Mr Whitehead formed Goldman Sachs Asset Management. A relatively small division in the mid-1990s, Corzine and Paulson encouraged its development and over four years, the number of employees had quadrupled to over 1000 in 1998. The investment banking side of the business benefited from the boom in IPOs and M&As. Finally, GS re-emerged as the market leader in block trading, due largely to the profitable disposal of $5 billion worth of British Petroleum shares on behalf of The Kuwait Investment Agency, followed by two more successful large block disposals.

Mergers in the investment banking sector continued apace in 1995–97. GS realised that without capital, it could fall behind. Proprietary and block share trading demanded large amounts of capital. Competitors such as Merrill Lynch and Salomon Brothers were able to put up billions to purchase other firms such as Mercury Asset Management and the bankrupt Japanese securities firm, Yamaichi Securities.

In January 1996, Corzine and Paulson, and the executive committee (except for John Thain, the youngest member of the committee and the chief financial officer), proposed that GS seek a public listing. The operating and partnership committees consisted of 40 senior partners just below the executive committee. An independent compensation specialist hired by them reported that the top 5–10 partners would improve their compensation if GS went public, but the next 150 partners would actually be worse off. Based on these findings, nearly 100% of these two committees rejected the idea.

Nonetheless, a fortnight later, the matter was put to all the partners, to be debated over a weekend meeting. Not only was the financial compensation unattractive to most partners, but just as in 1986, non-financial issues were raised such as moral obligations to earlier generations, and perceived problems of recruiting top staff. It was clear by Friday night that there would be a substantial no vote if one was held; as a result, the motion was withdrawn.

The meeting did give Corzine a mandate to improve the firm's corporate governance.[15] He did this by getting rid of the title of partner. Partners and long-standing senior vice-presidents (not partners) would now be called managing directors. MDs who were not partners (no capital investment) would receive all the benefits of a partner – equal salaries, offices, attendance at partners' meetings and access to the partners' dining room. The *Annual Report* would not distinguish between the two types of MDs, meaning clients and potential clients could not distinguish between the two.

This change in governance gave former senior VPs greater influence with clients because there was a distinction between them and thousands of "junior" VPs who had been at the firm for about 4 years and done well. It would mean GS could compete more effectively for new staff. Other investment banks in the USA and Europe had been attracting Goldman's VPs with MD titles, stock options, etc. All Goldmans could offer a recruit from another firm was the VP title. It was hoped the reorganisation would help to keep employees who would never make partner but were productive members of the firm. Nor would the economic value of partnership be diluted. With a more equitable personnel structure, revenues should rise.

---

[15] *Corporate governance*, simply defined, describes the way a firm is managed.

In 1998, GS continued to do very well in all aspects of its business. Its strong performance, together with the rising stock market, made it likely that if GS went public, it would sell at 3.5 to 4 times its book value, compared to less than 2 times book value at the time of the 1996 disposal. Therefore, the financial arguments for an IPO were strong. Also, GS was quickly becoming the only privately owned major investment bank.

As before, there was a two-day weekend meeting of the partnership and operating committees. It was decided to put the plan for an IPO to the partners again, because GS needed capital if it was to continue its expansion. It ruled out merging with a large bank, as some of its rivals had done.

The partners' weekend meeting took place in June 1998. Unlike the previous 1986 and 1996 meetings, the newest partners stood to gain because they had one or two record years behind them, and though they would be disadvantaged compared to the senior partners, they would do very well out of it. While the economic arguments were compelling, there was concern about whether the loss of partnership would result in loss of teamwork. But by Monday, the committees were unanimous: the best way forward was an IPO. A detailed package was put together (10–15% of its common equity was to be sold) and partners voted over the summer of 1998. A large majority voted in favour of going public, and an IPO was planned for November.

Even as the partners were voting, stock markets began to decline in August because of a fear that the Asian crisis might spread to the west. At the end of August, Russia defaulted on its debt, accelerating the speed of the decline. By the third week in September, it was clear that Long Term Capital Management (LTCM), a New York hedge fund, was in trouble. On 28 September, a consortium of banks, including Goldman Sachs, rescued LTCM at a cost of $3.625 billion. Bank stocks were hit particularly hard as the stock markets continued to decline because of their exposure in Russian debt and LTCM. Based on the value of shares similar to GS, its market value declined to 2.5 times book value. Citing unstable market conditions, the co-chairmen of GS withdrew the planned IPO. Corzine, a trader, was associated with the trading side of the bank. There had been trading losses of about $1 billion in the second half of 1998. He resigned his executive role in January but stayed on as co-chairman to see the IPO through. It was claimed he was dropped from the executive committee because he was associated with the sort of hedging activity that caused LTCM's collapse.

In March 1999, GS announced it would sell 10–15% of its common equity. The actual sale finally took place in May 1999 – it raised $3.6 billion, and the market value of GS was $33 billion. It was considered highly successful given it was a non-technology IPO.

## 10.2.8. Organisational Structure Post-IPO

Even after going public, GS's corporate governance was largely determined by a privately run inner circle. The management committee (with 17 members) acts as the Executive, making it more tightly controlled than it was. In addition, at the time of the IPO:

- There was a less powerful group of 221 partners.
- 48.3% of GS was still owned by the 221 partners. Corzine and Paulson 0.9% and 0.88%, respectively. Partners were not allowed to sell shares for 3–5 years. In less than a year

GS announced a secondary offering to allow some of the "insiders" to sell some of their stock.

- 21.2% was owned by the non-partner employees.
- 17.9% was owned by retired partners, Sumitomo Bank and a Hawaiian concern, Kamehameha of Hawaii.
- Only 12.6% of the firm was publicly owned, and most of these shares were placed in the hands of its own customers and long-term investors. However, in July 2000, it was announced that some partners, together with Sumitomo and Kamehameha, would sell 40 million shares, or 7.6% of the bank to institutions. According to GS, the main reason was to increase the percentage of free floating shares in the public domain – the sale would raise it to 17.4% and wider ownership of common stock. They emphasised that the choice of selling existing stock (rather than a new share issue) demonstrated the sale was not designed to raise capital.

Immediately after it went public, its activities were divided into two segments.

## 1.   Global Capital Markets

Investment banking: financial advisory (M&As, financial restructuring, real estate), underwriting: equity and debt
Trading and principal investments: fixed income (bonds); equity, currency and commodities
Principal investment (net revenues from merchant banking investments).

## 2.   Asset Management & Securities Services

Asset management
Securities services (e.g. brokerage)
Commissions.

Some time in 2001/2, the structure was changed. The current structure consists of three segments:

## 1.   Investment Banking

Financial advisory (including mergers and acquisitions)
Underwriting.

## 2.   Trading and Principal Investments

Fixed income, currency and commodities (FICC)
Equities
Principal investments: net revenues from merchant banking investments.

## 3.   Asset Management and Securities

Asset management

Securities
Commissions.

The operating results for 2000 to 2002 are reported in Table 10.2.

Controversy broke out in 2002 beginning with an investigation of Merrill Lynch by the New York Attorney General,[16] Eliot Spitzer, and concluding in April 2003 when 10 of the top US investment banks settled with several regulatory bodies for just over $1.4 billion in penalties and other payments, for alleged conflicts of interest between banks' analysts and their investment bank divisions. The case is discussed in Chapter 1, but there was a potential conflict of interest because the profits of the investment bank financed banks' research departments. Thus, banks' analysts were under pressure to support a particular company which was also giving underwriting, consulting or other business to the banks' investment banking division. No bank, including Goldmans, admitted liability. In its *Annual Report*, GS refers to the incident as a "Research Settlement". It paid out a total of $110 million, broken down into (a) $50 million in retrospective compensation, (b) $50 million over 5 years to fund an independent research group, which will supply GS clients and the other

Table 10.2   Goldman Sachs: Operating Results ($m; year-end November)

|  | 2003 | 2002 | 2001 | 2000 |
|---|---|---|---|---|
| **Investment banking** | | | | |
| Net revenues | 2 711 | 2 830 | 3 836 | 5 371 |
| Operating expenses | 2 504 | 2 454 | 3 117 | 3 645 |
| Pre-tax earnings | 207 | 376 | 719 | 1 726 |
| **Trading & principal investments** | | | | |
| Net revenues | 10 443 | 5 249 | 6 349 | 6 627 |
| Operating expenses | 6 938 | 4 273 | 5 134 | 4 199 |
| Pre-tax earnings | 3 505 | 976 | 1 215 | 2 428 |
| **Asset management & securities** | | | | |
| Net revenues | 2 858 | 5 907 | 5 626 | 4 592 |
| Operating expenses | 1 890 | 3 794 | 3 501 | 3 008 |
| Pre-tax earnings | 968 | 2 113 | 2 125 | 1 584 |
| **Total** | | | | |
| Net revenues | 16 012 | 13 986/13 986 | 15 811/15 811 | 16 590/16 590 |
| Operating expenses* | 11 567 | 10 733/10 521 | 12 115/11 752 | 11 570/10 852 |
| Pre-tax earnings* | 4 445 | 3 253/3 465 | 3 696/4 059 | 5 020/5 738 |

* For 2000–03, the first number is operating expenses/pre-tax earnings as reported in the *Annual Report*, which includes expenses not incurred by any one sector, involving amortisation of employee IPO awards ($212, $363, $428 million in 2002, 2001, 2000, respectively) and acquisition expenses in 2000 (= $290 million). The second number is total operating expenses/pre-tax earnings, the sum of operating expenses/pre-tax earnings reported in each section.
( ): % of total pre-tax earnings based on the second number for total pre-tax earnings.
*Source*:  Goldman Sachs *Annual Report*, 2002.

[16] The New York Attorney General is also the state's securities regulator.

investment banks with independent research, and (c) $10 million to go towards investor education. The firm has also agreed to:

*"adopt internal structural and other safeguards to further ensure the integrity of Goldman Sachs & Co investment research."*[17]

# Appendix

## *Traditional Investment Banking*

What is now described as traditional "investment banking" consists of the following.

- *Underwriting*: The bank "underwrites" a share or bond issue by guaranteeing a certain price for the shares or bonds. For example, if a government wants to issue new bonds, it will hire an investment bank to underwrite and sell the issue on the government's behalf. The bank will guarantee the government a certain price, and hope to sell the bond at a higher price. Likewise with a share issue, or IPO, the bank will guarantee the firm a certain price for the share, and expect to place the share at or above that price. The bank earns a fee for the service. In addition, it earns the excess of a bond or share that is sold at a price higher than the amount it is underwritten for.
- *Mergers and Acquisitions*: The bank, for a fee, will act on behalf of one firm which is planning to merge or acquire another. For example, when Richard Branson wanted to sell Virgin Music in 1991, Goldman Sachs valued the firm at £500 million, and then set out to find a firm interested in acquiring it. Initially, no firm appeared willing to pay £500 million, but by negotiating with two rival buyers, Goldman Sachs was able to sell it for £560 million.

Any bank has to have a good reputation to engage in underwriting and mergers and acquisitions, which takes time to earn. Clients must be given top priority and the client relationship developed over time. For example, when Mr Whitehead set up the Investment Banking Services division, the sales people in the division focused on large numbers of companies in a defined geographical area assigned to them, with the plan to develop relationships over a long period of time. Likewise, Sidney Weinberg organised Ford's original share issue in 1956, but this was after years of cultivating a relationship with Henry Ford. Weinberg's reputation for being on more than 30 Boards of Directors was also motivated by the need to cultivate relationships. The advantage of relationship banking is obtaining information on the firm over a long period of time, and for the client, getting to know the banker well. The drawback of relationship banking is that it can give rise to opportunistic behaviour by either party, that is taking advantage of the trust gained as a result of the relationship. Goldmans was to suffer this as a consequence of its dealings with Robert Maxwell (see case).

## *Fixed income, Foreign exchange and Equities Trading*

This type of trading can be described as a *flow* business: On behalf of the bank's clients, which may include other market makers, the bank "makes markets": making bid (in the

---

[17] Source: Goldman Sachs, *Annual Report 2002*, p. 59.

case of a sale) and offer (when the asset is bought) prices for equities, bonds, foreign exchange or commodities. The firm is exposed to price or market risk because it is quoting bid and offer prices for the asset in question. The market risk is hedged through deals with other market makers. The trader profits from the difference between the bid and offer price. Given the small margins, the trader relies on large volumes to make a reasonable profit on the small margin between the bid and offer price for each transaction. Traders are backed up by a sales team, whose job it is to find clients for the equities, bonds, foreign exchange or commodities. A bank such as Goldman Sachs will also use its large client base from other parts of the firm (e.g. investment banking) to provide business for this trading.

### *Proprietary Trading*

With proprietary trading, the firm is trading on its own account: seeking to profit from trades. It is a logical extension of the traditional trading described above, because the firm is using the experience gained from the traditional forms of trading. Proprietary trading, if successful, can be very profitable but unlike the other types of trading, the capital of the firm is at risk. A bank engaging in proprietary trading will have two books, a banking book and a trading book. Though GS had engaged in some proprietary trading in the 1980s, it was after 1991 that the division began to make large amounts of money, after it hired a trader with a good track record, *Larry Beccerra* for the London office. Within 9 months, the trader had made a profit of $58 million for GS. This was followed by a profitable bet on interest rates prior to the election in April 1992 when the Conservatives won an unexpected victory. The price of government gilts (like US Treasury bonds) fell as the expectation of a Conservative defeat increased. The view of GS was that even if Labour did get in, they would use Conservative policies to manage the economy, and the decline in gilt prices was unwarranted, or put another way, the rising risk premium on UK government paper, too high. As most traders sold gilts, Henry Bedford held 5000 gilt contracts. The losses mounted as the election approached, but with the surprise victory, the $8 million loss on the day of the election turned into a $20 million profit within two days.

Unlike the other types of business, there is nothing to be gained by building up relationships[18] in proprietary trading, and it is very much a short-term activity. Some partners expressed concern at the break with the GS tradition, but proprietary trading was here to stay. However, proprietary trading brought with it a new set of problems. First, there were new potential conflicts of interest, part of the wider ***principal agent*** problem, or more generally, ***agency*** problems.

With proprietary trading, agency problems arise because it can undermine relationship banking because of the conflict of interest: a bank can advise clients to invest in certain stock when it has purchased a large amount in that same stock. Or when underwriting, encourage its own book to purchase shares.

*Example*: Goldmans had the Whitehall Street Real Estate LP Fund. It invested in assets of troubled real estate and property development firms. This fund that was largely responsible for forcing Cadillac Fairview, a Toronto property developer, into bankruptcy. There was a

---

[18] Though information is important for the traders, and the many clients GS was a good source of information.

serious conflict of interest because investors in Cadillac Fairview were also Goldman clients, which undermined Goldman's reputation as a "relationship" bank because it appeared to be more interested in acquiring assets at a discount.

The second problem aggravated (if not created) by proprietary trading related to staffing. Goldmans prided itself on offering lifetime employment to the best and the brightest. With the growth of this type of trading, many key staff were being brought in at relatively senior levels, without having served their time working their way up through the organisation. For example, Berrera had had a varied career when he was hired as a senior proprietary trader.

A second related problem was compensation. GS paid well but was not competitive with other banks because partnership was considered the ultimate reward. In many banks, compensation was an objective measure, based on contribution to profits: the greater the contribution, the higher the compensation. Goldmans shunned such an approach. To quote Mr Friedman,

> "No one at the trading desk gets a share of the profits. No one in mergers gets a share of the fee. We wanted everyone to think of the firm's interest, as opposed to their own personal interest" (Endlich, 1999, p. 168).

The problem with directly linking compensation to the trader's profitability is that it encouraged excessive risk taking and discouraged team effort. Nonetheless, GS began to lose some of its best people to other banks that rewarded individual effort.

## References

Endlich, L. (1999), *Goldman Sachs: The Culture of Success*, London: Little Brown and Company.

Freedman, R.D. and J. Vohr (1991), "Goldman Sachs/Lehman Brothers", Case Series in Finance and Economics, C50, New York University Salomon Center, Leonard N. Stern School of Business.

Goldman Sachs (2000/01/02/03), *Annual Report* for various years. Available on-line/in pdf format from www.gs.com

Heffernan, S.A. (1996), *Modern Banking in Theory and Practice*, Chichester, UK: John Wiley & Sons.

International Financing Review (2000), *Review of the Year*, London: Thomson Financial.

## Questions

1. Why is an investment bank called "a bank"? Illustrate using the Goldman Sachs case.
2. Explain the following terms, and how they relate to the case: (a) PE ratio; (b) bid–offer price; (c) relationship banking; (d) block share trading; (e) IPO; (f) proprietary trading; (g) corporate culture; (h) the difference between firewalls and Chinese walls.
3. What is the difference between traditional investment banking and "trading"? Why is there animosity between the two groups?
4. Define the "principal agent" problem, and illustrate how it can arise in (a) a bank owned by partners, such as Goldman Sachs; (b) a bank owned by shareholders, such

as American Express; (c) banks in relation to their customers; (d) bank management and employees.

5. Using the case, explain why reputation is important to the success of an investment bank.

6. Use the case to explain how volatile interest rates can affect the banks' trading income. What action did the firm undertake to minimise the chance of a similar event occurring in the future?

7. Goldman Sachs took a relatively long period of time to seek a public listing. Based on the GS experience, identify the conditions needed for a successful IPO (initial public listing).

8. What is corporate governance and how did it change over time at Goldman Sachs? How has going public affected corporate governance?

9. The current organisational structure at GS consists of three segments: investment banking, trading and principal investments, asset management and securities. The operating results for GS appear in Table 10.2. Work out the percentage contribution to pre-tax earnings for each of the three segments over 2000, 2001 and 2002. Which segments have increased their pre-tax earnings since 2000; which have decreased? Why?

10. (a) In 2002/3, Goldman Sachs was one of 10 investment banks to pay a total $110 million in fines and related payments to US regulatory authorities. Why? What implications, if any, does this incident have for the future of Goldman Sachs?

   (b) How will the Sarbanes–Oxley Act (July 2002) affect Goldman Sachs?[19]

11. Choose two other banks* which you consider to be major rivals to Goldman Sachs. Using their respective annual reports and sources such as *Bankscope* and *The Banker*, prepare a table comparing Goldman Sachs with the other firms for the most recent three years. Rank Goldman Sachs in terms of: total assets, net interest margin, return on average assets, return on average equity, and the ratio of operating expenses to net revenue (a measure of efficiency, sometimes called the ratio of cost to income).

   (a) Are these major rivals strictly comparable, and if not, why not? What problems, if any, did you encounter with some of these banks when compiling the data?

   (b) In recent annual reports (e.g. 2002), the banks report VaR figures for recent years. Briefly explain the meaning of value of risk, its advantages and limitations. Can the VaR figures reported by one bank be compared with those reported by the other two banks? If not, what are the differences?

*For example: Barclays Capital, Credit Suisse/Credit Suisse First Boston, Deutsche Bank, Dresdner Kleinwort Benson Wasserstein, HSBC, JP Morgan Chase, Lehman Brothers, Merrill Lynch, Morgan Stanley (Dean Witter), Schroder, Salomon Smith Barney, UBS Warburg.

---

[19] See Chapter 5. For more background reading see a brief symposium paper, "Can Regulation Prevent Corporate Wrong-Doing?" (pp. 27–42), "Rush to Legislate" (pp. 43–47) and "Sarbanes–Oxley in Brief" (pp. 48–50). These papers appear in *The Financial Regulator*, 7(2), September, 2002.

## 10.3. Kidder Peabody Group[20]

*Relevant Parts of The Text:* Chapters 1 (investment banks, financial conglomerates) 2 and 9 (synergy, strategy).

> "But Leo", said Alan Horrvich, a third-year financial analyst at General Electric Capital Corporation (GECC) in September 1987: "I don't know anything about investment banking. If I walk in there with a lot of amateurish ideas for what he ought to do with Kidder, Cathart will rip me apart. OK, you're the boss, but why me?"

> "Look Alan", replied Mr Leo Halaran, Senior Vice-President, Finance of GECC: "we've got ten thousand things going on here right now and Cathart calls up and says, very politely, that he wants somebody very bright to work with him on a strategic review of Kidder Peabody. You're bright, you spent a semester in the specialised finance MBA programme at City University Business School in London, you earned that fancy MBA from New York University down there in Wall Street, and you are available right now, so you're our man. Relax, Si isn't all that tough. If you make it through the first few weeks without getting sent back, you've got a friend for life...", he ended with a grin. "Me."

Mr Silas S. Cathart, 61, had retired as Chairman and CEO of Illinois Tool Works in 1986. He had been a director of the General Electric Company for many years and was much admired as a first-rate, tough though diplomatic results-oriented manager. After the resignation of Mr Ralph DeNunzio as Chairman and CEO of Kidder Peabody following the management shake-up in May 1987, Mr Cathart had been asked by Mr Jack Welch, GE's hard-driving, young CEO, to set aside his retirement for a while and take over as CEO of Kidder Peabody, to give it the firm leadership it needed, particularly now. Cathart had not been able to say no. His first few months were spent trying to get a grip on the situation at Kidder, which had been traumatised by the insider trading problems, and by management uncertainty as to what GE and its outside CEO were going to do to Kidder next. After reporting substantial earnings of nearly $100 million in 1986, Kidder was expected to incur a significant loss in 1987.

Technically, Cathart and Kidder reported to Mr Gary Wendt, President and Chief Operating Officer of General Electric Financial Services (GEFC) and CEO of GECC, but Alan understood everyone believed that old Si reported only to himself and Mr Welch. Mr Cathart wasn't going to be in the job for that long and could not care less about company politics. All he had to do was return Kidder to profitability, and set it on the right strategic course – one that made sense to both the Kidder shareholders and the GE crowd. After that, he could go back to his retirement and let someone else take over.

---

[20] This case first appeared in the New York University Salomon Center Case Series on Banking and Finance (Case 26). Written by Roy Smith (1988). The case was edited and updated by Shelagh Heffernan; questions set by Shelagh Heffernan.

Everyone Alan had talked to at GECC felt that the job would be very tough, and that Cathart might be at a big disadvantage because he did not have prior experience in the securities industry.

Alan's plan was to play it dead straight with Mr Cathart, to work most of the night getting the basics under his belt, and to consider Kidder's strategic position, and how to implement any proposed changes. If asked something he did not know, he would simply say he did not know but would try to find out. A chronology of significant events is summarised below.

## 10.3.1. Chronology of Significant Events, 1986–87

### April 1986

General Electric Financial Services agreed to pay $600 million for an 80% interest in Kidder Peabody and Company, leaving the remaining 20% in the hands of the firm's management. GEFS is a wholly owned subsidiary of General Electric Company. The price paid was about three times the book value – each shareholder was to receive a cash payment equal to 50% of the shares being sold, the remainder being paid out over three years. GEFS was to replace the shareholder capital with an initial infusion of $300 million, with more to follow. When the transaction closed in June 1986, GE and Kidder shareholders had invested more equity in the firm than previously announced – Kidder's total capital was boosted to $700 million.

Mr Robert C. Wright, head of GEFS, claimed the expansion of investment banking activities would mean GEFS's sophisticated financial products in leasing and lending could be combined with corporate financing, advisory services and trading capability at Kidders. There was no plan to institute any management changes.

Kidder ranked 15th among investment banks in terms of capital, and had 2000 retail brokers in 68 offices. The view was that it was too small to compete with the giants, but too large to be a niche player, making it an awkward size. Among analysts, it was generally accepted that Kidder had not been purchased for its retail network, but rather, for its institutional and investment banking capabilities.

Kidder initiated the talks with GE. It was believed the firm agreed to give up its independence as a means of using a more aggressive strategy to achieve a better image – there was a general perception that it was being left behind.

### October 1986

Mr Ivan Boesky was arrested for insider trading. He implicated Mr Martin A. Siegel, a managing director of Drexel Burnham Lambert, who had been head of Kidder Peabody's merger and acquisition department until his departure in February 1986 to join Drexel.

### December 1986

Kidder reorganised its investment banking division. Eighty-five professionals were transferred to the merchant banking division, 45 of whom were placed in acquisition advisory, and another 40 in the high-yield junk bond department. The group was headed by Mr Peter Goodson, a Kidder managing director, who at the time noted the move was a fundamental change in management structure. Mr Goodson did not anticipate any long-term effects from the insider trading scandal.

### February 1987

The 1986 Kidder Annual Report emphasised the importance of synergies apparent in the combination of Kidder Peabody and GEFS – it was believed the synergies far exceeded the firm's expectations. A source of new business at Kidder was existing customer relationships with hundreds of middle-sized American firms at GEF. Additional capital from GEFC allowed Kidder to provide direct financing, picking up a sizeable number of new clients.

The Kidder Annual Report also revealed Kidder's core business had been reorganised to reinforce competitive strengths and facilitate future growth. A global capital markets group was formed under Mr Max C. Chapman Jr (President of Kidder, Peabody and Co., Incorporated), to direct the investment banking, merchant banking, asset finance, fixed income and financial futures operations on a world-wide basis. Mr John T. Roche, President and Chief Operating Officer, Kidder Peabody Group Inc., established an equity group. Mr William Ferrell headed up a municipal securities group, formed from the merger of the public finance and municipal securities groups. The CEO, Mr Ralph DeNunzio, claimed these changes were made to ensure the firm was in a position to compete effectively in the global market place.

### February 1987

Mr Richard B. Wigton, Managing Director, was arrested in his office by federal marshalls on charges of insider trading. A former employee, Mr Timothy Tabor, was also arrested. Both arrests were the result of allegations made against them and Mr Robert Freedman of Goldman Sachs and Company by Martin Siegel, who, next day, pleaded guilty to insider trading and other charges brought against him. Kidder's accountants, Deloitte, Haskin and Sells, qualified Kidder's 1986 financial statements because they were unable to evaluate the impact of insider trading charges. Kidder reported earnings of $90 million (compared to $47 million earned in 1985); ROE was 27%.

The New York Stock Exchange fined Kidder Peabody $300 000 for alleged violations of capital and other rules. Two senior officials, including the President, Mr Roche, were fined $25 000 each for their role in these violations.

The *Wall Street Journal* reported that Mr DeNunzio had instructed Martin Siegel to help start a takeover arbitrage department in March 1984; Mr DeNunzio had indicated that the role played by Mr Siegel should not be disclosed publicly – there were inherent conflicts in having the head of mergers and acquisitions directly involved in trading on takeover rumours. A Kidder spokesman said the report was a "misstatement", and denied that Mr DeNunzio had ordered the formation of such a unit.

## May 1987

Mr Lawrence Bossidy, Vice-Chairman of GE and head of all financial services, announced a management shake-up at Kidder Peabody: Mr DeNunzio, Mr Roche and Kidder's General Counsel, Mr Krantz, would be replaced. Following the arrests, GE sent in a team to assess Kidder. The internal investigation revealed the need for improved procedures and controls. Mr Cathart was to take over as Kidder's CEO. GE men were also brought in to fill the positions of chief financial and chief operating officers, and a senior vice-president's position for business development. The board of directors was also restructured, to ensure GE had a majority of seats on the Kidder board. In the same month, charges against Messrs Wigton, Tabor and Freedman were dismissed without prejudice, though it was expected they would be charged at some future date.

## June 1987

GE required Kidder to settle matters with the Federal Prosecutor and the SEC. In exchange for a $25 million payment and other concessions, including giving up the takeover arbitrage business, the US Attorney agreed not to indict Kidder Peabody on criminal charges related to insider trading. Civil litigation against Kidder was still possible, though it would not have the same stigma as criminal charges and conviction. GEFS also agreed to provide an additional $100 million of subordinated debt capital to Kidder Peabody.

## July 1987

GE announced its first half results. At the time, GE said its financial services were ahead of a year ago because of the strong performance at GECC (GE Capital Corporation) and ERC (Employers Reinsurance Corporation), which more than offset the effects of special provisions at Kidder Peabody for settlements reached with the government. It was estimated that Kidder had lost about $18 million in the second quarter.

## September 1987

Mr DeNunzio retired from Kidder Peabody after 34 years of service. For 20 of these years, he had been Kidder's principal executive officer. The *Wall Street Journal* reported that morale at Kidder Peabody was improving, with GE and Kidder officials conducting a full strategic review of the firm. It was also announced that Kidder planned to establish a full service foreign exchange operation and would operate trading desks in London and the Far East.

## 1989–94

Mr Michael Carpenter joined Kidder as "head" in 1989, just as the bank was reeling from the insider trading scandal. In a deal negotiated with the SEC, Kidder was required to close down its successful risk arbitrage department. This was quite a blow to Kidder because its other businesses were only mediocre.

Kidder had an excellent reputation, but was saddled with high expenses and many unproductive brokers. Half of the firm's retail offices produced no profit at all. In 1989, a number of the productive brokers left Kidder because of dissatisfaction with the level of bonuses. These departures, together with the closure of the risk arbitrage department, resulted in a net $53 million loss in 1989, and a loss of $54 million in 1990.

Mr Carpenter's arrival resulted in millions of dollars and a great deal of management time had been spent nursing Kidder back to health. The bank was also building up its investment banking operations. Profits rose in 1991; in 1992 they peaked at $258 million.

Most of Kidder's profits came from its fixed income securities operations, the one area where it had managed to establish a lead over other investment houses. Underwriting and trading mortgage backed securities (MBSs) pushed Kidder up the underwriting league tables. During this time, the profits from mortgage backed securities were said to have accounted for about 70% of total profits.

Unfortunately, the sharp rise in interest rates at the start of 1994 hurt the mortgage backed business. The consequences of the "go for it strategy" with MBSs was seen in the first quarter of 1994 – Kidder lost more than $25 million.

The same year, Kidder took a loss of around $25 million on margin trades entered into with Askin Capital Management, a hedge fund group which had to seek protection from its creditors, because of trading losses.

Mr Carpenter's attempts to build Kidder's other businesses produced mixed results. By reducing costs and firing unproductive brokers, Carpenter succeeded in turning round the retail brokerage business – it was the most profitable business, after the fixed income department. But Carpenter's objective of achieving synergy between GE Capital and Kidder Peabody had been far from successful. There was a great degree of animosity between Mr Carpenter and Mr Gary Wendt, the CEO of GE Capital. It was reported that when clients wanted GE Capital to put up money for a deal, they would avoid using Kidder as their investment banker. Mr Welch was reported as saying, "The only synergies that exist between Kidder and GE Capital are Capital's AAA credit rating".

In April 1994 it was revealed that Kidder had reported $350 million in fictitious profits because of an alleged phantom trading scheme. Kidder blamed Mr Joseph Jett, who had been accused of creating the fictitious profits between November 1991 and March 1994. Kidder had to take a $210 million charge against its first quarter earnings in 1994. There was also the question of how a person with so little experience could have been appointed to a position bearing so much responsibility. This fiasco was reminiscent of a deal that went sour for Kidder in autumn 1993, which cost Kidder $1.7 million. The deal was headed by Mr Kaplan, who like Mr Jett, had insufficient experience.

Both the SEC and the New York Stock Exchange (NYSE) launched enquiries into the Jett affair. In a report prepared by Gary Lynch (who is a lawyer with the law firm that represented Kidder in an arbitration case against Joseph Jett), it was concluded that there was lax oversight and poor judgement by Mr Jett's superiors, including Mr Cerrullo (former fixed income head) and Mr Mullin (former derivatives boss). The report suspiciously supports Kidder's claim that no other person knowingly acted with Mr Jett. Kidder's top managers should have been suspicious because Mr Jett was producing high profits in government bond trading – never a Kidder strength. Some of the blame can be attributed to the aggressive corporate culture of Kidder. At an internal Kidder conference, Jett was reported to have told 130 of the firm's senior executives "you make money at all costs".

However, from details that have been revealed in the prepared reports, it is evident that there were problems at Kidder long before the Jett affair, indeed, even before Jett arrived. For example, in December 1993 Kidder had the highest gearing ratio of any bank on Wall Street, at 100 to 1. Mr Jack Welch of GE attempted to restore the reputation of GE by disciplining or dismissing those responsible. Mr Michael Carpenter was pressurised into resigning; both Mr Mullin and Mr Cerrullo were fired.

On 17 October 1994, GE announced GE Capital was to sell Kidder Peabody to Paine Webber, another investment bank. The sale included the parts of Kidder that Paine Webber wished to purchase. GE Capital also transferred $580 million in liquid securities to Paine Webber, part of Kidder's inventory. In return GE Capital received shares in Paine Webber worth $670 million. Thus GE received a net of $90 million for a firm that it had purchased for $600 million in 1986, though GE also obtained a 25% stake in Paine Webber.

## Questions

1. How might a conglomerate go about assessing the real worth of an investment bank when so many of the assets are intangible?
2. Identify the areas of potential "synergy" for Kidder and GEFS. In this context, explain the differences between synergy and economies of scale/scope.
3. Was the emphasis on developing investment banking and corporate finance rather than the use of Kidder's retail outlets a wise decision?
4. Given Mr Cathart's mission of restoring Kidder to profitability, what advice might Alan Horrvich give? What are the implications for each strategic alternative?
5. What in fact happened after 1987?
6. Summarise the various scandals associated with Kidder Peabody. What factors made this firm prone to scandals?
7. In 1994, GE divested itself of Kidder Peabody. The extent of the failure of this "match" is illustrated by the sale of Kidder to Paine Webber for a net of $90 million, compared to the $600 million price tag for Kidder in 1986.
   (a) Did GE pay too much for Kidder in 1986? Why?
   (b) How much is GE to blame for the subsequent problems at Kidder? Could these problems have been avoided?
8. Was GE wise to take a 25% stake in Paine Webber?

## 10.4. From Sakura to Sumitomo Mitsui Financial Group[21]

In 1991–2 Sakura Bank, the product of a merger between two other banks, was Japan's and the world's second largest bank in terms of assets, valued at $438 billion. It was also one of the largest measured by capitalisation of common stock ($41.4 billion). Roughly a decade later, it merged again to form Sumitomo Matsui Financial Group (SMFG), and while the new bank remains in the top 10 by tier 1 capital, it has dropped out of the top 25 in terms of market capitalisation.

Sakura Bank was formed through the merger of the Mitsui Bank, a distinguished Tokyo bank which dated back to 1683, with the Taiyo Kobe Bank, a regional, largely retail bank covering the region of Kansai, including Osaka, Kobe and Kyoto. The Taiyo Kobe Bank was itself the result of an earlier merger between the Taiyo Bank and the Bank of Kobe.

The merger took place in April 1990 – the new bank was to be called the Mitsui Taiyo Kobe Bank until the banks were properly integrated. At that time, it would be renamed the Sakura Bank, after "cherry blossom", a symbol of unity and grace in the Japanese culture. In April 1992, the merged bank became the Sakura Bank.

Japan's Ministry of Finance (MoF) is thought to have strongly encouraged the merger because, at the time, bank mergers in Japan were rare, and usually occurred between a healthy institution and an unhealthy one. These two banks were both financially sound, but when the MOF "encouraged", banks obliged. At the time, the MoF was a regulatory power house and had been since the end of the war. With its five bureaux (Banking, Securities, International Finance, Tax and Budget), it was the key financial regulator, engaged in all aspects of supervision: examination of financial firms, control of interest rates and products, supervision of deposit protection, and setting rules on the activities of financial firms.

The newly merged bank had the most extensive retail branch network of any bank in Japan, with 612 branches and 108 international offices. The merger took place for several reasons:

- To improve consolidation of the banking sector, so it is better able to compete in a deregulated market.
- To create a "universal" bank, providing high-quality management and information systems.
- To achieve greater economies of scale.
- To achieve a greater diversification of credit risk.
- To use the bank's increased size and lending power to increase market share.

Past experience had shown that Japanese bank mergers were rarely successful, because strong cultural links in each bank made it difficult to combine staff, clients and facilities. Furthermore, until the mid-1990s there was a reluctance to make anyone redundant from a

---

[21] This case first appeared as Case 25 of the New York Salomon Center Case Series in Banking and Finance, written by Roy C. Smith (1992). The case was subsequently edited and updated by Heffernan (1994). This version is a major revision and update of the 1994 case.

Japanese firm or to change those in authority. But the announcement, in April 1992, that the merged bank was ready to use its new name, Sakura, suggested these difficulties had been overcome, and well inside the 3 years management originally announced it would take.

## 10.4.1. Background on the Japanese Banking System

The Japanese banking system is described in Chapter 5 of this book. For many years it was characterised by functional segmentation and close regulation by the Ministry of Finance and the Bank of Japan. During the 1970s Japanese banks experienced a period of steady growth and profitability. The Japanese are known for their high propensity to save, so banks could rely on households and corporations (earning revenues from export booms) for a steady supply of relatively cheap funds. The reputation that the Ministry of Finance and Bank of Japan had for casting a 100% safety net around the banking system meant, *ceteris paribus*, the cost of capital for Japanese banks was lower than for major banks headquartered in other industrialised countries.

The global presence of Japanese banks was noticeable by the late 1970s, but in the 1980s their international profile became even more pronounced because of the relatively low cost of deposits, surplus corporate funds, and the increased use of global capital markets. Lending activities increasingly took on a global profile. Japanese banks were sought out for virtually every major international financing deal. For example, in the RJR Nabisco takeover involving a leveraged buyout of $25 billion, Japanese participation was considered a crucial part of the financing. The combination of rapid asset growth and an appreciating yen meant that by 1994, six of the top 10 banks, ranked by asset size, were Japanese. By the late 1980s, Japanese banks had a reputation for being safe and relationship-oriented, but nothing special if measured by profit or innovations.

The reputation for "being safe" was partly due to the MoF's determination not to allow any banking failures in Japan – there had been no bank failures in the post-war period. It was also known that Japanese banks had substantial hidden reserves. Furthermore, banks held between 1% and 5% of the common stock of many of their corporate customers; these corporates, in turn, owned shares in the bank. The cross-shareholding positions had been built up in the early post-war period, before the Japanese stock market had commenced its 30-year rise. These shareholdings and urban branch real estate were recorded on the books at historic cost, and until the 1990s, the market value was far in excess of the book value.

The Japanese banks' ratio of capital to assets in the late 1980s appeared to be low compared to their US or European counterparts, but such ratios ignored the market value of their stockholdings and real estate. Also, Japanese banks were less profitable than banks in other countries for three reasons:

1. The emphasis on "relationship banking" obliged these banks to offer very low lending rates to their key corporate borrowers, especially the corporates which were part of the same keiretsu.
2. Operating costs are relatively high.
3. The Ministry of Finance discouraged financial innovation because of the concern that it might upset the established financial system.

Japanese banks appeared prepared to accept the relatively low profitability, in exchange for the protective nature of the system.

As Japanese banks became more involved in global activities, either through international lending, through the acquisition of foreign banks, or by multinational branching, they began to learn about the financial innovations available by the early 1980s. At the same time, the MoF accepted the reality of **imported deregulation**, that is, the financial sector would have to be deregulated to allow foreign financial firms to enter the Japanese market. The pressure for this change came from the mounting trade surplus Japan had with other countries and a new financial services regime in Europe that would penalise countries that did not offer EU banks "equal treatment". The MoF agreed to the gradual deregulation of domestic financial firms, and to lower entry barriers for foreign banks and securities houses. The MoF lifted *some* of the barriers separating different types of Japanese banks and between banks and securities firms, and began to allow market access to all qualified issuers or investors. The tight regulation of interest rates was relaxed. Though the full effects of the reforms were not expected to be felt until after 1994, Japanese banks and securities firms realised they would have to adjust to the inevitable effects of deregulation. However, these reforms were relatively minor compared to what was coming (Big Bang in 1996) and, as can be seen in Table 5.8 (Chapter 5), the big changes in the structure of the Japanese financial system did not occur until close to the turn of the century.

## 10.4.2. Zaitech and the Bubble Economy

As was the case in the west, by the mid-1980s, large Japanese corporations realised that issuing their own bonds could be a cheaper alternative to borrowing from Japanese banks. Also, an investment strategy known as *zaitech* was increasing in popularity: it was more profitable for a Japanese corporation to invest in financial assets rather than Japanese manufacturing businesses. Early on, these firms borrowed money for simple financial speculation, but over time the process became more sophisticated. Non-financial firms would issue securities with a low cash payout and use the money raised to invest in securities that were appreciating in value, such as real estate or a portfolio of stocks, warrants or options.

The heyday of zaitech was between 1984 and 1989 – Japanese firms issued a total of about $720 million in securities. More than 80% of these were equity securities. Japan's total new equity financing in this period was three times that of the USA, even though the US economy was twice the size of Japan's and it too was experiencing a boom. Just under half of these securities were sold in domestic markets, mainly in the form of convertible debentures (a bond issue where the investor has the option of converting the bond into a fixed number of common shares) and new share issues. The rest were sold in the euromarkets, usually as low coupon bonds with stock purchase warrants attached (a security similar to a convertible debenture but the conversion feature, as a warrant, can be detached and sold separately). The implication of a convertible debenture issue is that one day, new shares will be outstanding, thereby reducing earnings per share. But shareholders did not appear concerned, and share prices rarely declined following an issue.

Japanese banks were keen supporters of zaitech financing, because:

- They could underwrite the new corporate issues.
- They acted as guarantors of the payment of interest and principal on the bonds being issued.
- They could buy the warrants to replace stock in customer holdings, which allowed profits from a portfolio to be freed up, to be reinvested on a more leveraged basis.
- Once the warrants were detached, the bonds could be purchased at a discount of 30% to 40%.

The bonds could then be repackaged with an interest rate swap, and converted into a floating rate asset to be funded on the London deposit market, and held as a profitable international asset.

Zaitech became extremely popular among banks, corporations and investors alike, for different reasons. The late 1980s came to be known as the "bubble economy" in Japan because of the frequency with which financial market speculation, usually financed by margin loans, occurred. The prices of all financial assets, especially real estate and stocks, rose at rapid rates, encouraging yet more speculative behaviour.

As a result of zaitech and financial surpluses, Japanese companies were no longer dependent on extensive amounts of borrowing. Bank borrowing was not attractive if firms could issue bonds, which would be redeemed by conversion into common stock in the future. The ratios of long-term debt to equity (book value) began to decline for companies listed on the Tokyo Stock Exchange, from more than 50% in 1980 to about 39.6% at the end of 1990. By 1990, only 42% of corporate debt outstanding, or 17% of total capitalisation, was provided by bank loans. Bank loans that were negotiated often supported zaitech corporations or investment in bank certificates of deposit, which, because of relationship banking, the borrower could maintain at virtually no cost.

The fall in the leverage or gearing of Japanese firms was far more pronounced if equity is measured using market prices. By 1989, Japanese debt to equity ratios were half those of their US counterparts. But although many companies used surplus cash flows to repay debt, others engaged in zaitech – increasing debt to invest in other securities.

Thus, the real measure of leverage (gearing) was the ratio of net interest payable (interest received minus interest paid) to total operating income. By this measure, Japanese manufacturing companies, in aggregate, fell from 30% in 1980 to −5.3% in 1990. Thus, the manufacturing sector had become deleveraged or degeared: if zaitech holdings (based on December 1989 prices) were sold, they would have no debt at all.

## 10.4.3. Problem Loans and the Burst of the Bubble

Japanese banks had entered the global lending markets in the early 1980s and, determined to capture market share, competed on interest rates. The competition was not only with foreign banks, but other Japanese banks. Japanese banks became highly exposed in foreign loans, beginning with Latin American debt – they held portfolios of Third World loans which they had lent at below market rates. The MoF discouraged banks from writing off this debt after the Mexican crisis of 1982 – it wanted them to learn from their mistakes and exercise more discipline, and also, to limit tax credits taken by these write-offs. If banks were to write off loans, they had to do it off the books, by using the capital gains from the sale of securities and applying them against bad debt. Effectively, the banks' hidden assets became their loan loss reserves.

The Nikkei index peaked in December 1989 having risen sixfold since 1979, and then fell steadily to less than 15 000 in 1992, a 62% drop from its high. The real estate market followed, resulting in large losses for many zaitech players. The value of their zaitech holdings declined, but there was no change in their loan obligations. By the first half of 1991, bankruptcies in Japan had risen dramatically, with liabilities of $30 billion, six times that of 1989.

As the problems escalated, companies were compelled to sell off relationship sharehold-ings, which forced down share prices still further and led to expectations of future falls, which, in turn, caused further falls in share prices. The share price of companies known to be deep into zaitech dropped even further. For some they were well below the exercise prices of the outstanding warrants and convertible bonds that had been issued. The expectation had been that these bonds would be repaid through the conversion of the securities into common stock. If the conversions did not take place when the bond matured, the companies would have to pay off the bondholders. Over $100 billion of warrants and convertibles maturing in 1992 and 1993 were trading below their conversion prices in late 1991.

When the bubble burst, the number of problem loans to small businesses and individual customers increased dramatically. The shinkin banks were the most highly exposed, and it was expected that few would stay independent – the MoF would force troubled banks to merge with healthy ones. The big banks were also in trouble, but the degree of their problems was difficult to assess because banks were not required to declare a problem loan "non-performing" until at least one year after interest payments had ceased. However, it was the long-term banks which were the most affected, because they had been under the greatest pressure to find new business as borrowing by large corporations began to fall. Two key rating agencies downgraded the bond ratings of 10 major Japanese banks in 1990, though most remained in the Aa category. The rating agencies noted Japanese banks were a riskier investment with questionable profitability performance, but were also confident the MoF would intervene to prevent bank failures or defaults on obligations.

## 10.4.4. Application of the Basel Capital Assets Ratio

International banks headquartered in Japan were required to comply with Basel 1. Banks had to meet these capital adequacy standards by the beginning of 1993. Subsequently, the banks would have to comply with the market risk amendment approved in 1996, to be implemented by 1998 (see Chapter 6).

The interpretation of what counted as tier 2 capital was partly left to the discretion of regulators in a given country. The MoF allowed Japanese banks to count 45% (the after-tax equivalent amount) of their unrealised gains as tier 2 capital, because these banks had virtually no loan loss reserves. As share prices escalated in the 1980s, the value of the tier 2 capital increased, and many banks took advantage of the bubble economy to float new issues of tier 1 capital. But after December 1989, stock prices fell, and so did tier 2 capital, thereby reducing the banks' risk assets ratios. Japanese banks came under increasing pressure to satisfy the minimum requirements.

## 10.4.5. Sakura Bank in the 1990s

Sakura was one of the weakest performers of all the major Japanese city banks in 1991 because of high interest rates, small net interest margins, and rising overhead costs. The bank's stated risk asset ratios were, in March 1991, 3.67% for tier 1 and 7.35% for tiers 1 and 2. The average for Japanese banks was, respectively, 4.35% and 8.35%. Sakura's general expenses as a percentage of ordinary revenues were, on average, higher than for other city banks in the period 1988–90. Its net profits per employee were lower.

In its 1992 *Annual Report*, Sakura Bank acknowledged the new pressures of the Basel capital adequacy requirements, and noted that in the current environment it would be difficult to rely on new equity issues to increase the numerator of the risk assets ratio. Sakura intended to raise capital through subordinated debt and other means, and to limit the growth of assets. The bank's strategy was to focus on improving the return on assets and profitability. In anticipation of deregulating markets, Sakura wanted to increase efficiency and risk management techniques.

At this time, analysts believed the positive effects of the merger were just beginning to be felt, with additional benefits expected to be realised over the next 3 to 5 years. The benefits would be created through integration of merging branch networks and computer systems, and a reduction in personnel. Though operating profits were recovering, they remained depressed.

Unfortunately, this was not to be, and like all money centre banks, Sakura faced problems with mounting bad debt throughout the 1990s. With the announcement of Big Bang in 1996 (see Chapter 5), it was clear all banks would have to adjust to a new regulatory regime and could no longer rely on "regulatory guidance", whereby the banks effectively did what was asked of them by the MoF in return for an implicit safety net and protection in the form of a segmented market that stifled competition. Recall that Sakura itself was created from the merger of two banks, after pressure from the MoF. As has been noted, the MoF, fearing corporate bankruptcies, discouraged Japanese banks from declaring bad loans (and making the necessary provisioning) in the early years after the collapse of the stock market in 1989. Failure to write off bad debt in the early 1990s contributed to an ever-growing debt mountain throughout the decade.

Since its creation in 1991, Sakura Bank has been largely focused on retail banking, with the largest number of branches among the commercial banks, and an extensive ATM network. For example, it frequently topped the mortgage league tables, though with a slump in property prices, a large portfolio of housing related assets is less than ideal. The bank has comparatively small operations in the fields of asset management and investment banking.

Sakura's retail operations compete head on with the Japanese Post Office (JPO), which has been subsidised for years. The JPO is the traditional means by which the government raises cheap funds to finance public institutions. Until 1994, deposit rates were regulated and higher than the rates banks could offer. In 1994 they were deregulated, and in 1995, the MoF lifted restrictions on the types of savings deposits private banks could offer. But since the Post Office is not constrained to maximise profits, it has continued to attract deposits by offering higher rates than banks. For example, its main product is the *teigaku-chokin*, a fixed amount savings deposit. Once the designated amount has been on deposit for 6 months, it may be withdrawn without notice. However, it can be held on deposit for up to 10 years, at the interest rate paid on the original deposit, compounded semi-annually.[22] Thus, for example, if a deposit is made during a period of high interest rates, that rate can apply for up to 10 years. In 1996, five of the major banks (including Sakura) offered a similar type of savings deposit. However, these banks had to respond to changes in market interest rates, and could never guarantee a fixed rate over 10 years. Also, the JPO enjoys a number of implicit subsidies:

- Unlike banks, the JPO does not have to obtain MoF approval to open new branches. The JPO has a branch network of 24 000; letter couriers are used to facilitate cash deposits and withdrawals in one day, through the two deliveries. By contrast, Sakura Bank had just under 600 branches in the early 1990s, but cost considerations led to closures, so by the time it merged with Sumitomo, the number had fallen to 462.
- The JPO is exempt from a number of taxes, including corporate income tax and stamp duty.
- It does not have to pay deposit insurance premia, nor is it subject to reserve requirements.
- JPO deposit rates are set by the Ministry of Posts and Telecommunications, rather than the BJ/MoF.

One estimate put the state subsidy to the postal system at ¥730 billion per year, equivalent to 0.36% on postal savings deposits.[23] The result is a disproportionately high percentage (35%) of total savings and deposits being held at the Japanese Post Office, earning relatively low rates of return. In Japan, 17.8% of personal financial assets are held as JPO savings deposits compared to 2.9% in the UK and 1.8% in Germany.[24]

In September 1998, Sakura issued preference shares worth ¥300 billion ($43.7 billion) to members of the Mitsui keiretsu and Toyota Motor Corporation. The market responded positively, and Sakura's share price rose, but even so, the value of the bank is 50% lower than what it had been 9 months earlier, and 10% below the value it was at the time it was created. Put another way, Sakura was one of the largest banks in the world (measured by assets), but of little significance in terms of market capitalisation.

In March 1999, Sakura was one of several banks to take advantage of a banking package which had been approved by the Japanese Diet in October 1998. Worth ¥43 trillion ($360 bn), it was to be used to revitalise the banking sector through a programme of recapitalisation and restructuring. Part of the package consisted of capital injections and Sakura accepted one worth ¥7.45 trillion – the government bought preference shares, which would convert to ordinary banking stock between 3.5 months and 5 years.

---

[22] See Ito *et al.* (1998), p. 73.

[23] Source: Ministry of International Trade and Industry, as quoted in Ito *et al.* (1998), p. 73.

[24] See Ito *et al.* (1998), p. 71.

Sakura's attempts to raise capital through share issues reflected the pressure the bank was under to boost its capital to meet the Basel 1 risk assets ratio minimum of 8%. Increasing provisions for non-performing loans and a slump in equity prices (cross-shareholdings were falling in value) had depleted the bank of capital, and reserves.[25] At the same time, Sakura, like most banks, is reluctant to offer new loans, making it difficult for the manufacturing and retail sectors to recover from prolonged recession. Mr Akishige Okada (President) told a press conference the fresh capital was to be used for more aggressive action against non-performing loans, and to boost the capital adequacy ratio to 10%.

Though known for its retail banking presence, Sakura is also the key bank in the Mitsui keiretsu, and was always obliged to grant loans to its keiretsu members at favourable rates. As a consequence of this "relationship banking", Sakura is heavily exposed in property and related loans. For example, in December 2000, Mitsui Construction requested debt forgiveness on ¥163 billion. As the lead creditor, Sakura had to write off a substantial proportion of this debt. Though its global exposure is less than other money centre banks, it was enough to give rating agencies cause for concern. By late 1998, Sakura was carrying ¥1.47 trillion ($18 billion) in problem loans. A total of $11.8 billion had been loaned to Asian firms, with its biggest exposures in Hong Kong, Thailand, Singapore, China and Indonesia. At the time, most of these economies had been severely affected by the rapid downturn associated with the Asian crisis. Sakura considered about 41% of these to be low risk because the loans were to Japanese affiliated companies, with parent company guarantees. Also, the bank said provisions for loan losses in Asia had been included in the ¥1.7 trillion of loan provisions made in March, 1998.

Though Sakura's performance was dismal throughout the 1990s, it was not all doom and gloom. In September 2000, the regulatory authorities approved a plan to create an internet bank, Japan Net Bank (JNB), by a consortium led by Sakura. Sakura was to own 50% of the new bank, and several commercial concerns put up the rest of the capital, including an insurance firm, Tokyo Electric Power and Fujitsu Ltd. JNB offers the standard retail banking services. Deposits and withdrawals of cash are through Sakura's ATMs, which exceed 100 000. All other transactions are conducted using the internet. For example, if a loan is approved, the borrower can withdraw the cash from the ATM. As was noted in Chapter 2, JNB is one of two relatively successful internet banks in Japan. Mutual funds and insurance are some of the non-bank financial services on offer to JNB customers, reflecting the new financial structure emerging in Japan as a consequence of Big Bang. It is an example of a financial institution crossing the old boundaries associated with the segmented markets pre-Big Bang (see Table 5.8).

In addition, in June 2000, it took a controlling stake in Minato Bank, a regional bank located in Western Japan. Shares were purchased from Shinsei Bank (formerly the Long Term Credit Bank of Japan) and other institutions, making Minato Bank a (*de facto*)

---

[25] In 1998, shares in other companies held by the banks were still valued at historic cost. However, the banks were aware that because of the regulatory reforms, they would have to deduct equity losses from capital from 2001 and mark to market by 2002.

subsidiary of Sakura. It strengthens Sakura's presence in its home area, the Osako–Kobe region of Japan.

However, given Sakura's profile at the onset of the new millennium, it was clear a new alliance was needed to boost its capital strength, and to avoid being left behind in the trend towards forming mega banks. Sakura was aware it might be hit by a withdrawal of deposits from the bank, because, at the time, it was thought that the 100% deposit protection on retail deposits would be phased out by 2001.[26] Sakura had hoped to interest Deutsche Bank, but after careful scrutiny of Sakura's strengths and weaknesses, the German bank declined to make an offer. Sanwa Bank and Nomura were named as possible suitors, until Sanwa revealed it was to merge with the Asahi-Tokai group. In October 1999 came the surprise announcement that Sakura was to merge with Sumitomo Bank, to take place by April 2002. Sumitomo was considered one of the relatively strong money centre banks, though this is by comparison with quite a lack-lustre lot. Like the merger which had created Sakura in 1992, it was completed a year early, by April 2001.

Their activities complement each other. Sumitomo's strengths were in wholesale securities and asset management. In 1999, Sumitomo and Daiwa Securities had agreed a joint venture, with plans to set up a ¥300 billion fund (with GE Capital) to finance corporate mergers and acquisitions in Japan. Daiwa Securities received a much needed capital injection, while Sumitomo could expand in investment banking. Sakura was an established retail banking presence, including the internet bank, Japan Net Bank, both relatively cheap sources of funds.

Unlike the other mega mergers, the bank holding company model was not used by Sumitomo and Sakura. The merger was more traditional with an exchange of shares, with Sumitomo absorbing Sakura. The new bank was called Sumitomo Mitsui, an immediate reminder that this merger involves two financial arms of competing keiretsu – Sumitomo and Mitsui. It will have a single chairman, with 30 directors. By contrast Mizuho planned to have three chief executives, two chairmen and one president, and most of these banks have boards in excess of 50 members. The plan was to begin providing joint services at retail outlets, through the ATMs and internet banking. The Sumitomo–Daiwa alliance will be integrated with the (relatively small) securities subsidiary owned by Sakura. Investment banking operations (e.g. M&As) were merged, along with trust banking and insurance operations. At the time the merger was announced, the plan was to shed 9000 jobs (about a third of the joint workforce) and close overlapping branches.

The merger has been described as a "defensive" one, for a number of reasons:

- At the time of the merger (2002 figures), Sumitomo Mitsui was the third largest bank in the world measured by assets, following Mizuho Financial Group and Citigroup. Both

---

[26] To stem the increasing tide of deposit withdrawals, in 1998 the government announced a temporary 100% retail deposit protection, replacing the maximum payout of ¥10 000 yen. When the full guarantee on time deposits ended in April 2002, it prompted large transfers of cash from time deposits to current accounts, cash or gold. To stop this from happening again, current accounts remained covered – until March 2003, and in 2003 the deadline was extended again.

recognised that Big Bang and other factors were changing the structure of Japanese banking, especially among the top banks – mega banks were fast becoming the norm. The Mizuho Financial Group was formed through the merger of Fuji, Dai-ichi Kangyo, and the Industrial Bank of Japan in September 2000. In late 1999, Sanwa, Asahi and Tokai banks proposed a merger, though Asahi later withdrew. Instead, the UFJ holding company was established in April 2001 with Sanwa Bank, Tokai Bank and Toya Trust Bank. At the same time, another holding company, the Mitsubishi Tokyo Financial Group, was created when the Bank of Tokyo Mitsubishi and Mitsubishi Trust & Banking merged.[27]

- Japan's regulatory authorities had nationalised a bankrupt Long Term Credit Bank of Japan. It was sold to a US investment group, Ripplewood Holdings, operating under the new name, Shinsei Bank. However, the sale has proved controversial. Ripplewood secured a government guarantee that if existing loans fell by more than 20% below their value at the time of the sale, the Deposit Insurance Corporation would buy them at the original price, thereby covering any losses, a luxury other banks do not enjoy.

- The Ripplewood deal signalled the government's willingness to allow foreign ownership of Japanese banks, bringing with them knowledge of innovative techniques (e.g. expertise in the derivatives markets) lacking among Japan's banks and increasing competition.

- The approach of 2001, when 100% protection on bank deposits was supposed to end.

Sumitomo Matsui Financial Group (SMFG) faces considerable obstacles to success at the time of writing this case. The financial centres of two rival keiretsu have merged, which could upset relationships in them. In the end, however, a much stronger (perhaps too strong) single keiretsu could emerge. Japanese mergers, including the one that created Sakura, have a poor history of overcoming cultural differences, and getting rid of employees. Both banks have serious problems with non-performing loans that have not gone away. There is also the challenge of integrating and upgrading their computer systems.

In 2003, it was announced that Goldman Sachs would take the equivalent of a 7% stake in SMFG, investing ¥150 billion ($1.3 billion) in return for convertible preferred shares, carrying a 4.5% cash dividend after tax. A capital injection for SMFG, it gives Goldman's access to SMFG's very large portfolio of distressed assets.

SMFG also attempted a bid for Aozora Bank, formerly Nippon Credit Bank, until Softbank decided to sell its holdings in early 2003. An American private equity firm Cerberus, which already had a 12% stake, successfully bid for the 49% stake giving it a controlling interest in the bank. Cerberus also announced that a US businessman was to be Chairman of Aozora Bank of Japan. The approval by the Japanese authorities is further evidence of the regulators' commitment to allow foreign ownership of Japanese banks. Aozora had a relatively clean balance sheet at the time of the bid, bad loans having been

---

[27] Around the same time, three trust banks merged: Mitsubishi Trust and Banking, Nippon Trust Bank and Tokyo Trust Bank.

written off in earlier years, and big loan loss reserves are in place for the remaining risk assets. In 2003, problem loans were less than 5% of total loans, about a threefold reduction since 2002, and its Basel 1 risk assets ratio is around 12% – about 2% higher than the top four Japanese banks. It also has close connections with regional banks.

The 2002 financial results of the big four banks were dismal, and came with an announcement of a large increase in non-performing loans, equal to ¥26 800 billion, compared to ¥18 000 billion in the previous financial year. As a result, all the big four reported pre-tax losses. At the time, they were confident they would be in profit by 2003. However, in 2003, pre-tax losses for the four mega banks amounted to ¥4000 billion ($31.7 billion). Of The Banker's top 1000 banks, three of these banks placed at the top for pre-tax losses. SMFG was in third place after Mizuho (first) and UFI (second).[28] The results were due to exceptionally high provisioning for non-performing loans, and the new mark to market regulations caused a 30% fall in share prices. Banks had been hopeful they could generate revenue through higher lending margins (the average interest rate on corporate loans fell), fee income (increased by just 1%) and trust income (fell by 7%). Cost cutting, in the form of job cuts and branch closures, will have to continue. Sumitomo Mitsui was considered to be somewhat unique, because its exposure to several large (e.g. construction, property) companies leaves it in a comparatively weak asset position, and could overwhelm the effects of improved revenues and cost-cutting. The table below suggests SMGF has some way to go on cutting costs. At the time of the merger it was announced that 9000 employees (one-third of its workforce) would be cut from the payroll.

|  | Branches | No. of employees |
| --- | --- | --- |
| **2003** | | |
| SMFG | 403 | 30 944 |
| **1999** | | |
| Sumitomo | 284 | 16 330 |
| Sakura | 462 | 14 995 |

Source: The Banker, July issues, 1999, 2003.

SMFG, along with the other mega banks, are predicting profits for 2004. Many analysts think the banks will be plagued by "massive" non-performing loans for at least another two years.

## Questions

1. In the context of this case, explain the meaning of: (a) imported deregulation; (b) zaitech; (c) the EU's application of "equal treatment" and its implications for Japanese banks; (d) "relationship banking" in Japan; (e) universal banking in Japan.

---

[28] They were in prestigious company: Credit Suisse Group, West LB, Abbey National and Dresdner were also in the bottom 10 banks measured by pre-tax losses. Source: The Banker (2003), p. 180.

2. (a) Why has the cost of raising capital on global markets traditionally been lower for Japanese banks than for banks headquartered in western countries?

   (b) Is this still the case? Give reasons for your answer.

3. Using the case and the description of the Japanese banking structure found in Chapter 5, answer the following:

   (a) Why would the merger of a regional bank and a city bank achieve a greater diversification of credit risk?

   (b) Did functional segmentation encourage zaitech?

   (c) Why were the long-term credit banks more heavily exposed in zaitech operations than other types of banks in Japan?

   (d) Why is the Japanese Post Office one of Sakura/SMFG's main competitors? Can it build a profitable retail banking business in the presence of the Japanese Post Office?

   (e) Is the "bubble economy" described in this case the same as Minsky's financial fragility, defined in Chapter 4?

4. (a) What role did the MoF play in shaping the competitive capabilities of Japanese banks?

   (b) How will Big Bang and the Financial Services Agency (FSA) affect the future structure of Japanese banking?

5. The main Japanese banks appear, in recent years, to be setting aside large provisions for their non-performing loans, even though this eats into their profits. Is this the correct strategy?

6. Achieving economies of scale and/or scope is normally cited as one of the key reasons why banks and other firms enter into a merger.

   (a) To what extent does this argument apply in the Sakura/Sumitomo merger?

   (b) What strengths/weaknesses do the two banks bring with them into the merger?

   (c) What are implications of this merger for the keiretsu system in Japan?

7. Using the July issues of *The Banker*, complete a spreadsheet on the performance of Sakura, Sumitomo, 1992 to the most recent year possible and Sumitomo Matsui Financial Group (SMFG), 2002 to the most recent year possible. For each year, report: tier 1 capital, assets, the ratio of capital to assets, pre-tax profits, the ratio of profit to capital, return on assets, the Basel 1 risk assets ratio (*The Banker* calls it the "BIS ratio"), the ratio of cost to income, and non-performing loans as a percentage of total loans. If some of the measures are not available (na), report them on the spreadsheet as such. This exercise should:

   (a) Explain the meaning and comment on the usefulness of each of these performance measures.

   (b) Compare the performance of Sakura, Sumitomo and SMFG before and after the merger.

   (c) Obtain the same financial ratios, etc. using the most-recent data for at least two other Japanese banks in the top 5 (measured by tier 1 capital), two of the top 4 US banks, and two of the top 4 UK banks. Comment on the performance of SMFG compared to these other banks.

   (d) Discuss the future prospects for SMFG. Will the merger succeed in creating a profitable bank, able to compete on global markets?

## 10.5. Bancomer: A Study of an Emerging Market Bank[29]

*Relevant parts of text:* Chapter 6 (currency, market, sovereign and political risk).

On 1 September 1982, following the moratorium on the repayment of foreign debt, a balance of payments crisis, the imposition of exchange controls and a substantial devaluation of the peso, President José Lopez Portillo nationalised Mexico's six commercial banks. Over the next 9 years, the government channelled savings from these depository institutions to finance the national fiscal deficit. The management teams of banks remained under state control and given very little discretion over investment and personnel decisions. There was little scope for strategic planning. Instead, management's focus was on making financial resources available to the government through deposit-gathering, in return for the right to levy fees and other charges on the bank's depositors. Most of their assets were government bonds. Mexican banks had ceased to be the primary provider of market-oriented financial services to the Mexican public. While under state ownership and control, the Mexican banks were well capitalised and noted for their overall stability, sustained growth and profitability.

By the beginning of the 1990s, the Mexican economy had largely recovered from the dark days of "default", when the country announced it could no longer service its sovereign external debt. The Baker and Brady plans, together with IMF restructuring, had resulted in more realistic external debt repayments, via, for example, Brady bonds (see Chapter 6), an economy more open to foreign competition, privatisation and fiscal reform. The inflation rate fell from 30% in 1990 to 7% in 1993–4, with a reasonable annual GDP growth rate of 3–4%. Exchange rate policy was moving in the direction of a more liberal managed floating regime, beginning with a fixed peg in 1988 to a crawling peg, and in 1991, a crawling trading band.[30] Net capital inflows in the early 1990s financed a current account deficit. President Carlos Salinas, elected in 1988 for a fixed 6-year term, took much of the credit for the economic transformation.

Given other sectors had undergone extensive economic reform, it seemed incongruous to have a state run banking system. The President was determined to introduce a range of financial reforms aimed at the development of a liberalised, market-oriented financial sector. In mid-1990, the Mexican Constitution was amended to permit individuals and companies to own controlling interests in commercial banks. A privatisation committee was created to oversee the sale of Mexico's banks to private investors.

The Mexican Banking Law was enacted to regulate the ownership and operation of commercial banks. Under the Financial Groups Law (1990), the universal banking model was adopted. A range of diverse financial activities (including commercial and investment

---

[29] This case first appeared in the New York University Salomon Center Case Series in Banking and Finance (Case No. 18). Written by Roy Smith and Ingo Walter (1992). It has been edited and substantially revised by Shelagh Heffernan. Questions by Shelagh Heffernan.

[30] The peso could fluctuate within a band. Peso appreciation was fixed, but peso depreciation could move within a band linked to the inflation rate. Source: Beim and Calomiris (2001), p306.

banking, stockbroking and insurance) would be conducted under a financial services holding company. The plan was to use universal banking to make the Mexican banking system more efficient and competitive. Financial institutions could achieve economies of scale and scope/exploit synergies, enter new markets and explore new growth and cross-marketing opportunities. The reforms would also help prepare the financial sector for expected increased competition after the North American Free Trade Agreement (1993) was reached between Mexico, Canada and the United States. In 1994, the authorities granted permission for the entry and establishment of 52 foreign banks, brokerage houses and other financial institutions. The foreign banks provided services for blue chips and large businesses. Mexican banks such as Bancomer would have to fight hard to retain some of this business.

## 10.5.1. Overview of Bancomer

Throughout its 60-year history, Bancomer's owners and management pursued a strategy which focused on growth in the retail and middle market sectors, with a strong marketing orientation, reflecting a willingness to respond to customer needs. It operated a decentralised management structure prior to nationalisation, which, it argued, made the bank highly responsive to community needs. Under nationalisation, decision-making became centralised and bureaucratic, in line with the objective of gathering deposits for investment in Mexican government securities.

With the announcement of pending privatisation, Bancomer reasserted these strategic objectives:

- Maintenance of a leading market position in retail banking and the middle market.
- Introduction of new financial products, and distribution of these products through an extensive branch network.
- Spreading financial risk through size, industry and geographic diversification of Bancomer customers and services.
- A willingness to hire qualified managers and consultants.
- Reinvesting in Bancomer's businesses, especially technology, branch expansion and personnel training.
- Maintaining conservative credit standards and diversifying risks, to ensure no single loan could have a significant effect on earnings.
- Maintenance of a strong capital base.

At the end of 1991, Bancomer's net worth was projected to be about $2 billion. It was well capitalised, and in a good position to take advantage of emerging opportunities in the Mexican market. Though the Mexican government might have been expected to be an aggressive seller, inviting as many potential bidders as it could, political supporters of President Salinas and the PRI (Institutional Revolutionary Party) were given special consideration when the banks were privatised.

By the time the privatisation of the banking sector had commenced, the basic banking skills of most banking staff were, at best, rusty, especially in the area of credit and risk assessment, since for many years banks had been the conduit for savings to finance the government's fiscal deficit. Even the key regulator, the Banco de Mexico, lacked the requisite skills and prudential rules to control bank risk taking.

Nonetheless, Bancomer undertook to improve its asset quality between 1989 and 1991. It absorbed a series of non-recurring charges and created reserves for loan losses which subsequently exceeded all the required regulatory levels. Bancomer's profitability during 1989–90 reflected these charges and reserves, as well as the costs of refocusing the business and the impact of recent declines in the Mexican rate of inflation. As shown in Table 10.3, in 1989–90, real profits fell by 22% but grew by nearly 66% between 1990 and 1991. In common with other Mexican banks, Bancomer had a growing asset base, reflecting, among other things, impressive growth in the Mexican economy, strong demand for credit in pesos and dollars, and Bancomer's increased market share in lending. As of 30 June 1991, assets totalled $24 billion.

Higher-quality credits made up 95% of Bancomer's portfolio as of 30 June 1991. Past-due, lower-quality credits made up 1.78% of the portfolio, compared to 2.79% the year before. Reserve coverage for lower-quality credits improved during the year. A credit review conducted by independent auditors concluded that Bancomer's portfolio was appropriately classified. Bancomer was also well capitalised. In June 1991, the bank's ratio of capital to weighted risk assets was 7.4%, exceeding the 6% minimum requirement for 1991 and the 7% minimum set for 1992. As can be seen from Table 10.1, the Basel ratio rose steadily throughout the 1990s.

In 1991, Bancomer's net income was forecast to grow to about $400 million, an increase of over 50% in real terms compared to 1990. Its return on average assets was 2.21%, up from 1.84% in 1990; return on average equity was 24%. The net interest margin increased from 7.22% in 1990 to 7.4% in 1991, reflecting a shift from lower-yielding government securities to higher-yielding private sector loans, together with lower-cost peso denominated deposits which made up a large portion of Bancomer's funding base.

When privatised in October 1991, Bancomer had about 760 branches and held 26% of Mexican deposits.[31] It was the second largest bank after Banamex when measured by tier 1 capital or assets. The government sold 51% (with an option to buy another 25%) to Valres de Monterrey S.A. (Vamsa), a publicly traded financial services holding company involved in financial leasing, factoring, warehouse bonding and broking, and one of the largest life insurance firms in Mexico. It was wholly owned by a very large Mexican conglomerate, Grupo Visa. Visa had a variety of holdings including a beverages company. PROA, a holding company, was controlled by the Garza Laguera family, which owned 86% of Visa. Another 11% of Visa shares were held by allied investors, and the remaining 3% by the Mexican public. The PROA group had experience, albeit dated, in banking, having owned Banca Serfin S.A., Mexico's third largest bank, before it was nationalised. The Visa management group believed ties between Vamsa and the Bancomer group could produce substantial synergies by combining their factor leasing, insurance and brokerage activities.

---

[31] "Mexico Sells 51 Per Cent Stake In Bancomer For $2.5bn", *Financial Times*, 29 October 1991.

When the Vesma/Visa group took over Bancomer, it was valued at $5bn, 2.99 times the bank's book value.

The Chairman of Bancomer's management group (Ricardo G. Touché) recognised the importance of retraining and cutting costs. A comprehensive programme of changes was drawn up after Mr Touché called in an international consulting group to advise and implement new procedures. As a result, by year-end 1991:

- Staff numbers were cut at all levels. For example, one individual might coordinate the business of six branches rather than having six branch managers. Employee costs were reduced between 24% and 30% in the branches and between 19% and 29% in regional centres.[32]
- In 1989, Bancomer adopted a strategy of segmenting its markets within a branch: VIP banking (high net worth), personal banking (affluent customers but not VIP), retail banking (for 90% of the customers) and middle market corporate banking.
- Lending was concentrated among middle market firms (companies with annual sales between $0.7 million and $39.7 million) and retail lending, including consumer, credit card and mortgage loans.
- An institutional banking division was created to include international banking, corporate banking, international finance and public finance.

Outside Mexico City, Bancomer had about a quarter of the deposit market and just under a quarter of the credit market, helped by its branch network and regional boards structure. Bancomer had a network of 750 branches; approximately 115 were in Mexico City. It controlled 42% of the ATMs operated in Mexico.

The government financial reforms implemented between 1991 and 1992 were far-reaching:[33]

- Controls on deposit and loan rates were lifted.
- Directed credit (where the state directs lending to specific sectors) was abolished.
- Since the bank privatisation programme favoured certain families, there was no uniform application of "fit and proper" criteria for management.
- All deposits were backed by a 100% guarantee, including wholesale (e.g. interbank) and even foreign deposits.
- Every bank paid the same deposit insurance premium, regardless of their risk profile, though this is the norm in most countries – the USA being a notable exception.
- Banks were not required to satisfy capital ratios that reflected their risk taking.
- Non-performing loans were recorded as the amount that had not been repaid over the previous 90 days, rather than the value of the loan itself.

In addition, a number of factors encouraged greater risk taking and/or compounded the problems of excessive credit risk:

---

[32] Source: "Bancomer Saves $100 million through Re-engineering for Quality", *International Journal of Bank Marketing*, **14**(5), 29–30.
[33] These points are from Beim and Calormiris (2001), p. 310.

- As the banks moved back into lending, the supervisory authorities were facing very large portfolios to be monitored at a time when they, like the banks, had little training or experience in risk management.
- There were no experienced credit rating firms that could rate individuals or firms. Nor was there much credit history available, since the banks had engaged in so little lending up to this point.

During the privatisation period in 1990–91, Mexico's business elite paid out $12.4bn for the banks – paying an average of 3.1 times book value – in the belief that the financial sector would grow by about 8% per year, double that forecast for the economy as a whole. Just as with Bancomer, most of the state owned banks were purchased by families owning large industrial concerns because they had the capital to pay out the 3 to 4 times book value for these banks. *Connected lending* was common given the wide network of firms they owned. In some cases, these loans were used as part of the capital to purchase the banks. To the degree that they were *de facto* undercapitalised, it aggravated the moral hazard problem – go for broke – especially in the period before, during and after the crisis. This group of industrialists also supported President Salinas and his liberalisation programme. Lax consumer lending would help create a feel good factor, which would be good for the PRI in the upcoming August 1994 election.

After the financial reforms but before currency crisis, all banks wanted to get on the credit bandwagon, causing loan rates to drop and rapid credit expansion in the household and business sectors. Loans to the private sector grew by 327% between 1989 and 1992.[34] Commercial bank loans amounted to 10.6% of GDP in 1988 but by 1993, reached 34.5%.[35] With virtually no economic growth, loan losses rose sharply, and provisioning increased. By 1993, there was mounting concern about the viability of the banks. Return on assets/equity remained positive but profits began to fall – Table 10.3 shows a 27% drop in real profits. A new competitive threat was the potential entry of Canadian and US banks (or subsidiaries of foreign banks based in these countries), which would be allowed to establish branches over 10 years, once the North American Free Trade Agreement was signed in 1993.[36]

The Mexican economy had slowed considerably in 1993. An uprising in the state of Chiapas, and two high level political assassinations of members of the PRI party (one was a presidential candidate) in 1994, intensified investor concerns about the country's political stability. By March 1994, there was a net outflow of capital. To discourage capital flight, the government replaced its cetes (the Mexican equivalent of government Treasury bills) with **tesobonos**, which, like cetes, were payable in pesos but indexed to the peso–dollar exchange rate. Effectively the government had assumed the currency risk related to holding their bills, and this helped to stabilise the markets until November 1994. By this time the currency regime had moved from a crawling peg (1989) to a crawling trading band, two

---

[34] Cost of Credit is still too high after Privatisation-Banking, *The Financial Times*, 10 November, 1993, p. 6.

[35] Source: Beim and Calormiris (2001), p. 310.

[36] In 1993 (pre-agreement), Scotiabank (Canada) owned 5% of Comermex-Inverlat; and two Spanish banks Banco Bilbao-Vizcaya and Banco Central Hispano had a 20% shareholding in, respectively, Mercantil-Pobursa; and Prime-Internacional.

steps in the direction of a more liberal managed float (see footnote 30). In November, capital outflows and sales of the peso began to rise, and foreign exchange reserves began to fall at an alarming rate, from $17.2 billion in November to $6.1 billion at the end of December. As Box 10.1 explains, the banks' tesobonos swaps prompted additional margin calls as the pesos came under increasing pressure and fears about the Mexican government's willingness/ability to service the tesobonos grew. The government discovered the banks were using tesobonos swaps and other financial engineering techniques to circumvent government limits (see below), the banks were told to buy dollars to cover their risks. Thus, the Mexican banks themselves were significant contributors to the downward pressure on the peso.

Table 10.3  Performance Indicators for Bancomer and Other Mexican Banks

| | Tier 1 capital ($m) | Assets ($m) | Pre-tax profits ($m) | Real profits growth (%) | ROA (%) | Cost to income ratio (%) | Basel risk assets ratio (%) |
|---|---|---|---|---|---|---|---|
| **Dec 1990** | | | | | | | |
| Banamex | 803 | 22 416 | 536 | 190.5 | 0.72 | NA | NA |
| Bancomer | 679 | 18 812 | 341 | −22 | 1.84 | NA | NA |
| Banca Serfin | 254 | 8 591 | 131 | −21.1 | 1.53 | | |
| **Dec 1991** | | | | | | | |
| Banamex | 1 181 | 30 788 | 662 | 4.9 | 2.15 | NA | NA |
| Bancomer | 952 | 30 067 | 664 | 65.6 | 2.21 | NA | NA |
| Banca Serfin | 347 | 22 191 | 122 | −46.3 | 0.55 | | |
| **Dec 1992** | | | | | | | |
| Banamex | 974 | 37 829 | 104.9 | 39.2 | 2.77 | NA | NA |
| Bancomer | 1 285 | 33 161 | 1 054 | 39.4 | 3.18 | NA | NA |
| Banca Serfin | 854 | 20 993 | 152 | 9.4 | 0.72 | NA | NA |
| **Dec 1993** | | | | | | | |
| Banamex | 2 429 | 43 012 | 1 058 | −8.4 | 2.46 | NA | 11.69 |
| Bancomer | 1 515 | 36 134 | 843 | −27.4 | 2.33 | NA | 14.84 |
| Banca Serfin | 862 | 21 390 | 376 | 94.8 | 1.76 | NA | NA |
| **Dec 1994** | | | | | | | |
| Banamex | 1 405 | 33 789 | 203 | −69.3 | 0.6 | NA | 10.15 |
| Bancomer | 1 232 | 28 466 | 171 | −65.3 | 0.6 | NA | 9.11 |
| Banca Serfin | 742 | 19 849 | 49 | −79.7 | 0.25 | NA | NA |
| **Dec 1995** | | | | | | | |
| Banamex | 1 174 | 25 882 | 240 | 26.1 | 0.93 | NA | 11.7 |
| Bancomer | 1 222 | 23 174 | 80 | −50.3 | 0.34 | NA | 11.51 |
| Banca Serfin | 594 | 19 525 | 35 | −79.7 | 0.18 | NA | 5.1 |

*(continued overleaf)*

Table 10.3    (*continued*)

| | Tier 1 capital ($m) | Assets ($m) | Pre-tax profits ($m) | Real profits growth (%) | ROA (%) | Cost to income ratio (%) | Basel risk assets ratio (%) |
|---|---|---|---|---|---|---|---|
| **Dec 1996** | | | | | | | |
| Banamex | 1 207 | 30 892 | NA | NA | NA | NA | 12.6 |
| Bancomer | 1 139 | 26 396 | 346 | 232.1 | 1.31 | 56.68 | 12.18 |
| Banca Serfin | 494 | 19 882 | −984 | −2234 | −4.95 | NA | NA |
| **Dec 1997** | | | | | | | |
| Banamex | 1 790 | 30 844 | 348 | NA | 1.13 | 58.4 | 18.5 |
| Bancomer | 1 659 | 26 956 | 291 | −27.8 | 1.08 | 69.7 | 14.08 |
| Banca Serfin | 912 | 18 115 | −203 | NA | −1.12 | 106.35 | NA |
| **Dec 1998** | | | | | | | |
| Banamex | 1 908 | 29 844 | 201 | −39.6 | 0.67 | 56.6 | 18.8 |
| Bancomer | 1 461 | 25 836 | 93 | −66.5 | 0.36 | 74.39 | 16.43 |
| Banca Serfin | 685 | 16 904 | −34 | NA | −0.2 | 105.3 | NA |
| **Dec 1999** | | | | | | | |
| Banamex | 3 431 | 26 724 | 726 | 265 | 2.72 | 51.26 | 21.6 |
| Bancomer | 1 564 | 22 490 | 334 | 260.7 | 1.48 | 62.29 | 18.7 |
| Banca Serfin | 856 | 15 803 | NA | NA | NA | NA | 16.7 |
| **Dec 2000** | | | | | | | |
| Banamex | 2 469 | 34 902 | 1 009 | 4.8 | 2.89 | 54.19 | 12.3 |
| BBVA Bancomer | 1 985 | 41 151 | 398 | NA | 0.97 | 68.13 | 7.83 |
| Santander Mexicano | 1 018 | 40 186 | 261 | 92.1 | 1.13 | 78.32 | 16 |
| **Dec 2001** | | | | | | | |
| Banamex | 3 096 | 40 186 | 468 | −58.3 | 1.17 | NA | NA |
| BBVA Bancomer | 1 986 | 41 151 | 398 | NA | 0.97 | 68.13 | 12.18 |
| Santander Serfin | 1 018 | 23 154 | 261 | 92.1 | 1.13 | 78.32 | 16 |
| **Dec 2002** | | | | | | | |
| Banamex | 3 469 | 36 374 | 1 335 | 60.8 | 3.67 | 55.02 | 20.10 |
| BBVA Bancomer | 3 179 | 46 546 | 1 067 | 136.9 | 2.29 | 60.25 | 15.66 |
| Santander Serfin | 1 527 | 21 583 | 595 | −4 | 2.76 | 55.13 | NA |
| **Dec 2003** | | | | | | | |
| Banamex | 3 469 | 36 374 | 1 335 | 60.8 | 3.67 | 55.02 | 20.10 |
| BBVA Bancomer | 3 206 | 44 475 | 974 | 2.7 | 2.19 | 54.45 | 16.36 |
| Santander Serfin | 1 934 | 21 870 | 612 | 7.3 | 2.8 | 60.71 | 11.6 |

*Source: The Banker*, July issues, 1991–2004.
NA: not available.

**Box 10.1    Tesobonos swaps: a lesson in market/political risk exposure[1]**

The Mexican government raised finance through the issue of peso denominated bond/bills known as *cetes*. In March 1994, confronted with a new outflow of capital, it began to issue *tesobonos*, which was debt payable in pesos but indexed to the peso/dollar exchange rate. This meant the government assumed any currency risk arising from a future decline in the value of the peso. By the end of November, they accounted for over half of all government debt outstanding. Most of it was short term, despite pressure from the IMF and Washington to issue longer term debt.

Since the early 1990s, banks' foreign currency denominated liabilities had not been allowed to exceed 15% of total liabilities. Sophisticated global banks came up with a solution for Mexican banks wanting to circumvent this rule – a *tesobonos* swap.[2] For example, a US bank swapped income from tesobonos in exchange for interest on a loan made by it plus collateral (in the order of $200 million) – the latter to cover the Mexican bank's obligations under the swap. The Mexican bank received dollar interest on the tesobonos, which was Libor plus 4% – reflecting the higher risk on the tesobonos. The American bank received loan repayments (based on Libor plus a premium of say, 1%). All was well while the peso was stable. The Mexican bank seemed to get a very good deal: access to dollars and a nice profit – the difference between what they paid the western bank for the loan, and the receipts from the tesobonos.

So what was in it for the global bank? The tesobonos covered the holders for any currency risk, but given Mexico's history of reneging on foreign debt agreements, there was concern that if the currency did fall, the government might have problems servicing the debt. The swap was a hedge against this eventuality, which is exactly what happened. Pressure on the peso resumed in March 1994 (see text), and continued off and on until the currency began its free fall, losing more than 50% of its value after it was floated in December 1994. The markets became increasingly concerned about whether the Mexican government would be able to service and/or honour its debt, especially the tesobonos because the debt obligation grew as the value of the peso declined. In the autumn of 1994, the yield on the tesobonos rose and their capital value collapsed. Under the swap agreement, the New York bank made an additional margin call, which meant the Mexican banks had to sell pesos for dollars. Added pressure came from the Mexican authorities – when they found out about the derivative deals (in September 1994) the banks were instructed to buy an estimated $2 billion to cover their risks, putting more pressure on the peso. These actions contributed to a further decline in the currency.

These swap arrangements provide another example of inappropriate risk taking, in this case, by the Mexican banks, whose employees lacked training in the basic rudiments of credit risk assessment, never mind derivatives. The ethics of the western banks is also questionable – they did very well out of it, buying tesobonos and hedging against the market risk associated with their falling value should the Mexican government encounter debt servicing problems. In fact the government never did default on tesobonos (possibly because of the prompt rescue package); market sentiment drove down their capital value. Some American economists had expressed concern that the peso was overvalued as early as 1992, and if American banks reached the same conclusion, they spotted an opportunity to enjoy fat fees from advising on and arranging the swaps, and cover their market risk at the same time.

The new President took office on 1 December but failed to announce a programme of reforms (e.g. of the banking system). Nor were interest rates increased. The markets quickly lost confidence and a run on the peso began. There was little choice but to allow a free float, which came on 22 December – the peso went into free fall. Mexico's close relationship with Canada and the USA meant a swift rescue package was forthcoming. It consisted of $18 billion from the US and Canadian governments, the Bank for International Settlements

---

[1] This account adapted from Beim and Calormiris (2001), pp. 313–314. See also Garber (1998).

[2] Tesobonos swaps were the principal method for getting round the foreign currency restriction. Similar instruments were offered to Mexican banks: equity swaps and structured notes. In an equity swap, the foreign bank buys Mexican equity and swaps the dividend payments with the Mexican bank. If it was $2 billion in equity, the Mexican bank is loaned $2 billion (secured by the stock plus collateral) and in exchange gets the dividends plus any change in currency value from the equity. The Mexican bank assumes the market risk related to the price of the equity: should it collapse in value, the bank gets higher margin calls, etc.

Structured notes were also issued: the Mexican bank buys a note from the foreign bank payable in US dollars but indexed to the peso/dollar exchange rate. The note pays principal interest if the peso does not devalue but very little if there is a large depreciation. The foreign bank buys cetes to hedge against its risks.

and several American commercial banks. A $50 billion rescue package soon followed, organised by the same parties plus the World Bank and IMF. A new recovery plan was announced in March 1995 which included a bank bailout fund (see below), fiscal cutbacks, wage controls and higher taxes.

In 1994, the official percentage of non-performing loans stood at 7.3%, but given the way they were calculated, this figure was a gross underestimate. Thus, on the eve of the peso devaluation, the banks were already in trouble, though delinquent loans were not their only problem. The top Mexican banks, including Bancomer, had been persuaded by US investment banks that they could circumvent a law that prevented them from holding more than 15% of their liabilities in foreign currencies. They did so by engaging in tesobonos and other swaps. While the Mexican economy and government were perceived to be stable by investors, the banks earned good returns on the swaps, and relaxed because they were hedged against currency risks. They apparently failed to appreciate that these instruments exposed them to a high degree of market risk, which would create problems as soon as investors grew concerned with the Mexican government's ability and/or willingness to repay its debt. For the detail on the losses incurred as a result of these swaps, see Box 6.1.

Within a few months of the peso being floated, it had lost half its value against the dollar. The banks really began to suffer when interest rates rose by more than 25% after the peso was floated, peaking at 80% in March 1995. Interbank rates hit 114% in the same month, reflecting the volatility and uncertainty of the markets, though they fell to 90% by the end of the month. The annual inflation rate was 101%. This high inflation, high interest (nominal and real), recessionary environment badly affected many businesses, especially the smaller ones, just when entry into NAFTA left them exposed to foreign competition. Households and businesses found it increasingly difficult to service their debt. The banks began to feel the strain of the rising non-performing loans. To make matters worse, some banks demanded repayment of credit denominated in dollars.

In January 1995, credit rating agencies downgraded the deposits and debt of Mexican banks, including that of Bancomer. The downgrading, it was feared, would precipitate a wholesale loss of confidence in Mexican banks and force them into bankruptcy. In the first three months of 1995, average non-performing loans (NPLs) as a percentage of total loans jumped 15% – an increase of about 45% compared to the period before devaluation. The banking sector, already fragile, immediately collapsed.

The Finance Ministry and central bank announced a rescue plan for commercial banks in March 1995. Problem loans were to be recalculated as investment units – *unidades de inversión* (UDIs) – the debt's principal was indexed to inflation, paying up to 12% in real interest rates.[37] It meant 14% of the banks' total loan portfolio, all non-performing, was removed from their balance sheet. Weaker banks were taken over, restructured, and sold or merged.

By December 1994, the signs of increasing problems were reflected in Bancomer's results. Table 10.3 shows a real profit decline of 65%. The bank cut back on its branch expansion

---

[37] Source: "Lifeline Cast to Mexico's Troubled Banks", *Financial Times*, 30 March 1995.

and slashed jobs again, by about 15%. However, Bancomer along with Banamex weathered the crisis better than other banks because both benefited somewhat from a flight to relative safety by depositors, worried their own banks could fail. At Bancomer, provisioning for bad debt was increased, to cover about 62% of its non-performing assets. Even though Bancomer's profits fell in 1994 and 1995, they recovered dramatically in 1996, only to decline again in 1997 (see Table 10.1). Bancomer's return on assets rose from 0.34% in 1995 to 1.31% in 1996. Compare these results with Banca Serfin, the country's third largest bank by tier 1 capital. In 1995, pre-tax profits stood at $35 million, and its ROA was 0.18%, with a Basel ratio of just 5%. By 1996, Serfin was reporting losses of just under a billion, had a negative return on assets of just under 5%, and did not report a Basel ratio. Serfin never did recover from its problems, and was effectively nationalised (see below).

Under the 1995 rescue scheme, Bancomer sold 15.6 billion pesos worth of NPLs to the government. Nonetheless, Bancomer's NPL stood at 9.2% in April 1996. Though much lower than the average NPL for Mexican banks, it was very high by international standards. The bank announced it had created extraordinary reserves (2.8 billion pesos) to provision for the full amount of its bad loans. It was the first bank to do so, Bancomer slipped into losses during the first quarter.[38]

As Table 10.1 shows, the cost to income ratio, a measure of efficiency, was not reported until 1996. Bancomer's rose from 1996 onwards, reaching a high of 74.4% in 1998 – a period during which it was trying to cut costs. Between 1998 and 1999, this ratio was reduced by 12%, only to rise again in 2000, the year it was taken over. From 1993 onwards, the Basel risk assets ratios for both Banamex and Bancomer were quite respectable, well above the Basel minimum of 8% and in double digits. But in the takeover year, Bancomer's dropped by nearly 11%, to 7.8% in 2000.

As part of the reform of the banking system, it was announced that the banks were to use US Generally Accepted Accounting Principles (GAAP) from 1997. The Bancomer announcement regarding its bad debts was in preparation for this, but it was not enough – when GAAP was applied, NPLs rose to 18% of capital and net income (1996) fell by nearly 70%. Bancomer and other banks would require a great deal more capital, and looked to foreign banks to invest in them. In 1996, the Bank of Montreal had purchased 16% of Bancomer, but the capital injection was not nearly enough to meet its needs.

At the end of March 1999, Bancomer and Banamex announced they had entered into talks about merging, and informed the competition authorities. This move reflected the continued weak state of the banking sector, despite attempts to revive it post-crisis. The government had absorbed a total of $65 billion of bad debt from the banks' balance sheets, and many weaker banks were taken over and/or restructured. From December 1998, foreign banks had been given the legal backing to take over the top three banks – up to that time they were limited to a maximum of 20% of the bank. Merger talks by the top two was a defensive action, based on the idea that being bigger would in some way resolve their joint problems of insufficient capital. They expected

---

[38] Crawford, L. (1996), "Bancomer in the Red After Provisions", *Financial Times*, 18 April 1996.

to make a saving of $700 million through cutting back on overlap, etc. This, the banks argued, together with their large size, would give them greater access to capital markets. However, if these two banks were to merge, they would have a 40% share of the deposit market, creating concerns about lack of competition and rising inefficiency. The authority monitoring anti-competitive practices was seen as weak because of the degree of monopoly power that had been allowed to prevail in other sectors of the economy. This raised fears about more cartel-like behaviour, pushing up what were already unusually high spreads, which were costly for both borrowers and savers. Furthermore, should this new large bank get into trouble, there would be serious systemic problems, a cause for special concern in a country with a past history of financial/banking crises. However, soon after the two banks declared their merger intentions, the head of the Federal Competition Commission announced he would prevent any merger from taking place.

Despite the economic recovery between 1995 and 2000, the inability of the banks to deal with their bad debt problems together with weak bankruptcy laws and the lack of protection of creditor rights meant virtually no new credit was extended over this period, Firms had to look elsewhere: through bond issues (if large enough), or seeking foreign or domestic investors willing to inject capital or make loans. However, it was clear Mexico needed a banking system willing to lend, prompting the government to take the initiative.

In 1998, the *punto final* was introduced, and was to be the last of a series of loan loss sharing agreements between the banks and government. Creditors and debtors were given a certain date to resolve their claims. If they did, creditors got up to two-thirds of the debt they were owed, and debtors were given the last opportunity to receive government support to pay off their debts. For example, there could be a write off of mortgages of up to 50%. These generous terms resulted in over a million claims being settled, mainly individual borrowers and small firms. Large debts remained outstanding – most banks thinking they could recover more than what they would get from the state.

The extent of ongoing problems in Mexico's banking sector, four years after the 1995 crisis, was made apparent when, in May 1999, the Institute for Protection of Bank Savings (IPAB) was established with a remit to deal with banks with ongoing problems. It quickly took control of Mexico's third largest bank, Serfin Bank. It was estimated at the time that the cost of supporting the troubled banking sector had reached $100 billion. The IPAB is similar to a "bad bank", but has the power to take over whole banks. It is estimated to have about $50bn of bad loans on its books, of which $12bn originate from Serfin. The IPAB reported that it could take up to 20 years to deal with this bad debt. It also began to dismantle the 100% deposit insurance scheme and instructed existing banks, including Bancomer, to raise more capital. In December 1999, Bancomer complied and sold off its insurance subsidiary. At the same time Bancomer announced the development of bancassurance, i.e. that insurance products would be sold through its bank branches. Normally banks expand into bankassurance *after* they acquire an insurance subsidiary or partner.

Despite the sale of the large insurance subsidiary and an earlier capital injection by the Bank of Montreal in 1996, the bank was still under pressure to find a capital rich partner. In March 2000, Banco Bilbao Vizcaya Argentaria (BBVA) of Spain and Bancomer agreed that

BBVA would take a controlling interest (30%) in Bancomer. The $1.2 billion deal would create the largest bank in Mexico. BBVA would also take responsibility for managing the bank, to be known as BBVA-Bancomer. BBVA had purchased Probursa Bank in 1995 at the height of the crisis, and it was intended to integrate the operations of BBVA-Probursa into BBVA-Bancomer.

The first hostile bid in Mexican history came in May 2000 when Banacci, the parent of Banamex, announced its intention to purchase 65% of Bancomer, in a $2.4 billion bid. This came as a surprise, especially after the Federal Competition Commission had declared it would block any merger of these two banks. Now, in an apparent U-turn, the authority announced it might allow it to proceed if the banks agreed to sell off parts where they had a clear monopoly, including credit cards and private pensions. Within a month, however, the competition authority appeared to revert to it original position, expressing concern about potential problems arising from too concentrated a banking industry.

Five weeks later, the Bancomer Board approved the BBVA bid, after it offered an additional $1.4 billion in cash, bringing the total capital raised to $2.5 billion, which is exactly what Bancomer needed given its bad debt problems. The bid meant BBVA would own 32% of the bank, which rose to 45% after buying up the Bank of Montreal's holding in April 2001, and again to 54% in November 2002. It intends to own up to 65% of the bank.

This friendly takeover of Bancomer was part of a trend of consolidation and increased foreign ownership of Mexico's largest banks. Spain's largest bank, Santander Central Hispano (SCH), had bought 30% of Bital Bank, which boasted the largest retail branch network, and in 2001 ING took a 17.5% stake in Bital. In May 2000 the IPAB, having cleaned up the balance sheet of the troubled Serfin, sold it to Spain's SCH for $1.5bn. The new bank was called Santander Mexicano. By 2001, Citigroup had taken control of Banamex. Mexico's banking system was now owned and controlled by giant foreign players.

Post-consolidation, it is hoped that two new banking laws will help ensure the stability of the banking system. In April 2000, a new bankruptcy code of practice was established, modelled after the US system of chapter 11 administration which gives the indebted firm an opportunity to restructure its loans for a specified period of time. The courts protect the firm from creditors in this period. A second law was enacted in 2000, which protects creditors' rights to collateral should a firm go bankrupt. In a judicial system which had always favoured debtors (a common feature in the legal systems of many merging markets), the two new laws went some way to redress the balance.

## Questions

1. Use the description of Bancomer as a nationalised bank to discuss the pros and cons of having a nationalised banking system. Is it a sound public policy objective?
2. In the context of the case, explain the meaning of:
   (a) financial leasing;
   (b) brokerage services;
   (c) factoring;

(d) warehouse bonding;

(e) correspondent banking.

(f) market segmentation within a retail branch.

3. What did the Visa group expect to gain from the purchase of Bancomer, one of the newly privatised major banks in Mexico?

4. Mexico is an emerging market economy. What factors are unique to banks in this type of economy? Did the new owners of Bancomer (Visa) address these issues? The answer should focus on the newly privatised bank's strategy in terms of human resources, segmenting its markets within a branch, loan policy.

5. Define "connected lending" and discuss whether it is likely to be a problem given Visa's complex ownership structure.

6. Why did the currency crisis of 1994–95 lead to a downgrading of Bancomer and other banks' credit ratings by private rating agencies?

7. (a) The government initiated a series of financial reforms between 1991 and 1992. To what extent were these reforms a contributory factor to the subsequent banking crisis?

   (b) Draw a list of financial reforms which might have reduced the chances of the Mexican currency crisis from turning into a banking crisis.

   (c) With the benefit of hindsight, how did Bancomer's strategic initiatives contribute to the problems the bank faced during the crisis?

8. Were New York banks hedging against market risk, political risk or both when they engaged in tesobonos swaps?

9. Using Table 10.1:

   (a) Compare the performance of Bancomer's risk assets ratio with the Basel minimum requirement.

   (b) After takeover, BBVA-Bancomer's risk assets ratio slumped from 18.7% in 1999 to 7.83% in 2000. Review the reasons why this ratio might have dropped so dramatically in a year.

   (c) Based on your observations in (a) and (b), is the Basel ratio a good measure of performance and/or the bank's risk profile?

10. By early in the new century, the Mexican banking system was largely owned and controlled by foreign banks.

   (a) Within 9 years of being privatised, Bancomer (and other key Mexican banks) had been taken over or sold off. Why? (Crisis, bad loans, not enough capital, banking law changed in 1998.)

   (b) Were there sound reasons for discouraging a merger between Banamex and Bancomer?

   (c) What are the advantages and disadvantages of foreign ownership of banks in emerging markets (see Chapters 1 and 6 for discussion).

   (d) How has BBBV-Bancomer performed since it was taken over in 2000? [Use *Bankscope* (if students have access to it) OR the July editions of *The Banker*.]

## 10.6. Crédit Lyonnais[39]

**Relevant Parts of the Text:** Chapters 5, 6 (political risk), Chapter 8.

*"Seldom in the field of finance has so much been squandered so quickly by so few."*[40]

On the last working day of 1992, Monsieur Jean-Yves Harberer, Chairman of Crédit Lyonnais (CL), once again reaffirmed his plan to transform CL from a staid, state-controlled French bank into a high-performance pan-European universal bank, a key player in both commercial and investment banking markets and a cornerstone of European finance by the turn of the century. January 1993 was the eve of the EU's first attempt[41] to achieve a single market in goods/services throughout Europe, including financial services. Monsieur Harberer could cite an important milestone in the road to this goal, achieving a controlling interest in Bank für Gemeinwirtschaft, giving CL a major stake in Europe's largest and toughest financial services market, Germany.

According to Harberer, the banks likely to be the future leaders in Europe were Deutsche Bank (Germany), Barclays Bank (Great Britain), Istituto Bancaira San Paolo di Torino (Italy) and Crédit Lyonnais of France. These leading banks would come to dominate the pan-European banking markets. They would possess the capital strength, the domestic market share and the intra-European networks to intimidate rivals and repel competitive threats from all sources. Few others, in the opinion of Harberer, had much of a chance.

Harberer had chosen the grandest strategy of all. It was a strategy designed to have enormous appeal to CL's sole stockholder, the French government, given its proclaimed vision that a few Euro-champions needed to be nurtured in each important industry through an aggressive "industrial policy" of protection, subsidisation, ministerial guidance and selective capital infusions. Each Euro-champion (as many as possible French) must be capable of conducting commercial warfare on the global battlefield. In financial services, according to Harberer, CL would be France's chosen instrument.

To achieve this objective, Harberer had three goals:

- To make CL very, very large, with 1% to 2% of all bank deposits in the 15 (25 since 2004) European Community countries. To achieve this goal, CL would have to capture significant market share in multiple areas of banking and securities activities at once. Given the competitive dynamics of the financial services sector, speed was of the essence. Acquisitions of existing businesses would be made in various countries on several fronts, simultaneously.
- CL needed to expand and operate Europe-wide. This meant going up against the entrenched domestic competition in most of the national EU markets simultaneously, either via aggressive expansion, strategic alliances and networks, or local acquisitions.

---

[39] A version of the first part of this case appeared as Case 40 in the New York University Salomon Center Case Series in Banking and Finance, written by Roy C. Smith and Ingo Walter (1993). The case that appears here has been extensively edited and updated by Shelagh Heffernan.

[40] Source: "Debit Lyonnais's Encore", *The Economist*, 25 March 1995, p. 18.

[41] Now, more than a decade later, Europe continues to strive for a single financial market. The latest plan is to dismantle all barriers under the Financial Services Action Plan, 2005. See Chapter 5 for more detail.

The strategy was clear, but no one tactic would be enough. Opportunism and flexibility were essential to success.

- Crédit Lyonnais had to exert significant control over its corporate banking customers, using strategies such as deep lending, "relationship" investment banking with key non-financial firms, and having ownership stakes in many of these same firms. Only in this way, he felt, could CL exert sufficient influence over their financial and business affairs to direct large and profitable businesses his way. Harberer called this *banque industrie*, a French version of the classic German *Hausbank* relationship. Unlike British or American banks, owning part or all of industrial or manufacturing concerns was the norm for the major German and French universal banks.

Crédit Lyonnais had to retain the confidence of the French government because the state owned the bank. The government was expected to inject a great deal of capital, and clear the way to ensure CL achieved its acquisition and ownership plans. It would also have to look beyond the inevitable accidents that occur on the road to greater glory. Crédit Lyonnais would have to become an indispensable instrument of French and European industrial policy. The special relationship between the government and CL would have to transcend all political changes in France, even those which involved the privatisation of CL and other state owned banks.

Little did he know that his strategy for CL would culminate in the bank being nicknamed "Debit Lyonnais",[42] the costliest single bank bailout in European history (estimates of between \$17 and \$30 billion), and a Los Angeles Grand Jury indicting[43] Monsieur Harberer, along with five other CL executives, for fraud.

## 10.6.1. Crédit Lyonnais and Le Dirigisme Français

Crédit Lyonnais first opened for business in Lyons in 1863 as a **banque de dépôts**, which collected deposits, made loans and underwrote new issues of debt and equity for its corporate clients. The bank extended its operations to London during the Franco-Prussian war and, in the 1870s, expanded throughout France and to the major foreign business centres. By 1900, it was the largest French bank, measured by assets.

During the First World War, many of the personnel from the large French banks were conscripted, and competition in French banking increased. Smaller banks took advantage of larger banks' staffing difficulties and expanded rapidly. From 1917, the Crédits Populaires, a new form of banking establishment, arrived, adding to domestic competition. The 1917 Russian revolution led to the withdrawal of many deposits by wealthy Russian nationals who had fled the country. Though it was profitable in the 1920s, CL was not making nearly the profits it had enjoyed before the Great War.

During the Great Depression of the 1930s, CL adopted a cautious approach, closing about 100 offices in France and abroad. With the onset of the Second World War, CL remained essentially apolitical, continuing the majority of its banking activities, although some of

---

[42] "Debit Lyonnais, Again", *The Economist*; 28 January 1995, p. 15.
[43] Under the US system, an indictment contains charges that an individual committed a crime, but all defendants are presumed innocent until proven guilty.

the foreign offices fell out of the control of Head Office during the German occupation. The restoration of peace in 1945 brought with it a number of events central to determining CL's future course.

## 1945

The French government nationalised the **banques de dépôts**, including Crédit Lyonnais, Société Générale, Comptoir National d'Escomptes de Paris (CNEP) and Banque Nationale de Commerce et d'Industrie (BNCI). In 1966, the government merged the two smaller banks, CNEP and BNCI, into Banque Nationale de Paris (BNP).

## 1970

The president of CL, François Bloch-Lainé, adopted a strategy of forming partnerships with other banks in the form of a Union des Banques Arabes et Françaises (UBAF) and Europartners.

## 1973

A law was passed allowing the distribution of shares to the employees of nationalised banks and insurance companies such as Crédit Lyonnais. The election victory of the Gaullists, led by Valéry Giscard d'Estaing, resulted in the appointment of Jacques Chaine to replace François Bloch-Lainé as chief executive of CL.

## 1981

The Socialists won a resounding election victory and François Mitterand became President of France. Jean Deflassieux, financial advisor to the Socialist party, was appointed to replace Jacques Chaine at CL.

## 1982

The ruling Socialists nationalised all the major French banks not already owned by the state. The declared objective of the government was to influence the functioning of banks to favour the small and middle-sized businesses, as well as to help define and implement a new and more interventionist industrial and monetary policy. For Crédit Lyonnais, the only effect was the renationalisation of shares sold to employees in 1973.

## 1986

The Gaullists took control of the French Legislative Assembly, and Jacques Chirac was appointed as Prime Minister. There was a period of "cohabitation" with President Mitterand. Jean Deflassieux was replaced as CL chief executive by Jean-Maxime Lèvêque, known for his advocacy of privatisation. A privatisation law authorised the public sale of 65 large industrial companies, though CL was not targeted in the first round. Both Groupe Financiére de Paribas and the Sociètè Gènèrale were successfully privatised.

### 1988

The Socialists regained power in the assembly. Privatisations were immediately suspended. Jean Yves Harberer replaced Jean-Maxime Lévêque as president of Crédit Lyonnais.

### 1992

The Socialists were locked in an election battle with a Conservative and neo-Gaullist coalition led by Edward Balladur and Valéry Giscard d'Estaing. This led to another period of cohabitation – election prospects looked bleak for the Socialists and French presidential elections were not due until 1995. The Conservative party platform promised a resumption of the privatisation programme, to include a broad range of state owned enterprises. Crédit Lyonnais was thought to be on the list.

The successive changes in chief executives at CL and other nationalised firms by incoming governments illustrates how CL and other state owned firms were subject to persistent intervention by the state, commonly known as *dirigisme*. After nationalisation in 1945, CL had experienced a reasonable degree of independence (most of the CL board remained intact), but the government became increasingly interventionist, defining the bank's strategic direction and the structure of its leadership, with a view to using the nationalised banks as a key tool of industrial policy.

Despite the political situation, the French financial system underwent substantial structural change and deregulation in the 1970s and 1980s. It was transformed from being highly concentrated and compartmentalised into an open, well-developed domestic capital market. The deregulation was a partial response to London's financial reforms, which the Paris financial markets had to keep up with; it was also due to changing political fashion. In particular, the financial reforms under the Chirac administration helped shift French corporate finance towards open capital markets and away from bank lending.

The major French banks and industrial enterprises remained tied together by strong, informal relationships, a cohesion that had its roots in the Grandes Écoles, attended by leading government officials and senior managers of state owned and private companies and banks. The best graduates became Inspecteurs des Finances, a special appointment for the brightest graduates of the elite École Nationale d'Administration. This virtually ensured instant prestige for an individual, lifelong admiration, and responsible employment in the French government or in government-controlled entities.

Jean Yves Harberer was a paragon of this system. He graduated first in his class at the École Nationale d'Administration and joined the French Treasury as an Inspecteur Général des Finances. He rose rapidly, becoming head of the French Treasury while still in his forties. In 1982 President Mitterand moved him from the Treasury to run the newly nationalised Paribas (Compagnie Financière de Paris et des Pays-Bas). Harberer was widely resented at Paribas, and was seen as the instrument of its nationalisation. During his leadership, Paribas suffered its worst fiasco – it acquired the New York stockbroker AG Becker, which it sold at a $70 million loss a few years later. When Paribas was reprivatised in 1986, Harberer was removed from office, but was subsequently appointed chief executive and president of Crédit Lyonnais in 1988.

Harberer was described as authoritarian, brilliant and intimidating. He was virtually friendless but was the Socialists' favourite banker, with long-standing ties to Pierre Bérégovoy (Minister of Finance, later Prime Minister) and Jacques Delors, President of the European Commission until 1994. On his appointment to CL in 1988, it was soon made clear that Harberer wanted to implement grandiose schemes which would not have survived board scrutiny or shareholder reactions in privately owned financial institutions. He was not popular in the banking world, where he was thought of as a gambler, who adopted "go for broke" tactics. It was thought that in the event of a Conservative victory in March 1993 he would be replaced – he was still disliked by the Right, for serving as a tool of the Left while at Paribas in 1982.

## 10.6.3. The French Banking Scene in the 1990s

The French domestic market for financial services in the 1990s had been a highly competitive one, characterised by both compartmentalised universal as well as specialised institutions, each targeting different financial activities, despite the fact that deregulation had removed many of the legal barriers. The French banking structure consisted of:

- The caisses d'epargne: dominated the liquid savings deposit market, accounting for over 30% of this type of deposit.
- The banques cooperatives: originated as a coop system, these banks are found primarily in the agricultural sector, especially Crédit Agricole.
- The banques de dépôts: active in short-term industrial finance, notably BNP and Société Générale. Crédit National was involved in longer term loans, and Crédit Foncier in mortgage credit. In March 1989, BNP and UAP had sealed a bancassurance alliance, including a 10% share swap, which gave BNP a FF5.3 billion capital infusion and UAP 2000 French banking outlets from which to sell insurance.
- The banques d'affaires: these banks' principal focus was on corporate finance, and they were both aggressive and competent, Paribas being a good example. They have more in common with large financial conglomerates than with traditional British merchant banks or US investment banks.
- The banques étrangers: these foreign banks were mounting fairly effective challenges in specific niches. Barclays Bank had moved into private banking; JP Morgan into the wholesale sector. Numerous foreign firms, including Deutsche Bank and Union Bank of Switzerland, were attracted to dynamic French markets.
- Non-bank competitors: the French postal savings systems, finance companies such as Compagnie Bancaire (an affiliate of Paribas) and the large insurance companies fall into this category. They were stepping up their challenges to the large universal banks.

The most intense battle Crédit Lyonnais faced at home was to attract retail deposits. Interest-earning chequing accounts had been prohibited since 1967, so SICAVs monétaires were used as instruments to attract savings – French banks had been pushing this form of investment aggressively. However, the result was that the cost of funds had approached the money market rate, severely penalising banks which had lived off cheap, unremunerated accounts. This was especially difficult, given the rising cost of technology as banks competed to develop computerised networks offering more electronic services such as ATMs and direct telephone transactions through the domestic Minitel network.

### 10.6.4. The Launching Pad

By the early 1990s, Crédit Lyonnais had become a highly diversified bank, offering a complete range of financial services to most client segments throughout most of Europe. CL had holdings in Asia and North America under its own name. In South America and Africa it generally operated under the name of either partially or wholly owned subsidiaries.

In its drive to be a universal bank, CL offered a broad spectrum of financial services. At the end of 1992, it had 2639 retail banking outlets in France, as well as an array of specialised financial affiliates such as the Paris stockbroker Cholet-Dupont Michaux, money management affiliates, and niche-type businesses such as leasing. It also offered a range of insurance services, and was notable for its life insurance. It maintained a large portfolio of holdings in different French and European companies.

For operational purposes, Crèdit Lyonnais was divided into six units.

- The *banque des entreprises* (business bank), which catered to the financial requirements of a broad spectrum of business and industry. The core function was commercial lending. For small and medium-sized businesses, Crédit Lyonnais also offered risk management products, including financial and foreign exchange options, other derivatives, asset management services covering a broad range of investments, and international development assistance, such as helping to initiate cross-border partnerships and alliances. For large companies, CL services extended from fund raising through to syndicated lending, euronote and eurocommercial paper, distribution to large and complex financing arrangements such as projects and acquisitions financing, mergers and acquisitions advisory activities and real estate financing. It also maintained leasing subsidiaries – Slibail, Slificom, Slifergie in France, Woodchester in Ireland and the UK, Leasimpresa in Italy.
- The *banque des particuliers et des professionels* (retail bank) serviced private individuals and professional clients, and carried out basic banking services such as deposits, payments services and personal loans. There had been a significant decline in demand deposit account balances in favour of interest-bearing accounts, but with intensified competition and changes in legislation, clients were increasingly opting for SICAVs – open-ended unit trusts, and especially money market funds or SICAVs monétaires. To attract and maintain retail clients, CL was forced to innovate and enhance retail banking services. Debit cards, ATMs and home banking through Minitel (the French interactive phone system) were introduced. CL used its Lion Assurances subsidiary to market personal lines of insurance (for example, automobile insurance), in addition to life assurance.
- For large individual and professional clients, CL provided private banking services and tailored insurance plans, as well as special financing arrangements, such as Inter-Fimo and Crédit Médical de France, which financed the purchase and installation of medical equipment.
- The *banque des marchès capitaux* (investment bank) was responsible for underwriting and distributing bonds and new equity issues. In global markets, Crèdit Lyonnais Capital

Markets International units (for example, Crédit Lyonnais Securities in London) assured the bank's presence in foreign financial centres, while the French markets were covered by affiliates such as Cholet-Dupont. In 1991, CL was ranked first in placing domestic and euro-franc bonds. In the derivatives sector, it accounted for about 10% of the volume on the MATIF, France's futures and options exchange.

- **Altus Finance**, a finance company and former finance subsidiary of Thomson, in which CL acquired a 66% interest in 1991. Harberer was its chairman until December 1993. During that year, using a front organisation, Altus bought a large portfolio of high-yield junk bonds from the failed American insurance company Executive Life, a position which amounted to one-third of CL's tier 1 capital. This purchase was to come back to haunt the key parties (see below).
- The **gestionnaire pour compte de tiers** (fund management group) was responsible for the management of private portfolios as well as the SICAVs in which private individuals held shares. CL had enhanced its offerings to include those guaranteeing capital, yield and global diversification.

As actionnaire des entreprises, Crédit Lyonnais had been increasing its shareholdings in other companies to further the concept of a universal bank. The notion was that, by holding substantial shares, especially in non-financial companies, CL would be able to develop a much better understanding of these companies' financial needs and influence its financial decisions. Its holding structures included the following.

- **Clinvest**: CL's banque d'affaires, with a diversified holding of French companies, which had been a highly profitable part of the bank.
- **Euro-Clinvest**: A Clinvest subsidiary, with a portfolio of shares of companies in eight European countries.
- **Clindus**: Established in 1991, had strategic and statutory holdings, principally in Rhône-Poulenc and Usinor-Sacilor, that were added to CL's balance sheet with the "assistance" of the government.
- **Innolion**: A high technology start-up venture capital fund operating in France.
- **Compagnie Financiére d'Investissement Rhône-Alpes**: which invested in the Rhône-Alpes region of France.
- **Lyon Expansion**: A development capital fund for small and medium businesses and industries.

Harberer considered CL's existing structure to be an ideal basis upon which to build his banque industrie concept of a pan-European universal financial institution, with enough capacity to launch a simultaneous multi-pronged attack on an array of national markets, financial services and client segments, and to do so rapidly.

## 10.6.5. The Pan-European Playing Field

The EU directives for achieving a single financial market were reviewed in Chapter 5. An important point is that once the minimum requirements of the EU passport are met, conduct of business rules will vary in each EU country. Financial firms which locate in other states will have to comply with the rules imposed by the host country. It will mean firms will have to deal with 16 different sets of rules (the 15 EU countries plus the euromarkets). This could raise costs of compliance to regulations for pan-European firms, and leaves open the possibility that host country regulations will be used to favour domestic financial firms over firms from other EU states. However, the general view is that these rules will converge over time, creating a level playing field throughout Europe, and creating the competition necessary to make Europe a key world financial market.

It was expected that the regulatory regime would evolve along the lines of a universal banking model. All types of financial institutions could compete in each others' financial markets geographically, cross-client and cross-product, including insurance, real estate and various areas of commerce. This environment could, in turn, provide a platform for European institutions to mount serious challenges in North American and Asian financial markets.

Indeed, some observers considered financial services one of the few sectors of the European economy where the regulatory bodies were sometimes well ahead of business in promoting competitive change. Though often resisted by market participants themselves, financial services deregulation in Europe, by the early 1990s, had produced intense competition and pricing rivalry in many markets, an erosion of boundaries between types of financial establishments, a proliferation of new technologies and improved access to capital markets, which shifted the balance of power away from banks in favour of their customers.

## 10.6.6. The Pan-European Building Blocks

By late 1992, Harberer had already developed the beginnings of a pan-European bank in the retail sector via an extensive cross-border branch network. He had been making systematic moves towards this goal since 1988. This was needed to meet his target of capturing between 1% and 2% of total retail deposits in Europe, to provide the cheap funding CL needed to finance all its other growth initiatives.

Several acquisitions and purchases of stakes in other banks had been undertaken in quick succession as CL bought local medium-sized financial institutions in Belgium, Spain, Italy and Germany. Between 1987 and 1992, the number of CL branches in Europe had increased threefold. By 1991, 47% of the bank's profits came from outside France, compared to 30% in 1987. It major acquisitions included the following.

- Belgium: CL had rapidly expanded its local presence via aggressive branching. It tripled the number of retail and private banking clients in 18 months with a new higher yield account called Rendement Plus. This offered 9% on savings deposits, compared to 3–4% offered by local banks. CL could offer these rates mainly because it did not have the cumbersome and expensive infrastructure of Belgian banks – it had just 960 employees for 32 branches in the country, three per branch. The three big Belgian banks had at least 10 employees per branch in over 1000 branches.
- Netherlands: CL had raised its stake in Slavenburgs Bank (renamed Crédit Lyonnais Bank Nederland NV) from 78% to 100%. In 1987, it had acquired Nederlandse Credietbank, a former subsidiary of Chase Manhattan Bank in the USA.

- Ireland: CL held a 48% stake in Woodchester, renamed Woodchester Crédit Lyonnais Bank, a leasing and financing company, which intended to acquire a total of 40 to 50 retail banking outlets.
- CL reinforced its position in the London market by buying Alexanders, Laing and Cruickshank after Big Bang in 1986. In 1989 it was renamed Crédit Lyonnais Capital Markets.
- Spain: CL's branches had been merged with Banco Commercial Español, and renamed Crédit Lyonnais España SA, complemented by the acquisition of the medium-sized Banca-Jover in 1991.
- Germany: CL completed a deal in 1992 to purchase 50% of the Bank für Gemeinwirtschaft (BfG), ending a 5-year search for a viable presence in the most important European market outside France.

Harberer viewed the acquisition of BfG as a key achievement. Not only was Germany the largest European banking market, it was also the most difficult to penetrate. Others had tried, and many had failed. Those who succeeded had done so by buying niche-type businesses, often with indifferent results. None was taken seriously as major contenders alongside the three Grossbanken, the large regional and state-affiliated banks, and the cooperative and savings bank networks. With the acquisition of the BfG, Crédit Lyonnais expected to break the mould.

In 1990, the second largest German insurance group, AMB (Aachener and Münchener Beteiligungs GmbH), had negotiated with the state owned French insurer AGF (Assurance Générales de France) about a partnership arrangement. Besides the attractiveness of the German market, AGF was watching strategic moves by its arch-rival, the state owned insurer UAP – its expansion into Germany had come by way of the acquisition of a 34% stake in Groupe Victoire (from Banque Indosuez), a major French insurer which had earlier purchased a German insurer, Colonia Versicherungs AG.

AGF had bought 25% of AMB stock, but it was limited to only 9% of the voting rights by the AMB board, using a special class of vinculated shares. It was clearly concerned that a French company, twice its size, was out to control and eventually swallow it. Alongside the AGF acquisition of AMB stock, Crédit Lyonnais had bought a 1.8% stake in AMB as well. As part of its defensive tactics, AMB arranged for an Italian insurer, La Fondaria, to acquire a friendly stake, amounting to 20% of AMB shares. AGF then fought a historic shareholders' rights battle in German courts against the AMB board and a German industrial establishment instinctively distrustful of hostile changes in corporate control. The defence was further bolstered by the fact that 11% of AMB stock was held by Dresdner Bank, and 6% by Munich Re. Allianz, the largest German insurer, was a major shareholder in both Dresdner Bank and Munich Re. Harberer took it as a sign of the times that AGF had prevailed in the German courts and, with the help of CL's AMB shares, was able to obtain AGF recognition of its voting rights – no doubt the basis for future AGF share acquisitions, possibly the La Fondaria stake.

The AGF–AMB battle provided Harberer with the opening he was looking for. AGF proposed that Crédit Lyonnais buy AMB's bank, the Bank für Gemeinwirtschaft, which AMB was keen to dispose of and which had been up for sale for some period. BfG was the bank of the German Labour movement, plagued by poor management, periodic large losses and scandals, and a down-market client base. Nevertheless, BfG had some 200 well-situated branches throughout the country and presented a rare opportunity to buy a major German bank. AMB had already made great strides in turning BfG around, but a loss of 400 million Deutsche marks in 1990 and a meagre profit of only 120 million Deutsche marks in 1991 indicated that a major capital infusion would be required in 1993. AMB was hardly interested in supplying it, and a takeover by Crédit Lyonnais was seen by AMB as a welcome opportunity to divest itself of an albatross. CL valued BfG at 1.8 billion Deutsche marks; AMB valued it at 2.6 billion Deutsche marks. AMB suggested part of the deal could be the 1.8% AGF stock held by CL. In November 1992, it was agreed that CL would buy 50.1% of BfG for 1.9 billion Deutsche marks, effective at year-end.

Of course, acquisition battles like BfG were only the first and perhaps the easiest part of the building process. Certainly not all of CL's acquisitions had been easy to digest. Its purchase of the Slavenburgs Bank in the Netherlands, for example, had been the source of many headaches. Beyond a troublesome clash of corporate cultures, there had been a serious problem in maintaining supervision. Slavenburgs Bank (or CL Nederland) was responsible for making large loans to Giancarlo Parretti for the purchase of MGM shares in the USA (see below) – loans which CL's Paris head office later claimed it was not aware of until it was too late.

Besides outright acquisitions and aggressive expansion in the important European markets, CL also employed a strategy of engaging in strategic alliances and networks. One of the older of these, Europartners, was set up as a loose association between Crédit Lyonnais, Commerzbank, Banco di Roma, and Banco Hispaño Americano (BHA), based on a plan to extend banking networks into neighbouring countries and set up new joint operations. The idea was to provide a cheap way of allowing each of the partners' customers access to basic banking services in other countries.

It was not long before strains began to appear in Europartners. Over the years, Commerzbank had tightened its relations with its Spanish partner, and in 1989, BHA agreed to swap an 11% interest in its shares for a 5% stake in Commerzbank. The 1991 merger of BHA and Banco Central into Banco Central-Hispaño diluted Commerzbank's share to 4.5%. At the same time, there was a dispute over CL's expansion into Spain with the purchase of Banca Jover in the summer of 1991. A year earlier, Crédit Lyonnais had tried to purchase a 20% stake in Banco Hispaño Americano and was flatly rejected. BHA perceived the new action as a threat of direct competition in its home market, and suspended its relationship with CL.

Rebuffed in Spain, CL had also been thwarted in its attempt to deepen the Franco-German part of the Europartners agreement. In 1991, CL discussed swapping shares with Commerzbank, the smallest of the three German Grossbanken, thought to have involved 10% of Commerzbank's equity for 7% of CL's equity. Discussions broke down over German fears that the French bank had more in mind than cementing the Europartners alliance. Commerzbank did not want to become the German arm of a French bank. There was also the matter of price. Based on comparative figures, Commerzbank wanted a 10% for 10% share swap, even though the French bank was twice its size, because it considered itself to have a much better future in terms of earnings and market potential.

By the end of 1991, Europartners was effectively dead, though this did not preclude other strategic alliances as a future option for Crédit Lyonnais. Other partnerships had been more stable, including:

- The Banco Santander–Royal Bank of Scotland agreement, cemented by a share swap, to create a link-up through which clients could conduct cross-border transactions at terminals located at either bank's branches. Crédit Commerciale de France had signed up to join this alliance.
- There was the proposed BNP–Dresdner deal, a cooperative agreement that involved 10% cross-shareholdings and each bank continuing to run its existing operations, with reciprocal access to branch networks but with a programme of opening joint offices elsewhere, including Switzerland, Turkey, Japan and Hungary.

## 10.6.7. The Government Link

Over the years, French economic and financial policy has been highly changeable. When François Mitterand was elected President in 1981, his approach was to reflate the economy by increasing the size of the public sector, reducing the number of hours in the working week, and nationalising 49 key industrial and financial firms. These policies led to increased imports and a deterioration of both the trade balance and international capital flows. Under these conditions, the possible solutions were either to devalue the franc and take it out of the European Monetary System's Exchange Rate Mechanism, or to seriously reduce monetary expansion, reduce the fiscal deficit (which would involve cuts in spending) and stimulate the private sector.

The latter option was chosen. Taxes were cut, capital markets deregulated, and the French economy boomed throughout the 1980s. The Finance Minister, Pierre Bérégovoy, the driving force of fiscal prudence, maintained a franc fort, low inflation policy throughout the period and committed the country to partial privatisation, starting with the sale of minority stakes in Elf Aquitaine, Total and Crédit Locale de France in 1991.

On the other hand, the Socialists had not only nationalised the big banks in 1981 when they came to power, but had continued to influence their activities since then. For example, in 1992, BNP was asked to acquire an equity stake in Air France, and Crédit Lyonnais was "encouraged" to buy into the large integrated steelmaker Usinor-Sacilor, both of them inefficient state owned firms making large losses. By linking together the state owned equity portfolio and the equity holdings of state owned banks, the government could maintain control even if the non-financial companies were partially privatised. There was considerable debate whether any new government taking office in 1993 would have a programme of aggressive privatisation with non-intervention in the strategic direction of the operations of banks and industry – that is, whether the micro-intervention of the past was a "socialist" or "French" attribute.

In addition to its direct and indirect equity holdings, the French government kept tight control through "moral suasion", a tradition of political meddling by bureaucrats who considered themselves able to come up with better economic solutions to national needs than the interplay of market forces. On a European level, beyond the tampering with free competition of the past and a highly protectionist stance within the EU decision process on matters of industrial and trade policy, there was concern that the French government would continue its *dirigiste* role and even try to extend it to the cross-border relationships of French firms and banks.

Harberer saw the role of the state in France as a two-edged sword. At times, it could thwart the achievement of his objectives, but state backing gave CL access to deep pockets and political support to overcome obstacles and setbacks that would stop ordinary banks in their tracks. To maximise the advantages and minimise the disadvantages, strong backing by key government mandarins was crucial.

The value of the government link became obvious in several accidents that befell CL in its drive for growth. Specifically in wholesale lending; balance sheet expansion could be achieved rapidly but growth meant narrower lending margins. As the European recession began to bite during 1990 and 1991, most banks retrenched to weather the storm. Crédit Lyonnais, on the other hand, announced that it would maintain its set course and "buy" its way out of the recession. The bank had taken on much riskier projects than many of its competitors – the list of CL's lending problems in the early 1990s included:

- Robert Maxwell, credit losses were significant (see the Goldman Sachs case and Box 1.1 in Chapter 1).
- Hachette, the French publisher, whose television channel, La Cinq, went bankrupt.
- Olympia and York, the Canadian real estate developer, which failed. CL was the second largest European creditor of the firm's Canary Wharf project in London.
- Loans of over $1 billion to Giancarlo Parretti, an Italian financier (later accused of fraud) for his purchase of the Hollywood film studio MGM/UA Communications.
- Loans to the Italian Florio Fiorini, who ran SASEA, a Swiss holding company that collapsed in 1992.

CL's rapid expansion in 1991 and 1992 provided a significant increase in its net banking income. In 1990, CL achieved a net profit of FF 3.7 billion, a 20% increase over 1989, although a major proportion of this increase was attributable to Altus Finance. However, there was an equally large increase in provisions because of the long list of bad debts. By the end of 1991, CL's profits fell to FF 3.16 billion, and provisions increased from FF 4.2 billion to FF 9.6 billion.

At 1.6% of total loans, CL's provisions were precarious when compared to those of other French banks. They were three times those of its main French competitors, but still better than most UK banks. However, Moody's Investor Services downgraded CL's bond rating from Aa1 to Aa2 because of the MGM/UA controversy and CL's increasing exposure to risky loans, even though the French government, which owned the bank, had an Aa rating.

CL's interest margins continued to decline as competition for deposits increased. At the same time, costs were rising as investment in technologies became increasingly necessary to keep pace with competition, and difficulties were encountered in curbing escalating personnel costs. Assuming that margins were unlikely to improve and cost pressures would be difficult to reverse, CL would have to rely far more heavily on commission income in the future than it had in the past.

In September 1992, Crédit Lyonnais announced its group profits had fallen by 92% to FF 119 million in the first half, compared to FF 1.6 billion the year before. Once again, this dramatic fall in profits was due to an increase in provisions for bad debts, from FF 3.4 billion for the first half of 1991 to FF 6.3 billion for the first half of 1992, even as net banking income grew by 16% and gross operating profit before provisions increased by 33% in the same period. Forty per cent of the bad debt provisions were attributed to CL Bank Nederland, the Dutch subsidiary, in connection with the MGM/UA Communications loans. In December 1992, Moody's downgraded CL debt again, to Aa3, citing "higher risk in both the loan portfolio and the bank's strategy" (*Euromoney*, March 1993).

All of these problems notwithstanding, its owner, the French government, seemed satisfied with CL's performance – evidently growth was deemed to be more important than profits. But the issue of capital adequacy could not be avoided, either under the Basel 1 risk assets ratio or the EC Capital Adequacy and Own Funds directives. As a state owned bank, Crédit Lyonnais could not raise equity capital independently. Only 5% of CL's capital was owned by shareholders, in the form of non-voting certificats d'investissement. The rest belonged either to the government or government-controlled companies. Thus any new capital infusions would have to come from the state.

From 1989 to 1991, the French government made complicated arrangements with five state-controlled companies to bolster CL's capital base and at the same time, solve certain industrial problems. In November 1989, CL raised FF 1.5 billion by selling shares to the Caisse de Dépôts et Consignations. In February and December 1990, share swaps with Thomson brought in FF 6.4 billion. A deal with Rhône-Poulenc raised another FF 1.7 billion in 1990.

In 1991, at the request of Prime Minister Edith Cresson, Crédit Lyonnais invested FF 2.5 billion in Usinor-Sacilor, and gained a 10% stake. The bank also swapped 10% of Usinor's shares for 10% of new Crédit Lyonnais shares, thereby boosting CL's shareholder equity by about FF 3 billion. This allowed Crédit Lyonnais to consolidate its share of Usinor-Sacilor's profit and losses. The deal diluted CL's earnings but provided a temporary solution to the problems of the troubled steelmaker.

By late 1992, about 28% of CL's capital base consisted of shares in state owned firms. In all of the share swaps, other parties paid much higher than book value. These agreements had the effect of linking the fate of the bank to the success of the companies concerned, and also represented a powerful incentive to support these same companies in the future, in the face of uncertain profitability. But the resulting capital infusions were insufficient to meet the bank's needs, and the question remained as to what the implications of these crossholding arrangements would be if and when some of these firms were privatised, especially Thomson and Rhône-Poulenc. The rest of the badly needed equity would have to be injected by the government.

## 10.6.8. The Grand Design

Harberer's mosaic seemed to be coming together much faster than anyone could have predicted when he took control in 1988. The key achievements were:

- The bank's balance sheet had grown enormously under his leadership. CL had penetrated all of the European markets in significant ways, including the most difficult of all, Germany.
- CL had maintained its close relationship to its shareholder, the French government, which had shown its willingness to inject capital and to tolerate even serious setbacks on the road to greater financial prominence. The bank's rapid growth and European cross-border market penetration was well suited to the French government's industrial policy objective of having one large French firm as a leader in every major sector of the European economy.
- CL's shareholdings in industrial companies had grown from FF 10 billion in September 1988 to FF 45 billion in early 1992, and it accumulated significant equity stakes in key French industrial companies. This put CL in a position to influence strategies and financing activities of these corporations. At the same time, it had provided the government with a durable industrial influence, even if the affected firms were to be privatised.

According to Harberer,[44] the CL strategy was to build a large, profitable, European banking group. He treated Western Europe as the domestic market of EU banks for the next decade. The bank was looking beyond the 1993 single market, to the market as it would be by the turn of the century. He accepted that CL's location in key financial centres did not matter for major corporate clients, but it was important for small and medium-sized corporations and individuals, which required a local presence.

However, the strategy was considered highly controversial, and various commentators identified a number of weaknesses in it:

- Harberer had ignored the possibility that EU partners would object to the French government tampering with market competition in their countries by using CL to acquire local banks.
- Harberer had not adequately addressed the problem of how to expand rapidly without buying excessive quantities of low-grade paper. He was creating such a weak loan portfolio that even the government was growing alarmed.
- Harberer's strategies were likely targets for the political infighting that would follow the French presidential election in 1995. Time was running short for Harberer to accomplish all he was hoping for.
- Harberer had neglected the investment banking and capital markets side of the business. CL had holdings in many companies which, given a sufficiently high credit rating, would prefer to use the capital markets rather than bank loans to satisfy their financing requirements.

Some critics combined all of these points to form a gloomy picture of CL in the late 1990s:

- It was viewed as a bank with important industrial shareholdings in companies that were looking to the capital markets to meet most of their financing needs. CL also

---

[44] Reported in *The Euromoney Supplement*, March 1991.

had numerous acquisitions and alliances with foreign banks whose clients were likewise defecting to the capital markets.

- In its quest for rapid growth, CL had accumulated many bad loans, leaving the bank with a weak loan portfolio and vulnerable to recession. By early 1994, the sluggish French economy, together with high interest rates, caused a marked deterioration in the French property market, and the bankruptcy of many small and medium-sized firms.

- Crédit Lyonnais reported escalating losses in 1991, 1992 and 1993. In 1993, Mr Harberer was dismissed, and Mr Jean Peyrelevade took over as CEO. Harberer became the head of Crédit National, but under public pressure was sacked from this post after CL's 1993 results were publicised.

## 10.6.9. The State Rescue of Crédit Lyonnais

In March 1994, CL reported 1993 losses of FF 6.9 billion ($1.2 billion), substantially higher than the 1992 losses of FF 1.8 billion. In late March, the government announced the first of four rescue plans. FF 23 billion ($4 billion) of new capital was injected into CL, on condition it sell off some of its assets and cut costs, mainly by reducing the number of employees. However, CL, under the new chairman, M. Peyrelevade, was slow to put its affairs in order. Administration costs fell by 3% in the first half of 1994, due mainly to staff cuts, but little progress was made on the sale of assets. CL chose to dispose of non-core activities, such as:

- The bank's stake in the FNAC retailing chain.
- The Meridian hotel chain.
- TFI, a television channel.
- Adidas, the German shoe company.

The bank raised about FF 20 billion from these disposals. In late 1994, CL sold a 57% stake in Banca Lombarda, an Italian bank, but still owned another sizeable bank in Italy and a majority stake in the German bank, BfG. Mr Peyrelevade aimed to sell an additional $20 billion in assets to shed troubled businesses and boost the bank's efficiency. However, little was done to reduce the bank's expanding pan-European banking network. On the contrary, CL announced its future growth would come from CL's remaining retail banking operations in Europe.

After the 1994 bailout, a French parliamentary commission investigated and reported on CL's affairs on 12 July 1994. The Commission concluded CL had lacked a risk management system capable of controlling the risks it took. Many of the problems originated with one or another of its four subsidiaries: Crédit Lyonnais Bank Nederland (CLBN), Altus Finance, Société de Banque Occidentale (SDBO) and International Bankers. For example, one of SDBO's clients was Bernard Tapie, a heavily indebted left-wing businessman, convicted in 1994 of rigging a crucial football game. CLBN, the Dutch subsidiary, had loaned $1.3 billion to an Italian, Sgr Giancarlo Parretti, to buy the Hollywood giant Metro-Goldwyn-Mayer (MGM). After Sgr Parretti was ousted, Crédit Lyonnais assumed direct control of MGM and injected more money into it, hoping to find a buyer and recover the funds it had invested. Eventually (1996) MGM was sold with its cinema chain to Virgin for $1.6 billion, recouping less than half of CL's total investment.[45]

In 1994, CL's losses nearly doubled to FF 12.1 billion mainly because of a decline in the domestic retail banking business. New account openings were down by 20% in 1994. Roughly a year after the first rescue plan, the bank was seeking a new capital injection. The government had little choice but to oblige or risk prompting a run on deposits. The *second rescue* was announced in March 1995, and involved the creation of a "bad bank". Recall the creation of a bad bank was discussed in some detail in Chapter 8 (see Box 8.1). These "bad banks" or asset management companies assume some or all of the bad debt, cleaning up the balance sheet of the troubled bank. The French equivalent was the Consortium de Realisation (CDR), to be financed by a new state entity, the EPFR,[46] which in turn was backed by a 20-year loan (FF 145 billion) from Crédit Lyonnais, and guaranteed by the French government. The CDR would sell the bad assets it had taken from CL, saving the bank from having to make substantial provisions and write downs. Put simply, the CDR, indirectly financed (via the EPFR) by a loan from CL, was to use the money to purchase CL's bad assets!

Under the second rescue plan, CL moved $27 billion from the CL balance sheets to the CDR, including key dud assets:

• $8.5 billion in problem real estate loans.
• $4 billion exposure from the ownership of MGM studios.
• $9 billion in equity holdings.

Since the second rescue plan involved a government subsidy (estimated to be worth $9.4 billion) to a state owned entity, it had to be approved by the European Competition Commission, which it was, in July 1995. However, the Commission threw out the CL's assertion that it should decide on which bad assets were to be sold, nor was CL to be allowed to buy back any of these bad assets. The Commission also specified that by the end of 1998, at least 35% of its assets outside France had to be sold off, worth FF 300 billion – over the previous 17 months, CL had only managed to sell FF 15 billion worth of assets. Meanwhile, *The Banker* reported (May 1995, p. 22) that CL was effectively bankrupt, because losses (equal to FF 50 billion) exceeded its capital base.

1996 was a bad year all round. The Paris head office of Credit Lyonnais was almost completely gutted in a mysterious fire, which spread to the archives and destroyed many documents that would have been of use to the official French investigation into how the bank got into such a big mess. By late summer, it was apparent that a third bailout would be necessary because of problems arising from the second rescue plan, especially the loan CL made to set up the bad bank. CL had been obliged to make the loan at below market rates, but deep recession hit the French economy, with knock-on effects in the French banking market. Interest rates collapsed, and the amount of the loan outstanding was much higher than had been forecast, as was the cost of financing it – CL was receiving just 2.975% on

---

[45] Source: "Banking's Biggest Disaster", *The Economist*, 5 July 1997, pp. 69–71.
[46] The Etablissement Public de Financement et de Restructuration (EPFR) was created to fund the selling off of the bad assets (worth about FF 190 billion) that the state had "bought" from CL.

the loan but paying 5.8% on its own debt. Also, CL's bad debt situation was worse than it might have been because the government pressured the bank to keep lending to prevent bankruptcies and therefore loss of jobs in a recession. Though the bank had always denied it was subject to interference by the state, M. Harberer (the former chairman) claimed that CL was frequently pressed to support key industrial companies in an attempt to boost economic growth and reduce the unemployment rate.

CL was set to lose another FF 3.9 billion ($762 million) in 1996. The European Commission agreed to a *third rescue*: FF 3.9 billion as "emergency" state aid.[47] In 1997, the French government injected an additional FF 3 billion without the Commission's approval, raising the total amount to FF 6.9 billion.

The EC was irritated by the failure of CL to adhere to the conditions of the earlier rescue plan. Nonetheless, in May 1998, the European Commission approved a *fourth rescue* plan. The EPFR was to pay the market rate on the loan from CL. Also, CL could swap shares with EPFR to buy back the original loan, but the shares had to be sold on the open market.[48] CL was required to make a minimum dividend payout on these shares of 58% of net profit through to 2003.

Other explicit EC requirements were:

- That CL sell FF 675 billion worth of holdings including Crédit Lyonnais Belgium, Asian banks and Bank für Gemeinwirtschaft, Harberer's German prize.
- Crédit Lyonnais was to divest itself of all its retail holdings outside France.
- The bank's growth rate was subject to limits until 2014.
- Between 1998 and 2000, 78 of its 1923 branches must be closed.
- The state owned 82% of CL but it must be fully privatised by 1999.
- The Commissioner was to receive quarterly reports to ensure France was complying with the rules.[49]

## 10.6.10. The "Bad Bank" Bungle[50]

The state owned bad bank, CDR, was a miserable failure in contrast to most of the "bad banks" (e.g. the United States, Scandinavia and Korea) set up to dispose of dud assets. Why? There are a number of reasons. First, both CL and the government were anxious to give the impression that CL was financing its own rescue, and did this by having CL make a loan to the EPFR, which was funding the CDR. However, as has been noted, the below market rate on the loan caused even more problems for CL, and was a contributory factor to a third rescue plan. When the rate was raised to a market rate, it meant the CDR (via the taxpayer) was injecting money into CL. Second, it wasn't just bad assets the CDR took on. Assets in some healthy French firms were also transferred: it was reasoned that if the CDR could sell some good assets, it would reduce its overall losses. But their transfer to the bad bank immediately lowered the market value of these assets. As a result, the CDR recouped

---

[47] The details reported in this paragraph are from "Banking's Biggest Disaster", *The Economist*, 7 May 1997, pp. 69–71.

[48] This effectively privatises part of CL.

[49] This summary of conditions is from "The Bitter End", *The Economist*, 23 May 1998, p. 67.

[50] This account is from "Crisis and More Crisis", *The Economist*, 7 May 1997, p. 17.

far less than had been expected when they were sold. The treatment of certain dud assets was also questionable. The troubled subsidiary of CL, the Société de Banque Occidentale, was transferred to the CDR, its bad assets sold off and new capital injected, only to be sold back to CL rather than being sold on the open market. Société Générale complained to the European Commission, claiming it never had an opportunity to buy SBO, though the CDR denied this, saying there was no market interest in it. Third, after the European Commission insisted the CDR be independent of CL, the government announced that the CDR was to sell 80% of its assets within 5 years. The target effectively forced the CDR to sell at even heavier discounts because buyers knew it was under pressure to offload its portfolio. Finally, one of the bad assets the CDR took on in 1996, Executive Life, eventually implicated it in a criminal prosecution in the United States – see below.

## 10.6.11. Return to Profit and Privatisation[51]

Having offloaded its bad assets, the bank had returned to profit in 1997, reporting pre-tax profits of $702 million and in 1998, $588 million. The year the bank was privatised, 1999, profits were $1.1 billion.[52] Yet its cost to income ratio remained stubbornly high, at 79% in 1997, 76% in 1998 and 75% in 1999, compared to an average of 64% for the Crédit Agricole Group. In most years CL's ratio was well above those of its key competitors, suggesting this bank had done little to cut costs or improve efficiency.

The French government announced the plans for privatisation in March 1999 – 33% was to be sold to a group of institutional investors, 4.3% to employees and 51.8% to retail investors. The government would keep a 10.9% stake. At the end of June 1999, the share price was announced: 26.2 euros ($27.33) per share. The sale was completed in early July. It was 30 times oversubscribed by institutional investors: the final group consisting of several firms led by Crédit Agricole, and including Crédit Commercial de France, Commerzbank, BBV of Spain, Allianz, AXA, AGF (a French insurer) and Bank Intesa. No institution could buy more than 10% of the total shares. They also agreed not to sell their shares (up to July 2003) to an outsider until they had been offered to another institutional investor within the group of seven. The individual investor sale was three times oversubscribed.

Mr. Peyrelevade stayed on as chairman. The next issue was what the bank was going to do with the government stakeholding, which, under the Commission agreement, it had to sell off. For many months, negotiations had been going on between Crédit Agricole and the government, and it was widely assumed this bank would buy the government stake in a private deal. In a surprise move, the French Finance Minister, M. Mer, apparently frustrated by the slow progress of the negotiation, announced, in November 2002, that the government was to sell the shares by auction to the highest bidder, including any foreign bank – bids had to be in within 22 hours. BNP Paribas won, having bid 49% over the going market price. Crédit Agricole, having refused to pay €44 ($44) per share in the private deal, apparently offered this amount in its bid, only to lose out to the €58 offered by BNP Paribas.

---

[51] Sources for the statistics reported in this subsection: Lanchner, D. (2003), "Agricole's Carron goes Courting", *Institutional Investor*, **37**(1), 14 and "Farmer's Folly", *The Economist*, 21 December 2002, p. 103.
[52] Source: *The Banker*, July issues, 1997, 1998.

By mid-December, it was all change again. Crédit Agricole was stung by losing the government shares to BNP. The bank's unusual corporate structure was a key reason why it was slow to reach an agreement with the government. Crédit Agricole SA is a listed company, but 70% of it is owned by 45 regional mutual banks – the Fédération Nationale du Crédit Agricole. The Chairman of CA SA (M. Bué) had dithered over whether or not CA SA should buy the shares. When the auction was announced and CA lost out to BNP Paribas, there was great consternation, which galvanised the regions into action. M. Bué stepped down and M. Carton (Chairman of Fédération Nationale du Crédit Agricole) became Chairman of CA SA. Within a fortnight, M. Carton bid for Crédit Lyonnais. The bid was worth €16.5 billion ($17 billion), or €56 per share, 2 euros less than the BNP bid for the government shares. This was equivalent to 22.5 times CL's estimated 2002 earnings.

Not all the regional mutuals supported the bid, but most recognised that the alternative (BNP Paribas taking over CL) would put them at a considerable disadvantage. The takeover meant the combined assets of the new bank, called Credit Agricole, were €716.8 billion, only slightly smaller than BNP Paribas (€759.4 billion). For the first time, Agricole was represented in the urban areas, where CL had a 10% market share. Peyrelevade was concerned that if BNP bought CL, there would be large job losses, because of the high degree of urban overlap between the two banks. At the retail level, the new bank had a 30% market share. The plan is to maintain separate retail branches, similar to the strategy adopted by NatWest and The Royal Bank of Scotland. However, it is hoped some cost cutting will be possible through the integration of back office operations.

There are some tricky issues related to the integration of the two banks. The bank estimated that it can gain €760 in synergies, but by the spring of 2004, it had managed just 5% of that estimate.[53] The fact that Crédit Agricole has a complex ownership structure does not help, nor do the problems with top management at Caylon – created to run CA's corporate and investment banking business. Caylon is supposed to be the source of two-thirds of the synergies, which translates into job cuts. The new chief executive, from Crédit Agricole, is known for making efficiency gains but has no experience in investment banking. The atmosphere at Caylon is grim, and its two rivals, BNP Paribas and Société Générale, have been quick to poach key staff.

The total cost of bailing out Crédit Lyonnais was put at $17.25 billion by the chairman, M. Peyrelevade in June 2003. Other estimates in 1997[54] put it as high as FF 170 billion, about $22 billion at current (2003) exchange rates. While Japan's recent problems involve numerous banks and will leave it with a much higher bill (up to $580 billion – see Chapter 8), CL stands out as the most costly *single* bank rescue in history.

## 10.6.12. Executive Life: An Expensive Ghost from the Past

In 1998, following a tip-off from a French informant, the US regulatory authorities began to investigate the claim that Crédit Lyonnais had used a front organisation to bypass laws

[53] Source: "French Banking – Town and Country", *The Economist*, 13 March 2004, pp. 92–93.

[54] Charles de Courson, a deputy in the French parliament who became an expert on CL documentation – cited in "Banking's Biggest Disaster", *The Economist*, 7 May 1997, pp. 69–71.

prohibiting banks operating in the USA from engaging in certain activities. M. Peyrelevade, CL's chairman, admitted to a breach of US banking laws by Crédit Lyonnais, but claimed no knowledge of the affair at the time. He pointed the finger at M. Harberer because it was all done in the heyday of CL's expansionist strategy under him.

In 1991, a Californian life insurance company, Executive Life, was insolvent. Its two main assets were a junk bond portfolio worth about $6 billion (trading at half its face value) and life insurance contracts. American regulators insisted that the buyer of the junk bond portfolio also find a firm to take on the insurance contracts. CL's subsidiary, Altus Finance, specialised in high risk financial deals. Altus wanted the junk bonds, thinking of potential profits once the junk bond market recovered. As a subsidiary of a bank, Altus would be breaking US law if it owned an insurance firm. Harberer had an idea – to set up a front which, in French circles, was euphemised as a *portgage* (parking agreement). Cash and commissions were used to persuade some loyal CL clients to purchase the life insurance firm. Executive Life was renamed Aurora, and purchased by the consortium of investors.[55] They had duped the authorities into thinking they were the genuine owners when in fact, Altus had given them the cash to purchase the firm, and an undertaking to buy it back. The deal was completed in September 1993.

Altus Finance bought the junk bond portfolio in March 1992. However, some of these bonds were being converted to equity by the issuers. Again, Altus was running up against American laws: banks cannot own non-banks. Harberer persuaded one of its major borrowers, M. Pinault, owner of a French retail giant, to buy the junk bond portfolio and transfer it to Artemis, a firm controlled by Pinault. At the time Pinault had debts of FF 21 billion, which he was struggling to service, most of it in the form of loans made by CL. In November 1992, CL gave him a new line of credit and cash to purchase the junk bond portfolio.

Recall Altus had agreed to buy back Executive Life/Aurora, but if it did, Altus would be in breach of US banking law. To prevent this, Artemis was to buy the life insurance firm too, with cash from Crédit Lyonnais. By August 1995, Artemis owned 67% of Executive Life. The rest of it was owned by SunAmerica, a US insurance firm – it had no knowledge of the French antics.

By this time CL had a 24.5% stake in Artemis, in breach of at least two US laws, since it indirectly owned part of the junk bond portfolio and a life insurance firm. A detailed document outlining all these arrangements was faxed to Mr. Peyrelevade's office in December 1993, a month after M. Peyrelevade had become chairman. During the US investigation, M. Peyrelevade claimed he had no knowledge of the document, and even threatened to sue *The Economist*[56] for claiming he either did, or should have known about the deals. Many more documents were to follow, Crédit Lyonnais having left a long paper/electronic trail which provided rich pickings for the US prosecutors. In 1998, M. Pinault, in exchange for handing over documents, negotiated immunity from criminal prosecution by the US authorities.

---

[55] Including MAAF, a leading French insurance firm.

[56] *The Economist* was one of the first newspapers to uncover a trail of documents that showed the extent of Peyrelevade's knowledge and involvement. See, for example, "Executive Briefing" and a "New Scandal at Crédit Lyonnais" in *The Economist*, 7 May 1997, pp. 67–70.

Then came their Waterloo:

- June 2003: M. Harberer was fined and received a suspended prison sentence by a French court for failure to disclose the extent of CL's losses. He has said he will appeal.
- September 2003: M. Peyrelevade resigned as Chairman of Crédit Lyonnais, which had been taken over by Credit Agricole in December 2002.
- December 2003: The US Department of Justice announced plea and settlement agreements with Crédit Lyonnais, the bad bank, CDR (which had taken over the assets of Executive Life in 1995), MAAF Assurance (one of the leading members of the consortium paid to buy Executive Life, renamed Aurora, with an agreement that it would be sold back to Altus) and MAAF's chairman. All agreed to plead guilty to a criminal charge of making false statements to US regulators in the acquisition of the junk bond portfolio and life insurance business of Executive Life. These parties, and Artemis, are to pay fines totalling $771.75 million, believed to be the largest settlement of a criminal case in the USA.
- A Grand Jury indicted a number of individuals on several counts of fraud, and criminal violation of the Bank Holding Company Act, including Harberer, Peyrelevade, M. Henin (managing director of Artemis) and three other French nationals. They are to be tried in February 2005, though US attorney D. Yang has said there could be an out of court settlement before then.[57]

## 10.6.13. Conclusion

M. Harberer's expansionist vision for Crédit Lyonnais began when he was appointed chairman in 1988. It was two years after London's Big Bang, the culmination of a series of reforms aimed at ridding the City of restrictive practices, and giving its financial institutions a favourable, free market environment balanced with regulation. There were some celebrated banking disasters, such as BCCI and Barings, but the majority of London's banks have been highly successful. In France, the attitude could not have been more different. M. Harberer belonged to a meritocratic elite committed to the French government's belief that the state knew more than the markets. France was one of the democratic countries that suffered a prolonged bad dose of this disease, which is more frequently observed in communist or fascist states. Crédit Lyonnais's existence as an independent bank ended just short of its 140th birthday, though its state bank status had denied it true independence for some time. The case study illustrates how a bank can end up a costly failure because of meddling by the government while attempting to achieve so-called "national economic objectives". Egocentric executives lent enthusiastic support to the state's plans, envisioning a French global economic empire, with banks and other institutions dominating the European Union. Previous cases have illustrated the need for close supervision of banks, but that is quite different from state ownership, which encourages greater mistakes and risk taking. If governments must own banks, they should be left to sink or swim in a free market where they are treated on a par with private banks.

---

[57] Source of information on the settlement and indictments: press release from the US Department of Justice, D.W. Yang, US Attorney, Central District of California, 18 December 2003.

## Questions

1. Using the case, explain the meaning of:
   (a) banque industrie;
   (b) German hausbank;
   (c) dirigisme;
   (d) SICAVs monétaires;
   (e) French universal banking, as compared to British universal banking;
   (f) The declaration by Crédit Lyonnais (CL) that it would "buy" its way out of the 1990–91 recession.
2. What is the principal difference between state owned (nationalised) public and shareholder owned public banks?
3. What should be the criteria for taking a decision to become a pan-European bank? Was this the criteria used at CL?
4. (a) Do you agree that capturing 1% to 2% of European deposits is the key to becoming a pan-European bank?
   (b) What is meant by pan-European retail banking? Is it a feasible strategy?
5. In Chapter 5, it was noted that there are obstacles that may inhibit the completion of the single banking market. In this regard, what problems does the CL case highlight?
6. Was Harberer qualified to run Crédit Lyonnais?
7. Is an industrial policy of protection, subsidisation, ministerial guidance and selective capital infusions the optimal way of ensuring certain domestic firms are able to compete on global markets?
8. What are the conditions under which a state owned nationalised bank will be an efficient competitor, able to penetrate foreign markets?
9. Harberer's expansion into Europe was undertaken to gain a foothold in key EU states. Identify which ventures (if any) were consistent with sound financial principles.
10. To what extent did the changing political environment affect CL decision-making? Is this ever a problem for private or shareholder owned public banks?
11. To what extent did poor risk management contribute to the near collapse of CL?
12. In the context of the CL case, discuss the extent to which a trade-off exists between balance sheet growth and profitability?
13. (a) What factors caused the near collapse of Crédit Lyonnais in 1994, and the need for four rescue packages?
   (b) Could a privately owned bank ever get into a situation like this?
   (c) Was the French government (or succession of governments) correct to bail it out?
   (d) Why did the European Commission insist that CL be privatised?
14. Explain the meaning of "good bank/bad bank". Why did the CDR (the equivalent of a "bad bank") fail when similar arrangements in other countries (e.g. the USA, Korea) proved so successful? (See Box 8.1 in Chapter 8 for help with this answer.)
15. (a) What problems did Crédit Agricole face when in the process of taking over Crédit Lyonnais?
   (b) Are there any reasons for thinking the integration of CL into Crédit Agricole might be problematic?
16. (a) With reference to the Executive Life affair, what US banking laws were broken by (i) Altus Finance and (ii) Crédit Lyonnais?
   (b) If this situation had arisen in 2000, would Altus Finance and Crédit Lyonnais still be breaking any US banking laws? (See the section on US regulation in Chapter 5 to answer these questions.)
17. In the 1980s, France opted for nationalised banks as an integral part of its national economic plan. Around the same time, the UK had embarked on a number of financial reforms, culminating in "Big Bang", 1986. Both nations subsequently suffered some highly publicised bank "failures" in the 1990s. In view of this, was one system better than the other? (See the section on UK regulation in Chapter 5, and the description of the BCCI and Barings bank failures in Chapter 7.)

# 10.7. Continental Illinois Bank and Trust Company[58]

**Relevant Parts of the Text:** Chapters 5 (US regulation) and 7.

The collapse of Continental Illinois was one of the bank failure cases discussed in Chapter 7. This case study provides more detail on the collapse, and asks some broadly based questions which may be answered in conjunction with the material in Chapter 7.

## 10.7.1. A Detailed Summary of the Collapse of Continental

### 31 December 1981

At the end of December 1981, Continental had assets totalling $45.1 billion, making it the sixth largest bank in the USA. It had received favourable assessments from the Office of the Comptroller of the Currency (OCC) between 1974 and 1981. In 1978, Dun's Review listed it as one of the five best managed corporations in the USA. Energy loans amounted to 20% of loans and leases.

### 30 June 1982

Continental was holding $1.1 billion of loans purchased from Penn Square Bank of Oklahoma City, representing 3% of total loans and leases.

### 5 July 1982

Penn Square Bank failed. Continental placed $20 billion of collateral with the Chicago Federal Reserve, in anticipation of a run. It was not used, but Continental lost access to Federal Reserve (Fed) funds and the domestic certificates of deposits (CD) market. It replaced the lost deposits with eurodollar borrowing in the interbank market. By the end of July, it was apparent Continental had survived the run in both the US and euromarkets.

### 31 December 1982–31 March 1984

Non-performing assets more than trebled. The bank had loans outstanding to International Harvester, Massey-Ferguson, Braniff, the Alpha Group of Mexico, Nucorp Energy and Dome Petroleum.

### February 1984

To maintain its dividend, Continental sold its credit card business to Chemical Bank.

---

[58] This case first appeared in the New York University Salomon Center Case Studies in Banking and Finance (Case 41), by Richard Herring (1991). The case was edited and updated by Shelagh Heffernan; questions set by Shelagh Heffernan.

### 16 March 1984–4 May 1984

Seven small banks were closed, using a new "payout–cash advance" procedure, giving rise to losses on uninsured creditors.

### 9 May 1984

Rumours began to circulate in Tokyo that Continental was about to file for protection under chapter 11 bankruptcy law. A run on deposits began in Tokyo when traders received the news, and the run followed the sun west, as western financial markets began to open.

### 10 May 1984

The OCC issued a special news release that it was not aware of any significant changes in the operations of Continental, as reflected in published financial statements. The OCC said Continental's ratios compared favourably with those of other key multinational banks. The statement was an attempt to quash the rumours which had initiated the run.

### 11 May 1984

Continental borrowed about $3.6 billion (later rising to $4 billion) from the Chicago Fed, almost half the daily funding requirement.

### 14 May 1984

It was announced that a consortium of 16 major US banks would provide Continental with a 30-day $4.5 billion line of credit. During the week, the spread between CDs and T-bills widened from 40 basis points to 130 basis points.

### 17 May 1984

The Federal Deposit Insurance Corporation (FDIC) with the Fed and OCC guaranteed all depositors and general creditors of the bank. The guarantee was accompanied by a capital infusion of $2 billion (from the FDIC and a group of commercial banks) and a credit line from 28 banks of $5.5 billion. The Fed announced it was prepared to meet any extraordinary liquidity demands.

### Mid-May 1984

There was a further run on deposits, amounting to $20 billion, less $5 billion in asset sales. It was covered by borrowing $5 billion from the Fed, $2 billion in subordinated notes placed with the FDIC and domestic banks, and $4.1 billion from another 28 banks in the safety net arrangement. An additional $4 billion came from some banks in the safety net.

### *1 July 1984*

Officials admitted the run had continued, forcing the bank to sell another $5 billion in assets.

## 10.7.2. The Resolution

- Continental was divided into a "good" bank and a "bad" bank.
- The FDIC paid $2 billion for problem loans with a face value of $3 billion. The "bad" bank was to be managed for the FDIC by a newly formed service subsidiary of Continental. Any loans to sovereigns or guaranteed to sovereigns were exempted. The FDIC committed itself to assume as much as $1.5 billion in other troubled loans over a 3-year period. The purchases would take place at book value.
- The FDIC assumed Continental's $3.5 billion debt to the Reserve Bank of Chicago rather than paying cash. The FDIC was to repay the Chicago Fed over 5 years.
- The FDIC was to provide a $1 billion capital infusion in return for preferred stock, convertible into 80% of Continental's common stock.
- The FDIC replaced the Continental board and management team.

## 10.7.3. A Review of How the Problems at Continental Arose

Between 1974 and 1981, Continental grew rapidly, acquiring many loans that ultimately resulted in losses. The period 1982–84 was the aftermath of what happened once significant loan problems had been uncovered. The discussion is largely with reference to the bank, not the bank holding company.

Mr Roger E. Anderson became Chairman and Chief Executive Officer in 1973. He and a management team set strategic goals, the objective of which was to transform Continental from a midwestern country bank to a world class bank.

Between 1974 and 1981, Continental's assets grew by an average of over 13% per year. In 1984 it had $45.1 billion in total assets, making it the sixth largest bank in the USA, up from the eighth largest in 1974. Continental grew faster than any other wholesale bank in this period. In 1973, Continental had launched an aggressive campaign on segments of the banking market to increase market share. It rapidly built up its consumer loan portfolio.

A private placement unit was created that secured a foothold in the market by arranging placements of debt for small companies. It expanded globally by structuring syndicated eurodollar loans, making advances in direct lending to European multinational companies, and becoming active in project financing.

Like most banks, Continental suffered during the collapse of the real estate investment trust industry in the mid-1970s. Continental's management, however, handled the problem well – its recovery from the real estate problems was more successful than most other large banks with similar problems. As a result, Continental remained active in property lending throughout the period.

The recession of 1974–75 saw Continental emerge with one of the best loan loss records of its peer group, suggesting management knew how to deal with economic downturns. Some of Continental's main competitors had suffered financial problems, which enabled the bank to take advantage of a competitive opportunity and become the premier bank in the midwest.

The OCC conducted eight examinations of the bank during the period 1974–81, all of which were favourable. The bank's handling of its problem loans following the 1974–75 recession was considered superior to most other wholesale money centre banks.

In 1972 the bank had expanded the individual lending officers' authority and removed the loan approval process from a committee framework. In 1976 the bank reorganised itself, eliminating "red-tape" from its lending procedures. Major responsibility was delegated to lending officers in the field, resulting in fewer controls and levels of review. The idea was to provide lending officers with the flexibility to quickly take advantage of lending opportunities as they arose. While decentralised lending operations were common among money centre and large regional banks, Continental was a leader in this approach. Management believed such an organisational structure would allow Continental to expand market share and become one of the top three banks lending to corporations in the USA.

In light of this rapid growth, the OCC examiners stressed the importance of adequate controls, especially in the loan area. The examiners noted certain internal control problems, especially the exceptions to the timing of putting problem loans on the bank's internal watch list. However, given the bank's historical loan loss experience and proven ability to deal with problem situations, supervisors were not seriously concerned about the weaknesses they had reported.

Management implemented new internal controls, in response to the OCC report, including computer-generated past due reports and a system to track exceptions in the internal rating process.

In the period 1974–81 Continental sought to increase loan growth by courting companies in profitable, though in some cases high-risk, businesses. Lending officers were encouraged to move fast, offer more innovative packages, and take on more loans. This aggressive lending strategy worked well for the bank: its commercial and industrial loan portfolio grew from $4.9 billion in 1974 to $14.3 billion in 1981. It expanded its market share in the late 1970s (rising from 3.9% at the end of 1974 to 4.4% at year-end 1981), when many other money centre banks were losing out to foreign banks, the growing commercial paper market and other non-traditional lenders.

As part of its corporate expansion, Continental was very aggressive in the energy area. In the early 1950s it had created an oil-lending unit and was, reportedly, the first major bank to have petroleum engineers and other energy specialists on its staff. The economic consequences of the 1973 oil embargo and the resulting fourfold increase in world oil prices meant energy self-sufficiency became a top priority on the national political agenda. Various administrations and Congress launched initiatives to increase domestic production and reduce energy consumption. Continental, having cultivated this niche from the 1950s, became a key energy sector lending bank.

The commercial and industrial loan portfolio (including its energy loans) produced high returns for Continental – average returns were consistently higher than those of other wholesale money centre banks. The financial markets reacted favourably to the aggressive loan strategy adopted by Continental.

Analysts noted its stable assets and earnings growth, its excellent loan loss record, and its expertise in energy sector lending. In 1976, Continental Illinois Corporation's ratio of market price to book value began to rise – up to this date, it had lagged behind other money centre banks.

The rapid growth in its assets was funded by the purchase of wholesale money, including federal funds, negotiable certificates of deposit, and deposits from the interbank market. It had limited access to retail banking markets and core deposit funding because of state regulations in Illinois which effectively restricted the bank to unit bank status. Purchased funds made up 70% of the bank's total liabilities, substantially higher than the peer group average.

In the 1976 inspection by the OCC, examiners expressed concern about the bank's liquidity and its reliance on Fed funds, foreign deposits and negotiable CDs. By the summer of 1977, the bank had improved its liquidity and enhanced its monitoring systems. OCC examiners concluded that the bank was adequately monitoring its funding, and maintaining control. However, the bank was requested to submit quarterly status reports on classified assets over $4 million, and also to submit monthly status reports.

Continental's heavy reliance over this period on purchased money, which had a higher interest cost on retail deposits, offset much of the gain that accrued from the higher loan yields. Higher funding costs reduced Continental's net interest margin to a level well below its peer group. However, the bank was able to maintain its superior earnings growth because of low overheads (due to the absence of domestic branches and few foreign branches compared to its peer group) and non-interest expenses. Continental's ratio of non-interest expenses to average assets was far below its peer group average.

Throughout the late 1970s the OCC expressed concern not only about asset quality, but about capital adequacy as well. During the 1976 examination, the OCC pointed out the absence of a capital growth plan by Continental, which was unlike most other large national banks. In response, the bank prepared a 3-year capital plan and took immediate measures to increase capital, including cutting the size of its 1976 dividends to the holding company by $15 million. The bank holding company issued debt and used the proceeds to inject $62 million into the bank's surplus account. However, asset growth outpaced capital growth, and capital declined throughout 1980.

The 1979 OCC examination noted the continued improvement in Continental's asset quality. Classified assets had declined from 86% to 80% of gross capital funds. Liquidity was also considered adequate. The OCC did note some problems in the bank's internal credit review system – deficiencies were cited in the identification and rating of problem loans and in the completeness of credit files. OCC examiners also stressed the importance of a strong capital base, in light of Continental's rapid asset growth rate.

The 1980 examination drew similar conclusions. Liquidity was considered acceptable. Asset quality continued to improve – classified assets as a percentage of gross capital funds declined to 61%. This figure was lower than the average for other money centre banks.

Management was encouraged to organise an on-site review of information submitted to the loan review committee, such as periodic visits to foreign offices and other loan origination sites. Capital was considered adequate, even though it was not keeping pace with asset growth. It was thought Continental had sufficient capacity to meet external pressures and to fund projected growth.

In response to the 1980 examiner's report, Continental's management indicated that although they believed the existing internal credit review system was adequate, they were exploring ways of conducting on-site examinations in a cost effective way. An experimental field review was subsequently conducted.

Historically, Continental had made loans to energy producers that were secured by proven reserves or by properties surrounded by producing wells that were guaranteed to produce oil and gas. As part of management's intensified commitment to energy lending in the late 1970s, the bank had begun expanding its energy loan portfolio, including making loans secured by leases on underdeveloped properties with uncertain production potential. This change occurred at a time when energy prices were increasing rapidly and drilling and exploration activity booming. The bank also became particularly aggressive in expanding loans to small independent drillers and refiners.

By 1981, Continental's exposure to the energy sector was very pronounced. Management was unconcerned because it was confident about the strength of the sector and its knowledge of specific oil fields and companies. It was believed the bank had found a good way to leverage (gear) its expertise in the oil industry.

During the 1981 examination, the OCC placed special emphasis on the review of Continental's energy and real estate loan portfolio. The bank's energy portfolio was 20% of its total loans and leases, and 47% of all its commercial and industrial loans. The energy portfolio nearly doubled from 1979 to 1980, and increased by 50% in 1981. Losses from Continental's energy loans consistently averaged less than half the net loan losses from non-energy loans.

The 1981 OCC examination relied on information as of April that year. The examiners noted a significant level of participations from Penn Square that were backed up by letters of credit. Extra time was spent examining these loans because they were large relative to Penn Square's size. The OCC concluded the standby letters of credit were issued by banks other than Penn Square, including several money centre banks, alleviating the OCC's concerns. Only two of Continental's oil and gas loans had been classified, and neither loan had been purchased by Penn Square.

In the 1981 examination, the OCC continued to look at the quality of the credit rating system. Classified assets as a percentage of gross capital increased from 61% to 67%. This trend was common to other large banks and the OCC judged it to be due to declining macroeconomic conditions rather than a worsening of credit standards. The internal loan review system of the bank was also reviewed. It was noted that about 375 loans (totalling $2.4 billion) had not been reviewed by the rating committee within 1 year; 55 of these had not been reviewed over 2 years. Management admitted to being aware of these exceptions and noted it was in the process of reassessing its loan review system.

At the 1981 examination, the OCC was satisfied with Continental's quality and consistency of earnings. Though holding down dividends had resulted in a steady source of capital augmentation, capital still needed to be brought in line with asset growth. Liquidity was considered adequate to meet any external pressures. The OCC reported that suitable systems of managing funding and rate sensitivity were in place.

In response to the 1981 examination, the management at Continental denied there was a problem with the quality of the loan portfolio, given the state of the economy at the time, especially record high interest rates. But they stated that close, continued attention would be provided to the quality of the loan portfolio. Improvements were to be made to ensure loans were reviewed on schedule.

Throughout 1981, financial analysts believed that Continental would continue to exhibit superior growth because of its position as prime lender to the energy industry, its potential for an improved return on assets, and its record of loan losses. Continental was complimented for its choice of energy lending as a niche market.

## 10.7.4. The Demise of Continental: January 1982–July 1984

To fully understand Continental's demise, it is necessary to review the history of Penn Square Bank's involvement. Penn Square was one of the most aggressive lenders in a very active drilling part of the country – Oklahoma City. Its loan-generating ability exceeded its legal lending limit as well as its funding ability, so Penn Square originated energy loans and sold them to other banks, including Continental and Seattle First National Bank.

Although Continental began purchasing loans from Penn Square as early as 1978, significant growth in loan purchases did not occur until 1981. At the end of the 1981 OCC examination, Penn Square loan purchases were in excess of $500 million; at the start of the 1982 examination, they had risen to a total value of $1.1 billion. At their peak in the spring of 1982, loans that originated at Penn Square represented 17% of Continental's entire oil and gas portfolio.

The OCC made a quarterly visit to Continental in March 1982, ahead of their main examination. The energy sector was in decline, but even so, bank officials said they were comfortable with their expertise in the area. In the May 1982 examination, the OCC planned to focus on the energy portfolio – a specialist was assigned to the OCC to assist in the examination. OCC's concerns heightened when it was found, at the OCC examination of Penn Square, that Continental had purchased a significant quantity of bad loans from Penn Square. The OCC informed Continental of the serious situation at Penn Square and extended their examination to November, working closely with internal auditors at Penn Square and independent accountants to assess the damage.

On 5 July 1982, Penn Square failed. Continental was directed by the OCC to implement a number of corrective measures; the bank complied. In August, the OCC informed management of its intention to formalise these directives by placing the bank under a Formal Agreement: the Comptroller and OCC staff met with senior management at Continental to discuss the bank's condition and the impending agreement.

Continental moved quickly to determine the extent of its exposure in loans origi-nated by Penn Square, to assess the amount of loan loss provision necessary for the second quarter, and to stabilise funding. The OCC also scrutinised the Penn Square loan purchases carefully, assessing the effect on Continental's loan portfolio and the provision for loan losses.

The 1982 OCC examination determined that many of the purchases from Penn Square, especially in the months just prior to Penn Square's failure, had failed to meet Continental's typical energy lending standards. Many were also poorly documented and were, therefore, not being internally rated in a timely manner. Thus, an increasing number of these loans appeared on Continental's late rating reports. Also, numerous loans had appeared on the bank's internally generated collateral exception report. Recall that, in previous years, the reliability of Continental's internal reporting systems had been questioned. As a consequence, officers from the Special Industries division who were purchasing the loans from Penn Square were able to persuade senior officers to disregard the internal reports. As a result, any internal warning signals were either missed or ignored.

During the OCC's 1982 inspection, the examiners learned that a team of internal auditors had been sent twice in 1981 by Executive Vice-President Bergman, head of Continental's Special Industries group, to review the Penn Square loans being purchased by Continental. The internal auditors singled out several items for special attention, including incomplete and inaccurate records, questionable security interests, and the high level of loans to parties related to Penn Square. However, the Special Litigation report issued by Continental's board of directors in 1984 concluded that his audit report, although submitted to Mr Bergman, had not been seen by senior management at Continental prior to the collapse of Penn Square.

In December 1981, Continental's bank auditors submitted a written report of their findings of a second visit to Penn Square. They expressed concern about:

- Loans secured by Penn Square, consisting of standby letters of credit, representing one-third of Penn Square's equity.
- Questionable lien positions (arrangements whereby collateral is held until a debt is paid).
- Several loans in which Continental had purchased more than Penn Square's current outstanding balance.
- $565 000 in personal loans from Penn Square to Mr John R Lytle, manager of Continental's Mid-Continent Division of the Oil and Gas group, and the officer responsible for acquiring Penn Square loans.
- The Special Litigation Report indicated that while senior Continental management did receive news of these loans to Mr Lytle, they had not received the full auditors' report from the December review of the Penn Square lending operations. No action was taken by Continental to remove or discipline Mr Lytle until May 1982.

After the collapse of Penn Square in July 1982, Continental sent a staff of experienced energy lenders to Oklahoma City to review Penn Square's records and assess the dimensions of the problem. Each of the loans purchased from Penn Square was reviewed during the first two weeks of July. After analysing the probable risk associated with each credit, senior

Continental officers recommended an addition to loan loss reserves of $220 million. The OCC and Continental's accountants, after a review, accepted this figure as realistic. It was published on 21 July along with a full statement of Continental's second quarter results.

Continental's auditors, supported by accountants from Ernst and Whinney, remained in Oklahoma City reconciling Continental's records with Penn Square data, assisting in the Penn Square portfolio assessment programme and preparing loan workouts. In late August and early September, each loan purchased from Penn Square was reviewed by OCC examiners, who discussed their findings with the senior management at Continental before the third quarter results were released. The review resulted in $81 million being added to the bank's provision for loan losses in the third quarter, as reported in Continental Illinois Corporation's 14 October, 1982 press release. It also indicated that non-performing assets had risen to $2 billion, up $700 million from the previous quarter.

Simultaneous with the credit review, Continental undertook an extensive review of the people involved in the Penn Square relationship and lending policies, procedures and practices. Based on the recommendations of an independent review committee appointed by Continental's board of directors, Mr Lytle, Mr Bergman and his superior, Mr Baker ceased to work for the bank. Other bank personnel were reassigned.

The internal review committee, in the second phase, recommended:

- Codification of bank lending policies and procedures.
- Enhancement of secured lending and related support systems.
- Improvement in cooperation between loan operations and the line.
- Revision of loan operations activity to improve its reliability and productivity.
- Formulation of a credit risk evaluation division, as had been recommended by the OCC, to strengthen the bank's credit rating system and enhance credit risk identification, evaluation, reporting and monitoring.

Following the Penn Square collapse, the domestic money market's confidence in Continental was seriously weakened. The bank's access to the Fed Funds and domestic CD markets was severely restricted – Continental lost 40% of its purchased domestic funding in 1982.

Continental moved quickly to stabilise and restore its funding. Meetings were held with major funds providers, ratings agencies and members of the financial community. Public disclosures were periodically issued to correct misinformation. In the autumn of 1982, liquid assets were sold or allowed to mature. As the domestic markets for funds dried up, Continental shifted to the European interbank market. Foreign liabilities began to approach 50% of the bank's total liability structure.

Continental's parent holding company maintained its 50 cents per share dividend in August 1982. The earnings level did not warrant a dividend of this size, but the holding company management felt it was a necessary step to restore confidence and to raise capital in the market place.

Despite these actions, Continental's condition deteriorated throughout 1982. Many of its energy loans that had performed well and had been extremely profitable in the 1970s until well into 1981 were now seriously underperforming or non-performing.

At the holding company level, non-performing assets grew to $844 million at the end of the first quarter of 1982. While most of these had been concentrated in real estate loans and non-energy-related corporate loans through the first quarter of 1982, in the following quarters, a large number of energy loans became non-performing. By the end of 1982, close to half (over $900 million) of Continental's non-performing assets were energy-related. Net loan losses reached $371 million by December 1982, a near fivefold increase over losses for the previous year. Though the economy improved in 1983, losses at Continental remained high.

While oil and gas loans made up about 20% of Continental's average total loan portfolio in 1982 and 1983, they represented about 67% of its June 1982–84 losses. Most of these losses were a direct result of its purchase of loans from Penn Square. Although loans purchased from Penn Square averaged less than 3% of total loans over the past 2.5 years, they accounted for 41% of the bank's losses between June 1982 and June 1984. Penn Square loans had resulted in nearly $500 million in loan losses for Continental. Most of the loan losses originated in 1980 and 1981.

The loan quality problems caused Continental's earnings to collapse. The bank's provision for loan losses consumed 93% of its 1982 operating income, reaching $476.8 million. Net income fell from $236 million in 1981 to $72 million at year end.

The collapse of Penn Square and the energy industry forced Continental's management to reassess the bank's overall direction. Continental's Credit Risk Evaluation division, which had been created in the autumn of 1982 on the OCC's urging, was strengthened in early 1983 to provide improved risk evaluation and report regularly to senior management and the board of directors. The division also monitored the effectiveness of Continental's early warning credit quality system and provided an important check on corporate lending activities.

The Formal Agreement, signed on 14 March 1983, covered asset and liability management, loan administration and funding. It required the bank to continue to implement and maintain policies and procedures designed to improve performance. In addition to quarterly progress reports on how the bank was complying with the terms of the Agreement, Continental was also required to make periodic reports to the OCC on its criticised assets, funding and earnings.

Continental submitted the first quarterly compliance report required by the Formal Agreement to the OCC in March 1983. It indicated that appropriate actions required by the Agreement were being taken by the bank.

In April 1983, OCC examiners visited Continental to review the first quarter financial results. Non-performing assets, at $2.02 billion, were higher than anticipated by the bank, but market acceptance had improved and premium on funding instruments had declined.

Continental's 1983 recovery plan called for a reduction in assets and staff and a more conservative lending policy. Two executive officers, Mr David Taylor and Mr Edward Bottum, were appointed to Continental's board of directors in August 1983. Immediately after their appointment they instituted key management and organisational changes to aid in the bank's recovery. External market conditions during the second half of 1983, however, slowed Continental's recovery. Increasing interest rates squeezed net interest margins, loan demand was weak, and non-performing energy loans rose further as the energy industry continued to decline.

The general sentiment of bank analysts towards Continental was negative after Penn Square. It had become apparent to bank analysts by early 1983 that Penn Square wasn't Continental's only problem. Most analysts believed that Continental's stock would not recover in the short-term.

At the time of the 1983 examination, the condition of Continental had further deteriorated since the 1982 examination. Asset quality and earnings remained poor. Capital was adequate on a ratio basis, but under pressure due to asset and earnings problems. Funding had improved, but was still highly sensitive to poor performance and other negative developments. The bank was found to be in compliance with the terms of the Formal Agreement. In December 1983, the OCC examination was completed and the Comptroller and senior OCC staff met Continental's board of directors to discuss the findings.

A revised recovery plan for 1984 called for a further reduction in assets, enhanced capital-raising efforts, and a reduction in non-interest expenses and staff. Non-essential businesses, such as real estate and the bank's credit card operation, were to be sold to improve capital and refocus the bank on wholesale banking. Merger alternatives would be pursued with the assistance of Goldman Sachs, which had been retained in September 1983. Plans were also accelerated to transfer additional responsibilities to Taylor and Bottum.

In February 1984, Mr Taylor replaced Mr Roger Anderson as Continental's CEO; Mr Bottum was elected President. External events in the first quarter of 1984 produced further problems for the new management team. Asset quality continued to deteriorate and Continental recorded an operating loss for the first quarter of 1984.

Continental's condition as of 31 March 1984 remained poor. An OCC examination began on 19 March and targeted asset quality and funding. It concluded that continued operating losses and funding problems could be anticipated unless the bank's contingency plan to sell non-performing assets was successful. But details of this plan were not available at the completion of the examination on 20 April.

The Comptroller and his staff met with Continental's Chairman, CEO and President on 2 May to discuss the bank's dividend policy and contingency plan for selling non-performing assets. Following the meeting, the Comptroller concluded that the OCC's approval of the payment of the second quarter dividend to the holding company in part depended on the successful implementation of provisions contained in the contingency plan, specifically, the sale of non-performing assets.

Later that month, market confidence in Continental deteriorated still further – rumours of the bank's impending bankruptcy were fuelled by two erroneous press reports on 8 May that concerned the purchase of or investment in the bank. From that point on, the OCC was in continual contact with the bank and other bank regulatory agencies, especially the FDIC. On 10 May the OCC took the unusual step of issuing a news release stating that its office had not requested assistance for or even discussed Continental with any bank or securities firm. Additionally, it was noted, the OCC could find no basis for the rumours concerning the bank's fate.

On 10 May 1984, OCC examiners established an on-site presence in Continental's trading rooms in Chicago and London so they could closely monitor the bank's rapidly deteriorating funding situation. Initial reports from OCC examiners indicated that major providers of overnight and term funds were failing to renew their holdings of the liabilities of the bank and the bank holding company, Continental Illinois Corporation. The bank was forced to repay the deposits in eurodollar and domestic markets. In the absence of other funding sources, Continental was forced to approach the Federal Reserve Bank of Chicago.

From 12 to 14 May, a safety net of 16 banks put together a $4.5 billion line of credit for Continental. By 15 May, the safety net began to unwind because of a lack of confidence. On 16 and 17 May, the Comptroller and staff held meetings with Continental, other money centre banks and regulatory agencies in Chicago, New York and Washington to consider alternatives. A temporary assistance package was drawn up.

On 17 May the Comptroller, the Federal Deposit Insurance Corporation (FDIC) and the Federal Reserve Bank announced a financial assistance programme. The package had four features. First, there was a $2 billion injection of capital by the FDIC and seven US banks, with $1.5 billion of this coming from the FDIC. The capital injection took the form of a subordinated demand loan and was made available to CI for the period necessary to enhance the bank's permanent capital, by merger or otherwise. The rate of interest was 100 basis points above the 1-year Treasury bill rate. Second, 28 US banks provided a $5.5 billion federal funds back-up line to meet CI's immediate liquidity requirements, to be in place until a permanent solution was found. It had a spread of 0.25% above the Federal funds rate. Third, the Federal Reserve gave an assurance that it was prepared to meet any extraordinary liquidity requirements of CI. Finally, the FDIC guaranteed *all* depositors and other general creditors of the bank full protection, with no interruption in the service to the bank's customers.

In return for the package, all directors of CI were asked to resign and the FDIC took direct management control of the bank. The FDIC bought, at book value, $3.5 billion of CI's debt. The Federal Reserve injected about $1 billion in new capital. The bank's holding company, CI Corporation, issued 32 million preference shares to the FDIC, that on sale, converted into 160 million common shares in CI and $320 million in interest-bearing preferred stock. It also had an option on another 40.3 million shares in 1989, if losses on doubtful loans exceeded $800 million. It was estimated they exceeded $1 billion. Effectively, the bank was nationalised, at a cost of $1.1 billion. A new team of senior managers were appointed by the FDIC, which also, from time to time, sold some shares to the public (Kaufman, 2002, p. 425).

Over the next two months, the regulators held meetings with both domestic and foreign financial institutions and other parties interested in merging with or investing in Continental. Early on, it was apparent that it would be difficult to achieve a private sector solution. But any private sector/government-assisted transactions were likely to be too costly for the FDIC. Throughout this period, the OCC held several meetings with senior bank management and various members of the bank's board of directors. There were also numerous internal planning sessions. Intensive monitoring of the bank's funding continued and a joint OCC/FDIC review of the loan portfolio was conducted.

On 26 July the long-term solution was announced, subject to shareholder approval on 26 September. It was intended to restore Continental to health and to allow it to continue to operate without interruption. Two key elements made up the plan: changes in top management and substantial assistance. The solution resulted in the creation of a smaller and more viable bank. Management was removed, and shareholders incurred substantial losses, but all depositors were protected. Major disruption to the financial system was avoided. Upon implementation of the long-term solution, Continental would be well capitalised, with stronger assets and management. It was to be returned to private ownership at the earliest possible date. According to Kaufman (2002), by 1991 it was back in private hands, and in 1994 it was taken over by BankAmerica Corp.

## 10.7.5. Concluding Remarks

Continental Illinois got into problems for a number of reasons. First, it lacked a rigorous procedure for vetting new loans, resulting in poor quality loans to the US corporate sector, the energy sector and the real estate sector. This included participation in low quality loans to the energy sector, bought from Penn Square. Second, CI failed to classify bad loans as non-performing quickly, and the delay made depositors suspicious of what the bank was hiding. Third, the restricted deposit base of a single branch system forced the bank to rely on wholesale funds as it fought to expand. Fourth, supervisors should have been paying closer attention to liability management, in addition to internal credit control procedures.

Regulators were concerned about CI's dependence on global funding. This made it imperative for the Fed and FDIC to act as lender of last resort, to head off any risk of a run by foreign depositors on other US banks. Continental Illinois was also the first American example of regulators using a "too big to fail" policy. The three key US regulatory bodies were all of the view that allowing CI to go under would risk a national or even global financial crisis, because CI's correspondent bank relationships left it (and the correspondent banks) highly exposed on the interbank and Federal funds markets. The regulators claimed the exposure of 65 banks was equivalent to 100% of their capital; another 101 had between 50% and 100% of their capital exposed. However, Kaufman (1885, 1994) reports on a Congressional investigation of the collapse, which showed that only 1% of Continental's correspondent banks would have become legally insolvent if losses at CI had been 60 cents per dollar. In fact, actual losses turned out to be less than 5 cents on the dollar, and no bank suffered losses high enough to threaten their solvency. *The Economist* (1995) argues that regulators got their sums wrong, and reports that some privately believed the bank did not need to be rescued. However, it is worth noting that the correspondent banks were not privy to this information at the time of the crisis, and would have been concerned about any losses they incurred, even if their solvency was not under threat. Given the rumours, it was quite rational for them to withdraw all uninsured deposits, thereby worsening the position of CI.

Furthermore, the episode did initiate a too big to fail policy, which was used sporadically throughout the 1980s. Some applications were highly questionable. For example, in 1990 the FDIC protected both national and off-shore (Bahamas) depositors at the National Bank of Washington, ranked 250th in terms of asset size. The policy came to an end with the 1991 FDIC Improvement Act (FDICIA), which required all regulators to use prompt corrective action and the least cost approach when dealing with problem banks. However, the "systemic risk" exception in FDICIA has given the FDIC a loophole to apply too big to fail.[59]

## Questions

1. In the context of this case, explain the meaning of:
   (a) "an aggressive lending strategy";
   (b) safety net;
   (c) lifeboat rescue operation;
   (d) the case for 100% deposit insurance;
   (e) a policy of "too big to fail";
   (f) regulatory forbearance, with reference to the OCC.
2. Do you agree that a bank should exploit a situation where its competitors are suffering from financial distress?
3. Why was Continental's ratio of non-interest expenses to average assets and net interest margin below that of its peer group average?
4. Does the Continental case demonstrate there is no place for niche markets in banking?
5. List the (a) managerial factors, (b) macroeconomic factors and (c) other factors which contributed to the collapse of Continental. Rank these factors in order of importance and give reasons for your ranking.
6. With respect to the various runs on Continental:
   (a) Why did the bank experience a run in 1982 and how did it manage to survive without recourse to official assistance?
   (b) Why was the run in 1984 more devastating, ultimately leading to the demise of Continental as it was known?
7. After the break-up of Continental, the Bank of America became the subject of market rumours reminiscent of the Continental case. Why was the Bank of America able to withstand these rumours but not Continental?
8. Explain how the following regulatory changes might have prevented the collapse of Continental:
   (a) The Federal Deposit Insurance Corporation Act, 1991.
   (b) The Riegle–Neale Interstate Banking and Branch Efficiency Act, 1994.

---

[59] See Chapter 5 for more detail on the FDICIA.

## 10.8. Bankers Trust: From a Commercial/Investment Bank to Takeover by Deutsche Bank[60]

**Relevant Parts of the Text:** Chapters 1, 2, 3, 5, 9.

By the end of 1987, Mr Alfred Britain III retired after 12 years as CEO of Bankers Trust. His successor, Mr Charles S. Sanford Jr, based on results, believed that the bank had fully completed the transition from a money centre commercial bank to a global wholesale financial services company, able to compete with the best of the international merchant and investment banks. The stock yielded a 41% return on equity before extraordinary allowance for credit losses, up from 34% in 1984, which, at the time, was already the highest of all money centre banks.

In the late 1980s, media and analyst attention was fixed on BT's remarkable performance, focusing on how a mediocre money centre bank could transgress commercial banking standards to earn such extraordinary returns. Most of the financial press and Wall Street believed that BT had done a wonderful thing. Analysts from two investment banks at the time characterised BT as the most sophisticated US merchant bank, claiming the bank "epitomizes the dedication to merchant banking that its peers and competitors will have to strive to attain", and from another investment bank: "Bankers Trust is positioning itself to be a true investment bank". One of the well known specialist banking news journals said "Bankers Trust Co has one of the most clear cut images in banking – a big time, self-created international merchant bank, financier of leveraged buy-outs, underwriter of corporate bonds, invader of Wall St turf."

These plaudits were consistent with Mr Sanford's beliefs. But like any other successful institution, BT was not without its critics. BT's reputation for being one of the most aggressive financiers of leveraged deals (about $3 billion in LBO debt in the 1980s), with a substantial portfolio of real estate and LDC loans, triggered many arguments that its real credit exposure had been masked by exceptional, yet possibly tenuous, trading profits. Some of this cynicism was related to actions taken in the second quarter of 1987 when, in line with other New York banks that wrote their Latin American exposure down to 75% of book, BT increased its allowance for credit losses by $700 million. However, it still earned an overall profit, because of trading.

The critics' fears were heightened in 1987, following an earnings announcement, when BT's share price dropped substantially. Concerns were again raised in 1989, profits of 1988 turned to losses of $980 million because of an additional $1.6 billion provision against Third World debt and $150 million charge for bad credits. Based on 1989 earnings, and its competitive bearing in investment banking, some critics were of the view that BT had made insignificant progress since 1984 on its declared road to becoming a global merchant bank.

There is little doubt that BT had established itself as a visionary in the field of banking, but its aggressiveness in volatile high margin businesses, coupled with its decentralised structure, left BT vulnerable. Notwithstanding the protests of BT's management, who insisted they

---

[60] The first part of this case originated from the New York University Salomon Center Case Series in Banking and Finance (Case 07), authored by A. Sinclair, R. Smith and I. Walter. It was revised and updated by S. Heffernan for her 1996 book, and it has been revised again for *Modern Banking* (2004).

"never bet the bank", not all observers believed the BT strategy had maximised shareholder value-added. The jury was still out on whether BT had achieved its goal of becoming a global merchant bank. It would be important to observe BT's performance when the chips were down: the bank had not yet been tested in a recession.

This case is about the trials and tribulations of Bankers Trust through the 1990s, culminating in its being acquired by the German power house, Deutsche Bank. How did a bank which had, apparently, transformed itself into a new breed of investment bank (in all but name) end up being taken over? Has it been a good acquisition for Deutsche Bank? In answering these questions, students will see how events of the 1980s and 1990s transformed the US and global banking scene.

## 10.8.1. The Evolution of Bankers Trust

In the late 1970s, BT was a typical money centre bank,[61] strapped with credit losses arising from recession and the Real Estate Investment Trust crisis. It continued to operate a pro-gressive retail and commercial domestic banking business, with an international focus. But capital requirements, together with provisioning for bad debt, meant the bank would be con-strained in any attempt to operate in all markets. BT emerged from the 1970s wounded but still viable, and this position had a profound effect on its strategic focus. BT was placed fifth in the New York market. It had a 200-plus retail bank network, but it was widely accepted that to remain competitive over the next decade, BT would require a substantial investment in new technology, such as ATMs and information systems, and human resources. A retail banking network would be a source of low-cost funding for the bank, though ceilings on deposits rates were, officially, to be phased out by 1986, and they had already become largely ineffective. For these reasons, BT decided to focus on wholesale and corporate banking.

To disengage itself from retail banking, BT sold off its metropolitan retail branches, its credit card business, and four upstate New York commercial banking subsidiaries (which also had branches) between 1980 and 1984. These operations represented $1.8 billion in assets and were profitable at the time they were sold. BT earned $155.3 million, which it invested in its merchant banking business.

The bank was reorganised around four core businesses:

- Commercial banking;
- Corporate finance;
- Trust services;
- Resource management.

Each of these new businesses was headed by an executive vice-president, who reported to a new "Office of the Chairman", shared by Mr Sanford (president), Mr Al Brittain (chairman) and Mr Carl Mueller (vice-chairman). BT itself was divided into two principal

---

[61] The term "money centre commercial bank" was used to describe large (in terms of assets) US commercial banks that were headquartered in a key city – mainly New York (e.g. Chase Manhattan, Citibank) but also in Chicago (Continental Bank) and Los Angeles (at the time, Bank of America). Their main business was retail and wholesale banking. There were no banks with a nation-wide branch network because of restrictions (at the time) on inter- and even intrastate branching. By the late 1990s, the term had disappeared, due to changes in US regulation and structure (see Chapter 5).

units, Financial Services and ProfitCo (see below). The shift from money centre commercial banking to international merchant banking prompted changes in the way BT approached its business, especially in terms of management of the balance sheet, funding, costs and investment philosophy.

In the middle was the merchant bank – its balance sheet relationship was shared with commercial banking, but the bank's origination and distribution functions were more common to investment banking. The model adopted by BT was to combine deposit-taking and lending functions, and the broad relationship list of a commercial bank with the origination and distribution functions of an investment bank. BT had implemented several changes to achieve this objective.

- Marketing efforts were targeted at the institutional sector, redirecting resources to large and middle market corporations, financial institutions and governments.
- BT initiated an aggressive commercial origination and loan-sale programme to control balance sheet growth, emphasise fee-driven business and distribute risk.
- An investment banking emphasis was placed on corporate finance activities.
- A target of 20% return on equity was established as a benchmark to monitor corporate performance and measure risk-adjusted return in all business segments.
- A new incentive compensation scheme was developed to motivate employees to seek out new businesses and profit opportunities in line with corporate goals.
- Organisational changes relating to client and interdepartmental relationships, risk-taking, management hierarchy and business development were implemented.

## 10.8.2. The Organisational Framework

In 1984, BT was divided into two main units – Financial Services and ProfitCo.

### *Financial Services*

The merchant bank, with about 5500 employees, was headed by Mr Ralph MacDonald. It consisted mainly of three functional units.

- Corporate finance: headed by Mr David Beim, it provided merchant banking services to clients in the USA and Western Europe.
- Emerging markets: headed by Mr George Vojta, it provided merchant banking services in Latin America, Eastern Europe, Africa and the Middle East.
- Global markets: headed by Mr Eugene Shanks, it had world-wide responsibility for capital market based businesses and products. Securities dealing, foreign exchange, interest rate protection and similar areas all came under global markets, as did merchant banking in Asia/Pacific and Canadian markets.

Some interdisciplinary functions, such as loan distribution, reported jointly to corporate finance and global markets. Financial services did not handle either deposits or operating services, which were dealt with by ProfitCo. Another 1000 staff were attached to the corporate staff and 3000 employees were based outside the USA. The corporate level was responsible for:

- Treasury – BT's own funding and risk management.
- Credit policy – controlled credit risk in all business lines and provided some administrative support activities.

## *ProfitCo*

ProfitCo offered transaction processing, fiduciary and securities services, investment management and private banking. About half of BT's staff (6500) worked for ProfitCo.

BT's Fiduciary Services Department was reorganised into ProfitCo in 1984, as part of BT's decentralisation plan. Staff functions were shifted to line functions, with responsibility for earning profit. This elicited a process which effectively created many separate and divisible business segments; for each segment, it was possible to measure profitability against some external measure. It was believed this "profit centre" approach would improve the competitiveness of the service business by allowing BT to attract and motivate high-quality personnel. The entrepreneurial structure was supposed to encourage staff to achieve management responsibility, though it did put pressure on line management personnel to support their existence.

ProfitCo consisted of four departments:

- *FastCo*: Offered institutional fiduciary and securities servicing to both domestic and overseas clients. Within FastCo, there existed several groups which engaged in traditional trust business:
    - Investment Management Group: managed several billion dollars in pension, thrift and employee-benefit plan assets. It ranked as one of the top US firms in custody and clearing.
    - Employee Benefit Group: the largest provider of non-investment services, such as administrative and record-keeping services for pension and employee benefit plans.
    - The Trust and Agency Group: served as a trustee for public bond issues, and offered other services. Operation of the Securities Processing Group was a marked departure from customary trust activities.
- *Investment Management*: This department was concerned with institutional money management, especially in the passive investment area. There was a considerable advantage for clients in having both corporate trust and investment management centralised with the same provider. It made BT one of the largest US institutional money managers.
- *Private Banking*: This department targeted high net worth individuals, offering traditional trust services and other commercial banking services. The objective was to offer banking services to upscale customers, cross-marketing a range of fiduciary, banking and investment services. The emphasis was on personal service, offering high-quality investment-related products to clients. It had six New York City branches, one upstate New York branch and one branch in Florida.
- *Global Operations and Information Services (GOIS)*: GOIS offered funds transfer, cash management, trade payments and related informational services to world-wide institutional clients. It was extensively involved in dollar-related clearing services, and

in trade-related and securities-related payments. As part of its strategy to encourage entrepreneurship, GOIS was treated as a separate business with a separate sales force, product management capabilities and guidelines for profit. GOIS effectively centralised BT's transactions processing, and was kept separate from the commercial banking function.

Each business within ProfitCo was characterised by a strong level of recurring income. They were similarly organised with a sales/relationship manager, product managers who were involved in marketing, and an attendant product delivery function. The banking segment was a good source of business – products and services were cross-marketed to institutions and clients who were being serviced by other parts of BT. Though each business was operated independently within BT, ProfitCo operated the bank's back office systems, especially global market activities. ProfitCo provided the data centre for most of BT's business segments.

## 10.8.3. Bankers Trust: Activities

### *Resource Management (RMD)*

Located on Wall Street, RMD can be traced back to 1919, when BT was successful in the bond business. The Glass Steagall Act largely put an end to BT's underwriting activities. The bank was limited to underwriting and dealing in US government securities and general obligation bonds issued by state and local governments. BT continued to underwrite allowable securities and manage its own portfolio of government securities. This portfolio had made up a large part of BT's asset base, and was a major source of liquidity. However, in the 1960s, BT, like many commercial banks, began to rely on short-term borrowed funds such as negotiable CDs, bankers acceptances and commercial paper as a source of funds and liquidity.

Short-term funding was handled within the global markets group. The corporate treasurer managed aggregated risks involving both interest rate sensitivity and liquidity on a global basis. Capital budgeting decisions were reviewed at the highest level and ALM conducted on an aggregate basis, bringing people from each business segment together to communicate actual and prospective trends in the corporate risk profile. Often, however, the aggregate risk profile was very different from the individual parts because some risk was diversified away through position taking within each business. The emphasis was on slow balance sheet growth, encouraging an integrated approach to balance sheet funding.

Preceding organisational changes within the fiduciary function, RMD was preparing to compete with investment banking firms for both business (trading securities and underwriting) and people. Mr Charlie Sanford was placed in charge of the department and created a plan to compete on a par with investment banking firms. Traders and other professionals were hired and by 1980, Mr Sanford believed he had a top-rated trading capacity.

## Trading

Proprietary trading was the key capital market activity which helped BT sustain a record of positive profits for nearly two decades without a single quarterly loss in the foreign exchange or securities trading markets. By the end of the 1980s, management estimated that 60% of the bank's assets were liquid. The objective was to raise that figure to 80%.

Proprietary trading, and trading on behalf of BT customers, added a new dimension to the challenge facing management regarding long-term profitability and success. Consistent with its organisational layout, the trading function was operated very much like a business. Each trading division was structured to promote profitable activities and was supported by sophisticated information systems, large geographically dispersed staffs, and an emphasis on communication. Management believed constant communication provided the opportunity for new avenues of profit, with risk diversification the underlying objective. Additionally, the goal of consistent profitability was to generate asymmetric profit and losses. The management directive was twofold: (i) losses should be taken early – as soon as they were evident and (ii) when gains were made, they should be protected.

At the same time, management gave traders who proved themselves full rein to play their positions. In theory, no trader could commit more than a predetermined level of capital, but once that capital was earned back, the trader could play his/her position to amounts limited by accumulated profits. This meant there were single positions which exceeded a billion dollars. BT's reputation for taking the right positions encouraged herd instinct behaviour: traders at rival firms would take the same positions, which would magnify the extent BT moved the market.

## Commercial Paper

Mr Sanford believed part of the BT strategy should be to offer a wide range of institutional financial services on a global basis. The execution of this strategy involved BT's participation in the domestic commercial paper market, an area normally reserved for investment banks. In 1978, BT began to act as an agent for corporations issuing commercial paper, thereby challenging Glass Steagall – the bank convinced the Federal Reserve that commercial paper was a short-term loan, not a security.

## Derivatives and Risk Management

In 1978, BT improved on its internal risk management by establishing the Bankers Trust Futures Corporation. It operated on the emerging futures and options markets, to provide innovative hedging programmes to customers. It was the second subsidiary of a US banking company to receive full certification as a futures commission merchant.

Mr Sanford introduced RAROC, or risk-adjusted return on capital, defined as total risk-adjusted returns divided by total capital (see Chapter 3), a risk measurement system. The idea was to have a common measure of risk for all BT operations, thereby ensuring an efficient allocation of capital. A risk factor was assigned to each category of assets based on the volatility of the asset's market price. For example, a CD trader who ended the day with a long position in 60-day paper would be assigned a risk-adjusted amount of capital based on the risk factor for this maturity. Performance was assessed by dividing the trader's profit by the amount of capital allocated. An example of the distribution of capital appears below:

| Division | Amount ($mn) | % of total |
|---|---|---|
| Global Markets (credit) | 211 | 4.9 |
| Global Markets (market) | 206 | 4.8 |
| Other (credit) | 2 811 | 65.3 |
| Other (non-credit) | 1 080 | 24.1 |

In addition to being at the centre of a framework for risk management, RAROC was also used for:

- Comparison of the performance of different parts of the BT business.
- Portfolio management for determining areas that appeared most appropriate for investment or divestment.

## Corporate Finance

BT had shifted its focus to wholesale corporate banking and the institutional market, and needed to develop a competitive corporate finance capability that would make up the core of the merchant bank. The corporate finance department's reorganisation began in 1977. Two individuals with extensive Wall Street experience were hired, Mr Carl Mueller and Mr David Beim.

The corporate finance division had five lines of business.

- *The Capital Market Group*: This section acted as financial advisor or agent for corporations in the private placement of their securities with insurance companies, pension funds and other financial institutions. The group was strongly affiliated with global markets and BT's London merchant bank, Bankers Trust International. It maintained a role in eurosecurities offerings and dealt extensively with interest rate and currency swaps.
- *The Lease Financing Group*: Arranged large leases, placing the assets with other institutions and within BT. It served as an advisor to the lessor and/or lessee in transactions.
- *The Venture Capital Group*: This group made equity and other investments for the holding company (Bankers Trust New York Corporation). Most of the transactions were part of the leveraged buyouts and expansion financing, rather than *de novo* financing of companies. BT developed a special product niche in structuring leveraged buyouts.
- *The Public Finance Group*: This group acted as a financial advisor, underwriter or sales agent of tax-exempt financing for public and corporate issuers.
- *Loan Sales*: In 1984, as part of its merchant banking strategy, BT expanded its loan sales programme. One of the first commercial banks to be actively engaged in *securitisation*, the bank believed that in some cases, it could achieve superior returns on equity by originating and selling loans, rather than holding them on its own books. Loan securitisation also helped to stabilise balance sheet growth, maintain high liquidity levels, and meant the

bank could provide more services to major corporations. The timing of this effort was coincidental with BT's emphasis on the build-up of mergers and acquisitions advisory capacity, which in turn related very well to the growing "leveraged buyout" (LBO) phenomenon, and ensured a superior return on equity.

Mr Beim followed an employment policy of hiring the best and paying accordingly. Traditional domestic corporate lending was de-emphasised in favour of initiating and completing highly leveraged deals and other specialised lending operations.

By early 1985, BT had placed several groups of asset product managers and sales officers in New York, Tokyo, London and Hong Kong. The asset product management group worked with account officers to design the loan sale structure and related documentation. Most of the business was directed at large companies seeking substantial funding and broad access to the financial markets. The group could recommend financing programmes to improve the market access of such companies. Corporate finance product specialists might also be involved, so the bank provided credit expertise, technical advice and sales knowledge when working with customers.

Sales officers targeted investors as potential purchasers of the loans, and kept in close contact with them. Loans were sold to foreign banks, pension funds and insurance firms. Sales officers would spend weeks educating potential investors. The whole process ensured that a high proportion of the BT loan portfolio was in liquid form.

The "tactical asset and liability committee" was BT's policy-making body for loan sales. It met on a weekly basis to decide on the quarterly pricing of loan sales. The Committee focused on credit risk, market conditions and liquidity needs; it also sought out new opportunities for the loan origination function.

## Credit policy

In line with the greater emphasis on merchant banking and the loan sale programme, credit management procedures at BT were also tightened. The old credit review system had required loan approval by at least two account officers. The new process required at least one signature to be from a credit officer. Thus, credit officers became lending officers.

Line management was responsible for the credit approval process. Each department had to write a credit policy statement and specify lending authority for its line and credit officers. For example, division managers would be given a credit approval limit. Loan amounts within this limit could be approved with the signature of an account officer and the division manager. Larger loans required the signature of the group credit head and the loan officer. Loans larger than the group head's credit limit went to the department credit officer. Loans in excess of $200 million required the signature of the department head or the chief credit officer.

Using RAROC, management could assess the amount of credit risk embedded in all areas of the bank. Risks were placed in 60 industry categories, which were graded according to expected performance. The ranking was based on variables such as technical change, regulatory issues, capacity constraints, business cycle sensitivity, ability to protect pricing and margins, and structural stress. These variables were considered important because of their effect on growth and cash flow variability over both near and intermediate term horizons.

## Global markets

Global markets were considered to be of increasing importance. For example, foreign exchange facilities were expanded to provide 24-hour market-making capacity with 10 geographic locations. The bank was actively involved in the global syndicated loan euronote market and equity-linked derivatives.

Global markets was a functional division under the financial services side of BT. It had seven divisions. Half dealt with market-related activities, such as short-term funding and foreign exchange. The rest were concerned with financing activities, such as public fixed income markets, private placements, commodities, short-term and variable rate finance, and multiple currency derivatives. The objective was to assist clients in the management of their own risk positions and to establish product areas whose profitability was uncorrelated, to achieve a natural diversification and sustain profitability, no matter what the market situation.

The seven divisions had 60 profit centres, globally organised across time zones, which helped interaction. Customer, product and geographic variables were connected through a process of synergy. Employees of "global markets" numbered about 2200 and made up about 20% of the BT payroll. They were located in seven countries and 10 cities, including all the major world financial centres.

The nature of the divisional organisation emphasised a global product focus across time zones, at the expense of a more client-oriented regional focus. The system did appeal to large corporate clients wanting to structure multi-market financing for a cross-border acquisition. However, the organisational structure discouraged the development of local client relationships – BT acknowledged that the local clients had to be sold the approach by being shown the superiority of the product. There was an ongoing debate about whether the lack of strong client relationships would undermine the attempt to establish a leadership position BT had in financial engineering, deal making and trading.

BT had very little in the way of a distribution and sales network typical of most Wall Street houses. To maintain a competitive edge, the bank increasingly looked to financial engineering or structured finance, inventing complex and often lucrative products for specific clients. BT normally relied upon other firms to provide the distribution and sales functions it needed.

## Management style

The organisational changes at BT were designed to promote cooperation among BT business units, so as to provide a high-quality, innovative service to its clients. For this reason, it moved from a hierarchical structure typical of a commercial bank to the horizontal structure of most investment banks. However, there was hostility to the change among long-time BT employees, who were concerned with the stress on entrepreneurial initiative.

BT modified relationship banking by requiring staff to delve into product specialities and relate these to business lines required by each customer. Staff moved between the main centres loosely assigned to institutional clients, improving, it was hoped, organisational agility and fostering innovation and creativity. The approach should sustain enough flexibility in the organisation to allow BT to take advantage of new market opportunities immediately, whether in the form of a long-term relationship or a one-off profit-making opportunity. Though employees were encouraged to foster relationships with clients, they were also advised to look for opportunities to assist with an individual transaction.

Thus, the BT banking style differed from that of investment banks, where employees were rigidly assigned to either corporate or institutional customers, and from commercial banking, which tended to rely on "hands off" relationships to generate spread income.

To attract the top people into the organisation, BT dispensed with the standard commercial bank compensation scheme. Incentive compensation was introduced in the resource management department (RMD), then extended to other parts of BT. Traders were paid according to their performance, as measured by a high risk-adjusted rate of return on capital, as opposed to limits. The top performers received bonuses of 100% or more. In the corporate finance department, BT also linked compensation to performance, but, unlike RMD, bonuses were based both on the profitability of a new business and the degree to which the officer cooperated with others in the organisation to foster "excellence through common purpose". For example, in commercial banking, bonuses could now exceed 100% of salary (compared to a previous limit of 50%). The size of the bonus pool was not just a function of a department's profitability, but of total profits generated throughout BT.

### *Trouble with Swaps: 1993–98*

In 1993, net profits at BT were $1.07 billion, $596 million of which came from proprietary trading and advising corporations on the management of different types of market risk, such as currency and interest rate. The bank congratulated itself for being a model modern investment bank with a performance-driven culture and innovative trading strategies such as the use of derivatives to manage risk on BT's own trading book, and for its corporate clients, too.

However, in the spring of 1994, this part of BT was suddenly faced with serious problems. Several firms announced losses arising from swaps sold to them by Bankers Trust, New York. In March 1994, Gibsons Greetings Inc. announced losses amounting to $19.7 million from leveraged interest rate swaps, and in September of that year, commenced legal action – suing BT for $23 million to cover its derivatives losses, and $50 million in punitive damages. The case was settled out of court in January 1995 – BT paid $14 million to Gibson Greetings, after a tape revealed a managing director at Bankers had misled the company about the size of its financial losses. Bankers Trust had already (in December 1994) paid a $10 million fine to US regulatory authorities in relation to the affair. It was also required to sign an "agreement" with the Federal Reserve Bank of New York, which required BT to:

- Allow the regulator to monitor and closely scrutinise the leveraged derivatives business at Bankers Trust.
- Ensure clients using these complex derivatives understood the associated risks.
- Fund an independent investigation into the affair, to be undertaken by an experienced counsel.

Two other firms also announced large losses from BT's swaps. They also accepted out of court settlements – $67 million to Air Products and $12 million to Federal Paper Board Company. At this point BT had paid out over $100 million in the settlements and fines relating to improper behaviour by its leveraged swap group. The bank sacked one manager, reorganised the leveraged derivatives unit and reassigned staff to other jobs.

However, another big loser appeared determined to have their day in court. In April 1994, the chairman of Procter and Gamble (P&G) announced losses of $157 million on leveraged interest rate swaps. In 1993, the corporate treasurer at Procter and Gamble had purchased these swaps from Bankers Trust. One of the swaps was, effectively, a bet and would have yielded a substantial capital gain for Procter and Gamble had German and US interest rates converged more slowly than the market thought they would. In fact, the reverse happened, leading to large losses. The second swap was known by both parties as the "5–30 swap", and involved P&G receiving a fixed rate pegged to the 5-year US Treasury note and the 30-year Treasury bond and paying a floating rate pegged to the commercial paper rate. According to P&G, Bankers Trust guaranteed P&G would pay 40 basis points below the commercial paper rate. However, short-term rates fell relative to long rates, so P&G ended up facing a loss. Procter and Gamble refused to pay Bankers Trust the money lost on the swap contracts. P&G claimed it should never have been sold these swaps, because the bank did not fully explain the potential risks, nor did the bank disclose pricing methods that would have allowed Procter and Gamble to price the product themselves. Bankers Trust countered that P&G owed the bank close to $200 million. The question is why these instruments were being used for speculative purposes by a consumer goods conglomerate, and whether the firm had been correctly advised by Bankers Trust.

In late 1994, BT set aside $423 million as a provision for derivatives contracts that might prove unenforceable; $72 million was written off immediately. This provisioning suggested BT could lose over $500 million. Furthermore, the bank's trading division was bound to see a decline in business because so much of it depended on reputation and clients' trust in the bank – trading had already experienced a steep decline in profits. Bankers Trust faced potential severe financial difficulties and even collapse because of this derivatives-related scandal.

The publication of internal tapes which revealed a cynical attitude in the treatment of customers was unhelpful for the bank. In one video instruction tape shown to new employees at the bank, a BT salesman mentions how a swap works: BT can "get in the middle and rip them (the customers) off... take a little money", though the instructor does apologise after seeing the camera. Another explained how he would "lure people into that total calm, and then totally f- - - - them".[62] Further revelations came to light in pre-trial hearings, with, for example, a reference to an acronym used by BT derivatives staff: "ROF", for *rip-off factor*.

Several rulings were made by the judge[63] over the two years leading up to the trial:

- P&G's argument that swaps came under federal jurisdiction was rejected, as was their claim that BT has a fiduciary duty to P&G.
- P&G had to prove the bank had committed fraud before it could ask the courts to judge whether BT had engaged in racketeering.[64]

---

[62] Source: *The Economist*, "Bankers Trust-Shamed Again", 7 October 1995.

[63] US District Court Judge John Feikens.

[64] In the USA a firm or individual found guilty of racketeering (running a dishonest business) faces enormous fines and often jail.

- The judge ruled that P&G knew the risks associated with one of the contracts and, unless it could prove otherwise, should assume financial responsibility for that contract.
- However, the court also ruled that Bankers Trust had a duty of good faith under New York State commercial law. Such a duty arises if one party has superior information and this information is not available to the other party.[65]

Even though the judge appeared to be favouring Bankers Trust, if it went to court, the trial would be by jury, and US banks often lose cases because juries see them as unscrupulous profit machines. Both companies also had reputations to maintain. BT's reputation had already suffered and losing a court case would make matters worse. For Procter and Gamble, if the details of the case were discussed in open court, they could reveal that P&G, an enormous conglomerate, had a financial team with little understanding of financial derivatives.

More than two years after P&G announced its losses, and 11 days before the trial was due to begin, the two parties reached an out of court settlement. It came after new rulings by the judge, who dismissed or ruled against more allegations against BT made by P&G. P&G agreed to pay Bankers Trust $35 million in cash, and the bank was to absorb the rest of the amount ($160 million) in the dispute. P&G would also transfer $14 million worth of securities to Bankers Trust in relation to another derivatives transaction, which P&G claimed was not part of the law suit.[66]

Recall one of the conditions set by US regulators: that the affair was to be investigated by independent counsel. The report, co-authored by a regulator and a lawyer, was published in July 1996, after the law suits had been settled. It cleared Bankers Trust of any intention to defraud when it sold risky derivatives investments. However, it criticised the bank for failing to hold the derivatives section under senior management control. Certain employees had created an environment focused solely on profit at the expense of good risk management controls. The report called for disciplinary action to be taken against certain individuals (not named) who had failed to meet their responsibilities and/or engaged in misconduct with respect to these derivatives. By this time, most of the management team connected to these incidents had left the bank. In response to the report, Mr Newman noted that the entire section had been revamped with state of the art risk management techniques.

In 1994, derivatives sales and trading were the firm's most profitable business by a long way. Bankers Trust had excelled at selling derivatives to companies for hedge purposes (to protect firms from fluctuations in interest rates, foreign currency values and commodity prices) and to speculate, or bet on moves in these rates and prices. The bank also profited from proprietary trading. The scandals not only undermined BT's reputation, but the bank also lost its main source of profits.

To avoid future law suits, BT decided to send product contracts to several members of a client firm, not just the finance officers. In February 1995, a senior committee was formed to look at ways of improving BT customer relations, including employee compensation

---

[65] A third criterion for duty of good faith was noted by the court: the informed party knows the other party is acting on the basis of misinformation, though the duty would arise even if this did not apply.

[66] Source: Lamiell, P. (1996), "Analysts: Both Sides are Winners in Derivatives Settlement", *The Associated Press*, 9 May.

schemes that emphasised the importance of teamwork and longer-term client relationships, not just high sales. Also, new information systems were introduced. In May 1995, Mr Sanford announced his resignation as chairman, effective in 1996.

## 10.8.4. New Chairman. . . New Strategy

In April 1996 Frank N. Newman (a former deputy secretary of the US Treasury) was named as the new chairman of Bankers Trust, succeeding Mr Sanford. He had been president and chief executive officer of Bankers Trust for a short time before being made chairman. The appointment was a clear signal that the bank was determined to put its house in order, especially in the area of risky derivatives. It is no coincidence that the P&G case was settled a month after his appointment. Newman's job was clear cut – he had to restore the bank's reputation, and ensure adequate risk management schemes were in place. Mr Newman also decided to reduce the banks' dependence on risky derivatives, and not only because of the 1994 leveraged derivatives fiasco. In July 1996, the risk management services group lost $22 million (up from a loss of $9 million the previous year) due to losses in commodity derivatives after copper prices plunged in June. In Newman's view, a more diversified bank was a safer, more profitable bank. In several statements, Newman made it clear that rather than being known solely for its expertise in proprietary trading and foreign exchange operations, the bank had to develop a high reputation and be able to offer a full range of investment banking services to global customers in the developed and emerging markets. He appeared to be backed up by the figures. In the second quarter of 1996, BT's profits were largely due to the investment banking division.

An important move to boost investment banking was the acquisition, in late 1996, of a niche investment bank, Wolfensohn & Co., for $200 million in BT stock. The firm was known for its mergers and acquisitions and corporate advisory services. Its chairman, Mr Paul Volcker, agreed to stay on. A former Chairman of the Federal Reserve, he would help to improve BT's reputation as a reformed bank, unlikely to repeat earlier mistakes. In early April 1997, BT announced that the highly respected and oldest US investment bank with a retail stock broking interest, Alex Brown and Son Ltd, was to merge with Bankers Trust. This was the first merger between a US securities house and a commercial bank. At the time Alex Brown was a highly reputed stockbroker based in Baltimore. A stock swap (1 Alex Brown share for 0.83 shares of BT) valued the acquisition at roughly $1.7 billion. According to the BT chairman, the bank would gain strength from Alex Brown's US equity markets, research, institutional investor sales, high income retail[67] and distribution underwriting. Its blue chip reputation would also help BT. Alex Brown would have access to syndicated lending derivatives, and risk management.

The purchase reflected the changing scene in US financial services from a regulatory standpoint. Congress was proving very slow in repealing the Glass Steagall Act, which since 1933 had separated commercial[68] (BT) from investment banking (Alex Brown). The courts

---

[67] Alex Brown's had 460 brokers who focused on high income clients.

[68] As explained in Chapter 5 (see section on US regulation), a reinterpretation of section 20 of the Glass Steagall Act made it possible for commercial banks to engage in investment banking operations provided the revenues

and regulators responded with more lenient treatment of commercial banks that wanted to test the boundaries. The purchase of Alex Brown is a good illustration of this point.[69] The deal was possible under section 20 of the Act because the revenues earned from Alex Brown would amount to about 20% of BT's total earnings in underwriting. Under the old regulations (limit of 10%) the merger would not have been allowed. However, this limit had been raised to 25% earlier in 1997, which meant there was no violation of section 20 of the Glass Steagall Act. It is interesting that at this juncture, Bankers Trust was, for regulatory purposes, classified as a commercial bank, even though the strategy was to transform it into an investment bank.

Bankers Trust opted to buy a highly reputable investment banking businesses instead of organic growth. The jury is still out on which option is superior, if either. Other commercial banks, including some foreign ones such as Union Bank of Switzerland, had committed themselves to building up investment banking expertise over time. In the UK, attempts by the large commercial banks (Barclays, Midland, National Westminster Bank) to take advantage of regulatory reform ("Big Bang", in 1986) and move into investment banking (whether through organic growth or purchase of existing investment banks) largely failed and by the late 1990s, some of these banks had largely divested themselves of their investment banking business.

It was not expected the merger would result in a high number of redundancies or cost savings because the two firms' activities complemented each other. BT Alex Brown kept its headquarters in Baltimore. The firm handled IPOs for small companies, specialising in technology, retail, communications and health care. It also had a fund management group and offers stock brokerage services to high income individual investors.

In the same month, BT announced it had acquired NationsBank's institutional custody business, which increased the bank's total global assets under custody by just over $130 million to roughly $2000 billion. BT also acquired National Westminster's equity underwriting business in 1998. These acquisitions – Wolfensohn, Alex Brown, equity underwriting and a bigger custody business – showed how Mr Newman was changing the strategic direction of Bankers Trust. The bank was in a position to offer a broad range of investment banking/wholesale commercial banking products, though it remained in the second tier and was vulnerable to takeover by one of the major global players.

In March 1997, Bankers Trust signalled a substantial commitment to emerging markets when it announced the formation of a new subsidiary: Emerging Europe, Middle East & Africa Merchant Bank (EEMA), to be managed from London. The idea was to consolidate its trading and investment banking activities in Central and Eastern Europe, the Middle East and Africa. London was to run BT's offices in the Czech Republic, Greece, Hungary, Poland, Turkey, Russia, South Africa, Bahrain, Egypt and Israel.

---

from the securities activities were limited to some percentage set by the Federal Reserve, and appropriate firewalls were in place to keep areas where there might be a potential conflict of interest separate.

[69] In February 1997, Morgan Stanley, the investment bank with big corporates as their clients, merged with Dean Witter Discover, a largely retail brokerage and credit card company. The more liberal interpretation of the Glass Steagall Act began in 1984 when the Supreme Court used section 20 of the Act to rule that the Bank of America could buy a discount brokerage house (Charles Schwab) – it has since been sold. See Chapter 5 for more detail on section 20 subsidiaries.

## 10.8.5. New Problems and Merger Talks

Unfortunately, less than a year after Mr Newman had singled out emerging markets as part of BT's new diversified strategy, the company announced a major reduction in its emerging market operations, and any remaining emerging market activities were integrated into its core businesses. BT had been hit hard from its exposure in Thailand and Indonesia, where it reported trading losses, due to the Asian crisis. The bank lost about $72 million in both the last quarter of 1997 and the first quarter of 1998. However, in the investment banking business, net income more than doubled to $177 million, reflecting the success of its merger with Alex Brown. It also benefited from increased sales and trading in its New York office. Income from European emerging markets, Africa and the Middle East also improved.

By September 1998, matters looked more serious. Many western banks were caught out by the suddenness and magnitude of the Russian crisis (see Chapter 6), when Russia declared a moratorium on its foreign debt. But Bankers Trust faced problems on several fronts. First, its exposure to Russia was large relative to its size. In July and August of 1998, trading losses from its Russian exposure hit $260 million, bringing total trading losses to $350 million. BT's other sources of income had slowed. High-yield corporate (junk) bonds were hit by the Asian and Russian crises. Also, BT Alex Brown Inc. was suffering from the slowdown in initial public offerings and other equity underwriting. For these reasons, it posted a net loss for the third quarter of 1998, of $488 million.[70] This came soon after a report in the *Financial Times* (October 1998) that BT was in merger talks with Deutsche Bank (DB). By November, rumours were rife that the two banks were close to reaching a deal.

The merger talks indicated that after the enormous third-quarter loss, the senior executives at Bankers Trust concluded that a strategy of diversification, with a number of different specialised businesses (which should have ensured the bank could weather downturns), had not worked. As a mid-sized player with large losses, they appear to have decided that it was important to build up its capital base through a merger with a large financial institution. Better to choose the partner than to risk being taken over. It was well known that Mr Rolf Breuer, chief executive of Deutsche Bank, had been looking for a suitable US bank so DB could expand its investment banking business and become one of the world's leading banks. In November 1998 the rumours were confirmed when the *Wall Street Journal*[71] reported the lawyers from the two banks were meeting in New York. In late November 1998, the two banks announced a merger agreement had been reached, which, at the time, created the world's largest bank, with about $840 billion in assets.[72] Bankers Trust was also a bargain, having lost more than 42% of its value between July and October 1998, though the share price had recovered somewhat on rumours of a takeover. The $9 billion sale price was 2.1 BT's book value and a 43% premium over BT's share price at the time of the announcement.

---

[70] In the fourth quarter the firm managed a profit of $133.1 billion, so annual losses from 1998 were lower than expected- BT lost $6 million. A strong showing in the fourth quarter was particularly important for the $133.1 billion-asset company. In the third quarter – before that deal was reached – Bankers Trust posted a $488 million loss.

[71] "Deutsche Bank, Bankers Trust Near Pact – Deal for About $9.7 Billion Would Create Largest Financial-Services Firm", *The Wall Street Journal*, 23 November 1998, p. A2.

[72] At the end of 2003, Deutsche Bank ranked 12th out of 1000 banks in terms of tier 1 capital, and 6th if measured by assets. Source: *The Banker*, July 2004, p. 211.

## 10.8.6. An Odd Couple or Good Match?

On the face of it, the marriage seemed an odd one. Deutsche had been trying to build up its investment banking business – spending $3 billion[73] on it over the last decade. Bankers Trust own strategy of moving into investment banking had not worked very well. However, Deutsche (especially the chairman, Herr Rolf Breuer) thought a move into investment banking essential because of the change in how corporate clients financed their activities. Most were no longer looking to save or borrow, but instead wanted direct access to the capital markets. Hence the bank needed to refocus its activities on arranging, acting as lead managers, underwriting issues, brokering, advising and fund management.

At the time of the merger Herr Breuer spoke of a target ROE of 25% by 2001, up from 6.4% in 1997. The cost of "restructuring" was estimated at $1 billion, to pay for redundancies in overlapping areas. Just under 6% of employees, mainly based in London and New York, would be made redundant in areas of overlap: IT, operations, global markets and global equities.

Herr Breuer was keen to see Bankers Trust absorbed into Deutsche's investment and global operations as quickly as within three months of the takeover. This attitude was in marked contrast to when Deutsche took over Morgan Grenfell in 1989 but the firm continued to operate under its own name for nearly a decade. DB appeared to have learned a lesson from the Morgan Grenfell experience: the firm was given a great deal of autonomy which made the task of integrating it into the DB culture very difficult. The name, Alex Brown, was kept – Deutsche Alex and Brown was to run the US investment banking and equity businesses.

From a regulatory standpoint, there do not appear to be any major problems. Bankers Trust is a wholesale commercial bank with few retail consumers. Though Deutsche, as a universal bank, had commercial interests, regulation K allows foreign banks operating in the USA to keep these interests, provided a minimum of 50% of the bank's profits and assets come from outside the USA. Approval of the acquisition had to come from the European Commission, The New York State Bank Regulator and the Federal Reserve Bank. Approval was forthcoming from the Fed, the last of the regulatory hurdles, in May 1999. The merger took place in June 1999, a good 18 months after the acquisition plan was announced.

In March 1999, Bankers Trust was in the press again, for all the wrong reasons. It pleaded guilty to a felony in US District Court for misappropriation of client funds, and was fined $60 million. Dating back to 1996 (pre-Newman as chairman), it involved the client services processing division which misappropriated $19.1 million of client funds from dividend cheques sent out to shareholders but not cashed. Apparently the money was used to fund parties, offset expenses, or to make it look like the division was earning more income than it really was. Deutsche Bank was lucky: the US Department of Labor allowed Deutsche Bank to continue to manage pension assets despite an admission of fraud by its newly acquired US operation.

---

[73] Peterson, T. (1998), "Bankers Trust is the Last Thing Deutsche Needs", *Business Week*; 2 November, p. 52.

The question was whether the acquisition was going to work. To quote *The Economist*:

*"Take a transatlantic combination of a lumbering, accident-prone universal bank with a prickly, free-wheeling investment bank, and only the foolhardy would bet on success."*[74]

A $400 million retention or "handcuff" fund was set aside to retain the best of the DB and BT staff. Deutsche proved successful in retaining some staff, but lost some key players. Mr Newman resigned because he had been promised a seat on the Deutsche management board at the time of the acquisition agreement, only to be refused membership after the merger took place. However, many in the bank were content to see him go, though it was an expensive departure – Newman collected up to $67 million.

There were others Deutsche definitely wanted to keep on board. In 1998 (before the takeover announcement), Frank Quattrone left, taking about 100 of the technology group he had built up with him. The chief financial officer at BT, Richard Daniel, went in June 1999, despite being offered a $9m retention bonus. Other department heads and deputies left around the same time, and the CSFB poached all the staff working in the US health care area. Several top Deutsche staff also departed the bank. In July 1999, a small but profitable team of index fund managers joined Merrill Lynch. 1999 also saw the loss of some senior experts in the leveraged finance/junk bond area, and Alex Brown lost a few stars. The defections raised questions about what DB stood to gain from the acquisition: in the absence of expertise, areas such as high-yield bonds, asset management, custody and high-tech IPOs could flounder.

Breuer's key objective was to create a new type of universal bank with strengths in both wholesale commercial and investment banking, de-emphasising the traditional holdings of commercial concerns in Germany. Deutsche's $22 billion of German industrial and commercial holdings were hived off to a separate profit centre, making it possible they would be sold off at a future date.[75]

Analysts had thought Deutsche would lose many American clients post-acquisition, but they were proved wrong. 1999 turned into a record year for underwriting high-yield debt, equities and eurobonds, though the bank made few inroads into the M&A business. In 2000, Herr Breuer announced that the bank was to merge with the second largest German bank, Dresdner. Many of DB's investment bankers in London and New York were against the deal because Dresdner was perceived as old-fashioned, and very weak in investment banking. Dresdner pulled out of the deal after senior investment bankers persuaded Breuer that if the merger did go through, Dresdner's investment bank should be shut down.

The London office proved instrumental in DB's success in investment banking. Two names stand out. Mr Mitchell joined Deutsche Bank in 1995 from Merrill Lynch, and Mr Ackermann arrived in 1996 from Credit Suisse. Mitchell managed to attract hundreds of employees from other top investment banks. Though Ackermann avoids publicity, he too helped build up the London office. By this time, the acquisition of Bankers Trust was being seen in a new light: it had given Deutsche a foothold in the US securities markets just before one of the greatest bull runs in stock market history. Profits from investment banking rose to

---

[74] "Because it was there", *The Economist*, 28 November 1998, p. 73.
[75] If they were sold off, Deutsche would be the first German universal bank to end the tradition of holding equity shares in commercial outfits.

$3.7 billion in 2000, up from $1.3 billion in 1998. The London office began to have a great deal of power because by 2000, 60% of the bank's profits came from investment banking. Ironically, Herr Breuer, who had always declared a move into investment banking as the key strategy, saw his position being marginalised by the brash traders of the London office.

In early 2001, Breuer appeared to favour scaling down Deutsche Bank's emphasis on investment banking. Substantial job cuts in this area were announced, with 2600 staff made redundant, mainly in Frankfurt, though London and New York were also affected. A potential source of worry was a comment by the chairman, who admitted there were weaknesses in their investment banking business that could not be overcome through an acquisition. Herr Breuer revealed a new strategic focus: to increase profits in asset management and private banking – Breuer himself took control of the new division. There were also indications the bank wanted to increase its presence in retail asset management, having purchased an American on-line brokerage firm in December 2001. However, Breuer's new division soon lost money due to costly hiring and reduced equity purchases by retail clients.

Meanwhile, investment banking continued to make some impressive deals in 2001, and investment banking revenues were higher at Deutsche than at Goldman Sachs or Morgan Stanley. Over 80% of these revenues came from outside Germany, indicating the bank was well diversified in this area.

In May 2002, Mr Josef Ackermann was set to take over from Herr Breuer as head of the Vorstand, or management board. The German management system was beginning to become an issue for the bank, especially after it listed on the New York Stock Exchange in late 2001, which meant adopting US accounting standards. Under the German system the Vorstand can overrule the head, and there were pressures from senior management, most of whom are not German nationals, to replace this German style of management with the American system which has a chairman and CEO. Mr Ackerman supported the move to cut the size of the Vorstand in half, so it will have just four members. The official language of communication was changed to English in 2002.

## 10.8.7. Deutsche Weathers a Banking Storm in Germany

Mr Ackerman, a Swiss national, succeeded Breuer as head of Deutsche Bank in the summer of 2002. It is not just his background that will make it likely investment banking will continue to be given priority. German bankers called 2002 their "annus horribilis" because of the record number of corporate insolvencies and the decline in their investment portfolios due to the sharp drop in the stock market.[76] However, the Deutsche Bank weathered the storm better than other commercial banks in Germany. In a year where the pre-tax profits for the other three major commercial banks were negative, Table 10.4 illustrates that not only was Deutsche Bank in the black, its real profits were up on 2001. Deutsche Bank has remained profitable because it is far less dependent on the German markets than the other commercial banks at a time when Germany was suffering its worst recession in post-war history. For example, Commerzbank was in the red in 2002 and 2003, with the size of negative pre-tax profits rising over the two years. The same was true for HypoVereinsbank

---

[76] Wagner, J. (2003), "Getting Back in the Black", *The Banker*, March 25–27, p. 26.

and Dresdner Bank. By contrast, Deutsche's international operations in both investment banking and funds management ensured the bank remained profitable, though profits were slightly down in 2003. Deutsche also managed to cut its cost to income ratio from 90% in 2001 to 79% and 81% in 2002 and 2003, respectively. HypoVereinsbank Commerzbank have also kept costs down – their ratios of cost to income dropped from 69% to 64% and 77% to 73%. Dresdner, by contrast, has seen costs soar from 71% in 2002 to 117% in 2003 – in other words, cost exceeded income.

Unlike other European countries, these big commercial banks lack a strong retail presence – each has about 5% of the deposit market, at most. The state owned regional

Table 10.4   Annual Results for Deutsche Bank and Bankers Trust

| | Capital ($m) | Assets ($m) | Pre-tax profits (%) | Real profits growth (%) | C:I (%) | ROA (%) | ROE (%) | Basel 1 (%) |
|---|---|---|---|---|---|---|---|---|
| *Deutsche Bank* | | | | | | | | |
| Dec-90 | 10 413 | 267 702 | 1 631 | −32.8 | Na | 0.61 | Na | Na |
| Dec-91 | 11 258 | 296 266 | 2 280 | 36.9 | Na | 0.77 | Na | |
| Dec-92 | 11 303 | 303 840 | 2 315 | 3.9 | Na | 0.76 | Na | 10.5 |
| Dec-93 | 11 723 | 322 445 | 2 664 | 18.3 | Na | 0.83 | Na | 11.3 |
| Dec-94 | 13 089 | 368 261 | 2 049 | −33 | Na | 0.56 | Na | 10.4 |
| Dec-95 | 18 937 | 503 429 | 2 487 | −1 | Na | 0.49 | Na | 10.1 |
| Dec-96 | 18 571 | 569 906 | 3 145 | 35 | 71.7 | 0.55 | Na | 9.9 |
| Dec-97 | 17 371 | 581 979 | 1 140 | −59 | 68.51 | 0.2 | 6.4 | 10.6 |
| Dec-98 | 18 680 | 732 534 | 4 713 | 282.1 | 78.1 | 0.64 | Na | 11.5 |
| Dec-99 | 17 418 | 843 761 | 4 106 | 0.9 | 72.1 | 0.49 | 11.1 | 12 |
| Dec-00 | 20 076 | 874 706 | 6 261 | 61.6 | 74.5 | 0.72 | 20.1 | 12.6 |
| Dec-01 | 21 859 | 809 220 | 1 589 | −73.9 | 90.45 | 0.2 | 7.1 | 12.1 |
| Dec-02 | 23 849 | 795 255 | 3 722 | 94.3 | 78.75 | 0.47 | 10.2 | 12.3 |
| Dec-03 | 27 302 | 1 104 845 | 3 481 | −23.2 | 81.81 | 0.34 | 5.2 | 13.9 |
| *Bankers Trust* | | | | | | | | |
| Dec-90 | 2 616 | 62 854 | 819 | Na | | 1.33 | Na | Na |
| Dec-91 | 2 987 | 63 684 | 857 | 0.4 | | 1.35 | Na | Na |
| Dec-92 | 3 637 | 72 172 | 925 | 4.8 | | 1.41 | Na | 13.89 |
| Dec-93 | 4 846 | 92 082 | 1 566 | 64.4 | | 1.7 | Na | 14.46 |
| Dec-94 | 5 010 | 97 016 | 901 | −43.9 | | 0.93 | Na | 15.37 |
| Dec-95 | 5 262 | 104 002 | 350 | −62.2 | | 0.34 | Na | 14.18 |
| Dec-96 | 5 929 | 120 235 | 897 | 149.1 | 84.2 | 0.75 | Na | 13.3 |
| Dec-97 | 6 431 | 140 102 | 1 259 | 40.4 | 85.69 | 0.9 | Na | 14.1 |
| Dec-98 | 5 399 | 79 996 | −52 | −104.1 | 105.2 | −0.04 | Na | 14.11 |

Capital: Tier 1; C:I: cost to income; Basel 1: risk to assets ratio; ROA: return on assets; ROE: return on average equity.

*Source: The Banker*, July editions, 1991–2004; ROE: Deutsche Bank (2003), *Annual Review*.

(landesbanken) and local savings banks have about 80% of the retail deposit and loan market. They also enjoy a state guarantee[77] and thus an AAA rating, meaning they can attract deposits and make loans at lower rates. The savings banks have remained profitable during the recession because of their dominance in the retail and corporate markets. For this and other reasons, they are resisting the Chancellor's call for them to merge with private and cooperative banks, a strategy which has been so successful in France and Italy over the last few years. The Federal government has little control over their actions because they are owned and controlled by state governments. The result is over-banking in the German market, which keeps margins thin. Another important player in the retail market is Postbank, a bank operated by the German Post Office. It has about 6% of bank deposits and was privatised in June 2004. The Post Office, which was privatised in 2000, maintains management control, because 49% of Postbank was sold off. Deutsche Bank acted as lead manager of the IPO and, reportedly, turned down an approach by the government to block buy the shares because the bank considered the shares to be overpriced, and probably balked at the idea that they would not have management control.[78] Had DB been interested, there would have been a tricky conflict of interest to resolve. Should one of the commercial banks eventually take over Postbank, it would give it about an 11% share of deposits, making it a potentially serious competitor, especially after protection of the savings and regional banks is withdrawn.

Deutsche is now considered an investment bank, and it continues to cut back on its relatively small amount of corporate lending in Germany, though it has kept its domestic retail branch network. In 1999, DB integrated its on-line banking service with its retail banking department. The on-line system had attracted half a million customers (though it is unclear how many were already DB clients) and it was hoped the combination will allow customers to pick and choose on-line and off-line services according to their tastes. DB has even offered to share its on-line facility with other banks.[79]

In October 2003, Deutsche Bank received *The Banker*'s country and Western Europe awards, and was recognised as the top investment bank for interest rate swaps. The awards are based on 2002 results, so the country award comes as no surprise. It was named the "Bank for Western Europe" because of the big reduction in its operating costs (see the cost to income ratios in Table 10.4), and took the number one spot for fund management in Europe, placing in the top five globally. It was also the leading equities house in Europe. It attracted 500 000 new business and private clients in Europe.[80] Thus, by 2003, it had become the leading European investment bank. While it continues to be outclassed by

---

[77] An agreement with the EU means the guarantee must be phased out by July 2005.

[78] This proved correct when in the end, the shares were sold at about 3 euros less (€28.50) than the Chief Executive of Deutsche Post had been hoping to get. The shares are split between German retail and institutional investors; about 48% of the shares sold went to foreign investors.

[79] Its German rivals have adopted other strategies to return to profit. Dresdner is focusing on bancassurance (it purchased the failing insurance giant Allianz) and niche investment banking through its London outlet, Dresdner, Kleinwort Wasserstein. HVB is looking to Eastern Europe (through its ownership of Bank Austria and offering retail banking services in Northern Germany). Commerzbank looks the most vulnerable, hoping to gain from Deutsche's withdrawal from corporate lending. See Wagner, J. (2003), "Getting Back in the Black", *The Banker*, March 25–27, p. 27.

[80] *The Banker Awards 2003*, September.

many of the US banks on the global front, it seems that Deutsche Bank has achieved what Bankers Trust set out to do at the beginning of the case study: to move away from traditional core banking and into investment banking. The only major difference is that it has opted to keep its retail network in Germany. After BT sold its retail network, it became a wholesale commercial bank, with expertise in trading and risk management advice. However, that was not enough to keep its independence, and the name is all but forgotten in the new century. As Deutsche Bank strives to become a top tier global bank, what does Mr Ackerman and the Vorstand have to do to ensure its continued independence?

## Questions

1. In the USA, what is the difference between a money centre commercial bank and an investment bank?
2. Why has the term "money centre" largely disappeared in the USA?
3. In the first paragraph of the case, it was noted that in 1987 "the stock yielded a 41% return on equity before extraordinary allowance for credit losses...".
   (a) Is ROE a good indication of the success of the new strategy at Bankers Trust?
   (b) Identify other ways of measuring the success (or otherwise) of this bank.
4. The case revealed, either directly or indirectly, the multifaceted nature of BT's strategy. Answer the following questions:
   (a) Why did BT sell its retail banking network? Given that retail banking is usually one of the most profitable areas of banking, was it the right decision?
   (b) Why were "section 20" subsidiaries seen as a means of bypassing the Glass Steagall Act? Why was it important in BT's acquisition of Alex Brown?
   (c) Explain the meaning and consequences of a global product focus at the expense of a regional client focus.
   (d) What effect would the absence of a distribution and sales network have on BT operations?
   (e) Explain why BT's loan securitisation programme would stabilise balance sheet growth, increase liquidity and earn a higher return on equity.
   (f) What is RAROC? Identify the key problem associated with RAROC.
5. To fulfil the objectives of its new strategy, BT had to change its management style and employee compensation. Explain the meaning of the following terms, and discuss how they might encourage BT staff to achieve BT's strategic goals:
   (a) A horizontal management structure and how it differs from management style at commercial banks.
   (b) "Excellence through common purpose".
   (c) Incentive compensation and the bonus system.
6. What are the main lessons to be learned from the 1994 swaps debacle?
7. What were the main contributory factors to BT's acquisition by Deutsche Bank?
8. What are the advantages and disadvantages of absorbing a well-known bank name after a takeover? Why did Deutsche Bank erase the Bankers Trust label within weeks of takeover but keep the Alex Brown name, and for a decade, Morgan Grenfell's name?

9. (a) What actions did Mr Newman take to improve BT's bottom line and its status as an investment bank?

(b) According to Mr Newman, a diversified bank makes for a stronger, more profitable bank. So what was wrong with the strategy he devised for Bankers Trust?

10. With reference to becoming a successful investment bank, why did Deutsche Bank succeed where Bankers Trust failed?

11. Deutsche Bank is now a leading *European* investment bank but it is best described as a universal investment bank. Why? Is this a good strategic position for a bank wanting to be a leading global player?

# REFERENCES/BIBLIOGRAPHY

Abassi, B. and R.J. Taffler (1982), "Country Risk: A Model of Economic Performance Related to Debt Servicing Capacity", The City University Business School, Working Papers Series No. 36.

Acharya, V. (2002), "India: Crisis Reform and Growth In the Nineties", Stanford Center for Research on Economic Development and Policy Reform, Working Paper No. 139.

Acharya, V., I. Hasan and A. Saunders (2002), "Should Banks be Diversified? Evidence from Individual Bank Loan Portfolios", BIS Working Papers No. 118, September.

Adams, J.R. (1991), "The Big Fix: Inside the S&L Scandal; How an Unholy Alliance of Politics and Money Destroyed America's Banking System", Journal of Finance, Mar, 457–459.

Aharony, J., A. Saunders and I. Swary (1985), "The Effects of the International Banking Act on Domestic Bank Profitability and Risk", Journal of Money, Credit and Banking, 17(4), 493–511.

Ahluwalia, M. (2002), "Economic Reforms in India Since 1991: Has Gradualism Worked?", Journal of Economic Perspectives, 16(3), 67–88.

Aigner, D., C. Lovell and P. Schmidt (1977), "Foundation and Estimation of Stochastic Frontier Models", Journal of Econometrics, 6, 21–37.

Akerlof, G. (1970), "The Market for 'Lemons' ", Quarterly Journal of Economics, 84(3), 488–500.

Akerlof, G. and P. Romer (1993), "Looting: The Economic Underworld of Bankruptcy for Profit", Brookings Papers on Economic Activity, 2, 1–73.

Akhavein, J., A. Berger and D. Humphrey (1997), "The Effects of Megamergers on Efficiency and Prices: Evidence from a Bank Profit Function", Review of Industrial Organisation, 12, 95–139.

Alchian, A. and H. Demsetz (1972), "Production, Information Costs and Economic Organisation", American Economic Review, 62, 777–795.

Alford, A., P. Healy and N.K. Hwa (1998), "The Performance of International Joint Ventures: A Study of the Merchant Banking Industry in Singapore", Journal of Corporate Finance, 4, 31–52.

Aliber, R.Z. (1984), "International Banking: A Survey", Journal of Money, Credit and Banking, 16(4), 661–695.

Allen, F. and D. Gale (2000), "Bubbles and Crises", The Economic Journal 110(460), 236–255.

Allen, F. and G. Gorton (1993), "Churning Bubbles", Review of Economic Studies, 60, 813–836.

Allen, L. and A. Rai (1996), "Operational Efficiency in Banking: An International Comparison", Journal of Banking and Finance, 20, 655–672.

Altman, E.I. (1968), "Financial Ratios, Discriminant Analysis, and the Prediction of Corporate Bankruptcy", Journal of Monetary Finance, 23(4), 589–609.

Altman, E.I. (1977), "Predicting Performance in the Savings and Loan Association Industry", Journal of Economics, Oct, 443–466.

Altman, E.I. (1983), Corporate Financial Distress: A Complete Guide to Predicting, Avoiding and Dealing with Bankruptcy, New York: John Wiley & Sons.

Altman, E.I. (1985), "Managing the Commercial Lending Process", in R.C. Aspinwall and R.A. Eisenbeis (eds), *Handbook in Banking Strategy*, New York: John Wiley & Sons, pp. 473–510.

Altunbas, Y. and P. Molyneux (1994), "The Concentration Performance Relationship in European Banking – A Note", Institute of European Finance Research Papers in Banking and Finance, RP 94/12, pp. 1–12.

Altunbas, Y. and P. Molyneux (1996), "Cost Economies in EU Banking Systems", *Journal of Business and Economics*, **48**, 217–230.

Altunbas, Y., M. Liu, P. Molyneux and R. Seth (2000), "Efficiency and Risk in Japanese Banking", *Journal of Banking and Finance*, **24**, 1605–1628.

Altunbas, Y., L. Evans and P. Molyneux (2001a), "Ownership and Efficiency in Banking", *Journal of Money, Credit and Banking*, **33**(4), 926–954.

Altunbas, Y., E. Gardener, P. Molyneux and B. Moore (2001b), "Efficiency in European Banking", *European Economic Review*, **45**, 1931–1955.

Aluwalia, M.S. (2002), "Economic Reforms in China Since 1991: Has Gradualism Worked?", *Journal of Economic Perspectives*, **16**(3), 67–88.

Amato, J. and C. Furfine (2003), "Are Credit Ratings Procyclical?", BIS Working Papers No. 129, February.

Anderson, R. and B. Rivard (1998), "The Competition Policy Treatment of Shared EFT Networks", in Federal Reserve Bank of Chicago (ed.), *Proceedings of the Bank Structure and Competition Conference*, Chicago, pp. 174–198.

Andersson, M. and S. Viotti (1999), "Managing and Preventing Financial Crises – Lessons from the Swedish Experience", *Sveriges Riksbank Quarterly Review*, 1/1999.

Andreades, A. (1966), *A History of the Bank of England, 1640–1903*, 4th edn, London: Frank, Cass and Company.

Andrews, D. (1985), *Real Banking Profitability*, London: IBCA.

Angelini, P. and N. Cetorelli (2003), "The Effects of Regulatory Reform on Competition in the Banking Industry", *Journal of Money, Credit and Banking*, **35**(5), 664–684.

l'Anson, K. and A. Fight (2002), *Bank and Country Risk Analysis*, London: Euromoney.

APACS (Association of Payments and Clearing Services) (2003), *UK Payment Markets Trends and Forecasts*, available on line from www.apac.org.uk

Archer, S. and T. Ahmed (2003), "Emerging Standards for Islamic Financial Institutions: A Case for Accounting and Auditing Organization for Islamic Financial Institutions", Mimeo, World Bank.

Ardnt, H.W. (1988), "Comparative Advantage in Trade in Financial Services", *Banca Nationale Del Lavoro*, **164**(Mar), 61–78.

Argy, V. (1987), "International Financial Liberalisation: The Australian and Japanese Experiences Compared", *Bank of Japan Journal of Monetary and Economic Studies*, **5**(1), 105–167.

Arshadi, N. and E.C. Lawrence (1987), "An Empirical Investigation of New Bank Performance", *Journal of Banking and Finance*, **11**, 33–48.

Avery, R.B. and A.N. Berger (1991), "Risk-Based Capital and Deposit Insurance Reform", *Journal of Banking and Finance*, **15**(4/5), 847–874.

Avery, R.B. and G.A. Hanweck (1984), "A Dynamic Analysis of Bank Failures", in *Bank Structure and Competition Conference Proceedings*, Chicago: Federal Reserve Bank of Chicago.

Bae, K.-H., J.-K. Kang and C.-W. Lim (2002), "The Value of Durable Bank Relationships", *Journal of Financial Econometrics*, **64**, 181–214.

Bagehot, W. (1873), *Lombard Street: A Description of the Money Market*, reissued in 1962 by Richard D. Irwin, Homewood, IL and in 1999 by John Wiley & Sons, Chichester, UK. [The quotes in Chapter 7 come from the 1962 reprint.]

Bainbridge, A., D. Meere and P. Veal (2001), "Web Only and Traditional Banks Need to Sharpen Migration Skills", *The American Banker*, 17 August, p. 8.

Balen, M. (2002), *A Very English Deceit*, London: Fourth Estate/Harper Collins.

Balkan, E.M. (1992), "Political Instability, Country Risk, and the Probability of Default", *Applied Economics*, **24**, 999–1008.

Baltazar, R. and M. Santos (2003), "The Benefits of Banking Mega-mergers: Event Study Evidence from the 1988 Failed Mega-Merger Attempts in Canada", *Canadian Journal of Administrative Sciences*, **20**(3), 196–208.

Baltensperger, E. (1980), "Alternative Approaches to the Theory of the Banking Firm", *Journal of Monetary Economics*, **6**, 1–37.

Bank of England (1978), "The Secondary Banking Crisis and the Bank of England Support Operations", *Bank of England Quarterly Bulletin*, **18**(2), 230–239.

Bank of England (1980), "Measurement of Capital", *Bank of England Quarterly Bulletin*, **20**(3), 324–330.

Bank of England (1983), "The International Banking Scene: A Supervisory Perspective", *Bank of England Quarterly Bulletin*, **23**(2), 61–65.

Bank of England (1984a), "International Debt – Thinking About the Longer Term", *Bank of England Quarterly Bulletin*, **24**, 51–53.

Bank of England (1984b), "The Business of Financial Supervision", *Bank of England Quarterly Bulletin*, **24**, 46–50.

Bank of England (1985a), "Change in the Stock Exchange and Regulation of the City", *Bank of England Quarterly Bulletin*, **25**(4), 544–550.

Bank of England (1985b), "Managing Change in International Banking", *Bank of England Quarterly Bulletin*, **25**(4), 551–558.

Bank of England (1986), "Developments in International Banking and Capital Markets", *Bank of England Quarterly Bulletin*, **27**(2), 234–236.

Bank of England (1987a), "Japanese Banks in London", *Bank of England Quarterly Bulletin*, **27**(3), 518–524.

Bank of England (1987b), "Supervision and Central Banking", *Bank of England Quarterly Bulletin*, **27**(3), 380–385.

Bank of England (1992a), "Financial Regulation, What are We Trying to Do?", *Bank of England Quarterly Bulletin*, **32**(3), 322–324.

Bank of England (1992b), "Major International Banks' Performance", *Bank of England Quarterly Bulletin*, **32**(3), 288–297.

Bank of England (1993a), "The Bank of England's Role in Prudential Supervision", *Bank of England Quarterly Bulletin*, **33**(2), 260–264.

Bank of England (1993b), "The EC Single Market in Financial Services", *Bank of England Quarterly Bulletin*, **3**(1), 92–97.

Bank of England (1994a), "The Pursuit of Financial Stability", *Bank of England Quarterly Bulletin*, **34**(1), 60–66.

Bank of England (1994b), "The Development of a UK Real-Time Gross Settlement System", *Bank of England Quarterly Bulletin*, **34**(2), 163–171.

*The Banker* (1987), "Top 100 By Size: Importance of Capital", July, 153–172.

*The Banker* (1991–2004), "Top 1000 Banks", July issues of each year, 102–207.

*The Banker* (2004), "Reality Check on Basel II", July, 154–165.

Bannock, G. (2002), "Financial Services Regulation: Controlling the Costs", *The Financial Regulator*, **6**(4), 31–35.

Barker, D. and D. Holdsworth (1994), "The Causes of Bank Failure in the 1980s", Federal Reserve Bank of New York, Research Paper No. 9325.

Barnard, G. and P.M. Thomsen (2002), "Financial Sector Reform in Russia: Recent Experience, Priorities, and Impact on Economic Growth and Stability", available from www.imf.org/moscow

Basel Committee on Banking Supervision (1988), *International Convergence of Capital Measurement and Capital Standards*, Basel.

Basel Committee on Banking Supervision (1993), *The Prudential Supervision of Netting, Market Risks and Interest Rate Risks* (Consultative Proposal by the Basel Committee on Banking Supervision), Basel.

Basel Committee on Banking Supervision (1996), *Amendment to the Capital Accord to Incorporate Market Risks*, Basel.

Basel Committee on Banking Supervision (2001a), *Overview of New Capital Accord*, Basel. Can be downloaded from www.bis.org

Basel Committee on Banking Supervision (2001b), *Results of Second Quantitative Impact Study*, Basel. Can be downloaded from www.bis.org

Basel Committee on Banking Supervision (2003a), *The 2002 Loss Data Collection Exercise for Operational Risk: Summary of the Data Collected*, Basel. Can be downloaded from www.bis.org

Basel Committee on Banking Supervision (2003b), *Overview of the New Basel Capital Accord*, Basel. Can be downloaded from www.bis.org

Basel Committee on Banking Supervision (2004), *International Convergence of Capital Measurement and Capital Standards: A Revised Framework*, Basel. Can be downloaded from www.bis.org

Batchelor, R.A. (1986), "The Avoidance of Catastrophe: Two Nineteenth-Century Banking Crises", in F. Capie and G.E. Wood (eds), *Financial Crises and the World Banking System*, London: Macmillan.

Batunaggar, S. (2002), "Indonesia's Banking Crisis Resolution: The Way Forward", Mimeo, Banking Crisis Resolution Conference, Centre for Central Banking Studies, December.

Bauer, P., A. Berger, G. Ferrier and D.B. Humphrey (1998), "Consistency Conditions for Regulatory Analysis of Financial Institutions: A Comparison of Frontier Efficiency Models", *Journal of Economics and Business*, **50**, 85–114.

Beaver, W.H. (1966), "Financial Ratios as Predictors of Failure", Empirical Research in Accounting: Selected Studies, Supplement to *Journal of Accounting Research*, 71–111.

Beder, T. (1995), "VAR: Seductive But Dangerous", *Financial Analysts Journal*, **51**, 12–24.

Beim, D. and C. Calomiris (2001), *Emerging Financial Markets*, New York: McGraw Hill.

Beitel, P., D. Schiereck and M. Wahrenburg (2003), "Explaining the M&A – Success in European Bank Mergers and Acquisitions", *European Financial Management*, **10**(1), 109–140.

Bennett, R. (1993), "The Six Men Who Rule World Derivatives", *Euromoney*, **Aug**, 45–49.

Benston, G.J. (1965), "Branch Banking and Economies of Scale", *Journal of Finance*, **20**, 312–331.

Benston, G. (1973), "Bank Examination", *Bulletin of the Institute of Finance, Graduate School of Business Administration, New York University*, May, 89–90.

Benston, G.J. (1985), *An Analysis of the Causes of Savings and Loans Association Failures*, Monograph Series in Finance and Economics, New York: New York University.

Benston, G.J. (1989), *The Separation of Commercial and Investment Banking: The Glass Steagall Act Reconsidered*, New York: St Martins Press.

Benston, G.J. (1990a), *The Separation of Commercial and Investment Banking, The Glass–Steagall Act Revisited and Reconsidered*, New York: Oxford University Press.

Benston, G.J. (1990b), "US Banking in an Increasingly Integrated and Competitive World Economy", *Journal of Financial Services Research*, **4**, 311–339.

Benston, G.J. (1992), "International Regulatory Coordination of Banking", in J. Fingleton (ed.), *The Internationalisation of Capital Markets and the Regulatory Response*, London: Graham and Trotman, pp. 197–209.

Benston, G. and G. Kaufman (1986), "Risks and Failures in Banking: Overview, History, and Evaluation", *Federal Reserve Bank of Chicago Staff Memoranda*, 1–27.

Benston, G., R. Eisenbeis, P. Horvitz, E. Kane and G. Kaufman (1986), *Sage and Sound Banking*, Cambridge, MA: MIT Press.

Benston, G., W. Hunter and L. Wall (1995), "Motivations for Bank Mergers and Acquisitions: Enhancing the Deposit Insurance Put Option versus Earnings Diversification", *Journal of Money, Credit and Banking*, **27**(3), 777–788.

Bentley, R.J. (1987), "Debt Conversion in Latin America", *Columbia Journal of World Business*, **Fall**, 37–49.

Berger, A.N. (1993), "'Distribution Free' Estimates of Efficiency in the US Banking Industry and Tests of Standard Distributional Assumptions", *Journal of Productivity Analysis*, **4**, 261–292.

Berger, A.N. (1995), "The Profit Structure Relationship in Banking – Tests of Market Power and Efficient Structure Hypothesis", *Journal of Money, Credit and Banking*, **27**(2), 404–431.

Berger, A. (1998), "The Efficiency Effects of Bank Mergers and Acquisition: A Preliminary Look at the 1990s Data", in T. Amihud and G. Miller (eds), *Bank Mergers and Acquisitions*, New York: Kluwer Academic Publishers.

Berger, A.N. (2003), "The Economic Effects of Technological Progress: Evidence from the Banking Industry", *Journal of Money, Credit and Banking*, **35**, 141–176.

Berger, A.N. and T.H. Hannan (1989), "The Price–Concentration Relationship in Banking", *Review of Economics and Statistics*, **74**(May), 291–299; also, their "Reply to a Comment" by W.E. Jackson (1992), *Review of Economics and Statistics* (May), 373–376.

Berger, A. and T. Hannan (1998), "The Efficiency Cost of Market Power in the Banking Industry: A Test of the 'Quiet Life' and Related Hypotheses", *Review of Economics and Statistics*, **80**, 454–465.

Berger, A. and D. Humphrey (1991a), "The Dominance of Inefficiencies Over Scale and Product Mix Economies in Banking", *Journal of Monetary Economics*, **28**, 117–148.

Berger, A. and D. Humphrey (1991b), "Megamergers in Banking and the Use of Cost Efficiency and an Antitrust Defense", *The Antitrust Bulletin*, **37**(3), 541–600.

Berger, A. and D. Humphrey (1997), "Efficiency of Financial Institutions: International Survey and Directions for Further Research", *European Journal of Operation Research*, **98**, 175–212.

Berger, A. and L. Mester (1997), "Inside the Black Box: What Explains Differences in the Efficiencies of Financial Institutions", *Journal of Banking and Finance*, **21**, 895–947.

Berger, A. and L. Mester (2003), "Explaining the Dramatic Changes in the Performance of US Banks: Technological Change, Deregulation, and Dynamic Changes in Competition", *Journal of Financial Intermediation*, **12**(1), 57–96.

Berger, A., W. Hunter and S. Timme (1993), "The Efficiency of Financial Institutions: A Review and Preview of Research Past, Present, and Future", *Journal of Banking and Finance*, **17**, 221–249.

Berger, A., D. Humphrey and L. Pulley (1996), "Do Consumers Pay for One-Stop Banking? Evidence from an Alternative Revenue Function", *Journal of Banking and Finance*, **20**, 1601–1621.

Berger, A.N., R.S. Demsetz and P.E. Strahan (1999), "The Consolidation of the Financial Services Industry: Causes, Consequences, and Lessons for the Future", *Journal of Banking and Finance*, **23**, 135–194.

Berlin, M., A. Saunders and G.F. Udell (eds) (1991), "Deposit Insurance Reform", Special Issue, *Journal of Banking and Finance*, **15**(4/5), 733–1040.

Bernanke, B. and M. Gertler (1990), "Financial Fragility and Economic Performance", *Quarterly Journal of Economics*, **105**(1), 87–114.

Bernanke, B. and M. Gertler (1995), "Inside the Black Box: The Credit Channel of Monetary Policy Transmission", *Journal of Economic Perspectives*, **9**(4), 27–49.

Bernard, H. and J. Bisignano (2000), "Information, Liquidity, and Risk in the Interbank Market: Implicit Guarantees and Private Credit Market Failure", Bank for International Settlements Working Papers No. 86, March.

Bhattacharya, S. and U. Patel (2002), "Financial Intermediation In India: A Case of Aggravated Moral Hazard?", Stanford Center for Research on Economic Development and Policy Reform, Working Paper No. 145.

Bhattacharya, S. and U. Patel (2003), "Reform Strategies for the Indian Financial Sector", Stanford Center for Research on Economic Development and Policy Reform, Working Paper No. 208, February.

Bhattacharya, S. and P. Pfleiderer (1985), "Delegated Portfolio Management", *Journal of Economic Theory*, **36**(1), 1–25.

Bikker, J. and K. Haaf (2002), "Competition, Concentration, and their Relationship: An Empirical Analysis of the Banking Industry", *Journal of Banking and Finance*, **26**, 2191–2214.

BIS (1990), *The Lamfalussy Report*, Basel: Bank for International Settlements.

BIS (1999), "Strengthening the Banking System in China: Issues and Experience", BIS Policy Papers No. 7, October. Can be downloaded from www.bis.org

BIS (2000a), *Quarterly Review*, Basel: Bank for International Settlements.

BIS (2000b), "Sound Practices for Managing Liquidity in Banking Organisations", February, Basel: Basel Committee on Banking Supervision. Can be downloaded from www.bis.org

BIS (2000c), *Statistics on Payment Systems in the Group of 10 Countries*, Basel: Committee on Payments and Settlements Systems. Can be downloaded from www.bis.org

BIS (2001), "The Banking Industry in the Emerging Market Economies: Competition, Consolidation, and Systemic Stability", Bank for International Settlements Papers No. 4.

BIS (2003a), *Overview of the New Basel Capital Accord*, April, Basel: Basel Committee on Banking Supervision.

BIS (2003b), *Quantitative Impact Study 3 – Overview of Global Results*, May, Basel: Basel Committee on Banking Supervision.

BIS (2003c), *New Basel Capital Accord Consultative Document*, April, Basel: Basel Committee on Banking Supervision.

BIS (2003d), *73rd Annual Report*, Basel: Bank for International Settlements.

BIS (2003e), *Credit Risk Transfer*, Basel: Bank for International Settlements.

BIS (2003f), *Payment Systems in the Euro Area*, Basel: Bank for International Settlements.

BIS (2004a), *74th Annual Report*, Basel: Bank for International Settlements.

BIS (2004b), "Bank Failures in Mature Economies", Basel Committee of Banking Supervision Working Paper No. 13, April.

Bisignano, J. (1992), "Banking in the European Community: Structure, Competition and Public Policy", in G.G. Kaufman (ed.), *Banking Structures in Major Countries*, Dordrecht: Kluwer Academic Publishers.

Black, F. (1975), "Bank Funds Management in an Efficient Market", *Journal of Financial Economics*, **2**(Sept), 323–339.

Blair, M. (1998), *Blackstone's Guide to the Bank of England Act*, London: Blackstone Press.

Blake, D. and M. Pradhan (1991), "Debt Equity Swaps as Bond Conversions: Implications for Pricing", *Journal of Banking and Finance*, **15**(1), 29–42.

Bliss, R.T. and R.J. Rosen (2001), "CEO Compensation and Bank Mergers", *Journal of Financial Economics*, **61**, 107–138.

Boddy, M. (1980), *The Building Societies*, London: Macmillan.

Boleat, M. (1982), *The Building Society Industry*, London: Allen & Unwin.

Bollard, A. (2003), "Bollard Refocuses New Zealand Banking Supervision", *The Financial Regulator*, **8**(2), 17–18.

Bond Markets Online (2002), "European Securitisation Issuances Hits €92.4 billion through September", *Newsletter Online*, available from www.bondmarkets.com

Bonin, J. and Y. Huang (2001), "Dealing with the Bad Loans of the Chinese Banks", *Journal of Asian Economics*, **12**, 197–214.

Bordo, M., B. Eichengreen, D. Klingebiel and M. Soledad Martinez-Peria (2001), "Is the Crisis Problem Growing More Severe?", *Economic Policy*, **32**(Apr), 51–82.

Boreo, C. (2003), "Towards a Macroprudential Framework for Financial Supervision and Regulation", BIS Working Papers No. 128, February.

Bouchet, M. and H. Clark (2004), *Country Risk Assessment*, Chichester, UK: John Wiley & Sons.

Bourgheas, S. (1999), "Contagious Bank Runs", *International Review of Economics and Finance*, **8**, 131–146.

Bovenzi, J.F., J.A. Marino and F.E. McFadden (1983), "Commercial Bank Failure Prediction Models", *Federal Reserve Bank of Atlanta Economic Review*, **Nov**, 14–26.

Boyd, G.H. and M. Gertler (1994a), "Are Banks Dead? Or are the Reports Greatly Exaggerated?", in *Federal Reserve Bank of Chicago Conference Proceedings*, 'The Declining Role of Banking', 30th Annual Conference on Bank Structure and Competition, Chicago, May, pp. 85–117.

Boyd, G.H. and M. Gertler (1994b), "The Role of Large Banks in US Banking Crisis", *Federal Reserve Bank of Minneapolis Quarterly Review*, **18**(1), 2–21.

Boyd, J.H. and S.L. Graham (1991), "Investigating the Banking Consolidation Trend", *Federal Reserve Bank of Minneapolis Quarterly Review*, **15**(2), 3–15.

Boyd, T. (1998), "Nikkei gets a Boost from Bank Rescue", *Australian Financial Review*, **1**(9), 36.

Brainard, L.J. (1991), "Reform in Eastern Europe: Creating a Capital Market", in R. O'Brien and S. Hewin (eds), *Finance and the International Economy: 4 The Amex Bank Review Essays*, Oxford: Oxford University Press, pp. 8–22.

Brewer, T.L. and P. Rivoli (1990), "Politics and Perceived Country Creditworthiness in International Banking", *Journal of Money, Credit and Banking*, **22**(3), 357–369.

Briault, C. (2000), Draft Paper, "FSA Revisited and Some Issues for European Securities Markets Regulation", London: Financial Services Authority, December.

British Bankers Association (2002), *Annual Abstract of Banking Statistics*, London: British Bankers Association.

Brozen, Y. (1982), *Concentration, Mergers, and Public Policy*, New York: Macmillan.

Brunner, K. and A.H. Meltzer (1990), "Money Supply", in B.M. Friedman and F.H. Hahn, *Handbook of Monetary Economics, Volume 1*, New York: Elsevier, pp. 557–398.

Buch, C. (2000), "Information or Regulation: What is Driving the International Activities of Commercial Banks", Kiel Working Paper 1101, Kiel Institute of World Economics.

Buckle, M. and J. Thompson (1998), *The UK Financial System: Theory & Practice*, Manchester: Manchester University Press.

Building Societies Association (2000, 2001), *Annual Report*, London: Building Societies Association.

Burton, F.N. and H. Inoue (1987), "A Country Risk Appraisal Model of Foreign Asset Expropriation in Developing Countries", *Applied Economics*, **19**, 1009–1048.

Buser, S., A. Chen and E. Kane (1981), "Federal Deposit Insurance, Regulatory Policy, and Optimal Bank Capital", *Journal of Finance*, **36**, 51–60.

*Business Week* (1974), "Franklin Faces a Long Summer", May 25, 53–54.

*Business Week* (1974), "Money and Credit: What Went Wrong at Herstatt", August 3, 13–14.

REFERENCES/BIBLIOGRAPHY

Butt-Philips, A. (1988), "Implementing the European Internal Market: Problems and Prospects", Royal Institute of International Affairs, Discussion Paper 5, London.

Cagan, P. (1965), *Determinants and Effects of Changes in the Stock of Money 1875–1960*, Washington: National Bureau of Economic Research.

Calomiris, C. (1998), "Blueprints for a New Global Financial Architecture", Mimeo (unpublished), New York: Columbia Business School. Cited in Fischer (1999), *op. cit.*

Calomiris, C. and D. Beim (2001), *Emerging Financial Markets*, London: McGraw Hill/Irwin.

Calomiris, C. and A. Meltzer (1999), "Fixing the IMF", *The National Interest*, **56**(Summer), 88–96.

Calomiris, C. and A. Powell (2000), "Can Emerging Market Bank Regulators Establish Credible Discipline? The Case of Argentina, 1992–99", National Bureau of Economic Research, Washington, Working Paper No. 7715.

Calverley, J. (1990), *Country Risk Analysis*, London: Butterworths.

Camerer, C. (1989), "Bubbles and Fads in Asset Prices: A Review of Theory and Evidence", *Journal of Economic Surveys*, **3**, 3–41.

Cameron, R. (1967), *Banking in the Early Stages of Industrialization*, New York: Oxford University Press.

Cameron, R. (ed.) (1972), *Banking and Economic Development: Some Lessons of History*, New York: Oxford University Press.

Campbell, T. and W. Kracaw (1980), "Information Production, Market Signaling, and the Theory of Financial Intermediation", *Journal of Finance*, **35**, 863–882.

Capie, F. (2002), "The Emergence of the Bank of England as a Mature Central Bank", in P. O'Brien and D. Winch (eds), *The Political Economy of British Historical Experience, 1688–1914*, Oxford: Oxford University Press (for the British Academy), pp. 295–318.

Caprio, G. and D. Klingebiel (2003), "Episodes of Systemic and Bordeline Financial Crises", Mimeo, World Bank.

Carbo, S., E. Gardener and J. Williams (2000), "Efficiency and Technical Change in Europe's Savings Banks Industry", *Revue de la Banque*, **6**, 381–394.

de Carmoy, H. (1990), *Global Banking Strategy*, Oxford: Basil Blackwell.

Carrow, K.A. and R.A. Heron (1998), "The Interstate Banking and Branching Efficiency Act of 1994: A Wealth Event for the Acquisition Targets", *Journal of Banking and Finance*, **22**, 175–196.

Carver, N. (2003), "Credit Derivatives", *Financial Regulator*, **8**(1), 17–19.

Casserley, D. and G. Gibb (1999), *Banking in Asia: the End of Entitlement*, Chichester, UK: John Wiley & Sons.

Caves, R. (1974), "Causes of Direct Investment: Foreign Firms Shares in Canadian and UK Manufacturing Industries", *Review of Economics and Statistics*, **56**, 279–293.

Caves, R. (1982), *The Multinational Enterprise and Economic Analysis*, London: Cambridge University Press.

Cebula, R. (1999), "New Evidence on the Determinants of Bank Failures in the US", *Applied Economic Letters*, **6**, 45–47.

Cecchini, P. (1988), *The European Challenge: 1992*, London: Wildwood House.

Centre for Economic Business Research (2003), *The City's Importance to the UK Economy*, London: Corporation of London, January. Also available at www.cityoflondon.gov.uk

Centre for the Study of Financial Innovation (2001), *Bumps on the Road to Basel: An Anthology of Views on Basel 2*, London: Centre for the Study of Financial Innovation

Centre for the Study of Financial Innovation (2001), *Sizing up the City – London's Ranking as a Financial Centre*, London: Corporation of London, June. Also available at www.cityoflondon.gov.uk

Chakravarty, S.P., E.P.M. Gardener and J. Teppett (1995), "Gains from a Single European Market in Financial Services", *Current Politics and Economics of Europe*, **5.1**, 1–14.

Chamberlain, G. (1980), "Analysis of Covariance with Qualitative Data", *Review of Economic Studies*, **47**, 225–238.

Chang, R. and A. Velasco (1998a), "The Asian Liquidity Crisis", National Bureau of Economic Research Working Paper No. 6796.

Chang, R. and A. Velasco (1998b), "Financial Crises in Emerging Markets", National Bureau of Economic Research Working Paper No. 6606.

Chew, D. (ed.) (1991), *New Developments in Commercial Banking*, Oxford: Basil Blackwell.

Chionsini, G., A. Foglia and P. Reedtz (2003), "Bank Mergers, Diversification and Risk", Mimeo, Banca d'Italia, March.

Choi, S.-R., D. Park and A.E. Tschoegl (1996), "Banks and the World's Major Banking Centres, 1970–1980", *Weltwirtschaftliches Archiv*, **122**, 48–64.

Chong, B.S. (1991), "The Effects of Interstate Banking on Commercial Banks' Risk and Profitability", *Review of Economics and Statistics*, **73**(1), 78–84.

Citigroup Smith Barney (2003), "Basel II-Strategic Implications", Citigroup Smith Barney, October.

Clark, J. (1988), "Economies of Scale and Scope at Depository Financial Institutions: A Review of the Literature", *Federal Reserve Bank of Kansas City Economic Review*, Sept/Oct, 16–33.

Clarke, G., R. Cull, M. Peria and S. Sanchez (2001), "Foreign Bank Entry: Experience, Implications for Developing Countries, and Agenda for Further Research", Background Paper for the World Bank, World Development Report 2002: Institutions for Markets, October.

Coase, R.H. (1937), "The Nature of the Firm", *Economica*, **4**, 386–405.

Colwell, R.J. and E.P. Davis (1992), "Output, Productivity, and Externalities – the Case of Banking", Bank of England Discussion Paper No. 3.

Compton, E. (1981), *Inside Commercial Banking*, London: John Wiley & Sons.

Cooke, W.P. (1983), "The International Banking Scene: A Supervisory Perspective", *Bank of England Quarterly Bulletin*, **23**(1), 61–65.

Cooke, W.P. (1985), "Some Current Concerns of an International Banking Supervisor", *Bank of England Quarterly Bulletin*, **25**(2), 219–223.

Cooper, J. (1984), *The Management and Regulation of Banks*, London: Macmillan.

Cornett, M. and H. Tehranian (1992), "Changes in Corporate Performance Associated with Bank Acquisitions", *Journal of Financial Economics*, **31**, 211–234.

Corrigan, G. (1990), "The Role of Central Banks and the Financial System in Emerging Market Economies", *Federal Reserve Bank of New York Review*, **15**, 2–17.

Corvoisier, S. and R. Gropp (2002), "Bank Concentration and Retail Interest Rates", *Journal of Banking and Finance*, **26**, 2155–2189.

Coulbeck, N. (1984), *The Multinational Banking Industry*, London: Croom Helm.

Courtis, N. (2002), "Endgame in Basel", *Financial Regulator*, **6**(4), 26–30.

Cowling, K. and P.R. Thomlinson (2000), "The Japanese Crisis – A Case of Strategic Failure", *The Economic Journal*, **110**(464), F358–F382.

Craig, V.V. (1999), "Financial Deregulation in Japan", *FDIC Banking Review*, **11**(3).

CreditMetrics (1997), *Technical Document*, New York: JP Morgan (for updates see the website: http://riskmetrics.com/).

Crouhy, M. (2004), *The Essentials of Risk Management*, New York: McGraw Hill.

Crouhy, M. and D. Gali (1986), "An Economic Assessment of Capital Adequacy Requirements in the Banking Industry", *Journal of Banking and Finance*, **10**, 231–241.

Crouhy, M., D. Gali and R. Mark (2000), *Risk Management*, New York: McGraw Hill.

Cruickshank (2000), *Competition in UK Banking*, Norwich: The Stationary Office.

Cumming, C. (1987), "The Economics of Securitization", *Federal Reserve Bank of New York Quarterly Review*, **11**(3), 11–23.

REFERENCES/BIBLIOGRAPHY

Cumming, C. and L.M. Sweet (1988), "Financial Structure of G10 Countries: How Does the United States Compare?", *Federal Reserve Bank of New York Quarterly Review*, **12**(4), 14–25.

Curry, E.A., J.G. Fung and I.A. Harper (2003), "Multinational Banking: Historical, Empirical, and Case Perspectives", in Mullineux and Murinde, *op. cit*, pp. 27–59.

Cybo-Ottone, A. and M. Murgia (2000), *Journal of Banking and Finance*, **24**, 831–859.

Dale, R. (1992), *International Banking Deregulation*, Oxford: Basil Blackwell.

Damanpour, F. (1986), "A Survey of Market Structure and Activities of Foreign Banking in the US", *Columbia Journal of World Business*, **21**(4), 35–45.

Daniel, K., D. Hirshleifer and A. Subramanyam (1998), "Investor Psychology and Security Market Under-Reaction and Over-Reaction", *Journal of Finance*, **53**, 1839–1886.

Danielsson, J. (2000), "VaR: A Castle Built on Sand", *The Financial Regulator*, **5**(2), 46–50.

Danielsson, J. (2002), "The Emperor has no Clothes: Limits to Risk Modelling", *Journal of Banking and Finance*, **26**(7), 1273–1296.

Danielsson, J. and C. de Vries (1997), "Beyond the Sample: Extreme Quantile and Probability Estimation", Tinbergen Institute Discussion Paper No. 98-016/2, Rotterdam.

Dar, H.A. and J.R. Presley (2003), "Islamic Banking", in Mullineux and Murinde, *op. cit*, pp. 191–206.

Darby, M.R. (1986), "The Internationalisation of American Banking and Finance: Structure, Risk and World Interest Rates", *Journal of International Money and Finance*, **5**(4), 403–428.

Davis, E.P. (1992), *Debt, Financial Fragility and Systemic Risk*, Oxford: Oxford University Press.

Davis, E.P. and R.J. Colwell (1992), "Output, Productivity and Externalities: The Case of Banking", Bank of England Working Paper No. 3, August.

Davis, P. (1999), "Institutionalisation and EMU: Implications For European Financial Markets", *International Finance*, **2**, 33–61.

Davis, S. (1983), *The Management of International Banks*, London: Macmillan.

Davis, S. (1985), *Excellence in Banking*, London: Macmillan.

Davis, S. (1989), *Managing Change in the Excellent Banks*, London: Macmillan.

Davis, S. (2000), *Bank Mergers: Lessons for the Future*, London: Macmillan.

Davis, E.P. and K. Touri (2000), "The Changing Structure of Banks' Income – An Empirical Investigation", Mimeo.

Deane, M. (2001), "Basel II: Limping Towards Completion", *The Financial Regulator*, **June**, 20–21.

De Bandt and E.P. Davis (2000), "Competition, Contestability and Market Structure of European Banking Structures in the European Banking Sectors on the Eve of EMU", *Journal of Banking and Finance*, **24**, 1045–1066.

De Gregorio, J. (1999), "Financial Integration, Financial Development and Economic Growth", *Estudios de Economica*, **26**(2), 137–161.

DeLong, G. (2001), "Shareholder Gains from Focusing versus Diversifying Bank Mergers", *Journal of Financial Economics*, **59**, 221–252.

DeLong, G. (2003), "The Announcement Effects of US versus Non-US Bank Mergers: Do they Differ?", *Journal of Financial Research*, **XXVI**(4), 487–500.

Demirguc-Kunt, A. (1988), "Deposit-Institution Failures: A Review of Empirical Literature", *Economic Review – Federal Reserve Bank of Cleveland* (4th Quarter).

Demirguc-Kunt, A. and E. Detragiache (1998), "The Determinants of Banking Crises: Evidence from Developing and Developed Countries", *IMF Staff Papers*, **45**(1), 81–110.

Demirguc-Kunt, A. and R. Levine (1999), "Bank Based and Market Based Financial Systems: Cross-Country Comparisons", World Bank Policy Research Working Paper No. *2143*.

Demsetz, R. and P. Strahan (1995), "Diversification, Size, and Risk at Bank Holding Companies", Federal Reserve Bank of New York Research Paper, 95-06.

de Pauw, X. and W. Ross (2000), *Introduction to Securitisation*, London: Merrill Lynch.

Derivatives Policy Group (1995), *A Framework for Voluntary Oversight*.

Dermine, J. (ed.) (1993), *European Banking in the 1990s*, 2nd edn, Oxford: Basil Blackwell.

Dewatripont, M. and J. Tirole (1993), *The Prudential Regulation of Banks*, London: MIT Press.

De Young, R. (1997), "Bank Mergers, X-Efficiency, and the Market for Corporate Control", *Managerial Finance*, **23**, 32–47.

De Young, R. (2001), "The Financial Performance of Pure Play Internet Banks", *Economic Perspectives – Federal Reserve Bank of Chicago*, **25**(1), 60–83.

De Young, R. and K. Roland (1999), "Product Mix and Earnings Volatility at Commercial Banks: Evidence from a Degree of Leverage Model", Federal Reserve Bank of Chicago Working Paper, 99-6.

Diamond, D.W. (1984), "Financial Intermediation and Delegated Monitoring", *Review of Economic Studies*, **51**, 393–414.

Diamond, D.W. (1991), "Monitoring and Reputation: The Choice Between Bank Loans and Directly Placed Debt", *Journal of Political Economy*, **99**(4), 689–721.

Diamond, D. and P. Dybvig (1983), "Bank Runs, Deposit Insurance, and Liquidity", *Journal of Political Economy*, **91**, 401–419.

Dimson, E. and P. Marsh (1993), "The Debate on International Capital Requirements: Evidence on Equity Position Risk for UK Securities Firms", London Business School, June.

Dirienzo, T. and K. Hanson (1994), "Global Cash Management Security", in B. Welch (ed.), *Electronic Banking and Security: A Guide For Corporate and Financial Managers*, Oxford: Blackwell Business.

Dmitriev, M., M. Matovnikov, L. Mikhailov, L. Sycheva and E. Timofeyev (2001), "The Banking Sector", in B. Granville and P. Oppenheimer (eds), *Russia's Post Communist Economy*, Oxford: Oxford University Press.

Dotsey, M. and A. Kuprianov (1990), "Reforming Deposit Insurance: Lessons from the Savings and Loan Crisis", *Federal Reserve Bank of Richmond Economic Review*, **76**(12), 3–28.

Dowd, K. (1993), *Laissez-Faire Banking*, London: Rutledge.

Dowd, K. (1999), *Too Big to Fail? LongTerm Capital Management and the Federal Reserve*, Washington, DC: Cato Institute.

Drake, L. (1992), "Economies of Scale and Scope in UK Building Societies: An Application of the Translog Multiproduct Cost Function", *Applied Financial Economics*, **2**, 211–219.

Drake, L. and T.G. Weyman-Jones (1992), "Technical and Scale Efficiency in UK Building Societies", *Applied Financial Economics*, **2**, 211–219.

Drake, L. and R. Sniper (2002), "Economies of Scale in UK Building Societies: A Reappraisal Using an Entry/Exit Model", *Journal of Banking and Finance*, **26**, 2365–2382.

Drehmann, M., C. Goodhart and M. Krueger (2002), "The Challenges Facing Currency Usage: Will the Traditional Transaction Medium be Able to Resist Competition from the New Technologies?", *Economic Policy*, **34**(Apr), 193–227.

Dreze, J. and A. Sen (1995), *Economic Development and Social Opportunities*, New Dehli: Oxford Economic Press.

Dunbar, N. (2000), *Inventing Money – The Story of Long-Term Capital Management and the Legends Behind It*, Chichester, UK: John Wiley & Sons.

Earle, J. and S. Estrin (2001), "Privatization and the Structure of Enterprise Ownership", in B. Granville and P. Oppenheimer (eds), *Russia's Post Communist Economy*, Oxford: Oxford University Press.

Easterbrook, F.H. (1997), "International Corporate Differences: Markets or Laws", *Journal of Applied Corporate Finance*, **9**, 23–29.

Eaton, J. and M. Gersovitz (1979), "LDC Participation in International Financial Markets: Debt and Reserves", *Journal of Development Economics*, **7**, 3–21.

Eaton, J. and M. Gersovitz (1981a), "Debt With Potential Repudiation: Theoretical and Empirical Analysis", *Review of Economic Studies*, **48**, 289–309.

Eaton, J. and M. Gersovitz (1981b), "Poor Country Borrowing in Private Financial Markets and the Repudiation Issue", *Princeton Studies in International Finance*, **47**, June.

Eaton, J., M. Gersovitz and J.E. Stiglitz (1986), "The Pure Theory of Country Risk", *European Economic Review*, **30**, 481–513.

*The Economist* (1988), "French Bank Deregulation: Telling Tales from the Wrong Bank", 24 September, 122–125.

*The Economist* (1992), "Wish You Hadn't Asked?", 8 August, 77–78.

*The Economist* (1993a), "New Rules For Banks: Keep Them Minimal", 8 May, 20–21.

*The Economist* (1993b), "The Sum, Not The Parts", 11 December, 97–98.

*The Economist* (1994a), "Japanese Banks Tough on the Tax Payer", 26 February, 96–97.

*The Economist* (1994b), "American Banking Regulation: Four Into One Can Go", 5 March, 104–107.

*The Economist* (1994c), "Indigestion Strikes Europe", 12 March, 38–39.

*The Economist* (1995a), "Please, Governor, Can you Spare a Billion?", 25 March, 79–81.

*The Economist* (1995b), "Other People's Money, A Survey of Wall Street", 15 April.

*The Economist* (1999a), "Loud and Clear", 23 January, 80–81.

*The Economist* (1999b), "Frozen Liabilities", 27 February, 91.

*The Economist* (2000a), "Mr. Tanigaki's Augean Stables", 4 March, 110.

*The Economist* (2000b), "A Survey of On-line Finance", 1 May, 43.

*The Economist* (2000c), "E-money Revisited", 22 July, 106.

*The Economist* (2000d), "Japanese Insurers-Endgame", 2 September, 98.

*The Economist* (2003a), "As Good as it Gets", 5 December, 67–68.

*The Economist* (2003b), "Special Report – Bank Lending", 16 August, 61–63.

Edgeworth, F.Y. (1888), "The Mathematical Theory of Banking", *Journal of the Royal Statistical Society*, **51**, 113–127.

Eichengreen, B. and P.H. Lindert (eds) (1989), *The International Debt Crisis in Historical Perspective*, Cambridge, MA: MIT Press.

Eichengreen, B. and R. Portes (1986), "The Anatomy of Financial Crises", Centre For Economic Policy Research, Discussion Paper Series No. 130.

Eichengreen, B. and R. Portes (1988a), "Foreign Lending in the Interwar Years: The Bondholders' Perspective", Centre For Economic Policy Research, Discussion Paper Series No. 273.

Eichgreen, B. and R. Portes (1988b), "Settling Defaults in the Era of Bond Finance", Centre For Economic Policy Research, Discussion Paper Series No. 272.

Eichgreen, B. and R. Portes (1989), "Dealing With Debt: The 1930s and the 1980s", Centre For Economic Policy Research, Discussion Paper Series No. 300.

El-Hawary, D., W. Grais and Z. Iqbal (2004), "Regulating Islamic Financial Institutions: The Nature of the Regulated", World Bank Policy Research Working Paper No. 3227, March.

Ellis, D.M. and M.J. Flannery (1992), "Does the Debt Market Assess Large Banks' Risk? Time Series Evidence from Money Centre CDs", *Journal of Economics*, **30**, 3.

Ely, B. (2000), "Calling Time on Fannie and Freddie", *Financial Regulator*, **5**(1), 30–33.

Ely, D. and M. Song (2000), "Acquisition Activity of Large Depository Institutions in the 1990s: An Empirical Analysis of Motives", *The Quarterly Review of Economics and Finance*, **40**, 467–484.

Ely, D. and N. Varaiya (1996), "Opportunity Costs Incurred by the RTC in Cleaning up S and L Insolvencies", *Quarterly Review of Economics and Finance*, **36**(3), 291–310.

Emerson, M., M. Aujean, M. Catinal, P. Goybet and A. Jacquemin (1989), *The Economics of 1992: The EC Commission's Assessment of the Economic Effects of Completing the Internal Market*, Oxford: Oxford University Press.

Endlich, L. (1999), *Goldman Sachs: The Culture of Success*, London: Little Brown and Company.

Engelen, K. (2001), "Eichel's Shock to the System", *The Financial Regulator*, 5(4), 38–42.

Englund, P. (1999), "The Swedish Banking Crisis: Roots and Consequences", *Oxford Review of Economic Policy*, 15, 3.

Eppendorfer, C., R. Beckman and M. Neimke (2002), *Market Access Strategies for EU Banking Sector*, Berlin: Institut fur Europaische Politik. Can be downloaded from www.zew.de/erfstudyresults

Espahbodi, P. (1991), "Identification of Problem Banks and Binary Choice Models", *Journal of Banking and Finance*, 15, 53–71.

Esty, B., B. Narasimham and P. Tufano (1999), "Interest Rate Exposure and Bank Mergers", *Journal of Banking and Finance*, 23, 255–285.

Evanoff, D.D. and D.L. Fortier (1988), "Re-evaluation of the Structure–Conduct–Performance Paradigm in Banking", *Journal of Financial Services Research*, 1(3), 375–390.

Evanoff, D.D. and P.R. Israilevich (1991), "Productive Efficiency in Banking", *Economic Perspectives*, 15(4), 11–32.

Evans, H. (2000), "Plumbers and Architects: A Supervisory Perspective on International Architecture", Financial Services Authority Occasional Paper, January. Available on FSA website: www.fsa.gov.uk

Evenett, S.J. (2003), "The Cross Borders and Acquisitions Wave of the Late 1990s", National Bureau of Economic Research Working Paper No. 9655. Available from www.nber.org/papers/w9655

Fama, E.F. (1970), "Efficient Capital Markets: A Review of Theory and Empirical Work", *Journal of Finance*, 25, 383–417.

Fama, E.F. (1980), "Banking in the Theory of Finance", *Journal of Monetary Economics*, 6, 39–57.

Fama, E.F. (1985), "What's Different about Banks?", *Journal of Monetary Economics*, 15, 29–39.

Fama, E.F. (1991), "Efficient Capital Markets II", *Journal of Finance*, 46(5), 1575–1617.

Farrant, R. (2000), "Cruickshank Three Months On", *The Financial Regulator*, 5(2), 41–43.

Farrell, M. (1957), "The Measurement of Productive Efficiency", *Journal of the Royal Statistical Society, Series A*, 120(3), 253–291.

Federal Deposit Insurance Corporation (1997), *History of the Eighties – Lessons for the Future: An Examination of the Banking Crises of the Early 1980s and 1990s*. Available on-line at: http://www.fdic.gov/bank/historical/history/index.html

Federal Deposit Insurance Corporation (1998), *Managing the Crisis: The FDIC and RTC Experience*. Available from the FDIC website: http://www.fdic.gov/bank/historical/managing/contents.pdf

Federal Reserve (1993), "Interstate Banking: A Status Report", *Federal Reserve Bulletin*, 79(12), 1075–1089.

Federal Reserve Bank of Chicago (1980), "The Depository Institutions Deregulation and Monetary Control Act of 1980: Landmark Financial Legislation for the Eighties", *Economic Perspectives, Federal Reserve Bank of Chicago*, Sept/Oct, 3–23.

Federal Reserve Bank of New York (1987), "Capital Requirements of Commercial and Investment Banks: Contrasts in Regulation", *Federal Reserve Bank of New York Quarterly Review*, **Autumn**, 1–10.

Ferri, G., T.-S. Kang and I.-J. Kim (2001), "The Value of Relationship Banking During Financial Crises: Evidence from the Republic of Korea", World Bank Working Paper No. 2253.

Field, K. (1990), "Production Efficiency of British Building Societies", *Applied Economics*, 22(3), 415–426.

Financial Services Authority (2000), "A New Regulator for the New Millennium", January, http://www.fsa.gov.uk/

Financial Services Authority (2002), "Investment Research: Conflicts and other Issues", FSA Discussion Paper No. 15, http://www.fsa.gov.uk/

Financial Services Authority (2003), "Investment Research: Conflicts and other Issues", FSA Consultation Paper No. 171, http://www.fsa.gov.uk/

Financial Stability Forum (2001), "Report of the Multidisciplinary Working Group on Enhanced Exposure", available at www.fsforum.org – click on publications.

*Financial Times* (2000), "Life on the Net-Banking", 5 September.

Fingleton, E. (1994), "Nomura Aims To Please", *Institutional Investor*, October, 99–102.

Fisher, A. (1987), "Banks Facing up to Foreign Competition", *The Banker*, January.

Fisher, I. (1932), *Booms and Depressions*, New York: Adelphi.

Fisher, I. (1933), "Debt Deflation Theory of the Great Depression", *Econometrica*, 337–357.

Fisk, C. and F. Rimlinger (1979), "Non-Parametric Estimates of LDC Repayment Prospects", *Journal of Finance*, **34**(2), 429–438.

Fitch Ratings (2003), *Global Credit Derivatives: Risk Management or Risk?*, London: Fitch Ratings.

Flannery, M.J. (1982), "Retail Bank Deposits as Quasi-Fixed Factors of Production", *American Economic Review*, **72**(Jun), 527–536.

Flood, M.D. (1992), "Two Faces of Financial Innovation", *Federal Reserve Bank of St Louis Review*, **74**(5), 3–17.

Flood, R.D. and P.M. Garber (1994), *Speculative Bubbles, Speculative Attacks, and Policy Switching*, Cambridge, MA: MIT Press.

Focarelli, D., F. Panetta and C. Salleo (2002), "Why Do Banks Merge?", *Journal of Money, Credit and Banking*, **34**(4), 1047–1066.

Folkerts Landau, D. and A. Steinherr (1994), "The Wild Beast of Derivatives: To be Chained up, Fenced in or Tamed?", in R. O'Brien (ed.), *Finance and the International Economy*, Vol. 8, Oxford: Oxford University Press, pp. 8–27.

Fordyce, J.E. and M.L. Nickerson (1991), "An Overview of Legal Developments in the Banking and Financial Services Industry in Canada", *The International Lawyer*, **25**(2), 351–369.

Francis, J. (2000), "The Bahamas Perspective", *The Financial Regulator*, **4**(4), 27–33.

Frank, C.R. and W.R. Cline (1971), "Measurement of Debt Servicing Capacity: An Application of Discriminant Analysis", *Journal of International Economics*, **1**, 327–344.

Frankel, A.B. and J.D. Montgomery (1991), "Financial Structure, An International Perspective", *Brookings Papers on Economic Activity*, **1**, 257–310.

Frankel, A.B. and P.B. Morgan (1992), "Deregulation and Competition in Japanese Banking", *Federal Reserve Bulletin*, **78**(8), 579–593.

Freedman, C. (2000), "Monetary Implementation: Past, Present, and Future – Will Electronic Money Lead to the Eventual Demise of Central Banking?", *International Finance*, **3**(2), 211–227.

Freedman, R.D. and J. Vohr (1991a), "American Express", Case Series in Finance and Economics, C49, New York University Salomon Center, Leonard N. Stern School of Business.

Freedman, R.D. and J. Vohr (1991b), "Goldman Sachs/Lehman Brothers", Case Series in Finance and Economics, C50, New York University Salomon Center, Leonard N. Stern School of Business.

Freeman, D.G. (2002), "Did State Bank Branching Deregulation Produce Large Growth Effects?", *Economic Letters*, **75**, 383–389.

Friedman, B. (1999), "The Future of Monetary Policy: The Central Bank as an Army with only a Signal Corps", *International Finance*, **2**(3), 321–338.

Friedman, M. and A. Schwartz (1963), *A Monetary History of the United States, 1867–1960*, Princeton, NJ: Princeton University Press.

Friedman, M. and A.J. Schwartz (1986), "Has Government any Role in Money?", *Journal of Monetary Economics*, **17**, 37–62.

Fry, M. (1995), *Money, Interest and Banking in Economic Development*, 2nd edn, Baltimore, MD: Johns Hopkins University Press.

Fu, X. (2004), "Competition and Efficiency in Chinese Banking", PhD Thesis, Cass Business School, City University, London.

Furfine, C.H. (1999), "Interbank Exposures: Quantifying the Risk of Contagion", BIS Working Papers, June.

Furst, K., W. Lang and D. Nolle (2000), "Who Offers Internet Banking", *Quarterly Journal – Office of the Comptroller of Currency*, **19**(1), 1–22.

Gallo, J., V. Apilado and J. Kolari (1996), "Commercial Bank Mutual Fund Activities: Implications for Bank Risk and Profitability", *Journal of Banking and Finance*, **20**(7), 1775–1791.

Gates, B. (1995), *The Road Ahead*, New York: Viking.

Gennotte, G. and D. Pyle (1991), "Capital Controls and Bank Risk", *Journal of Banking and Finance*, **15**(4/5), 805–824.

Gerber, P. (1998), "Derivatives in International Capital Flows", Working Papers No. 6623, Washington: National Bureau of Economic Research.

Germany, J.D. and J.E. Morton (1985), "Financial Innovation and Deregulation in Foreign Industrial Countries", *Federal Reserve Bulletin*, **7**(10), 743–753.

Ghosh, A., T. Lane, M. Schulze-Ghattas, A. Bulír, J. Hamann and A. Mourmouras (2002), "IMF-Supported Programs in Capital Account Crises", IMF Occasional Paper No. 210, February, Washington: International Monetary Fund.

Gilbert, E.W. and W.L. Scott (2001), "The Financial Modernisation Act: New Perspectives for the Finance Curriculum", *Financial Services Review*, **10**, 197–208.

Gilbert, R.A. (1984), "Bank Market Structure and Competition: A Survey", *Journal of Money, Credit and Banking*, **4**, 21–36.

Gilbert, R.A. (1991), "Do Bank Holding Companies Act as Sources of Strength for Their Bank Subsidiaries?", *Federal Reserve Bank of St Louis Review*, **73**(1), 3–18.

Gilligan, T. and M. Smirlock (1984), "An Empirical Study of the Joint Production of Scale Economies in Commercial Banking", *Journal of Banking and Finance*, **8**, 67–78.

Goldberg, L.G. and G.A. Hanweck (1991), "The Growth of the World's 300 Largest Banking Organizations by Country", *Journal of Banking and Finance*, **15**, 207–223.

Goldberg, L.G. and A. Rai (1996), "The Structure–Performance Relationship for European Banking", *Journal of Banking and Finance*, **20**, 745–771.

Goldman Sachs (2000/01/02/03), *Annual Report* for various years. Available on-line/in pdf format from www.gs.com

Goldstein, M. (1998), *The Asian Financial Crisis: Causes, Cures, and Systemic Implications*, Washington: Institute for International Economics, 55, June.

Goodard, J.A., P. Molyneux and J.O.S. Wilson (2001), *European Banking: Efficiency, Technology and Growth*, Chichester, UK: John Wiley & Sons.

Goodhart, C.A.E. (1974), *Money, Information and Uncertainty*, London: Macmillan.

Goodhart, C.A.E. (1988), *The Evolution of Central Banks*, Cambridge, MA: MIT Press.

Goodhart, C.A.E. (1996), "Some Regulatory Concerns", *Schweizerische Zeitschrift fur Volkswirtschaft und Statistik/Swiss Journal of Economics and Statistics*, **132**(4/2), 613–635.

Goodhart, C.A.E. (2000), "Can Central Banking Survive the IT Revolution?", *International Finance*, **3**(2), 189–210.

Goodhart, C.A.E. and H. Huang (2000), "A Simple Model of an International Lender of Last Resort", *Economic Notes by Banca Monte dei Paschi di Siena, SpA*, **29**(1–2000), 1–11.

Goodhart, C.A.E. and D. Schoenmaker (1995), "Should the Functions of Monetary Policy and Banking Supervision be Separated?", *Oxford Economic Papers*, **47**, 539–560.

Gordon, J. and P. Gupta (2003), "Understanding India's Services Revolution", paper prepared for IMF-NCAER Conference, *A Tale of Two Giants: India's and China's Experience with Reform*, New Delhi, 14–16 November.

Gorton, G. (1988), "Banking Panics and Business Cycles", *Oxford Economic Papers*, **40**, 751–781.

Goryunov, Y. (2001), "The Russian Banking Sector in 2000", BIS Papers No. 4, 123–127.

Gowland, D.H. (1991), "Financial Innovation in Theory and Practice", in C.J. Green and D.T. Llewellyn (eds), *Surveys in Monetary Economics*, Vol. 2, Oxford: Basil Blackwell, pp. 79–115.

Gowland, P. (1994), *The Economics of Modern Banking*, Aldershot: Edward Elgar.

Granville, B. and P. Oppenheimer (eds) (2001), *Russia's Post Communist Economy*, Oxford: Oxford University Press.

Gray, S. and J. Place (1999), *Financial Derivatives*, Bank of England, Centre for Central Banking Studies, Handbooks in Central Banking, No. 17.

Greenbaum, S. (1967), "Competition and Efficiency in the Banking System – Empirical Research and its Policy Implications", *Journal of Political Economy*, **75**, 461–481.

Greenspan, A. (1994), "Optimal Bank Supervision in a Changing World", in *Federal Reserve Bank of Chicago, Conference Proceedings on The Declining Role of Banking*, 30th Annual Conference on Bank Structure and Competition, May, pp. 1–8.

Griffiths, B. (1970), "Competition in Banking", Hobart Paper No. 5, London: Institute of Economic Affairs.

Grigorian, D. and V. Manole (2002), "Determinants of Commercial Banks in Transitions: An Application of Data Envelope Analysis", World Bank Policy Research Working Paper No. 2850, June.

Gros, D. and A. Steinherr (2004), *Economic Transition in Central and Eastern Europe*, Cambridge: Cambridge University Press.

Group of 10 (2001), *Report on Consolidation in the Financial Sector*, Basel: Bank for International Settlements. Available from www.bis.org/publ/

Group of 30 (1993), *Derivatives: Practices and Principles – Special Report by the Global Derivatives Study Group*, Washington: Group of 30.

Group of 30 (1994), *Derivatives: Practices and Principles: Follow Up Surveys of Industry Practice*, Washington: Group of 30.

Gual, J. and D. Neven (1992), "Deregulation of the European Banking Industry (1980–1991)", Centre for Economic Policy Research, Discussion Paper No. 703.

Gup, B.E. and J.R. Walter (1991), "Profitable Large Banks: the Key to Their Success", in D. Chew (ed.), *New Developments in Commercial Banking*, Oxford: Basil Blackwell, pp. 37–42.

Gurley, J.G. and E.S. Shaw (1956), "Financial Intermediaries and the Savings–Investment Process", *Journal of Finance*, **11**, 257–276.

Guttentag, J. and R. Herring (1983), "The Lender of Last Resort Function in an International Context", Essays in International Finance No. 151, International Finance Section, Department of Economics, Princeton University.

Guttentag, J. and R. Herring (1986), "Disaster Myopia in International Banking", Essays in International Finance No. 164, International Finance Section, Department of Economics, Princeton University.

Hadlock, C., J. Houston and M. Ryngaert (1999), "The Role of Managerial Incentives in Bank Acquisitions", *Journal of Banking and Finance*, **23**, 221–241.

Haldane, A., G. Irwin and V. Saporta (2004), "Bail Out or Work Out? Theoretical Considerations", *The Economic Journal*, **114**(March), C130–C148.

Hall, M.J.B. (1985), "UK Banking Supervision and the Johnson Matthey Affair", Loughborough University Banking Centre, Research Paper Series No. 8, May.

Hall, M.J.B. (1993), *Banking Regulation and Supervision*, Aldershot: Edward Elgar.

Hannan, T.H. (1979), "The Theory of Limit Pricing: Some Applications to the Banking Industry", *Journal of Banking and Finance*, **3**, 221–234.

Hannan, T.H. (1991a), "Foundations of the Structure–Conduct–Performance Paradigm in Banking", *Journal of Money, Credit and Banking*, **23**(1), 68–84.

Hannan, T.H. (1991b), "The Bank Commercial Loan Markets and the Role of Market Structure: Evidence from Surveys of Commercial Lending", *Journal of Banking and Finance*, **15**, 133–149.

Hao, J., W.C. Hunter and W.K. Yang (2001), "Deregulation and Efficiency: the Case of Private Korean Banks", *Journal of Economics and Business*, **53**, 237–254.

Hardwick, P. (1989), "Economies of Scale in Building Societies", *Applied Economics*, **21**, 1291–1304.

Hardwick, P. (1990), "Multi-Product Cost Attributes: A Study of UK Building Societies", *Oxford Economic Papers*, **42**, 446–461.

Hardy, D. and E. Patti (2001), "Bank Reform and Bank Efficiency in Pakistan", IMF Working Paper WP/01/138.

Hassan, T. (2002), "Islamic Banking in Pakistan", *The Financial Regulator*, **7**(2), 70–74.

Hausman, J. (1978), "Specification Tests in Econometrics", *Econometrica*, **46**(6), 1251–1271.

Hawke, J. (2001), "Internet Banking: Challenges for Banks and Regulators", *Financial Regulator*, **6**(1), 16–19.

Haynes, M. and S. Thompson (1997), "The Productivity Effects of Bank Mergers: Evidence from UK Building Societies", Mimeo.

Heffernan, S.A. (1986a), "Determinants of Optimal Foreign Leverage Ratios in Developing Countries", *Journal of Banking and Finance*, **3**(Suppl.), 97–115.

Heffernan, S.A. (1986b), *Sovereign Risk Analysis*, London: Unwin Hyman.

Heffernan, S.A. (1992), "A Competition of Interest Equivalences for Non-Price Features of Bank Products", *Journal of Money, Credit and Banking*, **24**(May), 162–172.

Heffernan, S.A. (1993), "Competition in British Retail Banking", *Journal of Financial Services Research*, **7**(3), 309–332.

Heffernan, S.A. (1994), "Competition in the Canadian Personal Finance Sector", *International Journal of the Economics of Business*, **1**(3), 323–342.

Heffernan, S.A. (1996), *Modern Banking in Theory and Practice*, London: John Wiley & Sons.

Heffernan, S.A. (2001), "Japan: A Case for Financial Reform and Monetary Stimulus", *Annual Survey of Supervisory Developments*, London: Central Banking Publications.

Heffernan, S.A. (2002), "How do UK Financial Institutions Really Price their Banking Products?", *Journal of Banking and Finance*, **26**, 1997–2006.

Heffernan, S.A. (2003), "The Causes of Bank Failures", in Mullineux and Murinde, *op. cit.*

Heggestad, A.A. (1979), "A Survey of Studies on Banking Competition and Performance; Market Structure, Competition, and Performance", in F.R. Edwards (ed.), *Issues in Financial Regulation*, Maidenhead: McGraw Hill, pp. 449–490.

Heggestad, A.A. and J.J. Mingo (1976), "Prices, Nonprices, and Concentration in Commercial Banking", *Journal of Money, Credit and Banking*, **8**, 107–117.

Heggestad, A.A. and J.J. Mingo (1977), "The Competitive Condition of U.S. Banking Markets and the Impact of Structural Reform", *Journal of Finance*, **32**(3), 649–661.

Heinemann, F. and M. Jopp (2002), *The Benefits of a Working European Retail Market for EU Financial Services*, Berlin: Institut fur Europaische Politik. Can be downloaded from www.zew.de/erfstudyresults/

Hermes, N. and R. Lensick (eds) (2000), *Financial System Development in Transition Economies*, Special Issue, *Journal of Banking and Finance*, **24**(4), 507–524.

Herring, R. (1984), "Continental Illinois", Case Series in Finance and Economics, C41, New York University Salomon Center, Leonard N. Stern School of Business.

Hertig, G. and R. Lee (2003), "Four Predictions about the Future of EU Securities Regulation", *Journal of Corporate Law Studies*, **3**(2), 150–165.

Hey, J.D. (1989), "Introduction: Recent Developments in Microeconomics", in *Recent Issues in Microeconomics*, London: Macmillan.

Hill, G. (1975), *Why 67 Insured Banks Failed, 1960–74*, Washington: Federal Deposit Insurance Corporation.

Hirtle, B. (1991), "The Factors Affecting the Competitiveness of Internationally Active Financial Insitutions", *Federal Reserve Bank of New York Quarterly Review*, **Spring**, 38–51.

Hoggarth, G. and F. Soussa (2001), "Crisis Management, Lender of Last Resort, and the Changing Nature of the Banking Industry", in R. Brealey, A. Clark, C. Goodhart, J. Healey, D. Llewellyn, C. Shu, P. Sinclair and F. Soussa (eds), *Financial Stability and Central Banks*, London: Routledge.

Hoggarth, G., J. Reidhill and P. Sinclair (2003), "Resolution of Banking Crises: A Review", *Bank of England Financial Stability Review*, **15**(December), 109–123.

Honohan, P. and D. Klingebiel (2003), "The Fiscal Cost Implications of an Accommodating Approach to Banking Crises", *Journal of Banking and Finance*, **27**, 1539–1560.

Hoshi, T. and A. Kashyap (1999), "The Japanese Financial Crisis: Where Did It Come From and How Will It End?", National Bureau of Economic Research, Working Paper 7250, July. Available from http://www.nber.org/papers/w7250

Hoti, S. and M. McAleer (2003), "An Empirical Assessment of Country Risk Ratings and Associated", Mimeo, Department of Economics, University of Western Australia, June.

Houston, J. and M. Ryngaert (1994), "The Overall Gains from Large Bank Mergers", *Journal of Banking and Finance*, **18**, 1155–1176.

Hovaguimian, C. (2003), "The Catalytic Effect of IMF Lending: A Critical Review", *Financial Stability Review*, Bank of England, December, pp. 160–169.

Howells, P. and K. Bain (1998), *The Economics of Money, Banking and Finance, A European Text*, Harlow, UK: Pearson Education.

Howells, P. and K. Bain (2000), *Financial Markets and Institutions*, 3d edn, Harlow, UK: Financial Times/Prentice Hall, Pearson Education.

He, Q. and H.P. Gray (2001), "Multinational Banking and Economic Development: A Case Study", *Journal of Asian Economics*, **12**, 233–243.

Humphrey, D.B. (1987), "Cost Dispersion and the Measurement of Economies in Banking", *Federal Reserve Bank of Richmond Economic Review*, May/June.

Humphrey, D. (1992), "Flow Versus Stock Indicators in Bank Output: Effects on Productivity and Scale Economy Measurement", *Journal of Financial Services Research*, **6**, 115–135.

Hunter, W.C. and S.G. Timme (1986), "Technical Change, Organisational Form, and the Structure of Bank Production", *Journal of Money, Credit and Banking*, **18**, 2–66.

Hunter, W.C., S.G. Timme and W.K. Yang (1990), "An Examination of Cost Subadditivity and Multiproduct Production in Large US Commercial Banks", *Journal of Money, Credit and Banking*, **22**, 504–525.

Hwang, D.-Y., C.F. Lee and K.T. Liaw (1997), "Forecasting Bank Failures and Deposit Insurance Premium", *International Review of Economics and Finance*, **6**(3), 317–334.

International Financing Review (2000), *Review of the Year*, London: Thomson Financial.

International Monetary Fund (2002), "IMF-Supported Programs in Capital Account Crises", Occasional Paper No. 210.

International Monetary Fund (2003), "IMF Reviews the Experience with the Financial Sector Assessment Programme and Reaches Conclusions on Issues Going Forward", available from www.imf.org

Iqbal, Z. and A. Mirakhor (2002), "Development of Islamic Financial Institutions and Challenges Ahead", in S. Archer and R. Karim (eds), *Islamic, Growth and Innovation*, London: Euromoney.

Ischenko, D. and S. Samuels (2001), "Time to Catch Up – Basel II – Modern Capital for Modern Banks", Industry Report, London: SchroderSalmonSmithBarney.

Ischenko, D. and S. Samuels (2002), "Basel II – Winners and Losers", *Financial Regulator*, **6**(4), 6–7.

Isik, L. and M.K. Hassan (2002), "Technical Scale and Allocative Efficiencies of Turkish Banking Industry", *Journal of Banking and Finance*, **26**, 719–766.

Ito, T., K. Takuma and H. Uchibori (1998), "The Impact of the Big Bang on the Japanese Financial System", Fuji Research Paper No. 9, Tokyo: Fuji Institute Research Corporation.

Jackson, W.E. (1992), "The Price–Concentration Relationship in Banking: A Comment", *Review of Economics and Statistics*, **74**, 291–299; also "Reply" by Berger and Hannan, 373–376.

Jagtiani, J., A. Saunders and G. Udell (1993), "Bank Off-Balance Sheet Financial Innovations", New York University Salomon Center (Stern School of Business), Working Paper S-93-50.

James, C. (1991), "The Losses Realised in Bank Failures", *Journal of Finance*, **Sept**, 1223–1242.

Jayaratne, J. and P.E. Strahan (1997), "The Benefits of Branching Deregulation", *Economic Policy Review – Federal Reserve Bank of New York*, **3**(4), 13–39.

Jayaratne, J. and P.E. Strahan (2002), "The Finance–Growth Nexus: Evidence from Bank Branch Deregulation", *Quarterly Journal of Economics*, **111**, 639–670.

Jiang, C. (ed.) (2001), *The Banking Industry in China, 2001*, Beijing: China Financial Publishing House.

John, K., T.A. John and L.W. Senbet (1991), "Risk Shifting Incentives of Depository Institutions: A New Perspective on Federal Deposit Insurance Reform", *Journal of Banking and Finance*, **15**(4/5), 895–916.

Jorion, P. (1997), *Value at Risk*, New York: Irwin.

Jorion, P. and N. Taleb (1997), "The Jorion–Taleb Debate", *Derivatives Strategy*, available from www.derivativesstrategy.com

JP Morgan (1994), *Riskmetrics – Technical Document*, 2nd edn, November, New York: JP Morgan.

Kahn, C., G. Pennachi and B. Sopranzetti (2000), "Bank Consolidation and Consumer Loan Interest Rates", Wharton Financial Institutions Center WP 01–14.

Kane, E.J. (1984), "Technology and Regulatory Forces in the Developing Fusion of Financial Services Competition", *Journal of Finance*, **39**(3), 759–772.

Kane, E.J. (1985), *The Gathering Crisis in Federal Deposit Insurance*, Cambridge, MA: MIT Press.

Kane, E.J. and M.T. Yu (1994), "How Much Did Capital Forbearance Add to the Tab for the FSLIC Mess?", in *Federal Reserve Bank of Chicago, Conference Proceedings on The Declining Role of Banking*, 30th Annual Conference on Bank Structure and Competition, May.

Karim, R.A. (2004), "Islamic Banking", *The Financial Regulator*, **9**(1), 44–48.

Kaufman, G. (1984), "Measuring and Managing Interest Rate Risk, A Primer", Federal Reserve Bank of Chicago, Economic Perspectives, pp. 16–19.

Kaufman, G. (1985), "Implications of Large Bank Problems and Insolvencies for the Banking System and Economic Policy, Federal Reserve Bank of Chicago, Staff Memoranda, 85-3.

Kaufman, G. (1988), "Securities Activities of Commercial Banks: Recent Changes in the Economic and Legal Environments", *Midland Corporate Finance Journal*, **5**(4), 14–21.

Kaufman, G. (ed.) (1992), *Banking Structures in Major Countries*, The Netherlands: Kluwer Academic Publishers.

Kaufman, G. (1994), "Bank Contagion: A Review of the Theory and Evidence", *Journal of Financial Services Research*, 123–150.

Kaufman, G. (2002), "Too Big to Fail in US Banking: Quo Vadis?", *Quarterly Review of Economics and Finance*, **Summer**, 423–436.

Kay, J. (1991), "Economics and Business", *The Economic Journal*, **101**(Jan), 57–73.

Kay, J. (1993a), *Foundations of Corporate Success*, New York: Oxford University Press.

Kay, J. (1993b), "The Structure of Strategy", *Business Strategy Review*, **4**(2), 17–37.

Kay, J. and J. Vickers (1988), "Regulatory Reform in Britain", *Economic Policy*, **7**(Oct), 286–351.

Keeley, M.C. (1990), "Deposit Insurance, Risk, and Market Power in Banking", *American Economic Review*, **80**(5), 1183–1200.

Kendall, S.B. and M.E. Levonian (1991), "A Simple Approach to Better Deposit Insurance Pricing", *Journal of Banking and Finance*, **15**(4/5), 999–1018.

Keynes, J.M. (1930), *Treatise on Money*, London: Macmillan.

Khan, M.S. (1987), "Islamic Interest-Free Banking: A Theoretical Analysis", in S. Khan and A. Mirakhor (eds), *Theoretical Studies in Islamic Banking and Finance*, Houston: The Institute for Research and Islamic Studies, pp. 15–35.

Khan, M.S. and A. Mirakhor (1987), "The Framework and Practice of Islamic Banking", in S. Khan and A. Mirakhor (eds), *Theoretical Studies in Islamic Banking and Finance*, Houston: The Institute for Research and Islamic Studies, pp. 1–14.

Kim, H.Y. (1987), "Economies of Scale in Multi Product Firms: an Empirical Analysis", *Economica*, **54**, 185–206.

Kim, M. (1986), "Banking Technology and the Existence of a Consistent Output Aggregate", *Journal of Economics*, **18**, 181–195.

Kindleberger, C.P. (1978), "The Debt Situation of Developing Countries in Historical Perspective", in S.H. Goodman (ed.), *Financing and Risk in Developing Countries*, London: Praeger.

Kindleberger, C.P. (1978, 2000), *Manias, Panics and Crises*, New York: John Wiley & Sons [the fourth edition, referred to in this book, was published in 2000].

Kindleberger, C.P. (1984), *A Financial History of Western Europe*, London: George Allen and Unwin Publishers Ltd.

Kindleberger, C.P. (1993), *A Financial History of Western Europe*, 2nd edn, Oxford: Oxford University Press.

Kindleberger, C.P. and J.P. Laffargue (eds) (1982), *Finanical Crisis: Theory History and Policy*, New York: Cambridge University Press.

King, K.K. and J.M. O'Brien (1991), "Market Based Risk Adjusted Examination Schedules for Depository Institutions", *Journal of Banking and Finance*, **15**(4/5), 955–974.

King, M. (1999), "Challenges for Monetary Policy: New and Old", in *New Challenges for Monetary Policy, Symposium Proceedings*, Kansas City: Federal Reserve Bank, pp. 11–57.

Kiyotaki, N. and J. Moore (1997), "Credit Cycles", *Journal of Political Economy*, **105**(2), 211–249.

Klein, B. (1974), "Competitive Interest Payments on Bank Deposits and the Long Run Demand For Money", *American Economic Review*, **64**(6), 931–949.

Klein, M.A. (1971), "A Theory of the Banking Firm", *Journal of Money, Credit and Banking*, **3**, 205–218.

Klein, M.A. and N.B. Murphy (1971), "The Pricing of Bank Deposits: A Theoretical and Empirical Analysis", *Journal of Financial and Quantitative Analysis*, **6**, 747–761.

Koskenkylä, H. (1994), "The Nordic Banking Crisis", *Bank of Finland Quarterly Bulletin*, 8/94.

Koskenkylä, H. (2000), "The Nordic Countries' Banking Crises and Lessons Learned", Bank of Finland Working Paper 6/00.

Krueger, A. (2002), *A New Approach to Sovereign Debt Rescheduling*, Washington: IMF.

Krugman, P. (1994), "The Myth of Asia's Miracle", *Foreign Affairs*, **73**(6), 62–78.

Krugman, P. (1999), "Balance Sheets, the Transfer Problem and Financial Crises", Mimeo, MIT.

Kupiec, P. (1995), "Techniques for Verifying the Accuracy of Risk Management Measurement Models", *Journal of Derivatives*, **3**, 73–84.

Kupiec, P. and J. O'Brien (1997), "The Pre-Commitment Approach: Using Incentives to set Market Risk Capital Requirements", Washington: Board of Governors of the Federal Reserve System, 1997-14.

Kwast, M. and S. Passmore (1998), "The Subsidy Provided by the Federal Safety Net: Theory, Measurement, and Containment", in *Conference Proceedings on Bank Structure and Competition*, Chicago: Federal Reserve Bank of Chicago.

Lamfalussy, A. (2000), *Financial Crises in Emerging Markets*, London: Yale University Press.

Lannoo, K. (2002), "The Structure of Financial Market Supervision in the EU and the Required Adaptions in View of Market Integration", Background Paper for F. Heinemann and M. Jopp, *The Benefits of a Working European Retail Market for EU Financial Services*, Berlin: Institut fur Europaische Politik. Can be downloaded from www.zew.de/erfstudyresults/

La Porta, R., F. Lopez-de-Silanes, A. Shleifer and R.W. Vishny (1997), "Legal Determinants of External Finance", *Journal of Finance*, **52**, 1131–1150.

Lascelles, D. (2001), "Waking up to the FSA: How the City Views its New Regulator", London: Centre for the Study of Financial Innovation, May.

Lawrence, C. (1989), "Banking Costs, Generalised Functional Forms, and Estimation of Economies of Scale and Scope", *Journal of Money, Credit and Banking*, **21**, 368–379.

Leach, J.A., W.J. McDonough, D.W. Mullins and B. Quinn (1993), *Global Derivatives: Public Sector Responses*, Washington: Group of Thirty, Occasional Paper 44.

Leland, H. and D. Pyle (1977), "Information Asymmetries, Financial Structures and Financial Intermediaries", *Journal of Finance*, **32**, 511–513.

Lewis, M.K. (1991), "Theory and Practice of the Banking Firm", in C. Green and D. Llewellyn (eds), *Surveys in Monetary Economics*, Vol. 2, Oxford: Basil Blackwell, pp. 116–159.

Lindgren, C.-J., T.J.T. Balino, C. Enoch, A.-M. Gulde, M. Quintyn and L. Teo (1999), *Financial Sector Crisis: Lessons from Asia*, Washington: International Monetary Fund.

Llewellyn, D.T. (1985), "The Evolution of the British Financial System", *Gilbart Lectures on Banking*, London: The Institute of Bankers.

Llewellyn, D.T. (1991), "Structural Change in the British Financial System", in C. Green and D. Llewellyn (eds), *Surveys in Monetary Economics*, Vol. 2, Oxford: Basil Blackwell, pp. 210–259.

Llewellyn, D.T. (1992), "Competition, Diversification, and Structural Change in the British Financial System", in G.G. Kaufman (ed.), *Banking Structures in Major Countries*, Dordrecht: Kluwer Academic Publishers, pp. 429–468.

Lloyd-Williams, D.M., P. Molyneux and J. Thornton (1991), "Competition and Contestability in the Japanese Commercial Banking Market", Institute of European Finance, Research Papers in Banking and Finance No. 16, Bangor: University of Wales.

Logan, A. (2000), "The Early 1990s Small Banks Crisis; Leading Indicators", Financial Stability Review, December, London: The Bank of England, pp. 130–145.

Madalla, G. (1988), *Introduction to Econometrics*, New York: Macmillan.

Manasse, P., N. Roubini and P. Schimmelpfennig (2003), "Predicting Sovereign Debt Crises", IMF Working Paper WP/03/221.

Marshall, A. (1860/1961), *Principles of Economics*, New York: Macmillan.

Martin, D. (1977), "Early Warning of Bank Failure: A Logit Regression Approach", *Journal of Banking and Finance*, **15**, 53–71.

Mathur, S. and A. Kenyon (1997), *Creating Value: Shaping Tomorrow's Business*, Oxford: Butterworth Heinemann.

Matten, C. (2000), *Managing Bank Capital*, Chichester, UK: John Wiley & Sons.

McFadden, D. (1974), "The Measurement of Urban Travel Demand", *Journal of Public Economics*, **3**, 303–328.

McIntosh, J. (2002), "A Welfare Analysis of Canadian Chartered Bank Mergers", *Canadian Journal of Economics*, **35**(3), 457–475.

McKinnon, R. (1973), *Money and Capital in Economic Development*, Washington: Brookings Institution.

McKinnon, R. and H. Pill (1996), "Credible Liberalizations and International Capital Flows: The 'Overborrowing' Syndrome", in I. Takatoshi and A. Krueger (eds), *Financial Deregulation and Integration in East Asia*, Chicago: Chicago University Press.

Mendes, V. and J. Rebelo (2003), "Structure and Performance in the Portuguese Banking Industry in the Nineties", *Portuguese Economic Journal*, **2**, 53–68.

Mertens, A. and G. Urga (2001), "Efficiency, Scale and Scope Economies in the Ukrainian Banking Sector in 1998", *Emerging Markets Review*, **2**, 292–308.

Merton, R.C. (1990), "The Financial System and Economic Performance", *Journal of Financial Services Research*, **4**(4), 263–300.

Mester, L. (1987), "Efficient Production of Financial Services: Scale and Scope Economies", *Federal Reserve Bank of Philadelphia Business Review*, **15–25**(Jan/Feb), 83–86.

Meyer, P.A. and H.W. Pifer (1970), "Prediction of Bank Failures", *The Journal of Finance*, **Sept**, 853–868.

Milbourn, T., T. Boot and A. Thakor (1999), "Megamergers and Expanded Scope: Theories of Bank Size and Activity Diversity", *Journal of Banking and Finance*, **23**, 195–214.

Miller, E.A. (2001), "Yes! There are Limits to Arbitrage: Lessons from the Collapse of Long Term Capital Management", *The Journal of Social, Political and Economic Studies*, **26**(1), 321–328.

Milne, A. (2003), *"Basel Lite": Recommendations for the European Implementation of the New Basel Accord*, London: Centre for the Study of Financial Innovation.

Minsky, H.P. (1977), "Theory of Systemic Fragility", in E.I. Altman and A.W. Sametz (eds), *Financial Crises: Institutions and Markets in a Fragile Environment*, New York: John Wiley & Sons, pp. 138–152.

Minsky, H.P. (1982), "The Financial Instability Hypothesis: A Capitalist Process and the Behaviour of the World Economy", in C.P. Kindleberger and J.P. Laffargue (eds), *Financial Crisis: Theory, History and Policy*, New York: Cambridge University Press, pp. 13–41.

Minsky, H.P. (1986), *Stabilizing and Unstable Economy*, London/New Haven, CT: Yale University Press.

Mohan, R. (2004), "Globalisation: The Role of Institution Building in the Financial Sector: The Indian Case", *Reserve Bank of India*, **Feb**, 117–150.

Molyneux, P. (2003), "Technical Change, Costs, and Profits, in European Banking", Working Paper 03–21 for European Integration, Financial Institutions and Performance, Maastricht: United Nations University, Institute for New Technologies. Available from http://ideas.repec.org/p/dgr/unutaf/eifc03-21.html

Molyneux, P. and W. Forbes (1995), "Market, Structure, and Performance in European Banking", *Applied Economics*, **27**, 155–159.

Molyneux, P., P. Lloyd-Williams and J. Thornton (1994), "European Banking: An Analysis of Competitive Conditions", in J. Revell (ed.), *The Changing Face of European Banks and Securities Markets*, New York: St Martins Press.

Molyneux, P., Y. Altunbas and E. Gardener (1996), *Efficiency in European Banking*, Chichester, UK: John Wiley & Sons.

Monti, M. (1972), "Deposit, Credit, and Interest Rate Determination under Alternative Bank Objective Functions", in G.P. Szego and K. Snell (eds), *Mathematical Methods in Investment and Finance*, Amsterdam: North Holland, pp. 430–454.

Moody's Investors Service (2001), "Culture or Accounting: What are the Real Constraints for Islamic Finance in a Riba-Based Global Economy?", Special Comment, January.

Moran, T. (2003), *International Political Risk Management The Brave New World*, Vol. 2, Washington: World Bank.

Morishima, M. (1993), "Banking and Industry in Japan", London School of Economics Financial Markets Group, Special Paper No. 51, January.

Mullineux, A. and V. Murinde (eds) (2003), *Handbook of International Banking*, Cheltenham: Edward Elgar.

Nathan, A. and E.H. Neave (1989), "Competition and Contestability on Canada's Financial System", *Canadian Journal of Economics*, **22**(3), 576–594.

Nathan, A. and E.H. Neave (1991), "Reply to Perrakis", *Canadian Journal of Economics*, **24**, 733–735.

Nathan, L. (1999), "Community Banks are Going on-Line", *Communities and Banking – Federal Reserve Bank of Boston*, **27**(Fall), 2–28.

Nelder, M. (2003), "Competition Necessarily Tends to Produce Excess: The Experience of Free Banking in Switzerland", *German Economic Review*, **4**(3), 389–408.

Nellis, J. (1999), *Time to Re-think Privatization in Transition Economies?*, International Finance Corporation, Washington: World Bank.

Nickell, P., S. Perraudin and S. Varotto (2000), "Stability of Ratings Transition", *Journal of Banking and Finance*, **24**, 203–247.

Niehans, J. (1978), *The Theory of Money*, Baltimore: The Johns Hopkins University Press.

Nigh, D., K.R. Cho and S. Krishnan (1986), "The Role of Location Related Factors in US Banking Involvement Abroad: An Empirical Examination", *Journal of International Business Studies*, **17**(3), 59–72.

Nippani, S. and K.W. Green (2002), "The Banking Industry after the Riegle–Neal Act: Restructure and Overall Performance", *The Quarterly Review of Economics and Finance*, **42**, 901–909.

Obay, L. (2000), *Financial Innovation in the Banking Industry: The Case of Asset Securitization*, London: Garland Publishing.

Obstfeld, M. (1986), "Rational and Self-fulfilling Balance of Payments Crises", *American Economic Review*, **76**, 72–81.

Obstfeld, M. (1996), "Models of Currency Crises with Self Fulfilling Features", *European Economic Review*, **40**, 1037–1048.

OECD (1991), *Bank Profitability and Statistical Supplement*, Paris: OECD.

OECD (1992), *Economies of Scale and Scope in the Financial Services Industry: A Review of the Recent Literature*, Paris: OECD.

Ofek, E. and Richardson, M. (2003), "DotCom Mania: The Rise and Fall of Internet Stock Prices" (with Eli Ofek), *Journal of Finance*, **58**, 1113–1138.

O'Hara, M. and W. Shaw (1990), "Deposit Insurance and Wealth Effects: The Value of Being Too Big to Fail", *Journal of Finance*, **45**(5), 1587–1600.

O'Keefe, J. (1990), "The Texas Banking Crisis: Causes and Consequences, 1980–1989", *FDIC Banking Review* **3**(3), 2–3.

Pandit, N., G. Cook and G.M. Swann (2001), "The Dynamics of Industrial Clustering in British Financial Services", *The Services Industries Journal*, **21**, 31–61.

Pantalone, C. and M. Platt (1987), "Predicting Commercial Bank Failure Since Deregulation", *New England Economic Review*, **Jul/Aug**, 37–47.

Panzer, J. and J. Ross (1987), "Testing for Monopoly Equilibrium", *Journal of Industrial Economics*, **35**, 443–456.

Peek, J. and E. Rosengreen (1997), "The International Transmission Mechanism of Financial Shocks: The Case of Japan", *American Economic Review*, **87**(4), 495–505.

Peek, J. and E. Rosengreen (2003), "Unnatural Selection: Perverse Incentives and the Misallocation of Credit in Japan", National Bureau of Economic Research Working Paper 9643, April. Available from www.nber.org/papers.w9643

Perrakis, S. (1991), "Assessing Competition in Canada's Financial System: A Note", *Canadian Journal of Economics*, **24**(3), 727–732.

Pesek, B. (1970), "Bank's Supply Function and the Equilibrium Quantity of Money", *Canadian Journal of Economics*, **3**, 357–385.

Pesek, B. and T. Saving (1969), *Money, Wealth, and Economic Theory*, New York: Macmillan.

Pesola, J. (2001), "The Role of Macroeconomic Shocks in Banking Crises", Bank of Finland Discussion Papers, No. 6/2001.

Pilloff, J. (1996), "Performance Changes and Shareholder Wealth Creation Associated with Mergers of Publicly Traded Banking Institutions", *Journal of Money, Credit and Banking*, **28**(3), 294–310.

Platt, N. (2002), "PayPal Threat should Spur Bankers to Find P to P Payment Partners", *American Banker*, **167**(75), 7–8.

Porter, M. (1990), *The Competitive Advantage of Nations*, London: Macmillan.

Porter, M.E. (1998), "Clusters and the New Economics of Competition", *Harvard Business Review*, **Nov/Dec**, 77–90.

Posen, A.S. (2002), "Unchanging Innovation and Changing Economic Performance in Japan", in R. Nelson, B. Steil and D. Victor (eds), *Technological Innovation and Economic Performance*, Princeton: Princeton University Press.

Prager, R. and T. Hannan (1998), "Do Substantial Horizontal Mergers Generate Significant Price Effects? Evidence from the Banking Industry", *Journal of Industrial Economics*, **46**(4), 433–453.

Price Waterhouse (1988), "The Cost of Non Europe in Financial Services", in *Research of the Cost of Non Europe*, 19, Brussels: Commission of the European Communities.

Pyun, C.S., L. Scruggs and Nam, K. (2002), "Internet Banking in the US, Japan, and Europe", *Multinational Business Review*, **10**(2), 73–81.

Radelet, S. and J. Sachs (1998a), "The Onset of the East Asian Financial Crisis", Consulting Assistance on Economic Reform II, Harvard Discussion Paper No. 27, April, pp. 1–58.

Radelet, S. and J. Sachs (1998b), "The East Asian Financial Crisis: Diagnosis, Remedies, Prospects", Consulting Assistance on Economic Reform II, Harvard Discussion Paper No. 29, July, pp. 1–75.

Radelet, S. and W.T. Woo (2000), "Indonesia: A Troubled Beginning", in W.T. Woo, J.D. Sachs and K. Schwab (eds) *The Asian Financial Crisis*, London: MIT Press, pp. 165–183.

Rangan, N., R. Grabowski, H. Aly and C. Pasurka (1988), "The Technical Efficiency of US Banks", *Economic Letters*, **28**, 169–175.

Rangan, N., R. Grabowski, C. Pasurka and H. Aly (1990), "Technical Scale and Allocative Efficiencies in US Banking: an Empirical Investigation", *Review of Economics and Statistics*, **52**, 211–218.

Rees, R. (1985), "The Theory of Principle and Agent Parts 1 and 2", *Bulletin of Economic Research*, **1/2**, 3–95.

Reid, M. (1982), *Secondary Banking Crisis in the UK*, London: Macmillan.

Resti, A. (1998), "Regulation can Foster Mergers, Can Regulation Foster Efficiency? The Italian Case", *Journal of Economics and Business*, **50**, 157–169.

Revell, J. (1980), *Costs and Margins in Banking: An International Survey*, Paris: OECD.

Revell, J. (ed.) (1994), *The Changing Face of European Banks and Securities Markets*, Basingstoke: Macmillan.

Rhoades, S. (1993), "Efficiency Effects of Horizontal (In Market) Bank Mergers", *Journal of Banking and Finance*, **17**, 411–422.

Rhoades, S. (1994), "A Summary of Merger Performance in Banking, 1980–93 and an Assessment of the 'Operating Performance' and 'Event Study' Methodologies", Federal Reserve Bulletin, July.

Riskmetrics™ (1994), *Technical Document*, New York: JP Morgan. Available at http://riskmetrics.com/

Rivoli, P. and T. Brewer (1997), "Political Instability and Country Risk", *Global Finance Journal*, **8**(2), 309–321.

Rosen, R.D. and R. Murray (1997), "Opening Doors: Access to the Global Market and Financial Sectors", in M.E. Graham and A. Vourvoulas-Bush (eds), *The City and the World: New York's Global Future*, New York: Council on Foreign Relations.

Rosse, P.S. and J.C. Panzer (1977), "Chamberlain vs Robinson: An Empirical Test for Monopoly Rents", Bell Laboratories, EDP No. 90.

Rybczynski, T. (1997), "A New Look at the Evolution of the Financial System", in J. Revell (ed.), *The Recent Evolution of Financial Systems*, London: Macmillan.

Sachs, J.D. (1986), "Managing the LDC Debt Crisis", *Brookings Papers on Economic Activity*, **2**, 397–440.

Sachs, J. and W.T. Woo (1994), "Structural Factors in the Economic Reforms of China, Eastern Europe and the Former Soviet Union", *Economic Policy*, **18**(Apr), 101–146.

Sachs, J., A. Tornell and A. Velasco (1996), "Financial Crisis in Emerging Markets, Lessons from 1995", *Brookings Papers*, **27**(1), 147–199. Also appears as National Bureau of Economic Research, Working Paper No. 5576, May.

Salop, S. and J. Stiglitz (1977), "Bargains and Ripoffs: A Model of Monopolistically Competitive Price Dispersion", *Review of Economic Studies*, **4**, 493–510.

Sandal, K. (2004), "The Nordic Banking Crisis in the early 1990s – Resolution Methods and Fiscal Costs".

Santomero, A. (1979), "The Role of Transaction Costs and Rates of Return on the Demand Deposit Decision", *Journal of Economics*, **5**, 343–364.

Santomero, A. (1984), "Modelling the Banking Firm", *Journal of Money, Credit and Banking*, **16**(4), 576–602.

Santomero, A. and P. Hoffman (1998), "Problem Bank Resolution: Evaluating the Options", The Wharton School Financial Institutions Center Discussion Paper No. 98-05.

Santomero, A. and J.D. Vinso (1977), "Estimating the Probability of Failure for Commercial Banks and the Banking System", *Journal of Banking and Finance*, Sept, 185–205.

Santos, N. and M. Woodford (1997), "Rational Asset Pricing Bubbles", *Econometrica*, **65**, 19–57.

Sapienza, P. (1998), "The Effects of Banking Mergers on Loan Contracts", Working Paper, Northwestern University, Evanston, IL.

Saunders, A. (1994), "Universal Banking and the Separation of Banking and Commerce", Special Issue, *Journal of Banking and Finance*, **18**(2), 229–420.

Saunders, A. (1999), *Credit Risk Management*, New York: John Wiley & Sons.

Saunders, A. (2000), *Financial Institutions Management*: London: McGraw Hill.

Saunders, A. (2002), *Credit Risk Measurement: New Approaches to Value at Risk and other Paradigms*, 2nd edn, New York: John Wiley & Sons.

Saunders, A. and M. Cornett (2003), *Financial Institutions Management*, London: McGraw Hill/Irwin.

REFERENCES/BIBLIOGRAPHY

Schull, B. and L.J. White (1998), "Of Firewalls and Subsidiaries: the Right Stuff for Expanded Bank Activities", in *Payment Systems in the Global Economy: Risks and Opportunities*, 34th Annual Conference on Bank Structure and Competition, Federal Reserve Bank of Chicago, May, pp. 509–530.

Schwartz, A. (1986), "Real and Pseudo-Financial Crises", in F. Capie and G.E. Wood (eds), *Financial Crises and the World Banking System*, London: Macmillan, pp. 11–40.

Scott, D. (2002), "A Practical Guide to Managing Systemic Financial Crises; A Review of the Approaches Taken in Indonesia, the Republic of Korea, and Thailand", World Bank Working Paper No. 2843.

Scott, H.S. (1992), "Supervision of International Banking Post-BCCI", *Georgia State University Law Review*, **8**(3), 487–509.

Scott, H.S. and S. Iwahara (1994), *In Search of a Level Playing Field: The Implementation of the Basel Capital Accord in Japan and the United States*, Washington: Group of Thirty.

Sealey, C.W. (1983), "Valuation, Capital Structure and the Shareholder Unanimity for Depository Financial Intermediaries", *Journal of Finance*, **38**, 857–871.

Sealey, C.W. and J.T. Lindley (1977), "Inputs, Outputs, and a Theory of the Production and Cost at Depository Financial Institutions", *Journal of Finance*, **32**, 1251–1266.

Shaffer, S. (1982), "A Non-structural Test for Competition in Financial Markets", in *Bank Structure and Competition – Conference Proceedings*, Federal Reserve Bank of Chicago, pp. 225–243.

Shaffer, S. (1990), "A Test of Competition in Canadian Banking", Federal Reserve Bank of Philadelphia, Working Paper No. 90-18, July.

Shaffer, S. and E. David (1991), "Economies of Superscale in Commercial Banking", *Applied Economics*, **23**, 283–293.

Shapiro, A.C. (1988), *Multinational Financial Management*, Boston: Allyn and Bacon.

Shaw, E. (1973), *Financial Deepening in Economic Development*, New York: Oxford University Press.

Shea, T. (1993), "Reforms to Banking Regulation in Eastern Europe and the CIS", Mimeo (unpublished), November.

Sheffrin, H. (2000), *Beyond Greed and Fear: Understanding Behavioural Finance and the Psychology of Investors*, Boston: Harvard University Press.

Shepard, W.G. (1982), "Economies of Scale and Monopoly Profits", in J. Craven, *Industrial Organisation, Antitrust, and Public Policy*, Boston: Kluwer Nijhoff.

Sherwood, D. (1992), "Process Re-engineering in the Banks", *Banker's Digest*, 12–13.

Shin, H.S., F. Muennich, C.A.E. Goodhart, P. Embrechts, J. Danielsson and C. Keating (2001), "An Academic Response to Basel II", Financial Markets Group Special Paper SP#130, May.

Shleifer, A. (2000), *Inefficient Markets: An Introduction to Behavioural Finance*, Oxford: Oxford University Press.

Shleifer, A. and R. Vishny (1997), "The Limits to Arbitrage", *The Journal of Finance*, **LII**(1), 35–55.

Siems, T. (1996), "Bank Mergers and Shareholder Wealth: Evidence from 1995's Mega Merger Deals", *Financial Industry Studies of the Federal Reserve Bank of Dallas*, 1–12.

Silber, W. (1975), "*Towards a Theory of Financial Innovation*", in W. Silber (ed.), *Financial Innovation*, Lexington: Heath.

Silber, W.L. (1983), "Recent Structural Change in the Capital Markets: The Process of Financial Innovation", *Annual Economic Review (Papers and Proceedings)*, **73**(2), 89–95.

Silverman, G. (2003), "JP Morgan Admits to Poor Credit Management", *The Financial Times*, 3 May.

Simons, K. and J. Stavins (1998), "Has Antitrust Policy in Banking become Obsolete?" *New England Economic Review*, Federal Reserve Bank of Boston, 13–26.

Sinclair, A., R. Smith and I. Walter (1991), "Bankers Trust", Case Series in Finance and Economics, C07, New York University Salomon Center, Leonard N. Stern School of Business.

Sinkey, J. (1975), "A Multivariate Statistical Analysis of the Characteristics of Problem Banks", *Journal of Finance*, **30**(March), 21–36.

Sinkey, J. and R. Nash (1993), "Assessing the Riskiness and Profitability of Credit Card Banks", *Journal of Financial Services Research*, **7**, 127–150.

Sinkey, J. (2002), *Commercial Bank Financial Management – Into the Financial Services Industry*, 6th edn. New York: Macmillan, p. 306.

Slatz, I. (1997), "Federal Deposit Insurance Coverage and Bank Failures: A Co-integration Analysis with Semi-Annual Data, 1965–1991", *Journal of Economics and Finance*, **21**(3), 3–9.

Smirlock, M. (1985), "Evidence of the (Non) Relationship Between Concentration and Profitability in Banking", *Journal of Money, Credit and Banking*, **17**, 69–83.

Smith, R.C. (1988a), "American Express and Shearson Lehman Brothers", Case Series in Finance and Economics, C20, New York University Salomon Center, Leonard N. Stern School of Business.

Smith, R.C. (1988b), "The Kidder Peabody Group", Case Studies in Finance and Economics, C26, New York University Salomon Center, Leonard N. Stern School of Business.

Smith, R.C. (1992), "Sakura Bank Ltd.", Case Series in Finance and Economics, C25, New York University Salomon Center, Leonard N. Stern School of Business.

Smith, R.C. and I. Walter (1992), "The Privatisation of Bancomer", Case Series in Finance and Economics, C18, New York University Salomon Center, Leonard N. Stern School of Business.

Smith, R.C. and I. Walter (1993), "Crédit Lyonnais", Case Series in Finance and Economics, C40, New York University Salomon Center, Leonard N. Stern School of Business.

Smith, S. (1998), "Internet Payments: Momentum or Muddle?", *Journal of Internet Banking and Commerce*, **3**(3), 1–3.

Soifer, R. (2001), "US Banking Regulation: Gramm Leach Bliley", in N. Courtis and A. Milne (eds), *Annual Survey of Supervisory Developments*, London: Central Banking Publications, pp. 77–84.

Solow, R.M. (1982), "On the Lender of Last Resort", in C.P. Kindleberger and J.P. Laffargue (eds), *Financial Crises: Theory History and Policy*, New York: Cambridge University Press, pp. 237–255.

Spady, R. and A. Friedlaender (1978), "Hedonic Cost Functions for the Regulated Trucking Industry", *Bell Journal of Economics*, **5**(9), 159–179.

Staikouras, S. (forthcoming), "Multinational Banks, Credit Risk, and Financial Crises: A Qualitative Response Analysis", *Emerging Markets, Finance and Trade*.

Stamoulis, D.S. (2000), "How Banks Fit in an Internet Commerce Business and Activities Model", *Journal of Internet Banking and Commerce*, **5**(1), 1–4.

Standard and Poor's (1997), *Ratings Performance 1996: Stability and Transition*, New York: Standard and Poor's.

Stiglitz, J.E. and A. Weiss (1981), "Credit Rating in Markets with Imperfect Information", *American Economic Review*, **71**(June), 393–410.

Stiglitz, J.E. and A. Weiss (1988), "Banks as Social Accountants and Screening Devices for the Allocation of Credit", Working Paper No. 2710, Washington: National Bureau of Economic Research.

Stuart, C. (1975), *Search and Organization of Market Places*, Malmo: Lund Economic Series.

Sun, Q., W. Tong and J. Tong (2002), "How Does Government Ownership Affect Performance? Evidence from China's Privatization Experience", *Journal of Business Finance and Accounting*, **29**, 306–321.

Suominen, M. (2001), "E-Banking in the Nordic Countries – Its Emergence and Prospectives", in J. Krumnow and T.A. Lange (eds), *Manangement Handbuch eBanking*, Stuttgart: Schaffer-Poeschel-Verlag.

Suzuki, Y. (1987), "Financial Reform in Japan: Developments and Prospects", *Bank of Japan Monetary and Economic Studies*, **5**(3), 33–47.

Sweeney, P. (2000), "Small Banks, Big Plans", *US Banker*, **May**, 51–54.

Sykes, A. (2002), "Delivering the Benefits", *The Financial Regulator*, **6**(4), 36–37.

Taffler, R.J. (1983), "The Assessment of Company Solvency and Performance Using a Statistical Model", *Accounting and Business Research*, **Autumn**.

Taffler, R.J. (1984), "Empirical Models for the Monitoring of UK Corporations", *Journal of Banking and Finance*, **8**, 199–227.

Taffler, R.J. (2002a), "What Can We Learn From Behavioural Finance? (Part 1)", *Credit Control*, **23**(2), 14–17.

Taffler, R.J. (2002b), "What Can We Learn From Behavioural Finance? (Part 2)", *Credit Control*, **23**(4), 27–30.

Taleb, N. (1997), "The World According to Nassim Taleb", *Derivatives Strategy*, available from www.derivativesstrategy.com

Talwar, S.P. (2001), "Competition, Consolidation, and Systemic Stability in the Indian Banking Industry", in *The Banking Industry in the Emerging Market Economies: Competition, Consolidation, and Systemic Stability*, BIS Papers No. 4, Basel: BIS, pp. 75–79.

Tan, S.J. and I. Vertinsky (1987), "Strategic Management of International Financial Centers: A Tale of Two Cities", in S.J. Khoury and A. Ghosh (eds), *Recent Developments in International Banking and Finance*, Vol. 2, Lexington: Lexington Books.

Taylor, J. (2002), *Sovereign Debt Rescheduling: A US Perspective*, Washington: US Treasury.

Taylor, O., J. Beaverstock, G. Cook and N. Pandit (2003), *Financial Services Clustering and its Significance for London*, London: Corporation of London, February. Also available at www.cityoflondon.gov.uk

Ter Wengel, J. (1995), "International Trade in Banking Services", *Journal of International Money and Finance*, **14**(1), 47–64.

Terrell, T.S. (1986), "The Role of Domestic Banks in Domestic Banking Markets", in H.S. Cheng (ed.), *Financial Policy and Reform in the Pacific Basin Countries*, New York: Lexington Books.

Thornton, H. (1802), *An Enquiry into the Nature and Effects of the Paper Credit of Great Britain*, New York: Kelley (1965).

Tirole, J. (1985), "Asset Bubbles and Overlapping Generations", *Econometrica*, **53**, 1499–1528.

Tobin, J. (1963), "Commercial Banks as Creators of Money", in G. Horwich (ed.), *Banking and Monetary Studies*, Homewood: Irvine, pp. 408–419.

Tomkin, N. and C. Baden-Fuller (2000), "The Mondex Case Study", European Case Clearing House.

Tschoegl, A.E. (2000), "International Banking Centers, Geography, and Foreign Banks", *Financial Markets, Institutions and Instruments*, **9**(1), 1–32.

Tweedie, D. (2001), "Accounting for the World", *Financial Regulator*, **6**(2), 28–32.

Vander Vennet, R. (1996), "The Effects of Merger and Acquisitions on the Efficiency and Profitability of EC Credit Institutions", *Journal of Banking and Finance*, **20**, 1531–1558.

Wallison, P. (2003), "Freddie Mac – What Happens Now?", *The Financial Regulator*, **8**(2), 25–31.

Walter, I. and A. Saunders (1991), "National and Global Competitiveness of New York City as a Financial Center", New York University, Occasional Paper No. 11.

Ward, W. and S. Wolfe (2003), "Asset Backed Securitisation, Collateralised Loan Obligations, and Credit Derivatives", in Mullineux and Murinde, *op. cit.*, pp. 60–101.

Whalley, J. (2003), "Liberalization of China's Key Service Sectors Following WTO Accession: Some Scenarios and Issues of Measurement", National Bureau of Economic Research, Working Paper 10143, Washington: NBER. Available from www.nber.org/papers/w10143

Wheelock, D. and P. Wilson (2000), "Why do Banks Disappear? The Determinants of US Bank Failures and Acquisitions", *The Review of Economics and Statistics*, **82**(1), 127–138.

White, E.N. (1986), "Before the Glass–Steagall Act: An Analysis of the Investment Banking Activities of National Banks", *Explorations in Economic History*, **23**, 33–55.

White, L.J. (1991), *The S&L Debacle: Public Policy Lessons for Bank and Thrift Regulation*, New York: Oxford University Press.

Williams, J. and E. Gardener (2003), "The Efficiency of European Regional Banking", *Regional Studies*, **37**(4), 321–330.

Williams, M. (2000), "International Challenges to the Offshore Sector", *The Financial Regulator*, **4**(4), 20–26.

Williamson, O. (1981), "The Modern Corporation: Origins, Evolution, Attributes", *Journal of Economic Literature*, **19**, 1537–1568.

Wong, Y.C.R. and M.L.S. Wong (2001), "Competition in China's Domestic Banking Industry", *Cato Journal*, **21**(1), 19–41.

Woo, W.T., J.D. Sachs and K. Schwab (eds) (2000), *The Asian Financial Crisis*, London: MIT Press.

Wood, D. (2002), "CRO Profile: Christine Hayes – Egg", in *Erisk*. Available at www.erisk.com/portal/community/viewpoint/comm_viewpoint2002-01-14.asp

Wood, D. (2003), "Competition, Regulation and Financial Stability", in P. Booth and D. Currie (eds), *The Regulation of Financial Markets*, London: Institute of Economic Affairs, pp. 63–83.

Wood, G.W. (2000), "The Lender of Last Resort Reconsidered", *Journal of Financial Services Research*, **18**(2/3), 203–208.

Wood, G. and C. Staikouros (2004), "Non Interest Income, Balance Sheet Structure and Interest Rates", in C. Zopoundidis (ed.), *New Trends in Banking Management*, Berlin: Physica-Verlag.

World Bank (2002), *Transition: The First Ten Years*, Washington: World Bank.

World Savings Banks Institute and European Savings Banks Group (2003), "The Russian Banking Sector and the Leading Role of Sberbank", *Perspectives*, **45**, 14-11-2003.

Wriston, W. (1981), "Hearings before the Senate Committee on Banking, Housing, and Urban Affairs", *Testimony*, Part 2, 97th Congress, 29 October, pp. 589–590.

Wu, F. (2001), "China's WTO Membership: Implications for Macroeconomic Outlook and Financial Sector", *Asian Profile*, **29**(5), 363–378.

Wu, X. (1998), *China's Financial Industry in the New Stage of the Reform*, Tianjin: Tianjin People's Press.

Xu, J. (1996), "An Empirical Estimation of the Portfolio Diversification Hypothesis: the Case of Canadian Banking", *Canadian Journal of Economics*, **29**(Apr), S19.

Young, A. (1995), "The Tyranny of Numbers, Confronting the Statistical Realities of the East Asian Growth Experience", *Quarterly Journal of Economics*, **110**, 641–680.

Zaik, E., J. Walter, G. Kelling and C. James (1996), "RAROC at the Bank of America: From Theory to Practice", *Journal of Applied Corporate Finance*, **9**(2), 83–93.

Zhang, H. (1995), "Wealth Effects of US Bank Takeovers", *Applied Financial Economics*, **5**(5), 329–336.

# INDEX